ENCYCLOPEDIA OF
NORTH AMERICAN
INDIANS

ENCYCLOPEDIA OF NORTH AMERICAN INDIANS

FREDERICK E. HOXIE

EDITOR

HOUGHTON MIFFLIN COMPANY

Boston   New York

For information about this and other Houghton Mifflin
trade and reference books and multimedia products, visit
the Bookstore at Houghton Mifflin on the world Wide Web at
http://www.hmco.com/trade/.

LIBRARY OF CONGRESS CATALOGING-IN-PUBLICATION DATA

Encyclopedia of North American Indians / Frederick E. Hoxie, editor.
p. cm.
Includes index.
ISBN 0-395-66921-9
1. Indians of North America—Encyclopedias.   I. Hoxie, Frederick E.
E76.2.E53 1996
970.004'97'003—dc20   96-21411   CIP

Book design by Anne Palms Chalmers (Potawatomi ancestry)

Printed in the United States of America

HWK 10 9 8 7 6 5 4 3 2 1

The ornaments in this book are from *American Indian Design & Decoration* by
LeRoy H. Appleton, Dover Publications, Inc., New York, 1971. Page i, Seminole
beadwork: rainbow *(top)* and Arapaho beadwork *(bottom)*; p. ii, General
Pueblo pottery decoration: turtle; p. iii, Yuchi beadwork: centipede *(top)*, Mimbres pottery painting *(middle)*, design based on Cheyenne motif *(bottom)*; p. v,
Haida totem pole symbol: footprint; p. vi, Zuni woven sash; p.vii, Navajo, edge
of woman's blanket; p. 713, Winnebago beadwork; p. 715, Eskimo carved ivory
work bag fastener; p.727, Arapaho symbol for rocks; p. 728, General Pueblo
pottery decoration; p. 730, Ojibwa woven bag. Space breaks based on Cherokee
motif. Ornaments at letter headings: A: General Pueblo pottery decoration,
cloud serpent; B: Mimbres pottery decoration, bird; C: Nez Perce woven bag; D:
Florida Gulf Coast incised pottery; E: Hidatsa painted buffalo robe; F:
Potawatomi woven bag; G: Yuchi beadwork, storm clouds; H: Delaware quill
embroidery on hide; I: Menominee woven bag; J: Blackfoot quillwork; K:
Iriquois incised pottery pipe design; L: Delaware quill embroidery on hide; M:
Acoma woman's dress border; N: Pueblo pottery; O: Tlingit basketry, scoopnet;
P: Potawatomi beadwork; Q: General Pueblo pottery; R: Dakota beadwork on
hide; S: Mississippian incised pottery decoration; T: Eskimo carved bone needle
case; U: Zuni pottery decoration, deer; V: Sauk and Fox beadwork; W: Lillooet
basketry, mountains with lakes; Y: Santa Ana pottery; Z: Pueblo pottery.

CONTENTS

MAPS

INDIAN CULTURES OF NORTH AMERICA

INTRODUCTION

THOUGH CURIOSITY about Native American people began with Columbus, distortions and misperceptions have an equally long history. The admiral began it all by miscalculating his position and calling his hosts "Indians." Over the centuries others compounded his errors by arguing with straight faces that Native Americans were the descendants of wandering Israelites, members of a separate branch of creation, or humans who had sunk into "stupid repose" because they lived in a hostile wilderness.

Happily, a tradition of scholarship has struggled to replace such myths with more plausible explanations. A century ago anthropologists began a systematic effort to record Native American languages, excavate ancient Native American settlements, and understand Native American traditions. In the decades since World War II other disciplines have joined the effort. Historians developed a more sophisticated method for presenting Indian experiences from an Indian perspective. Sociologists crafted models of cultural adaptation that avoided the religious and political moralism of the past. Literary scholars, taking seriously the indomitable creative energy of Indian communities, have begun to include native artists in the academic canon. In recent decades students and researchers from many disciplines have also begun to collaborate with one another and, most important, increasing numbers of American Indians have joined their ranks and taken leadership roles in the academic enterprise. Unfortunately, however, most of this innovative scholarship has remained beyond the reach of the general reader. The result is a remarkably persistent state of public ignorance.

Descriptions of Native American life have long been simplistic. George Washington, for example, could decipher British military intentions, but he viewed the nation's Indians — people who stopped his army dead in its tracks in Ohio — as "wolves." Thomas Jefferson struck a more sympathetic pose, but he spent a remarkable amount of time insisting that the corn-producing tribes of the Southeast and Midwest settle down and learn to farm. Theodore Roosevelt was similarly unconcerned with the details of tribal life, claiming at one point that the enemies of American expansion were so foolish that they would probably be willing to "abandon Arizona to the Apaches." Such self-serving and racist thinking persists in our insistence that "wild" Indians not "wander off the reservation" and in our remarkable tolerance for public caricatures, mascots, and slurs that would be condemned were they attached to any other racial or ethnic group.

When discussing Indians, most Americans do not worry much about facts. A joint French-Indian raid on the village of Deerfield, Massachusetts, in 1704 was quickly labeled a "massacre," yet a brutal assault on a village of friendly (and sleeping) Cheyennes in 1864 was celebrated in the streets of Denver as a victory over "hostiles." A few years later the U.S. Supreme Court announced that Indians could not vote because they had neither been born in the United States nor "naturalized" like their immigrant neighbors. More recently, Hollywood producers have cast Italians to play Apaches and proudly falsified the life of Pocahontas — defending themselves in both instances by protesting that they meant no harm.

As appalling as the errors themselves is the fact that much of this historical distortion has been undertaken with the best of intentions. Columbus himself reported that the Arawaks who greeted him in the Caribbean were "guileless" and "generous." In the next century the French essayist Michel de Montaigne established the ideal of the Noble Savage in Western thought by routinely declaring European "civilization" to be inferior to "simple" Indian "barbarism." As imperial settlement and expansion gathered steam in the eighteenth and nineteenth centuries, other writers repeated this romantic theme. Alexander Pope rhapsodized about Indians who saw "God in clouds," while America's James Fenimore Cooper drew an enduring portrait of an imaginary Mohican, a man who was "an unblemished specimen of the noblest proportions of man." In our own time, unhappy city dwellers flock to ersatz tribal ceremonies hoping to relieve their distress by connecting with environmental virtue and ancient spiritual teachings. Some are content with expensive weekend workshops and designer leather costumes; others want to "become" Indian by locating a Native American ancestor or inventing a new identity out of whole cloth.

This history of ignorance, distortion, and well-intentioned stereotyping cries out for a corrective: a book filled with facts and well-informed interpretations. It should contain, as this one does, descriptions of Indian origins (from both an anthropological and a traditional Native American perspective), battlefield techniques, agricultural practices, and courtroom struggles. It should also explain Hollywood's congenital fascination with Native Americans and tell us something about the fakes and imposters who have pretended to be Indians. A curative and informative book published at the end of a generation of scholarly activism should also draw on the ideas of experts who have blossomed in all corners of the academic landscape in the past twenty-five years, attempting — as this book does — to condense their most interesting findings into brief essays that are buttressed with references to recently published books.

Because even reliable "facts" about Indians have found their way into nonsensical interpretations, a book that hopes to broaden and illuminate the public's understanding of Native American life should illuminate a few central ideas that non-Indians frequently forget. Four common themes run through the 447 entries in this book:

Indians Are People. Neither relics of a lost past nor forerunners of a utopian future, Native Americans are three-dimensional human beings who have been brilliant and brave as well as cruel and foolish. This book's entries acknowledge this fact, both in their descriptions of Indian actions in war and peace and in their multifaceted portrayals of cultural traditions and cultural leaders. Indian art is discussed in terms of individual artists as well as tribal traditions; political leaders are presented with all their various qualities — from the stubborn resistance of the Shawnee warrior Tecumseh to the political flexibility of the Crow tribe's Robert Yellowtail.

Indians Change. Entries in this book describe people and cultures over time. Tribal life is constantly adapting to new circumstances, and adapting to new technologies, and Native Americans have made choices about their futures and acted to alter both their history and the histories of their neighbors. Tribal entries generally include descriptions of migrations and internal divisions as well as a portrait of contemporary life among the group being discussed (one group, the Cheyennes, has two entries, reflecting their separation into northern and southern divisions more than a century ago). Other entries sustain this historical perspective. The essay on literature, for example, discusses some of the newest figures on the literary scene, the entry on art describes the evolution of new techniques and materials, and the essay on intermarriage discusses different features of that phenomenon through time. The biographies in the book describe innovators such as the Oxford-educated author John Joseph Matthews as well as defenders of tribal tradition like the Creek leader Chitto Harjo.

Indians Are a Permanent Part of American Life. Though they are often thought to have vanished completely or to be present only in scattered and isolated communities, Indians — the original inhabitants of the American continents — have survived repeated historical upheavals, participate in every aspect of modern life, and live in every corner of North America. Entries in this volume on major events such as the Civil War or on pivotal individuals like Joseph Brant and Alexander McGillivray make clear that Native North Americans are not bit players in the story of Canada and the United States, but people with a vital and continuing role in these nations' histories. Essays on religious freedom and contemporary arts point to the continuing relevance of Indian ideas and concerns in many parts of contemporary society.

Indians Have Voices. Whether cast in bronze or gazing quietly from sepia photographs, Native Americans in popular culture are usually mute. In the worlds of education and policymaking, there are those who continue to believe that decisions can be made without substantial Indian involvement. Equally disturbing are those who assert that a single Indian voice pronouncing "approval" of some travesty can somehow end all debate; they assume that any Native American is interchangeable with any other member of the group and that Indian communities and organizations cannot (or need not) be consulted. Though confined to print, this book has tried to battle this legacy of silence and simplification with dozens of entries written by Native Americans themselves.

Nearly half the tribal entries — from Creek to Hopi to Iroquois to Navajo to Zuni — were prepared by tribal members; all were written to present the group's view of itself and its history as well as to convey the basic facts of location, history, and principal defining traditions. Native American authors are indeed present throughout the volume, and a special effort was made to have the biographies of prominent individuals prepared by people from their tribes or families (see, for example, the portraits of Jim Thorpe and Levi General), and to have people who have been personally involved with certain topics write about those topics. Susan Williams, for example, a Sioux attorney who litigates water-rights cases across the West, explains water rights, while Osage scholar George Tinker, a professor of theology, presents religion, and Richard West, the Southern Cheyenne director of the Smithsonian's National Museum of the American Indian, examines repatriation.

———◆◆◆———

Faced with the experiences of millions of people in hundreds of communities over some forty thousand years of history, it is perhaps inevitable that a wary editor will emphasize the volume's educational ambition rather than its universal coverage. This book acknowledges the size and complexity of its subject and covers it as fully as is possible in a single-volume work, but it does not claim to tour every point on the "circle" of Native American experience. *Encyclopedia of North American Indians* strives instead to introduce, to teach, and to invite further inquiry. It seeks to accomplish that goal with four types of entries.

First, there are descriptions of one hundred tribes, providing coverage of all major contemporary groups. Smaller native communities such as those around Puget Sound, in the Midwest and the plateau region, in the pueblos of the Rio Grande, and in California are discussed in regional entries that balance particular descriptions with discussions of common themes. Five entries on major languages (Lakota, Navajo, Cherokee, Cree, and Ojibwa) and four entries on major language groups (Algonquian, Iroquoian, Pueblo, and Salishan) supplement this tribal coverage, as does a general entry on American Indian languages.

Second, the book contains one hundred biographies, selected to provide representation from different regions and eras as well as to introduce readers to the many arenas in which American Indians have had significant careers. Readers will find biographies of familiar (though frequently misrepresented) figures such as Sitting Bull, Pocahontas, and Geronimo as well as profiles of the baseball star Charles Bender, diplomats and reformers such as Sarah Winnemucca and Charles Eastman, artists like María Martínez, and scholars as various as the

Cherokee linguist Sequoyah and the modern anthropologist and novelist D'Arcy McNickle. Though a number of modern figures are represented, no living people are included among the subjects of the biographies.

Third, this encyclopedia draws people and places together around nearly one hundred interpretive entries that present brief overviews of significant topics, historical eras, and cultural traditions. Topics range from "African Americans and American Indians" to "Alcoholism" to "Beads and Beadwork" to "Bible Translations" to "Dreams" to Indian-white relations in a variety of eras in both Canada and the U.S. to "Voting." Like others in the volume, the entries in this third category have largely been produced by Indian and non-Indian people who have devoted years to the topic and written books on it, and who can therefore present both essential information and an introduction to major interpretive issues. Thus the "Treaties" entry, by a Native American law professor, explains why these frequently forgotten documents are so important to contemporary Indian people; "Birth," by a Lakota anthropologist, describes both the rituals associated with childbirth and the meanings attached to the event; and "Diseases," by a pioneering scholar in the field of historical demography, presents the evidence for what some have called the American "holocaust" that followed the introduction of European pathogens into the Western Hemisphere.

A final category of entries provides definitions for terms and events that are frequently mentioned and often misunderstood. Readers of these entries can learn about dozens of topics, including black drink, cradleboards, grass houses, peyote, and the White Dog Ceremony. Included in this category readers will also find entries on a dozen major treaties and several famous battles. It should be noted that many of these entries were drafted by Native American graduate students who took on the assignments as part of their scholarly training.

Acknowledging the limits of both space and imagination that confine any work of this kind, most entries conclude with suggestions for further reading. These bibliographical references have been selected to favor books that are relatively easy to find over arcane scholarly articles and works that are rare or out of print. In addition, the entry on bibliographies, prepared by a distinguished Navajo librarian, features titles that will enable serious readers to supplement the references provided with individual entries.

The four types of entries make up a work containing

447 separate listings. Two hundred sixty authors prepared the signed entries; short, unsigned entries reflect the work of nearly two dozen others. The editor encouraged each contributor to share his or her special insights and interpretations while providing readers with the facts and figures they would expect to find in a reference work of this kind. As a result many entries speak with the distinctive voice of their author. Ottawa historian Cecil King, for example, combines the tribal stories of origin with conventional historical information, while Lakota linguist Albert White Hat writes with great passion about the contemporary significance of his tribal language as well as its history and principal characteristics. Beginning with "Abenaki," and ending with "Zuni," the *Encyclopedia of North American Indians* contains both a wide array of topics and a symphony of voices.

The outstanding scholars who prepared the entries for this work deserve thanks both for their effort and their good humor. To reduce a life's passion to fifteen hundred words is no easy task, particularly if one is writing in a contentious academic setting or trying to create a portrait of a respected community figure that will be recognizable to neighbors and relatives. Virgil Vogel's "Place Names" entry stands out in this regard. Drawn from his several books on Indian place names in particular states, and submitted only days before his death, the entry is both a wonderful summary of a subject that engaged Professor Vogel for many years and an invitation to others to explore the topic further. In addition I am particularly indebted to the Native American authors who agreed to write descriptions of their tribes or relatives knowing from the start that completing the task to everyone's satisfaction would be impossible.

The *Encyclopedia*'s advisers — JoAllyn Archambault, Joy Harjo, Nancy Lurie, Peter Nabokov, Alvin M. Josephy, and Vine Deloria, Jr. — have provided steady encouragement throughout the project. Agreeing first that this book was a good idea and then worrying with me over entry lists, authors, and gaps in coverage, they have provided an essential source of advice and criticism. Several of them also allowed themselves to be recruited as authors and in that capacity made additional valuable contributions to the final product.

Supporting my efforts throughout this project has been the Newberry Library, a unique research library with spectacular holdings in American Indian history and culture and a tenacious commitment to public service and innovative scholarship. Work on the *Encyclopedia* began in 1992 when I directed the library's D'Arcy McNickle Center for the History of the American Indian and ended not long after I had been reincarnated as Vice President for Research and Education. Running steadily through this transition have been the generous support of the institution's leadership, particularly President Charles T. Cullen and senior research fellow Richard H. Brown, as well as the wise counsel and guidance of my valued colleagues John Aubrey, James Grossman, Craig Howe, Harvey Markowitz, and Helen Hornbeck Tanner.

Finally, to take a project of this size and complexity from pipe dream to publication in less than four years requires a steady team effort. Four stalwart individuals have seen me through the wilderness of entry lists, lost authors, and orphaned topics. In Chicago the superb work of Bonnie Lynn-Sherow, Rebecca Bales, and Amanda Seligman kept the paper flowing, the authors reasonably happy, and the pretension level low, while back at headquarters in Boston, senior editor Borgna Brunner and the staff at Houghton Mifflin set a standard of efficiency, accuracy, and insightfulness for us all to aim at. Special thanks go to assistant editors Holly Hartman and Amy K. Smith, designer Anne Chalmers, picture researcher Margaret Anne Miles, production supervisor Beth Rubè, proofreader Diane Fredrick, editor David Pritchard, and Carl Walesa, whose careful copyediting and deep involvement in the project provided a pleasant voice downstream telling us all that we were on the right track.

FREDERICK E. HOXIE

ENCYCLOPEDIA OF
NORTH AMERICAN
INDIANS

ABENAKI

By the time Europeans first saw northern New England, various groups of loosely related Algonquian-speaking peoples had inhabited the area for thousands of years. These Indian groups came to be known collectively as Abenakis, a name referring to their eastern location as "people of the dawn land." Their homelands stretched from Lake Champlain in the west to Maine's Atlantic Coast, and from the St. Lawrence Valley in Quebec to northern Massachusetts. The Abenakis included the Sokokis on the middle and upper Connecticut River, the Cowasucks farther upriver, the Missisquois on the northern shore of Lake Champlain, the Pennacooks of New Hampshire's Merrimack Valley, the Pigwackets in the White Mountains, the Androscoggins of western Maine, and the Penobscots, Norridgewocks, Wawenocks, and Kennebecs farther east. Anthropologists distinguish between the Eastern Abenakis of Maine and the Western Abenakis of Vermont, but the lines of separation are neither rigid nor clear, and rest on linguistic affiliation rather than political division. A more appropriate way of distinguishing between the two groups might be to regard as Western Abenaki those peoples who viewed the Champlain Valley, the scene of their creation stories, as the center of their universe, and to include as Eastern Abenaki groups who looked to the spiritual power of Mount Katahdin in Maine—although these were not the only sacred markers in the Abenaki homeland.

The French called them Abenaquis, Oubenaquis, or sometimes, when less certain as to their identity, Loups—a word they also applied to some other Indian peoples. English colonists often called all Indians they dealt with in Maine eastern Indians. By the late eighteenth century, British and Americans alike tended to label the Western Abenakis "St. Francis Indians," after the inhabitants of the village of Odanak, or St. Francis, in Quebec. The Abenakis' name for themselves was and is *Wabanaki*, although the Wabanaki Confederacy also includes the Passamaquoddies, Maliseets, and Micmacs, of northern Maine and the Maritime Provinces.

Abenaki peoples were hunters, and early Europeans saw no crops growing north of the Saco River. However, in the Champlain and Connecticut Valleys, the Abenakis grew corn centuries before Europeans arrived. In most areas, Abenaki people developed a diversified economy that combined hunting and gathering with fishing and corn agriculture on a seasonal basis. The Abenakis tended to locate their villages in river valleys, to take advantage of fertile bottom lands and spring fish runs, while forested mountains provided rich hunting territories. In the east, they harvested the marine resources offered by the Atlantic Coast. Community life varied with the seasons and their associated subsistence activities. Villages came to life when bands of related families congregated for spring fishing or planting, late summer harvesting, and winter stories and ceremonies; villages often disappeared when families dispersed into hunting territories in the fall.

The Abenakis did not operate, or deal with Europeans, as a single "tribe." Abenaki political and social structure was fluid and flexible. The family band was the core social unit, and leaders usually were heads of lineages rather than tribal chiefs. Europeans on the coast of Maine in the first decades of the seventeenth century referred to chiefs with great power, but leadership in Abenaki society seems more normally to have depended upon persuasion, example, and charisma and to have involved obligations to one's followers as much as authority over them.

As Europeans began to penetrate the Abenaki homeland in the seventeenth century, Abenaki people confronted a changing world. Europeans imported new diseases, new religions, and new technologies. Thousands of Abenakis died from epidemics such as the plague that swept the coast of Maine in 1617 and the smallpox epidemic of 1633–34 on the Merrimack and Connecticut Rivers. Many converted to Catholicism as Jesuit priests, promising salvation and coming hard on the heels of devastating diseases, established missions in their villages. Many Abenaki people received French surnames when they were baptized. The oldest Catholic cemetery in New England, dating from 1688, is at the Penobscot community on Indian Island, near Old Town, Maine. The Pennacooks and other groups closer to the English colonies came under the influence of Puritan missionaries. All Abenakis adopted some of the manufactured goods European traders filtered into their world.

But the Abenakis also shaped the new world that was emerging in New England. Europeans found inland travel made easier by Abenaki moccasins, canoes, and snowshoes; they learned Abenaki hunting and horticultural practices; they borrowed Abenaki words, sought out Abenaki healers, and sometimes spent much of their lives in Abenaki country. Abenaki communities came to include French missionaries, English captives, and those who simply preferred Abenaki society to life in colonial New England or New France. Captives who were adopted and stayed added an English strain to Abenaki society. Some of those who returned to English settlements retained strong attachments to Abenaki culture, and Abenaki parents continued to visit their adopted "children."

As competition mounted between England and France for control over North America, Abenaki homelands became war zones. Some Abenakis had felt the repercussions of King Philip's War in 1675–77 and knew well that English expansion threatened their lands and their way of life. The French seemed content with beaver pelts and baptisms, while the English demanded land cessions and cultural capitulation. Most Abenakis found the French to be more acceptable allies. Beginning in the late seventeenth century, as English settlers pushed northward, many Abenakis began to retreat, and some took up temporary or permanent residence at French mission villages like St. Francis and Bécancour on the banks of the St. Lawrence. Some Abenakis migrated to the Midwest, settling in the area south of the Great Lakes. Abenaki communities also received refugees from other Indian groups throughout New England. As they confronted the challenge of English expansion and escalating imperial rivalry, many of the people inhabiting Abenaki villages also were remaking their communities and rebuilding their lives.

Abenaki warriors frequently fought alongside the French during the so-called French and Indian Wars of the eighteenth century, but they also fought independently and for their own reasons. Many of their raids took them south to territory they regarded as rightfully

theirs and against settlers they regarded as thieves and trespassers. Abenaki villages fell to English assault in 1724, when the English and their Indian allies destroyed Norridgewock and killed and scalped the Jesuit missionary Sebastian Rasles, and in 1759 when Robert Rogers's Rangers torched St. Francis. For the most part, however, the Abenakis avoided such costly encounters. Their usual strategy was to raid the English frontier, elude pursuing militia, and evacuate their villages when danger threatened. Such tactics kept battle casualties to a minimum and kept English settlement pinned to the peripheries of Abenaki territory for the best part of a century.

The fall of New France in 1760 cost the Abenakis their French allies and opened a new era. British settlers moved onto Abenaki lands in unprecedented numbers, felling trees and building farms, mills, roads, and bridges. British soldiers stood behind these advances, and the British Indian Department tried to restrain the Abenakis by centralizing its relations with them at St. Francis. Rather than contend with their aggressive new neighbors, many Abenaki families retreated deeper into their territory, ignoring British directives to stop "wandering" and settle in one place.

The outbreak of the American Revolution brought agents and emissaries to Abenaki communities as both sides tried to recruit Abenaki warriors. Colonel John Allan, appointed by the Continental Congress as agent to the "eastern Indians," secured a measure of support from Indian groups in Maine and Nova Scotia for American efforts in the area, and the Penobscot chief Joseph Orono was sympathetic to the American cause. However, British pressures and threats prevented full-scale or consistent commitment. As in the French and Indian Wars, Abenaki neutrality was not a viable option. Instead, some Abenakis fought on each side in the Revolution. They usually served as scouts or rangers, a role that enabled them to keep the war away from their homes.

Though some Abenaki groups supported the American cause during the Revolution, all Abenakis suffered the consequences of American victory as individual states opened up Abenaki country to settlers and land speculators. Flouting the Indian Trade and Non-Intercourse Act of 1790, which required that Congress approve transfers of Indian land, Massachusetts made treaties with the Penobscots and Passamaquoddies that robbed them of huge amounts of territory. Logging companies and paper mills began operations on the rivers of northern New England. With the fur trade all

Abenaki women in Old Town, Maine.

but exhausted and their traditional patterns of subsistence disrupted, many Abenakis tried to maintain traditional ways of life in the poorer areas of their once-productive lands. Others worked as day laborers, or made and peddled baskets and birch-bark containers designed for American rather than Abenaki use. Some, like the Penobscots Joe Polis and Joseph Attean, who guided Henry David Thoreau on his treks through the Maine wilderness, worked for American travelers and tourists. Many Abenakis avoided identifying themselves as Indians, often passing as French Canadians. The U.S. Census of 1900 recorded 798 Indian people in Maine, 22 in New Hampshire, and 5 in Vermont! These figures reflected the myopia of the census takers and the fears and choices of Abenaki people in an envi-

ronment hostile to Indians. The Abenakis survived in far greater numbers, but most kept a low profile, often living in remote areas of northern New England. To their American neighbors, they seemed invisible. They were truly vanishing Americans.

The Abenakis refused to vanish, however. Through the hard times of the nineteenth and early twentieth centuries, many Abenaki people kept alive—and kept secret—stories, beliefs, basket-making skills, and community relations that defined them as Abenaki in their own eyes even as they appeared unidentifiable as Indians to outsiders. Not until 1954 did the state of Maine lift restrictions that prevented its Indian citizens from voting. As the social and political climate mellowed in American society in the later twentieth century, the

Abenakis ceased being invisible. They stepped forward to be counted and began to take increasing control over their own affairs. The Penobscots and Passamaquoddies brought suit against the state of Maine for the return of lands taken in contravention of the Trade and Non-Intercourse Act. After a protracted legal battle, the Maine Indian Land Claims Settlement Act of 1980 granted the tribes $81.5 million. The money has not brought the tribes economic independence but the victory boosted their efforts to rebuild their communities and revive their cultures. The tribes were able to repurchase some three hundred thousand acres of forestland. The injection of unprecedented amounts of capital enabled the Penobscots to create jobs, construct housing, invest in educational programs, and attract tribal members back to the community. In 1983 the Passamaquoddies bought the Dragon Products Company, New England's only cement maker, and then sold it in 1988, more than tripling their investment. They also bought a large blueberry farm near Machias, which they continue to operate as a tribal business.

Meanwhile, in Vermont, under the aggressive leadership of Chief Homer St. Francis, the Western Abenakis, who had never signed a treaty with the United States, began the long and tortuous process of trying to secure federal recognition of their status as an Indian tribe. Centered around Swanton, near the site of the ancient village of Missisquoi, the Vermont Abenakis also have worked to preserve ancient burials sites, have tackled the state head-on in fishing-rights cases and other issues affecting their sovereignty, and have produced educational programs to promote awareness of Abenaki presence and heritage in the state.

At Odanak in Quebec, the Abenaki inhabitants are recognized as "status Indians" by the Canadian government. In 1982, the community established the Mikwobait Cultural Association to help preserve Abenaki culture and heritage. A year later it started a profit-making corporation to create employment for craftworkers by selling their goods through outlets in Quebec, Montreal, and various cities in the United States.

After almost five hundred years of contact, Abenaki people in Quebec, the Acadia region of Canada, Maine, Vermont, and New Hampshire are still working out relations with non-Indian neighbors. These relations are not always smooth. Outsiders might criticize Abenaki actions and even question their identity as Indians, but the Abenakis have dispelled the illusion that they are a vanishing people. U. S. Census takers, who counted 5 Indians in Vermont in 1900, recorded 1,696 in 1990.

Calloway, Colin G., *The Western Abenakis of Vermont: War, Migration, and the Survival of an Indian People* (Norman: University of Oklahoma Press, 1990); Haviland, William A., and Marjory W. Power, *The Original Vermonters: Native Inhabitants Past and Present* (Hanover, N.H.: University Press of New England, 1981); Morrison, Kenneth M., *The Embattled Northeast: The Elusive Ideal of Alliance in Abenaki-Euramerican Relations* (Berkeley: University of California Press, 1984).

COLIN G. CALLOWAY
University of Wyoming

ADOBE WALLS, BATTLES OF

The Battles of Adobe Walls (1864 and 1874) get their names from a trading post established on the north side of the Canadian River in present-day Hutchinson County, Texas, in 1840 by Bent, St. Vrain and Company to attract the trade of the Kiowas and Comanches. Unable to make a profit, William Bent and his partner abandoned Adobe Walls by 1843.

The First Battle of Adobe Walls (November 25, 1864) was fought amid the crumbling ruins of Bent's isolated outpost. Earlier that year, General James H. Carleton, commander of the Department of New Mexico, determined to punish hostile Plains tribes. After subduing the Navajos, Carleton ordered Colonel Christopher (Kit) Carson to attack Kiowa and Comanche camps along the Canadian River near the Texas border. Carson's force of 335 soldiers, including 72 additional Utes and Jicarilla Apaches, initiated the battle by ambushing a Kiowa village. The startled warriors fled, regrouped near the abandoned trading post, and counterattacked. An overconfident Carson blindly pursued the Kiowas, failing to realize that Indian reinforcements had surrounded him. Grasping the gravity of the situation, Carson sought shelter in the ruins of Adobe Walls. The contingent from Fort Bascom, New Mexico, escaped certain death by retreating, thanks to two massive howitzers Carson employed to confuse his attackers. Carson claimed victory, but the First Battle of Adobe Walls was actually a draw. The battle did, however, succeed in reducing the frequency of Indian raids along the Santa Fe Trail.

The Second Battle of Adobe Walls (June 27, 1874) took place at a new trading post, also called Adobe Walls, located one mile south of the original post. By the summer of that year the post had become the center of buffalo hunting in Texas. Embittered Cheyennes, Kiowas, and Comanches cautiously watched as hide hunters from Dodge City, Kansas, slowly inched their way toward tribal hunting grounds. The tribes recognized that something had to be done to drive out the invaders, whose activities threatened to decimate the dwindling bison herds.

During a Sun Dance held in the spring of 1874, Quanah Parker, the war leader of the Kwahadi Comanches, urged the Indians to join forces and drive out the invaders. A short time later Parker, together with Lone Wolf (Kiowa), Woman's Heart (Kiowa), Big Bow (Comanche), Stone Wolf (Cheyenne), and White Shield (Cheyenne), agreed to attack Adobe Walls, the southernmost of the buffalo hunters' camps. Just before sunrise on June 27, 1874, Parker led the charge against the isolated outpost. During the daylong engagement, the hunters used their long-barreled buffalo guns to pick off charging warriors at long range with deadly accuracy. The Indians attacked the post throughout the day, but they failed to capture Adobe Walls. The Pan-Indian effort to prevent the wanton slaughter of the buffalo and drive the encroachers from the region had failed.

AFRICAN AMERICANS AND AMERICAN INDIANS

"Don't call us black. We are black, all right . . . [but] when you refer to us in the Seminole Nation, refer to us as freedmen. . . . Every black is not a freedman. . . . It's a distinct category." These words, spoken in 1993 by Lawrence Cudjoe, a representative of the Seminole Freedman band, illustrate the difficulties and the questions surrounding the Seminole Freedmen's search for cultural identity. The term *Seminole Freedmen* was first used in an 1866 Seminole treaty to designate "persons of African descent and blood." To assert that freedmen are a category distinct from other blacks is not to diminish their affiliation with the black community; rather, it is an attempt to illuminate a sparsely researched and barely written chapter of American history.

Relationships between African Americans and American Indians date to the first African arrivals in the English colonies at the beginning of the seventeenth century. Close proximity and shared situations of invasion and enslavement served to bridge cultural and linguistic gaps between the two groups. Although an awareness of their interconnected history exists in the significant portion of the modern African American community that also shares Indian ancestry, scholarship has thus far failed to document this experience. Rather than a simple connection between two imperiled communities, their shared history is the story of a combined quest for freedom, cultural identity, land, and ultimately self-determination.

Complexities surrounding the issue of mixed racial identity have arisen in both the black and Indian communities. What determines membership or identity in either group? What cultural, linguistic, physical, or ceremonial markers are necessary? For blacks, the "one-drop rule" has traditionally determined their racial identity. As noted by the historian Paul Spickard, even when individuals had ancestors that were overwhelmingly nonblack, law and custom dictated that one drop of black "blood" would make someone African American. On the other hand, the federal government as the arbitrator of Indian affairs has dictated that some tribal benefits be allocated only to those individuals at least one-fourth of whose ancestors are descended from a single federally recognized tribe. Thus Indians must struggle to prove their tribal affiliation, whereas blacks are arbitrarily and often superficially designated as African Americans.

Historically, further confusion arose from unions between blacks and Indians. Much of the intertwined history of these two groups unfolded in the colonial Southeast and along the eastern seaboard in the late eighteenth and early nineteenth centuries, when European powers were vying for control over indigenous people and their land. With the infusion of a market economy that thrived on the importation of black slaves, the number of Africans increased as warfare and disease decimated Indian populations. In a polarized and violent era, the lack of available partners for both blacks and Indians led to relationships between the two groups.

The tendency of Indians and blacks to form interracial communities also reflected the resistance of some whites to the idea of intermarriage with either group. This hostility was not reflective of earlier colonial periods, however, when racial categories and attitudes were less rigid and gender imbalances created opportunities for such unions. From the New York and New Jersey areas, examples of communities featuring mixed black, Indian, and white unions included Jackson Whites, Shinnecocks, Poosepatucks, and Montauks. Other seaboard communities formed similar groups, including the Narragansetts in Rhode Island, the Mashpees and Gay Heads in Massachusetts, the Melungeons in Ten-

Crow policemen of Crow Agency and Pryor, Montana: Smokey Wilson (1855–1936), left, and Yellow Worm Bear Crane. Photograph by Fred E. Miller (1868–1936).

nessee, the Brass Ankles in South Carolina, and the more numerous Lumbees in North Carolina. These and other groups are often described as "triracial isolates" because of their infusion of black, white, and Indian heritages and their practice of settling on the fringes of black or white areas.

For some of these triracial isolates, the process by which they designated their racial and ethnic backgrounds was often a response to external forces rather than an internal decision. To distance themselves from black communities, they focused on aspects of their Indian heritage—a practice that reflected the eastern and southern racial hierarchy that relegated blacks to the bottom of the social order, Indians close to that, and mixed-race people somewhere between Indians and whites.

On the other hand, a rather lax attitude toward runaway slaves prevailed in Spanish Florida, an area that provided sanctuary and fertile ground for the emergence of separate settlements comprising blacks and Indians. In Florida, both blacks and Indians needed military allies to thwart the advances of white settlers into the region. The historian Daniel F. Littlefield, Jr., even asserts that General Andrew Jackson's Florida invasion was not aimed at the Seminoles but was instead intended to break up the Maroon settlements that attracted runaway slaves.

Fears of cooperation between blacks and Indians fueled many attempts by whites to drive wedges between these groups and to create an atmosphere of suspicion that would prevent future alliances. For example, whites urged southeastern Indians to accept their views of slaveholding. Earlier forms of Indian slavery, both of Indians and of blacks, often served to replace tribal members lost in wars or epidemics. As their land base in the Southeast decreased, Cherokee Indians became more sedentary and introduced plantation-style agriculture, which benefited from large groups of slaves. Observing white slaveholders' treatment of their slaves as inferiors, these Indians were encouraged to create legal distances from their own slaves. By the 1820s, Cherokee and Creek Indians had, as part of their constitutions, enacted strict slave codes that forbade intermarriage between Indians and blacks, prohibited blacks from owning weapons, and ordered the two races to live in separate towns.

The African-American historian Kenneth Wiggins Porter wrote extensively in the 1930s and 1940s of the cooperation between blacks and Indians on the American frontier. He noted that the delineation and the structure of the frontier often promoted collaboration between the two groups. Without that cooperation the U.S. Army would have more swiftly routed southeastern Indians in Georgia and Florida for removal to Indian Territory. It was such an alliance that prompted army officers to offer bribes and promises of freedom to blacks affiliated with the southeastern tribes. This tactic produced tensions between former black and Indian allies.

Elsewhere in the continent, blacks encountered and befriended American Indians in the context of the fur trade. James Beckwourth, for example, a freedman from Virginia, spent several years as a Rocky Mountain trapper before moving on to California and producing his memoirs *(The Life and Adventures of James P. Beckwourth)* in 1856. Other blacks went west with wagon trains and military columns and made common cause with the Indians they encountered there.

Following the forced removal of southeastern tribes to Indian Territory in the 1830s, the remaining tenuous associations between blacks and Indians were tested by external factors such as the Civil War, slave raids, and the allocation of land to blacks and Indians—events that drove the groups further apart. The opening of Oklahoma Territory to settlement by black and white settlers following the Civil War was often regulated by black soldiers, who won the hatred of local tribesmen. Rifts between blacks and Indians were heightened by the black cavalrymen called Buffalo Soldiers, who aided the federal government in the divestiture of tribal lands.

In testimony before Congress in 1906, the Creek leader Chitto Harjo expressed sentiments felt by other Indians as well: "I hear the government is cutting up my land and giving it away to black people. I want to know if this is so. . . . These black people, who are they? They are Negroes that came in here as slaves. They have no right to this land." Chitto Harjo raised an important question: Who are they? Are they members of the tribe? Are they members of the black community? Are they black Indians?

The 1866 treaties negotiated between the federal government and the so-called Five Civilized Tribes following the Civil War provided tribal citizenship to all persons of African descent who were formerly associated with those tribes. However, this provision left room for many abuses and inaccuracies, and many eligible freedmen were denied full tribal membership. In addition to restricting tribal status, curtailed membership resulted in reduced land allotments. Oral interviews collected by the Works Progress Administration in the 1930s revealed that one man, Henry Battiest, of Indian and black heritage, reported that he "came to enroll with [the Dawes Commission] as my father was an Indian, but the Dawes Commission did not put me on the rolls . . . as an Indian but put me on the rolls as a freedman, so I selected forty acres of land as a freedman." Had his Indian ancestry been recognized, he would have received 160 acres.

Although all of the Five Civilized Tribes signed the 1866 treaties, some never did adopt the freedmen or extend political and civil rights to their former slaves. Neither the Choctaws nor the Chickasaws adopted freedmen as citizens, and the Cherokees extended treaty provisions only to freedmen who had resided in the Cherokee Nation prior to the war and who had remained there through 1866. Those who had fled the

war and returned later were disenfranchised. The Seminoles were the first to sign the 1866 treaty and to grant citizenship, voting rights, and positions on the tribal council to freedmen. Today the Seminole Nation is the sole tribe of the five to retain freedmen on its council, as stipulated in the most recent Seminole Constitution, amended in 1969.

For many black and Indian groups, their racial formation is reflective of their group identity. Even though their origin is complex and in many cases lost to historical evidence, there is a memory of what the sociologist Brewton Berry called "an unbroken thread which binds them to the past." For the Lumbees of North Carolina, names common to their group denote that past. For others, such as the Jackson Whites of New Jersey, their origin speaks of a shipload of British women, purchased to satisfy soldiers, who died and were replaced with African women. The women and children from those unions later removed themselves from main populations and intermarried with other displaced groups. Official records have obscured this history by means of arbitrary designations on census documents and by deliberate acts designed to marginalize and separate the groups.

The necessity to provide a historical context for relationships between blacks and Indians is only one part of an attempt to provide direction for a quest for identity and to build a healthy basis for future interactions between the two groups. For those who have shared ceremonies, language, customs, and marriage, the connections between them should be greater than their distances. Illuminating the history of black and Indian alliances provides the initial step toward a more comprehensive understanding of their separate and combined histories.

See also Intermarriage with Non-Indians.

Forbes, Jack D., *Africans and Native Americans: The Language of Race and the Evolution of Red-Black Peoples* (Urbana: University of Illinois Press, 1993); Littlefield, Daniel F., Jr., *Africans and Seminoles: From Removal to Emancipation* (Westport, Conn.: Greenwood Press, 1977); Root, Maria P. P., ed., *Racially Mixed People in America* (Newbury Park, Calif.: Sage Publications, 1992).

MELINDA MICCO (Seminole/Creek/Choctaw)
Mills College

AGRICULTURE

The agricultural history of Native Americans on the North American continent is the story of profound achievement prior to contact with European civiliza-

Sioux women and children guarding corn against blackbirds in August 1862.

tion; thereafter, it is a chronicle of decline and failure. Before the Christian era many Indian cultural groups of North America cultivated plants of Mesoamerican and indigenous origin. By A.D. 1000 corn (maize), beans, and squash were their most important cultivated food plants. Although other crops, such as cotton in the Southwest and wild rice in the Great Lakes region, remained important locally, the "three sisters" provided the nutritional base and chief source of subsistence and trade from agriculture until the twentieth century.

Native American farmers became skilled plant breeders. They carefully practiced the art of selection and adaptation to develop varieties for specific areas, such as corn that matured in sixty days near the Canadian border, where a cool, short growing season limited agriculture, as well as varieties for the hot, dry Southwest. Native American farmers also developed many varieties of beans and squash to meet local environ-mental conditions. Indian women were the primary agriculturists among most cultural groups, the peoples of the Southwest being an exception.

Indian farmers cultivated the rich, friable soils of the river valleys and flood plains, where wooden, stone, and bone hoes easily stirred the soil. In the uplands, grass-covered and heavy clay soils could not be tilled with these implements. East of the Mississippi River, Indian farmers girdled trees to help prepare the land for crops by eliminating unwanted shade. They used hoes and fire to remove brush. By burning weeds and the remains of the past season's crops they added potash, calcium, phosphorus, and magnesium to the soil, but they did not intentionally fertilize their croplands. A sharp-pointed digging or dibble stick served as the common tool for opening the soil to plant seeds. Some cultural groups such as the Mohawks soaked their seeds in a potion of hellebore to poison crows, while the Navajos sprinkled squash plants with a mixture of urine and goat's milk to protect against damage by chinch bugs and cockroaches. Indian farmers also picked insects and worms off plants with their fingers.

Native American farmers used a peg to help remove the husks from ears of corn, and some may have used shells to loosen the kernels from the cob. Women used a gathering stick, called a hoop, and a knife to harvest wild rice. They also used sticks, pestles, and mortars to thresh corn, beans, and other crops. Indian women used baskets to winnow the threshed corn and beans. In the North, Native American farmers also used baskets to store corn in their houses. Some cultural groups in the South stored their corn in roofed granaries to protect it from the weather and rodents. In the Midwest and West, many farming peoples dug storage pits, called caches, to preserve their corn, beans, and squash from spoilage and to protect their foodstuffs from thieves.

In the present-day eastern United States, Native Americans developed two forms of land tenure, one communal and the other individual. The village or cultural group claimed sovereignty over a particular area, and individual women controlled the use of specific fields. As long as a woman used a portion of land for agriculture, she had the continuing right of usage. If she stopped cultivating that land, however, either someone else would take the plot or it would revert to communal or village control. If the village moved, the headmen allotted new lands to the women in each lineage or family for cultivation. No fixed rules determined the size of a plot or the amount of land that an individual could claim. Each woman, sometimes aided by the men in the household, could clear as much land as she needed. While land could be inherited matrilineally, no one could claim absolute right to it. Land ultimately belonged to the village that owned or controlled it. In the Southwest, land-tenure customs differed from those of the East and Great Plains. There, individual males could own land and inherit it. Rights of communal and individual use were similar to eastern practices, although inherited land sometimes passed from father to son—that is, patrilineally—as among the Pimas, Papagos, and Yumas. Matrilineal inheritance and usage rights prevailed among the Pueblos, while the Navajos practiced shared use and inheritance customs.

Native Americans, then, recognized a group right to uncultivated land and individual rights to cultivated land. They did not believe that land could be bought or sold, because it did not belong to the present generation. Rather, Native Americans considered themselves trustees of the land for future generations. Because land belonged only temporarily to the generation inhabiting it, Native Americans could not accept the white man's concept of sale and absolute ownership. After European contact, Native Americans soon learned that land ownership for white farmers did not depend on use but rather on signed pieces of paper that could pass easily from person to person, the possession of which gave the holder exclusive right to the land described on it. This new cultural system of land ownership ultimately ended Native American agricultural practices east of the Mississippi River by the mid-nineteenth century.

European settlers on the eastern coast of North America learned to raise corn from the Indians, but no evidence exists that proves the Indians also taught them to fertilize with fish. At the same time that the Native Americans shared their agricultural traditions with the Europeans, they also adopted European agricultural practices, such as raising wheat and livestock, using the plow, and producing for a market economy.

When white settlers began to occupy lands in the trans-Mississippi West, the federal government adopted a reservation system to limit Indian land claims so that white agriculture could expand. Government officials and friends of the Indians believed that acculturation and assimilation could be achieved only when Native Americans learned to farm in the white tradition and own their own lands. This idea achieved partial fruition with the passage of the General Allotment Act in 1887, which provided for the allotment of Indian lands to individual Indian farmers. Few Native Americans, however, had access to the education, science, technology, or capital necessary to begin farming and achieve economic independence. Although federal agricultural policy was based on good intentions, it proved detrimental to the Indians. The allotment process enabled whites to gain control of Indian lands both legally and illegally. Between 1887 and 1934, the Indian land base declined by 90 million acres.

During the administration of Franklin Delano Roosevelt, John Collier became Commissioner of Indian Affairs. Collier supported the Indian Reorganization Act (1934), which ended the practice of allotting Indian lands, and he worked to improve the livestock and farming practices of Native Americans. Not all Indians, however, agreed with his policy, which required stock reductions to conserve the rangelands. Although Collier expanded the Indian land base, Congress failed to provide funds to establish the educational and credit programs necessary to support the development of Indian agriculture to the level of its white counterpart and thus to permit economic assimilation.

After World War II environmental limitations in the West, coupled with government policy designed to make Native Americans into small-scale subsistence farmers in the white tradition, prevented Indian agriculturists from becoming commercial farmers. Indian farmers continued to lack the scientific, technological, and financial resources to become independent agriculturists, and many Native Americans preferred to rent or sell their lands to white farmers in order to earn income. In 1950, Indian farmers averaged five hundred dollars in income annually, compared with twenty-five hundred dollars for white farmers. A decade later, less than 10 percent of Native Americans practiced agriculture, down from 45 percent in 1940. At the same time, approximately 70 percent of Native Americans lived in rural areas, although they composed less than 1 percent of the total population. Native Americans could not meet their subsistence needs by farming, and they had no possibility of competing with white agriculturalists on a commercial scale because of inadequate capital resources, technical skills, and managerial abilities. By the mid-1960s, each Indian who remained on the reservations earned an average of only $1,888 annually, while non-reservation Indians had annual incomes averaging $5,710. Federal agricultural policy had utterly failed to acculturate Native Americans and assimilate them into white culture and society. In addition, federal termination policy, designed to end tribal reliance on the federal government, further hindered the development of a strong agricultural base for Native Americans.

In the twentieth century, as white farmers began using western lands more intensively, they threatened Indian water rights, and the contest between Native Americans and whites over who owned and controlled the western waters became increasingly entangled in the courts. During the 1970s, white challenges to Indian water rights further threatened Native American agriculture. With water their most important natural resource, and with much of their land unsuitable for agriculture without it, water rights became the most significant issue related to Indian farming after 1970. Although Native Americans had used the courts to maintain their water rights since the Winters decision (1908), the federal judiciary has not yet quantified Indian water rights nor determined whether the government or the tribes reserved the water rights on reserva-

tions created by treaties. In the western United States urban demands for water have placed Native American water rights in jeopardy.

By the late twentieth century, Native Americans controlled 52 million acres of land, 42 million under tribal ownership and 10 million owned by individuals. Federal programs provided little aid specifically for Indian farmers, although Indian agriculturists could participate in a variety of programs offered by the Agricultural Stabilization and Conservation Service, the Commodity Credit Corporation, and the Farmers Home Administration. Yet Native American farmers had so little land under their control and so little capital that participation in federal agricultural programs proved impossible or impractical for most, because these programs were designed to aid commercial agriculturalists who operated on a relatively large scale.

By the early 1980s, the U.S. Census Bureau counted only 7,211 Native American farmers. Each of these agriculturalists usually cultivated or raised livestock on fewer than five hundred acres, a scale too small in the semi-arid and arid lands of the West to permit commercial production. Subsistence agriculture prevailed in the best circumstances, and most Native American farmers lived below the poverty level, earning less than ten thousand dollars annually from agriculture. Of these Indian farmers, only about two thousand operated as full-time farmers, and they averaged 50.4 years of age. By the 1987 census only 7,134 Native American farmers remained, and only 2,289 earned more than ten thousand dollars from the sale of agricultural commodities. The federal government stopped counting Indian farmers as a separate category for the 1992 agricultural census, because their number had become insignificant.

Although the Navajos and several other cultural groups were exceptions, by the late twentieth century most Native Americans did not have sufficient land or financial means to live independently as farmers. Federal Indian policy had failed to acculturate the Indians and assimilate them into white society by making them small-scale farmers. Although Native Americans had once been the most skilled agriculturists on the North American continent, their agricultural achievements lay in the past, and they had little hope for an agricultural future.

See also Food and Cuisine; Water Rights.

Hurt, R. Douglas, *Indian Agriculture in America: Prehistory to the Present* (Lawrence: University Press of Kansas, 1987); Will, George F., and George E. Hyde, *Corn among the Indians of the*

Upper Missouri (Lincoln: University of Nebraska Press, 1964); Wilson, Gilbert L., *Buffalo Bird Woman's Garden: Agriculture of the Hidatsa Indians* (St. Paul: Minnesota Historical Society Press, 1987).

R. DOUGLAS HURT
Iowa State University

AKIMEL O'ODHAM (PIMA)

The Akimel O'odhams (River People), formerly known as the Pimas, are some of the oldest residents of the American Southwest. Approximately 14,400 Piman-speaking people live in Arizona on the Salt River and Gila River Indian reservations just beyond the Phoenix city limits. The Akimel creation stories tell how the River People inherited the pre-Columbian culture of the Hohokams and developed agricultural villages along the perennial Gila and Salt Rivers. Spanish missionaries first contacted the Gila River people in the 1690s. Although never under Spanish rule, the Akimels demonstrated their business acumen in trade with the presidio at Tucson. They also cooperated with the Spanish against the Yavapai and Apaches.

In the early 1800s, the Akimels welcomed the migrating Maricopas into the Gila River valley. The two groups formed a strong defensive alliance, and today they still peacefully share the Gila River and Salt River reservations.

Travelers to the California goldfields described the Akimel villages as an oasis. The River People enjoyed a brisk business in selling food and animals to the forty-niners. With federal troops diverted elsewhere during the Civil War, the territorial government relied for protection on the River People under the Akimel leader Antonio Azul.

In 1859 the U.S. government established the Gila River Reservation but failed to protect the Akimels' water supply as settlers upstream diverted the Gila River. Even though most Akimels and Maricopas stayed on the Gila River, some moved to the Salt River, where a second reservation was established in 1879. During the second half of the nineteenth century the Akimels went from being prosperous farmers and businessmen to working as dependent laborers for Anglo-American settlers. The Presbyterian missionary Charles Cook stepped into this unstable situation, and by the turn of the century most Akimels had converted to the Protestant faith.

No longer self-supporting, the Akimels referred to the period from the 1870s through the early twentieth century as "the years of famine." The situation worsened in the late 1910s, when the Bureau of Indian Affairs allotted each tribal member only ten acres of irrigable land (when there was any water). In the 1930s, an overly paternalistic BIA superintendent inadvertently damaged the quality of the soil when he leveled the Akimels' farms in an effort to improve irrigation.

The situation improved only when the River People reasserted control over their future. As early as 1911 a tribal member, Kisto Morago, organized a "business committee" to investigate issues affecting the Akimels. The group successfully forced a reservation agent to resign. The Akimels' potential for self-rule increased with the organization of a tribal government in 1936 in accordance with the Indian Reorganization Act of 1934. Returning World War II veterans used the Akimel government to promote tribal enterprises that could take advantage of the nearby Phoenix market. Successful ventures include the Gila River Farms, Gila River Telecommunications, Firebird International Raceway, and two industrial parks that by 1977 had attracted sixteen firms; recently, the Gila River Casino has opened for business. To help preserve Akimel culture, the tribe established the Gila River Arts and Crafts Center. The tribal constitution was amended in 1962 to increase the Akimel government's responsiveness to the River People's wishes.

Problems still exist. A settlement in 1978 from the Indian Claims Commission was far from satisfactory, and the Akimel community is still negotiating the return of an adequate water supply. Urban problems are also encroaching on the reservation. Nevertheless, the River People's prospects have improved now that the community is united in its desire to control its future.

See also Tohono O'odham (Papago).

Dobyns, Henry F., *The Pima-Maricopa* (New York: Chelsea House Publishers, 1989); Russell, Frank, *The Pima Indians* (1904; reprint, Tucson: University of Arizona Press, 1975); Webb, George, *A Pima Remembers* (Tucson: University of Arizona Press, 1959).

PETER MACMILLAN BOOTH
Purdue University

AKWESASNE

A Mohawk community straddling the New York–Ontario border, Akwesasne is called the St. Regis

Reservation by some non-Indians. The community of Akwesasne, whose name means "Land Where the Partridge Drums," was established in 1755 near the site of a Jesuit mission at the confluence of the St. Lawrence, St. Regis, Raquette, Grass, and Salmon Rivers. It is the only American Indian reservation with lands in both the United States and Canada. As a result, sovereignty issues involving Akwesasne have at times been particularly problematic, causing the Akwesasne community to maintain two separate councils for dealing with the U.S. and Canadian governments.

As part of the Iroquois League, the people of Akwesasne have continually asserted their sovereignty. For example, in 1917, when the United States declared war on Germany, the Iroquois Council also declared war as one of the allied nations. Somewhat surprisingly, the most direct assault on the community's life and prerogatives did not appear until the 1950s. During that decade the construction of the St. Lawrence Seaway — which diverted the course of the St. Lawrence River to allow large ships to sail farther inland — industrialized the area surrounding Akwesasne and created horrific environmental pollution. This degradation destroyed the fishing and dairy industries of Akwesasne and hence dramatically undermined the self-sufficiency of the Akwesasne Mohawks. In addition, toxic levels of polychlorinated biphenyls (PCBs), mercury, and other pollutants have undermined the health and safety of Akwesasne residents. Further, by the 1970s the legal fight against industrial polluters had nearly bankrupted the Mohawk Council of Akwesasne.

Its tradition of asserting sovereignty across the international boundary, together with its struggle against pollution and economic exploitation, has often propelled Akwesasne to the forefront of Indian activism. For example, after the construction of the Cornwall-Massena International Bridge at Akwesasne as part of the St. Lawrence Seaway project, the Canadian government attempted to extract customs duties and tolls from Akwesasne residents using the bridge. In 1968, Akwesasne people, supported by the Indian Defense League of America, blockaded the bridge to protest these restrictions, and in February 1969 the Canadian government agreed to duty-free status for Akwesasne's residents.

The bridge blockade led to the founding of the monthly newspaper *Akwesasne Notes,* a journal that often employed the rhetoric of 1960s activism to press for the resolution of long-standing disagreements between the various Indian nations and the U.S. and Canadian governments. Its editors supported the occupation of Alcatraz in 1969, the Trail of Broken Treaties in 1972, and the occupation of Wounded Knee in 1973. It also published several important documents, including *Basic Call to Consciousness,* a presentation made by Iroquois elders to the United Nations in 1977, and *Wounded Knee: In the Voice of the Participants.* The editor of *Akwesasne Notes,* Doug George, has also been a leading opponent of the construction of a high-stakes gambling casino at Akwesasne since the 1980s.

See also Mohawk.

ALABAMA-COUSHATTA

In the beginning the People lived in a great underground cavern. One day they came to the surface and found a large tree standing at the cave's entrance. As they exited, the stream of people divided. Those going to one side became the Alabamas; those to the other, the Coushattas. (The Coushatta people speak Koasati, and frequently refer to themselves as Koasatis; however, their official name is Coushatta.)

Of Muskogean stock and members of the Upper Creek Confederacy, the Alabamas and Coushattas have intertwined histories. Their languages are mutually intelligible, and there has been frequent intermarriage. Inhabiting the hospitable southeastern woodlands, they enjoyed a high standard of living. In 1541, when they first encountered Europeans, they resided in adjacent areas of what is today Alabama. In the early eighteenth century congenial relations were established with French traders, leading in 1714 to the construction of Fort Toulouse.

In 1763 the British assumed control of the former French territories, and with encouragement from the French, the Alabamas and Coushattas began migrating west. They crossed the Sabine River into East Texas in 1780. The Alabamas established towns on the Angelina and Neches Rivers, and the Coushattas settled along the Trinity River. In 1809 they had a combined population of approximately 1,650.

Although both tribes remained neutral in the 1836 settlers' rebellion against Mexico, they fed Anglo refugees who passed through their towns. In gratitude, the Republic of Texas Congress granted four leagues of land to the two tribes in 1840, but title was never issued because the land had already been claimed by Euro-Texans. In 1854 the state of Texas purchased 1,110.7 acres for an Alabama reservation, and approximately five hundred tribal members moved onto the land. The Coushattas joined the Alabamas there in 1858.

After playing a minor role with the Confederacy during the Civil War, the two tribes were increasingly forgotten in the decade of the 1870s. This trend culminated in 1878 with the abolition of the state Indian agent post. The economic situation improved significantly in 1881 with the construction of the Houston-Shreveport railroad, providing employment in logging and saw-milling industries, but the tribe was largely invisible to outsiders. Alabama and Coushatta volunteers during World War I were barred from serving because they were Native Americans.

In 1928 the federal government purchased an additional 3,071 acres for the tribes' reservation, bringing the total to 4,181.7 acres. A charter for the newly incorporated Alabama-Coushatta Indian Tribe of Texas was ratified on October 17, 1939. In 1954 the federal government relinquished trusteeship of the reservation, and that responsibility was assumed by the state. Federal recognition was restored on August 18, 1987. Today the reservation is home for approximately six hundred Alabama-Coushattas.

The tribes are organized in a matriarchal system of twelve clans; elders are consulted on important issues, and they participate in formal activities such as the inauguration of a new chief. Although the traditional stomp dance is no longer celebrated, other cultural expressions such as pine-needle basket weaving are maintained. Powwows became regular events in the 1960s and continue to be held monthly. The annual powwow in June attracts participants from across the country. Alabama-Coushatta dancers have toured widely, traveling as far as Australia and Egypt. Other cultural expressions are being increasingly pursued. In 1993 the tribe won a federal court case allowing children to wear long hair in their school as an act of religious expression. This victory was the result of a combined effort on the part of youth, parents, the tribal council, and elders.

Martin, Howard N., "Polk County Indians: Alabamas, Coushattas, Pakana Muskogees," *East Texas Historical Journal* 17, no. 1 (1979): 3–23.

JONATHAN B. HOOK (Cherokee)
Houston, Texas

ALASKA
See Indian-White Relations in Alaska.

ALCATRAZ, OCCUPATION OF

In 1964 six Lakota men occupied the former federal prison on Alcatraz Island in San Francisco Bay. They claimed that under the terms of the 1868 Fort Laramie Treaty between the Sioux and the United States, an abandoned federal facility must revert back to Indian ownership. The federal government and the media treated the occupation as a joke, but the event set the precedent for a later occupation that began in 1969 and lasted nineteen months. This second occupation made headlines throughout the world. The 1969 campaign was planned in response to the Indian Office's efforts to relocate Indians to cities, as well as to protest poor reservation conditions. The occupiers, led by Adam Fortunate Eagle, the leader of the Bay Area United Council, and Richard Oakes, an Indian student at San Francisco State University, drew up a "Proclamation for the Indians of All Tribes" that offered to pay "twenty four dollars ($24) in glass beads and red

A famous November 1969 photo of some of the American Indians who occupied Alcatraz for nineteen months.

cloth" for the island, a reference to the seventeenth-century purchase of Manhattan. Their goal was to establish an educational and cultural center in the abandoned prison.

Proclamation in hand, seventy-eight Native Americans arrived on Alcatraz in the early morning of November 20, 1969. During the first few months of the occupation, Alcatraz was a rallying point for Native Americans from both urban areas and reservations. Island residents performed ceremonial dances, taught their children traditional art forms, and created a safe atmosphere for sharing cultural ideas. Despite this spirit, however, constant food and water shortages hampered the occupiers' ability to function. Dissension between the island residents and activists on the mainland further undermined efforts to sustain the group's sense of purpose.

Alcatraz remained Indian land until twenty armed federal marshals forcibly removed the fifteen remaining inhabitants on June 11, 1971. Although their original goals were not realized, the occupiers, representing numerous tribes, successfully brought Native American issues to the forefront of American politics during a highly volatile time in American history.

ALCOHOL AND INDIANS

Indians in eastern North America possessed no alcohol at the beginning of the colonial period. By 1800, so much alcohol flowed through the Indian villages east of the Mississippi that each community was forced to a decision: would its members drink, or would they abstain? No other European-produced commodity created the difficulties among Indians that alcohol, particularly rum and brandy, caused throughout the East. What is more, when the descendants of the colonists moved westward, they brought liquor, and its often tragic consequences, along with them.

There were, to be sure, Indians who produced and consumed alcohol long before Europeans brought beer, rum, and brandy to the Western Hemisphere. In the Southwest and throughout Central America, Indians fermented local plants to produce alcohol. But no such customs existed in eastern North America when the earliest recorded instances of drinking among Indians occurred during the sixteenth century. No substantial trade in alcohol had yet arisen; Europeans still provided wine only to select Indians. The few Indians who drank, according to observers, did so to the point of intoxication, an experience they apparently enjoyed; one European writer noted that the Indians came back for more. But not all Indians wanted alcohol or the experience it brought. Pierre Pastedechouen, a Montagnais, told Jesuits in the early 1630s that Indians had earlier believed that French explorers "were dressed in iron, ate bones, and drank blood." It is impossible to know how many Indians shared the revulsion that some felt against wine.

In British North America, the alcohol trade began in earnest after 1650, or about one to two generations after the establishment of permanent settlements by the English along the Atlantic Coast. The trade started then because colonists in the West Indies recognized the profits that could be made from transforming sugar into rum. After 1650, distillers in the Caribbean and on the mainland began to produce increasing quantities of rum. Enterprising colonists, many of them town dwellers who otherwise had limited contact with Indians, began to sell rum to Indians. By the beginning of the eighteenth century, more or less full-time traders began to transport liquor farther into the hinterland of colonial settlements. These colonists were responsible for hauling liquor to many Indian communities and to colonial trading posts, where Indians came to purchase it. With the expansion of white settlement westward during the nineteenth century, descendants of Europeans came to dominate the liquor trade even in regions where Indians had a tradition of fermenting local beverages.

Though it is often impossible to determine why Indians chose to drink, surviving evidence provides compelling clues. In the first place, Indian communities in early America had suffered a series of destabilizing shocks long before the liquor trade began. Epidemic diseases had decimated their communities, and colonists quickly tried to gain their lands, a process that at times became violent. These crises preceded the liquor trade, and quite possibly made Indians more inclined to drink. If Indians chose to drink out of frustration and despair, they were not alone; as social scientists have made clear, whenever Western societies undergo periods of rapid transition, rates of drinking increase. Perhaps many Indians chose to drink because they welcomed the respite from the disorienting forces that constantly besieged their world. Documentary evidence also suggests that some Indians enjoyed the heightened sense of power that seemed to accompany drunkenness.

A nineteenth-century engraving depicting a settler plying an Indian with drink.

Yet many Indians in eastern North America also welcomed the sensations of drunkenness for other reasons, and even felt it necessary to share these feelings with others. Some believed—as did Indians in the Southwest and Mexico—that the disorientations of intoxication had sacred dimensions. Some Indians in the Great Lakes region, for example, integrated alcohol into their existing ceremonies, notably mourning rituals. Other groups recognized the importance of alcohol by including it in hospitality rituals. This is exactly what Powhatan did when, after encountering some colonists in the 1610s, he pulled out a valued bottle of sack and doled out precise amounts to his visitors. Widely divergent groups—including the Montagnais in the St. Lawrence Valley, the Passamaquoddies in Maine, and the Teton Sioux—thought alcohol possessed spiritual power or came from supernatural forces.

Recognizing alcohol's power did not mean liking its taste. Some Indians complained about the taste of alcohol, and, as one colonist wrote in 1697, "they wonder much of the English for purchasing wine at so dear a rate when Rum is much cheaper & will make them sooner drunk." For Indians in seventeenth- and eighteenth-century America, the primary reason to drink was to get drunk. On occasion groups of Indians who did not possess enough alcohol to get everyone drunk gave their liquor to a few individuals to ensure that at least some would become intoxicated.

However welcome drunkenness was to some, almost all observers recognized that intoxication was dangerous. As soon as the liquor trade began in earnest, Indians throughout the eastern woodlands knew that such commerce could destroy their communities. Time and again, according to countless Indians who bore witness to drinking parties, members of Indian communities drank to the point of intoxication and then proceeded to act violently. Surviving records reveal that Indians killed one another when inebriated and wounded each other in drunken melees. Families also suffered, especially when young men sold the furs and skins from the hunt for alcohol, thereby impoverishing their relatives, who needed food and durable goods. Domestic violence, accidental falls into fires or off cliffs, and bouts of exposure when the inebriated passed out in cold weather all contributed to the suffering of Indian communities.

Given the varied ravages associated with alcohol, it was not surprising that Indians from throughout the eastern woodlands approached colonial officials to protest the trade. The officials, almost always wanting to maintain good relations with nearby Indians, made efforts to prevent traffic in alcohol. Virtually every colony outlawed the commerce at one point or another, although the laws were often short-lived. But the lack of any effective constabulary force limited colonists' attempts at preventing the trade, a fact that traders knew well when they transported their wares to remote Indian villages. Even some Indians became carriers of alcohol, often transporting it long distances to remote villages.

The success of the trade depended, of course, on the desire of Indians to drink. If community leaders, men and women, could have convinced the young men who drank most often to quit, the trade could have been eliminated. Some groups managed to ban it from their towns, threatening to destroy any casks of rum that traders brought. But in spite of the horrors associated with liquor, prohibition never occurred in any widespread, organized form. From the time the trade began until the present, Indians from a wide variety of villages and cultural backgrounds have chosen to drink. For liquor sellers, the profits on the trade were always worth any risks. And the trade was profitable, especially when traders added water to the alcohol before selling it. From the colonial period into the twentieth century, there has never been a shortage of people willing to engage in the traffic even when it was illegal.

Ever since the colonial period, efforts by Indians and whites to stop the trade have failed. President Thomas Jefferson, recognizing that federal laws could prevent the trade only in federal territory, asked territorial and state governors to ban the commerce in 1808, but his efforts made little difference to the trade. Various acts by the federal government throughout the nineteenth century and into the twentieth also failed to stop the

liquor trade. Even when government officials succeeded in banning alcohol on reservations, their reports noted that local Indians traveled beyond the limits of the reservation to purchase alcohol and that some of these western Indians, like Indians in the colonial period, brought alcohol back to their communities to resell it. In 1953, during the age of termination, the federal government removed the surviving prohibitions on Indian drinking; thereafter reservation governments possessed the power to ban sales in their communities.

Tribal governments also often failed to stop drinking in territory under their jurisdiction. The availability of alcohol on reservations remains a source of controversy today. Yet even though many communities realize its dangers, the commerce in alcohol continues. The three centuries or so of the alcohol trade suggest only one scenario: if Indians want liquor, then someone will be willing to sell it to them even if such sales are illegal or dangerous.

See also Alcoholism, Indian.

MacAndrew, Craig, and Robert B. Edgerton, *Drunken Comportment: A Social Explanation* (Chicago: Aldine, 1969); Mancall, Peter C., "'The Bewitching Tyranny of Custom': The Social Costs of Indian Drinking in Colonial America," *American Indian Culture and Research Journal* 17, no. 2 (1993): 15–42; Waddell, Jack O., and Michael W. Everett, eds., *Drinking Behavior among Southwestern Indians: An Anthropological Perspective* (Tucson: University of Arizona Press, 1980).

PETER C. MANCALL
University of Kansas

ALCOHOLISM, INDIAN

The "drunken Indian" has been a subject of continuing concern in the United States from the earliest contacts between Europeans and Indians down to the present day. Popular notions about the nature of alcohol and excessive drinking, however, have changed radically over the years. During the seventeenth and eighteenth centuries it was thought that the "savage" nature of Indians was expressed without inhibitions under the effects of alcohol. From the nineteenth century until the present, the idea that Indians are physiologically unable to handle alcohol as well as white Americans has become increasingly popular and is, indeed, a belief subscribed to by many Indians themselves. On the other hand, most contemporary studies of American Indians attribute deviant behaviors such as alcohol abuse to social disorganization and the stress of acculturation. A number of deprivations, including confinement to reservations and federal wardship, are cited as causes for many Indians to feel inadequate. Alcohol, according to this view, has been the easiest and quickest way to deaden the senses and to forget the feeling of inadequacy.

With few exceptions, the Indians of America north of Mexico had no knowledge of alcohol prior to contact with Europeans. In consequence, the drinking behaviors observed since the nineteenth century can be traced directly to the contact situation. In the Southwest, the Akimel O'odham (Pima), Papago (Tohono O'odham), and River Yuman peoples did make wine from the saguaro cactus as well as from the agave and mesquite. However, the alcoholic content of these beverages was quite low—between 3 and 4 percent—and their nutritional value was significant. Agave wine, for example, was rich in sucrose and vitamins B_1 and C. It was also an important source of comparatively safe liquid in areas where drinking water was scarce or contaminated. In the east, the Cherokees and Catawbas made a wine from persimmons.

The Pimas and Papagos made large quantities of saguaro wine in July, following the harvest of the first crops. During a saguaro ceremony all adults drank copiously, believing that, as humans saturated themselves with the wine, so the earth would be saturated with rain. Informal and secular use of alcohol appears to have been relatively infrequent so that, prior to the coming of the Europeans, none of the tribes of America (north of Rio Grande) had a well developed "drinking ethic" to prepare them for the advent of beverages with high alcoholic content.

It is difficult for the contemporary reader to fully appreciate the drinking practices in the United States during the nineteenth century. We are apt to compare descriptions of early drinking by Indians or frontiersmen with the more familiar drinking habits of the urbanized, largely middle-class society of the late twentieth century. The consumption of alcohol in nineteenth-century America, however, was unlike anything twentieth-century Americans are likely to experience in their own lives. Between 1790 and 1840, Americans drank more alcoholic beverages—nearly half a pint of hard liquor per adult male each day—than at any other time in our history. The most popular beverages were cider and whiskey. Water was usually of poor quality, milk was scarce and unsafe, and coffee, tea, and wine were imported and expensive.

When the frontier moved west of the Appalachians, settlers were cut off from the East and were forced to develop their own markets. Land transportation was too expensive for the bountiful corn crops to be hauled over the mountains. Whiskey was widely produced because it was easily preserved and traded, and it soon became the medium of exchange on the frontier.

During the colonial period there were already two distinct styles of drinking distilled spirits. Many Americans took small amounts of alcohol daily, either alone or with the family at home. "Drams" were taken upon rising, with meals, during midday breaks, and at bedtime. Ingesting frequent but small doses develops a tolerance to the effects of alcohol, and this style of drinking did not generally lead to intoxication. The other style of drinking was the communal binge, a form of public drinking to intoxication, and practically any gathering of three or more men provided an occasion for drinking vast quantities of liquor.

Although consumption declined for the nation as a whole during the latter half of the nineteenth century, binge drinking spread to the western frontier and became an integral part of the periodic gambling, fighting, and whoring sprees engaged in by trappers, miners, soldiers, and cowboys. Thus, western Indians had as tutors some of the heaviest drinkers in the nation at the time of their most disruptive contacts with Anglo-Americans. And Anglo-Americans, for a variety of reasons, encouraged this style of drinking among the western Indians. Fur companies, for example, preferred to pay trappers, white as well as Indian, with liquor rather than money so that they would drink up their profits and be forced to trap the next year. Not only did the Indians learn the binge style of drinking from observing those who introduced liquor to them, they also found the white man's notion that a man was not responsible for actions committed while intoxicated consonant with their own notions of possession by supernatural agents. Supernatural power was obtained in dreams or induced trance states that resembled the intoxicated state. Over the years the nation became increasingly urbanized, and drinking styles changed radically after national prohibition. Drinking on Indian reservations, however, continued largely unchanged due to their relative isolation from the larger society.

Today we are told that Indians and Alaska Natives die from "alcoholism" at almost five times the overall rate for the nation. Such statistics not only give cause for concern but also shape how the problem of Indian drinking is perceived. Moreover, the manner in which the data on Indian drinking is presented reflects our assumptions about the nature of alcohol as well as our image of the American Indian and of ourselves as a people. Because many believe that homicide, suicide, and accidents are strongly associated with alcohol, deaths from these "related" causes are often lumped together with deaths directly the result of drinking, such as alcoholic cirrhosis. But whether this image and our concern are directly related to an objective assessment of the Indians' use of alcohol or to more subtle involvements between whites and Indians is difficult to say.

The populations of most Indian tribes are so small that the relatively small number of occurrences of deaths from alcoholic cirrhosis or suicide will vary widely from year to year. The need to avoid bias caused by these fluctuations and to use population denominators of sufficient size to obtain statistically meaningful results leads most investigators to aggregate data for "all Indians" or Indians of a particular administrative region and to compare them to national averages. These practices, however, obscure the considerable differences in culture, environment, and interethnic relations among the many Indian groups. Obscured also are the considerable differences in mortality rates among regions of the nation as well as rural and urban non-Indian populations.

Today the southern states along with those of the Rocky Mountain West have relatively high rates of death from what have come to be thought of as alcohol-related causes, a circumstance often attributed to our frontier heritage. During the 1980s, for example, the average annual age-adjusted mortality rate from "selected alcohol-related causes" for twenty-one northern states was forty-five deaths per 100,000 population. By contrast the eight mountain states averaged sixty-six deaths, a rate nearly 50 percent higher.

In general, urban areas have lower mortality rates from alcohol-related causes than do rural areas, and regional differences are even greater in rural areas because of the persistence of older cultural factors as well as certain environmental variables. When rural areas of the northern and southern mountain region are compared, the northern tier has considerably lower mortality rates than the southern. For example, in 1987 and 1988 the rural populations of the northern mountain states had an annual death rate from alcoholic cirrhosis of 11.6 per 100,000 population—slightly above the national average of 10.6—compared to the southern states of Arizona and New Mexico with an average rate of 25 and Nevada with 43.8.

Western Indians live almost entirely in rural areas and may be expected to have death rates from alcohol-related causes more in line with those of the rural populations of the states in which they live. This is in fact the case for the Navajo tribe, which is the largest single tribe in the nation. When death rates for cirrhosis, suicide, homicide, and accidents among rural Navajos and Anglos in Arizona were compared, they were found to be virtually the same with the exception of deaths from accidents. There is also evidence to suggest that the proportions of these deaths due to alcohol abuse are virtually the same in the two groups. The higher rate of deaths due to accidents is due to environmental differences rather than to a higher proportion of alcohol-related accidents.

Tribal differences continue to be large, however, and the situation found among the Navajos cannot be generalized to all tribes. The Pueblos of New Mexico, for example, seem to have lower rates of alcohol-related deaths than do rural Anglos, while the tribes of the northern plains appear to have rates higher than those of their non-Indian neighbors.

Statistical data on drinking patterns often fail to reflect the distinctive nature of Indian society. The Indian style of binge drinking would be considered alcoholic by most measures used in studies of the subject. Withdrawal symptoms, generally thought to be a certain sign of physiological addiction, were reported by over 50 percent of drinkers in one study of 67 Navajo men and 45 women conducted from 1966 through 1990. Yet most of these drinkers became abstinent by the time they were thirty-five or forty years of age, a circumstance one would not expect if they had been addicted to alcohol. It seems likely that much of the explanation involves the characteristic style of drinking that takes place in Indian communities. The reservation style of drinking among the Navajos, for example, fosters sudden withdrawal. After ingesting large mounts of alcohol at one time, drinkers most frequently pass out or find their supply exhausted. Especially on reservations, there are no easily available supplies to help a drinker taper off. In towns bordering the reservation, drinkers may get arrested or wake up after drinking with no money. Social and legal prohibitions against drinking, the absence of a ready supply, and the fact that Indians who drink in public or in bars in off-reservation border towns are often arrested all foster sudden withdrawal and, in consequence, a high incidence of hallucinatory experiences.

Alcohol use and abuse is a heterogeneous phenomenon both among and within various tribes, and no global explanation, either racial or social, appears to account for it. As the number of Indian deaths from infectious diseases has decreased over the past thirty years, the Indian Health Service and Indian communities themselves are turning their attention more to the chronic disorders associated with aging as well as to such social pathologies as alcohol abuse. It is to be hoped that this will lead to a better understanding of the phenomenon and ultimately to more effective prevention and treatment programs.

See also Alcohol and Indians.

Kunitz, Stephen J., and Jerrold E. Levy, *Drinking Careers: A 25 Year Study of Three Navajo Populations* (New Haven: Yale University Press, 1994); MacAndrew, Craig, and Robert B. Edgerton, *Drunken Comportment: A Social Explanation* (Chicago: Aldine, 1969); Rorabaugh, W. J., *The Alcoholic Republic: An American Tradition* (New York: Oxford University Press, 1979).

JERROLD E. LEVY
University of Arizona

ALEUT

Scholars typically describe the indigenous groups of Alaska as Indians, Eskimos, and Aleuts. Most people are aware that the term *Indian* would never have been used to describe the indigenous peoples of the Americas if Columbus hadn't been a half a world off in his calculations, and many people are aware that the term *Eskimo* would not be in use if the first Europeans to come in contact with the indigenous peoples of the North American Arctic had not mispronounced the word *assime·w,* which the Algonquian Indians used to describe their neighbors to the north. But few seem aware that the name *Aleut* also came from external sources.

Aleut is the term usually used to describe the people of the Aleutian Islands on one hand, and the people of Kodiak Island, the lower Alaska and Kenai Peninsulas, and Prince William Sound on the other. While there are considerable similarities between these two groups of indigenous peoples, they represent separate cultures, with different languages. At the time of contact, they were traditional enemies as well as trading partners. Their principal similarity lies in the fact that they are both primarily coastal peoples who have always relied on the sea to provide their food.

In the 1740s, when the first Russian hunters and fur traders came to the Aleutian Islands, they assumed that the people living there were Aliutors—a coastal indigenous group they had previously encountered on the Kamchatka Peninsula. Ironically, the name *Aliutor* had been applied to this coastal group by another Kamchatkan group, the interior-residing Chavchuvs. According to modern researchers, the Aliutors were unlike the Chavchuvs; they lived in semi-subterranean sod houses, ate raw fish, and hunted small whales from skin boats. Their subsistence pattern was characteristic not only of coastal people in Kamchatka, but also of people from places as nearby as Attu and as distant as Prince William Sound. As the Russians left the Kamchatkan coast and moved out into the North Pacific, they continued to come across people who lived like the Aliutors, and they began to refer to all such sea-mammal-hunting peoples as *Aliut.*

The first people the Russians encountered as they moved eastward were the residents of the Near Islands, who called themselves *Sasignan.* These people were part of the larger group that resided from there to Port Mollar on the Alaska Peninsula and who did, and still do, call themselves *Unangan* (singular *Unangax*). There are several subgroups of the Unangan. Moving eastward from the home of the *Sasignan* are the *Qax̂un, Naahmiĝus, Niiĝuĝis, Akuuĝun, Qawalangin, Qigiiĝun,* and *Qagaan Tayaĝungin.* While the most common self-designation by the Aleutian Island people today may be *Aleut,* the name *Unangan* is well known, and some believe it should return as the name of preference.

As the Russians, together with their Unangax̂ guides, moved to the east from the Aleutian Islands, they encountered the people the Unangan called *Kanaaĝin.* Apparently the Russians transcribed the initial short a sound of this word as an unaccented Russian o. (Unaccented o and short a sound very much alike in Russian.) When Americans picked up the term from the Russians, they retained the Russian o, although Russian o and English o are very different sounds. Thus, the Unangax̂ word *Kanaaĝin* was modified to *Koniag.* The Russians, however, continued to refer to both groups as Aleuts. The people called *Kanaaĝin* by the *Unangan* called themselves *Sugpiat,* meaning "the real people" (the singular, *Sugpiaq,* means "a real person"). They in turn referred to the Unangan as *Tayaut.*

The Sugpiat are closely related linguistically to all the peoples of the coastal areas to the north, including the Yupiks of western Alaska and eastern Siberia, the Inupiat (singular *Inupiaq*) of Arctic Alaska, and the Inuits of Arctic Canada and Greenland. They are divided into regional subgroups, with these groups being further divided by groups at the village level. The village name is used followed by *miut,* which means "people who live at or belong to a particular location."

The Unangan and the Sugpiat both resisted the initial Russian invasion, but superior weaponry and the Russian practice of taking hostages brought both peoples under Russian rule, where they remained for nearly a century. During that time their numbers were drastically reduced by previously unknown diseases, and their cultures underwent significant changes as they adopted many Russian customs. Then, in 1867, the occupation rights to Alaska were purchased by the United States, and a new acculturation process began. To this day, however, the Russian influence is very noticeable in Unangax and Sugpiaq villages. The most conspicuous evidence of this influence is the omnipresence of the Russian Orthodox Church, which is the center of the social life in each community.

"Big Mike" Hodikoff, chief of the Aleut tribe in Atta, Alaska, photographed with his family in front of their house in 1934.

During the twentieth century these coastal groups came into contact with a new group of people, anthropologists. The newcomers recognized that while both groups now called themselves Aleuts, they were different from each other in many ways—including language. The anthropologists decided that the people of the Aleutian Islands were the *real* Aleuts, while the people of Kodiak Island and Prince William Sound were actually Eskimos. The anthropological literature began referring to the second group with such terms as *Pacific Eskimos* and *Pacific Yupiks*. This practice caused a strained relationship between many Sugpiat and anthropologists, since the Sugpiat had never identified themselves as Eskimo and did not care to begin doing so. It was then that the term *Alutiiq*, while apparently used sparingly in the past, became preferred for self-designation. *Alutiiq* (plural *Alutiit*) is simply the word *Aleut* in Sugcestun, the language of the Sugpiat. There are now those, however, who would prefer to return to using the term *Sugpiaq*. Nina Olsen, who grew up in Afognak village near Kodiak Island in the 1920s and 1930s, said, "When I was growing up in Afognak, I don't remember that we used the terms *Aleut* or *Alutiiq* to describe ourselves. We said *Sugpiaq*. Sugpiaq—'a real person.' I think we should go back to calling ourselves Sugpiaq. It has so much more meaning."

A defining event in the recent history of the Unangan and the Sugpiat, as it was for other Alaska indigenous groups, was the passage of the Alaska Native Claims Settlement Act in 1971. The new law established an additional identity for these groups when they became shareholders in regional corporations established to manage community land and resources. The corporations created for the Unangan and Sugpiat are the Aleut Corporation, for the Aleutian Islands region; Koniag, Inc., for the Kodiak Island area; Chugach Alaska Corporation, for Prince William Sound and the lower Kenai Peninsula; and the Bristol Bay Native Corporation, which, while serving a predominantly Yupik population, also works with four Sugpiaq villages on the Alaska Peninsula. Each of these geographical areas also has its own not-for-profit corporation that provides health, social, and political-advocacy services to the people. Those corporation are, respectively, the Aleutian/Pribilof Islands Association; the Kodiak Area Native Association; Chugachmiut, Inc.; and the Bristol Bay Native Association. Each Unangax and Sugpiaq village is governed by a tribal council, and each has the political status of "Indian tribe" and maintains a special relationship with the federal government.

Both the Unangan and the Sugpiat have conscious efforts under way to revitalize their cultures. Particular emphasis has been placed on language preservation. In spring 1994 construction was begun on a native museum and cultural center in Kodiak, and one is in the planning stages for Unalaska, in the Aleutians. Both groups hope that these efforts will result in the development and maintenance of strong ethnic and cultural identities that will make it clear to local residents and outsiders alike that the term *Aleut* cannot describe the region's varied people or their traditions.

See also Eskimo (Yupik/Inupiat/Inuit); Indian-White Relations in Alaska.

Bergsland, Knut, and Moses L. Dirks, eds., *Unangam ungiikangin kayux tunusangin-unangam uniikangis ama tunuzangis: Aleut Tales and Narratives* (Fairbanks: Alaska Native Language Center, University of Alaska at Fairbanks, 1990); Fitzhugh, William W., and Aron Crowell, eds., *Crossroads of Continents: Cultures of Alaska and Siberia* (Washington: Smithsonian Institution, 1988).

GORDON L. PULLAR (Kodiak Island Alutiiq [Sugpiaq])
University of Alaska at Fairbanks

ALGONQUIAN LANGUAGES

The Algonquian linguistic family encompasses those languages spoken aboriginally and currently in regions stretching from the plains to the eastern seaboard, as far south as present-day North Carolina and as far north as the Canadian Subarctic. Two languages spoken in California, Wiyot and Yurok, have distant linkages to Algonquian as well.

Linguists generally divide Algonquian languages into three regional groupings: the Plains Algonquian languages, which include Blackfoot, Cheyenne, and Arapaho-Atsina-Nawathinehena; the Central languages, which comprise Cree-Montagnais-Naskapi, Ojibwa, Potawatomi, Menominee, Sauk-Fox-Kickapoo, Miami-Illinois, and Shawnee; and the Eastern languages, which include Micmac, Maliseet, Passamaquoddy, Etchemin, Eastern Abenaki (of which the modern representative is Penobscot), Western Abenaki (sometimes called St. Francis), Loup A and Loup B, Massachusett (less accurately called Natick), Narragansett, Mohegan-Pequot, Montauk, Quiripi, Unquachog, Mahican, Munsee, Unami, Nanticoke, Powhatan, and Carolina Algonquian. Most Algonquian languages are or were represented by two or more dialect variants as well. Historically, speakers of one Algonquian language were often fluent in one or more additional languages. Many Menominee speakers, for example, have spoken (or do speak) Ojibwa.

Of the more than thirty languages within this family recorded since the seventeenth century, only Arapaho, Blackfoot, Cheyenne, Cree-Montagnais-Naskapi, Ojibwa, Potawatomi, Menominee, Sauk-Fox-Kickapoo, Maliseet-Passamaquoddy, and Micmac currently have significant numbers of speakers, and many of these are elderly. The majority of extinct Algonquian languages were spoken in the Northeast and along the Atlantic seaboard.

Techniques of historical linguistics suggest that the parent language of the Algonquian linguistic family, known as Proto-Algonquian, came to be spoken between three thousand and twenty-five hundred years ago. Reconstructed Proto-Algonquian terms for various animals and plants indicate a homeland for that language in the region between Georgian Bay and Lake Ontario. Other evidence suggests that relatively soon after the emergence of Proto-Algonquian in this area, its speakers fragmented into ten increasingly differentiated speech communities corresponding to the three Plains Algonquian languages and the six (later seven, when Potawatomi and Ojibwa separated) Central languages, as well as into an eastern community, speaking a language known as Proto–Eastern Algonquian. Isolated from the Central languages by the intervening Iroquoian language–speaking peoples of the Saint Lawrence drainage and what is now New York and western Pennsylvania, speakers of Proto–Eastern Algonquian ultimately split into the twenty or more distinct speech communities whose languages make (or made) up the Eastern Algonquian subgroup.

Although differing from one another in numerous ways, all Algonquian languages share basic patterns of inflection. Algonquian words were once described by the linguist Edward Sapir as resembling "tiny imagist poems." Sapir's analogy aptly captures the remarkable flexibility and specificity made possible by Algonquian morphological and syntactic structures. Algonquian languages mark grammatical categories of gender based not on biological sex, but rather on a distinction roughly corresponding to that in nature between living and nonliving entities—categories labeled *inanimate* and *animate* by linguists. Animate nouns include persons, animals, spirits, large trees, some fruits, some body parts, feathers, and tails, as well as pipes, snowshoes, and kettles. The assignment of nouns to animate and inanimate categories is not entirely transparent, however. For example, Munsee *lehlokíhlas,* "raspberry," is animate, while *wtéhim,* "strawberry," is inanimate.

Algonquian languages, like English, also mark number (singular and plural) and person (first, second, and third), although Algonquian languages make an additional distinction between the first person plural in which the hearer or addressee is included (first person plural inclusive) and the one in which the hearer is not included (first person plural exclusive). A further distinction is made between two third persons referred to in the same context. The further, or obviative, is marked by inflectional endings that distinguish it from the nearer third person, referred to as the proximate, as in the Cree sentence *Nāpēw atimwa wāpamēw,* "The man [*nāpēw;* proximate] saw the dog [*atimwa;* marked by the obviative ending -*a*]." Another important feature of Algonquian languages is the presence of "direction markers," which, in the absence of strict rules of word order, help to clarify the relationship between actor (or subject) and goal (object or patient) in a given sentence.

Algonquian nouns consist of stems to which both prefixes and suffixes may be added to indicate gender, number, person, and possession. Similarly, Algonquian verb stems are inflected for person, number, gender, and direction. For example, the Fox expression *newapamawa,* "I see him," inflects the stem *wap-,* "see") for person (marked by the prefix *ne-*), direction (with the direction marker -*am-*), and the gender and number of the goal (marked both by the direction marker -*am-* and by the suffix -*awa*). These and many other fascinating features of Algonquian languages have made them influential in the development of descriptive and theoretical linguistics in the United States and elsewhere.

Translations of Western religious works, particularly the Bible, have been made into various Algonquian languages since the seventeenth century. The earliest Bible printed in North America was in the Massachusett language, and was published in 1663. Although unwritten before European contact, all currently spoken Algonquian languages, and some that are now extinct, have had orthographies and/or syllabaries developed for them, and several are the focus of active reading and writing programs today. Algonquian languages such as Cree and Ojibwa still serve the needs of large communities of speakers, and many of the surviving languages such as Maliseet-Passamaquoddy are now the subject of revitalization programs designed to bring the languages back into use among younger speakers.

See also Languages.

Bloomfield, Leonard, "Algonquian," in *Linguistic Structures of Native America,* ed. Harry Hoijer (New York: Johnson Reprint, 1971); Goddard, Ives, "The Algonquian Independent Indicative," in *Contributions to Anthropology: Linguistics, I (Algonquian),* Anthropological Series no. 78, National Museum of Canada Bulletin no. 214 (Ottawa: National Museum of Canada, 1967); Wolfart, H. Christoph, and Janet F. Carroll, *Meet Cree: A Guide to the Language* (Lincoln: University of Nebraska Press, 1973).

KATHLEEN BRAGDON
College of William and Mary

AMERICAN INDIAN DEFENSE ASSOCIATION

Founded in 1923, the American Indian Defense Association (AIDA) was an organization of middle- and upper-class white people dedicated to Indian rights. The social worker John Collier served as the AIDA's executive secretary from 1923 until 1933, when Franklin Roosevelt appointed him Commissioner of Indian Affairs. Under Collier's leadership the AIDA was praised for its advocacy of native interests and decried by its critics as a group of hopelessly romantic "do-gooders." Collier, the principal organizer of the group, created the AIDA because of a need to consolidate the plethora of Indian interest groups that had arisen in the 1920s to defend various Indian groups, most prominently the Pueblo people, who opposed legislation that promised to undermine their landholding. Because of Collier's strong public-relations skills, many white progressives joined the AIDA. By 1932 the organization reported a membership of seventeen hundred.

During the 1920s, the AIDA maintained an office in Washington, D.C., where Collier and a team of professionals lobbied Congress to address problems associated with Indian poverty, to grant Indians greater cultural and religious freedom, and to recognize tribal organizations as legitimate actors in policymaking. Beginning in 1925 the AIDA issued *American Indian Life,* a periodic newsletter that was frequently critical of federal actions. Following Collier's appointment to the Indian Office, the association found it difficult to criticize the government. In 1936 it merged with the National Association of Indian Affairs to form the Association of American Indian Affairs, an advocacy group still in existence.

AMERICAN INDIAN MOVEMENT (AIM)

The American Indian Movement (AIM) was founded in Minneapolis, Minnesota, in 1968 by Dennis Banks, Clyde Bellecourt, Eddie Benton-Banai, and George Mitchell. Russell Means later become one of its most visible spokesmen.

The organization grew out of the civil rights struggles of the late 1960s; its original focus was to protect the rights of urban native people faced with poverty and police oppression. AIM evolved into an organization that called attention to a wide range of issues important to the native community: economic independence and control over native natural resources, the political autonomy of tribal reservations, the revitalization of traditional culture and spirituality, and the education of young Indian children. The latter often takes the form of challenges to the public school system to employ more native teachers, abandon stereotypical "Indian" portrayals in American history courses, and consult with elders over curriculum issues.

AIM has led several national protests including the occupation of Alcatraz Island (1969–71); the 1972 March on Washington to protest treaty violations, which resulted in the takeover of BIA headquarters; the 1973 occupation of the town of Wounded Knee, South Dakota; the 1978 "Longest Walk" from San Francisco to Washington to focus attention on the plight of American Indian people; and the 1981 occupation of the Black Hills to press demands for this sacred area to be returned to the Lakota people. More recently, AIM has led national efforts that seek to remove inappropriate names of native origin from sports teams.

AMERICAN INDIAN POLICY REVIEW COMMISSION

The American Indian Policy Review Commission, created by an act of Congress on January 2, 1975, was charged with reviewing federal policy toward Indians and making recommendations "by Indians for Indians" to Congress. The commission, which consisted of three members of the Senate, three Congressmen, and five Native Americans—three from federally recognized tribes, one from a non–federally recognized tribe, and one from an urban area—appointed a staff and set up eleven task forces. Each task force conducted an extensive review of a particular policy area and reported

its findings to the commission. The commission's major recommendations, submitted to Congress in May 1977, were to replace the Bureau of Indian Affairs with an independent Indian agency and to contract directly with tribes for services then being provided by the BIA.

Although the legacy of the commission continues to be debated, the two-year policy review increased the participation of congressional legislators in Indian affairs, began the process of limiting the role for the Bureau of Indian Affairs, and promoted the idea of tribal self-governance. Unfortunately, however, Congress did not enact the commission's recommendations. This failure was due in part to the departure of key legislative sponsors (such as James Abourezk of South Dakota) and backlash from western legislators who feared that greater tribal autonomy would anger their constituents. Nevertheless, by the late 1980s Congress had authorized a Tribal Self-Governance Demonstration Project, which transferred significant administrative functions (and funds) from the BIA to selected tribes. This project implemented the original thinking of the commission. Thus, despite its lack of immediate results, the commission set forth a new vision of the federal-Indian relationship that continues to attract political support.

ANTHROPOLOGY AND INDIANS

American anthropology as a science was founded upon the study of American Indians with their cooperation and sometimes collaboration. In some instances American Indians, watching the transformation of their societies, guided the research of anthropologists, who could record cultural practices in danger of extinction. In the late nineteenth century the sense that American Indian cultures were likely to be totally lost in the process of assimilation was shared by anthropologists and many Indians. That this prediction proved to be false does not alter the fact that thousands of cultural experts from many tribes cooperated with anthropologists, some of whom were themselves Native Americans, to record for posterity information about their lifeways. In a period when American mainstream opinion saw little or no value in native cultures, anthropologists were among the appreciative few who documented them for an unknown future.

American anthropology as a science was founded with the publication of *League of the Ho-de-no-sau-nee, or Iroquois* in 1851 by Lewis Henry Morgan. It remains the best description of the Iroquois, but what is not often appreciated is the fact that Morgan had an Iroquois collaborator who provided him with much of the information that appeared in this work. Ely S. Parker (1828–95), a Seneca from the Tonawanda Reservation, became acquainted with Morgan while still a teenager and provided him with information about the structure and workings of the Iroquois League. Morgan acknowledged Parker's contributions in the preface to *League,* and in its dedication referred to the book as "the fruit of our joint researches." However, in keeping with the notions of authorship at the time, Morgan did not list Parker as coauthor, in contrast to what is sometimes the practice today. By all indications Parker found his collaboration with Morgan to be personally satisfying and politically useful. Parker was charged with helping the Tonawanda Senecas retain their land, which was threatened by a dubious treaty, and his relationship with Morgan (an attorney) enabled him to call on his services as an expert witness. That Parker did not feel slighted by Morgan's claim to single authorship can be surmised by the fact that both men continued their mutually beneficial relationship after the publication of *League.*

By 1879—the year of the establishment of the Smithsonian Institution's Bureau of American Ethnology, dedicated to the study and documentation of American Indian cultures—American anthropology was developing a body of basic concepts about culture that was to be its principal contribution to international scholarship. Kinship, cultural development, and culture areas are but a few of these abstractions; almost all of the basic research that underlay this conceptual development was done in Indian communities with native collaborators who were interested in the investigation for their own reasons. Over the next fifty years thousands of native individuals were involved in some fashion with the ongoing study of their communities by a relatively small number of professional anthropologists, some of whom were themselves Indian. Indian people were hired as translators and as cultural experts, and were paid for their time. The income was probably an important rationale for their cooperation, but it is an insult to the collective intelligence of these men and women to claim that they cooperated only for the money, an assertion that has been made by some contemporary critics of anthropology.

By 1910 anthropology was in the process of becoming a university-based discipline, and Franz Boas was its acknowledged leader. The great majority of professionally trained anthropologists worked in North America studying some aspect of American Indian culture, although there were already anthropologists working in other parts of the world as well. Museums were funding fieldwork to gather information and material objects for their permanent collections, and there were a small but important number of professional Indian anthropologists who were publishing their own research. Francis La Flesche (1857–1932), an Omaha, began as an assistant to Alice Fletcher and J. O. Dorsey about 1882, learning linguistics and research techniques from them. He developed a close relationship with Fletcher, ultimately being adopted by her as a son, and was her collaborator for the rest of her life. He was publishing his own research by 1885 and continued his research and writing for the rest of his career. Another Indian anthropologist was Arthur C. Parker, (1881–1955), a Seneca, a grandnephew of Ely S. Parker, and eventually the director of the Rochester Museum in New York State. He published, was active in Indian political affairs, and was an important museum professional of his time. A third native anthropologist was Ella Deloria (1889–1971), a Yankton Sioux and a student of Franz Boas at Columbia. She spent her life actively researching and publishing, and was deeply involved with Lakota education and community affairs. These three are representative of a larger number of American Indians who participated in numerous ways in anthropological research in their own communities. There were many others. People like J. N. B. Hewitt (Iroquois), Jesse Cornplanter (Seneca), Essie Parrish (Pomo), John Joseph Mathews (Osage), William Jones (Fox), James R. Murie (Pawnee), and George Hunt (Tlingit) all contributed to the documentation of their societies as part of a shared vision that their cultures be preserved for future generations.

By World War II anthropology had shifted its primary emphasis from examining U.S. Indian cultures to studying the cultures of Africa, Asia, and Hispanic America, which included native communities. Paradigms had changed, and the faithful recording of cultural details was no longer fashionable. Indian anthropologists like Deloria and Parker continued to be active in the profession, but there were few to take their place when they retired.

The 1960s and 1970s were a time of intense public scrutiny and criticism of virtually all American institutions, and anthropology was no exception. There were many critiques generated from within and outside the discipline, and exploitation of native people was a frequent charge. There is no doubt that such exploitation by anthropologists has occurred in some cases, but to characterize all fieldwork and publication as exploitative is to deny the ability of native peoples to make their own judgments about their self-interest. Simultaneously, many American Indians began to redefine their relationship to anthropology and to question whether "outsiders"—non-Indian anthropologists and other researchers—should have the right to interpret native culture. The dialogue has been acrimonious at times and is still evolving. Control over access has been secured by some tribes, who have instituted a policy requiring all researchers to secure permission from a tribal committee before proceeding with their work, but for the most part individual researchers still make their own arrangements.

Since 1960 the number of non-Indian professional anthropologists whose geographical specialty is North America has declined in three of the four subfields of the discipline (cultural, physical, and linguistic anthropology). Only the fourth subfield, archaeology, has witnessed a growth in practitioners as a result of laws passed that safeguard archaeological resources. In contrast, the number of professional anthropologists who are of Indian descent has increased from less than twenty to eighty, most of them concentrated in cultural anthropology with a strong applied focus.

Simultaneously there has been a substantial increase in Indian interest in museum and archival collections of original materials as they relate to history and cultural practices. Many tribes have established their own museums and archives, and have secured copies of original documents first collected by anthropologists in the nineteenth and early twentieth centuries. These documents, often rich in linguistic and cultural detail, are proving to be treasure-troves for Indian people eager for such information. There are numerous examples of tribes that have rediscovered cultural practices described by anthropologists in archival or museum collections and have subsequently incorporated the information into current usage. Some professional Indian anthropologists are using these materials for their own scholarship. Work done by earlier generations of anthropologists and their Indian collaborators is finding a new audience today in the collaborators' descendants—the best evidence of the enduring value of anthropology for American Indians.

See also Deloria, Ella (Anpetu Waste); La Flesche Family; Origins: Anthropological Perspectives; Parker, Arthur C.; Repatriation.

La Flesche, Francis, *The Osage Tribe,* Annual Reports of the Bureau of American Ethnology, 1914–1928 (Washington, D.C.: Smithsonian Institution); Liberty, Margot, ed., *American Indian Intellectuals* (St. Paul, Minn.: West Publishing Company, 1978); Parker, Arthur C., *The Constitution of the Five Nations,* New York State Museum Bulletin no. 184 (Albany, 1916).

JoAllyn Archambault (Standing Rock Sioux)
National Museum of Natural History
Smithsonian Institution

Apache, Eastern

In 1541 Spanish explorers probably saw ancestral Eastern Apaches on the Great Plains using pack dogs to move hide tipis and other possessions. These Plains Apaches killed bison, deer, and antelope during communal hunts. They reckoned descent through women; men avoided their mothers-in-law.

Spaniards colonized the upper Rio Grande in 1598, and Plains Apaches soon acquired horses. Armed with lances, mounted Apaches expanded over the southern plains after 1620. Tribes differentiated from one another. Judging from linguistic evidence, one tribe split into the historic Lipan and Kiowa Apache groups.

Mounted Comanches with guns defeated Plains Apache tribes around 1718, forcing them to retreat. About that time, Wichitas and Pawnees forced Paloma Apaches to flee from their homeland north of the Platte River to the middle Arkansas River. Penxayes Apaches gardened along the Purgatoire River tributary of the Arkansas. By 1730, the Paloma, Arkansas River, and Carlana tribes had united into eastern-band Llanero Jicarillas. By 1750, western-band Ollero Jicarillas lived at Taos Pueblo, growing crops along the Rio Grande. Numerous Eastern Apaches amalgamated into three post-1750 southern Plains tribes: Jicarillas; Lipan Apaches *(see entry under Lipan Apache),* and Mescaleros.

Mescalero Apaches ranged from Jicarilla country to colonial El Paso del Norte on the lower Rio Grande. They alternately traded with or raided Spanish villages until 1775, when they negotiated peace. Mescalero warriors then served the Spaniards as scouts against other natives. Living mainly on rations, bored Mescalero women learned to play Spanish card games, gambling as Apaches always had. Mescaleros learned the Spanish language and adopted Spanish clothing, except moccasins. Soon after Mexico gained independence in 1821, it stopped issuing rations to the Mescaleros, who resumed raiding in order to survive.

Early in the nineteenth century the Kiowa Apaches still ranged with the Kiowas on the central plains near the confluence of the Platte and Missouri Rivers. Thus they escaped Spanish colonial domination, only to find themselves in the path of westward U.S. expansion. By midcentury they had participated in treaty councils in Kansas and Indian Territory.

In 1851 Mescalero and Jicarilla Apache chiefs signed a peace treaty with New Mexico's American governor. Having rustled horses from a U.S. Army command at El Paso late in 1847 during the war between the United States and Mexico, hungry Mescaleros continued raiding until January 1856, when U.S. troops decisively defeated them. In November of that year, the Indian agent Michael Steck began issuing them provisions and clothing at Fort Stanton.

In 1849, the Jicarillas made themselves the most hated natives in New Mexico when Jicarilla warriors killed half a dozen male travelers and captured the wife and daughter of one of them. Would-be rescuers watched a Jicarilla woman kill the captive woman as she tried to escape. The daughter and two African-American servant women disappeared. Still, federal agents thereafter issued rations to Jicarillas, who hunted and sold pots to villagers in order to live.

Early in the Civil War, Union forces abandoned southwestern military posts and Apaches resumed economic raiding. In 1862, Union volunteers from California took control of New Mexico, interning most Mescaleros, together with thousands of Navajos, at Bosque Redondo on the Pecos River. Union officers recruited Jicarillas to fight other Plains tribes. On November 3, 1865, the last Mescaleros fled Bosque Redondo. Mescaleros remained hidden from official view until 1870, when some began trading with J. H. Blazer near their former agency at Fort Stanton.

After the war, the United States settled Kiowa Apaches and Kiowas with Comanches on a large reservation in western Indian Territory. Jicarillas drew federal rations where Utes did, and the two peoples began to intermarry.

On May 29, 1873, the U.S. president reserved Tularosa River watershed lands for Mescaleros, but the reservation provided little protection. Outlaws rustled Mescalero livestock, and federal troops occupied their reserve, murdering scores of men.

In 1876, the government sent Jicarillas to Fort Stanton, but few stayed. In 1883, the government sent the Jicarillas to the Mescalero Reservation, but two hundred of them fled back to Santa Fe in 1886. In 1887, the president reserved for them lands in north central New Mexico. There Jicarillas built homes, using lumber from a reservation sawmill. Colonists harassed them, too, as they sold pots and baskets to raise money to buy sheep.

In 1887 Congress passed the General Allotment Act, which accelerated the transfer of reserved lands from natives to newcomers and initiated a period of intense native suffering. The termination of communal land management shattered traditional governance throughout Indian Territory. In 1900, Congress approved allotting 320 acres to each Comanche, Kiowa, and Kiowa Apache, and selling the "surplus" reserved acres.

In New Mexico, demoralized Mescaleros dwindled in numbers. Then in 1905, 37 Lipans moved from Mexico to the reservation. In 1913, 187 Chiricahua ex–prisoners of war moved from Fort Sill to the reservation. Finally the birth rate began to exceed the death rate. In the north, the Jicarilla population dropped from 995 in 1905 to 588 in 1920, when about 90 percent of the schoolchildren had tuberculosis.

During the allotment era, Bureau of Indian Affairs personnel tried to force Eastern Apaches to farm, speak English, cut their long hair, wear ready-to-wear clothes, and convert to Christianity. Ironically, the bureau financed its program of forced Mescalero cultural change with income from reservation timber sales and grazing leases.

When President Franklin D. Roosevelt launched the Indian New Deal in 1934, no reservation population took better advantage of the reforms than the Mescaleros. The new Mescalero Reservation Business Committee canceled grazing leases so Indians could run cattle on their reservation. Net annual income from cattle rose in three depression years from $18,000 to $101,000. The reservation government prospered along with families. In 1963, the business committee's president, Wendell Chino, borrowed money from New Mexico banks to purchase the Sierra Blanca ski resort. Later, the reservation government constructed a fish hatchery, a resort hotel, golf courses, and an industrial park.

The Jicarillas organized their elective government in mid-1937, as authorized by the 1934 Indian Reorganization Act. Petroleum-company exploration fees boosted family and government incomes in the 1950s. The

Jicarilla Tribal Council began publishing a newspaper in 1962. In 1963, a liquor store opened in Dulce; two years later an alcoholism program started.

The Comanche, Kiowa, and Kiowa Apache Business Council, established after the 1936 Oklahoma Indian Welfare Act, reflected the pre-1900 tri-tribal reservation. Following three decades of intertribal disputes, the Comanches in 1966 left that council, claiming that the other two groups had worked against them.

See also Apache, Western; Lipan Apache.

Gunnerson, Dolores, *The Jicarilla Apaches* (DeKalb: Northern Illinois University Press, 1974); Melody, Michael E., *The Apache* (New York: Chelsea House, 1988); Sonnichsen, C. L., *The Mescalero Apaches* (Norman: University of Oklahoma Press, 1972).

HENRY F. DOBYNS
Tucson, Arizona

APACHE, LIPAN
See Lipan Apache.

APACHE, WESTERN

There are six major divisions of the Apaches: the Western Apaches, the Chiricahuas, the Mescaleros, the Jicarillas, the Lipans, and the Kiowa Apaches. The westernmost Apache groups found in Arizona—excluding the Chiricahuas, who were originally in southeastern Arizona—are called the Western Apaches. They comprise five major subtribes: White Mountain, Cibecue, San Carlos, and Northern and Southern Tonto.

How long the Apaches have been in the Southwest is uncertain, but it is clear that they arrived before the Spanish explorations of 1539–42. Apache oral traditions contain some references to the north, but religion, ritual, religious practices, and sacred locales described in oral traditions are all located in the Southwest and northern Mexico, indicating ancient familiarity with the area. Oral traditions recount a long period of residence in northern Arizona and gradual movement south. Early Apache sites are hard to identify, and consequently the archaeological record is poor. Evidence from some archaeological sites suggests a date around A.D. 1450 for the entry of Athabaskan peoples into the Southwest, but some scholars call for earlier dates.

The historical home territories of the Western Apaches ranged from south of modern-day Flagstaff, near Sedona; along the drainages of the Verde River, across the Mogollon Rim into the White Mountains, and on to the Arizona–New Mexico border; and through the Gila River valley and portions of the Salt River valley to the Santa Catalinas, south to the Pinaleño or Graham Mountains, and as far south as the San Pedro River valley. Raiding, warfare, and their seasonal round of hunting and gathering took them into northern Mexico as well.

Today most Western Apaches live on two reservations. The White Mountain Apache Reservation and the San Carlos Reservation each are home to more than ten thousand tribal members who live in communities that cover just under 2 million acres of land. One other small reservation exists in Arizona near Payson for the Tonto Apaches, and some Apache people live on several of the small Yavapai reservations.

The Apache language belongs to the Southern Athabaskan language family and is related to other Athabaskan languages spoken on the Pacific Coast and in Canada. Western Apache and closely related Navajo are considered to be two distinct languages, each with multiple dialects. These languages belong to a greater grouping known as the Na-Dene phylum. Both languages are still spoken, with most speakers bilingual in English, but there is concern that younger people are not learning them.

Prior to European contact, the Western Apache economy was based on hunting and gathering, supplemented by gardening (horticulture), trade with more-settled agricultural peoples, and raiding. The Western Apaches were mobile people who moved in a seasonal round, covering millions of acres as they collected wild plants and hunted game from favored campsites. They were the most agricultural of all of the Apache groups.

The Western Apaches were primarily mountain and upland people who preferred cool, timbered locations. Their rugged, beautiful environment provided outstanding biodiversity. Agave (mescal), a large desert succulent plant with a tuberlike heart that could be roasted, was a favored staple plant food, as were cactus fruits (tunas), acorns, black walnuts, and pine nuts (piñons). These foods are still eaten, especially on ceremonial occasions. Agricultural sites in drainages near heads of creeks, rivers, or springs were the primary home bases. Here Apache families planted corn, beans, pumpkins, and other crops. Sometimes they left the crops alone or in the care of the elderly, the disabled, and the young while they went out to hunt and gather. Only planting and harvesting required a presence at the farm sites. Women were the primary farmers and men the hunters, but both sexes participated in large tasks that required many hands.

Winter was the primary hunting season as well as the time in which small parties embarked on raids. Winter camps moved every two weeks or so; favored sites were the Nantanes Plateau, the lower slopes of the Pinaleño or Graham Mountains, the Gila Range, and the Santa Theresa and Turnbull Mountains. Trade was carried on with more-settled groups such as the Pueblo Indians. Meat, skins, and other animal products as well as salt and other wild harvested products were traded for agricultural products such as corn, beans, squash, and cotton clothing. Apaches visited settled Pueblo communities and sometimes spent the winters camped outside pueblos. Apache tradition also tells of Apache people living in some Pueblo sites and building Pueblo-style structures at different times and places.

There were two types of groupings into which Western Apache society was organized: those based upon territoriality, and those based upon kinship. Individuals belonged to groups of both kinds at the same time. Local groups, bands, and subtribes were based upon territoriality. Matrilineages (matrilineal extended families), clans, and unnamed phratries were based upon kinship and marriage. Local groups occupied the farm sites, had rights to hunting territories, and were named for the farm sites. The local groups were made up of smaller, matrilineal-matrilocal family units, with multiple households organized around a woman, her husband, her married daughters and their families, and unmarried daughters and sons, all residing close to or with each other. A few Apache males were permitted more than one wife, normally sisters. Local groups in the same general watershed were known as bands. Anthropologists call groups of bands "subtribes."

Clans consisted of groups of people who considered themselves related and descended from a single female ancestor. They were often named for their place of origin. They served to unite Apaches in local groups, to regulate marriage through clan exogamy (which prohibited the marriage of members of the same or closely linked clans), and to carry out joint ceremonial obligations such as the puberty ceremony. In the nineteenth century there were over fifty named clans. Certain prototypical personality types and behaviors were said to be associated with each clan. Closely related clans were further grouped into unnamed units, called "phratries"

by scholars. Today clans and phratries have declined somewhat in importance, and matrilocal residence is less likely. The old territorial units, though disrupted by the reservation system, continue to provide the nucleus of some reservation settlements and political alignments.

People became leaders through force of personality, example, wealth, and prestige. Families had headmen and local groups had chiefs, normally male, but Apache leaders could not compel their followers except in situations of warfare. Leadership was normally achieved through experience and deed but often did run in families. Leaders were expected to provide for their followers by using their personal wealth.

Traditional Apache religion focuses on curing, puberty ceremonies, hunting and agricultural rituals, personal power and protection, and guidance for a moral life. Spiritual leaders, often referred to as medicine men and medicine women, have access to greater power than that possessed by ordinary individuals, who may also have some special gifts. These shamanic spiritual leaders provide healing and counseling and conduct ceremonies. Many Apaches consult these spiritual leaders. The Apache religion has been renewed through prophets and their teachings, the most important of whom in this century was Silas John Edwards. His trained disciples conduct ceremonies at consecrated holy grounds.

The most important and frequent community ceremony is the girl's puberty ceremony, called *Na'ii'es* in Apache and the Sunrise Ceremony or Sunrise Dance in English; it normally takes place in the summer months of the year after a girl's first menstruation. The *gaan* or mountain spirits, associated with mountain caves, appear as masked dancers during puberty ceremonies and are important in curing. The Apache religion is undergoing a resurgence at the present time, although some ceremonies are no longer conducted.

The Apache reservations were heavily missionized, first by the Evangelical Lutherans as part of the federal "Peace Policy" to convert and assimilate the western Indians. Other groups followed: Catholics, Mormons, Baptists, adherents of the pentecostal Miracle Church, and others. Some Apache people are exclusively Christian; others are Christian and also participate in the Apache religion; and some practice the Apache religion exclusively. Since 1989 the San Carlos Tribal Council has repeatedly opposed telescope development on Mount Graham, which contains Apache sacred sites. The Apache Survival Coalition has led an international battle to preserve these sites—a struggle that has received worldwide attention.

Although primarily peaceful, the Apaches were successful in resisting the Spanish, never permitting the establishment of settlements north of Tucson. After Mexico achieved independence from Spain in 1821, the Mexican government targeted the Apaches in an unsuccessful policy of extermination and slavery.

The Southwest became a part of the United States as a result of the Treaty of Guadalupe Hidalgo, which ended the war with Mexico, and the Gadsden Purchase of 1853. Initial contacts with Americans were peaceful, but this soon changed because of the failure of the Americans to recognize Apache rights to customary territories and the tribe's pattern of hunting and gathering over a broad area. Increasing numbers of American miners and settlers arrived in the Arizona Territory who had little respect for Apache rights to land and water. A series of incidents in which Americans pretended friendship but killed or poisoned Apaches ensued, and this treachery eventually ignited the Apache wars, which lasted from the 1850s until 1886.

Gradually, army posts were established in Apache territory, and rations were provided to the Apaches to compensate them for lost hunting, gathering, and farming opportunities. By 1870, the first reservations had been set up in areas not yet desired by the Americans. Many Apaches voluntarily moved to these reservations because the alternatives were extermination or starvation, but others were forcibly removed from their territories by the military. The reservations became giant concentration camps, with Indians from a number of different bands and territories crowded together. Food supplies were inadequate, and the army exercised total control.

The White Mountain Apache Reservation, centered on Fort Apache, was established informally in 1870 and formally by presidential executive order in 1871. In 1871 the Camp Grant Reservation was established for the Arivaipas, Pinals, and other Apache Indians, but was soon abolished. That same year a group of eighty people, primarily women and children, from the peaceful Arivaipa band were massacred by southern Arizonans while under the protection of the military, and twenty-eight children were kidnapped. This event, sometimes referred to as the Camp Grant Massacre, is remembered today by the tribe on Apache Memorial Day. In 1872, the San Carlos division of the White Mountain Apache Reservation was established, and

other Apache reservations were abolished. Displaced Apaches from different bands, groups, and subtribes, including the Chiricahuas, as well as Yavapai from the Verde River area, were all placed on the reservation, causing great hardship, overcrowding, and starvation. These conditions were made worse by constant reductions in the land area of the reservation by presidential executive orders in 1873, 1876, and 1877 following the discovery of valuable resources such as copper, silver, coal and timber on portions of the reservation. These reductions led to frequent outbreaks and military action, resulting in continued sporadic warfare between the Apaches and the army. Later reductions were made by presidential executive order to provide farmland, timber, and water to whites. By 1886 the government had placed all Apaches on reservations or imprisoned them.

In 1896 the reservation was formally split into two reservations, the northern section above the Salt River known as the Fort Apache or White Mountain Apache Reservation and the remainder as the San Carlos Apache Reservation. Rationing was eventually ended and troops were removed from the reservations, but Apaches still had no effective control of their lands and resources, and no economy. Many Apaches and most of the Yavapai were forced to work off-reservation as wage laborers in order to survive. Indian agents served as labor contractors, hiring out groups of Apaches for road construction, mining, and farm labor at off-reservation sites. From 1906 to 1930 many Apaches worked on the construction of dams on the Salt and Verde Rivers, and on Coolidge Dam. By 1926, 96 percent of the San Carlos grasslands were completely utilized by white cattlemen, but tribal herds began to increase slowly until 1935 and then more rapidly when the tribe regained some control over its lands. The White Mountain Apaches also had little control over their grazing. Both tribes had little self-determination until the passage of the Indian Reorganization Act of 1934, which led to the creation of tribal councils and the beginnings of self-government in 1935–37. Still, a great amount of control remained with the Indian agents and superintendents and the Bureau of Indian Affairs well into the 1970s. Many of the off-reservation jobs that Apaches had utilized began to disappear as the effects of the Great Depression hit Arizona in the 1930s, and neither cattle raising nor farming provided a strong enough base for the reservation economy, given the limited conditions on the reservation.

The San Carlos Reservation, which is primarily desert, has remained one of the poorest places in the entire United States and still suffers from very high unemployment and an inability to create new jobs, given its lack of resources, infrastructure, and capital and its remote location. Principal economic revenues today come from federal programs, cattle raising, timber sales, recreation (including fishing and hunting), limited farming, the mining of peridot (a green semiprecious stone), and a casino, which opened in 1994.

On the White Mountain Reservation the world's largest stand of ponderosa pine was sold and logged by white companies that utilized only small amounts of Apache labor. Still, the extensive forest and mountain environment has led to a stronger economy, with timber and recreational opportunities including a ski resort and many fishing lakes and streams on the reservation. Farming and cattle raising are also practiced. The tribe opened a casino, which doubled in size in 1995. Economic development continues on both reservations, but differences in environment and resources have led to very different outcomes. Western Apaches remain a culturally distinct population, poorly understood and still struggling to attain the economic levels enjoyed by other Americans.

See also Apache, Eastern; Lipan Apache.

Melody, Michael, *The Apache* (New York: Chelsea House Publishers, 1994); Perry, Richard J., *Apache Reservation: Indigenous People of the American State* (Austin: University of Texas Press, 1993); Perry, Richard J., *Western Apache Heritage: People of the Mountain Corridor* (Austin: University of Texas Press, 1991).

ELIZABETH A. BRANDT
Arizona State University

APESS, WILLIAM

(1798–1839)
Pequot preacher and writer; leader of the "Mashpee Revolt."

William Apess's newspaper obituary makes its judgment summarily: "In New York, it appears that for some time past, his conduct had been quite irregular, and he had lost the confidence of the best portions of the community. . . . He has occasionally indulged much too freely in drink, and would take frolics that would continue for a week or two." His death at forty-one seems to have been the direct result of alcoholism.

Born in a tent in the woods in late January 1798 somewhere around Colrain, Massachusetts, Apess had a beginning that appears consonant with his end. His father, also named William, was a man of mixed race, part Pequot and part white; his mother, Candace (her last name is unknown), was probably a slave, quite possibly part African American. These were people at the bottom of every social hierarchy—poor, without a stable homestead, a mixture of the two races most despised by other Americans. Nothing in the world to which he was born promised young William tolerance or support.

Thus begun and ended, William Apess's life might seem scripted on the most blinding stereotypes about Indians. Yet his books and his promotion of Indian rights justify our attention, in part because of their subversion of all such stereotypes. A knowledge of the circumstances of his birth and death, and of the fact that he was nearly beaten to death by his maternal grandmother when he was four, complicates most categories of racial or ethnic identity, as does what we know of the rest of his life.

At age five he was bound out to a neighboring white family, the Furmans, in Colchester, Connecticut. Raised by them until he was eleven, during which time he received his only formal education—six "winter" terms—Apess then had his indenture successively sold to two elite gentry families in the area. In April 1813 he ran away from the second of these, the William Williamses, to New York City, where he joined a militia company and served in the War of 1812. Being forbidden to attend Methodist camp meetings had precipitated Apess's decision to abandon his master and join the army. He mustered out in 1815, and spent the next eighteen months working a variety of jobs in Canada—all the while struggling to overcome a serious drinking problem that had become established when he was in the militia. Determined to break the habit, Apess decided to return "home"—to Connecticut, to his natal family, and to his people, the Pequots, from whom he had been separated for all of his formative years.

In the course of these experiences Apess forged a powerful identity as a Pequot, despite the trauma of having been beaten by his Pequot grandmother and brought up in apparent isolation from other Pequots. Just as remarkably, he made himself, with at best a modest formal education, into a writer of notable polemical power; he became a canny critic of white Europeans' use of history and Christianity to justify their racism against Indians. His autobiography, *A*

Son of the Forest (1829; 2d ed. 1831), is the first published autobiography actually written by an American Indian.

A Son of the Forest tells the story of a life of abuse and oppression, and tells it without either self-pity or an insistence on its author's exceptional nature. Produced for a world of white readers in which Indians existed only as stereotypes—stereotypes so pervasive and tenacious that the actualities of Indians' lives and histories could not be successfully represented—Apess's first book uses irony, as well as direct address, in a remarkable attempt to communicate very different understandings of Indians' lives.

Apess's own life after he returned to Connecticut from Canada in 1816–17 changed in ways that both confounded the stereotypes and made possible the assertion of his Pequot identity. Two important events marked the first years after his return. Apess once again attended Methodist camp meetings, drawn not simply to Christianity, but to a church that then had a special appeal to the lowly and dominated. Its egalitarianism had special power for those, like Apess, who had experienced the worst of the prejudices of the culture, enabling an affirmation not only of one's own spiritual worth, but also of one's own kind: "I felt convinced that Christ died for all mankind—that age, sect, color, country, or situation make no difference. I felt an assurance that I was included in the plan of redemption with all my brethren." He experienced conversion and was baptized in December 1818.

He also met Mary Wood of Salem, Connecticut, at a camp meeting. Herself apparently of mixed racial parentage, Mary Wood had also been a bound servant. They were married in December 1821 and lived together until Apess's death. They had at least three children, the oldest a son, Elisha or William (?), and two daughters (their names are unknown, though they married brothers, the Chummucks of Mashpee, Massachusetts).

Throughout the 1820s Apess grew more confident that God had called him to preach the Gospel. Refused ordination by the Methodist Episcopal Church—because, in his view, of its prejudice against Indians—he was ordained in 1829–30 by the Protestant Methodist Church, a more egalitarian Methodist group.

Apess's ordination inaugurated a brief but brilliant public career as a preacher to Indians, African Americans, and whites throughout New England and New York. An itinerant, following Methodist practices of the day, Apess was able to become knowledgeable about the conditions and needs of his fellow Indians throughout the region. He seems to have increasingly seen himself as their advocate. It was in this role that he first visited Mashpee, the largest of the surviving Indian towns in Massachusetts. The Mashpees had long been struggling to achieve full self-government, free from the paternalism of state-appointed white overseers and a minister chosen by Harvard College. Apess's arrival in 1833 was catalytic. The Mashpees made him one of their leaders. His polemical skills were at their sharpest in the several manifestos he produced, powerful enough to persuade Levi Lincoln, the rather hysterical governor of the state, that he faced a full-fledged armed rebellion—thus the name "the Mashpee Revolt" for what was a peaceable demand for all the rights of self-government belonging to any citizen. Apess's account, *Indian Nullification of the Unconstitutional Laws of Massachusetts* (1835), his fourth publication, remains the best source of information about the incident.

The controversy over Mashpee briefly made Apess a national and regional figure—and earned him many enemies. The Mashpees won most of their demands and, possibly for this reason, drew away from Apess's leadership. His last known public appearance came in Boston in early 1836, when he gave his "Eulogy on King Philip." It generated enough controversy that he was asked to repeat the address a second time. Only his obituary gives us any information about his final years.

Brief though it was, as hard as it began and ended, Apess's life was filled with achievement. His five publications represent the most substantial body of work by a Native American writer prior to the twentieth century. In them and in his life he demonstrated that in New England, and in the United States in general, Indian peoples persisted in forms and cultural identities far more complex and diverse than white people realized. His writing continues to teach by provoking a steady examination of the differences between Indian peoples' actual lives and the Euro-American culture's ongoing misrepresentations of them.

Krupat, Arnold, *Ethnocriticism: Ethnography, History, Literature* (Berkeley: University of California Press, 1992); Murray, David, *Forked Tongues: Speech, Writing and Representation in North American Indian Texts* (Bloomington: Indiana University Press, 1991); O'Connell, Barry, ed., *On Our Ground: The Complete Writings of William Apess, a Pequot* (Amherst: University of Massachusetts Press, 1992).

BARRY O'CONNELL
Amherst College

ARAPAHO

The Arapahos probably moved onto the western plains from the woodlands area near the Great Lakes, for they exhibit many traditions similar to Algonquian-speaking groups of that region. When they made the move is unknown. During the eighteenth century there were several divisions of Arapahos, which ranged from the Saskatchewan River south into Colorado and perhaps Oklahoma, west to the foothills of the Rockies, and east into western South Dakota and Kansas. The northernmost division, the Gros Ventres, settled in Montana. Two other main divisions are the Northern and Southern Arapahos. American traders adopted the Crow Indians' name for these people, which sounded like "Arapaho."

About 1730 the Arapahos began to hunt bison using horses acquired from Comanches who lived within reach of Spanish settlements. Horses enabled greater mobility, larger residence groups, and more elaborate rituals, and also led to wealth inequalities based on horse ownership. From the bison, the Arapahos obtained food, clothing, shelter, tools, and weapons. To accommodate seasonal movements of the bison, Arapaho bands (residence groups) were flexible in composition. A large network of kin facilitated cooperation in hunting.

A men's lodge organization promoted band cooperation, particularly for military purposes. This organization consisted of two youths' and five men's lodges, or ceremonial societies, each of which had specific political and ritual duties. Men earned their way through the entire series of seven lodges as they aged, through completion of initiation rites that involved apprenticing themselves to the next higher lodge. The lodges were ranked by members' age, the members of the old men's lodge having the most prestige and authority. A group of male and female priests directed the lodge rituals, which ensured the survival of the Arapahos.

During the 1850s, immigrants moving west to California and Oregon occasionally stopped in Colorado, in the heart of Arapaho hunting territory, to mine for gold, in violation of a treaty the Arapahos had signed with the federal government in 1851. In addition, immigrants disturbed the game and attacked the Arapahos. Troops did not distinguish one Indian from another when retaliating for Indian attacks on trespassing settlers. In the aftermath of the worst violence—the so-called Indian War of 1865–68—the Arapahos moved to reservations, where they thought they would be safe from further attacks.

About one thousand Northern Arapahos settled on the 2.3-million-acre Shoshone Reservation in Wyoming in 1878; they received individual allotments of land there in 1900. In 1937, the name of the reservation was changed to Wind River. Until 1947, when tribal leaders gained control over the tribes' mineral resources and instituted per capita distribution of several million dollars in income, the Arapahos struggled to sustain themselves on government rations, occasional wage work, and lease income from land allotted to individuals. After 1947, 15 percent of the income from mineral royalties was used for community services; the remaining 85 percent was distributed in monthly per capita payments.

Congress required the consent of tribal leaders, or "councilmen," on leases of tribally owned land, and the councilmen tried to use these moneys to improve living conditions. Elderly male and female ritual leaders supervised the actions of the councilmen. Leaders of all ages tried to mitigate the federal government's "civilization" policy by promoting changes that simultaneously reinforced traditional values and customs and indicated a desire to cooperate with federal officials.

In Oklahoma, about sixteen hundred Southern Arapahos settled on the Cheyenne-Arapaho Reservation, established by President Ulysses S. Grant in 1869. Federal officials pushed a "civilization program," and important headmen began building cattle herds and supervising labor on large gardens and hay fields. The federal government, under political pressure to open Oklahoma reservation lands to settlement by non-Indians, forced a cession from the Cheyennes and Arapahos in 1891. Individuals were allotted 160 acres, and the remainder of the 4-million-acre reservation was opened to settlement. Non-Indian settlers trespassed on Indian farms and ranches, stealing stock, equipment, wood, and other property. Pressure for land continued unabated, and in 1902 and 1906 Congress passed legislation that encouraged the sale of allotted Indian lands. Increasing poverty led to further land sales, so that today only about seventy-five thousand of the half million acres originally allotted remain in Arapaho hands.

Unable to support groups of followers and ignored by the federal government, political leaders lost authority. Peyote rituals were introduced to the Cheyennes and Arapahos in the late 1890s by Native Americans living to the south. The elderly leaders of the Arapaho ceremonial organization did not initiate successors, so that by the onset of World War II the Southern Arapahos had to apprentice themselves to the Northern Arapahos.

Today the Northern Arapahos number four thousand. A six-member elected business council oversees tribal operations, represents the tribe in dealings with the local and federal governments, and meets with the Shoshone council on matters of joint interest. There is no constitution and by-laws; rather, the business council attempts to operate by consensus, and a general council composed of eligible voters reserves veto power over their actions.

In 1975 Congress passed Public Law 638, which enabled tribes to contract for grants and programs formerly administered by federal agencies. This change allowed the business council to seek and control money for social programs. Families have continued to rely on the monthly per capita payment, for despite jobs created by the establishment of tribally owned businesses, unemployment remains high.

The three thousand Southern Arapahos have a few tribally owned oil wells on tribal land, but the income from these is sufficient for only a nominal annual per capita payment. Unemployment is lower than it is among the Northern Arapahos, because jobs in Oklahoma City and other urban areas are within commuting distance.

The Southern Arapahos agreed to form a joint constitutional government with the Southern Cheyennes in 1935. Today, tribal members elect four Arapahos and four Cheyennes to the Cheyenne-Arapaho business committee, which contracts for a number of social programs and oversees tribal businesses, including bingo, cigarette sales, and commercial farming.

For most Arapahos, religious life revolves around the Sun Dance Lodge, an annual ceremony of sacrifice and renewal. Ceremonial leaders are to be found only in Wyoming, although some curing and associated ceremonies have been delegated to a few Southern Arapahos. There are Christian churches and peyote meetings in both Wyoming and Oklahoma, the members of which may also participate in the traditional Arapaho religion.

Berthrong, Donald J., *The Cheyenne and Arapaho Ordeal: Reservation and Agency Life in the Indian Territory* (Norman: University of Oklahoma Press, 1976); Fowler, Loretta, *The Arapaho* (New York: Chelsea House Publishers, 1989); Trenholm, Virginia Cole, *The Arapahoes, Our People* (Norman: University of Oklahoma Press, 1970).

LORETTA FOWLER
University of Oklahoma

ARCHAEOLOGY AND INDIANS

The people who populated what we now call the Americas probably sailed or walked across the Bering Strait several thousand years ago—considerably before the Norsemen who discovered "Vineland" and long before Columbus arrived. Only sixty miles of open water separate Alaska from Russia; the strait freezes from time to time, enabling people to walk across it. We do not know who these people were or what they called themselves. But European explorers found them from the Bering Strait to Tierra del Fuego. It is unfortunate that the people Columbus encountered continue to be classified as a homogeneous group called Indians. Native scholars use the terms Indian and Native American reluctantly.

The field of archaeology is a discipline that has been little understood in the Native American community. Digging about in the ancient tombs and robbing graves are activities Native Americans associate with witchcraft and consider to be fraught with the danger of contamination and death. Traditionally, most Indian people would not consider digging up another human being's remains. However, times change.

The European explorers were fascinated by the native people they encountered in North America. Who were they? The ten lost tribes of Israel? Were they human? Non-Indians sought answers to these questions by excavating ancient settlement and burial sites. And from the first, they turned to Indian laborers to assist them. But native people have long since outgrown their status as mere informants or laborers for anthropologists. They have over the past fifty years become literate and are now ready to take an active role in the wider subject of human studies. They are no longer content to be examined, poked, dissected, analyzed, and interpreted by outsiders. They now request—no, they demand—that they be allowed to take an active role in the study of their people and their cultures.

The A:shiwi, or Zunis, have since the 1960s sponsored their own archaeological programs. The Hopis also have their own cultural-resources program. The Navajos have an exceptional resource-management department, and the Mashantucket Pequots of Ledyard, Connecticut, are designing and financing their own archaeological museum. Archaeology is helping them to rediscover their identity.

In the past, anthropologists ("the ones who ask foolish questions") would arrive in native communities every spring. They would flock into Indian villages with hard candy for the native children, small cameras, notebooks, and short, stubby pencils. (They always had short, stubby pencils.) Today there is not much flocking, but the anthropologists still arrive with their laptop computers, phone hookups, and grant money. However, they don't stay long. And there is no hard candy for the children.

The archaeologists were altogether a different breed. They hired field crews for pick-and-shovel duties and to provide information. They came in a large flock and camped out in the ruins they were excavating. And they stimulated little interest among Indians.

Traditionally, archaeological field parties hired their field workers from the nearby communities, with the intention of having them do all the major digging. Fieldwork crews at most of the major cities—Chaco, Hawikuh, Mesa Verde, Pecos, and Aztec, to name a few—were recruited from Navajo and Zuni groups. Some native families have provided stabilization-crew members for the National Park Service for over forty years. In the language of the Zunis and Navajos, archaeologists are called "the ones who dig up bodies or bones."

Therefore, although archaeology does not deal exclusively with digging up human remains, the implications of exhumation are so strong that there are very few tribal members willing to go into this line of work. So how can one explain why Indian people would work on an excavation crew? Some say it is all right to dig up human remains as long as one is doing the bidding of the person in charge. In other words, the workmen are not doing the digging on their own; they are doing it for pay. Therefore, they are not subject to spiritual danger and cannot be accused of witchcraft. And if a question of danger or contamination does arise, there is always the purification ceremony (the expense of which is so great that the rite is performed only in the case of real danger.) Others rationalize their activities by saying that they are not digging up their own and that even if they are digging up their own, they are doing so with respect for the human remains and not for "power."

Indian archaeologists also argue that most tribes do not have a very strong historical ethic, that they are very present-minded. Tribes look on the past in terms of events and happenings and look upon certain traditions in terms of the "here, now, and always." All their prayers, for example, start with the phrase, "Here, now, this day." They have a very strong present and future orientation but a weak historical perspective. As

one elder said, "Why dwell on the past? We have already been there . . . and we can't do anything to change it."

Today, there are more Indians with degrees and credentials from various universities than ever before. While gaining an education, however, these Native Americans are often losing ground culturally. Native cultures are suffering the same ills that confront small towns and large cities in America. What does all this have to do with archaeology or Indian archaeologists? A great deal. There has been a deep-seated change in cultural attitudes toward the very serious taboos concerning death and spiritual contamination, and toward ideas about witchcraft. Most of the Indians who are going into the field and who are pursuing professional degrees began as paraprofessionals in summer field schools and contract archaeology projects. And because they were not exposed to the deep cultural conditioning of the older generation, they do not dwell on cultural restrictions.

The law says that all federally funded construction projects, as part of the plan of work, must have an archaeological survey and must develop a data-recovery plan. Today, these projects are carried out by private contractors who hire local people as field-survey crews and as salvage, data-recovery, and excavation crews. Most of the work consists of resource management, surveying and mapping, mitigation programs, and repatriation activities. This is where all or most Indian archaeologists are involved. They are for the most part not directly in charge of excavations, simply because they have not had the advanced classroom training necessary. Furthermore, they are usually working in subject areas not directly associated with their own tribe.

Despite the growing participation of Indians in archaeology, some feelings of apprehension and anxiety persist, based on the old taboos. Consider the Zuni Archaeological Program (ZAP). Most, if not all, of the field programs sponsored by the ZAP are headed by non–tribal members, assisted by paraprofessional tribal field leaders. The latter are given the opportunity to participate in the production of field reports for publication. A recent statement by the only Indian archaeologist in the Bureau of Land Management working in the Great Basin reflects this mixture of scientific and tribal viewpoints. "I've never worked in a burial, and I wouldn't disturb one unless it was an emergency," he declared. "And then I'd have a medicine man there to bless the bones and the archaeologist. . . . We may be tainting our souls by messing with the dead." As a scientist and an Indian (Paiute), he lives in and between both worlds. He would like to see more Indian archaeologists, who, he feels, would be helping their people.

EDMUND J. LADD (Shiwi)
Museum of New Mexico
Santa Fe, New Mexico

ARCHAIC INDIANS

While always retaining an essential "Indianness," Native American cultures adapted over many centuries to regional extremes of temperature and climate, to the mountains, the deserts, the woodlands, and the prairies of the North American continent. Native Americans would eventually occupy one-quarter of the world's habitable surface, spreading to every terrestrial habitat in the Americas. As time passed, the increasingly varied Indian cultures would presage the extraordinary diversity that was to become America. Archaeologists use the term Archaic to refer to the nonagricultural human adaptations that once flourished across large parts of native North America. Although the *Archaic* adaptations spanned ten thousand years and an entire continent, certain key characteristics tie them all together.

The term *Archaic* was initially employed by archaeologists during the 1930s to designate a preceramic, preagricultural culture discovered in New York State. The absence of pottery was considered the hallmark of this cultural period. Over the years, as archaeologists expanded their excavations, they came to realize that similar "Archaic" materials could be found throughout North America. Today, *Archaic* has taken on two rather different meanings.

In eastern North America, *Archaic* defines a specific period of time between the earlier Paleo-Indian cultures and the later Woodland cultures (generally distinguished by ceramics, mound building, and agriculture). But through much of western North America, where the subsequent Woodland adaptations did not develop, *Archaic* refers to a more generalized, nonagricultural way of life. In ancient California, the Northwest Coast, and the intermountain West, such lifeways lasted perhaps ten thousand years—well into the period of initial European contact—and never represented a reliance on agriculture in any meaningful way.

There is every reason to believe that Indians of the Archaic period descended directly from Paleo-Indian ancestors. But the extinction of the Pleistocene mega-

fauna and the spread of the modern deciduous forest produced such significant environmental changes that Archaic people were required to adopt lifestyles rather different from those of their Paleo-Indian predecessors.

As Archaic people spread, they learned to live off the land, and they prospered. Some Archaic groups, particularly those living in high latitudes, depended heavily on hunting for their livelihood. Others, such as the Northwest Coast groups, became experts at fishing. Some, like the Native Americans in the eastern woodlands, would eventually discard their Archaic lifeway in favor of farming. Each tradition of the Archaic is adapted to its particular corner of America.

As the post-Pleistocene climate turned warmer and the vast desert lakes began to dry out in the American West, people of the Desert Archaic tradition began using the emergent marshes to their advantage, collecting bulrushes, cattails, and insect larvae, and fishing the rivers during rich spawning runs.

Other Desert Archaic people quit the disappearing lakes altogether, moving into upland mountain valleys. Here they hunted bighorn sheep and collected plants in the ever-changing post–Ice Age landscape. These Archaic uplanders survived by pursuing a scheduled seasonal round, commonly moving several times each year.

Survival in these harsh desert conditions required an extraordinary degree of cooperation. The Desert Archaic lifeway must have revolved around the nuclear family, the basic and irreducible unit of survival, which was characterized by a simple division of labor according to gender.

Unlike their Paleo-Indian forebears, who tended to focus most subsistence efforts on a few select species, Archaic people in California exploited an immense array of environments. This broad-based lifeway served them well because no single resource held the key to their survival. The resulting lifeway survived for millennia, shifting with changing conditions but always maintaining the balance between people and the land.

Californians found plentiful sources of protein-rich seeds in the chaparral, where they also hunted deer and smaller mammals. Along the Pacific coastline they harvested countless species of fish, shellfish, seals, and even whales that periodically became beached. The mountains provided deer, bear, and elk, plus the plant foods that became available by midsummer. The major rivers served up huge quantities of spawning salmon, trout, and eel.

Archaic Californians managed their homeland with a gentle hand. Lightning fires have always been a threat to the indispensable acorn harvest, and Archaic people clearly understood the principles of fire ecology. They knew that the chaparral became ecologically unstable when it was overly mature. When fire finally did erupt, it could be catastrophic. They took preventive action by deliberately setting brushfires to burn off older growth, litter, and seedlings. Periodic torching of the underbrush eliminated the danger of the destructive crown fires that all too often darken today's California summer sky.

Californian Archaic people also understood that a managed burn of chaparral vegetation promoted new growth. Tender new sprouts appeared within a month of a spring burn, providing attractive browse for deer; fall burning was certain to provide springtime fare for the Indian people. Judicious burning also increased the available grazing lands for deer, elk, and antelope and facilitated the gathering of acorns, which ripened after the burning took place. Fires were sometimes deliberately set in oak groves to clear the ground for easier acorn gathering, to decrease the effects of pests such as the acorn weevil, and to kill other kinds of tree seedlings that could eventually crowd out the valuable oaks.

On the Great Plains—a flat land of cold winters and hot summers, of sparse and unpredictable precipitation—the Paleo-Indian ancestors had hunted mammoths and other now-extinct Ice Age game. Then at the end of the Pleistocene the primeval northern conifer forest was gradually replaced by deciduous woodland. Sometime between 8000 and 6000 B.C. these woodlands were in turn replaced by a postglacial vegetation cover of perennial grasses. Trees occur today only in stream valleys, scarp lands, and hilly localities.

Plains Archaic people prospered here for hundreds of generations by following their natural cycle of hunting game of all kinds and gathering seeds, tubers, nuts, and berries. While the Plains Archaic lifeway emphasized variety and broad-based subsistence, bison hunting was always critical for survival.

Long before European horses came to the Great Plains, Archaic hunters developed highly successful ways of harvesting buffalo. Although they sometimes hunted these huge beasts individually, they learned the hard way that driving a stone-tipped arrow or spear through the tough buffalo hide was no easy task. Many arrows were lost before one struck home. This is why the Plains Archaic hunters developed the art of "buffalo jumping," a cleverly successful way to take large numbers of buffalo without the dangers and uncertain-

ties of individual stalking. Buffalo jumps employ a highly sophisticated hunting technique, and archaeologists are only beginning to understand their complexity.

Perhaps the most spectacular expression of the eastern Archaic lifeway can be seen at Poverty Point, an archaeological site in Louisiana constructed between about 1800 and 500 B.C. Poverty Point is best known for the striking earthworks still visible there: one large mound and three smaller ones, interrelated to six concentric low ridges arranged in the shape of a partial octagon. The largest mound looks like a bird with wings outspread; it measures 710 by 640 feet and stands 70 feet high. Although the smaller, conical mounds superficially resemble the burial mounds of the subsequent Woodland cultures, no human burials have been found in the Poverty Point mounds.

Millions of cubic feet of earth were required to construct the six concentric ridges, the outermost having an exterior diameter of two-thirds of a mile. So extensive are these earthworks that, when they were first reported in 1873, investigators thought they were natural levee formations. Only when archaeologists took to the air, in the 1950s, was it discovered that these embankments were man-made artificial ridges. Some of the embankments had houses built on top of them, while others seem to have served only to connect the mounds or perhaps to mark alignments of some sort.

The artifacts from Poverty Point not only demonstrate a high degree of craftsmanship, but also establish a pattern of long-distance trade: copper from the Great Lakes, lead ore (galena) from Missouri, soapstone (steatite) from Alabama and Georgia, and various tool stones (used for dart points and knives) from Arkansas, Tennessee, Mississippi, Alabama, Kentucky, Indiana, and Ohio.

Poverty Point has long posed a problem for American archaeologists. In the traditional view, Native Americans during this time period are believed to have been nomadic hunters and gatherers, living in small bands or rudimentary tribes. Such "unsophisticated" people were thought to have been incapable of joining together for large-scale community projects such as the huge earthworks at Poverty Point. According to this conventional wisdom, such monumental construction efforts would be possible only after relatively large human populations had started living in permanent villages, which would in turn have been supported by a food-producing, fully agricultural economic base. Because Poverty Point appears to satisfy neither condition, it has become "enigmatic."

Many archaeologists now question this view. Some think that the distinctive Poverty Point lifeway might have arisen without any agricultural base. Others think that the Poverty Point people did farm, but that they farmed in a different manner from most American Indian groups. Instead of producing maize (an import from Mexico), perhaps the fields supporting Poverty Point contained plants native to the Southeast, like sunflowers, sumpweed (marsh elder), and goosefoot. Some evidence also suggests that Poverty Point groups might have cultivated small garden plots of bottle gourd and squash, both for use as containers and for their edible seeds.

Poverty Point was until recently viewed as a cultural isolate. But today more than one hundred Poverty Point sites are known in Louisiana, Arkansas, and Mississippi; so-called Poverty Point influences can be traced as far as Florida, Tennessee, and Missouri. Clearly the Poverty Point phenomenon existed over a huge region, encompassing many people and multiple sites. Granted, the Poverty Point site itself remains unusual, but it is no longer the archaeological mystery it was three decades ago.

Poverty Point people were by no means homogeneous; rather, they were divided into a number of politically, socially, ethnically, and linguistically distinct groups, sharing a set of distinctive artifacts: Poverty Point objects, clay figurines, micro-flints, plummets, and extraordinarily well crafted stone beads and pendants. These objects' common denominators include a preponderance of exotic materials and, especially in the case of ornaments and other emblems of status, of ground and polished stone.

Poverty Point was eventually abandoned, and a thousand years would pass before eastern North America again saw such elaborate ceremonial spaces. But Poverty Point remains important because it shows the degree to which Native American creativity of later periods was anchored in the long-standing lifeway of the Archaic people, from the desert foragers of the West to the forest dwellers of the Southeast, from the acorn harvesters of California to the buffalo hunters of the Great Plains, from the whale hunters of the Olympic Peninsula to the precocious mound builders at Poverty Point.

Some would dismiss these Archaic people as simply "primitive," irrelevant to modern concerns because they did not become farmers and live in cities. Today, some think that to be "primitive" is to be backward, shabby, ailing, and famished.

Western civilization has constructed its own past, a perception of history based on platitudes projected backward in time. Nineteenth-century scholars wrote of the three major stages of human culture: a progression from "savagery" to "barbarism" and finally to "civilization." Later social historians characterized the technological innovations of the past as somehow "rescuing" human beings from the "pressures" of simpler lifestyles and "permitting" new, more progressive customs to unfold. This view assumes that people must always attempt to get ahead, to wrest an edge. It assumes that people must invent agriculture as a natural culmination of human evolution. But does this "civilized" lifestyle necessarily bring with it improvements in health and well-being? Does this really imply "progress"?

The Native American Archaic past tells us that the answer is no. Today's shortsighted view of "progress" ignores the fact that specialization can itself be destabilizing. How many people realize that farmers often must work much harder than hunters, gatherers, and fishing people? Typical preindustrial farmers spent four to six days per week working the fields. The California foragers may have needed to work only two days a week to feed their families. Farming people usually require that their children help out in the fields. Children in foraging societies have not typically been part of the labor force.

Native people of California achieved the highest aboriginal population density in North America without an agricultural base. The nonagricultural people of the Great Plains crafted ecologically viable alliances capable of weathering the long-term storm. Desert Archaic people maintained a virtually unchanged adaptation to the harshest of environments for ten thousand years.

We have much to learn from nonagricultural foraging people. These nonspecialized economies have a demonstrated longevity and a degree of long-term cultural stability and survival unknown in today's world.

See also Mound Builders; Paleo-Indians; Woodland Phase Indians.

Frison, George C., *Prehistoric Hunters of the High Plains,* 2d ed. (San Diego: Academic Press, 1991); Kirk, Ruth, with Richard D. Daugherty, *Hunters of the Whale: An Adventure in Northwest Coast Archaeology* (New York: William Morrow and Company, 1974); Thomas, David Hurst, "Spreading across America," in *Exploring Ancient Native America: An Archaeological Guide* (New York: Macmillan, 1994).

DAVID HURST THOMAS
American Museum of Natural History

ARCHITECTURE

More than constraints of climate or technology dictated the size and shape of American Indian homes, camps, and towns. Indian architectural traditions also reflected the diversity of tribal economic patterns, social organizations, historical experiences, religious systems, and worldviews. American Indian societies were no slaves to necessity, and in any particular region any one of a number of determinants could have the greatest impact.

In the Northeast, for instance, neither natural limitations of building materials nor climate forced Iroquois tribespeople to build bark-covered, barrel-roofed *long-houses* up to four hundred feet long. Length was determined by the social code, which required all members of the same (matrilineal) clan to live under one roof. Similarly, on the opposite coast, the Salish-speaking people of Puget Sound chose to construct equally lengthy, shed-roofed structures of cedar planks to shelter, in some cases, entire villages within a single structure. On the other hand, their northern neighbors along the British Columbia coast preferred separate wood structures so that more prestigious lineages might be immediately recognized by their "noble" houses, which often carried their own proper names.

To the general public the subject of Indian architecture conjures up the stereotypical trio of *igloo, tipi,* and *wigwam*. Across North America, however, Indian builders created dozens of different structures for multiple purposes using the bark, wood, rocks, reeds, grass, earth, snow, and other natural materials at hand.

Up and down the Atlantic Coast one basic structural system—pole frames sheathed with bark or reeds—produced a wide spectrum of building types. In the Canadian Maritimes and the eastern subarctic, tipi-shaped wigwams were made of conical groupings of fir uprights rigidified with supporting hoops. For their covering, birch-bark sheets were sewn into long scrolls with root fibers and stiffened at the end with battens. Once the sheets were draped over the frame, external poles kept them from blowing off in heavy winds. Inside these cozy shelters the floors were softened with interwoven sweet-smelling spruce boughs; furs provided added warmth and comfort.

For more permanent settlements along the Mid-Atlantic Coast, Algonquian-speaking tribes bent their saplings into rounded shapes, which were then shrouded with various barks. Known by the generic Algonquian term for "dwelling," the one- or two-family *wig-*

wam was hemispherical. But the frame could also be elongated, creating an aisle of hoops for a barrel-roofed "longhouse" that could shelter numerous families. John White's sketches of the North Carolina native settlements he visited in 1585 show villages with and without protective log palisades, longhouses of different sizes (probably reflecting social status), a pointy-roofed "temple" structure, clearly delineated dance and ritual grounds, central "streets," and lookout stands on stilts for deterring crows from corn fields.

Along the St. Lawrence River were found the most elaborate bark buildings—Iroquois longhouses. Celebrated in native myth and oratory as well as in social and political history, these structures at one time extended hundreds of feet in length, depending on the population of the resident clan. Their roofing frames of bent (or perhaps prebent) saplings were lashed atop vertical upright posts. Roofed with elm-bark slabs, a clan totem emblazoned by the doorway, such a structure could be expanded when a new husband married into the building's social unit. Within the building, bunklike compartments lined both sides, with families sharing cooking fires that were spaced down the central corridor and from whose pots any house resident was free to partake. Occupied year-round, in the seventeenth century some larger Iroquois villages contained dozens of such structures.

In the Great Lakes and across the subarctic, bark technology produced a host of structures. Among the Winnebagos and Ojibwas, oral traditions perpetuated the making of over half a dozen building types. There were small domical wigwams, roofed with birch bark but often walled with reed mats for easy rain runoff. To clamp the bark roofing in place, heavy poles were leaned around the building, or an exoskeleton of saplings was bound tightly over it. Decorated woven mats were hung inside for insulation. For their great medicine-lodge ceremonies, extended domical structures were constructed, with the framing left open, the side walls of leafy boughs or bark, and the interior appointed to meet ritual requirements. But for divination rituals they also constructed telephone-booth-sized structures, popularly known as "shaking tents," in which shamans hid themselves to divine the whereabouts of lost objects or desired game.

Winter buildings also included not only small conical wigwams but extended conical or tentlike structures inhabited by a handful of families. In extremely cold weather their outside, slanting walls might be banked with snow and the interior would be floored with

Blackfeet women raising tipi poles on the northern plains circa 1900.

springy evergreens. For summer usage families often moved into airier, gable-roofed houses, cooking outside beneath attached arbors whose roofs could also serve as drying racks for firewood or vegetables.

In the Far North a time-honored mode of fighting extreme cold was to burrow into the ground. Semisubterranean houses framed with whale ribs or stacked vertebrae, corbeled driftwood or flat rocks and covered with turf or sod are found in encampments built by most circumpolar peoples. Their dropped floors allowed for maximum natural insulation, their ramplike entry tunnels often featured cold traps, their thick walls and roofs — with thermal effectiveness usually enhanced by a padding of thick snow — contained the meager heat

provided by oil lamps and human bodies, and their raised interior sleeping and working decks kept occupants off the cold floor and as close as possible to trapped, rising heat.

The elaboration of the snow igloo (from Canadian Inuit *iglu*, "house"), a catenary arch composed of a spiraling of snow blocks preferably cut from a fresh drift, was in fact limited to the central Canadian Inuit peoples. With an ice window cut from a frozen stream placed over the entryway tunnel, walrus hides toggled inside for additional insulation, and furs thickly spread on sleeping areas, these structures kept occupants comfortable during the harshest season. When a number of igloos were linked by windproof tunnels, a central,

Teenagers in front of a pueblo in Taos Pueblo, New Mexico, in 1990.

domical roof might be constructed for communal games and feasts. Up to thirty feet in diameter, such roofs were strong enough to support trapezes on which shamans might display their powers.

At the opposite end of the climate range, across the southeastern portion of North America, tribes like the Cherokees, Creeks, and Choctaws clustered around "towns," reflecting the region's pre-Columbian civic heritage of ceremonial centers containing plazas geometrically flanked by earthworks that supported temples or chiefly residences. Early Spanish and British chroniclers verify that Hopewell and Mississippian archaeological traditions were reflected in the settlements of their historical-period successors. Domestic structures, built around a superstructure of hardwood posts and peak-roofed with a thatch covering, were walled with cane wattle and clay daub. Around the exterior might be applied a whitewash colored by finely ground oyster shells.

Most southeastern towns also featured an open-air court for playing ball games and a ceremonial "square ground," flanked by arbors, with assigned seating for dignitaries and clan members. Most important was the winter "townhouse," called by the Creeks *chakofa,* with its steep conical roof that white visitors often likened to a sugar loaf. Used for ritual gatherings, tribal deliberations, and diplomatic negotiations, Cherokee council houses contained bleachers that could seat five hundred occupants and a centrally placed sacred fire fed by appointed tenders.

On the Great Plains the early architectural tradition of rectangular earth lodges persisted into historic times, although the buildings gradually turned circular in form. Found within sedentary villages occupied by gardening-and-hunting tribes in both the central plains and the Middle Missouri, the structures featured partially excavated floors and were framed with cottonwood side posts, central pillars, and roofing rafters. A

A San Carlos Apache wickiup photographed in 1905.

matting of grass or bark, earth or sod was heaped and smoothened over the buildings, which in this damp climate usually required refurbishment or replacement every dozen years.

As the Pawnee peoples of Nebraska's Republican River and Loup River areas rounded their earth-lodge corners and added entryway tunnels of extended length, they ceremonially encoded the building members with cosmological symbolism. Key posts were associated with celestial dieties, earth-lodge construction became a sacred ritual, and the buildings featured shrines at the western end opposite the main entrance and were used for astronomical observations through the centrally located smoke hole and the doorway.

Along the upper Missouri River the Mandans and Hidatsas also shifted from rectangular to circular earth lodges shortly before white contact. Mandan villages were oriented around plazas in whose center sat a barrel-shaped shrine to Lone Man, the culture hero who had introduced most of their tribal institutions—including architecture. Under the direction of women who "owned" the rights to construction and control of domestic space, men performed the heavy construction work on buildings, which used four main central posts—unlike the Pawnees' buildings, which customarily used eight—and which might extend ninety feet in diameter.

As horses increased mobility on the Great Plains, the tradition of conical tents whose semicircular covers could be packed onto triangular frames for easy trans-port gained heightened utility. Newly mounted tribes could now fully exploit the lengthy, lightweight lodgepole pine for framing. Their portable buildings—generally known today as *tipis,* from the Lakota word meaning "to dwell"—soon trebled in height, allowing families to quickly erect and break them down on fast-moving buffalo hunts or to pitch them proudly in huge circles during religious festivals or at formal summertime gatherings when entire tribes convened.

On their carefully tailored covers of sinew-sewn, tanned, and smoked buffalo hides were often painted key symbols associated with the vision experience of a leading male occupant—even though these dwellings also fell under female dominion. The Kiowas of the southern plains and the Blackfeet far to the north were best known for these heraldic "murals in the round." Painted tipis were prominently displayed during annual Sun Dance gatherings, when clans or warrior societies pitched their tipis in time-honored locations around the central Sun Dance Lodge frame made of saplings radiating from a sacred forked cottonwood post.

The most elaborate wood architecture in North America appeared along the northern Pacific Coast. Peoples such as the Kwakiutls, Tsimshians, and Haidas split huge red-cedar trunks using stone mauls and elk-horn wedges and then thinned the rough boards with "elbow adzes" edged with razor-sharp giant mussel shells—and later with metal obtained in exchange for sea-otter pelts. Around heavy post-and-beam frames, these wide boards were either slung vertically, shiplap fashion, with the help of supple withes, or else fixed horizontally around the front and sides. Shingling on the shallow gable roofs was of shorter split-cedar slabs. Inside the house were one or more rectangular tiers supporting the sleeping booths, while a fire pit burned in the earthen center of the building.

Seaside villages were composed of a line or two of such houses facing the Pacific Coast fjords and inlets, with the most favorable locations found near river mouths. Among the Kwakiutls and Tsimshians, facades of elite buildings, generally positioned at the center of a string of houses, were elaborately painted with stylized renderings of clan ancestors. For the Haidas, the crest or "totem" pole associated with their distinctive six-beam house generally carried these "autobiographies" of the houses and their mythic pedigrees, and facades were commonly unpainted.

For the best example of the general priority of sociocultural determinants of the shape and look of American Indian–built forms, one might compare the southwestern Pueblo house cluster with the neighboring Navajo homesteads. The older Pueblo Indian structures of New Mexico and Arizona saw greater use of adobe in the east, where the Rio Grande provided ample water, and more common employment of workable sandstone in the more arid, western mesa country of modern-day Arizona. Generally piling their three-to-five-story house clusters protectively around ceremonial plazas, the occupants used the roof terraces as work spaces for drying venison, vegetables, and firewood as well as for viewing platforms from which to watch the communal harvest dances of summer and the winter animal dances. Completing the spatial ensemble would be the men's social-religious meeting spaces, known generically by the Hopi word *kiva*. In form they were either circular free-standing structures, as one still sees today among the eastern Pueblos, entered by means of ladders jutting from the central smoke hole, or attached rectangular structures, as are still used at Acoma, Zuni, and the Hopi villages.

When ancestors of the present-day Navajos and Apaches entered the region, however, they eschewed the Pueblo clustering idea in favor of dispersed family homesteads. Closely associated with Navajo identity is the centerpiece of these Indian ranches, the *hogan,* of which there are male and female types. Although Navajo builders have proved highly adaptive, constructing their hogans from cedar logs, rocks, railroad ties, cinder blocks, or two-by-fours, these structures share the basic requirements of being east-facing single-room homes with centrally placed cooking and heating sources.

In addition to these buildings, Indians also improvised more temporary structures for many social and ceremonial occasions. Wherever coolness or shade was desired, arbors were often built from available materials. Throughout the diverse architectural inventory of California Indian peoples, such shades or *ramadas* were extremely common, along with earthen pit houses, conical thatch houses, and two-pitch redwood plank houses. These arbors could be rudimentary structures, such as those that northern Plains groups built of pole uprights and crosspieces with flat roofing of leafy cottonwood boughs. Some were more elaborately constructed, such as Yokuts shades, which could provide a second roof over a row of smaller, grass-covered buildings.

In other corners of Native America arbors were the preferred spaces for summer living, such as the shades built by Kiowas from bent hickory frames and thatched with willow boughs. When extra coolness was desired, the leaves would be dashed with buckets of water so that the subsequent evaporation would cause temperatures inside to drop on even the hottest days.

See also Grass Houses; Hogan; Longhouse; Tipi; Wigwam.

MacDonald, George F., *Haida Monumental Art: Villages of the Queen Charlotte Islands* (Vancouver: University of British Columbia Press, 1983); Morgan, Lewis Henry, *Houses and the House-Life of the American Aborigines* (Chicago: University of Chicago Press, 1965); Nabokov, Peter, and Robert Easton, *Native American Architecture* (New York: Oxford University Press, 1989).

PETER NABOKOV
University of Wisconsin at Madison

ARIKARA (SAHNISH)

> There is but one supreme being of power and wisdom, the Chief Above (Neshanu Natchitak). He rules the world. But he gave Mother Corn authority over all things on earth. Neshanu Natchitak is above all, but he made Mother Corn intermediary with human beings on earth. Reverence and gratitude are due from mankind to Nishanu Natchitak for all the good things which we have, and to Mother Corn, through whose mediation we enjoy all these benefits.
>
> *Albert Simpson, Arikara*

For Arikaras, the Mother Corn Ceremony, a ritual which centered on the theme of world renewal, linked the universe, through Mother Corn (represented by a cedar tree), to the keepers of sacred bundles and their kin. Each of the twelve Arikara village bands that lived along the Missouri River in what is now South Dakota had a sacred bundle associated with the Mother Corn rites. Bundles, whether personal or group, provided an object-based connection with powers that, though beyond the realm of daily life, were needed to exist in the everyday world. In matters of daily life, Mother Corn instructed the people in the right ways of living in the world, instilling in them respect for plants and animals, and imparting knowledge of the arts and of housing construction. Through this knowledge, ceremonial lodges become symbolic of the structure of the world.

The Arikaras, who refer to themselves as the Sahnish people, lived for centuries in earth-lodge dwellings in semisedentary horticultural communities. The central earth-lodge or holy lodge was a ceremonial structure that mirrored Arikara cosmology and in which various bundle rites were performed. Though the ancestors of the Arikaras originated in present-day eastern Texas and adjacent portions of present-day Oklahoma, Arkansas, and Louisiana, their knowledge of earth-lodge construction and maize agriculture developed during their later residence in the central Great Plains, primarily Nebraska.

Arikaras are closely related to Skiri Pawnees from whom they split while both groups were settled along the Loup River in present-day Nebraska. Both groups share linguistic features of the Caddoan language family. Archaeological and oral historical information indicates the Arikaras migrated northward along the Missouri River until they reached what is now South Dakota. By the time European travelers encountered them, they had already suffered major population losses from smallpox epidemics (which ravaged many native villages throughout the eighteenth and nineteenth centuries). The remaining Arikaras continued northward along the Missouri and eventually settled south of Mandan and Hidatsa villages north of present-day Bismarck, North Dakota, where they maintained an active trade of agricultural products with other Plains groups.

Despite the devastation of disease and subsequent population losses, the earth-lodge villages of the Arikaras, Mandans, and Hidatsas remained a central destination for Euro-Americans in their increasing westward expansion. A major smallpox epidemic decimated all three riparian settlements in 1837, however, and by 1856, the remaining Arikaras had joined with Mandans and Hidatsas at Like-A-Fishhook Village. The Fort Berthold Reservation in North Dakota was established by executive order in 1891, at which time the Arikaras were forced to resettle there along with the Mandans and the Hidatsas.

The first cession of Arikara lands by treaty took place in 1851 at Fort Laramie. The treaty negotiated there designated more than twelve million acres of reservation land between the Yellowstone and Missouri Rivers. Through subsequent treaty abrogations, the indigenous land base of the Mandans, Hidatsas, and Arikaras was reduced to 640,000 acres by 1910. Cultural adjustments in the early reservation period included the reversal of some gender-based occupations; for example, men were taught Euro-American techniques of farming, thereafter encroaching on what was traditionally women's domain. By 1920, Arikaras were successfully competing in the farming and ranching economies in North Dakota, especially in what is now the White Shield District of Fort Berthold, where they benefitted from the agriculturally rich land. Under the 1934 Indian Reorganization Act, the Arikara Nation merged into a single political body with the Hidatsa and the Mandan Nations, collectively known as the Three Affiliated Tribes.

No synopsis of Arikara cultural history would be complete without emphasizing the devastating effects of the construction of the 1951 Garrison Dam, built in a post–World War II development effort to harness hydroelectric power on the Missouri River. The benefits of this project remain few for Fort Berthold people. The Garrison Dam fragmented the reservation land base and divided communities along geopolitical boundaries. While Arikaras live throughout the Fort Berthold Reservation, the most concentrated tribal community remains at White Shield, near early reservation settlements and cultural sites. Among these important sites is the Old Scouts Cemetery, where the famous Arikara scouts who fought with General George Custer and their descendants mark a place of remembrance in Arikara history.

Arikara political and social life mirrors the cosmological ordering of the Arikara world, which in pre-reservation times was tightly structured and hierarchical. Chieftainships were hereditary and sanctioned by ritual authority. Today, the relationships between cosmology, tribal leadership, and social organization are influenced by hereditary class positions and kinship ties that link individuals to extant ceremonial offices. The importance of renewal ceremonies in reaffirming kinship relations is evidenced at various points in the life cycle, such as when a child receives an Arikara name, and in the funerary rites known as the After-Feed which mark a person's passage to the next world.

Despite Arikara population losses resulting from smallpox epidemics, Euro-American conquest, and the dispossession of native lands, ritual life continues to be practiced with modified regularity among contemporary Arikaras, most of whom identify with the Awahu band and trace their ancestry to the Arikara chief, Sitting Bear. While some Arikara elders refer to tribal genealogical associations as "clans," these groupings do not parallel the clan constructs of Mandans and Hidatsas, with whom many Arikaras have intermarried. All three tribes ascribe to classificatory ways of reckoning generational kin, with continuing bias toward matrilineality and matrifocality.

Today, the White Shield District is home to a range of community organizations and programs that celebrate Arikara culture. Among these is the annual powwow, the White Shield Celebration. The Dead Grass Society Singers, the resident drum group for White Shield, actively maintains and creates Arikara songs, which are integral to Arikara traditions. In addition, through the efforts of the Sahnish Cultural Society and Fort Berthold Community College, the Arikara language has been incorporated into the community-based educational curriculum. Through these and other efforts, the Sahnish people are working toward cultural survival and community empowerment.

See also Hidatsa; Mandan.

Gilmore, Melvin R., The Arikara Genesis and Its Teachings. *Indian Notes 3*: (1926): 188–193; Parks, Douglas R., *Traditional Narratives of the Arikara Indians*. 4 Vols. (Lincoln: University of Nebraska Press, 1991); Rogers, J. Daniel, *Objects of Change. The Archaeology and History of Arikara Contact with Europeans* (Washington: Smithsonian Institution Press, 1990).

TRESSA L. BERMAN
Arizona State University West
and National Museum of Natural History

J. DANIEL ROGERS
National Museum of Natural History

ARROWHEADS

Arrowheads—or, more properly, projectile points—are the stone, metal, bone, or antler components of prehistoric weaponry designed to penetrate and impart a lethal wound. Most of them were made of stone, manufactured by means of percussion and pressure flaking. The process of stone flaking (or knapping), in which a stone is gradually diminished in size until the desired shape is obtained, required great skill, which could be developed only through long practice.

Smaller numbers of projectile points were made from other raw materials. Slate projectiles were ground to the desired shape by Eskimo hunters. Bone and antler, used in many instances, were shaped by cutting and abrasion. Antler tips were used in rare cases, and needed only a hole drilled in the cut end before they were ready to be fitted over the end of a wooden shaft. Metal points were known only rarely in prehistoric times; they were shaped from native copper and were limited to copper sources, especially in the vicinity of the Great Lakes. In some cases a projectile point was not used at all, and a wooden shaft was simply brought to a sharp point; an enlarged piece of wood (or bunt point) was used effectively on birds and small mammals. Iron projectile points were introduced in protohistoric times by European traders, and some Native American groups salvaged metal discarded by the Europeans and forged it into projectile points.

Prehistoric Native Americans expended surprising amounts of time and effort in acquiring the best of stone-flaking materials. When surface materials were exhausted, quarrying became necessary. Trenches, shafts, and open quarries have been found at all known sources of good flaking materials. Lacking metal tools, Native Americans operated these mines with relatively simple tools and techniques. One well-known source of flaking materials in Wyoming was called the Spanish Diggings by the early pioneers because, not believing that Native Americans could have dug the trenches, pits, and shafts that they found there, the settlers attributed the excavations to Spaniards searching for gold.

Projectile points are commonly referred to as the guide fossils for archaeologists. Fortunately for archaeology, each prehistoric cultural group manufactured its projectile points within well-defined limits of size, shape, and technology—to the extent that the presence of a particular cultural group can be determined through its projectile points. Archaeologists group projectile points into types, and each type can be assigned to a past cultural group and time period. Projectile points changed gradually over time, and although some types are often difficult to distinguish, if a large sample of points is recovered in a good geologic context and can be assumed to have been made by one cultural group, an archaeologist can usually determine, within limits, both the culture and the time period represented. Although some other tool types may also be culture and time specific, many tools have experienced no changes in shape for thousands of years and cannot be used as reliable chronological indicators.

The oldest recognized type of projectile point known to have existed in North America dates from just over eleven thousand years ago. Known as the Clovis projectile point (fig. a), this well-designed piece of weaponry has been found in all of the forty-eight contiguous states as well as in Central America and Mesoamerica. Its ability to penetrate and kill a mammoth has been demonstrated through experiments on African elephants. Contemporary with the chipped-stone Clovis points are elongate cylinders with sharp points carved from mammoth or mastodon bone and ivory, which may have been used as projectiles.

In the period between the Clovis era and about eight thousand years ago, cultural groups known as the late

Paleo-Indians used a number of projectile-point types. These points demonstrate technological and morphological changes that can be assigned to a number of different cultural groups. A stemmed type known as Eden (fig. b), named after a nine-thousand-year-old site in western Wyoming, indicates a change in the method of attaching or hafting stone points to wooden shafts. A highly developed stone-knapping technology is demonstrated in all Paleo-Indian projectile points, which also show evidence of concerted efforts to acquire the best of raw materials, some from distances of several hundred kilometers.

After about eight thousand years ago, the notching of projectile points became popular (fig. c), although unnotched types did recur. Notching made it easier to attach a point to a wooden shaft, but it also weakened the point, and breakage was common across notches. Variations in the notching process are time specific and aid the archaeologist in chronological placement. Large notched and unnotched projectile points were mounted on short shafts (called *foreshafts*) that were in turn inserted into tapered holes in a longer shaft (called a *main shaft*). They were propelled by an *atlatl*, a stick held in one hand that acts to lengthen the arm of the user. A hook in the end of the atlatl engages with a small hole or cup in the proximal end of the main shaft.

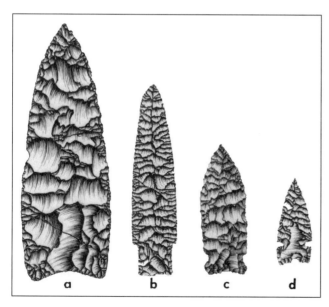

Arrowheads, or projectile points, used by prehistoric Native Americans: Clovis (a), 11,000 years old; Cody Complex (b), 8,000 years old; Archaic side-notched (c), 6,500 years old; bow-and-arrow side-notched (d), 800 years old.

The sharp end of the projectile point penetrates an animal's hide, and the sharp blade edges cut a hole large enough to allow entry of the entire foreshaft. Feather fletching improved the accuracy of the long shaft.

After about two thousand years ago, the size of projectile points decreased noticeably (fig. d), a trend that coincided with the appearance of the bow and arrow. Attached to a shaft of smaller diameter and shorter length, the smaller points compensated for their lack of weight by the higher velocities they could attain. Another advantage of the bow and arrow was that less raw stone-flaking material was needed for the manufacture of projectile points. Although these small projectile points are often referred to as bird points or small animal points, thousands of them have been recovered on the Great Plains at sites of buffalo jumping and trapping during the bow-and-arrow period, a fact that demonstrates the lethal qualities of such points on large animals.

A question that inevitably arises is why these projectile points were not retrieved and reused. Many were in fact reused, and broken parts that could be reshaped into functional weaponry were commonly so treated. However, reshaped projectile points are of little interest to archaeologists because in the reshaping process, a point's original configuration becomes altered to such a degree that, unless the point has been found together with something that can be dated, type identification and chronological placement become difficult if not impossible.

See also Paleo-Indians; Woodland Phase Indians.

GEORGE C. FRISON
University of Wyoming

ART, VISUAL (TO 1960)

Native Americans regard art as an element of life, not as a separate aesthetic expression. In aboriginal societies, public life brings together dancing, poetry, and the plastic and graphic arts, uniting them in a single function: ritual as the all-embracing expression of life. Art is indispensable to ritual, and ritual represents the Native American concept of the whole life process.

Aboriginal philosophy does not separate art from healing or spirituality. Most of the healing disciplines came originally from religious beliefs and the practices of spiritual leaders. Trance, dance, painted drums, and painted shields were central to early shamanism, as they are to the continuing practice of this art and of other forms of Indian spirituality today.

In the hundreds of Native American languages there is no word that comes close to the meaning of the Western word *art*. Art, beauty, and spirituality are intertwined in the Native American routine of living.

Native Americans freely use symbols of the spiritual and physical worlds to enrich their daily lives and ceremonies. Symbols are protectors and reminders of the living universe, bridging the gap between the spiritual and physical realms. Symbols are used in ritual performances to portray the power in the cosmos. A common visual symbol used for healing in many American Indian societies in the past and also today is the mandala. The mandala represents the cosmos in miniature and, at the same time, the pantheon. Its construction is equivalent to a magical re-creation of the world. The mandala is in essence a schematic diagram showing the

Chilkat frontlet mask (Alaska, late nineteenth century) of carved and painted wood, operculum shell, human hair, and sinew cord, said to have belonged to Skundoo, a Chilkat shaman.

balance of forces in the symbolic universe. Native Americans have created mandalas in Navajo and Pueblo sand paintings, on Plains war shields, and on rock paintings throughout North America; they have also projected the mandala into space and time in the form of medicine wheels.

The medicine wheel, a mandalic art form and religious symbol, is common to many tribes. It consists of a circle, through the center of which are drawn horizontal and vertical lines and at the center of which an eagle feather is usually attached. The circle represents the sacred outer boundary of Earth; the vertical and horizontal lines represent the sun's and humanity's sacred paths; the crossing of the lines indicates Earth's center; the eagle feather is a sign of the Creator's power over everything. The medicine wheel is often marked with the four sacred colors common to indigenous people throughout North and South America— black, white, red, and yellow—representing the four cardinal directions, the four symbolic races of humanity, and other fourfold relationships.

It is difficult to discuss traditional Native American visual arts, especially prehistoric art, in terms of isolated objects categorized as paintings, sculpture, and so forth. For example, in many native cultures masks form part of a whole complex encompassing music, dance, drama, and poetry. In the setting of a modern museum or gallery, the essence of the aesthetic of such masks is lost.

In the area now called the United States, the indigenous populations were, and still are, extremely varied. Attempts to classify or order this diversity are complex. A common method used by scholars is the concept of "culture areas," geographical regions occupied by peoples with a significant degree of similarity among themselves and a significant amount of dissimilarity from the cultures of peoples in other areas. For the purposes of this essay, then, the *East* will be considered to have the Atlantic Coast as its eastern boundary and to be bordered on the west by the Great Plains. (At times the art of the *Southeast* will be discussed separately.) The *Plains* will include the prairies of the Midwest, most of the states of Michigan, Illinois, and Missouri, and the western parts of Arkansas and Texas, and will have the Rocky Mountains as its western boundary. The *West* will include southern California, the Great Basin, and the Plateau—all of the United States west of the Rocky Mountains with the exception of the Northwest Coast and the Southwest. The *Northwest Coast* will include

San Ildefonso Pueblo polychrome storage jar, circa 1925, by María Martínez (1886–1980), designed by her husband, Julian Martínez (1897–1943). María Martínez, with the help of her husband, was responsible for the revival of traditional pottery styles.

the Pacific Coast from southern Alaska to northern California. And the *Southwest* will encompass most of Arizona and New Mexico, southeastern Nevada, southern Utah, and southwestern Colorado.

Eastern Art

Prehistoric symbolism increased in the eastern United States around 1000 B.C., when the Woodland cultures began to take shape, particularly along the lower Mississippi River and the lower Ohio River. Although the people continued some modes of Archaic subsistence, horticulture had begun to emerge and Indians began manufacturing elaborate objects to be used in ceremonial and artistic contexts. During the Woodland period, pottery was manufactured all over the eastern United States. Techniques for carving stone and hammering copper were also developed. The animal symbolism used in embellishing these objects (buzzards, falcons, owls, eagles, frogs, serpents, and turtles) became widespread among indigenous people now called southeastern Indians.

Design elements included an emphasis on raptorial birds with curved beaks and talons. Birds and other creatures either were depicted in a split representation, in which the creature is shown split down the middle, so that both its left and right sides are depicted, or were represented in opposition or conflict. Design elements also included geometric forms such as circles and four-sided figures. Such geometric motifs were incised on stone and ceramics that were used to form mounds and earthworks. Earth mounds in the shape of animals and in geometric shapes were built up over the remains of the dead.

Around A.D. 800 southeastern Indians began practicing maize agriculture. Accompanying this horticultural development was the introduction of a widespread symbolic system that art historians call the Southern Cult or Southeastern Ceremonial Complex, which appears to have had links to Mesoamerica. Vessels and effigy jars excavated in southern Missouri, Arkansas, and Louisiana resemble similar items found in Veracruz and Zacatecas, Mexico. Clay and shell engravings found in the Southeast also carry motifs that resemble Mexican designs, such as the winged serpent and the eagle warrior. Eye-in-hand and wide-jawed-skull symbols found on objects recovered from Moundville, Alabama, are associated with the Aztec god Mitlantecutli, the Death God of the Aztec codices. When Spanish explorers came to the South in the sixteenth century, the Moundville complex was flourishing. However, European diseases caused a population collapse and societal deterioration. Many symbols associated with Moundville were no longer in use when the English arrived on the Atlantic Coast a century later.

British and U.S. dominance of the eastern art area led to disease, warfare, land loss, and the disruption of traditional cultures. The 1830s, an era of forced removal to Oklahoma for many eastern groups, were a particularly troubling time. One effect of all these changes was a marked decline in pictorial and sculptural traditions. However, the decorative arts associated with clothing still flourished. European-introduced glass beads replaced quills and shells in beadwork. Although some European-derived design elements such as floral motifs and curvilinear patterns were incorporated in clothing decorations, there still persisted decorative symbols that had existed since precontact times.

Plains Art

In prehistoric times some Plains people lived a hunting-gathering life that had been practiced for thousands of years, while others lived in agricultural communities along major waterways and had a lifestyle similar to that of Eastern Woodlands cultures. Art activity was minimal, and the only known paintings scholars have found are in the form of rock art. However, the introduction of the horse in the eighteenth century and the westward migration of other tribes fleeing European settlers caused a shift in customs. Many Plains peoples adopted a nomadic lifestyle and encouraged individuality and group assertiveness within their communities. Personal honor became a significant goal for many people.

These aspects of life influenced Plains art, which became portable and was intended to display the courage, war heroism, and prestige of the owner. The decorative arts were expressed in fine clothing and in horse regalia through the use of porcupine-quill embroidery, shells, and glass beads. Geometric motifs dominated, with white and bright colors used in small designs against a dark background. Women were responsible for decorating clothing and household items.

Art created by men was mnemonic, detailing a man's conquests in war and on the hunt; it often incorporated symbols derived from vision quests and dreams. Hide paintings that recorded tribal events were made to be displayed on the ground, surrounded by viewers. Prior to the 1800s humans were depicted as stick figures and animal forms were formalized, with minimal detail. Greater naturalism in the depiction of people and animals occurred in the mid-1800s as a result of interaction with European and American artists such as Karl Bodmer and George Catlin, who visited and pictorially documented the Plains tribes. Hide paintings gradually became replaced by ledger-book drawings and paintings, which also recorded historical events. Most ledger books (account books obtained from whites and filled with drawings) date from the last quarter of the nineteenth century, but some were produced as recently as the first decade of the twentieth century. In some books each page was equivalent to a section of a hide painting, while in others the format used was based on European spatial illusionism and perspective. Unlike art from other cultural areas, Plains art was predominantly the result of the cultural changes that began with the onset of Western expansion and the Plains peoples' consequent exposure to European art.

Western Art

Pictographs and petroglyphs were the only found pictorial art in the Great Basin and Plateau. Between the Sierra Nevada and the Pacific Ocean, on the other hand, pictorial traditions focused on basketry and rock art. With the exception of indigenous southern Californians, western Native Americans had no contact with Europeans until after the middle of the nineteenth cen-

tury, at which point many of them experienced extermination or dislocation. Indians living in southern California missions had their lives totally disrupted during the post-1848 mining boom; as a result, 90 percent of them died. Contact with whites caused near-total destruction of all western indigenous art.

Northwest Coast Art

Because of regional isolation and an unusual ecological situation, Northwest Coast cultures were very different from other indigenous groups. Stress was placed on kinship ranking and a hierarchical social system, expressed visually in village architecture and in outward signs of wealth through artworks such as heraldic wood carvings, decorated utensils, totem poles, kinetic masks, and blankets.

Professional artists supported by an elite ruling class created prestigious items such as monumental sculptures celebrating the owner's family history and ceremonial masks used in dramas to enact a lineage's history and achievements. Architectural carving followed the vertical, columnar qualities of tree trunks; the dominant color schemes included the four sacred colors: red, yellow, black, and white. Unlike the masks of most Native American tribes and nations, Northwest Coast masks were highly naturalistic, often portraits of specific individuals. Most masks were equipped with moving parts, giving rise to a distinct, sophisticated illusionistic theater art.

In the nineteenth century the European fur trade had devastating effects on the arts of the Northwest Coast. Trade upset the social, political, and economic life of the region, and European diseases and warfare reduced the population. Christian missionaries outlawed giveaway ceremonies and other traditional institutions that supported artistic development. By the end of the century, many aspects of traditional Northwest Coast culture had been eroded, but communities continued to practice their traditional crafts. When government policies began to change around the middle of the twentieth century, Northwest Coast peoples quickly reestablished their spiritual traditions and fostered a cultural renaissance.

Southwestern Art

Three great sedentary cultures developed in the Southwest, primarily after 300 B.C. In the southern Arizona desert area the *Hohokam* peoples lived in agricultural villages where they cultivated corn, beans, and squash. They created distinct pottery styles and used shells to make jewelry; their cultivation of cotton gave rise to experimentation in clothing design. The *Mogollon* peoples of southwestern New Mexico also lived in permanent homes and produced pottery, jewelry, and woven cloth. Their use of the kiva or underground ceremonial room indicates contact with the *Anasazi* culture. That culture was centered in the Four Corners area of the Southwest—the point at which Arizona, New Mexico, Colorado, and Utah meet. Developing somewhat later (A.D. 1100–1300), the Anasazi displayed their creativity through architecture. They constructed cliff, mesa, and valley pueblos equipped with kivas. Murals were painted on kiva walls using a dry fresco technique. Color was applied in flat, even tones. Imagery included representational forms such as masked supernatural beings, beings with zoomorphic and anthropomorphic characteristics, plant life, and natural phenomena such as clouds, lightning, and astral forms. The Anasazi also created distinct pottery styles, basketry, textiles, and personal adornments.

The richest artistic contribution of all three groups was the ceramic traditions they developed. The Hohokam peoples concentrated on red-on-buff styles, the Mogollon peoples emphasized black-on-white color schemes, and the Anasazi used shapes and designs that were reflective of their basketry.

Because of its geographical location, "advanced" civilization, and similarities with Mexico in areas such as masonry, painted pottery, cloth weaving, rain ceremonies, and the priesthood, the Southwest is often regarded as the passageway for the flow of culture from Mesoamerica to other parts of the North American continent. Many scholars believe that the concept of Father Sky and Mother Earth, which spread to many areas in North America, developed in Mesoamerica.

Although 1540 is the date often used by scholars to mark the termination of North American prehistoric cultures, in the Southwest there is little evidence of a break in craft expression at that time. Artistic traditions continued to flourish, with little noticeable change. With the advent of the railroad in the region in the 1880s, native crafts people adapted their works to meet the needs of Anglo tourists, sometimes incorporating new materials such as silver or commercial dyes. However, despite slight modifications in styles and materials, native artistic traditions continued.

The use of the arts for healing has also continued in the Southwest, remaining almost unchanged since European contact. The most well known example of art in the service of healing is the Navajo sand-painting ritual, in which a patient lies on the ground while a medicine man–singer chants and blows colored sand onto the patient and onto the ground. Cultural symbols that are related to specific myths, deities, illnesses, and so forth are created by the medicine man during such ceremonies. Sand paintings are created and then destroyed each time a ceremony is performed. Over one thousand images and songs are associated with Navajo sand-painting ceremonies.

Traditional pictorial arts of the Southwest were ancient and varied. Some were purely decorative; others, featuring representational images, tended to be used for ritual purposes. This practice, with modifications, continues today.

———◆◆◆———

Five hundred years after the arrival of Columbus in the New World, the cultural influences acting on Native American art remain varied and complex. Many aesthetic changes have taken place in the twentieth century as native peoples have participated more fully in the dominant culture and incorporated artistic traditions from the United States, Europe, and other parts of the globe into their own traditions. Native American artists are in the process of developing new definitions of Indian art. Any insistence that Indian art remain "traditional" as a way of preserving culture is a form of cultural discrimination, because cultures are dynamic, not static.

Some modern writers have categorized the dominant styles of twentieth-century Native American art into four schools: historic expressionism, traditionalism, modernism, and individualism. *Historic expressionism* follows the techniques and design conventions of nineteenth-century tribal aesthetics while incorporating new themes. It is a reinterpretation of ancient conventions. *Traditionalism* retains a flat, shaded treatment of historic native imagery. This style is identified in the public's mind as "real Indian art" and is associated with the Santa Fe Studio of Dorothy Dunn and the "Kiowa movement." It was the style encouraged in the Philbrook Art Center's earlier competitions, held in Oklahoma beginning in 1946. Celebrated artists of this style such as Gilbert Atencio, Andrew Tsinahjinnic, Archie Blackowl, Harrison Begay, Fred Kabotie, Stephen Mopope, Ma Pe Wi, and Pablita Velarde created a rich legacy. Unfortunately, some conservative scholars and collectors have canonized this heritage as the only legitimate Indian art. *Modernism* experiments with mainstream contemporary art techniques but maintains a visible Native American imagery. *Individualism* refers to work that is indistinguishable from mainstream contemporary art and does not show an obvious allegiance to Indian social movements or ethnic identity.

Artists such as Oscar Howe (Yanktonai Sioux, 1915–84), Al Houser (Chiricahua Apache, 1914–94), R. C. Gorman (Navajo, 1932–), and others helped bridge the gap between so-called traditional American Indian art and mainstream art. These artists opened new, expressive avenues for Indian artists that went beyond the meticulously detailed, yet frozen realism of traditional Indian painting. With neo-cubism, Howe recast traditional Indian imagery into structured planes and dramatic color combinations centered on heroic, mystical views of Indians. Howe's 1954 painting *Victory Dance,* influenced by European cubism, is a transitional work that retains the mystic nature of Howe's vision while at the same time imparting an experimental thrust to Indian painting. R. C. Gorman was the first Indian to paint nude figures and the first Indian to own a successful commercial gallery. Sculptor Al Houser's work spanned six decades, and he used styles ranging from the figurative to the surreal and abstract. No matter what the style or period, most Native American art emphasizes Indian values of beauty, balance, and harmony.

Although contemporary Native American culture has lost some of its early symbolism and rituals because of cultural change and assimilation, its essence remains. Native American thinking has not ever separated art from life, what is beautiful from what is functional. Art, beauty, and spirituality are intertwined in the routine of living. The Native American aesthetic has survived colonialism, servitude, racial discrimination, and rapid technological change.

See also Basketry; Beads and Beadwork; Howe, Oscar; Martínez, María; Moundville; Pictographs; Sandpainting; Textiles.

Brody, J. J., *Indian Painter and White Patrons* (Albuquerque: University of New Mexico Press, 1971); Wade, E., ed., *The Arts of the North American Indian: Native Traditions in Evolution* (New York: Hudson Hills Press, 1986); Wade, E., and R. Strickland, *Magic Images: Contemporary Native American Art* (Norman: University of Oklahoma Press, 1981).

PHOEBE FARRIS-DUFRENE (Powhatan)
Purdue University

ARTS, CONTEMPORARY (SINCE 1960)

The early 1960s marked the start of a transition from an Indian art era circumscribed predominantly by non-Indian "experts" to a time when Native American artists began to shape and define their own visual, written, and performing arts. The decade of the 1960s also was the demarcation point between the federal Indian policies of termination and self-determination, producing a mix of programs that promoted both the assimilation of Indians into the dominant society and their cultural distinctiveness from it. Public and private support for contemporary native arts fostered a similar mix of freedom from stylistic and content constraints and a desire to respond to new audiences and marketplace opportunities. It was a period that saw the highest federal concentration on the economic advancement of artists since the government's Indian arts projects of the New Deal era.

During the Kennedy administration, established and emerging Indian artists received heightened visibility, beginning with the commissioning of a work for the new president's inauguration by the Creek painter Solomon McCombs. McCombs, like other artists of his generation such as the painters Fred Beaver (Creek-Seminole) and Archie Blackowl (Cheyenne), was schooled in the "traditional Indian painting" technique at Bacone College in Muskogee, Oklahoma. Its arts programs were run from the 1930s into the 1970s by the senior painters Acee Blue Eagle (Creek), Woody Crumbo (Potawatomi-Creek), and Terry Saul (Choctaw-Chickasaw), and the painter-sculptor W. Richard West, Sr. (Cheyenne), who also taught at another arts center, the Haskell Institute in Lawrence, Kansas, and who revived the art of Plains wood sculpture.

Three contemporaries of the Bacone artists, in terms of age and stylistic training, who were prominent in the 1960s were the sculptor-painter Allan Houser (Chiricahua Apache) and the painters Pablita Velarde (Santa Clara Pueblo) and Oscar Howe (Crow Creek Sioux). They had studied the flat-painting style at the Santa Fe Indian School's studio and quickly departed from the confines of the form. Houser would set the standard for Indian sculpture in that decade, as his son Bob Haozous would in the 1980s and 1990s. Mentor to hundreds of accomplished artists, including his apprentice sculptor Craig Goseyan (White Mountain Apache), Houser was awarded France's Palme Académique in 1992 and the National Medal of Arts, the only Indian ever to be so honored. Velarde's blend of traditional imagery, natural materials, and modern painting techniques has influenced generations of Southwest painters, her daughter Helen Hardin and Tony Da (San Ildefonso Pueblo) among them.

Oscar Howe's new work so startled the experts that his painting was rejected as nontraditional by the jury for the 1958 competition at the Philbrook Art Center in Tulsa, Oklahoma. In response to artists' demands, arts competitions subsequently changed their rules, and Howe's work swept the Philbrook's top awards in 1960 and 1961. Howe's success and his style were catalytic. He and such peers as W. Richard West, Sr., and Blackbear Bosin (Kiowa-Comanche) energized younger painters like Doc Tate Nevaquaya (Comanche), Joan Hill (Creek-Cherokee), Ruth Blalock Jones (Delaware-Shawnee, and Bacone's first woman art director), and Howe's students, who would become influences in their own right: the painter and sculptor Fritz Scholder (Luiseño); and the Oglala Sioux painters Arthur Amiotte and Donald Montileaux. In 1981, two years before he died, Howe said he had been "labeled wrongfully a Cubist. The basic design is *Tahokmu* [spider web]. From an all-Indian background, I developed my own style."

In 1962, a federal focal point for native arts development was established in Santa Fe with the founding of the Institute of American Indian Arts (IAIA), which would be partially privatized in 1988, as the Institute of American Indian and Alaska Native Arts and Culture Development. The IAIA plan was advanced early in the Kennedy administration by the Rockefeller Foundation–funded Southwest Indian Arts Project (1958–61), by the Indian Arts and Crafts Board (IACB), and by the poet-writer John Collier, the Indian Commissioner who had initiated the IACB in 1935. Pivotal to these developments was Lloyd Kiva New (Cherokee), a designer-educator named to the IACB in 1961 and its chair from 1971 to 1995, who taught at the IAIA from its inception and was its president from 1967 to 1978.

In 1964, as the IAIA was organizing, the IACB sponsored a series of key shows, starting with its first annual Invitational Exhibition of Indian Art in Washington, D.C. Among the featured artists was the self-taught painter-sculptor Jerome Tiger (Creek-Seminole), whose ethereal depictions of tribal life and simplicity of form commanded top honors in major competitions. One of Tiger's last group exhibits was the Smithsonian Institution's *America Discovers Indian Art Show* in 1967, the year in which a shooting accident ended his brilliant five-year career and life at twenty-six.

Among other artists who rose to prominence in the 1960s and remained influential were George Morrison (Grand Portage Chippewa) and R. C. Gorman (Nava-

jo). Morrison, a painter shaped by abstract expressionism and surrealism in New York City and France from 1946 to 1963, taught art at the Rhode Island School of Design and the University of Minnesota in his home state, where he also gained fame for his sculpted and collaged wood constructions and totems. Gorman, whose painting was informed by his father, the painter Carl Gorman, and by muralists whose work he studied in Mexico, was the first living native artist whose works were shown in the Metropolitan Museum of Art. Also a master of marketing, he opened his still-successful gallery in Taos, New Mexico, in 1968 as his lyrical portrayals of Navajo women became pop icons and as he gained celebrity status.

Indian musicians and performers also made their mark in the 1960s. The recording artists Patrick Sky (Creek) and Buffy Sainte-Marie (Cree) were leading folksinger-songwriters, often performing in Greenwich Village coffeehouses. Sainte-Marie, whose protest songs became anthems of the era, later gained fame as a *Sesame Street* regular and Academy Award–winning songwriter. Works of the composer Louis Ballard (Osage) were widely produced, notably *The Gods Will Hear,* a cantata with lyrics by Lloyd Kiva New, which was performed by the National Symphony Orchestra.

Jesse Ed Davis (Kiowa) was a top rock guitar player from the 1960s through the 1980s, first with Taj Mahal and Leon Russell and later as a studio musician whose riffs became rock-and-roll staples. The saxophonist Jim Pepper (Creek and Kaw) developed a unique mix of jazz and tribal music, a first usually attributed to jazz great Miles Davis, who credited Pepper with it. Muriel Miguel (Kuna/Rappahannock) made theater history as an actor with the leading experimental repertory group of the period, Joe Chaikin's Open Theatre, and would later be acclaimed as a director and innovator in women's theater.

During the 1960s native images, words, and music were emblematic of the counterculture movement, which denounced the country's genocidal and ecocidal history and focused attention on ongoing Indian resistance. Native portrayals in pop, poster, and T-shirt art and in theater, movies, and music were metaphors for causes of the day, the good-stereotype versions of Indian mascots and slogans in the sports world. The proliferation of Indian imagery encouraged many Indian artists to try to clear away the underbrush of stereotypical depictions, to rescue their symbols and history, to tell their own story, although some simply cashed in on the trend with their own Indian kitsch or became copy artists of those who drew inspiration from native peoples.

Out of this swirl, native artists and would-be artists gravitated to the IAIA from reservations and urban areas, from traditional and assimilated upbringings. The IAIA's most prominent teacher, Allan Houser, gave instruction in sculpture, painting, and design from 1962 to 1975 and helped put the school on the art world's map. In addition to developing skills in his students, he imparted the value of traditional and historical knowledge and cultural metaphor, elements his students cite as essential to their artistic and human growth at the IAIA. Houser also opened doors globally for younger artists and was responsible for the categories of sculpture and monumental sculpture being added to the Santa Fe Indian Market's national arts competition. In 1992, when the IAIA Museum opened, its permanent outdoor exhibition space was named the Allan Houser Art Park.

Fritz Scholder taught at the IAIA from 1964 to 1969, arriving with a solid reputation as an excellent colorist in expressionist/pop art. He learned alongside and

Looking *(1995), by the Luiseño painter-sculptor Fritz Scholder (b. 1937).*

from IAIA students and faculty as they together developed new directions in Indian art that began to emerge in 1965, the year in which Scholder started to paint Indian subjects and T. C. Cannon (Kiowa and Caddo), started his two-year term of study there. Cannon (Pai-doung-u-day), a painter-poet-musician, was the unrivaled school star, a natural and original artist, who shared with Scholder a penchant for image busting. Cannon, like several of his fellow students, went on to study at the San Francisco Art Institute and to serve in Vietnam; others took time away from the IAIA to fight the Indian wars at home.

Among other IAIA student innovators of the 1960s, some of whom would later teach there, were Larry Ahvakana (Inupiaq), Earl Biss (Crow), Parker Boyiddle (Kiowa-Wichita), Bennie Buffalo (Cheyenne), Sherman Chaddlesone (Kiowa), Don Chunestudey (Cherokee), Karita Coffey (Comanche), Grey Cohoe (Navajo), Larry DesJarlais (Turtle Mountain Chippewa), Earl Eder (Sioux), Phyllis Fife (Creek), Henry Gobin (Tulalip), Benjamin Harjo, Jr. (Seminole-Shawnee), Doug Hyde (Nez Perce), Bruce King (Oneida), King Kuka (Blackfeet), Linda Lomahaftewa (Hopi and Choctaw), Bill Prokopioff (Aleut), Kevin Redstar (Crow), Bill Soza (Cahuilla), Richard Ray Whitman (Euchee and Pawnee), Ray Winters (Oglala Sioux), and Alfred Youngman (Cree).

In 1969, N. Scott Momaday (Kiowa) rose to world prominence with his Pulitzer Prize in Fiction for his first novel, *House Made of Dawn* (1968), which he soon followed with *The Way to Rainy Mountain*. Momaday (Tsoai-talee), a writer-poet-painter with scores of books and exhibits to his credit, spawned a generation of native writers; he remains a professor of English and the most highly acclaimed Indian literary figure. Also in 1969, the lawyer-historian Vine Deloria, Jr. (Standing Rock Sioux), published his best-selling popular history, *Custer Died for Your Sins,* which became the thesaurus of Indian political issues of the time, as did his second book, *We Talk, You Listen.*

The singer-activist Floyd Westerman produced a record album, the title and themes of which were taken from Deloria's *Custer,* that became an anthem of Indian activism of the early 1970s. The most successful of the Indian musicians of the era, though, were the rock groups Redbone and XIT. Westerman (Crow Creek Sioux) and American Indian Movement leaders of the period—Dennis J. Banks (Leech Lake Chippewa), Russell Means (Oglala Sioux) and John Trudell (Santee Sioux)—would gain fame as actors in the 1990s in films, including some about their own activities in the 1960s and 1970s.

As Indian activism captured world attention, beginning with the 1969 takeover of Alcatraz Island, blockbuster movies and books about Indians generated increased interest in the "Indian story." Notable among these were the book *Bury My Heart at Wounded Knee* (1970) and the films *Soldier Blue* (1970) and *Little Big Man* (1971). The latter featured Dan George (Squamish), whose portrayal of a Cheyenne chief during the 1880s won the Best Supporting Actor award of the New York Film Critics. Will Sampson (Creek) received an Academy Award nomination in the same category for his performance as an asylum inmate in the 1975 film *One Flew Over the Cuckoo's Nest*. Although some documentaries and short films by native filmmakers such as Sandy Johnson Osawa (Makah) were produced in the 1970s, Indian producers would not come into their own until the 1980s. As of the time of this publication, no major film has been directed or produced by a native person.

Starting in 1971, native theater companies formed and stage productions flourished. The most significant companies of the decade were Muriel Miguel's native women's improvisational group, Spiderwoman Theater Company, in New York; the American Indian Theater Company (AITC), also in New York; the Native American Theatre Ensemble, in Tulsa; and the Red Earth Performing Arts Company, in Seattle. Significant productions included *Body Indian* (1972), *Foghorn* (1972) and *49* (1975), all developed by the AITC and shaped by the director Hanay Geiogamah (Kiowa-Delaware); *The Indian Experience* (1975) by John Kaufman (Nez Perce); and the artist-writer Bruce King's play about Vietnam, *Dust Off*, first produced in Santa Fe in 1978.

In 1972, the Smithsonian Institution's National Collection of Fine Art in Washington, D.C., opened an exhibition, titled *Two American Painters*, of works by T. C. Cannon and Fritz Scholder, which toured European capitals in 1973. Hailed as exquisite, witty, and biting, their images became a measure of truth of the Indian past and metaphors for modern turbulence. Both artists skyrocketed to stardom in the visual arts and popular culture, a status enjoyed by Scholder through the present. Cannon's artistic influence continues, although his life ended in a car wreck in 1978, when he was thirty-two.

The six-day takeover of the Bureau of Indian Affairs building in 1972 in Washington, D.C., and the seventy-one-day occupation of the Oglala Sioux Reservation village of Wounded Knee in 1973 presented major energizing forces and images for native artists for that time and afterward. During the 1972 takeover, some IAIA students and graduates found tangible proof that their designs and artwork had been used and marketed without their consent or any compensation to them, also finding that among the most prominently displayed paintings identified as native work were a few by artists known to have been white people posing as Indians. The reaction by native artists to both situations was vigorous, beginning with the removal of the IAIA-student-designed drapes from the BIA Commissioner's office and ending with the slashing of the pseudo-Indian paintings and the imprinting of the word *fake* on the canvases.

The style and success of *Two American Painters*—along with the international attention focused on conditions in U.S. Indian country—provided inspiration for native artists in all mediums and opportunities for grants, commissions, and shows. Among those whose careers were launched or received a boost beyond the decade were Harry Fonseca (Nisenan Maidu), Richard Glazer-Danay (Mohawk), Conrad House (Navajo and Oneida), Michael Kabotie (Hopi), Frank LaPena (Wintu-Nomtipom), George C. Longfish (Seneca/Tuscarora), Bill Reid (Haida), Juane Quick-to-See Smith (Salish), John Wilnoty (Cherokee), and Duffy Wilson (Tuscarora). Wilson, a sculptor, later directed the Native American Center for the Living Arts in Niagara Falls, which was codesigned, in a turtle shape, by a preeminent native architect, Dennis Sun Rhodes (Arapaho).

Among artists who developed during the 1970s in the IAIA tradition were Delmar Boni (San Carlos Apache), David P. Bradley (White Earth Chippewa), Barry Coffin (Potawatomi-Creek), Anthony Gauthier (Winnebago), Bill Glass, Jr. (Cherokee), John Hoover (Aleut), Dan Namingha (Hopi), and Roxanne Swentzell (Santa Clara Pueblo). Several artists accomplished in both the written and visual arts also developed at IAIA during the 1970s, including Barney Bush (Shawnee-Cayuga), Grey Cohoe (Navajo), Alex Jacobs/Karoniaktatie (Akwesasne Mohawk), and Harold Littlebird (Santo Domingo Pueblo).

In 1982, two events highlighted natives in the visual and performing arts and at the same time created a controversy that rocked the Indian and arts worlds. *Night of the First Americans* and *Art of the First Americans*—a glitzy stage and art show at the Kennedy Center and the follow-up exhibit at the Smithsonian—

featured appearances and works by some artists who falsely claimed to be native people. Several native artists and tribal leaders lodged complaints on Capitol Hill and with the press, generating investigations, exposés, marketplace reforms, and a new law. In 1989, the Indian Arts and Crafts Act of 1935 was updated to protect native artists and consumers of Indian products, imposing stiff penalties for those fraudulently selling or promoting work as Indian produced. The amendments were sponsored by Senator (then Representative) Ben Nighthorse Campbell (Cheyenne), the only Indian and only producing artist in Congress.

During the 1980s and into the following decade, among the brightest lights in the visual arts were David P. Bradley, Bob Haozous, Hachivi Edgar Heap of Birds (Cheyenne), Conrad House, Jean LaMarr (Paiute/Pit River), James Lavadour (Umatilla), Truman Lowe (Winnebago), Jack Malotte (Western Shoshone), and Susan Stewart (Crow). Bradley and House, admired as painters' painters and for their versatility, consistently captured honors in Indian art shows, such as the Santa Fe Indian Market, where Bradley was the only artist to take the top awards in both painting and sculpture and House in both painting and textile design. Bradley also was one of the leading artists behind the first state law (New Mexico's) protecting Indian art and artists, as well as a similar 1989 national law.

LaMarr, widely recognized as an impeccable printmaker and painter, was included in a prestigious 1987 exhibit at the Museum of Modern Art, *Committed to Print: Social and Political Themes in Recent American Printed Art.* Malotte, respected among other artists for his graphics and painting, produced works of social and political commentary that became symbols of numerous human-rights and environmental causes in his home state of Nevada and nationwide. Lavadour, known for his large-canvas oils, and Stewart, known for her acrylics and installations, also have concentrated their work in their reservation communities in Oregon and Montana, respectively, training and promoting other Indian artists locally. Lowe, acclaimed for his sculptures and installations, also is an educator and the first native artist to chair a major art department, at the University of Wisconsin at Madison.

Haozous, who often showed with Allan Houser in the prior decade, took center stage in the 1980s among contemporary sculptors, particularly with his massive works in steel, with each new piece greeted as a significant event in the art world into the 1990s. Among his masterworks are *Apache Holocaust,* a thirty-seven-foot-high painted and rusted-steel sculpture with graffitied Apache names ascending the structure and a bound Apache man in traditional dress atop it. Heap of Birds, among the world's top conceptual artists, produces textual art, as well as paintings, prints, and installations. Also a professor of art at the University of Oklahoma, he is the most widely exhibited of native artists. He gained international attention in 1983 with his *In Our Language*—computerized light messages in Cheyenne and English carried on the famous Times Square billboard usually reserved for breaking news.

Other visual artists who emerged in the 1980s and took their place among the leading and most innovative of native artists in the 1990s included the painters Tony Abeyta (Navajo), Dan Lomahaftewa (Hopi and Choctaw), Judith Lowry (Mountain Maidu), Mateo Romero (Cochiti Pueblo), Kay Walkingstick (Cherokee), and Emmi Whitehorse (Navajo); the ceramicists Anita Fields (Osage) and Peter B. Jones (Seneca); the glass potter-sculptor Tony Jojola (Isleta Pueblo); the clay potter-sculptor Diego Romero (Cochiti Pueblo); the sculptor Bently Spang (Cheyenne); the beadworker–conceptual artist Marcus Amerman (Choctaw); the doll maker Donald Tenoso (Hunkpapa Lakota); the photographers–multimedia artists Shelley Niro (Mohawk) and Jolene Rickard (Tuscarora); and the installation and performance artists James Luna (Luiseño) and Nora Naranjo-Morse (Santa Clara Pueblo). Of these, the most well known is Luna, who has exhibited himself on a sawhorse in *End of the Trail,* in a museum case in *The Artifact Piece,* and as a new-age profit prophet in *Shame-Man.*

Among the innovators in Indian music in the 1980s were the poet John Trudell and the musician Jesse Ed Davis, whose 1986 recording *aka Graffiti Man,* produced by Davis, was lauded in *Rolling Stone* by singer-songwriter Bob Dylan as the best record of the year. Following Davis's death in 1987, Trudell teamed up with a new band that included the traditional singer-drummer Quiltman (Warm Springs) and, with musical and promotion assistance by singer-songwriter Jackson Browne, produced records into the 1990s, most recently under the band name Bad Dog. Trudell immersed himself in poetry following the 1979 deaths of his wife, three children, and mother-in-law in a fire of suspicious origins. He also turned to film acting, debuting in the 1988 *Pow-Wow Highway,* with the actor Gary Farmer (Cayuga), and appearing in the 1992 *Thunderheart,* with Graham Greene (Oneida) and Sheila Tousey (Menominee/Stockbridge-Munsee), in which he played an activist being tracked by the FBI on the Oglala Sioux Reservation in the early 1970s, a role he had lived. He appeared as himself in the producer-actor-director Robert Redford's 1992 documentary about Leonard Peltier's case, *Incident at Oglala.*

The movie that heightened the visibility of natives in film, and in all the Indian arts, was the producer-actor-director Kevin Costner's *Dances with Wolves,* which swept the Oscars for 1990 and earned a Best Supporting Actor nomination for Graham Greene, who (like Gary Farmer) was an accomplished stage and film actor trained in the European classics. Opportunities for native actors, technicians, and consultants became more abundant. Films and television movies, including the megahit Disney cartoon *Pocahontas* (1995), a raft of TBS productions, and the popular CBS series *Northern Exposure,* offered a seemingly endless source of employment in all but the decision-making capacities in the 1990s. The 1992 version of *The Last of the Mohicans* and its cast, including Dennis J. Banks and Russell Means, prompted the comedian Charlie Hill (Oneida) to quip, "AIM leaders in that movie would be like the Black Panthers starring in a remake of *Little Black Sambo.*"

During the 1990s the combination of the 1992 Columbus quincentenary and the financial success of Indian-theme films and television shows also opened doors for native producers, writers, and directors working on their own films, many of whom had struggled for backing and a forum for a decade or more. Sandy Johnson Osawa (Makah), the head of Upstream Productions in Seattle and a longtime producer-writer, became the first Indian producer to have a documentary aired by a major network, NBC, in prime time: *The Seventh Fire,* a half-hour special on tribal fishing-rights struggles, was premiered in 1992. Also that year, PBS aired a two-hour special on Pueblo-European contact and relations, *Surviving Columbus,* directed by Diane Reyna (Taos Pueblo), written by Simon Ortiz, and produced by George Burdeau, Edmund Ladd (Zuni Pueblo), and Phil Lucas (Choctaw).

In 1993, Robert Redford's Sundance Institute began a five-year program to promote native filmmakers, directors, and screenwriters, selecting at least two each year for its coveted program-development slots. Films by and about natives were featured throughout the 1994 Sundance Film Festival, which kicked off with a press conference on the native film project. Among the first selected to participate in the project were the young filmmakers Chris Ayer (Cheyenne and Arapaho)

and Sherman Alexie (Coeur d'Alene). Also in 1994, the Scottsdale Center for the Arts and two Indian arts groups, Atlatl, and the Native American Producers Alliance, presented a native film and video festival in Scottsdale, "Imagining Indians," named after a film by the alliance's president, Victor Masayesva (Hopi). The festival featured Masayesva's film as well as *Everything Has a Spirit* by Ava Hamilton (Arapaho) and *Navajo Talking Pictures* by Arlene Bowman (Navajo), and highlighted native film luminaries as panelists and performers.

The Spiderwoman Theater Company continued into the 1990s as the Indian theater group in greatest demand. Its founder, Muriel Miguel, codirected a 1993 production in New York of *Rez Sisters* by the Canadian playwright Tomson Highway (Cree), whose *Dry Lips Oughta Move to Kapuskasing* was given a dramatic reading there in 1994. Miguel's one-woman show, *Hot and Soft,* was produced off-Broadway in 1994; *Princess Pocahontas and the Blue Spots,* a play by Miguel's niece, was produced in New York in 1991. A new native theater ensemble, Chuka Lokoli, developed in the early 1990s, and one of its improvisation pieces, *In the Spirit,* was produced in 1992; this work and *Sneaky,* by William S. Yellow Robe, Jr. (Assiniboine), were selected for the 1993 New Work Now! Festival at the Public Theater in New York.

With the 1990s popularity of poetry slams and raging—the raucous styles of performance competitions and opening acts for rock and alternative music productions—several native poets set distinctive styles in the growing circuit, most notably ASH (Cheyenne and Hodulgee Muskogee), Lance Henson (Cheyenne), Alex Jacobs (Akwesasne Mohawk), and Simon Ortiz (Acoma Pueblo). The poet Joy Harjo (Muskogee) also turned to performance with her jazz/reggae band Poetic Justice, in the words-with-music style of John Trudell; she plays saxophone and performs her poetry, accompanied by the noted lawyer Susan M. Williams (Sisseton-Wahpeton Sioux) on drums, the tribal judge Willie Bluehouse Johnson (Isleta Pueblo and Navajo) on guitar, John Williams (Sisseton-Wahpeton Sioux) on bass, and Frank Poocha (Hopi-Pima) on keyboards. Several singers who developed in the earlier folk/ballad style performed and recorded in the 1990s, including Delmar Boni, Sharon Burch (Navajo), Paul Ortega (Mescalero Apache)—all of whom sing in their own languages and in English—and Joanne Shenandoah (Oneida). In 1993, Buffy Sainte-Marie was instrumental in introducing a Music of Aboriginal Canada category for the Juno music awards; the first such honor went to Lawrence Martin (Cree) of the group Kashtin for its platinum hit, "akua tuta."

Among the native music innovators in the 1990s were Red Thunder, a native rock band of Apache, Pueblo, and Mayan musicians blending rock and tribal instruments and music, including a trap-set of traditional Indian drums. Red Thunder has commanded the largest viewing audience of any contemporary Indian music group. Cary Morin (Crow) and his group the Atoll rose to prominence with their reggae releases, including *Dream Marquee* in 1993, and Robby Bee and the Boyz from the Rez proved to be crowd pleasers throughout the Southwest with their mix of hip-hop, rap, and native beats. The flute player R. Carlos Nakai (Navajo-Ute), an established musician of the 1980s, became a highly successful recording artist in the New Age music market of the 1990s.

The 1992 Columbus year provided the greatest number of exhibition and sales opportunities of any in the century. Some exhibitions offered commentary on the quincentenary itself, such as Atlatl's *Submuloc Show/ Columbus Wohs* at the Minneapolis Institute of Arts and *We're Still Here* at the American Indian Community House Gallery/Museum in New York City. Others ignored the topic, presenting fine art as its own statement—for example, The Morning Star Foundation's *Visions from Native America: Contemporary Art for the Year of the Indigenous Peoples,* which was the first native art show of national scope ever presented on Capitol Hill, in the House and Senate rotundas. The historic exhibition included paintings, sculpture, and mixed-media works by Tony Abeyta, Larry Ahvakana, Marcus Amerman, David P. Bradley, Barry Coffin, Steve Deo (Yuchi/Creek), Dennis R. Fox, Jr. (Mandan/Hidatsa), Bob Haozous, Sharron Ahtone Harjo (Kiowa), Hachivi Edgar Heap of Birds, Valjean Hessing (Choctaw), Conrad House, Doug Hyde, Jean LaMarr, Linda Lomahaftewa, Jack Malotte, George Morrison, Stan Natchez (Shoshone/Paiute), Lillian Pitt (Wasco/Yakama), Martin Red Bear (Sicangu/Oglala Lakota), W. Richard West, Sr., Emmi Whitehorse, and Richard Ray Whitman.

Also in 1992, the IAIA opened its museum in Santa Fe with a stunning exhibit, *Three Decades of Contemporary Indian Art at the Institute of American Indian Arts,* curated by the museum's founding director, Richard Hill, Sr. (Tuscarora). Hill, an accomplished photographer and painter, later joined the staff of the National Museum of the American Indian, working with the National Museum's director, W. Richard West, Jr. (Cheyenne), to guide the new museum to its official opening, and three major exhibits of works from the collection and a contemporary collaboration. The opening took place at the Custom House, a historic building in New York City and the home of the museum's permanent exhibit there, in late 1994, attracting the most press and public attention internationally of any native arts event. It is the new museum that holds the potential for being a major boon to all native arts, as well as the educational focal point in the United States regarding native peoples generally, into the twenty-first century.

See also Art, Visual (to 1960); Movies; Music; Textiles.

SUZAN SHOWN HARJO
(Cheyenne and Hodulgee Muskogee)
The Morning Star Institute
Washington, D.C.

ASSINIBOINE

Closely related linguistically and culturally to the eastern and middle Dakotas, the Assiniboines are a Siouan-speaking people who initially inhabited the woodlands and parkland prairie regions southeast, south, and southwest of Lake Winnipeg. Assiniboine is an Algonquian word meaning "those who cook with stones." It is the prevailing interpretation today that the Assiniboines, who were distinct by A.D. 1550, may have come from the Sandy Lake and Duck Bay archaeological cultures found along the forest's edge in the period A.D. 1250 to 1500. (However, the *Jesuit Relation* of 1640 reported an earlier fission among the Dakotas that resulted in the Assiniboines' social formation.) This division occurred through adversarial pressures from the neighboring Algonquian groups to the north and west, probably the protohistoric Cheyenne and Atsina-Arapaho groups. The Assiniboines were allies of the western Crees and later the western Ojibwas, and enemies of other Algonquian groups, including the Blackfoot Confederacy, and of the Siouan-speaking Dakota/Lakota Sioux and Hidatsas.

In 1658 Europeans first encountered the trade canoes of Assiniboines on the north shore of Lake Superior and in the vicinity of Lake Nipigon. By the late seventeenth century most Assiniboines were concentrated within the southern Lake Winnipeg region, between the Assiniboine River and the valley of the Red River. The remaining Assiniboines relocated their trade routes away from the western Great Lakes to the competing English and French trading posts on Hudson Bay and eventually to the interior. In this same period they made regular trade expeditions to Missouri River tribes' villages, the major market of the northern plains. Subgroups among the Assiniboines fulfilled the specialized role of middlemen, while others seasonally exploited the rich environment of this region. A minority of individuals became trading captains and organized seasonal expeditions to transport furs to Hudson Bay, imitating the practice of the Crees and Ojibwas. Trade interactions united the allies militarily, and eventually religiously, politically, and socially as well.

In the regions southeast of Lake Winnipeg, the Assiniboines continued to rely upon a seasonal round of wild-rice harvesting; to the southwest they procured buffalo by trapping them in pounds. They eventually expanded their procurement cycle to the regions beyond the Souris River basin to the upper Missouri River, and from the Qu'Appelle Valley to the Cypress Hills. Assiniboines suffered massive population reductions from smallpox epidemics in 1737, 1780–81, and 1837–38, each of which required major reconstitutions of their society.

In 1826 a U.S. Indian agent was assigned to the Assiniboines on the upper Missouri River. Three years later, the American Fur Company built Fort Union at the confluence of the Missouri and Yellowstone Rivers. The fort dominated the southern trade relations of the Assiniboines until the late 1850s. The Fort Laramie Treaty of 1851 designated Assiniboine lands south of the soon-to-be-surveyed border between the United States and British North America, and the 1855 Isaac Stevens Treaty with the Blackfeet declared the entire northern tier north of the Missouri in present-day Montana to be a hunting ground for Blackfeet and "other Indians." In 1866 Assiniboines living in the vicinity of the recently abandoned Fort Union agreed to come under the protection of Fort Buford, in modern-day North Dakota. In 1869 the Milk River Agency was established near present-day Chinook, Montana; it was later moved to a trading post called Fort Peck, purchased by the trading company of Durfee and Peck in 1874. However, hostilities increased among the various Indians within the jurisdiction of the agency, and a new agency called Fort Belknap was established for the Atsina Gros Ventres and the upper Assiniboines in 1873, and the agency at Fort Peck was moved to Poplar River in 1877, where the lower Assiniboines shared the agency with Yanktonais and Sisseton-Wahpeton Dakotas.

The Cypress Hills massacre in 1873, in which Assiniboines led by Little Soldier were attacked and killed by wolfers and whiskey traders, brought the new Dominion of Canada into the region of the Canadian west known as Whoop-Up country. A constabulary known as the North-West Mounted Police was established as a direct result of this violence, and the Canadian government established posts at Fort McLeod and at Fort Walsh in the Cypress Hills. This effort to protect both Indians and non-Indians was also an effort to enforce the international border. As the buffalo herds began to disappear, the Cypress Hills, Wood Mountain, and the Moose Mountains increasingly became refuges to starving Indians, the Assiniboines among them.

The Numbered Treaties, signed in Canada in the 1870s, resulted in reserves being surveyed for the bands of treaty signers. Treaty 4 was signed by bands in present-day southern Saskatchewan; Treaty 6 at Forts Carleton and Pitt in central Saskatchewan; and Treaty 7 at Fort McLeod in southern Alberta. Assiniboines eventually took reserves in Saskatchewan and Alberta. By the 1890s and early 1900s a number of reserves had been reevaluated, and in several cases Assiniboine reserves or portions of lands were seized as part of the Canadian policy of "developing" the prairies by filling them with new settlers.

The U.S. reservation boundaries of Fort Belknap and Fort Peck were fixed by 1889. Throughout the 1890s much of the land on these reservations was leased to large cattle operators. Lands were first allotted at Fort Peck in 1909, and at Fort Belknap in 1921, fostering protected ownership of individual lands. The allotting of lands ended with the Indian Reorganization Act in 1934; Fort Belknap accepted the new law and organized a tribal government under it, whereas Fort Peck did not.

The first decades of the twentieth century were difficult ones for both U.S. and Canadian Assiniboines. Subsistence farming was both encouraged and discouraged as government policies fluctuated. Children were often sent away to either government or church-operated residential schools that purposely discouraged adherence to Indian culture. Limited governance, in the form of either chiefs and councils or business committees, was gradually allowed, but Indian agents or superintendents dominated most aspects of tribal life. Men served in the armed forces of both nations in the two world wars and returned to pursue greater freedoms and responsibilities for themselves and their relatives.

In Canada, the Assiniboine reserves in Saskatchewan are Carry the Kettle, Pheasant Rump, and Ocean Man, with Assiniboines represented as a minority on the Mosquito, Red Pheasant, Grizzley Bear's Head, Kawacatoose, Cowessess, Little Black Bear, and White Bear reserves. The Alexis, Paul, Wesley, Big Horn, and Eden Valley reserves are in Alberta (where Assiniboines are known as Stoneys); descendants of the Sharps Head band were scattered onto several other non-Stoney reserves in Alberta. In Montana, Assiniboines reside on the Fort Belknap and Fort Peck reservations, shared respectively with the Atsina Gros Ventres and with descendants from all three divisions of the Sioux.

Contemporary Assiniboine accomplishments include increased economic development, success in pursuing land and other claims, and innovative political and service structures. Though language loss is at a critical stage, many cultural traditions remain strong, with participation by all generations. For example, there is a vibrant network of participants in the Medicine Lodge religion (called the Rain Dance in Canada). Assiniboines are also active participants in the northern plains powwow circuit.

See also Indian-White Relations in Canada, 1763 to the Present.

Ray, Arthur, *Indians in the Fur Trade: Their Role as Hunters, Trappers, and Middlemen in the Lands Southwest of Hudson Bay, 1660–1870* (Toronto: University of Toronto Press, 1974); Russell, Dale R., *Eighteenth-Century Western Cree and Their Neighbors,* Archaeological Survey of Canada, Mercury Series Paper no. 143 (Hull: Canadian Museum of Civilization, 1991).

DAVID REED MILLER
Saskatchewan Indian Federated College
University of Regina

ASTRONOMY

Like other peoples of the world, North American Indian groups have developed organized explanations for celestial appearances—the sun, moon, and stars and their cyclical movements across the dome of the sky. They have created a rich, evolving celestial lore and constructed elaborate calendars to organize and guide their activities. Both literally and figuratively, the sky has given direction to their lives and influenced earthly behavior. For example, the Apaches, Navajos, and Plains Indians participate in the rhythms of their celestial environment by systematically entering their lodgings while walking in the sun-wise, or clockwise, direction. In contrast, Euro-Americans tend to move counterclockwise.

Only recently have scholars attempted a systematic study of the astronomical knowledge and worldview of the North American Indian. Individuals from a wide assortment of disciplines have used a variety of evidence—archaeological research, interviews, oral histories, folklore, mythology, and studies of ceremony and ritual behavior—to support their efforts. Scholars designate the study of the astronomy of historic cultures *ethnoastronomy*; they term the study of the astronomy of prehistoric cultures *archaeoastronomy*. In the Americas, because remnants of pre-Columbian cultural practices have survived into historic times, the study of archaeoastronomy is enormously enhanced by the ability to question historic descendants of pre-Columbian peoples about their own astronomical interests and customs.

Although the variety and complexity of Native American tribes prevents detailed generalizations about their approach to the earth and sky, Native American tribes share a belief in the essential oneness of the cosmos. All things, including plants and trees, rocks and streams, animals, insects, sea creatures, people—even the sun, moon, and stars—are related to one another. They further share a belief that the elements of the cosmos are not static, but in constant motion or transformation. Not only do beings move within the realms of the earth and sky; they move between the two realms. Some are capable of transformation. Occasionally, supernatural sky creatures come to the earth and those of the earth travel to the sky. For the Pawnees, the Bella Coolas, and many other groups, the sky is the source of life itself. In contrast, the Kiowas, Navajos, and Pueblo peoples tell of their emergence from the underworld yet also look to the sky for worldly guidance.

For the most part, traditional Native American thinkers regard the sky as a source of stability and regular motion and the source of principles by which to live. They determine the four primary directions—east, south, west, and north—by observing the sun, moon, and stars. In contrast to the orderly sky, events on the earth are capable of breaking into chaos at the slightest provocation. As Native American myths illustrate, Coyote and other tricksters have an enormous capacity for irregular behavior that upsets an orderly progression of earthly events. Sometimes they introduce a measure of irregularity even into the sky. In one version of the Navajo myth of creation, Coyote scatters the stars that Black God has been carefully placing in the dark sky. In a Hopi myth in which Coyote begs to carry the sun disk, he strays off the path and causes chaos on earth. To guard against such deviations from order, many American Indian groups have developed ceremonies to assist the continuation of stable, predictable movements, lest the sky beings fail to take their usual paths. In other words, the rituals mediate between earth and sky. For example, part of the Hopi winter solstice ceremony includes a mock battle between a participant representing the sun and a group of singers who constrain the indecisive sun to remain on his proper yearly track. In this they are responding to an observable phenomenon: that the sun changes position along the horizon from day to day throughout the year.

The stories and myths that explain celestial phenomena also set a moral tone for life on earth. For instance, one Lakota Sioux myth illustrates proper behavior by describing a chief's selfish actions and their consequences. The constellation known to the Lakotas as the Hand, composed of most of the stars of the European constellation Orion, represents the hand the chief lost when the "Thunder Beings" of the sky tore off his arm and serves as a nightly reminder both of the story and of the consequences of selfish behavior.

Each tribe places a different emphasis on observations of the celestial sphere for the yearly calendar. Tribes with a dominant agricultural tradition, such as the Pueblo tribes, closely monitor the yearly path of the sun along the horizon to learn the right periods during which to plant and harvest and also, more importantly, to determine the proper days for holding ceremonies. Their Anasazi ancestors of the twelfth and thirteenth centuries apparently also carefully followed the sun's motions, incorporating architectural features into their buildings that would remove the guesswork from setting the yearly calendar. The Cahokians of the same era, who lived along the Mississippi, organized their mounds and their city along the cardinal directions and also developed a sophisticated solar calendar.

Some groups, such as the Chumashes, Navajos, and Pawnees, tend to emphasize stellar observations. The Navajos have used the seasonal position of the constellation Revolving Male (the Big Dipper) to determine planting times. In the spring, the Skiri Pawnees watched for the first appearance of the constellation Swimming Ducks, which signaled the appropriate time to begin the spring thunder ritual. The Mescalero Apaches time the nightly phases of the girls' puberty ceremony by carefully following the position and orientation of certain bright stars.

The changing form of the moon, occurring in a cycle that approximates a woman's menstrual cycle, makes it a prime subject for myth and for devising a convenient monthly calendar. However, the fact that the moon's cycle is incommensurate with the yearly cycle of the sun causes difficulties in achieving harmony with the solar calendar and has induced some Native American groups to correct for the discrepancy by adding a month every three years.

The planets wander along the ecliptic (the apparent yearly path of the sun), appearing in different parts of the sky during the year. Venus and Mercury stay relatively near the sun, whereas Mars, Jupiter, and Saturn can appear anywhere along the ecliptic. Although the planets' relatively erratic motions (compared with those of the stars) have long been observed, only the Skiri Pawnees and a few California groups are known to have studied these motions. Solar and lunar eclipses, fireballs, meteors, and comets were and still are seen as irregular sky phenomena that portend ominous happenings on earth.

One of the most important recent developments in ethnoastronomy is the realization that gatherers and hunters, as well as agricultural peoples, depended on a celestial calendar for following the seasonal round and for predicting the proper times for ceremonies. For example, the Cahuillas, Chumashes, Gabrielinos, and other California tribes made extensive use of solar, lunar, and stellar observations but practiced little agriculture. They used their astronomical knowledge to predict the ripening of certain foods and the arrival of fish and game at favorite fishing and hunting grounds.

When carefully read, myths and traditional stories provide considerable insight into tribal views of the sky. The Alabama Indian myth about a celestial skiff seems to encode a keen knowledge of the night sky, particularly the motions of the Big Dipper as it rotates about the pole, nightly swinging down to earth and rising up in the morning during the summer months. The Alabamas linked this celestial appearance to their ball game, their summer ceremonial dances, and the green corn ceremony, in which they celebrated the ripening of the corn. The Navajos see a hogan in the sky with the nightly rotation of Revolving Male (the Big Dipper), Revolving Female (Cassiopeia), and North Fire (the North Star). In summary, Native American groups not only used the sky for calendrical and directional applications but also incorporated aspects of the sky into their daily lives.

Williamson, Ray A., *Living the Sky: The Cosmos of the American Indian* (Boston: Houghton Mifflin, 1984; reprint, Norman: University of Oklahoma Press, 1987); Williamson, Ray A., ed., *Archaeoastronomy in the Americas* (Los Altos, Calif.: Ballena Press, 1981); Williamson, Ray A., and Claire R. Farrer, eds., *Earth and Sky: Native American Cosmovision* (Albuquerque: University of New Mexico Press, 1993).

RAY A. WILLIAMSON
Office of Technology Assessment
U.S. Congress

BASKETRY

Basketry is one of the oldest and most widespread American Indian arts. Archaeological sites have yielded basketry specimens over ten thousand years old. Native peoples from the Atlantic to the Pacific, and from the Aleutians to the Everglades, still create and use baskets today. Like their makers, American Indian baskets are remarkably diverse; manufacturing techniques, weaving material, shapes, and designs vary from tribe to tribe.

Generally, basketry was a women's art, but among some Indian peoples, such as the Pomos and the Yupiks, men wove as well, creating sturdy baskets that saw hard use as fish traps or pack baskets. Younger family members learned this skill from their elders, observing, copying, being gently corrected, and improving over years of practice until they, in turn, taught others.

Basket makers harvested, processed, and used a wide variety of native plants, ranging from large swamp canes to tall saguaro cactuses, from fine rye grass to sturdy black ash trees. In doing so, they utilized many different plant parts: stems, roots, bark, wood, shoots, leaves, and needles. The wealth of time, specialized knowledge, and skill necessary for gathering and preparing weaving material is an essential, but often unappreciated, component of American Indian basketry. As my grandmother, the Pomo weaver Lucy Smith, told me, "You just can't go to the store and get these things!"

Gathering basketry materials was usually a communal affair; families and friends talked and laughed while digging roots or stripping bark. Weavers collected limited amounts, taking care to leave enough behind to ensure plant regeneration for future harvests. People always gave thanks for what was taken; they said prayers, sang songs, or left small gifts of food or tobacco. The Pomo weaver Elsie Allen recalls that her mother "always approached sedge grass very slowly. She'd come and stand and say a prayer. . . . She'd always ask the Spirit to give her plenty of roots. Then she'd say, 'Thank you, Father,' before she dug."

Weavers gathered basketry materials at specific times of the year, carefully choosing materials with particular characteristics. Willow shoots, for instance, were harvested in early spring after the buds had broken, but before they had fully leafed, when they were flexible and the bark slipped off easily. Only willow shoots that were long, straight, slender, and free of lateral branches were suitable.

Basket makers utilized a number of horticultural methods, including pruning, controlled burning, soil cultivation, and weeding, to optimize the production of desirable plant features. These practices, necessary to produce usable basketry materials, also benefited plants. Pruning redbud, for example, increased its vigor and productivity and curbed insect infestations, while stimulating the growth of long, straight, strong shoots. Basketry plants flourished generation after generation precisely because of human manipulation, rather than by purely natural growth processes. These horticultural techniques demonstrate weavers' intimate knowledge of the plants around them, and are but one example of the sophistication of Native American land use and management.

Once gathered, basketry materials were cleaned and prepared for use through various techniques including debarking, splitting, soaking, dyeing, pounding, sun bleaching, drying, steaming, boiling, cooking over fires, and baking in earth ovens. Weavers had to size their materials so that they were uniform in width and diameter, an exacting and time-consuming task necessary to ensure the regular and even appearance of the finished basket.

Most baskets were decorated, often with elaborate geometric designs depicting various environmental features, such as quail topknots, lightning, or shark's teeth. The finished basket, with its complexities of spacing, balance, symmetry, and placement of design elements onto a three-dimensional framework, had to be conceptualized at the start. Nothing was written; the weaver carried this intricate image in her mind even as she focused on the technical demands of basket construction.

Native American peoples utilized three general basket-construction techniques—plaiting, twining, and coiling—in a vast and varied array. In plaiting, the warp and weft elements pass over and under each other at right angles. In twining, two or more horizontal weft elements are twisted around vertical warp elements. In coiling, the foundation continuously spirals upward while being bound together by a sewing element.

Aboriginally, basketry was imbued with great economic and social significance, and baskets proved indispensable to everyday life. They were necessary in gathering, preparing, storing, cooking, and serving food; there were berry baskets, eel baskets, cornmeal sifters, mush-boiling baskets, water jugs, and food platters. Nuu-Chah-Nulth (or Nootka) babies napped in basketry cradles; Western Apache children played with toy baskets; Yokuts women gambled with walnut dice on basketry trays. A Navajo bride and groom ate cornmeal from a special basketry tray; Hopi women threw baskets to ob-

The Pomo basket maker Elsie Allen (1899–1990) outside her home in Pinoleville Rancheria, Ukiah, California, in December 1981. Photo by Scott M. Patterson.

servers as they danced in the village plaza; Tlingit shamans stored eagle down in cylindrical baskets.

With increasing white contact, European manufactured items, generally easier to obtain than baskets, began to replace baskets in everyday native life; pots, pans, boxes, plates, and gunnysacks became ubiquitous domestic utensils. In turn, some weavers incorporated European goods into their basketry, ornamenting baskets with glass beads, coloring weaving material with aniline dyes, or using wool yarn and silk embroidery floss as decorative weaving elements. European goods also inspired new designs and forms. Weavers shaped baskets in the form of top hats, teakettles, and wine goblets; they included flour-sack fabric motifs, china patterns, and English letters in their basket designs.

White contact also introduced native peoples to a cash economy. Due to white interest in native arts, a commercial market for "Indian curios" made it possible for native weavers to earn money selling their baskets to nonnatives. This market reached its apex from 1890 to 1910. Collecting Indian baskets was a popular middle-class hobby, and it was fashionable to have "a number of Indian baskets strewn around the parlor," as one enthusiast wrote. Tourists often purchased these baskets while traveling through "Indian country," whether via steamship in Alaska or the railroad in the Southwest.

At a time when Native women had few choices of occupation, basket making provided a welcome and significant source of income. It also allowed weavers to preserve and practice important cultural traditions in the midst of tremendous cultural change. Prior to the commercial basket market, weavers produced only what was needed for their families' use. The extensive nonnative demand for Indian baskets, however, caused a surge in basket production. Contrary to dealers' rhetoric, Indian basketry at this time was not a "dying art" but thrived as never before.

Weavers created baskets using new techniques, new forms, and new designs, expressly to appeal to nonnative tastes and needs. In some cases, weavers created new types of functional baskets for white buyers, such as the potato-harvesting splint baskets woven by the Micmacs. More commonly, however, the main function of commercial Indian baskets was aesthetic, not utilitarian, and buyers valued them as objects of beauty and curiosity. Miniaturized versions of traditional baskets became especially popular with both weavers and buyers, requiring less time and material to make, while being less expensive and easier to transport.

World War I and the Great Depression led to a marked decline in the American Indian basketry market. For several decades there was a hiatus in basket making as native women turned to other means of livelihood, and few had time to learn and undertake the demanding process of weaving baskets.

Recently, Native American basketry has experienced a resurgence, the result of a renewed admiration of American Indian art by nonnatives, and of American Indian peoples' rekindled pride in their heritage. A new generation of weavers is learning the old skills, revitalizing the craft in places where it had virtually disappeared.

Contemporary native weavers are creating baskets as much to express ethnic identity and cultural heritage as to earn money. Baskets today are woven as gifts for family and friends, for display or use around the house, and for use in traditional ceremonies, which are themselves being revived. The California weaver Jennifer Bates declares, "Making baskets is a way I can help my family maintain their heritage as Miwok Indians. Gathering the different plants, at places where my relatives always have, gives us a tangible link with our ancestors. Knowing the correct time of the year to gather each different plant keeps us aware of the changing seasons of the earth, just as our ancestors were aware of them. Making the baskets gives us time to spend together as a family, remembering the past and planning for the future."

Currently, American Indian basketry faces a number of challenges. Many native peoples live in cities and pursue professional careers, making it difficult to obtain basketry materials and to find the time to weave. Modern land use threatens the future of Indian basketry through the destruction of native basketry plants' habitats: building development, overgrazing, logging, agriculture, and gravel mining have destroyed gathering sites used by generations of basket weavers, while air, water, and ground pollution damage remaining plants.

As plants become more scarce, weavers must travel greater and greater distances to collect materials. Surviving concentrations of basketry plants frequently exist on nontribal lands, either public or private, where pesticide and herbicide spraying are common practices. Weavers often do not know if, or when, a gathering area has been sprayed, and many fear becoming seriously ill from working with toxic plant materials, since these sprays contain known carcinogens. In addition, traditional collecting practices, like controlled burning, often conflict with property restrictions.

American Indian basket makers are facing new challenges with remarkable creativity. Some weavers transplant and raise basketry plants in backyard suburban gardens. Many are joining together to form organizations, such as the Maine Basketweavers Alliance and the California Indian Basketweavers Association, to recognize and support both experienced and beginning weavers, as well as to educate land-use agencies.

American Indian basketry has survived for thousands of years in an unbroken continuity of practice, a vital artistic tradition incorporating both traditional values and social change. Indian baskets, no less than the peoples who create them, are beautiful and enduring.

Ortiz, Beverly R., "Contemporary California Indian Basketweavers and the Environment," in *Before the Wilderness: Environmental Management by Native Californians,* ed. Thomas C. Blackburn and Kat Anderson (Menlo Park, Calif.: Ballena Press, 1993); Porter, Frank W., III, ed., *The Art of Native American Basketry: A Living Legacy* (New York: Greenwood Press, 1990); Turnbaugh, Sarah Peabody, and William A. Turnbaugh, *Indian Baskets* (West Chester, Pa.: Schiffer Publishing, 1986).

SHERRIE SMITH-FERRI
(Dry Creek Pomo/Bodega Miwok)
Grace Hudson Museum
Ukiah, California

BEADS AND BEADWORK

The oldest bead made by American Indians is of bone. It was recovered from a Folsom site near Midland, Texas, and is 10,900 years old. The second-oldest bead is made of oil shale, is 10,100 years old, and was found at a site in Colorado. Both are very small. The bone bead measures 1.6 mm; the shale bead is even smaller. The bone bead is as finely made as the best hishe beads (disk-shaped shell beads with a single hole in the middle) created by contemporary Indian bead makers using modern equipment. Because both of these examples are so small and well made, it is reasonable to assume that bead manufacture was already an ancient art one hundred centuries ago.

Beads have been recovered archaeologically from every area of North America, and they were made from a wide variety of natural materials. By the fifteenth century these included shells, stones, precious and semiprecious gemstones, horn, teeth, ivory, fired clay, gold, silver, copper, pearls, seeds, wood, fruit pits, tree sap, vegetal fibers, and porcupine quills.

That beads were significant in American Indian social life is indicated by their mention in some tribal oral traditions as a supernatural being or part of a deity's name. In the historic period in the American Northeast, Iroquoian and Algonquian tribes made belts from shell beads (wampum) to record important political and diplomatic events. Another gauge of the importance of beads is their placement in large quantities in the graves of high-status individuals such as can be found at Cahokia, a twelfth-century Mississippian site near present-day St. Louis. Recently in the Lambayeque Valley of coastal Peru the excavation of three royal Moche-period (A.D. 100–800) tombs has revealed some of the most beautiful and technically sophisticated beads in the Americas, and perhaps in the world. Made from gold and silver and fashioned in the shapes of spiders, human heads, peanuts, felines, and owls, these beads are by their very nature proof of the prominent role they played in the social and ritual life of the Moche kingdoms.

Because Europeans had traded manufactured glass beads with great success in Africa and the Far East, it is not surprising that beads were among the items Columbus carried to the Americas on his first voyages. Caribbean native peoples traded locally made items for the glass beads, representative samples of which have subsequently been found in archaeological sites. Glass beads became staple items in the stock of trade materials carried everywhere in the Americas, in part because of their light weight, but also because they were popular and profitable.

American Indians incorporated glass beads into their aesthetic and technical systems, and in some places replaced native-made beads with the new trade versions. Beads were strung, sewn, netted, woven, and used as inlay, and these techniques continue to be of primary importance today. The fibers used to attach beads to objects were initially made by natives from vegetal fiber or mammal sinew, but once it appeared, manufactured thread tended to replace these materials. When European traders introduced a variety of colors in their bead stock, tribes developed preferences for particular colors, and the wise trader provided his customers with the hues of their choice. It is evident that in some places, such as the American plains and woodlands, indigenous aesthetic and technical systems influenced the development of beadwork as a new art form. In these areas it is relatively easy to identify some beaded designs as having originally been executed in porcupine quillwork. Similarly, some bead techniques are visual replacements for earlier quillwork techniques.

Networks of trade and exchange are ancient in the Americas, and the adoption of glass beads and other exotic trade materials by American Indians created conditions for a realignment of traditional exchange relationships. Once beads (and other items such as guns, metal tools, etc.) became necessities rather than luxuries, Indians were tied irretrievably to a network of reciprocal exchanges with Europeans.

By 1850 almost all Indian communities were eager to acquire glass beads and were experimenting with new techniques and artistic approaches made possible by the new medium. In some areas native artists preferred working with the new materials to engaging in more labor-intensive, indigenous crafts (e.g., porcupine quillwork) and stopped using the older decorative techniques, while in other areas artists continued to use both.

Beadwork worn by the wife of a Kiowa chief during a festival in Gallup, New Mexico, in August 1970.

By the twentieth century beadwork using glass beads had become one of the hallmarks of American Indian arts and, in the minds of many non-Indians, the emblem of Indian ethnicity. Most bead artists have been and continue to be women, and they have been very creative in the development of new techniques, styles, and aesthetics, as well as extremely productive. With the exception of ritual material, beadwork that has found its way into museum collections was generally made by women—a fact not often recognized. In many areas the money earned by women through the sale of their beadwork made a major contribution to the family economy, and this is still true today. Income realized through the sale of beaded items continues to be an important element in the lives of many Indian families, whose members often collaborate in the manufacture of beadwork for sale. Some families travel the powwow circuit, selling directly to the public, while others sell their work to middlemen. Some types of modern beadwork are more valuable than others, and artists can thus realize a greater return for their labor. Very fine hishe-bead necklaces handmade from shell and turquoise by Pueblo artists can sell for thousands of dollars in fine jewelry stores. In contrast, most glass beadwork made in the plains, although its manufacture is as labor-intensive as is the making of hishe-bead necklaces, yields only the basic minimum wage for its creators.

Notwithstanding the economic importance of beadmaking, a significant portion of all glass beadwork is made for personal or family use, to be worn within the context of modern Indian social life.

There is still some production of beads from natural materials, particularly in the American Southwest, where beadmakers use shell, coral, and turquoise for hishe necklaces that are principally sold to a non-Indian market. On the other hand wampum, made in the Northeast, and shell and soapstone beads, made in California, are intended for Indian consumption.

Traditionally, beadworking was learned within a family setting, and that is still the case for the majority of modern bead artists. However, the establishment of arts-and-crafts programs in both urban and reservation settings created new opportunities for instruction beginning in the 1960s.

There are tens of thousands of contemporary bead artists who create original items and infuse this ancient art form with renewed energy. One of the best known is Vanessa Paukeigope Jennings of Anadarko, Oklahoma, who received a National Heritage Fellowship from the National Endowment for the Arts in 1989 in recognition of her mastery of all of the traditional Kiowa art forms. She is representative of a generation of beadworkers who, having learned their art from their grandmothers, remain committed to the traditional forms but reinterpret them with new vision.

Today, modern communication, transportation, and Native American competitive art shows contribute to increased levels of intertribal artistic exchange. Tribally distinct styles have largely given way to regional styles, with a few exceptions. Bead artists are embracing visual influences from many sources including popular culture, advertising logos, movies, comic books, and, more recently, computer-generated designs. The marketing of beadwork is fully subsumed in the national economy: one-of-a-kind high-fashion items are available for a select clientele; less distinctive items appear in mail-order catalogs and in thousands of retail stores throughout the United States.

Like artists everywhere, beadworkers have continually invented and reinterpreted their own visual culture and incorporated their new ideas into local traditions. The thousands of contemporary beadworkers working today are making their own contributions to an art form and a heritage that is more than ten thousand years old.

Orchard, William C., *Beads and Beadwork of the American Indians* (New York: Museum of the American Indian, Heye Foundation, 1975); Smith, Monte, *The Technique of North American Indian Beadwork* (Ogden, Utah: Eagle's View Publishing Company, 1983).

JOALLYN ARCHAMBAULT (Standing Rock Sioux)
National Museum of Natural History
Smithsonian Institution

BENDER, CHIEF

(1883–1954)
Ojibwa professional baseball player and coach.

Charles Albert "Chief" Bender was one of the finest pitchers in major-league baseball during the first two decades of the twentieth century—a period that put a premium on outstanding pitching. His teammates included the future Baseball Hall of Fame pitchers Rube Waddell, Herb Pennock, and Eddie Plank, while surrounding him in the big leagues shone such stars as Christy Mathewson, Walter Johnson, Cy Young, "Three-Finger" Brown, and "Iron Man" Joe McGinnity. Connie Mack, the longtime Philadelphia manager for whom Bender played twelve seasons (1903–14), wrote in 1950 that Bender was one of the top half-dozen pitchers in the history of the game; Mack is also reported to have said that Bender was the greatest "money pitcher" he'd ever coached.

Like many American Indian athletes (the most famous of whom was Jim Thorpe), the Minnesota-born Bender graduated from Carlisle Indian Industrial School. He was the son of a German-American farmer father and an Ojibwa mother. After Carlisle he attended Dickinson College, also in Carlisle, Pennsylvania, though not for long. At the age of twenty, and without a day in the minor leagues, Bender began pitching for Connie Mack's A's in 1903, the third year of the new American League.

Although baseball was enormously popular in the early decades of this century, the reputation of the game, and particularly that of baseball players, was not terribly respectable. While Christy Mathewson—or "the Christian Gentleman," as he was known—was the best-known exception to this rule, Chief Bender also belonged to the small group of unusually upstanding players. Suspended briefly in 1911 for having succumbed to the hard-drinking atmosphere of professional baseball, the pitcher mostly appears to have resisted such pressure.

His onetime roommate on the A's, the pitcher Rube Bressler, described Bender as "one of the kindest and finest men who ever lived," and credited the veteran with helping him face the inevitability of defeat early in his career. Others described Bender as "classy," or "one of the nicest people you'd ever meet." As a result, in an era peopled by such characters as John McGraw, Ty Cobb, and Rube Waddell (Bender's teammate and one of the strangest people ever to play professional baseball), little attention has been paid to Bender as a person.

Bender was not the first American Indian to play in the major leagues. That honor goes to Lou Sockalexis, who played just three years for Cleveland in 1897–99 (and is considered by some to be the inspiration for the club's name in later years—the Indians). Several dozen American Indians came into the big leagues in the next two decades, and although Jim Thorpe was certainly the best known of these, Chief Bender was the finest baseball player of the group, and the only one in the Baseball Hall of Fame.

It is worth pointing out that while American Indian ballplayers were nearly always called "Chief," this nickname was used much less often among Indians themselves. John "Chief" Meyers, for example, a Mission Indian who played against Bender, referred to him as Charlie.

At least in baseball, the question of discrimination directed at American Indians in the early twentieth century is not entirely simple. On the one hand, according to one historian of the game during those years, Indian ballplayers received "substantial attention" in the press for two reasons. First, they were unusual. But at the same time, the game's promoters emphasized the Indians' background to argue—falsely—that baseball was a genuinely democratic sport.

To further complicate matters, some managers tried to sneak African-American ballplayers into the segregated game by calling them Indians, Cubans, or Mexicans. In 1901, for example, Giants manager John McGraw claimed that his new second baseman, Charlie Grant, was an American Indian, and gave him the name Chief Tockahama. McGraw's rival manager Charles Comiskey blew the whistle on what had become an open secret, and Grant's career in the majors was finished before it started. Bender's friend Chief Meyers (who played for McGraw's Giants) had to endure taunts of "nigger" from fans who thought him black.

Bender himself seems not to have suffered this fate. He explained once:

> The reason I went into baseball as a profession was that when I left school, baseball offered me the best opportunity both for money and advancement. . . . I adopted it because I played baseball better than I could do anything else, because the life and the game appealed to me and because there was so little of racial prejudice in the game. . . . There has been scarcely a trace of sentiment against me on account of birth. I have been treated the same as other men.

There was in fact an enormous amount of racial prejudice in major-league baseball. The game had successfully banished African Americans from playing, and some of its biggest stars, such as Ty Cobb, were vicious racists. Bender, however, generally somewhat quiet and aloof, was well known for handling racial taunts gracefully. When fans heckled him or greeted him with war whoops on the field, he would answer them by cupping his hands around his mouth and shouting, "Foreigners! Foreigners!"

Although Bender rarely led his league in pitching statistics, he played key roles in five Philadelphia pennants and pitched extremely well in the World Series. In ten games he compiled a six-four record, with fifty-nine strikeouts, just twenty-one walks, and an excellent 2.44 earned run average.

Bender left the A's in 1914 to join the upstart Federal League club in Baltimore; the following year he came back to Philadelphia, where he played with the Phillies for his last two seasons in the majors, 1916–17. In 1918 he worked in World War I shipyards. Thereafter he either played, managed, coached, or scouted in baseball (mostly in the minors, but occasionally in the majors) until his death in 1954 at the age of seventy-one. Bender married Marie Clements in 1904. They had no children. His sister Elizabeth married the Winnebago educator Henry Roe Cloud, linking the ballplayer to another prominent Native American from the early twentieth century. Bender was elected to the Baseball Hall of Fame in 1953, a year before he died.

See also Thorpe, Jim.

James, Bill, *The Bill James Historical Baseball Abstract* (New York: Villard Books, 1988); Reiss, Steven A., *Touching Base: Professional Baseball and American Culture in the Progressive Age* (Westport, Conn.: Greenwood Press, 1980).

WARREN GOLDSTEIN
State University of New York
College at Old Westbury

BERDACHE

Berdache is the term that non-Indians used to refer to individuals in native societies who exhibited cross-gender behavior, including dress. The term is derived from an Arabic word meaning "sex slave boy." In general, berdaches were individuals who had male bodies but chose to participate in traditionally female roles within the Indian community. From an Indian perspective, berdaches rested somewhere on a gender continuum. The existence of the berdache makes it clear that Indian societies did not conceive of humanity as being sharply divided into two genders.

Berdache refers mainly to men-as-women because outsiders tended to focus on men as the important figures in native society. Thus early literature makes little or no mention of women-as-men (those with female bodies who fulfilled traditionally male roles). Because the first non-Indian visitors to a tribal group were usually male, and sought sexual relations with native women, encounters with men-as-women were more common than with women-as-men. Most Indian societies believed that berdaches were in touch with sacred powers and deserved a prestigious position within tribal society. As contact with whites increased, berdaches

were forced underground, altering their appearance as they experienced ridicule and ostracism by whites.

See also Gender.

BERING STRAIT THEORY

Most anthropologists today believe that the ancestors of all American Indians immigrated from northeastern Asia across the Bering land bridge during the Ice Age, between 12,000 and 60,000 years ago. Known as the Bering Strait theory, this idea is supported by archaeological, biological, and geological evidence.

As water became locked up in the polar ice caps, sea levels dropped as much as 300 feet. The Bering Sea between Siberia and Alaska is no more than 180 feet deep and would have been dry land at those times. The land bridge, called Beringia, was open several times in the last sixty thousand years: 50,000 to 60,000 years ago, 40,000 to 45,000 years ago, 28,000 to 33,000 years ago, and 13,000 to 23,000 years ago. During each of these periods, central and northwestern Alaska were ice free, and for 80 percent of the period from 10,000 to 30,000 years ago there was an ice-free corridor between the eastern (Laurentide) and western (Cordillerran) North American ice sheets that linked Alaska to the American Great Plains.

Biologically, American Indians are quite similar to the peoples of eastern Asia. They share a number of physical similarities—in teeth, skeletal features, coloration, hair type, and lack of body hair, as well as less visible characteristics—that set them apart from other humans in Europe and Africa.

Some scholars have suggested prehistoric migrations to North America from northern Europe, the Middle East, Africa, or Polynesia. Little or no evidence supports these theories, however. Many American Indians, in contrast, believe their people were divinely created in the Americas.

See also Origins: Anthropological Perspectives.

BIBLE TRANSLATIONS

The history of American Indian Bible translation is part of the broader history of Christian mission, which dates to the earliest days of the church. It is as much the story of the methods and assumptions of individuals and groups involved in this ministry as it is a chronicle of the products of their efforts.

Since these efforts began in the seventeenth century, the Bible has been translated in its entirety into six North American Indian languages. Printed in 1663, John Eliot's Bible for the "praying communities" of Massachusett Indians near Boston and Roxbury was not only the first such translation but the earliest complete Bible published in North America. Governor John Winthrop and the General Court of Massachusetts Bay considered Eliot's work as a partial fulfillment of the colony's agreement with their sovereign and sponsors to "gospel" and "civilize" the New World's "savages." Though many historians now question the sincerity with which most of the colonists entered into this compact, the depth of Eliot's commitment is witnessed by the fifteen years he toiled in learning Massachusett and devising an orthography to transcribe the Bible. Eliot viewed this difficult undertaking as "a sacred and holy work, to be regarded with fear, care, and reverence." Historians now deem it a turning point in the history of Christian missionary work. As one scholar has stated, Eliot's Massachusett Scriptures were "without precedent in modern times, for there was no tradition of such Bible translation for missionary purposes, except for versions of the almost legendary figures of the Early Church—Ulfilas, Mesrop, and Cyril and Methodius."

Even though Indian translations of portions of the Bible continued to appear during the seventeenth and eighteenth centuries, two hundred years were to elapse between the Massachusett Bible and the next complete translation, a version in Western Cree published in 1862 by associates of the British and Foreign Bible Society (BFBS). These second Indian Scriptures were followed in relatively rapid succession by versions in Eastern Arctic Inuit, published in 1871 by the BFBS; Dakota or Eastern Sioux, financed by the American Bible Society (ABS) and printed in 1880; and Gwich'in (a subarctic Cordilleran language), completed in 1898 by associates of the BFBS. The Navajo Bible, published in 1985 after forty-one years of collaborative effort by the Wycliffe Society and the ABS, is the latest version to contain the complete text of the Jewish and Christian Scriptures. Although not always accorded the credit they were due, Indian speakers provided the insiders' knowledge and insights without which none of these translations would have been possible.

In addition to six unabridged Bibles, translations for portions of the Hebrew and Christian Scriptures now exist in at least forty-six Indian languages. To these should be added numerous "Bible histories," which, while not technically translations, summarize the Bible in whole or in part in Native American tongues.

Considering that the effort to produce American Indian Bibles has been under way for nearly three and a half centuries, the accomplishments of this ministry may seem modest at best. Such an appraisal, however, must be weighed against the tremendous problems involved in translation, biblical or otherwise. One of the primary obstacles facing any translator is the great difficulty entailed in learning the lexicon and syntax of another language. Linguistic plurality poses further complications. For instance, many of the metaphors and narrative forms found in the Bible are so culture-bound that, even where feasible, a literal translation would render them misleading or nonsensical to non-Western peoples. What possible meaning could a verbatim translation of the expression "Lamb of God" hold for a society without a pastoral tradition and unfamiliar with the cultural, theological, and emotional significance attached to the term *lamb* in Western Christology? In the past, translators tended to attribute such difficulties to what they saw as the intellectual and spiritual inferiority of Indians and other non-Western groups. However, modern translators, rejecting this interpretation as ethnocentric, instead search for parallels of biblical concepts within the spiritual traditions of the peoples with whom they are working.

In addition to problems of method, differences among denominations and church societies regarding the importance of biblical translation in missionary work have also affected the pace and number of translations. It is significant, for example, that the work of translating the Bible has been an overwhelmingly Protestant endeavor. At least two causes exist for this fact. In the first place, because of the primacy of the sacraments in Roman Catholicism, Catholic missionaries have traditionally placed more stress on producing native-language versions of these rituals than on translating Bibles. As a result, Indian-language versions of the Lord's Prayer, the rite of confession, and the Mass exist for many groups among whom Catholic missions have been active. Secondly, in the centuries preceding the Second Vatican Council in 1962, the magisterium—the officials invested with the teaching authority of the Catholic Church—discouraged the dissemination of Bibles among the laity, believing that laypeople lacked the proper hermeneutical and theological training to achieve correct interpretations of biblical texts. Church officials instead encouraged the production and distribution of Bible summaries that supplemented catechisms in edifying readers with what they believed were proper lessons in faith and morals. Translations of both these summaries and catechisms now exist in many American Indian languages.

In contrast with its Catholic counterpart, the abiding tenet of Protestant missiology has been that contact with God's word is the major avenue by which grace effects salvation, and many Protestant churches and missionary agencies have for years directed their monetary and human resources toward translating the Bible into Indian languages.

Associates of the American Bible Society, the Canadian Bible Society, and the Wycliffe Society's Summer Institute of Linguistics are currently involved in at least twenty projects among Native Americans in the United States and among First Nations in Canada. These include translations for portions of the Scriptures into Western Keres, Zuni, Havasupai, Ute, Crow, Cheyenne, Mesquakie, Choctaw, Inupiatun, Siberian Yupik, Carrier, Naskapi, Micmac, and Dogrib. In addition, a new version of the Navajo Christian Scriptures, one that will be more in keeping with the tribe's contemporary language and culture, is currently in preparation. Finally, work is under way on a Central Yupik version of the Hebrew Testament. When this work is finished, a complete Bible will exist in that language, making it the seventh American Indian Scriptures.

Eames, Wilberforce, "Bible Translations," in *Handbook of American Indians North of Mexico,* ed. Frederick W. Hodge (Washington, D.C.: Government Printing Office, 1912); Hutchison, William R., *Errand to the World: American Protestant Thought and Foreign Missions* (Chicago: University of Chicago Press, 1987).

The author wishes to thank David Kenderick and Leanna Lupas of the American Bible Society and J. David Myers of the North American Branch of Summer Institute of Linguistics for their contributions to this article.

HARVEY MARKOWITZ
D'Arcy McNickle Center for the
History of the American Indian
Newberry Library

BIBLIOGRAPHIES

American Indian voices have been heard throughout history. Oral tradition was and still is a major method used to hand down histories, cultural traditions, and worldviews. In the preservation of tribal histories, the sacred scrolls of the southern Ojibwas tell of the Midewewin. Dakota records called *winter counts* carry Dakota history through paintings on buffalo robes. The Tohono O'Odhams marked their history on calendar sticks, while knots tied in string kept the biographical records of the Interior Salish.

All these are reminders of times past, and together they weave a history of Native Americans. Using these devices, American Indians kept alive the identity of their nations with richness and separateness. Unfortunately, written literature fails to touch on the essence of the heartbeat that keeps American Indians proud of their nations and participating in their traditions. Many of the early written sources portray the stereotypic romantic notion of the doe-eyed princess or the savage heathen that is still a part of contemporary literature. It is important, therefore, for students of Native American life to approach written literature on that subject cautiously. The best tool for linking the native peoples who continue to sustain their oral traditions to the world of the written word is the bibliography.

Bibliographies identify, locate, and provide access to information resources in a variety of formats. Bibliographies serve as maps for the novice researcher as well as for the seasoned scholar, guiding both through a maze of information. Bibliographies lay the groundwork for assessing who did what, where, how, when, and how well through formats that include school and library catalogs, journal articles, bibliographical essays, encyclopedias, handbooks, and almanacs.

However, researchers need to examine bibliographies carefully if they are seeking an American Indian perspective; bibliographers often mix Indian-authored works with efforts of non-Indian writers, burying the native voice.

The earliest published work by a Native American in the present-day United States was the Mohegan missionary Samson Occom's *A Sermon, Preached at the Execution of Moses Paul, an Indian,* printed in 1772 by Thomas and Samuel Green in New Haven, Connecticut. The works of early American Indian writers have been given due credit in various bibliographies — most comprehensively in Daniel Littlefield and James Parins's *Bibliography of Native American Writers, 1772–1924* (1981) and its supplement (1985).

It was not until 1873 that the first purely Indian bibliography was published, Thomas Warren Field's *An Essay Towards an Indian Bibliography.* This work, published in New York by Scribner, Armstrong, and

Company, was actually a sales catalog of the author's personal library. Nevertheless, the Field bibliography is recognized as a standard source for pre-1873 literature and serves as a reminder of early scholarly interest in American Indians.

The identification of bibliographies is not always an easy task. The subject entry to look under in most library catalogs is "Indians of North America—Bibliography." Most libraries use the Library of Congress (LC) system or the Dewey Decimal system to classify their holdings. The Dewey system uses numbers, 016.97 being the class where Indian bibliographies are located. The LC system assigns a combination of alphabetical and numeric characters; Indian bibliographies are found in the Z1209–Z1210 classes. Marilyn Haas's *Indians of North America: Methods and Sources for Library Research* provides a more detailed description of these classification systems. More library holdings are available on-line, and search by subject is the most beneficial. Be aware, however, that some information sources do not necessarily follow these classification schemes.

Examining bibliographies produced in different time periods conveys a general idea of the development and progression of guides to American Indian topics. A search of the OCLC national library database produced a list of 144 works classified as American Indian bibliographies published before 1896. (However, it should be kept in mind that the computer cannot differentiate original works from variant editions, facsimiles, reprints, and translations.) From 1896 to 1901 letters from the missions to the Jesuits were published in seventy-three volumes as *The Jesuit Relations and Allied Documents* by the Burrows Brothers Company in Cleveland. Thereafter, 54 titles were added to the roster of bibliographies before 1930. More interest in American Indians came to light between 1931 and 1950, as witnessed by the 75 bibliographies published during that period. In the years from 1961 to 1970 there were a total of 217 entries, 66 of which were produced in 1970 alone. In 1975 there appeared 87 of the 590 bibliographies compiled in the years 1971 to 1980. In the next thirteen years, 581 bibliographic titles were produced.

Several significant works from this roster deserve specific discussion. For example, in 1941 George Peter Murdock compiled his *Ethnographic Bibliographic Bibliography of North America* in 168 pages. Published by the Human Relations Area Files Press of New Haven, Connecticut, it is a standard bibliography for American Indian studies. Subsequent editions include the second edition in 1953 with 239 pages and the third edition in 1960 with 393 pages. In 1975, Murdock collaborated with Timothy O'Leary and produced the fourth edition in five volumes. The five volumes of the original publication are arranged according to geographic areas, complete with area maps; the entries are subdivided by tribe. Its 1990 supplement is arranged by author, with extensive subject and tribal indexes. Entries are not annotated, but the supplement includes relevant subject headings within the main entries.

The Education of the American Indians: A Survey of the Literature by Brewton Berry was prepared for the Special Subcommittee on Indian Education of the Senate Committee on Labor and Public Welfare and published by the Government Printing Office in 1969. This unprecedented document covered a wide range of subjects, many of which were historical. The very broad, general headings for the 708 titles are "Histories," "Problems," "Causes," and "Indian College Students." Because of the congressional audience, this bibliography has been used as a source for many subsequent works in education.

The Educational Resources Information Center and the Clearinghouse on Rural Education and Small Schools, commonly referred to as ERIC/CRESS, published *American Indian Education: A Selected Bibliography* in 1969 and issued nine supplements over the next decade. The intent of this series was to provide a guide to the latest in resources and educational research and/or development.

In the 1960s the National Indian Education Association (NIEA) identified the need for a comprehensive catalog addressing American Indian media materials, with pertinent bibliographic information. Project MEDIA (Media Evaluations and Dissemination by Indian Americans) was established in 1973 with the goal of identifying, acquiring, reviewing, and evaluating print and nonprint media materials. The results were then compiled into a catalog and disseminated to those responsible for fulfilling the educational needs of American Indians. *Native American Evaluations of Media Materials* (fall 1977) and *Media Evaluations and Dissemination by Indian Americans* (2d ed., summer 1978) were two of the publications produced by this endeavor. The evaluation process set up by the project was an important achievement because American Indians were involved throughout to assure high quality, accurate and unbiased information. Although the project was short-lived, it provided a framework for citation entry and demonstrated the evaluative skills of native people.

The Newberry Library Center for the History of the American Indian (subsequently named for its founding director, D'Arcy McNickle), introduced its bibliographic series with titles that compile information by subject, geographic area, and tribe. Under the editorial leadership of William R. Swagerty and Francis Jennings, thirty-one topical bibliographies had been compiled by 1987. Significant features of this series include bibliographical essays and a list of recommended works organized by scholastic levels. The McNickle Center also supported Francis Paul Prucha's *A Bibliographic Guide to the History of Indian-White Relations in the United States* (1977); Prucha published a supplement to this work in 1982. In 1995 the University of Oklahoma Press published *Writings in Indian History, 1985–1990* for the center. Edited by Colin G. Calloway, Jay Miller, and Richard A. Sattler, the bibliography seeks to continue Prucha's work. In addition, Colin Calloway has edited a collection of bibliographic essays, published for the McNickle Center by the University of Oklahoma Press as *New Directions in American Indian History* (1987).

In 1980 Scarecrow Press began its Native American Bibliography series under the general editorship of Jack W. Marken. The seventeen volumes that appeared by 1994 cover tribal groups, subjects, and geographic areas. Compiled by distinguished experts, these bibliographies are intended to be comprehensive, with annotations accompanying the important entries. More recently, Frederick E. Hoxie and Harvey Markowitz compiled a general bibliography entitled *Native Americans: An Annotated Bibliography* (1991), which is selective rather than comprehensive in scope. Together these works are useful to students of American Indian studies and library science because they provide a balanced guide to the literature while fulfilling the guidelines for a bibliographic work.

In 1991, Duane Kendall Hale wrote *Researching and Writing Tribal Histories*. In it, Hale asserted that there are 341 known published bibliographies. He noted that these titles, other than general compilations, tend to be tribal, geographic, or subject oriented, and more likely to be a combination. Interestingly, Hale observed that several tribes have had fewer than sixteen books written about them and noted that 127 tribes have yet to be described in book form. These inadequacies make geographic and subject bibliographies that much more useful, since a seasoned researcher may identify tribal information in a work that a bibliographer may have categorized simply as regional.

The information explosion of the 1960s and 1970s created many new bibliographic sources. Whereas authors like Murdock incorporated the use of computers early on in their work, many of the titles mentioned earlier were researched by traditional methods: searching card catalogs, reviewing previously published materials, collecting reading lists, or simply compiling lists of materials that attract one's fancy. With the advent of electronic technology, CDs, and on-line databases, there has been an even more massive information explosion, and the need for bibliographic control has increased. This need is particularly important in a time of tribal self-determination and self-sufficiency.

Today, Indian people are eager to take advantage of the information superhighway. Like the ancestors who gave direction and guided their communities with their wisdom, Indian bibliographies can be pathfinders that teach us to tread steadfastly while remaining alert and curious. When bibliographies are representative of the true Indian experience and provide a forum for learning, the circle will be complete.

VELMA SALABIYE (Navajo)
American Indian Studies Center
University of California at Los Angeles

BIRTH

Birthing among most American Indian and Alaska Native groups was a very natural and normative event. Yet in descriptions of native women one frequently reads that women "would leave the march when camps were moving, give birth, and run with the newborn child to rejoin the band." In the more contemporary reports of public-health workers, it is frequently noted that native women seldom cry out during the birth process. What these stereotypic descriptions indicate is that many people view Native American birthing practices through the lens of romance and imagination. Such views also prompt the curious to explore the ethnographic facts that surround the act of childbirth and to reflect upon the traditions that operated within American Indian societies and separated them from other peoples.

Because many recent studies of North American cultures present a typical life cycle within each community, birthing information is readily available for groups as diverse as the Inuits of the Arctic, the Haidas and Tlingits of the Northwest Coast, the Pomos of California, the Zunis of the American Southwest, and many others. Although each group maintained specific rituals that set it apart from others, several general trends can be seen, most of which are apparent in the case of the Lakota peoples of the Great Plains. The following discussion presents Lakota birthing practices as typical of such practices among North American Indians.

As was true of many other tribes, the Lakotas did not surround the period of pregnancy with restrictive taboos or practices. Women who were pregnant might avoid certain foods and be excluded from certain ceremonies, but they would otherwise function within the community as they always had. When a woman went into labor, soft skins were arranged within a lodge and the individual was instructed to kneel in the center of the area and grasp a tipi pole for support. The prospective mother was assisted by a group of experienced, elder women; young girls and males were excluded. Elder women would oversee the birthing process, occasionally placing their arms around the mother's midsection if difficulties arose. Following the birth, these same elders would assist in the expulsion of the placenta and would be responsible for severing the umbilical cord. A six-inch section of the cord would be saved by these midwives, to be dried and placed in a special pouch usually made in the shape of a turtle or lizard. These shapes were seen in the various constellations of the prairie sky, and the pouches were believed to call down protective spirits to stand watch over the child.

Following the birth, Lakota children were generally anointed with bear grease that had been scented with beaver castor. Elders believed that the ceremony would instill the strength of the bear and the industry of the beaver in the child's character. The Lakotas would also place a leather cap decorated with quillwork on the infant's head for protection and to ensure the proper closing of the fontanel. Brown powder from a prairie mushroom was used as a diaper substitute. Other tribes used moss or other absorbent substances to provide a sanitary method of disposing of bodily wastes. The child was then placed in a cradleboard made of wood or rawhide that was covered with skins. Though most frequently noted on the Great Plains among groups like the Lakotas, cradleboards were observed in many parts of the continent, from the Southwest to the Great Lakes and the Northeast. Even where cradleboards were not used (as in the Arctic, where wood was in short supply), children were typically swaddled to induce quiet and to free mothers so they might fulfill their many other responsibilities.

Following the birth, Lakota mothers were given special herb teas and a nutritious broth made from buffalo meat. They did not immediately nurse the baby, because the first milk was thought not to be healthy. Instead, a well-respected elder was invited to remove the first milk. To be invited to perform this service was considered a great honor to both the elder and the child, as the Lakotas believed that in this way the character of the elder would be transferred to the newborn child. Afterward the elder would be presented with gifts and the child would be free to nurse from the mother.

After the child was placed in the cradleboard, he or she would be presented to the father and his extended family. A respected man or woman would later be invited to present the child with a name at a public ceremony that was generally followed by gift giving and feasting. The Lakotas would then declare the child to be one of the *pte oyate* (buffalo people). Other tribes would perform similar ceremonies to welcome the newborn into their communities. These generally involved naming, the honoring of elder relatives, and community celebration. The birth and welcoming of a child were heralded events. The Lakotas called children *wakan yesha,* "like the sacred," reflecting the extent to which the arrival of a new life was associated with the mystery of life and death and was a reminder of how closely human beings lived to spiritual power and spiritual forces.

Although childbirth was frequently described, lactation is not a firm part of the ethnographic record. Despite the fact that most early research was carried out by men who were either uninterested in childbirth or unable to collect information on the subject, it is known that nursing often continued for five or six years. This practice may have been encouraged by the difficult conditions many Native Americans endured, particularly in hunting and gathering societies, or perhaps because women who nurse become pregnant less frequently, and it also had the benefit of extending the intervals between the birth of children in a family.

See also Child Rearing.

BEATRICE MEDICINE (Lakota)
Wakpala, South Dakota

BLACK DRINK

Black drink was the name given by the English and Americans to a ritual beverage brewed traditionally by the Indians of the southeastern United States. They prepared it from the roasted leaves and stems of the yaupon holly (*Ilex vomitoria*), native to the Atlantic and Gulf Coasts. The active ingredient is caffeine. Black drink was used as a substitute for coffee and tea by southern colonists under the name *cassine*.

Prior to the nineteenth century, this beverage was consumed during the daily deliberations of the village councils and at all other important council meetings. Creeks, Cherokees, Choctaws, and others believed it purified the drinker and purged him of anger and falsehoods. Black drink was prepared by special village officials and served in large communal cups, frequently made of conch shell. The men in council were served in order of precedence, starting with important visitors. They consumed large quantities at a sitting. Afterward, they purged themselves by vomiting.

The name *black drink* was also applied to a variety of other ritual beverages prepared by the southeastern Indians from other plants. In the 1830s, the use of the black drink was abandoned when the tribes removed to Oklahoma, where the yaupon holly does not grow. Still, other ritual beverages (sometimes also referred to as "black drink") continue to be used in traditional rituals in both the Southeast and Oklahoma.

BLACK ELK

(1863–1950)
Oglala Lakota holy man, traditional healer, and visionary.

Black Elk was born in December 1863 on the Little Powder River, west of present-day South Dakota. He was the son of the elder Black Elk and White Cow Sees Woman. Black Elk was the fourth person in his family in as many generations to bear this name.

Black Elk was a man seasoned with a lifetime of idiosyncrasies. He experienced the tail end of the U.S. and Sioux wars and the beginnings of U.S. oppressive policies toward his people. He also lived during the early reservation period, before the Indian Reorganization Act of 1934 took full effect. He was three years old when the Fetterman Battle was fought, five years old during the signing of the 1868 Fort Laramie Treaty, not quite a teenager during the Battle of the Little Bighorn, and a young man of twenty-seven when Chief Big Foot and his band were massacred at Wounded Knee Creek in December 1890. This latter event occurred just eight miles from where Black Elk made his home on the Pine Ridge Indian Reservation. He spoke candidly of these events in interviews with the poet John G. Neihardt.

During Black Elk's young adulthood, missionaries attempted to convert the Oglala Lakotas to Christianity, and not many escaped the intense measures inflicted upon those who resisted. Black Elk was no exception. He attempted to understand Christianity after he was subjugated to it, and was baptized Nicholas Black Elk on December 6, 1904, at the Holy Rosary Mission near present-day Pine Ridge, South Dakota. Although the role of staunch Catholic was forced upon him, he played it well to appease his oppressors.

Black Elk's Lakota spirituality remained strong throughout his life. He was part of the underground traditional religious movement, which began shortly after the U.S. government banned native religious practices. These underground activities became a vital part of his life, as did his visible life as a staunch Catholic. He mastered both, but he feared that U.S. policies would overcome the Lakota Nation and destroy his community's identity. Many of the Lakota traditional holy men and healers of that time shared that basic philosophy. Some chose to record the Lakotas' sacred knowledge and information via non-Indian writers in the hopes of preserving it for future generations of Lakota people.

Remarkably, Black Elk committed himself to this task. During the summer of 1930 he dictated his life story to John Neihardt, and the resulting book, *Black Elk Speaks,* appeared in 1932. Reprinted many times, the work was widely circulated and read by the general public. The positive aspect of his decision to go public was that his story offered an understanding of the history of his people and a sense of hope for the future not only of the Lakotas, but of all humankind.

Black Elk's vision eventually became a message to the Lakota Nation—a warning that, should the Lakota people cross over into total assimilation and acculturation, they would lose their rich traditions and cease to exist as a unique nation. This message was evident in his final words, arranged by Neihardt but spoken by Black Elk: "There is no center any longer, and the sacred tree is dead."

As an elder, Black Elk entertained the general public in the summer months by reenacting the traditional La-

Black Elk (1863–1950) at Maderson, South Dakota, in 1947. Photograph by Joseph Epes Brown.

kota life at Duhamel's Sioux Indian Pageant in the Black Hills. This was his means of informing them of Lakota history and also of earning money during the Great Depression. The remainder of his time was spent with his family and friends on the Pine Ridge Reservation, where he often served as guest speaker at various gatherings.

The passage of the Indian Religious Freedom Act in 1978 lifted the fear of federal prosecution and allowed the Lakota Nation free expression and open practice of its centuries-old religion. The combination of this legislation and the popularity of Black Elk's teachings created a renaissance of Lakota spirituality. This new movement has resulted in decreased membership in Christian faiths and declined attendance of Lakotas at Christian services across the reservation. In attempts to maintain and gain membership, some Christian churches have incorporated minimal Lakota traditions, but the move toward true Lakota traditional spirituality has continued to grow, particularly among the younger generation.

The movement of current generations of Lakota people, inspired by Black Elk's words, is to reverse the process that, within a century, transformed their culture. The first step toward the regeneration of the culture has involved a psychological healing from a century of oppression, in addition to a relearning of Lakota identity. Black Elk's warnings about eventual genocide have been heeded.

Black Elk's legacy is that of courage and inspiration to the Lakota Nation. He provided leadership in the acceptance of Christianity for a peaceful coexistence with the dominant society while simultaneously remaining a Lakota traditionalist at heart.

Black Elk lived through a trying and tumultuous period of Lakota history. One can change the appearance of a man and have him act in a prescribed manner in the shadows of oppression, but one cannot change the thousands of years of ingrained, culturally fostered spirituality that can be found only in a man's heart and mind.

See also Sioux.

Black Elk, *Black Elk Speaks,* as told through John G. Neihardt, with an introduction by Vine Deloria, Jr. (Lincoln: University of Nebraska Press, 1979); Black Elk, *The Sixth Grandfather: Black Elk's Teachings Given to John G. Neihardt,* ed. Raymond J. DeMallie (Lincoln: University of Nebraska Press, 1984); Rice, Julian, *Black Elk's Story: Distinguishing Its Lakota Purpose* (Albuquerque: University of New Mexico Press, 1991).

KAREN D. LONE HILL (Oglala Lakota)
Oglala Lakota College
Kyle, South Dakota

BLACKFOOT

The Blackfoot, or Blackfeet, are the children of people put on earth by Apistotokiwa, the Maker. The Nizitapi, or Real People, as they call each other, originated on a homeland covering today's southern Alberta, western Saskatchewan, and central Montana. Today, the tribe resides on a reservation in Montana, adjacent to Gla-

Sampson and Leah Beaver with their daughter, Frances Louise, in 1907.

cier National Park and the U.S.-Canadian border. The Blackfeet belong to a confederacy that originally included the Blood, North Piegan, and Siksika tribes of Alberta and the Small Robes, who were the southernmost band in the Blackfoot confederacy. The Small Robes, two thousand strong in 1835, were exterminated in the nineteenth century by smallpox and warfare.

When the artist George Catlin visited the Blackfeet in 1832, he estimated the confederacy's population at 16,500. The German prince Maximilian zu Wied and Karl Bodmer, an artist, visiting a year later, put the population at closer to twenty thousand. Catlin called the Blackfeet "the most powerful tribe of Indians on the continent." In 1837, a smallpox pandemic scourged the upper Missouri River homeland of the Blackfeet, and

the tribe was decimated. Its survival and recovery speak of an enduring people.

The name Blackfoot is an exclusively English term. In the tribal language, the name is Amskapi Pikuni. *Pikuni* derives from an old form meaning "spotted robes." Occasionally, elders will use *Sokeetapi*, or "Prairie People," and *Apikunipuyi*, "Speakers of the Same Language," as descriptive names.

A popular anthropological theory has the Blackfeet moving onto the plains of what is now Montana in 1750. This idea derives from the naive academic notion that the tribe was migrating southward when contact with westward expansion was made. Recent archaeological discoveries, and Blackfoot origin tradition, confirm the tribe's residency in its homeland for thousands of years.

The Blackfeet were people of the plains and buffalo. They never used canoes or ate fish. To the Blackfeet, rivers and lakes hold a special power because they are inhabited by the Suyitapis, the Underwater People. Painted lodge covers, medicine bundles, and other sacred items were transferred to the tribe from the Suyitapis. In turn, their power and domain are respected by the tribe. Today, the reservation waterways and lakes are touted as premier fishing spots. Yet most tribal members maintain the traditional ban on fishing.

In 1896, at the urging of George Bird Grinnell, founder of the Audubon Society, the tribe, then reduced to fourteen hundred members, signed a $1.5-million agreement with the federal government relinquishing its western territory. The relinquished area became Glacier National Park on May 11, 1910. Transcripts of the meeting include a closing speech by White Calf, leader of the tribe. In it, he referred to Ninastako, Chief Mountain, a sacred place of the tribe, stating, "Chief Mountain is my head. Now my head is cut off. The mountains have been my last refuge." The speech echoes the history of the tribe's relationship with an encroaching new order.

The Blackfoot Indian Reservation today is a fifty-mile square of mountains and foothills, lakes and rivers falling eastward onto the plains. The 1,525,712-acre reserve is but a portion of the 26-million-acre tribal homeland recognized by the federal government in 1855. The population today is approaching the numbers reported by Catlin and Prince Maximilian, and half of the fifteen thousand enrolled tribal members live on the reservation. Enrollment in the tribe is set forth by a rule inspired by the Bureau of Indian Affairs. Only those with the requisite "blood quantum" (today, people with one-fourth degree, or more, blood lineage) can be tribal members. Enrolled members are issued identification cards indicating their blood quantum degree and enrollment number. Membership in the tribe entails a variety of tribal rights and responsibilities, ranging from use of communal lands to serving on the governing body, the Blackfoot Tribal Business Council.

Tribal headquarters are located at the Blackfoot Indian Agency in Browning, Montana, the largest of five reservation communities. Legend has it that the wife of the agency officer, D. M. Browning, selected the current site: overwhelmed by the beauty of acres of wildflowers alongside Willow Creek, she convinced her husband to move the agency there. Actually, the decision was made by the Great Northern Railroad, whose tracks pass nearby.

With the extermination of buffalo in 1883, the Blackfeet were left without food, and a large number starved to death the following winter. The Starvation Winter is the darkest period in the history of the tribe. Another dark time was Baker's Massacre. In the freezing dawn of January 23, 1870, the Second United States Regiment of Cavalry, under Major Eugene Baker, massacred Heavy Runner's camp at Willow Rounds, Montana. A total of 173 Blackfeet were killed, mostly women and children, and 140 were taken prisoner. The prisoners, many with smallpox, were chased onto the freezing prairie and abandoned. Descendants of the victims recount the event as part of tribal and family histories.

Much of the foundation for contemporary Blackfoot life was laid between 1884 and 1910. During that period, the tribe's exceedingly high death rate began to decline and the population began to grow. Catholic and government boarding schools were built on the reservation. The schools exerted enormous effort to separate students from their tribal language and cultural ways. Government officials and teachers emphasized vocational training and "civilized" behavior.

Today, the tribe seeks to recover its heritage so that the group might flourish in a more tolerant world. The Blackfeet are revitalizing their tribal language, culture, and identity in the belief that strength comes from a healthy self-image. The return to the native language and culture is viewed as a healing movement rather than a retreat into an unhappy past.

Dempsey, Hugh A., and Linda Moir, *Bibliography of the Blackfoot* (Metuchen, N.J., and London: Scarecrow Press, 1989); Farr, William E., *The Reservation Blackfeet, 1882–1945: A Photographic History of Cultural Survival* (Seattle: University of Washington Press, 1984); Schultz, James Willard (Apikuni), *Blackfeet and Buffalo: Memories of Life among the Indians* (Norman: University of Oklahoma Press, 1962).

DARRELL ROBES KIPP (Blackfoot)
Piegan Institute
Blackfoot Indian Reservation

BLACK HAWK (MAKATAIMESHEKIAKIAK)

(1767–1838)
Sauk war leader and spokesman.

Born at Saukenuk, the largest Sauk village, near the mouth of the Rock River in northwestern Illinois, Black Hawk grew to manhood at a time of great change for tribal people in the upper Mississippi Valley. British victory in the Seven Years' War had ousted France from North America, but French traders remained active among the Mississippi Valley peoples as they and the British and Spanish competed for Indian trade and alliances. By 1804 the Spanish had left Louisiana and the British retreated into Canada, leaving many northern tribes at the mercy of the Americans. During his adult life Black Hawk watched with growing impatience and anger as the Sauks had their economy weakened, their mobility limited, and their lands taken by the advancing United States. In the face of these fundamental shifts he spoke for Sauk traditions; he opposed the pioneers and rejected their claims to tribal lands. His unbending resistance eventually brought disaster to his followers. Nevertheless, his life exemplified traditional Sauk values. A village war leader who hoped for better times, he helped to foster resistance to unavoidable, if painful, changes in tribal life.

In a world of rapidly changing political and economic allegiances, the Sauks suffered a continuing decline in their standard of living. As pioneers hurried west into the Mississippi Valley and south of the Great Lakes, Indians in these regions faced continuing pressures to cede part or all of their land holdings. The same population pressures forced more competition among neighboring tribes as they strove to maintain their hunting, trapping, gathering, and farming subsistence cycles. When available game diminished, the villagers had few options. They could travel farther from home to hunt, or shift to other economic activities. The Illinois Sauks rejected the latter option, and, as a result, their hunting parties met spirited resistance from the Cherokees in the south and the Osages to the west.

Young Black Hawk developed his skills as a warrior and leader during the late eighteenth century as the Sauks and their allies the Mesquakies (Fox) carried out repeated raids against neighboring tribes. (Before Black Hawk reached adulthood, his father died while fighting against the Cherokees.) Nevertheless, the Sauks engaged in diplomacy as well as warfare. Until 1804, when Americans supplanted the Spanish at St. Louis, Black Hawk looked upon the Spanish as friends and allies. He felt the same way about the British. As late as the 1820s, large groups of Sauks traveled north and east to the Canadian post at Malden, just across the border from Detroit, to receive annual presents and assurances of English goodwill.

The Americans were different. From the first Sauk contacts with federal officials, Sauk leaders felt threatened or dissatisfied. To them the Americans seemed to favor their Osage enemies and to ignore or look down upon the eastern tribes. This perception led to violence, and in 1804 the Indians killed several settlers. The pioneers demanded that the Sauks be punished, and when a small delegation of tribal village leaders visited St. Louis in 1804, federal officials there persuaded them to sign a treaty ceding all tribal lands east of the Mississippi River. For nearly three decades, that agreement brought continuing friction and misunderstanding between the tribe and the United States. It was a direct cause of the Black Hawk War.

It took some years for the main body of Sauks to learn about the 1804 treaty, and from the start the majority of villagers rejected it because it had not been ratified. While not a political leader, Black Hawk spoke against the treaty repeatedly. As a mature adult he came to see all actions by the Americans as suspect and as aimed at harming or disrupting Sauk life. An outspoken traditionalist, he rejected payments of treaty annuities from U.S. officials. His world centered on the village of Saukenuk. It was there that he had grown to manhood, participated in the annual ceremonies, and recounted his victories over tribal enemies. It was also the burial place of his friends and family members. At the outbreak of the War of 1812 the forty-five-year-old warrior urged his tribesmen to join the British and fight American expansion.

During the war Black Hawk led hundreds of Sauk warriors east to Detroit, where they campaigned with the British in Michigan, Indiana, and Ohio. By late 1813 the warriors had returned home only to learn that the village elders had chosen young Keokuk as the war leader for the community. Much to Black Hawk's consternation, Keokuk's superior oratorical and political skills allowed him to dominate Sauk affairs for the next several decades. While Keokuk stood at center stage, the older and more experienced Black Hawk led a successful attack on American shipping on the Mississippi. In May 1814 the warrior defeated a force of over four hundred soldiers and militiamen commanded by Major Zachary Taylor, who had been sent north to punish the Sauks for their anti-American acts.

In 1816 Sauk and Mesquakie leaders signed treaties ending hostilities. From then until the late 1820s the villagers continued their precarious occupation of the Mississippi Valley in the face of ever-increasing numbers of settlers. By 1831 Black Hawk had come to be recognized as the spokesman for a motley grouping of Sauks, Mesquakies, and other Indians who continued to refuse to migrate west beyond the Mississippi.

The following year Black Hawk led the so-called British Band east across the Mississippi into Illinois. He and his followers hoped to establish a new village and begin farming again. This action set off loud protests from pioneers and politicians, and President Andrew Jackson ordered federal troops into action. By late April 1832, American regulars and Illinois militiamen began chasing the Indians up the Rock River valley into southern Wisconsin and then west toward the Mississippi. They overtook the exhausted band at the mouth of the Bad Axe River, slaughtering many of them. This crushing defeat persuaded other midwestern tribes to accept removal to the West and ended Black Hawk's public career. After being imprisoned in Virginia for some months, he was sent back to his tribe in disgrace. He died in 1838.

Black Hawk's career illustrates the divisions within tribal and village groups as they sought to deal effectively with the United States. Some leaders recognized the need for accommodation with the powerful Americans. Others rejected such action, turning to native religion and even denial in hopes of retaining traditional practices and locations. Black Hawk provided a powerful symbol of cultural pride for the Sauks and Mesquakies during an era of constant disruption and hardship. He based his actions on Sauk practices and beliefs, but by 1832 the crush of frontier settlement had made such ideas impossible to maintain.

See also Sauk.

Nichols, Roger L., *Black Hawk and the Warrior's Path* (Arlington Heights, Ill.: Harlan Davidson, 1992); Nichols, Roger L., "The Black Hawk War in Retrospect," *Wisconsin Magazine of History 65* (summer 1982): 238–46.

ROGER L. NICHOLS
University of Arizona

BOARDING SCHOOLS

Beginning in the nineteenth century, boarding schools played a fundamental role in the programs designed by the U.S. government to foster the assimilation of native peoples into the mainstream of American society. Reformers and politicians who favored the policy of reservation allotment also advanced the concept of placing Indian children in residential schools where they would speak English, learn a vocation, and practice farming.

Advocates of boarding schools argued that industrial training, in combination with several years of isolation from family, would diminish the influence of tribalism on a new generation of American Indians. For fifty years after the first federally administered residential school was established in 1879 at Carlisle, Pennsylvania, thousands of Native American children and youth were sent to live, work, and be educated in the schools.

Prior to Carlisle, most American Indians had little experience with the boarding-school concept. Some had attended mission schools, and three unique institutions had developed earlier in the century: the Choctaw Academy and the Cherokee Male and Female Seminaries. The Choctaw Academy in Kentucky, founded in 1825, was a male boarding school that Indian and white children attended. The academy was funded by proceeds from Choctaw land cessions in the Southeast during the 1820s. By 1851, the Cherokees in Oklahoma had opened male and female seminaries near Tahlequah to educate members of their nation. Cherokee students studied a curriculum that was patterned after that of Mount Holyoke Seminary in Massachusetts.

Boarding-school attendance increased dramatically when Congress increased funding for Indian education in the 1870s. The Indian Industrial School at Carlisle was the most well known of the Indian boarding schools, and developed a reputation for athleticism and winning football teams. Jim Thorpe, the most famous Native American athlete of the twentieth century, was a student at Carlisle when he won the decathlon and pentathlon during the Olympic Games in Sweden in 1912. Indian students like Thorpe were recruited to Pennsylvania from many tribes and regions in the West. Carlisle's founder, Richard Henry Pratt, a former officer in the U.S. military, designed the simple boarding-school program. Ideally, students were to spend half the day in the classroom and the remainder in manual labor. The vocationally oriented "outing program" was also a trademark of Pratt's that many other schools adopted. His goal was encapsulated in the phrase "Kill the Indian and save the man."

By 1899, twenty-five residential schools had been established in fifteen states with a total enrollment of twenty thousand students. Tremendous tribal diversity was reflected in the boarding-school population. In 1917, the final year Carlisle was in operation, fifty-eight tribes were represented in the student body, with Ojibwa students in the majority. The Haskell Institute in Lawrence, Kansas, founded in 1884, was a very intertribal school, with students enrolled from the

"Before" and "after" photographs of three Pueblo boys—Watte, Keise-te-Wa, and He-Li-te—who, upon attending the Carlisle Indian Industrial School, became Sheldon Jackson, Harvey Townsend, and John Shields. Such photographs were used to advance the idea that American Indians could be culturally transformed through boarding-school education.

Midwest, the Southwest, and Oklahoma. Hundreds of Cherokee students attended the Chilocco Indian School in Oklahoma, though the institution also recruited from a wide range of tribes. Not all Indian boarding schools were as diverse as Carlisle, Haskell, and Chilocco. The Santa Fe Indian School, opened in New Mexico in 1890, primarily educated Pueblos and youths from other tribes in the Southwest. Reservation boarding schools, like Riverside in Oklahoma and Keams Canyon in Arizona, served more local Indian populations.

The transition to boarding-school life seldom came smoothly for Indian children. The experience was punctuated by the trauma of separation from family and community, severe bouts of homesickness, and a difficult period of adjustment to a new environment. The loneliness students experienced was compounded by harsh policies that strictly regulated visits home. Officials limited the frequency and duration of children's visits to their families, contending that relatives and other community members would hinder the work of assimilation, or that newly reformed and educated students would lapse into their former "degraded" lifestyles. For Indian children, this often meant an extended stay of four years or more at school. Inflexible boarding-school regulations developed into a source of conflict between parents and school officials. As one mother complained to a school superintendent at the Flandreau Boarding School in South Dakota, where her daughter resided, "It seems it would be much easier to get her out of prison than out of your school."

The boarding-school setting also proved to be conducive to the spread of disease. Many of the Indian deaths during the great influenza pandemic of 1918, which hit the Native American population hard, took place in boarding schools. At Haskell alone, over three hundred students grew critically ill, and many died. In the early twentieth century trachoma, a contagious and painful eye disease, afflicted nearly half of the boarding-school population.

Tuberculosis was also commonplace in government boarding schools, where diseased and healthy students intermingled. Little effort was made to provide afflicted children with special care or enriched diets. In letters to their family members, students sometimes complained of poor health. In 1924 a young student from Ashland, Wisconsin, requested that she be sent to a tuberculosis sanatorium rather than attend school while suffering the effects of the disease. The girl, miserable because of painful lesions on her legs that refused to heal, complained about the constant drilling and marching that was so much a part of the boarding-school regimen. The student tried to reason with her superintendent when she said: "How do you expect me to learn and study when I suffer so [?] . . . Would you rather have me go away to a sanatorium and get well and where I can learn and be happy or, Have me going to school and suffer?" By 1924, when this letter was written, students with tuberculosis had long been "officially" excluded from attending government boarding schools.

Native American parents often charged government boarding schools with ravaging the health of their children. In letters to school superintendents and sometimes to the Indian Office in Washington, parents complained about the outing programs, the long days, the work details, and the fact that boarding schools relied heavily on unpaid student labor for their operation. Some parents grew so concerned about the deteriorating health of their children that they refused to return them to boarding schools. The father of another student wrote to Flandreau in 1913 to explain his son's absence in September. The man, a cattle rancher, simply said he "preferred to have a live cowboy rather than a dead scholar." Unfortunately, hundreds of Native American children did not survive the boarding-school experience. Many Indian schools, including Haskell, Carlisle, Chemawa (in Oregon), and others, maintained cemeteries to bury the many Indian children who succumbed to sickness and disease.

The Meriam Report, a major investigation into Indian affairs that was published in 1928, confirmed the complaints Indian families and students had been making for years. It asserted that government boarding schools needlessly separated families and that children were often malnourished, sick, insufficiently clothed, overworked, harshly punished, and poorly trained. During John Collier's long tenure as Commissioner of Indian Affairs from 1933 to 1945, many government boarding schools closed or changed to day schools. Ironically, attendance rose during the same period because of Indian poverty during the Great Depression. Despite Collier's wishes, government boarding schools were never completely abandoned. A few schools remained operational at midcentury. Haskell Institute converted to the Haskell Indian Junior College in 1964, Chilocco closed in 1980, and the Phoenix Indian School ceased operating late in the Reagan era. Some institutions continued as boarding schools but hired new administrators and instituted more contemporary policies. The Santa Fe Indian School, founded in 1890 to educate Indian children in the Southwest, is operated today by the All Indian Pueblo Council in New Mexico.

The boarding-school concept had many shortcomings, but the institutions are credited with cultivating "Pan-Indianism," an important part of native identity in the twentieth century. People formerly separated by language, culture, and geography lived and worked together in residential schools. Students formed close bonds and enjoyed a rich cross-cultural exchange. Graduates of government schools often married former classmates, found employment in the Indian Service, migrated to urban areas, or returned to their reservations and entered tribal politics. Countless new alliances, both personal and political, were forged in government boarding schools.

See also Carlisle Indian Industrial School; Chemawa Indian School; Education; Flandreau School; Hampton Institute; Phoenix Indian School; Santee Normal Training School.

Lomawaima, K. Tsianina, *They Called It Prairie Light: The Story of Chilocco Indian School* (Lincoln: University of Nebraska Press, 1994); Trennert, Robert A., Jr., *The Phoenix Indian School: Forced Assimilation in Arizona, 1891–1935* (Norman: University of Oklahoma Press, 1988).

BRENDA J. CHILD (Red Lake Chippewa)
University of Wisconsin at Milwaukee

BOUDINOT, ELIAS

(1804?–1839)
Cherokee editor, signer of the Treaty of New Echota.

Elias Boudinot (or Boudinott; he was also known as Buck Watie or Galagina [Kiakeena]) epitomizes the generation of Cherokee leaders who guided their people through a profound cultural transformation. Born at Oothcaloga in the Cherokee Nation, now northwest Georgia, in about 1804, Boudinot entered a world that already was changing. His father, Oo-watie, and uncle, the Ridge (or Major Ridge, as he later would be known), had left their compact, traditionally organized town of Hiwassee in about 1800 to settle on widely dispersed farms. This decision reflected a shift away from the communitarian values of traditional Cherokee society to a more individualistic worldview. Oo-watie and the Ridge had taken one of the first steps toward the "civilization" that U.S. Indian policy promoted from the 1790s to the late 1820s. This policy encouraged native people to become culturally white—that is, to cultivate the soil like white men, to learn to read and write English, to convert to Christianity, and to establish a republican government with written laws.

Oo-watie and the Ridge took another step when they sent their children to a Moravian mission school. Buck Watie, as Boudinot was known to the missionaries, enrolled in school in 1811, and he proved so apt that a representative of the American Board of Commissioners for Foreign Missions, an interdenominational organization headquartered in Boston, invited Buck, his cousin John Ridge, and another boy to attend the Foreign Mission School in Cornwall, Connecticut. Oo-watie agreed, and Buck went north with American Board representatives in 1818. On their way to Connecticut, they stopped in New Jersey to visit a man named Elias Boudinot, who had served in the Continental Congress and presided over the American Bible Society. Young Buck Watie was so impressed with their host that he enrolled at the Foreign Mission School as Elias Boudinot (although he often spelled his last name "Boudinott" to distinguish himself from the elder Boudinot).

Boudinot's intellect and (after his conversion in 1820) piety so impressed the faculty at Cornwall that they arranged for him to enter Andover Theological Seminary in 1822, but poor health prevented his enrollment. He returned home, but he had left his heart in Cornwall. In fact, both Boudinot and his cousin John Ridge had fallen in love with New England women. In 1824, Ridge's marriage to the daughter of the school's steward provoked a firestorm of protest because the bride, as the local newspaper editor wrote, "has thus made herself a *squaw*, and connected her race to a race of Indians." When Elias Boudinot married Harriet Ruggles Gold, the daughter of a Cornwall physician, in 1826, agents of the school described the marriage as "criminal" and closed the Foreign Mission School.

This experience in Connecticut marked both men: though committed to "civilization" and Christianization, they also doubted that a white society obsessed with race would ever accept Indians as equals.

Despite his misgivings about whites, Boudinot ardently promoted Cherokee "civilization." As clerk of the Cherokee Council from 1825 to 1827, he contributed to the Cherokees' achievement of the "civilization" program's political goal: in 1827, they wrote a republican constitution patterned after those of the states. He participated in Bible and temperance societies and promoted plans, never realized, for a lending library and museum. In 1826, he embarked on a lecture tour of major American cities to raise funds for a printing press and for type in the Cherokee syllabary, which had been devised in the early 1820s by Sequoyah. When the press and the type arrived, he became editor of the bilingual *Cherokee Phoenix*. He also sought to promote Christianity among his people by translating the religious tract *Poor Sarah, or The Indian Woman* into Cherokee and collaborating with the American Board missionary Samuel Austin Worcester on translations of the New Testament and Christian hymns.

As white pressure for the Cherokees to move west mounted, Boudinot became one of the most eloquent defenders of Cherokee rights. The Cherokees, he wrote, "live on the land which God gave them—they are surrounded by guarantees which this Republic has voluntarily made for their protection and which once formed a sufficient security against oppression. If those guarantees must now be violated with impunity for purposes altogether selfish, the sin will not be at our door, but at the door of our *oppressor* and our faithless *Guardian*." He found the arrest of Worcester for violation of a Georgia law requiring white men in the Cherokee Nation to take an oath of allegiance to the state particularly galling. The U.S. Supreme Court's decision in Worcester's favor in 1832 brought hope, which Georgia's refusal to comply with the decision dashed. At this point, Boudinot began to have misgivings about the Cherokees' refusal to negotiate a removal treaty.

Sentiment in favor of negotiation coalesced around the leadership of Boudinot, John Ridge, and Major Ridge. Because most Cherokees opposed removal and it was feared that whites might interpret any dissent as weakness, the Cherokee government prohibited debate of the issue in the *Phoenix*. Boudinot indignantly resigned. He did agree to serve on delegations to Washington in 1834 and 1835, however, in order to try to convince Principal Chief John Ross to negotiate. Despite the suffering of the Cherokees at the hands of invading whites, Ross remained steadfast in his opposition to negotiation. In December 1835, members of the party advocating a treaty met in Boudinot's house at New Echota and signed a treaty that provided for the exchange of the Cherokee country in the east for lands west of the Mississippi. Although these men lacked any authorization from the Cherokee government, the U.S. Senate ratified the document—the Treaty of New Echota—and in 1838–39 the Cherokee people moved west in an agonizing journey known as the Trail of Tears.

Denounced by most Cherokees, Boudinot moved west in 1837 and settled at Park Hill, Cherokee Nation (modern-day northeastern Oklahoma). In 1839, a party of unknown men attacked and killed him as he walked from his home to a nearby mission to get them medicine. His cousin and uncle died the same day. All paid the prescribed penalty for violating the Cherokee law prohibiting the unauthorized cession of land. Despite his ignominious demise, however, Elias Boudinot had helped foster adaptability and resilience among the Cherokees, qualities that enabled his nation to survive the trauma of removal, to rebuild in the West, and to endure to the present.

See also Cherokee; Ridge, Major; Ross, John; Treaty of New Echota (1835).

Perdue, Theda, *Cherokee Editor: The Writings of Elias Boudinot* (Knoxville: University of Tennessee Press, 1983).

THEDA PERDUE
University of Kentucky

Boy Scouts and Indians

The Boy Scouts of America is an offshoot of the British Boy Scout Association, founded in 1908 by Lord Robert S. S. Baden-Powell (1857–1941), First Baron of Gilwell, and British general. Known as "the Hero of Mafeking," Baden-Powell became famous for his participation in the Boer War, where he first witnessed African military scouts engaged in outdoor skills. Upon returning to England, he founded Scouting, soon to become the largest international youth organization.

At the turn of the twentieth century a number of youth organizations also flourished in the United States, all of which employed "Indian lore" as the focal point of their programs. Of particular importance were the Sons of Daniel Boone, founded in 1900 by Daniel Beard (1850–1941) of Cincinnati, an artist, outdoorsman, author of children's books, and close friend of Mark Twain. Equally significant was the Woodcraft League of America, established in 1902 by Ernest Thompson Seton (1860–1946), a Canadian naturalist, author, and illustrator. Seton (who had changed his name from Ernest Seton Thompson in 1901) was married twice, his second wife being Julia M. Buttree, who wrote *The Rhythm of the Red Man* (1930), one of the earliest books on American Indian music and dance to be adopted by the Scouts.

The Boy Scouts of America was founded in 1910 by James E. West, a prominent Washington, D.C., attorney, at which point the organizations established by Beard and Seton merged with the BSA. West was named first chief Scout executive, and Beard and Seton were elected to Scouting's national council.

The outdoor skills originally inspired by African scouts easily became transformed into a camping program much of which was based on a romantic study of American Indian cultures. One year after the BSA's founding, the Indian Lore merit badge was created and proved to be one of Scouting's most sought-after awards. The establishment of this merit badge was perhaps the first straightforward attempt in the United States to teach young boys about the native history of their own regions, as well as something about native material culture, songs and dances, and languages.

In their formative years, Scouting and America's infatuation with Indian cultures grew hand in hand. According to Scouting officials, Indians became a major "lure" to recruit boys into the movement. In 1927, the first official *Handbook for Boys,* second in popularity in the United States only to the Bible, contained a section called "American Indian Craft," which instructed readers on how to make a tipi, moccasins, tom-toms, and bows and arrows.

This chapter was written by Dr. Ralph Hubbard, son of Elbert Hubbard ("Message to Garcia"), who forsook a career in biology to create one in Indian lore. Part Cherokee himself, Hubbard began teaching Indian dancing in 1913 on his ranch at Ten Sleep, near Boulder, Colorado. In 1920, he organized the American Indian activities at the first World Scout Jamboree in England. These were considered one of the most dramatic elements in the program and were included each year thereafter. He also organized the Indian program at the first American Boy Scout Jamboree. Hubbard later built two Indian museums: one at Wounded Knee,

South Dakota, which was destroyed during the occupation of 1973; and a second at Medora, North Dakota, a community he was identified with until he died.

Although Indian lore is taught to Cub Scouts and Boy Scouts, by far the most influential Scouting program has been the Order of the Arrow, founded in 1915 by E. Urner Goodman and Carroll A. Edson at Treasure Island Scout Camp, near Philadelphia. The "Arrow," comprising older Boy Scouts who are elected to this national camping fraternity by their nonmember cohorts, continues to focus on Indian themes at biennial conferences, where local lodges compete against each other during an Indian pageant. Initiation into the Arrow is secret and is usually done at summer camp, where boys physically tapped out by an Indian runner are required to stay in the woods alone as part of their initiation.

Exploring, the program for older boys and girls, also has had an impact on the study of Indian lore, some posts specializing in Indians of their region. The most famous example of such focus was the Koshare Indian Dancers of LaJunta, Colorado, organized by Buck Burshears, a Scout leader.

Although Indian Lore was popular among tens of millions of youth and adults, several Scout leaders stand out as major figures. The most sophisticated book on Indian crafts, *The Book of Indian Crafts and Indian Lore* (1928), was written by a Scout executive, Julian H. Salomon. Walter "Whittlin'" Ben Hunt wrote *Indiancraft* (1942) as well as numerous articles in *Boys' Life,* the official Scout magazine, a position he shared with other prominent authors such as the ethnologist George Bird Grinnell and the Dakota physician Charles A. Eastman (Ohiyesa). Bernard S. Mason, whose Camp Fairchild became the center of Indian activities for Wisconsin Scouts, wrote the influential *Dances and Stories of the American Indian* (1944) and *The Book of Indian Crafts and Costumes* (1946). For over forty years during the early twentieth century another Scouter, Carl Parlasca, directed an Indian pageant, based on Longfellow's poem "The Song of Hiawatha," at Elgin, Illinois.

In the 1930s and 1940s, many Scouts became disenchanted with the limitations Scout officials had placed on the "authentic" study of Indian lore and formed their own organizations, soon to be called "hobbyist" groups. A number of new publications appeared, beginning with *The American Indian Hobbyists* (1954), established by Norman Feder; *American Indian Tradition* (1960), under the editorship of Richard R. McAl-

lister, followed, as did *Powwow Trails* (1964), founded by William K. and Marla N. Powers; *American Indian Crafts and Culture* (1967), edited by Tyrone H. Stewart; and finally, *Whispering Wind* (1967), edited by Jack Heriard and still in circulation. All were founded by former Scouts.

In the 1970s, many Scout and hobbyist organizations were criticized by American Indians for the performance of religious dances by whites, leading to a reevaluation of the Indian lore program and a new emphasis on contemporary Indian powwow singing and dancing. During this same decade, the BSA also placed some emphasis on employing American Indian paraprofessionals to organize Scouting on Indian reservations and communities. A national council on Scouting continues to promote Scouting for Indians. Among those prominent American Indian leaders serving on the National Committee on Scouting for American Indians in the past have been the Honorable Brantley Blue (Lumbee), commissioner of the Indian Claims Commission; Louis Bruce (Lakota-Mohawk), the first American Indian to serve as Commissioner of Indian Affairs; and the Honorable Ben Reifel (Lakota), the first American Indian to serve as a U.S. congressman.

Scouting continues to flourish among American Indian youth, and at least on some Indian reservations the program is well attended.

See also Eastman, Charles (Ohiyesa); Reifel, Ben.

Mason, Bernard S., *Dances and Stories of the American Indian* (New York: Ronald Press, 1944); Powers, William K., "The Indian Hobbyist Movement in North America," in *Handbook of North American Indians,* ed. William C. Sturtevant, vol. 4, *History of Indian-White Relations,* ed. Wilcomb E. Washburn (Washington: Smithsonian Institution, 1989); Powers, William K., *Here Is Your Hobby: Indian Dancing and Costumes* (New York: G. P. Putnam's Sons, 1966).

WILLIAM K. POWERS
Rutgers University

BRANT, JOSEPH

(1743?–1807)
Mohawk soldier and statesman.

One of the most versatile and remarkable men in American history, Joseph Brant (Thayendanegea, "He Places Together Two Bets") is best remembered as a Loyalist military leader during the American War of In-

A watercolor of Joseph Brant, circa 1785, possibly by James Peachey. Brant holds a friendship belt and a peace calumet. A large marine-shell gorget or "moon" hangs from his neck, as well as a (probable) King George III silver medal.

dependence, the promoter of a pan-tribal confederacy to defend Indian land in postrevolutionary years, and the founder of an Indian community on the Grand River in Ontario.

Brant was born in Ohio, the son of Tehonwagh-kwangeraghkwa of Canajoharie, New York, and his wife, Margaret. Joseph took his last name from his stepfather, Brant, a Mohawk sachem, and gained from connections with the British after his sister, Mary (Molly), became mistress to Sir William Johnson. He acquired a facility in English at Eleazar Wheelock's

school in Lebanon, Connecticut (1761–63), and after returning to Canajoharie to farm in the European fashion he assisted Christian missionaries and the Johnsons—Sir William's nephew, Guy, succeeded his uncle as Superintendent of Indian Affairs—as a translator, interpreter, and aide.

Although personally indebted to the British, and a man with a foot in both the Indian and white cultures, Brant grew concerned about the threats to Indian land before the outbreak of the American Revolution. After a visit to London in 1775–76, during which he was received by George III and patronized by such luminaries as James Boswell, he attempted to break the Iroquois Confederacy's policy of neutrality, convinced by British pledges of support and future protection. Raising a party of Indian and white volunteers, he goaded the powerful Senecas into supporting him in a bloody ambush of American militia at Oriskany, New York, on August 6, 1777, and for five years operated with outstanding military talent against the Americans in New York and Ohio.

Brant was not the head war chief of Britain's Iroquois allies, as is sometimes represented. He owed his influence to his abilities, the support of his sister, Mary (whose influence was reckoned "far superior to that of all the chiefs put together"), and later to his marriage to Catherine, sister of the leading Mohawk sachem, and to a captaincy in the British Indian Department. Undoubtedly his services were of strategic value to the British. Cooperating with other Loyalists and Indians, he struck unpredictably across a wide front, helping to paralyze superior bodies of militia, destroy provisions and settlements, and divert Continental troops from the east. In 1781 he and his troops frustrated an expedition against Detroit. Despite his battlefield successes, however, Brant's cause was doomed. The war divided the Iroquois Confederacy and wasted Iroquois villages. Worse, Britain abandoned its Indian allies in the Treaty of Paris (1783), when it ceded the Crown's claim to land south of the Great Lakes and accepted peace terms that contained no mention of native rights.

After the war Brant moved quickly to represent all the king's late Indian allies. In 1784 a large and fertile tract on the Grand River in Ontario was awarded to his people. Almost two thousand Indian Loyalists, principally Iroquois, ultimately settled the grant; the Mohawks settled at the site of modern-day Brantford. In another visit to London in 1786 Brant further secured financial indemnification for losses suffered by the Mohawks in the war.

Brant urged the Indians south of the Great Lakes to resist the pretensions of the United States to have won land north of the Ohio River by conquest, and under his guidance they formed a pan-tribal alliance at a congress upon the Sandusky in 1783. Embracing Indians from the Great Lakes and Ohio regions, and even southern Creeks and Cherokees, this grand and unprecedented confederacy upheld the old Indian boundary line along the Ohio established at the Treaty of Fort Stanwix in 1768. British fears of losing Indian support had led to their retention of western posts such as Detroit and Niagara, in contravention of the Treaty of Paris, and they continued to provision the Indian confederacy and supply it with ammunition. Brant regarded armed resistance as a last resort, however, and hoped that Indian solidarity would force the United States to negotiate and recognize a permanent Indian claim in Ohio. Unfortunately, the Americans exploited divisions among the Indians to secure recognition of their aspirations in treaties at Fort Harmar (1789). Nevertheless, the young (and weak) U.S. government was brought to repudiate the principle of conquest and to accept that lands should be acquired by purchase and treaty.

Thereafter Brant yielded his leadership of the confederacy to the Shawnees, Delawares, and Miamis, but he continued to urge both the Indians and the United States to settle their differences in Ohio with a compromise boundary based upon the Muskingum River. Both sides held out for total victory, and the Indians were defeated at the Battle of Fallen Timbers in 1794, but the pan-tribal ideals Brant had nurtured influenced history until the death of Tecumseh in 1813.

At his new home on the Grand River, Brant exhibited the ambiguities of a man rooted in contrasting cultures. He encouraged the Indians to improve their economy, adopt Christianity, and support British schooling. His translations of Saint Mark's Gospel and the Book of Common Prayer into Mohawk were published in 1787. He associated with the elite on both sides of the Atlantic, lived in European style at his house at Burlington, Ontario, attended by liveried servants, and sat to the fashionable portrait painters of the day. Yet he remained fiercely proud of his Indian ancestry, encouraged many aboriginal ceremonies, and was doubtful about wholesale acculturation. Comparing British and Iroquois societies, he remarked, "After every exertion to divest myself of prejudice, I am obliged to give my opinion in favor of my own people."

Brant's most disastrous policy was his sale or lease of land on the Grand to invest in stocks for an annuity for the Indians. Despite resistance from British officials, who denied that the Indians held the tract in fee simple, in 1798 Brant alienated some 350,000 acres for sums that ultimately yielded the Indians little benefit. He thus encountered the frustrations of grappling with the problem of creating a satisfactory livelihood for people whose land resources had been reduced.

Joseph Brant was tall, muscular, and fine featured. Ambitious and vain, he was also generous, humane, and dedicated not only to the Mohawks but also to Indians in general. Equally at home on the battlefield or in council, he was a man of rare energy and vision. He was thrice married, but had only one wife at a time. Nine of his children reached maturity; one, John (1794–1832), distinguished himself in the War of 1812 and briefly took a seat in the Upper Canadian House of Assembly. Joseph Brant died at Burlington on November 24, 1807.

See also Iroquois Confederacy; Mohawk.

Graymont, Barbara, *The Iroquois in the American Revolution* (Syracuse, N.Y.: Syracuse University Press, 1972); Kelsay, Isabel Thompson, *Joseph Brant, 1743–1807: Man of Two Worlds* (Syracuse, N.Y.: Syracuse University Press, 1984); Stone, William Leete, *Life of Joseph Brant, Thayendanegea*, 2 vols. (1838; reprint, St. Clair Shores, Minn.: Scholarly Press, 1970).

JOHN SUGDEN
Hereward College
Coventry, England

BUREAU OF INDIAN AFFAIRS

The Bureau of Indian Affairs (BIA, periodically referred to during its history as the Indian Bureau, the Indian Office, the Indian Service, and the Indian Desk) is responsible for administering the United States's overall relationship with more than five hundred tribes and Alaskan communities. Each tribe, depending on its history, treaties, and applicable congressional laws and legal decisions, maintains a separate and unique relationship with the United States. For many tribes the bureau has represented mistrust, fraud, and cultural destruction; for the national government it has represented both the goal of fair dealing and the reality of mistreatment.

In the colonial era, Britain, France, Spain, and their colonies courted the Indian nations as trading partners and military allies. In North America, tribes of the Iroquois Confederacy as well as Cherokees, Creeks, and others adeptly played one competitor against another, negotiating trade and friendship treaties to their advantage. Following the American Revolution, the new nation's internal growth and development hinged on its ability to obtain new lands from these same tribes for white settlement. The country's international security depended upon its ability to prevent alliances between Indian nations and European powers. To attain these vital national objectives, the newly formed federal government assumed from the individual colonies total control over Indian affairs. Federally appointed Indian agents and superintendents, working closely with territorial governors and reporting to the secretary of war, handled the government's relations with tribes. Guided by the Trade and Intercourse Acts, these individuals were responsible for promoting "civilization," restricting the liquor trade, issuing trade licenses, and detailing Indian activities to the War Department.

In 1824, Secretary of War John C. Calhoun administratively created within the War Department the Bureau of Indian Affairs. Calhoun appointed Thomas McKenney as the bureau's first head and instructed him to oversee treaty negotiations, manage Indian schools, and administer Indian trade, as well as handle all expenditures and correspondence concerning Indian affairs. In 1832, at the behest of McKenney, Congress formally mandated the bureau and approved the appointment of a Commissioner of Indian Affairs, under whose authority rested the management and direction of all Indian affairs.

By the mid-1830s, the tribes' relationships with the United States had changed dramatically. The defeat of Great Britain in the War of 1812 and the United States's annexation of Spanish Florida deprived the Indian nations of powerful European allies. No longer concerned with the tribes' military power or their potential for collaboration with Europeans, President Andrew Jackson viewed the tribes solely as obstacles to American expansion. The Indian Removal Act and other federal legislative initiatives sought to separate Indians from the path of settlement. By 1840, the bureau and the American military had relocated more than thirty tribes west of the Mississippi. During the 1850s the number of Indians under bureau control more than doubled as Congress organized the territories of Texas, Oregon, California, Arizona, and New Mexico.

In 1849, shortly before this expansion in bureau responsibilities, Congress shifted the Indian Office from the Department of War to the newly created Department of the Interior. This structural change also symbolized a new federal objective in Indian relations. Led by Commissioners Luke Lea and George Manypenny, who served, respectively, from 1850 to 1857, the bureau energetically espoused the "civilization" of Indians through the creation of the reservation system. By negotiating treaties with tribes for their settlement on reservations, the Indian Office hoped to protect tribes from whites and to offer alternatives to traditional lifeways.

The Civil War disrupted the bureau's agenda and services to tribes. Many tribes, especially those in and around Indian Territory, were drawn into the conflict. With the war's end in 1865, the bureau embarked on an ambitious program to dismantle tribal governments and assimilate Indian people into the American mainstream. In a policy strongly supported by Ely S. Parker, a Seneca who served as the first Indian commissioner of the bureau, the government initiated a series of reforms designed to decrease corruption within the bureau and to Christianize and civilize Indians as quickly as possible. In 1869, Congress created the Board of Indian Commissioners, staffed with unpaid businessmen, to supervise bureau expenditures. In a further move to stem mismanagement and speed assimilation, the bureau, acting on initiatives begun with President Ulysses S. Grant, turned over the administration of many functions to religious denominations. Church and religious lay leaders filled the posts of schoolteachers and superintendents and worked as Indian agents.

As Indian agents increased their control over the distribution of rations, goods, and lands, tribal leaders were divested of their authority. The establishment of Indian police forces in 1878 further undermined the traditional role of clans and leaders in resolving disputes. Other federal regulations forbade the practice of Indian ceremonies and required Indians to perform manual labor for their rations.

The passage of the General Allotment (or Dawes) Act in 1887 paved the way for an attack on the last cultural mainstay of tribal existence—communal ownership of land. Directed to break up the tribal land base, bureau agents surveyed reservations, divided them into individual parcels, and assigned lands to individual Indians. The agents also oversaw the sale of what were labeled "surplus" lands to white settlers. Over the next four decades, the Indian Office allotted and issued patents to more than 7 million acres, a process that ultimately reduced Indian landholdings from 138 million acres to 48 million.

THE REASON OF THE INDIAN OUTBREAK.
General Miles declares that the Indians are starved into rebellion.

An 1890 cartoon depicting the graft and corruption of Indian agents, who enriched themselves at the expense of their Indian wards.

As the government sought to destroy the tribal community and provide care to its individualized wards, the bureau's responsibilities, personnel, and budget increased dramatically. Its bureaucratic structure, which since 1846 had contained a Land Division, a Civilization Division, and a Finance and Records Division, had by the 1890s grown to include a Medical and Education Division and a Depredations Division.

In 1901, the Board of Indian Commissioners emphasized that the Indian Office's purpose was "to make all Indians self-supporting, self-respecting, and useful citizens of the United States." Taking this mandate to heart, Commissioner Cato Sells in 1917 issued a "Declaration of Policy" that announced the bureau's intention to sever all ties to "competent" Indians. "Competents" would be Indians of less than one-half native ancestry, or those holding high school diplomas. These individuals would cease to be federal wards. They would receive a fee patent for their land allotments, would not be eligible for any federal services, and would be divested of their share in tribal property.

Commissioner Sells's enthusiastic pursuit of improved health care for Indians proved more beneficial than his policy declaration. As detailed in a 1912 survey, Indians suffered from high rates of tuberculosis, poor nutrition, high infant mortality, and blindness from trachoma. Sells increased appropriations for the Medical Division and focused attention on health issues, but improvements were minimal. In 1928 the Meriam Report detailed continuing inadequate services and expenditures in all areas of bureau administration, especially health care, housing, and education.

In 1933, the social worker John Collier replaced Charles Rhoads as commissioner. For the first time, tribes had a head of the bureau who was both knowledgeable and respectful of tribal cultures and values. Supported by the reform momentum of Franklin Roosevelt's "New Deal," Collier successfully stopped the allotment of Indian lands, improved Indian education programs, and sought to restore tribal political authority through the passage of the 1934 Indian Reorganization Act.

Collier's campaign to restore authority to the tribes incurred considerable hostility from the American public. The commissioner was heavily criticized during the later years of his twelve-year tenure in office, and in 1948, the Hoover Commission, reporting to a Republican-dominated Congress, asserted that the assimilation of Indian people into American society must once again be the dominant objective of federal policy. Toward this end, the bureau implemented a number of bureaucratic reforms designed to speed the entry of Indians into the mainstream. Congress also terminated bureau responsibility over more than one hundred tribes and bands, a move that ended both government control and government protections for these communities.

The termination era of the 1940s and 1950s magnified what had evolved into a love-hate relationship between Indians and the bureau. From the perspective of Native Americans, the bureau, for all its ineptitude and maladministration, embodied the federal government's trust obligation toward tribes. Severing the bureau's responsibilities deprived tribes of a visible acknowledgment of their rights and status as quasi sovereigns vis-à-vis the American political system.

Opposition to the Indian Bureau's terminationist tendencies took many forms—petitions, lobbying, and militant protests such as the takeover of the bureau's offices in Washington, D.C., in November 1972. These efforts achieved success in the mid-1970s with the passage of significant legislation such as the Indian Self-Determination and Educational Assistance Act and the Indian Child Welfare Act, which directed the bureau to shift its efforts from paternalism and control to service to tribes in their quest for self-determination. This new policy was put into effect by a bureau work force that

was increasingly (and, by the mid-1970s, predominantly) Indian. In 1934, when Indian hiring preference was first legislated, Indians made up 34 percent of the bureau's employees. By 1980, this figure had risen to 78 percent. And since 1966, with the appointment of Robert Bennett, an Oneida from Wisconsin, as commissioner, Indians have held the top leadership positions in the bureau through both Republican and Democratic administrations.

Currently the Indian Bureau is formally committed to allowing tribes to assume responsibility for the administration of programs and services funded by the federal government. In 1991 Congress passed the Tribal Self-Governance Demonstration Project Act, raising to thirty the number of tribes who are in the process of assuming total control from the bureau of all local programs and services. Despite bureaucratic foot-dragging and tribal concerns that self-determination may revive congressional support for termination, the bureau's relationship with Indian nations is coming full circle. The bureau is slowly returning to its original role as the government's negotiator with and protector of more than five hundred inherently sovereign political communities that maintain a special relationship with the United States.

Prucha, Francis P., *The Great Father: The United States Government and the American Indians*, 2 vols. (Lincoln: University of Nebraska Press, 1984); Taylor, Theodore, *The Bureau of Indian Affairs* (Boulder, Colo.: Westview Press, 1984).

SHARON O'BRIEN
University of Notre Dame

BURNETTE, BOB

(1926–84)
Sicangu (Brulé) Sioux political leader.

Known nationally from the 1950s to the 1980s as a political fighter for Indian civil rights and tribal self-determination, Robert Phillip Burnette was born in Rosebud, South Dakota, on January 26, 1926. His parents, Grover and Winnie Rogers Burnette, were members of a family of Sioux ranchers and farmers in the White River area of the Rosebud Reservation.

Political activism came almost naturally to Burnette. His grandfather and father had both been prominent in reservation politics, representing their districts on the tribal council, and had also been active in Democratic Party politics on the state and national levels. One of Burnette's earliest memories was of his own campaigning at the Rosebud Boarding School when he was eight years old, opposing his tribe's acceptance of the Indian Reorganization Act of 1934 because it withheld from Indians the right of self-government.

Burnette received all his formal education at the Rosebud Boarding School. In 1943, when he was seventeen years old, he enlisted in the Marine Corps and served with an antiaircraft unit in the Pacific. During World War II, he saw San Diego, Los Angeles, San Francisco, and other off-reservation places for the first time, observing the better material standards of living enjoyed by non-Indians and persuading himself that after the war the government would see to it that Indians on reservations also had a better life.

Yet when he returned to Rosebud in 1946, he found things the same, or even worse. At first he joined his father in farming and ranching, and in 1947 he married Beatrice E. Briggs of the Rosebud Reservation community of Okreek, with whom he eventually had nine children. But anti-Indian prejudice, discrimination, and the policies of the Bureau of Indian Affairs still presented everyday problems for the Sioux people. Earlier, government allotment policies—which resulted in the breaking up of Sioux cattle associations, whose members had grazed their stock in common on tribal lands—had forced Indian ranchers to confine their cattle to their own small allotments. This change had driven many Sioux out of ranching and had caused others, including Burnette's family, to curtail their operations and rent grazing lands from others.

Now there were new problems. Pressed by whites who wanted the Indians' lands, the termination-minded Bureau of Indian Affairs in 1950 raised the Indian ranchers' rents and adopted other policies designed to force the Sioux to sell or lease their allotted lands to the whites. The economic squeeze and the loss of reservation lands to whites angered Burnette, who blamed much of what was happening on collusion between corrupt tribal officials and the Bureau of Indian Affairs. In 1952, after a hard-fought campaign, he won election to the Rosebud Tribal Council, representing the reservation's Swift Bear community. Two years later, at the age of twenty-eight, his dynamism and commitment to reform led to his election as tribal president. He served in that capacity for eight years, being reelected in 1956, 1958, and 1960.

By the late 1950s he had won widespread attention as a combative Indian leader, representing his tribe in national and regional Indian organizations, helping organize Indian intertribal councils in Arizona and California, and gaining support for Indian causes from many prominent non-Indians who in time would include the philanthropist Doris Duke, John and Robert Kennedy, and Martin Luther King, Jr. In 1961, backed by a reform faction of tribal leaders and believing that he could better serve his people by working on the national level, he resigned from the presidency of his tribe and assumed the duties and responsibilities of executive director of the National Congress of American Indians (NCAI) in Washington, D.C.

There, working with legislators on Capitol Hill and with Secretary of the Interior Stewart Udall and other government officials, he struggled to bring about reforms at all levels of Indians affairs. Many of the causes for which he fought, including self-determination and an Indian civil rights act (one finally passed in 1968, though it was largely nullified by the U.S. Supreme Court in the 1978 *Santa Clara Pueblo* v. *Martinez* decision), were aimed at ending collusion on reservations between dictatorial government agents and corrupt tribal officials, and inevitably Burnette's championing of these causes made him powerful enemies as well as friends.

Meanwhile, conditions among his own people on the Rosebud Reservation had continued to concern him, and in 1964, feuding with Cato Valandra, his successor as tribal president, he retired from his position with the NCAI and returned to his own people. In the following two decades, he continued to battle for self-determination, sovereignty, and other Indian causes both on the national scene and on his reservation. Backed largely by young Indians, as well as by elders, full bloods, and other traditionalists, he ran repeatedly for the tribal presidency, losing several times through what he charged were fraudulent actions by his opponents, but winning in 1974. At the same time, he played leading roles, sometimes as a mediator and advocate of nonviolence, in some of the historic Indian activist events of the late 1960s and early 1970s, including the takeover of the Bureau of Indian Affairs building in Washington, D.C., and the 1973 siege at Wounded Knee. Documenting the Indians' struggles, he published *The Tortured Americans* in 1971 and coauthored *The Road to Wounded Knee* in 1974.

Burnette's last years were marked by bitter political fights stemming from his attempts to gain an independent tribal judiciary at Rosebud that would enable Indians to rein in the powers of corrupt tribal officers. Trumped-up charges of misconduct in office were leveled against him, and he was denied the right to seek office again. He fought the charges and was cleared by the tribal court. But it was too late. On September 12, 1984, preparing once again to run for president of his tribe, he died of heart failure.

In a time of great change in the relations between Indians and the rest of the American people, Burnette's significance lay in the crusading role he played in Washington and among non-Indian, as well as Indian, friends and supporters that helped to turn public opinion and the federal government away from the 1950s policy of terminating reservations and, by the 1970s, toward one of recognizing the Indians' right of sovereignty and self-determination. A memorial card printed for his funeral read, "One man, with the courage of his convictions, is a majority" — a sentiment that to many reflected his qualities of perseverance and commitment.

See also Herding and Ranching; National Congress of American Indians; Wounded Knee Takeover, 1973.

Burnette, Robert, *The Tortured Americans* (Englewood Cliffs, N.J.: Prentice-Hall, 1971); Burnette, Robert, and John Koster, *The Road to Wounded Knee* (New York: Bantam Books, 1974).

ALVIN M. JOSEPHY, JR.
Greenwich, Connecticut

CADDO

The Caddo people originally occupied the Red River bend region of present-day Arkansas, Oklahoma, Texas, and Louisiana. In 1994 the Caddo Tribe of Oklahoma numbered thirty-two hundred enrolled members, with headquarters on a thirty-seven-acre reservation at Binger, Oklahoma, forty miles southwest of Oklahoma City. Caddo tradition recounts the emergence of the first man and woman from below ground near the Red River, the man bringing with him a pipe and flint pieces, and the woman carrying seeds of corn and pumpkins. The Caddos' first village, Tall-Timber-on-the-Hill, was located near present-day Caddo Lake on the Louisiana-Texas border.

The name *Caddo* is adapted from the term *Kadohadacho,* signifying "the real chiefs," a name formerly referring only to the community dwelling at the bend of the Red River near present-day Texarkana, Texas. But in American usage the term *Caddo* includes descendants of about twenty separate communities that existed in the seventeenth century.

The Caddo people formed the most western of the chiefdoms that attained peak development in the southeastern United States from the tenth to the thirteenth century. Living in dispersed hamlets surrounded by fields, they raised the basic Indian crops—corn, beans, squash, and pumpkins—as well as sunflowers, melons, tobacco, and gourds. Their forty-foot-high circular houses were thatched with straw, creating a bee-hive appearance. Buffalo hunters set out annually for three- or four-month expeditions to eastern Oklahoma or the Texas plains.

Caddo women employed a special technique for dying doeskin shiny black for fringed garments decorated with white seed beads, and wove vegetable fibers into cloth. High-ranking members of society wore cloaks decorated with turkey feathers. Principal trade items were bows and bow wood, and exceptionally fine pottery that reached the Illinois country and Indian towns along the Gulf Coast. Craftsmen made ornaments from Great Lakes copper and engraved marine shells with symbolic figures similar to Mexican designs.

The hierarchical government of the Caddo people was headed by a priestly ruler, the *chinesi,* who presided at ceremonies held in a temple set atop a platform mound. Parallel organizations existed among the Kadohadacho group on the Red River and the geographically separated Hasinai in East Texas. Women as well as men held important hereditary offices. Second in line were the *caddi,* who governed the individual communities; they were assisted by tamas, who handled daily administrative tasks such as calling people together for meetings and announcing the arrival of returning war parties or visiting delegations.

The Caddos had no sustained contact with Europeans until the development of the French fur trade in the eighteenth century. In 1542, Luis de Moscoso led the remnants of the de Soto expedition on a loop through the Caddo country, leaving little damage and no epidemic disease. The first Spanish expedition from Mexico City, headed by Domingo Téran do los Ríos, was welcomed in 1691 by the chinesi at the temple mound site near modern-day Alto, Texas. Since the Indians kept repeating their greeting *tejas,* meaning "friends," Spanish authorities gave this name to the province, later spelled "Texas." Epidemics brought from Mexico reduced the Caddo population from an estimated eight thousand to only four thousand by the turn of the eighteenth century. From 1690 to 1773, Spanish missions existed intermittently among the Caddos of East Texas (Hasinai).

The Caddos became linked to the French fur trade following the arrival of Louis Jucherau de St.-Denis at Natchitoches in 1699 and the construction of a French fort there in 1713. Their skills in pottery making had declined by 1750, after they acquired metal kettles as trade goods. Although the Spanish established a post, Los Adaes, near modern-day Robeline, Louisiana, in 1721, it was ineffective in curtailing trade between Spanish Texas and French Louisiana.

The Caddos' role in intertribal affairs became more evident after Spain acquired that part of Louisiana Territory west of the Mississippi by terms of the Treaty of Paris in 1763. In cooperation with Athanase de Mézières, a son-in-law of St.-Denis who was serving as a Spanish agent at Natchitoches, Caddo leaders in the 1770s secured formal alliances for the Spanish with tribes to the west and north in order to oppose aggressive Osage warfare. Punitive raids by the Osages, traditional Caddo enemies, beginning suddenly in 1770, combined with population loss due to smallpox epidemics, forced the Kadohadacho to retreat down the Red River closer to modern-day Shreveport, Louisiana, in the 1790s.

Caddo leaders continued their diplomatic role with neighboring tribes after the American acquisition of Louisiana in 1803. When the U.S. Indian agent John Sibley held his first major intertribal council at Natchitoches in 1807, the Caddos brought in leaders from northwestern tribes, including the Wacos, Taovayas, and Tawakonis (later collectively called the Wichitas), as well as the Comanches of West Texas. That same year, the Caddo leaders brought the first Cherokees into Texas and arranged for peace with the Choctaws, concluding a fifteen-year period of hostilities. Sibley reported that the Caddo leaders controlled the entire region between the Mississippi River and the Rio Grande through their alliances.

The Kadohadacho ceded their Louisiana territory to the United States by the Treaty of 1835 and moved to lands of their Hasinai relations in Texas, a province of Mexico since the end of the Mexican Wars for Independence (1810–21). Shawnees, Delawares, Kickapoos, and Cherokees, allied with the Caddos against the Osages, had already moved into the Red River borderlands. With the addition of various Choctaw, Creek, and Seminole immigrants, the Caddos became but one coalition in a group of over twenty tribes represented in East Texas by the time of Texas independence from Mexico in 1836. The Caddos were dislodged from their entire home country as a consequence of anti-Indian warfare in Texas beginning in 1839–40. For about twenty years, Caddo people were dispersed. Some moved into Oklahoma, where their traditional hunting grounds had been assigned to the Choctaws and Chickasaws by the American government. Others fled to the hill country of West Texas or accepted the invitation of the Mexican government to cross the Rio Grande into Mexico, where they were close to Cherokee and Kickapoo refugees for about seven years before returning to the Brazos River region of Texas.

Following the American annexation of Texas in 1846, the federal government established a reservation for the Caddos and their allies on the upper Brazos River in 1854, where they were harassed by new settlers with strong anti-Indian sentiments. Moved to action by the murder of sleeping members of a family hunting party, Indian agent Robert S. Neighbors led the Caddos on an emergency flight across the Red River to Oklahoma in August 1859. Neighbors was murdered on his return to Texas; the Caddos still make pilgrimages to his grave.

In Oklahoma, the tribe was split by the Civil War, some members fleeing as far as Colorado. All were assigned to a reservation in 1872. The Ghost Dance religion, spreading in the 1880s, made many converts among the Caddos, who sang some of the songs associated with the ritual at their dance grounds as late as the 1940s. The Caddo people retain a rich musical tradition, attaching special importance to the Turkey Dance, performed only by women and always before sundown. The songs of this dance trace tribal history, with added songs recalling the days of Osage warfare.

Glover, William B., "A History of the Caddo Indians," *Louisiana Historical Quarterly* 18 (1935): 873–946; Newkumet, Vinola Beaver, and Howard L. Meredith, *Hasinai: A Traditional History of the Caddo Confederacy* (College Station: Texas A&M University Press, 1988); Tanner, Helen Hornbeck, "The Territory of the Caddo," in *Caddo Indians IV* (New York: Garland Publishing, 1974).

HELEN HORNBECK TANNER
Newberry Library

CAHOKIA

Cahokia was a major Mississippian urban center located in what is now Collinsville, Illinois, across the river from St. Louis, Missouri. Occupied between about A.D. 700 and A.D. 1250, the core of the site covered more than two hundred acres and was surrounded by a wooden palisade containing in excess of twenty thousand logs. The city contained more than one hundred mounds, the largest of which rose over one hundred feet above the countryside and covered sixteen acres at its base. Many mounds served as bases for elite residences and public buildings, which were erected on their summits. Cahokia contained plazas, residential districts, a large circular wooden-post monument, and elite burials containing burial goods drawn from the Gulf of Mexico, the Rockies, the southern Appalachians, and the Great Lakes. It was unquestionably the largest prehistoric urban center north of Mexico.

The people of Cahokia subsisted primarily by farming corn, beans, and squash, along with other starchy-seeded plants. They supplemented this diet by hunting and fishing. The site was surrounded by hundreds of smaller settlements, which stretched for about one hundred miles along the Mississippi. These smaller settlements contributed to Cahokia's support. Cahokia also engaged in, and to some extent controlled, wide-ranging trade that extended from the Pacific Northwest to Florida and from the western Great Lakes to the Gulf Coast.

At its peak (A.D. 1000–1150) Cahokia was home to a highly centralized theocracy, which controlled a large area along the Mississippi containing a population of at least thirty thousand to forty thousand. Archaeological evidence for Cahokia's influence can be traced from the Atzalan site of Wisconsin in the north to the Gulf Coast in the south and from the middle Missouri River of the Dakotas in the west to the Macon Plateau of Georgia in the east. The Cahokia elite were not able to maintain their control over this territory, however. After 1150, the central Mississippi Valley was occupied by smaller, less centralized chiefdoms, and the city began to lose people and influence. When Europeans arrived, Cahokia had been abandoned for nearly four centuries.

See also Mississippians.

CAHUILLA

The Cahuillas are Takic-speaking peoples who reside in Southern California in what are now Riverside and San Diego counties. Many, but not all, of the Cahuilla peoples live on reservations—Cahuilla, Agua Caliente, Santa Rosa, Torres-Martinez, Cabeson, Morongo, Los Coyotes, Ramona, and Saboba. These reservations were established after many years of conflict with local and federal authorities in the 1870s. Today the Cahuillas number about twenty-four hundred people. Prior to European intrusion, however, when they occupied the better part of Riverside County and the northern portion of San Diego County, they numbered from six thousand to ten thousand people.

Within their language-speaking group, the Cahuillas were divided into about a dozen independent clans containing five hundred to twelve hundred people each. These clans controlled separate territories of several hundred square miles each and maintained their own political authority. Each clan was allied through ritual systems that provided political stability and networks for economic exchange. Each clan was dialectically different from the others.

Community beliefs were clearly stated in various song cycles (epic poems) and historical accounts that described a clan's sacred and secular history and provided guidelines for behavior. These beliefs were reinforced on a regular basis, usually annually, in clan ritual centers where the texts of the song cycles were presented in their entirety—a process requiring several days to complete. The most important parts of these gatherings were the nukil ceremonies, which honored those members of a clan who had died since the last *nukil* ritual had been performed.

For the Cahuillas, cosmological values and concepts were established when the world was created by Mukat. The Cahuilla creation story tells of the origin of the world, the death of god (Mukat), and the consequences of that death for humans (e.g., the need for death, social roles, and so forth). It also describes the basic concepts of supernatural power and its proper use in the contemporary world.

Initially, the Cahuillas were not affected by the Spanish mission system. On the other hand, they were very much affected by the economic systems imposed on their homelands. They engaged in wage labor for the Spanish and Mexicans and became an integral part of the labor force in Southern California. When the Americans arrived in the 1850s, the Cahuillas signed a treaty with the U.S. government, but the agreement was not ratified. As a result the Cahuillas were left without a legal land base until the 1870s.

Remarkably, however, the arrival of the Spanish and the Americans did not obliterate the Cahuillas' own political, legal, and religious systems. The most damaging effects the Europeans had were in losses of Cahuilla land, the death of perhaps 80 percent of the Cahuilla peoples from European diseases, and the gradual loss of Cahuilla political autonomy.

Today, most of the descendants of the Cahuillas are residents of reservations where, until recently, the people engaged in agriculture, viticulture, cattle raising, and wage labor. Today some reservations also earn income from tourism. A new, important economic activity on several reservations (e.g., Morongo and Cabeson) is gaming. Other reservations are planning gaming facilities. Such enterprises are providing a significant new economic base for the people.

Modern-day Cahuilla reservations are administered by elected tribal councils. Some reservations are allotted to individuals, while on others the land is held in common. Issues of health, education, and welfare are matters of concern for the state of California, since California Indians were partially terminated from federal agencies in the 1950s. However, with the new income from gaming, many problems arising from a lack of funds have now been or soon will be somewhat alleviated.

The traditional language is still routinely spoken by some several dozen elders, and some traditional music and dance persist in the song-and-dance cycles referred to as the *bird songs,* and in the hand game locally known as *peon.* Classes in language, cultural history, and crafts are being held for young people on several reservations.

A fiesta system, thought for a time to have been a lost tradition, was revived in 1964 by the Malki Museum on the Morongo Indian Reservation. This museum was the first Indian museum established on a California Indian reservation. Now several reservations (e.g., Agua Caliente, Cabeson, and Pala) have established museums and sponsor fiestas each year. The latter offer important opportunities for intertribal interactions. The music and dance traditions of many tribes are featured, and artists have venues for displaying their works. In addition, these events provide Indian organizations with the chance to publicize their programs.

Cahuillas have been active in political protests for many years. At first (1840–91) they confederated into quasi-military groups under the leadership of generals—men such as Juan Antonio, Cabeson, and Antonio Garra—not only to defend themselves from the encroachments of Europeans but also to demand various political and economic rights. After reservations were established (c. 1891), these confederations disappeared, but within several decades the Cahuillas had formed their own protest organizations or joined others, such as the Mission Indian Federation. These protest organizations arose in response to oppressive practices by Indian Service personnel, and they became significant vehicles for political protests against the federal government's policies regarding the management of Indian affairs. These organizations were pivotal in the redressing of economic, political, and legal grievances from 1919 until the early 1960s.

Today a strong sense of history prevails among the Cahuillas. Several reservations have developed museums and cultural centers (e.g., the Malki Museum on the Morongo Indian Reservation, the Agua Caliente Cultural Center on the Agua Caliente Indian Reservation, and the Cupeno Cultural Center on the Pala Indian Reservation) and have established cultural and educational programs for young people, elders, and visitors. Educational achievement is a high priority, and the Cahuillas are rapidly progressing in this regard. Cahuillas have been and are actively engaged in teaching and publishing works about their traditional culture and history.

See also California Tribes.

Bean, Lowell John, *Mukat's People: The Cahuilla Indians of Southern California* (Berkeley: University of California Press, 1972); Bean, Lowell John, Sylvia Vane, and Jackson Young, *The Cahuilla Landscape: The Santa Rosa and San Jacinto Mountains* (Menlo Park, Calif.: Ballena Press, 1991); James, Harry C., *The Cahuilla Indians* (Banning, Calif.: Malki Museum Press, 1969).

LOWELL JOHN BEAN
California State University at Hayward

CALIFORNIA TRIBES

Aboriginal California encompassed hundreds of thousands of peoples in thousands of villages speaking over one hundred separate languages with many more derivative dialects. The tribal groups spanned a multitude of environmental conditions, from deserts in the south to mountains along the coastline to the great valley in the central part of the region. First-contact experiences also varied widely, from brief contacts with European ships in the early sixteenth century to the gold rush in the Sierra Nevada in the latter half of the nineteenth century. This land, cut off on all sides by mountains, deserts, and ocean, has always been dramatically different from any other part of native North America and is known to the present day for its distinct regional identity.

Before contact with Europeans, California communities were located in small, relatively isolated areas with populations ranging from less than 100 to over 1,000 people, averaging 250 per group. Groups often lived in close proximity to other people who spoke a different language, so it was beneficial to understand and speak at least one foreign language. Largely patrilocal in residence, village society was organized on the basis of kinship, with each village consisting of extended relatives in one or two families, lineages, or clans. In times of need, the regional political system allowed for the formation of temporary alliances, which changed in composition according to changing circumstances.

Aboriginal California's subsistence economies did not fit the usual hunter-gatherer or agricultural typologies, instead representing a hunter-gatherer-harvester system in which the social group mobilized to harvest seasonal crops such as acorns. Natural harvests were processed and stored, with surpluses being utilized in regional trade networks that gave geographically distant groups access to a variety of foods and a multitude of exotic materials.

Societies were religious by nature and in structure. Social control was achieved through a code of moral laws, and conflicts were handled more often through moral sanctions than through confrontation and warfare. Infractions were mediated by leaders of families, villages, and tribes. If the offense was severe or covert, medicine people had the moral training to resolve it. Group warfare existed but was rare, usually reserved for retaliation against an offense to the religious order, which often took the form of a disruption in the food supply.

Early historic contact occurred in different parts of California in different decades and even centuries, with non-Indian peoples who had differing approaches to dealing with Indians. The Spanish and Mexican invasion occurred in the southern and coastal areas. In the Spanish-Mexican period, Indians were valued as an essential economic work force that sustained the missions, presidios, and pueblos. Under the Spanish and, later, Mexican systems, Indian people were permitted to live in tribal communities on or near the missions and ranchos. As a result, survivors of original communities stayed together for decades after the American period.

In the coastal regions of Spanish occupancy from 1769 to 1848, the local Native American population was reduced by 90 percent. Epidemic diseases such as measles, cholera, and smallpox ravaged the vulnerable Indian people. The crowded missions were an ideal incubating ground for disease, resulting in an extremely high death rate for the biologically vulnerable, the old, the young, pregnant women, and so on.

The Russians occupied a limited land base on the north coast and on the northern offshore (Farallon) islands for several decades in the early nineteenth century. They also used the Indian people as an economic asset—as a work force around the fort and trading post at Fort Ross, and as hunters on offshore ships. Agents of the British Hudson's Bay Company entered the northern river valleys from Oregon in the early 1800s, but found little of economic value. They had little social or economic impact themselves, but left in their wake a malaria epidemic that decimated thousands of Indian people in the contacted areas of the Sacramento Valley. American trappers and explorers arrived in the mid-1800s and hunted mainly in the northern part of the state, outside of Mexican-controlled areas. They moved through Indian country quickly.

Government Indian policies in California rarely resembled those in other parts of North America. In 1850, the new California legislature passed the Government and Protection of the Indians Act, which provided for the indenture of loitering, intoxicated, or orphaned Indians and regulated Indian employment. The law was amended ten years later to expand the scope of slavery to include adults. The state policy resembled the "black codes" adopted by slave states as a means to control both free blacks and bondsmen. The state government also subsidized military campaigns against Indians, allowing for the indiscriminate killing of Indian women and children, as well as men, and justifying the slaughter as protecting settlers from Indian threat. A program of genocide, called "extermination" in the California press, was carried out by a group calling itself the California Volunteer Militia and by temporary bands of miners and ranchers—all organized for the purpose of killing Indians. Between 1845 and 1870, the Indian population in California declined by 80 percent, from 150,000 to 30,000 people. As many as 40 percent of these deaths were the result of extermination killings. Only a few native Californians survived the removal and extermination campaigns of the 1850s. These survivors found an uneasy refuge at the seven military reservations created to protect them. California operated the reservation system beginning in 1853, when Congress appropriated $250,000 to establish the first five reservations; all the reservations were closed in 1864. Later, Congress passed the Four Reservation Act, which authorized the creation of the Hoopa Valley, Tule River, and Round Valley reserves in California (no fourth reservation was ever completed).

In the late nineteenth century California contained many tribes and few reservations. As a result, people from various tribal communities were taken to reser-

The Cupeño tribe of southern California during its forced removal to a reservation in 1903. Indian removal was not limited to the eastern and southern regions of the United States, but extended across the continent—and into the twentieth century.

vations where they were unfamiliar with the resident Indian population and were not able to exploit local natural food resources. This disruption of the social and political fabric of aboriginal life led to tension, desperation, and feuding. At the same time, Indian labor, especially prized during the early gold-rush years, was becoming irrelevant to the state's agricultural economy. There was a constant demand for Indians to work as domestic servants, however, and by the 1880s, as fruit growers and specialty farmers expanded their operations, a new demand for cheap labor had arisen.

As the native population declined in the late nineteenth century, Indian groups reactivated traditional alliances and partnerships. A group under threat would move to the territory of an alliance partner, where it would be taken in, fed, and protected. The alliances of this period were structured along old patterns of political organization such as marriage, extended family, shared religious system, and language group. When native communities were forced to fragment or disperse, they divided along family lines through kinship and intermarriage. Therefore, though

whole communities may not have been allowed to survive, their structural segments lived on. For example, the Redwood Creek people moved to Hoopa Valley to live with their kinfolk.

As Indian communities developed new kinds of Euro-American-style political organizations, the role that leaders played as spokespeople to outsiders became important. These leaders—mostly men at first—aroused suspicion in the outsider population and became targeted for isolation (jail) and destruction (murder). In many cases, the position of tribal spokesperson became so dangerous for men that women, less likely to be the objects of violent attacks, began coming forward to assume such positions.

Thus the men, who had traditionally been hunters, fishermen, religious participants, and political leaders, were now denied access to subsistence resources and to positions of political and economic power. They were forced to find work on the farms, ranches, and mines of white owners. Religious leaders were not allowed to go into the hills, and therefore could not feed the spiritual beings in the mountains. The world that they had nourished for centuries through ritual activities, songs, stories, dances, and prayers began to starve and deteriorate.

At the same time a new generation of half-Indian children were born to Indian women who had been raped or taken as wives by the Spanish, Mexican, and American invaders. These women and children, occupying a new place in a social structure, became marginalized as not fully Indian and not fully white.

California Indian survivors used multiple strategies to maintain their cultures in this shifting and hostile environment. Some hid in the foothills, while others lived quietly so as to minimize the chances of retaliation. Leaders, both male and female, took on the internal role of coordinators in the community, maintaining heritage and traditions. Some Indian people married non-Indians who could offer protection. Others moved to population centers and entered the non-Indian society and economy, cutting traditional family ties. Indian boarding schools socialized children in an environment absent of traditional cultural influences or parental interaction. Young people at the boarding schools often married members of other tribes, with the women moving away from their homes forever. The men would return with wives who knew nothing of local culture, and the next generation of children would be raised without knowing their culture.

In the early twentieth century, a number of civic organizations, including the Sequoya League, the Mission Indian Federation, and the Indian Board of Cooperation, were formed to improve the social and economic conditions of California Indians. Indians themselves played an important role in the structure and activities of these organizations. The Indian Board of Cooperation, for example, encouraged Indians to undertake self-determination on their own terms by securing educational and financial opportunities and benefits. All the Indians of California were eligible to join these organizations.

California Indians and their allies went to court to win compensation for lands taken in the nineteenth century. One case concerned compensation for reservations promised in early, unratified treaties but never granted, and a second concerned compensation for the rest of California's land that had not been promised as treaty reservations. The settlement of these cases extinguished the aboriginal title claims that California Indians could make to aboriginal territories, but established a clear relationship between the state's native communities and federal officials. By 1950, 117 Indian communities had been established in California by the federal government either on lands set aside from the public domain or on lands purchased with federal funds.

In the 1950s, California witnessed a number of changes. Under the federal government's termination policy, thirty-six small reservations (called *rancherias*) exchanged official community existence for individual title to land and a distribution of money. During these same years, a federal program of relocation moved unemployed Indians and Indian veterans from their home communities to urban areas. This program moved California people to the state's cities and drew thousands of non-California Indians to cities such as Oakland and Los Angeles.

During the second half of the twentieth century two Indian worlds have emerged in California: that of traditional reservation life, and that of urban immigrant life (largely involving non-California Indians). These two worlds often compete for non-Indian support as the urban Indians seek funds as "ethnic groups" while California tribes maintain their government-to-government relationship with the United States, which brings them money and services. Beginning in the 1960s, the federal "war on poverty" increased the amount of money going to reservations, and urban-development programs often supported the rise of native leaders in cities. These two arenas supported one another as city-trained activists returned home to become tribal leaders and both urban and rural activists combined their efforts in organizations such as the American Indian Movement (AIM).

In the 1970s and 1980s, California tribes became increasingly involved in the struggle to control Indian education. The California Indian Education Association was formed in 1972, and soon afterward DQU University (an Indian-run institution) was established on federal land near Sacramento. In the mid-1970s, departments of Native American studies were instituted at several California state universities and colleges. Publishing also became a focus of activity. The Indian Historian Press and the Malki Museum Press (on the Morongo Reservation) were founded in the 1970s, and cultural centers and tribal museums appeared. In 1976 American bicentennial moneys went to the construction of the Hoopa Tribal Museum and the rebuilding of three Hupa villages abandoned sixty years before.

The 1980s, an era of burgeoning tribal self-government and economic development, brought progress for many California Indian communities. A court decision in 1983 reversed the termination of seventeen California rancherias, and many Indian leaders became involved in the formulation of state and federal programs. At the end of the twentieth century, there are more Indian tribes in California seeking recognition by the federal government than there are in the rest of the United States—some thirty California tribes. Their tenacity, together with the persistence and inventiveness of their reservation and urban-based counterparts, bears powerful witness to the survival of native culture in the nation's most populous state.

Cook, Sherburne F., *The Conflict between the California Indian and White Civilization* (Berkeley: University of California Press, 1976); Editors of Time-Life Books, *The Indians of California* (Alexandria, Va.: Time Life, Inc., 1994); Heizer, Robert F., ed., *California,* vol. 8 of *Handbook of North American Indians,* ed. William C. Sturtevant (Washington: Smithsonian Institution, 1978).

LEE DAVIS
National Museum of the American Indian
Smithsonian Institution

CALUMET

In the North American context the term *calumet* (from the Norman French *chalumet,* a shepherd's pipe) technically refers to the shaft of a Native American ceremonial pipe. In common usage, however, the term more often refers to the entire pipe.

Though each Indian nation has its own formula for sanctifying and decorating the calumet, some universals do appear. The shaft is generally decorated with symbols and symbolic objects such as feathers and pieces of fur. It is often painted in colors appropriate to the pipe's function.

Pipes are smoked as sacred "signatures" to important events such as peace or alliance making, the undertaking of war, or success in the hunt. By passing through the calumet, smoke is sanctified. Once rendered sacred in this way it becomes the medium by which the prayers, wishes, or promises of the smoking parties are carried to the deities. Calumets—and the events solemnized by their use—are held in the highest sacred regard by those nations that employ them.

Today Indians of all regions use the calumet, although its use was historically most widely reported among the indigenous peoples of the eastern woodlands and Great Plains.

CANADA
See Indian-White Relations in Canada, 1763 to the Present.

CANOES

Canoes are the most common type of boat used by Indians. Long and narrow, with generally rounded bottoms and no keel, they taper toward the bow and stern. They are generally propelled by paddles or by poling.

North American Indians made two basic types of canoes. In the eastern woodlands and along the Pacific Coast, they crafted dugouts made from large logs that had been hollowed out and shaped by steam. In the subarctic and Arctic, as well as on the plateau and in the northern portions of the eastern woodlands, native people built wooden frames for their canoes and covered them with bark or animal hides. Eastern Indians generally covered their canoes with birch or elm bark. In the West and in the Arctic, canoe builders used animal hides, such as caribou, moose, and walrus, to cover the frames. Both types of canoes ranged in size from small boats eight to ten feet long, designed to carry one to three people, to much larger boats capable of carrying more than forty people.

Canoes were used everywhere in North America except in the arid regions of the Great Plains, the Great Basin, the Southwest, and the interior of California. They provided an efficient means of transportation in areas that abounded with streams and lakes and along the coasts. Their shape and relatively shallow draft made them easy to navigate. Frame canoes were also lightweight and easy to portage between streams and rivers. Even smaller canoes could carry up to a ton of cargo and be navigated by a single person. The large dugout canoes in the East and on the Pacific Coast could sail in the open sea and were sometimes used to hunt whales, as well as for trading and warfare.

As they became heavily involved in the European fur trade, many northeastern tribes replaced their heavy dugouts with lighter, more easily navigable frame canoes. By the late nineteenth century, most Eastern Indians had ceased using canoes, except in parts of the Northeast, the upper Great Lakes, Florida, and parts of Louisiana. Today, native canoe building is largely confined to the subarctic, the upper Great Lakes, and the Northeast. Elsewhere, canoes have been replaced by manufactured boats and other modern forms of transportation.

CAPTIVES

On March 31, 1799, Richard J. Cleveland, a twenty-five-year-old entrepreneur from Salem, Massachusetts, cruised through the southern Alaskan waters around Sitka on the *Dragon,* trying his luck with the local Tlingits in hopes of making a killing in the sea otter trade. Cleveland had left the South China coast on a fifty-ton English cutter with a dubious crew bound for the Northwest Coast. Later, writing of his exploits in his *Narrative of Voyages and Commercial Enterprises* (1850), he described his impressions of the natives of southeastern Alaska: a "more hideous set of beings, in the form of men and women I had never before seen," with some groups looking "as if they had escaped from the dominions of Satan himself."

Cleveland's adventures were successful from the commercial perspective, but at several points along the area of Norfolk Sound he ran into trouble. On May 6 near Chilkat (Tlingit) land, about five hundred natives arrived in long canoes with between twelve and twenty-eight people in each, "armed with muskets, spears, and daggers." Cleveland's ship was becalmed in Chatham's Straits, and the captain and crew feared capture. They were convinced that "death was greatly to be preferred to falling into the hands of these barbarians." Cleveland's response was to order up the ship's full array of cannons, arms, and pikes. He later discovered that not long before another English ship, fearing attack, fired on and probably killed natives.

More than 100 years before Cleveland's voyage, the first account of an attack by indigenous people on an English settlement and subsequent capture opened with the following alarm: "On the tenth of February, 1675 came the Indians with great numbers upon Lancaster." In her narrative, The Sovereignty and Goodness of God (1682), Mary White Rowlandson, the wife of a Puritan minister, described an attack on a frontier town west of Boston and traced an earthly adventure with a spiritual significance: her thirteen weeks among the Narragansetts and Wampanoags during King Philip's War.

These two accounts—one a seaman's adventure story, the other the record of a minister's wife's captivity—contain the major themes of capture by Indians found in a variety of English and American writings in early America. First, there is the description of indigenous people as ugly, satanic, brutal, and nonhuman; "ravenous bears," Rowlandson once called the Narragansetts. Second, there is a stated or implied allegation of Indian irrationality and unpredictability—

the presupposition that "wild Indians" might attack, capture, or kill for no reason at all; there is no sense of the possibility that a set of grievances had preceded the attack, that negotiations had broken down, that whites had overrun native lands, that, as in the case of Alaska Natives, lives had been lost and justifiable compensation or retribution was being sought. Third, commercial motives are downplayed, and justified if not glamorized. Thus in Captain John Smith's account of his capture, we lose touch with the fact that Smith and his men arrived in what we now call Virginia not for a pleasure trip but to lay the groundwork for a major English commercial enterprise. In Cleveland's account, the potential capture of his men comes out of some irrational action by the natives, not out of any objection of theirs to the exploitation of their resources. Fourth, gender colors and shapes descriptions of capture: when white men are in danger of capture, their stories become high adventure; white women's experiences are usually tales of woe and victimization. Finally, capture is seen in a much more ambiguous light in these writings than the accounts themselves explicitly contend. Within Rowlandson's narrative we find a friendship formed between the captive Rowlandson and King Philip or Metacom, the Wampanoag sachem. Other accounts describe men and women escaping from "civilized" circumstances to live as "white Indians."

Any discussion of captives must acknowledge that the topic has been shaped by a set of racial, entrepreneurial, religious, and gender assumptions that suggest that the world was or should have been a European or American oyster. On the other hand, there is an earlier, precontact history of prisoners of war among indigenous peoples.

Capture was a widely used tactic of warfare in North, South, and Central America before 1492. Although first described by the Spaniards to justify their own conquest of Mexico, the Aztecs' frequent use of captives as slaves and religious sacrifices undermined their regime and contributed to its demise.

In northeastern North America from approximately 1550 through the American Revolution, death, torture, adoption, or ransom awaited native men captured in wartime. Accounts from colonial times by British, French, and American survivors testify to white comrades and native enemies alike being beaten, tortured, and either burned to death or accepted into indigenous societies. Father Isaac Jogues's account (1643–46) was one of many depicting the capture and torture of priests and Hurons alike among the Iroquois. Similar accounts can be found for the Southwest and the Northwest Coast. Adoption was a common result of capture among Indians east of the Mississippi, from the Hurons and Iroquois in the North to the Cherokees in the South, and among the Great Lakes Ojibwas and the Santee Sioux as well.

In the seventeenth and eighteenth centuries, Northeast native women were powerful determinants of the fate of war captives. Among the Iroquois, the taking of captives to assuage the loss of kin was an accepted reason for warfare. Female elders decided whether the men would go to war, and a wife or mother who had lost a son, husband, or daughter in war could choose a captive man or woman to adopt into her family. Either sex could be substituted for a lost relative. The scene described by Captain John Smith of Pocahontas saving him in early Virginia (1607) was probably the product of a cultural misreading by him of the accepted powers of leading women to save prisoners. So common was this practice in the eighteenth century that Lewis Henry Morgan claimed that the Iroquois would have died out because of disease and warfare had they not taken captives into their midst.

The sex and age of a prisoner of war was important in determining his or her treatment. Among many indigenous nations of the Northeast (and well into Canada), men went to war knowing that if they were captured, a trial involving torture and possibly death was likely. Adoption was possible if the man could endure his trials, but this meant becoming one with the enemy. In Morgan's words, if the victim made it through a gauntlet of a "long avenue of whips," running naked to the waist, he would be "treated with the utmost affection and kindness." Those who did not pass this test were "led away to torture, and to death." On the other hand, native women and small children, although at times psychologically terrorized and frequently traumatized by the death of parents, relatives, and friends, or by scenes of torture inflicted on loved ones, might be treated gently in preparation for their ultimate integration into enemy tribal, village, and family life. Mary Jemison, captured by French and Shawnees in 1758 during the Seven Years' War in southwestern Pennsylvania, was adopted into Seneca society after marrying one of its members. She refused repatriation to white society.

Although the lore of Indian-white relations is filled with tales of Indians capturing hapless white victims, the record shows that when war or profit was involved, this kind of "savagery" was not limited by color or cul-

ture. Europeans themselves frequently captured indigenous peoples. European "explorers" and fishermen kidnapped native people in early America, bringing them back to Europe as showpieces. From the 1600s to the nineteenth century, as disease and overwork decimated New World natives, Africans by the millions were captured and brought to the New World to replace the indigenous labor force. Spanish explorers forcibly took more than a thousand southeastern Indians to the West Indies. Early French attempts at abduction also began in the sixteenth century. Participants included Verrazano's French-sponsored expedition in 1524 and Cartier's in 1534–35. In the early eighteenth century the French encouraged the capture of indigenous women in Canada for forced resettlement downriver in Louisiana; approximately eighty of these female Indians died in transit. On the northern Spanish frontier, slaving expeditions were practiced by Nuño de Guzman, the first governor of Mexico, who in the 1530s took twenty Acoma captives and sentenced them to servitude, and Governor Juan de Eulate (1618–25) sold Indians into slavery by shipping them to New Spain.

After the Pequot War (1637) in southern New England, the British joined the effort, enslaving forty-eight native women and children in the Massachusetts Bay Colony and exchanging Pequot warriors for African slaves in the West Indies. At the time of Rowlandson's capture in 1675–76 during King Philip's War, Richard Waldron of Marblehead captured four hundred Abenakis and had them sold into slavery. During the Tuscarora Wars (1711 and 1713) more than four hundred Indian slaves were sold by the colonial government of North Carolina. In the Yamasee War that followed, South Carolina became a leader in Indian slaving.

Although indigenous people were subject to capture and genocidal treatment, it is the fate of Euro-American captives that has held the imagination of the American and European public in thrall from the days of Captain John Smith and Mary Rowlandson. Stories of the Indian enemy opposed to the brave white male captive and the long-suffering or fainting white female captive became favored material in American sermons, history books, fiction, and film.

While attacks and captures by Indians were not everyday experiences along the Atlantic plains or Pacific frontiers, they were not uncommon. In New England between 1675 and 1763, an estimated 1,641 white captives were taken. Although capture was a central piece of the indigenous system of making war—earlier inflicted on native people by other indigenous enemies—Puritan sermons in early New England like those of Cotton Mather described the experience as an act of Providence sent down upon them by an angry God: punishment for the sins of the new Zion gone astray in the wilderness. Based upon actual events during the colonial Indian wars of the seventeenth and early eighteenth centuries, the writings of Puritan ministers and captives evolved from descriptions of religious experiences into, in the nineteenth and twentieth centuries, works of ethnography, propaganda, and popular culture.

Propagandistic and racist elements appeared in these narratives from the outset, with New England natives being called "savages," "wolves," and "furious Tawnies." Indians were often cast as barbarous devils and contrasted with "civilized" whites. Their use of capture, attack, and torture was seen as a justification for Euro-American warfare, expropriation of land, and extermination.

Although the Puritan narratives relied on biblical citation and didacticism, by the eighteenth and early nineteenth centuries the captivity narrative itself evolved into a form of patriotic gore, folklore, and wild fiction. By 1800 Mary Rowlandson, Captain John Smith, and Father Isaac Jogues were joined by other figures such as John Williams, Eunice Williams, Hannah Dustan, Mary Jemison, and Daniel Boone and his daughter Jemima as well-known subjects of captivity literature. These narratives became further exaggerated and modified in fictional works such as *The Last of the Mohicans* (1824) and dime novels like Ann Sophia Stephens's *Malaeska, the Indian Wife of the White Hunter* (1860), the story of a supposed Indian woman who was in fact a white captive. Captivity themes also became a staple of American art and popular culture. In the nineteenth century they were used in the creation of works of art by John Vanderlyn, Asher Durand, Erastus Dow Palmer, and Charles (Carl) Wimar. In the mid- to late-twentieth century popular films such as *The Searchers, The Emerald Forest, Dances with Wolves,* and *The Last of the Mohicans* have portrayed white men, women, and children captured in war and transformed into Indians.

But captivity accounts offer more than propaganda or a good read. Some contain accurate ethnographic information. Still others argue directly or indirectly for better Indian-white relations. As politics and history, a select number of these narratives provide early windows into Anglo-American, Indian, and French interaction in North America. The narratives of John Gyles, Mary Jemison, Colonel James Smith, John Dunn Hunter, and John Tanner depict Euro-Americans captured in war, all of whom lived at length with Indians and were sympathetic and objective enough to offer up to Anglo-American readers information about the native societies in which they lived. Sarah Wakefield, captured in the Dakota War of 1862, argued in her account that government mismanagement and greed brought on that disastrous Indian war.

From adventure to spiritual testimony to omitted and distorted accounts, the depiction of capture and Indian-white encounters through European and American eyes left a formidable imprint on American history and politics, on notions of gender, race, and ethnicity, and on the arts and popular culture.

Axtell, James, "The Scholastic Philosophy of the Wilderness" and "The White Indians of Colonial America," in *The European and the Indian: Essays in the Ethnohistory of Colonial North America* (New York: Oxford University Press, 1981); Namias, June, *White Captives: Gender and Ethnicity on the American Frontier* (Chapel Hill and London: University of North Carolina Press, 1993); Washburn, Wilcomb E., ed. *The Garland Library of Narratives of North American Indian Captivities.* 111 vols. (New York: Garland Publishing, 1976–83).

JUNE NAMIAS
University of Alaska at Anchorage

CARLISLE INDIAN INDUSTRIAL SCHOOL

Formally opened in 1879 on the site of an abandoned military base in Pennsylvania, Carlisle was the first nonreservation boarding school established by the U.S. government for the exclusive use of native children. Its first director was Richard Henry Pratt, an army officer who had experience in running an Indian prisoner-of-war camp in St. Augustine, Florida. Pratt convinced government officials and humanitarian reformers that education was the solution to the "Indian Problem."

The objective of Carlisle's curriculum was, in Pratt's words, to "kill the Indian and save the man." The school set out to teach boys skills in the mechanical and agricultural arts; girls were trained in sewing, cooking, laundry, and general housework. The English language was considered a strong "civilizing" force at Carlisle, and the use of native languages was strictly forbidden. Further attempts to break tribal ties included placing children with white families for the summer months, dressing students in military uniforms, and encouraging them to find permanent employment away from their home reservations.

By 1900, Carlisle had over twelve hundred students from seventy-nine tribes. Nevertheless, rising costs, resistance from parents, a preference for institutions closer to Indian populations, and World War I led to the decision to close the school in September 1918. The Indian Office returned the school buildings to the army.

See also Boarding Schools; Education.

CASA GRANDE

Casa Grande is a late Hohokam archaeological site on the Gila River near Florence, Arizona. The site itself consisted of a large four-story multiroom structure and numerous outbuildings, as well as relic irrigation canals. Today the outbuildings have disappeared and the central building rises only twenty to twenty-five feet, with a thirty-five-foot central tower. This structure, which has adobe walls three to five feet thick, has five rooms on the ground floor and presumably had a similar number of rooms on each of the others.

The site was occupied between A.D. 1200 and A.D. 1450, at which time the Hohokams were in decline. The Anasazi peoples to the north and east began exerting considerable influence among the Hohokams at this time as well. The architecture of Casa Grande illustrates this influence, as it more closely resembles Anasazi dwellings than it does earlier Hohokam villages. The site apparently was abandoned prior to the arrival of the first Europeans.

CATAWBA

On November 29, 1993, the Catawba Indian Nation formally reached a settlement with the state of South Carolina and the government of the United States in a land dispute that had begun more than 150 years earlier. Chief Gilbert Blue, in a public ceremony at the tribe's new cultural center, signed a document on behalf of the tribe's fourteen hundred members in which the Catawbas agreed to give up their claim to lands taken from them by South Carolina in the Treaty of Nation Ford on March 13, 1840. In return, the Catawbas received federal recognition as an Indian tribe, along

with $50 million for land purchases, economic development, social services, and education.

This agreement signaled a new chapter in Catawba history. And yet, as important as it was, the agreement is only one in a long series of turning points for the Catawbas. The first came perhaps one thousand years ago, when Siouan-speaking people headed east across the Appalachian Mountains. By the time Spanish explorers visited the southeastern interior in the mid-sixteenth century, the descendants of these first settlers, divided into many tribes, had spread across the southern piedmont. Among the most prominent of these piedmont peoples were the Catawbas, living beside the river that today bears their name.

With the arrival of strangers from Europe and Africa the Catawbas, like all Native Americans, faced a world every bit as new as the "new world" confronted by the transatlantic travelers. The contours of the Catawbas' new world were shaped first and most profoundly by imported diseases. In 1698, 1718, 1738, and 1759 epidemics tore through Catawba villages, reducing the nation's population from perhaps five thousand in 1690 to less than five hundred in 1760. In order to survive, during the early eighteenth century Catawbas incorporated neighboring Indian groups—Waterees, Cheraws, Pedees, Saponis, and others—in similar straits. So successful was this strategy that a visitor in 1743 heard more than twenty different languages spoken in the nation's six towns.

While rebuilding their society, Catawbas also learned the wisdom of befriending Anglo-America. We "cannot live without the assistance of the English," one leader admitted to colonists in 1715. By then, a generation of trade with Anglo-America had left Catawbas dependent on these outsiders for weapons and other necessities. Unable to live without the English, Catawbas learned to live with them, even serving as allies against the French in the Seven Years' War.

Such accommodation was not surrender, however. Though colonists boasted that Catawbas were "directed intirely by the Government of So. Carolina," in fact these Indians made the most of their precarious position in the new American world. Led by chiefs such as Hagler (1750–63), the nation developed a strategy of playing rival interests off against each other that had several provinces courting its favor. "Those Indians," noted one colonial observer in 1757, "seem to understand well how to make their Advantage of" such attention. Through such negotiations Catawbas acquired an abundant supply of European goods and, during a drought in the late 1750s, hundreds of bushels of corn.

The late 1750s, however, brought another terrible test to the nation, and again the Catawbas relied on Anglo-America to meet that test. In the fall of 1759 a smallpox epidemic killed two of every three Catawbas. At the same time, colonial settlers moving into Catawba territory frequently clashed with the Indians. In response, surviving Catawbas went through provincial authorities to acquire from King George III in 1763 a 144,000-acre reservation along the Catawba River. Secure in this legal protection, the Catawbas learned to get along with their new neighbors. Catawba women sold them traditional pottery; Catawba men caught runaway slaves and sold deerskins; Catawba leaders rented out reservation land. The nation's support of the rebels in the American Revolution secured its reputation as a steadfast friend of the piedmont's new rulers.

Their reputation as potters and patriots did not make Catawbas immune to the powerful forces pressing after 1800 for Indian exile. Though the nation escaped the spate of removals during the 1830s, removal came at last when in 1840 Catawba leaders sold the entire reservation to South Carolina, receiving in return promises of cash and a new reservation elsewhere in the Carolinas. These were the terms of the Treaty of Nation Ford, which, unfulfilled by the state and never ratified by the U.S. Senate as federal law requires, nonetheless drove the Catawbas from their homeland.

In exile for several years, by 1850 Catawbas had begun to drift back to their ancestral territories, taking up residence on 640 acres that South Carolina agreed to buy for them with some of their treaty money. Ever since, this state reservation has been at the core of Catawba identity.

A second pillar of modern Catawba identity has been the Mormon Church. Missionaries from the Church of Jesus Christ of Latter-day Saints first arrived on the reservation in 1883. They enjoyed immediate success, in part because Indians had a central role in Mormon theology. An added attraction was that neighboring whites hated Mormonism; thus converts to the new faith had a way to channel resistance to their conquerors. Mormonism revitalized Catawba life. Teachers, preachers, and a new social code became important forces in the nation, just as the Mormon church was the largest building on the reservation.

In the twentieth century outsiders have often predicted the Catawbas' imminent demise as Indians. Catawba children have grown up knowing only English, and the last speaker of Catawba, Samuel Blue, died in 1959; intermarriage with whites has become increasingly common, and the last alleged Catawba "full blood," Hester Louisa Blue, died in 1963; finally, in 1962 the federal government terminated the Catawba tribe, giving official sanction to what appeared, in other ways, to be the end of a long road.

In fact, neither Mormonism nor English, neither termination nor intermarriage, has spelled the Catawbas' doom. The reservation has remained—a tangible symbol of the Catawbas' special status. Enduring, too, has been the pottery tradition, passed from one generation of women to the next. Finally, Catawbas have never wavered in the pursuit of their land rights, a long campaign that culminated in the ceremony at the Catawba Cultural Center in November 1993.

That campaign and that agreement are part of a larger revitalization of Catawba life that includes an annual festival, pottery classes, and a language program based on tapes made by the tribe's elders two generations ago. Contemporary Catawbas, listening to those voices from the past speak once again, are akin to their more distant ancestors crossing the Appalachian range a millennium ago. Like those pioneers, Catawbas today are poised on the frontier of a new world filled with challenge and promise.

See also Hagler.

Brown, Douglas Summers, *The Catawba Indians: The People of the River* (Columbia: University of South Carolina Press, 1966); Hudson, Charles M., *The Catawba Nation, University of Georgia Monographs,* no. 18 (Athens: University of Georgia Press, 1970); Merrell, James H., *The Indians' New World: Catawbas and Their Neighbors from European Contact through the Era of Removal* (Chapel Hill: University of North Carolina Press, 1989).

JAMES H. MERRELL
Vassar College

CAUGHNAWAGA

The Indian settlement of Caughnawaga was established in 1667 when a French Jesuit, Father Pierre Raffeix, persuaded a group of Oneida Indians to take up permanent residence alongside several French immigrant families at La Prairie, on the south bank of the St. Lawrence across from present-day Montreal. This original mixed group of Indians and French habitants was soon joined by a much larger group of Mohawks from the south (New York State.) The Caughnawaga settlement moved several times over the years, finally settling on its present site near St. Regis in 1755.

The Mohawk-speaking inhabitants of Caughnawaga allied themselves with their French neighbors, and many were converted to Catholicism, most notably Kateri Tekakwitha. The Iroquois at Caughnawaga fought alongside the French in all the major colonial wars. At the conclusion of the American Revolution, it was clear that Loyalist Indians were no longer welcome in the United States, and by 1777 nearly all of the Mohawk-speaking Iroquois had immigrated to British North America and settled on reserves in Quebec and Ontario. In 1890, Caughnawaga contained approximately 25 percent of the Mohawks in North America.

As a result of Caughnawaga residents' long association with the Catholic Church, their involvement in the fur trade, and the Canadian government's assimilationist policies, old Mohawk religious practice and longhouse ritual lapsed. In the 1920s, however, traditional Mohawk religion and political structure were reintroduced at Caughnawaga, and the settlement is now affiliated with the Six Nations Confederacy of Canada.

In 1989, the Mohawks living in Quebec and upper New York State, particularly those at Oka Reserve across the St. Lawrence from Caughnawaga, captured international attention in a military standoff with Quebec's provincial police. A dispute over a parcel of land claimed by the Mohawks at Oka but slated for development by provincial authorities as a municipal golf course escalated into armed confrontation between the Sûreté du Québec and a band of Mohawk "warriors." In an attempt to storm the barricades set up by the Mohawks, a provincial policeman was accidentally shot and killed. It is still unknown which side fired the fatal bullet. Negotiations continued for more than a year, starkly revealing a surprising level of anti-Indian sentiment by local non-Indians and insensitivity to Indian land claims by provincial and federal government officials. For Native Canadians, Oka was a victory because it made the average Canadian aware of native issues and was a primary step in raising official responsiveness and avoiding conflict in the future.

See also Indian-White Relations in Canada, 1763 to the Present.

CAYUGA

The Cayugas form one nation of the Iroquois Confederacy. With the Oneidas, they are the Younger Brothers of the league, having reciprocal relations vis-à-vis the Elder Brothers: the Mohawks, Onondagas, and Senecas. They have ten sachemships (matrilineally inherited chieftainship positions) within the confederacy.

At the time of first contact with Euro-Americans, the Cayugas occupied three main agricultural villages in what are now Cayuga and Seneca counties in western New York State. Cayuga hunting territory ranged north to Lake Ontario and south to the Susquehanna River.

From 1641 to 1684 the Cayugas warred with other Iroquois against nations to the northwest, west, and south of Iroquois country and incorporated captives from these groups into their communities. Because the French were allied with their enemies, relations were strained with Europeans until neutrality with both France and England was established in separate treaties in 1701.

In the eighteenth century, the Cayugas continued their policy of incorporation, taking in Tutelos, Saponis, Nanticokes, and Conoys, all of whom joined the League of the Iroquois as nonvoting members under Cayuga auspices in 1753.

Although the Cayugas were officially neutral during the Seven Years' War (1756–63) between France and England, Cayuga warriors often joined the French. Most Cayugas, alarmed by the encroachment of English colonists into Indian country after the defeat of the French in 1763, allied themselves with the British during the American Revolution against land-hungry Americans. Cayuga villages were destroyed by American forces in 1779. After the war, New York State acquired the homeland of the Cayugas in negotiations that took place from 1789 through 1807.

Many Cayugas moved to the Six Nations Reserve in Ontario, Canada, where they joined other Iroquois displaced by the war. Most practice the Longhouse religion instituted by the Seneca prophet Handsome Lake between 1799 and 1815, and accept the authority of the hereditary Confederate Council. Some of the leading Iroquois ritualists of the 1990s are Cayugas living at Six Nations Reserve.

After the American Revolution, other Cayugas settled with Senecas at Buffalo Creek (near present-day Buffalo, New York), where they, too, were exposed to Handsome Lake's teachings. Although some Cayugas in modern-day communities are Christian, missionary efforts among them met with less success than they did among other Indian nations. Buffalo Creek was ceded at the Treaty of Buffalo Creek in 1842. Cayugas there then moved with Senecas to the Cattaraugus Reservation. In 1848, the people of Cattaraugus and the Allegany Seneca Reservation joined politically to form the Seneca Nation, with an elective system of government.

As a result of the Buffalo Creek treaty, a few Cayugas, along with some Senecas, moved to Kansas. Although most returned, a very small number stayed, eventually receiving allotments of land.

Another band of Cayugas settled on the Little Sandusky River in Ohio between 1807 and 1817; from there they moved to Oklahoma in 1831–32. From 1887 to 1903, most Iroquois land in Oklahoma was allotted to individuals, though some was kept as tribally owned property for ceremonial and burial grounds. In 1934, the Oklahoma group adopted the name "Seneca/Cayuga Tribe of Oklahoma" and established an elective council.

Although the Cayugas are without their original homeland, they have not given up hope of reclaiming it. An official land claim was initiated in the late 1970s and was still being negotiated in the mid-1990s. The Cayugas have very persuasive arguments, the strongest being that, contrary to federal law, their land was acquired through treaties conducted by New York State rather than by federal officials.

MARY DRUKE BECKER
Iroquois Indian Museum
Howes Cave, New York

CHEMAWA INDIAN SCHOOL

Established in February 1880 as the Training School for Indian Youth, the Chemawa school for Indians is an off-reservation boarding school located in Oregon that serves tribes throughout the Pacific Northwest and Alaska. At the time of its founding in Forest Grove, Oregon, the school offered Indians the opportunity to earn an education and assimilate into mainstream society. Over time, however, its primary goal became providing training in vocational skills that would serve graduates both on and off the reservation.

Fire destroyed most of the original school in 1885, which prompted a move to a new location at Chemawa, Oregon, and the renaming of the facility. Students took an active role in rebuilding and caring for the school, and by 1922 enrollment had climbed to over one thousand students. In 1927, Chemawa became a fully accredited four-year high school.

Chemawa's focus has changed in the past century. It began as a coercive and authoritarian institution, be-

came vocationally oriented in the early twentieth century, and later tried to incorporate native traditions into a general academic curriculum. Though initially unpopular with native students, Chemawa has survived various attempts by the Bureau of Indian Affairs to close it, thanks mainly to the support of Northwest tribes who have taken pride in the school's accomplishments and for whom it assumed an important role in the education of their children.

See also Boarding Schools; Education.

CHEROKEE

At the time of European contact, the Cherokees numbered about twenty-two thousand and controlled more than forty thousand square miles of land. Their homeland consisted of parts of eight present states: the Carolinas, the Virginias, Kentucky, Tennessee, Georgia, and Alabama. The original holdings were gradually eliminated by more than three dozen land cessions with the British and the United States between 1721 and 1835. By 1819, Cherokee territory included only the adjacent mountainous areas of North Carolina, Tennessee, Georgia, and Alabama. In December 1835, the Treaty of New Echota ceded the last remaining territory east of the Mississippi. In exchange the Cherokees received equivalent holdings in what is now northeastern Oklahoma.

Numerically, the Cherokees constitute the largest Indian tribe in the United States. In the 1990 census, 308,132 people identified themselves as Cherokees. More than half of these are federally recognized members of either the Eastern Band of Cherokee Indians, in western North Carolina, or the Cherokee Nation of Oklahoma. The Eastern Band has more than ten thousand members, who are descended from approximately one thousand Cherokees who avoided forced removal in 1838 by claiming North Carolina citizenship under an earlier treaty or by taking refuge in and near the Great Smoky Mountains. Enrollment in the Eastern Band requires one-thirty-second degree of Cherokee blood through descent from an enrollee on the 1924 Baker roll. Membership in the Cherokee Nation of Oklahoma requires proof of descent from an ancestor on the 1906 Dawes Commission roll. There is no minimum blood quantum requirement—a policy that has resulted in a rapid expansion of tribal membership, which has grown from slightly more than fifty thousand in 1980 to more than one hundred seventy-five thousand in 1995, with tens of thousands of applications still pending. The Cherokee Nation of Oklahoma is now the largest federally recognized tribe in the United States. The United Band of Keetoowahs was organized among the Oklahoma Cherokees in the 1930s as a political entity and has held federal recognition since 1946. Two other Oklahoma Cherokee groups, neither of which is a political entity, also use the name Keetoowah. In addition to the three federally recognized groups, more than fifty other organizations in at least twelve states claim Cherokee descent.

The Cherokee Nation of Oklahoma

Cherokees residing on land ceded by the Treaty of New Echota, signed in 1835, were given two years to voluntarily remove to the West. When the time period expired in May 1838, only about two thousand Cherokees had left their homes. To complete the removal, seven thousand federal and state troops were sent to the Cherokee Nation. Between June 1838 and April 1839, fifteen thousand Cherokees were forced to emigrate to the Indian Territory.

The forced removal of the Cherokees in 1838–39 marked the beginning of a new era in Cherokee history. This rebirth was signified by the adoption of a new constitution shortly after the majority of Cherokees arrived in the Indian Territory in 1839. The Cherokees brought to Oklahoma their concept of democratic government, their churches and schools, their newspapers and books, and their businesses. Tahlequah became the new capital and the center of business activity, and Park Hill emerged as a cultural oasis in Indian Territory. Two bilingual publications, the *Cherokee Advocate* and the *Cherokee Messenger,* became, respectively, the first newspaper and the first periodical in the new territory. In addition, the presses churned out hundreds of religious and secular tracts printed in the Cherokee syllabary, which had been introduced by Sequoyah in 1821. Before long, the Cherokees' educational system had grown to include 144 elementary schools and two institutions of higher education, the Cherokee Male and Female Seminaries.

Despite the losses experienced during removal, the Cherokees regained their prominence by adopting a progressive outlook toward the future. The years between removal and the 1860s were called the Cherokees' golden age, a period of prosperity that ended with the devastation of the American Civil War. Like residents of most border areas, Cherokees were divided in their loyalties. One-third of the Cherokee population either died or moved away during the war. After the war, Cherokee land was again taken, this time to accommodate other tribes displaced by the U.S. government. At the turn of the century most of the remaining tribal land was parceled out to individual Cherokees in allotments. Final eligibility for allotments was determined by the Dawes Commission rolls of 1906. The surviving original enrollees and their descendants make up the tribal membership of today's Cherokee Nation of Oklahoma.

The Cherokee Nation is a source of pride and identity for its members, many of whom live in the original territory of the Cherokee Nation, which is located in fourteen counties of northeastern Oklahoma. Today this land is not a reservation, but a jurisdictional service area. The tribal structure was reorganized in the 1970s, and since then the Cherokee Nation has become a leader in education, health care, housing, vocational training, and economic development in northeastern Oklahoma. The nation currently employs 940 people on staff and in its business enterprises, and its annual payroll exceeds $13 million.

The assets of the Cherokee Nation include ninety-six miles of the Arkansas River bed and more than sixty-one thousand acres of tribal land. Over the past fifteen years, the Cherokee Nation has posted dramatic and steady financial growth while increasing its asset base. The annual operating budget exceeds $50 million, with the funds provided by federal programs and generated from tribal sources.

The responsibilities of the Cherokee Nation tribal government are divided into three major areas: social programs, development and special services, and tribal operations. Among tribal business enterprises are Cherokee Nation industries, two arts-and-crafts outlets, a utility company, and ranching, poultry, and wood-cutting operations. In November 1990 the Cherokee Nation opened its first gaming facility, Bingo Outpost, at Roland, Oklahoma.

In addition to the decision to enter the bingo market, other recent initiatives of the tribal government include the approval of a tax code and the tribe's bid to enter the self-governance program. In February 1990 the tribal council approved the Cherokee Nation Tax Code, which allows the tribe to tax businesses on tribal lands, including smoke shops. The Cherokee Nation applied for direct funding for tribal programs and services for fiscal year 1991 as part of its aggressive push for increased self-governance. The agreement, approved by

An 1886 political cartoon depicting the Cherokee nation as Gulliver immobilized by an assortment of Lilliputian white exploiters, among them railroads, courts, and oil tycoons.

the U.S. Congress, authorizes the tribe to plan, conduct, consolidate, and administer programs and receive direct funding to deliver services to tribal members.

The Eastern Band of Cherokee Indians

Modern Eastern Cherokees trace their origins to about one thousand Cherokees who managed to avoid removal. One-third of these—some fifty-seven families—were living outside the Cherokee Nation on the Oconaluftee River in the early nineteenth century and claimed U.S. citizenship under the treaties of 1817 and 1819. Living on nontribal land, these families were not subject to the Treaty of New Echota. They were referred to as the Oconaluftee Citizen Indians by the U.S. Army, which made no attempt to remove them. These Indians were joined in November 1838 by refugees from the Nantahala River area.

Other Cherokees who remained in North Carolina included those living in the village of Cheoih, near Robbinsville, which had a close alliance with local whites. A number of families along the Valley River were also left behind. They were headed by white males, and the army was unable to obtain a clarification of their status. Other Cherokees who remained in the East came from such places as Turtle Town and Duck Town in Tennessee, Fighting Town in Georgia, and Shooting Creek and Hanging Dog Town in North Carolina.

The fate of the North Carolina Cherokees remained in question for several years following removal. By 1848, however, the U.S. Congress agreed to recognize the rights of the North Carolina Cherokees on the condition that the state recognize their rights as permanent residents. Acknowledgment was not forthcoming until after the Civil War. During the war the Eastern Cherokees sided with their white neighbors and the Confederacy. Many enlisted in the Sixty-ninth North Carolina Infantry, which was commanded by William Holland

Thomas and became known as the Thomas Legion. After the war, the Cherokees faced the prospect of losing their land again. Title to their land was held by Thomas, their trusted friend and attorney. He had invested heavily in the Southern cause and was now impoverished and mentally unstable. His creditors obtained sheriff's deeds to all his property, including the Cherokees' land. In 1866, the state of North Carolina finally recognized the Cherokees as permanent residents and the federal government allowed money promised under the previous treaty to be used to pay Thomas's debts to insure that the tribe would not be dispossessed.

With questions about their residency and legal status resolved, the Cherokees began to reorganize their tribal government. On December 9, 1868, a general council of the Eastern Cherokees was held at Cheoih in Graham County. In the first election since removal, Flying Squirrel was chosen principal chief and was inaugurated on December 1, 1870. The Qualla Boundary, also known as the Eastern Cherokee Reservation, was soon established, and the limits were marked in 1876 by the Temple Survey. The Qualla Boundary had a population of 835 in 1880; another 189 Cherokees lived in Graham County, 83 in Cherokee County, and 12 in Macon County. In the 1880s, many of the Cherokees living in Macon and Cherokee Counties moved to Qualla to take advantage of its newly established school and to give themselves a chance to become more involved in the community.

The Cherokees became incorporated under the laws of North Carolina in 1889 and began conducting business as the Eastern Band of Cherokee Indians. Title to tribal lands previously held by the Commissioner of Indian Affairs was transferred to the corporation. By 1890 an incipient cash economy had developed. Unfortunately, the advent of the timber industry, which operated on Cherokee land for a few decades, resulted in the deforestation of the mountains.

In 1919, Cherokee veterans of World War I were made citizens of the United States. In 1924, all American Indians received U.S. citizenship. Also in that year, Cherokee land was placed in federal trust, with the guarantee that the land would always remain in Cherokee possession.

The opening of Great Smoky Mountains National Park in 1940 changed the long-term focus of the Cherokee economy. After World War II, the scenic wilderness of the park began to draw hundreds of thousands of visitors annually. The Cherokee Historical Association was organized in 1948 and premiered its outdoor drama, *Unto These Hills,* two years later. In 1952, the association opened the Oconaluftee Indian Village. Today tourism is the primary industry in the Qualla Boundary area, providing jobs for about 65 percent of the local population.

Lands currently held by the Eastern Band of Cherokee Indians include 56,572.8 acres in five counties of western North Carolina and 76.3 acres in two counties in eastern Tennessee. In North Carolina, tribal holdings include fifty-two tracts or boundaries, which are contained in thirty separate bodies of land. The majority of the land is in Jackson and Swain Counties. A small strip of land is in Haywood County, and scattered residential tracts are in Graham and Cherokee Counties. Possessory title to approximately 80 percent of tribal land is held by individuals, who can transfer land only to other tribal members. Of the more than ten thousand Eastern Cherokees, about sixty-five hundred live on tribal lands.

In 1984, the Eastern Band of Cherokee Indians and the Cherokee Nation of Oklahoma met in a joint council session for the first time in nearly 150 years. Joint sessions now meet every two years and deal with issues that affect both groups. Both groups take pride in their common history and have developed cultural attractions both in North Carolina and in Oklahoma that share the story of the Cherokees with the public. The re-created villages, museums, and outdoor dramas provide employment for Cherokee people, promote the continuation of traditional arts and crafts, strengthen tribal identity, and provide important educational services. About fourteen thousand people speak Cherokee as a first language, making them the seventh-largest group of speakers of a native language north of Mexico.

Today, the Eastern Band of Cherokee Indians and the Cherokee Nation of Oklahoma are prosperous and vibrant communities that share a deep appreciation for the past and great optimism about the future.

See also Cherokee Language.

King, Duane H., ed., *The Cherokee Indian Nation: A Troubled History* (Knoxville: University of Tennessee Press, 1979); Mooney, James, *Myths of the Cherokee,* Bureau of American Ethnology, 19th Annual Report (Washington: Govt. Printing Office, 1900); Woodward, Grace, *The Cherokees* (Norman: University of Oklahoma Press, 1963).

DUANE H. KING (Cherokee)
Southwest Museum, Los Angeles

CHEROKEE LANGUAGE

Cherokee is spoken today by about fourteen thousand people in western North Carolina and northeastern Oklahoma. At the time of European contact, three major dialects were recognized. These corresponded roughly to the three main geographical divisions of the Cherokee Nation. The Lower or Elati dialect was spoken in what is now northwestern South Carolina and the adjacent area of Georgia. The Middle or Kituhwa dialect was spoken in most of western North Carolina. The Overhill or Otali dialect was spoken in all the towns of East Tennessee and in the towns along the Hiwassee and Cheowa Rivers in North Carolina, as well as in northeastern Alabama and northwestern Georgia during the late eighteenth and early nineteenth centuries.

Cherokee became a distinct language about thirty-five hundred years ago. It is most closely related to the Iroquoian languages spoken today by members of the Mohawk, Oneida, Onondaga, Cayuga, Seneca, and Tuscarora communities of New York and Ontario. Cherokee is also related to a number of Iroquoian languages that became extinct during the historic period.

Even with the great temporal and spatial separation between Cherokee and the other Iroquoian languages, they do share some common features that led writers, as early as the eighteenth century, to suggest intrafamilial relationships. For example, the Iroquoian family is one of the few language families in the world that has no bilabial stops (*b* and *p* sounds). This characteristic is quite distinct from neighboring Algonquian and Muskogean languages. Also, the Iroquoian pronominal prefixes, which are employed in every Cherokee sentence, share some easily recognizable cognates.

Cherokee has a relatively small inventory of sounds, with only seventeen meaningful units—eleven consonants and six vowels. In addition, two prosodic features, vowel length and pitch accent, also affect meaning. The absence of bilabial stops and of labio-dental spirants (*f* and *v* sounds) leaves the bilabial nasal *m* sound as the only consonant requiring lip articulation. The *m* sound has very limited distribution, occurring in fewer than ten aboriginal words. All of these are uninflected nouns with uncertain etymologies, suggesting that the *m* sound is a relatively recent addition to Cherokee. As a result, Cherokee does not have the staccato sound of English or German. All other meaningful units of sound, or *phonemes,* constitute regularly occurring correspondences with sounds of other Iroquoian languages.

Structurally, Cherokee is a polysynthetic language. As in the case of German or Latin, units of meaning, called *morphemes,* are linked together and occasionally form very long words. Cherokee verbs, constituting the most important word type, must contain as a minimum a pronominal prefix, a verb root, an aspect suffix, and a modal suffix. For example, the verb form *ke:ka,* "I am going," has each of these elements. The pronominal prefix is *k-,* which indicates first person singular. The verb root is *-e,* "to go." The aspect suffix that this verb employs for the present-tense stem is *-k-.* The present-tense modal suffix for regular verbs in Cherokee is *-a.* Verbs can also have prepronominal prefixes, reflexive prefixes, and derivative suffixes. Given all possible combinations of affixes, each regular verb can have 21,262 inflected forms.

The pronominal prefixes convey the person, number, and, in some cases, gender of both the subject and object of the verb. Except in cases where the subject and object are of the same person and number, the agreement rule serves to clarify the grammatical functions of nouns, as in the following sentences: *takhe:hi atshuhtsa ki:hli,* "The boy is chasing the dogs," and *anikhe:hi atshuhtsa ki:hli* "The dogs are chasing the boy." In the first sentence *ta-,* the pronominal prefix of the verb, indicates that the subject of the verb is singular and the object of the verb is plural. *Atshuhtsa,* "boy," is a singular form, whereas *ki:hli,* which does not have a distinct plural representation, can mean either "dog" or "dogs." Therefore the subject of the first sentence can only be "boy." By the same reasoning the subject of the second sentence must be "dogs," since the pronominal prefix *ani-* indicates that the subject is plural and the object is singular.

Five categories of aspect suffixes are discernible in Cherokee grammar: present, imperfective, perfective, imperative, and infinitive. The present-aspect suffixes indicate that the action of the verb is happening at the time of the utterance. The imperfective suffixes convey noncompletive action in either the future or past. The perfective suffixes convey completive action either future or past. The imperative suffixes are employed for immediate past action. The infinitives have no temporal association.

A modal suffix occurs in final position in all Cherokee verbs. With the exception of the suffixes added to the present and imperative stems, no class distinction is recognized by the modals. Seven of the eleven modal suffixes can be added to either the perfective or imperfective stems. Two of these distinguish between actions witnessed by the speaker and those reported to him. Others relate habitual action, intentive action, participle forms, and so forth. Cherokee also has classificatory verbs that convey not only action but the nature of the object or recipient of the action—for example, whether that object is round, flexible, long and rigid, liquid, or animate. More than forty sets of classificatory verbs have been identified.

All words that contain two or more morphemes are subject to morphophonemic rules. The most important of these is the epenthesis rule, which breaks up impermissible consonant or vowel clusters. Cherokee sentences are also subject to numerous syntactic rules. One rule, found in every sentence, requires that the pronominal prefix of the verb agree in person and number—and gender, when applicable—with both the subject and the object. Because of this rule, word order is not as rigid in Cherokee as in English.

The Cherokee writing system was devised by Sequoyah, the only person in recorded history to accomplish such a task without first being literate in at least one language. Seventy-eight of the eighty-five symbols in written Cherokee represent consonant-vowel combinations; the remainder represent the six vowels and the consonant *s*.

Today, the Overhill dialect is maintained by about thirteen thousand people in northeastern Oklahoma. The Middle dialect is now spoken by about seven hundred people on the Qualla Boundary in North Carolina. The Lower dialect is extinct; its last speaker was encountered by the ethnologist James Mooney on the Qualla Boundary in 1888. Another dialect, which shows characteristics of both the Overhill and Middle dialects, is spoken today by about three hundred fifty people in the Snowbird Community near Robbinsville, North Carolina. Cherokee speakers constitute the seventh largest group of speakers of native languages north of Mexico, and in some communities in eastern Oklahoma and western North Carolina, Cherokee is used by speakers of all ages.

See also Cherokee; Languages.

Chafe, Wallace, "Siouan, Iroquoian and Caddoan," in *Current Trends in Linguistics 10*, ed. Thomas A. Sebeok (The Hague: Mouton, 1973); King, Duane Harold, "Who Really Discovered the Cherokee-Iroquoian Relationship?" *Journal of Cherokee Studies* 2, no. 4 (1977): 401–4; King, Duane Harold, "Cherokee Classificatory Verbs," *Journal of Cherokee Studies* 3, no. 1 (1978): 40–44.

DUANE H. KING (Cherokee)
Southwest Museum, Los Angeles

CHEYENNE, NORTHERN

Oral tradition tells of a time when the people who called themselves *Tsetschestahase,* and are now called by others "Cheyenne" (probably from a Sioux word meaning "crazy talkers"), were fishermen, living in a marshy area by a large body of water, living probably very much like their more easterly Algonquian relatives. Next, they were villagers who lived in earth lodges, planted corn, and hunted without horses. Later, after migrating westward onto the Great Plains, they received from the Sacred Mountain (modern Bear Butte, South Dakota) the buffalo and developed the lifeway for which they are best known today: the classic horse-buffalo-tipi complex of the high plains. Archaeology confirms the transition from semisedentary earth-lodge villages to high-plains life, and the reinvention of Cheyenne culture in the new environment. This transformation, which probably took place in the mid–seventeenth century, included an encounter with and the incorporation of the Suhtai people. Tsetscheschahase and Suhtai, according to oral history, were able to understand each other's (Algonquian) language, and so recognized their kinship and joined together. The Suhtai brought with them their culture hero, Erect Horns, and his teachings, as well as the Sun Dance and the Sacred Hat medicine bundle that figures prominently in it. Like other tribal ceremonies, the Sun Dance was banned in the early part of this century, but was never completely lost and has undergone a modern revival. The Sacred Hat is kept today by Northern Cheyennes of Suhtai descent; it remains the preeminent spiritual icon of the Northern Cheyenne people. From the Sacred Mountain came the teachings of the culture hero Sweet Medicine and the four Sacred Arrows, now kept in Oklahoma by the Southern Cheyenne people. The famous Cheyenne Council of Forty-four also developed during the classic high-plains period. Its fame derives from the fact that, unlike many other Native American governments, the council was a vaguely representative body with conventional rules of procedure that non-Indian people could comprehend.

Today, most of the more than six thousand Northern Cheyenne people live on the reservation in southeastern Montana; others live off-reservation in urban or rural areas around the country. Though federal officials have long sought to subdue the Northern Cheyennes and settle them on a joint reservation with some other group (the Sioux, the Crows, the Southern Cheyennes), the ancestors of present-day Northern Cheyennes have always insisted on official recognition of their separate identity. The Reservation, on the Tongue River, represents their victory. The people there have held on to their native lands more tightly than most other tribes. Ninety-seven percent of the land within the reservation remains in tribal hands, most of it held in common by the tribe and in trust with the federal government.

The Northern Cheyennes were among the last Indians to accept allotment, doing so only in 1926, just eight years before the Indian Reorganization Act ended this practice for all tribes. The reservation consists of some 460,000 acres of prairie grassland and rolling timbered hills, unsuited for farming but ideal for cattle grazing. The land is rich in high-quality, low-sulfur coal. The tribe is known for its strong opposition to large-scale coal development, its communal holding of mineral rights, and its steadfast defense of the quality of its land, air, and water—as well as its quality of life—in the face of coal development in surrounding areas. The tribe is also careful to manage its timber resources by selectively harvesting trees and by repairing any forest-fire damage.

The Northern Cheyenne Reservation is divided into five districts, each of which sends representatives to a tribal council. Northern Cheyenne tribal offices and Bureau of Indian Affairs offices are located in Lame Deer, the largest town on the reservation. Dull Knife College, one of the more than two dozen tribally controlled colleges, is located in Lame Deer, as is the Northern Cheyenne public elementary school and the new Morning Star High School. Other programs such as Head Start, the tribal ambulance service, and the tribal police are also headquartered in Lame Deer. Annual events hosted by the tribe are the spring rodeo and the Memorial Day and July 4th powwows.

Though other tribes signing the Fort Laramie Treaty of 1868 gained recognition for their reservations thereby, the Northern Cheyennes did not. Their tiny original reservation on the Tongue River was created by executive order on November 26, 1884, by which time Congress had unilaterally declared an end to treaty making with Indians. The reservation's boundaries expanded to their present size as a result of another executive order, signed on March 19, 1900. Although the reservation lies within their plains homelands, the Northern Cheyenne people have not escaped dislocation and removal. Indian success in the Battle of the Little Bighorn made federal officials anxious about the continued presence of Northern Cheyenne people in the area. Pressure was brought to remove them to Oklahoma,

The Northern Cheyenne leaders Dull Knife, seated, *and Little Wolf in 1873.*

where Southern Cheyenne relatives were already situated on a reservation they shared with the Southern Arapahos. For a time the Northern Cheyennes resisted removal and amalgamation, but, with the threat of military encounter if they refused, 937 of them began a trip southward from the Red Cloud Agency on May 28, 1877, with the understanding that they would be able to return north if they were unhappy in Indian Territory. They traveled under cavalry "escort" to join the Southern Cheyennes.

Northern and Southern Cheyennes had separated earlier in the nineteenth century, mostly for reasons of trade. The Cheyenne people, however, had sustained (and continue to sustain) linguistic, cultural, and spiritual bonds through continual visits and joint ceremonial activities, and think of themselves as kin who share a common cultural tradition.

From the outset, things did not go well in Oklahoma. Provisions were inadequate to support the increased number of people on the reservation, and the Northern Cheyennes suffered from disease (within two months of their arrival, nearly two-thirds of them became sick with malaria) as well as from the heat. Northern Cheyenne chiefs asked that the people be allowed to return north, but government officials refused their persistent demands. The situation continued to deteriorate, and the people determined that they would rather die trying to return home than languish in Indian Territory. Little Wolf and Morning Star led most of the Northern Cheyenne people as they fled the Cheyenne and Arapaho Agency in 1878. As they traveled they divided into ever smaller groups to increase the likelihood that some would reach their northern homeland. They suffered great losses against huge odds—the worst coming when a captured group under Dull Knife were massacred in an attempt to escape from Fort Robinson, Nebraska—but some two hundred succeeded in returning home and winning their own reservation.

The transformation in Northern Cheyenne community and culture in the late nineteenth century is only one of many transformations that have taken place throughout Northern Cheyenne history. The people continue to change, but also to maintain both roots in and spiritual connections with their own history. Their resilience and their ability to sustain community through the incorporation of new ideas and new peoples continue to serve them well. Today, as in the past, there are many different ways of being Cheyenne, but the shared language and shared history, the Old Man Chiefs, the military societies, the Sun Dance, the Sacred Hat, and the Sacred Arrows continue to symbolize and sustain Northern Cheyenne culture.

Stands-in-Timber, John, and Margot Liberty, *Cheyenne Memories* (New Haven, Conn.: Yale University Press, 1967); Svingen, Orlan J., *The Northern Cheyenne Indian Reservation, 1877–1900* (Niwot, Colo.: University Press of Colorado, 1993).

RUBIE SOOTKIS (Northern Cheyenne)
Native American Producers Association

TERRY STRAUS
University of Chicago

CHEYENNE, SOUTHERN

Modern Tsetschestahase (Southern Cheyennes) trace their origins to the "ancient time" when they occupied the upper reaches of the Mississippi River. There they thrived on crops and woodland animals, fish and fowl.

Before 1700 an unknown disease greatly reduced their numbers, and other groups preyed upon them. Shortly after 1700 (the time of the dogs), the Tsetschestahase moved from the woodlands to the prairies of present-day eastern North Dakota. There they practiced agriculture and lived in earthen lodges.

By the mid-1750s the Sioux increased their pressure on the numerically inferior Tsetschestahase, who again headed west. In their flight, so one story goes, they destroyed one of their enemies, an unknown group of Siouan-speaking people. One captive, the wife of a slain chief, explained to the Tsetschestahase her tribe's form of government. The Tsetschestahase respected her and followed her guidance in devising their present-day form of government, a council of chiefs (initially forty-four in number) selected for their bravery, appearance, and wisdom. These chiefs represented the eleven bands of Tsetschestahase, each band electing four representatives. These leaders made important decisions regarding camp locations, intraband disputes, religious ceremonies, and war.

In the Third Age, the time of the buffalo, the Tsetschestahase adapted to the short-grass plains by hunting bison. However, they suffered more attacks from the Sioux and took refuge near the Black Hills. During this time of trouble, Maheo (Sweet Medicine) climbed Howahwas (Bear Butte), and there Maiyun (a powerful spirit) taught him. Maiyun allowed Maheo to take the Mahuts (four medicine arrows: two man arrows and two buffalo arrows, for success in defense and sustenance), the most sacred possessions of the Tsetschestahase to this day. The Mahuts, a gift from Maheo (the ruling spirit of the universe), guided and protected the Tsetschestahase on the high plains. The Mahuts command respect, and the Tsetschestahase "renew" the arrows in times of trouble, when in need of support, or to purify their nation. Once an infrequent occurrence, the Arrow Renewal Ceremony has become something of an annual ritual timed near the summer solstice.

The Tsetschestahase represented and re-created the great circle of life through their ceremonies. They divided the circle into the four directions of the universe, each representing a spiritual helper of Maheo, and the four great men's societies: initially the Kit Fox Men, the Elk (Horn) Scraper Men, the Dog Men, and the Red Shield Men, and now the Bowstrings, the Elk Horns, the Kit Foxes, and the Dog Soldiers. The Tsetschestahase have always formed gender-specific societies—for example, the Medicine Women. They performed their own rituals and ceremonies for making tipis and other medicine. The societies took their members from all the bands, and when the bands were united, the societies guided tribal affairs.

The Tsetschestahase symbolized their sense of family in the circular arrangements inside their lodges, in the circle of the ceremonial lodges, and in the great circular setting of a village. Pairs of forces (male and female, life and death, light and darkness, hot and cold) moved in seasonal cycles, and they represented, and still represent, these forces in their ceremonies. Time and life moved in great cycles balanced by countervailing forces.

Around 1800 the Tsetschestahase merged with the Suhtais; the two groups had been enemies until each recognized a common identity in their similar languages. The Suhtais, bison hunters, instructed the Tsetschestahase, who had acquired the horse. The Tsetschestahase, now a horse-borne bison-hunting culture, abandoned nearly all of their agriculture. The Suhtais also taught the Tsetschestahase the Oxheheom (the Sun Dance ceremony), and the rituals and sacred traditions associated with the teachings of Tomsivsi (Erect Horns) about the Issiwum (Buffalo Cap). As the Tsetschestahase moved west they encountered the people who were to become one of their principal allies, the Arapahos. These two peoples, while sharing and maintaining a defensive and trade alliance, retained separate identities, and even pitched their lodges in different camp circles when occupying the same ground.

Between 1810 and 1830 the Hevatanui band moved from the Black Hills to the Arkansas River valley, while the Omisi band and the Suhtais remained north of the Platte River. The Hevatanui band became the Southern Cheyennes. Though retaining a strong identification with their northern brothers and sisters, they took on a distinct identity. For example, the northerners kept the Issiwum, while the southerners held the Mahuts, and both practiced the Oxheheom. Between 1830 and 1840, the southerners dominated the central high plains between the South Platte and Arkansas Rivers. They fought the Pawnees to the east, the Utes to the west, and the Comanches, Kiowas, and Plains Apaches to the south. In 1840, the Southern Cheyennes and Arapahos negotiated a peace with their southern foes. The terms established a prolific trade in horses, guns, mules, manufactured goods, furs, and whiskey among themselves, Americans, and the *comancheros* (New Mexican traders).

At the conclusion of the Mexican-American war, the Tsetschestahase faced new difficulties. In 1849 a cholera epidemic swept through the population, killing perhaps half of the tribe. Increased traffic on the Santa Fe Trail and in the watersheds of the Smoky and Republican Hill Rivers destroyed winter-camping and hunting grounds. The Tsetschestahase, especially the Dog Soldiers society, fought to save their land, while the peace chiefs desperately tried to reach some means of accommodation with representatives of the U.S. government. The Fort Laramie Treaty of 1851, known among the Tsetschestahase as the Big Treaty or the Fitzpatrick Treaty, formally recognized the Tsetschestahases' range and promised annuities and army protection from depredations as long as the Tsetschestahase allowed immigrants safe passage. However, by the 1850s the decline of the bison, the destruction of their winter-camping grounds, and the flourishing of the whiskey trade had reduced the Tsetschestahase to near starvation.

Some Tsetschestahase, led by Black Kettle and Yellow Wolf, secured federal help to return to farming in the Fort Wise Treaty of 1861. The Civil War resulted in a poor effort by the Bureau of Indian Affairs to build an irrigation system and plant crops. Funding evaporated, and the Tsetschestahase never derived any benefit from this operation. As conditions deteriorated, the Dog Soldiers continued their depredations on Americans and other tribal peoples. The result was tragedy when on November 29, 1864, Colonel John M. Chivington and his Colorado volunteers needlessly attacked the peaceful Tsetschestahase (led by Black Kettle, Yellow Wolf, and One Eye) and the Southern Arapahos (led by Left Hand) at Sand Creek. No one knows exactly how many Tsetschestahase were massacred; perhaps as many as 160 perished.

The Tsetschestahase continued to suffer in a pattern of assaults, followed by negotiations. The Little Arkansas River (1865) and Medicine Lodge (1867) treaties were followed by General Winfield Hancock's campaign in 1867 and Custer's attack on Black Kettle's peaceful village encampment on the banks of the Washita River in present-day western Oklahoma in November 1868. By 1869 the U.S. Army had defeated the Dog Soldiers under the leadership of Tall Bull, which ended the confrontations between the army and the Tsetschestahase.

The Bureau of Indian Affairs placed the Tsetschestahase on what was initially a 5-million-acre reservation in present-day Oklahoma. Based at Darlington, the agent John D. Miles attempted to convert the Tsetschestahase to Christianity, ranching, farming, freighting, and American notions of education. Missionaries, too, soon arrived to "save" the "savages."

However, educational gains often proved intangible. Tsetschestahase trained in the manual arts lacked job opportunities, and women trained according to middle-class domestic values had little use for such skills in their reservation homes.

The Tsetschestahase had some success in the freighting business, and despite being poorly supplied by the federal government, they prospered at cattle ranching. However, competition for grazing land led a Texas drover to kill Running Buffalo, an influential Dog Soldier who opposed Texan leasing operations on the Cheyenne Reservation. Only the appearance of federal troops prevented further bloodshed. Tsetschestahase even fought among themselves. Their reservation lands came under assault with the passage of the Dawes Severalty Act in 1887, which allotted 160 acres to each Tsetschestahase. In the early 1890s the federal government surveyed the reservation, and in April 1892 Anglo-Americans began buying the "surplus" lands. By 1900 "reform" had failed as only 15 to 18 percent of the Tsetschestahase were practicing farming; Chief White Shield's band of 186 people were still living in tipis and tents at the Red Moon district near Hammon.

The Tsetschestahase had reached their cultural nadir. They no longer practiced their Corn Dance, a ceremony largely conducted by women. In the 1890s a few practiced the Ghost Dance, and others who explored the religious use of peyote encountered frequent arrests and trials. American teachers forced Tsetschestahase children to speak only English, and Christian missionaries discouraged traditional religious ceremonies, social practices, and beliefs. In 1927 the Tsetschestahase performed the last Massaum ceremony, an ancient dance perhaps predating their woodland origins.

Still, in the first half of the twentieth century young Tsetschestahase proved resilient by adapting to a new set of social circumstances. The young received counsel such as "Go to school. Learn to provide for your family." And many attended church-related schools that had ties to the religious mission to the Tsetschestahase. In the 1930s the Tsetschestahase formed a business council in keeping with Commissioner of Indian Affairs John Collier's reforms during the New Deal. The Tsetschestahase served proudly in the U.S. armed forces during both world wars and in Korea, Vietnam, and the Gulf War. At the same time, they withstood Bureau of Indian Affairs attempts to terminate their tribe and relocate them to large urban areas.

In the 1960s, stimulated by the civil rights movement, the Tsetschestahase actively asserted themselves. Today, they proudly celebrate religious ceremonies like the Sun Dance and the Arrow Renewal Ceremony. They also engage in elaborate giveaways and powwows in which the sealing of position and leadership results in people giving away their possessions to those in need while others shower an "honored" one with gifts in recognition of that person's high status. The Tsetschestahase are actively working to recover their culture through community efforts and activities. In the summer of 1992, under the Native American Graves Protection and Repatriation Act, Tsetschestahase repatriated remains stored at the Smithsonian Institution, some of which belonged to identified victims of the Sand Creek massacre.

The Tsetschestahase are still working to overcome numerous threats to their identity and culture. Many fail to graduate from high school and often find themselves in legal and economic difficulties. Others face serious drinking and drug problems. Nonetheless, Tsetschestahase show remarkable resilience in the face of nearly overwhelming discrimination and economic obstacles. Youths often excel in public schools, colleges, and universities and work with adults to maintain the "Cheyenne way." The Tsetschestahase continue to renew themselves, their families, and their ways in the great circle of life.

Berthrong, Donald J., *The Southern Cheyennes* (Norman: University of Oklahoma Press, 1963); Berthrong, Donald J., *The Cheyenne and Arapaho Ordeal: Reservation and Agency Life in the Indian Territory, 1875–1907* (Norman: University of Oklahoma Press, 1976).

JAMES E. SHEROW
Kansas State University

SAM HART (Southern Cheyenne)
El Reno, Oklahoma

CHICKASAW

The story of the Chickasaws begins somewhere in the dim past, perhaps in what is now Mexico. According to legend, the people followed a sacred leaning pole, which they erected each day. When the pole no longer leaned, they knew they had found their new home. The land occupied by the Chickasaw Nation once comprised tens of thousands of square miles in the southeastern United States.

This land was coveted by the North American colonial powers—Spain, France, and England—and alliances and battles were joined and fought with the

Chickasaws and other tribal nations throughout the seventeenth century. The United States entered this mix in the eighteenth century and eventually consolidated its power enough to significantly influence the Chickasaws and other southeastern tribes.

With increasing white settlement during the early part of the nineteenth century, the U.S. government forced the southeastern tribes to move to the West on the Trail of Tears. Some forty-nine hundred Chickasaws and eleven hundred of their slaves settled in the Choctaw Nation (in what is now Oklahoma) until the tribe received sufficient government annuities to buy land immediately west of the Choctaws. In 1856 the Chickasaw leadership drafted and ratified a constitution at the tribe's new capital, Tishomingo. The first Chickasaw governor was Cyrus Harris, who had been born in Mississippi.

The next challenge to the Chickasaw Nation came in the latter part of the nineteenth century, by which time white settlers outnumbered Chickasaws on their own land many times over. This time Congress, instead of forcing the tribe to move again, carved up the Chickasaw Nation into individual allotments, in violation of treaty agreements. Although the tribe resisted this idea, land allotments proceeded after the turn of the century. Congress effectively gutted Chickasaw tribal government by 1906—except for the federally appointed governor and tribal attorneys to preside over what was intended to be a final liquidation.

That liquidation never happened. Douglas Johnston, the twelfth Chickasaw governor, dutifully protected the tribe's interests until his death in 1939. Ten years later, Congress finally appropriated $8.5 million for the tribe and its Choctaw Nation partners for their jointly owned 350,000 acres of coal- and asphalt-rich land and $3.5 million for some disputed land called the "leased district." Most of this money was dispensed to tribal members as a per capita payment.

By 1950, however, grassroots movements within the old Chickasaw and Choctaw Nations had sprung up, calling for democratic forms of tribal government. The leader of the movement in the Chickasaw Nation, Overton James, was appointed governor in 1963. Starting with virtually no records and assets, James began building a tribal government just as the federal government began funneling millions of dollars to tribes to bolster tribal governments and social and economic services to tribal members. In 1971, in the first federally recognized Chickasaw tribal election since 1904, James was elected governor.

In 1979 the Chickasaw Nation adopted a new constitution establishing a three-branch government. After some court challenges by tribal members, a modified form of the constitution was ratified by the members and approved by the U.S. government in 1983. After twenty-four years as governor, Overton James retired in 1987, and his lieutenant governor, Bill Anoatubby, was elected to replace him.

Early Chickasaw tribal life was matrilineal and clan centered. A mixed economy based on corn agriculture also included warfare and trade as principal pursuits. Prosperous fortified towns featured both open-sided summer houses and comfortable wattle and daub winter dwellings. Healing ceremonies called pashofa dances and annual green corn renewal observances were held to ensure tribal harmony and well-being. Stickball, a rough-and-tumble game related to lacrosse, was played to help settle community differences, and was sometimes used as a substitute for war. Warfare was highly regarded, and Chickasaw forces dominated much of the mid-South region.

Today the government of the Chickasaw Nation is composed of executive, legislative, and judicial departments that provide economic, social, educational, and cultural services to thirty-five thousand tribal members. Located in thirteen counties in south central Oklahoma, the Chickasaw Nation as of August 31, 1994, had assets totaling $35 million.

GARY WHITE DEER (Chickasaw)
Ada, Oklahoma

CHILD REARING

In spite of the wide diversity of Native American cultures, early accounts reveal numerous cross-cultural similarities in Native American perspectives on child rearing. These include: allowing children to learn through their own observations; relying strongly on nonverbal cues rather than verbal directions; engaging the spiritual world in the child-rearing process by praying, chanting, and singing, as well as by conferring special names to give children guidance and power; educating children for their future roles by including them from infancy in all social, economic, and ritual activities; giving children the same range of freedom of behavior as adults; using stories to provide an understanding of the world and its relationships, both those between individuals and that between man and nature;

Cheyenne girls circa 1900 playing with dolls and miniature tipis. With these models, mothers prepared their daughters for the tasks of adult life—which for women included tipi construction.

respecting the individuality and desires of children to the same degree that those are respected in adults; teaching children their responsibilities to each member of their kinship group; allowing children to fulfill their physical needs such as sleeping, eating, and physical activity with minimal adult direction or restraint; impressing children with their roles in society through marking their passage into new stages of development with public ceremonies, especially at puberty.

Underlying these characteristics is a view of children, from birth, as full participants in society, with a standing equal to that of adults. This attitude is a reflection of the religious orientation of Native Americans, in which all things in nature are accorded equal respect, be they inanimate or animate. Consequently, children

were not expected to be supervised by adults but to be free like their elders, their freedom limited only by social obligations. As a result, child-care practices emphasized a responsiveness to the wishes of the child. For example, children were usually toilet trained when they were ready, and not according to a schedule based on adult needs, and in some societies children nursed for as long as five to seven years. Thus Native Americans allowed children to fit themselves into the social order, rarely using corporal punishment or other coercive methods to force conformity.

At the time of contact with Europeans, most Native Americans lived in face-to-face communities where people knew one another. Child training was aided by shared values and an extended kinship system that tied an individual to all members of the society, either by descent or marriage, or through formal religious or social affiliations. As a consequence, all adults shared some responsibility for socializing the society's children.

While Native American societies shared a broadly common orientation, nomadic hunting and gathering societies expressed these general values more fully than sedentary, horticultural societies, which had larger populations and more hierarchical social structures, and in which survival required more difficult and time-consuming work. However, most societies, regardless of their economic systems, were organized for subsistence, requiring all people to contribute to the group according to their ability. Children represented the continuation of society, and their accomplishments signified the group's potential to endure. The importance and centrality of children was reflected in the public celebration of events in a child's life, such as a child's first steps, a girl's first menstrual cycle, or a boy's search for his spiritual helper at puberty.

In native societies, the adults primarily responsible for child care were often not the parents. In hunting and gathering societies, it was more practical for grandparents to rear children too young to participate in economic activities. For example, among such tribes as the Arapahos, Gros Ventres, Blackfeet, and Sioux of the northern plains, grandparents prepared and cooked the food, did the household chores, and took care of the children. Grandparents were also repositories of cultural knowledge and wisdom, which they passed on to their grandchildren through instruction and stories. In these societies, children's individuality was allowed maximum expression and child training was minimally coercive. Strong emotional ties and intimate, teasing relationships also tended to develop between these children and their grandparents.

Although men in northern Plains cultures were frequently expected to be warriors and hunters, they spent a great deal of time with their children when they were at home, especially with their sons. In societies that placed a premium on individual initiative and personal skill, they taught young boys to make tools such as spears, shields, and bows and arrows, and encouraged them to practice by hunting small animals around their village. Thus from early childhood, boys' play activities helped prepare them for their adult roles.

In these societies, as soon as they were old enough, girls were taught by their grandmothers and mothers to make moccasins, clothing, and lodge coverings, and to participate in daily chores such as preparing food and carrying water. Girls were also responsible for the care of their younger siblings, and strong emotional attachments developed between younger and older siblings, who spent a great deal of time in each other's company. Girls and boys were generally allowed to interact until they reached puberty. At puberty, girls were secluded in a menstrual hut and female relatives instructed them in homemaking skills and proper behavior. At the end of this time, girls were ready for marriage.

Among such tribes as the Blackfeet and Crows, there are also accounts of men having strong and loving relationships with favorite daughters, whom they would take with them on hunting and raiding forays. As a result, some girls became proficient in male activities and a few women became noted warriors and leaders.

In some nomadic societies, children went to live with other relatives; most often boys went to live with uncles. Children were sometimes given in adoption to other families who had lost children, or to older people who had no descendants to take care of them. In the fluid world of hunters and gatherers, adoption of both children and adults was frequent, and adoptees were accepted as fully as if they had been born into the family.

Horticultural societies such as the Pueblos and the Iroquois frequently traced kinship through mothers. These matrilineal kinship systems assigned the mother's brother the task of training male children. In these societies, children belonged to the mother's kinship group, and the father belonged to another clan (his mother's clan). It was thus necessary for a male from the mother's clan (the mother's brother) to be responsible for training boys to assume their responsibilities in the clan. For example, among the Hopis, the men cultivated the fields owned by their wife's clan. Around the age of ten, sons began to learn to cultivate crops by working alongside their fathers. But it was the maternal uncle who was primarily responsible for socializing children, especially boys. The maternal uncle educated boys to fulfill their obligations to other members of their kinship group, preparing them for the ritual roles of their clan and for initiation into social fraternities. Maternal uncles were also the primary disciplinarians of Hopi children and as a result were the most respected and sometimes feared members of a child's kin group. The Hopi father-son relationship was more relaxed and affectionate.

Hopi girls had a close relationship with their mothers, who trained them in their household duties. Grinding corn, the food that was most central to their survival, was the most time-consuming and difficult work they had to do. Nevertheless, instruction was not didactic but cooperative. Women and girls sang songs as they ground their corn, sharing a common burden, the women teaching by example. Not surprisingly, corn grinding was also one of the main components of the girls' ceremonies at puberty and marriage.

In many societies, it was believed that children were reincarnated ancestors and that if they were not treated well, they would leave. In such societies, coercive methods were avoided for fear the child would die. However, there are Native American examples of coercive methods, including corporal punishment. Parents who exercised this type of control were likely to deflect their children's frustration and anger from themselves by telling them that a spirit would take them away if they did not do what they were told. Among the Hopis, it was primarily the mother's brother who punished children for misbehavior. Men dressed as kachinas, powerful beings in Hopi mythology, also whipped children of both sexes in their first initiation ceremony, which took place when they were from six to ten years of age. Among the Nez Perces, there was a "Whipperman" who disciplined children by switching them in groups. The most severe example of parental control of children's behavior was the Ojibwa enforcement of ritual fasting, which children were made to undertake periodically for a day at a time beginning around the age of four or five to prepare them psychologically for the scarcity of food that occurred during the winter.

Because parents did not usually take on disciplinary tasks, Native American societies often relied upon peer pressure to control children's behavior. In most societies, a child was a member of an extended family and was usually raised in the company of many peers. If a child did things to bring attention to himself, peers shamed him into conformity. When corporal punishment was used among the Hopis and the Nez Perces, children were usually disciplined in peer groups, even though only one child might be guilty of misbehavior. By punishing an entire group, adults could rely on children to control each other's behavior.

The basic values underlying traditional cultural approaches to child rearing are still evident in Native America. This fact is particularly evident where people have remained in their own communities and traditional religious practices have persisted. However, contact with nonnative influences has tended to dilute these perspectives, undermining community standards. Today the contrast between native and European childrearing strategies is not as strong as it once was. Many

social workers assert that the disjuncture between traditional practices and contemporary conditions has contributed to social and educational difficulties.

See also Birth; Families.

Landes, Ruth, *The Ojibwa Woman* (New York: AMS Press, 1969); Sandoz, Mari, *These Were the Sioux* (New York: Hastings House, 1961); Simmons, Leo W., ed., *Sun Chief: The Autobiography of a Hopi Indian* (New Haven, Conn.: Yale University Press, 1942).

MARILYN G. BENTZ (Gros Ventre)
University of Washington

CHILOCCO INDIAN SCHOOL

Chilocco was an Indian boarding school established in 1884 by the U.S. government to educate children of the nomadic tribes of western Oklahoma. The original school was built on 8,320 acres purchased from the Cherokees, in modern-day Kay County, near the Kansas border.

At its opening, the school offered education through the eighth grade. The school was based on the "industrial" plan, which offered a half day of instruction in academic subjects and a half day of vocational instruction and work. Boys primarily studied agricultural pursuits, and girls learned domestic arts. Under this plan, the school produced most of its food and many other items it needed.

The school soon expanded to include all Indian children in Indian Territory except those of the Five Civilized Tribes, and grew from one building in 1884 to thirty-five buildings in 1907. After 1910, Chilocco also admitted children from the Five Civilized Tribes. By 1916, the school offered education through the tenth grade. In the late 1930s the lower elementary grades had been eliminated, though junior and senior high school education continued. Instruction was cut back to high school classes only after World War II. Between 1930 and 1959, the school's annual enrollment averaged between eight hundred and twelve hundred students. Chilocco closed in June 1980, amid considerable opposition from Indian parents.

Ironically, although it was intended to transform nomadic Indians into "civilized" American farmers and citizens, Chilocco actually reinforced Indian and tribal identity among its students. It trained leaders of the western Oklahoma tribes for almost a century and created bonds of friendship between children of different tribes. Chilocco helped create a Pan-Indian identity among the Indian people in Oklahoma.

See also Boarding Schools; Education.

CHIPPEWA
See Ojibwa.

CHOCTAW

The Choctaws have two stories about their origins in their traditional homeland in central Mississippi. One is that their ancestors came from west of the Mississippi River and settled in what is now the homeland. The other is that the tribe is descended from ancestors who were formed by a spirit from the damp earth of Nanih Waiyah, a large mound in northeastern Mississippi.

The stories correspond in some details with evidence from archaeology and history. Some of the ancestors of the Choctaws probably lived in northwestern Alabama in a large village that archaeologists now call Moundville. By the late 1500s, the people of this community had moved on to other places because their homeland could no longer produce sufficient food. Most probably lived along the Tombigbee River in what is now northeastern Mississippi.

Other ancestors of the Choctaws probably did come from west of the Mississippi. During the eighteenth century people moved regularly back and forth across the river, and by the early nineteenth century a number of Choctaws lived in the west near the Arkansas River. The differing origins of the Choctaws probably explain why their territory comprised three districts, each with its own chief; the three chiefs governed jointly.

Both in Mississippi and later in the West, the Choctaws were farmers whose villages were composed of log houses surrounded by cornfields. Men hunted, and women raised the crops, although men sometimes helped with clearing the fields. Each village had a chief who met with a council of elders and experienced men in a square at the center of the village. The younger men made up the hunters and warriors of the tribe. They defended their territory against the Chickasaw tribe in the north, whose language was very similar to theirs but who considered themselves very separate from the Choctaws, and from the Creeks on the east.

Conflicts between villagers, and sometimes with other tribes, were generally settled by sport rather than war. The stickball game (a forerunner of the modern game of lacrosse) pitted teams from different villages against each other. Winning was a matter not only of skill but of the power of the villages' spiritual leaders to influence the outcome through their prayers and powers.

The Choctaws's major deity was the sun, a spiritual being whose earthly representative was fire. Their form of burial of the dead was to expose the body on a raised platform, where it decayed, offering its essence back to the sun. The *alikchi* were men with individual spiritual powers. They could foretell the future and affect people's lives by curing illness. They were also often suspected of using their power for evil ends.

Choctaw society was organized in two major divisions, or *iksas*—the kashapa okla or Imoklasha, and the okla in holahta or *hattak in holahta*—that regulated marriage. Children belonged to their mother's *iksa,* and people were required to marry into the opposite *iksa.* Political power passed through the woman's line as a chief's nephew, his sister's son, generally inherited his power.

The Choctaws met their first Europeans in 1541. Between 1539 and 1541 Hernando de Soto and some six hundred Spanish soldiers traveled from Tampa Bay to the Mississippi River, where de Soto died of a fever and his body was thrown into the river. Although the contact was limited, it probably introduced European diseases that had an effect on the population and location of Choctaw villages.

The next European immigrants into Choctaw territory were representatives of French and English colonial governments who appeared at the end of the seventeenth century. Choctaw men discovered that the deerskins that their women tanned were desirable trade items for European men. Throughout the Choctaw territory, men began to trade skins for cloth, weapons, ammunition, and iron cooking utensils.

These trade relationships and attempts by colonial agents to secure military alliances with the Choctaws ultimately led to a division within the tribe of those villages that traded with the French and those that traded with the English. A civil war led to a final victory for the villages allied with the French, and peace was restored by 1750. But the French ultimately lost their war with the British in the Ohio Valley (the French and Indian War of American history), and they were forced to give up their claims in America (and their alliance with the Choctaws) through the Treaty of Paris in 1763.

The English now controlled the trade with tribes in the Southeast, but American settlers, who were moving steadily westward from North Carolina and Kentucky, entered Choctaw territory and added another element to tribal life. They married Choctaw women and produced mixed-blood families. They also introduced domesticated cattle and established trading posts that attracted other white men into Choctaw country. The cattle reduced dependence on deer meat for those who raised them. The trading posts changed the Choctaws's dependence on skins for clothing to a dependence on cloth as skins became the marker of trade value.

During the Revolutionary War, Choctaw leaders remained largely neutral, although some agreed to report the movement of English forces along the Mississippi River. Although American colonists won the war against their British governors, the Spanish still controlled the land below the thirty-first parallel in Florida and all the lands west of the Mississippi River. The Choctaws quickly signed treaties both with the American government in 1786 and with the Spanish in 1784 and 1793. This new balance of power did not last long, however, for by 1803 Thomas Jefferson had negotiated the purchase of the Louisiana Territory from France, which had acquired it from Spain two years before. The Louisiana Purchase isolated the Choctaws from many Spanish allies and set off an American campaign to remove all the Indian nations east of the Mississippi River to the western lands.

The Choctaws had seen the impact of white settlement on their territory since colonial times. War with the Creek Indians on their eastern boundary had led to the decline of the deer population and a loss of hunting lands. The development of cotton growing in the rich Mississippi Delta region began to cut off their access to hunting in that area. In 1805, the Choctaws signed a treaty ceding a stretch of land that bordered on Spanish territory in Florida. The fledgling U.S. government was anxious to secure its borders against the threat of Spanish intervention in the South and was happy to separate tribes like the Choctaws from potential international patrons.

In 1816 Choctaw leaders signed a treaty ceding land along their eastern boundary, the Tombigbee River. The cession was small, but the implications were important. The annual income from that treaty provided partial support for schools established by the American Board of Commissioners for Foreign Missions. Tribal leaders and white men with Choctaw families supported the idea of education because they believed it would improve the Choctaws's ability to deal with the U.S. government and with the white people who were settling in the surrounding territory.

If the Choctaws saw education as providing an opportunity to live with their white neighbors, the federal government saw it as a way of assimilating Indians into white society. Those who would not learn white ways could be moved to the western territory beyond the Mississippi. Choctaws, however, lived and farmed on both sides of the river. Government agents tried to convince the Choctaws to sign a treaty giving up their lands east of the Mississippi. When they refused, Andrew Jackson, chief negotiator for the United States, threatened to make a treaty only with the western Choctaws, who were by this time quite a separate group.

In 1820, Choctaw leaders acknowledged Jackson's threats and signed a treaty ceding their lands in Mississippi in exchange for approximately 13 million acres in what is now the state of Oklahoma. Although the 1820 treaty called for them to move to the western lands, most Choctaws remained in Mississippi. By 1825, white settlers were moving onto the western lands, and a group of Choctaw leaders went to Washington, D.C., where they signed a treaty agreeing to an adjustment that moved the eastern border of these lands, in what was then Oklahoma, to its present location along the eastern border of the state.

When it became obvious, however, that most Choctaws would not voluntarily leave their homes in Mississippi, government agents again put pressure on tribal leaders to sign a treaty agreeing to move west. Tribal leaders were deeply divided over the prospect of removal. A power struggle broke out in the northeast district of the tribe between David Folsom, son of a Scotch Irish father and a Choctaw mother, and Mushulatubbee, the last of the full-blood chiefs of the tribe (Pushmataha and Apuckshanubbee, the other two full-blood chiefs, had died during the 1825 trip to Washington). At a council in 1826, David Folsom and the chief of the southern district agreed to step aside in favor of the election of Greenwood LeFlore, son of a French father and a mixed-blood Choctaw mother, as sole leader of the Choctaws. LeFlore personified the effect of European influence on the Choctaws. He supported missionaries and education. His position as sole chief represented the influence of white society upon the tribe and the decline of the traditional tripartite leadership. The council also adopted a written constitution calling for a form of elected, representative government, a significant change from the custom of councils composed of all the adult men of the tribe.

This change from the traditional three divisions of leadership almost led to a civil war. This conflict gave Andrew Jackson the opportunity to convince a small group of Choctaw leaders to accept removal. In September 1830, near Dancing Rabbit Creek in northeastern

Mississippi, Indian Office officials held a treaty council. After most of the Choctaws at the treaty ground had rejected the idea of removal and gone home, this group of leaders signed a treaty in which they agreed to move from the state and go to the western lands.

The Treaty of Dancing Rabbit Creek set most of the Choctaws on what is now called the Trail of Tears—a trip, often reluctantly taken, to the Mississippi and along the rivers that led into Indian Territory. It was a time of great suffering for most of those who traveled from Mississippi. The majority made the trip in the winter of 1831–32, a time of bitter cold. Almost a quarter died along the way from exposure to the weather and outbreaks of cholera. When they settled in the new homeland along the western banks of the Arkansas River, they did not have adequate supplies of food or medicine, and after they had planted corn the following spring, the river flooded, destroying the crops.

Despite the hardships, the Choctaws reestablished their tribal government in the West. They wrote a new constitution in 1834. The missionaries who had established their schools in Mississippi accompanied them, but by 1842 the Choctaw government had taken control of the schools, although missionaries still staffed them. By 1861, the Choctaws had a representative form of government, and Cyrus Kingsbury, head of the Choctaw Presbyterian mission, described the tribe as Christianized in its practices, although church membership was far from universal. Choctaw was still the working language of the tribe, and many people still hunted as well as farmed.

Not all the Choctaws left Mississippi in 1831–32. The Treaty of Dancing Rabbit Creek had included a provision to appeal to its signers, the fourteenth article: any Choctaw who did not want to move west could remain in Mississippi, register with the government agent for an allotment, receive title to the land, and remain as a citizen of the state. Yet very few of those who stayed behind actually received title to their lands. They became sharecroppers and wage laborers and sustained their communities through traditional stickball games, funeral ceremonies, and attendance at Christian church ceremonies, where Choctaw ministers preached in their language and where they could sing their hymns in Choctaw.

In 1887 Congress passed the General Allotment Act, which would end the communal land-holding patterns of Indian tribes and give individual tribal members title to their lands under the legal system of the United States. Under that act, the lands of the Choctaw tribe in Oklahoma were divided, and in 1907, when Oklahoma became a state, the right of the tribe to govern itself ended.

In 1903 the Dawes Commission, which was overseeing the allocation of land to individual Choctaws, encouraged those tribal members still living in Mississippi to move to Oklahoma. About three hundred did so, but about one thousand stayed behind. In 1918, Congress finally appropriated funds to buy lands in Mississippi so the remaining Choctaws could have their own homeland once again.

The Choctaw Nation of Oklahoma and the Mississippi Band of Choctaw Indians today have separate governments, a heritage of their separate historical experiences. They are now beginning to establish a sense of their shared origins.

The Mississippi Band of Choctaw Indians has, since the 1970s, been able to attract manufacturing firms to their reservation lands. The reservation population is now about five thousand. In Oklahoma, the tribal government runs a resort area on Lake Texoma. The tribal governments, so long separated by the terms of a treaty, have reestablished contact to talk about their mutual projects. The Oklahoma tribe sponsors regular bus trips to Mississippi for tribal members who want to rediscover their heritage in the east.

See also Five Civilized Tribes; Trail of Tears; Treaty of Dancing Rabbit Creek (1830).

Debo, Angie, *The Rise and Fall of the Choctaw Republic* (Norman: University of Oklahoma Press, 1934); DeRosier, Arthur H., Jr., *The Removal of the Choctaw Indians* (New York: Harper & Row, 1972); White, Richard, *Roots of Dependency: Subsistence, Environment, and Social Change among the Choctaws, Pawnees and Navajos* (Lincoln: University of Nebraska Press, 1983).

CLARA SUE KIDWELL (Choctaw/Chippewa)
University of Oklahoma

CHUMASH

The Chumash Indian culture of south central California was actually a network of seventy-five to one hundred hunting, fishing, and gathering communities who spoke eight related languages and numbered between twenty thousand and thirty thousand members on the eve of Spanish arrival. These politically independent Chumash villages of various sizes were concentrated in three regions spread over an area encompassing seven thousand square miles.

Most numerous and largest were the coastal Chumash villages dotting 250 miles of shoreline between present-day San Luis Obispo and Oxnard, with creek mouths and estuaries the most desirable locations. There were the island Chumashes, occupying the four channel islands of Santa Cruz, Santa Rosa, San Miguel, and Anacapa. Finally, there were the interior settlements, located up to seventy-five miles into the mountainous valleys of present-day Santa Barbara County. At the conceptual center of this landscape was Mount Pinos, the Chumashes' sacred 8,831-foot peak just to the east of the present-day city of Santa Barbara.

Chumash culture developed over many hundreds of years. Archaeologists identify the so-called Millingstone Indians of about ten thousand years ago as probable Chumash ancestors. Over time their egalitarian way of life produced the most complex, stratified society of hunters and gatherers in California. By the sixteenth century the spread-out Chumash communities were knit together by common customs and shared symbols, similar social and political systems, a far-reaching trade network, and a sense of national identity.

Every Chumash village was governed by its *wot*, or chief—a position that generally was inherited through the male line. Among the *wot's* principal duties was caring for the indigent and elderly among his people. A larger community—such as Syuhtun, at present-day Santa Barbara, or Shisholop, at present-day Ventura—might have several *wots* whose other duties included assigning hunting and foraging areas, passing on requests from other Chumashes to gather food in their territory, and making sure that sufficient supplies were set aside for religious and social festivals.

A typical Chumash village would feature fifteen to fifty tallish, bowl-shaped tule-thatched houses roughly aligned along a street. Inside the houses were woven mats, fur blankets, beautiful handmade hardwood bowls, and elegant soapstone pots decorated with shell beads. Paths led to other special-use areas, such as the community's game-playing field for intervillage tournaments and sacred enclosures for rituals. Beside many houses stood a *temascal*, a mud-coated, dome-shaped cleansing sweat bath that most Chumashes enjoyed daily. Close by the *wot's* house was a granary for stockpiling food for distribution among his neediest people.

Since Chumash society was patrilineal and patrilocal, all of any village's married women would have come from other villages, thereby producing kinship connections across village lines. Chumash society was divided into three classes, with craft specialists organized into guilds on one rung, astrologers and priests on another, and on top the *wot* lineages. These chiefs were assisted by their special messengers, the *ksen,* and assisting them in meeting their responsibilities was the community *paxa,* a ceremonial official who oversaw key religious rites, such as the fall's acorn harvest festival and the winter solstice rites.

Performers at these collective ceremonies belonged to the prestigious *antap* ritual society. Their members were recruited from high-born families and initiated as children by learning secret dances and songs. In addition the Chumashes had shamans who mediated between tribal members and the spirit world. They cured the sick, interpreted dreams, and guided vision seekers during *toloache*-drinking rituals, when the highly dangerous hallucinogenic was used to enable Chumashes to make direct appeals to their spirit helpers.

It is often suggested that the celebrated rock art of the Chumashes was applied during these *toloache* rites. Located throughout sandstone rock shelters and valley caves in the interior valleys, and generally near freshwater sources, Chumash rock paintings featured animal-like beings, fishes and birds, and what look like astronomical phenomena—stars and planets. Chumash rock art stands out in its varied palette and stylistic complexity. Pulverizing various colored rocks produced red, white, blue, green, yellow, gray, and brown, with black coming from charcoal. Animal fat or milkweed sap bound the colored powders together before they were applied with stiff feathers or fiber brushes.

Benefiting from their exceedingly rich, varied habitat, Chumash hunters, fishermen, and foragers fully exploited their marine, coastal, and river resources. In unique redwood-planked boats known as *tomols,* lashed together with thongs and waterproofed by the natural asphalt that leaks out of the region's beaches, they regularly conveyed resources from their offshore islands to the mainland. Known as the Brotherhood of the Tomol, these mariners imported specialized stone blades and drills manufactured on the islands, plus marine resources such as shark, bonito, and halibut.

On the open sea and along the rivers, Chumash fishermen used a variety of nets, traps, baskets, hooks, spears, and plant poisons to catch or stun fish and catch seals and sea otters. On the coast they collected abalone and mussels, while inland they hunted small animals, deer, bear, and mountain lions. Foremost among the nuts and seeds they gathered in season was the staple of the Chumash diet, oak acorns, which were processed using a variety of baskets. Indeed, Chumash basketry rivals any in California, with women employing coiling, twining, and wickerwork techniques to create gift baskets, grinding baskets, and storage baskets that can hold five to six gallons of water when protected by linings of natural asphalt.

On the mainland the Chumash trade network passed to the interior raw marine materials such as fish, whale bones, and oils. Black soapstone, quarried from Santa Catalina Island, changed hands eastward to the Colorado River in exchange for materials made or harvested by Yuman-speaking peoples. Chumash shell beads, cut and smoothened from purple Olivella shells, were sent north to the Salinans, east to the Yokuts, and south to the Mohaves.

Although the Portuguese conquistador Juan Rodriguez Cabrillo first encountered the Chumashes in 1542, it was not until 1772 that five Catholic missions were established within the Chumash Nation; Mission Santa Inez was the last to be built, in 1808. But the Chumashes bristled at the harsh Spanish regime and staged short-lived rebellions in 1824 at Santa Inez, La Purissima, and Santa Barbara. After the secularization of the missions in 1833, the Chumash population fell into severe decline, with 250 Indians left around the outskirts of Mission Santa Barbara by 1839. In 1901 the U.S. government allocated seventy-five acres along Zanja de Cota Creek near Mission Santa Ynez to the surviving Chumash community. Over the following decades the tribe's numbers steadily increased. Today the Chumashes have their own business council, a thriving bingo operation, and a federal housing program on their small reservation; there are approximately five thousand people who now proudly identify themselves as Chumash Indians.

See also California Tribes.

Blackburn, Thomas C., *December's Child: A Book of Chumash Oral Narratives* (Berkeley, Calif.: University of California Press, 1975); Hudson, Travis, and Thomas C. Blackburn, *The Material Culture of the Chumash Interaction Sphere* (Ramona, Calif.: Ballera Press and the Santa Barbara Museum of Natural History Cooperative, 1979).

PETER NABOKOV
University of Wisconsin at Madison

CIGAR-STORE INDIAN

Because of the general illiteracy of the populace, early store owners used descriptive emblems or figures to ad-

vertise their shops' wares. Indians and tobacco had always been associated, and the depiction of native people on smoke-shop signs was inevitable. As early as the seventeenth century, European tobacconists used figures of Indians to advertise their shops. Because European carvers had never seen a Native American, these early cigar-store "Indians" looked more like black slaves with feathered headdresses and other fanciful, exotic features. These carvings were called "Black Boys" or "Virginians" in the trade. Eventually, the European cigar-store figure began to take on a more "authentic" yet highly stylized native visage, and by the time the smoke-shop figure arrived in the Americas in the early eighteenth century, it had become thoroughly "Indian." The early cigar-store Indians could be purchased as either male or female and were fashioned both in wood and cast iron. In the early years the female figure (with or without papoose) was by far the more popular, outnumbering male figures four to one. Occasionally, the female figure was adorned with a headdress of tobacco leaves in place of the more standard feathers. By the late 1800s the cigar-store Indian was doomed to extinction, relegated to the museum and the antique shop by new sidewalk-obstruction laws and the need for sidewalk space for venders of fruit and other goods. To all but the serious collector or museum curator, the cigar-store Indian is today considered the native equivalent of the black lawn jockey — a stereotypical and thus demeaning portrayal of Native Americans.

THE CIVIL WAR
IN INDIAN TERRITORY

The Civil War in Indian Territory was in reality two wars. It was a war between pro-Northern and pro-Southern factions among the so-called Five Civilized Tribes. Among the Creeks and the Cherokees, however, it was also a continuation of the conflict between those factions that had supported removal and those that had been opposed. It was this second element that made the war such a destructive and bloody conflict.

The Five Civilized Tribes had strong ties with the South. Transportation and trade linked them with the Southern states. Among all of the tribes, except the Seminoles, there was the presence of a large, politically important group of slave owners dependent upon plantation agriculture. At the outbreak of the Civil War, federal troops were withdrawn from Indian Territory, opening the way for Confederate agents. In the summer of 1861, treaties of alliance with the Confederacy were signed by the Creeks, Choctaws, Chickasaws, Seminoles, Quapaws, Senecas, Caddos, Wichitas, Osages, and Shawnees. In October, Chief John Ross of the Cherokees abandoned his initial position of neutrality and also signed a treaty with the Confederacy. In these treaties the Confederacy promised to assume former federal obligations, to protect the tribes from invasion, and to invite Indian representation in the Confederate Congress. In turn the tribes were to provide troops for their own defense.

In compliance with these treaties, tribal governments organized three Indian regiments: (1) a Choctaw-Chickasaw regiment, (2) a Creek-Seminole regiment, and (3) a Cherokee regiment. The latter regiment, under Colonel John Drew, was composed primarily of supporters of Chief Ross. Independently, Cherokee colonel Stand Watie organized a second, anti-Ross regiment, which brought the total to four regiments comprising five thousand Indian troops. These forces were placed under the command of Colonel Douglas Cooper, a former Choctaw agent. At this time the smaller tribes were not asked to provide troops, but by the end of the war men from all tribes would be involved, with over ten thousand Indian troops under arms.

Although the Confederacy had treaties with the tribal governments, popular support for the Confederacy varied. Among the Five Civilized Tribes, the Choctaws and the Chickasaws were the most enthusiastic Secessionists, while the majority of full bloods among the Cherokees, Creeks, and Seminoles initially favored neutrality. In the late fall of 1861 the Creek leader Opothle Yoholo called on all of the Indians favoring neutrality to join him in his camp at Deep Fork. Fearing this movement, Confederate Indian forces, supported by a detachment of Texas cavalry, moved to disperse Opothle Yoholo's growing following. Moving slowly north toward Kansas, the Neutrals repulsed the attacking Confederate forces at the battles of Round Mountain and Chusto Talasah. At Chusto Talasah some of Drew's Cherokee troops deserted and joined Opothle Yoholo. However, the Neutrals were now low on ammunition, and on December 26 the Confederates defeated them and captured most of their wagons, supplies, and livestock at the Battle of Chustenahlah. With little more than the clothing on their backs, the survivors then fled on foot through the snow to Kansas, where they became refugees.

The Confederate defeat in March 1862 at the Battle of Pea Ridge in Arkansas ended the threat of a Southern invasion of Missouri and opened the way for a federal thrust into Indian Territory. Watie and Drew's Cherokee regiments returned home from Arkansas to prepare for the coming battle. In Kansas, Union officers had organized two Indian regiments from among the growing number of Creek, Seminole, and Cherokee refugees and deserters. In June 1862 the Indian Expedition—the two Union Indian regiments, together with several regiments of Kansas and Wisconsin volunteers invaded the Cherokee Nation, capturing both the capital at Tahlequah and Fort Gibson. Chief Ross declared his support for the Union, and most of Drew's regiment surrendered and joined the Union Army. However, fearing an attack by Watie, the expedition quickly withdrew to Kansas.

With the Indian Expedition's withdrawal, a chaotic period ensued in which the Confederate Cherokees attacked Ross's supporters in the Cherokee Nation and even raided as far north as Fort Scott, Kansas. Thousands of Union Cherokees fled to Kansas, where most of the men were recruited by Colonel William Phillips into the Indian regiments (there were now three) which formed the Indian Home Guard.

In 1863 the Union Cherokees held the Cowskin Prairie Council, in which they disavowed the treaty with the Confederacy, denounced Stand Watie, abolished slavery in the Cherokee Nation, and elected Thomas Pegg as acting chief. In the spring of 1863, Colonel Phillips, commanding the Indian Home Guard and supported by other federal troops, invaded Indian Territory again, recapturing Tahlequah and Fort Gibson and driving the Confederate Indian forces south and west of the Arkansas River.

In July the Confederates massed a force of almost five thousand Choctaw, Chickasaw, Creek, Seminole, and Cherokee troops, together with some Texas cavalry, near Honey Springs, Creek Nation, in preparation for an attack on Fort Gibson. On July 17, they were attacked and defeated by an army of almost three thousand federal troops. In August, a force of forty-five hundred Union soldiers crossed the Canadian River and destroyed the important Confederate munitions depot at Perryville, Choctaw Nation, before recrossing the river. On September 1, Union troops captured Fort Smith, Arkansas, cutting off supplies flowing into the territory from the east. In February 1864, fifteen hundred troops made a quick strike down the Texas Road—the main trail to Texas from Missouri—

through the Choctaw Nation almost to the Red River. Colonel Phillips had his men systematically destroy everything in their path, telling them, "I do not ask you to take prisoners."

The war now entered its final and most destructive phase. Union forces settled in north of the Arkansas and Canadian Rivers, in the Cherokee, Creek, and Seminole Nations. Sixteen thousand pro-Union Indian refugees moved south from Kansas to new camps near Fort Gibson, where they lived off rations issued by federal troops. At the same time, the Confederate forces were reorganized. The Creek, Seminole, and Cherokee units became the First Indian Cavalry Brigade, commanded by Stand Watie, now a brigadier general. The Chickasaw and Choctaw units became the Second Indian Cavalry Brigade.

In the region controlled by the Union, pro-Union Indians, supported by federal troops, began wreaking vengeance on Southern sympathizers. They burned homes, stole livestock, and murdered many who opposed them. Thousands of Creek, Cherokee, and Seminole families fled south. By the fall of 1864 almost eleven thousand pro-Confederate Indians were living in disease-ridden camps along or near the Red River, while thousands more had fled farther south into East Texas.

Poorly armed and short of supplies, Watie and his Confederate allies responded with highly effective guerrilla raids into Northern-held areas. Watie's main target was the long federal supply line from Kansas, which was critical not only for providing troops, but also for provisioning the large camps of Union refugees. Most of these raids were carried out by small cavalry units, but Watie would attack federal forces whenever he found a good opportunity. In June 1864 he captured the supply steamboat J. R. Williams on the Arkansas River. In September, he struck just south of the Kansas line, capturing a supply train of 240 wagons and 740 mules at Cabin Creek Crossing. Watie also ordered the burning of Tahlequah as well as the plantation home of John Ross at Park Hill. Many of his men took vengeance on pro-Union families whenever they encountered them.

As the war approached its end, anarchy prevailed throughout most of Indian Territory. Union and Confederate "deserters," Indians and non-Indians alike, formed outlaw gangs and roamed the countryside, indiscriminately killing, burning, and looting. In the last months of the war, some of the high-ranking Union officers joined in the lawlessness, stealing over three hundred thousand head of Indian-owned cattle and driving them to Kansas.

The Civil War in Indian Territory ended on July 14, 1865, when the Chickasaws and the Caddos surrendered. The war had been fought at an incredible cost. Estimates of those who were killed or died of war-related causes range as high as 25 percent for the Creeks, Seminoles, and Cherokees. Other estimates show that out of a total population in excess of sixty thousand for the Five Civilized Tribes, over six thousand and possibly as many as ten thousand died. The economy of Indian Territory was totally destroyed; almost every house, barn, store, and public building had been burned. The vast majority of Indian families had been reduced to impoverished, homeless refugees. Nevertheless, there was one more blow yet to fall. Even though as many members of the Five Civilized Tribes had served in the Union Army as had served in the Confederate Army, the federal government declared its treaties with the tribes to be void and forced the tribes to negotiate new treaties that ceded the western part of Indian Territory to the United States.

See also Five Civilized Tribes; Indian Territory; Opothle Yoholo; Ross, John; Watie, Stand.

Abel, Annie Heloise, *The American Indian as Slaveholder and Secessionist* (Cleveland: Arthur H. Clark Company, 1915); Abel, Annie Heloise, *The American Indian as Participant in the Civil War* (Cleveland: Arthur H. Clark Company, 1919); Fischer, LeRoy H., ed., *The Civil War Era in Indian Territory* (Los Angeles: Lorrin L. Morrison, 1974).

GARRICK BAILEY
(Euro-American, Cherokee, and Choctaw)
University of Tulsa

ROBERTA GLENN BAILEY
Tulsa, Oklahoma

CLOUD, HENRY ROE

(1884–1950)
Nebraska Winnebago educator, political leader, and Indian Service employee.

Wa-Na-Xi-Lay Hunkah was born on December 28, 1884, along the Missouri River on the Winnebago Reservation in Nebraska. He was given the name Henry Clarence Cloud by educators at the Genoa, Nebraska, government boarding school, who found his Indian name too cumbersome. Cloud later transferred to the Santee Normal Training School, a mission-run Indian school on the nearby Santee Indian Reservation. At Santee, which was primarily a vocational high school, Cloud trained as a printer and blacksmith. At the Santee school, Cloud also converted to Christianity, a commitment that continued and was a major force throughout his life. At the urging of one of his teachers at Santee, Cloud applied and was accepted at Mount Hermon School in Northfield, Massachusetts. Mount Hermon served as a college preparatory school, and many of its graduates went on to Ivy League schools. Cloud graduated in the summer of 1906 as salutatorian of his class, and entered Yale University that fall.

In the spring of 1907, Cloud met the missionaries Walter and Mary Roe when they came to speak at Yale. The Roe family was actively involved in missionary activities among the Southern Cheyenne and Arapaho Indian tribes at Colony, Oklahoma. Cloud, as a sign of respect and affection for this couple and especially for Mary Roe, soon began using "Roe" as a middle name. During summer vacations, Cloud joined the couple in their missionary efforts at Colony and, at Cloud's urging, on the Winnebago Reservation in Nebraska.

By the time Cloud graduated from Yale with a Bachelor of Arts degree in psychology and philosophy in 1910, he was gaining national exposure. Cloud played an active role in the famous Lake Mohonk Conferences and in 1910 was one of the keynote speakers. Cloud also became a strong advocate for the return and the allotment of the Apache prisoners held at Fort Sill, a cause that he helped lead until the remnants of the tribe were freed in 1913.

After Yale, Cloud continued his education. He attended Oberlin College in Ohio for a year and then attended Auburn Theological Seminary in New York State, where he was ordained as a Presbyterian minister in 1913. While doing his seminary work, Cloud had also undertaken graduate studies at Yale, receiving a master's degree in anthropology from that school in 1912.

Cloud added to his national reputation by becoming one of the early members of the Society of American Indians, a Pan-Indian reform group founded in 1911. Cloud held several offices in the SAI and participated in most of its annual conferences until 1920. At the 1914 SAI conference in Madison, Wisconsin, Cloud met Elizabeth Bender, a Minnesota Ojibwa who had attended Hampton Institute and was also active in SAI affairs. Bender was the sister of Charles "Chief" Bender of baseball fame. Cloud and Bender were married on June 12, 1916, and had five children: Elizabeth Marion

(1917–91), Anne Woesha (1918–73), Lillian Alberta (1920–57), Romana Clark (1922–72), and Henry Roe Cloud II (1926–29).

After seminary, Cloud focused more and more on the development of his own school for Indian youth. Cloud started working with the Roes on plans for the school as early as 1908, and between 1913 and 1915 he identified potential sponsors, board members, and sites for the school. In the fall of 1915, the Roe Indian Institute, so named to honor Walter Roe, but later renamed the American Indian Institute, opened in Wichita, Kansas. Cloud's goal was to run a "Mt. Hermon of the West" to prepare Indian men for college. Cloud acted as president, chief fund-raiser, teacher, principal, and in many other capacities during the sixteen years he ran the school. Leading the only Indian-run high school in the country only added to Cloud's growing national reputation.

In 1914 and 1915, Cloud investigated the Indian school system for the Phelps-Stokes Fund, a New York–based philanthropic organization devoted to improving minority educational opportunities. Secretary of the Interior Hubert Work chose Cloud to be one of the "Committee of 100," a group that was formed in 1923 to advise the administration on Indian affairs. In 1926, Lewis M. Meriam picked Cloud to be one of the principal investigators for the Meriam Commission, which sponsored the now-famous survey by the Institute for Government Research on the conditions of the Indian tribes and field administration. This investigation led to the publication of *The Problem of Indian Administration* in 1928. As a result of his role in the nationwide survey of the Indians, his position at the American Indian Institute, and his vital writing and public-speaking career, Cloud received wide recognition from both Indians and whites as an expert on Indian affairs, especially in the area of Indian education.

Cloud began his almost twenty-year career in government in late August 1931 as a field representative at large, with duties relating to Indian education. Cloud's appointment was widely covered in the press, and it was reported that he was the first Native American to fill the post of field agent in the Indian Service. Cloud's duties in his early years of government service ranged far beyond Indian education as he conducted investigations at Indian agencies around the country. In 1933, Commissioner of Indian Affairs John Collier appointed Cloud superintendent of the Haskell Indian School in Lawrence, Kansas, perhaps the the most visible and prestigious position in Indian education.

Cloud had served at Haskell for less than one year when Collier asked him to help lead the fight for the acceptance of the Wheeler-Howard Act. Cloud traveled and spoke widely among the Indians, especially those of North and South Dakota, garnering support for the bill and later helping tribes organize under its provisions. In recognition of Cloud's prominence, in 1935 the Indian Council Fire chose Cloud to receive the Indian Achievement Award, its highest honor. In 1939, Cloud accepted the position of superintendent of the Umatilla Agency near Pendleton, Oregon. Cloud was a strong advocate for the tribes assigned to his agency, fighting for increased New Deal dollars and helping the tribes prepare for the many changes that the huge hydropower dams along the Columbia River would bring to these salmon-fishing people. In 1948 Cloud was reassigned to the Portland-area office of the BIA, where he was given the task of untangling the heirship records of the Grande Ronde–Siletz Agency as part of an Indian Claims Commission settlement. Cloud died on February 9, 1950, in Siletz, Oregon.

Crum, Steven J., "Henry Roe Cloud, a Winnebago Indian Reformer: His Quest for American Indian Higher Education," *Kansas History* 2, no. 3 (autumn 1988): 171–84; Sorci, Thomas, "Latter Day Father of the Indian Nations," *The News* (Northfield Mount Hermon School) 27, no. 3 (summer 1988): 17–19.

JASON TETZLOFF
Western Washington University

COCHISE

(c. 1810–74)
Chiricahua Apache war chief and leader.

A Chiricahua Apache of the Chokonen band, Cochise (or Goci—"his nose"—referring to his prominent nose) was born about 1810, probably in southeastern Arizona. During his first twenty years his people maintained a precarious truce with Mexico, which issued rations to obviate Apache raiding. In 1831 Mexico curtailed this practice, and the famished Apaches went to war. Cochise likely participated in a three-day battle, beginning on May 21, 1832, with Mexican troops near the Mogollon Mountains in New Mexico, during which both sides suffered heavy casualties. In February 1835 he led a war party into Sonora, Mexico. Soon afterward a desperate Mexico turned to deceit and chicanery, placed a bounty on Apache scalps, and hired mercenaries to exterminate Apaches. This hostility

served to further exacerbate the situation, for revenge was an important factor in Chiricahua warfare. A mercenary force massacred a score of Apaches on April 22, 1837, in southwestern New Mexico; Sonoran troops killed another hundred Apaches near Janos, Chihuahua, in August 1844; and Anglo-Mexican scalphunters left 148 Apaches dead at Galeana, Chihuahua, on July 7, 1846, a bloodletting to which Cochise's father likely fell victim. After these incidents, it was war to the knife between the Chiricahuas and Mexico.

During the late 1830s Cochise married Dos-teh-seh, a daughter of Mangas Coloradas, thus forming a Chiricahua alliance that lasted for twenty-five years. Taza, his eldest son, was born about 1842, and a second son, Naiche, about 1856. By another wife, he had two daughters born in the 1850s.

Cochise began to emerge as the principal leader of the Chokonen band of Chiricahuas in the late 1840s and early 1850s. On June 21, 1848, he led an assault on Fronteras, Sonora, and was captured. He remained a prisoner for six weeks, until the Indians exchanged eleven Mexican captives for him. In his prime, he stood five feet ten inches tall and weighed about 175 pounds. One American described him as "exceedingly well built, of manly and martial appearance, not unlike our conception of the Roman soldier." His hair was black, and he wore it, in the traditional Apache style, to his shoulders. He had a high forehead, a strong Roman nose, and prominent cheekbones. Usually serious and formal when discussing tribal matters, he was also celebrated for his truthfulness and integrity. He told one American that a "man should never lie" and said to another, "If a man won't tell the truth he should be put out of the way." On December 30, 1858, he met Southern Apache agent Michael Steck at Apache Pass and assured him that he wanted peace with Americans. For the next few years a tenuous truce prevailed, with Steck issuing rations and Cochise continuing to raid unimpeded into Mexico.

Relations became strained in 1860 before finally hitting rock bottom in February 1861, when Lieutenant George Bascom met Cochise at Apache Pass and accused him of capturing a boy whom other Apaches had taken. When Bascom, who had invited Cochise into his tent, told him that he would hold him prisoner until the boy was returned, the chief cut through the tent and escaped. But Bascom's troops soon captured five members of Cochise's family, and within days Cochise attacked, killing several Mexicans and capturing four Americans, whom he offered in exchange for his relatives. Bascom refused. Cochise, frustrated, tortured his prisoners to death. Bascom retaliated and hanged Cochise's brother and two of his nephews. The Americans later released Cochise's wife and child.

After what the Apaches called the "Cut the Tent" incident, Cochise's indomitable spirit and fierce, uncompromising hatred of his enemies dominated the Chiricahuas. Normally reserved, almost provincial in nature, he now sought tribal influence to avenge his relatives' deaths. Initially he raided and killed for revenge; later, as his rage abated, he continued to wage war as the conflict evolved into a bloody cycle of revenge, American counterstrikes, and Apache retaliation. During the first five years of his eleven-year war (1861–72) Cochise was the aggressor—a war chief sufficiently bold and influential to attract followers from the four Chiricahua bands and recruits from Western Apache groups. Cochise and Mangas Coloradas joined forces and attacked Americans throughout 1861 and 1862. They ambushed several parties at Cook's Canyon, New Mexico, during the summer of 1861. On September 27, 1861, they openly assaulted the mining town of Pinos Altos, New Mexico, but the miners repulsed them with cannon fire. The Apaches audaciously fought American troops to a stalemate at Apache Pass on July 15, 1862, until howitzers forced their retreat. Cochise's passionate hatred of Americans was aroused again in January 1863 when Americans duped Mangas Coloradas to a parley and subsequently executed him—which, to the Chiricahuas, was the greatest of wrongs. In 1865 he was as bellicose as ever, vowing that he would never make peace with the Americans.

In his day Cochise embodied the essence of Apache warfare. One American remarked that Cochise "never met his equal with a lance," while another claimed that no Apache could "draw an arrow to the head and send it farther with more ease than him." He was also an accomplished horseman. During one fight an American scout tried in vain to kill Cochise, who was able to "slip over to the side of his horse, hanging on the horse's neck." His courage in battle was legendary; he regularly led his men into combat. An American officer wrote that many efforts were made to kill Cochise, who "with his mounted warriors" led several charges. During a fight Cochise had complete control of his men. "A private soldier would as soon think of disobeying a direct order of the President as would a Chiricahua Apache a command of Cochise," one observer noted.

From 1866 until 1868 Cochise divided his time between Arizona and Mexico, carrying on guerrilla warfare against both. In late 1868 a Sonoran campaign drove him into Arizona, and the next fall American troops doggedly pursued him, forcing him into two major fights and several skirmishes in the Chiricahua Mountains that cost several Apache lives. By 1870 he understood that peace was necessary to ensure the survival of his people. Cochise conferred with Americans at Camp Mogollon, Arizona, in August 1870 and at Cañada Alamosa, New Mexico, on October 20, 1870. He remained distrustful of the Americans, however, and soon returned to his ancestral home in Arizona. Troops hunted him during 1871, giving him, in Cochise's words, "no rest, no peace" and compelling him to return to Cañada Alamosa on September 28, 1871. He remained there until late March 1872, when he heard that the Americans were relocating the reservation. He returned to Arizona and resumed hostilities until General Oliver Howard, helped by Thomas Jeffords, found him in the Dragoon Mountains on October 1, 1872, and agreed to Cochise's request for a reservation in southeastern Arizona. Cochise kept the treaty and maintained the peace until his death in the Dragoon Mountains on June 8, 1874.

See also Apache, Western; Mangas Coloradas; Wars: 1850–1900.

Sweeney, Edwin R., *Cochise: Chiricahua Apache Chief* (Norman: University of Oklahoma Press, 1991).

EDWIN R. SWEENEY
St. Charles, Missouri

CODE TALKERS

During World War I and World War II, many Indian languages were used by the U.S. military as secret codes, and most of these codes were transmitted and received by Native Americans. The Choctaws offered their expertise in both world wars, and the Comanches, Creeks, Menominees, Ojibwas, and Hopis all contributed to the effort as code talkers in World War II. Though each of these groups developed a code, they typically kept their communications close to a straight translation of English into their own language. Because the codes were relatively modest, all were eventually broken.

However, one code resisted all enemy efforts to break it. In 1941, Philip Johnston, a long-time Navajo Reservation resident, approached the U.S. Army Signal Corps with an idea for a new secret code. He proposed not only that the Navajo language be used, but also that a set of code words be devised in this unique and difficult language. After a series of successful demonstrations, the U.S. Marine Corps recruited twenty-nine Navajo communication specialists to conceive and transmit the code. Eventually, the marines recruited more than four hundred Navajos as code talkers. Johnston was also inducted into the corps as a trainer. Several hundred words were used that either corresponded to a particular military expression or to a letter in the English alphabet, since more difficult words had to be spelled out. Though the code was used in Africa and Europe, it was most often heard in the Pacific theater and was the only spoken code used by the marines at Iwo Jima.

COEUR D'ALENE

The Schitsu'Umish (Coeur d'Alenes) are a Salishan-speaking Plateau people whose original homeland encompassed over 4 million acres of camas-prairie, mountain, lake, and riverine habitat in the northern panhandle of Idaho and in eastern Washington. Relatively isolated until the mid–eighteenth century and dependent primarily upon the aquatic resources of Lake Coeur d'Alene and the Coeur d'Alene and St. Joe Rivers feeding into it, the tribe was divided into three or four divisions and occupied more than thirty villages.

By the mid–eighteenth century, the Coeur d'Alenes had adopted the horse and were hunting buffalo on the plains, increasing their contact and warfare with other tribes. By 1850, however, epidemic diseases had reduced their numbers to five hundred from an estimated precontact population of three thousand. Nevertheless the Coeur d'Alenes remained fiercely independent and maintained a reputation for sharp bargaining with early fur traders, who named them Coeur d'Alenes (from the French for "heart like an awl").

In 1842 the Coeur d'Alenes welcomed Jesuit missionaries led by Father Pierre DeSmet to live with them. Under the long tenure of Father Joseph Joset, many Coeur d'Alenes became Catholic and settled near the Sacred Heart Mission, on the north bank of the Coeur d'Alene River, where they were encouraged to learn English and to farm.

When he came west to establish American authority in Oregon Territory in 1855, Governor Isaac Stevens failed to make a promised treaty with the Coeur d'Alenes. The tribe lacked protection against the incursions of miners and white settlers, and responded by attacking U.S. troops in the brief Steptoe/Wright War of 1858. Gradually, however, conditions improved. Efforts to secure compensation for ceded lands and to gain a reservation—created by executive order in 1873—encompassing all of Lake Coeur d'Alene and the lower Coeur d'Alene and St. Joe Rivers, at first appeared successful. But by 1890 the tribe had been forced to cede the northern portion of the lake and the site of the Sacred Heart Mission to non-Indians. A reservation was finally established in 1891, but it covered only 345,000 acres.

In the 1860s and 1870s, the Idaho gold rush and traffic across the Mullen Road had persuaded tribesmen to move themselves and the mission to the rich lands of the camas prairie. By 1900, many Coeur d'Alenes had become prosperous farmers and ranchers there, with Victorian-style houses, large horse herds, and up to twelve hundred acres each under plow. As a consequence the tribe became a target of the General Allotment Act, which reduced Coeur d'Alene tribal lands to 58,000 acres.

Although the Coeur d'Alenes initially rejected the Indian Reorganization Act, the tribe now has an elected tribal council that has struggled to recoup nineteenth-century losses and to stimulate economic development. In 1958, 12,878 acres of unsold surplus land were returned to the tribe, and in 1959 the tribe won a settlement of $4 million from the Indian Claims Commission. By the 1990s the tribe had developed a 6,400-acre tribal farm, a shopping center, a medical center, tourist accommodations, and a gaming complex. At the same time, the tribe is actively working to preserve the Coeur d'Alene language and culture, to enlarge the Coeur d'Alene land base through land acquisitions, and to protect the tribe's natural resources and rural environment.

JACQUELINE PETERSON
Washington State University

COLUMBIAN EXCHANGE

In 1972, the historian Alfred W. Crosby, Jr., proposed that Christopher Columbus's voyages to the New World produced even greater consequences biologically than they did culturally. The *Columbian Exchange* is the term Crosby coined to describe the worldwide redistribution of plants, animals, and diseases that resulted from the initial contacts between Europeans and American Indians. This process had a profound impact on both societies. Columbus brought the first horses and pigs to the Americas; both animals became integrated into many Indian societies. Likewise, the new plant and animal species that Columbus and other explorers encountered in North America (such as tobacco, corn, and turkeys) presented a challenge to traditional Christian conceptions of the world and opened new opportunities for European farmers and businesspeople.

Perhaps the most powerful currency of the Columbian Exchange, however, was epidemic disease. Everyday European diseases were unknown in North America before Columbus's arrival. The New World provided virgin soil for epidemics. The natives' lack of immunity to European diseases resulted in decreases among native populations that reached as high as 90 percent. Although scholars debate the number of indigenous lives lost in particular areas, the social implications of this phenomenon are well documented. Political and spiritual leaders died and left traditions in disarray; subsistence cycles were disrupted; family life was devastated. These losses put American Indians at a disadvantage when they fought to protect their lands or attempted to negotiate treaties with imperial powers. Largely immune to the diseases that corroded native life, Europeans were able to take and hold an advantage over the tribes, turning their attention to learning to use the domesticated animals and plants they encountered in the New World.

See also Diseases.

COLVILLE TRIBES

The peoples now constituting the Colville Confederated Tribes and Reservation in north central Washington State aboriginally occupied the tributaries of the upper half of the Columbia River. Downriver were the Sahaptians, now at Yakima, and the Chinooks, decimated by 1830.

Starting from the north the Colville tribes, speakers of closely related Interior Salishan languages, were the (Arrow) Lakes, Colviles, Sanpoils, Nespelems, southern Okanogans, and Met-hows of one dialect chain, and then the Chelans, Entiats, Peskwaws (Wenatchis), and Columbians, who lived in the Big Bend of the Columbia River.

Before Europeans arrived the Colville tribes organized themselves by language, drainage, and winter village, each with a leader advised by an assembly of married adults. During winter families lived in pit houses or communal mat lodges; the rest of the year they camped in skin or mat tents. Throughout the year families moved to resource locations to harvest roots, berries, game animals, and, most important, salmon. Before each of these foods was gathered, a special feast was held to thank it for sustaining humans yet again. During the winter, dances were held so everyone could sing and worship the spirits who took care of the land and assured continued bounty.

People were most busy between May and August, the fishing season. In addition to sturgeon, the anadromous runs of five kinds of salmon (a few weighing as much as one hundred pounds) and of trout provided the Plateau regional staple. Every possible fishery was used, with large gatherings at river mouths and especially at Kettle Falls, under the direction of a salmon priest and a divider, both of whom made sure that all salmon speared or trapped were shared with everyone in the camp and fully utilized.

Colville shamans had long made a practice of transplanting certain plants (roots, herbs, willows, and so forth) to places where they would be most useful. Therefore, when fur traders introduced corn, potatoes, and other crops, chiefs and shamans took the lead in establishing communal tribal gardens on lakeshores.

American and British traders built fur posts at Fort Spokane (1810), Fort Okanogan (1811), and Fort Colville (1825). Goods introduced at these locations added to the changes already introduced by the arrival of the horse around 1740. By 1800, Columbian groups traveled regularly to hunt bison in Montana. The newcomers also brought epidemics, which depopulated whole watersheds. The United States forced many Washington tribes to accept treaties in 1855, but ancestors of only half the modern Colvilles attended the meeting at Walla Walla. During the subsequent Treaty War (1856–58), Colville tribes continued to avoid confrontations. Finally, however, an executive order established their reservation in 1872. In 1885, Chief Joseph and those survivors of his Wallowa Nez Perce band who were under indictment in Idaho for killing settlers joined the Colville Reservation. Later, a group of Sahaptians from southeastern Washington also settled there.

In the late nineteenth century, demands by gold miners and mineral prospectors began to diminish Colville lands. A northern tier of lands was removed in 1892, and the rest was allotted in 1905. In the 1930s, dams along the Columbia and increased American settlement further eroded Colville authority. In 1938, the tribes set up an elected business council and established four voting districts—at Inchelium, Keller, Nespelem, and Omak.

At present, the reservation manages logging, mining, recreational, and investment industries, along with bingo, sports, and gambling facilities. Most Colvilles are Catholics, served by Jesuits who have maintained a strong intellectual tradition of learning native languages, respecting native rituals, and working closely with the community.

Miller, Jay, ed., *Mourning Dove: A Salishan Autobiography* (Lincoln: University of Nebraska Press, 1990); Ray, Verne F., *The Sanpoil and Nespelem: Salishan People of Northeastern Washington,* University of Washington Publications in Anthropology, no. 5 (1933; reprint, New Haven: Human Relations Area File, 1954); Walker, Deward, ed., Plateau, vol. 12 of *Handbook of North American Indians,* ed. William C. Sturtevant (Washington: Smithsonian Institution, 1994).

JAY MILLER (Lenape)
Lushootseed Research

COMANCHE

Since the mid-1600s, if not earlier, Comanches were exploiting the northwestern buffalo plains. By the early 1700s, some Comanches had begun to move south, where, after contact with Apaches and Spaniards in New Mexico, they adopted horses and a horse-mounted lifestyle. By the second decade of the nineteenth century, most Comanches had been forced south of the Arkansas River by the advancing Cheyennes and Arapahos.

The Shoshonean-speaking Comanches were among the first of the Plains peoples to take up the horse-mounted lifestyle so familiar from the modern stereotype of American Indians. In the eighteenth and nineteenth centuries they comprised several culturally similar but politically independent tribal divisions, each composed of residential groups of extended family units, linked into wider groupings by kinship, sodality, and political ties. The number of these tribal divisions depended on the domestic and political resources that were available at any one time. In the eighteenth century there were three divisions: Yamparika (Root Eaters), Jupe (Timber People), and Kotsoteka (Buffalo Eaters).

By the mid-nineteenth century the Comanches had reorganized into six divisions, including two—the Yamparika and Kotsoteka—from the previous century, along with four new divisions, the Tenewa or Tenema (Downstream People), Penateka (Honey Eaters), Nokoni (Wanderers), and Kwahada (Antelope).

The foundation of the Comanche domestic economy was the buffalo, obtained by both individual stalking and group hunting methods. The Comanches also traded the animal products of the Great Plains with neighboring peoples for agricultural products and, in postcontact times, for Euro-American manufactured goods. In addition, Comanche groups maintained political relations with various Euro-Americans—Spaniards, Mexicans, Anglo-Americans, Yankees, and Confederates—through which they obtained important but often short-lived political resources. Ensuring the continuation of and controlling the access to these resources—the buffalo, trade, and Euro-American relations—was an important aspect of Comanches politics and the political economy.

The most important treaties the Comanches negotiated with the United States were the 1865 Treaty of the Little Arkansas River, signed mainly by Yamparikas and establishing a reservation that encompassed much of the Texas Panhandle, and the 1867 Treaty of Medicine Lodge Creek, signed by representatives of all Comanche divisions except the Kwahadas, whose chiefs were visiting Santa Fe at the time of the council. While reducing the size of the Little Arkansas reservation, the Medicine Lodge agreement provided for schools, houses, farming instruction, and annuities for twenty-five years. It also confederated the Comanches with the Kiowas and Plains (Kiowa) Apaches, and it established the basis for continuing Comanche–U.S. relations during most of the next century. In 1963 Comanches separated from the Medicine Lodge confederation and established a single political organization, the Comanche Tribe of Oklahoma.

Between 1901 and 1906, the Kiowa-Comanche-Apache Reservation was allotted to individual Indians, each receiving a 160-acre tract; the "surplus lands" were thrown open to white settlement. As a result, modern Comanches live in a relatively populated area surrounded by non-Indians. Many are active (although sometimes only partial) participants in the Anglo-American economy. As a corporate tribal community, the Comanches have few independent resources; these include a bingo operation and, along with the Kiowas and Apaches, a recreational water park.

Comanches have been important in the spread of several ceremonials throughout the Great Plains. The eastern Shoshone Sun Dance was based on ceremonies taught by a Comanche in the late eighteenth century. In the late 1880s, drawing on Lipan Apache antecedents, Comanches developed the ceremonies associated with the Native American Church, and began actively proselytizing the new religion. In the twentieth century Comanches received the modern powwow, and have played an important role in developing its southern plains variations.

Identity as a member of the Comanche community is maintained by participation in Comanche activities. There are a number of active Native American Church congregations. Similarly, there are a number of Christian congregations that use traditional Comanche symbols and metaphors in the composition of hymns, sermons, and services.

From the 1890s, when Comanches volunteered to join a U.S. Army scouting company at Fort Sill, Comanches have continued a military involvement with a particularly Comanche flavor. During World War I, Comanche army recruits were sent off and welcomed home again to the strains of men's-society songs. In World War II, many Comanches, along with other Oklahoma Indians, enlisted in the Forty-fifth "Thunderbird" Division. Even before the war, a squad of Comanches was specifically recruited into the Fourth Signal Company, Fourth Infantry Regiment, Forty-fifth Division, to use the Comanche language as the basis of a signal code. Veterans from both World War II and the Korean War were welcomed home with Victory Dance celebrations. The celebration in 1952 for the returning Korean War veterans has continued in the form of the annual Comanche Homecoming powwow, expressing an explicit Comanche identity. The Little Pony Society was revived in 1972 to honor returning Vietnam War veterans. In 1976 the Tuwhi (Black Knives) were revived as a specifically Yamparika organization. Other modern societies include the Comanche Indian Veterans Association and the Comanche War Dance Society, which was given the rights to perform the Osage Heluska Society's "Straight" war dance.

The Gourd Dance ritual, used by the Little Ponies, Comanche Gourd Clan, and Comanche Indian Veterans Association, is both a point of articulation with other tribes and a means for communicating a Comanche identity. In this sense, the Gourd Dance is as much a tribal as a Pan-Indian ritual.

The tribal center is just north of Lawton, Oklahoma. Local benefit and honoring powwows are held throughout the year. The annual Comanche Homecoming is held each year in mid-July in Walters, Oklahoma. From a low of less than two thousand in 1900, the population has grown to approximately nine thousand registered Comanches in 1990.

THOMAS W. KAVANAGH
Mathers Museum, Indiana University

COMANCHEROS

The Comancheros were an active group of New Mexican traders of mixed ethnic origin, numbering as many as one thousand at a time, who operated on the southern plains, exchanging goods with the Comanches and other groups. This trade started in 1786, following a peace treaty between the Spanish and the Comanches, and the term *Comanchero* began to appear after 1843 when Josiah Gregg's *Commerce of the Prairies* called the Comancheros traders who came from the "rude classes of the frontier."

Throughout the nineteenth century, the Comancheros were an elusive and disruptive part of frontier life. Characterized variously as harmless drifters or lawless villains, they threatened Texas cattle herds and provided refuge to runaways and criminals.

During the early nineteenth century, Comanchero traders exchanged bread, flour, and cornmeal for horses, mules, buffalo robes, and meat. After the Mexican-American War the Comanches frequently opposed American settlement, drawing the Comancheros into military diplomacy and negotiations over trade relations. The withdrawal of U.S. soldiers from the region at the beginning of the Civil War allowed the trade to flourish again. The nature of the trade was also modified. A new trade arose in powder, lead, guns, and whiskey—all frequently exchanged for stolen cattle.

Comanchero trade faded away between 1867 and 1880. Permit restrictions, the extension of legal institutions, and military intervention disrupted the activity, and the surrender of the last large group of independent Comanches in 1875 dramatically reduced the base for trade. The final blow came with the destruction of the buffalo in 1879. After that date the Comanchero traders became a part of frontier history and raw material for novelists and filmmakers.

COOLIDGE, SHERMAN

(1862–1932)
Native American leader and minister.

Every now and then an individual of remarkable accomplishments and unique experience is forgotten as history is recorded. Such is the case with Sherman Coolidge. Coolidge's life is a story of irony and contrast that unfolded during a critical period for American Indian populations.

Runs-on-Top, later to be known as Sherman Coolidge, was born in 1862 near Goose Creek, in the Wind River country of Wyoming. His parents, Banasda (Big Heart) and Ba-ahnoce (Turtle Woman), were Arapahos. The Arapahos were almost continually at war with the Shoshones and Bannocks while also being involved in conflicts with federal troops. When Runs-on-Top was seven years old, his father was killed by a war party of Bannocks who were attempting to steal horses. Runs-on-Top, his younger brother, and his mother escaped by crawling under their tipi cover and hiding in the brush until the fight was over.

In the spring of 1870, the Arapahos were attacked by a large contingent of Shoshones and Bannocks near the present site of Lander, Wyoming. Runs-on-Top and his younger brother were taken captive during the raid, but their mother escaped. Eventually, the boys were given to American troops by the Shoshones and Bannocks. Their mother, after learning where the boys were, decided to leave them in the care of the military for their safety. The two youngsters remained with the army at Camp Brown, Wyoming, and were taken in by military families. The younger brother, Little One-Who-Dies-and-Lives-Again, was cared for by Captain Laribee and renamed Philip Sheridan, after the famous general. Runs-on-Top was befriended by the Camp Brown surgeon, Dr. Shapleigh, and was renamed for William Tecumseh Sherman. Young William Sherman caught the eye of Captain and Mrs. Charles A. Coolidge, who were childless, and in late 1870 the pair adopted him. William Sherman became Sherman Coolidge.

Coolidge was treated well by his foster parents, who encouraged his education and rapid assumption of white ways. Over time, the boy began to mirror the dress, habits, and manners of white children from fine families. At the age of nine, he was baptized by the Episcopal bishop, the Reverend Southgate, and was enrolled at the Shattuck Military School in Faribault, Minnesota. An exemplary student, he consistently ranked in the upper quarter of his class.

As Coolidge grew, his memories of his early life among the Arapahos faded. His foster parents encouraged him to perform to the best of his abilities and to strive for perfection. The Coolidges knew that segments of the white community would resent Sherman because of his Indian ancestry, but they hoped that a good education would enable him to overcome these prejudices. Ironically, Sherman accompanied his adoptive father west in 1876 while Captain Coolidge was involved in campaigns against the Sioux. It was during that same year that Sherman began to consider becoming a missionary among the western tribes. Initially the Coolidges tried to discourage him, but they eventually enrolled him in the Seabury Divinity School, near Chicago. In 1884, Coolidge graduated with a Bachelor of Divinity degree and later that same year was ordained a deacon in the Episcopal Church by Henry B. Whipple. Shortly thereafter, Coolidge proceeded to the Wind River Reservation in Wyoming to undertake his first church assignment.

The Wind River Reservation was originally established for the Shoshones. Later, the Arapahos were placed on the reservation with their old adversaries, and the two groups occupied opposite ends of the reserve. Upon his arrival at Wind River, Sherman was greeted by his mother, Ba-ahnoce, who had learned of his impending return from a local missionary. After so many years of separation, Coolidge felt somewhat alienated from his mother, but the two maintained cordial relations and he eventually persuaded her to convert to Christianity. During his first years at Wind River, Coolidge worked as a mediator between the tribal factions and helped secure a tentative peace between the groups.

In 1887, Coolidge enrolled at Hobart College in Geneva, New York, to continue his theological studies. He completed his courses in 1889 and was ordained to the priesthood before returning to the Wind River Agency. Back in Wyoming, he ministered to the needs of Indians and whites alike and traveled extensively to perform services for outlying communities. While Coolidge was engaged in his church work, he met Grace Wetherbee, the daughter of an affluent New York City couple, who was visiting an old school friend. Grace was also interested in church work, and the two began a long-term relationship that would culminate in their marriage in October 1902. Numerous people had counseled against a mixed-race marriage. Yet when an announcement of the marriage appeared in the *New York Times,* headlined "Indian Husband

Approved," the opening line read: "Father of Miss Wetherbee who married Arapaho, gave full consent."

Grace Coolidge worked hand in hand with her husband as he ministered to the needs of the Wind River community. She began to write about her experiences on the reservation, and many of these stories were published in *Collier's Weekly* and the *Outlook*. Sherman worked diligently on behalf of American Indians and in 1911 became one of the founding members of the Society of American Indians. The society was the first prominent Indian-controlled rights organization in the country, and Sherman remained an influential figure in the group for a number of years. Grace's writing led to the publication of *Teepee Neighbors* in 1917, a collection of touching vignettes of life on the Wind River Reservation in the early twentieth century. The Coolidges raised two daughters, Sarah and Rose, and adopted a number of Indian children. Sometime after World War I Sherman transferred to Colorado Springs, Colorado, and served in churches in that state. He died on January 24, 1932, and Grace died five years later, in 1937.

See also Arapaho.

GEORGE L. CORNELL (Sault Ste. Marie Chippewa)
Michigan State University

COPWAY, GEORGE

(1818–69)
Mississauga Ojibwa writer and lecturer.

With the publication of his autobiography, *Life, History, and Travels* (1847), George Copway (Kahgegagahbowh, "Firm Standing") became one of the best-known American writers of his day. Three more books, completed in 1850 and 1851, and his publication of a newspaper, *Copway's American Indian*, in 1851, gave the young man access to America's highest social and literary circles. He was one of the first North American Indians to have his writings published and widely read.

In his autobiography Copway described his childhood on the north shore of Lake Ontario, in the Rice Lake area of Upper Canada, today's Ontario, from his birth in 1818 to his departure as a Methodist Church worker in the church's Lake Superior District. His parents had educated him in the Ojibwa tradition until their conversion to Methodism in the late 1820s. After they became Christians their son attended the mission school at Rice Lake.

None of the details of Copway's early life, until he left for Lake Superior in 1834, can be verified by other sources. Regardless of the lack of confirming accounts, however, the story he tells in his autobiography rings true. The Ojibwas in Upper Canada did indeed face enormous challenges in the 1820s as a result of the influx of tens of thousands of British immigrants onto their hunting grounds. The newcomers inadvertently brought disease, and traders introduced an abundance of alcohol. The Ojibwas—or Mississaugas, as the settlers called the Ojibwas on the north shore of Lake Ontario—suffered great population loss, and alcohol abuse became endemic. After Mississauga Christians led by Peter Jones, a bilingual and bicultural preacher from the Credit River, reached them in 1826 and 1827, many Rice Lake Mississaugas embraced Christianity.

Copway gave special attention in his autobiography to his family's conversion. The common human values shared by the Indian and Christian faiths attracted his parents, as did the Methodists' abstention from alcohol. Visions and dreams played an important role in his family's and his own acceptance of Methodism. His later life indicates that his desire to achieve equality with the newcomers also motivated him to join the church.

The new convert's two or three years at the Rice Lake Methodist school gave him enough knowledge of English to act as an Ojibwa interpreter for the nonnative missionaries. The bright young man moved quickly through the ranks in the Lake Superior District as his abilities in translating became well known. After three years as an interpreter, schoolteacher, and preacher, the Illinois Conference of the Methodist Church sent him and two other young Ojibwa converts to the Ebenezer Manual Labor School at Jacksonville, Illinois. Two years of study there prepared them for ordination.

Copway's close contacts with nonnatives led him to adopt much of their outlook. As he wrote in his last book, *Running Sketches of Men and Places* (1851), "Man is the one for whom this world is made." He accepted many of the values of the larger society and distanced himself from those Native American spiritual beliefs that did not place human beings in the center of the universe.

His marriage brought the Indian minister ever closer to the dominant society. On a short visit to Upper Canada in early 1840 he met Elizabeth Howell, a young Englishwoman whose family farmed in the Toronto area. They married in June 1840, just before Copway traveled to Minnesota to take up his first posting as an Indian missionary. But they would not spend long in the United States. When his nonnative Methodist colleagues declined to treat him as an equal he became frustrated and unhappy. Finally, in 1842, he left the United States for Upper Canada, where he served at the Ojibwa Methodist mission at Saugeen on Lake Huron.

Finances proved the young native minister's undoing. He spent band funds freely, without always obtaining council approval to do so. In early 1846 two Upper Canadian bands, those of Saugeen and his own Rice Lake, accused him of embezzlement. As a result of the charges the Indian Department put him in jail, where he remained for several weeks. The Canadian Conference of the Wesleyan Methodist Church expelled him. Alienated and bitter, Copway and his family returned to the United States after his release from prison.

In terms of his career, his expulsion from the Methodist Church proved a blessing in disguise, for it forced him into a new field of endeavor: he became a celebrated author and lecturer. How Copway succeeded in writing his life story while, in one observer's words, "going from place to place, without much of steady employment, for 6 or 8 months, and perhaps more," remains a mystery. No doubt his well-educated wife helped. Curiously, his autobiography resembles the African slave narratives then available, as well as the works of writers of spiritual confessions. As one might expect, he makes no mention of his short stay in a Canadian jail, or of his expulsion from the Canadian Conference of the Wesleyan Methodist Church.

Copway's *Life, History, and Travels* proved an instant success. It had gone through seven printings by the end of 1848. As the newly acclaimed author spoke well, a lecturing career opened up to him. Large numbers of Americans came to his lectures to see and hear "the noble Christian convert." New writing projects followed: his *Traditional History and Characteristic Sketches of the Ojibway Nation* (1850), the first history of a North American Indian nation in English by an Indian; and *Running Sketches of Men and Places* (1851), an account of his European travels in 1850. He also published an epic poem, *The Ojibway Conquest* (1850), although Julius Taylor Clark, a former Indian agent, later claimed to have written it. Apparently Clark gave the manuscript to Copway to publish on the understanding that Copway would use the money earned to promote the creation of an Indian territory west of the Mississippi.

In the May 31, 1851, issue of the *Literary World,* the magazine's editors, Evert and George Duyckinck, de-

scribed George Copway as "a shrewd, wide-awake man, with a knowledge of the world which few of the white race could overmatch." Yet events would prove this assessment premature. Copway's inability to enlarge upon his writing themes and his constant need to solicit money caused his downfall. Within half a year after the Duyckincks' reference, Copway was indeed overmatched. His newspaper folded, and gradually thereafter he lost his audience.

Little is known about Copway's life after 1851. Scattered references exist to lectures he presented throughout the eastern United States (one was canceled in Boston in 1858 because of poor attendance). During the Civil War he worked as a recruiter of Canadian Indians for the Union Army. After the war, in 1867, he surfaced as a root doctor in Detroit. One year later he appeared in Canada, without his wife and infant daughter, at the Lake of Two Mountains (Oka) Reserve, just west of Montreal. There he declared himself a "pagan," eager to join the Roman Catholic Church. The one-time Methodist preacher, author, lecturer, and herbal doctor died at the Lake of Two Mountains Reserve early in 1869, just before his First Communion.

Smith, Donald B., "The Life of George Copway or Kahgegagahbowh (1818–1869)—and a Review of His Writings," *Journal of Canadian Studies* 23, no. 3 (fall 1988): 5–38.

DONALD B. SMITH
University of Calgary

CORNPLANTER

(1740?–1836)
Seneca war chief and statesman.

Cornplanter (Kaiiontwa'ko^n, "By What One Plants") was born at Canawagus on the Genesee River in present-day New York State around 1740. His father was an Albany trader named John Abeel or O'Bail, and Cornplanter was known to the English as John O'Bail or Captain O'Bail. His half brother Handsome Lake was an Iroquois Confederacy chief, as was a nephew who was known as Blacksnake or Governor Blacksnake.

During the American Revolution, Cornplanter was chosen at a gathering of warriors (along with the respected Seneca war chief Old Smoke) to lead the Iroquois warriors in support of the British. Cornplanter had at first vigorously opposed Iroquois participation in the war on either side and had admonished his warriors against fighting, stating, according to Governor Blacksnake, "war is war Death is the Death a fight is a hard business." Governor Blacksnake also stated that at the end of this speech Joseph Brant, the war chief of the Mohawk Valley Mohawks, who had earlier traveled to England to cement his ties to the Crown, accused Cornplanter of cowardice. Cornplanter eventually led fighters against the Americans throughout the course of the war.

Cornplanter was second in command of the Indian fighters at the Battle of Wyoming in June 1778. More than 300 Americans were killed in this action (and fewer than ten Indians and Rangers) while eight forts and a thousand dwellings were destroyed. On August 2, 1780, Cornplanter, Brant, Old Smoke, and the Cayuga war chief Fish Carrier led about four hundred Indians and Tories on a scorched-earth campaign against the Canajoharie District in the Mohawk Valley. Approximately fifty to sixty prisoners were taken, while two forts and fifty-three houses were destroyed. Among the houses burned was that of John Abeel, who was captured and then recognized as Cornplanter's father. Cornplanter apologized intensely for burning his father's home and offered to take his father home to the Seneca country or, if he preferred, to send him back to his white family. Abeel chose the latter.

In October 1780, Cornplanter was among the leaders in a series of attacks on forts and settlements in the Schoharie Valley in what is now eastern New York State. This action was in response to the Clinton-Sullivan campaign of the previous year that had resulted in the destruction of two hundred Iroquois houses and an estimated 150,000 bushels of grain in addition to some forty Iroquois dead and more than sixty captured. The counterattack prompted New York Governor George Clinton to comment that New York's western frontier was now at Schenectady.

At the end of the Revolutionary War Cornplanter organized and led a delegation to Fort Stanwix, where in 1783 a treaty was negotiated between the United States and the Six Nations Iroquois Confederacy. While embraced by the United States, the treaty made such sweeping concessions of Iroquois land that, when presented to the government of the Confederacy, it was deemed unacceptable. The Six Nations Grand Council never ratified it. In a speech delivered to President Washington at Philadelphia, Cornplanter stated: "When our chiefs returned from the treaty at Fort Stanwix, and laid before our council what had been done there, our nation was surprised to hear how great a country you

had compelled them to give up to you, without your paying to us any thing for it. . . . We asked each other, what have we done to deserve such severe chastisement?" Cornplanter participated in a series of treaties in 1784, 1789, 1794, 1797, and 1802, all of which ceded large areas of Seneca territory to non-Indians. Because of these cessions he became extremely unpopular among his own people and at one point stated "[t]he great God, and not man, has preserved the Cornplanter from the hands of his own nation."

In 1790 Cornplanter and several other Seneca chiefs met with George Washington to protest the terms of the Fort Stanwix Treaty, stating "you demand from us a great country, as the price of that peace which you had offered us; as if our want of strength had destroyed our rights. . . . Were the terms dictated to us by your commissioners reasonable and just?" The Senecas went on to say that there was no reason why further land cessions should be expected.

Cornplanter subsequently became a faithful ally of the new United States and was probably influential in persuading George Washington to adopt treaty making as the preferred method of dealing with Indian tribes while urging fair and honest treatment of the Indians generally. Congress passed the 1790 Non-Intercourse Act with the intention of upholding President Washington's promises that the federal government would protect Indian lands against fraud and theft.

On November 4, 1791, the United States suffered what was probably its worst military defeat at the hands of Indians; 630 soldiers under General Arthur St. Clair were killed in a complete rout by the Shawnees and their allies on the Ohio-Indiana border. Subsequent attempts to arrange peace negotiations with these Indians were not successful, and George Washington now turned to the Six Nations to act as intermediaries. The following year Cornplanter, at considerable risk to his own life, led a Six Nations delegation to a meeting on the Glaize (now Auglaize) River in an effort to reach an accommodation with the victorious Shawnees on behalf of the United States. Cornplanter's delegation met with the Indian forces that had defeated General St. Clair and found them in a less than conciliatory mood. They treated Cornplanter and his delegation with contempt for what they saw as their subservience to the Americans and issued a demand that white settlers evacuate the lands they were occupying northwest of the Ohio River. Although he was not completely successful in this peace initiative, Cornplanter received a grant of one square mile of land from the State of Pennsylvania for his efforts and for his assistance in dissuading the Iroquois Confederacy from joining the Shawnees in the fighting in Ohio.

He was living on this "Cornplanter Grant" in June of 1799 when his half brother Handsome Lake, who was living in the same house, arose from a coma and announced he had experienced a vision. The two men continued to live there until 1803 when a dispute with Handsome Lake sent the latter to Coldspring on the Allegheny Reservation, where he embarked on his lifelong mission to revive the ancient ways and values while adapting to the new world of the reservation. Cornplanter continued to live on his Pennsylvania grant for the rest of his life.

Cornplanter died on February 18, 1836, and was buried at the Cornplanter Grant. In 1964 the cemetery where he was buried was moved to higher ground to make way for the reservoir that would be created by construction of the nearby Kinzua Dam.

See also Cayuga; Handsome Lake; Seneca.

Abler, Thomas S., *Chainbreaker: The Revolutionary War Memoirs of Governor Blacksnake as told to Benjamin Williams* (Lincoln: University of Nebraska Press, 1989); Graymont, Barbara, *The Iroquois in the American Revolution* (Syracuse, N.Y.: Syracuse University Press, 1972); Sword, Wiley, *President Washington's Indian War: The Struggle for the Old Northwest, 1790–1795* (Norman: University of Oklahoma Press, 1985).

JOHN C. MOHAWK (Seneca)
State University of New York at Buffalo

CRADLEBOARDS

Cradleboards are objects in which babies are carried. Traditionally they have been made and used by most tribes in North America, especially nomadic tribes. Tribes in the Arctic and the southeastern United States did not use cradleboards, although these objects have been found in both places archaeologically. Though most cradleboards appear remarkably similar, they are made from local materials that differ from location to location. The back of the cradleboard, flat and oval or rectangular in shape, is often made of wooden slabs or tree branches, or woven from reeds or other materials. The child is swaddled and placed on top of the backing, tucked into a pouch made from animal skins and/or cloth. A protective arch, usually fashioned from a willow branch, reeds, or carved wood, hangs over the child's head.

Cradleboards serve several functions within a tribal group. Cradleboards were and are utilitarian; they transport babies safely and free a mother's hands for chores. Psychologically, a baby in a cradleboard feels safe and secure; he or she is swaddled and held close to the mother. Cradleboards are objects of beauty and are a personal expression of the maker. Depending on the tribe, they can be decorated with beadwork, quillwork, weaving, woodwork, and/or ribbon and cloth designs. Cradleboards may also be decorated or designed with sacred symbols, colors, or objects to bring good life and luck to the child. For this reason family members choose carefully who is to make a cradleboard for their child. In some tribes, if an infant dies, the cradleboard will not be used again.

See also Child Rearing.

CRAZY HORSE (TASUNKE WITKO)

(1840-77)
Oglala Lakota warrior and political leader.

Crazy Horse! The name stirs the imagination and a sense that we should know who and what he was. Some of us may indeed know the legend surrounding the man, but not many know the flesh-and-blood, caring, thinking, feeling, human being that was Crazy Horse.

He was of Oglala and Mniconju stock, born near Bear Butte, in the Black Hills of what is now South Dakota, in the Winter the Oglala Took One Hundred Horses from the Snakes (according to the winter count of the Bad Face band of the Oglalas), or 1840.

His father, the second Crazy Horse (his grandfather was the first) was Oglala Lakota and his mother, Rattling Blanket Woman, was Mniconju Lakota. As a boy he was known as Light Hair and Curly. In his mid to late teens he was called His Horse Stands in Sight. It was probably before his twentieth year that he was given the name Crazy Horse, becoming the third, and the last, in his family to carry it.

Crazy Horse is most often remembered as a warrior and leader of warriors, riding into battle with loose, waist-length hair flowing in the wind. While this is a true image, there were other sides to his identity: he was a son, a pupil, a brother, a loner, a husband, a thwarted lover, and a father. The way of the warrior was a societal role preordained for males in traditional Lakota life. Young men, however, often sought a vision

A Sioux drawing of Crazy Horse, foreground, *during the Battle of the Little Bighorn. No photographs exist of the Sioux leader.*

to clarify their specific paths and seek spiritual connection to help them on that path. Crazy Horse had such a vision as a boy. In it he saw a warrior mounted on a horse that changed colors, riding through hail and lightning, and through the arrows and bullets of enemies as his own people tried to hold him back. The vision revealed his destiny, giving him a clarity of purpose that few men or women in any culture have had.

Two incidents during his boyhood helped form his attitude about white people. They occurred about a year apart, and both involved the U.S. Army. In the first, in 1854, a brash young officer underestimated the resolve and fighting ability of Lakota warriors when he insisted that they return a diseased and abandoned cow they had captured. The confrontation set off an encounter that resulted in the deaths of an entire detachment of thirty soldiers. The second incident occurred when the army retaliated about a year later and wiped out most of an unsuspecting Lakota village, killing women and children as well as warriors. Both incidents taught Crazy Horse that white people could be cruel and were not to be trusted. It was a lesson he never forgot.

As a warrior Crazy Horse earned recognition and many battle honors. In 1866, for example, his actions as a decoy leader helped to lure a contingent of eighty soldiers from Fort Phil Kearny (in what is now north-central Wyoming) into a trap set by Lakota and utter defeat by Lakota, Cheyenne, and Arapaho warriors. That engagement was called the Battle of the Hundred in the Hands by the Lakotas, and the Fetterman Battle or the Fetterman Massacre by the whites. Because of such deeds Crazy Horse became a war leader by his mid-twenties, though he did not seek that role or its accompanying status.

In Lakota tradition the people selected leaders by consensus, basing their opinions on the qualities, virtues, and actions that set a person apart. Crazy Horse certainly set himself apart as a courageous warrior, and as a quiet, humble, caring man away from the warpath. In fact, he was one of the youngest Lakota men in memory to receive one of the highest honors and responsibilities accorded to males: the title of Shirtwearer.

A Shirtwearer was expected to be an ultimate provider and protector of his people and to lead an exemplary life as a role model. When Crazy Horse was caught trying to steal another man's wife, he was forced to give up the shirt and the role. But because of his considerable stature as a warrior and war leader, the people continued to look to him for overall leadership—a fact that fomented jealousy among his rivals and may ultimately have led to his death.

Crazy Horse was a quiet, introspective, and very shy man. He dressed plainly and rarely spoke in public or participated in public ceremonies. He did not recount his war deeds, nor did he wear or display the symbols of achievement accruing to him because of those deeds. Such reticence was not the custom of Lakota warriors.

He had three wives during the course of his life. The first was Black Buffalo Woman, whom he had loved since boyhood. Though she had married another, she left her husband (a privilege allowed in Lakota tradition) and eloped with Crazy Horse. But her jealous husband followed them and nearly killed Crazy Horse. Black Buffalo Woman finally returned to her husband, mainly to avoid bloodshed among her own people. His second wife was Black Shawl. His third wife was Nellie Laravie (or Larrabee), given to him five months before his death. Of the three, only Black Shawl bore him a child, a daughter. Black Shawl was the wife with whom he lived through much of his adult life; she died in 1920. Their daughter, named They Are Afraid of Her, died at the age of three, probably of cholera.

In 1876 Crazy Horse was the battlefield leader in two engagements considered by the U.S. Army to be among the most pivotal and important in what they termed "the Indian Wars." At the Battle of the Rosebud he and his forces fought General George Crook to a standstill. And eight days later on the Greasy Grass (Little Bighorn) River he led Lakota and Cheyenne warriors again in a decisive victory against Lieutenant Colonel George Custer's Seventh Cavalry. Unfortunately, however, those victories served only to motivate the army to step up its campaigns against the last free-roaming bands of Lakotas. In May of 1877 Crazy Horse's band indicated it would surrender. His was among the last of the Lakotas to come in.

Crazy Horse intended to settle at one of the other agencies in Dakota Territory, but he was persuaded at the last minute to take his people to Fort Robinson, Nebraska, with the understanding that he would be allowed to have his own agency there. That never happened.

Several months after his arrival at Fort Robinson, the commanding general attempted to take Crazy Horse into custody, because of rumors of Crazy Horse plotting against the government. Crazy Horse resisted the attempt and in the ensuing panic a guard stabbed him twice with a rifle-mounted bayonet. Crazy Horse died that night, September 5, 1877. He was thirty-six years old, the victim of his own stature and the jealousy and fear of lesser men. His life coincided with and symbolized the last years of the great buffalo hunting culture of the Lakotas.

As a leader, Crazy Horse kept the interests of his people before him. He provided for them and protected them from harm. He signed no treaties, and he surrendered only because he did not want his followers to suffer depravation, cold, and hunger. Even in his dying moments he thought of his people. For all of those reasons, it is easy for the Lakotas to remember him and say his name as if it were a prayer. *Crazy Horse!*

See also Little Bighorn, Battle of; Red Cloud; Sioux; Sitting Bull.

Hardoff, Richard G., *The Oglala Lakota Crazy Horse: A Preliminary Genealogical Study and an Annotated Listing of Primary Sources* (New York: Carroll & Company, 1985); Sandoz, Mari, *Crazy Horse, the Strange Man of the Oglalas* (New York: Knopf, 1945).

JOSEPH M. MARSHALL III (Sicangu Lakota)
American Indian Nations Arts and Cultural Organization
Santa Fe, New Mexico

CREE

While Europe was establishing its philosophical traditions, political institutions, and social framework, the Cree people of Canada were building a nation that extended from the boreal forests of Quebec to the foothills of the Rocky Mountains. In the process of nation building, they explored new lands and engaged in extensive trade with their aboriginal neighbors. Quick to adapt to new experiences, they took from other cultures what was useful in their own lives and ignored the rest. Theirs is a unique story in that they also developed several distinct cultural subgroups, beginning with the James Bay (Eastern) Crees and culminating in the establishment of the Plains Crees. In 1534, when Jacques Cartier was trying to find a short route to the Orient through the St. Lawrence River valley, the Eastern Crees were extending their culture westward from Quebec into the lands of present-day Ontario. As the French and later the English established fur-trade colonies in the seventeenth century, they met the Swampy and Plains Crees, who were accustomed to trade and aware of its usefulness in furthering national aspirations. The histories of the Crees and of the European colonizers have been intimately linked for nearly five hundred years.

Two important facets of Cree life should be noted: the vast expanse of land that they have occupied historically and occupy at present; and the various cultural subdivisions that have emerged through time. Over the years, the Crees, originally an Eastern Woodlands people (the James Bay Crees) have spread out, becoming, in turn, a Western Woodlands people (the Swampy Crees) a Parklands people (the Woods Crees), and a people with a Plains way of life (the Plains Crees). Since the late nineteenth century, they have also adopted the ways of the industrial and agricultural world. Each subgroup also encompasses several divisions. The Plains Crees, for example, comprise the Calling River People, the Rabbit Skin People, the Cree-Assiniboin People, the Touchwood Hills People, the House People, the Willow People, and the Beaver Hills People. The result is that one overall national designation covers several geographically and culturally distinct groupings that occupy homelands in Quebec, Ontario, Manitoba, Saskatchewan, Alberta, British Columbia, and the Northwest Territories in Canada, and in Montana in the United States.

The Cree story has its beginnings in the woodlands around James Bay in what is now northern Quebec. In prehistoric times, game was plentiful around the bay, and Cree "stewards" who cared for and hunted on territories in excess of five hundred square miles were common. Each "steward" was responsible for his territory and the animals on it, a practice that has continued to the present day. Each hunting territory could support three to five extended families. It was only in the spring that the people would gather in larger groups to fish at selected places near the mouths of the many rivers that empty into James Bay. Some of these spring meeting places remained in constant use up to 1975, when they were flooded by the construction of Hydro Quebec's La Grande hydroelectric dam. Because of their practice of living in groups of less than fifty during the winter and gathering in slightly larger groups during the summer, the James Bay Crees did not find it necessary to develop the social and political institutions favored by Europeans. What they did develop was the ability to range over large territories and, as their numbers grew, to expand into nearby regions. In so doing, they began the growth process that was to mark their subsequent history.

A rich archaeological record indicates that as the James Bay Crees moved, their population grew and they developed trade relations with distant communities. The artifacts they left behind also indicate that they did not wander aimlessly but rather expanded their sphere of interests because of increased population pressures and the attraction that new experiences and lands held out to them. Theirs was a good life, even if the climate was difficult and game was sometimes scarce. Today James Bay Crees continue to have an intimate relationship with the land, even though Hydro Quebec's extensive damming of rivers and flooding of historic Cree territories has undermined a number of traditional activities. Despite this damage, however, some of the Crees continue to engage in traditional hunting, fishing, and trapping, while others have diversified their economic base into airlines, construction, and other business ventures. The result is a people who maintain many traditions despite the stress of poverty and land loss.

As the French and later the English expanded slowly westward after 1600, they entered the Swampy Cree world. The French called these people the Cristinaux (from an Ojibwa word denoting a member of a band living south of James Bay), a term that came to be used in its shortened and altered form to refer to all Crees. The Crees have as many words to refer to themselves as there are different Cree peoples, but in most cases these terms are not translatable, and the people themselves have chosen to use the word Cree as well. In 1640, when the Swampy Crees were first mentioned by the Jesuits, they were living in the region around Lake Nipigon and Moose River and along the East Main River in present-day Ontario. They lived in much the same way as their relations in Quebec and were quick to realize the advantages of English fur-trade practices. Unwilling to risk the voyage into the hinterland, early Hudson's Bay Company traders remained confined in their forts and waited for the "Indians" to come to them. The Crees, long accustomed to trade, soon became the middlemen in the trade and, by diligent use of trade items, especially the gun, established treaties with other First Nations, notably the Plains Assiniboins and the Blackfeet. At the same time, they began moving onto the western parklands and woodlands and later onto the plains themselves. However, most of the early Swampy Crees continued to maintain their habit of living on the coast of Hudson's Bay during the summer and inland in the winter, a practice that was well suited to their culture and to the trade that they carried on with their neighbors and, sometimes, their enemies.

In the eighteenth century, as the Crees were approaching the plains and the endless numbers of buffalo to be found there, they also met up with the horse, which had traveled north from Mexico. Making use of the trade habits of the Hudson's Bay Company for their own interests, the Crees traded guns to the Blackfeet for the horses they needed to become successful Plains people. At the same time, the guns allowed the Blackfeet the upper hand in dealing with their Shoshone and Crow enemies to the south, who had horses but no guns. The result was a Blackfoot buffer zone between the Plains Crees to the north and east and the hostile Shoshones and Crows to the south.

By 1800 the Crees were established on the Great Plains and had fully adapted to the equestrian way of life. The Plains Crees also continued their close relations with the Assiniboins, to the extent that many Crees and Assiniboins intermarried, thus providing large kin groups as well as allies who would protect Cree lands from attack. At this time the Crees also waged war against the Sioux, Gros Ventres, and other peoples to the south who were being forced north and west by American expansion across the Missouri River. By 1867, when Canada united into a single nation, the Plains Crees were deeply entrenched in the West, even though they had been decimated by recurrent epidemics of smallpox and impoverished by the drastic drop in the number of buffalo as well as the relocation of the fur trade to the Far North. Faced with such difficult problems after 1870, Cree leaders such as Big Bear, Poundmaker, Little Pine, and Paipwat began to work toward the creation of a safe Cree haven in a rapidly changing world.

As Canadian treaty commissioners moved out of Red River (Winnipeg) in 1871, the Plains Crees began bringing together other plains First Nations to discuss the creation of an "Indian" territory in southern Saskatchewan where aboriginal law would prevail and where "Indian" people could begin the practice of farming and ranching. Canadian authorities rejected this proposal, preferring small reserves where the "Indians" could be Christianized, civilized, and assimilated into the Euro-Canadian mainstream. Long-standing differences between the aboriginal nations also helped to put the Cree proposal at risk. When the Métis under Louis Riel took up arms to defend their homes in 1885, Canada responded by sending in approximately ten thousand troops to subdue about three hundred Métis

as well as to disarm and dismount the local Cree bands. Cree leaders were arrested, and the bands were forced onto reserves.

Not all of the Cree Nations were forced onto reserves, however, and until recently, many of the more northerly Cree people were left to their own devices. But as large-scale oil and forest utilization developed after 1960, the Lubicon Cree Nation in northern Alberta and the James Bay Crees in Quebec were uprooted and marginalized. This process of sudden resource extraction and consequent Cree impoverishment and displacement occurred with increasing frequency after 1970, causing a politicization among Crees that has led to a Canada-wide renewal of Cree culture as well as a renewed determination on the part of Crees to fight for their lands.

Today there are more than sixty thousand Cree peoples and their allies living in six of the ten provinces of Canada, in the Northwest Territories (north of the western Canadian provinces), and on the Rocky Boy reservation in Montana and in other areas in the United States. There are still many Crees, especially older people in the northern areas, who speak their ancestral tongue. Cree schools in Quebec and in western Canada are reviving interest in ancestral native languages by the younger generation of Crees, while several Canadian universities are recording and publishing traditional Cree stories and teachings. The Sun Dance drum is again being heard on a regular basis, and traditional Cree elders are once more taking their rightful place in Cree communities.

The long and continuing story of the Cree Nation extends far beyond written history in Canada. One result of this history is that current land-claims negotiations between the Crees and the provincial and federal Canadian governments are ongoing, despite determined Canadian efforts to control the process. Cree professionals, as well as skilled and unskilled workers, abound in western and eastern Canada and are at the forefront of the push toward self-determination. The recent decision by the Department of Indian Affairs to turn over control of Indian affairs to the First Nations in Manitoba is being led, in large part, by Cree politicians, elders, and the people themselves. In the final analysis, it is they who possess the wisdom and knowledge to determine their fate and the role they see for themselves in Canada, a role that they have been practicing successfully since long before the first Europeans imagined they had "discovered" a new world.

See also Fur Trade; Indian-White Relations in Canada, 1763 to the Present.

Milloy, John S., *The Plains Cree: Trade, Diplomacy and War, 1790–1870.* (Winnipeg: University of Manitoba Press, 1988); Richardson, Boyce, *Strangers Devour the Land* (Toronto: Douglas and McIntyre, 1991).

FRED J. SHORE
University of Manitoba

CREEK (MUSKOGEE)

Today thirty-seven thousand people identify themselves as members of the Muskogee Nation, better known as the Creeks. This sense of tribal unity was not always the case. At the time of European contact in the seventeenth century, the native inhabitants of the Southeast had no single name for themselves and no inclusive social or political identity. Their allegiance was primarily to their particular town, or *talwa*. Fifty to eighty such towns and villages, made up of at least twenty separate ethnic groups speaking several distinct languages, dotted the region of modern-day Georgia and Alabama. British traders from the newly founded settlement of Charleston, South Carolina, called the Ochese people of this region "Ochese Creeks," presumably because they lived along the waterway now known as the Ocmulgee River. This term was eventually shortened to "Creeks" and freely applied to the various other groups the colonists met inland. The proper modern-day designation, however, is *Muskogee* (also spelled *Muscogee*), being the term contemporary members use in referring to themselves and their culture.

The present-day capital of the Muskogee Nation is Okmulgee, Oklahoma. The tribal government boasts a revised constitution, extensive health-care services, educational and employment services, and housing for low-income members. Business ventures include smoke shops and high-stakes bingo in Tulsa and Okmulgee. In 1991 the nation took another step forward with the election of a woman as second chief. But despite three hundred years of conquest, accommodation, and change, many customs have remained constant within the Muskogee community. District representatives still meet in national council to handle tribal affairs. Members still attend ceremonial stomp dances, take medicine (a religious ceremony involving scratching, bathing, and imbibing a root drink that serves as an emetic), identify themselves by town affiliation, and

come together to elect their leaders. Parents continue to teach children the various dialects of the Muskogee language.

The oral tradition surrounding the origin of the Muskogees holds that the ancestors came from the west, migrating eastward over hazardous terrain, warring with those in their way and incorporating the people they conquered. Some of the migrants eventually settled in Cusseta and Coweta, along the Chattahoochee River on the present-day Alabama-Georgia border, while others settled in Abihka and Tuckabatchee, fifty miles to the west along the Coosa and Alabama Rivers.

Anthropological evidence points to the Mississippian civilization as the source of Muskogee life and culture. When Hernando de Soto encountered it on his inland expedition in search of treasure in 1539, the Mississippian culture was already in decline, and it quickly collapsed as war and disease killed some 90 percent of the population. Survivors moved into the Southeast from all directions and regrouped to start new traditions. Friendly overtures and offers of protection encouraged groups to settle near the original Muskogee towns of Cusseta, Coweta, Abihka, and Tuckabatchee.

In the eighteenth century, the ancestors of the modern Muskogees made up the core of a large, multivillage confederacy, held together in part by the Muskogee language, which was spoken, albeit in a variety of dialects, in most of the towns. As colonial expansion grew more threatening, the confederacy banded more closely together to defend its boundaries and protect its independence against claims by outsiders. After its struggles proved unsuccessful and federal authorities forced its members to move west to Indian Territory, the confederacy evolved into a single tribe, calling itself the Muskogee Nation.

Throughout this period of conflict and relocation, the town remained the primary social and political unit, and town identity continued to be the central element of the Muskogee experience. *Talwa* (town) signified "tribe," meaning that people regarded each town as a distinct political entity retaining its autonomy, its special identity, and its control over local affairs. Today more than forty towns in Oklahoma still maintain their separate identities, and the 1975 Muskogee constitution touched off a controversy because government representation was no longer based on towns but on eight legislative districts.

Initially, the Muskogee Confederacy was a loose alliance of towns. Only the prospect of war brought the towns together to resist the Europeans. Gradually, the confederacy grew as towns met in councils to discuss affairs with their European neighbors. For example, a group of towns met in 1734 to select an ambassador to England. In addition, geography created a subdivision within the alliance. Towns on the Chattahoochee, Ocmulgee, and Flint Rivers (Lower Towns) met together, while towns on the Coosa, Tallapoosa, and Alabama Rivers (Upper Towns) convened a separate council. This geographic grouping of towns eventually grew into a dichotomy unique to the Muskogee Nation.

A town's political autonomy was virtually sacred. Individual towns could reject the regional council's suggestions. Each town selected at least one *micco*—or headman, to Europeans. Some towns had more than one *micco*. *Miccos* conducted all town affairs, including diplomacy with other towns and Europeans. A *micco*'s leadership depended upon his capacity to persuade through charisma and experience. A *micco* wielded power only as long as he held the respect of many people.

A *micco* met with his advisers to discuss suggestions and make decisions for the town. When threatened with war, each town decided how fully to participate and whom to send into battle; the confederacy never required towns to participate. More than half the confederacy opted out of most conflicts. For example, in 1796, when the confederacy was at war with the Chickasaws, the town of Cusseta refused to take part because it regarded the Chickasaws as friends. (Following removal to the West and the growth of the unified Muskogee Nation, many tribal members continued to value the principle of town autonomy.) Factionalism became a dominant characteristic of the nation's political landscape. *Miccos* who could exploit the situation grew strong in popularity, military success, and wealth.

During the eighteenth century, differing experiences with Europeans generated tension between Upper Towns and Lower Towns. Lower Towns, located on the Georgia frontier, prospered from active trade with British colonists. Upper Towns preferred French and Spanish traders. Trade with the British colonists made the Lower Towns wealthy and powerful; they began to assimilate English values and customs as they enjoyed the results of trade. During the American Revolution, the Lower Towns remained neutral in hopes that the old arrangements would continue. But Upper Towns— alienated from Charleston and its traders—allied themselves with the British.

Even though the Creeks—like other neutral or pro-British tribes — suffered in the aftermath of the Revolution, they united in the face of a growing American nation. The Treaty of Paris (1783) put the confederacy within the boundaries of the newly created United States. In response, the Muskogees adopted a defensive attitude, seeking to preserve territory and culture. In this atmosphere, Alexander McGillivray, a mixed blood from Ochiapofa, rose to prominence as he pushed towns to develop a unified foreign policy and cleverly juggled the interests of traders, constituents, and foreign diplomats. His leadership contributed to the growth of an active central council and culminated in the Treaty of New York (1790). In this treaty the United States pledged to protect the confederacy from outside settlement, while it made McGillivray an American brigadier and compensated the Creeks for their loyalty. That loyalty, however, lasted only until the tribe realized that the United States was allowing Georgians to continue settling in Muskogee territory.

During the War of 1812, ongoing tensions between Upper and Lower Towns broke into violence. Led by William Weatherford, Peter McQueen, Menawa, and the prophet Josiah Francis, twenty-four Upper Towns took up the "Red Stick" of war (runners carrying red sticks spread the news of war from town to town) to purge their territory of American influences. In contrast, William McIntosh, *micco* of Coweta, led a force of Lower Towns to side with the Americans. The ensuing Creek Civil War (1813–14) set twenty-five hundred Red Sticks against a combined force of fifteen thousand Indians and Americans under the command of Andrew Jackson. The pivotal battle took place on March 27, 1814, at Tohopeka, located on a horseshoe-shaped bend of the Tallapoosa River. The Red Sticks fought valiantly in the Battle of Horseshoe Bend, but nine hundred of them died as the Americans crushed them. Altogether, nearly three thousand Upper Town members died in the war.

In the aftermath of the war, the confederacy evolved into the Muskogee Nation. *Miccos* sought to preserve culture and land from the onslaught of Manifest Destiny, and villages came to see the advantages of unity as more attractive than local autonomy. Beginning with the decision to execute William McIntosh, Jr., for signing the 1825 Treaty of Indian Springs without the council's permission, *miccos* began to pursue a unified course against claims on their territory. During the 1820s, however, the confederacy's leaders reluctantly acknowledged that absolute resistance was impossible and that removal was inevitable. In 1832, Opothle Yoholo, the *micco* of Tuckabatchee, led ninety *miccos* in signing a treaty that outlined the terms for removal. Those who wanted to could stay in Alabama, but most emigrated west.

The geographical grouping of Creek social life into towns continued as many village groups resettled intact. As these towns started over in the new land, they also re-created the Upper and Lower Creek councils, the former led by Roley McIntosh and the latter by Opothle Yoholo. Contact between the two councils was rare until 1839, when they merged into a single national body, presided over jointly by McIntosh and Opothle Yoholo.

Eventually, the Muskogees' struggle to survive in Oklahoma brought the towns together under a new constitutional government with elected leaders and town representatives. The new constitution of 1860 centralized the political process, codified laws for everyone, and authorized a national council to act on behalf of all towns. Members now viewed themselves as part of a unique new entity—the Muskogee Nation.

But this unity was short-lived. During the U.S. Civil War, old factional tensions erupted again and nearly destroyed the fledgling nation. In 1861, Daniel N. McIntosh, youngest son of executed William McIntosh, organized the First Creek Regiment, whose purpose was to fight Union-sympathizing Creeks, led by the aged Opothle Yoholo. Opothle Yoholo led about two thousand warriors and their families north to Kansas for protection. Their exodus was slow because they took household goods, cattle, horses, and sheep with them. The Confederate Creeks harassed the northern cavalcade. Opothle Yoholo organized a rear guard to protect their flight. The First Regiment engaged the Union Creeks in three battles, fueling the urgency to reach Kansas. Eventually a blizzard took a severe toll on the cavalcade. Many people froze to death, their bodies abandoned in the snow. Union forces could not provide relief. Opothle Yoholo's people continued to die from exposure and starvation once they reached their Kansas sanctuary. Opothle Yoholo died as well and, like the hosts of unknown who had perished on the trek west from Georgia and during the flight north, was buried in an unmarked grave.

Surprisingly, when the war ended, rival groups within the tribe were able to bridge their differences and to unite again as one people. The Treaty of 1866 and the reconstruction process blurred the geographic divison. Peace and friendship again characterized the Musko-gees, and they were once again united as the Muskogee Nation. In 1867, a revised constitution created a government that resembled the government of the United States. It had a two-house legislature, a court system, and a chief executive. Though the constitution was revised again in 1975, the earlier government remains intact.

Within the reunited Muskogee Nation, however, conflicts continued to arise. The most famous of these were the Sands Rebellion (1871), the Green Peach War (1882), and the Crazy Snake movement (1900–1909). In each instance, people frustrated by the changes forced on them by outsiders gathered around charismatic indigenous leaders who advocated the restoration of traditional culture.

At the end of the nineteenth century, the Dawes Severalty Act brought the most serious external challenge to the Muskogee Nation. Most members opposed the idea of dividing their common lands into individual parcels. Six political parties ran candidates for principal chief in the election of 1895, and all opposed allotment. Nevertheless, even though the national council refused to permit the allotment surveys to begin, the Dawes Commission opened a land office anyway. It began work at Muskogee on April 1, 1899, allotting Muskogee lands to individual members. Resigned to the inevitable, most members selected their allotments. By the spring of 1900, the process of land divisions was largely complete.

Designed as a strategy for assimilation, allotment nearly destroyed Muskogee life, even though it did not assimilate tribal members into "mainstream" society. In 1934, the Indian Reorganization Act halted this failed policy, and the tribe was able to win some recognition for its political institutions. In 1972, the transition to full control occurred when Claude Cox was elected principal chief by tribal members. Although lacking a communal land base, the Muskogee people were a sovereign nation again.

Some Creeks remained in the Southeast, where they were frequently swindled out of their lands and declined to the station of sharecroppers. In 1962 the survivors of this remnant group organized for recognition as a tribe, and in 1980 the United States accepted them as the Poarch Creek band of Creeks. As a result, several hundred members still live in the traditional homeland of the Muskogee Nation.

The obvious links of contemporary Muskogee culture with the past are stomp dances, called *busks* by historians and other outsiders. Fourteen stomp grounds operate throughout northeastern Oklahoma, attracting thousands of members each year. Stomp dances are held monthly from May to September, the largest being the Green Corn Ceremonial in July. Not to be confused with a powwow, the Green Corn is a celebration for the new harvest, a time to praise the All-Supreme, and a time for atonement. At this gathering the Muskogee language is spoken in its different dialects. Men and women share traditional communal duties. Fasting and stickball play remain important elements of the ceremonials. Ceremonial fires burn atop ceremonial ashes carried from the homeland during the removal. Stomp dances, particularly the Green Corn Ceremonial, continue to keep Muskogee culture and identity intact despite two centuries of pressures to assimilate.

See also McGillivray, Alexander; McIntosh, William, Jr.; Opothle Yoholo; Red Stick War.

Debo, Angie, *The Road to Disappearance: A History of the Creek Indians* (Norman: University of Oklahoma Press, 1941); Green, Michael D., *The Creeks* (New York: Chelsea House, 1990); Martin, Joel W., *Sacred Revolt: The Muskogee's Struggle for a New World* (Boston: Beacon Press, 1991).

KENNETH W. MCINTOSH (Muskogee)
University of Tulsa

CREE LANGUAGE

The Cree language (in Plains Cree, *nêhiyawêwin*) is spoken by about fifty thousand people in six Canadian provinces and territories and in the state of Montana. A member of the Algonquian family of languages, it is closely related to the Montagnais language of Quebec and Labrador, from which it separated at least five hundred years ago, and more distantly to Ojibwa (Chippewa), Shawnee, Blackfoot, Cheyenne, Micmac, Delaware, and others; speakers of these other languages may sometimes recognize individual Cree words but cannot understand whole sentences, nor can Cree speakers understand the languages these other people speak.

Cree has a relatively simple sound system compared with other languages of the world. Most Cree dialects have only ten distinct consonants: *p, t, k,* and *c* (which varies in pronunciation from *ts* as in *cats* to *(t)ch* as in *catch*); *s* and *h; m* and *n;* and *w* and *y.* Most have seven vowels: short *a, i,* and *o* and long *â, ê, î,* and *ô.* Eastern dialects also have the consonants (English *sh*), and some dialects also have *r, l,* or *ð (th* as in *this*).

Five dialect divisions can be identified by their pronunciation of certain words. The Atikamekw dialect of southwestern Quebec has *r* in words like *iriniwak,* "people," and *kîr,* "you"; Moose Cree, at the southern end of James Bay, has *l,* as in *ililiwak* and *kîla;* Swampy Cree, spoken by many people in northern Ontario and Manitoba, substitutes *n,* as in *ininiwak* and *kîna;* the Woods Cree dialect of northwestern Manitoba and northeastern Saskatchewan has *ð (th),* as in *iðiniwak* and *kîða;* and Plains Cree, spoken by a large number of people across Saskatchewan and Alberta, and in neighboring parts of the Northwest Territories and Montana, substitutes *y,* as in *iyiniwak* and *kîya.* The dialects also sometimes use different words to express the same idea, and in some cases have different inflections and sentence structures. The examples that follow are drawn from Plains Cree.

English distinguishes first person (*I;* plural *we*), second person (*you*), and third person (*he, she, it;* plural *they*). However, English *we* is ambiguous: it may mean "you and I" ("*We're* friends, aren't *we*?") or "I and they" ("*We're* going, but you must stay"). Cree has two distinct forms: the inclusive *kîyânaw,* "we (you and I)," and the exclusive *nîyanân,* "we (but not you)." In the second person Cree has two separate pronouns: *kîya,* "you (singular)," and *kîyawâw,* "you (plural)." Some speakers of English similarly contrast *you* (singular) and *youse* or *you-all* (plural).

In the third person singular, English has three categories—*he, she,* and *it*—but *he* and *she* refer only to humans and a few other nouns. In French and Spanish all nouns are either masculine (*he*) or feminine (*she*); in Cree all nouns are either animate (*he, she*) or inanimate (*it*). Nouns referring to humans and other animals are inherently animate in gender; also animate are words for trees and some other plants (e.g., corn, tobacco, raspberries), and, unpredictably, a few other words (e.g., kettle, smoking pipe, fingernail, snowshoe, car). All other nouns are inanimate in gender.

The animate/inanimate gender distinction is fundamental to Cree grammar: there are separate verb stems and different inflections for intransitive verbs depending on the gender of the subject; for example, *ayôskanak wîhkitisiwak,* "raspberries taste good," but *otêhimina wîhkasinwa,* "strawberries taste good" (*-w-* is the third-person ending on intransitive verbs, and *-ak* and *-a* indicate animate and inanimate plural, respectively). Transitive verbs have different stems depending on the gender of the direct object, and different inflections to indicate every possible combination of subject and object; for example, *ayôskanak niwîhkispwâwak*, "I like the taste of raspberries," but *otêhimina niwîhkistên*, "I like the taste of strawberries."

In Cree only one third-person participant in a sentence (and, often, in a whole paragraph) can be treated as central. All other third-person participants are marked as obviative, a category sometimes called "the other third person" or even "fourth person." For example, if we are talking about a boy and his dog, the boy will be third person (as in English) but the dog will be obviative, as in *otêma*, "his dog" (*-a* indicates the obviative), or *nâpêsis kî-wâpamêw anihi atimwa*, "the boy [*nâpêsis*] saw that dog [*atimw-*]"; simply by changing the ending on the verb—*nâpêsis kî-wâpamik anihi atimwa*—we can reverse the meaning to "that dog saw the boy." If we were focused on the dog rather than the boy, we could also say *atim kî-wâpamêw anihi nâpêsisa*, "the dog saw that boy (obviative)"—or *anihi nâpêsisa kî-wâpamêw* or *anihi kî-wâpamêw nâpêsisa*, "he saw that boy," since Cree word order is quite free.

The obviative allows Cree to avoid some of the ambiguities inherent in a language like English. As soon as it is clear in a discourse which participant is third person and which is obviative, the nouns can be omitted: after saying *nâpêsis kî-wâpamêw anihi atimwa*, "the boy saw that dog," for instance, we could add *ê-kî-pimipahtâyit wîkihk*, "he was running along by his house"; the ending *-yit* shows that the subject of the verb "run" is obviative (the dog), whereas the form *wîkihk*, "his house," instead of *wîkiyîhk* shows that the house is the boy's, not the dog's.

Like all other indigenous languages of North America, Cree is in danger of extinction: the number of Cree speakers has been declining in recent years as many children grow up speaking only English. Some schools have introduced Cree language programs, but typically only a few hours a week are devoted to Cree; the rest of the time the children hear and speak English at school, and at home they watch English-language television. However, in the more remote communities at least, there are still children learning Cree as their mother tongue, so it is likely to survive as a spoken language for the foreseeable future.

See also Languages.

Ahenakew, Freda, *Cree Language Structures: A Cree Approach* (Winnipeg: Pemmican Publications, 1987); Ahenakew, Freda, ed., *Wâskahikaniwiyiniw-âcimowina / Stories of the House People*, told by Peter Vandall and Joe Douquette (Winnipeg: University of Manitoba Press, 1987); Wolfart, H. C., and Janet F. Carroll, *Meet Cree: A Guide to the Cree Language*, rev. ed. (Edmonton: University of Alberta Press; Lincoln: University of Nebraska Press, 1981).

FREDA AHENAKEW (Plains Cree)
University of Manitoba

DAVID H. PENTLAND
University of Manitoba

CROW

The Crow Tribe of Indians is currently located in southeastern Montana. The Crows are of Siouan origin, speaking a language classified as Siouan. The tribe is directly descended from the Hidatsa tribe of present-day North Dakota, sometimes called the North Dakota Gros Ventres. The separation of the Crows from the Hidatsas is placed at 1400–1500 by anthropologists, and at A.D. 900–1000 by linguists, whose estimates are based on the age of glottal development and the variance of the Crow language from that of the parent tribe.

There were originally three bands of the tribe: the River Crows, who inhabited the territory along the Musselshell and Yellowstone Rivers south of the Missouri River; the Kicked-in-the-Bellies, the band that frequented the area now known as the Bighorn Basin in northern Wyoming; and the Mountain Crows, also known as the Main Camps, who frequented the area of the Upper Yellowstone River and the Bighorn Mountains. Among the stories told concerning the separation of the Crows from the Hidatsas is that of No Vitals and his search for the sacred tobacco.

No Vitals and his brother were on a vision-quest fast, during which they experienced very similar visitations of the supernatural. The brothers' shared vision was said to be of corn, which was already grown by the Hidatsas. But in No Vitals's vision he also saw wild mountain tobacco growing in the foothills of mountains. Thus began the separation on the Missouri River of No Vitals and his followers from the rest of the Hidatsas. No Vitals and his small band of followers embarked on the first of two odysseys, which saw them journey to the eastern slopes of the Canadian Rockies, in present-day Alberta, to the upper reaches of the Arkansas River. To this day the Crows still sing lullabies of the mountains of Glacier Park and the fowl of the Arkansas. Not finding any tobacco on the first odyssey, the No Vitals band returned to the Missouri to pursue the vision again. When they finally did find wild tobacco (*Nicotiana multivalvis* and *N. quadrivalvis*), it was growing among the foothills of the Bighorn Mountains, and the small band relocated to the valleys of the Bighorn and Yellowstone Rivers. The Crows quickly became nomadic hunters, their activities ranging from stalking large game to trapping small animals to staging elaborate buffalo jumps.

The Crows are matrilineal; clan lineage is traced through the mother. The present-day clan system is derived from the thirteen original clans of the tribe. Today there are ten clans, two in each of five kinship groups. Discussions of the origin of the clans go back to Old Man Coyote, the trickster character in ancient stories of the tribe. It is said that Old Man Coyote characterized clans as similar to driftwood in that they belonged to whichever group happened upon them. To this day, Crows are identified by clan, in keeping with the characteristics and personalities generally associated with that clan through the ages and generations.

The Crows' yearly cultural round was similar to that of other Indian tribes of the northern Great Plains. Spring, considered the beginning of the cycle, was perhaps the most significant of the seasons. First thunder was a signal to discontinue the winter's activities such as storytelling and to take up tools and revive the tribal ceremonies. This activity coincided with the birth of new birds and animals. Adoption and initiation ceremonies were begun, and a new perspective on life blended with new plant growth and the coming abundance of the warm seasons.

Summer was a time of gathering the fruits of Crow country. Fresh berries, roots, and other items of subsistence were plentiful. It was time to enjoy the pure waters and cool winds of the mountains. Autumn was a time to harvest necessities and prepare for the winter. Traditional war parties were forgone to intensify the hunt for prime animals and the gathering of other necessities. Meat, berries, and other supplies were accumulated and prepared for the winter ahead. Winter was a time to retreat to the sheltered valleys and to strengthen family and tribal ties. After the first snow, storytelling began, and continued until the first thunder of spring.

The worship system of the Crows' parent tribe, the Hidatsas, was carried on by the Crows; some forms have persisted to the present day. The tribe also copied, adopted, and adapted worship practices and ceremonies from other tribes. Fasting for divine guidance as practiced by the Hidatsas was retained by the Crows, as were wound healing and other ceremonies for health maintenance, and the sweat lodge. The Crow Sun Dance, a communal worship of the sun, was banned by federal authorities in the late 1800s, but the Shoshone Sun Dance came to the Crows in 1941 and became a popular feature of tribal life. The peyote ceremony also came from the tribes of Oklahoma in the early twentieth century.

The original ceremony of the tribe is known as the Tobacco Ceremony (sometimes mistakenly called the Beaver Dance). This ceremony surrounds the harvesting, cultivation, and keeping of the sacred tobacco seeds first identified in No Vitals's vision. No Vitals believed that by practicing the Tobacco Ceremony, the Crows would multiply and grow stronger.

The Crows' leadership roles generally resembled those of the Hidatsas. Warlike endeavors were key to becoming a chief and leader. Four acts of bravery and display were considered prerequisites for leadership; their achievement reflected divine guidance and grace. First, one had to be the first to strike or touch the enemy in battle. There could be only one first striker in a battle, and the race to attain that honor created the fury of the attack on the enemy. Second, one had to take a weapon from the enemy in battle. With the coming of gunpowder, the taking of a rifle was a prime honor. Third, one had to take a horse in battle, either from the enemy horse herd or, better, from the doorway of the owner's lodge. Fourth, one had to lead a successful war party and demonstrate leadership prowess in a demanding situation. The achievement of all these honors qualified one to be a chief, but it remained for the camp, the clan, the band, or other group to select its leader from the pool of eligible candidates. The head or principal chief was selected by a council of chiefs.

Women played a significant role in practically every phase of Crow culture. They fashioned objects of worship and well-being. They were the eyes and ears for their husband, whether or not he was a chief. They related the feelings and talk of the camp, band, and tribe. As such, women reflected the mood of the tribe and discussed tribal direction and options with the men.

The Crow Reservation was first defined by the treaties of 1851 and 1868, negotiated with representatives of the United States at Fort Laramie, Wyoming. Reduced by subsequent land sales, the reservation is today significantly "checkerboarded," with Indian and non-Indian lands interspersed. Almost half of the reservation is technically owned by Indians and held in trust by the federal government, but land use by tribal members is minimal. Indian lands have been sold and/or leased to nonmembers to such an extent that the overwhelming majority of Crow Indian land is under the control of white farmers and ranchers. The populations of Indian and non-Indian residents on the reservation are about equal.

The Crows began as an agricultural and quasi-sedentary tribe. They became a nomadic, hunting tribe, and today they constitute a rural community occupying a federal Indian reservation, but with members both on and off the reservation. Until the 1930s the majority of tribal members spoke only the Crow language, but today the majority speak English. Contemporary lifestyles and mores are intermeshed with ancient Crow culture, tradition, and systems of worship.

BARNEY OLD COYOTE (Crow)
Little Big Horn College
Crow Agency, Montana

CURTIS, CHARLES

(1860–1936)
Kaw attorney, congressman, senator, and vice president of the United States.

Born in North Topeka, Kansas, on January 25, 1860, Charles Curtis is the only person of documentable Indian blood quantum to be elected to the second-highest office of the land. On his maternal side he was one-eighth Kaw (or Kansa, as the tribe was known by Euro-Americans prior to 1850). Through the marriage of his great-great-grandfather to an Osage woman, he claimed a modest blood quantum of this tribe as well. Curtis's father was Orren Arms Curtis, a non-Indian who migrated to Kansas Territory from Indiana just prior to the Civil War.

Following the untimely death of his quarter-blood mother, Ellen, in 1863, young Curtis was placed in the home of his white grandmother, Permelia Hubbard Curtis. A stern person who insisted that the Methodist Church and the Republican Party were the keys to salvation, she exerted a considerable influence on Curtis's education. At age six Curtis went to live with his Indian grandmother, Julie Gonville Pappan, on the Kaw Reservation near Council Grove, Kansas, where he attended the Friends Mission School. But the removal of the Kaws to an Indian Territory reservation prompted his return, in 1868, to the home of his grandmother Curtis in North Topeka.

While attending elementary school, the young mixed blood worked weekends as a hack driver and produce peddler at the railroad station near his grandfather's hotel and bar in North Topeka. He also rode as a jockey in Kansas, in Indian Territory, and in Texas during the summer months of 1869–75. Following high school he read law under the Topeka attorney Aderial H. Case, and at age twenty-one he was admitted to the Kansas bar. He married Anne E. Baird of Topeka on November 27, 1884, and they had three children: Permelia, Harry, and Leona.

According to the terms of the Kansa Treaty of 1825, Curtis's grandmother Pappan was granted a fee-simple 640-acre allotment on the north bank of the Kansas River in North Topeka. Most of this allotment was sold to land jobbers, but a forty-acre tract was willed to Curtis and his sister upon the death of their mother. Utilizing his legal expertise, Curtis turned their forty-acre inheritance into a profitable enterprise, and in later years proudly cited his business acumen as proof that the allotment of Indian reservations was a powerful instrument in the assimilation of Indian people.

Curtis's formal political career began in 1885, when he was elected county attorney for Shawnee County; the county seat, Topeka, was also the state capital. Kansas had amended its constitution in favor of prohibition five years earlier, and the young attorney made the most of it. Contrary to the expectations of most Democrats and not a few Republicans, a zealous Curtis closed down most of the bootleg bars in the county, including those operating within the shadow of the state capitol. With his reputation thus established, Curtis was elected to Congress in 1892. According to William Allen White, who knew Curtis well, issues did not really bother the Kaw politician. His small talk of local affairs, family, and the weather was rendered all the more effective by his penetrating eyes, his engaging smile—and his Indianness, at a time when most whites nostalgically anticipated the demise of Indian America.

Because he failed to move to the Kaw Reservation in Indian Territory (Oklahoma) or take part in tribal affairs, the Indian Office removed Curtis's name from tribal membership in 1878. Yet as a member of committees dealing with tribal finances, Indian Territory legislation, and public lands—and, after 1903, as chairman of the House Committee on Indian Affairs—Congressman Curtis eagerly assumed a leadership role in the future of the American Indian. He sponsored the Curtis Act of 1898, which abolished tribal courts, established the legislative machinery for dissolution of the Five Civilized

Senate Majority Leader Charles Curtis, right, *riding with President-Elect Calvin Coolidge and his wife in the 1924 inaugural parade. Four years later Curtis became vice president of the United States under Herbert Hoover.*

Tribes, and paved the way for Oklahoma statehood. He championed the rights of Indian orphans and women even as he advocated the interests of the oil, gas, and coal companies that were cheating tribal governments of their natural resources. And he played a personal role in the allotment of his own tribe, returning to tribal membership in time to share in a lucrative distribution for himself and his children in 1902.

For his long hours and party dedication, including what one pundit termed his trinitarian support of the tariff, the GOP, and the GAR (Grand Army of the Republic), Curtis remained in the House until 1907, when he was selected to fill the unexpired term (1907–13) of Kansas senator Joseph R. Burton. Curtis was returned to the Senate by popular vote in 1914, where he served continuously until he became Herbert Hoover's vice president in 1929. In the Senate he headed the Rules Committee, served as party whip, and generally supported conservative farm policies, high tariffs, diplomatic isolation, veterans' benefits, prohibition, and the economic interests of his native state.

Following the death of Henry Cabot Lodge in 1924, Curtis was selected majority leader of the Senate. It was his finest hour. Yet he soon cast longing eyes on the White House—seeing the presidency as, if nothing else, a reward for his tireless service to the GOP. But when Hoover won the nomination on the first ballot at the Republican Convention in Kansas City, Curtis had to satisfy himself with the number-two spot on the ticket.

As vice president, Curtis called for improving the life of American Indians, yet he provided no details as to how this was to be accomplished. Ignoring a call for reform by John Collier, the Commissioner of Indian Affairs, Curtis cast his lot with assimilationist organizations such as the Exposition of Indian Tribal Arts (over which he proudly served as honorary chairman), a group of Southwest artists who attacked Collier's proposal for a national Indian Arts and Crafts Board on the grounds that it would lower the value of Indian products and stifle individual initiative.

Frustrated with the routine duties of the vice presidency, Curtis grudgingly wielded the Senate gavel and busied himself by decorating his office with Indian artifacts and hosting hundreds of official dinners. He attended cabinet meetings, yet his advice was seldom sought; perhaps, as one critic noted, he had little to offer.

The victory of Franklin D. Roosevelt in 1932 ended Curtis's political career. Even his home state of Kansas went for FDR, a rejection that loomed large in his decision to establish his legal residence in the District of Columbia. He retained a nominal association with a law firm in Topeka, but after 1933 his main interest was the Washington law office he had established, where Republican stalwarts gathered to discuss the future of the party and of the nation. On February 8, 1936, Curtis was found dead of a heart attack in his Washington home. Following memorial services in Washington and Topeka, Curtis was interred in a North Topeka cemetery not far from where he had been born three-quarters of a century earlier.

Seitz, Don C., *From Kaw Tepee to Capitol: The Life Story of Charles Curtis, Indian, Who Has Risen to High Estate* (New York: Frederick A. Stokes, 1928); Unrau, William E., *Mixed-Bloods and Tribal Dissolution: Charles Curtis and the Quest for Indian Identity* (Lawrence: University Press of Kansas, 1989).

WILLIAM E. UNRAU
Wichita State University

D

DALLES, THE

The Dalles is located in north central Oregon on a section of the Columbia River characterized by a series of steep, sloped rapids and known for its abundance of salmon. Because of the strong rapids, salmon swimming upstream stop to rest in the eddies, allowing fishermen an easy catch. In precontact times, the Dalles was a center of heavy trade and a favorite destination for annual fishing expeditions for tribes throughout the Pacific Northwest. Various native groups traded dried and fresh salmon, animal pelts, dentalia and other shells, dried plant food, and even slaves. The Wasco-Wishrams dominated the Dalles and enjoyed an extensive and lucrative trade network.

As a result of this extensive network, European trade items found their way into the economies of the Northwest tribes even though white traders themselves did not discover the Dalles until well after 1800. The fur trade quickly brought the Dalles tribes into extensive contact with whites. Fort Vancouver, established in the 1820s by the Hudson's Bay Company, served as the principal source of trade goods at the Dalles. This shift in economic power set the stage for the removal of local tribes by the United States to reservations in Oregon and Washington.

Nevertheless, treaty stipulations assured the continued access of the tribes to their traditional fishing spots at the Dalles. Challenges to those rights have punctuated the twentieth century, but the region's tribes are using the courts to ensure their present and future access to the area's rich natural resources.

See also Fishing; Fishing and Hunting Rights.

DANCE

American Indian dance exists everywhere in North America and in every venue, from the most traditional and private spaces to the most public and accessible. Thousands of dancers perform every day in out-of-the-way places—not to satisfy paying audiences or patrons, but to assure the continuation of ancient lifeways, to honor deities and each other, to associate with friends and kin, and to affirm their Indian identities. Others showcase Native American dance on the stage, using the worlds of ballet and modern dance or performing abridged versions of traditional dances.

Most Indian dance events are noncommercial and succeed with nothing but word-of-mouth advertising. The best performers and leaders (or choreographers) rely on time-tested notions of space, time, music, dress, adornment, and steps to create dance events. Although many dances and ceremonies are performed regularly by Indians living on or near reservations in the United States and Canada, new contexts—like urban Indian gatherings and powwows—foster the composition, change, and continuation of dance traditions. Music and dance are frequently shared across tribal boundaries in an ever-expanding circle of tradition.

Looking at the ancient art of the Americas, it is possible to imagine many dances dating back to prehistoric times. In the fall in North America, stately dancers in feather cloaks and engraved shell jewelry perform a harvest dance. In the winter, storytellers entertain young and old alike with legends of animals who can dance, talk, and sing. In the spring, dancers celebrate the cleansing of the earth and its waterways after a long winter. In the summer, children perform animal dances and games. All these activities existed when North America was inhabited only by native peoples. Some of these dance traditions still exist today.

After European contact, many Indians were dispersed from aboriginal lands to new homelands, cities, or reservations. At the same time, Indian religious practices—the nexus for most dances—became a focus of contention. When the Pueblo Indians of New Mexico and Arizona revolted in 1680 and forced the Spanish south to El Paso, they gained concessions regarding taxation, governance, and the moderation of religious persecution from the Europeans. After the revolt, na-

Crow dancers, circa 1900. At the left is a man dressed as a clown to amuse the audience.

tive religions and dances were often practiced alongside Catholic rituals. Though the U.S. government's nineteenth-century ban on Indian religions targeted the Sun Dance and Ghost Dance in particular, it affected all other facets of native religion as well. In Canada, the government seized many beautiful ceremonial objects and much dance regalia when Northwest Coast Indian potlatches became illegal. In the twentieth century, economic necessity and a U.S. government relocation program compelled many Indians to migrate to cities. Their creative solution for surviving urban alienation has been to start powwow clubs with other Indian community members, with Plains Indian music and

dance dominating regardless of the multiplicity of club members' tribal heritages.

From prehistoric evidence, early-contact drawings and paintings, and verbal descriptions from today's Indians (the keepers of tribal memory), we know something of early ceremonies, dances, and musical instruments. Dancers performed to both vocal and instrumental music, the latter featuring a variety of instruments. The musicians set the beat and marked the changes with both kettle and frame drums; hand-held rattles of gourd, rawhide, horn, and turtle shell; animal-tooth, turtle-shell, shell, and deer-hoof strung rattles worn on various parts of the dancers' bodies;

conch-shell trumpets; bird-bone whistles or trumpets; cane and ceramic flutes and whistles; striking sticks; struck logs; rasps; musical bows; and other, similar instruments. The various rattles enriched the sound by underscoring important words, keeping the beat, and adding sonic layers to the texture of the music.

Many of these instruments have survived. Furthermore, some important new additions to the catalog of instruments and dance regalia have evolved, arising from the substitution of metal rattles and bells for ones formerly made of natural materials. Tin-can leg rattles, for example, have substituted for rattles made from turtle shells, and metal saltshakers have sometimes replaced the hollow-gourd rattles used in the Gourd Dance. Sequins, trade beads, plastic bones, and other mass-produced items adorn today's dance outfits.

Dance still occupies an important place within many modern Indian groups. Many traditional dances, often tied to seasonal or life-cycle events, are regionally or tribally specific; the singers usually perform in native languages, and the ceremonies unfold according to ancient calendars and belief systems. Few traditional dances offer individual freedom of expression. Rather, each dancer expresses himself or herself within the bounds of prescribed physical action. In addition to public dances, there are private and semipublic dances for curing, prayer, initiation, storytelling, performing magic, playing games, courting, hunting, and influencing nature. In performing traditional songs, dances, and rituals, the Indians of today reaffirm their ties to a living culture.

Dance forms vary because Native Americans are different not only from other peoples, but from each other as well. One finds few solos, yet many ensemble forms. Many of the latter have a leader and chorus. Some are unison groups; others, groups with featured soloists. A few include dancers with individualistic styles. Sometimes one finds multipart dances, with the dancers occupying a variety of roles. Not all Indian people dance to a drum. Often the dancers themselves, activating the rattles and bells that adorn their dance clothes, set the beat.

Indian dance is not particularly acrobatic. It is in fact somewhat restrained, with the dancers staying close to the earth, for practical as well as philosophical reasons. Dancers usually take small steps—because of space, the number of participants, or the need to conserve their strength in order to dance for long periods of time (sometimes all day or night). Some dancers mimic animals or birds, or the work of hunting, fishing, planting,

harvesting, and preparing food, or other occupations, or warfare. The largest motions are in the torso and head, with very few twists of the dancer's body. Feet, when they are extended, act as a unit with the legs, and hands with the arms. Small movements of the forearms and wrists occur when the dancer shakes an implement such as a rattle, stick, or branch. Some expressions in dance require crouching or bent-over postures, which do not usually lend themselves to quick movements. Although individual expression can be a part of most North American Plains dances, Pueblo dances require unison and strict rules of motion, broken up from time to time by the relatively free movements of the clowns. The Hoop Dance, a modern "show dance" of many tribes, is one of the most individual; it features a dancer's manipulation of a dozen or more hoops over and around his or her torso, legs, and arms to form a variety of geometric shapes.

Frequently the directions of the dances, the words that accompany the music, the number of repetitions of a dance sequence, the choice and manufacture of instruments, the dress and bodily adornment, and the interactions of performers are symbolic in nature and cannot be properly appreciated unless the observer is familiar with the community's beliefs. Indeed, in Indian life the dance is inextricably bound to the belief systems and the music, and the belief systems and the music can hardly exist without the dance.

With American Indian dance, unlike most Euro-American classical and folk dance, it is often not possible to predict certain elements: the exact length of a dance, the number of beats before a turn, the number of dancers required, the exact time of the performance, or even whether a rehearsal will be held. Although many Indian communities offer songs and dances from ancient times, even some of these older ceremonies require new compositions each season—such as the Turtle Dance *(Okushare),* Cloud Dance *(Pongonshare),* and Basket Dance *(Tunshare)* of San Juan Pueblo. Though the ancient standards and beliefs are upheld, new words and tunes appear within that framework, and each season the dancers must rehearse anew with the singers.

Other forms—like the Stomp Dance of the Cherokees, Creeks, Yuchis, and other tribes that formerly inhabited the southeastern United States—offer infinite variation within a set framework. No two Stomp Dances would ever be identical. The song/dance leader begins with a standardized introduction, with the chorus echoing him in call-and-response fashion. Then he chooses from among the many songs in his repertoire, stringing them together in a cycle. Each song and each section in the song vary in length and number of beats from time to time, whether because of inspiration, the introduction of words, or individual artistry. Since the dancers, singers, and instrumentalists (women dancers wearing turtle-shell leg rattles) all dance with and follow the leader, the improvisatory style is exhilarating, not problematic. The leader gives a hand signal for a subtle change of beat, the dancers slow or stop, and all make the transition to the next song, sometimes marking it with a group shout.

In the early stages of ethnographic research, many researchers sought out the oldest dancers and singers, hoping to find "pure" art forms. In this search for purity, researchers ignored the fact that Indian people have the creativity and ability to change their music and dance over time. Although the repetition of ancient songs, dances, and ceremonies is necessary to maintain social, religious, and curing ceremonies, the creation and performance of new songs and dances is equally necessary to ensure sustained interest and continuity. It is commendable to reenact a dance from the nineteenth century about a war expedition, but it is equally important to compose new songs and dances for modern events, as some Oklahoma Kiowas have done for the 1991 Operation Desert Storm.

New dances and genres continue to arise, with new words, melodies, steps, and regalia. For example, the women's Fancy-Shawl and Jingle-Dress competitions feature many innovations, particularly in freedom of movement. The contemporary revival of many Indian dances has also fostered a healthy controversy over authenticity of versions; proper instrumentation and dress; suitable venues; ownership of songs, dances, and ceremonies; and even whether some dances should be revived at all.

In the future, social dances will likely survive, but less communal and more specialized dances—ceremonial dances and curing ceremonies—may not outlast their specialist practitioners. If people continue to live out of the mainstream in rural pockets, native people will persevere in carrying on their language, music, dance, and ceremonies. If community life disintegrates further because of economic or political necessity, music and dance may also perish.

The value of Indian dances to the peoples who created them and still use them cannot be overestimated. The importance of American Indian dance is found not only in its impact on modern society, but also in the traditions and values it expresses to and for Indian peoples. Native peoples' relationships to their creators, to their fellow humans, and to nature are what American Indian dance really celebrates.

See also Music.

Heth, Charlotte, ed., *Native American Dance: Ceremonies and Social Traditions* (Washington, D.C.: National Museum of the American Indian, Smithsonian Institution, 1992; Golden, Colorado: Fulcrum Publishing, 1992); Kurath, Gertrude Prokosch, *Half a Century of Dance Research* (Flagstaff, Ariz.: Cross-Cultural Dance Resources, 1986).

CHARLOTTE HETH (Cherokee)
National Museum of the American Indian
Smithsonian Institution

DAWES ACT

Named for its sponsor, Massachusetts senator Henry L. Dawes, the Dawes Act or General Allotment Act of 1887 attempted to establish private ownership of Indian lands by initiating government partitions of reservations. Under the act, each Indian family head was to receive 160 acres, and all other individuals over the age of eighteen were to receive 80 acres each. Individuals would be allowed to select their allotments, but a tribe that had been marked by the Indian Office for allotment could not stop the process. Subsequent amendments gave the secretary of the interior the authority to sell or lease these allotted lands. The allotment process began soon after the passage of the act and continued until it was formally ended by the 1934 Indian Reorganization Act.

The Dawes Act reflected both the assimilationist tone of the late nineteenth century and non-Indians' belief in the "civilizing" power of land ownership. Although not all tribes and reservations came under the jurisdiction of the act, the allotment process deprived Indian people of more than 90 million acres of land—or around two-thirds of their total land base.

DEATH

In the early spring of 1832 a prominent Mandan woman died. She had lived in an earth-lodge village located on the Missouri River near present-day Bismarck, North Dakota. She had many children and during her lifetime had been a member of the White Buffalo Cow Society and had participated in its powerful animal-calling rituals; she had also held rights in one of the important Holy Women bundles. As a consequence of her relation to this bundle, she had a reputation as a powerful healer. Her relatives immediately began to make preparations, dressing the woman in her finest clothes and placing her favorite gardening stick with her body. She was oiled and her face painted red; then her body was wrapped in a bison hide and the entire bundle was secured with leather thongs.

The body was carried to an area within sight of the village and placed on a four-post scaffold. Relatives expressed their grief by clipping their hair, sometimes gashing themselves with knives or cutting off a finger joint. For some days afterward, her husband, her children, and other relatives would go to the site, often lying under the scaffold, mourning their loss. On the fourth day after the death, a ritual was performed that released her spirit, allowing it to travel to the earth-lodge village of the dead located downstream on the Missouri River.

After the scaffold had rotted, all of her bones except the skull were placed in a bundle and buried in the village refuse pile. The skull was lovingly placed, along with others, in a large circle outside the village. All of the skulls faced the center, and each rested on a bed of sage. On a small mound in the middle were two bison skulls, one male and one female. When the weather was pleasant, one of the woman's daughters might be seen sitting beside the skull, chatting pleasantly with her mother about events of the past few days.

While the Mandan ritual of releasing the spirit was taking place, half a continent to the west another person had died. This man was a prominent member of Tlingit society and had lived in a village located on the southwestern coast of Alaska. After his body was washed and his face painted, the knees were drawn up and tied; the corpse was wrapped in blankets and was placed in a sitting position at the back of a house. Surrounding his body were crests symbolizing his status in the community. After a wake of eight days, the body was cremated and the remains placed in a box that was taken to a grave house belonging to his relatives. One or more years later a memorial potlatch was held. This ritual honored the ancestor, legitimated the social status of his kin group, and reaffirmed that group's sacred traditions. At the conclusion of this ritual process, the man's bones were placed in a new mortuary box.

Across the continent, to the north of Lake Ontario, another ritual was taking place in a Huron village. Many kin had died during the past eight years, and it was time to place their bones in a communal grave. Because some of these persons were prominent, much property had been gathered in anticipation of the ritual of resuscitation that was about to unfold. At the end of this ritual, the dead gained new life as others took their names and responsibilities, some of the names of important chiefs becoming clan or lineage titles.

These descriptions are composite portraits of mortuary practices in three different societies based on observations made during the eighteenth and nineteenth centuries. Among other Native Americans at about the same time period, images and practices surrounding death were as vivid, concrete, and different. These cultural differences were rooted deep in the pre-Columbian past. Comprehending this diversity for the whole of North America is impossible, but some generalizations can be made on the basis of what is known about particular peoples. In addition to the mortuary rituals and practices that have been illustrated, Native American peoples had traditions explaining how death originated; they projected various notions of how the body was animated; and they maintained complex traditions about a land of the dead.

The Mandan creator, Lone Man, decreed that human beings should not live longer than one hundred years, but elsewhere on the Great Plains there were different views. Among the Blackfeet on the northern plains, Napi or Old Man argued with Old Woman concerning whether people should die or live forever. After some discussion, Old Woman threw a rock in the water, saying that if it floated people would come back to life after four days; if it sank people would die forever. In that primordial time, as a consequence of this act, death became an inalterable part of human destiny. Similar traditions were told elsewhere on the northern plains as well as on the southern plains, but the actors had different identities. Among the Apaches the two major figures responsible for the origin of death were Coyote and Raven; and in Caddoan death traditions, Coyote was a prominent figure.

Words translated as "soul," "spirit," or "ghost" both reveal and conceal Native American understandings of death. According to the view of many North American peoples, there were at least two souls or spirits. One animated the body, while the other traveled in dreams and visions. It was this latter spirit that sometimes joined the body spirit and became identified with the personality that survived after death. Among the Naskapis on the Labrador peninsula and the Cherokees in the Southeast, notions of the soul or spirit were associated with the identity of the individual, and included both intellectual and emotional dimensions.

Mandans thought that humans possessed four spirits. A white spirit was associated with the white sage plant. The second spirit was light brown and was associated with the meadowlark. The third spirit was identified more closely with the particular dwelling place of the dead person. The fourth spirit was black and was associated with a ghost that might frighten the people. The white and brown spirits united after death, traveling to the village of the dead, while the third spirit remained near the lodge where the person had died.

After death occurred, an individual's spirit traveled to a land of the dead. In some groups there were rituals that released the spirit for its journey; and in other groups, such as the Lakotas, spirits of relatives were kept for a time in a sacred bundle before being released. Spirits often traveled along particular roads or paths that followed some feature of the natural terrain, such as a stream or river. Many groups believed that the dead traveled along a sky road, the Milky Way.

While there was probably no Native American understanding of a place of eternal damnation, there were some spirits who had a more difficult time entering the land of the dead or who did not arrive at their destination at all. The Hidatsas, who lived near the Mandans on the Missouri River, believed that murderers became restless spirit wanderers, never to rejoin their kin in the land of the dead. The Mandans believed that babies who died before being named were not yet part of the community; their spirits returned to a place known as the Baby Hill, to be reborn at a later time.

The land of the dead was imagined in very different ways, but in many instances spirits lived there in much the same way as they had in the land of the living. For the Blackfeet, this land was in the Sand Hills, a place somewhere out on the plains away from the camps of the living. Some Hidatsas thought it was under Devil's Lake in eastern North Dakota, while others thought there was a sky country where the dead lived again. The Naskapis also thought the dead lived in the sky. There the dead often danced, illuminating the horizon as the northern lights. In the Northwest the Sanpoils believed the dead lived on an island in the middle of a great river. For many Pacific Coast peoples, the land of the dead was located far out in the sea, beyond the western horizon. The Laguna Pueblo people believed that ancestors became clouds or kachina spirits, bringing life-giving rain to the people.

Because of government attempts to assimilate Native American peoples, and a long history of Christian missionary activities, some indigenous traditions and practices surrounding death have disappeared. Others continue to evolve and shape the experience of many present-day Native American peoples. For example, indigenous traditions about death still persist among some Northern Cheyennes. The spirits of most people who die travel to a land of the dead located at the end of the Milky Way. The spirits of persons who have violated the Cheyenne way may become lost or reincarnated as animals. Since for many Northern Cheyenne people separation and loneliness are greatly feared, a good death is viewed as one that allows the person to rejoin his or her spirit kin. Among the Tewas of San Juan Pueblo, Catholic symbolism informs some of the rituals surrounding death, but encompassing the Catholic motifs is an overarching Tewa world, rich with traditional religious symbolism and practice. A survey of many other contemporary Native American societies would show similar patterns of continuity and discontinuity, as indigenous traditions surrounding death and dying continue to be preserved as well as changed.

Hultkrantz, Åke, "The Soul and the Life Hereafter," in *The Religions of the American Indians* (Berkeley: University of California Press, 1979); Kan, Sergei, *Symbolic Immortality: The Tlingit Potlatch of the Nineteenth Century* (Washington: Smithsonian Institution, 1989).

HOWARD L. HARROD
Vanderbilt University

DEGANAWIDA

An Iroquois spiritual figure, Deganawida (the name means "Two River Currents Flowing Together"), according to Iroquois tradition, joined Hiawatha to form a political and social confederation of five Iroquois tribes.

The traditional historical narratives of Deganawida's life do not always agree. Some claim that he was born into the Huron tribe to a virgin mother who attempted to drown him. Others chronicle Deganawida's Huron origins but mention nothing of this calamity, and still others say he was born into the Onondaga Nation and was later adopted by the Mohawks. All accounts agree that Deganawida felt predestined to unite the Iroquois tribes living south of the Hurons. The Iroquois also credit Deganawida's considerable diplomatic skills with establishing the confederacy of the Senecas, Cayugas, Oneidas, Onondagas, and Mohawks and with laying down the confederacy's laws, regulations, and principles. Interestingly, it is also claimed that Deganawida was a poor public speaker; Hiawatha is credited with giving life to Deganawida's visionary plans through his oratorical skills.

DELAWARE

The Delawares—known to themselves as Lenape or Lenni Lenape (People Who Are the Standard)—spoke a language belonging to the eastern branch of the Algonquian or Algic stock. Until the late seventeenth and early eighteenth centuries their homeland was the drainage of the Delaware River and all of its tributaries, along with the lower portion of the Hudson River. At least three dialects of Delaware were spoken: northern or Munsee, southern or Unami, and a coastal one later called Unalachtigo (Those Who Left the Waves Behind). The geographical break between speakers of Munsee and Unami came at the Lehigh River below the Delaware River Water Gap. These dialects became the basis for later tribal identifications when European pressures forced the Delawares to consolidate into political entities.

Aboriginally, the Delawares were divided into numerous groups identified with their own village, hunting territories, and river tributary. Their tribal identity was based in the traditional religion, particularly its rituals. According to traditional belief, Lenapehaking (Delaware land) was thought into being by a male Creator, who caused a giant turtle to rise from the primordial sea before a great cedar grew at the center of its shell to produce the first man and woman, who were the parents of all other life.

The major Delaware ritual, the Gamwing (Big House Rite), defined the larger communities within Delaware society. The principal towns had special gabled longhouses where this ceremony was held every autumn to give thanks for the harvest of corn, beans, squash, sunflowers, and other crops and to pray for successful hunting. In all, the rite expressed the mutual dependence of men and women on each other, as expressed through a necessary joint reliance on crops and meat,

summer and winter, and day and night. During the two weeks of the rite, the world was renewed and all within the region confirmed their personal ties with local spirits as each, in turn, sang his or her own song of power during night gatherings.

Generally, Delaware men were hunters, making their weapons and tools of stone and wood, and women were farmers, producing pots, baskets, and leather clothing. Women worked together, but men hunted alone except when everyone helped during fall fire surrounds to capture and kill deer herds.

Like their immediate neighbors—the Mahicans, Mohawks, and Oneidas—the Delawares had three clans. The Delaware clans were called Wolf or Round Foot, Turkey, and Turtle or Concave Foot. Since the Delawares traced kinship and clan membership through the mother, periodic ceremonies, owned by clan leaders, were held in the farming town belonging to that clan. These important rites, which involved masked men representing the spirits of Mother Corn or game animals, brought family members together and attracted huge gatherings. Smaller rites in honor of sacred dolls, bears, and otters were sponsored by the women of particular households, for the local community.

This mixed economy of hunting and farming required seasonal movements from the large summer farming towns filled with bark-shingled longhouses and the summer resorts along the Atlantic shore to upland camps for fall hunting. Each of these areas was managed by the inhabitants and users. For example, hunting lands were burned over in the fall to increase visibility and to encourage fresh growth in the spring. The shells of clams and oysters were piled in middens along the shore to create well-drained platforms for campers. In addition, a far-flung trade network brought exotic goods like shell, mica, and copper to religious centers at the Falls (modern Trenton) and Minisink Island (upriver). The center at the Falls maintained trading ties with the Illinois Hopewells and, perhaps, with later Mississippian mound builders. These distant links were used as the basis for claiming settlements in Ohio and Indiana when Delaware refugees began moving westward.

Contacts with Europeans (Basques, English, Spaniards) began before 1524, when Giovanni da Verrazano was greeted in New York Harbor without awe. Despite their self-confidence, however, the Delawares soon learned what damage European epidemics could wreak upon them. By the seventeenth century many Delawares were angry and discouraged; some of them attacked Henry Hudson's ships when he appeared in 1609. In 1624, daily contacts with Europeans began when Dutch Walloons (French-speaking Protestants) settled on Burlington Island in the lower Delaware River. As trading for corn, other crops, and wampum beads developed, a special trade vocabulary or jargon, based on uninflected Unami words, arose and soon spread throughout the Northeast when the Walloons were resettled at New Amsterdam (modern New York) in 1626. The Swedish colony in modern Delaware State also used this jargon. The trade in beaver pelts soon dominated the lives of Delaware men, whose families were eager for guns, metal pots, machined cloth, axes, needles, and china.

European rivalries and conflicts (which had allowed the Delawares to play all sides off against each other) eventually allowed the English to take over the Dutch colonies in 1655. Aided by their Iroquois allies, the English forced land-cession treaties on various Delaware enclaves. From their homeland, most Delawares moved into Pennsylvania, where the last group to live on their namesake river was defrauded of their land by the Penn family during the infamous Walking Purchase of 1737.

Pressed by white settlers, the Delawares moved to the Tuscarawas branch of the Muskingum River in Ohio. There the American Revolution overtook them. The Delawares divided into neutrals in Ohio, pro-Americans at Pittsburgh, and pro-English Loyalists in northwestern Ohio. (During this time the Delawares occupied the symbolic position of "women" or peace-keeping matrons in an intertribal league fostered by the Dutch and British in which the Iroquois were the "men." In addition, the other Algonquian tribes addressed the Delawares as "grandfather" at formal gatherings. While these kinship uses were consistent with native practices, they baffled many colonial white officials.)

During the 1790s, most of the pro-British Munsees went to Canada, where they remain. The Unamis continued west, settling in Indiana (1800–1820), Missouri (1821–29), and Kansas (1830–67) before finally accepting a reservation in Oklahoma (1867 to present). Along the way, a bewildering number of splinter groups were left at each location or set off on their own. Prominent among these were some Unamis who left Indiana and settled along the Mississippi in 1789, allied themselves with the Caddos in Texas, and fled with them to central Oklahoma in 1869.

Even while moving, again and again, to avoid colonial malice, numbers of Delawares were the victims of repeated atrocities, including the massacres at Pavonia (1643), Paxtung (1763), Gnadenhutten (1782), and Moraviantown (1813).

After experiencing depopulation, dislocation, and distress in their homeland, the Delawares regrouped in Ohio under the able leadership of Netawatawas (or Newcomber). Later, in Indiana, a woman prophet reframed their rituals to reconstitute the kind of ceremonially based congregation that had aboriginally defined membership in the greater Delaware community. She gave women a more prominent role at the start and finish of the Gamwing and encouraged young men to take leadership positions. As a consequence of this regrouping, several Delawares were executed for sorcery, as well as for their pro-American and Christian stances.

Although the Delawares were exposed to Lutheran missionaries during the days of the Dutch and Swedish colonies, few listened and fewer converted. An active mission began when Moravians, a sect of pietistic Protestants from central Europe, founded Bethlehem, Pennsylvania, in 1740 and converted Delaware refugees in the area. In Ohio separate Delaware and Mahican mission towns shared the Tuscarawas with followers of the Gamwing and other rites. Over ninety members of Gnadenhutten, a Christian Delaware town, were massacred by American soldiers in 1782, and the survivors left the United States for Canada, settling Moraviantown on the Thames River. That village was in turn attacked by American forces during their invasion of Canada in 1813. Another Moravian mission was attempted in Indiana, but failed in the aftermath of the prophet-led religious fervor.

In 1833, a few of the Canadian Moravian Delawares rejoined the majority in Kansas but, feeling unwelcome, went back to the Thames. In Kansas, Baptists and Methodists began to convert those Delawares who were living as rural farmers so that, by the time these Unami Delawares moved to Oklahoma, the traditionalists or "Big House people" were in the minority, continuing to hold the Gamwing every year until 1924, with a brief attenuated revival during World War II. By then, these traditionalist families were involved in the Native American church or the peyote religion; the latter had a particular appeal because John Wilson (Moonhead), whose father was Delaware, composed the original songs and conducted meetings of the longer Big Moon Way. Over time, however, the Delawares have adopted the forms of the shorter Little Moon Way of Quanah Parker and the Comanches, Caddos, and Kiowas. Little Moon is now the preferred practice of the Oklahoma Delawares.

Today, aside from those Munsees living with the Stockbridge-Munsees of Wisconsin and with a tiny Ojibwa community in Kansas, most Munsees live in Ontario, where Delawares share the Grand River Reserve of the Six Nations under the sponsorship of the Cayugas, who loaned them the use of their longhouse when their own Big House was abandoned. Along the nearby Thames River, there are two communities: Moraviantown, founded in 1792; and Munceytown, settled in the 1830s by Munsees who converted to Methodism. In 1900, over six hundred people identified as Munsees; by 1950, there were about one thousand.

The majority of Unami Delawares are in eastern Oklahoma, where they purchased rights in the Cherokee Nation in 1867 but were not recognized as Cherokee citizens until 1890. By 1900, tribal governance shifted from selected chiefs to an elected business council. The Delawares suffered allotment after 1902, along with the other Oklahoma tribes. This process ended in 1907, and the tribe's remaining land was sold, except for cemeteries held in trust. Poverty became common. The Dust Bowl and the Great Depression drove many Christian Delawares to California, where the tribal language was used for hymns and sermons until midcentury. In 1900, about one thousand people identified as Delawares, but by 1980 the tribal roll, which recognizes only descent, not blood quantum, included almost ten thousand, many of them recruited by land-claim settlements in 1963, 1969, and 1971 (although the money was not released until a 1977 court order).

The Delawares in western Oklahoma, who moved from Missouri into Texas and lived with the Caddos until forced to Anadarko in 1859, are the only federally recognized Delaware community in the United States, although for much of this century they were submerged under the official designation of Wichitas and Affiliated Bands.

Most Delawares have historically worked as unskilled laborers, but increasing numbers are becoming professionals. Many are nurses and teachers, and a few are doctors, accountants, lawyers, businesspeople, and professors. Those near urban centers like Tulsa, Oklahoma City, and London, Ontario, have been better paid and employed, particularly in the oil and cattle industries. Payment for land claims provided each enrolled member with a modest sum, with 10 percent of the total reserved for various tribal enterprises. A tribal or band business council now governs each community.

Oklahoma groups have also generated tribal income from bingo and the sale of tobacco products.

For the Delawares, the highlight of recent decades has been a series of events bringing together leaders and others from their many communities. In March 1983, these leaders dedicated a Munsee exhibit at Katonah, New York. In June 1987, they gathered again to rebury the bones of an ancestor found during the renovation of Ellis Island. In 1988, 1990, and 1992, civic leaders of New Philadelphia, Ohio, hosted academic and social gatherings celebrating the Delawares and legally chartering a modern version of the Delaware Nation Grand Council of North America, incorporated in August 1992.

Naming ceremonies continue to be held, but without their ancient religious context. Native kin terms, polite phrases, and food names remain in use, but the language is moribund, with few fluent speakers. Each summer, every Delaware community hosts a tribal powwow, when Woodland-style outfits are still worn and widely scattered families gather at the current home of their clan or tribe.

Goddard, Ives, "Delaware," in *Handbook of North American Indians,* ed. William C. Sturtevant, vol. 15, *Northeast,* ed. Bruce Trigger (Washington: Smithsonian Institution, 1978); Miller, Jay, and Nora Thompson Dean, "A Personal Account of the Delaware Big House Rite," *Pennsylvania Archaeologist* 48, no. 1–2 (1978): 39–43; Weslager, C. A., *The Delaware Indians: A History* (New Brunswick, N.J.: Rutgers University Press, 1972).

JAY MILLER (Lenape)
Lushootseed Research

DELORIA, ELLA (ANPETU WASTE)

(1889–1971)
Yankton Sioux linguist and author.

A member of a prominent Sioux family, Ella Deloria was one of the first truly bilingual, bicultural figures in American anthropology. She translated thousands of pages of ethnographic texts written in the Sioux language, wrote in both the Lakota and Dakota dialects herself, and compiled a Lakota grammar and dictionary. These activities helped insure the survival and continued strength of the Sioux language.

The familial nature of Deloria's biculturalism can be traced to her grandfather, François Des Lauriers, who served the Yankton Sioux both as a traditional spiritual leader and as a political intermediary in negotiations with the federal government. Her father, the Reverend Philip Deloria, and her brother, the Reverend Vine Deloria, Sr., were native clergymen who between them brought thousands of Sioux Indians into the Episcopal Church. Her nephews Vine Deloria, Jr., and Philip S. Deloria have also played prominent roles in Indian affairs since the 1960s.

Ella Deloria was born on January 31, 1889, in the White Swan district of the Yankton Sioux Reservation in South Dakota. The following year the family moved from Yankton to the St. Elizabeth's mission at Wakpala, on the Standing Rock Reservation. Between home and mission, Deloria grew up speaking all three of her language's dialects—the Lakota, Dakota, and Nakota variations—and possessing a fluent knowledge of the subtleties of Sioux culture. Deloria proved equally adept at her non-Indian, religious education. She excelled at both the St. Elizabeth's mission school and, beginning in 1902, the All Saint's School in Sioux Falls, South Dakota, where she performed well enough to win a scholarship to Oberlin College. After two years at Oberlin, Deloria transferred to Columbia University in New York, where in 1914 she graduated with a B.A. in education.

While at Columbia, Deloria gave public lectures on Indian subjects, demonstrated Dakota dances, and worked with school and Campfire Girls groups to develop a wider appreciation of native cultures. Equally important, she began working for the anthropologist Franz Boas, translating the manuscripts of George Bushotter, a Lakota who had collaborated with the anthropologist James Dorsey in 1887 and 1888 and who had left behind over a thousand pages of material written in the Lakota dialect. In 1914 Deloria returned as a teacher to the All Saint's School while her sister Susan finished her studies. Two years later, with their mother seriously ill, the two returned home to Wakpala. Their mother died shortly thereafter, and the sisters remained at home in order to assist their father. Although Deloria had become comfortable in the non-Indian world of New York City, she plotted her life in terms of her Dakota kinship obligations to her family.

In 1923, at age thirty-five, Deloria embarked upon her own career, becoming a physical-education instructor at the Haskell Institute in Lawrence, Kansas. Working conditions at Haskell proved to be less than satisfactory, however, and when Boas contacted her in 1927 about continuing the translation of the Bushotter materials, she moved back to New York. Over the next decade Boas and Deloria established a close profession-

al relationship, with Deloria working in the field—collecting language materials and ethnographic information in South Dakota—and then traveling to New York for the more collaborative work of translation and synthesis. In 1932 she published *Dakota Texts*, which consists of sixty-four oral narratives recorded in Dakota with both literal and free English translations.

Deloria found working for Boas intellectually challenging, but she constantly teetered on the brink of economic disaster, frequently having to plead for more work and better compensation. She had skill and practical experience equal to that of any of Boas's famous protégés, but she barely received a research assistant's wage. At one point she and her sister lived out of a car while gathering material for Boas. Deloria's obligations to her father, who had suffered a series of strokes, complicated matters still further. Funding for her research was always sporadic, and in 1938 it dried up almost completely. She patched together periods of employment with a private group studying Navajo affairs, with the Episcopal Church, and, in 1940, with the Farm Security Administration.

Deloria's diminishing economic reliance on Boas (who died in 1942) forced her to assert herself as a scholar in her own right. In 1943 and 1944 she received research grants from the American Philosophical Society that allowed her to begin an ethnographic study of the Dakotas, *Camp Circle Society*. In 1944 she published a popular book, *Speaking of Indians*, and in 1948 she received a grant from the Wenner-Gren Foundation to continue her research. During this period she also completed the manuscript for *Waterlily*, an "ethnographic novel" that paints a precontact Dakota world through the eyes of native women.

The same sense of obligation—part Dakota kinship, part Christian religious training—that had led her to tend her parents at the expense of her career reemerged in 1955 when she reluctantly agreed to take over the school at her father's mission. In 1958, however, she vowed to devote more time to *Camp Circle Society*, and again pieced together part-time museum and lecture work. In 1961 Deloria was appointed assistant director of the W. H. Over Museum at the University of South Dakota at Vermillion, where she began assembling a lexicon of Siouan language material. The following year, at age seventy-three, Deloria and the university's Institute for Indian Studies received a large National Science Foundation grant to compile a Sioux dictionary. This long-awaited triumph was tempered, however, by the death in 1963 of her sister and lifelong companion, Susan.

After months of grieving, Deloria returned to the dictionary, the project having been continued (although without additional funds) through 1968. In 1966 and again in 1968, Deloria spent two months of the year teaching Sioux language and culture at St. Mary's Indian School for Girls in Springfield, South Dakota. She remained active in the late 1960s, conducting workshops for the Nebraska Teacher Corps and working for six months on a claims report for the Yankton tribe. Ella Deloria continued working on her dictionary, publishing articles, and giving lectures until shortly before her death on February 12, 1971.

Deloria overcame numerous difficulties—her lack of an advanced degree, constant economic hardship, and race, gender, and age biases—to produce an astonishing body of work. The Bushotter manuscript and others by George Sword and Jack Frazier, which make up a significant part of the corpus of Lakota-Dakota ethnography, owe their existence in English translation to Ella Deloria, as do numerous other documents. The Deloria-Boas grammar has become a standard source in Lakota linguistics, and the Deloria dictionary is being reworked for publication. In addition, through her practice of teaching and writing in Siouan dialects and encouraging teachers to use their native tongue, Deloria not only protected the language but, as the author Julian Rice has recently argued, *projected* a native-language literature decades before a readership existed. Her personalized efforts to instruct non-Indians in Sioux culture fulfilled the familial mission of bridging the two cultures. Deloria's literary and anthropological legacy is only now beginning to find a wider audience—both Indian and non-Indian—through publication, republication, and critical analysis.

Deloria, Ella, *Waterlily* (Lincoln: University of Nebraska Press, 1988); Rice, Julian, *Deer Women and Elk Men: The Lakota Narratives of Ella Deloria* (Albuquerque: University of New Mexico Press, 1992).

PHILIP J. DELORIA (Lakota ancestry)
University of Colorado at Boulder

DELORIA, VINE, SR.

(1901–90)
Standing Rock Sioux (Fort Yates) priest and leader.

The Deloria family has produced several distinguished religious leaders. The family name is derived from the name of a French trapper, Des Lauriers, who had been taken into the tribe sometime in the eighteenth century. Vine Deloria, Sr.'s paternal grandfather, Saswe or François, was a Yankton subchief and medicine man who underwent a conversion to Christianity in the 1860s, an event one writer has called "legendary," and the story of which is still told and discussed among the Sioux. An enthusiastic Christian, François welcomed the missionaries who took up residence on the Yankton reservation and sent his children to their school. His son Philip Deloria was a particularly good student. He attended both local and off-reservation boarding schools and was ordained as a priest in 1892. He remained in charge of the Standing Rock Mission until 1925. Philip Deloria was one of the first Sioux Indians to become an Episcopal priest. While he was in charge of the North Dakota Episcopal Mission, he supervised the construction of St. Elizabeth's School.

Vine Deloria, Sr.'s mother, Mary Sully, was the granddaughter of an army-post marriage between General Alfred Sully and a Yankton woman during the 1860s. Vine Victor was the youngest child of Philip and Mary Sully Deloria. He was born on October 6, 1901, in the village of Wakpala, on the Standing Rock reservation.

Vine Deloria's birth occurred eleven years after the massacre at Wounded Knee and less than a decade after Frederick Jackson Turner announced the close of the American frontier. Deloria grew up in the Standing Rock vicarage, but he was familiar with life on a variety of Dakota reservations. His childhood took place during a time of momentous transition as the Sioux adjusted to the end of buffalo hunting and the onset of assimilation. Tribespeople reeled under the multiple impacts of allotment, the sale of reservation lands, the suppression of traditional culture, and the shattered dreams of a failed tribal cattle industry.

When his mother died in 1915, Deloria entered Kearney (Nebraska) Military Academy, an Episcopal educational institution. Although he could not speak English and had never before had a long-term stay away from home, he did well in school. In 1921 he graduated as a cadet major. He enrolled in St. Stephen's College, a predecessor of Bard College, in Annandale, New York. Deloria was a renowned college athlete, and in 1922 Walter Camp named him an honorable mention all-American back. He graduated from St. Stephen's in liberal arts in 1926.

For brief periods, Deloria worked as boy's athletic adviser at the Fort Sill (Oklahoma) federal Indian boarding school and then as a Colorado coal miner before acceding to his father's wish and entering General Theological Seminary in New York City in 1928. He returned to South Dakota in late April 1931 to be ordained as an Episcopal deacon in his father's church. Shortly thereafter his father died. Deloria returned to the seminary and graduated. His first assignment was at the Pine Ridge Mission, where he served under the well-known pioneer Episcopal missionary Father Neville Joyner. In 1932 Deloria married Barbara Sloat Eastburn of New York. That May he was ordained as a priest. They had three children: a daughter, Barbara Sanchez, and sons Vine, Jr., and Sam.

In the 1870s Philip Deloria had been one of the three founders of the Brotherhood of Christian Unity, formerly called the Planting Society. An interdenominational Christian fellowship, it is the oldest continuous all-Indian organization in the United States. When Vine Deloria entered the ministry, he worked diligently in the BCU, serving frequently as an elected officer. He served with distinction during forty active years, seeing ministerial duty on all South Dakota reservations before spending 1951–53 in Dennison, Iowa. He ministered to reservation and urban Indians, mixed congregations, and white parishioners. Because he was fluent in all three Sioux dialects, he preached in the native tongue of his congregations, as well as in English. He served a church in Durant, Iowa, beginning in 1958, and then returned to South Dakota in 1961 to be archdeacon of the Niobrara Convocation, encompassing the Sioux, who made up the largest single ethnic minority within the Protestant Episcopal Church in the United States. From 1954 to 1958 he worked at the national headquarters of the Episcopal Church as executive secretary for Indian work; he was the first American Indian to be appointed to a major national church position. From 1965 to 1967 he was the vice-chair of that church's National Advisory Committee on Indian Work. His efforts paved the way for the formation two years later of the church's National Committee on Indian Work. During his retirement in South Dakota, Deloria worked in the BCU, taught, and provided ministerial assistance when needed.

Because both of his parents had been previously married and widowed, Deloria had several half-brothers and -sisters. Among the other children of Mary and Philip, however, was Ella Deloria (1889–1971), who graduated from Columbia University in 1914, later studying anthropology with Franz Boas. Among her publications are *Dakota Texts* (1932) and *Speaking of Indians* (1944). Following gradually declining health,

Vine Deloria, Sr., died on February 26, 1990, in Tucson, Arizona, at the age of eighty-eight. His years of service, his devotion, and his example of selfless giving were honored with addresses, the presentation of gifts to guests, and a memorial dinner at the 118th annual meeting of the Niobrara Convocation in June of that year.

See also Deloria, Ella; Sioux.

Deloria, Vine, Sr., "The Establishment of Christianity among the Sioux," in Raymond J. DeMallie and Douglas R. Parks, eds., *Sioux Indian Religion: Tradition and Innovation* (Norman: University of Oklahoma Press, 1987); "Deloria, Vine, Sr.," in *The Encyclopedia of Native American Religions,* Arlene Hirschfelder and Paulette Molin, eds. (New York: Facts on File, 1992); Sneve, Virginia Driving Hawk, *That They May Have Life: The Episcopal Church in South Dakota, 1859–1976* (New York: Seabury Press, 1977).

C. B. CLARK (Muskogee)
Oklahoma City University

DISEASES

Contagious diseases that originated in the Old World have had an overwhelming impact on the post-Columbian biological history of native North Americans. Ancestral Native Americans migrated over the Beringian land bridge before most of the lethal pathogens preying on human populations evolved. Consequently, the Native American population increased for thousands of years, free from the selective biological pressure of the contagious diseases that evolved in the Old World. The examination of naturally mummified remains of Native Americans who lived several thousand years ago has revealed that the original migrants must have carried with them across Beringia several intestinal parasites common to all humankind.

Born parasite free, human infants ingest parasites with food or from feces when they begin to move about and explore their environment. A child's intestinal parasites become life threatening at the time of weaning, when the child's metabolism must adjust to a solid diet while supporting the always hungry parasites. Weanling diarrhea, causing fatal dehydration, kept Native American infant mortality rates high, thus slowing population growth.

A heavy intestinal parasite load can cause anemia in persons who survive this "weaning-walking crisis." As long as native North Americans lived on fish, game, and wild plant products, their high animal-protein intake helped them prevent serious anemia. When native North Americans shifted to horticultural food production, maize, beans, squash, and other cultivated foods provided them with calories that fueled a rapid population increase. Anemia then became a more serious problem for their well-being, because the proportion of iron in their diet decreased. The effects of anemia are discerned in many pre-Columbian native North American skeletons in a characteristic loss of eye-socket bone.

In addition, Native Americans either brought with them or encountered in their new environment the pathogens that infect open wounds and those that cause dental caries. Bone changes in the skeletons of prehistoric Americans show that many suffered from arthritis.

Analysis of blood groups indicates that all Native Americans descended from only a few original ancestors. Native Americans in 1490 were significantly less diverse genetically than were Old World peoples. This genetic unity militated against Native American biological survival when the Columbian Exchange—the transfer of people, their pathogens, animals, and plants—began in 1492. Pathogens preying on human beings typically increase in virulence as they reproduce in persons of the same genotype. A child catching measles from a family member is twice as likely to die as a child catching the same disease from someone else.

In broader demographic terms, a virus transmitted from one Native American to another has only a 68 percent chance of encountering a new histocompatibility antigen. The same virus transmitted from one African to another has a 99.5 percent chance of encountering a new histocompatibility antigen. In other words, the virus is far more likely to be preadapted to a new Native American host than it is to one of Old World descent.

European invaders and their African slaves transmitted all of the most contagious diseases that had evolved in the Old World to Native Americans. Most scholars now agree that as a consequence, the number of native Mesoamericans alive in 1619 was but 5 to 10 percent of the number alive in 1519.

There is less consensus concerning the consequences of the Columbian Exchange for native North Americans, because documentary records of disease epidemics and native population trends in North America cover much shorter periods there than do records for quickly colonized Mesoamerica. Nondocumentary evidence indicates that Old World pathogens did not wait

for literate observers before spreading from one Native American ethnic group to another. The research question always is whether the pathogen that caused known epidemic mortality to the south spread to and across North America.

The second Columbian voyage to Hispaniola, in 1493, initiated the epidemic disease sequence. Most likely, domestic animals transported by Columbus's colonizing fleet harbored an influenza virus that spread among island natives, with catastrophic consequences. Native canoe crews could have carried the virus to Cuba and Florida; currently, there is no way to verify whether they did so.

Smallpox broke out on Hispaniola in 1518. Mayan-language annals indicate that native canoe traders transmitted the disease to Yucatecans before Spanish invaders transmitted it to Mesoamerica in 1520. Archaeological evidence of a population crash at that time on the Columbia Plateau near the Canada-U.S. border indicates that the virus spread northward through all of the intervening native populations.

Measles attacked Mesoamericans with high mortality in 1531–33, and Spaniards reported the epidemic from the province of Sonora, immediately south of Arizona. From there, the virus probably spread farther north. In 1539–43, a large Spanish military expedition marauded from peninsular Florida to northern Arkansas and eastern Texas. The Spaniards reported visiting populous native statelets or chiefdoms throughout what became the southeastern United States. Originally commanded by Hernando de Soto, one of the conquerors of the South American Inca empire, the expedition inflicted significant casualties on several native polities. Today scholars suspect that the expedition also transmitted one or more Old World diseases to the native peoples it encountered.

In 1560, Spaniards attempted to colonize Pensacola Bay. Short of food, they sent parties north to seek supplies from some of the powerful polities de Soto had visited. They did not succeed: the kind of polities de Soto encountered no longer existed; the populations had been decimated. The prime suspect today is the lethal epidemic that killed millions of Mesoamericans from 1545 to 1548. Probably a combination of pneumonic and bubonic plague, the disease could have been typhus. The Spanish Pensacola colonists themselves almost certainly transmitted to native North Americans the influenza virus that became epidemic in the Caribbean and Mesoamerica in 1559 after sweeping across Europe two years earlier.

French records of an abortive Florida colonization attempt in 1564 indicate that an unidentified pathogen was then epidemic among native Timucuan-speakers. By the time the Spaniards ceded Florida to England in 1763 and evacuated the peninsula, only a few hundred Timucuans survived. Transported in Spanish ships to the disease-ridden tropical coasts of Mexico and Cuba, that remnant also perished.

An English reconnaissance party on Roanoke Island in 1585 transmitted to its hosts an unidentified pathogen that killed scores of natives in each of the island's villages. Inasmuch as the islanders regularly communicated with relatives on the mainland, they surely carried the disease there; the question is how far it spread.

The diseases crossing the ocean during the sixteenth century usually caused so-called virgin-soil epidemics, because every Native American with whom they came in contact was susceptible. Those natives who survived the 1520 smallpox epidemic became immune to that virus, and it seems not to have recurred until 1562. Smallpox immunity protected no one against measles, plague, or influenza, however. Often entire families perished during virgin-soil epidemics because all members were stricken simultaneously, leaving no one capable of fetching water or preparing food.

One general native therapy for pre-Columbian ailments called for perspiring in a heated sweat lodge and then plunging one's body into cold water. Unfortunately, this treatment weakened or killed patients with the high fevers typical of contagious Old World diseases.

European colonists on the Atlantic Coast during the seventeenth century left written records of the principal contagious disease epidemics that decimated nearby Native Americans. In 1613–17, bubonic plague halved Florida's missionized native population. By 1619, the epidemic had spread northward to New England. So many Massachusetts died that the Pilgrims, who arrived in 1620, persuaded themselves that God had destroyed the natives to open their territory to European colonists. This self-serving "cant of conquest," as the historian Francis Jennings called it, had fundamental psychological consequences for later relations between natives and newcomers. It still reverberates through time.

In 1633, measles (or smallpox, or both) struck native peoples of New England and the Great Lakes area. In 1637, a different pathogen (most likely scarlet fever) swept through the same peoples. Two years later, smallpox spread through them. The combined mortality of the three epidemics caused a precipitous decline in na-tive population and military manpower just when European colonists began moving inland.

Smallpox recurred in 1649, 1662, 1669, and 1687. A person who survives a smallpox attack acquires life-long immunity to the virus. Children resist the small-pox virus better than teenagers or adults. The more frequently smallpox invades a given population, there-fore, the sooner it becomes a childhood disease causing relatively low mortality. Immunity to smallpox does not protect a person against other viruses or bacteria, though, and other pathogens spread to Native Ameri-cans between smallpox epidemics. Measles struck in 1658 and 1692, influenza in 1647 and 1675, and diph-theria in 1659. Debilitating malaria reached southern North America no later than the 1690s.

Thirteen known epidemics decimated native peoples in North America during the seventeenth century. The lack of records of natives living far from the colonial frontiers makes it impossible to determine how far each pathogen spread.

Old World pathogens continued to reach epidemic proportions during the eighteenth century. Smallpox spread at least from Texas to New England in 1715–21; apparently across the continent in 1729–33; from Texas to Hudson Bay in 1738–39; across New England in 1746; from Texas to the Great Lakes in 1750–52, 1755–60, and 1762–66; clearly over all North America in 1779–83; in Alaska and Canada in 1785–87; and among the Pueblo Indians in 1788. Measles struck New England and Great Lakes peoples in 1713–15; perhaps spread across the continent in 1727–28; struck southwestern U.S. peoples in 1768–70; and spread from Texas to Hudson Bay in 1776–78. Influenza spread across North America in 1761; diph-theria became epidemic among New England tribes in 1735–36. Thus sixteen major epidemics swept away natives in all or large portions of North America during this century.

Another major Old World disease attacked native North Americans for the first time during the nine-teenth century. Transmitted by passengers on fast-mov-ing ships, cholera reached North America in 1832. It caused widespread although spotty native mortality. In 1849, forty-niners infected with cholera spread the dis-ease to Plains peoples and other Native Americans liv-ing along the routes to California.

Major smallpox epidemics affected the Pueblo and Plains peoples in 1815–16; Plains and Great Lakes tribes in 1831–34; native peoples from Alaska to the Pueblos in 1836–40; the Aleut to the Plains peoples in

1843–46; Plains and Plateau peoples in 1848–50; Columbia River basin peoples disastrously in 1852–53; Plains tribes in 1854–57; natives across the United States between 1860 and 1867; natives from the St. Lawrence River to the Northwest Coast in 1876–78; and tribes from California to Arizona, New Mexico, and Oklahoma in 1896–99. Federal Indian Service records show that 74 percent of the Hopis who refused Western medical attention died during the latter epidemic, grim proof of how lethal earlier smallpox epidemics must have been. Measles appears to have become a childhood disease among Native Americans, typically contracted from nearby colonists as the latter spread rapidly across the continent.

Some native ethnic populations began to recover late in the nineteenth century, though handicapped by virtually epidemic tuberculosis. Others started to increase in the first decades of the twentieth century. The 1918–19 influenza pandemic took a significant toll among isolated native groups.

After World War II, at just about the time new medicines had been developed to control tuberculosis and trachoma, diabetes emerged as the major disease killing and maiming native North Americans. This development seems to have been caused by Native Americans' abandoning traditional foods in favor of a low-quality version of the diet of other North Americans. As Native Americans become increasingly integrated into the general society today, they suffer from the same diseases as other North Americans, including AIDS.

See also Population: Precontact to the Present.

Crosby, Alfred W., Jr., *The Columbian Exchange: Biological and Cultural Consequences of 1492* (Westport, Conn.: Greenwood Publishing Company, 1972); Dobyns, Henry F., *Their Number Become Thinned: Native American Population Dynamics in Eastern North America* (Knoxville: University of Tennessee Press, 1983); Thornton, Russell, *American Indian Holocaust and Survival: A Population History since 1492* (Norman: University of Oklahoma Press, 1987).

HENRY F. DOBYNS
Tucson, Arizona

DODGE, HENRY CHEE

(1857?–1947)
Navajo political leader.

Henry Chee Dodge, better known as Chee Dodge, was born at Fort Defiance, Arizona, to a Navajo-Jemez mother of the Coyote Pass clan, probably in 1857. The exact year of his birth, as well as the identity of his father, is uncertain. Documentary evidence suggests that Dodge's father was a white Indian agent or army officer, possibly Henry L. Dodge, for whom the young Dodge was named. His mother was killed by the Hopis during the Christopher "Kit" Carson military campaign against the Navajos in 1864. Dodge was subsequently adopted by a Navajo family and accompanied them on the long walk to Fort Sumner and the Bosque Redondo Reservation in eastern New Mexico. After surviving four years of incarceration at Bosque Redondo, Dodge returned to Fort Defiance with his family in 1868. Back in Arizona he was reunited with an aunt married to a white agency employee, who taught the boy English. A few years later Dodge went to live with the family of the Indian agent William F. N. Army and enrolled in the Fort Defiance Indian School, where he learned to read and write. Dodge quickly found employment as the official interpreter at the Navajo Agency in Fort Defiance. He later translated for Washington Matthews, the pioneer ethnographer of the Navajos, at Fort Wingate. Dodge helped Matthews write two of his classic works on the mythology and ceremonialism of the tribe: *Navajo Legends* and *The Night Chant*. In 1884, Matthews arranged for Dodge to accompany a delegation of medicine men to Washington, D.C.—the first of many trips Dodge would make to the nation's capital on behalf of his people.

The years following the Navajos' return from Bosque Redondo were characterized by tension, conflict, and occasional bloodshed as the Navajos competed with their white neighbors for ownership and use of the land. The reservation created by treaty in 1868 soon proved to be far too small to meet the needs of the Navajo people and their rapidly expanding herds of sheep, goats, cattle, and horses. Neither the Navajos nor white stockmen respected the reservation's official boundaries, and clashes often occurred over grazing and water rights. A second potentially explosive source of problems was the presence of white prospectors searching for gold within the reservation's borders. When the U.S. Army seemed reluctant or unable to evict these trespassers, the Navajos took matters into their own hands. At the same time, Navajos who ventured across the reservation's borders to white settlements were commonly beaten, robbed, and sometimes murdered. Each new incident threatened to ignite a general outbreak of hostilities.

Increasingly, Dodge found himself called in to help investigate such incidents and to serve as a mediator. The intelligence, courage, and interpretive skills demonstrated by the young man soon caught the attention of government officials. In 1884 Dodge, still in his twenties, was named by the agent Dennis Riordan as chief of the Navajo police force. Later that same year he was named by Riordan as "head chief" of the Navajo tribe.

In the beginning the Navajos were reluctant to follow a mixed-blood leader who had been chosen by the federal government. Over time, however, Dodge won the trust and respect of his people. Although he moved easily in white society, he continued to live something of a traditional lifestyle. Most important, he followed the Navajo custom of plural marriage, eventually taking perhaps as many as eight wives. In keeping with Navajo tradition, most of these women were clan sisters. Other marriages may have been arranged to enhance ties with local headmen. Whatever their motivation, Dodge's marital arrangements served to strengthen his identity and status within the tribe.

In 1890 Dodge formed a partnership with a white trader, Stephen E. Aldrich, and opened a trading post at Round Rock, a small settlement located in the geographical center of the vast Navajo Reservation. He remained partners with Aldrich for over a decade. During this time he played an important role in promoting Navajo arts and crafts, and was especially active in sponsoring talented silversmiths.

In 1892 Dodge's Round Rock Trading Post served as the stage for a historic confrontation between the Indian agent Dana Shipley and a powerful headman named Black Horse. The cause of this conflict was Black Horse's resistance to Shipley's forced recruitment of Navajo children for the Fort Defiance school, an institution that had earned a notorious reputation for its alleged mistreatment of students. Black Horse and his followers dragged Shipley from the building and beat him severely. Dodge, a trader named Charles Hubbell, and three Navajo policeman were able to rescue the battered agent, providing him refuge inside the trading post until the military arrived. Dodge then skillfully negotiated a peaceful end to the explosive affair.

Dodge realized only modest profits from his trading business and eventually dissolved his partnership with Aldrich. Meanwhile, he had invested heavily in livestock. Reportedly, Dodge began with two sheep issued to him by the government upon his return from Bosque Redondo. Through selective breeding, he was able to increase and upgrade his herd, eventually developing sheep that produced a high yield of mutton and wool.

In time, the livestock industry brought great wealth to Dodge, and he adopted a lifestyle befitting a man of money and prestige. With a passion for fine clothes and the best horses, the tall, handsome, and charismatic Dodge possessed all of the qualities needed to emerge as his tribe's leading modern-day politician.

In 1923 Chee Dodge was selected to be the first chairman of the newly formed Navajo Tribal Council, a position he held until 1928. For the next two decades he remained the dominant figure in Navajo politics. Dodge generally trusted the federal government and supported most of its policies toward the Navajos. His loyalty to the government, however, was pushed to the limit during the New Deal years when Commissioner of Indian Affairs John Collier initiated an unpopular mandatory livestock-reduction program to address soil erosion on the reservation, which federal officials believed was caused by overgrazing. In the end, Dodge was able to provide only a lukewarm endorsement of what proved to be a disastrous and failed program.

In the arena of tribal politics, Dodge became the acknowledged leader of a faction known as the traditionalists, a position that placed him opposite the reformist and assimilationist Jacob C. Morgan. The two men remained bitter personal and political enemies for many years.

In 1942, at an age when most men have long retired, the venerable and snowy-haired Dodge was elected tribal chairman for another term. He was reelected in 1946 but contracted pneumonia soon after the election and was never able to take office. Dodge died on January 7, 1947, well into his eighties.

Dodge was survived by five of his six children, including Tom Dodge, who himself served a term as tribal chairman, and Annie Dodge Wauneka, who became the first woman to be elected to the Navajo Tribal Council and was eventually awarded a Presidential Medal of Freedom for her work in improving health care on the Navajo Reservation.

The death of Henry Chee Dodge ended a public life that spanned not only decades but eras. Dodge formed a bridge between the contrasting worlds of the Navajo and the white man, and in doing so he, more than any other leader, was responsible for his people's successful transition into the contemporary era.

See also Navajo.

Bailey, Garrick, and Roberta Glenn Bailey, *A History of the Navajos: The Reservation Years* (Santa Fe, N. Mex.: School of American Research Press, 1986); Brugge, David M., "Henry

Chee Dodge: From Long Walk to Self-Determination," in *Indian Lives: Essays on Nineteenth- and Twentieth-Century Native American Leaders,* ed. L. G. Moses and Raymond Wilson (Albuquerque: University of New Mexico Press, 1985).

STEVE PAVLIK
Chinle High School
Chinle, Arizona

DOZIER, EDWARD P.

(1916–71)
Santa Clara Pueblo anthropologist.

Edward Pasqual Dozier wrote, in an article about values, "Man and the universe are conceived to be in a kind of a balance . . . [and] honest dealings, generosity, hospitality, deference to the old and a mild and uninitiating demeanor receive high value in the [Pueblo] culture." He emulated these qualities both personally and professionally. His personal life influenced and enriched his professional life, as this article will demonstrate.

Edward Pasqual Dozier was born in Santa Clara Pueblo, New Mexico, on April 23, 1916. Because he was the youngest of his siblings by five to eighteen years, he was showered with love and attention. His parents were Thomas Sublette and Leocadia Gutierrez Dozier. Leocadia could not speak English, and Thomas could not speak Tewa; they managed to communicate with the broken Spanish they each spoke. Young Edward spoke Spanish to his father and Tewa to the rest of his family; he did not learn English until he was twelve.

Dozier grew up primarily in Santa Clara. Since his siblings were so much older than he, his playmates were often his cousins and friends. They were kept busy with chores, such as hauling water and taking care of chickens and gardens, but also had time to play and explore. Always—whether he was alone, with family, or with friends—his favorite activities were hiking and fishing in the mountains surrounding the pueblo.

Dozier's father died when he was nine, after which his older brothers supported the family with various jobs (loading freight cars, farming, and carpentry). Although Dozier did poorly in elementary school, his brothers (most of whom did not even finish the fourth grade) worked to send him to a Catholic high school in Santa Fe.

In 1935, during the summer after he graduated from high school, Dozier participated in a study of traditional medicinal plants. Designed to encourage young Pueblo men to talk with their elders about traditions, it was never completed. Nevertheless, Dozier's experience with it may have added to his awareness of the unique knowledge of the Santa Clara elders, as well as giving birth to his respect for ethnography.

For Dozier, the years between 1935 and 1941 were devoted to a mixture of school, work, and travel. He attended the University of New Mexico but often had to take time off to earn tuition money. One summer he hitchhiked across the country (not a dangerous activity in the 1930s, he later said). He attended Georgetown University, in Washington, D.C., for a year. In Washington, he would force himself to listen and talk to his housemates so he could learn to use the English language the way native speakers did. Once he was back in New Mexico, his formal studies took second place to what he was learning about life outside the pueblo.

In 1941 Dozier was drafted and served as a sergeant in intelligence for the Army Air Corps. Again his interest in anthropology became apparent, and while he was stationed in Saipan, he received permission to do a small ethnographic study. On leave from the army in 1943, Dozier married Claire Elizabeth Butler, a woman he had met years before in Washington, D.C. A year later, their daughter, Wanda Marie, was born. In 1945 Dozier was discharged from the army and brought his new family home to Santa Clara. The marriage didn't last, however, and Wanda was raised by Dozier's family.

Under the GI Bill, Dozier reenrolled at the University of New Mexico, where he did some work for the anthropologist Willard W. Hill, an expert on Navajo culture. His experience with Hill deepened his interest in anthropology. Focusing on linguistics and cultural anthropology, he completed his B.A. in 1947 and his master's degree in 1949. When he received his doctorate in 1951, he became the first person to receive a Ph.D. in anthropology from UCLA.

Before leaving the University of New Mexico, Dozier had met Marianne Fink, who was studying psychology and anthropology there. In 1950 they married and spent a year on the Hopi Reservation, where Dozier finished the fieldwork for his dissertation. Dozier taught classes at the University of Oregon for a year while writing his dissertation.

In 1952 the Doziers began to build their own house near Albuquerque. Their dream was to be close to both the University of New Mexico and Santa Clara. In

1953, however, Dozier accepted a position at Northwestern University, in Evanston, Illinois, where he and Marianne lived until 1958. He taught during the school year, and the Doziers spent summers working on their house in New Mexico, visiting family in Santa Clara, and camping in the mountains on the reservation. During the summer of 1955, their son, Miguel Thamu, was born.

Dozier was a fellow at the Center for Advanced Studies of the Behavioral Sciences at Stanford University in 1958–59. Their daughter, Anya, was born in 1959, and three months later the family moved to the Philippines where Dozier conducted research among the Kalingas of northern Luzon.

Dozier soon became tired of living far from home, and in 1960 the family moved to Tucson, Arizona (just a day's drive from Santa Clara). Dozier was hired by the Department of Anthropology at the University of Arizona as a full professor. He designed the university's American Indian Studies program, which is still in place today. He was a popular teacher and remained at the university until he died on May 2, 1971. During his time at the university, he continued his research in the pueblos and in the Philippines.

Dozier's research was funded by grants from numerous foundations. He wrote four books (*The Hopi-Tewa of Arizona; Hano: A Tewa Indian Community in Arizona; Mountain Arbiters: The Changing Life of a Philippine Hill People;* and *The Pueblo Indians of North America*) and many articles, which appeared in various scholarly journals and books. He was recognized both nationally and in the pueblos for his sensitive, insightful research.

Dozier was also a member of many professional organizations. It was important to him to take part in groups that influenced policies about American Indians, and through such connections he worked with other Indian scholars such as D'Arcy McNickle, Bea Medicine, Alfonso Ortiz, and David Warren. On a personal level, Dozier encouraged other Indian people to get college degrees. Furthermore, his commitment to Santa Clara is evidenced, in part, by the fact that all three of his children live or work in the pueblo.

Dozier always remembered how it felt to be a newcomer to a culture (even if the culture was simply that of the university) and knew how to make people feel at home. After all, what first drew him to anthropology was its promise to help people move from one culture to another with ease. He constantly worked to make transitions easier for those around him.

Dozier, Edward P., "The Value and Moral Concepts of Rio Grande Pueblo Indians," in *Encyclopedia of Morals,* ed. Vergilius Ferm (New York: New York Philosophical Library, 1956); Gridley, Marion E., "Edward P. Dozier," in *Indians of Today,* 4th ed. (n.p.: ICFP, 1971); Sando, Joe S., "Some Who Shaped Pueblo History," in *Pueblo Nations: Eight Centuries of Pueblo Indian History* (Santa Fe, N.M.: Clear Light Publishers, 1992).

ANYA DOZIER ENOS (Santa Clara Pueblo)
Santa Fe Indian School

DREAMS

Dreams have played a central and determinative role in the formation of the religious and spiritual worlds of most Native American groups. As early as 1623, dreams were recorded among the Hurons by the French Catholic Recollect brother Gabriel Sagard. These accounts were then expanded by the writings of the Jesuit priest Jean de Brébeuf, who lived with the Hurons around Georgian Bay (1634–36). According to these writings, young Huron and Iroquois men would fast for extended periods, either in a partitioned rear section of their longhouse or in a specially made shelter. These fasts could last as long as thirty days and were undertaken so that the young men would have a vision or powerful dream that would enhance their abilities in hunting, warfare, or healing. The records of Brébeuf also include dramatic accounts of dreams and visions that came spontaneously to women and played a role in determining those women's participation in various ceremonial rites.

If the dreamer was successful, he would obtain a vision of a dream spirit who would give him a specific ability or power and show him how to solicit that power through special songs and ritual activities. Among most native groups, the dream spirit would then become a lifelong protector and helper whose aid and abilities could be solicited through prayer and tobacco offerings. In dreams, the dreaming soul—that aspect of self that travels in visions away from the body—could contact the dream spirit and receive instructions. Dreams were considered by many native groups to be the most valid means for communicating with the spiritual powers and the primary basis of religious knowledge. Advanced dreamers who became religious specialists would interpret dreams in order to diagnose illness, foretell the death or return to health of the sick, predict the outcome of expeditions in hunting and warfare, as well as which objects could be substituted for those things appearing in dreams which were difficult or impossible to procure for carrying out dream induced rituals.

Many ceremonies were attributed to dream origins. Foundational dreams would be transmitted through kinship groups, who held an exclusive knowledge of the dream and of the correct ritual for its enactment. The dream was usually owned by the head of the family and passed on through special ceremonial rites. However, additional dreams, especially by those who were recognized religious leaders, could modify and change the ceremonial patterns. A unique aspect of the Iroquois dreaming traditions was the dream-guessing feast, when dreamers would join together and go from longhouse to longhouse in entranced states induced by their dream spirits. Handling red-hot coals and dancing and singing, each dreamer would ask that his or her "dream desire," narrated in the form of a riddle, be guessed by other members of the longhouse. When the riddle had been correctly solved, gifts would be given to the dreamer to satisfy the dream desire. A failure to receive the correct gifts could indicate the coming death of the dreamer.

Southeastern sources clearly show the centrality of dreaming in the religious worlds of most native groups in that region. Dreams were actively sought, both in regular sleep and in special fasting, and the songs and powers given through them became an intrinsic feature of the social and religious life of the dreamer. Dreams revealed the existence of a spirit world that had continuity with and similarity to the world of the living and that could be visited through dreams. Among the Choctaws, Creeks, and Cherokees, certain dreamers could travel to a village of the dead and there converse with their former relatives. Dreaming thus gave an experiential confirmation of the existence of other worlds, including that of the dead. Among the Cherokees, dream interpreters would seek out the "seat of pain" for those who were ill by asking them extensive questions about their dreams ranging back over months and sometimes over a period of years. Dream typologies were developed by means of which particular types of animals, actions, or various other dream images were given specific meanings and used diagnostically to predict future events or indicate cures that would bring the dreamer back into harmony with the dream spirits. The creation of the Cherokee syllabary by Sequoyah allowed many of the Cherokee spiritual leaders to record in the indigenous language a variety

of formulaic prayers and ritual songs—most of which originated in dreams that had been passed on through oral tradition until they were written down by native practitioners in the old Cherokee language.

The most well known dreaming practices are those of the native peoples of the Great Plains. With her research, conducted in the 1920s, Ruth Benedict set the stage for interpreting Plains dreaming as the primary means by which a particular group reinforced its "culture pattern." Dreams were seen as stereotypical in reproducing similar content that supported the religious worldview of the dreamer. However, alternative research later done by many native ethnographers showed clearly that dreaming was not stereotypical, that every dream had many unique and divergent qualities, and that no two dreams were ever identical. The distinction between dreams and visions was not considered significant; the primary criteria for evaluating the sacred power of a dream or vision depended upon the degree to which the subject could reproduce a visible, positive result as a consequence of his or her following either a dream had while sleeping or a waking vision attained while fasting or praying. Only those dreams or visions that resulted in a direct manifestation of power were considered sacred.

On the Plains, dreams were acquired in two basic ways: either they came spontaneously or they were sought ritually. A majority of the dreams and visions collected in the ethnography were spontaneous; acquired without conscious effort, they nevertheless made a lasting and lifelong impression on the dreamer. Spontaneous dreams were common for women under specific circumstances, such as during times of mourning for the recent dead, when Plains women would often slash their legs and arms and wander away from camp crying to the sacred powers. Domestic quarrels and conflicts among close kin groups could also result in a woman's wandering away from camp and then having a remarkable visionary experience. Women who were captured by enemy warriors and later escaped to wander over the plains for many days without food, seeking their home tribe, often had visions. Dreams also came unsought during periods of illness. Such was the case with the famous dream of the Oglala Sioux holy man Black Elk, which occurred to him in 1872 at the age of nine.

The more structured vision quest or dream fast was usually undertaken by Plains men, and sometimes women, during adolescence, but it was sometimes repeated among certain groups throughout life. Young men went to experienced elders, usually relatives, to receive instructions for carrying out a proper dream fast. They would undergo various purification rites and then go to a nearby hill, on the top of which they would either make a circle within which they remained or dig a pit in which they stayed throughout the fast. Dressed in a minimum of clothing, with long hair unbraided, carrying only a pipe and a robe, they would pray continually to the holy powers to grant them a powerful dream. After as many as ten days of fasting, a successful dreamer might come down from the hill and relate his dream to elders in a sweat lodge. Or he might wait a specific number of days before approaching a leader of a dream society, whose members held rituals related to a particular dream spirit, like the buffalo or bear, and ask to join the dream society based on his successful vision.

Successful dreams were enacted, and the power of the dream had to be demonstrated for the dream to be accepted as an authentic gift from the dream spirits. Successful dreamers were expected to demonstrate remarkable or powerful abilities as a sign of a power-granting dream. Dreamers used a variety of objects to hold the power given to them in the dream, and would paint themselves and their horses according to dream experiences. The dream objects were kept within sacred bundles, which were unwrapped only under ritual circumstances, during which the dream was often narrated. In using the dream objects, dream songs were sung; these songs epitomized the heart of the dream recreation. Dream images were painted on tipis, robes, and other gear to empower those objects. Women would use dream images as a source for designs in crafts as well as in quill and bead work and other types of clothing ornamentation. The designs of the famous Ghost Dance shirts used during the religious revival that began in the 1890s were all said to have originated in visionary dreams. In Plains culture, dreams were central and a primary means for innovation and change in religious and social practices.

Dreams played a powerful social role among Northwest Coast peoples as well as among many Inuit groups. Franz Boas (1925) collected an entire volume of Kwakiutl dreams, showing the rich and complex dream symbolism that completely pervaded the Kwakiutl spiritual world. Sometimes a dream spirit would embed a dream crystal—a valuable source of power—

in the body of the dreamer. The possession of such a crystal was a sign of a dreamer's initiation into advanced dreaming practices. Many flying dreams have been recorded; they signify the dreamer's ability to explore hidden dimensions of the religious cosmology. Dreams among Northwest Coast peoples as well as subarctic peoples indicate a strong belief in reincarnation. Many dreamers have claimed to know about their past lives through dream experiences, and there are records of women who dreamed of giving birth to someone who had recently died in the community. Certain dream spirits might send negative or frightening dreams, such as Stimsila among the Bella Coolas. On the other hand, certain dream spirits were regarded as protectors and accompanied the dreamer throughout life, revealing in dreams future events, matters pertaining to secret societies, and other critical life experiences.

Among the Pueblos, Navajos, and Apaches of the American Southwest, dreams were of much less significance. The highly structured ritual life of the Pueblo people and the complex healing rites of the Navajos did not normally allow for innovation through dreams. Traditional knowledge was transmitted through learning the rites and songs of the ceremonies and not through dreaming practices. Dorothy Eggan (1949) collected Hopi dreams and noted how they function in a personal way for the dreamer. But, she found, they are not usually connected to religious sanctions, nor are they considered necessary for becoming a participant in communal rites. However, Hopis evaluate dreams as either good or bad and take appropriate actions to counteract the effects of negative dreams. Among the Zunis, dreams are also evaluated, and only bad dreams are shared. For the Navajos, dreams may determine what type of diagnostician the dreamer may become, and they play a role in determining the causes of illness.

Benedict, Ruth, "The Vision in Plains Culture," *American Anthropologist* 24 (1922): 1–23; Irwin, Lee, *The Dream-Seekers: Native American Visionary Traditions of the Great Plains* (Norman: University of Oklahoma Press, 1994); Tedlock, Barbara, *Dreaming: Anthropological and Psychological Interpretations* (Cambridge: Cambridge University Press, 1987).

LEE IRWIN
(Mohawk-Delaware Ancestry)
College of Charleston

E

EASTERN UNIVERSITIES AND INDIANS

THE COLLEGE OF WILLIAM AND MARY

The College of William and Mary's experiment in American Indian education attempted to convert natives from a traditional way of life and thought to a new one. Despite the pious intentions of Virginia's earliest English arrivals, the establishment of a Native American school in the colony was not realized until February 8, 1693, when James Blair, Virginia's commissary, received a royal charter from King William III and Queen Mary for "a place of universal study" for American Indian and English youth in Virginia. During his trip abroad, Blair also arranged to have rents from the Brafferton estate, purchased by the Irish-born scientist Robert Boyle's executors, bankroll the Indian school that was to be part of the new educational institution.

William and Mary opened its doors to native pupils in 1700, only to discover that tribal elders refused to relinquish their beloved children to the care of strangers. Hesitant tribal leaders perceived the Williamsburg school to be nothing more than an elaborate ruse designed to secure an ample supply of Indian slaves. As a result, chieftains sent captured enemies to the college in place of their own children.

Native enrollment at the college—much of it enforced—peaked during periods of Indian and white conflict. The natives' presence in Williamsburg acted to deter potential Indian enemies from attacking Virginia's frontier settlements for fear of reprisals. During the Tuscarora War (1711–13), twenty Nansemond, Nottaway, Merherrin, Chickahominy, and Pamunkey children attended the school. In 1715 a visiting Catawba delegation agreed to dispatch to Williamsburg two children from each of their towns as hostages during the Yamasee War. After each crisis passed, captive students returned home.

As the clouds of war appeared on the horizon in 1750, Virginians recruited Iroquois and Cherokee students for the college, hoping thereby to prevent those two powerful Indian confederacies from becoming French allies. Iroquois representatives, however, refused to send their sons to Williamsburg. Canasatego, an Onondaga, recalled that educated natives "were absolutely good for nothing." Although able to read and write, he continued, English-educated pupils did not know the "true method for killing deer, catching Beaver, or surprizing an enemy." The Onondaga diplomat did, however, agree to receive "a dozen or two English youth" and "make men of them."

Negotiations with the Cherokees fared much better. Eight Cherokee students attended the school from 1753 to 1756. These scholars, however, did not like the confinement of school life. Governor Robert Dinwiddie informed Old Hop, the Cherokee chieftain, that the young men were well cared for but could not be reconciled to their books and "went away of their own accord."

By 1760 few natives attended William and Mary. The majority were hostages dispatched to Williamsburg as part of complex treaty agreements or, like four Shawnee pupils enrolled in 1774, prisoners of war. After fighting erupted between the British and Americans in April 1775, the Boyle legacy was transferred to the West Indies, where it was used to educate black slaves. Lacking financial resources to continue, the Indian school at the college closed its doors in 1777.

JON L. BRUDVIG
The College of William and Mary

DARTMOUTH COLLEGE

New Hampshire's Dartmouth College, according to its charter, was created "for the education and instruction of Youth of the Indian Tribes in this Land in reading, writing and all parts of Learning . . . as well as in all liberal Arts and Sciences; and also of English Youth and any others." The charter was granted in 1769 to Eleazar Wheelock, an evangelical Congregational minister who since 1754 had been attempting to Christianize Indians at his Moor's Indian Charity School in eastern Connecticut. In the 225 years since Wheelock received the charter, Dartmouth has concentrated mostly on the education of those "English Youth and any others." The college has, however, a long history of involvement with Indian education and, in a 1969 "refounding," instituted what has proved to be a very successful Native American academic and social program.

The pre-1969 involvement with Native Americans took several forms. Wheelock used money raised in England by Samson Occom (Mohegan) to finance the first Dartmouth buildings. Wheelock brought Moor's Indian Charity School with him to New Hampshire and used it as both a college preparatory school for whites and a place to educate natives. His successors continued to support Moor's, in part because Indian education was funded by a Scottish trust. The number of Indians enrolled was never large, however, and the school was closed in the 1850s. For the next century most of the few Indians seeking education at Dartmouth were either rejected, shipped off to neighboring academies, or—before 1900—accommodated in the college's associated programs in agriculture, medicine, and science. Only a handful ever enrolled in Dartmouth's core liberal-arts college. Researchers disagree over the precise number of Native Americans attending the school between founding and refounding, but there weren't many. The best guess for the two-hundred-year period is about 120 students in the various schools. Only nine appear to have graduated from either Dartmouth or its associate schools. One of these graduates was Charles A. Eastman (Ohiyesa), a member of the class of 1887. The college's main commitment to things native was through an increasing institutional use of racial symbols. For example, by the 1920s most college intercollegiate athletic teams were known as the Dartmouth Indians.

The 1969 refounding, announced by the college's newly appointed president, John Kemeny, in his inaugural address, brought dramatic change. The college set a goal of 3 percent Indian undergraduate enrollment (about 120 in a student body of 4,000), instructed admissions officers to recruit qualified Native American students, and provided money for support services, both academic and social. Progress was slow but steady. The class of 1991 was the first to reach the hoped-for thirty matriculants. The graduation rate for Indians attending Dartmouth increased steadily to over 70 percent. Native American Studies, begun as an experimental interdisciplinary program in 1972, became a permanent program in 1980; under the leadership of Michael Dorris it attracted hundreds of students of all races to its many course offerings. The college provided living and social quarters, financial aid, internships, and staff for Native American activities. Despite opposition, especially from older college alumni, the use of Indian symbols declined. The college insisted that athletic teams stop using them entirely.

Dartmouth today is firmly committed to the education of American Indians. Since 1970 enrolled members of 111 different tribes have attended the college. Graduates, many of whom have obtained professional degrees, serve Indian peoples in multiple ways. The annual Dartmouth Powwow has become a major social event in New Hampshire and Vermont. It has taken a while, but Dartmouth College is finally doing something significant "for the education and instruction of Youth of the Indian Tribes in this Land."

JERE DANIELL
Dartmouth College

HARVARD UNIVERSITY

Although Harvard University enjoys a worldwide reputation for academic excellence, its founding purpose—to educate American Indian youths—is little known. Drawn up in 1650, shortly after the Pilgrims arrived in the New World, Harvard's original charter states that the college was established for "the education of the English and Indian youths of this country in knowledge and godliness."

In 1654, the enthusiasm for Harvard's founding purpose by the Society for the Propagation of the Gospel Among the Indian and Others (also known as the New England Company) led to the construction of a two-story brick structure in Harvard Yard known as the Indian College. By 1665, however, there were no longer any Indian students at Harvard. By the end of the seventeenth century, only eight Indian students had attended the college, and just one, Caleb Cheeshahteamuck, had graduated.

Because no Indian students were attending Harvard at the time, the Indian College was used to board English youths from 1665 until 1693, when, with the permission of the New England Company, administrators decided to demolish the building with the provision that "in case any Indian should hereafter be sent to the College, they should enjoy their studies rent-free." In this way, the New England Company's legacy of providing for Indian students persisted, although the physical structure of the Indian College did not. Thus, in just fifteen years after Harvard's founding there were no Indian students attending the college, and within fifty years of Harvard's founding, its mission to educate and Christianize Indians had nearly been forgotten.

Little is known about Harvard's history regarding native peoples between 1693 and the 1950s. What is clear is that Harvard's commitment to native education lay dormant for some three hundred years. Although the "rent-free" status of Indian students had been forgotten, an increase in native-student enrollment occurred in the 1960s, mostly at the law school and the Graduate School of Education (GSE). This increased Indian-student presence, and its attendant activism, paved the way for a rebirth of Harvard's obligation to Indian education with the founding in 1970 of the American Indian Program at GSE. The program received a grant from the federal government to fill the void of trained American Indian and Alaska Native professionals in the field of education and to recruit Indian students to GSE. The program, renamed the Harvard Native American Program in 1991, has been instrumental in supporting Native American students, who since its inception have earned 182 advanced degrees in education. As of 1995, GSE had conferred 156 master's degrees, 22 certificates of advanced study, and 19 doctorates on Native Americans.

Today there is a sense that Harvard has begun to renew its commitment to providing education to native peoples. A prominent example of this commitment is the John F. Kennedy School of Government's Project on American Indian Economic Development. This project's central, continuing activities include comparative and case research and the application of that research in services to native nations. Furthermore, the enrollment rate of native students at Harvard is slowly increasing. In 1995, forty undergraduates and seventy-three graduate students at the university identified themselves as Native Americans—0.6 percent of the total student body. These activities and changes demonstrate that Harvard continues its struggle to fulfill one of its original missions: the education of the native peoples of North America.

MANLEY A. BEGAY, JR. (Navajo)
Harvard University

PRINCETON UNIVERSITY

The first instance of federal aid to education in the newly independent United States was very probably the congressional subvention voted in 1779 for the education of three Delaware Indians in Princeton, New Jersey. John Witherspoon, president of the College of New Jersey (later Princeton University), admitted them to preparatory studies in the Princeton grammar school that year. Only one of them was to matriculate in the college: George Morgan White Eyes (1770?–1798) of the Princeton class of 1789, son of a sachem loyal to the American cause whose unjust murder by an American officer motivated this congressional largess.

White Eyes was preceded at the college by two other Delaware students several decades earlier: Jacob Wooley (born 1743?), of the class of 1762; and Shawquskukhkung (Wilted Grass), also known as Bartholomew Scott Calvin (1756?–1840), class of 1776. White Eyes was in Princeton when the college temporarily became the capital of the United States for four months in 1783. While it was meeting there, the Continental Congress, undoubtedly under the urgings of White Eye's namesake, the Indian agent George Morgan, became the scene of deliberations of fundamental legislation concerning the relationship of the American Indian and the nation. None of the three Delaware undergraduates at Princeton in the eighteenth century completed work for their baccalaureate degree.

More than half a century was to pass before the next group of Native American students arrived on the Princeton campus, all of them capable, this time, of bridging the extraordinary transcultural chasm. They were three Cherokees who had prepared at the Lawrenceville School: John McDonald Ross (1820–42) of the Princeton class of 1841; William Potter Ross (1823–91), class of 1842; and Robert Daniel Ross (1826–63), class of 1843. All were nephews of John Ross, the principal chief of the Cherokee Nation. William Potter Ross, who served as a lieutenant colonel in the Confederate Army, succeeded his uncle as principal chief in 1861 and went on to become one of the Cherokee Nation's leading statesmen. His brother Robert Daniel Ross earned a M.A. from Princeton in 1846 and received his M.D. degree from the University of Pennsylvania in 1847, becoming one of the first Indians to practice European medicine.

The class of 1863 included Allan McFarlan, a Choctaw from Indian Territory who, according to class records, "disappeared at the end of the Sophomore year, in the midst of the war excitement."

In the first half of the twentieth century only three Native Americans are known to have matriculated at Princeton University: Howard Edwards Gansworth (1876–1956), a Seneca (and a descendant of Red Jacket) who graduated with the class of 1901; John Gibson, a Pima who studied briefly with the class of 1920; and

J. Paul Baldeagle (1897–1970), a Lakota who received his A.B. degree with the class of 1923.

Almost another half century was to pass before Indians were again to be found among the student body: in 1970 a Hopi man and a Lakota woman entered as freshmen. They were the first of a small but extraordinary group of American Indian students at Princeton in the 1970s. In this single decade at least twenty-four students with genuine ties to Native American communities studied at Princeton. Some indication of the quantum leap of cultures these students achieved is suggested by the fact that at least five of them were raised by parents who were monolingual speakers of their native languages. Two-thirds of them were from reservations. All of the reservation Indians eventually returned home to responsibilities in their own communities.

ALFRED BUSH
Princeton University

YALE UNIVERSITY

At the time of its founding in 1701 as the Collegiate School of Connecticut (soon to be renamed Yale College in honor of Elihu Yale, a wealthy benefactor), both the faculty and students at Yale showed great interest in "saving" Indians by converting them to Christianity. Abraham Pierson, the father of the first rector of Yale, had served as a preacher to the local Quinnipiac Indians in the late 1650s. Among the college's early alumni who became missionaries to tribes in the Northeast were John Sergeant (1710–49) and David Brainerd (1718–47), both of whom preached to Indians in the area between Stockbridge, Massachusetts, and Albany, New York. The Reverend Jonathan Edwards (1703–58), probably Yale's most brilliant graduate in the eighteenth century, also served as a missionary in the same area for a few years.

Given the highly charged religious atmosphere, it is not surprising that in 1754 Eleazar Wheelock, another Yale-educated minister, founded Moor's Indian Charity School in Lebanon, Connecticut. Wheelock was impressed by the promise of his Indian students (among whom was the future Mohawk leader Joseph Brant), but especially by a Mohegan convert, Samson Occom, whom he had tutored privately from 1743 to 1747. With Occom's help he secured funds from England that allowed him in 1769 to found Dartmouth College, originally intended as a school for Indian youths.

Although no Indian youth attended Yale in the eighteenth century, the fascination with Indian tribes and their leaders persisted. During the era of the American Revolution and afterward, Yale graduates John Trumbull (1756–1843) and Jeremiah Evarts (1781–1831) and former students James Fenimore Cooper (1789–1851) and Jedidiah Morse (1761–1826) developed deep interests in both Indian life and Indian affairs.

Later in the nineteenth century, Senator Henry L. Dawes of the Yale class of 1839, while wishing to help "the red man," was responsible for the controversial Dawes Severalty Act of 1887, which promised homesteads for individual Indians in an effort to make them farmers and therefore assimilated Americans. Meanwhile Frederic Remington, a graduate of the Yale Art School, was busy painting Indians as romantic but tragic figures.

It was not until 1906 that Yale admitted its first Indian American, Henry Roe Cloud, a Winnebago from Nebraska, as a student. After receiving his B.A. in 1910, Cloud continued his studies at Oberlin and Auburn Theological Seminary and was ordained as a Presbyterian minister in 1913. Subsequently he returned to Yale to take an M.A. degree. Cloud was an effective representative before Washington officials on matters of policy, and in 1915 he founded the Roe Indian Institute (named for the white missionary couple who had adopted him). Cloud served as superintendent of his own institute for many years. Equally important during the late 1920s, Cloud coauthored the famous Meriam Report of 1928, which called for a complete overhaul of federal Indian policy.

In the twentieth century two fundamental shifts in the perception of Indian Americans and their culture occurred at Yale and other institutions of higher learning. First, beginning in 1900, Yale's Peabody Museum of Natural History acquired major collections of Pacific Northwest, Plains, Seminole, and northeastern Indian artifacts. Noted anthropologists such as Clark Wissler, Edward Sapir, and Keith Basso joined the Yale faculty and offered courses on Indian societies. Similarly, the archaeologists Hiram Bingham, Irving Rouse, Michael Coe, and others taught courses at Yale on Indian prehistoric societies in Central and South America.

Second, the university admitted a growing number of Indians to Yale College and to its graduate and professional schools. Recent students have included Indians from Alaska, the Navajo Nation, and the Sioux and Iroquois reservations, among them Claudia Emmanuel (a descendant of Joseph Brant) and Sam Deloria. Both are now lawyers. Dr. Joseph Jacobs, a Mohawk, who graduated from the Yale School of Medicine, heads the National Institutes of Health program for alternative medicine. In 1994 Philip Deloria, of Sioux descent, and Brian Wescott, of Tlingit descent, received their Ph.D.'s in American Studies. By the fall of 1994 some thirty-two Indian students were enrolled in Yale College alone. A number of Yale University graduates, both Indian and non-Indian, now teach Indian history and studies in other schools, work on reservations or for the federal government, serve as legal counsel for tribal groups, or pursue special studies of Indian culture and crafts. Ironically, the greatest change in Yale's nearly three centuries of concern for Indians has occurred only in the last four decades. As one faculty member put it, "We have learned to listen in order to learn."

See also Education.

HOWARD R. LAMAR
Yale University

EASTMAN, CHARLES (OHIYESA)

(1858–1939)
Wahpeton and Mdewakanton Dakota (Sioux) medical doctor, government employee (agency physician, surnames translator, U.S. Indian inspector), writer, lecturer, and reformer.

Charles Alexander Eastman's mother died several months after his birth, which resulted in his childhood name, Hakadah, "Pitiful Last" (child); at age four he was given the name Ohiyesa, meaning "the Winner," in honor of his village's having won a lacrosse game with a neighboring village. He was raised by his paternal grandmother, and during the Minnesota Dakota conflict of 1862, she fled with him and others along with the headman Standing Buffalo onto the prairies of the Dakota Territory and eventually into Canada. Ten years later his father, Jacob Many Lightings Eastman, who had been presumed killed in the conflict, sought out his son in southeastern Manitoba, brought him to his homestead at Flandreau, South Dakota, and started him on the road to Euro-American learning by sending him to Santee Normal School. It was there that Ohiyesa adopted the name Charles Alexander Eastman, the Eastman coming from his father, who had taken the surname of his deceased wife's father, the military officer and artist Seth Eastman. Eastman went on to the preparatory school of Knox College, then to Kimball Union Academy and to Dartmouth College, from which he graduated in 1886; he graduated from the medical school of Boston College in 1889.

Eastman's educational achievements attracted the attention of the reformers who favored an Indian policy dedicated to the incorporation of Indians into American society. Eastman sought a position as an agency physician with the Bureau of Indian Affairs and was assigned to the Pine Ridge Agency in the fall of 1889. He arrived amid the Ghost Dance revitalization movement that authorities were calling an "uprising" and that ended tragically in the Wounded Knee massacre the following year. Eastman was the first physician to reach the killing field, and the experience affected him deeply. During these first weeks he also met and subsequently married the young reformer Elaine Goodale, who at the time they met was the Superintendent of Indian Education for the reservations within the Dakota Territory.

Eastman began his literary career when his wife urged him to write stories of his childhood for his own children. He later sent the stories to *St. Nicholas: An Illustrated Magazine for Young Folks*. His writings became popular with adults as well, and this success convinced him to write a range of books and to become a lecturer on the Chautauqua circuits. *Indian Boyhood* (1902) and *From the Deep Woods to Civilization* (1916) make up his autobiographical works. His stories for children include *Red Hunters and the Animal People* (1904), *Old Indian Days* (1907), *Wigwam Evenings* (1909), *Indian Child Life* (1913), *Indian Scout Talks* (1914), and *Indian Heroes and Great Chieftains* (1918). His philosophical works include *The Soul of the Indian* (1911) and *The Indian Today* (1915).

Having become increasingly disillusioned with the U.S. Indian Service, Eastman left Pine Ridge in 1893. Later, after several years of private medical practice in St. Paul, Minnesota, he became an organizer of YMCA chapters on reservations and reserves in the United States and Canada. By 1898 he had joined his brother, the Reverend John Eastman, as a lobbyist for the restoration of Santee Sioux treaty rights; he also became briefly associated with Carlisle Indian Industrial School. In 1900 he was appointed a physician at the Crow Creek Agency in South Dakota. Three years later he left that position and was engaged on a contract basis to translate surnames for the Dakota and Lakota Sioux agencies. He carried out this task while continuing his literary pursuits and public presentations. By 1910 he was seeking to renew himself and reconnect with his childhood by arranging to spend a summer traveling among Indian peoples in northern Minnesota and southern Ontario. He returned from this journey to write *The Soul of the Indian*. At this time, Charles and his wife acquired property in southern New Hampshire and began a summer camp for girls. In the off-seasons, when he was not on lecture tours, Eastman spent time at the camp. In 1923 he accepted a three-year appointment as a U.S. Indian inspector. He was by that time considered one of the foremost educated Indians; he was active in the Society of American Indians, was an appointee to the Committee of One Hundred to advise the Coolidge administration on Indian policy, and was a national spokesperson for Indian concerns and aspirations. From that point until his death in 1939 Eastman lived in Detroit, advising hobbyist groups and telling his stories to interested audiences.

Eastman's life was remarkable because of the transformation he made from one way of life to another. He translated significant Indian ideas and values for the larger population. After having written first for children, the weight of his many frustrating life experiences pressed him into explaining the contributions Indians had made. In the process, he became a public figure and educator. By the 1930s Eastman, who had been considered by many early reformers to be a testament to acculturation, had become a romantic and was considered completely out of step with the New Deal reform program of Commissioner of Indian Affairs John Collier. Late in his life, some felt Eastman had become a folksy caricature playing to popular stereotypes. His writings remain his most important contributions, however, while the contextual details of his life demonstrate that non-Indian reformers' programs were never easy for Indians to live.

Miller, David Reed, "Charles Alexander Eastman, the 'Winner': From Deep Woods to Civilization," in *American Indian Intellectuals*, ed. Margot Liberty (St. Paul, Minn.: West Publishing Company, 1978); Ruoff, LaVonne Brown, introduction to *Old Indian Days*, by Charles Alexander Eastman (reprint, Lincoln: University of Nebraska Press, Bison Books, 1991); Wilson, Raymond, *Ohiyesa: Charles Eastman, Santee Sioux* (Urbana: University of Illinois Press, 1983).

DAVID REED MILLER
Saskatchewan Indian Federated College
University of Regina

EDUCATION

Education is the process by which a culture teaches its ways to ensuing generations. Education has also been an area of continuous conflict in the history of relations between American Indians and outsiders. From the 1500s forward, native perceptions of education have undergone immense changes, but core precepts have held. As a consequence, native beliefs regarding education influence nonnative people today.

Long before outsiders left their drifting pieces of Turtle Island (Europe, Africa, and Asia) to cross the waters, the First Americans were teaching their children the ways of the people. Whether they were Lenni Lenape (Delaware), Nimiipu (Nez Perce), or Diné (Navajo), native communities saw education as intrinsic to their cultural continuity. In the hundreds of native groups populating the continent and speaking more than 250 different languages, children were a focus of concern. Infants received even greater care, for, as the Haudenosaunee (Iroquois) noted, "an infant's life is as the thinness of a maple leaf." Valued as future bearers of culture, children received guidance and affection through internal networks composed of families, clans, and subsocieties, all linked within the community by common language, religion, economic needs, and worldview.

The continent spawned tremendous diversity in cultures, a diversity echoed in their means of education. Nonetheless, similarities suggest some common themes. Native communities taught their children three dimensions of maturity: survival, spirituality, and ethics. Children's instruction came from multiple sources, including parents, elders, and spiritual leaders. On the Columbia River plateau boys learned to fish the rivers crowded with salmon each spring; in the fall they hunted for bear, deer, and elk. Girls smoked salmon, gathered roots and berries, wove baskets, and sewed clothing and moccasins. Both went on vision quests. In the high-desert Southwest, Anasazi boys learned to raise corn, beans, and squash in an arid land, to hunt and to weave cotton, and to understand the nature of their spiritual role. Girls cared for the home, ground corn and cooked, and participated in the seasonal ceremonies. Both learned that the village was of greater importance than the individual. Since native groups living between the Rio Grande and the Arctic relied exclusively on oral learning, storytelling was ubiquitous. Figures such as Raven and Coyote taught lessons, often through humor, and sometimes through negative example.

Each group created incentives for maturity. Training began with the cradleboard, which provided security and discipline for infants; older youths were molded by the authoritative presence of masked figures or the ridicule of "joking cousins," who were obligated to keep them humble with barbs and pointed jokes. Since maturity assumed endurance and an imperviousness to pain and hardship, corporal punishment was rare.

Education reinforced the First Americans' unique economic and spiritual link with the land, a connection that was maintained through an ongoing symbiotic relationship. Countless generations carrying on the precepts and traditions of that ancient heritage are a testimony to educational success.

The outsiders sailing to North America brought with them their own forms of education. Like the First Americans, they represented diverse cultures, with equally diverse approaches to education. Whether Spanish, Dutch, African, French, Russian, or English, they also taught their children skills and knowledge in the areas of survival, spirituality, and ethics. Although many immigrants reflected a Judeo-Christian tradition, their faiths were as varied as those of the First Americans, and they represented an equally broad spectrum, extending from African tribal religions to numerous varieties of Christianity.

The outsiders perceived the land and people of the Americas through many worldviews, which ranged from medieval to Enlightenment to protocapitalist. Despite this diversity, those who came from Europe also brought specific values that molded their approach toward native people. Two dimensions of their worldview—their perception of land as commodity and their view of religion as a precept that must be taught to those who did not share similar beliefs—had a profound impact on the education of native children.

These twin goals—land acquisition and religious conversion—guided their approach; their methods were more problematic. Beyond warfare, a staple solution to crisis, Europeans relied on the weapon of education to persuade tribal people that European worldviews were superior. Viewing adults as less malleable, they saw native children as vessels of change. Children could be molded toward the values of land ownership, individualism, and some form of Christianity, especially if they were removed from their community.

Tribal people viewing this approach began to perceive European education as compartmentalized learning. Although Europeans, like tribal groups, taught their children at home, some sent them away to special dwellings for further instruction. There they sat on wooden benches and recited before an elder or learned numbers from talking leaves or memorized the spiritual book they called the Bible. Gradually tribal people called this form of learning "white man's education."

From the early seventeenth through the mid-nineteenth century most Indian children had little contact with "white man's education." Those few who did learned in day or boarding schools from "Black Robes" or Protestant ministers or schoolmasters. In the Southwest, Franciscan padres taught Pueblo children; in the northeastern woodlands, Protestant schoolmasters, some of them American Indian, taught Algonquin or Iroquois youth. In 1663 several Algonquins and the Congregationalist John Eliot published the first North American Bible, in Massachusett and English. Before the American Revolution a small number of Indian students attended eastern colleges such as Harvard and Dartmouth.

When it was not fighting the Indian nations, the young republic relied on "white man's education" to attain Euro-American goals of land acquisition, individualism, and religious conversion. Bypassing the Constitution's mandate for the separation of church and state, Congress endorsed a partnership between the federal government and church organizations through a contractual relationship formalized in the Indian Civilization Fund Act (1819), which provided federal funding for "benevolent societies" to instruct Indians in agriculture and Indian children "in reading, writing and arithmetic." Moreover, more than one-fourth of the treaties negotiated between Indian tribes and the federal government included schooling provisions.

Although these measures reached only a small percentage of Indian children, many of those were members of the Southeast tribes removed to Indian Territory in the 1830s along the Trail of Tears. Prominent among these were the Cherokees, whose commitment to change led to strong support for schooling. Once settled in the West, the so-called Five Civilized Tribes controlled their own schools until Congress passed the Curtis Act in 1898, which dissolved all their governmental institutions, including schools.

Although Indians had attended boarding schools for many generations before the 1870s, this traumatic form of education took on new life after the wars in the trans-Mississippi West were over and the last treaties were signed. The chasm that divided the Navajo surrender at Canyon de Chelly (1863) and the Indian victory at Little Bighorn (1876) from today's Indian world was first crossed when relatives of the Navajo headman Manuelito and the Lakota leader Spotted Tail boarded the train for Carlisle Indian Industrial School in Pennsylvania.

Brought into being in 1879 by Richard Henry Pratt, an army officer and educator, Carlisle epitomized "white man's education" (and continued to do so long after it was closed in 1918). By 1900, twenty-four clones of Carlisle, including Haskell, Chemawa, Flandreau, Albuquerque, and Chilocco, had opened in the West, but Carlisle clung to its legendary status, becoming a source of pride to Indians, who rooted for its football teams and athletes like Jim Thorpe.

Thousands of Indians learned their three R's and a vocational skill at Carlisle and other boarding schools, yet their motivations and reactions remained mixed. Luther Standing Bear, a Lakota, recalled, "This chance to go East would prove that I was brave if I were to accept." Zitkala Ša (Gertrude Bonnin), a Yankton, liked the incentives: "big red apples," and riding "on the iron horse." Others were sent by their tribes in order to become cultural brokers between their communities and outsiders. Some were enrolled because they were orphans or lived in poverty, and the schools promised food, clothing, and shelter.

Between 1879 and the 1930s the Bureau of Indian Affairs often failed to fulfill this promise. Federal schools often scrimped on food, and relied on the students' skills in sewing, farming, cooking, cobbling, and carpentry to operate the institutions. Yet the harsh conditions, the severe punishments for speaking a native language or running away, the military discipline—"You lined up and marched, to almost everything you did," recalled a Tulalip—and the rigid pressure to be like whites failed to prevent students from forging a Pan-Indian identity, or from recalling their school days with nostalgia.

During the 1930s Commissioner of Indian Affairs John Collier modified the assimilationist image of BIA schools, but trends in schooling outside the BIA had already irrevocably altered the shape of "white man's education." Federal reimbursement to public schools for the enrollment of Indian pupils was already in place by 1900, and by 1928 the majority of Indian schoolchildren attended public school. World War II increased this trend dramatically. Military service and war work drew thousands of Indians to urban areas. The war also revolutionized American Indian attitudes toward schooling. Indian veterans relied on the GI Bill and urged support for schooling. The BIA opened programs for Navajo and Alaska "overage" youths to learn the three R's and undertake job training. The Indian Claims Commission, established in 1946, granted monetary awards that were used by some tribes for scholarship funding. The term "white man's education" had become an anachronism, and Indians replaced it with "Get an education." Education had come to mean a high school diploma, a ticket to a job.

Federal Indian policy of the postwar years exerted another pressure for schooling. As tribes resisted the extension of states' legal authority and the unilateral termination of tribal relationships with the federal government, Indians realized that the battle of wits demanded even more schooling. By the 1960s the goal of a high school diploma was expanding toward college and, for some, graduate school. The law served as a magnet: it offered a powerful weapon to deal with legal claims, state governments, the BIA, and Congress.

The political climate of the 1960s stimulated the drive for more schooling; it also introduced the idea of an Indian voice in federal policymaking and public discussion of native issues. In this tumultuous era American Indians moved to complete the circle that would eventually lead them toward the holistic education once central to their societies.

The persistent onslaught by Euro-Americans had taken its toll. Disease, warfare, removal, land theft, and schooling had persuaded some native survivors to adopt the Euro-American values of land ownership, individualism, and Christianity. The 1960s saw a widespread questioning of this trend among schooled Indians—both urban and reservation—who began to campaign for self-determination and treaty rights through resistance measures like the Pacific Northwest fish-ins.

As these struggles became diversified in a milieu dominated by the civil rights movement and Lyndon Johnson's Great Society, they incorporated a new approach to schooling. The congressional battles over Indian control of schooling, which led to the passage of the Indian Education Act (1972), the Indian Self-Determination and Education Assistance Act (1975), and the Tribally Controlled Community College Assistance Act (1978), reflected the combined efforts of Indian lobbying groups and liberal members of Congress. This legislation has brought some Indian control over programs for the 85 percent of all Indian children who are in public school, along with direct contracting and other forms of control for BIA-funded schools.

A pivotal decade, the 1960s reintroduced some balance to Indian education. In precontact times education was sustained by family and community; by the mid–twentieth century it had splintered between the native community and nonnative schools. The 1970s legislation provided a means for tribal people to reconnect the values taught in their communities with those introduced in school. In the long run, this might lead toward the integrated education that had once been central to native communities.

The decade of the 1960s also altered the balance between education influenced by Euro-Americans and education influenced by Indians. Although most outsiders had ignored what American Indians could teach them, some nonnative people had always been receptive to tribal worldviews. From the 1960s forward this receptivity expanded as Americans confronted issues such as pollution and diminishing natural resources. Recent decades have raised questions on both sides of the cultural divide: nonnatives have begun to listen to the teachings of tribal people; American Indians have been searching for connections between high school and college diplomas and the ancient core of their education.

See also Boarding Schools; Carlisle Indian Industrial School; Chemawa Indian School; Child Rearing; Chilocco Indian School; Eastern Universities and Indians; Flandreau School; Missions and Missionaries; Phoenix Indian School; Santee Normal Training School; Standing Bear, Luther; Zitkala Ša (Gertrude Bonnin).

Hyer, Sally, *One House, One Voice, One Heart: Native American Education at the Santa Fe Indian School* (Santa Fe: Museum of New Mexico Press, 1990); Szasz, Margaret Connell, *Education and the American Indian: The Road to Self-Determination since 1928* (Albuquerque: University of New Mexico Press, 1977); Szasz, Margaret Connell, *Indian Education in the American Colonies, 1607–1783* (Albuquerque: University of New Mexico Press, 1988).

MARGARET CONNELL SZASZ
University of New Mexico

ELDERS

Elders played vital roles within tribal cultures in family and camp life, political organizations, social and economic activities, and religious ceremonies. Among most tribes, aging was considered a sign of favor by supernatural spirits that enabled a person to acquire wisdom, knowledge of the world and its creatures, and tribal lore. Older people immersed in the oral history of their people have provided us with most of what we know about tribes prior to the arrival of European visitors.

Within extended families elders performed many functions. Regardless of whether they resided in a small wickiup or a large longhouse, elders were respected, loved, and considered useful. Older men no longer fit for warfare or hunting made bows, arrows, shields, and other implements, while older women, although not freed as early in life from their routine duties, turned to weaving baskets or cloth or continued their bead and quill work. Elderly Navajo and Pueblo silversmiths and potters still produce exquisite metal and earthen wares despite some loss of dexterity. Grandparents were the first teachers and companions of boys and girls, creating lasting bonds of respect and affection. A child was deemed unfortunate if he or she had no grandparent to act as a counselor and protector. In many tribes such as the community of Taos Pueblo, the requirement that young parents travel great distances to find work has often heightened the importance of grandparents as caretakers. Traditionally, male youths learned tribal lore as they listened to their grandfathers and their companions recount migrations, myths, and conflicts with enemies. If a family wanted entertainment for an evening, an old man skilled in storytelling was invited to eat with the family and guests.

Respect was not limited to elderly males. Senior women were often the social arbiters of family problems and activities. If a divorce occurred in a Navajo family, the husband departed from the camp and senior women maintained lifelong control of their sheep flocks. Even in tribes considered male dominated, women ran camps, and political leaders were careful not to incur the displeasure of elderly women, who were capable of ridiculing a chief at public gatherings.

Respect and love for elders did not deter their abandonment by some western tribes. Before acquiring horses, the Blackfeet routinely left their old, enfeebled people behind when camps moved. Elderly Kiowas were "thrown away" because those about to die were thought to be possessed by evil spirits. When non-Indians intervened to rescue such people, the "victims" were displeased because they had accepted their family's decision. Among the Western Apaches of east-central Arizona, whose environment required them to move seasonally, the aged lacked prestige because they could no longer accumulate property. Aged family members received less desirable clothing, bedding, and food portions. Old persons no longer able to walk or ride were given a supply of food and water and told that their family would return after several days; but the family never returned. In the contemporary era, however, pensions and government benefits mean that the elderly are no longer the poorest family members, and they are given more adequate attention.

Tribal elders perform a number of social functions. They teach younger generations the moral principles by which they should live and urge intratribal sharing of material goods. They set an example of living as much as possible without conflict and, if conflict occurs, of settling differences according to tribal custom or law. Older people are expected to remember complex family relationships so that individuals contemplating marriage within exogamous clans can be warned against marrying someone too closely related.

In tribes with age-graded men's societies, the oldest men formed the most prestigious society. At the top of a tribe's hierarchy were, for example, the Pueblo priesthoods or the seven Arapaho "water-pouring old men" or the ten Kiowa men of Koitsenko society. Only invited old women could belong to the Kiowa Calf Old Women society. Other Plains tribes had women's societies that were secular in function, being devoted to quilling, tipi making, or tipi decorating. A younger woman desiring to join such a society applied to an old society member, who instructed her in the techniques of the craft. In the 1930s, when federal programs were established to revive tribal crafts, older women taught their juniors tanning, beading, basketry, and other crafts. Today, older men and women are the ones who are fluent in their tribal language, a critical element in the transmission of tribal culture, and it is they who are deeply concerned that ceremonies are not being performed properly or "the way they used to be."

Until the late 1800s elders were simultaneously religious and political leaders. A priest-chief and his elderly companions supervised the six great Cherokee ceremonies; some of those ceremonies marked periods of the agricultural cycle, while others offered individual and collective spiritual renewal. Among the Osages were men, as described by John Joseph Mathews, whose "fires of mating and hunting and war had been banked," and they were known as the Little Old Men. Early in the tribe's history they devised the tribe's formal religion, established the pattern of male descent, and issued the rule of exogamy. Before induction into membership, Little Old Men received seven years of ceremonial training. Arapaho elders, as ritual leaders, have retained significant power. Down to the 1890s, seven elderly priests, the "water-pouring old men," directed all tribal rituals and dominated politics. When candidates for this highest Arapaho priesthood could not attain the necessary qualifications, the qualifications were lessened, and eventually "four old men" were chosen to function instead of the seven water-pouring old men. Today the "four old men" and a Sun Dance chief wield ceremonial authority and are very influential in all tribal activities.

Another group of holy men, known as shamans or medicine men, were generally but not exclusively elderly men. On the Great Plains, a wise, elderly shaman assisted youths during their vision quest. After fasting and sacrifice induced a vision, the old man interpreted the vision, prescribed conduct, including taboos, and assembled the youth's medicine bag. When a man had a vision indicating that he could become a shaman, he sought out an older practitioner, who instructed him in the art of healing with herbs, roots, and rituals. Upon a man's becoming a shaman, his wife became his assistant and acquired knowledge of healing. But there were also medicine women who were known as healers independent of male validation. Shamans were also accomplished sleight-of-hand artists or conjurors who seemingly drew from patients' bodies objects alleged to cause disease.

In tribal government, elders exerted enormous influence. Until 1827, when Cherokees adopted a constitution and a representative form of government, elders led by priest-chiefs dominated politics in the autonomous Cherokee towns. The priest-chiefs were assisted by seven elders representing the seven Cherokee clans, and all other elderly men, who were designated "beloved men." Cherokee elders also used their influence to restrain younger warriors from undertakings likely to endanger a town's population. By persuasion elders gained support from more impulsive youths for solutions to perplexing issues, because unanimity, or at least acquiescence, was required for harmony within the town. The Cherokee Nighthawk Society still assumes that elders should restrain young people from unwise actions.

Through most of the 1800s, the Osage Little Old Men controlled important aspects of tribal life. While younger chiefs dealt with other Indians or non-Indians, the Little Old Men decided upon peace or war, where the village would be relocated, when a buffalo hunt would be conducted, and who would become Osage chiefs. Until the reservation era, the Little Old Men formed village councils, and the assembled members of these councils, representing all twenty-four Osage clans, constituted the tribal council.

Arapaho elders have been successful in maintaining their political power. Until the late 1800s, the water-pouring old men selected chiefs, who followed the elders' guidance in diplomacy and the internal governance of the tribe. The "four old men," the successors of the water-pouring old men, have, by maintaining ceremonial dominance, by being receptive to change, and by retaining the support of elderly men and women, kept their position as arbiters of Arapaho politics and society.

The prominence of the Navajo Tribal Council and its officers masks the strength of elders in local Navajo political organizations. Despite efforts to centralize Navajo politics by federal officials, the Navajos use chapter organizations founded in 1927 to maintain local control of key political and economic issues. Influential local headmen still play crucial roles in the Navajo Tribal Council. In chapter meetings a group of elders seated before the moderator's place are called upon to speak and lead discussions. They function as an elders' council whose views are respected and whose votes establish the chapter's course of action.

Although elderly chiefs no longer dominate tribal relations with the federal government as they did until the early 1900s, present leaders seek the opinion of elders before they meet with federal officials. Pan-Indian organizations such as the American Indian Movement and the National Indian Youth Council, led by younger people, incurred some suspicion on the part of elders, resulting in a limited following and effectiveness on many reservations. Since the 1930s, tribal business committees when representing their tribes are on firmer ground when they accept guidance from elders. In the 1950s, when Native Americans decided to revive tribal ceremonies that had been suppressed for decades by government regulations, it was elders who searched for information to restore ceremonial rituals. In domestic life, many tribes have developed day-care facilities to accommodate working parents and have worked to incorporate elders into these centers' programs and activities. Despite dramatic changes in ways of life, the wisdom of elders is still respected in Native American tribes and communities.

DONALD J. BERTHRONG
Lafayette, Indiana

ENGLISH LANGUAGE AND INDIANS

The relationship between Indians and the English language has been a difficult one, as English has been used to enforce conformity to Euro-American society and to obliterate ancestral languages. Nevertheless, Indians have contributed to English, and they have made it their own by adapting it as a means of their own cultural expression.

There are about one thousand English words (not including toponyms) that have North American indigenous languages as their source. The practice of borrowing these words and incorporating them, often in a highly modified form, began in the sixteenth century and continued into the twentieth, although the major periods of transfer occurred in times of earliest contact. There are two major areas in which such words were borrowed. One is the terminology used for the native fauna and flora of North America (for example, *raccoon, opossum, geoduck, hickory, squash*), and the other is the terminology for items of Indian culture (for example, *toboggan, tipi, wigwam, potlatch, wampum*).

Somewhat surprisingly, the reverse has not been true. North American indigenous languages have been fairly resistant to borrowing vocabulary from the languages of the European invaders. Many speakers assiduously eschew mixing in English words and phrases while speaking their languages, while others use them parsimoniously and with no adaptation so that they function as foreign words rather than loan words. Trade items and features of the postcontact Indian culture are generally designated with colorful and descriptive native neologisms. In Lakota, for example, "chair" is *čaŋʔakaŋyaŋkapi* (literally, "they sit on wood"), "clock" is *mazaškaŋškaŋ* (metal in continuous motion), and "fry bread" is *wigliʔuŋkagapi* (they make it with oil). The purism of North American languages contrasts sharply with their Mesoamerican counterparts, which are often heavily larded with Spanish.

The most widely used North American Indian language today is the English vernacular sometimes called Red English or Indian English. Comparable to Black English but entirely distinct from it, Indian English is a strong and positive linguistic expression of modern Indian identity. Like Black English, it shows both regional and social variation. The latter is particularly significant, as variations range from the highly colloquial speech forms of many traditional older Indians to the colorful expressions of Indian teenagers to the slight coloration in pronunciation of Standard English spoken by acculturated Indian professionals. In addition, there are identifiable tribal varieties of Indian English, with features in some cases relatable to ancestral languages—whether or not these are known by the speakers.

The literary expression of the forms and diction of Indian English may be seen in the works of modern Indian Anglophone writers such as N. Scott Momaday, Leslie Marmon Silko, Louise Erdrich, and James Welch. The anthropologist Anthony Mattina has advocated colloquial Indian English as the form of English into which to translate traditional oral narratives from their original indigenous languages.

See also Languages; Place Names; Words That Have Entered English Usage.

Bevington, Gary, *Where Do Words Come From? An Introduction to Etymology* (Dubuque, Iowa: Kendall/Hunt, 1995); Leap, William L., *American Indian English* (Salt Lake City: University of Utah Press, 1993).

GARY BEVINGTON
Northeastern Illinois University
and NAES College

ERIE

The Eries, known also as the "cat" or "raccoon" nation, were an Iroquoian-speaking people who, until their dispersal in 1657, occupied the Lake Erie shore from modern Buffalo, New York, to Erie, Pennsylvania. Since no Europeans are known to have visited Erie towns, there is little documentary evidence about these people. Instead, scholars have relied heavily on the archaeological remains of the Eries and the cultures from which they originated, as well as on information about better-known peoples with whom they shared cultural traits, such as the Hurons and the Five Nations Iroquois.

The Eries emerged from an earlier culture known by its archaeological remains to have been centered in southern Ontario. By the early sixteenth century the production of corn had become basic to a settled way of life based on a gender division of labor within semi-permanent villages, and local populations were growing steadily larger thanks to reliable supplies of plant foods as well as fish and game. This rise in population also contributed to persistent, low-level warfare between the Eries and neighboring peoples—a practice associated with resource competition as well as with the Iroquoian tradition of the "mourning war," whereby enemy captives were sought to replace dead kinfolk, assuage grief, and thus maintain both harmony and the social fabric.

By the time the French learned of them in the early seventeenth century, the Eries appear to have been organized as a loose ethnic confederacy consisting of three, perhaps four, clusters of villages concentrated in what is now southwestern New York State. French estimates that the Eries could field two to three thousand warriors suggest a total population of from eight to twelve thousand in the 1640s.

The destruction of the Eries was part of a larger pattern of warfare in the Northeast linked to the arrival of Europeans along with their weapons, materials, and diseases. In an effort to secure access to valued European goods as well as to replace mounting losses from infectious diseases, the Five Nations Iroquois systematically attacked and dispersed rival peoples during the late 1640s and early 1650s. Dispersal of the Hurons by 1649 was followed by a similar campaign against the Neutrals of Ontario, whose trading partners included the Eries.

By 1654 the Eries had also become a target of Iroquois raids, principally from the Seneca towns at the western end of the Five Nations territory. The Eries's location astride the Lake Erie plain put them in a position to block Iroquois efforts to reach rich hunting grounds in the Ohio Valley and thus made them an object of concerted Iroquois attack. Weakened by epidemics, including smallpox, in 1637 and again in 1639–41, and lacking the firearms acquired by the Iroquois from Dutch traders, the Eries succumbed to a series of onslaughts culminating in their dispersal in 1657.

Some Eries may have fled to the Carolina lowlands and formed the group known in the 1670s as Westos. One band is known to have remained in the Ohio Valley until 1680, when it finally surrendered to the Senecas. This band and other Erie captives were adopted by the Iroquois, and their descendants were undoubtedly among those Senecas who began to resettle in the upper Ohio Valley in the 1740s.

Richter, Daniel K., *The Ordeal of the Longhouse: The Peoples of the Iroquois League in the Era of European Colonization* (Chapel Hill: University of North Carolina Press, 1992); Trigger, Bruce G., "Early Iroquoian Contacts with Europeans," in *Handbook of North American Indians,* ed. William C. Sturtevant, vol. 15, *Northeast,* ed. Bruce Trigger (Washington: Smithsonian Institution, 1978); White, Marian E., "Erie," in *Handbook of North American Indians,* ed. William C. Sturtevant, vol. 15, *Northeast,* ed. Bruce Trigger (Washington: Smithsonian Institution, 1978).

MICHAEL N. MCCONNELL
University of Alabama at Birmingham

ESKIMO (YUPIK/INUPIAT/INUIT)

The Eskimo and Aleut peoples occupy the northern North American coastline and nearby islands from Prince William Sound in south central Alaska westward and northward in Alaska, across the Bering Sea to St. Lawrence Island and eastern Siberia, and around the continental Arctic coast eastward across Canada to Quebec, Labrador, and on to Greenland. With the exception of the southernmost areas in Alaska, this region is icebound for nine to ten months of the year, and in most areas, treeless tundra predominates in the interior. The Eskimo cultural tradition evolved during the first millennium a.d. in the Bering Strait region, developing into the Thule culture, which spread rapidly to the north and east across the continent and to Greenland. This highly productive maritime culture focused on the harvest of large sea mammals, particularly the bowhead whale, utilizing toggle harpoons and open skin boats as well as kayaks, sleds, and dog teams; it is associated with semisubterranean houses and larger village settlements.

The eastward expansion of Thule culture is associated with a warming trend that occurred after A.D. 900, reducing the Arctic ice pack and establishing open sea conditions suitable as a summer habitat for the bowhead whale. A cooling period began after 1200, culminating in the little ice age of 1650–1800, during which increased sea-ice accumulation brought about a decline in whaling activities and gave rise to regional variations and diversification in subsistence patterns. Disruptions were most severe in the central Arctic, where people became more dependent on the ringed seals that lived and bred along the ice edge. Although the ice house or igloo is the most common image of Eskimo society, the use of this residential structure was limited (except for emergencies) to the central Canadian Arctic region and represents an adaptation to these cooling environmental conditions.

The Eskimo-Aleut language family consists of two long-separated but related branches, Eskimo and Aleut. The Eskimo language is further divided into two principal groups, the northern Inupiaq/Inuit and the more southerly Yupik. The Inupiaq and Inuit people speak localized dialects that stretch in a continuum from Norton Sound in Alaska northward and all the way across the continent to Greenland. The Yupik language includes five distinct sublanguages or dialects, of which three are represented in Alaska: Siberian Yupik, on St. Lawrence Island and the Siberian coast; Central Yupik, in southwestern Alaska; and Alutiiq, in the northern Pacific area (Kodiak Island and Prince William Sound). Together with their Aleut neighbors to the west, the Alutiiq people inhabit a warmer, wetter, and largely ice-free maritime zone significantly different from that of

the northern Eskimos. The Aleut and Alutiiq peoples shared certain cultural features not found among northern Eskimo groups, most notably open-sea hunting techniques involving the use of a barbed harpoon dart; extremes of social differentiation, including the use of slaves; and, particularly among the Aleuts, matrilineal social organization. The Alutiiq Eskimo culture also reflects influences from the maritime Pacific Northwest coast Indian cultures to the south. The major Eskimo cultural divisions are shown in Table 1.

Alaskan Eskimo groups were subdivided into territorial groups, or "societies," which at the local level comprised a number of smaller associations of extended family groups, or bands. The location and composition of modern villages and communities often reflect these traditional territorial associations, although the history of interaction with commercial whalers, traders, missionaries, and government schoolteachers is also a factor. Throughout Eskimo country, before the adoption of Western-style housing, members of the extended family usually lived together under one roof. Household size varied considerably depending upon population density and the availability of resources; the largest such groupings were found in Northwest Alaska. Today the residential group is the conjugal family, but the extended family continues to be the principal social unit, cooperating in the production, distribution, and consumption of foods and materials, even though the constituent households may be geographically dispersed in the community.

Kinship is the basic organizing principle of Eskimo society. Like the American system, Eskimo kinship is bilateral, placing equal emphasis on relationships on both the mother's and father's sides of the family. Relationships within extended families (grandparents, parents, brothers, sisters, aunts, uncles, cousins, nieces, and nephews) are particularly important, as is an individual's kindred—the larger set of consanguineal relationships that can be traced on both sides up and down through three generations. The Siberian Yupik communities on St. Lawrence Island, where larger patrilineal descent groups function as political and economic units, is an exception to this Eskimo pattern. The scope of Eskimo kinship is maximal; that is, it recognizes more distant or affinal (related by marriage) relationships. This was important in the precontact period, when the ability to establish a kinship connection in a distant community meant the difference between life and death for the "stranger." In contemporary communities, where social life is often highly interactive, much

Eskimo women photographed in Alaska in 1903.

daily association and interchange is structured according to these relationships, particularly among the households within extended families.

Other social practices establish "quasi-kinship" relationships that also serve to link separate households and older and younger members of extended families. These traditional practices, while undergoing some changes, have been continued in modern communities. For example, adoption is widespread in Eskimo communities: single and multiple adoptions are common, as are adoptions of a grandchild by the grandparents. Special relationships are recognized between individuals with the same name, and between surviving relatives and the namesake when another namesake is deceased. Newborn babies are usually given the name of a recently deceased person and are seen as vessels for the rebirth of the spirit of the late individual, most often a member of the grandparental generation. Formal trading partnerships once provided a further means of establishing long-term relationships between members of different communities and between coastal and interior groups. While this custom is no longer practiced today, the institution of friendships between members of different extended families in the community is common.

Alaskan Eskimo communities frequently included men of influence who headed extended family groups, organized trade, led hunting groups, and were ceremonial leaders. In the north, men who captained whaling crews held the greatest wealth and influence, having acquired or inherited significant wealth in the form of whale boats and equipment, which helped them to provide economic support for their crews. Formerly, the members of each whaling crew were associated with a men's house (*karigi*), headed by the captain (*umaelik*), who also led associated hunting rituals and sponsored trading expeditions. While members of the captain's extended family provided the core of this group, the crew also included non-kin, and sons often joined the karigi of their father. These karigi associations provided an additional degree of community integration in the larger whaling villages. Modern umaelit own the whaling boat and equipment, are responsible for supplying the crew while out on the ice, and often provide access to hunting equipment and other assistance to their crew during the remaining part of the year.

Eskimos follow a scheduled annual round of subsistence activities often correlated with the presence of animals during their seasonal migrations. They harvest sea mammals including bearded, spotted, ringed, and harbor seals, bowhead and beluga whales, walrus, narwhals, sea lions, and sea otters. They also utilize other marine resources such as polar bears, crabs, smelt, and herring. During warmer months, inland resources including caribou, ducks, geese, fish (especially whitefish, char, and salmon), and plant foods are important. Families are often absent at various times in the warm season as they disperse to hunting and fishing camps on the land. Variations in ecology and the availability of animals have resulted in regional differences in subsistence practices, and both coastal and interior adaptations have arisen. For example, while most Eskimo communities focus on marine mammals supplemented with caribou, waterfowl, and fish, some inland groups in Alaska and Canada depend upon caribou as their primary resource, while in Southwest Alaska salmon is the major resource for the interior, riverine Yupik Eskimos.

Modern subsistence hunters use aluminum skiffs and outboard motors (or larger boats), snowmachines, sleds, rifles, CB radios, fish nets, and camping equipment, and they must provide for supplies and equipment repair. Spring whaling entails additional efforts to establish camps on the ice at the edge of the shore-fast ice leads and supply a skin boat (*umiaq*), shoulder and darting guns, harpoons, and food and supplies to support a crew, while fall whaling involves open-sea hunting using motorboats. Whaling involves year-round

preparatory efforts; besides getting equipment ready, the skins of bearded seals (or walrus on St. Lawrence Island) must be acquired for skin boats, and sufficient meat and fish must be accumulated to provide for the crew. Employment is necessary to support these subsistence activities, and in most communities wage-work opportunities are limited. Although female hunters are not unknown, a division of labor is maintained: men do the hunting and fishing, while women are responsible for processing and distributing the catch within the extended family (after primary distribution within the hunting party by the men). Bowhead whales are butchered, and their meat is distributed to the participating crews and the community, according to formal, prescribed rules.

The International Whaling Commission (IWC) imposed a quota on the 1978 harvest of bowhead whales that affected the eight whaling communities in Alaska. In response, the Alaska whalers formed the Alaskan Eskimo Whaling Commission to represent themselves before the IWC and to seek an increase in the harvest quota, with notable success. Similar associations have been formed with regard to other animal resources, such as the Eskimo Walrus Commission, the Sea Otter Commission, and the International Porcupine Caribou Commission. A contemporary concern is the presence of trace metals and industrial pollutants in the organs of marine mammals in the Arctic. In addition to monitoring the levels of such pollutants, Eskimos have been developing cooperative agreements across state and national boundaries for the management and protection of shared animal populations, including waterfowl, polar bears, and walrus.

Whaling is associated with a significant round of ritual and community ceremonial activity. Preparatory efforts include specific activities that show respect for the whale, and a whale captain's wife follows behavioral prescriptions during the hunt that are believed to be pleasing and not cause alarm to the spirit of the whale. It is she who pours fresh water into the whale's mouth after it is caught, an activity thought to help the whale's soul return to the spirit world. Ceremonial distributions of whale meat and *maktak* (skin and blubber) are made to the community—initially by the captain's wife, and later by the captain himself at the Nulakataq celebration, when the successful whaling captains host a community feast followed by a blanket toss, in which a person is propelled high into the air by the coordinated action of people pulling on a large piece of ugruk skin. Captains also contribute portions of whales and

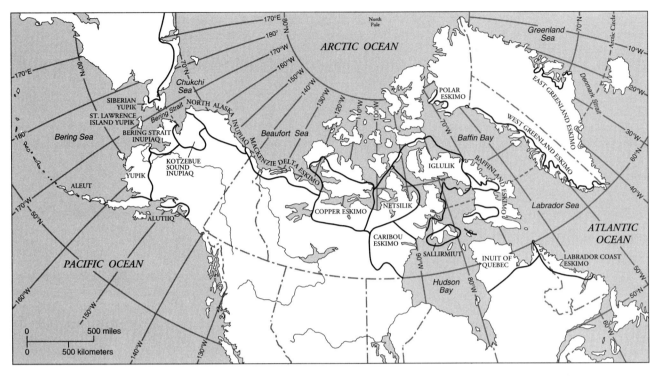

ARCTIC TRIBAL TERRITORIES

other animals to the large annual community feasts at Thanksgiving and Christmas.

Alaskan Eskimos used to celebrate the Messenger Feast during midwinter. This was a large ceremonial gathering organized by the heads of extended families (or, in the north, by an *umaelik*), who sent messengers to invite designated persons (usually trading partners) from other communities. The feasting was accompanied by elaborate gift giving, competitive games, and feats of strength, as well as singing, dancing, and storytelling. According to report, the last of these gatherings in North Alaska, there called Kivgiq, occurred in 1915 in Wainwright. Under the influence of missionaries, this ceremony gradually declined and was discontinued in the early twentieth century throughout Alaska. This tradition was revived several years ago in Barrow and is now a regular ceremonial event involving all North Slope (the northern Alaska region) communities each year. According to one anthropologist, a comical dance involving men and women is the most important contemporary annual community ceremonial event among the Yupik on Nelson Island, in which some of the gift-giving elements of the Messenger Feast survive.

The Yupik Eskimos formerly celebrated the Bladder Feast, which was a propitiation and a demonstration of

respect for the seals caught during the year. It was believed that the spirits of the seals moved into their bladders when they were killed, and the bladders of harvested seals were inflated and hung in the men's house throughout the year; the spirits of the seals were feasted and entertained during the annual ceremony, at the end of which the bladders were released into the sea to help the spirits return to their ocean home, where they could be reborn. Seal parties, during which seal meat and numerous small household items are given away, are another common ceremonial event; these are given by the woman of the household in the spring when the men and boys bring home their first seals of the year.

Beliefs in the spirituality of the natural world were very salient in Eskimo culture. Animals were thought to resemble humans in having souls or spirits that could think, feel, and talk. Eskimos believed that animals would give themselves voluntarily to the hunter who acted properly toward them, and the purpose of many ritual practices was in fact to show respect for and give thanks to the spirits of animals taken for food. Across the Arctic, Eskimos gave a drink of water to dead seals, whales, caribou, and waterfowl after they had killed them. If humans did not show their appreciation, or if they acted improperly, animals could prevent themselves from appearing in physical form, and humans might starve. Another Eskimo belief was that the spirits of whales, after spending time in the human community, returned to their home under the sea and reported on the human behaviors they had observed to the other whales; their reports, in turn, had an effect on the spring whale hunt. When respect was shown to the spirits of the whale and harmonious behavior was present in the community, whales would return and allow themselves to be harvested in the following spring. Eskimos believe in reincarnation and the recycling of both human and animal souls. They also believed that rocks, mountains, and other features of the landscape had spirits. Contemporary Eskimos believe in supernatural beings with whom ordinary people interact. These beings include caribou people, miniature people, invisible people, mermaids, and trolls, and may be present to assist people in hunting efforts and at times of distress; there are even reports of marriages between humans and caribou people.

MAJOR CULTURAL AND LINGUISTIC DIVISIONS OF ESKIMO PEOPLES

Yupik
    Alutiiq or North Pacific Eskimo (Koniag and Chugach Eskimo)
    Central Alaskan Yupik
    Siberian Yupik (St. Lawrence Island and eastern Siberia)
Inupiaq/Inuit
    Northwest and North Alaskan Inupiaq
        Bering Strait
        Kotzebue Sound
        Coastal North Alaskan Inupiaq (Taremuit)
        Interior North Alaskan Inupiaq (Nunamuit)
    Canadian Inuit
        MacKenzie Delta
        Central Arctic Inuit
            Copper
            Netsilik
            Igulik
            Caribou
            Baffin Island
        Quebec
        Labrador Coast
    Greenlandic Inuit
        Polar (Thule) Eskimo
        West Greenland
        East Greenland

See also Aleut; Indian-White Relations in Alaska; Indian-White Relations in Canada, 1763 to the Present.

Brody, Hugh, *Living Arctic: Hunters of the Canadian North* (London: Faber and Faber, 1987); Damas, David, ed., *Arctic*, vol. 5 of *Handbook of North American Indians*, ed. William C. Sturtevant (Washington: Smithsonian Institution, 1984); Fienup-Riordan, Ann, *Boundaries and Passages* (Norman: University of Oklahoma Press, 1994).

CHARLES W. SMYTHE
Smithsonian Institution

ETOWAH

Located in northwestern Georgia near the city of Rome, Etowah is a large Mississippian archaeological site. It covers fifty-two acres and contains three large mounds that surround a central plaza, as well as numerous smaller mounds, many of which served as the bases for elite dwellings and public buildings. The largest mound, larger than a football field at its base and sixty feet high, sits south of the plaza. Two principal mounds stand twenty-five feet high on the east and west sides of the plaza. Another, larger plaza, about three hundred feet square, lies east of these mounds and is plastered with specially prepared clay.

About 350 elite burials have been found in one of the central mounds. These burials were accompanied by extensive grave goods made of exotic materials, such as copper, greenstone, mica, and marine shell. The central site was surrounded by a moat and a wooden palisade.

Originally excavated in the nineteenth century, Etowah has been the site of numerous other excavations, and research has continued there to the present day. Occupied between A.D. 900 and A.D. 1500, Etowah was the capital of a large theocratic chiefdom that reached its peak in the late fifteenth century. It controlled or influenced much of northern Georgia, northeastern Alabama, eastern Tennessee, and the western Carolinas at that time. Its location allowed it to exploit and control the flow of resources from four physiographic provinces as well as sources of copper, greenstone, and mica, which were widely exported. The people of Etowah manufactured numerous finely crafted artifacts using these and other exotic materials, most of which served as markers of elite status.

Etowah was abandoned and then reoccupied by a much smaller village in the late fifteenth or early sixteenth century. Chronic warfare, probably with another chiefdom centered at Moundville in eastern Alabama, has been suggested as a factor in its decline. Although the site never regained its earlier grandeur, the Etowah chiefdom was ancestral to the Coosa chiefdom described by the early Spanish explorers and to some of the later Creek Indian towns.

See also Mississippians.

EUROPE, INDIANS IN

Over the past five centuries, thousands of American Indians have come to Europe. Although they did not come as conquerors, and often arrived rather as members of conquered peoples, their impact on Europeans goes far beyond the limited scope of their physical transatlantic presence. Stereotypical images of the "Indian," ranging from the noble savage to the savage brute, were created in Europe only in small part on the basis of personal encounters with Native Americans; for the most part they were adapted from classical and medieval views of cultural "otherness" according to their creators' ever-changing needs. American Indian visitors to Europe were more affected by European visions of the "Indian" than they were effective in creating those visions.

Columbus was only the first explorer to abduct American Indians and present them in Europe as proof of his transatlantic discoveries and of the potential usefulness of these people to Europeans. In 1501, the king of Portugal was reportedly pleased at the sight of a group of above-average-sized natives of Newfoundland, whom he intended to use as slaves. Hundreds of Native Americans were shipped to Europe for that very purpose in the first decades of the sixteenth century. The practice was largely abandoned when American Indians turned out to be especially susceptible to European diseases, but the trade continued into the seventeenth century. In 1614, for example, the ship captain Thomas Hunt kidnapped twenty-four native New Englanders, including the famous Squanto, and sold them in Málaga to the Spaniards.

Others were carried to Europe to document the need to "civilize" and convert the aboriginal North Americans, or to arouse European interest in the New World's resources, and thus to support the colonial enterprise. Jacques Cartier, the French explorer of the St. Lawrence River, specifically trapped the Iroquois chief Donnacona on his ship in 1536, "that he might relate and tell to the king all he has seen in the west of the wonders of the world." At the same time it was hoped that Native American visitors to Europe would be favorably impressed by the splendors of the Continent and the power of its monarchs. As Indians themselves became increasingly curious about the land whence the white men had come, it was no longer necessary to forcibly take them abroad.

After the sixteenth century, Native Americans were also brought to Europe to receive an education that would enable them to act as teachers and diplomats. Some were trained in Rome for the priesthood in order to become missionaries among their own people. In the twentieth century, American Indian soldiers fighting in the Great War against the German "Huns" were sometimes cited as an example of how other savages had already been redeemed by civilization.

In the eighteenth century, Native American politicians began to visit Europe regularly. Three Mohawks and a Mohegan touted as "the Four Kings of Canada" paid a much publicized visit to Queen Anne in 1710. With the end of the French and British colonial empires in America such visits became less common, though they have continued into the twentieth century. After failing to obtain British support in the struggle of the hereditary chiefs of the Six Nations against the Canadian government, the Cayuga chief Deskaheh in 1923 submitted "The Redman's Appeal for Justice" to the recently established League of Nations in Geneva. Canadian Indian representatives traveled to England to lobby for native rights when the Canadian constitution was "repatriated" in the 1980s. Since the 1980s, Geneva has become a meeting ground for (generally self-appointed rather than elected) American Indian politicians in connection with the sessions of the United Nations Working Group for Indigenous People. These sessions also draw delegates from the numerous European groups supporting Native American political causes.

Whatever the reasons for their visits to Europe might have been, American Indians quickly found themselves treated as objects of curiosity. They were made to paddle their canoes on local ponds, demonstrate other notable skills, or simply let themselves be looked at for their strange attire or able (if exotic) bodies. The landlord of an establishment that was housing a Cherokee delegation visiting London in 1762 charged admission to the Indians' dressing room, "which gave them [the Indians] the highest disgust, these people having a particular aversion to being stared at while dressing or eating."

The commercialization of cultural differences reached its peak in the nineteenth century, when competing entrepreneurs brought American Indians and other exotic groups to Europe. During his eight years' residence in London and Paris, the American artist George Catlin promoted interest in his gallery of American Indian paintings by employing Native American dance troupes. By far the most successful of these showmen, however, was "Buffalo Bill" Cody, whose Wild West show helped to establish the Sioux as the epitome of "the American Indian" in Europe. The participants in such shows—who had suffered military defeat and were facing economic deprivation on their reservations, and whose numbers included Black Elk, Iron Tail, and some of the leaders of the Ghost Dance movement—were given an opportunity for gainful employment by exhibiting aspects of their traditional culture in front of an enthusiastic and sympathetic audience.

Since a certain conformity with the prevalent stereotype of "the Indian" generally helped showpiece Indians convince their audiences of their authenticity, impostors were often more successful in this business than true Native Americans. William Augustus Bowles, an American loyalist who often dressed as "commander-in-chief of the Creek and Cherokee" Nations, was lionized by London society in 1791; in the 1920s Edgardo Laplante, an Italian American from New York posing as the Iroquois chief White Elk on his way to Geneva, was cheered by the Italian public and received by Mussolini, but was later imprisoned for fraud. Some of the "Indian medicine men" who since around 1980 have begun to fill their European customers' needs for expensive healing ceremonies, sweat lodges, and even Sun Dances, have not always been what they were claiming to be.

By far the largest number of Indians in Europe in the twentieth century, however, have come from the ranks of the "Indian clubs" that have flourished from England to Russia and from Scandinavia to Italy. These clubs represent the "tribalization" of European Indian hobbyism—the attempt to emulate American Indian philosophy and life-styles, an effort that is rooted in a long-standing Western primitivist reaction to industrialization and urban life. During colonial times, French *coureurs du bois* and British army officers stationed at frontier posts often dressed as Indians and married Native American women. German mercenaries in the American Revolution were surprised to find some of their countrymen installed as Indian chiefs in Nova Scotia and in Florida. Around 1910, the Englishman Archibald Belaney began his transformation into Grey Owl, whose books on nature and conservation made him perhaps the most popular "Indian" in Europe of the 1930s. At the same time Club Manitou was founded in Dresden as one of the first hobbyist groups. Members still meet on weekends or in summer camps, are quite successful in the replication of nineteenth-century Plains Indian costumes, and often explain their hobby by claiming a special mystic relationship between their own people and the American Indians.

Dickason, Olive Patricia, *The Myth of the Savage and the Beginnings of French Colonialism in the Americas* (Edmonton: University of Alberta Press, 1984); Feest, Christian F., ed., *Indians and Europe: An Interdisciplinary Collection of Essays* (Aachen: Rader Verlag, 1987); Foreman, Carolyn T., *Indians Abroad: 1493–1938* (Norman: University of Oklahoma Press, 1943).

CHRISTIAN F. FEEST
Johann Wolfgang Goethe–Universität
Frankfurt, Germany

❖❖❖F❖❖❖

FAKES AND IMPOSTORS

Euro-Americans have been adopting Native American identities for more than five centuries. Non-Indians' motives for posing as native people, however, have changed according to popular perceptions of indigenous life. Indian *impostors*—persons who have falsely claimed Indian parentage, birthplace, and upbringing in order to pass as Indians in mainstream society—are a more recent phenomenon related to the growth of consumer culture in the United States. During the colonial period, the material culture of many native societies resembled that of white frontier communities, and there existed a fluid exchange of people between cultures as they traded, fought, and intermarried with one another. This interchange dropped dramatically after the American Revolution as Indian people played a reduced economic and military role in affairs.

Despite their disappearance from everyday life, however, Indians continued to be icons of American exceptionalism for novelists and artists, who exploited white stereotypes of Indians in a nationalistic effort to define American culture. Romantic authors like Henry Wadsworth Longfellow (*The Song of Hiawatha*, 1855) and James Fenimore Cooper (*The Last of the Mohicans*, 1826) successfully captured the imaginations of Euro-Americans and made the "noble savage" a permanent feature of a distinctly American identity. Similarly, the careers of the artists Charles Bird King, John Mix Stanley, and, most prominently, George Catlin rested on curiosity about Indians and the popular belief that native people would soon disappear. The American fascination with Indian culture reached its apex during the 1890s, when most tribes had been confined to reservations and popular entertainers like P. T. Barnum and Buffalo Bill Cody played to the public's nostalgic fascination with the "vanishing" Red Man.

By the beginning of the twentieth century, some flamboyant individuals had chosen to exploit the Indian's romantic appeal for commercial gains by posing as Native Americans. The difference between European adoptees of Indian culture before 1890 and these later impostors can be found in their audiences. Early white settlers, traders, and explorers who adopted Indian identities did so in order to be accepted into native society and to serve as intermediaries between the worlds of Indians and Europeans. Commercial exploiters of Indian identities, however, wished to be accepted as Indians in Euro-American society as part of a self-serving public-relations strategy.

One singularly successful impostor, Chief Two Moons Meridas, faked an Indian identity for more than three decades, building a commercial empire through the sale of his "bitter oil," which he claimed had "made [his] race so healthy for generations." Born in 1888, Meridas was, a Bureau of Indian Affairs investigation into his application for Indian status revealed, of Mexican or African-American descent. Peddling his patented formula in New York City and Connecticut from 1914 until his death in 1933, Meridas made frequent visits to the Pine Ridge Indian Reservation in South Dakota to bolster his commercial image—even employing reservation Indians in his factory in Waterbury, Connecticut. Invariably dressed in Plains Indian regalia in his advertisements and in his travels throughout the United States and Europe, Two Moons was described by one reporter as "Head of all the Sioux Tribes" and the "World's Greatest Herbalist . . . beloved by all Indians immaterial of boundary reservations."

In the racist and nativist atmosphere of the early twentieth century, an Indian identity was preferable to the social and economic limitations white Americans imposed on anyone suspected of any other non-European heritage. This was the motivation behind one of the best-known impostors of this century, Chief Buffalo Child Long Lance. The child of former slaves who shared some Indian and white ancestry, the well-built, physically handsome Sylvester Long was not content to languish in the segregated atmosphere of the black community in Winston-Salem, North Carolina. With the help of his parents and high school principal, Long was admitted to Carlisle Indian Industrial School in 1909 as an "Eastern Cherokee."

Carlisle was the perfect training ground for Long's future career as an Indian impostor. After failing his admittance exams to West Point and serving a stint in the Canadian armed forces, "Chief Long Lance" took up newspaper reporting in western Canada. Reinventing himself once again as an Oklahoma Cherokee (and later as a Blackfoot), Long Lance reported on reserve conditions throughout Canada, absorbing all he could about Plains Indian culture. His 1928 autobiography, hailed by Paul Radin, a respected anthropologist, as one Indian's "authentic account of childhood and early manhood," was an imaginative compilation of characters and stories Long had acquired at Carlisle and in his travels throughout Canada and the United States.

Long Lance's celebrity reached its apex in 1930, when he was given the lead role of an Indian warrior in the motion picture *The Silent Enemy*. Even before the film's release, however, Long Lance's flamboyant personal style and inconsistent stories about his past fed suspicions about his native heritage, and he began to fear eventual exposure as a non-Indian impostor—or, worse, as a member of the black community of Winston-Salem. Unable to confide in anyone about his true identity, addicted to alcohol and bereft of family and friends, a despondent chief Long Lance took his own life in California in 1932.

Contemporary with Long Lance, the Englishman Archie Belaney, or "Grey Owl," similarly wished to escape his past. Belaney's career as an Indian impostor began innocently enough. Deeply impressed as a child with stories of "Red" Indians by Ernest Thompson Seton (*Two Little Savages*, 1903), Belaney was determined to someday live in the Canadian wilderness. In 1910, he emigrated from his native England and apprenticed himself to a trapper in Temegami, Ontario. There he was accepted into a local Ojibwa community and married Angele Egwana. Their daughter, Agnes, was born in 1911. Three years later, overwhelmed by this new responsibility and fearful of the ridicule of his white neighbors for having married an Indian, Belaney abandoned his family, fled to Quebec, and enlisted in the Canadian Army. It was during his stint in the army that Belaney first pretended to be an Indian, claiming that his father was a Scots trader who died a Texas Ranger in Mexico, leaving behind his Apache wife and infant son. In reality, Belaney's mother, an unwed teenager at his birth, had abandoned her son, leaving

him to be raised by two maiden aunts—a fact that he tried desperately to escape for the rest of his life.

Wounded in France, Belaney was discharged to Canada in 1917. There he resumed trapping and pretended to be an Indian while guiding tourists on canoe expeditions. In 1925, at the age of thirty-six, and despite the fact that he was still married to Angele, he married Gertrude Bernard, nineteen, a peripheral member of a prominent Mohawk family. Anahareo, as he renamed her, convinced him of the cruelty of trapping beaver, and Belaney became an outspoken opponent of no-limit trapping and leg traps. Belaney made public recompense for his former involvement in the industry by hand-raising two beaver kits whose mother had died in a trap. To make ends meet, Belaney began to write articles for *Country Life* and other magazines in 1929 under the name "Grey Owl," and in 1931, at his publisher's insistence, he published *Men of the Last Frontier*, an alleged autobiography in which he told the story of his life as an Indian.

Capitalizing on Grey Owl's powerful public image as an Indian and as a wildlife conservationist, the Canadian Forest Service hired him as a spokesman for the country's national parks, and the tall, hawk-faced Englishman in braids became the darling of conservation circles for the next seven years, until his death in 1938. Unlike Long Lance, Belaney did not make a concerted effort to conceal his true identity; park workers and his adopted family in Ontario knew Grey Owl as Archie Belaney. Instead, a widely accepted paternalism toward Indians in Canada allowed that, so long as Grey Owl was a positive role model for Indians and conformed to romantic white stereotypes, his impostor status could be overlooked and even lauded.

In the wake of economic depression and war in the 1940s, romantic celebrities like Long Lance and Grey Owl were forgotten. Beginning in the 1960s, however, a time of youthful discontent with conventional society and the rediscovery of "other" cultures, a new generation of impostors emerged. Probably the best known of these new Indian fakes was Jamake Highwater. Also known as Gregory Markopoulos of Toledo, Ohio, or Jay Marks, as he called himself between 1954 and 1970, Highwater became a well-known spokesperson for the "native" perspective both in print and on film. His best-known literary effort, *The Primal Mind: Vision and Reality in Indian America* (1981), was made into a Public Broadcasting Service documentary in 1985, and Highwater followed up this success with a round of television interviews. The Indian critics who exposed Highwater as an impostor blamed his ability to pass as an Indian on the media, "who are quick to publicize Indian stories from those who have a quick access to the media by virtue of their being articulate in the ways of White society." Highwater himself attempted to obscure his non-Indian origins by calling into question the validity of cultural identity in modern society, even as he continued to write books and articles based on native social and religious life. A volley of accusations that Highwater had faked both his Indian heritage and his university credentials (he falsely claimed to have advanced degrees from the University of California at Berkeley and the University of Chicago) followed the 1985 PBS broadcast.

Among his other accomplishments as an Indian impostor, Highwater won a Newbery Honor Award for children's literature (*Anpao*, 1977). In 1991, another author of children's literature was similarly revealed as an impostor. Forrest Carter's *The Education of Little Tree* (1976) was not a commercial success when it was first published, but it rebounded onto the best-seller list in 1990, winning the American Booksellers Award. Upon its reissue in 1986, *Little Tree* was advertised as the true story of an orphaned Cherokee boy raised by his grandparents to follow "the way." Filled with comforting Indian stereotypes of a culture in harmony with the natural environment and pithy reflections on mainstream white society, it was embraced by educators and parents who wanted to inculcate children with a more holistic and socially inclusive perspective. *Little Tree* was actually written by Asa Earl Carter, a former speechwriter for Alabama governor George Wallace and a member of the Ku Klux Klan. Even more disconcerting, Carter, who died in 1979, was attributed with having written Wallace's infamous inaugural speech, in which he promised, "Segregation now! Segregation tomorrow! Segregation forever!"

Little Tree fooled both literature experts and native writers. While parts of the story echo current and past Cherokee tradition, its primary pitch was not to Indians but to a self-conscious generation of non-Indians seeking Native American insights on modern society. Although the true story behind *Little Tree* was galling to native people and embarrassing to publishers, critics concede that there is little that can be done to prevent impostors from exploiting the stereotypical appeal to white society of "the Indian" as philosopher and storyteller.

While the media may be ungovernable in terms of regulating authenticity, some Indian leaders have called upon the legal system to ensure that commercial artists posing as Indians be prevented from passing off their work as authentic American Indian craftsmanship. To this end, the Indian Arts and Crafts Act was passed by Congress in 1990. According to its preamble, the law is designed to "expand the powers of the Indian Arts and Crafts Board" and to prevent criminal and civil violations against American Indian craftsmanship. While providing for the support of authentic Indian artists, the primary purpose of the act is to prevent non-Indian works of art—paintings, crafts, pottery, and textiles—from being marketed as Indian produced. Contention has arisen among some native groups as they struggle to define what constitutes "native" art and search for ways to enforce the provisions of the act in the marketplace.

The history of Indian impostors clearly reflects the presence and power of Indian stereotypes in white American society. Indian impersonators also raise questions of cultural identity and ownership. How should Indian identity be determined? Laws are inevitably inadequate to this task. Better arbiters are the traditions and perceptions of native people themselves. How to interpret these traditions and perceptions is, of course, quite difficult. While simple answers are not likely to appear in the near future, the lack of a precise definition of what constitutes Indian identity and culture will not diminish Indian peoples' sense of injustice when they discover that yet another cultural pirate is at large.

Dippie, Brian, *The Vanishing American* (Middletown, Conn.: Wesleyan University Press, 1982); Smith, Donald B., *From the Land of Shadows: The Making of Grey Owl* (Saskatoon, Saskatchewan: Western Producer Prairie Books, 1990); Smith, Donald B., *Long Lance: The True Story of an Impostor* (Lincoln: University of Nebraska Press, 1983).

BONNIE LYNN-SHEROW
Kansas State University

FAMILIES

Because the word *family* carries meanings in English that are largely European, the idea of marriage might serve better as a basis for understanding relationships among Native American husbands, wives, and children. Minimally, a native family consisted of a mother and her children sharing the same fireplace and eating meals together most of the time. Only among hunting tribes of the North and West did a married couple occupy a single tent or house. Otherwise, among farmers and people living in bountiful regions like the Northwest Coast, such conjugal units shared a communal home. Sometimes, each family had a fire, but more usually the two families on either side shared the same hearth.

Marriage was an alliance between families, extending a network of kin and caring for children, both natural and adopted. Rank was always a factor in these arrangements, because every society had proper and disorderly members. Stable, supportive marriages were a mark of status and rank, while casual liaisons were considered lowly behavior. Members of leading families intermarried so that their homes could provide

community support as havens for the orphaned and displaced. Among such prominent families, marriages were carefully arranged, sometimes before birth. Since a leading family was both wealthy and generous, hosting and labor demands encouraged the taking of multiple spouses. Most often, there were women, usually sisters, married to the same man, who was a good provider. In a few cases, as among Great Basin Numics, a woman might marry several men, often brothers.

Marriages were shaped both by taboos (for example, a universal ban on incest) and by incentive, such as a desire to match talents, careers, and personalities in a couple. For example, the families of shamans tended to intermarry. Cultural considerations were also important.

A Bannock family at Medicine Lodge Creek, Idaho. The photograph was taken by William Henry Jackson on June 11, 1871.

Each culture defined the individual "person" according to existing social institutions and beliefs about the sources of life. Often, each of the parents contributed a different "substance" or component to their child. For example, a mother provided the flesh and blood, while the father enabled the bone to develop into the skeleton. The soul or souls came from various ancestors or spirits, while the spark of life came from a godlike Creator. Among Navajos and other Athabaskan speakers, a holy wind infused the baby at birth, leaving its tracks in the whorled ridges at the ends of the fingers and toes. After birth, names were supplied by certain relatives, reflecting the gender, kin affiliations, and other memberships of the baby. Girls' names were usually pretty and recalled flowers, while boys' names were expressions of courage, valor, or fortitude. Before puberty, children would quest for a personal spirit or guardian, who helped them succeed at a career.

Kinship terms, taught within the family, were applied throughout the cosmos. Terms for "mother" and "father" applied to a broad range of individuals, only some of them human; all were equally persons in native belief. Thus, the earth and other sustaining forces were addressed as "mother" in prayers, while "father" indicated the sun and various supernatural beings who instructed and protected a child. Grandparent terms were used to express the warm, close bonds that skipped generations, since grandparents often raised their grandchildren while the parents obtained and processed food.

The house itself was viewed as another kind of person, its door a mouth, its walls like skin, its central fire a heart, and its framework a skeleton. Membership in a household depended on the same kinds of considerations as did the definition of a person. Indeed, residence was the principal means of defining social institutions such as clans, cults, and voluntary organizations. Aside from the single-family dwellings of the hunters, most householders belonged to the same extended, culturally defined family.

Household memberships depended on the size and density of the population, which itself reflected the local economy and available resources. Families meshed into larger kinship networks of two types. One included only about three generations and focused around a set of individuals forming a kindred, a unit also found in modern American society. Members of a *kindred* were traced through both the mother and the father as far as memory allowed. Among tribes, therefore, kindreds could be huge. In practice, however, kin-

dreds functioned in terms of significant individuals who guided and directed the membership. Most commonly, a nodal kindred formed around a married couple, and, after their death, around a cluster of their children, together with *their* spouses and children. In cases where an office (such as that of caribou-hunt leader), object (a sacred fetish bringing good fortune), or career (a shamanistic practice for curing illness and fighting off malice) was passed down through the kindred, the inheritors formed a line of descent defining a *stem kindred*.

More complicated were populous societies where kinship was traced only through the father, only through the mother, or through each parent for different purposes. In these cases, families were submerged within lineages, links through fathers and sons or through mothers and daughters forming parts of larger institutions. Often, lineages shared the same household. But patrilineages and matrilineages were not mirror images of each other, because men took the public positions of leadership in both cases. In other words, while men were both leaders and kinsmen because of who their fathers were in a patrilineage, in a matrilineage kinship depended on mothers but leadership passed from brothers to nephews through the common link of a woman who was sister to the officeholder and mother to the inheritor.

The classic, often cited example of a matrilineal society is the New York Iroquois (Haudenosaunee), where the matrilineage is called *ohwachira* and the cross-generational groupings of mothers and daughters are led by brothers and sisters. Another famous example is the Hopis of Arizona, where certain matrilineal households take leading roles in public ceremonies because the matron or senior woman inherits from her mother the custodianship of carved fetishes of animals, plants, and humans that protect the entire pueblo.

Lineages are, in turn, components of larger groupings such as clans, phratries, and, sometimes, moieties. While lineages rarely have a name of their own, all of these larger units are named. Lineages form strands within a clan. For both patriclans and matriclans, real or metaphorical kinship is traced among all clan members; for this reason, these members cannot marry one another. For example, when a member of the Wolf clan travels, he or she will receive a warm welcome and open hospitality in any Wolf clan household, even of another tribe. The virtues of this mystical bond of clanship, therefore, are readily apparent because of the wide range of kin, mutual caring, and supportive pro-

The Lupe family, White Mountain Apaches, in front of their home in Whiteriver, Arizona, in 1993.

tection that are automatically assumed between clanspeople. In the event that someone is hurt, injured, or killed by another, men of the same clan as the victim have the obligation to take revenge.

Clans, in turn, organize into clusters called *phratries,* often on the basis of some logical comparison. Thus, clans called Crane, Frog, Sand, and Willow will belong to a Water phratry. Among the Hopis, phratries function as a way for rituals, owned by clans, to be passed on when a clan becomes extinct. In this event, the last official of the clan will teach the ritual to a man in another clan within the phratry, whose clan will then inherit the necessary fetish and take over the sponsoring of the rite. Often, members of the same phratry believe they share a common substance of personhood and so forbid intermarriage as incestuous.

Birth is not the only means by which a person can belong to a clan or phratry. Some people are adopted, either because they had no clan to begin with (perhaps

because they had been a captive or had married into the community) or because they were in such personal turmoil that a shaman decided that adoption would provide another set of relatives to help these people. Sometimes a person has conveniently "forgotten" that he or she belongs to another clan and is given a new clan membership; in any case, he or she is usually delighted at having even more relatives.

Moieties, whether composed of phratries or only of basic households, represented two halves of a community. For example, many of the Siouian tribes of the Great Plains had moieties of Sky and Earth, each composed of a number of clans. In addition, the Earth moiety included Land and Water phratries. Among the Creeks (Muskogees) of the Southeast, Red-War and White-Peace moieties consisted of both clans and phratries. The Tsimshians of the Northwest divided their moieties in half again to distinguish Killer Whale and Wolf from Raven and Eagle.

The Tewa Pueblos of New Mexico, however, had only Summer and Winter moieties. To keep these two halves integrated, ranks of priesthoods at "the middle" coordinated town activities. During games and other competitions, teams were formed of the married versus the unmarried to randomize the selection and mix the moieties. The Keresan Pueblos just west of the Tewa had a double descent system in which clans passed though the mother and moieties went through the father.

All of these institutional considerations affected marriage choices in Native America, and are reflected in six kinship types based on how "cousins" (using the American English term) are classified. Each type, named for the culture in which it was first identified, fits into a scale of increasingly complex considerations. The Hawaiian type does not recognize any distinctions except that of siblings, "brother" and "sister," so everyone in your generation is either one or the other. Similarly, everyone in the older generations is "father" or "mother," and "grandfather" or "grandmother." Eskimoan, like modern American society, has separate terms for siblings and for cousins, as well as for parents and for uncles and aunts. Iroquoian makes the fine distinction between siblings and cross-cousins, the children of your parents' opposite-gender siblings (father's sisters and mother's brothers). The children of your parents' same-gender siblings were parallel cousins (children of father's brothers and mother's sisters). Since your male parent and his brothers were all called "father" and your female parent and her sisters were all called "mother," Iroquoians called parallel cousins "brothers" and "sisters," reserving their "cousin" term for cross-cousins. The Sudanese type carefully distinguishes siblings from cross-cousins *and* from parallel cousins.

Most complex are the Crow (Crowan) and Omaha (Omahan) types, which involve clans, matrilineal for Crows and patrilineal for Omahas. Sometimes, to allow for affiliation with the father's clan among Crows or mother's clan among Omahas, a child will be described as born *of* the proper clan and *for* the clan of the other parent. In addition to sibling and cousin terms, a special transgenerational term sorts out the linkage and clan of the other, or the "for," parent. For the Crows, this term applies to a father's sisters and all the women who pass on his clan and matrilineage. For the Omahas, the term is "mother's brothers," who do the same for her clan and patrilineage. Often, among leading families, marriage between the same two clans

will be perpetuated in each generation to maintain a position of power and influence.

In clan societies, marriages are carefully arranged among leading families, often with clan meetings along the way to decide on the best choice for their young members and to collect the goods to be given away at the wedding. In addition to the parents, or the clan parent, of a child, town leaders must also approve of the marriage. While the couple will court alone, the marriage must have public sanction. Among ranking families, of course, it is possible that the couple will not have seen each other previously since elite marriages also constituted political alliances over a large region.

Weddings involved a series of visits and exchanges. The mother of the groom or her representative would bring meat and other "male" foods to the bride's family, returning with small gifts. Then the bride's mother would come to the groom's family with plant and other "female" foods to show that her daughter knew how to take care of a family. Finally, when all was ready, the couple would be joined together at a public gathering, where the leaders lectured them on family virtues and everyone feasted. Sometimes, as in the Northwest, the bride brought a dowry of slaves and luxuries with her to pass on to her children. In other cases, as with the Crows and Apaches, the couple lived with the bride's family, the husband hunting and working for his in-laws until their children were born and they moved into a place of their own. A young couple "respected" their in-laws in various ways. Among the Apaches and some Plains tribes, parents-in-law were avoided after the marriage. Even though they were living in the same house, for example, a husband could not speak to, look at, or mention his mother-in-law. During an emergency, each might speak to the air or some object to convey necessary information, but never to each other directly.

For the duration of the marriage, the in-law families constantly exchanged food and gifts to show that they cared for each other and shared the same grandchildren.

At death, because the family or clan of the deceased was plunged into grief, as a final gesture of respect, the in-laws would take over the funeral, ready to condole, cook food, sing dirges, attend the wake, dig the grave or set up a scaffold, wash the body, make a coffin, divide the deceased's property among nonrelatives, and care for the survivor until he or she remarried. In this way, families sustained their members and contributed to the institutions of the larger culture. Such practices also encouraged a belief in the permanence of "family" throughout the stages of life.

See also Child Rearing.

Eggan, Fred, ed., *Social Anthropology of North American Tribes* (Chicago: University of Chicago Press, 1955); Fox, Robin, *Kinship and Marriage* (New York: Penguin Books, 1967).

JAY MILLER (Lenape)
Lushootseed Research

FETTERMAN FIGHT

The Fetterman Fight occurred on December 21, 1866, near Fort Phil Kearny just south of present-day Sheridan, Wyoming, between eighty-one U.S. cavalry and infantry troops and an estimated two thousand Lakota, Cheyenne, and Arapaho warriors. It was known to the Indians as the Battle of the Hundred Slain. Fort Phil Kearny had been established in July 1866 as one of the three forts designed to protect travelers on the Bozeman Trail, which had been established in 1862 and ran from the Oregon Trail to the goldfields in southwestern Montana. The trail ran through the fine Powder River hunting grounds, and its use was strongly opposed by the Lakotas under the leadership of the Oglala chief Red Cloud. Captain William J. Fetterman, hotheaded and contemptuous of Indians, had boasted that he could ride through the whole Sioux nation with eighty men. On December 21, a Sioux, Cheyenne, and Arapaho party including Crazy Horse drew eighty men under Fetterman's command out of the fort to defend a wood-cutting party. Fetterman disobeyed explicit orders not to pursue the Indians beyond Lodge Trail Ridge. Once he and his men had ridden beyond the ridge, they were ambushed. Within forty-five minutes they were all dead. Indian casualty estimates have ranged from ten to one hundred killed, with between sixty and three hundred wounded. The battle was a turning point in the Bozeman Trail War (also known as Red Cloud's War). In 1868 the Fort Laramie Treaty called for the abandonment of the three forts and the withdrawal of protection from the Bozeman Trail.

See also Red Cloud.

FILMS
See Movies.

FISHING

Natural-resource use has been a contentious issue throughout the history of the American Indian. While probably the most serious conflicts in recent years have involved native fishing practices, there is a paucity of information both on traditional methods of fishing and on the role of native people in the development of the fishing industry of North America.

Fishing was a dominant means of subsistence on the Northwest Coast but also played an important role in the economic life of native peoples of the Arctic, Subarctic, Northeast, Southeast, California, Great Basin, and Plateau cultural areas. As a general rule, where there were edible fish in sufficient numbers, native peoples utilized them. The manner of fishing covered the widest array of technologies conceivable, and most of these techniques are still employed today.

History
Indian fishing can be traced through four stages that occurred throughout North America but took place at different time periods and at varying paces. Initially the use of fisheries resources was part of the traditional round of subsistence activities. Access, control, and distribution of fisheries resources varied according to cultural custom. For example, in some areas of the Pacific Northwest fishing locations were owned by families or clans, whereas in the Great Lakes area fishing locations were generally open to all. During the early phase of European contact these traditional systems persisted. Even when the Europeans were interested in exploiting the Indians' fisheries, native systems of allocation and European concepts coexisted.

As the European populations grew and demands on the fisheries resources increased, native people were initially incorporated into the commercial fishing industry as suppliers or as workers. This second period lasted just a few years in some areas, whereas in other areas, such as parts of Alaska, it is still evident. It was generally ushered in with the intensive development of fisheries resources, and the native people were often in a position, as fishers and processors, to provide the knowledge and labor necessary to effectively utilize resources on a large scale.

The third period can be characterized as a time of marginalization. In most areas, increasing technological sophistication and increased capitalization worked to exclude Native Americans from participation in commercial fisheries.

Finally, native people have sought to bring about a fourth phase by gaining reentry into the fisheries through legal channels. This process has been facilitated by litigation and some of the most controversial court decisions in recent history.

Methods

The traditional methods of Indian fishing varied depending upon the species, the natural environment, and customary usage. Fishing technology can be categorized into several general areas, based on increasing technological sophistication. Many of these techniques are still used in Indian fisheries, and all have their analogues in modern fisheries, both Indian and non-Indian.

The simplest techniques were also the most widely used. Spears, harpoons, gaffs, and dip nets were commonly found where fishing was less important to the total subsistence base, but were also found for specialized use in areas where other forms of fishing were practiced. Examples include the Sahaptin dip-net salmon fishery of the Columbia Plateau and the spear fishery of the Anishinabe and others in the lakes of Minnesota and Wisconsin.

Hook-and-line fishing, including trolling, were commonly employed in large bodies of water, especially in

American Indians gaffing salmon out of the rapids at Celilo Falls, Oregon, circa 1900. The Celilo Falls and Dalles areas of the Columbia River together formed a fourteen-mile-long series of cascades and waterfalls that offered excellent fishing. People from all over the plateau region and from the coast would fish, trade, and socialize here.

the marine environment. The Chumashes of California trolled for pelagic species such as tuna, and the peoples of the Arctic commonly fished for char and other species with hook and line through the ice in winter.

Fish poisoning was most effective where fish were concentrated and the water was still or slow moving. Poisonous plants, such as buckeye or soaproot, were used by native groups in California and the Great Basin to catch trout and suckers.

The use of traps and weirs required the cooperation of large numbers of people. Weirs were generally latticework devices that were set across streams. As fish passed through openings in the weir they could be easily captured in traps of open basketwork manufacture. Larger traps of stone or pilings were used separately from weirs usually along inshore environments, where tidal waters would carry the fish—generally schooling species such as smelt—into the impoundments. The Micmacs of the Canadian Maritimes used weirs to fish herring and salmon. Traps were employed by a number of northern Indian groups such as the Crees of the Subarctic.

Net fishing involved the use of two main types of nets: gill nets, which capture by entangling fish; and seines, which capture by surrounding them. Gill nets were constructed by tying twine into specific mesh sizes designed to catch certain species. Seines merely needed to have mesh smaller than the fish they were designed to capture. Gill nets were widely distributed, although there is some disagreement over whether they were endemic to some areas, such as the Subarctic, or introduced early in the contact period. Seines were most effective in shallow water with few obstructions. The Chinooks, fishing the sandy shoals of the lower Columbia River, used seines reaching lengths of six hundred feet that required dozens of people to operate.

Other, more specialized fishing devices had limited distribution. Herring rakes, used along the Northwest Coast, were long wooden slats with needle-shaped bone tines placed along one edge. As they were stroked through the water, the herring were impaled on the tines. Trawls were mostly found in the central Northwest Coast area. Baglike devices upward of forty feet in length, they were towed midwater to capture schooling species such as salmon. Perhaps the most sophisticated fishing technology was reflected in the reef net, utilized by the Straits Salishes of the Gulf and San Juan Islands area of the Northwest Coast, specifically for sockeye salmon. Reef nets were long, stationary nets, anchored to the sea bottom at the forward end and tied between the bows of two canoes at the back end. A smaller net was strung between the two canoes. Sockeye salmon, swimming along the sea bottom, followed the long net up (as if swimming over an underwater reef) and into the smaller net, where they would be hauled aboard the canoes.

The recent assertion of aboriginal fishing rights by many tribes and bands may stimulate increased scholarly interest in American Indian fishing technology. Certainly the role native peoples played in the commercial development of fisheries resources deserves attention.

See also Dalles, The; Fishing and Hunting Rights.

Boxberger, Daniel, *To Fish in Common: The Ethnohistory of Lummi Indian Salmon Fishing* (Lincoln: University of Nebraska Press, 1989); Rostlund, Erhard, *Freshwater Fish and Fishing in Native North America,* University of California Publications in Geography no. 9 (Berkeley: University of California Press, 1952); Stewart, Hilary, *Indian Fishing: Early Methods on the Northwest Coast* (Seattle: University of Washington Press, 1977).

DANIEL L. BOXBERGER
Western Washington University

FISHING AND HUNTING RIGHTS

Fishing and hunting have been at the core of many American Indian cultures since precontact. Indian hunting and fishing were conducted then—as they are now—not for sport, but for food and for a livelihood. This was well understood by the early colonists and later by the U.S. government. Thus, many of the treaties negotiated between the federal government and Indian tribes in the nineteenth century contained provisions guaranteeing rights to hunt and fish. But the growth of the white population, and with it the proliferation of fenced lands, the destruction of natural habitat, and often the destruction of wildlife itself, drastically curtailed the Indians' ability to carry on these activities.

By the end of the nineteenth century, state governments had responded to growing numbers of sports hunters and outlawed the sale of almost all game meat, so that hunting was reserved for recreational purposes. Fishing was also reserved for sport—except in the Pacific Northwest, where a burgeoning fishing industry had begun in the mid–nineteenth century. But even there, Indian fishermen found their activities severely restricted by state laws that placed their traditional fisheries out of bounds and allocated the resource to commercial and sport fishermen.

Inevitably, Indians who attempted to carry on their traditional hunting or fishing activities found themselves in collision with state laws: trespass laws, licensing laws, laws prohibiting the sale of game or fish, closed seasons, catch limits, prohibited gear, closed areas, and the like. This problem occurred even though, in many cases, hunting and fishing were protected by federal treaty.

Although the rights set forth in the treaties were in theory guaranteed by the federal government, the government rarely intervened on behalf of Indian hunters and fishermen. State courts routinely rejected assertions of treaty rights: some ruled that treaty guarantees made prior to statehood were nullified by the admission of the state to the Union; others held that such rights were superseded by state laws enacted for fish and game conservation; and still others interpreted treaty language in such a way as to conclude that Indians received no rights different from those of other citizens. The result was that Indians were regarded as poachers; they fished or hunted at the risk of being arrested and jailed. There were exceptions, however: on the isolated occasions when the federal government interceded on behalf of Indians, particularly in the federal courts, Indian hunting and fishing rights received judicial recognition.

In the second half of the twentieth century, Indian hunting and fishing rights were aggressively litigated, not just by the federal government, but often by the Indians themselves. Out of this struggle grew a well-developed body of law defining the scope of Indian hunting and fishing rights in the United States.

Fishing and Hunting Within Indian Reservations

It has become established law that states may not regulate Indian tribes or their members within a reservation's boundaries. Thus, on-reservation Indian hunting and fishing have generally been free from interference by state officials and are regulated by the tribes themselves. However, some federal conservation laws do apply to Indians hunting on the reservation. For example, the Eagle Protection Act has been held to supersede the relevant treaty hunting right. In other cases, where it appears that Congress so intended, it has been held that federal conservation laws do not override Indian treaties.

The issue of non-Indians hunting and fishing on the reservation presents more complex problems. Tribes have the authority to require tribal permits and licenses from non-Indians, but do not always have the ability to bar non-Indians from hunting and fishing on lands within a reservation that are not owned by Indians or the tribe. States have the ability to regulate such non-Indian reservation hunting and fishing, and in many cases the tribe and the state both regulate such hunters and fishermen. Non-Indians hunting or fishing without tribal consent may be prosecuted by the federal government under federal trespass laws.

Off-Reservation Fishing and Hunting

Where reservations are without sufficient game resources, Indians hunt on ceded lands outside the reservations lands historically held by the Indians but at some point ceded by them to the United States in treaties or agreements.

The existence and scope of off-reservation hunting rights is governed by treaties. Under the U.S. Constitution, treaties and executive agreements ratified by Congress have the force of federal law and supersede state laws. Many treaties reserved Indian hunting rights over "open and unclaimed lands." When an Indian is hunting in the exercise of a treaty right, he is not subject to state hunting laws. The treaty hunting right does not extend to private, developed, or cultivated lands. However, lands that are otherwise open to hunting are subject to Indian treaty hunting.

The courts have held that, even in the absence of a treaty right, tribes may hunt on lands aboriginally held by them, so long as their aboriginal right has never been extinguished by Congress or expressly given up by the tribes.

Pacific Northwest Indian Fishing

Treaties made with Pacific Northwest tribes and bands in 1854 and 1855 guaranteed the tribes' right to take fish at their "usual and accustomed places." This treaty promise induced the tribes to cede their lands and settle on distant reservations.

By the 1870s, the perfection of the canning process had led to the industrialization of the salmon fishery. Indians were soon crowded out by commercial fishermen fishing in marine waters and intercepting salmon before they could reach the areas where the Indians traditionally fished.

With the coming of state government, state laws prohibited net fishing on the rivers in favor of marine fishing. Thus, the Indians were prohibited by state law from fishing at their "usual and accustomed places."

Indians were forced either to abandon their treaty rights or to risk arrest.

In 1954, Indians began to challenge the validity of such state laws. In 1974, after years of conflict, sometimes breaking out into violence, the federal courts ruled that the treaties with the Indians required the states to limit sport and commercial harvests so as to allow the Indians to take up to 50 percent of the runs of fish destined to pass through the Indians' usual and accustomed grounds. And in 1979, a U.S. Supreme Court decision settled the legal issue in favor of the Indians.

These court decisions brought about a revival of the area's Indian fishing economy, which had been moribund for over one hundred years.

The Great Lakes

After 1966, when stocks of salmon were successfully planted in the Great Lakes, conflict arose between sport fishermen and Indians. In 1979, a federal court ruled that Indians had reserved the right to fish and hunt in an 1836 treaty and that the state of Michigan had no power to regulate Indian fishing and hunting.

Similar litigation in Wisconsin on behalf of the bands of Chippewa (or Ojibwa) Indians in northern Wisconsin, northeastern Minnesota, and the Upper Peninsula of Michigan resulted in a 1983 federal-court ruling that the Indians' rights to hunt and fish were protected from interference by the state of Wisconsin.

Both the Michigan and Wisconsin fishing controversies aroused bitter hostility from non-Indian sports interests, culminating in riots. In 1991, the state of Wisconsin and the Lake Superior Chippewas agreed on a management plan for the lake fishery that seems to be alleviating some of the tensions.

In 1994, the Mille Lacs band of Chippewas won a Federal District Court decision upholding hunting, fishing, and gathering rights reserved for them by an 1837 treaty to an area in east central Minnesota. The Fond du Lac band of Chippewas continue to litigate for hunting and fishing rights to an area north of Lake Superior.

Indian hunting and fishing litigation has established some principles of federal law that protect Indian hunting and fishing. Unless abrogated by Congress, Indian treaties remain valid and supersede state law. The treaties will be construed by the courts as the Indians understood them at the time they were negotiated. Indians are entitled to adapt their traditional hunting and fishing techniques to modern methods and to conduct hunting and fishing for commercial purposes. The treaty right belongs to the tribe and not to the individual, and the tribe has the right to regulate the treaty hunting and fishing activities of its members.

Tribes and their members share the same concerns over conservation of fish and game that state governments do, and it is becoming clearer with each passing year that preservation of these resources requires close cooperation between tribal, state, and federal governments to ensure that fish and game will be available to future generations of Americans, Indian and non-Indian.

See also Fishing; Hunting.

Cleland, Charles E., *Rites of Conquest* (Ann Arbor: University of Michigan Press, 1992); Cohen, Fay G., *Treaties on Trial* (Seattle and London: University of Washington Press, 1986); Cohen, Felix S., *Handbook of Federal Indian Law*, ed. Rennard Strickland and Charles F. Wilkinson (Charlottesville, Va.: Michie Bobbs-Merrill, 1982).

ALVIN J. ZIONTZ
Seattle, Washington

FIVE CIVILIZED TRIBES

The term *Five Civilized Tribes* is the name commonly given to the five major tribes of the southeastern part of the United States: the Cherokees, Chickasaws, Choctaws, Muskogee Confederation (Creeks), and Seminoles. These tribes came into contact with Europeans early in American history and adapted quickly to new conditions. Intermarriage between the tribes and whites produced a number of tribal leaders as well as established planters and prosperous businessmen within these communities. The tribes also developed their own constitutions, law codes, judicial systems, and other facets of "civilization," and by the early nineteenth century had come to be called "Civilized Tribes."

As early as 1808 the Cherokees were codifying their laws. The "civilization" of the Cherokees was enhanced when Sequoyah developed the Cherokee syllabary, which reduced the Cherokee language to eighty-five written characters. By the 1820s the syllabary had spread throughout the Cherokee Nation East. Newspapers and books were being printed using the Cherokee syllabary, and in 1821 *The Laws of the Cherokee Nation* was published, the first printed law code of a Native American tribe. A national government, complete with legislative, judicial, and executive branches, was organized in 1827. In 1828, the *Cherokee Phoenix,* the first Indian newspaper, appeared. Following Cherokee removal to Oklahoma, a national printing press was established at Tahlequah. It, along with the Park Hill Mission Press, printed an abundance of books and periodicals. Schools were opened throughout the nation, and the Cherokee Female Seminary and Cherokee Male Seminary provided a college-level education to promising Indian leaders.

By the beginning of the eighteenth century the Chickasaws had established extensive trading relations with European colonists. Missionary work among the tribe was well under way by the 1820s, and in 1844 the Chickasaws' first written law was printed. It appropriated funds for a tribal academy, the Chickasaw Manual Labor School. Several other educational institutions were established, including Wapanucka Institute, Bloomfield Academy, Collins (Colbert) Institute, and Burney Institute. In 1848 the tribe adopted its first written constitution.

In 1824 the Choctaws opened their first school, Choctaw Academy, at Blue Springs, Kentucky, and in 1842 the tribe established a series of boarding schools —Spencer, Fort Coffee, and Armstrong academies, and Goodwater, Ianubbi, Chuwahla, Wheelock, and New Hope seminaries—that were funded by the tribe. In 1838 the Choctaw Council established twelve local schools, with the teachers' salaries to be paid by the tribe. In 1834 the Choctaws produced the first written constitution adopted within present-day Oklahoma.

The Muskogee Confederation, commonly called the Creeks, first adopted written laws in 1817, and in 1839 organized a tribal government, whose structure was based on a series of tribal towns. As early as 1835 books were being published in the Creek language, and in 1842 the Koweta Mission school was opened. Several other schools soon followed, and by 1896 the Creeks were funding seventy local schools and six boarding schools—Eufaula, Wealaka, Nuyaka, Wetumka, Euchee, and Coweta—as well as the Creek Orphans Home, the Pecan Creek Colored Boarding School, and the Colored Creek Orphans Home. In addition a number of other local schools were funded by the tribe for Creek freedmen.

The Seminoles were the most traditional of the Five Civilized Tribes. Following their removal they were settled with the Creeks, where they were allowed to establish town governments under Creek law. In 1856 the tribes separated and the Seminoles formed their own government, consisting of an elective principal chief, a second chief, and a national council. The council also served as the judicial body. A company of lighthorsemen, with an elected captain, enforced tribal laws. Missionaries were active among the Seminoles after their removal, and in 1844 the first tribal school—Oak Ridge Mission—was opened. By 1868 four schools—Wewoka Mission, Sasakwa Female Academy, Mekasukey Academy, and Emahaka Academy—were in operation.

FLANDREAU SCHOOL

An off-reservation Indian boarding school in South Dakota located between Sioux Falls and Brookings, Flandreau is the oldest boarding school in continuous operation in the United States. The Bureau of Indian Affairs established Flandreau in 1893 in the expectation that off-reservation education would break down tribalism and assimilate Indian youth.

Today, the state of South Dakota accredits Flandreau as a high school, although the school remains totally funded by the Bureau of Indian Affairs. One hundred sixty resident employees provide housing and care for Flandreau's students for 175 days each year. In 1993 three administrators and forty-three teachers served 556 students at the school. The student body is diverse, representing sixty-three tribes and bands from thirty-four states.

See also Boarding Schools; Education.

FOOD AND CUISINE

The wealth of the Americas in 1492 was not in gold and silver, as Europeans thought, but in the variety of foods that grew in American soils. Pineapples, avocados, chocolate, chilies, tomatoes, and peanuts are all familiar American foods today. Corn, beans, squash, pumpkins, and potatoes are also important.

Throughout the Americas, native people utilized an amazing variety of wild and domesticated plants. From upstate New York through the Ohio River valley, people gathered a wide variety of wild foods—fruits (grapes, plums, thorn apples, bearberries, cherries, blackberries, blueberries, elderberries, sumac berries) and nuts (acorns, butternuts, hickory nuts, walnuts, hazelnuts, and beechnuts). The Iroquois ceremonial cycle included a strawberry festival that celebrated the small, new wild strawberries that were a particular delicacy and a harbinger of spring. Their juice is still drunk at ceremonies in contemporary Iroquois communities.

In the northeastern part of North America, native people domesticated sunflowers (*Helianthus annuus*) and their associated tubers, now known as Jerusalem artichokes (*Helianthus tuberosus*) although they are more like a radish than an artichoke. They also cultivated sumpweed (*Iva annua* var. *macrocarpa*), goosefoot (*Chenopodium bushianum* Aellen), maygrass (*Phalaris caroliniana* Walt.), and giant ragweed (*Ambrosia trifida* L.). These plants could withstand a wide range of environmental conditions and spread readily (qualities that today lead them to be classified as weeds).

Fresh berries provided energy and assuaged thirst. Dried, they served as thickeners and flavorings. Mixed with fat and dried meat, they were an essential ingredient of pemmican (an Algonquian language term), a very concentrated food source for travelers.

Seeds, the stored energy that produces new life, were an essential part of native foods. Wild rice, technically a grass (*Zizania aquatica*), was and is an important staple for Indians in the upper Great Lakes, where it grows extensively in shallow lakes. It stores an exceptional amount of nutritional value, probably the greatest of any grain used by Native Americans.

Wild rice is still a staple of the diet of Indian people in the Great Lakes area. Its Ojibwa name is *manoomin*, "good seed." It is harvested in the late summer, usually at the end of August and the beginning of September. The green grain is then dried, threshed and winnowed. It can be ground into a kind of meal and used for making bread; like corn, it can even be popped.

Wild plants provided not only seeds and roots but also tender greens in the spring. The first shoots of dandelions, milkweed, pokeweed, lamb's quarters, mustard, dock, and watercress were gathered by the Delaware Indians in the nineteenth century. They were parboiled and then cooked with meat. The tender green fiddleheads (tightly curled fern fronds) that are eaten as a delicacy during the early New England spring today were probably enjoyed by New England Indians before European settlers arrived.

Corn is generally regarded as the greatest agricultural contribution of American Indians to the world's diet. It was the major food source for many native groups throughout North and South America. Corn is de-

scended from teosinte, a wild grass that some eight thousand to fifteen thousand years ago began to be modified by human selection. It was probably domesticated in northern Mexico and introduced into the American Southwest by about 4000 B.C. It was a relative latecomer in the Midwest, appearing sometime around 200 B.C.

Domestication creates a symbiotic relationship between humans and plants. A plant's primary form of energy storage is the seed. Wild plants reproduce by being able to scatter their seeds freely; however, humans who collect seeds want them to stay in one place, and they favor plants whose seeds stay attached to the plant. But because humans must then remove the seeds from the plants, the plants become dependent on humans to disperse the seeds so they can reproduce. This is what happened with teosinte, whose seed cases modified into rigid containers characteristic of the kernels of maize. Although the process of human selection was not systematic in the beginning, it became deliberate, and it altered the structure of the corn plant.

Humans altered food plants in other ways. The Hopis produced a corn plant whose seed is adapted to the arid growing conditions of their mesas. The taproot is very long, to reach down to the underlying subsurface moisture, and the seedling adapted to growing a long way under the soil before breaking through and putting out its first leaves. The colors of Hopi corn—red, white, blue, and yellow—are the result of selection and the careful preservation of seeds.

Corn, beans, squash, and deer meat fed as many as ten thousand people in the Chaco Canyon region of western New Mexico around A.D. 1100. For Pueblo people in the Southwest, corn is both food and religion. Ceremonies mark the beginning and end of planting seasons. The Hopis celebrate the Niman Kachina Ceremony in June to bid good-bye to the Kachina spirits who have lived with them during the winter and spring and who must now go to their homes in the San Francisco Mountains to plant their own crops.

When children are born in traditional Pueblo communities, they are presented to the sun with two perfect ears of corn, their corn mothers. These ears represent the ideal relationship between human beings and the corn plants upon which they depend for their existence. The Iroquois (and many other eastern tribes) celebrated the Green Corn Ceremony in the early spring. It marked the emergence of the first ears of corn. The immature "milk" corn was scraped from the cob and made into puddings.

A married woman grinding corn while a single woman (identified as such by her hairstyle) bakes bread at Tewa (Hano) Pueblo, New Mexico, in the winter of 1892–93.

Squashes and gourds (*Cucurbita pepo*) were domesticated in the Southwest. Tepary beans (*Phaseolus acutifolius* var. *latifolius*) were also domesticated as an important source of protein.

Corn, beans, and squash became an important triad of domesticated crops throughout North America. A Navajo planting song tells how the spirits of the corn, beans, and squash enjoy being together. In the Northeast, among the Iroquois, these spirits — and the crops they represented — were called the "three sisters," and myths tell of three beautiful maidens seen walking by moonlight around the fields that bordered the villages. Mohawk women planted corn seeds in holes poked into the ground with digging sticks. When the corn had

sprouted, they piled earth around the base of the stalk to discourage hungry animals, and close by they planted bean seeds, whose sprouts climbed the corn stalks to reach the sun. Squash seeds were sometimes planted around the base of the plants as well; the broad squash leaves served to keep the soil moist under their shade. Native people processed some of the corn they grew by boiling it with wood ash. The Iroquois cooked corn with beans because the spirits of the sisters wanted to be together. Scientific nutritional theory explains that the amino acids in corn and beans complement each other to produce complete protein.

Sweeteners for food included wild honey, dried and fresh fruit, and maple sugar, produced by sugar maple trees, which were found from Alabama to the northern Lake Superior region. Maple sugar was used most extensively by native people around the Great Lakes region—Menominees, Potawatomies, Ojibwas, Fox, and Sauks. The sap develops in freezing temperatures during late winter as the tree rests, and rises during early spring when the temperatures are warm enough to thaw the sap.

Fish and game provided protein. An estimated 45 million buffalo and probably as many deer and antelope roamed the Great Plains by the time Europeans arrived. On the Northwest Coast, salmon and halibut fillets were dried in the smoke from common cooking fires that rose to the rafters of the longhouses. Whole halibut were dried in the sun on the roofs. Whole salmon had to be smoked slowly in small, closed huts because of their rich oils. On the East Coast, lobsters, clams, and mussels abounded, although lobster was used mainly as bait for bass and cod. In the Southeast, Indians ate deer, wild geese, gar, crabs, bass, and squid. Deer were abundant, and flocks of wild turkeys hung around Indian villages scavenging the kitchen middens; the birds were small, very fast, and probably quite tough unless one got a young one.

Animal fats and oils provided seasoning and texture for food. Bears were widespread throughout North America, and fat was commonly rendered from their meat. On the Great Plains, the rich hump meat of buffalo also provided fat. The whales and seals of the Northwest Coast offered the local Indians a rich source of oil.

Native people in North America did not domesticate animals for food. The abundance of wild game probably made it unnecessary. The only domesticated animal in North America, the dog, was, however, used for food on some ceremonial occasions. One part of the Iroquois midwinter ceremony involved the killing and cooking of a white dog. Feasting was an essential part of many ceremonies. On the Great Plains, Lakota women boiled buffalo tongues for a feast during the annual Sun Dance.

Indian meals generally consisted of a soup or stew cooked and eaten out of a single pot, most often with the fingers. Some sort of bread made out of ground meal and water and cooked on a hot, flat stone was used to dip food from the pot and sop up juices. Food was readily available throughout the day.

Cooking techniques included roasting meat or fish over an open fire. On the Northwest Coast, salmon were roasted in a latticework of cedar splints held in a split stake that was driven into the ground facing a bonfire of cedar or alder wood. Boiling was done in pottery vessels in the Southwest and on the East Coast, and, on the Great Plains, in the cleaned paunch of a slaughtered buffalo suspended on a framework of sticks and filled with water heated by dropping red-hot stones into it. Root vegetables (like the camas root, the bulb of a species of lily used widely by the Nez Perces in Idaho) were often buried in pits lined with hot coals and leaves and left to steam for a day until tender. In the Southwest, young Navajo women ground corn into meal to be mixed with water and cooked in a pit oven overnight. The act was part of a puberty ceremony. The more corn the girl could grind, the more successful her life as an adult woman would be.

Traditional native foods, both animals and plants, largely disappeared as European settlers moved into Indian territories. Indian people came to depend on the foods used by Europeans. During the reservation period beginning in the 1850s, government rations of beef replaced buffalo and deer meat, sugar replaced wild honey, wheat flour substituted for cornmeal, and coffee became part of the diet on Indian reservations. These were the rations provided to Indians in exchange for the land that their leaders signed away in treaties. Today, however, in native communities, wild rice, wojape (Lakota grape dumpling stew), grilled salmon on the Northwest Coast, and piki bread in Hopi communities still are markers of tribal identity.

Cooking food is an activity that transcends culture. The ways in which food is cooked, and the ingredients, depend on the environment. The ceremonies that surround its cooking and its eating are very much a product of human culture. Native American cuisine is a product of basic human needs, a wide range of environmental conditions, and a cultural understanding of how people relate to their environments in practical and ceremonial ways.

See also Agriculture; Fishing; Hunting.

Foster, Nelson, and Linda S. Cordell, *Chilies to Chocolate: Food the Americas Gave the World* (Tucson and London: University of Arizona Press, 1992); Hurt, R. Douglas, *Indian Agriculture in America: Prehistory to the Present* (Lawrence: University Press of Kansas, 1987); Yarnell, Richard Asa, *Aboriginal Relationships between Culture and Plant Life in the Upper Great Lakes Region*, Anthropological Papers, Museum of Anthropology, University of Michigan, no. 23 (Ann Arbor: University of Michigan, 1964).

CLARA SUE KIDWELL (Choctaw/Chippewa)
University of Oklahoma

FORT DEARBORN MASSACRE

The Fort Dearborn Massacre, in which approximately five hundred Potawatomis, Kickapoos, Sauks, and Winnebagos killed more than sixty Americans and Miamis leaving the future site of Chicago, took place early in the War of 1812. As it became clear that Britain and the United States would go to war, Indians debated whether alliance with the English or the Americans could halt further white encroachment on their lands. The Potawatomis, whose security had been threatened by the building of Fort Dearborn at the mouth of the Chicago River in 1803, were sharply divided on the question. Some followed the Shawnee Prophet (Tenskwatawa), who urged an alliance with the British, while others supported neutrality or alliance with the United States.

On August 9, 1812, the American general William Hull at Detroit sent word to Fort Dearborn that Fort Michilimackinac had fallen to the British. He ordered Captain Nathan Heald to evacuate immediately. Leaders of Indian villages along Lake Michigan headed for Fort Dearborn. Sensing danger, Heald refused to depart. On August 13, William Wells, a former white captive and an adopted son of the Miamis, arrived with a party of his Miami kinsmen to escort the residents of the fort through Potawatomi territory and on to safety at Detroit. On August 15, news that General Hull was losing ground farther east encouraged local Potawatomis to attack the departing group of ninety-six men, women, and children. In the ensuing battle, Wells, along with approximately fifty-three soldiers, two white women, twelve white children, and fifteen Potawatomis, died. The next day, General Hull surrendered the Detroit garrison, leaving the entire Great Lakes under the control of the Americans' British and Indian adversaries.

FOX/MESQUAKIE

Officially known as the Sac and Fox of Iowa, the Mesquakies are the only Native American tribe in Iowa today. The tribe still owns land it purchased from the state of Iowa in 1857 and owns and operates businesses near the community of Tama in the central region of the state.

The key to understanding the tribe is to follow its tracks through history. How the tribe came to take on the name Mesquakie reveals much about the people, who have always been tenacious in their self-determination and resistance to Anglo-American acculturation. Such resistance can be seen in their refusal to accept tribal names given to them by outsiders. It was the French who first labeled the tribe the Fox when they encountered them in the 1600s, and two hundred years later the U.S. government renamed them "the Sac and Fox of Iowa." Yet for all intents and purposes the tribe has always recognized itself and its members as the Mesquakies (Red Earth People) or derivatives thereof.

Some scholars suggest that prior to European contact the Mesquakies lived near what is now the St. Lawrence Seaway but were forced into the western Great Lakes region by the Iroquois. Jean Nicolet, a Frenchman who at the time was mapping a route down the Great Lakes waterway into the North American interior for French Governor Samuel de Champlain, was reputedly the first European to meet the Mesquakies, in 1634. In 1667 a French Jesuit missionary, Claude Allouez, recorded seeing a thousand Mesquakies near the Wolf River in Wisconsin.

During this time, the Mesquakies lived primarily in the Green Bay region on the southern rim of Lake Superior. The tribe's culture was then primarily like that of other hunting and horticultural peoples of the Great Lakes area. The people lived in villages, usually named after their band's leader, during the warmer seasons, occupying permanent lodges that were made of poles and elm bark. Each lodge housed anywhere from five to thirty people.

The women raised corn, beans, squash, pumpkins, and melons in communal garden plots near the villages. They also gathered such foods as nuts, berries, honey, beeswax, and tubers. Women were responsible not only for growing and gathering food, but also for caring for children, keeping the lodges maintained, and tanning hides. The men hunted deer and other fur-bearing animals for food, clothing, and articles of trade. They also designed and carved canoes and flatboats for transportation. After the horse was introduced in the eighteenth century, men also made saddles and tended the family herds.

In the fall and winter seasons, the Mesquakies migrated to the prairies for hunting. Winter-camp lodges were small and made of cattail mats and poles. These oval-shaped structures housed from one to five people and were designed for frequent moves. Trading was done in the winter, when encampments were often large, but in the fall and spring seasons the camps would disperse into smaller groups to ease the hunt for game.

During the early 1700s the Mesquakies controlled the main Wisconsin portages that covered the routes from Green Bay to the Mississippi. Demanding fees from those who wanted to travel the routes, the Mesquakies angered the French, the English, and other Native American tribes. For thirty years the tribe fended off these groups, but in 1730, in an effort to salvage what was left of their group, the Mesquakies formed a close alliance with the nearby Sauks. This alliance was strong because both tribes were culturally and linguistically similar. The Mesquakies and the Sauks, along with another woodlands tribe, the Kickapoos, speak varying dialects of an Algonquian language called Sauk-Fox-Kickapoo. Early studies suggest that the three tribes lived in close proximity before European contact and had learned to rely on each other in defending their lands. It was not surprising, then, that the Mesquakies fled to the Sauk tribe and blended easily with them. But this amalgamated group still could not fend off the encroaching Anglo-Americans. Both groups were forced to migrate south, finally settling in an area near the confluence of the Rock and Mississippi Rivers in present-day Iowa and Illinois.

In 1804 a few Sauk Indians ceded most of their lands to the Americans in a treaty that would further disrupt the Mesquakies. One Sauk band, whose leader was accused of instigating the treaty, broke away from the tribe and became officially recognized by the Americans as "the Sac [a corruption of *Sauk*] and Fox of the Missouri." Concurrently the remaining group was named "the Sac and Fox of the Mississippi."

Between 1832 and 1842 the U.S. government forced the Mississippi Mesquakies to cede their lands and move to a reservation in east central Kansas. After nearly ten years of living on the reservation, a group of Mesquakies separated from the Sac and Fox and returned to Iowa, where they purchased land in Tama County. The members pooled money from annuity payments, the sale of their horses, and the sale of personal items to acquire the property. More land has been purchased since that time.

Building on their strong traditions—they once controlled a major waterway during westward U.S. expansion and survived near extinction—the Mesquakies have retaken their name and reclaimed their proud heritage. During those long years of battle, forced communion with the Sauks, removal, and oppression on the reservation, the Mesquakies fiercely maintained their culture and their spiritual beliefs. Since then a culture nearly destroyed has, like the phoenix, emerged from the ashes intact and in every way entirely Mesquakie.

See also Sauk.

Callender, Charles, "Fox," in *Handbook of North American Indians,* ed. William C. Sturtevant, vol. 15, *Northeast,* ed. Bruce G. Trigger (Washington: Smithsonian Institution, 1978); Hagan, William T., *The Sac and Fox Indians* (Norman: University of Oklahoma Press, 1958); Joffe, Natalie F., "The Fox of Iowa," in *Acculturation in Seven American Indian Tribes,* ed. Ralph Linton (New York: Appleton-Century, 1940).

SUZANNE HECK
Central Missouri State University

FRENCH-INDIAN RELATIONS
See Indian-White Relations in New France.

FUR TRADE

For as long as people have lived in the Americas, they have sought out the furs and hides of land- and sea-based animals. Most were acquired for personal use in clothing, shelter, and watercraft. Even after contact with Europeans, the majority of furs and hides taken by Native Americans from North America's abundant wildlife populations were put to domestic use. Some tribes had better access to fur-bearing animals than others; moreover, some groups were less interested in specializing in hide procurement than in other activities. Furs were but part of the elaborate trade networks that developed from this continent's ancient system of commodity exchange. Most often tribes in linguistic affiliation with each other traded on a regular and continuous basis, sending relatives back and forth between villages or camps.

The entry of Europeans into native trade and social systems occurred in stages. The first European-Indian fur trade began as an offshoot of European interest in the cod fisheries of the North Atlantic from the 1490s through the 1580s. To Europeans, whose wildlife had undergone heavy population reductions to serve their own tables and wardrobes, North America appeared a treasure trove. In the early days of the fur trade, European fishermen wanted only "fancy furs," such as sable, mink, otter, and ermine, used for the finest coats and collars or trimmings both back home and in Asia.

As the market for these furs expanded, less desirable pelts also grew attractive. By the mid–sixteenth century, itinerant French corsairs sailing along the southern Atlantic seaboard began taking on board large quantities of marten pelts and deerskins, obtained from Coastal Algonquians in exchange for metal hardware, cloth, and what most Europeans thought of as baubles and trinkets.

As the deerskin trade took hold in the Southeast, beaver (*Castor canadensis*) joined the list of fancy furs in the Northeast and in the interior. The stimulus was European induced. Beaver had been reported in abundance from Jacques Cartier's expeditions to the St. Lawrence (1534–43), and hatmakers in Paris became eager to import increasing quantities of the marvelous furs, which were sturdy, flexible, and resistant to both water and wind. European felt makers preferred North American beaver because the underhairs of this well-insulated animal could be bound together fairly consistently to make a very high grade of hat.

At first all beaver skins were procured by Indians. White trappers and hunters avoided competing with native hunters and their trading partners in order to maintain good relations with their trading allies. This understanding did not last long in most theaters of the North American fur trade, however, and mercantile interests, determined to make their presence felt beyond coastlines, soon penetrated to new territories. Seeing greater profits to be gleaned from the interior, Europeans leveraged their way past powerful Indian middlemen and trading tribes and sought direct contact with the native people who had access to furs.

The result of this commercial expansion was the disruption of traditional alliances and the escalation of inter-Indian rivalries. In the Northeast, the first product of this change was the era of the protracted Iroquois Wars in the mid–seventeenth century. During that period the Hurons, the major middlemen of the Great Lakes, were nearly destroyed by the Iroquois and their Dutch and English trading partners. Farther north, the royal chartering of the Hudson's Bay Company in 1670 brought the English into the subarctic region, where they hoped to wrest profits from the westward-expanding French based in Montreal. For the next century, the French and English were at each other's throats across western Canada as they vied for native allegiance and trade.

Responding to the English challenge, the French sent explorers, missionaries, and *coureurs du bois* (licensed traders) into uncharted western lands. The scheme worked. By 1680, an estimated eight hundred French traders were gathering furs in the interior for transshipment back to Montreal. In the eighteenth century the French continued this expansion, building posts at strategic junctions such as Detroit (1701) and intermarrying with Indian women. Both policies served them well: by 1763 the French had acquired the major share of furs harvested in North America.

The French were less successful in wresting allegiance and furs from the Indians who traded at Hudson's Bay. Some furs trickled down to them from the James Bay Crees and other tribes of the interior; most did not. As long as the HBC did not tamper with middlemen, especially the Western Crees and Assiniboins, furs continued to be brought to the company, ultimately arriving at York Factory for shipment by water to London. In 1713, at the Treaty of Utrecht, the French conceded Hudson Bay to the English, but they would continue to tap a percentage of the interior trade until New France fell to the British in 1763.

Unlike the French, who wove diplomatic and imperial considerations into their business decisions, the Hudson's Bay Company traders were interested only in remaining profitable. And that they did from 1713 to 1763. After 1763 the HBC faced new competition from old French firms in Montreal, now reincarnated as the North West Company. Led by a mix of English, Scottish, and New England merchants and traders, this company saw opportunity in continuing the old French system and drawing on the experience of French Canadians. From the late 1770s up through the War of 1812, the North West Company moved rapidly and aggressively deep into the North American interior and on to the Pacific Coast, mapping the land, building new posts, and securing Indian friendships among tribes through the inclusion of native provisioners and hunters in all operations.

The success of the North West Company forced the HBC to give up its complacent perch on Hudson Bay. For the next forty-seven years the two clashed, each trying to drive the other out of preferred Indian trade zones. Finally, in 1821, after absorbing all rivals, the two companies merged, retaining the older name of Hudson's Bay Company.

During the early nineteenth century, as environments changed with wildlife reduction, Indian households took on new looks. Traders introduced new goods and foodstuffs that enabled Indian families to spend more time in fur production and less time making tools, utensils, and clothing. Copper kettles, metal awls, files,

Cree trappers trading beaver skins at Fort Pitt, Saskatchewan, in 1885.

knives, hatchets, and axes as well as guns, spear points, fishhooks, blankets, commercial rope and netting, and clothing became standard in Indian households. This path was an irreversible one, but it did not lead immediately to complete dependency on white traders. During this intermediary stage of the trade, Indians still controlled their lands and retained (but rarely used) the power to evict white companies.

Several factors encouraged stable relations between Indians and their trading partners. Most Indians were not politically unified or confederated, and so were not inclined to challenge the European system as a whole. Moreover, following the example of the French, many British and Scottish traders had married into Indian families, and the offspring of these unions formed a new people, the Métis, who served as a constant bridge between the Indian and white worlds. Of equal importance to material and biological fusion was the weakening effect wrought by the fur trade on tribal lifeways.

Alcohol, for example, was a constant presence. Many Indian groups came to expect liquor as a present prior to commencing trade. Brandy and furs became inseparable early in the trade on the East Coast and remained the pattern as the trade expanded westward. More serious was a new element the Europeans could not effectively control—disease. Lacking immunity or resistance to many communicable germs, trading Indians seldom escaped outbreaks of epidemics such as measles, mumps, and influenza. Of these and many others, by far the greatest killer was smallpox, which reached every fur producing region of North America between 1760 and 1890.

Between HBC reorganization in 1821 and Canadian Confederation in 1867, an event that prompted the final withdrawal of the HBC from posts south of the present U.S.-Canadian border, Indians faced new challenges across North America. In the eastern interior, Americans continued the colonial practice of buying raccoon, deer, and muskrat pelts from both Indians and whites for very little money. Many small firms competed with each other and with the American Fur Company, a New York–based giant of the industry, founded in 1808 by John Jacob Astor, who planned to build a chain of posts from the Great Lakes to the Pacific. Although few Indians worked directly as wage earners for Astor or any other company, they continued to be the major procurers of furs on their own lands. Whites who trapped on their own did so at their peril. Most tribes had sanctions by species, by gender, and by season on which animals could be asked to give up their lives for humans. White trappers scoured many regions of North America indiscriminately, creating confrontation and stimulating a native need for more furs and more guns to protect their interests. Beaver pelts from the Rocky Mountains and the northern plains continued to be in great demand, but they grew increasingly difficult to find and became less marketable than South American nutria (*Myocastor coypus*) skins and silk. By 1835, beavers had been superseded in number and in importance by raccoons in the Old Northwest (raccoon had become the dominant fur in the American trade by the 1840s) and by bison in the western territories.

Elsewhere, on the Pacific Coast and in the Far North, the fur trade brought parallel distress to animals and to dependent human populations during the eighteenth and nineteenth centuries. Many species of pelagic mammals were hunted to near exhaustion. Sea otters, used by the Chinese as status symbols in garments, once graced the Pacific in large herds. Vessels from many nations partook of the bounty of sea otters, fur seals, walruses, and whales while they lasted. Among humans, the Aleuts suffered the most. Beginning in 1762, Russians colonized Alaska, employing well-tested policies of taking hostages in exchange for servile labor. Several generations of Aleuts labored as hostage slaves for Russian masters, supplying countless furs from the continental shelf and offshore islands to keep relatives alive. Along the coast of British Columbia, native traders continued to dictate terms of the trade as the volume and variety of foreign vessels in their home waters escalated. The Haidas, Nootkas, Bella Coolas, and Makahs witnessed fierce international competition for their resources, beginning with Spanish and English voyages to the region in the 1770s. Superb whalers and fishermen as well as keen traders and power brokers, these tribes were represented by headmen not to be outdone by foreign ship captains. Although that reten-

tion of control eroded across time, it remained a hallmark for this region well into the second half of the nineteenth century.

In 1846, the fur trade took on features that reflected modernization and shifting international boundaries. The HBC and the American Fur Company continued to purchase furs from Indians on both sides of the international boundary, but the California and Fraser River gold rushes, as well as the rapid movement of settlers into the western territories and states, forced a diversification of local economies. In the United States, many trading posts were sold to the U.S. Army; others were abandoned. In Canada, the British retreated to Vancouver Island and the Arctic interior, leaving many unresolved land and wildlife problems to a largely unsympathetic populace eager to acquire gold, farms, and the commercial fisheries.

By the mid–nineteenth century the United States was wrestling unsuccessfully with the legacy and continued practice of exploitation of resources on Indian lands by private parties. The Dominion of Canada did better, regulating settlement in an orderly manner by law and, to a degree, by practice. The Indian Act of 1868 levied strict penalties for trespass on Indian lands and was enforced through a national police force. A series of treaties created reserves, reducing the native land base but guaranteeing subsistence and trapping activities on Crown (public) lands as well as the parcels set aside for natives only. These treaty rights applied to most Indians in western Canada and were later extended to tribes across the country.

After 1867, entrepreneurs from Britain, Canada, and the United States expanded their activities in the Far North, tapping into the rich wildlife of the High Arctic, the Yukon, and Alaska. The Pribilof Islands yielded over 100,000 fur-seal pelts per year and contributed to a rise in volume and in value of furs processed in the United States up to 1890, when the seal population was recognized as nearly depleted. Skunk and mink joined fur seals and bison as major U.S. exports to Great Britain during this period. The completion of transcontinental railroads in the United States after 1869 and in Canada after 1885 heralded a new era in Indian-white relations. Agrarian interests and the fur trade did not mix well. In western North America, canids—wolves, coyotes, and foxes—as well as bears, cougars, and badgers faced farmers, rangers, and townspeople eager to see their end. In the twentieth century, the demand for fancy coats and hats in eastern and European cities kept Canadian hunters busy in the Far North, where the HBC faced challenges from itinerants and large merchants with easy access to the new railway lines connecting Edmonton and Winnipeg with Vancouver and Montreal. The Yukon and Northwest Territories served as new wildlife frontiers, but stiff competition and native determination to harvest selectively kept many species viable in the mixed economy of the twentieth century. By 1932, the HBC's share of the Canadian fur trade had declined to 42 percent. In 1957 York Factory closed its doors, and in the 1980s the HBC sold its Northern Stores subdivision, retaining only its retail department stores under the corporate name "The Bay."

See also Indian-White Relations in Canada, 1763 to the Present.

Phillips, Paul Chrisler, with J. W. Smurr, *The Fur Trade,* 2 vols. (Norman: University of Oklahoma Press, 1961); Van Kirk, Sylvia, *"Many Tender Ties": Women in Fur Trade Society, 1670–1870* (Winnipeg: Watson and Dwyer, 1980).

WILLIAM R. SWAGERTY
University of Idaho

G

GAMBLING

Native American Indians have endured centuries of institutional interference and promises of economic transformation. Tribal chance and tragic wisdom have nurtured trickster stories, but who could have imagined that casinos would rescue communities and reduce the chronic unemployment rates on reservations? This preposterous source of income has heartened the sense of survival in the face of domination.

Luther Standing Bear must have wondered about a civilization that would count coup with coins. He seemed to envision, on his way to a government school with other children, the contradictions that would follow upon the creation of casinos as well as the ensuing contention over tribal sovereignty on reservations. The Lakota activist and author was born around 1868 and was raised to be a hunter and warrior, but by then the federal government had nearly exterminated the buffalo, and it would soon remove tribal families to reservations. He was one of the first children to be educated at the Carlisle Indian Industrial School in Carlisle, Pennsylvania.

Describing his journey to Carlisle, Standing Bear wrote in *My People, the Sioux* that when "the train stopped" in Sioux City, "we raised the windows to look out." The "white people were yelling at us and making a great noise," and they

> started to throw money at us. We little fellows began to gather up the money, but the larger boys told us not to take it, but to throw it back at them. They told us if we took the money the white people would put our names in a big book. We did not have sense enough then to understand that those white people had no way of discovering what our names were. However, we threw the money all back at them. At this, the white people laughed and threw more money at us.

Five generations later, many of the same tribes that remember colonial cruelties and the miseries of hunger, disease, coercive assimilation, and manifest manners are now moneyed casino patrons and impresarios on reservations. Standing Bear would be astonished that white people are once more throwing money at the tribes. Millions of dollars are lost by gamblers each month at bingo, blackjack, electronic slot machines, and other games of chance at casinos located on reservation land. The riches, for some, are the new wampum, or the curious coup count of lost coins.

More than a hundred U.S. tribes are reported to have casinos or gaming facilities on and near reservations; the losses by the patrons at these operations, estimated to be several billion dollars a year, have become the extreme sources of tribal revenue. The ironies of Pan-Indian casino reparations could become the wages of sovereignty.

The Indian Gaming Regulatory Act, passed in 1988, recognized that the tribes have the "exclusive right to regulate gaming" if the activity is not prohibited by federal or state laws. The new gaming regulations established a National Indian Gaming Commission to meet congressional concerns and to "protect such gaming as a means of generating tribal revenue."

The new law established three classes of gaming: traditional tribal games; games such as bingo, lotto, and pull tabs; and, the most controversial, a class that includes lotteries, slot machines, blackjack, pari-mutuel betting, and other casino-type games. The tribes with the third class of games are required to negotiate with the state to enter into a "compact governing the conduct of gaming activities."

In the past few years there have been more news stories about tribal casinos than about any other tribal enterprises. The *New York Times* has published numerous reports on the enormous Foxwoods Casino, owned and operated by the Mashantucket Pequot Indians. Governor Lowell Weicker of Connecticut reached an agreement with the new casino to permit slot machines—an agreement required, in part, by the new federal gaming laws. The Pequot Indians agreed to contribute at least a million dollars a year in gambling profits to a fund to aid troubled cities and towns.

Minnesota has negotiated agreements with more than a dozen casinos on eleven reservations in the state. The *Minneapolis Star Tribune* reported that tribal gaming employed more people in the state than the United Parcel Service or the Burlington Northern Railroad: "Lump the six casinos together, and they are the twentieth-largest employer in Minnesota," with about five thousand employees. The Mystic Lake Casino, owned by the Shakopee Mdewakanton Sioux, seats more than a thousand people at bingo and operates at least as many slot machines. The Shooting Star Casino on the White Earth Chippewa Reservation cost more than $16 million to construct, and the tribe has plans to build an addition that would double the size of the original.

The Bureau of Indian Affairs reported in *Indian News* that in 1992 twenty tribes in two states, Michigan and Minnesota, provided close to eight thousand casino jobs, with an annual payroll of more than $90 million. The report indicated that the casinos generate more than $11 million in annual Social Security and Medicare tax revenue and more than $2 million in state and federal unemployment compensation. At the same time, the casinos have significantly reduced the cost of welfare in the two states. The number of Indian casinos and employees in the United States grows steadily, and the estimated several billion dollars in the losses of patrons has increased at a rate that could save several state budgets from ruin.

Anishinaabe singers are the heirs of a rich tradition of chance in their moccasin games. In one game, four objects are covered with two pairs of moccasins; one object is marked and gives rise to the chance of the game. None of these games is played without music and the beat of a drum. Memorable songs have been inspired by the chance inherent in moccasin games. The best moccasin-game songs were first heard in dreams and visions, and the songs, together with the beat of the drum—accented beats and then hesitation—enhanced the games, teasing the players into choosing the moccasins that covered the unmarked objects.

There are no traditional songs to tease the people playing the electronic machines; the coins are the sounds of technology. The tease of chance is in casino stories, not in songs. This chance has no association with communities, arises from no dreams of hidden objects.

The casinos have raised new contradictions, brought about the bereavement of traditional tribal values, and aroused the envy of outsiders. The more money that is lost at casino games, the greater the revenues, and because of the riches involved, the elections of tribal leaders become more hotly contested.

The Mohawks at Akwesasne, for instance, came to violence over the casinos located on their reserve. One side fought for casinos and sovereignty, while the other side, mainly the elected tribal leaders, opposed gambling operations in their communities. Two tribal people were killed and a casino was damaged before the onslaught ended.

"The allure of fast tax-free money inflamed and emboldened the Mohawks who entered the gambling business, even as it weakened those holding on to the old ways," wrote Rick Hornung in *One Nation under the Gun: Inside the Mohawk Civil War.*

> A new class of bingo chiefs were beating the odds, dealing with the white economy on favorable terms. The traditionalists counterattacked, claiming that Mohawk life was being corrupted by men who profit from games of chance rather than work. White bureaucrats and politicians, police and prosecutors initially saw this dispute as a brawl over gambling.

The Mohawks, however, saw this as a threat to their traditional way of life.

The Red Lake Band of Chippewa Indians in Minnesota and the Mescalero Apache Tribe of New Mexico have sued agencies of the federal government in an effort to have the new gaming laws declared unconstitutional and to prohibit the appointment of the National Indian Gaming Commission. The essential issue is tribal sovereignty.

The claim of the tribes is that the Indian Gaming Regulatory Act "violates their sovereign prerogatives to conduct affairs on their lands as permitted by treaties and the Indian Self-Determination Act," wrote William Thompson in *Indian Gaming and the Law.* Most tribes have either avoided or disputed the regulation that the third class of games, those that have raised the most revenue at casinos, must be negotiated with state governments. Tribal leaders maintain that casinos are located on sovereign tribal land, outside of state jurisdiction. Nonetheless, federal agents raided casinos and seized machines to enforce the gaming laws on five reservations in Arizona. The seizure was blocked by angry tribal people on one reservation until the governor agreed to negotiate the issue.

Tim Giago, the editor and publisher of *Indian Country Today,* said, "There is a lot of anger in Indian Country over this. The Indian nations are sick and tired of being treated like children. These are sovereign lands. Why in hell should these lands need the state's permission?"

William Thompson argued that the essential "control over Indian gaming should be national." The issues of tribal sovereignty, he wrote, "are difficult and they are clearly controversial. What is clear, though, is that the vast majority of tribes do not want any state regulation whatsoever. They should not be required to come under state regulations."

Tribal sovereignty is an essential right that has been *limited* but not *given* by the federal government. Congress negotiated the original treaties with the tribes and has the absolute power to terminate reservations. That tension, between the idea of limited sovereignty and assimilation, could be resolved in federal courts or by congressional action in favor of state governments. Casinos could be the last representation of tribal sovereignty.

Tribal sovereignty is inherent, and that sense of inherence, natural reason, tradition, and territorial power has been the defense of sovereignty on tribal land and reservations. Federal courts and congressional legislation have limited the absolute practices of sovereignty, such as certain criminal and civil responsibilities on reservations, but the inherence of sovereignty is sustained in the many interpretations of treaties with the federal government.

Alas, the Indian Gaming Regulatory Act has placed tribal sovereignty in competition with the sovereignty of the states. "The concept of sovereignty originated in the closer association of the developing state and the developing community which became inevitable when it was discovered that power had to be shared between them," wrote F. H. Hinsley in *Sovereignty*. "The function of the concept was to provide the only formula which could ensure the effective exercise of power once this division of power or collaboration of forces had become inescapable."

The Coalition to Protect Community and States' Rights has been active in the defense of state sovereignty. The stated mission of the coalition is to "seek clarification of the federal Indian gaming law so as to restore a level playing field between Indian gambling and other forms of legalized gambling, and to protect communities and states which oppose it from having unwanted and untaxed gambling thrust upon them." There is nothing in the coalition's stated mission, objectives, or proposed action that mentions treaties or the inherent sovereignty of the tribes.

Thus has envy of casino riches incited the enemies of the tribes and those who oppose the sovereignty honored for more than a century in treaties with the federal government. Such envy, of course, represents the manifest manners of dominance, of oppression, and of racism. Tribal sovereignty, in this sense, could be weakened only if the casino tribes were enervated by their own new wealth and were seen by the world as being both rich and without political power.

Standing Bear heard the voices of the Ghost Dance, worked at the famous Wanamaker department store in Philadelphia, toured with Buffalo Bill's Wild West show in Europe, and acted in western movies; these and other adventures endowed him with a wider vision of the world. He, and other tribal leaders who matured in the last century with a sense of tragic wisdom, might have advised the tribes to throw some of their casino millions to others as an association of power and as an honorable mandate of sovereignty.

To endure the adversities of political lobbies, the tribes must do more for others in the world than the federal government has done for them in the past. The rich casino tribes must demonstrate the inherence and the power of their sovereignty in the world. The tribes could name ambassadors to various nations and establish an international presence as a sovereign government; the creation of embassies would be a wiser test of sovereignty than casino riches. Tribal embassies could negotiate the liberation of hundreds of stateless families in the world.

The liberation of Kurdish, Tibetan, Haitian, and other families, for instance, would sustain the moral traditions of tribal cultures. The relocation of stateless families to reservation communities would assume an undeniable tribal sovereignty, and such an action in the cause of peace and survivance would earn international eminence.

Casinos are the wages of wealth, morality, and sovereignty, but tribal courage and an international presence could secure more than an envy of casino riches and the limited sovereignty determined by federal courts and state governments.

Eadington, William R., ed., *Indian Gaming and the Law* (Reno, Nev.: Institute for the Study of Gambling and Gaming, 1990); Hornung, Rick, *One Nation under the Gun: Inside the Mohawk Civil War* (New York: Pantheon Books, 1991).

GERALD VIZENOR (Anishinaabe)
University of California at Berkeley

GARRY, JOSEPH

(1910–75)
Coeur d'Alene national political leader and the most
prominent American Indian spokesman of the 1950s.

At a critical juncture in U.S.-Indian relations, Joseph
Richard Garry unified tribal leaders as a political force
to turn back the resolve of Congress to end federal
trusteeship. Handsome, personable, and articulate,
Garry won six consecutive terms (1953–59) as president of the National Congress of American Indians and
rallied the organization to reverse government efforts
to break up Indian land bases, destroy tribal identities,
and abandon federal treaties with native tribes. For the
Coeur d'Alenes, Garry fashioned model economic and
governance programs.

Garry was born on March 8, 1910, into his small, impoverished tribe in northern Idaho. His father, Ignace H.
Garry, was the last traditional chief of the Coeur
d'Alenes and the great-grandson of a noted chief, Spokane Garry. His mother, Susette Revais, was the granddaughter of a noted interpreter of treaty-making times.

Ignace Garry and his family performed in native costumes as token Indians for dignitaries visiting the nearby city of Spokane, often at the famed Davenport Hotel. Young Joe liked demonstrating Indian ways, liked
the spotlight, and found that life at the hotel stirred his
ambition.

After completing the two-year commercial course at
the Haskell Institute, Garry enrolled at Butler University, in Indianapolis, Indiana, thinking he would become
a forest botanist. As the sole Indian student at Butler,
he was happy to be a campus personage. He taught Indian lore at boys' summer camps. But Garry could not
afford to complete his studies, and he entered the Indian Service as a clerk-typist, transferring after four years
to the Navy Department in Washington, D.C. Superiors invariably praised Garry's harmonious relations
with coworkers. "A boy of very fine personality," one
wrote on Garry's evaluation.

Garry returned home to marry — it was to be a short-
lived union — as World War II broke out. He served as
an infantry sergeant and after the war returned home
to establish a small cattle herd and study animal husbandry briefly at Washington State College. He was
eventually recalled to fight in Korea.

In 1950 the Coeur d'Alene tribe filed a claim for lost
aboriginal lands with the Indian Claims Commission.
Garry joined tribal leaders, who had barely started to

plan for economic development when in 1953 Congress resolved to end trusteeship. Meanwhile the Internal Revenue Service relied on a recent court ruling to
charge eighteen members of the tribe, including Garry,
with failing to pay taxes on income from allotted lands.
For years such income had been presumed tax-exempt.
The tribe dispatched Garry to solicit defense funds
from other tribes and to promote united resistance to
federal encroachment on Indian rights.

With a portfolio and a mission, Garry traveled widely through the western states, appealing for united
opposition to government policy. The Ninth Circuit
Court eventually overturned the attempt to tax tribal
incomes. Garry turned his pilgrimage into the presidency of the Affiliated Tribes of the Northwest, and he rapidly developed the constituency that elected him to the
presidency of the National Congress of American Indians (NCAI) at its Phoenix convention in 1953.

Garry warned that Indians had to hold on to their
lands to achieve economic independence, declaring,
"Indians are hard to get rid of as long as they have their
land." He demanded an Indian voice in federal deliberations affecting Native Americans.

Shortly before Garry's election by the NCAI, Congress endorsed House Concurrent Resolution 108,
which declared that Indian tribes and individuals
should rapidly be "freed" from federal supervision. Indians cried that Congress would thus destroy Indian
tribes. On the heels of his election, then, Garry convened an NCAI emergency conference of forty-three
tribes from twenty-one states and Alaska, which met in
Washington, D.C., in February 1954 to declare united
resistance to termination. The conference enunciated an
Indian policy: "Congress should not enact legislation
affecting Indian property or other rights without . . .
consent of the Indian tribes concerned."

Thereafter, Garry traveled constantly, speaking to Indian tribal councils, service clubs, and civic organizations to justify Indian opposition to government policy.
He testified at congressional hearings and lobbied individual congressmen. Nearly six feet tall, of light copper
complexion, dressed in a business suit, Garry made an
impressive advocate. He spoke lucidly, in a rich bari
tone. He was soon the best-known Indian spokesman
in America.

His was not the only voice. Helen L. Peterson, the
tireless executive secretary of the NCAI, and tribal
leaders also made themselves heard. Peterson reprinted magazine articles for a large mailing list. Her
small staff analyzed bills in Congress affecting Indi-

ans and counseled tribes on lobbying. The NCAI fought termination, state control of Indian tribes, the practice of stripping tribal members of less than half Indian blood of their lands—all while working on a shoestring. In Garry's time, the NCAI's annual budget rarely exceeded twenty-five thousand dollars. By 1958 the federal government had backed away from ending trusteeship without consent and all but abandoned termination.

While he presided over NCAI, Garry was also elected chairman of the Coeur d'Alene tribe and set about planning an economic resurrection of his people. In 1957 and 1959, he was elected to the Idaho House of Representatives, the first Native American in that state's legislature. And he continued as president of the Affiliated Tribes of the Northwest.

On May 6, 1958, the Indian Claims Commission awarded the Coeur d'Alenes $4.3 million. The tribe named Garry program director to plan for using the award. A dissident clique resisted the plan that Garry proposed, alleging that he—and his wife, Leona, the tribal secretary—had turned dictatorial, and they carried their discontent to the NCAI. No doubt Garry did dominate, believing himself to be the most experienced manager on the tribal council. He relinquished the presidency of the NCAI in 1959 to run unsuccessfully for the U.S. Senate, and could not rebuild his constituency when he attempted to take back his old post.

During the 1960s, Garry applied himself to tribal development, completing a new constitution and a law-and-order code for the Coeur d'Alenes in 1962. He counseled other tribes. The Coeur d'Alenes improved sanitation and housing. In 1967 Garry gave up the chairmanship of the tribal council to serve in the Idaho Senate, where he championed Indian and veterans' concerns.

But once he was out of the national limelight, his political base slipped away. A beloved daughter died. Garry's health broke. He sometimes turned to alcohol and memories: he had been chosen the Outstanding Indian of North America in 1957 and 1959, had won the National Indian Council Fire Achievement Award in 1973, and had received accolades of achievement from dozens of community-service and Indian organizations.

Garry lost his bid for reelection to the tribal council in 1972, a bitter defeat. He died on the last day of 1975 and was buried with a military honor guard in the mission cemetery at DeSmet, Idaho. The executive board of the NCAI at the time summed up Garry's contribution to Native Americans: "[he] was responsible for the

Indians holding on to their land base, and he invented tribal government, as we know it."

See also Coeur d'Alene.

Bernstein, Alison R., *American Indians and World War II: Toward a New Era in Indian Affairs* (Norman: University of Oklahoma Press, 1991); Cohen, Felix S., "Erosion of Indian Rights, 1950–53," *Yale Law Journal* 62 (February 1953): 348–90; Fixico, Donald L., *Termination and Relocation: Federal Indian Policy, 1945–1960* (Albuquerque: University of New Mexico Press, 1986).

JOHN FAHEY
Eastern Washington University

GENDER

Gender is a culturally constructed category of social analysis whose meaning varies from one group of Native American peoples to the next. Within each cultural tradition meanings and values are given to sexual behaviors and perceptions. For example, the Cheyennes maintained strict codes for proper sexual behavior. Loss of power for males was attributed to loss of semen; continence was therefore associated with strength. Proscriptions and prescriptions of gender are therefore tied to beliefs that are based on group norms. All cultures define appropriate sex roles and formulate gendered meanings for the actions of males and females as they pass through the life cycle. Cultural constructions allow both for the perception of biological facts and for the interpretation of behaviors that are linked to those facts.

Cultural systems of meaning explicate gender categories and thereby interpret group behavior. For example, the term *berdache* first appeared in Jesuit writings about the aboriginal inhabitants of North America when the missionaries observed native men in Iroquois society who dressed and acted as women. The term stems from the Arabic *bardaj* and has entered into the social-science literature, where it has masked gender categories that exist in indigenous societies. Recently, native scholars have won acceptance for the term *two spirit* to denote bisexual or homosexual individuals, preferring it to *berdache* because it does not carry pejorative meanings from the past. In addition, the term allows students and scholars to press forward with their scholarship by eliminating culturally inappropriate usages.

Observers of Native American life have described gender identities in many settings, but these identities are not always accepted by Indian people. The group's role expectations may be accepted or rejected, and individual behaviors may inspire new categories. Thus, whereas every human society has designations to recognize phenotypic sex characteristics of male and female, a careful examination of the cultures of native North America reveals a wide variation in gender roles—for example, the *nadle* or *nadleeh* among the Navajos, the Mohave *hwame,* and the Tewa *kwedo,* all of which designate a person who has both male and female spirits within. Other groups did not have such social designations. Individual autonomy and personhood were also variable.

The origin stories and the underlying principles of proper behavior for both males and females and for gender-crossing males such as the Lakota *winkte* or Cheyenne *hemanah* were internalized in the socialization process of males and females. In many societies women followed well-defined norms for proper behavior that were supernaturally sanctioned and strictly enforced. Among the Lakotas, for example, virgins played a significant role in the Sun Dance ritual despite the fact that the traditional tribal culture maintained a gender-crossing role for males. Similarly, Lakota society limited male leadership to warriors or those with particular religious insights but did not stigmatize those men who followed women's roles.

Ethnographic studies of Native Americans, like studies produced by other branches of scholarship, reflect the prejudices and expectations of researchers and therefore have not always explored the range of gender categories that traditionally existed in indigenous societies. Over time, however, a more sophisticated view has become influential and gender studies have proliferated. At the same time, many groups argue that only a person who is a member of an indigenous nation can articulate the parameters of that unique culture. For this reason, the emphasis of this entry will be on the Lakota and Dakota manifestations of gender and on the meaning of the term *winkte,* a designation that has assumed an intertribal or Pan-Indian connotation.

The term *winkte* has traditionally been applied to a male "who wanted to be a woman." This term also has the connotation in traditional language usage of a man "who kills women." Many male researchers reject this second meaning, preferring the idea that *winkte* is simply the Lakota word for male homosexual. No analogous term that might be applied to lesbian behavior has

yet to appear in any traditional linguistic texts or the contemporary vernacular. This assertion is made even though the literary scholar Paula Gunn Allen believes that the Lakota word *koshkalaka* can be interpreted in the English vernacular as "dyke." This term, however, simply refers to "male youth" (or postpubescent male), much as the female equivalent, *wikoshkalaka,* means "young woman" or postmenarche female. (The prefix *wi* carries the meaning of "female"; *winyan* means "woman.") These examples highlight the danger of observers who lack native-language skills using native terms to describe gender categories.

It has recently become evident that there is a great deal that scholars and researchers do not understand about the construction of gender categories in American Indian societies and the behavioral implications of those categories. Following Gunn Allen's designation of *koshkalaka* as the Lakota term for "lesbian," for example, one Lakota lesbian has used the designation as a label for herself and her orientation. The study of gender construction thus becomes a self-serving mechanism, and traditional native perspectives or materials gathered by indigenous people themselves are constructed to meet this need.

The Lakota example also suggests that some nations of American Indians recognized an alternative gender role for one sex but did not recognize a complementary role for the other. Nor were gender roles necessarily viewed as equivalent. It would seem, therefore, that gender orientation was not necessarily a reflection of fitting into one or another social category, but was rather a product of one's evolving sense of personhood and a reflection of a society's worldview. Traditionally the Lakota term *bloka* is often described as meaning "sexually potent" and carrying connotations of masculine superiority akin to those carried by the Spanish term *macho.* In the precontact era, however, *bloka* was used to indicate those potent masculine powers that were often symbolized by the buffalo bull: strength, bravery, and aggressiveness. Such traits were useful in a nomadic society that was frequently in conflict with its neighbors. This earlier meaning also carried with it the notion that a person exhibiting *bloka* would be a generous provider who could be relied upon by his family, extended family *(tiospaye),* band, and nation.

In the 1950s, an era of reservation poverty and social disruption, the term *bloka* came to be used in a new way to describe a particular gendered behavior: women who managed to be good providers to their families through employment and ranching were often referred to as exhibiting *bloka*. Most recently, a new term has appeared—*bloka win*. This term refers to women who have achieved success in society. Similarly, a modern Lakota elder who knew of a member of her reservation culture who had "come out" as a lesbian in San Francisco referred to her as a *winkte win*, as the Lakota lesbian previously mentioned *now* calls herself *koshkalaka win*. These constructions of terms for gender categories that had not previously existed attest to the vibrancy and adaptiveness of contemporary carriers of the culture. These innovations reflect newly recognized behaviors, individual feelings attached to those behaviors, and an evolving community point of view. They also suggest that social and cultural categories are constantly being revised and negotiated by members of a community.

The case of the Lakotas indicates that in examining the concept of gender in Native America, the entire range of categories and behavioral expectations should be studied within their cultural context. At the same time, one should recall that after centuries of contact with non-Indians and adaptations to repressive legal actions and genocidal intrusions by native communities, the relationship between human actions and gender categories has grown increasingly complex. At present there is considerable erosion in the extent to which native communities accept traditional gender and sex roles as a part of their cultural fabric. Once one sets aside the stereotypical notion that there is some monolithic conception of gender that is uniform across American Indian communities, it is easier to detect and sustain particular conceptions and individual tribal practices. For example, although frequently cited by other Native Americans as exemplifying "Indian" gender conceptions, the Lakota people derive many of their cultural ideas and practices from the gift of the sacred pipe to the nation by White Buffalo Calf Woman. Told many times in various publications, this story has not been undermined by the advent of Christianity. It still gives meaning to life for the many Lakotas who believe in the gift and who understand its relationship to the tribe's seven sacred rites. Moreover, the story of White Buffalo Calf Woman sets in motion the proper behavior of males toward females and the deeply held ethic of reciprocity, respect, and honor. It also inspires important aspects of the Lakotas' commitment to four cardinal virtues: generosity, bravery, fortitude, and wisdom. Conceptions of gender remain a fascinating and largely unexplored aspect of Native American life.

See also Berdache.

Medicine, Beatrice, "Gender," in *Native America in the Twentieth Century*, ed. Mary B. Davis (New York: Garland, 1994); Medicine, Beatrice, "Warrior Women: Sex Role Alternatives for Plains Indian Women," in *The Hidden Half: Studies of Plains Indian Women*, ed. Patricia Albers and Beatrice Medicine (Landham, Md.: University Press of America, 1983); Williams, Walter, *The Spirit and the Flesh* (Boston: Beacon Press, 1986).

BEATRICE MEDICINE (Lakota)
Wakpala, South Dakota

GENERAL, ALEXANDER (DESKAHE)

(1889–1965)
Cayuga-Oneida political and religious leader.

During Alexander "Jack" General's lifetime, his community, the Six Nations, of the Grand River Reserve in southern Ontario, underwent tremendous social and political change. In 1889 the Six Nations Reserve was a multination farming community with a population of about thirty-five hundred. The forty-five-thousand-acre reserve appeared to the casual visitor to resemble the surrounding rural agricultural settlements. But a closer examination of the community revealed a rich Iroquoian history and culture that set it apart from its nonaboriginal neighbors.

Alexander General was the youngest of eight children born into a traditional Iroquois family. His parents, Lydia and William General, followed a conservative lifestyle as devout adherents to the Longhouse religion and raised their children to accept Iroquois cultural values. The family farmed and often supplemented their income by seasonal agricultural work off-reserve. They attended the annual cycle of Longhouse ceremonies, maintained their language, followed the matrilineal descent for clan affiliation, and supported the governing authority of the Iroquois Confederacy Council. As a child Alexander was given the clan name Shao-hyowa (Great Sky) by his mother's sister. He attended day school on the reserve, where he learned English and the three R's, but because of ill health and family moves off-reserve to participate in seasonal labor, Alexander's formal education was limited. His father died in a tragic gun accident in 1899, and following his mother's death several years later he became responsible for the family farm.

The Longhouse religion of the Iroquois is based on oral tradition, and it involves a great deal of speech-

Alexander General, left, *unveiling a monument in memory of his brother Levi General on September 12, 1960. Levi General's widow and Ray Fadden of the St. Regis Reserve are at the right.*

making. Each speech follows a prescribed format, but each speaker brings a unique voice to the role. The ability to deliver the various addresses, speeches, prayers, and invocations involved is considered a gift from the Creator. Young people with this talent come under the guidance of a main speaker, assuring a continuous source of qualified candidates for the role. Alexander regularly attended Sour Springs Longhouse and listened to the speeches. His keen interest was coupled with a natural speaking ability, and at about the age of eighteen he began to practice the Longhouse speeches in private. He memorized them, and the main speaker at Sour Springs encouraged him to train for the role. Throughout his life General was one of the principal speakers at Sour Springs Longhouse.

In 1918 an influenza epidemic spread through the reserve. General survived with the aid of Indian herbal medicine, but his Christian fiancée died. Over the years General's family continued to rely on traditional health systems and maintained membership in several medicine societies. General's political career had begun a year earlier when, at the age of twenty-eight, he

was appointed an assistant to his brother Levi, who had been selected to serve as Deskahe ("More Than Eleven"). This Cayuga title signifies that its holder is one of the fifty hereditary chiefs of the Iroquois Confederacy Council. Levi General (born 1873) was a devoted defender of Iroquois sovereignty. Levi's oratorical skill was recognized as outstanding, and he was appointed to the position of deputy speaker of the council in 1918 and official speaker in 1922.

The speaker played a powerful role in the daily administration of Confederacy Council business. Levi General took on international diplomacy as well when he traveled to Europe as the confederacy's representative, presenting the sovereignty case in London in 1921 and to the League of Nations in Geneva in 1923. The Confederacy Council had hired a lawyer to document the Iroquois position against the Canadian government's 1920 amendment to the Indian Act, which forced enfranchisement on Canadian Indians. The Confederacy Council maintained the position that the council was a sovereign entity exempt from Canada's laws, but the foreign governments Levi General met with failed to recognize that claim.

While Levi was overseas in October 1924, the Canadian government, with the support of a minority of Six Nations Reserve residents, imposed a new form of local government on the reserve. The Confederacy Council was abolished in favor of a democratically elected band council, and the chiefs were ousted from their council house at Ohsweken. Levi was unable to return to the Six Nations Reserve, and ill health kept him in hospital and at the home of friends in New York State. Alexander visited his brother and sought the assistance of traditional healers. On some occasions, however, his visits were prevented by border officials who chose not to recognize the Jay Treaty of 1794, which allowed North American Indians free passage between Canada and the United States. In spite of his failing physical condition, Levi made one last impassioned radio speech from Rochester, during which he told the listening audience about the right of the Six Nations to live under their own laws and to worship the Creator in their own way. Levi died three months later, in June 1925.

Alexander General was installed as Deskahe in December 1925 and immediately set to work reinstating the Confederacy Council as the legitimate government of the reserve. Although the chiefs had continued to meet, the day-to-day administration of the community was now under the control of the elected band council. At every opportunity General spoke out on behalf of the confederacy and its role in the historical development of North America. The confederacy chiefs and their Christian supporters, the Mohawk Workers, raised funds for legal assistance and for diplomatic trips to Ottawa and overseas. In 1930 General was delegated to go to England and on behalf of the confederacy to seek justice from the king. The chiefs believed that their historical ties to Great Britain remained in force because of the treaties signed between the Six Nations and the British monarch. The British government, however, viewed the matter as an internal Canadian dispute and refused to acknowledge the Iroquois claim of sovereignty. The only victory the Six Nations were able to claim from the trip was the fact that General traveled to England on a confederacy-issued passport.

Following his brother's death, Alexander General became a guiding influence in a newly formed Indian-rights organization, the Indian Defense League of America. Chief Clinton Rickard, a family friend from the Tuscarora Reservation in New York State, had founded the league with a group of like-minded people from reserves on both sides of the international boundary. The group demanded that the Jay Treaty be honored, and in 1928 it achieved its goal after taking the case to Washington. As a reminder to the public and the U.S. government, the league organized its annual Border Crossing Celebration at Niagara Falls to promote the right to cross the border. Throughout his life General actively supported the Indian Defense League and regularly participated in the Border Crossing events.

In 1949 a chapter of the Indian Defense League established an annual theatrical pageant at the Six Nations Reserve that depicted on an outdoor stage the dramatic history of the Six Nations of the Iroquois. General played an influential role as historical adviser and, on occasion, as production manager, director, and actor. The organization brought the history of the Six Nations alive for the volunteer cast as well as for the audience. Those reserve residents who participated as actors and stagehands were able to learn from General about the richness of Iroquois culture and history.

General made a conscious effort to promote the understanding of Iroquois culture and religion both on and off the reserve. From the 1930s until his death, he assisted the many anthropologists who visited the Six Nations Reserve on field trips, eagerly sharing his knowledge with them. As a fluent speaker of Cayuga and English he was able to explain the meanings of the complex speeches and ceremonies to the visiting scholars.

In 1932 a University of Pennsylvania professor of anthropology, Frank Speck, began a collaboration with Alexander on a study of the religious ceremonies at Sour Springs Longhouse. Working together until 1947, they produced the book *Midwinter Rites of the Cayuga Longhouse* in 1949. In the book the anthropologist gave the religious leader an opportunity to explain many of the complexities of traditional Iroquois ceremonies and in so doing promoted a greater awareness of his colleague's religious philosophy. General, recognizing the value of their work, allowed his voice to be preserved on tape and in written form. Not only did he assist anthropologists in their search for knowledge, he often allowed the local press to attend Longhouse functions at Sour Springs. The reporters were eager to write about the ceremonies, and the explanations General gave were often quoted at length. The media gave General the opportunity to promote the Confederacy Council as the rightful government at the Six Nations Reserve.

Despite his hospitalization for tuberculosis at the Brantford Sanatorium in 1955, General continued his duties as a religious leader. He shared his knowledge of Iroquois culture with everyone, information that was preserved in the writings of anthropologists, one of whom acknowledged General as "one of the most able interpreters of Iroquois ceremonial and ideology." General died at Brantford General Hospital in September 1965. The local newspaper reported that he was "one of the best known and respected residents of the Six Nations Reserve" and that he was "a progressive farmer and prominent in district affairs." He was buried at the Sour Springs Longhouse.

Shimony, Annemarie, "Alexander General, Deskahe," in *American Indian Intellectuals*, Proceedings of the American Ethnological Society (St. Paul: West Publishing Company, 1978); Speck, Frank G., in collaboration with Alexander General, *Midwinter Rites of the Cayuga Longhouse* (1949; reprint, Ohsweken, Ontario: Iroqrafts, 1987).

SHEILA STAATS (Mohawk)
Woodland Cultural Centre
Brantford, Ontario

GERONIMO (GOYATHLAY)

(c. 1829–1909)
Apache leader.

Goyathlay, or Geronimo, was born in about 1829. His kinship, cultural, and territorial ties transcended three Apache divisions—the Bedonkohes, Nednais, and

Geronimo, on horseback, left, flanked by his son Perico, holding a baby, on his left and his son Chief Naiche, on horseback, at right. Another Apache, Tsisnah, is at the far right. The photo, by C. S. Fly, was taken sometime before 1886.

Chiricahuas—and what became the U.S.-Mexican border. Following the Apache matrilineal custom, his father had moved from the Nednai homeland in the Sierra Madre of Mexico to an area near the headwaters of the Gila River, where his wife's people, the Bedonkohes, lived. Coming of age in that arid and mountainous terrain, Goyathlay learned how to worship Apache spirits, hunt, plant, and fight enemies. He also married a woman named Alope and had three children with her.

An 1858 episode of genocide in Mexico, together with U.S. expansion into the West, changed Goyathlay's life forever. In that year Mexican troops slaughtered many Bedonkohe women and children, including Goyathlay's wife, children, and mother, after which the Bedonkohes prepared to retaliate. Goyathlay was entrusted with the task of encouraging the other Apache bands to join the war. During subsequent years of fighting, Goyathlay avenged the death of his loved ones

many times over. He also acquired recognition among his people as an intrepid, if not reckless, fighter. His success in war was attributed to a mystical power that prevented guns and bullets from killing him. The Mexicans called him Geronimo, or Jerome, for reasons that are not entirely clear. Some claim it was a transcription of the Spanish attempt to pronounce the name Goyathlay; others believe that his enemies, when attacking his forces, appealed aloud to St. Jerome for assistance. In any event, the name stuck.

The details of Goyathlay's personal life during the 1860s and 1870s are obscure. After Alope's death, he apparently wed women from the Chiricahua and Bedonkohe bands. Though these marriages produced children, at least one child, along with its mother, was killed by the Mexicans.

Meanwhile, encroaching U.S. miners, settlers, and military men had begun to disrupt Apache life, taking land, instigating conflict, and subjecting the Indians to white laws. In 1863, when U.S. soldiers used force to establish a post in Chiricahua country and murdered Mangas Coloradas under a flag of truce, bloody warfare ensued. Goyathlay apparently fought under Cochise, Victorio, and others, but the Apaches were overpowered.

By the early 1870s, most Apache bands, threatened with extermination and starvation, had accepted peace terms and reservations. Yet many of them detested the new life. They were expected to become Christian farmers under deplorable conditions that included confinement, hunger, and white supervision. Soon after moving with his family to the Chiricahua Reservation, Goyathlay became a leader in opposing the planned dismantling of Apache culture. Goyathlay's reputation as a warrior, his oratory skills, and his wisdom enabled him to command a following and have a hand in matters of war and peace. His rising influence filled a void caused by the deaths of Cochise and other prominent Apaches. Conversely, other Apaches, who viewed armed resistance as a threat to the delicate peace, cooperated with U.S. military and civilian authorities, working as reservation policemen and scouts.

In 1876, Goyathlay protested the Chiricahuas' removal to the desolate San Carlos Reservation by fleeing with his family. Although captured, arrested, and transported to a San Carlos guardhouse, he did not end his opposition to the government's program. In 1878 Goyathlay and his supporters joined other Apaches in Mexico, but in the winter of 1880, tired of fighting, they returned to San Carlos. In September 1881 Goyathlay and others bolted after U.S. soldiers forcefully suppressed a religious gathering. Goyathlay and others stormed San Carlos the following spring and led hundreds of Apaches in a desperate bid for freedom.

During these outbreaks, defiant Apaches raided Mexican and U.S. settlements, fighting soldiers and settlers on both sides of the border. Though Mexicans and white Americans had been massacring Apaches for years, land-hungry settlers and government officials nevertheless branded the Apaches as murderous renegades who deserved death, imprisonment, or banishment. Goyathlay in particular became targeted for elimination.

Apache scouts under General George Crook, the commander of U.S. troops in Arizona, located the Chiricahuas in Mexico during the spring of 1883. Pursuant to an agreement reached with Crook, the Chiricahuas returned to San Carlos. In 1884, Goyathlay's followers were placed on Turkey Creek, within the San Carlos reserve, but they fled the following year with a small group of followers and their families after hearing rumors that their leaders would be executed. With five thousand U.S. troops, several hundred Indian scouts, and hundreds of Mexican soldiers in pursuit, the Chiricahua leaders surrendered to Crook, consenting reluctantly to live in Florida for two years. Before reaching San Carlos, however, Goyathlay and some thirty followers raced back to Mexico. Low on ammunition and not wanting to risk more deaths, they surrendered to General Nelson A. Miles, Crook's replacement, in September 1886.

U.S. soldiers quickly shipped the captives to three Florida internment camps, where other Apaches had previously been sent. Among the exiles, who eventually totaled 469 people, were Apache scouts and their families, people who had once provided invaluable assistance to the United States. Irrespective of which side they had fought on, the Apaches now not only were held as prisoners of war but also were expected to adopt white culture. Incarcerated at Fort Pickens away from their wives and children, several men, including Goyathlay, performed hard labor, sawing logs. Many Chiricahuas died from heat, humidity, and disease. The survivors were forced to cut their hair, wear Euro-American clothing, and send their children to distant boarding schools.

In 1887, military officials reunited the Apache families at Mount Vernon Barracks, Alabama. While there, one of Goyathlay's two wives received permission to move to the Mescalero Reservation in New Mexico Territory. She took their two children, Lenna and Robbie, with her.

In 1892, 388 survivors were shipped to Fort Sill, Indian Territory (Oklahoma). Once there, Goyathlay converted to Christianity, apparently without forfeiting his traditional beliefs and values. He sustained his family by ranching, farming, and selling autographed pictures of himself. He gained celebrity status, appearing at President Teddy Roosevelt's inaugural parade and the St. Louis World's Fair. He also told his experiences to S. M. Barrett, who recorded and edited his story in *Geronimo's Story of His Life,* published in 1907. Still a prisoner of war and longing for home, Goyathlay died of pneumonia at Fort Sill on February 17, 1909. He was survived by a daughter, Eva Geronimo, at Fort Sill and the two children at Mescalero.

Congress finally released the Apache prisoners in 1913. One hundred eighty-seven of them went to the Mescalero Reservation, and seventy-eight stayed in Oklahoma. By then, Goyathlay had become an American legend.

See also Apache, Western.

Barrett, S. M., *Geronimo's Story of His Life* (New York: Duffield & Co., 1907); Debo, Angie, *Geronimo: The Man, His Time, His Place* (Norman: University of Oklahoma Press, 1976).

JAMES RIDING IN (Pawnee)
Arizona State University

GHOST DANCE

The Ghost Dance is the popular name given to a pair of religious dances created in the late nineteenth century near the Walker River Reservation in Nevada. During the 1870s and again in the 1890s, Indians in western states adopted new ceremonies that centered on circular dancing and the hope that deceased ancestors and vanishing food sources would return to earth and revive Indian communities facing the domination of whites.

In the late 1860s, a Paiute named Wodziwob returned from a trance and declared that Indians could create a new paradise by performing a series of common rituals. Wodziwob's teachings spread westward among Indian groups living in California and Oregon, among them the Klamaths, the Miwoks, the Modocs, and the Yuroks. Although each group adapted the ritual to fit within its own traditions, the shared core was a dance in which participants joined hands and sidestepped leftward around a circle.

The 1870s Ghost Dance movement gradually subsided, but a new Ghost Dance attracted great attention in the 1890s. It began in 1889, when a Paiute named Wovoka fell into a trance and returned to consciousness preaching that by performing a circular dance and adhering to certain principles of virtuous and peaceful living, Indians could restore their lands and recover their own deceased ancestors. Aided by modern communication and rail travel, Wovoka's teachings spread quickly among tribes in the western United States. He gained followers among the Cheyennes, Arapahos, Sioux, Kiowas, Caddos, and Paiutes. Like the 1870s Ghost Dance, the new ceremony was performed in a circle. But Wovoka's followers performed the ritual for several days and sought visions as the culmination of the activity.

Among the Sioux, the Ghost Dance became a central focus of disaffected young men and women. Its spread to the Sioux reservations coincided with a period of intense suffering and led directly to the Wounded Knee massacre in December 1890. Nevertheless, Wovoka's Ghost Dance continued to prevail among some people,

The back of a Ghost Dance shirt collected at Wounded Knee.

and Wovoka remained a visible and influential prophet and shaman until his death in September 1932. Some Pawnees, for example, continued to practice the Ghost Dance into the early twentieth century. Other practitioners continued to follow Wovoka's teachings until the 1960s.

See also Wovoka (Jack Wilson).

GODFROY, FRANCIS (PALONSWA)
(1788–1840)
Miami war chief and trader.

Francis (or François) Godfroy was born near Kekionga (now Fort Wayne, Indiana) in 1788, the son of a French trader and a Miami woman. His Miami name, Palonswa, was the Miami approximation of the name *François*. The Miamis were involved in comparatively few frontier grievances in the period leading up to the War of 1812, but their resistance to further land cessions in Indiana Territory after 1809 led to American attacks on their villages along the lower Mississinewa River near today's Peru, Indiana. Francis Godfroy may have been one of the leaders in a Miami counterattack on an American army led by Lieutenant Colonel John Campbell in the Battle of the Mississinewa on December 17–18, 1812, but there is no firm evidence that he played such a role.

After the War of 1812, Godfroy turned increasingly to trade, in partnership with the Miamis' principal chief, Jean Baptiste Richardville. In 1823 he had a two-story trading post built at the mouth of the Mississinewa, which was kept well stocked with merchandise. Until 1827 he alternated residences between the post, known as Mount Pleasant, and his treaty reserve in today's Blackford County, Indiana. As a mixed-blood trader well aware of the value of land and merchandise, he became influential with Richardville in brokering the sale of tribal land at treaty councils held in 1826, 1834, and 1838. From 1818 to 1838, Godfroy was given a total of seventeen sections of land (10,880 acres) and $17,612 in payment for services as chief and for the debts of tribespeople to his trading post, as well as a house and other gifts.

Though Godfroy was well rewarded for his services as an intermediary between the Miami tribe and American officials, he was no mere pawn of American interests. Along with Richardville, he was able to frustrate the efforts of General John Tipton, Governor Lewis Cass, and various Indian agents to bring about rapid land cessions and Miami removal. In conjunction with traders such as the Ewing brothers, Godfroy and Richardville were able to wrest much larger payments for land ceded by treaty and to postpone the Miamis' removal longer than that of most other midwestern tribes. Godfroy, Richardville, and another Miami chief named Meshingomesia were able to get exemption from removal for their families. These small family groups of Miamis became the core population of today's Indiana Miami tribe.

In 1830, Francis Godfroy was elected war chief of the Miamis, though the post was largely honorary at that time. He died in May 1840 at his Mount Pleasant trading post and was buried nearby. The Godfroy cemetery continues as a Miami burial ground today. Through his two wives he left a large number of descendants. A large man, he dressed in a mixture of European and native clothing, often wearing a vest and waistcoat over a ruffled shirt, with a breechcloth, leggings, and moccasins. He was pictured by two amateur artists, James Otto Lewis and George Winter.

Godfroy was a key figure in the continuing persistence of the Indiana Miamis as a tribe through his landholdings and the leadership of his descendants. After his death, his treaty grant surrounding Mount Pleasant became a refuge for landless Miamis returning from Kansas after Miami removal in 1846. His youngest son, Gabriel (Wapanakekapwa, "White Blossoms"), became a leader of the Indiana Miamis until his death in 1910. His many children and grandchildren married among all the Miami kinship groups to the extent that over one-fourth of the current Indiana Miami tribe can claim descendancy from him. Later descendants have continued in leadership roles in the tribe to this day. Ira Sylvester Godfroy (Metocina, "Indian"), a great-grandson of Godfroy's, was a chief of the Indiana Miamis from 1938 to 1961, and was a leader in gaining tribal awards in Miami land claims. Another great-grandson, Clarence Godfroy (Kapapwah, "Looking over the Top"), was a noted Miami storyteller and one of the last fluent speakers of the Miami language. In 1977, in federal circuit court in South Bend, Indiana, another great-grandson, Oliver Godfroy (Swimming Turtle), won tax exemption on seventy-nine acres of remaining Francis Godfroy treaty ground.

See also Miami; Richardville, Jean Baptiste (Peshewa).

Anson, Bert, *The Miami Indians* (Norman: University of Oklahoma Press, 1970); Feest, Christian F., and R. David Edmunds, *Indians and a Changing Frontier: The Art of George Winter* (Indianapolis: Indiana Historical Society, 1993).

STEWART RAFERT
University of Delaware

GRASS HOUSES

Grass houses were most commonly constructed by Caddoan-speaking Indians of the southern plains, notably the Wichitas and Caddos. A grass house consisted of a frame of cedar poles arranged conically, with one end anchored in the ground and the tops bound together with sapling strips. Around this frame were tied stringers of saplings, which gave the frame additional strength. (The construction of the frame was the men's responsibility.) Finally, wheat grass, coarser and denser than regular prairie grass, was lashed to this frame in bunches beginning at the bottom and continuing in overlapping rows to the peak. The attachment of the wheat grass was done by women, one working inside the house and one on the outside, using a long cottonwood needle to pass a cord back and forth between them.

The traditional division of labor in the construction of a grass house was based on the legend of the Red Bean Man, to whom the builders prayed before selecting the materials for the house. Grass houses had ceased to be used by any tribe by the early twentieth century. The Wichita Indians of Oklahoma, however, have resurrected the art of building grass houses and today are actively engaged in passing on the tradition of the Red Bean Man and grass-house construction to the next generation.

See also Architecture.

GROS VENTRE

The Algonquian-speaking Gros Ventre Indian tribe occupies the Fort Belknap Reservation, which it shares with the Assiniboines in north central Montana. There are approximately three thousand enrolled Gros Ventres, with 1,385 members residing on the reservation. The tribe has been referred to by many inaccurate names throughout history, including Rapid Indians, Waterfall Indians, Big Bellies, Willow Indians, Atsinas, and Gros Ventres of the Prairie. Scholars and early explorers have often confused the Gros Ventres of the River, also known as the Hidatsas, with the Gros Ventres of Fort Belknap. The Gros Ventres of Fort Belknap refer to themselves as the A'ani', "White Clay People."

The religious structure of the A'ani' is similar to that of many tribes of the northern plains. Their most important ceremony, the Sun Dance, was held during the summer months. The introduction of Catholicism into the tribe devastated much A'ani' culture, with only a few remnants surviving today. Two pipes form the spiritual center of the tribe: the Flat Pipe and the Feathered Pipe. These have been regarded as communally sacred for centuries.

A'ani' and Arapaho oral tradition tells that the two tribes were once joined, living on the Canadian plains, and that they parted company around the Red River in 1700. The earliest known document describing contact of A'ani' with white traders dates from 1754 and establishes the tribe on the vast plains between the north and south branches of the Saskatchewan River. It was there that the A'ani' resided until the smallpox epidemic of 1780, which drastically reduced their numbers. At the same time the A'ani' were being pushed south by the well-armed Crees and Assiniboines. In 1793 and 1794 the A'ani' burned down two trading posts in their territory, hoping to cut off the flow of arms to the Crees and Assiniboines.

In 1826, half of the A'ani' rejoined the Arapahos and went south to trade with the Mexicans. After many skirmishes, these A'ani' returned to Montana. On their return trip, they rendezvoused with white trappers and Flatheads in southeastern Idaho. The trading among them had gone awry, and the A'ani' fought the trappers and the Flatheads at what today is known as Pierre's Hole.

After the tribe reunited in central Montana, several explorers and artists met the A'ani' and recorded their wealth. Prince Maximilian and the artist Karl Bodmer met them in 1833 at the confluence of the Arrow and Missouri Rivers, where Bodmer painted portraits of several A'ani' people.

The smallpox epidemic of 1837 was devastating for many tribes of the northern plains; fortunately, the A'ani' suffered relatively few losses because of their earlier exposure to smallpox. But the A'ani' were feeling increasing pressure from the Crows, and they decided to join forces with the Blackfeet. The Blackfeet and the A'ani' signed a treaty with the federal government in 1855 establishing common hunting grounds and a yearly distribution of provisions. The A'ani' later split with the Blackfeet, and in 1888 Fort Belknap was established as their home. In 1895, with the buffalo herds declining because of the railroads and the activities of white buffalo hunters, the A'ani' population reached its all-time low: 596 members.

In 1884, the first gold rush in the Little Rockies, which at the time were within the southern portion of Fort Belknap Reservation, took place. Pressure from non-Indian miners forced the tribes to cede the land in 1895. This area had long been sacred to the A'ani' people (and in fact many of them continue to make pilgrimages to these mountains today despite the ongoing mining activities).

The Jesuits first came to Fort Belknap to convert A'ani' in 1862 and built St. Paul's Mission in 1887. Because of increased pressure and economic hardship, many A'ani' converted. The dominance of Catholicism at Fort Belknap has resulted in the loss of many traditional ceremonies. Today the A'ani' of Fort Belknap are turning toward the culture and values of their ancestors and experiencing a cultural renaissance. Many of the old traditions and activities are being revived, including the use of the two sacred pipes.

Cooper, John M., "Religion and Ritual," in *The Gros Ventres of Montana,* ed. Regina Flannery, part 2 (Washington D.C.: Catholic University of America Press, 1957); Flannery, Regina, "Social Life," in *The Gros Ventres of Montana,* ed. Regina Flannery, part 1 (Washington D.C.: Catholic University of America Press, 1953); Horse Capture, George P., *The Seven Visions of Bull Lodge.* (Lincoln: University of Nebraska Press, 1992).

JOE D. HORSE CAPTURE (A'ani')
Bozeman, Montana

H

HAGLER (NOPKEHE)

(c. 1700–1763)
Catawba political leader.

Chief (in Catawba, *eractasswa*) of the Catawba Nation from 1750 until his death in 1763, Hagler has lived on in historical memory ever since. Catawbas "still speak of him with much feeling," noted a visitor to their small South Carolina reservation nearly a century after his death. "A Southern gentleman" is how one modern historian described him, noting Nopkehe's friendship with whites. "The outstanding chief in Catawba history" was the assessment of another.

Hagler was more controversial and more interesting in life than in death. A colonist wrote in 1755 that Catawbas despised Hagler and wanted to choose another leader. Nor was Hagler always a gentleman. One visitor to the Catawbas reported that Nopkehe "with much Assurance demanded" to know whether colonists were sending ammunition to the nation. "I told him I knew of none. He said the White People spoke much and performed but little." In 1759 Hagler had grown so tired of colonial company that he wondered whether "may be the white people would go away and leave us to our Selves."

A paucity of sources makes it hard to chronicle Hagler's life. Though he was a prominent warrior from the lineage that produced *eractasswas,* surviving records make no mention of him before he became chief. Nonetheless, it is possible to reconstruct the experiences that Hagler, as a person born in the Catawba Nation around 1700, likely had that would have shaped his years as chief. He knew, for example, that the Catawbas had lost a war against South Carolina in 1715 because colonists cut off trade and the Indians ran out of ammunition. Forty years later Hagler remembered this technological dependence, admitting that colonists "could make Cloaths to supply those they wore out . . . and the Indians could not do so." In addition, Hagler knew another sort of war, the long-range, small-scale conflict with the Iroquois that of-

fered warriors prestige but drained Catawba resources and people. Finally, Hagler watched colonial farmers invade the Catawbas' piedmont territory and calculated the consequences for his nation. "The White people were now seated all round them," he observed in 1756, "and by that means had them entirely in their power."

When Hagler became chief in 1750 these developments had combined to render the Catawbas' situation particularly desperate. Iroquois raiders "are so thick about us we cannot go from Home," the nation's leaders lamented. As if this were not serious enough, in the fall of 1749 disease and enemy attacks had killed Hagler's predecessor, Yanabe Yatengway, and fourteen other leaders. South Carolina governor James Glen, considering the Catawbas' predicament, feared "the Total destruction of that poor Nation."

Hagler was instrumental in preventing that destruction. One secret of his success was his skill at negotiating with colonial officials. Offering Catawba allegiance to the British against the French, he reaped rewards essential to Catawba survival: peace with the Iroquois in 1751; in 1763, a reservation to keep colonial farmers out; and, throughout his tenure, a steady flow of gifts—arms and ammunition, food and clothing—that helped the Catawbas survive severe drought and offset their declining trade in deerskins.

Hagler's negotiations might seem likely to have rendered Catawbas subservient to colonial masters. "The Corn was Given to them on Condition of their Good beheavour," one South Carolina agent bluntly reminded the Indians. Another claimed that the nation was "directed intirely by the Government of So. Carolina." Echoing this refrain, Hagler himself admitted that Catawbas were "intirely dependent on the Province of South Carolina." "My Skin is dark," he told colonists in 1762, "yet I look upon myself as a Whiteman."

The reality beneath this friendly rhetoric was more complicated. While Catawbas were indeed closely connected to South Carolina officials, skilled diplomacy also brought the nation attention (and gifts) from Virginia and North Carolina. Parts of those diplomatic conversations did consist of obsequious statements of Catawba dependence; but parts, too, were what Hagler called "strong" speeches in which he complained of colonial incompetence and issued veiled threats. Of course Catawba leaders favored peace with English America, he would say. But, he fretted to colonists, the Catawba "yong people who are Already greatly incenced [by Anglo-American misdeeds] perhaps May Not be prevaled Upon from Doing some great Mischief." In other "strong" speeches Hagler made clear the Catawbas' intention of charting for themselves a separate destiny. "We Expect to live on those Lands we now possess During our Time here," he told one colonial audience in 1754, "for when the Great man above made us, he . . . also made our forefathers and [us] of this Colour and Hue (Showing his hands and Breast) . . . and Ever since we Lived after our manner and fashion."

As Hagler's dramatic words suggest, while one secret of his success was his ability to manipulate colonists for the good of the nation, another was his determination never to stray too far from Catawba tradition. His talk of being a white man doubtless pleased colonists, but it also satisfied Catawbas, who understood a "white man" to be someone devoted to peace. Catawbas would have been happy, too, with Hagler's habit of working through a council (letters the nation sent to colonists bore not only his mark but those of a score or more councilors), as well as his insistence that his people would make peace with the Iroquois and war upon the French when they were ready, and not according to some colonial timetable.

Hagler's balancing act was by no means flawless. Not only did he frustrate Anglo-American officials eager to coax him to the treaty table or prod him into war, but he occasionally fell afoul of his own people. One 1757 attempt to negotiate with South Carolina on his own earned him a public rebuke from the nation's council, and for reasons unknown one war party he led went into battle without him when he abruptly headed home. More dangerous still, both for the *eractasswa* and for the nation, was James Bullen, the son of a Carolina trader and a Catawba woman, who sought to supplant Hagler. By 1755, a visitor to the nation reported, Bullen's many followers had created a "Dangerous Division" among the Catawbas, and civil war seemed imminent.

Hagler weathered this storm with his customary strategy of getting colonial authorities to confirm their support of him and ensuring that Catawba councilors

remained loyal. In that dual strategy lay the source of Hagler's accomplishments. At a time of crisis, he found a way to accommodate colonial powers without sacrificing Catawba autonomy. A look at the large number of Indian peoples living in Carolina at the time of his birth who, unlike the Catawbas, did not survive the colonial era reveals that this was no mean feat.

See also Catawba.

Merrell, James H., "'Minding the Business of the Nation': Hagler as Catawba Leader," *Ethnohistory* 33 (1986): 55–70.

JAMES H. MERRELL
Vassar College

HAIDA

The Haidas comprise an international tribe whose principal residences are in Masset and Skidegate, British Columbia; and in Hydaburg, Alaska. There are also many Haidas in various urban areas in the western United States and Canada. Before contact with Europeans in the late eighteenth century, the Haidas lived on what are now the Queen Charlotte Islands and the Alexander Archipelago off the northwest coast of North America. The locally reliable supplies of halibut and salmon, which formed the basis of their diet, supported the Haidas well. They lived in large cedar-plank houses and built fifty-foot-high totem poles at the fronts of the buildings. The Haidas' system of potlatch reinforced a social hierarchy based on rankings of both hereditary status and wealth. The northern and southern dialects of the Haida language are unrelated to any other known tongue.

The Haidas of Alaska traditionally lived in three villages on the west coast of Prince of Wales Island and in one village on the island's east coast. In 1911, with the encouragement and support of the U.S. government and the Presbyterian Church, the three Haida villages of Cordova Bay consolidated at Hydaburg. On June 19, 1912, President William Howard Taft signed Executive Order no. 1555, establishing the Hydaburg Reservation for the protection and civilization of the Haidas. Hydaburg was modeled on what would be known as the Metlakatla Plan, whereby the natives would be the developers and proprietors of the community and its enterprises, and would be treated as citizens of the United States while at home.

The Haidas have been involved in three distinct processes of adjudicating their aboriginal claims. In

1935 the Tlingit and Haida Indians brought suit against the United States in a court of claims case that awarded the Tlingit and Haida Indians of Alaska $7 .2 million for the taking of aboriginal lands by the United States when it established the Alexander Archipelago Forest Reserve (now known as the Tongass National Forest) in 1902. The Tlingit and Haida Central Council was designated as the administrator of funds and programs derived from the court of claims case.

In April 1938, the Hydaburg Cooperative Association became the first economic enterprise organized under the terms of the Alaska Reorganization Act. Shortly thereafter the association filed a petition with the Department of the Interior for a reservation and submitted to an adjudicative process for its creation. The reservation was subsequently established, but in 1952 the agreement that led to its creation was declared null and void by the U.S. District Court.

In 1971, the Alaska Native Claims Settlement Act was signed into law, authorizing the creation of for-profit corporations for each of the native villages in Alaska. Village corporations with significant Haida shareholders include Haida Corporation in Hydaburg, Kavilco in Kasaan, and Shaan-Seet in Craig. These village corporations incorporated under the laws of Alaska and received a total of 23,040 acres of land, much of it forest lands. The corporations are looking at ways to enter into various business opportunities on Prince of Wales Island such as forest-products, hospitality, charter-fishing, oil-products, and rock-crushing operations.

In contrast to the Haidas in Alaska, Haidas in the towns of Masset and Skidegate in the Canadian reserves were administered by the Canadian Department of Indian Affairs. In the twentieth century, Haidas in Masset continued to make their livings from fishing. Men worked as fishers and boatbuilders, while employed women worked in a cannery in nearby New Masset. Residents of Skidegate found work in the logging camps on their reserves. During the 1960s, when the Canadian authorities encouraged greater Indian participation in self-governance, the Masset and Skidegate Haidas renewed their traditional arts, including the erection of totem poles, the revival of dance, and the building of canoes. In the 1980s, the two villages formed the Council of the Haida Nation to support their political interests.

The issue most important to the modern Haidas continues to be the establishment of a governing body that will have political and economic control of their ancestral homelands. Problems with defining the role of an officially recognized Haida tribe are complicated by the Indian Reorganization Act, the Alaska Native Claims Settlement Act, and the institutions created under those laws.

ADRIAN LeCORNU (Haida)
Craig, Alaska

HAMPTON INSTITUTE

Founded as the Hampton Normal and Agricultural Institute, Hampton Institute is located near Hampton, Virginia. The American Missionary Association of New York bought the land in 1867 specifically to provide instruction for freedmen. The school opened in April 1868 and received a formal charter from the General Assembly of Virginia in 1870. The founder and first principal was General Samuel Chapman Armstrong, assigned by the Freedmen's Bureau and himself the son of missionary educators in the Hawaiian Islands.

Indian students first attended Hampton in 1878 when a group of Kiowa men who had been held as prisoners of war at St. Petersburg, Florida, were brought north as an experiment in Indian education. The first group's success led Congress to authorize its leader, Army captain Richard Henry Pratt, use of an abandoned army barracks at Carlisle, Pennsylvania, for an all-Indian institution. Pratt founded the Carlisle Indian Industrial School in 1879.

Some officials objected to the mixing of African American and Native American students, yet Hampton was much like other federal boarding schools for Indians. Generally, students learned domestic and agricultural arts and crafts and were then encouraged to return to their people as emissaries of Euro-American culture. Male students also received military training.

By the turn of the century nearly a thousand students were attending Hampton, of whom 135 were Native American. From that high point, the number of Indian pupils dwindled until 1923, when the program was discontinued.

See also Boarding Schools; Education.

HAND GAME

According to the anthropologist Stewart Culin, the Hand Game "is played by 81 different tribes from some 28 different linguistic roots. Although thought of as a Plains Indian game, it is actually played by native people in the western two-thirds of the North American Continent." The Hand Game is a guessing game played to music in which the hider conceals an object in each hand. Only one of the objects is marked. The guesser points to the hand he or she thinks contains the marked object. If the choice is correct, the guesser wins a counting stick; if not, the guesser loses a counting stick. When one team wins all the counting sticks, the game is over and that team claims the prize.

The Hand Game is often played by teams who stand or sit in rows across an open area five or six feet wide.

Individuals from each side take turns guessing. Their guesses are accompanied by elaborate hand movements, singing, and drumming. Teams play with elaborately carved sticks, and the stakes of victory are often quite high. Among some Plains tribes in former times, each stick represented a horse. The equipment for a Hand Game usually consisted of two "bones" (hiding sticks), eleven counting sticks, one drum, and one drumstick.

Originally only males could play the Hand Game. Females assisted with the singing and cheering. The female singers occupied the last row of players. Among some nations women could play this game with one an-

A team of four Shoshone women playing the Hand Game. The woman in dark glasses uses a blanket to conceal the two small bones with which the game is played.

other. There was always a strict division by sex of the actual players. However, in the modern game, females generally may participate as hiders or guessers. The drum is nearly always played by a male.

Today you will find professional Hand Game teams in various communities. They have team colors, jackets, songs, and other accouterments associated with athletic competition. Traditionally, this game was played day and night, nonstop, until one side ran out of goods to bet. Today tournaments are usually held in conjunction with a tribal celebration or powwow. The local committee offers cash prizes to the winning team. The winner is usually determined by the double elimination system, in which a team that loses twice is eliminated from the competition.

During the days of the buffalo, the Hand Game was a part of the intense good-natured rivalries that existed between warrior societies. Each club or society tried to outdo the other, not only to gain notoriety in the village, but also to become rich by winning the game prizes away from their opponents. Strong "medicine" was also used to assure success. An individual's spirit was called upon to assist in the correct guess or to foil opposing medicine.

Music is a major component of the Hand Game. Frances Densmore and other early ethnomusicologists transcribed a number of game songs at the turn of the century, and recordings of contemporary music are still available. One interesting feature concerning the fast, hard-soft drumbeat employed in the Hand Game is that its cadence is "against" the heart's rhythm. This counterpalpitation creates psychological excitement, confusing the guesser and adding to the general emotion of the game.

Despite its ancient origins, the Hand Game is not a thing of the past but a continuing, integral part of modern-day Native American culture. Each year the American Indian Higher Education Consortium of Tribal Colleges and Universities holds a series of intercollegiate competitions among its thirty-one members; usually the Hand Game is included in this annual event.

Culin, Stewart, *Games of the North American Indian* (1907; reprint, New York: Dover Publications, 1975); Densmore, Frances, *Music of the Teton Sioux, Smithsonian Institution,* Bureau of American Ethnology Bulletin 61 (Washington, D.C., 1918).

LOUIS GARCIA
Fort Berthold Community College
New Town, North Dakota

HANDSOME LAKE
(1735–1815)
Iroquois religious leader.

Handsome Lake (Sganyadai:yo) was born in 1735 at the village of Ganawagrahs, in present-day New York State. Born into the Wolf clan, he was later adopted by the Turtle clan. Relatively little is known of his earlier life. In July 1777 he and his half brother Cornplanter attended a great war council of the Iroquois Confederacy with the British at Oswego. Though the brothers initially argued for Seneca neutrality, they later fought alongside the British forces against the revolutionaries.

In 1780 Cornplanter and his followers moved to the Allegheny Valley; for the next decade, he traveled extensively among his people, counseling peace with the thirteen states, and went to Albany and Philadelphia to meet with the new state and federal governments. His brother Handsome Lake was described at the time as being a dissolute man, ravaged by drink. From 1795 to 1799, he lived as an invalid in Cornplanter's house, consumed by a wasting disease ascribed to his excessive drinking and to his having offended the Creator.

On June 15, 1799, Cornplanter, summoned urgently to his house, was told that his brother was dying. The unconscious Handsome Lake—in at least one account he was taken by his family for dead and dressed for burial—awakened some hours later and began to recount three visions he had had while he lay sick. In the first, he had been visited by three messengers, he said, handsome men dressed alike and carrying pronged blueberry saplings as canes, who at first prescribed medicine to cure him of his illness. He pledged to the messengers that, should he be allowed to walk on the earth again, he would repent of his sins. The messengers told him that the Creator had sent them to find him because he had been chosen for a mission. In his second vision a fourth messenger showed him the paths to heaven and hell and revealed the nail holes in his hands and feet. In his third vision the Creator's instructions were given to him. His recounting of these instructions came to be known as the Code of Handsome Lake:

- *Ohnega* (alcohol), the worst of evils, had been given to the white man to ease his labors but had been abused by all and had to be renounced.
- *Otgo* (witchcraft) was to be used by its practitioners not for evil purposes but for healing, and witches were to give freely of their good medicine.

- *Onohwet* (love medicine) "clouds the mind and sickens the body to the point of death." Those who did not repent of its use were on the path to hell.
- The blessings of marriage, family, and children were to be cherished so that the strength of the people could be renewed.

But Handsome Lake taught much more than abstinence, family values, and the continued practice of the ceremonies, songs, and dances of thanksgiving. He counseled his people to learn the white man's ways by sending some of their sons to school; he preached against vanity; he told his people there was nothing wrong with building and living in a white man's house, or farming as the white man did; he told them to keep their traditional clothing and wear it at ceremonies to give thanks; and he preached the confession of sin.

Faith keepers had special responsibilities for preserving the traditional ceremonies, prayers, and rituals. The code prescribed four sacred rituals: the Great Feather Dance, to honor children and life; the Drum Dance, to honor the spirit beings who watch over the Haudenosaunee; the Men's Chant, to honor the Creator; and the Peach Pit Bowl Game and the Sustenance Dance. All of these rituals were to be performed at midwinter ceremonies.

Handsome Lake warned against the Evil One, trying to turn the people away from sin. He told of how a child's love and encouragement relieved him of his own weariness and depression. And he made predictions about the future: that the Iroquois chiefs would argue among themselves and abandon the Great Council; that the people would cease their ceremonies and return to witchcraft; that a woman well past childbearing age would give birth; that a child would bear a baby. The fulfillment of these predictions and others would be a sign that the end was near. Then the four spirit beings would gather the young and old to the Creator to shield them from sadness, and the earth would come to an end.

Handsome Lake began his preaching in his home village of Cornplanter's Town, or Burnt House, on the Allegheny River, where he remained for some ten years. In 1802, he traveled to Washington, D.C., to meet with President Thomas Jefferson and Secretary of War Henry Dearborn, who said of the Iroquois prophet in a letter, "If all the red people follow the advice of your friend and teacher Handsome Lake, . . . the Great Spirit will take care of you." He later moved upriver to Cold Springs, where he spent two years before moving again to Tonawanda, where he lived for another four years.

At Tonawanda, Handsome Lake received emissaries from the Onondaga Nation inviting him to bring his message to their people. Shortly thereafter he had a vision in which he was advised by the three messengers that it was his duty to go to the Onondagas, but that he would meet there four messengers, who would lead him to the Sky Trail. Although after learning of this vision the Tonawanda people begged him not to go, Handsome Lake set out east for Onondaga territory, passing his abandoned birthplace at Ganawagrahs.

By the time Handsome Lake and his followers reached Onondaga (sometimes referred to as Onondaga Castle), near Syracuse, New York, Handsome Lake was very ill and weak. The Onondagas organized a lacrosse game, hoping to lift his spirits, but on August 10, 1815, he left this world to embark on the Sky Trail.

Almost a decade after Handsome Lake's death, his teachings were revived with the help of his grandson Jimmy Johnson and his nephew Owen Blacksnake. Since this revival, representatives from the Iroquois longhouse in Ontario and the one in New York State have met each autumn in Tonawanda to agree on a schedule of meetings at various reserves, where the people gather to reaffirm their faith in his teachings. The preaching of the Code of Handsome Lake, which embodies the most profound tenets of the Longhouse beliefs, remains the heart and soul of their faith, and sustains that faith as a living testament to Iroquois tradition.

See also Iroquois Confederacy; Seneca.

Wallace, Anthony F. C., *The Death and Rebirth of the Seneca* (New York: Knopf, 1969).

TED MONTOUR
Woodland Cultural Centre
Brantford, Ontario

HARJO, CHITTO

(1846–1909?)
Creek farmer, micco *of the Crazy Snakes.*

Chitto Harjo is symbolic of resistance and opposition to assimilation among members of the Muskogee Nation. His leadership is legendary among his people, his mystique heightened by his tragic, mysterious death. The name *Chitto* (pronounced *chit-toe*) is a form of the

Chitto Harjo, leader of the Crazy Snake movement.

Creek word meaning "snake." *Harjo* (pronounced *ha-cho*) is a common second name among the Creeks. It means "recklessly brave" or "brave beyond discretion." The English equivalent is "crazy." Consequently, among whites Chitto Harjo was renowned as Crazy Snake and his followers were called Crazy Snakes, or simply Snakes.

The Crazy Snake movement (1900–1909) marked a significant transition in Native American history. A minority of Creek Indians, mostly full bloods, ardently opposed the allotment of tribal lands during the first decade of the twentieth century. They sought to preserve their culture by demanding that their tribal government and the United States enforce the removal treaty of 1832 and abandon efforts to dissolve the Creek Nation. The Crazy Snake resistance to allotment resulted in the use of federal troops in 1901 and the Oklahoma National Guard in 1909, marking one of the last times the United States resorted to military force to resolve an Indian conflict.

Chitto Harjo was born in 1846 in Arbeka–Deep Fork, Indian Territory. His father, Aharlock Harjo, raised the boy to be a farmer. Harjo's influence began in 1899 when he was selected *heneha* (orator) of the town of Hickory Ground by its micco, Lahtah Micco. The Muskogee Nation valued oratory, and each town's *micco* (chief) delegated someone to make speeches on his behalf. When illness stranded Lahtah Micco in Washington, D.C., in 1900, Harjo assumed leadership of Hickory Ground and did not relinquish it until he was fatally wounded in 1909.

Hickory Ground Creeks adamantly refused to participate in the allotment process because it promised to break up the tribal domain, thereby violating the treaty of 1832. As far as the Hickory Ground Creeks were concerned, this was the only legal treaty between the Muskogee Nation and the United States. Throughout the summer of 1900, Harjo circulated among the seasonal stomp dances seeking pledges to oppose allotment. By the fall of 1900 he had united a group of Creeks who were willing to do battle against the allotment of their tribal land.

Disappointed that the Muskogee National Council was determined to proceed with allotment, the Hickory Ground Creeks, by then known as Crazy Snakes or Snakes, established their own government in the fall of 1900. The lighthorse, or police, enforced newly adopted Snake laws. Snake emissaries were sent to recruit members from other tribes. Dissident Choctaws, Cherokees, and Seminoles joined them. Afraid that the Hickory Ground crusade held the seeds of a revolutionary movement, Pleasant Porter, principal chief of the Muskogee Nation, turned to U.S. marshal Leo Bennett for help. Bennett warned federal officials that the Snakes were organizing a growing intertribal movement opposed to allotment. In January 1901, in a letter to President McKinley, the Snakes formally announced their campaign to stop allotment.

On January 25, 1901, Troop A of the Eighth U.S. Cavalry was sent from Fort Reno to arrest Snake leaders and disband the Snake movement. Commanded by Lieutenant H. B. Dixon, this force of sixty-five soldiers encamped near Henryetta. Two days later, U.S. deputy marshal Grant Johnson and interpreter Bernie McIntosh arrested the Snake leader at his home without resistance.

Nearly one hundred Snakes were arrested and transported to Muskogee, where they appeared in federal court before Judge John R. Thomas. They agreed to plead guilty to four charges in exchange for a suspension of fines and prison sentences. Thomas released them with a warning to cease their activities, but Harjo and some of the others resumed their resistance soon after they were freed. One year later, in February 1902, U.S. marshals rearrested Harjo and nine other Snakes, who were transferred to the federal penitentiary at Leavenworth, Kansas, to complete the remainder of their original two-year sentences.

The imprisonment of Harjo from March to November 1902 forced the Snake movement to change its tactics. The Snakes began to challenge allotment and other policies through political structures rather than militant demands. Snakes ran for Creek tribal political offices, circulated petitions, retained lobbyists in Washington, and corresponded with federal officials. In 1905, Harjo traveled to Washington to meet with President Theodore Roosevelt. The meeting was brief, and neither man had the language skills to make his points understood to the other. Harjo left Washington feeling confused about Roosevelt's position regarding allotment.

Prompted by Snake grievances, the U.S. Senate launched an investigation into matters related to the final disposition of the affairs of the so-called Five Civilized Tribes. On November 23, 1906, Chitto Harjo testified in Tulsa before a Senate select committee, eloquently petitioning the committee to recognize the treaty of 1832. His speech was a poignant plea for justice. Listeners characterized him as a "warrior-statesman," "a patriot like George Washington," "a man of strong magnetism," and "the most wonderful speaker I ever heard." However, despite his oratorical skills, the committee rejected Harjo's appeal. Disappointed, he then devised a plan to move his people to Mexico, but soon found that they had no interest in leaving their homes.

Although some whites praised Harjo for his stand against allotment, most continued to fear him and his followers. This fear erupted into deadly violence in the early spring of 1909. Harjo and other Snakes had given sanctuary to former black slaves who had been expelled from Henryetta once they were freed from their Creek owners. A few of the freedmen resorted to stealing farm goods in order to feed their families. Local peace officers formed a posse and set out for Hickory Ground to arrest the thieves. A shootout erupted, resulting in the deaths of an estimated fifteen men and the arrest of forty-two, including some Snakes. Harjo was at his home some twenty miles from the tent encampment of the freedmen, but Sheriff William L. Odum of

Checotah blamed the leader for the battle. Even though testimony from neighbors exonerated Harjo from any involvement in the battle, Odum soon sent four U.S. deputy marshals to Harjo's home to arrest him.

At sundown on March 27, the officers approached Harjo's cabin. As posted sentinels ran toward the cabin to sound the alarm, the officers opened fire. The sentinels returned fire, killing two of the marshals. The surviving officers gathered the dead and returned to Checotah, where a large posse was organized to arrest Harjo. Unknown to them, Harjo had been wounded in the gunfire, most likely fatally, and had fled. The posse returned to Harjo's cabin only to find he had disappeared. Frustrated, the posse looted his home and burned all buildings to the ground.

Fearing that the violence would spread and be turned against other Creeks, Governor Charles N. Haskell ordered the First Regiment of the Oklahoma National Guard to Hickory Ground to establish peace and arrest Harjo. But they failed to find him there. Harjo remained in hiding until his death.

Harjo's death remains shrouded in mystery. A persistent story maintains that he fled to Mexico, where he lived to be an old man. Another story asserts that he was burned to death in his cabin when the posse's rage erupted in a fiery blaze of revenge. Another account claims that Harjo was hanged in Okmulgee, Oklahoma, in 1910. Still another account has Harjo shot and drowned in the Canadian river. But documentation for all of these accounts is inadequate. According to the testimony of family and friends, what probably happened is that Harjo died from the gunshot wound at the home of a Choctaw friend, Daniel Bob, in the Kiamichi Mountains soon after the attack on his home.

Following Harjo's disappearance, Eufaula Harjo (no relation) infused the Snake movement with a new spirit of cooperation. During the summer of 1909, Eufaula Harjo forged the Snake movement into an official intertribal organization called the Four Mothers Nation. Recognizing that full bloods around the state shared common concerns and aims, the organization expanded to represent all full bloods under the coalition name the Indian Bureau. Political commonalities took precedence over religious, linguistic, and cultural differences. The spirit of intertribal advocacy and activism has continued throughout the twentieth century through numerous Indian organizations. The Crazy Snake movement continued until World War I, but its influence waned as the Indian Bureau organized collective political activism across Oklahoma.

See also Creek (Muskogee).

Bolster, Mel H., *Crazy Snake and the Smoked Meat Rebellion* (Boston: Brandon Press, 1976); Debo, Angie, *And Still the Waters Run: The Betrayal of the Five Civilized Tribes* (Princeton, N.J.: Princeton University Press, 1940); Debo, Angie, *The Road to Disappearance* (Princeton, N.J.: Princeton University Press, 1941).

KENNETH W. MCINTOSH (Muskogee)
University of Tulsa

HATATHLI, NED

(1923–72)
Navajo leader and educator.

Ned Hatathli was born on October 11, 1923, on Coal Mine Mesa, near the community of Tuba City, Arizona, on the western portion of the Navajo Indian Reservation. His father and grandfather were highly respected medicine men. Hatathli grew up in a traditional Navajo home, where he herded sheep, hauled water, and chopped wood. He was born into the Ashishi (Salt) clan.

The first school Hatathli attended was the Bureau of Indian Affairs boarding school at Tuba City. Hatathli graduated from Northern Arizona University in 1950 with a major in art and education. In 1951 he became director of the Arts and Crafts Guild in Window Rock, Arizona, where he developed a lifelong interest in and respect for Navajo crafts. Later, when he became a tribal councilman and eventually director of the Division of Natural Resources for the Navajo tribe, Hatathli developed community projects through which the women from his home community at Coal Mine Mesa would weave rugs and Hatathli would buy them for resale, paying a higher price than the women would ordinarily receive from traders. He developed the raised design now characteristic of Coal Mine Mesa weaving. Hatathli also used his own money to help his community: at Christmas, and on other occasions, he was known to buy food for everyone.

After retiring from his Arts and Crafts Guild leadership, Hatathli got involved in tribal politics. He was elected to the Navajo Nation Council in 1956. During his tenure on the council he introduced legislation that expanded the Navajo Scholarship Program, which encouraged Navajo young people to attend institutions of higher education. The tribal council in the 1950s had three college-educated members—Hatathli, Dillon

Platero, and Allan Yazzie—who did much to further the growth of Navajo education.

Hatathli eventually resigned from the tribal council and became the first director of the Natural Resources Division of the Navajo tribe. In that capacity he was instrumental in assuring Navajo participation in and benefit from the development of natural resources such as oil, gas, coal, timber, and uranium. Under his leadership the Navajo tribe built a modern sawmill at Navajo, New Mexico. Hatathli also served as chairman of the newly formed board of directors for the Navajo Forest Products Industry.

In 1966 Hatathli became the president of a group of three Navajo leaders called DINE (Demonstration in Navajo Education), Diné being the word the Navajos use to refer to themselves. The organization was responsible for directing and guiding the Rough Rock Demonstration School for its first three or four years. Rough Rock, the first Indian school in the United States to be totally controlled by Indian people, had as its goal the determination of whether Navajos who had little or no education could effectively control and direct their own school. The school was jointly funded by the Bureau of Indian Affairs and the Office of Economic Opportunity; the DINE board was the contracting entity: the bureau refused to enter into a contract with the Rough Rock community itself but was willing to enter into a contract with three articulate and educated Navajos. Hatathli and DINE were instrumental in assisting the local school board; eventually DINE ceased to exist and was replaced by a local all-Navajo school board. The school project proved highly successful and was visited by representatives from over seventy different Indian tribes from throughout the country. The Rough Rock Demonstration School was the first "contract school"—that is, a locally run school that contracts with the Bureau of Indian Affairs to provide educational services. In 1994 there were over seventy such contract Indian schools scattered throughout the United States.

In the 1960s Hatathli became an education specialist in the Bureau of Indian Affairs for the Navajo Agriculture Project, which was to bring under irrigation 110,000 acres of land south of Farmington, New Mexico. When this author was asked by the chairman of the Navajo tribe in 1968 to start what is now Navajo Community College, he approached Hatathli and offered him the position of executive vice president; a year later Hatathli became president of that institution. Gloria Begaye, Hatathli's oldest daughter, said in an

Ned Hatathli in 1954, when he served as director of the Arts and Crafts Guild in Window Rock, Arizona.

interview that her father stated that the field of education—specifically, his post as president of Navajo Community College—was where he wanted to be and where he intended to make his mark.

Throughout much of his life Hatathli felt that knowing the Navajo language and culture was a handicap. He did not want his children to suffer under such a handicap, and therefore neither Hatathli nor his wife, Florence, spoke Navajo to their children, nor did they teach them about traditional Navajo culture. His daughter Gloria declared, "One of the reasons we [Ned's children] don't speak Navajo is because he wanted us to speak English and be able to compete in the modern world." It was not until Hatathli became associated with Navajo Community College, founded

as it was on the idea of teaching a knowledge of and respect for Navajo culture and language, that he became convinced of the harm he had done to his children and apologized to them. In the following years Hatathli turned increasingly to his traditional culture. He had begun learning the Blessing Way, a Navajo healing ceremony, before he died.

On October 12, 1972, the eve of an important conference at Navajo Community College, Hatathli, while cleaning his gun, accidentally shot himself in the chest. Annie Wauneka, the revered grandmother of the Navajo tribe and a councilwoman at the time, cried out upon learning of Hatathli's death, "I wanted him to be chairman. Now he's gone. Heaven help the Navajo!"

Champagne, Duane, "Prominent Native North Americans," in *The North American Almanac*, ed. Duane Champagne (Detroit, Washington, D.C., and London: Gale Research, 1994); Gridley, Marion E., "Ned Hatathli," in *Contemporary American Indian Leaders* (New York: Dodd, Mead and Company, 1972).

ROBERT A. ROESSEL, JR.
Navajo Division of Education
Window Rock, Arizona

HAYES, IRA

(1923–55)
Native American war hero.

Ira Hayes returned a hero,
celebrated through the land.
He was wined and speeched and honored,
everybody shook his hand.
But he was just a Pima Indian,
no water, no home, no chance.
At home no one cared what Ira'd done
and when did the Indians dance?
Peter LaForge, "Ballad of Ira Hayes"

A media-created hero of World War II, Ira Hayes symbolized two postwar realities in American society: the return of thousands of veterans to civilian life, and the impoverished status of Indian peoples relative to Anglo-American prosperity. Ira Hamilton Hayes was born on the Gila Reservation in Arizona on January 12, 1923, to Joe and Nancy Hayes, both members of the Pima Indian tribe. Joe Hayes was a cotton farmer, and the family lived most of Ira's childhood in a traditional Pima adobe house in Bapchule, forty miles southeast of Phoenix. The oldest of four brothers, young Ira listened intently as older Pima men described their experiences during World War I. Many of the men of the reservation had served in the Arizona National Guard 158th Infantry in France, in spite of their military exemption as noncitizens.

In August 1942, Hayes enlisted in the U.S. Marine Corps Reserve. The night before his departure, Joe and Nancy Hayes hosted a community dinner in their son's honor. Each of the guests spoke to Ira about Pima honor, loyalty, and family. Upon his arrival in San Diego for basic training, the other recruits dubbed Hayes "the Chief." Upon his graduation, Hayes set his sights on becoming a marine parachutist and thus joining a new division of the Marine Corps. The training was especially rigorous, but at five-foot-seven and 135 pounds, Hayes was well suited for both the technical training and the "tumbling" (landing safely on the ground after a jump) that trainees were required to master before they were accepted into the outfit.

In December 1942, Hayes was promoted to private first class and assigned to the Third Parachute Battalion, Third Marine Division. Hayes's battalion sailed for the South Pacific in March 1943. Hayes's division joined forces with the U.S. Navy and allied forces in the Solomon Islands, a Japanese stronghold. The marines established a regular routine of training, assault, and training again for the next assault as they overtook the islands one by one. Hayes spent six months on New Caledonia and two weeks on Guadalcanal, and then trained for several weeks on the island of Vella Lavella. Hayes's unit finally saw combat in the assault on Bougainville, a disease-infested tropical island of dense foliage and regular monsoons. While in a foxhole, Hayes and a companion of his, William Faulkner, were surprised by a Japanese soldier who jumped into the hole—on top of Ira's raised bayonet.

In January 1944, the men of the Third Parachute Battalion were given a thirty-day leave and headed for San Diego. Hayes met his parents in Phoenix, his first visit in nearly a year. When he returned to duty, Hayes discovered that his battalion had been dissolved. The Marine Corps had decided that the extra pay paratroopers received was a luxury the corps could not afford. Hayes was reassigned to Company E "Easy," Second Battalion, Twenty-eighth Marine Division, as a rifleman and sent to Camp Pendleton near San Diego. In September 1944, Hayes's division embarked for Camp Tarawa on the big island of Hawaii. Life on the island was easy compared with his assignment in the South Pacific, and Hayes and his companions found time to explore the island on horseback. On January 7, 1945, Hayes's company disembarked for Maui, and by January 27 they had headed back to the South Pacific.

The marines' assault on Iwo Jima began February 20, 1945. Hayes's company was one of the first to land, and his division suffered heavy casualties. On February 23, the marines fought their way to the top of Mount Suribachi, the highest point on the island, and planted a small American flag. The next day, a detachment of six men, including Hayes, was sent to the summit to raise a larger, more visible flag. They were joined halfway by a civilian photographer, Joe Rosenthal. His picture of this second flag-raising became an instant classic and served as a model for a bronze statue in Arlington Cemetery that honors the marines who died in World War II.

Hayes was the last man in the photograph to be officially identified. By the campaign's end, three of the six marines captured in Rosenthal's photo had been killed in combat. The three survivors were hailed as heroes and sent on a big-city tour around the country to make speeches and reenact the now-famous flag raising in New York, Philadelphia, Rochester, Chicago, Detroit, and Indianapolis. A quiet, shy man, Hayes suffered terribly under the glaring lens of public attention and from a deep sense of guilt that he, and not his fallen comrades, should be so honored. By the end of the first week of his stay in Chicago, Hayes was drinking heavily. After only two weeks on the tour circuit, he was ordered back to his company, which was stationed in Hawaii. The war for Hayes and the other marines ended in August 1945 with the bombing of Hiroshima and Nagasaki.

In December 1945, Hayes was discharged and returned to his parents' farm in Arizona. Back on the reservation, he was dismayed to find his people, the Pimas, still without sufficient water for their crops and largely forgotten by mainstream American society. Hayes worked his father's twenty-acre farm and picked cotton at three dollars per one hundred pounds. He fell into a pattern of hard labor followed by drunken sprees that often landed him in jail.

Under the Indian Relocation Program, Hayes filed for relocation to Chicago, where he hoped racial prejudice and his notoriety as a war hero would not follow him. He was accepted into the program in 1953 and offered a job as a tool grinder at International Harvester. But there was no escape from publicity as Hayes was "officially" greeted at the Chicago train station by local Indian organizations proud to have the hero in their midst. Before long, Hayes was jailed once again for drunkenness and lost his job at Harvester. It was the height of Hayes's humiliation and the end of his earnest efforts at rehabilitation. Hayes soon returned to the Gila Reservation, and on January 23, 1955, his frozen body was discovered a mile from his parents' home.

Hayes's untimely death became symbolic of the failure both of the nation to meet the needs of veterans and of the Indian Relocation Program. Critics claimed that relocation was just one more government scheme to defraud Indians of their land by moving them into the cities and off the reservations forever. Supporters of the policy defended it as providing Indian peoples equal economic opportunity in postwar America. Indi-

ans themselves had mixed feelings about relocation. Some relocatees adjusted well to urban life but realized later that they had traded upward mobility for their tribal heritage on the reservation. Others used relocation as a means of visiting the city and had no intention of permanent relocation. Many Indian leaders wanted the monies that had been allocated for relocation to be used toward economic development on the reservations.

In many ways Ira Hayes's experience in the Marine Corps and afterward was not unlike that of other veterans. Return to civilian life after the violence of war was disorienting, and although most veterans made the transition successfully, some, like Hayes, were unable to cope with the sudden loss of belonging and purpose. The transition was particularly difficult for American Indians. In uniform they were treated with respect. But once they were back on American soil, ignored by the nation they had fought to preserve, Indian veterans were subjected to the sting of racial prejudice. Relocation was an inadequate solution to the problems faced by veterans like Hayes who needed the support of community as well as a job. Ira Hayes survived the war only to succumb to the ensuing peace.

Hemingway, Albert, *Ira Hayes, Pima Marine* (Boston: University Press of America, 1988); Van de Mark, Dorothy, "The Raid on the Reservations," *Harpers Magazine,* March 1956, pp. 48–53; Vogel, Virgil, *This Land Was Ours* (New York: Harper and Row, 1972).

BONNIE LYNN-SHEROW
Kansas State University

HEALTH AND HEALERS

The European conquest of the Americas was largely responsible for the deteriorating health status of the descendants of the native peoples. The long-term consequences of the devastating cycles of epidemics, dispossession, displacement, and poverty have still not been adequately measured, but there is no doubt that these historical experiences continue to affect the health of American Indians and Alaska Natives today.

While the health status of American Indians and Alaska Natives suffered as a result of European conquest, the nutritional and other resources of the native peoples contributed to the survival of many of the early European settlers in America. Some of these resources, such as the medicinal herbs of some native groups that have become a part of modern medicine, are still used. For example, at least 220 botanical drugs listed in the *Pharmacopoeia of the United States* and in the *National Formulary* were discovered and used by Indian tribes in pre-European times. Some of the more well known of these drugs are digitalis, quinine, belladonna, cocaine from coca leaves, curare, and ipecac.

Despite reports from early explorers regarding the excellent hygiene and robust health of native groups, diseases introduced by the Europeans decimated villages, altered the demography of tribes, and forever changed the lifestyles of the survivors. The epidemics also greatly diminished and in some cases completely destroyed the indigenous health resources of many native communities.

As the invasion of the New World continued, warfare, dispossession, and displacement also greatly affected the health resources of native peoples. For example, those removed from their ancestral land had no access to places where they gathered their traditional medicinal herbs. As the brutal depopulation by disease and warfare intensified, the healing abilities of some indigenous practitioners were suppressed or simply overwhelmed by the new diseases and the lethal tactics of the Europeans.

By the late nineteenth century, when the ravages of communicable diseases and warfare were less evident and most surviving tribes were confined to reservations, the federal government with the assistance of various organized religious groups redoubled its efforts to "civilize" and "Christianize" the natives. This attack on traditional native religions, however, also meant a renewed attack on indigenous health resources, because religious leaders in most tribes were also healers. Indigenous healers and their healing ceremonies were labeled primitive, evil, and pagan, and were viewed as barriers to civilization and assimilation. Little or no effort was made to understand traditional Indian religion or its role in the health care of tribal groups.

Although contemporary society is more open to cultural differences, only recently have the lifeways and beliefs held by native peoples become a concern to the non-Indian world. For example, it was not until Western-trained health-care providers realized the importance of culture and how culture colors the acceptance or nonacceptance of certain health-care interventions that culture became an important variable in the planning and delivery of health-care services to ethnically diverse populations.

Today health-care providers are attempting to learn about some of the basic health beliefs and practices of American Indians and Alaska Natives. In this endeavor, they have come to realize that many native health and treatment concepts are based on logical principles and the innovative use of plants and other available resources. For example, most American Indians and Alaska Natives have beliefs and traditional cultural practices that are oriented toward good health; many of the traditional tribal taboos focus on rules that reinforce disease prevention and healthy lifestyles. Unfortunately, many of these ideas and practices either are lost or have become drastically changed as a result of forced acculturation and poverty. Thus an increasing number of American Indians and Alaska Natives are having to rediscover that physical illness can affect a person's mental health, and that interventions must treat the whole person—mind, body, spirit, and emotions—to restore the balance, or harmony, between these elements. Moreover, these interventions must extend beyond the individual because, according to native beliefs, if certain health problems are left untreated, the unhealthy situation can affect family members and even the entire community. Thus, many healing ceremonies treat the whole family or the whole community in an effort to restore balance and harmony in the group.

To reestablish harmony, one must explore and correct that which caused the disharmony—that is, the *why* of the illness or misfortune. It is thought that by understanding the *why,* not only can similar conditions be prevented, but also further damage can be avoided. In contrast, the goal of modern medicine, from the perspective of most Native Americans, is to treat the symptoms; that is, modern medicine addresses *how* a disease occurred (for example, a viral or bacterial infection) but not necessarily *why*. Within the conceptual framework of most Indian tribes, the *why* of an illness or misfortune may be either natural or supernatural, and the treatment or intervention must therefore utilize either natural or—with the help of a healer—supernatural resources.

The concept of harmony is symbolized and conceptualized in healing ceremonies by various tribes in a number of different ways. Harmony and balance are often conceptualized as a circle; for example, human development is often represented as a circle and not as a linear progression from birth to old age. Harmony or interrelatedness may also be represented in the context of Native American religious beliefs—the four cardinal directions, the four winds, or the four directions marking the medicine wheel. These four elements are also often represented as sources of energy, power, and knowledge. Sometimes sacred colors may represent such elements as fire, wind, water, and earth.

Although most tribes have their own terms for their traditional healers, *medicine man, medicine woman, practitioner,* and *shaman* are generic titles used by non-Indians to describe indigenous healers. (For example, the word *shaman* was borrowed from the Siberian Tungusic word *šaman,* which translates as "spiritual medicine man" or "one whose practice is primarily within the realm of the supernatural.")

Most indigenous healers, however, utilize a variety of treatment modalities, depending on whether the source of the illness is natural or supernatural. In addition, there are other important specialists or subspecialists in most tribes—herbalists, midwives, and diagnosticians. Some aid the healers, and others practice independently and may be called upon because of their expertise in such procedures as setting bones, treating wounds, making diagnoses, assisting with births, and making herbal medicines. Although the introduction of modern medicine has all but replaced many of the functions of these subspecialists, diagnosticians, herbalists, and traditional birth attendants are still active in some tribes.

For different tribes, the traditional healing system may range from a highly organized structure headed by full-time healers who preside over and coordinate a variety of ceremonial activities to an informal arrangement whereby a healer works part-time and is employed in other occupations when not treating patients. Comparable to priests or ministers, indigenous healers not only are sought in time of illness, but also are utilized to ensure protection or to bless a happy occasion.

When treating a patient, most healers work in the patient's home, where the healing ceremonies may be less public and involve primarily the patient and the patient's family. Depending on the tribe, the type of illness, and the type of intervention, some healing ceremonies may require a few minutes, while others require days; or a series of different ceremonies may be called for that can extend over a period of one or two years. In some instances, the preparation for a healing ceremony, such as a Sun Dance, may take months. And depending on the nature of the rituals or healing ceremonies, there may be more than one healer or one patient involved. The ceremony may require singers, dancers, drummers, persons who prepare ceremonial objects, persons who serve as mentors, and elders, who may help prepare the dancers. The fees for these ceremonies vary, but friends, family members, and the community generally help with the cost.

How a healer becomes designated as such varies from one tribe to the next, but in most instances a healer learns healing skills by serving an apprenticeship or by gaining membership in a healing society. Some are born into these medicine societies, but most acquire the knowledge from a senior practitioner. Depending on the complexity of the ceremonies and the healing skills to be learned, the training period may last from two to twenty years. For example, among the Ojibwas it often takes over twenty years for a healer to become a full-fledged member of the Midewiwin (or Grand Medicine) Society—a society to which only the most senior and experienced healers belong. In addition to studying and training, the candidates for the Midewiwin Society are expected to lead blameless lives that exemplify values such as honesty, bravery, and humility.

While ministering to the sick is often considered a curative role, most healers in Indian communities view themselves as guides or catalysts in the healing process. For example, through prayers, songs, and other related activities, healers help create an appropriate curative environment. In some healing ceremonies the preparation of such an environment may include the symbolic presence of helping deities in the form of masked dancers or pictorial images—for example, sand paintings. The appropriate healing environment may also call for the wearing of special garments or the use of special items or instruments such as drums or flutes. These items may be used to invite, accompany, or thank the helping spirits. Similarly, burning sage and sweet grass or "doing a sweat" in a sweat lodge may be used to purify the healing environment in preparation for the arrival of the helping deities.

While the use of modern medicine is the norm for most American Indians and Alaska Natives today, the renaissance of indigenous medicine in many Indian communities has been fostered by the development of health problems that cannot be cured or successfully treated by modern medicine. The renewed use of traditional interventions has also led to the adoption and borrowing between tribes of some of the popular modes of treatment, such as the use of sweat lodges and of "talking circles" (group therapy).

The increasing presence of incurable chronic health problems among Indian people has been attributed to an unhealthy lifestyle and inappropriate behavior. The high rates of accidents, suicide, and homicide among Native Americans, for example, have been attributed in part to the excessive and unhealthy use of alcohol. In other instances, the increased sedentary lifestyle, combined with diets high in fat and cholesterol, is considered a major cause of health problems associated with obesity such as non-insulin-dependent diabetes mellitus (NIDDM), cancer, and heart disease. Diabetes is endemic in some Indian tribes, with some communities reporting a 60 to 70 percent incidence of NIDDM in the population over the age of forty-five. The human cost of this disease is staggering, especially since significant numbers of those with NIDDM develop vascular complications that lead to cardiovascular diseases, blindness, amputation of limbs, or renal failure.

Because many chronic diseases are the result of an unhealthy lifestyle, culture has become an important variable in helping patients to manage such diseases and to prevent further complications. It is important to note, however, that chronic diseases are a new experience for many Native Americans. In fact, most tribal concepts of illness have historically focused on acute illnesses. Thus, the notion of managing a lifelong disease is a difficult concept for Native Americans to comprehend or accept. Moreover, the treatment of a number of these diseases requires a change in lifestyle and eating habits—a measure that seems strange to some, who find it difficult to understand how certain foods can contribute to poor health.

The increased availability of indigenous healing interventions has had many positive consequences. Patients are better able to find answers to such questions as why the disease or disability occurred. Furthermore, appropriate healing ceremonies can be conducted which provide patients with the peace of mind necessary to accept and to cope effectively with chronic health problems. Such interventions help reestablish harmony so that the physical health problem does not cripple the mind, the emotions, or the spirit of the individual.

Understandably, the increased use of indigenous healing practices has also been sparked by resistance to a number of proassimilation government policies. Thus, native healing concepts are especially evident in Indian communities where tribes have developed or assumed management of their own health programs. These tribal health programs emphasize the integration and use of culturally relevant modalities and interventions along with those offered by modern medicine. Such approaches include a central role for indigenous healers and healing ceremonies. In many instances, the recognition and appreciation of indigenous healing ways are also encouraged and supported by non-Indian health-care providers who seek to incorporate these ideas and interventions into the fabric of modern medicine.

The growing popularity and use of indigenous treatments among non-Indians, especially by members of the New Age movement, has sparked a growing resentment among many tribes against the use of Sun Dances, vision quests, sweat lodges, and other ceremonies by these non-Indian therapists. This resentment has resulted not only because of the commercialization and misuse of the rites, but also because these treatments are used primarily for self-exploration rather than for healing and for the good of a group.

See also Diseases; Impact of American Indian Civilizations on Europe and the World.

Adair, John, and Kurt Deuschle, *The People's Health: Medicine and Anthropology in a Navajo Community* (New York: Appleton-Century Crofts, 1970); Bahr, D. M., J. Gregoria, D. Lopez, and A. Alvarez, *Piman Shamanism and Staying Sickness* (Tucson: University of Arizona Press, 1974); Vogel, Virgil, *American Indian Medicine* (Norman: University of Oklahoma Press, 1970).

JENNIE R. JOE (Navajo)
University of Arizona

HENDRICK

(c. 1680–1755)
Mahican-Mohawk leader.

Mahican by birth, Hendrick (this is the form of the name most often seen in English-language sources; he was also known as Tee Yee Neen Ho Ga Row, Teoniahigarawe, Tiyanoga, White Head, Hendrick Peters, and King Hendrick) advanced to leadership among the Mohawks after his adoption into the Wolf clan. He is notable in history chiefly for his undeviating support of New York and the British crown against New France. While still a boy, he adopted Protestant Christianity, and rejected the solicitations of Jesuit missionaries.

Hendrick became prominent in 1710 as one of the so-called four kings taken to London by Colonel Francis Nicholson and Peter Schuyler who hoped that a visit by pro-British Indians would generate support for an English invasion of French Canada. The Indians were the sensation of fashionable society. Dressed in formal costume, they were presented to Queen Anne and had their portraits painted. (On a second visit to England in 1740, Hendrick was received and patronized by King George II.) The queen donated a silver communion service for a Mohawk chapel at Fort Hunter, near the predominantly Protestant Mohawk town of Tiononderoge, and the Society for the Propagation of the Gospel sent a missionary. But various factors prevented the projected invasion from taking place. Among other problems, Hendrick's Mohawk warriors were double-crossed by the Onondaga chief Teganissorens, who kept French authorities well informed of the English military's every mishap. Not for the first or last time, the Mohawks and the Onondagas pursued different policies in the course of their rivalry with each other.

Hendrick rose to special authority after the appointment of the merchant William Johnson as New York's agent in charge of Indian affairs. The chief's violently anti-French attitude fitted Johnson's policies as well. The pair seduced the Mohawks into a disastrous campaign against Montreal in 1747. Other Iroquois nations, following the Onondagas' lead, refused to join this ill-advised raid, which lost heavily when ambushed by the French and their Indian allies. Johnson resigned his provincial post in 1750, but he continued to profit from trade, and he maintained close ties with leading Mohawk families, including Hendrick's.

With Johnson out of office, the Mohawks became alienated from the policies and personnel of New York's Indian-affairs office. Commissioners in Albany made the critical decisions, and they were more concerned with acquiring Mohawk lands than with establishing friendly relations with Indian people. (Johnson himself picked up millions of acres of Indian territory, but his methods were less crude than the commissioners', and he respected the property of his Mohawk neighbors.)

In 1753, Hendrick led an angry delegation to announce at Albany that the Covenant Chain alliance, linking the colony to its Iroquois allies, had been broken. His declaration made a serious impression on the Lords of Trade and Plantations in London, who ordered a new interprovincial treaty in the Crown's own name to redress Hendrick's grievances and renew the alliance. This new agreement took place at the Albany Congress of 1754.

Virginia stayed away, and New York's governor, James De Lancey, was able to seize control of the congress for his own purposes. The Crown's interests were forgotten. In this contentious and unsettled atmosphere, Hendrick took the opportunity to impress the colonial delegates by flaunting Mohawk leadership of the Iroquois League and denigrating the Onondagas.

The Albany congress's much-touted scheme of interprovincial unity proposed by Benjamin Franklin was approved by no colony and not even considered by the Crown. The most substantial victors of the congress were William Johnson, who emerged as the Crown's direct agent in Iroquois affairs, and Johnson's old ally, Hendrick, now the dominant chief in the Iroquois League.

Much of the Albany congress's real business took place "in the bushes"—separately from the formal sessions. Pennsylvania's Conrad Weiser and Connecticut's John H. Lydius persuaded an assortment of Iroquois chiefs into signing deeds for lands in dispute between the two colonies. With full knowledge that these procedures violated Iroquois custom, and in association with signatories who had no right or authority, Hendrick signed both deeds. His political motive is not evident. He seems to have been among the men described by Weiser as "greedy for money." In due course, the lands thus deeded became the scene of the Pennamite Wars between Pennsylvania and Connecticut in the Wyoming Valley of the Susquehanna River.

In 1755, William Johnson was commissioned to campaign against the French outpost of Fort St.-Frédéric at Crown Point on Lake George. As before, Hendrick recruited a Mohawk contingent and led them personally into battle. He was always renowned for personal bravery, and he had gained a self-conception of overpowering self-importance. "We are the six confederate Indian nations," he proclaimed, "the Heads and Superiors of all Indian nations of the Continent of America." However, the Lake George battle became greatly confused, and Hendrick had grown old and fat. When his horse was killed under him, he was unable to flee and was himself killed.

See also Mohawk.

Jennings, Francis, *The Ambiguous Iroquois Empire* (New York: W.W. Norton & Co., 1988).

FRANCIS JENNINGS
University of North Carolina at Chapel Hill

HERDING AND RANCHING

For many American Indian communities, the care of livestock has been central not only to the workings of their economies but to the functioning of their cultures. Livestock, in the form of horses, cattle, sheep, and goats, came with the Europeans, but the herding of animals preceded this incursion. Native peoples had had long experience in the stalking, hunting, and driving of various animals—including antelope and deer. Nevertheless, horses, sheep, and cattle transformed the lives of many Indian nations. Although the Europeans brought these animals to the Americas, they could not keep them to themselves. Nor, in some instances, did they wish to do so. Missionaries laboring in what would become the American Southwest, for example, encouraged the herding of sheep and cattle as part of their program of acculturation. In time, the Indians embedded the acquisition of these animals in their own creation stories. The gods or the holy people provided horses, they said—not the Spaniards or the French or the English. Cultural heroes made great journeys to acquire the horses. On the Great Plains, native peoples would tell stories about how the cattle were created because one day the buffalo would no longer be there.

Such accounts speak to the cultural integration of livestock into the Indian world and remind us that, since the time of contact with the Europeans, Indians have shown a consistent ability to incorporate the unfamiliar into their societies. Nonetheless, some accommodation had to take place—Indians had not owned the deer or the antelope or the buffalo.

At the same time, ownership, for the Indians, did not always have to rest with the individual or exist for the exclusive benefit of the individual. Indians frequently found alternative methods of exercising ownership and control of their livestock. Ownership was often shared with family members or members of a particular clan. Animals could also be used to express community values: cattle might be given to a newly married couple, or sheep might be entrusted to the stewardship of young children. The meat of the animals could be employed to

Oglala Sioux riders herding buffalo during the 1992 spring roundup on the Slim Butte Game Range in South Dakota.

feed relatives or guests at social or religious gatherings. Singers or shamans could be paid with meat or with the animals themselves. And in demonstrating an ability to ride a horse well or to raise top-quality livestock, Indians could achieve recognition of individual performance in a culturally approved arena. In each of these dimensions, animals were valued for more than their strictly economic utility.

In the late nineteenth century, military defeat and confinement to reservations signaled a traumatic shift for Indian nations. On one reservation after another, livestock offered a way for individuals and communities to maintain identities and forge new ties. In many instances, livestock had already become a central feature in the economy and culture of a particular group; in the case of other groups, new initiatives were needed before animal husbandry could take hold.

Although sheep came to be a part of many Indian cultures, they are associated especially with the Navajos or Diné. After the Navajos were resettled on their reservation in 1868, they succeeded in expanding their land holdings and the size of their flocks of sheep. This increase, applauded by government agents and operators of trading posts, eventually led to problems with soil erosion—especially when the land base could no longer be readily expanded. But in the first few critical decades after 1868, sheep had fueled a kind of renaissance. Navajo weaving entered into dramatic new stages of design, and sheep fed the people, paid the religious leaders, and helped the children become a part of the Navajo world.

Prior to the Civil War, horses had been adopted by Indian groups all over North America. They had been used for raiding, war, transportation, and hunting. The end of buffalo hunts and war did not mean for Plains Indian men a loss of interest in or love for horses. Nor did the surrender of Geronimo and the end of the old days for the Comanches curtail comparable emotions for the Apaches or the Comanches. How could a life out of doors, a life on horseback, be continued?

The answer for many Indian communities came in the form of cattle ranching. For the Comanches, leaders such as Quanah Parker led the way through the acquisition of and shrewd dealing in cattle. On the San Carlos and White Mountain (Fort Apache) Reservations in Arizona, federal agents worked with tribal members to develop native livestock associations. In addition, they worked to limit and then to reduce the amount of reservation land leased to outsiders. In the southern part of the state, the Tohono O'odhams (Papagos) also engaged

in cattle ranching. They, too, competed with non-Indians for access to rangeland. In each of these instances, Indian communities made the raising of cattle a central dimension of their economy and society.

In the northern plains country, Indian cattle ranching had to take a somewhat different course. Unlike the Southwest, which had relatively few Anglo-American residents in the late nineteenth century, the northern plains had been the destination for many Anglo-Americans who sought land for farming and ranching during this era. Their demands for acreage aided the movement to confine Indians on reservations. Their use of what had been native land allowed their industry to expand. And their continuing need for more land prompted the General Allotment or Dawes Act of 1887 and other measures that fractured the Indian estate.

Nonetheless, the late nineteenth and early twentieth centuries witnessed the advent of Indian cattle ranching on the northern plains. The various Sioux reservations in the Dakotas achieved some good results in this pastime. So, too, did such Montana tribes as the Blackfeet, Crows, Northern Cheyennes, and Gros Ventres. The Hidatsas in North Dakota also became involved, as did the Northern Arapahos and Eastern Shoshones in Wyoming. This progress was often achieved in spite of federal preference for farming rather than ranching as well as the complications inherent in managing a reservation occupied by more than one tribe halting the encroachments of Anglo cattlemen. Many Indian cowboys also worked for non-Indian ranchers, both on and off Indian lands.

Such involvement spurred the evolution of Indian participation in rodeo. On reservations, occasions such as the Crow Fair gave rise to Native American rodeo. And in the larger arena of national rodeo competition, bronc riders such as Jackson Sundown (Nez Perce) and Sam Bird-in-Ground (Crow) quickly made their mark. Will Rogers (Cherokee) began his entertainment career as a roper—a skill he had picked up on his father's ranch in Oklahoma. This tradition has been carried on to the present day. The Indian National Rodeo attracts top-notch Indian cowboys from all over North America, who compete for generous amounts of prize money as well as prestige. Local communities throughout Indian country continue to sponsor their own rodeos. Children still learn to ride and rope at an early age and remain conscious of carrying on in the footsteps of older male and female relatives.

Since the 1920s, Indian ranchers have known many of the same complications and difficulties as their non-Indian counterparts. Concern about overgrazing prompted restrictions for both groups in the 1930s. Urbanization in the post–World War II West has meant state legislatures dominated by urban interests and a new generation of westerners who know little about farming or ranching. On some reservations, both the number of livestock and the number of people engaged in ranching have declined. However, the tradition remains important. Indian livestock persists, the animals the symbols of cultural identity, indications that Indian communities are here to stay.

See also Horses and Indians.

Getty, Harry, *The San Carlos Apache Cattle Industry* (Tucson: University of Arizona Press, 1963); Iverson, Peter, *When Indians Became Cowboys: Native Peoples and Cattle Ranching in the American West* (Norman: University of Oklahoma Press, 1994).

PETER IVERSON
Arizona State University

HEWITT, J. N. B.

(1859–1937)
Tuscarora ethnologist and linguist.

John Napoleon Brinton Hewitt, the son of Harriet Brinton and David Brainard Hewitt, was born on December 16, 1859, on the Tuscarora Indian Reservation in western New York State. His mother was of Tuscarora, French, English, and Oneida descent. His father, of Scottish and English descent, had been orphaned as a boy, adopted into a Tuscarora family on the Tuscarora Reservation, and raised as an Indian. John was taught to read and write English by his parents, and although both parents spoke fluent Tuscarora, they did not teach it to their children. Not until he was eleven and entered the district school did John begin to learn the Tuscarora language from his classmates. Five years later, he entered the union school in Wilson, New York, where he studied for two years, and then the union school in Lockport, New York. Overstudy and a case of sunstroke, however, so affected his health that he was unable to finish his last term. He returned to the reservation, becoming a farmer and newspaper correspondent, and establishing a private night school for Tuscarora men. And on the reservation he might have remained had it not been for Erminnie A. Smith.

In 1880, supported by the Bureau of Ethnology (which later became the Bureau of American Ethnolo-

gy), Smith set out to study the Iroquois languages and to collect Iroquois myths and tales. On the suggestion of the noted anthropologist Lewis H. Morgan she went to the Tuscarora Reservation, where she met Hewitt and hired him as her assistant for the summer. He continued in that capacity for the next five years. After Smith died in 1886, Hewitt applied for a position at the bureau to complete the work he and Smith had been engaged in: a Tuscarora-English dictionary. He was hired as an ethnologist, and retained this title until his death fifty-one years later.

At the bureau Hewitt continued his study of Indian languages and myths, especially those of the Iroquois, begun under Smith. These were also the particular interests of John Wesley Powell, who had established the bureau in 1879 and was its director until his death in 1902. Powell saw the classification of North American Indian languages as one of the primary tasks of the bureau, and, not unexpectedly, a number of papers Hewitt wrote while Powell was director concerned this subject. In an unpublished one, written a year after his joining the bureau, Hewitt established the relationship of Cherokee to the Iroquois languages, a connection long suspected but not fully proven. In 1893 he wrote two papers, both also unpublished, on the relationship between the Sahaptian (Shahaptian), Waiilatpuan, and Lutuamian language families—what he termed the Shahapwailutan family (now known as Plateau Penutian). In another unpublished paper, he tested and rejected the idea of a relationship between the Mayan and Polynesian languages. For the anthropologist William John McGee, he compared Seri to the Yuman and Waicurian languages, finding no relationship between them. Among the other papers Hewitt published in his early years at the bureau are his neglected "Polysynthesis in the Languages of the American Indians" and, perhaps his best-known article, "Orenda and a Definition of Religion"; both appeared in the journal *American Anthropologist*. After Powell's death, much of the attention of the bureau staff was directed at completing the bureau's two-volume *Handbook of American Indians North of Mexico,* for which Hewitt wrote a number of entries.

Probably Hewitt's most significant contributions are his transcriptions in the Iroquois languages, and corresponding English translations, of the ritual speeches and traditions—the great oral texts—that serve to define the cultures of so-called nonliterate societies such as the Iroquois much as do written texts in "literate" ones. These include the Iroquois origin myth (the cosmology), the traditional account of the founding of the League of the Iroquois, and the speeches of the condolence ceremony held for the purpose of installing chiefs of the league. The two major publications resulting from Hewitt's interest in mythology are "Iroquois Cosmology" and "Seneca Fiction, Legends, and Myths." Both appeared in the *Annual Reports of the Bureau of American Ethnology;* the latter work, a collection compiled by Jeremiah Curtin and Hewitt, was edited by Hewitt.

Present-day linguists hold Hewitt's linguistic work in high regard. He was almost obsessive about being accurate, constantly revising his manuscripts. This quality drove him to an understanding of the Iroquois languages he might not have had otherwise. But it also made him notoriously slow to finish writing up his materials, and much of his research remains unpublished.

Consciously or unconsciously, he may have intended it to be so. Hewitt was, after all, an Indian living and working in the white world (most of the employees of the bureau were white) and writing about Indians. He was also a devout Christian studying non-Christian beliefs as a means of increasing the Indians' own sense of self-esteem. When he was hired by the bureau there were no anthropologists holding a Ph.D. in the discipline. This changed in the next few decades, and Hewitt found himself an "amateur" (without formal training) in a field dominated by "professionals" (those who had had graduate training). By continuing to study Iroquois languages and cultures, but not publishing his results, Hewitt solved—after a fashion—the dilemma of his situation. By recording Iroquois traditions, he preserved them; by not publishing them, he preserved them from criticism by others. (Hewitt's papers, including his unpublished manuscripts, are to be found in the National Anthropological Archives, at the Smithsonian Institution.)

Hewitt joined the Anthropological Society of Washington a year after moving to Washington, D.C.; he served as its treasurer from 1912 to 1926 and as its president from 1932 to 1934. He was a charter member of the American Anthropological Association and of the Society of American Indians. From 1918 until his death he was the Smithsonian Institution's representative on the U.S. Board of Geographic Names. Hewitt was a member of the Ingram Memorial Congregational Church until 1925, when he joined All Souls Unitarian Church.

Hewitt married twice, both times to non-Indian women. His first wife, whose name is not known, died in 1918. In 1925 he married Carrie Louise Hurlbut, who survived him. Hewitt died on October 14, 1937, at the age of seventy-eight.

See also Iroquoian Languages; Tuscarora.

Baldwin, Marie L. B., "John N. B. Hewitt, Ethnologist," *Quarterly Journal of the Society of American Indians* 2 (1914): 147–50; Swanton, John R., "John Napoleon Brinton Hewitt," *American Anthropologist* 40 (1938): 286–90.

ELISABETH TOOKER
Temple University

HIAWATHA

(flourished c. 1570)
Legendary Mohawk founder of the Iroquois Confederacy.

The first sketchy European references to Hiawatha date from the seventeenth century, but the earliest complete account of his life comes from the Mohawk leader Joseph Brant, who wrote about Hiawatha in the early nineteenth century. Since then, Iroquois storytellers have related many versions of the legend. Hiawatha's name was appropriated by Henry Wadsworth Longfellow in his 1855 poem *The Song of Hiawatha.* However, Longfellow's poem, set in the Great Lakes area, has almost nothing to do with the historic figure of Hiawatha.

There are dozens of stories recounting the founding of the Five Nations of the Iroquois. (The original Five Nations were the Mohawks, Oneidas, Onondagas, Cayugas, and Senecas. A sixth nation, the Tuscaroras, joined the confederacy in 1712.) Contemporary scholars date the beginning of the confederacy to the early to middle fifteenth century. According to one version, "Everywhere there was peril and everywhere mourning" in Iroquoia. "Feuds with outer nations and feuds with brother nations, feuds of sister towns and feuds of families and of clans made every warrior a stealthy man who liked to kill." Hiawatha was one such man. Living in isolation as a cannibal, Hiawatha waylaid unsuspecting travelers and ate their flesh. One day, as Hiawatha prepared another victim for his cooking pot, he glanced into the pot and saw a face in it. The face belonged to the spiritual figure Deganawida, who convinced Hiawatha to throw away the body of his victim and eat venison in its place. Hiawatha vowed to atone for the deaths he had caused by spreading Deganawida's message throughout Iroquoia.

Having experienced a spiritual and moral transformation, Hiawatha went among the Mohawks preaching a message of peace. He married and had a family. But he was opposed in his mission by the Onondaga leader Tadadaho. Tadadaho and others who were unconverted killed Hiawatha's daughters, and in his grief Hiawatha returned to the woods. Still accompanied by Deganawida, Hiawatha created a string of shells known as wampum. (In some versions, the string is made of elderberry rushes; in others, of bird quills.) Hiawatha's plan for Iroquois revitalization was symbolized by this wampum belt—a "chain" connecting the Five Nations. The wampum belt was used as a universal language by the Five Nations to convey messages of war and of peace.

Hiawatha again went among the people of the Five Nations, this time convincing them of the need to end blood violence among themselves and to join together in peace. Eventually, Tadadaho himself was convinced by Hiawatha and his converts to end the violence and to form a league based on internal peace and respect for ancestors, warriors, clan mothers, kin, and community. It was at Onondaga, Tadadaho's homeland, that the council fires of the Five Nations were eventually held. Besides the wampum belt, which depicted the Five Nations, with Onondaga at its center, the league was further represented by the longhouse; these structures housed the extended families of the various nations. Each longhouse provided shelter for a clan mother and her daughters and their families. Hence, the matrilineal/matrilocal clan was understood to be linked to the harmony and kinship of the various Iroquois nations.

Hiawatha's role as peacemaker also led him to devise a way for the Iroquois to ease their suffering during times of loss without resorting to revenge. He preached that a condolence ceremony should serve in place of violence to relieve the suffering of an affected family. According to the seventeenth-century Frenchman Joseph Lafitau, members of a deceased person's household were to cut their hair and smear their faces with dirt or ashes and engage in a ten-day ritual of mourning, during which time they would be "excused from every duty of civility and courtesy." The longer grieving process took a year. The principles of mourning required members of other clans to "cover" the grief of the afflicted family by conducting feasts and ceremonies and by giving gifts known as condolence presents.

If the condolence ceremony was not enough, another strategy was available—one that involved a "requickening" ceremony in which a deceased person's family would adopt someone in order to replace the loved one in the family. If the victim was someone of high status, someone of a lower rank from within the clan or village often would fill the vacant position. However, if the deceased was of lower status, family members would look outside the Five Nations for a replacement; hence emerged the *mourning war*, in which members of the Five Nations waged war on an outside group specifically to gain captives. Sometimes outside captives would be ritually killed to allow the bereaved family to vent its grief. At other times, the captives were "adopted" into the clan and given the name and social role of the dead family member. It is interesting to note that the adoptee did not need to be of the same gender as the deceased. One famous Seneca adoptee from the eighteenth century, Mary Jemison, was taken to replace a male in a clan. Jemison did not perform the social role of a male, however; she performed women's tasks.

Hiawatha's old age and death are unrecorded, but his strategies, in which warfare became a way of venting emotion and of replacing deceased members of Five Nations clans, lived on. They helped the Iroquois Confederacy become one of the most populous and most powerful indigenous groups in the eastern part of North America. The ethic of internal peace established by Hiawatha remained with the Five Nations (and, later, Six Nations) until the American Revolution split them apart. The Iroquois League presented a united front against European invaders throughout the era of colonization. In addition, the social and spiritual revitalization articulated by Hiawatha foreshadowed later Iroquois revitalizations, most notably the movement led by the Seneca prophet Handsome Lake in the nineteenth century.

The Iroquois nations have continually found ways to meet the challenges facing them. The founding of the Iroquois Confederacy under Hiawatha was the first of many such creative adaptations.

See also Deganawida; Iroquois Confederacy.

Parker, Arthur C., *Parker on the Iroquois* (Syracuse: Syracuse University Press, 1968); Richter, Daniel K., *Ordeal of the Longhouse: The Peoples of the Iroquois League in the Era of European Colonization* (Chapel Hill: University of North Carolina Press, 1992); Wallace, Anthony F. C., *The Death and Rebirth of the Seneca* (New York: Alfred A. Knopf, 1970).

KATHRYN A. ABBOTT
University of Massachusetts at Amherst

HIDATSA

The Hidatsas, or *Nuxbaaga* ("Original People" as they call themselves) of the main division of Hidatsas, trace their origins from the point of their emergence from what is now called Devil's Lake in eastern North Dakota. The archaeological record indicates that the Hidatsas had established settlements on the Knife River at its confluence with the Missouri by the early 1600s. The early semisedentary culture of these farmers and bison hunters rested on the cultivation of corn, beans, squash, and tobacco. These commodities marked the Hidatsa villages as major indigenous trading centers of the Great Plains. The first written accounts of Hidatsa life by nonnatives began with the geographer David Thompson's 1797 narratives, which were written after the Hidatsa "River Crows" split from the "Mountain Crows" of present-day Montana.

By 1804, the year Lewis and Clark visited the earth-lodge villages on the Upper Missouri, the Hidatsas distinguished among three independent groups: the Awatixas, the Awaxawis, and the Hidatsas proper. Of these, the Hidatsas proper occupied the largest village site on the Knife River; the Awatixas lived in a smaller settlement on the opposite side of the river. The Awaxawis, the smallest Hidatsa group, maintained an independent village several miles south of the other two groups. Distinctions among these autonomous groups had implications for exogamous social arrangements and trade relations. After population losses following an 1834 attack by the Dakota and a smallpox epidemic in 1837, the three Hidatsa groups merged with the Mandans at Like-A-Fishhook Village in 1845. The Arikaras joined them in 1856.

The Fort Laramie Treaty of 1851 described the boundaries of Hidatsa territory as reaching from the Missouri River as far west as the Yellowstone. By 1910, subsequent treaty abrogations reduced this land base to 640,000 acres. The Fort Berthold reservation was established by executive order in 1891, but it was not until the provisions of the 1934 Indian Reorganization Act that the Mandans, Hidatsas, and Arikaras incorporated as the Three Affiliated Tribes. Despite particular features of shared history, there remain distinct linguistic and cultural differences among the three tribes.

Hidatsa society is matrilineal. Hidatsas say that a person comes into the world through his or her mother's clan, and leaves through the father's clan. By this they mean that the mother's clan bestows membership and belonging, whereas the father's clan confers differential rights and responsibilities. In general, clan relations structure ceremonial and social behavior by prescribing individual participation in life-cycle events, such as naming ceremonies, funerals, and the War Bonnet Dances which involve selected clan children each spring.

Hidatsa kinship shares many features with Mandan social organization; Hidatsa and Mandan clans belong to one of two remaining divisions, the Three Clan (*Naginawi*) and the Four Clan (*Nagitopa*). Hidatsas generally agree that the Three Clan comprises the Knife, Alkali Lodge, and Low Cap clans and that the Four Clan is made up of the Waterbuster, Prairie Chicken, Wide Ridge (extinct), and Dirt or Mud Dripping clans. This system, described at length by the anthropologist Alfred Bowers, appears to be what remains of a moiety system that operated in the late eighteenth century as the thirteen-clan system of the Awatixas and the seven-clan system of the Awaxawis and Hidatsas proper. While Mandan assimilation with Hidatsa forms of social organization allows a treatment of the two divisions as a unitary system, tribal members distinguish between "Mandan" and "Hidatsa" cultural identity.

Among the Hidatsas, kinship is actively constructed to assert shared group identity and cultural history. Thus origin stories related to the thirteen-clan system, such as the story of Charred Body, are told as a means of relaying cultural history by establishing ancestral relationships to specific cultural and sacred sites in North Dakota. Society bundles, as representative objects that embody cultural origins, reinforce group identity and symbolically anchor kinship ties by marking and ceremonially activating ritual relationships. Cultural knowledge associated with these collective rites is carefully monitored and guarded.

In previous times, Hidatsa age-graded societies regulated the transmission of ritual knowledge and in general structured Hidatsa society by prescribing cultural norms. For example, the Black Mouth Society was a male warrior society whose members policed the activities of the village. Women's age-graded societies likewise directed the comportment of girls, who were inducted into one of the Holy Women societies at appropriate junctures in the life cycle. Contemporary Hidatsas abide by these rules in modified forms, and several societies, such as the Antelope, Kit Fox, and Enemy Women, remain active today.

The Hidatsas share common historical linkages with the Mandans and Arikaras, including twentieth-century upheavals and adjustments caused by construction of the Garrison Dam. Built in 1951 by the Army Corps of Engineers, this dam had an immense impact on the Three Affiliated Tribes, one nearly equal in severity to the 1837 smallpox epidemic that reduced the Hidatsas to near cultural extinction. In addition to flooding and destroying the three tribes' fertile bottomlands, the dam fractured communities and separated them across wide distances. People who were once neighbors now live surrounded by immense lakes that cut them off from one another. Nonetheless, Hidatsas continue to travel around the water from their communities in Mandaree, Four Bears, Shell Creek, Lucky Mound (Parshall), and New Town.

Community segments, such as those at Shell Creek and Mandaree, maintain distinct orientations as "Hidatsa" sites of residence and cultural history. Community celebrations at Mandaree (West Segment) and Little Shell (North Segment) attest to Hidatsa solidarity. Drum groups, such as the Mandaree Singers, affirm cultural continuity and innovation. The Hidatsas retain the most tribal members at Fort Berthold and actively speak their native language in the greatest numbers. Elder Hidatsa speakers teach language classes at Fort Berthold Community College, which also sponsors community mentor programs in tribal languages. In addition, the New Town public school offers computer-based Hidatsa-language instruction.

Recent gains in the legislative arena have added to a renewed sense of social and cultural revitalization. For example, testimonies given by tribal members as part of the 1986 Joint Tribal Advisory Committee provided evidence for just compensation awards for lands taken from the tribes for the Garrison Dam project. The 1988 Indian Gaming Regulatory Act made it possible for the Three Affiliated Tribes to open the Four Bears Casino at Fort Berthold in 1992. The revenues generated there are targeted for community-development programs that hold the promise of increasing economic autonomy and tribal sovereignty for the Hidatsa Nation and the Three Affiliated Tribes.

See also Arikara (Sahnish); Mandan.

Bowers, Alfred W., *Hidatsa Social and Ceremonial Organization* (Washington, D.C.: Smithsonian Institution, 1965; reprint, with an Introduction by Douglas R. Parks, Lincoln: University of Nebraska Press, 1993); Gilman, Carolyn, and Mary Jane Schneider, *On the Way to Independence: Memories of a Hidatsa Indian Family, 1840–1920* (St. Paul: Minnesota Historical Society, 1987).

TRESSA L. BERMAN
Arizona State University West
and National Museum of Natural History

HILL 57

Hill 57, named for a prominent local hilltop sign that advertised fifty-seven varieties of pickles, is located on the northwest side of Great Falls, Montana. It began as a squatters' village of mixed-blood Indians who moved to the area in search of work, but has persisted as the most visible community of "unrecognized" Indians in the United States. Never housing more than a few hundred people, Hill 57 came to symbolize urban Indian poverty and caused officials in Montana and elsewhere to rethink their support for the termination of federal relationships with native people.

The families who lived at Hill 57 came from two different refugee groups that migrated into Montana in the late nineteenth century. These groups were the Métis—mixed-blood Ojibwa and Cree societies descended from the fur-trader communities of eastern and central Canada—and the Little Shell band of Ojibwas, who migrated west from the Turtle Mountain Reservation in North Dakota.

During the 1940s and 1950s, the living conditions at the Hill 57 settlement were crowded and unsanitary, shocking local politicians, social workers, and journalists. Owning no land, controlling no resources, without schools, and discriminated against by the surrounding white and reservation communities, the families of Hill 57 struggled to survive in homemade dwellings. In 1957 Montana senator James E. Murray petitioned the Bureau of Indian Affairs to designate Hill 57 as a reservation, but federal officials replied that the people should enroll themselves at existing reservations or relocate to a different urban area. Eventually many of the families moved into the city of Great Falls or to other Montana towns. Today only a few families live on Hill 57, with their descendants once again scattered over Montana. Their presence continues to remind their neighbors of the Indian people who remain invisible to both government officials and the general public.

HISTORIANS AND INDIANS

Until quite recently, the concept of race has run through all histories of North American Indians. Invariably, scholars have portrayed Indians as inherently inferior to Europeans. This perceived inferiority is sometimes ascribed to divine predestination, sometimes to a lack of the capacity to learn the arts of civilization, sometimes to an inability to live in the presence of civilized Europeans. English writings labeled these variously conceived inferiorities first as heathenism, then as the legacy of hereditary race characteristics. Throughout this conceptual change, the idea persisted that Indians were savage creatures of the wilderness, in contrast and antagonism to the "civil" society of Europeans.

In its most mature manifestation, the theme of savagery versus civilization was expressed by the nineteenth-century amateur historian Francis Parkman, and later reduced to the formula of "the Frontier" by the leading professional scholar of the early twentieth century, Frederick Jackson Turner. Faith in native "savagery" persisted throughout much of the twentieth century in the compilations of frontier phenomena produced by Turner's disciple Ray Allen Billington and his successors.

The interpretation of established data is every historian's right and duty. Turner's method of interpretation, however, was to force facts to fit his preconceived notions of American development. Thus, for example, he included the state of Maine—the easternmost place in the United States—as part of his "Frontier West." Ignoring the multitude of data that show peoples of various cultures mixing, doing business and intermarrying with each other in vast frontier areas stretching across jurisdictions, Turner invented a barrier of perpetual hostility—"a line between civilization and savagery"—and sorted all those phenomena on one side or the other of the line. He called this imaginary construction "the Frontier," and the power of semantics is demonstrated by the way his invention displaced the facts. As a rationale and justification for European conquest, the general concept of a line between enemies long antedated Turner's formulation. In America this line traditionally separated European-based "civilizations" from native societies. Viewed in this way, Indian peoples were inevitably portrayed as less than human.

Not surprisingly, then, one can trace the abolition of Indian humanity back to Captain John Smith and the Reverend Samuel Purchas, whose seventeenth-century propaganda in behalf of the Virginia Company has been enormously influential among historians. Smith denounced the Chesapeake Powhatans as "cruel beasts" with "a more unnaturall brutishness than beasts." His comparison with predatory animals remains to the present day a favorite device to dehumanize Indians. Purchas went a step further. Before the Powhatans' 1622 uprising, he had boasted of how Virginians had conciliated the savages, but after hostilities erupted Purchas converted the Indians into nonpersons. They became "like Cain, both Murtherers and Vagabonds," and therefore, "I can scarcely call [them] inhabitants." This concept was so convenient for ideological purposes that it has been perpetuated in the concept of the "vanishing Indian."

One can also trace these concepts to Massachusetts's colonial governor John Winthrop, Sr., whose *History of New England* (2 vols., 1825–26) underlies most subsequent publications about that region. Winthrop believed that divine providence must be presented "according to truth with due weight," and he achieved due weight by omission of sources reflecting Indian understandings. Roger Williams deviated from Winthrop's war propaganda by writing *A Key into the Language of America,* which is still regarded as an excellent source for the culture and society of the Narragansetts. But Williams was exceptional in New England, where a litany of hate was continued by Judge Samuel Penhallow, somewhat cynically delivered by the Unitarian clergyman George Edward Ellis, and raised to a shriek of invective by Ellis's successor, John Gorham Palfrey.

Though less noticed, a countervailing tradition grew from Dutch sources in Albany and from the Quakers of Philadelphia. This alternative view of native life, exemplified by William Penn's accurate and still useful descriptions of the Delaware Indians, grew naturally out of the accommodationist policies in colonial New Netherland, New York, and Pennsylvania. The Moravian missionaries at nearby Bethlehem were also influential. The Moravians dealt with their Indian converts very differently from Massachusetts's self-centered proselytizer John Eliot, whose writings were designed to extract donations from English religionists. In contrast, the Moravian John Heckewelder's accounts of Delaware tradition were consulted and published by the American Philosophical Society and remain a reliable source of information.

Farther south, the Virginian William Beverley reported broken tribes in the eighteenth century with a notable degree of accuracy and sympathy. The South Carolinian John Lawson teased European men with accounts of susceptible Indian maidens in the Carolinas. James Adair traded from South Carolina among several tribes, his favorite being the Chickasaws, among whom he settled and married. Adair's *History of the American Indians* (1775) gives eyewitness testimony, but fits it into a thesis of Indians being the lost tribe of Israel.

In the nineteenth century these racist characterizations were given a scientific veneer as historians blended the pseudoscience of social Darwinism into their writings. Social Darwinism postulated that the races could be ranked (from greater to lesser levels of savagery or civilization) according to natural intrinsic qualities. Early anthropologists, assuming that their object of study was this hierarchy of "races," contributed heavily to the Spencerian project of distinguishing the "fit" from the "unfit" in the "struggle for existence."

Indians, of course, were determined to be unfit. Thus Lewis Henry Morgan, often called the founder of American anthropology, thought that Indians were so passionately devoted to "the hunter life" that "the red race has never risen, or can rise above its present level." Nature had created Europeans as "the highest type of mankind," which has "proved its intrinsic superiority by gradually assuming the control of the earth." Happily, anthropology matured, and under the tutelage of Franz Boas anthropologists became among the first to reject social Darwinism as a model for human evolution. Other social scientists were not so rigorous. Morgan was consulted avidly by the historian Francis Parkman, who was seeking "scientific" support for his white-supremacist doctrines, and by commentators like John Wesley Powell, who advocated mass irrigation projects to "develop" the "wastelands" then inhabited by western Indians.

By the late nineteenth century, writing about Indians was dominated by "reformers" who accepted the "savage" formulation but who campaigned to "save" the Indians through "assimilating" them to white standards. These scholars always demanded fair treatment for native peoples but never investigated how the Indians themselves understood the world. Prominent among writers of this genre was Helen Hunt Jackson, whose *Century of Dishonor* (1881) and the fictional *Ramona* (1884) substituted sentimentality and good intentions for reality and substantive engagement with native people.

Midway into the twentieth century, various influences created an explosion of new literature, only a small sampling of which can be given here. The 1950 "Needs and Opportunities" conference sponsored by the Institute of Early American History and Culture at Williamsburg, Virginia, directed historians' attention to the neglected arena of native scholarship. The American Society for Ethnohistory was founded soon after, in 1954, and has since published a quarterly journal and held annual conferences devoted almost exclusively to the American Indian. In 1972, the Newberry Library founded its D'Arcy McNickle Center for the History of the American Indian; aided by the National

Endowment for the Humanities, the center has supported research for dozens of books written by fellowship recipients. The Smithsonian Institution is gradually publishing *Handbook of North American Indians,* a "handbook" planned for twenty volumes, which when completed will be indispensable in its field. In addition, a number of universities have established Indian-studies centers, and the Smithsonian has committed itself to establishing a National Museum of the American Indian.

Notice must also be given to Oxford University Press for following the excellent example of the *Canadian National Biography,* which has taken pains to include native individuals in historical context; when completed, Oxford's *American National Biography* will include an unprecedented number of native profiles. Beginning publication in 1932, the University of Oklahoma Press's continuing series "The Civilization of the American Indian" now includes more than two hundred titles and has done for tribal cultures what other presses have done for native persons. This effort has been supplemented by additional focused series on the Indian past by the university presses of Nebraska and Arizona and by Cambridge University Press.

These new outlets demonstrate a radical change in scholarly outlook, exemplified further by whole new fields of study. The confirmable phenomena of cultures are replacing the malign inventions of race. In place of Samuel Purchas's dismissal of Indians as nonpersons, we now have demographers trying to estimate native populations before European invasion and what happened to those populations' descendants. Instead of tales of bloodthirsty savages, we now have studies of Indians' commerce, both intertribal and intersocial. Instead of being looked upon as "degenerate halfbreeds," the synthetic offspring of mixed liaisons appear in new studies of fur-trade society and of Canada's Métis population. People once thought to worship the devil appear today in studies of missions, native religions, and contextualized episodes of revival and religious renewal.

Instead of histories of savages who wandered over the land rather than inhabiting it, we have exhaustive accounts of land tenure and the purposeful manipulation of natural resources. And what were once considered mere savage "shacks" are now displayed as ingenious architectural responses to varied environments. Instead of an imaginary "Frontier," there now exist detailed studies of particular tribes and of complex interactions in the continent's many regions. Once thought to have "no government worthy of the name," Indian tribes are now studied intensively in relation to policies between themselves and Euro-American governments, allowing sovereignty to resurface publicly as a living issue.

Unfortunately, little of this deluge of new scholarship has made an impression on the historical profession at large or the authors of school history texts. The sheer bulk of this work calls mainstream historians with professional consciences to turn away from standard racist mythology and join in the construction of a history worthy of our collective past.

See also Native American Studies; Savage, Savages, Savagism.

Jennings, Francis, *The Founders of America* (New York: W. W. Norton and Co., 1993); Jennings, Francis, and William R. Swagerty, eds., Newberry Library Center for the History of the American Indian Bibliographical Series, 30 vols. (Bloomington: Indiana University Press, 1979–82); Hurtado, Albert L., and Peter Iverson, eds., *Major Problems in American Indian History* (Lexington, Mass.: D. C. Heath and Co., 1994).

FRANCIS JENNINGS
University of North Carolina at Chapel Hill

HOGAN

A traditional house of the Navajo Indians, the hogan exists in several different styles. The earliest type of hogan was called the *forked-stick hogan* and was made from wooden poles shaped in a conical form and covered with mud. Other styles include the rounded and the hexagonal hogan, which are usually made of wood and mud—resources the land can easily supply. The hexagonal hogan, which normally has six sides but can have as many as eight, started to appear around 1900. It emerged with the advent of railroads, which brought a ready supply of railroad ties to hogan builders. Whereas some hogans (especially those in Chaco Canyon) use stone, more permanent dwellings were not routinely adopted by a culture that frequently abandoned homes after the death of a family member or changed residences to exploit new grazing areas.

Hogans have one round room, usually not more than twenty-five feet in diameter. They are used not only for family housing but also for ceremonial purposes. Use is specifically prescribed by the Holy People, who built the first hogans of turquoise, white shell, jet, or abalone shell. The door must always face the rising sun, women must sit on the north side and men on the south, and medicine men and other dignitaries must sit at the west facing the door. Most hogans are consecrated with rituals and the sprinkling of corn pollen before they are used.

See also Architecture.

HOLE-IN-THE-DAY (BUGONAGESHIG)

(1828?–68)
Minnesota Ojibwa political leader.

Hole-in-the-Day was probably born at the Ojibwa village of Sandy Lake, in present-day Minnesota, to parents who exemplified the complex nature of Ojibwa political leadership. His mother, Josephine (?) (her Ojibwa name is not known), was a daughter of Broken Tooth, a Sandy Lake civil leader. His father, Hole-in-the-Day the Elder, was a war leader. The Ojibwas felt that civil leaders and war leaders served complementary functions, but they expected the unruly and confrontational war leaders to remain secondary in influence to the deliberative, responsible, elderly civil leaders.

Early in his life, Hole-in-the-Day gained an appreciation of the issues confronting the Ojibwas when he attended intervillage political meetings with his father in the 1830s and 1840s. These same issues would prove enduring, engaging Hole-in-the-Day's generation twenty years later as well. Relations with the United States preoccupied Ojibwa leaders of both generations. The Ojibwas had enjoyed friendly relations with the earlier French and British populations, based on the mutually satisfactory fur trade. Concerned Ojibwas realized, however, that the United States was committed to sedentary agriculture—a drastically different kind of land use that threatened their ability to retain control of their traditional homelands.

Ojibwa leaders believed they could avoid subordination to the United States by restructuring their economy to place more reliance on agriculture and less on hunting and trapping. Avoiding economic dependence would protect them from Euro-American pressures to cede additional land or remove themselves from Minnesota altogether. Cultural and political autonomy would flow from this position of economic strength.

With his father's death in 1847, Hole-in-the-Day emerged as a leader. He firmly supported the plan to restructure the Ojibwa economy and established his own farm. Very quickly, however, Hole-in-the-Day came to

Hole-in-the-Day in 1858.

view the U.S. federal Indian policy as misconceived, as creating conditions that sabotaged rather than supported the Ojibwa efforts at self-sufficiency.

Hole-in-the-Day's evolving thinking was reflected at the negotiations that produced the Treaty of 1855, by which the Ojibwas ceded the majority of their Minnesota lands for the generous-sounding sum of ten thousand dollars plus annual payments of twenty thousand dollars in cash, goods, and services for twenty years. Hole-in-the-Day fought hard for an alternative that he believed would lay the foundations necessary for the Ojibwas to reorient their economy. The Ojibwas, he argued, needed large lump sums that would enable them to build a costly and complex infrastructure of roads, houses, barns, and cleared fields. They needed farming equipment, plus knowledge of agricultural technology and animal husbandry. The government's offer amounted to only four dollars per person per year, a figure clearly inadequate for funding a major

economic transformation. Despite his forceful arguments, however, Hole-in-the-Day was unable to persuade the Euro-American negotiators to comply.

The Treaty of 1855 proved disastrous, as Hole-in-the-Day had foreseen. Euro-American settlement destroyed the habitat of game and fur-bearing animals, so the Ojibwas could neither feed themselves nor collect enough pelts to exchange for food. The remaining land base was broken up into small, separate reservations, inadequate for launching a farming revolution. The Ojibwas slid rapidly into poverty.

The disastrous effects of the 1855 treaty badly eroded Ojibwa confidence in their civil leaders. Hole-in-the-Day, who once observed that he had trouble sleeping because of his distress over the treaty's failure to provide economic security, also reevaluated existing Ojibwa policy. Increasingly, many Ojibwas advocated a more confrontational approach toward the United States; not surprisingly, many warriors supported this approach. In the calls for armed resistance, Hole-in-the-Day saw a strategy that, he hoped, would win for the Ojibwas what their treaties had not. He cultivated the support of the warriors, and began building a new political coalition. Central to his coalition were two influential groups: non-Indian fur traders, and the bicultural, bilingual mixed-blooded (or Métis) population.

On August 18, 1862, Hole-in-the-Day put his strategy to the test: he declared war on the United States. Ojibwa warriors targeted Euro-American property but avoided taking lives, a situation that distinguished them sharply from the Minnesota Dakotas, who also took up arms in 1862, and spilled American blood. The bloodlessness of the Ojibwa conflict seemingly explains the relatively mild American reaction, especially when contrasted to the vehemence with which they prosecuted Dakotas for alleged war crimes. Hole-in-the-Day's bicultural allies also figured importantly in the war's outcome, acting as liaisons with Euro-American officials, emphasizing Ojibwa forbearance but warning that American intransigence might compel them to follow the Dakotas' example. By this combination of efforts, the militant strategy succeeded. Supported by warriors representing several villages, Hole-in-the-Day negotiated a new treaty in 1864 meant to create the conditions the Ojibwas needed to underwrite their economic transformation. His success brought him enormous prestige and power. It also won for him the enmity of many civil leaders, who feared his personal ambitions. More significantly, many Ojibwas besides these civil leaders saw Hole-in-the-Day's warrior-dominated power base as an enormous threat to the very nature of the Ojibwa political order.

Hole-in-the-Day was assassinated on June 27, 1868, by warriors from the village of the Leech Lake. The assassins' identities were widely known, but they were never prosecuted. Evidently, Hole-in-the-Day's family feared that if they exacted kin revenge, they would touch off a dangerous cycle of retaliatory killings. (No American law at the time applied to Indian-Indian crimes.) Controversy has continued to surround Hole-in-the-Day's death, with allegations repeatedly surfacing that he was killed because he could not be bought or controlled.

Hole-in-the-Day married polygynously, the matches designed to create ties between important families. Four spouses can be identified with certainty; records regarding the children of these unions are contradictory. His first wife's name is unknown, and apparently none of the children of this marriage survived childhood. He also wed Jun-du-je-way-be-quay, or Mary Isabelle (?); their children probably were Isabella, Minogishig (Ignatius), O-be-sau (Ida), and Ke-we-to-be-quay (Lucy). His third wife was O-dun-ew, or Nancy, with whom he probably had three children: O-bim-e-ge-shig-o-quay (Louisa), Quod-ance (Julie), and No-din-e-gah-bow-eak (Rosie).

Hole-in-the-Day's most well-publicized marital alliance occurred in 1867, when he wed Ellen McCarty, a chambermaid at his Washington, D.C., hotel. Euro-Americans questioned the legality of the marriage, privately performed by an unidentified Chicago priest, but Hole-in-the-Day and the Ojibwas regarded the union as legitimate. The couple had one son, Joseph. It further seems likely that Hole-in-the-Day viewed this marriage as a conciliatory political gesture, an effort to reassure Euro-Americans of the basic commitment to amicable relations that underlay his willingness to resort to force of arms.

Diedrich, Mark, *The Chiefs Hole-in-the-Day of the Mississippi Chippewa* (Minneapolis: Coyote Books, 1986).

REBECCA KUGEL
University of California at Riverside

HOPI

Ancestors of the Hopi people and the extended families or clans that constitute today's Hopi Nation have lived in the greater Southwest for millennia. The word *Hopi* is derived from *Hopituh:* people who live according to the Hopi way. Hopi lands in northeastern Arizona cover more than 1.5 million acres. Land elevation ranges from five thousand to seven thousand feet, with an annual precipitation of eight to twelve inches. Living off land that is largely high desert plateau has resulted in a repertoire of farming technologies, food-crop selection and domestication, and a unique lifeway.

Corn is the principal crop raised by Hopi farmers. It is eaten fresh from the gardens during the first harvest. It is also dried and preserved in granaries for processing on an as-needed basis. To Hopi people, corn is life. It has sustained the people throughout their history. It is the first solid food fed to infants at their clan naming ceremony. *Piki,* a wafer-thin bread made from finely ground blue-corn meal, is prepared for daily consumption and for special occasions like feasts and weddings. It is also prepared for the deceased, to sustain their essences as they journey into the spirit world.

Part of the Hopi origin story recalls the time of emergence from a previous world into the present world. Those who emerged were invited to choose from a number of ears of corn. Some ears were large and hearty, indicating a life of bountifulness and material prosperity on this earth. Some were short, indicating that lessons in life would be learned from hardships but that overcoming hardships would make the people strong and enduring. Hopis chose to live the life of the short ear of corn and migrated to the lands upon which they built their enduring villages and culture.

Today Hopis blend their small-scale farming economy with wage labor and small-business economies. Crafting kachina dolls, silver jewelry, pottery, and baskets for the commercial art market is both a cultural and an economic activity. Other small businesses include hospitality and food service, ranching, and mercantile and technology-related enterprises. Hopi professionals participate in a variety of occupations. At the University of Arizona, for example, there are Hopis who serve in the professorial and administrative ranks. Hopis living much of the year away from the homeland probably have as much to do with the Hopi economy as those who live year round in the villages. All Hopis do what is necessary to contribute to the well-being of the Hopi homeland.

Throughout their history, Hopis have maintained political and social relationships with neighboring populations. Ancient trading ties between Hopis and Zunis, for example, continue to the present day. Military alliances with Hano- or Tewa-speaking populations

A Hopi woman firing pottery.

along the Rio Grande have taken different shape today, but the ties are nevertheless very strong. Some political relations have formed the basis for lawsuits and countersuits over mineral and land resources (such as the modern land dispute with the Diné, or Navajos).

Contact with Europeans began in the sixteenth century. Spanish colonization was severely stunted by the Pueblo Revolt of 1680 and its aftermath, but continued into the nineteenth century. The Hopis' participation in the revolt was a clear reassertion of their place on the landscape; there was little or no room for colonization and missionization. Their actions and voices were heard loud and clear by officials of the Spanish government. Jurisdiction over the area passed to the United States in 1848 with the signing of the U.S.-Mexican Treaty. In 1882 the Hopi Indian Reservation was established by executive order of U.S. president Chester A. Arthur. The Hopi Tribal Council and Government was organized in 1935, and its constitution was approved

by the U.S. secretary of the interior in 1936. Today the tribe is federally recognized as "the Hopi Tribe."

Hopis educate their members in two ways: through formal education, and through traditional education within cultural institutions known as *kivas*. Hopi education is provided by five systems: local public schools, federally funded government schools, village contract schools, private schools, and kivas. For many years Hopi students had to leave home to attend high school at off-reservation U.S.-government-operated or private boarding schools. In 1985 the new Hopi junior and senior high school was opened to all students in the region. Having a year-round population of teenage Hopis on the reservation has had a very positive impact on tribal culture, because it allows young people to participate in the annual cycle of ritual and ceremonial life in their villages.

At about age eight, Hopi boys and girls begin a prescribed series of initiation rites that guide them from

childhood through adolescence and into young adulthood. They are taught many principles and ethics of
being a Hopi. They are also instructed according to the
teachings of the kachina spirits, with whom they form
lifelong friendships. They learn the value of family and
kinship systems and the centrality of reciprocity in
Hopi life. They also receive the tools and strategies for
meeting and dealing with hardships. Prowess in athletics, especially long-distance running, is viewed as an essential part of this process. In the end they become
adults and teachers to the next generation of youth.
The Hopi language is also maintained by these processes, as well as in the home.

Arizona's state universities are developing a Hopi
syllabary or writing system, and the University of Arizona is managing the implementation of the syllabary
program at the Hopi high school. Currently the Hopi
dictionary contains over thirty thousand terms. The
dictionary project is part of a larger effort by Hopi officials and Hopi religious leaders to preserve many aspects of Hopi culture.

The Hopi Foundation, based at the village of Bacavi
on Third Mesa, has led a nongovernmental approach to
cultural preservation. Comprising Hopi professionals
and laypersons, the Hopi Foundation seeks to contribute to and improve the quality of Hopi life. The
Hopi Foundation has explored ways to employ solar energy to electrify homes, to restore traditional clan houses, to make college fellowships available to students,
and to respond to individual and village proposals.

The Hopi Way has its basis in the origin story of the
people, which calls on the people to fulfill the covenant
between the deity Masawu and the first Hopis. The
Hopi Way requires people to know the cultural and
physical landscape of the homeland and to call upon
aunts, uncles, clan mothers, and kiva and religious
leaders for inspiration and guidance. The Hopi Way
calls on community members to learn and practice self-
discipline, cooperation, and reciprocity. The Hopi Way
is clearly not for everyone, but it is the way of the *Hopituh*.

James, Harry C., *Pages from Hopi History* (Tucson: University of
Arizona Press, 1974); Qoyawayma, Polingaysi, *No Turning
Back,* as told to Vada Carlson (Albuquerque: University of New
Mexico Press, 1964); Secakuku, Alph H., *Following the Sun and
Moon: Hopi Kachina Tradition* (Flagstaff, Ariz.: Northland
Press, 1995).

HARTMAN H. LOMAWAIMA (Hopi)
Arizona State Museum
University of Arizona

HORSES AND INDIANS

Thousands of years passed before they were finally
united, but horses and Indians were made for each
other. In the 450 years since horses and Indians were
first brought together, many nations have had a presence in North America. Some, like the Spaniards, used
the horse to establish a stronghold, while others—the
French and English—saw their power washed away.
Throughout the course of these changes, the connection between Indians and horses remained strong. Visit
any Indian reservation—particularly on the plains,
where hunters once relied on their mounts—and the
continuing relationship between Indians and horses is
illustrated in celebration parades, in the presence of
horse herds in fields along the highways and back
roads, and among schoolchildren who write and draw
pictures of nothing else.

The horse was brought to North America by Spanish
exploratory expeditions. Many have speculated about
how the horse first came into the Indians' possession. It
was once thought that horses from the Francisco Coronado expedition may have been taken by Indians in
1541, but careful analysis lends greater credence to another theory. It is most likely that horses were obtained
by Indians in a gradual process. The transfer probably
began as the Spanish conquistadors taught the Indians
the art of horsemanship in return for logistic support.
Later, trained Indian horsemen transferred horses to
other Indians through trade and raiding.

The first tribes to have horses in their possession
were those who came in contact with the Spaniards. In
the early period the number of horses in North America was small, and it was not until greater numbers arrived that their mass diffusion took place. Herds established in South America were the first to become large
enough to be considered abundant. Horticultural tribes
probably had a limited interest in horses and acquired
them in limited numbers. Most used the horse primarily as a pack animal at first, as they used the dog, converting only after some time to mounted use. After
mastering the art of horsemanship these tribes acted as
intermediaries in the dispersal of the horse culture to
other Indians.

Obviously, Indian tribes carried out an active trade
in horses, since many were skilled in training and rearing horses prior to contact with non-Indian explorers.
Each tribe acquired such skills during the trading
process, enabling various tribes to utilize the horse
quickly. The Plains Indians have the image of having

Roping horses on the Arapaho Ranch, Thermopolis, Wyoming.

been closely associated with the horse, yet it is likely that the wide-scale diffusion of the horse among them did not occur until between 1640 and 1885. The horse had certainly spread to the northern reaches of the Great Plains by 1750. In 1754, Anthony Hendry, a Hudson's Bay Company employee, met horse-mounted Indians in what is now Saskatchewan who were skilled in buffalo-hunting horsemanship. By 1885, reservation life had become the only option for all the tribes, and intertribal diffusion of the horse came to an end.

The anthropologist John C. Ewers has traced the diffusion of the horse among the Plains Indians. He cites Santa Fe, New Mexico, as a distribution center. The horse trade moved in a northern direction over the plains. Southern tribes such as the Kiowas, Comanches, Arapahos, and Cheyennes obtained the horse well before the northern tribes. The southern tribes brought the horse northward; numerous tribal histories note

this fact. The Shoshones are credited by the Blackfoot, Flathead, and Nez Perce tribal oral traditions as having delivered the first horses to them.

Later, tribes such as the Nez Perces, Flatheads, Pend Oreilles, and Kootenays, located west of the Rocky Mountains, were noted for having large numbers of horses. Many of these horses crossed the mountains and contributed to the buildup of herds on the Great Plains. The Crows are often cited as having large herds of horses and distributing them to many neighboring tribes.

Undoubtedly, horses were at first distributed among the tribes according to established trade patterns. As tribes learned the value of the horse, more coercive measures were applied. Horse raiding became an accepted method of procurement as soon as men learned the basic elements of stealth horsemanship. Plains societies quickly developed such raids into an art form, if not an essential element in their lifestyle.

Certainly, word of the horse preceded its actual sighting and use. Tribal histories abound with stories of first sightings and initial possession, as well as many elaborate and mystical tales of how the horse came among the tribes. The tribal names given to the horse reflect the mystery associated with the animal. *Elk dog* and *big dog* are common names that remain today in the languages of many Plains tribes.

Many scholars believe that the horse radically changed the way of life of the Indian, but this is an overstatement. In fact, horses actually enhanced a preexisting way of life. For example, nomadic tribes were greatly influenced by the horse's ability to carry large loads. Such tribes could thus transport themselves farther, with less effort, which made life easier for the whole tribe. Farmers used horses primarily for personal transportation. Nevertheless, the effect of the horse may have been more profound for the horticultural tribes as these people came to realize that the animal would be of greater use in hunting. Hunting buffalo on horseback became a viable method of obtaining food. Many sedentary tribes were also encouraged to abandon their farms because the horse-based mobility of neighboring tribes placed them at risk to raiding parties.

Many universal elements of horse use were diffused along with the horses themselves—for instance, the practice of mounting the horse from the right side. Methods of breaking horses were also passed along. It was common practice to break wild horses by riding them in a lake or river or boggy area; later, experienced Indian horsemen employed the same methods used by horse trainers today. Another Indian practice was the use of a quirt instead of spurs. Perhaps the most surprising facet of Indian horsemanship was the fact that the animals received no branding or marking of any kind. Owners identified individual horses by sight, and their ability to do so was remarkable. Even if they owned large numbers of horses, they had no difficulty in keeping track of their herds by this method.

The Indian and the horse were compatible in every way. In 1910, older Blackfoot men lamented the loss of their horses more than the loss of their land. The affinity between horses and Indians remains one of the most powerful images in American history.

See also Herding and Ranching.

Ewers, John C., *The Horse in Blackfoot Indian Culture* (Washington: Smithsonian Institution, 1955).

DARRELL ROBES KIPP (Blackfoot)
Piegan Institute
Blackfoot Indian Reservation

HORSESHOE BEND, BATTLE OF

Horseshoe Bend, on the upper Tallapoosa River in Tallapoosa County, Alabama, was the site of an Upper Creek Red Stick village and the last battle of the Creek or Red Stick War of 1813–14. Upper Creek followers of the Red Stick prophets built the new town of Tohopika in a bend of the upper Tallapoosa in the summer of 1813. The site was quickly settled by people from towns of the Apihka division of the tribe. It was surrounded on three sides by the river and by a stout breastwork on the fourth.

Following a series of defeats by Americans and their Indian allies, Red Sticks from towns on the Coosa and upper Tallapoosa Rivers retreated to Tohopika early in 1814. In March of that year, the town held about four hundred women and children and one thousand warriors.

A force of fifteen hundred Americans with five hundred Cherokees and one hundred "friendly" Creeks under Andrew Jackson surrounded and attacked the town on March 27, 1814. Despite inferior numbers and a lack of firearms, the defenders held off the attack until some of the Cherokees forded the river and attacked from the rear. About eight hundred Red Stick warriors were killed and three hundred fifty women and children taken captive.

This final defeat broke the Red Stick rebellion. In its aftermath, about two thousand Creek rebels fled to Florida, where they joined the Seminoles. The remaining Creeks signed the Treaty of Fort Jackson in August 1814, officially ending the war with the United States and ceding 14 million acres to federal authorities.

See also Creek (Muskogee); Red Stick War.

HOWE, OSCAR

(1915–83)
Yanktonai Sioux artist, designer, university professor, and administrator.

At the end of his life, Oscar Howe had become the best-known and most highly regarded Sioux artist of the twentieth century. His paintings and other illustrations are represented in the collections of many museums and private individuals throughout the world, and special galleries in the Denver Museum of Natural History and the Oscar Howe Art Center, in Mitchell, South Dakota, feature his work.

Born in the community of Joe Creek on the Crow Creek Indian Reservation in South Dakota on May 13, 1915, Oscar Howe spent his childhood and preadolescent years faced with poverty, illness, and frustration. The son of full-blood Yanktonai parents, he was sent off to attend the Pierre Indian School, a government boarding school with a strict military regime. He spoke no English when he first went there and, like so many other children, was punished physically to discourage his reliance on his native language and culture. Forced acculturation was the policy of the day. In 1933 physical afflictions—an unidentified skin disease and trachoma—led to his being sent home. He worked determinedly to heal his afflictions and return to school; eventually he transferred to the Santa Fe Indian School and completed his high school education in 1938.

At the Santa Fe Indian School, Howe trained under the art teacher Dorothy Dunn Kramer. At the time of his graduation, several of his paintings were on exhibit at the Brooklyn Museum's Gallery for Living Artists and the San Francisco Civic Center, and several of his pieces joined exhibitions in London and Paris. A number of his works were reproduced in magazines.

Howe returned to the Crow Creek Reservation in 1938, and in the midst of the Great Depression he reevaluated his career. He knew he wanted to be an artist, but he recognized that his choice was not a practical one. In this atmosphere he decided to accept a position as an art instructor at the Pierre Indian School, receiving room and board as his only remuneration. By 1940 he had become associated with the South Dakota Artists Project, and in that year he was assigned to paint the interior dome of the Carnegie Public Library in Mitchell, South Dakota. Subsequently, he was sent to the Indian Art Center at Fort Sill, Oklahoma, to take a special course in painting murals, and upon his return he was assigned to paint ten large oil murals about the history of the Missouri River basin on the walls of the new civic auditorium in Mobridge, South Dakota. Just as he had started work on this commission he received his notice for military service. The authorities gave him two extra weeks to finish the work.

During World War II, Oscar Howe spent three and a half years in the U.S. Army and fought as part of the 442nd Anti-Aircraft Battalion in North Africa, Italy, France, and Germany. In 1945, at the end of his tour of duty, he met Adelheit Karla Margarete Anna (Heidi) Hampel in her father's clothing store in Biedenkopf, Germany. He soon returned to the United States with the rank of corporal and began his adjustment to civil-ian life. In 1947 Howe entered one of his paintings, Dakota Duck Hunt, in the second annual National Indian Painting Exhibition at the Philbrook Art Center in Tulsa, Oklahoma, and won the grand prize of $350. After several years of correspondence, Howe wrote to Heidi Hampel asking her to "take a chance" on him and be his wife. In July 1947 the two were married in Chicago. Heidi accompanied her new husband back to South Dakota, where she eventually became his business manager, publicity agent, and historian, documenting his works. Shortly after their marriage, Howe was commissioned to supply fifty illustrations for a two-volume work, North American Indian Costumes, published by the University of Oklahoma Press in 1952. The project involved both historical research and the production of the final illustrations. In June 1948 Heidi and Oscar's daughter, Inge Dawn, was born.

In the fall of 1948 Howe was invited to design the Corn Palace Civic Auditorium in Mitchell, South Dakota, and was also admitted to Dakota Wesleyan University in Mitchell, where he was given a special appointment as artist-in-residence and instructor in art. This recognition of and commitment to his potential gave him an institutional base from which to develop his creativity. Three years later he was awarded the Harvey Dunn Medal in Art. Upon his graduation from Dakota Wesleyan he went on leave from his instructional position with the university's art department to pursue graduate training at the University of Oklahoma. He received his Master of Fine Arts degree from Oklahoma in 1954 and returned to Dakota Wesleyan to be the head of the Department of Art. From September 1943 until his appointment as an assistant professor of fine arts at the University of South Dakota in 1957, he was also the director of the art program at the Pierre Indian School. The University of South Dakota was his institutional home from 1957 until the end of his life.

Besides his university duties, Oscar Howe devoted time to his art, working vigorously at it in the evenings, during summers, and while on vacation. In 1957 a major exhibition of his art was held in Santa Fe, New Mexico. His popularity as an artist increased as he incorporated into his style a fusion of Dakota themes and abstract innovations, demonstrating his ability to draw on native philosophies and new artistic techniques to further explore his themes and subjects. His abstract geometric designs continue to be used in the medium of split ears of corn in mosaiclike panels on Mitchell's Corn Palace. For a ten-year period Howe designed and supervised the execution of many of the panels, which were changed annually. The Howe designs are occasionally recycled today.

The intrinsic value of Oscar Howe's art continues to be recognized as his work appears in major surveys of North American Indian art and modern American art. He made innovative use of cubism, which he considered to be a logical parallel to Native American—and, specifically, Dakota—geometric traditions evident in the designs of painted parfleches, robes, and tipi liners as well as in clothing decorations done in painting, quillwork, and beadwork. Howe demythologized a romanticized aboriginal past and created artwork with a continuity and connection from past to present. He wanted his art to be seen and perceived as an informed whole that expressed his aesthetic and reflected his Yanktonai Sioux culture.

See also Art, Visual (to 1960); Arts, Contemporary (since 1960).

Agogino, George, "Oscar Howe: Sioux Artist," *Plains Anthropologist* 32 (116): 197–202; Dockstader, Frederick J., "The Revolt of Trader Boy: Oscar Howe and Indian Art," *American Indian Art* 8 (3): 42–51; Pennington, Robert, *Oscar Howe: Artist of the Sioux* (Pierre, S. Dak.: Dakota Territory Centennial Commission, 1961).

DAVID REED MILLER
Saskatchewan Indian Federated College
University of Regina

HUNTING

Hunting and gathering characterized the subsistence strategies of most Native Americans prior to European contact. The domestication of plants had early beginnings and eventually formed the economic base for several cultural groups in the Southwest and Mesoamerica. Some food plants—especially corn, beans, and squash—were adapted to climatic conditions in the more northerly areas and gradually became important in the economy of the Plains people dwelling along the upper Missouri River. Despite these achievements, however, the annual summer buffalo hunt remained an important event in the Plains Indians' economic, social, and religious life, and similar harvests continue to be important to other groups.

It is difficult at times to establish a strict boundary between hunting and gathering. The latter usually refers to the collection of plant resources, but the collection of some of the smaller mammals and reptiles falls more in the realm of gathering than of hunting. On the other hand, although collecting some of the smaller mammals used for food, such as squirrels and wood rats, requires considerable knowledge and skill, hunting usually brings to mind the pursuit and procurement of the medium- to larger-size grazing and browsing mammals such as pronghorn, deer, elk, bison, and mammoth and scavengers and carnivores such as the coyote, wolf, cougar, and bear.

Most traditional Native American hunting was aimed at provisioning the human group. Nevertheless, there were also ritualistic aspects to the hunt. For example, an Eskimo youth would kill a polar bear with a spear as a rite of passage to full status as an adult male. Moreover, most societies believed it was critical that they maintain a special relationship with animals. They believed that animals made themselves available to humans only for as long as animal spirits received proper treatment from hunters. This belief placed certain restrictions on hunting activities. For example, among some Eskimos, the same weaponry could not be used to hunt both land and sea mammals. Most important, the animal spirits had to be ritually treated so that they would return to the spirit world with a favorable report that would ensure future success for the hunters. This spirit relationship also provided an excuse for poor hunting results. The unsuccessful hunter could claim that someone had not treated the animal spirits properly and that, consequently, the spirit world was withholding the animals until the situation was corrected through proper rituals and observations.

Animal procurement usually involved most or all of the entire hunting group. In such communal efforts a religious specialist or shaman who was believed to have control over the animals directed the hunt. A classic example of this practice was the Plains Indian buffalo jump, where large numbers of animals were stampeded over high bluffs or were herded into corrals and killed. Throughout this group activity a shaman used spiritual power and ritual paraphernalia to draw the animals to their death. Another example of this ceremonial practice involved the Shoshoneans in the Great Basin, who were adept at communally trapping pronghorn herds. If for some reason a pronghorn shaman was not available, the entire trapping effort would be postponed until one could be found. Among the North Alaskan Eskimos, the first captured whale of the season was given special ritual treatment, and only after this ceremony could the regular whale hunt begin.

A Cherokee man and boy hunting with blowpipes in Tahlequah, Oklahoma, in 1992.

Spiritual intervention was invoked most prominently where the chances of failure were high. While the buffalo jump and the pronghorn trap served as focuses of religious activity, the communal rabbit hunts among the Great Basin Shoshoneans, which involved nets and large numbers of people, did not. In the latter case the behavior of the animals assured success, and supernatural assistance was not sought.

Any hunt involving medium- or large-size mammals had a strong possibility of failure. Success for the prehistoric hunter demanded that he learn many things. The most important aspects of hunting knowledge were (1) a thorough knowledge of the behavior patterns of the species being hunted, (2) familiarity with the hunting territory, (3) familiarity with the use and limitations of available weaponry, and (4) proper physical and mental conditioning on the part of the hunter. All of these factors required careful attention.

Every animal species demonstrates unique and ever-changing behavioral patterns. Some such patterns reflect physiological traits such as age, sex, breeding habits, and body condition. Others, external to the animal, include time of year, time of day, weather, feed conditions, distance to water, and whether the prey is alone, in a small group, or part of a large herd. Traditional American Indian hunters had to be aware of all of these conditions, to analyze them, and to quickly sort out the procurement strategy most appropriate to the situation. In order to acquire this body of knowledge, Native American hunters had to begin training at an early age.

A common misunderstanding about hunting is that there is a single hunting strategy that can be applied to any and all situations. In reality, hunters must develop a strategy each time they set out to hunt. Several species may be present in a given territory at the same time, but each will require a unique procurement strategy. Consequently, attempts to procure more than a single species at one time seldom meet with success.

The hunter also needs to be aware of the behavior of species other than those hunted. The reactions of birds and other animals can provide important information about the prey. Certain calls of a crow, magpie, or squirrel, for example, often reveal movements of the prey. The movements of such animals and of carnivores such as coyotes and cougars can also indicate the location and movements of the prey.

Native American hunters and gatherers recognized a home territory and resisted intrusions from other groups. Traditionally, however, boundaries were usually not as carefully defined as they became after the arrival of Europeans. It was common for one or more human hunting groups to cross territorial boundaries for communal hunting activities such as a buffalo jump or pronghorn trap, since these large operations typically produced surplus meat to be cured and stored for later use by all involved. Thus not only could several groups be provisioned at once, but sharing of food provided native people with a kind of insurance against future starvation. Those who invited others to hunt with them at a time of plenty could expect assistance from their neighbors during times of stress.

Prehistoric Native American hunting groups were usually patrilineal, and hunting was almost always a male pursuit. Gathering by females may at times have provided more food resources than hunting, but hunting was generally considered far more prestigious, and it typically established the ideology of the group. There was a strong motive for this patrilineality in hunting groups because in this type of social group, the male remained in his familiar hunting territory after marriage and could expect the maximum in hunting success. In patrilineal hunting groups, the men began the training of their male offspring at an early age. Males would marry females from other hunting groups if necessary in order to maintain continuity in the male line and avoid a situation wherein the male hunter would have to move to and become familiar with a different territory.

Different animal species exploit their territories in different but generally predictable ways. The hunter had to know what any particular animal was most likely to do if it moved beyond his range of vision, and therefore had to know the terrain and vegetative cover of the entire hunting area. This required continual monitoring of conditions within the hunting territory—conditions that changed continually and often

rapidly. Rainfall and, consequently, feed conditions could differ from year to year. A severe hailstorm or insect infestation might decrease the feed supply to such an extent that the animals would be forced to move to a different part of the territory. Water sources could often determine animal movements and thereby figured prominently in any procurement strategy.

Prior to the arrival of Europeans, a Native American hunter's weapons were part of his most prized possessions. They received more than merely functional care and maintenance. No hunter would consider using another person's weapons, because it was believed that in the process the weapons would lose their potency and even present a danger to the nonowner. Native Americans often engaged in the nonfunctional embellishment of weaponry, in the same way that a modern hunter decorates and polishes the wooden stock of a rifle and engraves the metal parts. What appear to be ownership marks are often found on wooden components of weapons that have survived into the present.

Native American weaponry had to be maintained in peak condition. Nothing would have been more frustrating to the hunter than to execute the flawless pursuit of an animal and then lose it at the last moment because of a faulty weapon. An undetected flaw in any of the early Native Americans' weaponry components, such as a fracture plane in a stone projectile point or a split in a throwing stick, bow, or arrow shaft, would have spoiled an otherwise successful hunting episode. Wooden components had to be kept dry and properly stored, and they required continual monitoring to prevent them from warping and twisting. A slight bend in the shaft of an arrow or dart could destroy accuracy and limit the weapon's lethal potential. The prehistoric hunter spent at least as much time in maintaining weaponry as in its manufacture.

Traditional Native American weaponry was based on one of three systems. The simplest was the thrusting or throwing spear, which consists of a long, heavy shaft with a projectile point on one end. The spear may be thrust directly into an animal while still in the hunter's hands, or thrown for a short distance. Because the velocity is low, it requires added force by the hunter to penetrate the hides of large animals. It proves effective provided the prey is close at hand, as in the case of a trapped animal.

A second system consisted of the throwing stick, or atlatl and dart. It was known in the Old World and is presumed to have come across the Bering Strait into North America with the earliest known Clovis hunters.

This device serves as an extension of the human arm and allows the application of kinetic energy directly to the end of a long shaft attached to a relatively heavy projectile such as a Clovis point. The shaft may be fletched to improve performance, although good results at short ranges can be obtained without fletching. The atlatl increases velocity, allowing for a lighter shaft and providing a longer-range weapon than a hand-held spear. In the hands of an expert, the atlatl and dart is a lethal weapon.

The bow and arrow is believed to have come into North America from northeastern Asia about two thousand years ago and rapidly replaced the atlatl and dart. The principles of operation of the bow and arrow are different from those of the other two systems in that the bow and arrow utilizes a smaller projectile point on a shorter and lighter shaft. While the other two weapon systems require direct kinetic energy from the hunter's arms, the bow and arrow utilizes the potential energy stored in the bow's arms at full draw position. The lighter, fletched shaft allows higher velocities and is accurate and effective at longer distances. The smaller projectile points used with a bow have been called bird or small-animal points because of their size, but they were lethal to animals as large as buffalo. All three weapon systems require constant practice in order to acquire and sustain any measure of proficiency in their use.

Finally, hunting requires the utmost in physical and mental conditioning. The better developed the hunter's senses of sight, hearing, and smell and the better his physical conditioning, the better are his chances of becoming really good. Mental attitude is also important. The successful hunter must be patient and able to maintain a sometimes uncomfortable position for long periods of time to avoid scaring away potential prey. Endurance is often needed to withstand bad weather and to pursue wounded animals.

The killing of the animal is only part of the hunting process. The best of meat can be ruined by improper handling, and, although the butchering and processing of meat products was usually delegated to the females, no true hunter would allow good meat to spoil through failure to properly field-dress the animal.

Traditional Native American hunting required the acquisition of a vast body of knowledge about the behavior of prey animals and the territory they inhabited as well as about the use, maintenance, and limitations of weaponry; it also required the development of the individual hunter's physical and mental powers. The hunter needed only to look outside the lodge on the day of the hunt in order to determine weather conditions and, by combining this with all of the other information at hand, to sort out the strategy that presented the greatest potential for success. The human hunter proved to be the most successful of all predators and could always devise a strategy to procure any animal species. Despite changes in technology and potential hunting area that occurred after the arrival of Europeans, these features of Native American hunting persisted and remain evident among some Native American hunters today.

See also Fishing and Hunting Rights.

Frison, George C., *Prehistoric Hunters of the High Plains,* 2d ed. (San Diego: Academic Press, 1991); Spencer, Robert F., *The North Alaskan Eskimo: A Study in Ecology and Society,* Smithsonian Institution, Bureau of American Ethnology Bulletin 171 (Washington, D.C., 1959); Steward, Julian H., *Basin-Plateau Aboriginal Sociopolitical Groups,* Smithsonian Institution, Bureau of American Ethnology Bulletin 120 (Washington, D.C., 1938).

GEORGE C. FRISON
University of Wyoming

HUPA

The Hoopa Valley Indian Reservation, in northwestern California, is 144 miles square, bisected by the Trinity River. The Hoopa Valley, surrounded by mountains timbered with pine, fir, and hardwoods, is the center of the Hupa world. (In Natinook, *Hupa* means "The Place Where the Trails Return.")

In small villages along the river, the Hupas built cedar-plank houses over oblong pits, with central hearths, earthen shelves along the walls, small round doorways at one corner, and stone-paved porches. Several of these houses are still standing, and continue to be used for ceremonies. In addition to family homes, where the women and children slept, each village had at least one sweat house, used by the males for daily sweating, as a "lodge" for teaching, storytelling, singing, and brotherhood, and as sleeping quarters for men and older boys. Each village also had a larger sacred house for gatherings and ceremonies such as the Brush Dance, a healing ceremony that is still practiced. The fire pit at one of these sacred houses has been radiocarbon-dated as being over seven thousand years old, indicating the maintenance of a building on this site "always," as legend holds.

Food resources were varied and abundant for the Hupas, although salmon, deer, and acorns provided the bulk of their diet. The generally mild climate made heavy clothing unnecessary, but ceremonial garb was lavishly fashioned of a wide range of natural materials. Women's bowl-shaped hats are just one type of the intricately woven basketry items still produced by Hupa women, who have long been recognized for this skill. Men excelled in woodworking, among many crafts. By redwood canoe and overland, the Hupas visited and traded with distant villages, necessitating proficiency in languages other than their own Athabaskan tongue.

Religious beliefs and practices were a crucial part of everyday life. The most significant segment of their religion encompassed two ceremonials, one serving to revitalize the world for the coming year, the other to ward off famine, disease, and other disasters. These were called, respectively, the White Deerskin Dance and the Jump Dance; they are still held biannually in September.

The Hupas remained undisturbed until the 1850s, when the discovery of gold brought hordes of would-be miners swarming into the area, wreaking havoc on the Hupas' villages, disrupting their subsistence cycles, and causing serious conflict. Treaties made with California's native people remained unratified and unfulfilled by the federal government. This neglect allowed depredations against the Hupas to proceed unchecked, even though Fort Gaston was established at Hoopa in 1858 "for their protection." The Interior Department established the Hoopa Valley Reservation in 1864 and a boarding school in 1893. The community established a business council in 1933 and created a constitution for its government and legal affairs. That same year a public school opened on the reservation.

Today the Hoopa Reservation is California's largest and most populous reservation. It is home to more than two thousand members and maintains the largest accumulation of tribal funds in the state. Much of its current prosperity is due to the post–World War II lumber boom, which created an abundance of well-paid jobs and profitable small businesses. In 1988 the tribe was selected by the Bureau of Indian Affairs to participate in the Tribal Self-Governance Demonstration Project and today is a model for other tribes in self-governance, economic development, natural-resource management, social services, and cultural preservation.

Tribal enterprises include a market, a motel, a restaurant, a museum, a post office, a radio station, a bingo hall, a clinic, a hospital project, a senior center, fisheries, a forestry corporation, and law-enforcement and tribal court systems. Tribal members, many with college degrees, hold most administrative and managerial positions for tribal operations, working as tribal-council members, college administrators, professors, lawyers, doctors, teachers, engineers, and foresters and in other degreed professions.

Goddard, Pliny Earle, *Life and Culture of the Hupa*, UCPAAE, vol. 1, no. 1 (Berkeley: University of California Press, 1903); Nelson, Byron, Jr., *Our Home Forever: A Hupa Tribal History* (Hoopa, Calif.: Hoopa Tribe, 1978); Wallace, William, Jr., "Hupa, Chilula, and Whilkut," in *Handbook of North American Indians,* ed. William C. Sturtevant, vol. 8, *California,* ed. Robert F. Heizer (Washington: Smithsonian Institution, 1978).

DAVID RISLING (Hupa)
University of California at Davis

LESLIE CAMPBELL (Hupa)
Hoopa, California

HURON/WYANDOT

The Iroquoian peoples whom the seventeenth-century French labeled Hurons (from the Old French *hure,* meaning "boar's head," referring to the male Hurons' bristly coiffure) lived between Lake Simcoe and the southeastern corner of Georgian Bay in today's Canadian province of Ontario. They called themselves *Wendat,* "Dwellers of the Peninsula" (or perhaps "Islanders"), referring to the fact that their territory was bounded by water on three sides. According to seventeenth-century estimates, they numbered between twenty and forty thousand and lived in eighteen to twenty-five villages clustered in an area that measured thirty-five miles east to west and twenty miles north to south. Immediately to the south were the very closely related Tionontatis (Petuns or Tobacco People, specialists in growing the sacred plant), whose population was estimated at about seven thousand.

Like all Iroquoian peoples, the Hurons were farmers who supplemented their crops with hunting. Archaeologists favor the theory that they began inhabiting their lands soon after the retreat of the glaciers, slowly evolving from hunter-gatherers into farmer-hunters.

Their own traditions have them arriving later, from the southeast. In any event, by A.D. 500 they were growing corn (the plant's northward spread from Mexico had been controlled by its capacity to adapt to shorter northern growing seasons). By 1500 the famous "three sisters" of Amerindian agriculture—corn, beans, and squash, grown together—were well established as the principal food crops. Tobacco had been cultivated long before the introduction of corn and was the responsibility of the men, whereas the food crops were the responsibility of the women.

The Huron villages were clustered close to each other, with their corn fields forming a surrounding belt. These fields were extensive; early in the seventeenth century, it was reported that they covered about seven thousand acres; one early visitor to Huronia, as the region occupied by the Hurons was known, said that "it was easier to get lost in a corn field" than in the surrounding forest. Not only did agriculture provide the Hurons with 80 percent of their diet, but its products were important for trade. Situated as they were at the northern limits for Stone Age agriculture, as well as at a crossroads of the region's trading networks, the Hurons were dominant not only in trade, but also in diplomacy and war. Socially, they were organized into eight matrilineal clans that arose from three phratries; for ceremonial purposes, the phratries were divided into two moieties.

Huron government was three tiered, including village, tribal, and confederacy levels; all operated on the principle of group consensus. By the beginning of the seventeenth century, the Hurons had formed themselves into a confederacy of four peoples, which according to their own oral history had originated at the beginning of the fifteenth century at the initiative of the Attignawantans, "People of the Bear," and the Attigneenongnahacs, "Barking Dogs." The Arendarhonons, "People of the Rock," joined about 1590, and the fourth group, the Tahontaenrats, "People of the Deer," joined about 1610. A possible fifth, the Ataronchronons, "People of the Marshes," does not appear to have attained full membership. If the Huron chronology is correct, their confederacy may have antedated that of the Five Nations (it will be remembered that Hiawatha, one of the founders of the Great League of Peace of the Iroquois, was said to be a Huron). The year in which the Arendarhonons joined, 1590, suggests that they were refugees from the St. Lawrence Valley, which was probably also the case for the Tahontaenrats. Their language differences were on the whole minor, so that all

Hurons could understand each other; theirs was the trade language of the North.

The first meeting with the French was at the initiative of the Arendarhonons, easternmost of the confederates. European goods had been filtering into the interior through Amerindian networks since the mid–sixteenth century; Outchetaguin, an Arendarhonon chief, wishing to get direct access to this new trade, joined with Iroquet, chief of the neighboring Algonquins, to meet Samuel de Champlain (c. 1570–1635) at Quebec in 1609. Out of this encounter developed the historic alliance of the French and Hurons. As the fur trade developed, bringing prosperity to both the Hurons and the French, the Five Nations, or Iroquois, to the south entered into a period of expansion. This growth appears to have been an aggressive reaction to a number of factors, such as the increasing intrusion of Europeans, tribal rivalries exacerbated by the fur trade, and above all social dislocations caused by European-introduced epidemics. The Hurons, isolated as they were from alternative sources of European trade, were affected by these changes particularly severely. For example, the French insistence on the introduction of the Jesuits in 1634 exposed them to a concentrated missionary campaign that weakened social solidarity to the point where Christianized Hurons refused to fight alongside their traditionalist fellow tribesmen. Escalating hostilities with the Iroquois finally resulted in the destruction of Huronia in 1649, and the dispersal of its once-powerful confederacy. The Iroquois capped their victory by attacking the neighboring Petuns during the winter of 1649–50. This was a move to prevent the Hurons from reforming their settlements around those of the Petuns, and perhaps reviving their confederacy. In spite of everything, groups of Petuns and Hurons succeeded in joining forces and retreating to the Windsor/Detroit area and northern Ohio. These groups became known as Wyandots (a variation of their traditional name for themselves).

However, most of the Huron refugees fled south to join the Iroquois, since many of them already had relatives among the Five Nations, a result of the Iroquois practice of adopting prisoners of war to replenish their own losses from fighting as well as from the epidemics. Another group of several hundred Hurons went east, to establish themselves in Loretteville on the edge of Quebec City, where their descendants have remained.

In their new homes, the Wyandots soon dominated intertribal politics; when they claimed a large part of present-day Ohio and a part of southwestern Ontario, they were recognized by neighboring tribes. Old colonial associations did not entirely disappear, however, and the Wyandots supported the French during the French and Indian War, and at first backed Pontiac during the 1763 uprising in the Ohio Valley. They sided with the British during the American War of Independence, and again lost out with the Treaty of Greenville, signed in 1795, when they were forced into the first of several land cessions to the United States. Eventually, in 1843, the Wyandots of the Midwest were resettled in Wyandotte County, Kansas. Regaining their tribal status in 1867, they were granted a tract of land in northeastern Oklahoma, where their descendants can be found today.

In southwestern Ontario, the Wyandots ceded their lands to the Crown in 1790. At first they retained two reserves, but soon lost those as well. In 1876, the remaining forty-one Wyandot heads of families applied for the right to vote, which was granted in 1880–81. Some of these families are still in the area.

Delâge, Denys, *Bitter Feast* (Vancouver: University of British Columbia Press, 1993); Heidenreich, Conrad, *Huronia* (Toronto: McClelland and Stewart, 1971); Trigger, Bruce G., *Children of Aataentsic*, 2 vols. (Montreal and London: McGill-Queen's University Press, 1976).

OLIVE PATRICIA DICKASON
University of Alberta

ILLINOIS

In the mid-1600s the Illinois were a populous group of tribes sharing the same language, culture, and traditions. Among the more important Illinois tribes were the Peoria, Kaskaskia, Tamaroa, Cahokia, Michigamia, Maroa, Tapouaro, Moingwena, Espeminkia, Chinkoa, Chepoussa, and Coiracoentanon. When first contacted by the French, the Miamis and Weas were considered part of this alliance, and the name *Ilaniawaki* reflects Miami pronunciation. *Ilaniawaki,* now pronounced *Illiniwek,* means something like "real or original ones" and quickly became the French term *Illinois.* In the Peoria-French dictionary compiled by the Jesuit Gravier, the natives' formal name for themselves was listed as *Inuka* (plural *Inuki*). While often spoken of as a confederacy, the Illinois never had the political cohesion of the Iroquois and Huron confederacies.

Numbering perhaps twenty-five thousand at the height of their power, the Illinois occupied the entire area between the Wabash on the east and a line about 150 miles west of the Mississippi (from the Illinois *Missi-sippiwe,* "Great River"). The northern border of their territory was in southern Wisconsin, and the southern border was the Ohio River. Their area included all of the present state of Illinois and parts of Wisconsin, Iowa, and Missouri, as well as the northeast corner of Arkansas. This great expanse of land the Illinois considered their traditional territory: *Ehi puniaminshi mishimaha Kashihiwia* ("Where the Creator placed them anciently," in Tamaroa).

The Illinois lived in a close relationship with their environment, utilizing various resources in a seasonal round of activities. Villages were often quite large and were located along major rivers, where the people could utilize their large dugout canoes (*misuri* is the Illinois word for "canoe"). Bark longhouses shared by six to ten families were usual. These large, permanent villages were where agricultural activity took place.

In the spring, garden plots were prepared for planting, weeds were burned, and the soil was worked up.

As soon as the danger of frost was over, planting began, the principal crops being corn, beans, and squash. When the corn was about a foot high it was mounded up with soil and climbing beans were planted. After the "hilling of the corn," most of the community left the village and went on a communal summer buffalo hunt. During July, women who had stayed behind went to harvest *apakwa* (cattails) and *anakan* (bulrushes). *Apakwa* were sewn together to make the weatherproof mats that covered the winter lodge, and *anakan* were woven into mats that were used on sleeping platforms.

When the summer hunt was over, the people returned to their village carrying dried and smoked meat and buffalo robes they had tanned. Every family had two or three canoes, thirty to forty feet in length, which were used to transport heavy loads back to the village. In the winter lightweight sledges called *shukwahagane,* "slides on its belly," would be used on the smooth ice of the rivers and streams.

Shortly after the return to the village, harvest would begin. In addition to their crops, the Illinois gathered wild foods such as *makupina,* "bear tuber" (the yellow pond lily), *piniki* (Indian potato), *piakimina* (persimmon), *assemina* (paw-paw), and *pakana* (pecan). Most of the crop would be dried and stored in deep pits called *akwanagane* (and referred to as *caches* by the French). When the harvest was complete, the Illinois left for winter hunting camps. The population would be widely scattered for the duration of winter, living in small groups of several families so that the hunters would be able to feed them without exhausting the deer population.

At the end of winter the Illinois moved back to their permanent villages. Some groups stopped at traditional maple-sugaring camps on the way, to make sugar for family consumption and trade. The first activity upon arriving back at the village was the opening of the storage pits. The Illinois were able to live on the dried buffalo meat and agricultural produce they had set aside until the summer hunt. With spring came the preparation of gardens for planting, and another cycle began.

Religious activity in Illinois villages was dominated by an organized shaman association that included some who had been trained since childhood. *Ireni mitewa*, "true *mite* person," was the Peoria term for a great shaman. Clan bundle feasts, naming and adoption rituals, funerals, and community-wide observances such as the Fish Dance at spawning time were held while the Illiniweks were in their main villages. The *mitewaki* organized public performances during which they exhibited their powers to the entire community. Lacrosse games, often held between tribes or other social groupings, were community events, accompanied by active betting. A variety of gambling and guessing games were popular, although compulsive gambling was considered a great fault.

Around 1650 refugee Eries and Tionontatis were taken in by the Illinois, these tribes having been defeated and dispersed by the Iroquois. Soon the Iroquois themselves arrived, beginning a war that lasted over fifty years. At first Illinois warriors were able to drive them back, but each year more Iroquois would arrive. Finally a large tribal village was surprised and destroyed. All who survived the attack were tortured and burned at the stake; the entire community was exterminated. When the other Illinois tribes learned what had happened, the panic-stricken communities fled west of the Mississippi. They were now intruding on the traditional hunting territories of other tribes, who promptly declared war on them. The most serious conflict was with the Sioux.

By the mid-1700s, a century of continual warfare had reduced the Illinois by 90 percent. As their numbers decreased, the Illinois became less and less able to defend themselves. Longtime allies of the French, they never reconciled themselves to British rule. During the Revolutionary War, the Illinois supported the Americans, furnishing them with scouts. General George Rogers Clark promised to protect the Illinois villages while Illinois men were accompanying his army, but the Americans failed to follow through on Clark's promise. In revenge for the Illinois' recognition of the United States and the assistance they were giving the American military effort, pro-English tribes launched a series of devastating attacks on the undefended villages. Large numbers of Illinois were killed, and many women and children were carried off.

After the conclusion of the Revolutionary War, a series of treaties, intended to transfer title of Illinois lands to the federal government, were enacted in 1803, 1818, and 1832. The last of the Kaskaskias and Peorias crossed the Mississippi and headed across Missouri toward Kansas. However, all the Illiniweks did not leave Illinois. The Tamaroas, led by Chief Black Wolf, accompanied by the Metchigameas, moved upriver to their traditional homeland, *Sisipiwe Shikiwe* (Two Rivers Land, between the Illinois and Mississippi Rivers) and refused to have any further dealings with the federal government. Many of their descendants still reside there. In the 1850s the surviving refugees who had gone west came together under the leadership of the Peoria chief Baptiste Peoria. Now officially known as the Peoria Indian Tribe of Oklahoma, they maintain tribal offices in Miami, Oklahoma.

Today the Illinois language is kept alive primarily through traditional naming rituals, prayers, and songs. The Jesuits compiled extensive manuscript dictionaries of the Peoria and Kaskaskia dialects in the 1700s, which have been used in the preparation of modern teaching materials. For the most part, there are only minor differences in pronunciation between the various dialects; for example, the word for "canoe" is *misoli* in Miami, *mitholi* in Wea, *misuli* in modern Peoria, and *misuri* in Tamaroa.

Four painted Illinois buffalo robes from the 1700s are on permanent exhibit in the Musée d'Homme in France, and robes painted in the ancient Illiniwek manner have been seen at powwows in Oklahoma and Illinois. Early examples of Illinois porcupine-quill work, weaving, and woodcarving can be found in museums in North America and Europe. Carved wood effigy bowls in the form of a beaver, closely resembling clay effigy bowls from the Cahokia mound complex near St. Louis, seem to have been an Illiniwek specialty. They are still used in the "ghost feasts" held to honor deceased friends and relatives.

In 1988 the Peoria Indian Tribe of Oklahoma and Illiniwek descendants took an active role in efforts to save the Grand Village of the Kaskaskias when it was threatened by the construction of a marina and condominium complex. They have also been active in attempts to prevent the destruction of archaeological sites and the desecration of graves. Currently, a revival of traditional culture is in progress. In 1993 the Peorias held their first South-Wind (or stomp) Dance in over a century, and they are planning on making this an annual event. In 1994 the Peorias, Kaskaskias, Tamaroas, and Metchigameas presented an altar cloth and votive wampum belt to the Church of the Immaculate Conception on Kaskaskia Island, Illinois. Founded by Père Jacques Marquette in 1675 as a mission to the Kaskaskias, the church was badly damaged in the Mississippi River flood of 1993.

JOHN K. WHITE (Cherokee and Shawnee)
Sangamon State University
Springfield, Illinois

IMPACT OF AMERICAN INDIAN CIVILIZATIONS ON EUROPE AND THE WORLD

In *The Wealth of Nations,* published in 1776, Adam Smith wrote that "the discovery of America, and that of a passage to the East Indies by the Cape of Good Hope, are the two greatest and most important events recorded in the history of mankind." Smith grasped the importance of the coming together of Europe, Africa, and Asia with the Americas well before the full consequences of that event could unfold.

The Indians gave to humankind—whether willingly, unwillingly, or inadvertently—the means by which the modern world came into being. The massive amounts of Indian gold and silver taken from Mexico, the Caribbean, and the Andes promoted the rise of the capitalist economy. Indian crops such as the potato and maize helped to shift the European balance of power away from the Mediterranean and toward the northern countries of Russia, Germany, and Britain. American Indian pharmacology together with the new Indian foods ignited a population explosion in Europe that quickly inflamed Asia and Africa as well. The new cottons, dyes, rubber, and some simple forms of Indian technology propelled a revolutionary mode of production, which led to industrialization. Indian stimulants and depressants, from chocolate and tobacco to peyote and coca, set off a world search for ever higher highs and ever lower lows. The American Indians, through their gifts to humanity, have participated in virtually every step of the creation of the modern world, but their contributions have been greatest in the areas of agriculture, medicine, and technology.

Agriculture and Food

Far beyond the value of the gold and silver or the furs taken from the Americas were the crops that the Indians gave to the world, and through which the Indians had their greatest global impact. Indian farmers of North and South America gave the world maize, potatoes, sweet potatoes, tomatoes, beans, pumpkins, squash, chocolate, vanilla, papayas, persimmons, jicama, pecans, chilies, hickory nuts, peanuts, sunflower seeds, maple syrup, tapioca, avocados, pineapples, and dozens of lesser-known foods.

The agricultural gifts of the Indians have spread from the farmers of America to farmers around the world. Through thousands of years of careful breeding, Indian farmers adapted corn to some of the coldest, hottest, wettest, and driest places in America. Today corn grows over a larger area than does any other cultivated food in the world. It grows virtually anywhere that farmers can cultivate crops.

Maize from Mexico and potatoes from the Andes made up what the French historian Fernand Braudel called "the miracle crops." Europe first benefited from the American largess when the white potato spread from its home in Bolivia and Peru through Ireland and on across the European continent to Russia. This new miracle tuber provided more calories and nutrition per acre than any form of grain, and it did so on land so poor that it would not even support oats. Even though most Europeans never learned to eat maize, they fed it to their chickens and pigs, and it thereby improved their diet by greatly increasing their supply of protein through eggs and meat.

Maize made an even bigger impact in Africa, where it supplemented traditional grains grown in temperate zones and spread into tropic zones. Together with the other American Indian crops of peanuts, cassava, and a wide variety of beans, maize allowed African nutrition to climb at such a rate that Africa's population survived and even increased despite the pernicious slave trade.

In Asia, the American sweet potato and maize grew in zones too cool or dry for rice. The introduction of maize and the sweet potato—along with peanuts, tomatoes, and chilies—permitted Chinese farmers to bring new areas of their continent into productive cultivation. The oils from sunflowers and peanuts as well as the protein from a wide variety of beans helped to feed the growing population of humans as well as their domesticated animals.

Chilies and avocados had a greater impact in India and southern Asia. Tomatoes and sweet peppers greatly improved diets in the Mediterranean and the Balkans. The pineapple greatly changed farming in the South Pacific, where it was introduced as a cash crop. Cacao and peanuts played similar roles in the economy of West Africa.

The economies of many nations now depend on these American Indian crops. Just as the United States leads the world in maize production and cotton production, Russia is the world's largest producer of potatoes and sunflowers. China leads in the production of sweet potatoes, India in peanut production, and the Ivory Coast in the production of cacao.

If we look at the larger population picture since the spread of American crops around the world, we see tremendous increases. In fact, improved nutrition accounts for most of the world's population growth prior to this century.

Medicine and Healing

At the same time that global trading routes spread American Indian crops around the world, they also spread a variety of new medicines that proved effective in treating some of the oldest diseases of humankind.

The Quechua-speaking Incas of the Andes understood well the medicinal properties of many plants growing not only in the Andes but in the Amazon jungle as well. One of these plants was a tree that grew at elevations of three thousand to nine thousand feet and produced the bitter-tasting quinine or "Peruvian bark" that could cure many ailments, including cramps, chills, and heart-rhythm disorders.

The introduction of quinine to Europe for the treatment of malaria marks the beginning of modern pharmacology. This seems to have taken place in about 1630; by 1643 the bark had gained mention in a Belgian medical text, *Discours et advis sur les flus de ventre douloureux,* by Herman van der Heyden. The new medicine made extensive European settlement of America possible. For example, records of Governor Berkeley of Virginia for 1671 show that before the introduction of quinine into Virginia one colonist in every five died from malaria within a year of settling there; after the incorporation of quinine, no one died from malaria. The change was dramatic and simple.

Two other American plants, related to the tree that provided quinine, helped treat amoebic dysentery, a lethal intestinal infection that produces high fever and bloody diarrhea following the ingestion of certain amoebas. Even today the disease ranks as one of the world's major killers of young children; if not treated, it can kill adults as well. The Indians of the Amazon cured this disease with medicine made from roots of three- to four-year-old specimens of the plants *Cephaelis ipecacuanha* and *C. acuminata.* The Indians called this medicine *ipecac.* One of its properties was that in certain doses it caused the patient to vomit. The Indians used it in this capacity both to expel unwanted substances such as poisons and as a way of ritually purifying the body. Poison clinics throughout the world still use ipecac for the same purposes; patients are given ipecac to induce vomiting after they have ingested a toxic substance.

When Francisco de Orellana made his voyages down the Napo River through what is now Ecuador and discovered the Amazon, Indians along the way frequently attacked his heavily armed band. The simple, wooden weapons of the Indians seemed to offer little threat to the sophisticated European arsenal of metal. The confidence of the Spanish suffered a serious challenge, however, when one of Orellana's men died from a minute Indian arrow that had barely pierced his skin. This unknown soldier of Orellana's became the first European victim of an arrow tipped with the powerful poison *curare.*

Initially, no one could imagine any practical application for such a powerful drug other than for illegal or unethical purposes, but doctors soon found that small doses of curare acted as a muscle relaxant. In this way it served as the first treatment for tetanus or lockjaw, which causes a severe cramping of the muscles of the throat and jaw; curare relieved the cramping by relaxing the affected muscles. Doctors soon gave it to patients going into abdominal surgery to relax the strong muscles that otherwise made operations in that area nearly impossible. Doctors also found that curare relaxed a patient enough to permit the insertion of a tube into the windpipe to facilitate breathing during operations. In due time curare was synthesized into a number of different muscle-relaxant drugs fulfilling a variety of medicinal purposes.

The Indians of northern California and Oregon gave modern medicine its most commonly used laxative or cathartic. They used the bark of the cascara buckthorne (*Rhamnus purshiana*) as a cure for constipation. The Old World already had a number of such medical cures, but the Indian remedy, as advertisers still stress today, acts in an exceptionally mild manner. Even though scientists have failed to synthesize it in the laboratory, it has spread to become the world's most commonly used laxative since its commercial introduction by the American pharmaceutical industry in 1878.

Indians in the northeastern United States treated intestinal worms with the vermifuge pinkroot (*Spigelia marilandica*), a plant with red and yellow flowers. Trees of the genus *Cornus* of North America, known as dogwoods, were used by the Indians to reduce fever. They had a number of emetics in addition to ipecac; these included bloodroot (*Sanguinaria canadensis;* also called puccoon) and lobelia. The Indians made a perspiration-increasing drug from the snakeroot *Aristolochia serpenteria,* an astringent from alumroot (*Heuchera americana*), and a stimulant from boneset (*Eupatorium perfoliatum*).

One of the most important, yet most abused, medicines came from the coca bush of South America. Coca had arrived in Europe by 1565, when Nicolas Monardes of Seville made the first scientific descriptions and drawings of it. Not until the late 1850s, though, did German chemists manage to isolate the active ingredient, which became known as cocaine. Its first major medical use, in the 1880s, was as an anesthetic for painful eye surgery and later for dental surgery and other kinds of operations. Eventually chemists synthesized cocaine to make procaine. Under the name novocaine, it continues today as one of the most important anesthetics in the world. Even though cocaine cured nothing, it launched the medical use of local anesthesia, which replaced the more common use of ether.

The Indian medicine coca formed the basis not only of cocaine and novocaine but of flavorings for wines and soft drinks as well. The history of the coca plant shows how easily the medicines of the Indians could be used for important medical purposes, as well as for more frivolous, and even dangerous, ones.

Crafts and Industrial Products

The Indians had many crops, such as cotton, henequen, and tobacco, that became a part of world agriculture and greatly stimulated industrialization. Asia had already produced some forms of cotton, but the long-staple varieties of the American Indians proved superior for weaving into soft cloth. The Mexican dye cochineal was used to lend fabrics the bright scarlet color that gave British soldiers the nickname "redcoats."

In the nineteenth century, rubber from the Indians of the Amazon was put to new uses by Europeans and became important in military gear and later in making tires for bicycles and, eventually, for automobiles. Rubber became one of the fundamental natural resources of the twentieth century, and its cultivation spread from the Amazon to much of southern Asia.

Nowhere in native America was there the attention to metal weapons manufacturing that was common in Europe, Africa, and Asia. American metal technology, however, was much more advanced in the decorative arts. Indians used the lost-wax technique for casting gold and silver. This art reached a particularly sophisticated level among the Chibchas of modern Colombia. Most of this decorative metalwork disappeared early on as a result of the extensive looting that took place in the early years of Spanish conquest and subsequently reappeared in the form of money and of decorations in European churches, palaces, and cathedrals.

In various parts of the Americas, Indians invented items as varied as the hammock, snowshoes, the bulb syringe, kayaks, and the process of using acid to etch designs onto shell. Indians invented the blowgun, developed animal and bird decoys for use in hunting, wove cloth from feathers, made rubber boots, and invented various musical instruments. The Indians developed a wide assortment of sports based around the rubber ball, and built numerous large courts for the playing of ball games. Some of these games, such as lacrosse, were taken over nearly directly from the North American Indians; others were changed and incorporated into Old World games using the Indian substance of rubber.

In general, Indian science and technology had considerably less impact on the world than Indian agriculture and medicines. This was not because the Indians' technology and science were inferior, but because the Europeans were often not at a level sophisticated enough to allow them to adopt Indian knowledge. For example, the Mayas used the concept of zero and place mathematics, and they had a more accurate calendar than that of the Europeans. The Spaniards did not adopt these superior systems because they did not understand them and saw no need to change their older but less accurate systems.

In addition to the many material contributions of Indians to world culture through their agriculture, medicine, and technology, they influenced the nonmaterial domains of culture as well. In areas such as spiritualism and in political ideology and practice, the Indians had a great impact on the Enlightenment in Europe and the development of democratic federalism in the United States. Such Indian influences as these have only just begun to have a widespread effect.

Crosby, Alfred W., Jr., *The Columbian Exchange* (Westport, Conn.: Greenwood Press, 1972); Driver, Harold E., *The Indians of North America,* 2d ed. (Chicago: University of Chicago Press, 1969); Weatherford, Jack, *Indian Givers: How the Indians of the Americas Transformed the World* (New York: Crown Publishers, 1988).

JACK WEATHERFORD
Macalester College

INDIAN RIGHTS ASSOCIATION

Formed in Philadelphia in 1882 by the Philadelphians Herbert Walsh and Henry Pancoast, the Indian Rights Association (IRA) was dedicated to providing the equal protection of the law, education, citizenship, and individual land title to Indians. It was also interested in civil-service reform and good administration in the Bureau of Indian Affairs. Believing that Indians should give up their "tribal relation," with the goal of complete assimilation through education as Christian agriculturalists, the reformers blamed avaricious whites and a corrupt and paternalistic government for the continuing existence of the "Indian problem." They saw themselves as advocating equal status for Indians, and to that end they organized branch associations in cities, sent representatives on fact-finding missions into Indian country, published pamphlets, maintained a highly public visibility through speeches and in the press, and kept a full-time lobbyist in Washington. So effective was the association that most of its program was enacted before 1900. Among the IRA's achievements were the passage of the General Allotment Act, which included allotments and citizenship, the formation of a comprehensive compulsory government school system, and the extension of civil-service rules to the Indian Office. After the turn of the century, the association began to lose its effectiveness in Indian-policy formulation. The tide began to turn against the failed allotment policy and in favor of Indian land consolidation, cultural retention, and self-government. The IRA opposed the Indian Reorganization Act and other reforms of the 1930s and bemoaned the decline of missionary influence in the Indian Office. Though no longer the power it once was, the association continued to be active. It warned against the rapid pace of the termination policy of the 1950s and supported the self-determination movement of the 1960s and 1970s. Yet after the Indian activism of the sixties and seventies, many of the older white reform organizations were weakened. By 1994, the Indian Rights Association had ceased to exist.

Groups such as the Indian Rights Association considered themselves the "friends of the Indian," but although they were well intentioned and some of their activities were beneficial, many of the policies they helped enact, such as allotment, were tremendously destructive to Indian people.

See also Reformers and Reform Groups.

INDIAN TERRITORY

Indian Territory was never a territory in the strict political sense of the term. For the entire period of its existence, it was an unorganized territory, meaning that there was never a territorial government or a federally appointed territorial governor. The only governments were those of the resident tribes. Thus Indian Territory was defined not by what it was, but rather by what it was not: Indian Territory was the Indian-occupied region of the central United States that was not part of any state or organized territory. As a result, its geographical boundaries were frequently ambiguous and periodically altered. For much of its history it was referred to not as Indian Territory, but rather as "the Indian territory."

Indian Territory was a product of Indian removal. With the purchase of Louisiana in 1803 the idea developed of resettling the tribes of the eastern United States on the new lands west of the Mississippi. Here, beyond the limits of white settlement, it was thought, the tribes could have permanent homes and live undisturbed. In 1804 Congress passed legislation authorizing the negotiation of removal treaties with the eastern tribes, and in the subsequent two decades several tribes or segments of tribes moved west. This first phase of removal was relatively voluntary. It was also piecemeal and chaotic, since white settlers were moving west of the Mississippi as well. In 1819 Arkansas Territory was established; in 1821 Missouri was admitted to the Union; and in 1824 the present western boundary of Arkansas was drawn. In 1825 the region west of Arkansas and Missouri and east of Mexican territory was defined as "Indian Country."

In 1830 Congress set out to finish the process of removal by adopting the Indian Removal Act, which provided for the exchange of the remaining Indian lands east of the Mississippi for new lands in Indian Country. The western boundaries of Missouri and Arkansas were to become what some foresaw as a "permanent Indian frontier," with the land beyond set aside by Congress for Indian use. After 1830 this land gradually became known as the Indian territory. In the fifteen years that followed the passage of the removal act, almost one hundred thousand eastern Indians were resettled west of Missouri and Arkansas. Following the boundary, which extended from the Red River north to the Missouri River, the federal Indian Office established an unbroken line of Indian nations or reservations. Many of the treaties that created these preserves used language similar to that contained in the treaty with the Cherokees, which stated that the new lands "shall, in no future time without their consent, be included within the territorial limits or jurisdiction of any State or Territory."

President Andrew Jackson foresaw the need for an officially defined Indian Territory as well as the need for some form of tribal confederacy to govern the territory. In 1834 he proposed the Western Territory Bill, which would have formally defined Indian Territory as that region bounded on the south by the Red River, on the north by the Platte and Missouri Rivers, on the east by the states of Missouri and Arkansas, and on the west by the international boundary with Mexico. So defined, this territory would have covered most of present-day Oklahoma and all of Kansas, as well as southern Nebraska and eastern Colorado. Although the bill was not enacted, in that same year Congress did pass legislation that defined "Indian Country" as that portion of the western United States that was not part of any state or territory. The new law also regulated certain activities of non-Indians within the region and established judicial boundaries: the northern portion of the region was to be under the control of the federal courts of Missouri; the southern portion (modern Oklahoma), under the federal courts of Arkansas.

The Indian population was not evenly distributed within the Indian territory during this early period. The most populous of the tribes—the Choctaw, Cherokee, Chickasaw, Creek, and Seminole Nations (the so-called Five Civilized Tribes)—were located in the southern portion. To the north, in present-day Kansas, were the reservations of numerous small midwestern and plains tribes.

A second removal and concentration of Indian populations occurred in 1854, when twelve treaties were negotiated with tribes living in the northern part of the territory. Together, these agreements opened 18 million acres of land for white settlement. That same year Congress created Kansas Territory, which encompassed the remaining tribes and their diminished reservations. Thus in 1854 the Indian territory was reduced to the area approximating present-day Oklahoma, with most of the land owned by the Five Civilized Tribes.

In 1865, because the governments of the Five Civilized Tribes had supported the South during the Civil War, the federal government declared its existing treaties with these tribes void. New treaties were negotiated the following year, in which the tribes either ceded the western portions of their lands to the federal

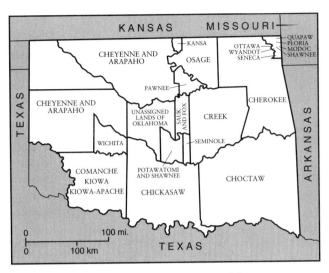

INDIAN TERRITORY IN 1889

government for the resettlement of "friendly Indians" or, in the case of the Cherokees, provided for the sale of their western lands ("the Cherokee Outlet") to friendly tribes. The Choctaw-Chickasaw treaty also included a plan to establish a territorial government for tribes, with the Commissioner of Indian Affairs assuming the position, and additional title, of Governor of the Territory of Oklahoma. However, these provisions were never implemented, and the Indian territory remained unorganized.

With these newly ceded western lands of the Five Civilized Tribes available for Indian settlement, a third wave of removals began as the government started moving the remaining tribes from Texas, Kansas, Nebraska, and elsewhere into the territory. Between 1866 and 1885, the Cheyenne and Arapaho, the Comanche, Kiowa, and Apache, the Wichita and Caddo, the Potawatomi and Shawnee, the Kickapoo, the Iowa, the Sauk and Fox, the Pawnee, the Oto and Missouri, the Ponca, the Tonkawa, the Kaw, the Osage, the Peoria, the Wyandot, the Eastern Shawnee, the Modoc, and the Ottawa Reservations were established in Indian Territory. At first the term *Indian Territory* was not applied to these new reservations. The Potawatomi treaty of 1867, for example, specified only that the new reservation would be "in the Indian country south of Kansas." It further stated that this land would "never be included within the jurisdiction of any state or territory, unless an Indian Territory be organized." No mention was made of Indian Territory in the 1868 treaty with the Cheyennes and Arapahos. However, the

Osage Reservation Act of 1872 stated that the reservation was located in "Indian Territory," and all subsequent tribal agreements, executive orders, and other federal actions relative to the region referred to the area as Indian Territory. Thus, starting in the 1870s, government officials increasingly treated the region as a territory.

By 1885 all of the land available in Indian Territory—except for a 2-million-acre tract in the very center, called the Unassigned Lands, and the westernmost portion of the Cherokee Outlet—had been assigned Indian tribes. In 1887, Congress passed the General Indian Allotment Act, which initiated the process of dividing tribal property and dissolving tribal agreements. Of the tribes in Indian Territory, only the Five Civilized Tribes and the Osages were exempted from its provisions.

In 1889 two significant events occurred. In March, Congress established a separate federal court at Muskogee for Indian Territory, and for the first time it officially defined the area's boundaries: Indian Territory was the area bounded by the states of Kansas, Missouri, Arkansas, and Texas and the Territory of New Mexico. On April 22 the Unassigned Lands were opened to settlement by non-Indians in the first of the famous land runs. Over fifty thousand homesteaders settled in the region on that day.

In May 1890 Indian Territory was divided into Oklahoma Territory and Indian Territory. Oklahoma Territory was defined as incorporating the Unassigned Lands and all reservations, with the exception of those of the Five Civilized Tribes and the small reservations in the extreme northeastern portion of Indian Territory. While all of the reservations in the Cherokee Outlet were to be part of Oklahoma Territory, that portion of the Outlet still owned by the Cherokee Nation would remain as part of Indian Territory until purchased by the government. Almost immediately a special commission was organized to negotiate the allotment of the reservations in Oklahoma Territory and the sale of "surplus" (unallotted) lands so that they could be opened for non-Indian settlement. In 1893 the Cherokee sold their remaining portion of the Outlet, which was immediately incorporated into Oklahoma Territory and opened for settlement. Thus by 1893 Indian Territory had been reduced to just the reservations of the Five Civilized Tribes proper and the small reservations in the northeast. In 1893 the Dawes Commission was created by Congress to negotiate agreements with the Five Civilized Tribes to allot their lands, and in 1898 the allotment process began in what remained of Indi-

an Territory. In a futile attempt to maintain some semblance of continued Indian separation, leaders of the Five Civilized Tribes organ-ized a constitutional convention in 1905, drew up a constitution, and asked to be admitted to the Union as the state of Sequoyah. Congress rejected the plan and in 1907 approved a statute that joined Indian Territory with Oklahoma Territory to create the new state of Oklahoma.

See also Civil War in Indian Territory, The; Five Civilized Tribes.

Foreman, Grant, *Indian Removal* (Norman: University of Oklahoma Press, 1932); Foreman, Grant, *The Last Trek of the Indians* (Chicago: University of Chicago Press, 1946); Wright, Muriel H., *A Guide to the Indian Tribes of Oklahoma* (Norman: University of Oklahoma Press, 1951).

GARRICK BAILEY
(Euro-American, Cherokee, and Choctaw)
University of Tulsa

ROBERTA GLENN BAILEY
Tulsa, Oklahoma

INDIAN-WHITE RELATIONS IN ALASKA

The earliest oral tradition recounting the arrival of Europeans in Alaska dates to 1786. The L'uknax̱.adi Coho clan, who had stopped at Lituya Bay on their way to trade with the Yakutat Tlingits, saw two ships, which they believed to be great birds with white wings. Historical records reveal that the ships were under the command of the French explorer La Pérouse. The written accounts indicate that the Russians were the first Europeans to reach Alaska, arriving in 1741. La Pérouse's record of his visit identifies two issues of significance to the Tlingits. The Tlingits sought to establish economic relations because they wanted to trade for iron. They also made it clear that they were the owners of the land, and they sold the French an island for their use. This encounter set the stage for the next two hundred years of Indian-white relations in Alaska, which—in addition to the Athabaskan, Tlingit, and Haida Indians—would involve the Inupiat and Yupiks and their ancestral cousins, the Aleuts.

Until the late 1800s, most of the encounters between native peoples and Europeans occurred in the southern coastal regions of Alaska. The Inupiat, Yupiks, and Athabaskans lived in the interior regions and along the western and northern coasts and had little or no contact with the Russians. They were unaware that their country had been claimed by the Russians and then sold to the United States.

Native-white relations in Alaska were structured by economic, political, religious, and educational activities. The objectives of Alaska Natives were fairly uniform. They wanted to maintain their traditional cultures, to protect ownership of their land, and to benefit from the technology and economic opportunities made available by the arrival of white people in Alaska. The Russian policy toward Alaska Natives, with the exception of the Aleuts, was generally consistent with these objectives. The Russians claimed Alaska through discovery, but they exercised little or no control over the land or its people. The Americans, however, changed this policy and set an intrusive course. The conflict between Native and American objectives led to open confrontations in Southeast Alaska and less than amicable relationships elsewhere.

Political Relations

Alaska Natives maintained their political independence during the Russian period (1741–1867). They never entered into any treaties with the Russians, nor did they sell them any land. They refused to pay the taxes that the Russians attempted to impose. For their part, the Russians gradually abandoned the effort to control Alaska Natives because it undermined their fur-trading enterprise. Attempts by the Russians to impose political authority over the Tlingits led to an attack on the Russian fort in Sitka in 1802. Natives who embraced Christianity were recognized as Russian citizens, with the same rights as other Russians. On the other hand, tribes that refused to acknowledge the Russians and practiced their ancient customs were classified as uncivilized. While shunned by official Russian authorities, these "uncivilized" people also lived free of outside constraints.

The 1867 Treaty of Cession, under which Alaska was ceded to the United States, provided that "the uncivilized tribes will be subject to such laws that the United States may, from time to time, adopt in regard to aboriginal tribes of that country." Nevertheless, the treaty appeared to confer citizenship upon the "uncivilized" tribes, because it made no legal distinctions among native tribes. Alaska Natives, on the other hand, did not acknowledge the legitimacy of the Treaty of Cession and in fact dispatched representatives to Washington to protest the sale, which they viewed as illegal. They argued that the Russians had been allowed to live in Alaska only with their consent and for the mutual benefit of both peoples.

The political authority of Alaska Natives went almost unchallenged during the initial period of U.S. administration, in part because of the small American population and the absence of civil law. In the southeast, the military supported Tlingit law as the most efficient way to ensure order in Alaska. Conflicts between the Tlingits and the military erupted only when native people applied their traditional laws to whites. In separate incidents, the military attacked native villages in Wrangell, Angoon, and Kake, burning and destroying the houses and canoes so essential to Tlingit livelihood.

It was not until the passage of the Organic Act of 1884, which established civilian rule in Alaska, and the subsequent influx of white settlers and American law into the territory that the political authority of Alaska Natives was seriously challenged. White businessmen and missionaries had led a well-organized effort to promote the passage of the act in order to expand their opportunities and to promote the "settlement" of the area.

While it is now recognized that the legal status of Alaska Natives is substantially the same as that of federally recognized American Indian tribes, their legal status in the early historic period was clouded by judicial action. Business interests opposed any special political status for Alaska Natives. They felt that the extension of American laws to Alaska Natives would undermine economic expansion by creating categories of "tribally owned" property and establishing specific rights for native groups. Through the decisions of one judge—Matthew Deady of the Portland federal district court, which had jurisdiction over Alaska until 1884—Alaska Natives were denied protection provided under U.S. Indian law and policy. Deady determined the legal status of Alaska Natives in a series of rulings inconsistent with existing federal Indian policy. The basic effect was that Alaska Natives were denied legal protection under both Indian law and territorial civil law. They had no legal recourse in resisting the ongoing encroachments into their territories and the appropriations of their land and resources. Reacting to the damage wrought on their communities by American law, Alaska Natives became convinced that they should become involved in politics. In 1924 they elected William Paul, a brilliant Tlingit lawyer, as the first Alaska Native representative to the territorial legislature. He was despised by many whites for his successful efforts, both in the legislature and in the courts, to eradicate discrimination. In 1945 the territorial legislature enacted an antidiscrimination bill. Upon the bill's passage, Paul observed that although it wouldn't end racist attitudes, it did outlaw discriminatory action.

Religion and Education

Religion and education were introduced simultaneously to Alaska Natives. Alaska is a vast territory, one-fifth the size of the continental United States. At the time of the Alaska purchase, thirty thousand Alaska Natives with six thousand children of school age lived in widely scattered villages inaccessible by regular means of travel. Early missionaries worked to divide the territory among the different Christian denominations, and virtually all operated schools. By 1903, eighty-two missions and mission churches were operating in Alaska. Sheldon Jackson, a Presbyterian missionary who served as the government's first Special Agent for Education, attempted to expand the scope of the twenty-five-thousand-dollar annual educational appropriation by using these funds to subsidize missionary schools. He believed it was necessary to separate native children from their parents, and urged the spread of boarding schools across Alaska. Children arrived in schools speaking only their native language, and they were routinely punished for failing to adopt English. Frequently they finished their schooling determined to abandon their traditions.

In 1905, the territorial government established a dual school system. White children and children who were of mixed blood and led a "civilized" life attended one school, while native children went to a separate school. *Civilized* was defined as having adopted the white man's way of life and associating with white people. Congress also expanded the authority of employees of the education service, allowing them to serve as peace officers. In addition to their educational responsibilities, they had the authority to arrest natives who violated the Criminal Code of Alaska. The segregated school system remained in operation until 1960.

Economic Relations

Economic relations between Alaska Natives and outsiders began in the eighteenth century. According to Tlingit oral traditions, the Russians were originally attracted to the shores of Alaska after they discovered a floating bundle of sea-otter pelts wrapped in halibut skins; news of the valuable cargo of furs was enough to encourage a rapid Russian economic expansion into Alaska. The Russians started in the western Aleutians, then moved east to Kodiak Island, and finally arrived on the shores of South Central Alaska and Southeast Alaska.

The Aleuts were the first to face the cruelty of the Russian commercial hunters. These hunters frequently held native women captive, leaving their husbands no alternative but to hunt for furs for the Russians. Aleuts were conscripted for hunts that extended along the coastal areas of southern Alaska and even to California. In addition, one group was forcibly relocated to the Pribilof Islands in the Bering Sea to harvest seals and prepare their pelts for export. The removal and loss of a large number of hunters from their communities, the brutality of the Russian traders, and the diseases and deprivation that ensued devastated the Aleuts. In little more than a century, their numbers were reduced from fifteen thousand to less than three thousand.

The Russian encounter with the Tlingits was different. Living in more concentrated settlements, and often familiar with Europeans, the Tlingits resisted every effort to enslave them. As a result, trading relations were established in the eighteenth century that were generally mutually beneficial to both the Tlingits and the Russians. As the sea-otter population began to decline, the Russians shifted their focus to the coast of western Alaska and along the Yukon and Kuskokwim Rivers. When the Russians left Alaska in 1867, the native population base in the southern coastal areas of the territory was less than half of what it had been when they first arrived. They had also nearly exterminated the sea-otter population. They left behind the Russian Orthodox religion, a faith that had been largely taken up by the surviving Aleuts.

The discovery of gold in Alaska and Canada in the 1890s changed the balance of power in the region. When the United States assumed jurisdiction of Alaska, the nonnative non-Russian population numbered less than five hundred. But with the prospect of instant wealth promised by the discovery of gold, thousands of prospectors flooded into the interior and western regions of Alaska. By 1900, the population of Nome, in northwestern Alaska, swelled to twenty thousand. By 1908, over $140 million in gold had been extracted from Alaska, but native people—the legitimate owners of the land—did not share in the wealth. In addition, the wildlife populations upon which natives were directly dependent were reduced by uncontrolled hunting and environmental destruction. Diseases accompanied by social vices also took their toll on the native population.

The first salmon cannery in Southeast Alaska was built in 1878. This institution brought with it a new cycle of expropriation of native land and resources that continued for more than a century. The industry quickly expanded into the entire south central region, to Kodiak Island, and then to the Alaska Peninsula and Bristol Bay. Without any regard for the native population, which depended on the salmon resources, the salmon industry ruthlessly took control of all the major salmon streams. Not only did this expansion prevent native people from fishing in their own streams, but it reduced those populations to poverty by refusing them employment in the canneries. Native appeals to the federal and territorial governments for protection were of no avail. Classified as "Alaskans" rather than "Indians," native people could find no legal basis for a claim of protection.

The Aleut, Yupik, and Inupiaq communities that depended upon sea mammals experienced the same fate as the fish-dependent natives in Southeast Alaska. During the years of rapid American expansion, commercial hunters nearly exterminated the walrus, whale, fur-seal, and sea-otter populations. In 1909 a former military officer observed that the effects of the activities of the whites on the native population could "only be viewed as disgraceful to a nation claiming to be civilized, humanitarian or Christian." He reported that indigenous food supplies had been destroyed for a price of $300 million in revenues, that the natives' environment had been altered and their lifestyle changed. And he posed a haunting question: "Will this nation pay its debt on this account?"

Land and Resources

The wholesale expropriation of native land and resources continued throughout the early twentieth century. The Alaska purchase had not extinguished the aboriginal title of Alaska Natives to their property, but federal authorities nevertheless withdrew huge tracts of land for forests, parks, and a large Arctic petroleum reserve. Military installations were established throughout Alaska on lands claimed by native groups. In 1891, still acting without authorization, Congress opened land for town sites and trading and manufacturing sites, timber reserves, and other public purposes. Ironically, the only native group to have land set aside for it was the Canadian Tsimshians: in 1887, Congress established an eighty-six-thousand-acre reservation for that group on lands owned by the Cape Fox Tlingits. The state of Alaska received the largest acreage granted by the federal government: under the Alaska Statehood Act of 1958, the state was allowed to select 108 million acres of Alaska's total acreage of 375 million acres for its own use. The state began its selection of land soon afterward. Much of the land selected was in areas frequently used by native people for hunting and fishing.

The state's selection of this land galvanized Alaska Natives into action. They formed a statewide organization, the Alaska Federation of Natives, to pursue the recognition and settlement of their aboriginal land claims. They were successful in convincing Secretary of the Interior Stewart Udall to impose a freeze on the state's selection of land. Oil discoveries on the North Slope of Alaska in 1968 only added to native determination to win control of their territory. Meanwhile, large energy corporations, eager to tap this resource but faced with both the land freeze and native claims to lands, sided with native people and agitated for a settlement of the land claims. The result was the enactment of the Alaska Native Claims Settlement Act (ANCSA) of 1971.

ANCSA recognized native lands but treated them in a new way. Unlike Indian reservation lands, which are held in trust by the federal government, native land in Alaska would be held under fee simple title. Congress required Alaska Natives to organize twelve regional profit-making corporations and approximately two hundred village corporations to manage this property. Under ANCSA, 44 million acres were conveyed to these regional and village corporations, along with $962.5 million in compensation for the extinguishment of aboriginal title to the remaining acreage of Alaska. All Alaska Natives were enrolled as individual shareholders of the ANCSA corporations. The intent was clear: Congress intended to promote economic development and the economic assimilation of Alaska Natives to the American mold. The results of this decision have been mixed. Some corporations became financially successful, while others remained inactive and a few faced bankruptcy.

ANCSA extinguished aboriginal hunting and fishing rights to "public lands," but subsequent congressional legislation restored protection of subsistence hunting and fishing for rural residents of Alaska. Alaska's state constitution provides for equal hunting and fishing rights for all Alaskans. The issue remains a source of contention between native and nonnative Alaskans and between urban and rural residents. Native people are fighting to protect their subsistence hunting and fishing, which they assert is necessary for their cultural survival.

From the first, outsiders and Alaska Natives have viewed the region and its cultures from very different—virtually opposite—perspectives. Newcomers have sought to "develop" and "civilize" a territory that the indigenous people have always seen as their home.

See also Fishing and Hunting Rights; Indian-White Relations in the United States, 1900 to the Present; Subarctic Tribes.

Case, David S., *Alaska Natives and American Laws* (Fairbanks: University of Alaska Press, 1984); de Laguna, Frederica, *Under Mount Saint Elias: The History and Culture of the Yakutat Tlingit* (Washington, D.C.: Smithsonian Institution Press, 1972); Landon, Steve J., *The Native People of Alaska* (Anchorage: Greatland Graphics, 1987).

ROSITA WORL (Tlingit)
Juneau, Alaska

INDIAN-WHITE RELATIONS IN CANADA, 1763 TO THE PRESENT

Following the British victory over French forces in North America at Quebec City in 1759, Indian-white relations moved into an era of exclusively British policy-making. That era began with the Royal Proclamation of 1763, which recognized Indian land rights and set the pattern for treaty making in the remainder of British North America to the present time. Historically, Canadian authorities have been ambivalent about treaties, viewing them as "mere promises" to peoples who were destined to disappear as a distinct population. Today, rejuvenated Indian Nations have successfully forced their concerns to the forefront of ongoing constitutional negotiations and, as a result, have assumed an increasingly prominent role in Canadian society.

It should be noted that the term *First Nation* has come to be widely recognized in Canada as a less stereotypical term than *Indian,* and therefore preferable. The term *aboriginal* has also received coinage, as a result of its usage in the Canadian Constitution. *First Nation* and *aboriginal* are inclusive of all concerned groups—Indians, Métis, and Inuits. Similarly, *settler* and *colonist* are preferable terms to *white,* which suggests homogeneity.

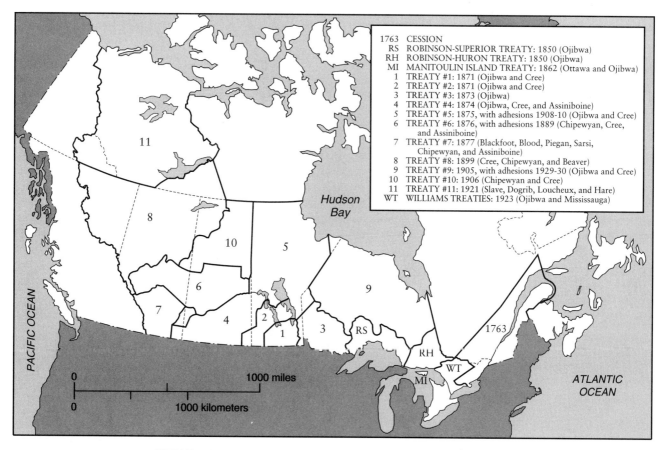

TREATIES WITH INDIAN NATIONS IN CANADA, 1763–1923

The Royal Proclamation of 1763

In 1763, nearly three centuries after Columbus's first voyage, North America was still largely unsettled by Europeans. The British and French were vying for influence over the continent. Indian Nations, who had initially welcomed and aided the European newcomers, had formed alliances with various powers (and each other) and played decisive roles in numerous struggles. Many Indian Nations in the interior remained unconquered.

The rivalry between the European powers was fierce, and the tenacity of the alliance that developed between the Indians and the French nearly toppled the British. Nevertheless, at Quebec City, in the heart of French territory, General Wolfe defeated General Montcalm on the Plains of Abraham in 1759 and the French era was over.

The suspicion toward the British of the Indians who had fought with the French led to "Pontiac's Rebellion," in which nearly a dozen forts were destroyed. The Royal Proclamation of 1763 was intended to make peace after the fighting and to consolidate the British hold on North America. Specifically, the proclamation recognized Indian ownership interests in all unsettled lands, and formalized the process of acquiring such lands from Indians. Settlers were prohibited from encroaching on unceded Indian territories. When it became necessary to negotiate with First Nations over territory, the British would convene a meeting at which terms of purchase would be agreed upon, and a commitment to peace and settlement would occur in the form of a treaty. When American independence was achieved, the royal proclamation ceased to apply to the new territory of the United States. However, it continued to set the pattern for treaty making in the remainder of British North America.

It should be borne in mind that despite European portrayals of First Nations as "savages," a strong tradition of covenant making already existed among them. Treatylike agreements fit well with Indian experience and were easily understood by native leaders. For First Nations, however, such agreements were more than simple political commitments; they were sacred covenants witnessed by the Creator. Indians believed that breaking such arrangements would bring dire spiritual repercussions.

Treaty Making with First Nations

The proclamation ushered in an era of treaty making as the official British policy for dealing with Indians in British North America. After the War of 1812, First Nations in eastern North America fell into decline as potent military forces. The need remained, however, to deal with them sensitively and judiciously, in order to avoid further unrest. As the British consolidated their territories north of the Great Lakes, they signed treaties with the Huron-Robinsons and the Huron-Superiors (both 1850). These treaties provided for the payment of annuities and recognized aboriginal hunting and fishing rights. Among the policy debates accompanying the treaty-making process was the question of whether Indians could adapt to white cultural norms. In 1830, Lieutenant-Governor Sir John Colborne set up the Coldwater experiment, which involved "collecting the Indians in villages and inducing them to cultivate the land." In contrast, in the late 1830s, Sir Frances Bond Head established Manitoulin Island as an isolated area, with the expectation that the Indians who lived there would slowly fade into extinction.

The next important era of treaty making came with the founding of Canada in 1867. Prime Minister Sir John A. Macdonald's "National Policy" led central Canada—Ontario and Quebec—to prosper and grow, as industrial centers in these areas catered to a burgeoning frontier in the West. The Canadian Pacific Railroad was built west as the Northwest Territories and British Columbia joined the Confederation in 1870. To deal with Indian claims in these new regions, new treaties were negotiated. Canadian officials saw these treaties as instruments to assist Indians in making a transition to a new mode of economy, particularly once it became apparent that the buffalo would quickly disappear. In addition to granting hunting and fishing rights and annual annuities (typically five dollars), the treaties also set aside lands for agricultural purposes—generally, one-fifth of a square mile per band member. Agricultural implements such as plows were to be provided. Other benefits included medical care, exemption from overseas war service, and tax immunity.

Although the approach of the treaty negotiators was extremely paternalistic, the Indians were aware of what was at stake and did not automatically accede to the treaty offers. For example, talks on one treaty dragged on for three years and resulted in an increase in amounts of annuities and land allotments. In drafting another, the negotiators were forced to include a famine clause, a far-sighted demand by the First Nations under the circumstances. Almost immediately after the treaties had been agreed upon, disputes arose as to what they meant. While the whites saw treaties as total surrenders of interest in the ceded lands, the Indians often maintained that they had surrendered these lands for agricultural purposes only and that they retained ownership over the animals, the waters, and the subsurface resources.

Ultimately, though, control over Indian affairs came not from the treaties, which were never fully ratified by Parliament, but from the federal Indian Act. This law underwent its first major consolidation in 1876. According to the new law, Indians were bound to their reserves as legal minors (until 1960, they were excluded from citizenship and denied the right to vote). The whole thrust of the act was to make Indians totally subservient to the Department of Indian Affairs, and to empower the department to undertake whatever measures were necessary to "civilize" them. Every effort was made to discourage and destroy all vestiges of Indian culture. The best hope held out to the Indians was for them to become "civilized" enough to qualify for enfranchisement. Under such an arrangement, the Indians would renounce their identity and ties to their community in return for the rights of ordinary citizens, such as the right to vote and own private property.

Despite the flurry of treaty making that accompanied the early period of Canadian expansion, close to half of Canada, primarily on the West Coast and in the Far North, remained unceded. In other words, the aboriginal claim of the First Nations had not been fully extinguished. The colony of British Columbia, however, took the position that it had unilaterally extinguished aboriginal title prior to joining Canada. Court challenges such as the *Calder* case (or *Nishga* case) in 1972 have forced provincial governments to address the issue, and this pressure has led to negotiations with groups such as the Crees in northern Quebec. Under the James Bay and Northern Quebec Agreement (1975), for example, the Crees gained control over 5,543 square kilometers of Quebec and received $233 million in compensation.

Canadian Policy Regarding First Nations

Up until recent times, Canadian policy toward First Nations could be summed up in three words: protection, civilization, and assimilation. British imperialist ideology held that Indian tribes were racially and culturally inferior to European—and, more specifically, Anglo-Saxon—cultural groups. As a result, although treaties were ostensibly made between two nations, their effect was simply to get First Nations out of the way of immigrant settlement and onto reserves, where the tribes would either "melt away" or become "civilized" enough to become Canadian citizens.

Substantial differences in interpretation emerged when opportunities arose to adjudicate the meaning of the treaties. The First Nations believed that, by virtue of the negotiations and the sacred ceremonies sealing the agreements, the treaties were binding. In the eyes of the courts, however, the treaties contained no more than "mere promises"; the government was bound only by its honor to uphold them. In 1918 Fred Loft, a Mohawk, helped to found the League of Indians of Canada, one of Canada's earliest national Indian organizations, to fight for treaty rights and land claims. Unfortunately, the Indian Department opposed the league at all turns, and, largely owing to Loft's ill health, the league soon disbanded.

In 1931, legal experts claimed that the Statute of Westminster, which saw the Canadian Crown replace the British Crown as sovereign of Canada, nullified the treaties with the Indians. Indians expressed their concern that by withdrawing its authority the British Crown was abandoning its responsibilities and "putting the fox in charge of the chicken coop." The long-term government stategy was in fact to eliminate Indians as a legally distinct people. In 1947, a government anthropologist, Diamond Jenness, actually presented a "Plan to Liquidate Canada's Indian Problem in 25 Years." His proposal appeared to have been adopted by the Trudeau government when it issued its White Paper Policy in 1969. Philosophically, the government talked about creating "equality" by removing the conditions that made First Nations different. But the policy amounted to a blueprint for termination: eliminating the treaties, Indian status, and Indian reserves. The policy provoked widespread Indian opposition, and led to the formation of the first truly national Indian political organization, the National Indian Brotherhood, in 1970.

Recent Constitutional Developments

First Nations had always felt somewhat excluded from the fabric of a country said to have only two founding nations—English and French. It was once believed that First Nations were biologically and culturally inferior, and were destined to fade into oblivion. But today, their population of approximately 1 million is among the fastest-growing segments of Canadian society. With no special representation in Parliament, however, First Nations remain politically insignificant. Although they represent approximately 4 percent of the population, dispersed in over two thousand communities across Canada, only 1 percent of the members of Parliament are First Nations. First Nations have had to use moral suasion and the media to assert their place as Canada's third "founding culture." That opportunity and challenge presented itself beginning with the patriation of the constitution in 1982, when the current Canadian Constitution replaced the British North America Act as the supreme law of the land.

Section 35(2) of this constitution recognized that "the 'aboriginal peoples of Canada' includes the Indian, Inuit and Métis peoples." The existence of varying degrees of status for persons of aboriginal ancestry in Canada has always been a complicating factor in government relations with the First Nations. "Status" or "registered" Indians are essentially those who are recognized under the Indian Act as being legally entitled to "special status." There were 543,000 Status Indians in Canada in 1993. Another significant group recognized in Section 35 were the mixed-blood "Métis," who descended from French-Canadian males and Indian females, were generally associated with the fur trade and tended to demonstrate mixed French and Indian cultural attributes. And the constitution also recognized the Inuits, otherwise called Eskimos, as a distinct aboriginal group. Section 35 also stated that "the existing aboriginal and treaty rights of the aboriginal peoples of Canada are hereby recognized and confirmed." These constitutional statements still lack legal clarity and definition. Some officials claimed that the only rights that existed were hunting and fishing rights. The constitution did, however, make a commitment to convene future constitutional conferences to define aboriginal matters.

The status of Canada's Indian treaties also became a point of debate. Indian delegations traveled to England to ask the queen to intercede as the original party to the treaties. The situation was referred back to Canada, however, and the recognition granted in Section 35 was eventually confirmed despite a concerted effort, particularly on the part of the provincial premiers, to exclude it. Despite the early victory, however, the constitutional talks on aboriginal matters in 1983 were disappointing. Quebec refused to participate, and there was wide disagreement over what constituted "existing aboriginal and treaty rights." The 1984 constitutional talks focused on the concept of "aboriginal self-government." Two very different approaches were espoused: First Nations advocated the recognition of a preexisting right to self-government as the starting point; the federal and provincial leaders, or "First Ministers," maintained that such self-government could come about only with legislative approval by their respective governments. In 1985, the federal and provincial gov-

A Mohawk Indian raising his rifle atop an overturned police car during the 1990 confrontation at the Kahnesetake Reserve near Oka, Quebec. Unresolved land claims are responsible for similar crises at First Nations communities across Canada.

ernments made a modified proposal: that aboriginal self-government be constitutionally recognized, but that its details be negotiated among all levels of jurisdiction. While this compromise proposal received wide support, it was not agreed to by the Assembly of First Nations, which represented Status Indians. A final conference in 1987 saw a further entrenchment of positions, and the constitutional conferences ended in deadlock, with no agreement in sight.

Disappointment over the failed First Nations negotiations was amplified by the central government's ready concession to Quebec's constitutional demands. The Meech Lake Accord was unveiled in 1987 by Prime Minister Brian Mulroney following low-profile meetings of the First Ministers. The accord's main intent was to recognize Quebec's "distinct society" culturally and jurisdictionally. The accord, which required unanimity in the assenting provinces, failed largely as a result of the Cree Indian Elijah Harper, who on June 23,

1990, refused to support the accord in the Manitoba legislature. His action was taken because of the sense that Quebec's French-Canadian interests, which had not been included in the original Canadian Constitution of 1982, were being taken into account at the further expense of First Nations.

The Oka conflict of 1990 epitomized the confusion and bitterness that First Nations were experiencing in their relationship with the rest of the country. Taking place forty kilometers (twenty-five miles) west of Montreal, the Oka conflict was rooted in over two hundred years of neglect. When a local government attempted to expand a golf course onto land claimed by the Mohawks, the Indians protested by blockading entry into the area. The Quebec police were called in. A decision by the police to storm the blockade on July 11 ended in the death of one officer in the ensuing gun battle. The situation shocked the country as the Canadian government called in thirty-seven hundred troops to surround the Mohawks. Although the Mohawks were eventually disarmed and bloodshed was narrowly averted after seventy-eight days of standoff, the conflict had a profound impact on the Canadian psyche, and burned into the country's consciousness the fact that First Nation issues could not continue to be neglected.

The 1993 Charlottetown Accord, a second attempt at national reconciliation, contained hard-won terms that First Nations had achieved in return for their support of the overall agreement. Among these was the constitutional recognition of First Nation self-government by federal and provincial governments. However, this accord was rejected in a national referendum by a public tired of constitutional haggling and more concerned about dealing with the economic problems plaguing the country.

Sovereignty remains central to the disputes between First Nations and the Canadian government. Federal and provincial officials have tended to resist the notion of native sovereignty, largely out of the fear of its implications for political power and revenue sharing. Nevertheless, recent developments—including the statement by the Royal Commission on Aboriginal Peoples that First Nation sovereignty exists in law even without constitutional guarantees, and the election in 1993 of a Liberal government that is receptive to this concept— give some cause for optimism. There has also been a recent flurry of modern-day treaty making. In 1991, an agreement with the Gwich'in of the Yukon gave them control over 15,000 square kilometers, and compensation of $75 million. A 1992 agreement to establish the territory of Nunavut has given the Inuits 350,000 square kilometers and $580 million. These modern treaties are not based on the premise that First Nations will disappear, but instead appear to lay the groundwork for a vibrant future. It appears that the nature of Canadian federalism is changing. Canadians are moving away from the "two nations" concept and toward the idea that their nation is a place where the diversity of First Nations and other cultures can be respected.

See also Eskimo (Yupik/Inupiat/Inuit); Subarctic Tribes.

Dickason, Olive, *Canada's First Nations* (Toronto: McLelland and Stewart, 1992); Morris, Alexander, *Treaties of Canada with the Indians of Manitoba and the Northwest Territories* (Toronto: Coles Publishing Co., 1979); Morse, B., ed. *Aboriginal Peoples and the Law: Indian Métis, and Inuit Rights in Canada* (Ottawa: Carleton University Press, 1985).

BLAIR STONECHILD (Plains Cree)
Saskatchewan Indian Federated College
Regina, Canada

INDIAN-WHITE RELATIONS IN NEW FRANCE

The oral traditions of the Montagnais hunters tell us that they lived at the site of present-day Quebec City until the French came looking for land. They gave the French permission to build a town there in exchange for guns and flour. But with time the French grew in numbers, while the Montagnais shrank and retreated into the hinterland. According to Ojibwa oral traditions, a shaman dreamed that men wearing hats would arrive downriver, and so he set out with some young friends to meet them. He thus helped his nation befriend these people, to whom they traded furs for axes, knives, beads, cloth, firearms, and alcohol. Later these people (the French) approached the shaman's people and concluded an alliance treaty with the Great Lakes nations. Oral traditions thus stress the precedence of the aboriginal occupation and the new era that began with the arrival of people bearing unfamiliar goods and tools but also taking over land. The result was an alliance-cum-invasion.

The primary and most tragic consequence of contact between Europeans and New World peoples in modern-day Canada was the devastation of the aboriginal population by epidemics introduced by the European newcomers. By 1611, Jesuit priests were reporting a decrease in the native population in Acadia coinciding with an increase in exchanges with the French. Toward the end of her life, Marie de l'Incarnation (1599–

1672), who founded the Ursuline order of nuns, wrote from her convent in Quebec City in 1664 that there were only one-twentieth the Amerindians there than had been present when she arrived in 1639. In 1721, the Jesuit historian Charlevoix spoke of the same ratio with regard to the Indians in the interior. Seventeenth-century Jesuit accounts referred to an infinity of native nations, while those of a century later described a deserted countryside with scattered populations and wide empty spaces.

Although they had come initially in the sixteenth century for the cod fishery in the Gulf of St. Lawrence, the French became more and more interested in the fur trade. The first recorded contact between Frenchmen and native people occurred in 1534, when Jacques Cartier traveled up the St. Lawrence. The French began to form alliances in Acadia in 1604 with the Maliseets, Abenakis, and Micmacs. They also forged alliances at Tadoussac in 1603 and at Quebec in 1608 with the Montagnais, Algonquins, Nipissings, and Hurons, creating a huge trade network covering the entire St. Lawrence and Great Lakes basin. These alliances also involved military obligations, which led to the French fighting the Iroquois, the traditional enemies of their allies. The Iroquois allied themselves first with the Dutch and then, in 1664, with the British.

The French-Indian alliance networks built up around the fur trade soon became a factor in the imperial struggles between France and Great Britain. Britain was more capitalistic and a greater naval power. Its colonies contained more immigrants and practiced greater religious tolerance, thereby opening the doors to large numbers of dissidents. Britain was therefore very successful at colonizing North America, building a population in its territories that was twenty to thirty times larger than that of the French colonies. At the end of the French regime, there were only about ten thousand French colonists in Acadia and about sixty thousand along the shores of the St. Lawrence from Montreal downriver, an area from which the sedentary aboriginal population had been largely wiped out in the sixteenth century. There were also a few thousand French, at the most, in the vast hinterland between Montreal and Louisiana. As a result, there were very few tensions with the Indians over land.

The sparseness of the French settlements explains the scope of the French-Amerindian alliance, which expanded to cover the whole interior of the continent. The Indian nations saw Britain's colonial success as a serious threat to their lands and therefore often preferred a tactical alliance with the French. There were other reasons as well, however. For one thing, the Montagnais, Algonquin, and Huron alliance network was much larger than that of the Iroquois. Also, the greater competitiveness of English goods prompted the French to court the Amerindians so they would not lose out on trade. Finally, the importance to France of the spreading of Catholicism meant that French missionaries ventured ever farther afield to live among the Indians.

The huge territory covered by the French-Amerindian alliance included the modern-day Maritime Provinces, the Gulf of St. Lawrence and the St. Lawrence River, the Great Lakes, and the Mississippi. The Amerindians living in this territory were allies of the French, not subjects, and they were indispensable to the French as both trade partners and military allies. This alliance was military, matrimonial, commercial, religious, and cultural in nature. The strength of the French empire rested primarily on the support of France's aboriginal comrades in arms. The French, however, although recognizing their partners' ally status, harbored the (frustrated) desire to reduce their allies to the status of subjects.

In North America, the diplomatic use of blood-tie metaphors defined the status, place, and role of allied partners. For example, the Dutch, and later the British, and their Iroquois allies called each other "brethren," indicating that they felt themselves to be on an equal footing. The same was true for the French and their Indian allies up to 1649. But, after the first major epidemics and the defeat of the Hurons and other French allies at the hands of the Dutch-backed Iroquois, the nations allied with France referred to the French governor as "father." Four Great Lakes nations (the Huron-Wyandots, Ottawas, Potawatomis, and Ojibwas) formed a council that, augmented by many other native nations, accepted their status as "children" of the French governor. The Amerindians living on lands near the colonized area downriver from Montreal also joined this new relationship.

For the Indian nations of New France, the native, and not the European, family was the point of reference. Traditionally, in northeastern North America parental authority was much less coercive than in Europe. In agreeing to call the governor their father, the native chiefs required that he be a provider and defender, allowing him to play a role much like that of an Indian chief. In other words, they expected him to be a leader who could rally everyone around him and yet act noncoercively. The French did not see things in this way. Their goal was to use the *father* title to impose upon their allies the European patrilineal kinship system, whereby the father had absolute authority over his children. Their attitude caused a great deal of friction, with one governor after another trying to give his "children" orders and the latter seeing these orders as proposals to be first debated and then agreed to or turned down. Throughout the French regime, the Amerindian interpretation largely prevailed over the European one.

Historical maps of seventeenth- and eighteenth-century North America reveal a continent divided between empires, with New France filling the whole interior from Quebec to New Orleans. These maps misrepresent the political reality, however. The French king's rule was confined to tiny colonial settlements near the mouths of the St. Lawrence and Mississippi Rivers, and it was only in these small areas that he could give orders, levy taxes, dispose of land, and enlist men in the army. The Amerindian allies of the French had not been subjugated; they were still practically sovereign, regardless of official pronouncements. Instead of showing the extent of the French empire, then, these maps depict the territory occupied by those nations that belonged to the French-Amerindian alliance.

The French and their Indian allies were economically dependent on each other. The French could not obtain the furs on which their economy was based without the technical know-how and trade networks of their allies, and the Indians could not produce iron, glass, or woolens on their own. The fur trade was not based on theft or plunder (although both occurred from time to time); it was based on stable networks and organized around biethnic pairs of Montrealers and Indians across the continent. Over the centuries, however, the fur trade gradually transferred wealth from native to European groups. This was basically due to the fact that the accumulation of capital was one-sided, with European businesspeople, companies, and governments reaping the benefits.

The French and Indian alliance was also a military one, and here too the allies had mutual needs and depended upon one another. The French could not hold their own in North America without the native warriors and their traditional ambush tactics, which relied upon individual autonomy and independent action. By the same token, the Indians could not resist the British takeover of their lands or hold back their aboriginal enemies without the gunpowder, firearms, and, eventually, cannon and mortar of the French or the intervention of the French Army. The French authorities were given permission to build forts on Indian land and later agreed to give their hosts annual gifts so that their "lease" to this land would be renewed. Once they had really settled in, however, the French could use the force that their forts allowed them to impose their wishes.

The official French position was always that French settlers were in North America on a religious mission. But this description did not prevent travelers or *coureurs des bois* from borrowing religious rituals from the Indians or eventually joining various nations on the continent once they adopted their religious beliefs along with other cultural traits. On the other hand, native conversion to Christianity cannot be seen merely as an effect of colonial expansion. The abolition of old boundaries and the intermarriage and overlapping of peoples that this expansion brought with it favored belief in a universal rather than an ethnic god. What is more, the horrendous impact of the epidemics and their selective nature (the Amerindian population was decimated, while whites were hardly affected) were often interpreted by the Indians according to the logic of their magical and spiritual universe and were thus seen as a sign that they had committed sacrilege and that their alliance with their gods had been broken. Some of them believed that they had to revive their traditional religion, while others felt that the Christian God offered believers greater protection.

There were massive cultural transfers within the alliance. The Amerindians acquired, among other things, writing, metal, gunpowder, fruit trees, hogs, cats, chickens, onions, and specialized types of fortifications, and the French and the French Canadians acquired knowledge of native geography and flora and fauna as well as familiarity with maize, squash, beans, the snowshoe, and the canoe. At a more fundamental level, their proximity to America's first inhabitants soon distinguished French Canadians from Frenchmen. The huge diversity of North American cultures promoted an attitude of cultural relativism that, bolstered by the Indians' criticism of Western society, was to feed debates at the end of the seventeenth century and during the eighteenth about the republican form of government, the rearing of children, and the ideals of freedom, equality, brotherhood, and the right to happiness. Obviously, native influences on North American culture were not the only ones, but they were powerful. They occurred in a colonial context, however. The French did not come as immigrants into Amerindian society, although there were some exceptions; rather, they came to found neighboring communities.

The long imperial conflict in North America between France and Great Britain culminated in the French and Indian War (1754–60). A key component of British strategy was an attempt to break the French-Amerindian alliance by preventing the French from supplying the Indians and by themselves concluding treaties with the Indians that were designed to bring about the neutrality of Indian nations in return for land guarantees. These tactics were largely responsible for the defeat of the French and their departure from North America in 1763. Insofar and as long as the British needed the Amerindians for the fur trade and the war against the thirteen American colonies, they adopted the policy the French had used earlier with regard to Amerindians.

Delâge, Denys, *Bitter Feast: Amerindians and Europeans in Northeastern North America, 1600–1664* (Vancouver: University of British Columbia Press, 1993); Trigger, Bruce G., *Natives and Newcomers: Canada's "Heroic Age" Reconsidered* (Montreal: McGill–Queens University Press, 1985); White, Richard, *The Middle Ground: Indians, Empires and Republics in the Great Lakes Region, 1650–1815* (Cambridge: Cambridge University Press, 1991).

DENYS DELÂGE
Laval University
Quebec City

INDIAN-WHITE RELATIONS IN NORTH AMERICA BEFORE 1776

The colonization of North America by Europeans decisively altered the histories of the continent's native peoples. But the scope and impact of these changes varied enormously from one place to another and from one period to another.

When Europeans began arriving in North America they encountered a land characterized by both continuity and change. For more than ten thousand years, kin-based communities had developed myriad ways of living off the land, of exchanging goods and otherwise interacting with one another, and of expressing themselves spiritually and aesthetically. This diversity was reflected in their societies, which ranged from small, mobile bands of a few dozen hunter-gatherers in the Great Basin to Mississippian temple-mound centers in the Southeast with thousands of inhabitants.

Indians in some areas were experiencing particularly pronounced changes during the fifteenth and sixteenth centuries. Inhabitants of Chaco Canyon, Mesa Verde, and other Anasazi centers in the Southwest had dispersed in the face of drought and political upheaval after the thirteenth century. Their descendants settled in pueblos on the Rio Grande and elsewhere and, by the sixteenth century, had begun trading with newly arrived Athabaskan-speaking Apaches and Navajos. In the Mississippi Valley, Cahokia and several other urban trade centers had collapsed in the thirteenth and fourteenth centuries, sending refugees in all directions and significantly reorienting exchange networks and alliances. Elsewhere in the eastern woodlands, a pattern of gradually increasing, intensifying conflict between communities was linked to the pressure of growing populations on resources and to competition for control of exchange networks.

The earliest contacts between Native Americans and Europeans began after the late tenth century as Norse settlers from Iceland established several settlements among Thule Eskimos in Greenland and, briefly, one among Beothuk Indians in Newfoundland. At first the newcomers exchanged metal tools and woolen cloth for animal pelts and ivory. But trade disputes, intensified if not caused by Norse attitudes of superiority, increasingly led to violence. Facing hostile natives and a gradually cooling climate, the Norse withdrew from America by the fifteenth century.

The Norse departure coincided with the beginning of more sustained European expansion. From the 1490s to the 1590s, Europeans, by various means, spread themselves, their material goods, and their microbes over the eastern subarctic coast, most of the eastern woodlands, and portions of the southwestern interior and the California coast. In the Northeast, some fishermen and whalers gradually turned to specialized trading of glass, cloth, and metal goods for beaver and other furs. Observing native norms of reciprocity, they succeeded where efforts to kidnap or dominate Indians failed. By the 1580s French traders returned regularly to clients on the Northeast Coast and in the St. Lawrence Valley. In the Southeast, initial Spanish efforts by Ponce de León, Narváez, de Soto, and others, as well as a chain of Jesuit missions on the Atlantic coast, failed because of Indian distrust and resentment. Expeditions from Mexico to the Southwest, led by Fray Marcos de Niza and Coronado, alienated Pueblos and other native peoples. As a result of all these encounters, many Indians were drawn toward European goods but their attitudes toward the newcomers themselves depended greatly on previous experiences. European diseases proved especially viru-

TRIBAL LANDS AT TIME OF CONTACT

lent in the Southeast where they undermined most Mississippian temple-mound centers.

During the early seventeenth century, Europeans made use of alliances and instabilities created by themselves and their predecessors to establish permanent colonies. English colonizers in New England and the Chesapeake took advantage of population losses from epidemics to establish themselves, as did the Spanish in renewing the expansion of Florida. Heavy Spanish levies on Pueblo corn in New Mexico caused the Apaches and Navajos to raid the Pueblos for what they formerly obtained by trade, forcing the Pueblos to rely on the Spanish for protection. The English and Spanish did not hesitate to use force to subdue natives they considered subjects. On the St. Lawrence, the exclusion by Montagnais and Hurons of the Five Nations Iroquois from direct contact with French traders generated a fierce rivalry. Upon founding New France in 1608, the French aligned themselves with the Montagnais and Hurons, both to garner the thick pelts of the Canadian interior and to protect these Indians from the Iroquois. In response, the latter began trading with the new colony of New Netherland at its headquarters on the Hudson River.

For the remainder of the century relations between natives and colonizers varied enormously from one area to another as groups sought to survive and flourish in a rapidly changing colonial milieu. The influx of settlers in several Atlantic coastal colonies led to violent conflicts over land in New England, New Netherland, and the Chesapeake. Native resentment against Franciscan missionaries and secular authorities led to several revolts by Indians against Spanish rule in Florida and to the massive Pueblo Revolt in New Mexico, in which the Spanish were driven entirely from the region for twelve years (1680–92).

During the same period, Indian-white relations in the northeastern interior centered on the struggle for control of trade on the St. Lawrence and the Great Lakes. During the 1630s both the Iroquois and the Indian allies of New France suffered losses of population in the face of epidemics and depletions of beaver due to overhunting. Amply supplied with Dutch guns and ammunition, the Iroquois escalated their raids in the 1640s and 1650s into the "Beaver Wars" in which the Five Nations destroyed the Hurons, Petuns, Neutrals, and Eries as political entities and adopted captives and refugees from these nations into their own ranks. Thereafter the Iroquois drove Algonquian-speaking peoples out of their homelands in the eastern Great Lakes, the Michigan Peninsula, and the Ohio Valley. Many of the refugees clustered in the western Great Lakes, where interethnic villages emerged to trade and ally with the French.

The Iroquois were weakened after 1664, when New Netherland was seized by the English. As France moved to arm its Indian allies to the north and as anti-Iroquois sentiment crystallized among eastern Indians from Canada to the Chesapeake, the Iroquois were obliged to subordinate their strategic goals to those of New York and the English empire. They helped defeat anti-English Indians in King Philip's War in New Eng-

land (1675–76) and then joined the colony of New York in a series of "Covenant Chain" treaties giving them a role overseeing subject Indians in several seaboard colonies. In the 1680s they launched a new round of wars against New France's western allies. After these conflicts merged in 1689 with the Anglo-French conflict known as King William's War, growing numbers of Iroquois found the English alliances less than effective in protecting them from devastating attacks. The growth of neutralist and pro-French sentiment finally led the Five Nations to sign treaties of peace and neutrality, known as the Grand Settlement, with both France and England in 1701.

In the meantime, the founding of Charleston in 1670 stimulated the rapid expansion of English trade and settlement in the Southeast. English traders supplied guns to Indians in exchange for deerskins and for captives sold as slaves, mostly to the West Indies. France's establishment of Louisiana in 1699 provided the Choctaws with a source of arms for resisting slave raids by Creeks and Chickasaws, but the Spanish in Florida were less inclined to distribute guns to Timucua, Guale, and Apalachee subjects, who frequently rebelled against Spanish rule. As a result, these peoples were the principal victims of the Indian slave trade. English abuses of their own allies finally led to a large-scale uprising by the Yamasees, supported by the Creeks and Catawbas, in 1715. Only the support of the Cherokees, who had suffered frequently at the hands of the Creeks, enabled the English to crush the Yamasees. Thereafter the Creeks, following the pattern of the Iroquois, pursued a policy of neutrality toward England, France, and Spain.

Indian life west of the Mississippi River also changed decisively during the late seventeenth and early eighteenth centuries, but along very different lines. Although the Spanish formally reconquered New Mexico after the Pueblo Revolt, their dependence on Pueblo support for defending New Mexico obliged them to rule with a lighter hand. In particular, the Franciscans were obliged to tolerate native religions. The colony also abolished the forced labor system known as the *encomienda*.

During the Spanish absence, Navajos captured many horses and sheep left behind and moved toward a more sedentary way of life based on herding. The Apaches focused more strictly on horses to improve their mobility during raids on the Spanish and the Pueblos. Navajos and Apaches also traded horses to neighboring peoples, including Utes and Shoshones, some of whom moved on to the southern Great Plains and became known as Comanches. Meanwhile, French traders in Canada and Louisiana extended their activities to the plains, often arming Indians in the process. The effect was to stimulate conflicts over hunting territory in which some Indians were forced from their homelands, such as the Lakota Sioux by bands of Ojibwas (Anishinabes). By midcentury many Plains peoples had incorporated guns and horses into their material and ceremonial lives. Some, such as the Pawnees, Mandans, Arikaras, and Hidatsas, retained their farming, village-oriented ways. Others, such as the Lakota Sioux, Cheyennes, Arapahos, Crows, and Comanches, developed more nomadic ways of life based on the movements of bison herds.

In eastern North America, the rapid growth of the British empire and its settler population was transforming Indian-white relations. Well before the middle of the eighteenth century, settlers occupied most lands east of the Appalachians, forcing peoples like the Housatonics of Massachusetts and the Catawbas of South Carolina to accommodate themselves to a white majority and producing extensive losses of land and autonomy. Others, such as the Delawares of Pennsylvania and the Tuscaroras of North Carolina, were forced from their homelands entirely. Most Delawares fled west toward the Ohio Valley, after the Pennsylvania government and the Iroquois used a fraudulent treaty as a basis for evicting them, while the Iroquoian-speaking Tuscaroras, driven out by force, found refuge as the sixth nation of the Iroquois Confederacy. Even the powerful Creeks were pressured into ceding land to the new colony of Georgia in 1733. (The process was largely, but not exclusively, English: in Louisiana, the French turned on their erstwhile Natchez allies in order to gain land for expanded tobacco production.)

English colonial expansion led to intensified Anglo-French imperial competition. By the late 1740s speculators in Virginia and Pennsylvania were eyeing the upper Ohio Valley as an area for future settlement. The region was inhabited by various Indian peoples, many of them refugees, who were nominally allied with the French but generally sought to remain independent of French, English, and Iroquois influence. Although they resented French efforts to exert more direct control over them, the Shawnees, Delawares, and other Indians were even more alarmed by British intentions. On July 9, 1755, they ambushed General James Braddock as his regular troops attempted to seize France's Fort Duquesne; then, along with the Cherokees to the south,

they attacked frontier settlements that were encroaching on Indian lands. But in 1758, fearing that the French had gained too great an advantage, the Shawnees, Delawares, and Iroquois agreed, in the Treaty of Easton, to support the English. Within a year, the British and their Indian allies had driven the French from Ohio, and in 1760 they seized New France. In the meantime British troops invaded Cherokee country, burning homes and crops and forcing the Cherokees to surrender in 1761.

The totality of the British victory and the withdrawal of the French from their posts on the Ohio and the Great Lakes stunned Indians in the area accustomed to "playing off" the two powers. Their astonishment turned to anger when the British commander, Sir Jeffrey Amherst, ordered a cessation of presents to allied Indians. Many natives heeded the message of Neolin, the "Delaware Prophet," who urged a rejection of all contact with Europeans and their goods as the means of restoring Indian autonomy and abundance. Others seized on rumors that the French would return if the Indians began an uprising against the British. In 1761 Indians mounted a series of loosely coordinated assaults on the British posts, since termed "Pontiac's Rebellion" after a prominent Ottawa participant. Amherst approved the presentation of smallpox-infested blankets to peace-seeking Indians at Fort Pitt, but the uprising was otherwise settled amicably when the British promised to protect the Indians from settler incursions. By the Proclamation of 1763, Britain established a line along the Appalachian crest, west of which Indians retained title to all lands not freely ceded and from which squatters, outlaws, and unauthorized traders were banned.

British efforts to enforce the new policies foundered on colonial resistance to the policies themselves, to the taxes imposed by the British to finance them, and to the prerogatives claimed by Crown and Parliament vis-à-vis the colonies. The encroachment of settlers on Indian lands continued and, in 1768, financially strapped Britain returned control of trade to the individual colonies. In the same year the British and Iroquois, in the Treaty of Fort Stanwix, ceded Shawnee, Delaware, and Cherokee lands in Ohio without those nations' consent. Tensions remained high along the frontier until the outbreak of the American Revolution. As war approached, the minority of Indians who were already subjects of colonial governments supported the rebels. Most others lined up with the British or sought to remain neutral, hoping thereby to maximize their political sovereignty and cultural integrity in a world radically altered during the preceding three centuries.

Merrell, James H., *The Indians' New World: Catawbas and Their Neighbors from European Contact through the Era of European Removal* (Chapel Hill: University of North Carolina Press, 1989); Richter, Daniel, *The Ordeal of the Longhouse: The Peoples of the Iroquois League in the Era of European Colonization* (Chapel Hill: University of North Carolina Press, 1992); White, Richard, *The Middle Ground: Indians, Empires, and Republics in the Great Lakes Region, 1650–1815* (Cambridge: Cambridge University Press, 1991).

NEAL SALISBURY
Smith College

INDIAN-WHITE RELATIONS IN THE UNITED STATES, 1776–1900

Between 1776 and 1900, relations between American Indians and the non-Indian majority in the United States were characterized by a growing imbalance of power between the two peoples, and by considerable misunderstanding. In the postrevolutionary period most Native American people, while cognizant of the growing political and military power of the new United States, remained politically autonomous. Most tribes east of the Mississippi were economically dependent upon trade with outsiders, but they maintained considerable political control over their lives. As the nineteenth century progressed, however, Indians became first economically more dependent on, and then politically subjugated by, white men and their governments. Meanwhile, federal programs designed to acculturate and assimilate Indian people into white society generally failed.

During the American Revolution most of the trans-Appalachian tribes supported the British. In the South, American military campaigns generally defeated the Creeks and Cherokees, but in the North the tribesmen carried the war to Kentucky, and by 1783 tribes such as the Shawnees remained on the offensive. Yet after the Treaty of Paris (1783) the Americans treated all tribes as defeated enemies and attempted to dictate policies to them. In the South, Alexander McGillivray centralized power within the Creek Confederacy, and by negotiating a series of diplomatic agreements between Spain, the federal government, and the state of Georgia he shrewdly, if temporarily, maintained Creek autonomy. North of the Ohio the federal government

claimed ownership of most tribal lands, and when the Indians refused to recognize that claim, federal officials entered into a series of spurious treaties disavowed by most of the tribes. When Indians resisted white settlement north of the Ohio River, federal officials dispatched two expeditions—one led by Josiah Harmar (1790), the other by Arthur St. Clair (1791)—against tribal villages along the Maumee watershed, but the tribesmen defeated both armies. Only in 1794, after Anthony Wayne's victory at Fallen Timbers, did the northern tribes sign the Treaty of Greenville, relinquishing their claims to most of Ohio.

Following the Treaty of Greenville, federal officials championed a "civilization program" designed to acculturate Indian people and transform them into small yeomen farmers. During the 1790s Congress passed the Indian Intercourse Acts, a series of laws designed to regulate trade and land transactions, codify legal relationships between Indians and whites, and provide goods and services that would facilitate the government's "civilization" program. Thomas Jefferson was particularly interested in promoting such programs, and during his administration such activity increased.

The programs generally were unsuccessful. Among the southern tribes some mixed bloods who embraced acculturation and established farms and plantations were praised by their agents, but elsewhere the programs floundered. With few exceptions, more traditional tribespeople resented ethnocentric efforts to transform them into carbon copies of white men. Meanwhile the fur trade declined, alcoholism increased, and Indians were repeatedly subjected to racial discrimination and injustice. Socioeconomic conditions among the tribes deteriorated, and tribes were forced to cede additional lands for dwindling annuity payments. In response, many turned to the nativistic teachings of the Shawnee Prophet (Tenskwatawa) and his brother Tecumseh, who offered both a religious deliverance and a unified political front against any further land cessions. During the War of 1812 warriors loyal to Tecumseh joined with the British, while hostile Creeks fought both their kinsmen and the United States. When the war ended Tecumseh had been killed and the anti-American warriors had been defeated.

In the postwar decade the pace of acculturation accelerated. The Bureau of Indian Affairs (BIA) was founded in 1824, and mixed-blood leaders among the southern tribes joined with Protestant missionaries to advocate Christianity, representative government, statutory laws, literacy, and plantation agriculture. North

A delegation of Sauk, Fox, and Kansa chiefs meeting with government officials in Washington in February 1867. This delegation signed a treaty (never ratified) in which they ceded their tribes' remaining lands in Kansas.

of the Ohio many mixed-blood leaders, modeling themselves after the creole French, pursued careers as entrepreneurs. After the election of Andrew Jackson, Congress passed the Indian Removal Act (1830), which was designed to remove the eastern tribes to the trans-Mississippi West.

Most of the tribes preferred to remain in their homelands. Warfare erupted in 1832 when Black Hawk led a large group of Sauks and Foxes back to Illinois, from which they had been forced to remove to Iowa; and the Seminoles fought a protracted guerrilla campaign (the Second Seminole War), which lasted from 1835 to 1842, before part of the tribe was removed to Indian Territory. The Cherokees fought removal in the federal court system, but when the U.S. Supreme Court ruled in their favor (*Worcester* v. *Georgia,* 1832), Jackson ig-

nored the decision and refused to protect the tribe from the state of Georgia. During the 1830s most of the tribes were removed to the West. These forced emigrations, often mismanaged and poorly financed, were disastrous for the Indians. Although some tribes arrived in Kansas or Oklahoma relatively unscathed, others suffered hardship and death. Historians argue over the final figures, but the Cherokees, for example, lost between two thousand and four thousand people from a total population of sixteen thousand.

In the West the removed tribes encountered opposition from Indians indigenous to the region (e.g., the Osages, Pawnees, and Dakotas), but after an initial period, most endured and some flourished. In Kansas, Potawatomi entrepreneurs sold food, livestock, and fodder to white travelers en route to Colorado and California, while the Cherokees, Creeks, Choctaws, Chickasaws, and Seminoles—a group known as the Five Southern Tribes—reestablished farms, plantations, schools, and tribal governments in eastern Oklahoma.

The Plains tribes fared less well. Their initial distance from white settlement and reliance upon the bison herds provided them with some political and economic autonomy, but during the late 1840s growing numbers of white Americans crossed their territories en route to Oregon and California. Although the popular media have emphasized unfriendly encounters between the Plains tribes and wagon trains, such confrontations rarely occurred. Sometimes Indians stole horses, or pilfered camp equipment, but more often warriors served as guides for wagon trains or traded game for flour, sugar, or other staples. Yet in order to minimize conflict, federal officials decided to concentrate the Plains tribes in areas that were well away from the emigrant trails. In 1851 they met with the northern Plains tribes at Fort Laramie, where most of those tribes agreed to remain north of the Platte River. In 1853, at Fort Atkinson, Kansas, the Comanches, Kiowas, and Apaches promised to stay south of the Arkansas. At times both Indians and whites violated the agreements, which became totally ineffective once the discovery of gold in Colorado and Montana in the late 1850s brought white miners into the area in unprecedented numbers.

During the Civil War the Five Southern Tribes split into pro-Northern and pro-Confederate factions. In most cases these divisions reflected old quarrels from the removal era more than political allegiance to either the North or the South, but the resulting conflict devastated the Cherokees and Creeks, where old animosities sparked particularly bitter warfare. When the conflict ended, federal officials used the pretense of disloyalty to seize lands from the Creeks and Cherokees for use as new reservations for tribes previously residing in other states and territories. Meanwhile, in Minnesota, the Eastern Dakotas rose in retribution for the government's inability to meet past treaty obligations (1862) but were defeated, and thirty-eight of their number were hanged at the largest mass public execution in American history. In Colorado, over one hundred fifty peaceful Cheyennes were massacred by militia at Sand Creek (1864), while in the Southwest James Carelton campaigned against the Apaches and Navajos, sending members from both tribes to a bleak reservation at Bosque Redondo (1863), in eastern New Mexico. Finally, as the Civil War waned, federal officials violated the 1851 Treaty of Fort Laramie and constructed forts

to protect the Bozeman Trail, a road that carried miners across Wyoming's Powder River country to the gold fields. Red Cloud led a successful Sioux resistance, then signed the Second Treaty of Fort Laramie (1868), a document in which the Sioux and other northern Plains tribes agreed to remain within well-defined borders in exchange for federal promises to protect both the tribes and their territories.

The Second Treaty of Fort Laramie foreshadowed President Ulysses Grant's "Peace Policy," which began in the 1870s. Influenced by reformers, Grant appointed a board of commissioners to oversee Indian policy and then assigned different Indian agencies to various religious denominations. Responding to charges of corruption, he replaced career bureaucrats with religious leaders and other reformers. Although the latter were motivated by high ideals, they often lacked experience, and after 1880 the policy was abandoned.

Ironically, the Peace Policy years also witnessed the last of the "Indian wars" that pitted soldiers against tribesmen who resisted confinement to reservations. Confrontations occurred between the government and the Modocs (1873), the Nez Perces (1877), and the Utes (1879), but the most notable clashes took place on the northern plains and in Arizona. In 1874, after gold was discovered in the Dakota Territory's Black Hills, miners invaded the region and the Sioux struck back, killing prospectors. Since the army could not keep miners from the Black Hills, federal officials violated the Second Fort Laramie Treaty, seizing the hills and demanding that all Sioux relocate onto new reservations. When several bands refused, military expeditions were dispatched, and on June 25, 1876, George A. Custer and 225 soldiers were defeated and killed at the Battle of the Little Bighorn. Within six months most of the Sioux were forced onto reservations. In the Southwest, Victorio, Nana, and Geronimo led an Apache resistance that extended from 1874 until 1886, when Geronimo finally surrendered.

The final two decades of the nineteenth century marked the nadir of Native American existence. Confined to reservation lands that whites considered undesirable, many Indian people existed through the acceptance of annuity payments or demeaning food rations. Although the Five Southern Tribes and a few other tribal governments still exercised some control over their constituents, most Indians were stripped of political power by military forces and federal bureaucrats. Some participated in government-sponsored agricultural programs, but most reservations were ill suited to farming.

Continuing a policy of mandatory acculturation, the BIA urged tribespeople to adopt white dress, economic skills, and domestic institutions and to speak English. Indian parents were forced to enroll their children in distant boarding schools, where the students were forbidden to speak their native languages and were taught to disdain their tribal heritage. Federal agents supported Christian missionary efforts but outlawed traditional religious practices, including dances, ball games, and other ceremonies. Meanwhile tuberculosis, trachoma, and other communicable diseases ravaged the reservations. By 1900 the Native American population in the United States had fallen to 237,196, the lowest figure ever reported in any recorded census.

In response, Indian people again turned to religion. Although some of the tribal religions, particularly in the Southwest, persisted, others were overshadowed by newer, more syncretic beliefs. The peyote faith, long a tradition among the Lipan Apaches, emerged among the tribes of southwestern Oklahoma. Combining traditional beliefs with Christianity, the "Peyote Road" offered Indian people a religious manifestation of Pan-Indian identity, but it was opposed by the BIA and missionaries. In the Northwest, revivalistic leaders such as Smohalla (1870s), Taivibo (1870s), and John Slocum (1880s) paved the way for Wovoka, a Paiute holy man whose vision in 1889 initiated the Ghost Dance, a ceremony promising that both the Indians' dead relatives and the bison would return to a world free of white men. The new faith spread to the northern plains, where it found willing converts among the Sioux, a people devastated by their reservation experiences. Tragically, the conversion of the Western Sioux threatened both the military and local Indian agents. In De-

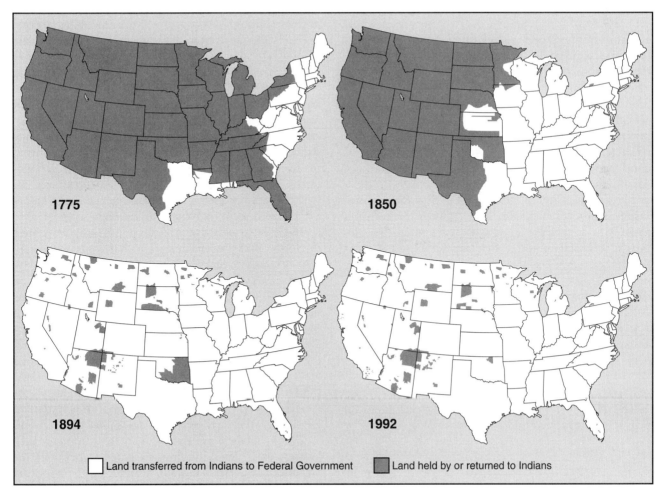

1775

1850

1894

1992

☐ Land transferred from Indians to Federal Government   ■ Land held by or returned to Indians

LAND LOSSES

cember 1890 American troops surrounded a party of Ghost Dancers led by Big Foot, and a scuffle led to the Battle of Wounded Knee, in which over one hundred fifty Indians and twenty-nine soldiers were killed.

Convinced that the reservations contributed to the Indians' "lack of progress," reformers such as Carl Schurz, Helen Hunt Jackson, and participants at the Lake Mohonk Conference (a meeting of religious and humanitarian leaders in New York State) petitioned Congress to abolish the reservation system. In response Congress passed the General Allotment Act in 1887, which instructed the BIA, upon the president's recommendation, to divide reservations into 160-acre plots, which would be assigned to individual Indians. The reformers believed that such legislation would provide each Indian with a small farm, strengthen the Indians' commitment to private property, and force Indian people to leave their communal tribal villages. Unfortunately, the act also was supported by special-interest groups who wished to gain access to reservation lands, since the surplus land left after allotment would be sold to white settlers. To prevent fraud, individual allotments supposedly would be held in trust by the government for twenty-five years, after which Indians would receive the allotments in fee simple.

Indian people overwhelmingly opposed allotment, but federal officials began to divide their lands anyway, concentrating first on those reservations that held good agricultural land. Although the Five Southern Tribes, the Osages, and a few other groups initially were exempt from allotment, other legislation soon made them eligible. Meanwhile, additional legislation altered the size of the allotments and limited the safeguards upon eligibility so that the actual administration of the allotment process was rampant with fraud. In 1887, prior to the act's passage, Indian people owned approximately 138 million acres. In 1934, when allotment finally ceased, they held only 48 million acres, half of which was either desert or semidesert. Obviously, by 1900 Indian people could look back over a "century of dishonor" and looked forward to an uncertain future.

Gibson, Arrell Morgan, *The American Indian: Prehistory to the Present* (Lexington, Mass.: D. C. Heath and Company, 1980); Hagan, William T., *The American Indian*, rev. ed. (Chicago: University of Chicago Press, 1993); Prucha, Francis Paul, *The Great Father: The United States Government and the American Indians,* 2 vols. (Lincoln: University of Nebraska Press, 1984).

R. DAVID EDMUNDS (Cherokee)
Indiana University

INDIAN-WHITE RELATIONS IN THE UNITED STATES, 1900 TO THE PRESENT

During the twentieth century, relations between Indians and non-Indians in the United States have been marked by an unfortunate series of misunderstandings caused by prejudiced minds and negative stereotypes. Overcoming these obstacles, the nation's 2.1 million Native Americans have proved their resilience by surviving in a world dominated by other races and cultures.

During the nineteenth century American Indians, by tradition a communal people, were forcibly separated from their native cultures and lands. By the turn of the century Native Americans held only 77,865,373 acres of land, of which 5,409,530 had been assigned by federal commissioners to individual Indians. The effort to individualize Indians and force them to forgo their tribal and traditional ways caused strife among tribal communities and provoked a growing Indian opposition. Events like the Crazy Snake Rebellion among the Creeks of Oklahoma and the formation of the Four Mothers Society by Cherokees, Creeks, Choctaws, and Chickasaws reflected a desire by some Indians to live according to old community ways. But the federal government insisted that all Indians conform to white ways. Indian Territory, designed always to belong to the Native Americans and containing sixty-seven different tribes, became settled also by Anglo-Americans, who pushed for statehood, achieving it on November 16, 1907, in spite of Indian opposition.

While America witnessed the populist movement in the farm states and the growth of European immigrant populations in eastern cities, American Indians were reduced in the public eye to the status of ancient relics. Most citizens were unaware, for example, that ten thousand Indian men were serving in World War I or that educated Indians were becoming teachers, farmers, and ministers. During the first decades of the century the gap between Indians and whites widened as, with a few exceptions, Native Americans continued to find the thinking of white Americans illogical. The exceptions were individuals like Charles Eastman, Luther Standing Bear, and others who had attended boarding schools and learned the ways of white society. In 1911 such "progressive" red Americans gathered to organize the Society of American Indians, promoting the adoption of white ways in place of tribal ways and the abolition of the Bureau of Indian Affairs (BIA). Federal officials continued to outlaw powwows and religious practices like the Sun Dance that they considered "heathen" and backward.

In the early twentieth century Indians continued to be the target of "civilization" efforts. The Carlisle Indian Industrial School in Pennsylvania, the Haskell Institute in Kansas, and the Chilocco Indian School in Oklahoma were instruments for eradicating Indian languages and lifeways. Only English was allowed in the schools, and classes sought to redirect the lives of the Indian youth with training in new vocations and trades. But they could not change the young people's innate feelings of being Indian. Housed with children from across the country, Indian students began to reflect a broad Indian consciousness that was developing in response to the attitudes of dominant society and the federal government. Similarly, common resistance to federal authority often united reservation communities and produced new leaders who spoke for the groups. Men like the Navajo Chee Dodge and the Menominees' Reginald Oshkosh spoke the white man's language but sought the allegiance of their elders and kinsmen and worked to defend their tribes' interests.

The popular image of the 1920s as an age of roaring automobiles and dancing flappers had little meaning for Indians. Despite the creation of the Committee of One Hundred to investigate Indian affairs in 1923, the administrations of Warren G. Harding and Calvin Coolidge made few changes in federal policy. Fraud and debauchery plagued the Five Civilized Tribes in Oklahoma as court-appointed guardians bilked Indian minors and elderly Indians out of their properties and money. The extreme was the circle of murders of members of the Lizzie Kyle family among the Osages in the early 1920s for oil head rights. In 1924 a federal law thrust U.S. citizenship upon the remaining Indian population, even though federal authorities permitted Arizona, Utah, and New Mexico to block Native Americans from voting for the next twenty years. The Indian Rights Association and the newly formed American Indian Defense Association stood ready to protect Indian rights—with the latter group becoming increasingly vocal—but the two organizations had a limited impact.

The plight of American Indians attracted little attention until 1928, when a shocking study, the Meriam Report, exposed the pervasiveness of Indian poverty and the failure of allotment's promises. The culmination of this new interest in reform was the so-called Indian New Deal, instigated by Secretary of the Interior Harold Ickes and Commissioner of Indian Affairs John Collier in 1933. Collier and the Interior Department's solicitor, the legal scholar Felix Cohen, drafted a radical new law that would restructure tribal governments and the administration of federal policies. The forty-eight-page bill became the Indian Reorganization Act of 1934. It introduced federal programs to support Indian agriculture, vocational education, and economic development, but its centerpiece was a provision allowing reservation communities to set up tribal governments patterned after local units of the American government. Although some critics of Collier and the BIA claimed that his determined pursuit of his goals perpetuated federal paternalism and undermined tribal traditions, the authority of Indian communities expanded during his tenure. The new Indian governments began to assert their rights and press local and federal officials to reverse the century-long decline in tribal sovereignty.

Popular images of Indians also began to shift during the 1930s. Dime novels, Wild West shows, and the early cinema reinforced the "savage" image of Indian people. But the new, pro-Indian effort in the Indian Bureau also brought new attention to Indian people. Indian writers faced the challenge of correcting stereotypes and presenting an Indian viewpoint. Prior to 1920, Alexander Posey, Charles Eastman, and Gertrude Bonnin (Zitkala Ša) had been pioneers in this effort. During the 1920s and 1930s new writers began to appear. They included Luther Standing Bear, John Joseph Matthews, Pauline Johnson, and D'Arcy McNickle. Their work in turn inspired a post–World War II generation of authors who burst on the scene in the 1960s and 1970s. These included N. Scott Momaday, whose *House Made of Dawn* won the Pulitzer Prize in 1969, James Welch, Vine Deloria, Jr., Leslie Marmon Silko, Paula Gunn Allen, Louise Erdrich, Wendy Rose, Linda Hogan, and Gerald Vizenor.

In spite of the early efforts of Indian writers, negative public images changed only marginally after World War II. Even though American Indians sent twenty-five thousand men and women to World War II, ten thousand to the Korean conflict, and forty-three thousand to Vietnam, their efforts did little to erase negative images of Indians. Such images have also persisted in federal policy. Following World War II the Bureau of Indian Affairs instituted a program to terminate the federal government's trust relations with many tribes. Officials proposed reducing federal expenditures and shrinking the federal bureaucracy by "getting out of the Indian business" and setting Indians "free" from federal support and protection. House Concurrent Resolution 108, passed in 1953, formalized the commitment and confirmed political support for termination. Dillon S. Myer, who headed the BIA in the Truman administration, favored the abandonment of tribal governments, and Utah senator Arthur Watkins, a favorite son of western business interests, worked simultaneously to eliminate the federal role in native life. A relocation program was instituted to recruit Indians to move to cities. Though many Indians migrated to cities successfully, the program was a disaster. After a period of subsidized "adjustment," Indian recruits were abandoned. Poverty and homelessness quickly produced frustration and anger, and these, in turn, produced additional problems: alcoholism, joblessness, and poverty.

The principal instrument for changing negative views of Indian people and for changing the policies was an upsurge in political activism by American Indians during the 1960s and 1970s. This Indian renaissance was produced by a complex combination of urban anger and tribally based assertiveness. For years the only national Indian voice was the National Congress of American Indians, a moderate group of tribal leaders who had begun meeting annually in 1944. A new voice began to be heard in 1961 when the American Indian Chicago Conference gathered to present an Indian agenda for the new Kennedy administration. After this meeting, the National Indian Youth Council formed as American Indian youth became more involved in national Indian issues. Additional examples of this new activism and militancy would include the founding of the American Indian Movement in 1968, the occupation of Alcatraz Island in 1969, the Trail of Broken Treaties march of 1972, and the armed occupation of Wounded Knee, South Dakota, in 1973. These and other actions produced a national and highly visible call for Indian self-determination.

Although Indian self-determination has been embraced as a goal by every president since Lyndon Johnson, congressional action has rarely matched presidential rhetoric. Congress and the Johnson administration were frequently preoccupied by the Vietnam War and social unrest at home. Change was more frequently inspired by journalistic efforts such as those of Carl Rowan in Minnesota, lobbying by the National Indian Youth Council and the National Congress of American Indians, and local protests such as the "fish-ins" in Washington State. Nevertheless, pro-Indian legislation did emerge during the 1970s. New laws included a settlement of land claims in Maine in 1978 and two pieces of landmark legislation passed the same year—the In-

dian Child Welfare Act and the American Indian Religious Freedom Act. The first established a role for tribes in the adoption of Indian children, and the second declared constitutional support for Native American religious freedom. Another law, the Indian Self-Determination and Educational Assistance Act, was passed in 1975 but only gradually became the basis of federal Indian policy. The Self-Determination Act stipulated that tribes could enter into contracts with the Indian Bureau to administer their own programs, from education to health care to housing. In 1978, Congress attempted to monitor the progress of the government in implementing this important measure by creating the American Indian Policy Review Commission to survey programs undertaken in tribal communities and funded by the federal government.

Because tribal governments increasingly operate as sophisticated business corporations, the future of Indian-white relations rests on Indian self-determination. Tribal leaders shoulder enormous responsibilities that include the protection of hunting and fishing rights, water rights, religious traditions, and cultural heritage. At the same time, modern tribal governments struggle to develop successful gaming operations, profitable industrial factories, and effective educational and social-welfare programs. Tribes that have fulfilled this ambition include the Mississippi Choctaws, Navajos, White Mountain Apaches, Oklahoma Cherokees, Pequots, and Oklahoma Creeks.

Accompanying changes in federal legislation have been victories in state and federal courts. From a low point in 1903 after the U.S. Supreme Court's decision in *Lone Wolf* v. *Hitchcock* permitted Congress to abrogate treaties, Indian interests have risen in the eyes of judges and legal commentators. In 1946 Congress authorized a general review of outstanding land claims by creating the Indian Claims Commission. Over its thirty-year term the commission reviewed hundreds of cases and recommended millions of dollars in awards. And beginning in the 1950s, assertive tribal governments and their attorneys brought a growing number of cases to the federal and state courts for review. Their efforts produced major victories in the areas of water, fishing, and mineral rights and in the legal prerogatives of tribal governments.

Despite the emerging partnership between tribes and federal officials, Indians and whites continue to occupy separate worlds. As much as 67 percent of the total Indian population of the United States lives in urban areas, a large part of this group having settled Indian communities in Chicago, Los Angeles, Seattle, Oklahoma City, Albuquerque, Detroit, San Francisco, and other major centers. American Indians live among, work with, and even marry non-Indians, but Indian communities and an "Indian" identity continue to exist. This identity is distinctive and enduring, even though it often differs from the ideas of Indians who have continued to follow the traditions of their individual tribes. A significant Indian population continues in modern America, even though so much of tribal culture has been lost that the "Indian way" is sometimes equated with Pan-Indian activities such as powwows, art shows, and dances.

The Indian renaissance of the 1990s has attracted a growing following for "Indianness," defined by many as an attitude of respect for the environment and for native spirituality. Because this new popularity of Indian values has accompanied the emergence of native-run casinos, there has been an unfortunate bandwagon effect as non-Indians and Indians who previously would not admit their native heritage suddenly seek to cash in by lobbying to become tribal members. Their appeals have created a new problem for the tribes. At the same time, the negative stereotypes of the past have dissolved in favor of a pro-Indian attitude cultivated by the non-Indian media and the movie industry. During the 1990s films and documentaries such as *Dances with Wolves,* *The Last of the Mohicans,* and *Pocahontas* produced generally positive portraits of native people but rarely delved into the complexity and detail of daily life. Despite great changes in law and policy, the non-Indian world continues to define what it means to be an Indian, and the responsibility to define and defend their interests remains with Indians themselves.

Cornell, Stephen, *The Return of the Native: American Indian Political Resurgence* (New York: Oxford University Press, 1988); Deloria, Vine, Jr., and Clifford M. Lytle, *The Nations Within: The Past and Future of American Indian Sovereignty* (New York: Pantheon Books, 1984).

DONALD L. FIXICO
(Seminole, Creek, Shawnee, Sac and Fox)
Western Michigan University

INTERMARRIAGE WITH NON-INDIANS

The marital union of Indians with non-Indians began in the early colonial period. Through marriage to Spanish explorers in the West and to French fur trappers and English colonists in the East, native inhabitants entered into economic, sexual, procreative, familial, and

social relationships with these newcomers. As a consequence of these interactions, groups of mixed ancestry became significant features of tribal life among the Cherokees and Creeks of the Southeast, the Ojibwas of the Great Lakes, and the Senecas of the Northeast. By 1900, nearly half of all Cherokees were married to whites and spoke English, while tribes in the western United States remained comparatively isolated from European contact and reported few instances of intermarriage.

With the arrival of Europeans and the introduction of trade goods came the concept of race, which ordered human variety and distinguished "superior" groups from "inferior" ones. From this perspective, American Indians, like other minorities, occupied the lower rung of development, and marital unions between Europeans and Indians were discouraged. Although the 1614 marriage of the English planter John Rolfe and Chief Powhatan's daughter Pocahontas provides a persistently popular example of intermarriage, such unions were not always welcome. In 1824, for example, the residents of Cornwall, Connecticut, burned in effigy the young Christian Cherokee student Elias Boudinot and his white fiancée to protest the couple's betrothal. The incident undermined support for the local Foreign Mission School, which Boudinot and other future Cherokee leaders had attended, leading directly to its closing.

Still, intermarriage continued. For many settlers and colonists, marital alliances with Indians generated goodwill and cemented trade relations. Free traders in the Great Lakes, the Rocky Mountains, and the Southeast who operated with few assets but their charm and wit found their native hosts eager to form bonds of kinship between their families and strangers who might serve as loyal partners and steady sources of weapons and tools. Other instances of intermarriage occurred when African slaves escaped and sought refuge with American Indians or when individual Europeans abandoned their settlements and sought to start new lives in native communities. Over the years social scientists have frequently voiced approval for these trends, arguing that intermarriage marks the last stage of the assimilation process. Some intellectuals, beginning with Thomas Jefferson and continuing into the 1930s with Franz Boas, even argued that intermarriage would eventually cause the Indian population to disappear.

By the end of the nineteenth century, Indians were coming into closer contact with non-Indians. Long-term affections developed from frequent contacts between Indians and government agents, traders, teachers, settlers, and military personnel, and intermarriage became commonplace in many areas. Indian women frequently married white settlers who leased Indian land or army personnel stationed at nearby military installations. The children of these mixed marriages often became important leaders because of their ability to stand between the white and Indian worlds and to act as culture brokers. For example, among the Navajos, Henry Chee Dodge (1857?–1947) became an interpreter for the government agent at Fort Defiance during his youth and later became the leader of the Navajo people largely on the strength of his mixed ancestry. Numerous instances of intermarriage between Indians and non-Indians also occurred at schools and missions established on Indian reservations. For example, the Sioux physician Charles A. Eastman (himself the grandson of an itinerant white artist) married a young New England woman who was teaching at the agency to which he had been assigned. Although these unions were accepted, objections were also voiced and epithets—like *squaw man* for white males involved with native females—were frequently heard.

In the provinces of Canada there were also instances of intermarriage, particularly between the Crees and the French. But rather than assimilating into the dominant Euro-Canadian society, the offspring of these unions ultimately identified themselves as a new group, the Métis. Recognized as a distinct community by colonial officials as early as 1690 and remaining so over time, the Métis migrated westward during the eighteenth and nineteenth centuries, playing a central role in the expanding fur-trade industry. In 1869 their ambitions came into direct conflict with the newly formed Canadian national government as the Métis leader Louis Riel struggled with the confederation to win formal recognition for the Métis but failed. Though they were granted land in the new province of Manitoba, Riel and his followers continued to resist the national authorities until the leader's execution following the 1885 Northwest Rebellion.

American Indians continued to experience the onslaught of Western civilization into the 1930s as new school facilities, medical clinics, and highways brought the outside world even closer to their doors. Though ten thousand Native Americans fought in World War I and twenty-five thousand joined the armed forces during World War II, many more thousands joined the war industry during the wars and left the reservations for urban communities. In the mid-1950s, the federal Indi-

an relocation program encouraged still more Indians to move en masse from reservations to metropolitan areas like Denver, Detroit, Chicago, Los Angeles, and Seattle to receive job training and education. In the 1970s, half of all American Indians lived in cities. These urban immigrants displayed demographic characteristics different from those of their rural, reservation cohorts: they had increased levels of income and employment, higher levels of education, lower rates of fertility, and higher rates of intermarriage. Although the effects of these events and programs on intermarriage rates and patterns have not been studied precisely, it would be safe to conclude that intermarriage with non-Indians increased significantly during this period.

In the United States, laws in at least four states (North Carolina, Nevada, Arizona, and Oregon) prohibited sexual relations between Indians and whites. Although these laws were not enforced with the rigor applied to similar statutes affecting African Americans, a 1967 ruling by the U.S. Supreme Court declared all such prohibitions unconstitutional. Until that time, discrimination and segregation played major roles in personal decisions regarding marriage outside one's race. During this period as well, the children of racially mixed parents were also forced to "pass" as members of the dominant race in order to avoid discrimination in schools and the workplace.

The 1970 U.S. Census showed that 33 percent of Indian men and 35 percent of Indian women had white spouses. In 1980, this figure increased to 53 percent among all Indians above age sixteen, in contrast to only 1 percent of Euro-Americans and 2 percent of African Americans married to members of other racial groups. In fact, American Indians are the most exogamous group in America today. These increased rates of intermarriage are an important barometer of social integration not only because such integration involves social intimacy among marital partners and their children, but also because it is likely to draw other extended family members and kin networks into regular contact.

According to the 1990 census, almost 80 percent of all Indians are of mixed ancestry and a similar percentage live in off-reservation communities. The intermarriage rate for American Indians continues to hover around 50 percent, and racially mixed Indian families continue to be better educated, to have more off-reservation experience, higher levels of social and economic well-being, lower fertility rates, and higher levels of labor-force participation, and to live more frequently in single households than endogamous American Indian couples.

Although viewing intermarriage as an indication of assimilation has been criticized as simplistic, this approach is still being widely used by social scientists conducting research on intermarriage today. The approach is questionable because the underlying assumption often made about marriages between Indians and non-Indians is that the exogamous marrying Indian spouse will abandon his or her indigenous language, culture, and identity and become absorbed into Euro-American culture. Such an argument suggests that Indians are passive and unconscious actors within American society and that "Indianness" is a function of genetics rather than of tradition and political affiliation. It reflects a belief that urban Indian immigrants and intermarried families have been stripped of their Indianness and have become part of the cultural mainstream. Recent research on intermarriage, on the other hand, views intermarried families as conscious actors who construct and negotiate their familial and cultural identities within their everyday lives. For example, scholars today examine how intermarried families and mixed-blood children construct their identities within particular situations and within a particular historical and cultural context. They also acknowledge that individuals move back and forth between cultural and social milieus and that non-Indian spouses frequently become incorporated into the rituals and activities of tribal cultures.

For most of the twentieth century, anthropologists and social scientists were predicting that American Indians would vanish as the result of poverty, disease, and assimilation into Western society. Yet Native Americans did not vanish. In response, scholars have begun to speculate on the consequences of intermarriage. Some researchers suggest that intermarriage, urbanization, and self-identification will create divisions among American Indians similar to the class divisions among African Americans. Other researchers predict that intermarriage will undermine Indian status; they suggest that biracial unions will accomplish the abolition of native cultures where federal policies of termination and relocation have failed.

Sandefur, Gary D., and Trudy McKinnell, "American Indian Intermarriage," *Social Science Research* 15 (1986): 347–71; Snipp, Matthew C., *American Indians: The First of This Land* (New York: Russell Sage Foundation, 1989).

BRENDA K. MANUELITO (Navajo)
University of New Mexico

IROQUOIAN LANGUAGES

The Iroquoian family consists of a group of languages all descended from a common ancestor known as Proto-Iroquoian. The modern daughter languages include Cherokee, now spoken primarily in North Carolina and Oklahoma; Tuscarora, near Niagara Falls, New York; Seneca, in western New York; Cayuga, at Six Nations in Ontario; Onondaga, in central New York near Syracuse; Oneida, near London, Ontario, and Green Bay, Wisconsin; and Mohawk, in Quebec, Ontario, and New York. The languages are not generally mutually intelligible, although their grammatical structures are similar.

Records exist of several more Iroquoian languages that are no longer spoken: Huron, Wyandot, Petun, Neutral, Erie, Susquehannock, Meherrin, and Nottoway. One of the first recorded North American languages was spoken by Iroquoian people who encountered Jacques Cartier in 1534 near the mouth of the St. Lawrence. Their language gave us a well-known place name: *kaná:ta'*, "settlement," now *Canada*.

Languages of the Iroquoian family differ in some fundamental ways from those of Europe. Their vocabularies and grammatical categories often encode slightly different concepts or features, and they offer their speakers different kinds of stylistic options. One obvious difference is the typical length of words. Consider the Mohawk *entsakwanenhstarón:ko'*, "we'll take the corn (back) off the cob." Such words are intricately constructed of many meaningful parts. This one begins with the prefix *en-*, specifying future tense, followed by the repetitive prefix *ts-*, "back," and the pronominal prefix *akwa-*, "we." The pronoun does not have the same range of application as English *we*. Mohawk speakers distinguish *inclusive* from *exclusive* we: inclusive forms include the listener ("you and I"); exclusive forms exclude the listener ("they and I"). The pronoun *akwa-* is exclusive; the speaker who used this word was describing family memories to people not in her family. If instead she had been proposing activities to her children, she would have used the inclusive *tewa-*, "you all and I." The Mohawk pronoun *akwa-* specifies another distinction not systematically expressed in English. It refers to three or more individuals: "they and I." If just two individuals had been involved, a dual pronoun would have been used: *akeni-*, "he and I" or "she and I."

Following the pronoun in this word is the noun stem *-nenhst-*, "corn," built on the root *-nenh-*, "seed."

Next is the verb root -ron-, "put on," then the reversive suffix -ko. The verb root and reversive combine to mean "un–put on" or "take off." The final glottal stop indicates that the speaker is referring to one complete event ("we'll take the corn off the cob") rather than to a series or an ongoing activity ("we'll be taking the corn off the cob").

This word, entsakwanenhstarón:ko', is a verb in Mohawk: it describes an action. Iroquoian nouns—like Mohawk o'tá:ra', "clay, pottery, chimney"; okónhsa', "face"; raksà:'a, "boy"; e-ksà:'a, "girl"—show different internal structure. They generally begin with just a prefix indicating gender and, for humans, number. The prefix o- on "clay" and "face" is neuter, the prefix ra- on "boy" is masculine singular ("he-child"), and the prefix e- on "girl" is feminine singular. Possession can be indicated by a prefix: Mohawk ak-i'tà:ra', "my-crock"; ako-'tà:ra, "her-crock." In English, several different kinds of possession are categorized grammatically in the same way, all with the same possessive pronouns: "my crock," "my face," "my grandfather." In Iroquoian languages, the three kinds are distinguished: Mohawk ak-i'tà:ra', "my-crock"; k-konhsà:ke, "my-face"; and rak-hsótha, "my-grandfather." One set of possessive pronouns is used with alienable possessions—that is, objects that may be acquired, given away, or lost, like a crock. Another set is used with inalienable possessions like body parts. Kinsmen are not categorized as possessions at all. The term rak-hsótha specifies a relationship: "he is grandfather to me" (rak-, "he to me"). The senior kinsman, here the grandfather, is the primary member. A different prefix appears in "my grandson": ri-aterè:'a, literally "I have him as a grandchild" (ri-, "I to him").

Although both Iroquoian languages and English distinguish verbs and nouns, usage of these two categories in speech does not match. Speakers of Iroquoian languages use a much higher proportion of verbs than do speakers of English. In Iroquoian languages, as in English, verbs are used to describe actions or states: ratákhe', "he's running"; iostáthen, "it is dry"; sahonwatihné:kanonte', "she gave them another drink." Because all verbs contain pronominal prefixes (ra-, "he"; io-, "it"; honwati-, "she/them"), they may stand alone as full sentences in their own right. Since they may contain so many meaningful parts, verbs can express complex ideas: sahonwatihnè:kanonte' is literally s-a-honwa-ti-hnek-nont-e'; that is, "again-[past tense marker]-she/him-[plural marker]-liquid-feed-completely." Iroquoian verbs are also often used to designate objects, serving the roles of nouns in other languages:

iontkonhsekowáhtha', "towel"; literally i-ont-konh-sekow-aht-ha', "one-self-face-wipe-with-habitually"; teiohnekahiò:tsis, "vinegar"; literally te-io-hnek-ahiò:tsis "change of state–it-liquid–sour/bitter is"; iotékha', "fire"; literally, io-ték-ha', "it-burn-s." With the descriptive power of Iroquoian verb structure, speakers have not needed to borrow many European words for introduced objects and concepts.

An interesting feature of Iroquoian languages is noun incorporation, the presence of noun roots inside of verbs, like -hnek-, "liquid," in "she gave them a drink" and "vinegar". Incorporation can be used to background information that is not particularly newsworthy. It can also serve to classify events or states. The noun root -'nikonhr-, "mind," for example, appears in many Mohawk verbs referring to mental phenomena: wake-'nikonhr-atshá:nih, "I am brave" ("my mind is strong"); wake-'nikonhr-áksen's, "I feel sad, disappointed" ("my mind is bad"); wake-'nikónhr-hens, "I forget" ("my mind has fallen"). The noun root -ia't-, "body," appears in many verbs describing physical phenomena: wat-ia't-á:ken, "I am conspicuous" ("I am bodily visible"); wat-ia't-áhton, "I'm lost" ("I am bodily lost"); ronwa-ia't-enhá:wi, "she's carrying him" ("she's body-carrying him"). The noun root -rihw-, "word, idea, matter," appears in many verbs describing verbal or abstract phenomena: wa'ke-rihw-ísa', "I promised" ("I word-finished"); wa'ke-rih-ón:ni', "I caused it" ("I matter-made").

Iroquoian languages offer their speakers many expressive options unknown in European languages, and their speakers in turn exploit them to their fullest. These speakers have long been respected for their stylistic skill and verbal wit in all settings, from formal oratory to animated conversation.

See also Languages.

Mithun, Marianne, "General Characteristics of North American Indian Languages," in *Handbook of North American Indians*, ed. William C. Sturtevant, vol. 17, *Languages*, ed. Ives Goddard (Washington: Smithsonian Institution, 1995); Mithun, Marianne, "Iroquoian," in *The Languages of Native America*, ed. Lyle Campbell and Marianne Mithun (Austin: University of Texas Press, 1979).

MARIANNE MITHUN
University of California at Santa Barbara

IROQUOIS CONFEDERACY

The Iroquois Confederacy is a political union of North American Indian nations who acted (and act) in war and peace, in trade alliances and treaties of goodwill, as a single nation. The term *Iroquois* was derived from the Algonquian word *Irinakhoiw,* which the French spelled with the suffix *-ois.* The word, which translates as "real adders," illustrates a common phenomenon in which a derisive term used by a native group's enemy becomes the accepted designation of the group in the European languages. The English knew them as the Five Indian Nations: the Mohawk, Oneida, Onondaga, Cayuga and Seneca. In 1722, when the Tuscaroras joined their league, the confederacy became known as the Six Indian Nations or Six Nations Confederacy. The people of the Six Nations designate themselves *Haudenosaunee,* which translates loosely as "people of the longhouse."

The confederacy was long in existence when Europeans arrived and became conscious of it in the early seventeenth century. No one knows the exact date of its founding, but a conservative estimate finds it in existence late in the fifteenth century. Some Iroquois oral tradition projects the founding date at several centuries earlier.

The oral tradition recounting the founding of the league is called the *Gayaneshakgowa,* or *Great Law of Peace.* This tradition identifies a Huron individual, Deganawida (known in Iroquois tradition as the Peacemaker), as a prophet who was inspired with a plan to end human beings' abuses of other human beings. This mission began at a time of great confusion and blood feuding, when assassinations and murder were common and when war parties were often dispatched to distant lands to avenge an act of violence, which then escalated into warfare between clans, villages, and whole nations.

The Peacemaker enlisted the assistance of a former Onondaga chief, Hiawatha, to carry his message to the nations. The message they brought was complex, and the tradition that relates it requires over a week in the telling. The Peacemaker proposed that the leaders of the communities organize for the purpose of creating a forum at which "thinking will replace violence." This assembly of leaders became the Grand Council, and eventually there were fifty sachems, or chiefs, from the various nations: nine Mohawks, nine Oneidas, fourteen Onondagas, ten Cayugas, and eight Senecas. They would assemble at Onondaga, at the geographical center of the country of the Five Nations, and would gather under what the Peacemaker called the Great Tree of Peace. There, reason would prevail.

The Haudenosaunee took their identity from their custom of building permanent towns and, within the towns, longhouses that served as communal dwellings and ceremonial buildings. The largest of these were about sixty feet wide by over a hundred yards long. The Peacemaker compared the Great League to a longhouse with the sky as its roof, the earth as its floor, and the fires of the nations burning within. The various nations had been organized into clans, and the Peacemaker adapted this tradition to the new political order, facilitating the renaming of the clans. There would be nine clans in all, but different nations would have different configurations. The clans are Turtle, Bear, Wolf, Heron, Hawk, Snipe, Beaver, Deer, and Eel. The women of the clans would meet under the leadership of a clan mother and select the men who would assemble as chiefs in the Grand Council. The Peacemaker proposed that the People of the Longhouse would be united in a brotherhood so strong that the people of the Turtle clan of the Senecas would view the people of the Turtle clan of the Mohawks as their own blood kin, and as such it would be unlawful for a person of one of these nations to marry a person of the other who was of the same clan, just as it would be wrong for a person to marry a sibling.

There was initial opposition to the plan of unity from a powerful Onondaga war chief whose name was Tadodaho. He was said to be the embodiment of evil, an individual who had woven snakes into his hair to intimidate all in his presence, and he had no interest in supporting a league dedicated to peace. The Peacemaker and Hayanwatah despaired of ever converting him until they voiced their concerns to Jikohnsaseh, a woman chief of the Cat (or Neutral) Nation. She suggested that he could be won over by being offered the chairmanship of the Great League. When the nations assembled to make their offer, Tadodaho accepted. Jikohnsaseh, who came to be described as the Mother of Nations or the Peace Queen, seized the horns of authority and placed them on Tadodaho's head in a gesture symbolic of the power of women in Iroquois polity.

The Grand Council was empowered to treat with foreign nations and peoples and to settle disputes among the Five Nations. The Iroquois Confederacy is divided into houses or, in their own parlance, "brotherhoods." The elder brothers are the Mohawks and Senecas. The younger brothers are the Oneidas, Cayugas, and, since 1722, the Tuscaroras. The Onondagas are known as the "Firekeepers." The Senecas and Mohawks confer as a "house," and the Cayugas, Oneidas, and Tuscaroras confer in a separate caucus, in a structure similar to that found in upper and lower houses in

Chiefs of the Iroquois Confederacy in the Council House at the Six Nations Reserve, circa 1910. The Onondaga chief holds wampum strings. Banners hanging at the left and right represent the Deer and Turtle clans.

some parliamentary systems. Issues that arise before the council are considered first by the Mohawk and Seneca "side," then by the Cayugas, Oneidas, and Tuscaroras in council. If these two "sides" are unable to reach agreement, the matter is sent to the Onondagas, who then cast the deciding vote. If the two "sides" reach agreement, the Onondagas have no veto power and must confirm the decision. In each of their deliberations there is an effort to reach unanimity, but when unanimity is impossible to achieve a vote is taken to determine the sense of the assembly. If the measure is favored by a significant majority, a second vote is taken at which those who dissented are expected to express solidarity with the others.

Continuous contact with a European nation commenced in 1609 when Samuel de Champlain led a

French force against a Mohawk military expedition in the Champlain Valley. This led to intermittent warfare between France and her Indian allies on one side and the Haudenosaunee on the other. This warfare was interrupted in 1624 with a peace arrangement that may be described as the first treaty between the Haudenosaunee and a European nation. The peace was short-lived, and intermittent hostilities continued. France had developed extensive alliances with Indian nations north of the St. Lawrence River and the Great Lakes, and the European introduction of the fur trade greatly enhanced competition among various Indian nations.

France and the Haudenosaunee concluded a treaty of peace in 1653, but war resumed in 1658, marking the beginning of a century during which the Haudenosaunee balanced their own interests in the context of the rivalry between England and France. The war was costly to New France, however, and in 1665 a military buildup in New France brought the two sides to negotiations and another treaty. Within months of the treaty France launched an invasion into Mohawk territory. One of the results of this exchange was that a Mohawk village was coerced into accepting French Jesuit missionaries. This village would eventually move under French protection to the St. Lawrence Valley, where its people would become known as the "French" or Caugnawaga Iroquois. They would eventually find their home in the oldest and largest Indian town established by Europeans—Kahnawake, Quebec—but they would be estranged from the confederacy from that time.

One of the first actions of the English after expelling the Dutch from the colony of New York was the establishment of formal relations with the Haudenosaunee in the form of a treaty with the Mohawks and Senecas in 1664. There were treaties of peace between the Haudenosaunee and other colonies during this period: with Massachusetts and Connecticut in 1677, with Maryland and Virginia in 1677, and another with Virginia in 1679.

Although they were arguably outnumbered and potentially surrounded by powerful enemies, the Haudenosaunee managed to sustain a measure of political and commercial hegemony among their Indian neighbors through the skillful and energetic use of diplomacy. Through a complex web of agreements and alliances they played a principal role in control of trade routes and in access to large but sparsely populated hunting territories shared by a number of Indian nations. Their strategic location—they were adjacent to both the French and English colonies—was a major factor that enabled them to exercise influence over international affairs far in excess of that afforded by either their numbers or their military prowess.

France continued to view the Haudenosaunee as a threat to their ambitions for economic hegemony over the Indian nations and lands around the Great Lakes and into the Ohio Valley. French efforts to establish economic and military alliances with the Illinois Nation led to tensions between France and the Haudenosaunee after the latter attacked the Illinois in 1680. In early 1684 Seneca warriors seized a French arms shipment and also attacked a French outpost on the Illinois River. New France's Governor La Barre sought and received permission to go to war. In July he set off with an army that was soon devastated by sickness, and he

was forced to abandon plans for attack. The next year France sent the Marquis de Denonville to accomplish the task of forcing the Haudenosaunee into submission. He launched an attack in the summer of 1687 during which French armies and their Indian allies invaded the Seneca country while most of the able-bodied Seneca men were pursuing military action against Indians in the Mississippi watershed. All the Seneca towns were burned, but the French were forced to withdraw and there was no decisive battle. Two years later Haudenosaunee forces attacked the French at Lachine on the St. Lawrence River and laid siege to nearby Montreal. Hostilities between the Haudenosaunee and France were to continue independent of France's struggle with England during the War of the League of Augsburg (which ended in 1697) until a peace treaty ending the war was signed in 1701.

From that time until France was expelled from North America in 1763, the Haudenosaunee maintained a position of neutrality in the wars between France and England, although they maintained closer cultural and economic relations with England. Following the Seven Years' War some Senecas joined Pontiac's campaign to drive English settlers out of the Ohio region, but Sir William Johnson was successful in keeping the Seneca Nation as a whole and the rest of the Haudenosaunee from joining Pontiac's forces.

During the American Revolution the Grand Council of the Haudenosaunee met and formally declared neutrality in the war between Britain and the American colonists. However, religious loyalties had invaded the Haudenosaunee communities and continued to work to their disadvantage. In 1776 many of the Mohawks in the Mohawk Valley were members of the Church of England, while a number of Oneida warriors were converts to the Bostonian puritanism of the Reverend Samuel Kirkland. Loyalties divided communities and families along these lines. At the same time, disaster struck Onondaga in 1777 in the form of a plague that rendered the Onondagas unable to host confederacy meetings at a critical moment in the war. In the absence of confederacy advice, significant numbers of Iroquois warriors joined the war effort in support of Britain. In retaliation, American forces invaded confederacy lands in 1779, burning crops and villages and scattering the population.

All in all, the American Revolution was a disaster for the Haudenosaunee. Following the war, treaties were signed that transferred ever larger areas of Haudenosaunee territory into the hands of New York State and a series of land speculators. Not even the Oneidas and Tuscaroras, who had supported the American revolutionaries, were spared. They lost most of their land in what are generally regarded as coercive or fraudulent treaties. Joseph Brant, the Mohawk war chief most responsible for persuading the warriors to support the British, negotiated lands in Canada, most notably a territory along the Grand River, in reparation for those lost in New York. In 1784, following the treaty that ended the war, many of the Haudenosaunee migrated there.

In the nineteenth century the Iroquois Confederacy continued as both a political alliance and a cultural entity. In 1799 the Seneca prophet Handsome Lake began his mission to restore the traditional practices of the Haudenosaunee and to lay the foundation of the modern Iroquois traditional religion. He also restored the Confederacy Council Fire to Onondaga in central New York State. Shortly thereafter the nations on the Grand River, unable to travel the great distance to Onondaga to conduct their governance, kindled a confederacy fire at their home in Canada. Since that time the confederacy has conducted Grand Councils in both longhouses. Although the two councils unite and act as one whenever business must be conducted that affects them both, the Grand River Council is the primary political organization in negotiations with Canada and its political subdivisions, while the Grand Council at Onondaga is the primary negotiator with the United States and its subdivisions.

Although there have been some changes, the chiefs of the confederacy continue to meet in council and to host gatherings at which the Great Law is recited, both at Grand River and at Onondaga. The political culture of the Haudenosaunee, now some five or more centuries old, continues to function to this day with a resilience that has enabled their continued existence as a distinct people.

See also Cayuga; Mohawk; Oneida; Onondaga; Seneca; Tuscarora.

Berman, Howard, "Perspectives on American Indian Sovereignty and International Law, 1600 to 1776," in *Exiled in the Land of the Free: Democracy, Indian Nations, and the U.S. Constitution* (Santa Fe, N. Mex.: Clear Light Publishers, 1992); Morgan, Lewis Henry, *League of the Ho-de-no-sau-nee, or Iroquois* (Rochester, N.Y.: Sage & Brother, 1851); Wallace, Paul A. W., *White Roots of Peace: The Iroquois Book of Life* (Philadelphia: University of Pennsylvania Press, 1946).

JOHN C. MOHAWK (Seneca)
State University of New York at Buffalo

ISHI

1860?–1916
Last survivor of the Yahi tribe.

In August 1911 a Yahi man about fifty years old came down out of the dense chaparral and rocky terrain of northeastern California's Lassen foothills. He had been living in those hills, in hiding with the last Yahi people, for some forty years. In the twenty-five-year period following the beginning of the California Gold Rush in 1849, most of the native people of northern California had been killed by Euro-Americans or their diseases, and those who remained were having a hard time surviving the miners' and settlers' impact on the land. The small Yahi tribe, known even before the arrival of whites for their fierce courage, was among the more effective groups in resisting the takeover, and they had suffered greatly.

In 1908 a group of men surveying for the Oro Light and Power Company inadvertently walked right into the hidden camp of the Yahis, whose population had by then been reduced to four. Three fled, leaving behind an old woman who couldn't walk. The surveyors left the woman unharmed, but took all the Yahis' possessions with them—blankets, acorns, salmon, traps, arrows, even a fire-making tool. Soon only one Yahi was still alive. Three years later he decided to join other humans, even though, given the facts of history, he probably expected to be killed.

The people who found the silent and acquiescent "wild man" called Sheriff J. B. Webber, who took him to the Oroville jail for his own protection. No one could communicate with him. Sam Batwi, one of the few remaining Yana people, was brought to try to talk with him because they were both Indians from the same general area. But although the Yahis were a part of the same linguistic group as the Yanas, their languages were not very similar, and the two men did not understand each other well. Reporters and newspaper publishers took full advantage of this mystery, and sensational stories soon reached San Francisco.

Alfred Kroeber and Thomas Waterman, anthropologists at the University of California, had heard about the surveying party's encounter with the Yahi people and had tried, without success, to find them. Hearing the news, they correctly guessed that the man was a Yahi. Kroeber, who had dedicated his considerable energy to "salvage anthropology"—that is, finding and recording what remained of native cultures before they

Ishi, the last of the Yahi people.

new life with curiosity, grace, and great generosity of spirit.

In 1914 Ishi developed a cough that soon proved to be a symptom of active tuberculosis. In 1916, while staying with the Watermans in Berkeley and working with the linguist Edward Sapir to record Yahi words and phrases, he died. After his death Saxton Pope, a doctor at the hospital next to the museum who had become a particular friend of Ishi's, wrote: "His were the qualities that last forever. He was kind; he had courage and self-restraint, and though all had been taken from him, there was no bitterness in his heart."

Nobody with any imagination can help but feel the immensity of this tragedy, so dense with irony, so loaded with universal symbols. And the symbolism has indeed become loaded for Native American people. Many non-Indians, cherishing the sterling qualities of Ishi's personality that Saxton Pope and others noted, see him as a romantic and nostalgic figure. Somehow, far too many people have come to believe that the "last wild Indian in North America," as he is called in the subtitle of Theodora Kroeber's *Ishi in Two Worlds*, was the last of the California Indians; plenty of California children from families that act Indian, feel Indian, are Indian, and are treated by their communities as Indian have had the puzzling experience of hearing in school that there are no more California Indians. How can this be? Maybe it's easier to think the excesses of history are all in the past and their victims extinct than it is to deal with the events of the past and their impact on the present. Despite this brutal history and subsequent efforts to downplay their traditions and sovereignty, California Indians are very much present, distinguished from the mainstream by the bits and pieces of their heritage they have been able to hold on to or salvage. In another twist of fate, the bits and pieces have often come from scholars who worked with people like Ishi, scholars who believed they were recording the last vestiges of cultures that would not survive.

Kroeber, Theodora, *Ishi in Two Worlds: A Biography of the Last Wild Indian in North America* (Berkeley and Los Angeles: University of California Press, 1967); Riffe, Jed, and Pamela Roberts, *Ishi, the Last Yahi* (Berkeley, Calif.: Rattlesnake Productions, 1992), videocassette.

JEANNINE GENDAR
News from Native California

disappeared completely—arranged to bring the man to stay at the university's anthropology museum in San Francisco. The man never told anyone his true name, and it was at the museum that people began to call him "Ishi," the Yahi word for "man."

As anthropologists, Kroeber and Waterman were thrilled with this opportunity to study a culture and language on the brink of disappearance. Over the next four years and seven months, as they learned to communicate with each other, Ishi gave them a vast and detailed body of information about Yahi life, even accompanying them in 1914 on a trip to his old home at Deer Creek. Meanwhile, visiting Ishi at the museum became a popular Sunday outing for families in the San Francisco Bay area. For his part, Ishi took up his

J

JOHNSON, PAULINE (TEKAHIONWAKE)

(1861–1913)
Mohawk writer and performer.

Born at Chiefswood on the Grand River Reserve of the Six Nations, near Brantford, Ontario, Emily Pauline Johnson was the daughter of George Henry Martin Johnson, Mohawk (Chief Teyonnhehkewea), and Emily Susanna Howells, English-born cousin of William Dean Howells. Johnson's father and paternal grandfather were strong influences on her life. The latter, John "Smoke" Johnson (Sakayengwaraton), was a hero of the War of 1812 and a renowned orator in the Iroquois councils. A gifted speaker in his own right, her father frequently made speeches on behalf of his people and served as a liaison between the Six Nations community and the outside world.

Johnson was reared at Chiefswood, the impressive house built by her father that became a gathering place for Indian and white visitors. She was primarily educated at home by her mother, who stimulated her children's love of literature by reading them works by the English romanticists. At age fourteen, Emily entered Brantford Collegiate Institute, where she remained until 1877. Her greatest pleasure there was performing in plays and pageants, although her parents opposed her desire to become an actress. After her return to Chiefswood, she devoted the next two years to visiting friends and writing poetry.

Not all of Johnson's childhood was idyllic. Because her father fearlessly tried to eradicate illegal traffic in alcohol and timber on the reserve, he was severely beaten in 1865, clubbed and shot in 1873, and assaulted again in 1878. George never fully recovered from these attacks; he died in 1884. The family then abandoned Chiefswood and a gracious lifestyle to live in nearby Brantford. After Smoke Johnson's death in 1886, Johnson assumed her great-grandfather Jacob Johnson's Indian name, signing all her poems "E. Pauline Johnson" and "Tekahionwake."

After the family was settled in Brantford, Johnson returned to writing poems, several of which were published in the *Week*, a Toronto journal. Johnson's public career began in 1892, when her recitation of her poem "A Cry from an Indian Wife" electrified a Toronto audience. Thereafter she supported herself primarily as an interpreter of her own works in Canada, Great Britain, and the United States. Often billed as "the Mohawk Princess," Johnson performed the Indian portion of her program in a fringed buckskin dress of her own design and the remainder in an evening gown. In 1894, Johnson traveled to London, where under the patronage of such prominent figures as Sir Charles Tupper, Canadian high commissioner to London, and Lady and Lord Ripon, former viceroy of India and Britain's colonial secretary, she met members of London society and gave recitals in their salons.

She also arranged for the publication of her first volume of poetry, *The White Wampum* (1895). Approximately half of the poems in the volume had Indian themes; many of these poems characterize Indian women. In reviewing the volume, the Canadian critic Hector Charlesworth called Johnson the most popular figure in Canadian literature and "in many respects the most prominent one." Critics were especially impressed by her "Song My Paddle Sings," a lyric later memorized by generations of Canadian schoolchildren.

The White Wampum's appearance greatly increased interest in Johnson's performances. In 1898, she became engaged to Charles Robert Lumley Drayton, whose parents strongly opposed their son's marriage to a mixed-blood older woman and stage performer. Drayton broke the engagement a year later. After her mother died in 1898, Johnson made Winnipeg her home. Vulnerable after her broken engagement and the loss of her mother, she may have become romantically involved with her unscrupulous manager, Charles Wurz (or Wuerz) in 1900–1901. She alludes to a tragic love affair in three of her best poems, unpublished in

Pauline Johnson on Christmas Day, 1897.

to retire from performing in 1909 and settle permanently in Vancouver.

During this period, she began her collaboration with Joe Capilano, a Squamish chief she had met during her 1906 visit to London. Her imaginative and dramatic re-creations of his Chinook stories were published as *The Legends of Vancouver* (1911), one of her best works. Here Johnson revealed an acute sense of the importance of setting, the interaction between storyteller and audience, and the act of storytelling. In 1912, Johnson published the poetry collection *Flint and Feather,* which included poems from her two earlier volumes as well as additional work. She died of cancer in Vancouver in 1913.

Two collections of her prose were published posthumously in 1913: *The Shagganappi,* boys' adventure stories; and *The Moccasin Maker,* which contains memorable portraits of Indian and non-Indian women on the frontier, a loving fictional account of her parents' courtship and marriage, and the essay "A Pagan in St. Paul's." *The Moccasin Maker,* which focuses on the role of Native American and white women on the frontier, is more important to the development of American Indian literature than is Johnson's poetry. The family focus in this book reflects the traditions of the women's domestic romances popular at the turn of the century; however, the heroines of such stories as "The Red Girl's Reasoning" and "As It Was in the Beginning" display far more independence and strength than the traditional heroine in the mainstream literature of the time.

Although critics have praised the lyricism of some of Johnson's poems, they have also noted her tendency to sentimentalism. Nevertheless, her *Flint and Feather* and *The Legends of Vancouver* have remained in print since her death. Johnson was the first American Indian woman to publish books of poetry and a collection of short fiction. She was also one of the first Native American authors to explore the theme of the mixed-blood Indian's search for identity, a dominant concern of twentieth-century Native American writers.

See also Literature by Indians.

Johnson, E. Pauline, *The Moccasin Maker* (1913; reprint, with an introduction and notes by A. LaVonne Brown Ruoff, Tucson: University of Arizona Press, 1987); Keller, Betty, *Pauline: A Biography of Pauline Johnson* (Vancouver: Douglas, 1981); McRaye, Walter, *Pauline Johnson and Her Friends* (Toronto: Ryerson, 1947).

A. LaVonne Brown Ruoff
University of Illinois at Chicago

her lifetime: "Morrow Land," "Heidelburgh," and "Song." Undoubtedly Johnson's grief over these relationships led to her frequent use in her writings of the theme of the betrayal of Indian women by white men. In 1901 J. Walter McRaye, with whom she had toured briefly in 1897, became her business partner and manager.

Her second book of poems, *Canadian Born* (1903), disappointed her critics because it included many poems written years earlier and because the new ones lacked the fresh voice of the earlier volume. In 1906, she traveled to Great Britain again, where she received rave reviews for her London performances and met such influential people as Algernon Swinburne. From 1907 to 1912, she frequently contributed stories and articles to *Mother's Magazine* and *Boys' World,* both published in the United States by the Cook Publishing Company. Her small income as an author enabled her

JONES, PETER

(1802–56)
Mississauga Ojibwa Methodist minister, chief of the
Credit River Mississaugas, and translator.

After his conversion to Christianity in 1823 Peter Jones
(Kahkewaquonaby, "Sacred Feathers") became the first
native Methodist missionary to the Ojibwas. He prepared, with the help of his brother John, translations of
the Bible from English into Ojibwa. As a chief of his
community, the Mississaugas of the Credit River, he
fought for over a quarter of a century for Mississauga
land rights and for those of other Ojibwa communities
throughout southern Ontario.

Peter Jones was born at the Head of the Lake (present-day Hamilton, Ontario) in 1802. His father, Augustus Jones, an American surveyor, had come to
Upper Canada, as Ontario was then known, fifteen
years earlier. In his work he had met a Mississauga
woman named Tuhbenahneequay, who became Peter's
mother. Since Augustus already had a Mohawk wife
and family he could not continue to live with his Mississauga companion, whom he left to raise young Peter
and their older son, John.

Tuhbenahneequay raised Peter and John with the
help of her parents and other band members. The boys
learned the religion and customs of their mother's people. Young Peter, a strong, hardy lad, earned the reputation of being an excellent hunter.

The late eighteenth and early nineteenth centuries
proved a difficult period for the Mississaugas, as the
settlers called the Ojibwas on the north shore of Lake
Ontario. Disease, chiefly smallpox, had made inroads
in their numbers, as had alcohol abuse. From approximately five hundred individuals in the late 1780s the
Mississaugas at the western end of the lake had declined to about two hundred by the early 1820s.

The war of 1812 led to great devastation at the Head
of the Lake, where a major battle occurred at Stoney
Creek in 1813 between the British and the American
invaders. Game also declined because of the increased
settlement in the area immediately after the war. When
Tuhbenahneequay's band appeared on the point of disintegration Augustus Jones intervened. In 1816 he took
his two Mississauga sons to live with him and his Mohawk family on the Grand River, thirty miles to the
west.

Peter benefited from two years of schooling in small
one-room schools. He learned English and, at home,
presumably some words of Mohawk, the language of

*Peter Jones holding a pipe tomahawk given to him by Sir Au-
gustus D'Este, Queen Victoria's first cousin. This picture, the
earliest surviving photograph of a North American Indian,
was taken in Edinburgh on August 4, 1845, during Jones's
tour of Scotland.*

his stepmother, half sisters, and half brothers. Augustus
taught his Mississauga sons how to farm and to care
for poultry and livestock. Peter also learned the carpentry skills needed to build houses and barns.

Christianity did not appeal to the young man. His father arranged to have him baptized in the Mohawk
Chapel, the local Anglican church, but the ceremony
meant nothing to him. He consented to it only because,
as he later wrote, "I might be entitled to all the privileges of the white inhabitants." At this stage of his life
he hoped to work in the fur trade as a clerk. As with
many of the English-speaking mixed bloods involved in
the fur trade, Peter apparently wanted to integrate him-

self into the British Protestant world, not that of the North American Indian. A visit to a Methodist camp meeting in 1823, however, would totally alter the direction of his life.

Peter attended the camp meeting at the request of his half sister Polly. He went without having any strong commitment to Ojibwa spiritual beliefs. Among his mother's people his religious education had been incomplete. Although he had gone on vision quests as a young man, he had never been blessed with a vision, with the presentation of a spiritual guardian. At the camp meeting, however, the ministers reached him. He became visibly affected. After four emotional days and nights of sermons and hymn singing he accepted Christianity.

Peter's conversion transformed him completely. He decided that he would devote his life to teaching the Ojibwas about Christianity. Able to speak Ojibwa, and knowledgeable about their culture, he made the new faith comprehensible. By 1825 the young native evangelist had led half of the Credit River Mississaugas into the Methodist Church. Moreover, on account of his skill in English, he and his white Methodist missionary allies successfully convinced the governor of Upper Canada to construct from the Mississaugas' own funds a permanent village on the Credit River. There the Methodists would teach religion as well as farming techniques. By the end of 1826 almost all of the remaining Credit River Mississaugas had become Methodists. The converts looked to Peter Jones for direction.

Over the next two decades Peter Jones evolved his plan of how to help the Upper Canadian Ojibwas. Contrary to what many colonists believed, the Mississaugas were not doomed to extinction. Jones believed that, by accepting Christianity and a settled agricultural way of life, they could survive and prosper even in the midst of the steadily growing settler community. In 1826–27 the Mississaugas established an agricultural village that quickly became the envy of other Ojibwa communities.

News of the Credit River mission spread throughout Upper Canada. To raise funds for this mission and the other Methodist Indian missions that followed, Peter Jones went on speaking tours throughout the colony and later to the United States and Britain. The highlight of his foreign trips came in 1838 when he was granted an audience with Queen Victoria at Windsor Castle. Jones made a great impression in Britain. An Irish clergyman described him as a man of "Saul-like stature, broad shoulders, high cheekbones, erect bearing, sleek jet-black hair, and fine intellect."

The native missionary acquired a lifelong ally in 1833 when he married Eliza Field, the daughter of a wealthy English soap and candle manufacturer. They had met and fallen in love during his first missionary tour of Britain in 1831. She helped him copy out his translations of the scriptures and Methodist hymns into Ojibwa, taught the Mississauga girls to sew, and instructed them in religion. She also strengthened him in his resolve to fully Europeanize the Credit River Mississaugas.

While Jones's work to protect the remaining land base of the Ojibwas met with strong support, a number of Mississaugas, perhaps as many as half of those at the Credit River mission, opposed his attempts to erase so much of the remaining Ojibwa culture and customs. He persevered in his attempts to introduce European-style discipline for the children, to promote residential schools, and to govern by voting on questions rather than by seeking consensus.

The Methodists' emphasis on Europeanization alienated many Ojibwas in other communities. This helped to check the Methodist advance in the mid-1830s, after approximately two thousand Indians in Upper Canada had joined the church. Splits among the Methodists themselves also hurt their missionary work; for seven years in the 1840s the Methodists in Upper Canada divided into two separate conferences. Increased competition from the Anglicans and especially the Roman Catholics also weakened the Methodists' outreach. Peter Jones's declining health in the late 1840s and early 1850s removed from active service the Methodists' leading native missionary.

At his death in 1856 Jones was survived by his wife, his aged mother, a half sister, and four sons. Eliza Jones collected his diaries and his notes for a history of the Mississaugas, invaluable primary source materials for a study of Christian Ojibwas in southern Ontario in the mid-nineteenth century. Both his *Life and Journals* (1860) and *History of the Ojebway Indians* (1861) were published posthumously.

See also Missions and Missionaries.

Smith, Donald B., "Peter Jones," in *Dictionary of Canadian Biography*, vol. 8, 1851–1860 (Toronto: University of Toronto Press, 1985); Smith, Donald B., *Sacred Feathers: The Reverend Peter Jones (Kahkewaquonaby) and the Mississauga Indians* (Lincoln: University of Nebraska Press, 1987).

DONALD B. SMITH
University of Calgary

JONES, WILLIAM
(MEGASIAWA; BLACK EAGLE)

(1871–1909)
Fox anthropologist.

Born on March 28, 1871, on the Sauk and Fox Reservation in Indian Territory, William Jones was the product of English-Welsh and Fox marriages. His grandfather, William Washington Jones, went west with Daniel Boone, fought in the Black Hawk War, and while in Iowa married Katiqua, daughter of the Fox chief Washi-ho-wa. Their son, Henry Clay Jones (Bald Eagle), married an English woman named Sarah Penny. She died when William was one year old, and the boy was raised by his grandmother Katiqua on the reservation, to which some of her people had been moved in 1870. Katiqua, of the Eagle clan, refused to speak English in the nine years she raised him.

Shortly after 1880, Katiqua died and the boy's father sent him to a Quaker boarding school for Indian children in Wabash, Indiana, where he remained for three years. He then returned to his father's house in Indian Territory and worked as a cowboy. Years later, shortly before his death, Jones recalled his teenage years with deep nostalgia: "I wish the Plains could have remained as they were when I was a 'kid.' . . . Did you ever behold clearer moonlight nights anywhere else? Did you hear the lone cry of the wolf and the yelp of the coyote? I wish you could have seen the long horn and the old-time punchers." In the fall of 1889 he entered Hampton Institute in Virginia; upon his graduation in 1892 he received two prizes for scholarship. Later that year he entered Philips Academy in Andover, Massachusetts, where he excelled in classical studies and began to formulate plans for studying medicine and returning to his people as a physician.

After graduating from Philips in 1896 Jones spent the summer with his father, who was commissioned to "collect" Indian students from Indian Territory for Carlisle Indian Industrial School in Carlisle, Pennsylvania. In the fall he entered Harvard College, and the following spring he met Frederic W. Putnam, a professor of anthropology and the director of the Peabody Museum of Archaeology and Ethnology at Harvard. Putnam turned Jones's interests and ambitions permanently away from medicine and toward anthropology. The Boston Folk-Lore Society sent him to the West in the summer of 1897, and he lived among the Sauk and Fox peoples in Tama, Iowa, his mother's hometown. The ease of his acceptance there confirmed his intentions.

Jones returned to Harvard in the fall, and over the next three years he joined several clubs (including the Folk Lore Club), wrote articles for and edited the *Harvard Monthly*, won the *Harvard Advocate* scholarship for excellence in English composition, and upon graduation in June 1900 was awarded honorable mention for his studies in American archaeology. He entered Columbia University the following fall, to work with Franz Boas as a President's University Scholar. By June 1901 he had a master's degree from Columbia and was headed again for fieldwork in the West. Boas instructed the young man to "collect as much information as possible on the language and customs of the Sac and Fox, and obtain as many specimens as you can illustrating the ethnology of the people." Jones spent the summer in Iowa and Oklahoma, returning later in the year to New York and Columbia. For the next several years Jones's life maintained this divided pattern as he sought to become an ethnographer for his own people. "The wind is wailing outside as it does on the plains," he wrote from his apartment in New York City, "and it strikes a chord of lonesomeness in my soul. The wind is always wailing, singing, screaming, and murmuring out there, and when once you get used to its sound you never forget it."

In the summer of 1902 Jones returned to the plains, staying late into the fall. "I meet up with old faces, faces that were full of life when I was a child, and are now on the other side of the hill of life—on the downward side of that hill," he wrote on October 1; and, six weeks later: "I am traveling north. . . . It is growing dark on the prairies, a sort of thing I like to see, because, somehow, it sets my mind to recalling past scenes of childhood when this country was worth while living in." After another winter at Columbia (1902–3), during which he worked chiefly on linguistics with a Kickapoo informant, Jones spent the summer traveling for the American Museum among the Indian peoples— mainly Sioux and Ojibwas—of the Great Lakes region and beyond, from Manitoba to the Dakotas. Again he stayed deep into the autumn: "September 29. The frost has nipped the birch and poplar and red oak, and I wish I could describe to you the beautiful soft yellow of the birch and poplar leaves, and how rich the crimson is on the leaves of the oak. We paddled by miles and miles of color on both sides of us. It has been a long time since I have eaten so much wild meat."

Jones received his Ph.D. in anthropology from Columbia in 1904. That summer he returned to the Canadian border to continue recording Ojibwa stories and linguistic texts. In November he stopped for a few weeks among the Sauk-Fox of Oklahoma to observe their customs and collect data and material artifacts. He continued his Ojibwa work for the next two years, always seeking, as he wrote, "wilder people who dance and do magic." He was also hoping to find a reliable position of employment so that he could, among other things, marry his fiancée, Caroline Andrus, of Hampton, Virginia. The position never developed; nor did the marriage. Instead, in the winter of 1906, George A. Dorsey of the Field Museum in Chicago offered Jones a choice of expeditions: Africa, the South Seas, or the Philippine Islands. Initially reluctant to postpone his North American work but without viable financial options, Jones chose the Philippines project. He moved to Chicago for a year, where he attempted to complete his Ojibwa work while preparing for the overseas expedition, which was being sponsored by industrialist R. F. Cummings. In July 1907 he visited Oklahoma; he sailed for the Philippines the next month.

During the fall of 1907 Jones made his way up the Cagayan River in northern Luzon Province, arriving among the head-hunting Ilongot peoples of that region in April 1908. There he remained, living in various villages, for nearly a year, experiencing, as Renato Rosaldo described it, a "profound ambivalence toward the Ilongots, shifting as it did between a love of their primeval beauty and a hatred of their primitive bestiality." On March 29, 1909, on the way downstream with his material culture collections, Jones, exasperated with Ilongot delays, verbally abused and threatened his carriers. They responded by attacking him with knives and spears, and he died within a few hours. His body was found face up in a balsa canoe.

The first Native American to receive an advanced degree in anthropology and undertake anthropological fieldwork in the United States, Jones abandoned that work—as he thought, temporarily—with the encouragement of his mentors and for lack of alternative opportunities in his chosen field. There is a deep irony in his fate: he, a Native American, was among the first professionally trained anthropologists to undertake fieldwork among native peoples of the first overseas colonial possession of the United States—and one of the first to die in such service. William Jones, Anglo-Indian son of the American prairies, lived a severely divided life as he underwent a process of personal acculturation that involved, above all, observing and recording the rapid and often tragic acculturations of others. He never returned to the United States or to his beloved Indian Territory. "I was born out of doors," he wrote from the Philippine jungle. "Now it looks as if I shall keep on under the open sky, and at the end lie down out of doors, which, of course, is as it should be."

Rideout, Henry Milner, William Jones: *Indian, Cowboy, American Scholar, and Anthropologist in the Field* (New York: Frederick A. Stokes Company, 1912); Rosaldo, Renato, *Ilongot Headhunting, 1883–1974: A Study in Society and History* (Stanford, Calif.: Stanford University Press, 1980); Stoner, Barbara, "Why Was William Jones Killed?" *Bulletin of the Field Museum of Natural History* 42, no. 8 (1971): 10–13.

CURTIS M. HINSLEY
Flagstaff, Arizona

JOSEPH (HEINMOT TOOYALAKEKT)
(1841–1904)
Nez Perce leader.

"Good words do not last long until they amount to something. Good words will not give me back my children. . . . It makes my heart sick when I remember all the good words and all the broken promises." These words spoken by Joseph (often known as Chief Joseph) reveal a personality that reflected the hardships that tribes such as the Nez Perces endured during contact with Western civilization. Understanding that personality requires an investigation of its past.

Heinmot Tooyalakekt was born in present-day eastern Oregon in 1841 to Tu-ya-kas-kas and a Nez Perce woman from the Grande Ronde Valley. Tu-ya-kas-kas was chief of the Wallamotkin band, which inhabited seven villages in the area. Tu-ya-kas-kas's village was called In-nan-toe-e-in. The tribal elders stated that he could speak some English and that he was half Cayuse and half Nez Perce. History has lost the Indian name of Chief Joseph's mother, but she was baptized by the Reverend H. H. Spaulding on May 14, 1843, and given the name Arenoth.

The marriage of Tu-ya-kas-kas and Arenoth produced four children. Their first child was a son named Sousouquee, the second was Heinmot Tooyalakekt, the third was a son named Ollokot (or Aloqat), and the fourth was a daughter named Ai-ai-tominee. From all accounts, Sousouquee was taller and even more handsome than his younger brothers; he was killed in 1865. Tu-ya-kas-kas accepted Christianity and had his family baptized in 1843. His baptismal name was Joseph; he

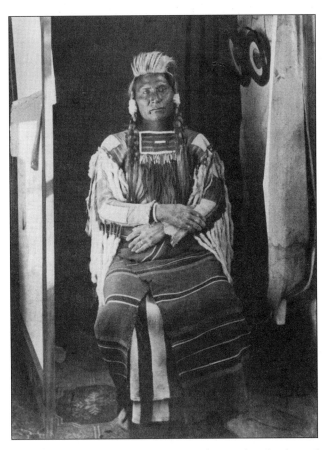

Chief Joseph in October 1877, just a few weeks after he and the Nez Perces surrendered. The photograph is by John H. Fouch.

was also known as Old Joseph. Tu-ya-kas-kas believed in the old Nez Perce traditions. After the signing of the Treaty of 1863, which reduced the size of the reservation, Old Joseph, very upset, and not understanding the division of his people, took his family to the buffalo country east of the Rockies.

After his father died in 1871, Heinmot Tooyalakekt, by this time known as Young Joseph, was given the chieftainship of the Wallamotkin band. Young Joseph married a Nez Perce woman known as Wa-win-te-pi-ksat. She was the daughter of Chief Whisk-tasket, of the Lapwai area. In 1865 they had a daughter named Kap-kap-on-mi. He later married another Nez Perce woman by the name of Springtime and had a second daughter, who was born at Tepahlewam in 1877. Throughout his life, Joseph had a total of four wives—the two already mentioned and two others, I-atu-ton-mi and He-yoom-yoyikt. He had a total of nine

children—five girls and four boys. All except Kap-kap-on-mi died before the age of two. Kap-kap-on-mi survived the Nez Perce War of 1877 and escaped to Canada. She later returned to Idaho, along with thirteen other Nez Perces, and changed her name to Sarah. On July 21, 1879, Sarah married a Nez Perce named George Moses. Sarah never had any children, and she never saw her father again. She died some years later. Sarah's mother lived until 1929; she died in February of that year at Nespelem, Washington.

Chief Joseph was well known to many of the settlers and soldiers in late-nineteenth-century Oregon, Idaho, and Washington. He has been described by numerous observers as a tall, straight, and handsome man with a dignified, quiet demeanor. The 1877 war brought changes not only to Chief Joseph, but to all the Nez Perces, Christian and otherwise. The conflict began when federal authorities ordered all of the chiefs whose bands resided outside the boundaries of the diminished reservation created by the Treaty of 1863 to be on the new reservation within thirty days. This smaller preserve had been created to accommodate miners and settlers who had streamed across the borders of the tribe's earlier (and larger) reservation in the early 1860s. The chiefs who were now "off" the reservation included Joseph as well as Looking Glass, White Bird, Tuhool-hut'sut, and Husis-kute.

In the course of their relocation, a group of warriors killed some white settlers. Fearing retaliation, the "off-reservation" chiefs fled eastward toward the continental divide. During the next four months Joseph, Looking Glass, and the others won several battles against the pursuing bluecoats as they traveled more than one thousand miles across Idaho and Montana.

The Nez Perce War, as it was later known, has been researched by numerous scholars and described in minute detail. Unfortunately, myths have also been created regarding the conflict. The greatest of these myths is that Joseph was a "war chief." This label was first applied by the soldiers that were involved in the campaign, the main contributors being General O. O. Howard and his aide-de-camp, Lieutenant C. E. S. Wood. It was the Nez Perce warriors that provided clarification on this topic. They said that Joseph was not a "war chief," but a "civil chief" charged with diplomacy and political leadership.

On October 5, 1877, Chief Joseph surrendered his rifle to Colonel Nelson Miles not far from the modern town of Chinook. By that time all chiefs were dead except for White Bird and Joseph. White Bird had escaped to Canada, and Joseph was alone. It was a moment that demanded all of Joseph's strength and wisdom. After the surrender, Joseph and all the Nez Perces were held as prisoners of war and sent to Fort Leavenworth, Kansas. They later were sent to Oklahoma. During this time, many of the tribe's women and children died of malaria. In 1879, Joseph and another leader, Yellow Bull, visited Washington, D.C., to argue for permission to return to the Pacific Northwest. They met with the Commissioner of Indian Affairs and with Secretary of the Interior Carl Schurz. They also made an attempt at winning congressional support, but western senators were able to prevent any positive action. Chief Joseph made such a favorable impression that the Indian Rights Association and several eastern philanthropists began to speak out on his behalf. Joseph's suffering became a national cause, and Joseph's speeches were circulated throughout the country. By May 1884, fourteen petitions had been received by Congress in support of Joseph. On April 29, 1885, the Commissioner of Indian Affairs ordered the tribe's guardians to move the Nez Perce back to the Northwest. On May 22, 1885, the Nez Perce boarded railroad cars in Arkansas City to return home to the reservation. The charisma and diplomacy of Chief Joseph had prevailed.

Unfortunately, Chief Joseph and 150 of his followers were sent to the Colville Reservation in central Washington. They were not allowed to return to the Wallowa Valley in eastern Oregon, the gravesite of Old Joseph. "He who don't love the grave of his father," Joseph said, "is worse than a wild animal." Again, Joseph made numerous trips east to gain support. In April 1897 he visited New York City, attending the dedication of Grant's Tomb as a guest of Buffalo Bill. Joseph never won permission to return to his beloved Wallowa Valley, but he did have the opportunity to visit his father's grave in 1900 on a trip with Indian Inspector James McLaughlin. He and his band became permanent residents of the Colville Reservation.

Chief Joseph was found dead in his tipi at Nespelem, Washington, on September 21, 1904. As related by Chief Red Star (Willie Andrews), "Chief Joseph was found dead in his blankets. His wife went to wake him for breakfast around seven or eight o'clock, but he did not move. Just as if sleeping he was dead. He had been unwell for some time but was up and around." His grave at Nespelem can still be visited.

See also Nez Perce.

Gidley, M., *With One Sky above Us* (New York: G. P. Putnam's Sons, 1979); Josephy, Alvin M., Jr., *The Nez Perce Indians and the Opening of the Northwest* (New Haven and London: Yale University Press, 1965); McWhorter, L. V., *Hear Me, My Chiefs!* (Caldwell, Idaho: Caxton Printers, 1983).

OTIS HALFMOON (Nez Perce)
National Park Service

JOURNALISM
See Newspapers, Magazines, and Journals.

KAMIAKIN

(c. 1800–1877)
Yakama and Palouse warrior and statesman.

On the snowy slopes of Mount Rainier, Kamiakin received his *tah* or spirit power when a buffalo came to him in a vision, sang a power song, and directed the young boy's life. Kamiakin's Sahaptin-speaking elders interpreted his vision, telling him that he would become a great warrior and leader but that his life would be tragic. He was told that he must be true to his course of action, because it was the right course. Kamiakin's life was set into motion by his vision quest, and the prophecy of the elders did come true. However, his destiny as a powerful Indian leader among the Yakamas, the Palouses, and other tribes of the Columbia Plateau was also determined by his familial ties. Years before Kamiakin's birth, two women traveled to the stars, marrying star men. One of the women returned to earth with a boy fathered by one of the star men. This boy became the patriarch of the Weowicht family, of which Kamiakin was a member.

Born around 1800, Kamiakin was the first son of Kamoshnite (Yakama) and Tsyiyak (Palouse-Spokane). Kamoshnite was the daughter of Weowicht and the sister of Owhi and Teias, two prominent Yakama chiefs. Kamiakin grew up in present-day central Washington, but he traveled to the Great Plains with his family, where he earned the distinction of becoming a warrior and buffalo hunter. He rose quickly as a tribal leader, and he was sufficiently wealthy to have five wives. His first wife was Sunkhaye, his cousin and the daughter of Teias. He broke social convention within the family by marrying four women from a rival family of Chief Tenax. These women had familial ties with the Salish-speaking Indians of the Northwest. By marrying them, Kamiakin incurred the wrath of his uncles but extended his power base among many Indians.

By 1853, when the United States split the Oregon Territory in two, creating Washington Territory, Kamiakin was the most prominent Yakama chief. He was not head chief of the Yakamas, because there were many chiefs, who led several bands. However, representatives of the U.S. Army and the Office of Indian Affairs noted in their documents that Kamiakin was the major political and military leader in the area. In 1853, President Franklin Pierce appointed Isaac Ingalls Stevens governor of Washington Territory and Superintendent of Indian Affairs. After completing a survey for the Northern Pacific Railroad, Stevens negotiated treaties with Indians of Puget Sound and on the coast. He was generally successful in forcing Indians to accept treaties that concentrated many tribes and bands onto relatively small reservations.

According to Indian and white accounts, Stevens forged the mark of Nisqually chief Leschi and his brothers on the Medicine Creek Treaty. Leschi was Kamiakin's distant cousin, and he visited the Yakamas to report on Stevens's deceptive treaty making. When Stevens's representative, James Doty, arrived in the Yakama country in early 1855, Kamiakin originally refused to meet him. Because of friction between Kamiakin and his uncles, Owhi and Teias, these two leaders asserted themselves by meeting Doty and agreed to attend the Walla Walla Council with Stevens. Reluctantly, Kamiakin also met Doty and agreed to meet Stevens in the Walla Walla Valley. Kamiakin carefully refused to accept tobacco from Doty, saying he would never accept anything from whites, because they might later claim that he took it in payment for his land. Kamiakin proclaimed that he would never sell his land.

In May and June of 1855, Stevens outlined American Indian policy to the Yakamas, Nez Perces, Umatillas, Cayuses, and Walla Wallas. Kamiakin listened patiently to the whites as they explained treaties, reservations, removal, and the governance of natives by the Office of Indian Affairs. Kamiakin said little during the council, but he opposed the Yakama Treaty, which created the Yakama Reservation. He originally determined to leave the council without signing, but Owhi, Teias, and others pressured him into signing as an act of peace and friendship. Kamiakin believed that war was inevitable, and he returned to the Yakama country to prepare for a fight and muster his allies. In July white miners discovered gold north of the Spokane River, and soon afterward Yakama warriors executed a few miners who had raped Yakama women and stolen horses. When Yakama agent Andrew Bolon investigated, two Yakamas murdered him, triggering the Yakama War of 1855–58.

Kamiakin fought against regular troops and volunteer militiamen, but because of divisions within the Yakama leadership and the successes of the U.S. soldiers, he soon left the Yakama country, never to return. He established a village along the north bank of the Palouse River among his father's people, the Palouses. From 1856 until his death in 1877, Kamiakin considered himself a Palouse chief. Kamiakin and his band may have fought Colonel Edward Steptoe when regular troops rode north of the Snake River, invading the Palouse Hills. Kamiakin did not instigate this fight, and if he was there, he played a minor role in defeating Steptoe. Kamiakin participated in the final episode of the Yakama War, fighting Colonel George Wright and his regulars at the Battles of Four Lakes and Spokane Plain. At Four Lakes a burst of cannon fire dropped a pine tree, which struck and injured Kamiakin. Colestah, Kamiakin's fifth wife and a warrior woman, rescued her husband before he could be captured.

The Indians lost these battles. Kamiakin considered negotiating with Wright but instead left the region, traveling to Canada and then to Montana, where he settled with friendly Flatheads. In 1860, Kamiakin returned to his home on the Palouse River, where he fished, hunted, gathered, and gardened. In 1864 Colestah died, and the next spring Kamiakin moved his village to Rock Lake. Cattlemen under William Henderson tried to drive Kamiakin from the region, but Superintendent of Indian Affairs Robert Milroy recognized Kamiakin's claim to the Rock Lake property and vowed to protect the chief from the Hendersons. Kamiakin lived out his days at Rock Lake. On two occasions Indian agents offered him food and clothing, but each time he refused. He died in 1877 and was buried near his village. White grave robbers stole his skull, but friends intervened and reburied his remains in an unmarked grave. Following his death, all of Kamiakin's family left their home at Rock Lake. Most moved to the Colville Reservation, where they reside to this day.

See also Yakama.

Schuster, Helen H., *The Yakima* (New York: Chelsea House Publishers, 1990); Splawn, Andrew Jackson, *Ka-mi-akin, Last Hero of the Yakimas* (Portland, Oreg.: Stationery and Printing Company, 1917); Trafzer, Clifford E., and Richard D. Scheuerman, *Renegade Tribe: The Palouse Indians and the Invasion of the Inland Pacific Northwest* (Pullman: Washington State University Press, 1986).

CLIFFORD E. TRAFZER (Wyandot)
University of California at Riverside

KEETOWAH

Keetowah, a Cherokee word, has various other spellings: Ketoowah, Kittuwa, Kituhwa, and Kittowa. The word derives from the name of a Cherokee settlement located near the Tuckasegee River, in present-day North Carolina. The settlement of Kituhwa was one of the "seven mother towns." The people were called Ani Kituhwagi or "People of Kituhwa." The settlement was responsible for the protection of the northern frontier of the Cherokee Nation. The Shawnees even referred to Cherokees as the Kituhwas.

After the Cherokee removal to Indian Territory and just prior to the Civil War, a secret society in the tribe adopted the name Keetowah. Nighthawk Keetowahs were strict traditionalists who wanted to preserve their culture in the new setting of Indian Territory. Just before the turn of the twentieth century they promoted opposition to the federal allotment policy that preceded Oklahoma statehood. Today the Keetowah Society continues to promote and preserve Cherokee traditions.

Separate from the Keetowah Society, another group of Cherokees formed the United Keetowah Band. This is a federally recognized group of Cherokees who believe it is they, and not the Cherokee Nation government, who should represent the Cherokee people.

See also Cherokee.

KELLOGG, MINNIE
(1880–c. 1949)
Oneida activist and writer.

Laura Minnie Cornelius Kellogg was born on the Oneida Reservation near Green Bay, Wisconsin, the daughter of Adam Poe Cornelius and Celicia Bread Cornelius, farmers. A descendant of central New York State Oneida Indians who followed an Indian missionary, the Reverend Eleazar Williams, into the Wisconsin territory in 1822, she was a baptized member of the Episcopal Church of the Holy Apostles. Included in her prominent lineage were Daniel Bread, a major nineteenth-century Oneida chief in New York and Wisconsin who was known for his powerful oratorical skills, and Skenandore, the last of the New York Oneida chiefs, who was one of the tribe's leaders during its migration to Wisconsin.

Unlike many of her contemporaries, Kellogg avoided attending distant Indian boarding schools. She was educated in the 1890s at Grafton Hall, an Episcopal boarding school largely for non-Indians located at Fond du Lac, Wisconsin. In the first decade of the twentieth century, she studied at Barnard College, Cornell University, the New York School of Philanthropy (later the Columbia University School of Social Work), Stanford University, and the University of Wisconsin, although she never received degrees from any of these institutions.

One of the best Indian linguists of her generation, Kellogg had a superior command of Oneida and Mohawk as well as English. But she gained national attention through her spellbinding oratory and her eloquent writing skills. As a public speaker, she told of the eighteenth-century League of the Iroquois, the lessons and wisdom of Indian elders, and the overriding concerns of the Iroquois to win back their lands, which she insisted had been taken fraudulently by New York State and by land speculators. She was equally accomplished with a pen, devoting herself to writing on behalf of Progressive Era reform causes such as women's rights as well as writing political tracts on Indian issues; she also wrote plays and short stories. Her writings include *Our Democracy and the American Indian* (1920) and *Indian Reveries: Gehdos of the Lost Empire* (1921).

In 1911 Kellogg joined with other well-educated Native Americans to found the Society of American Indians, a national reform-minded organization largely devoted to the acquisition of U.S. citizenship for Native Americans and the improvement of social conditions on reservations. She later served variously as secretary of the organization's executive committee and as its vice-president for education. Kellogg differed from the majority of her colleagues in the Society of American Indians, however, in her vehement opposition to the economic and educational policies of the Bureau of Indian Affairs. She was also more confident than other organization members that Native Americans could, without assistance, transform their reservations into self-sustaining communities. After her marriage on

April 22, 1912, to Orrin Joseph Kellogg, a non-Indian attorney from Minneapolis, she became even more isolated from the organization's leadership. Eventually, she broke with the Society of American Indians, outlining her views in *Our Democracy and the American Indian*, which drew significant inspiration from the Mormon economic model of community development and survival.

Kellogg and her husband spent much of the time before, during, and after World War I organizing a massive Iroquois land-claims suit. For this legal effort, they made exorbitant promises and collected funds from poor Indians in Iroquois communities throughout the United States and Canada. Their collection methods led to their arrests in Oklahoma (1913) and Montreal (1925), although they were never convicted of fraud. In 1927 the U.S. District Court dismissed their Iroquois land-claims suit, *Deere v. St. Lawrence River Power Company*, because of what it claimed was a lack of jurisdiction over the dispute.

Kellogg continued to exercise influence in Indian affairs into the 1930s, but her insistence on Indian self-sufficiency became less appealing during the New Deal era, when the government was providing tribes with economic assistance and promoting Indian languages and cultural traditions. By the 1940s she was a forgotten woman who had outlived her time. According to Oneida tribal sources, she died in obscurity in the late 1940s. Her death certificate and burial record have not been located.

Acknowledged as a pioneer of the land-claims movement and as a determined advocate of Indian education and economic development, Kellogg nevertheless has been accused by many Indian elders of fomenting divisions within Iroquois communities and of swindling Indians out of hundreds of thousands of dollars in her abortive efforts to litigate their land claims. Seeking to use her extraordinary abilities to help her people, she ended up condemned by many of them as a common thief.

Hauptman, Laurence M., "Designing Woman: Minnie Kellogg, Iroquois leader," in *Indian Lives: Essays on Nineteenth and Twentieth Century Native American Leaders*, ed. L. George Moses and Raymond Wilson (Albuquerque: University of New Mexico Press, 1985); McLester, Thelma Cornelius, "Oneida Women Leaders," in *The Oneida Experience: Two Perspectives*, ed. Jack Campisi and Laurence M. Hauptman (Syracuse, N.Y.: Syracuse University Press, 1988).

LAURENCE M. HAUPTMAN
SUNY College at New Paltz

KICKAPOO

When French fur traders first encountered the Kick-apoos in the 1600s, these Indians had already established a reputation for independence and mobility that has distinguished them ever since. Not long before initial contact with Europeans, the Kickapoos, or *ki-ikaapoa*—"people who move about"—relocated from villages west of Lake Erie to southern Wisconsin. By the mid-1700s they had resettled in Indiana and Illinois, with several bands claiming lands between the Vermillion and Wabash Rivers and others living along the Sangamon River to the west. By 1800 some bands began migrating to the Southwest, with many eventually settling in northern Mexico. During the 1820s most of the Sangamon River, or Prairie, bands relocated to southwestern Missouri, the result of a land-cession treaty with the U.S. government.

The Prairie bands' stay in Missouri was brief. In 1832 additional treaties resulted in the resettlement of the largest Kickapoo bands, the Prairie and the Vermillion, west of the Missouri River, near Fort Leavenworth, in present-day Kansas. Over the next three decades, ignoring instructions from U.S. officials, most of the Prairie Kickapoos moved south to join relatives already in northern Mexico. Throughout the rest of the century, these southern Kickapoos were notorious for plundering American ranches and settlements along the Rio Grande.

In 1873, the U.S. Army attacked a camp of Pota-watomis and Kickapoos in Mexico, capturing numbers of women and children. The following year, many Mexican Kickapoos reluctantly agreed to settle on a reservation, abandoning Mexico for a more secure life in Oklahoma. On American soil, however, they spent the following decades squabbling with American authorities, contesting land allotment and the government's civilization program.

Because of their frequent migrations and customary reticence toward outsiders, information on traditional Kickapoo customs, social organization, and religion has remained fragmentary. The Kickapoos shared cultural traits with the Fox, Sauks, Mascoutins, and Potawatomis, and they spoke one of three dialects that make up the Sauk-Fox-Kickapoo language.

Each Kickapoo band was autonomous, with its own headmen and their assistants as well as war chiefs and warriors. From spring through fall, each band stayed close to its village, the women maintaining the wicki-ups—brush-covered dwellings—and cultivating corn, beans, and squash and gathering edible plants, the men hunting game and defending the village against enemies. Following the harvest, they abandoned the village for the winter buffalo hunt. Over the decades the separate bands gained more autonomy as they adjusted to particular environmental factors, encountered missionaries, traders, and settlers, and interacted with and adopted the traits of other tribes.

Historically, status in patrilineal Kickapoo society was based on membership in such clans as Eagle, Bear, Water, Buffalo, Fox, and Thunder. These groups were further divided into moieties—the *oskasa,* or black, and the *kiiskooha,* or white—which formed the basis for competition in lacrosse and other games and determined seating at religious ceremonies.

The Great Manitou, or Creator, stood atop the Kickapoo spiritual hierarchy, with lesser manitous existing in the four winds, the sky, the moon and stars, and grandmother earth. Wisaka, son of the Great Manitou, created the earth and everything in it, including the Kickapoos. Wisaka also gave the Kickapoos the sacred bundles, the basis of Kickapoo ceremonialism. Possessing special powers, these animal-skin pouches contained sacred mementos and objects representing past glories. Medicine societies organized and performed the spring ceremonies centering on clan bundles. Selected members of each clan led the weeklong bundle ceremonies, which, along with the Green Corn Dance and Buffalo Dance, strengthened group cohesion and helped the Kickapoos maintain traditional ways.

An important member of most bands was the priest, or shaman, who was able to communicate with the spirit world. Followers believed a shaman could predict the future and cure the sick. Because one's personal welfare depended on relationships with the spirit world, individual Kickapoos facing uncertainty or grappling with a difficult decision often consulted a shaman, whose authority sometimes exceeded that of the chiefs.

The most influential Kickapoo shaman was Kenekuk (c. 1790–1852), of the Vermillion band. After settling in Kansas in 1833, Kenekuk, "the Kickapoo Prophet," instructed followers in a new religion combining traditional Kickapoo ceremonialism with Christianity. A central tenet of the religion was a strict edict against relinquishing lands to whites. Ordering adherents to put aside their clan bundles, to abstain from alcohol and other vices, and to live peacefully with whites, Kenekuk helped them adjust to a rapidly changing, white-dominated world and withstand efforts to expel them from

Kansas. Today, although few still practice Kenekuk's unique religion, the approximately thirteen hundred Kansas Kickapoos realize it was the prophet's example that enabled them to counter pressures to abandon their small reservation. Their resistance, however, came at a price; although they have been endeavoring to renew and abide by tribal customs, few, if any, speak their native tongue, and many of the old Kickapoo customs have been forgotten.

Other Kickapoo groups followed more traditional paths, rejecting white customs entirely. By the early 1890s, many Oklahoma Kickapoos demonstrated their disdain for U.S. policy and returned to Mexico, joining relatives who had stayed behind. By 1960 they had established a village near Eagle Pass, Texas, constructing wickiups out of cardboard and other scrap materials. In 1985 they received title to 125 nearby acres, and today modern housing has begun replacing the wickiups. Among the most traditional Indians in North America, the seven hundred Texas-Mexican Kickapoos adhere strictly to their ancient customs, earning a living as migrant laborers in Wyoming, Montana, and Colorado. Holding dual citizenship, they maintain a second village at Nacimiento, Mexico, their sacred religious ground.

In Oklahoma, about two thousand Kickapoos reside in Pottawatomie, Oklahoma, and Lincoln Counties. The long struggle by these Kickapoos to remain independent has proved difficult; the loss of tribal lands to allotment devastated the tribal economic base. Their resistance to governmental acculturation efforts and to formal schooling, moreover, has left them ill equipped to prosper in white-dominated society. They have nevertheless survived; perhaps the most traditional Indians in Oklahoma, they strictly adhere to their Kickapoo customs and language.

Defending ancient traditions has been a priority for Kickapoos regardless of band, clan, or place of residence. Although the Kansas Kickapoos have adopted the outward ways of European America, they have made a strong effort in recent years to reclaim their traditional religions and customs. Their relatives in Oklahoma, Texas, and Mexico never abandoned Kickapoo traditions, remaining proud and steadfastly independent.

Gibson, Arrell M., The Kickapoos: Lords of the Middle Border (Norman: University of Oklahoma Press, 1963); Herring, Joseph B., Kenekuk, the Kickapoo Prophet (Lawrence: University Press of Kansas, 1988); Latorre, Felipe A., and Dolores L. Latorre, The Mexican Kickapoo Indians (Austin and London: University of Texas Press, 1976).

JOSEPH B. HERRING
National Endowment for the Humanities

KING PHILIP
See Metacom (King Philip).

KINZUA DAM

Though its construction had been proposed as early as 1908, it wasn't until 1964 that the U.S. Army Corps of Engineers built Kinzua Dam to control flooding on the Allegheny and Ohio Rivers, to provide for pollution abatement, and to create recreation facilities. The dam's reservoir flooded Seneca lands in Pennsylvania and all of New York's Allegany Indian Reservation— more than nine thousand acres in all. It inundated the last tribal lands in Pennsylvania, the Cornplanter Tract, and destroyed the Senecas' spiritual center, the Cold Spring Longhouse. The project forced the relocation of 130 Indian families.

The Senecas sought an injunction to prevent construction, citing the Canandaigua Treaty of 1794 between the United States and the Iroquois, which guaranteed Seneca rights to the land. They lost their suit, but Congress did compensate the Seneca Nation with $15 million for direct and indirect damages and to fund a rehabilitation program.

The proposal, planning, and construction of Kinzua Dam went forward in the face of determined Seneca protests and in violation of the 1794 treaty. Its history demonstrates that Congress may unilaterally violate treaties made with Indian nations.

See also Seneca.

KIOWA

Kiowa, the only Kiowa-Tanoan Plains language, is distantly related to Tiwa, spoken at Taos Pueblo, although the Kiowas claim to have originated in the Yellowstone

River region of Montana, near their oldest friends, the Crows. In the Kiowa origin myth, Saynday, or Trickster, transformed the underground-dwelling Kiowas into ants, beckoning them to emerge to the earth's surface through a hollow cottonwood log. A pregnant woman blocked further passage of the *K'uato*, the "Pulling-out" People; that is why the nineteenth-century Kiowas numbered only about one thousand people.

By the mid–eighteenth century, the Kiowas and affiliated Plains Apache people acquired horses and began a southeastward migration. Between 1775 and 1805, they encountered the Lakota Sioux and Cheyennes near the Black Hills and were pushed farther south to the southern plains, where horses were more plentiful. Southern plains intertribal relations were unstable until the Kiowas made peace with the Comanches in 1790, the Osages in 1834, and the Cheyennes in 1840. By that time, the allied Kiowas, Comanches, and Plains Apaches (KCA Indians) hunted buffalo and foraged between the Arkansas and Red Rivers. Coalesced war parties raided west into present-day New Mexico, and south into Texas and Mexico, encountering Navajo, Ute, Mexican, and Texan enemies.

Landholdings of the KCA Indians began to shrink after the 1865 Little Arkansas Treaty, whereby the Kiowas and Comanches agreed to abandon lands in Kansas and New Mexico. Through the 1867 Medicine Lodge Treaty, the KCA Indians relinquished all lands except a tract in southwestern Oklahoma near the Wichita Mountains. Following the Red River War of 1874–75, the Kiowas remained on the KCA Reservation, where the Indian agents expected them to transform themselves from buffalo hunters and raiders into Christian yeomen farmers and ranchers; with exceptions, such changes did not occur. In 1892, the Cherokee Commission (or Jerome Commission) forced the KCA Indians into the allotment process, and on August 6, 1901, the former KCA Reservation was opened by lottery for homesteading. The Kiowas bitterly fought the opening, taking their case all the way to the U.S. Supreme Court, where they were unsuccessful in the case of *Lone Wolf* v. *Hitchcock*. They were eventually compelled to take individual 160-acre tracts of land. Today, most Kiowa allotments are north of the Wichita Mountains in Caddo and Kiowa Counties.

Nineteenth-century kinship was similar to the Hawaiian system whereby relatives were distinguished by sex and generation; hence all cousins were classified as "brothers" and "sisters." Extended family groups, or *kindreds,* led by the oldest of a group of brothers, were the building blocks of Kiowa society, subdivided through a class system into the most prominent families, the *ondedw,* or "rich"; the *ondegup'a,* "second best"; the *kwwn,* "poor"; and the *dapom,* "worthless." Prior to 1875, there were between ten and twenty prominent Kiowa kindreds coalesced with lesser-ranked kindreds to comprise the larger hunting bands. Each *topadoga,* or "band," was led by the most respected brother, or *topadok'i,* "main chief," of the kindred. The bands, not to be confused with the subtribes making up the Sun Dance circle, were divided into northern and southern groups, ranging between southwestern Kansas and the Texas Panhandle. After 1875, the *topadok'i* were regarded as mere "beef chiefs" by the Indian agents, who desired to disrupt tribalism. During allotment, the bands were further broken up as the Kiowas settled into geographic enclaves on their former reservation.

In Kiowa cosmology, *dwdw,* "power," a universal spirit force permeating the universe, was present in all natural entities, including the air, earth, mountains, water, plants, and animals. Souls or spirits inhabited these entities as well as natural phenomena such as the four directional winds, thunder, and whirlwinds. All spirits possessed *dwdw,* but the most powerful spirit forces were, respectively, Sun, Moon, Stars, Spirits in the Air, and Buffalo. From their youth, Kiowa men fasted on mountains and hilltops, where they endured vision quests to obtain *dwdw.* Few, however, were fortunate enough to receive *dwdw.* Many came away with nothing, although one could receive power through inheritance or purchase—most *dwdw* belonged to *ondedw* men—for men with power could give it to others. Those who received power became either great curers or warriors, and painted their power symbols on shields. Prior to the attenuation of war power that resulted from the cessation of warfare in 1875, there were several shield societies. There are still several Kiowa "Indian doctors."

The *talyi-da-i,* "boy medicine," or Ten Medicines, consisted of tribal medicine bundles whose *ondedw* keepers prayed for the well-being of the people and were consulted to settle civil disputes. The *taimo,* or Sun Dance bundle, contained the sacred doll used during the Sun Dance, the tribal ceremony that spiritually and socially united the people. Sun Dances, held in mid-June, but only if sponsored by prominent men, were conducted to renew the bison herds and the Kiowas. Because of government intervention, the Sun Dance was discontinued in 1890, the summer the Kiowas obtained the Ghost Dance ceremony. The short-lived Ghost Dance of 1890–91 gave way to the Ghost Dance movement of 1894–1916, which was eradicated by the Kiowa superintendent in 1916.

The peyote religion had made inroads among the KCA Indians by 1870. Today many Kiowas participate in Native American Church ceremonies, but the majority attend community Baptist, Methodist, and Pentecostal churches. The Kiowas readily accepted Christianity, claiming that they already knew how to pray when full-time missionaries arrived in 1887. Bundle inheritance has broken down in the twentieth century, but the eleven tribal bundles are still consulted with prayer requests. The Kiowas are very tolerant of religious diversity, for they believe that *Dwk'i,* "Power Man" or "God," is in everything. *Dwdw* still exists; it merely assumes different guises.

Many twentieth-century Kiowas have served in the U.S. armed forces. In 1957–58, veterans of World War II and the Korean War helped revive two sodalities: the Kiowa Gourd Clan and the Black Leggings Warrior Society. The Kiowas are very active in southern plains powwows—particularly where the Gourd Dance is performed, for they see its performance as an expression of their tribal identity.

Today there are approximately ten thousand enrolled Kiowas; about four thousand of them live near the Oklahoma towns of Carnegie, Fort Cobb, and Anadarko. Prominent contemporary Kiowas include N. Scott Momaday, winner of the 1969 Pulitzer Prize for literature for *House Made of Dawn,* and Everett Rhoades, former assistant surgeon general of the United States.

Mishkin, Bernard, *Rank and Warfare among the Plains Indians* (1940; reprint, with an introduction by Morris W. Foster, Lincoln: University of Nebraska Press, 1992); Mooney, James, *Calendar History of the Kiowa Indians* (1895–96; reprint, with an introduction by John C. Ewers, Washington, D.C.: Smithsonian Institution Press, 1979); Richardson, Jane, *Law and Status among the Kiowa Indians* (Seattle: University of Washington Press, 1940).

BENJAMIN R. KRACHT
Northeastern State University
Tahlequah, Oklahoma

KIVA

Since time immemorial the Pueblo tribes of the Southwest have had kivas, windowless sacred chambers where religious ceremonies are held. The kiva is the ritual center of Pueblo communities and serves as the meeting place between the sacred and the mundane, the spiritual and the physical. According to most Pueblo legends, the spiritual beings of the world below instructed the people of this world to construct the kiva in the shape of *sipapu,* the place where humans emerged into the world from their previous existence. The people entered the kiva from the top, descending a ladder, because kivas were built into the ground to bring the two worlds closer together.

With few exceptions, only men participated in the rituals and ceremonies held within the kiva. They also used the kiva for councils, social gatherings, ceremonial sweat baths, and sometimes as sleeping quarters for young men. The kiva housed ceremonial items, its walls were often elaborately decorated, and altars held fetishes representing animals and deities.

When the Spanish arrived in the Southwest in the sixteenth century, they insisted that the Puebloan peoples cease their religious customs, including kiva ceremonies, and practice the Christian religion in churches. Though some kivas were violated, many survived. It was not until the 1930s that Pueblo people could again practice their religion openly. Some Pueblo ceremonies practiced today can be viewed by outsiders; the kiva, however, can be viewed and used only by members of the Pueblo communities.

See also Architecture.

KLAMATH

Though proud of their ancient traditions, the Klamath tribes have been indelibly marked by their more recent history. In 1954 Congress terminated federal recognition of the Klamath people, thereby paving the way for the loss of the group's 862,662-acre reserve, which included vast stands of ponderosa pine. This disastrous action left the Klamaths virtually landless, socially ravaged, and disenfranchised. The group has only recently begun to recover from this tragic episode in its history.

The Klamath tribes, located in the high plateau region of south-central Oregon, are descended from the Klamath, Modoc, and Yahooskin bands of Indians, which European travelers first called Snakes or Paiutes. The Klamaths and Modocs shared a similar language and culture but had distinctive identities, as did the Yahooskins. The linguistic affiliation of the Klamaths and

Modocs is very close. Resemblances to Molala, Sahap-tin, and the California Penutian languages have been noted. Both tribes traditionally consisted of a number of small, distinct village-based political entities that acted as cohesive units when circumstances required them to do so. Leaders among both tribes were chosen for their demonstrated ability and for specific actions, beyond which their authority did not extend. In la-ter times, leadership roles were more long-standing. Among the Klamaths, women were sometimes recog-nized as chiefs. The Yahooskins (Paiutes) were a Sho-shonean-speaking people with a simple social organiza-tion adapted to their harsh natural environment. Their lifestyle was often nomadic, although they dwelled within fixed boundaries.

Prior to the arrival of Europeans, each of the Klam-aths' ancestor tribes existed as a sovereign entity. These groups resided in the lands of southern Oregon and northern California until 1864, when federal officials negotiated a treaty with them. The tribes reserved to themselves 1.18 million acres of resource-rich land from their aboriginal domain of more than 20 million acres. These lands, occupied for more than ten thou-sand years, were reserved as the groups' permanent homeland. The 1864 treaty was thus intended to secure peace and prevent encroachment on these lands in the future. It did neither.

Unbeknownst to government negotiators at the 1864 proceedings, another federal agent had negotiated an unauthorized treaty with the Modocs reserving their homelands near Tule Lake, California. Locating the Modocs and Paiutes on what had, since time immemo-rial, been "Klamath land" created predictable intertrib-al conflict.

In the aftermath of the 1864 treaty and the Modocs' unhappiness at being assigned to an Oregon reserve, conflict and violence broke out. In November 1872 Captain Jack (Kintpuash) and fifty-two other Modoc warriors and their families returned to their homelands in California, ignoring the fact that Congress had never ratified the treaty recognizing their reservation there. They occupied the lava beds near Tule Lake for nearly six months and held off approximately one thousand military personnel, a company of Oregon Volunteers, and seventy-eight Warm Springs Indian scouts. The war cost the federal government almost five hundred thousand dollars and over four hundred soldiers' lives. The Modocs lost thirteen warriors and the war. On Oc-tober 3, 1873, Captain Jack and three other leaders were hanged at Fort Klamath. Two of the remaining

captives were sent to Alcatraz Island military prison. The other 153 were removed to Fort Quapaw, Oklaho-ma. A generation later those who chose to do so were allowed to return to the Klamath Reservation in Ore-gon.

But before the tragedy of the "Modoc War," other confrontations disrupted the Klamaths' peaceful pre-serve. In 1871, the Klamath tribes protested the reser-vation boundary survey because it failed to honor the mountaintop-to-mountaintop provisions of their trea-ty. Repeated prodding produced a new survey, which confirmed the erroneous exclusion of 624,000 acres from the reservation. The tribes were paid less than 85 cents per acre for this land and nothing for its timber. Even before these negotiations, private citizens had been seen surveying the contested lands. Over tribal protests, unauthorized settlement continued through-out the nineteenth century. A court of claims decision in 1937 eventually awarded the tribe $7,291,778.56 for these and other losses, but over 27 percent of that sum ($1,978,431.24) was deducted to cover federal ex-penditures for the tribes dating back to the 1864 treaty.

The General Allotment Act of 1887 was intended to convert tribal members to farmers and open tribally held lands to non-Indian settlement. At Klamath, how-ever, most of the allotted lands were neither suited to agriculture nor large enough to support a small herd. Luckily, the tribes managed to retain their unallotted land with its vast timber holdings. The "competency" requirements for Klamaths to sell their allotments were seldom enforced, however, and by 1954 non-Indians had acquired over 114,515 acres of Indian-owned land within the reservation. By October 1957, less than half a century after the allotment process, 173,834 acres of timberland (over 70 percent of the allotted lands) had passed from Indian ownership.

In 1913, Klamath tribal members began receiving per capita payments for the sale of tribal timber. These sales rendered the tribes economically self-supporting. Congress required the tribes to use their timber pro-ceeds to finance the federal agency on the reservation, and no effort was made to prepare tribal members for personal or tribal self-sufficiency. As tribal members became aware of their timber wealth, some individuals petitioned federal officials to liquidate tribal property and turn the proceeds over to individual tribal mem-bers.

In spite of consistent tribal opposition to the termi-nation of federal supervision and overwhelming evi-dence that the action would be disastrous to the

Klamaths, Congress passed the Klamath Termination Act (P.L. 587) on August 13, 1954. Unlike other "terminated" tribes such as the Menominees of Wisconsin, the Klamaths were not allowed to retain any communally owned land or assets. During the 1970s the tribes used the courts to begin the process of rebuilding federal recognition of their rights. *Kimball v. Callahan* (*Kimball I*; 1975), *Kimball II* (1979), and *U.S. v. Adair* (1983) held that treaty rights to hunting, fishing, and gathering were retained by all tribal members within the original reservation boundaries and that Klamath water rights necessary to support treaty resources had not been terminated. These legal victories spurred a resurgence in tribal identity and pride.

By the 1970s it was apparent that the termination policy had been a complete disaster for the Klamath peoples. Between 1966 and 1980, 20 percent of deaths within the tribe occurred among people under twenty-five years of age, and 52 percent among people under forty. Forty percent of all deaths were alcohol caused or related. The infant mortality rate among the Klamaths was two and a half times as high as that of the general population of Oregon; 70 percent of Klamaths acquired less than a high school education, and three times as many Indians as non-Indians in Klamath County had incomes below the poverty level.

In 1985 the Klamath General Council voted to petition Congress for legislation that would restore federal recognition to the tribe. The act passed Congress without opposition in August 1986. Today the largely landless Klamath tribes hope to negotiate a land acquisition plan with the federal government. A first step in that process began on December 16, 1994, when Governor Barbara Roberts of Oregon signed a gaming contract that will enable the tribes to initiate their first major post-termination economic-development project.

Ray, Verne F., *Primitive Pragmatists: The Modoc Indians of Northern California* (Seattle: University of Washington Press, 1963); Stern, Theodore, *The Klamath Tribe: A People and Their Reservation* (Seattle: University of Washington Press, 1966).

KATHLEEN SHAYE HILL (Klamath Tribes)
Seattle, Washington

KWAKIUTL

We have been called the Kwakiutl ever since 1849, when the white people came to stay in our territories. In fact, the Kwakiutl only occupy the village now called Fort Rupert. The rest of us have our own names and our own villages. For example, the Gwawa'enuxw live at Hopetown. Collectively, we call ourselves the Kwakwaka'wakw—that is, all of the people who speak the language Kwakwala.

Archaeological evidence indicates that our people have occupied Vancouver Island, the adjacent mainland, and the islands between for about nine thousand years. Before the Canadian government contracted our traditional boundaries to enclose small reserves, each tribal group owned its territory, through which it moved seasonally. During the winter, each occupied a more permanent site, where the people engaged in intensive ceremonial activities while enjoying the abundant supply of foods from the sea and land that they had gathered earlier in the year.

With the introduction of European technology and food, much of the traditional subsistence cycle was altered. A variety of salmon and shellfish are still gathered and preserved by freezing, canning, or smoking, and the spring runs of eulachon (candlefish) in Knight and Kingcome Inlets are still harvested and rendered into oil.

Although the red cedar is no longer used for housing, clothing, and canoes, its bark is still processed to decorate items of ceremonial gear. Its wood is used to create masks and totem poles. In recent years, renewed interest in the construction of dugout canoes has created an additional demand for red cedar. The building of a sixty-foot canoe requires a carefully selected cedar log, and the search for such a log often reveals the extent of the problems created by the uncontrolled logging practices of large corporations. Suitable logs are difficult to find, and the success of any modern canoe gathering is a tribute to the determination and enthusiasm of those who participate.

The first anthropologist to come to our area, Franz Boas, arrived in 1886; since then countless books and papers have been written about what is called the *potlatch*, a ceremony practiced along the Pacific Coast from Alaska to northern California. The term comes from Chinook Jargon, a language developed during the early days of the fur trade, and means "to give." Each cultural group has its own word for the ceremony. In Kwakwala, the word is *pasa*, literally meaning "to flatten"—that is, to flatten one's guests under the weight of the gifts given to them. Potlatches are held to name children, mourn the dead, transfer rights and privileges from one generation to the next, and conduct marriage exchanges.

Participants at a winter feast of the Gusgimukw tribe, photographed at Fort Rupert, Vancouver Island, British Columbia, on November 25, 1894. Four dancers, their faces blackened with charcoal, sit on a platform above the others, flanked by two attendants. The dancers wear Hudson's Bay Company blankets and cedar-bark neck rings and head rings. Two of the women seated on the ground show the head deformation that indicated high rank among the Gusgimukw.

The first white people to settle in our territory did not interfere with the potlatch. Merchants profited by selling huge quantities of blankets, oak chests, glassware, sacks of flour, and other goods, which were distributed at potlatches. It was not until Christian missions and government agencies became established that opposition to the ceremony began. Although the government of Canada first enacted legislation prohibiting the potlatch in 1884, for several decades the law could not be enforced because it was so badly written. It was simply ignored by those who considered the ceremony a special gift from the Creator. Finally, in 1921, through the zealous efforts of the Indian agent William Halliday, forty-five of our highest-ranking chiefs and

their wives were arrested for violating the law by singing, dancing, and giving and receiving gifts, as well as making speeches. Twenty-two people were sentenced to prison terms of two to three months; the rest were given suspended sentences on the condition that their entire villages surrender their ceremonial treasures. These included coppers (our symbols of wealth), masks, rattles, whistles, and kerfed boxes. The collection was shipped to Ottawa, to what was then the Victoria Memorial Museum and has since become the National Museum of Man. Part of what became known as the Potlatch Collection was then transferred to the Royal Ontario Museum in Toronto. George Heye bought thirty-three objects for the Museum of the

American Indian/Heye Foundation in New York. This latter portion was then transferred to the National Museum of the American Indian.

During the years of potlatch prohibition, the ceremony simply went underground, with hosts carefully choosing villages that the police would have difficulty reaching in stormy weather. Our old people say that this is when our world became dark. Some of the Kwakwaka'wakw became Christians and their children attended missionary schools, with a resultant loss of language and of skills in harvesting traditional foods. More seriously, the knowledge the children should have been acquiring about their place in the potlatch system was lost.

In 1951, when the Canadian Indian Act was revised, the section prohibiting the potlatch was deleted, not repealed—as our people had continued to hope. Convinced that the surrender of our treasures had been illegal, we began in 1969 to negotiate with the National Museum of Man for the repatriation of its portion of these objects. By 1975, the museum had agreed to return our treasures on the condition that two museums be built to house them. The Kwakiutl Museum at Cape Mudge opened in 1979; the opening of the U'mista Cultural Centre in Alert Bay followed, in 1980. The Royal Ontario Museum returned its part of the collection in 1988, and in 1993 the National Museum of the American Indian repatriated some of our treasures.

In earlier days, people were sometimes captured by enemy tribes. The return home of the captives, either through payment of ransom or owing to a retaliatory raid, was called *u'mista*—that is, a special return. The U'mista Cultural Centre was named for the special return of our treasures from distant museums. Our *u'mista* also includes our return to the path our ancestors prepared for us. The center has produced a series of twelve Kwakwala-language books for use in schools, and two award-winning documentary films, *Potlatch . . . A Strict Law Bids Us Dance* and *Box of Treasures*. The collection of oral histories from our old people continues, as do programs for the teaching of language, dance, and song. Since it opened, the U'mista Cultural Centre has become a real focus for the strengthening of our cultural activities in Alert Bay and the surrounding communities.

The increasing number of potlatches held each year is indicative of the revitalization of our culture. Most of these events take place in the traditional big house located in Alert Bay, home of the 'Namgis, one of the seventeen contemporary bands that make up the Kwakwaka'wakw. Built in 1963, the big house accommodates about seven hundred people, and it is here that young singers and dancers proudly display their skills to their families and other guests. Their performances demonstrate the vitality and persistence of Kwakwaka'wakw culture, despite the efforts of white people to "civilize" us.

See also Potlatch.

Boas, Franz, *Kwakiutl Ethnography,* ed. Helen Codere (Chicago: University of Chicago Press, 1966); Aldona, Jonaitis, ed. *Chiefly Feasts: The Enduring Kwakiutl Potlatch* (Seattle: University of Washington Press, 1991); Macnair, Peter L., Alan L. Hoover, and Kevin Neary, *The Legacy: Continuing Traditions of Canadian Northwest Coast Indian Art* (Victoria: British Columbia Provincial Museum, 1980).

GLORIA CRANMER WEBSTER ('Namgis)
U'mista Cultural Centre
Alert Bay, British Columbia

L

LACROSSE

Lacrosse was one of many varieties of indigenous stick-ball games being played by American Indians at the time of European contact. Almost exclusively a male team sport, it is distinguished from the others, such as field hockey or shinny, by the use of a netted racket with which to pick the ball off the ground, throw, catch, and convey it into or past a goal to score a point. The cardinal rule in all varieties of lacrosse is that the ball, with few exceptions, must not be touched with the hands.

Early descriptions of lacrosse, from missionaries such as the French Jesuits in Huron country in the 1630s as well as English explorers such as Jonathan Carver in the mid-eighteenth-century Great Lakes area, are scanty and often conflicting. They inform us mostly about such matters as team size, equipment used, the duration of games, and length of playing fields, while telling us almost nothing about stick-handling, game strategy, or the rules of play. The oldest surviving sticks date only from the first quarter of the nineteenth century, and the first detailed reports on Indian lacrosse are from even later. George Beers provided good information on Mohawk playing techniques in his Lacrosse, published in 1869, while James Mooney in an 1890 issue of *American Anthropologist* described in detail the "[Eastern] Cherokee Ball-Play," including its legendary origins, its elaborate rituals, and the rules and manner of play.

Given the paucity of early data, we will probably never be able to reconstruct the history of the sport. Attempts to connect it to the rubber-ball games of Mesoamerica or to a perhaps older game using a single post surmounted by some animal effigy and played together by men and women remain speculative. As can best be determined, the distribution of lacrosse shows it to have been played throughout the eastern half of North America, mostly by tribes in the Southeast, around the western Great Lakes, and in the St. Lawrence Valley area. Its presence today in Oklahoma and other states west of the Mississippi reflects tribal removals to those areas in the nineteenth century. Although isolated reports exist of some form of lacrosse among northern California and British Columbia tribes, their late date brings into question any widespread diffusion of the sport on the West Coast.

On the basis of equipment, type of goal used, and stick-handling techniques, it is possible to discern three basic forms of lacrosse—the southeastern, the Great Lakes, and the Iroquoian. Among southeastern tribes (Cherokees, Choctaws, Chickasaws, Creeks, Seminoles, Yuchis, and others), a double-stick version of the game is still practiced. A two-and-a-half-foot stick is held in each hand, and the soft, small deerskin ball is retrieved and cupped between the sticks. Great Lakes players (Ojibwas, Menominees, Potawatomis, Sauks, Fox, Miamis, Winnebagos, Santee Dakotas, and others) used a single three-foot stick that terminated in a round, closed pocket about three to four inches in diameter, scarcely larger than the ball, which was usually made of wood, charred and scraped to shape. The northeastern stick, found among Iroquoian and New England tribes, is the progenitor of all present-day sticks, whether for box or field lacrosse. The longest of the three—usually more than three feet in length—it is characterized by a shaft that ends in a sort of crook and by the large, flat, triangular surface of webbing extending as much as two-thirds the length of the stick. "A wall woven of gut extends from the tip of the crook to meet the shaft and form the pocket of the stick."

Lacrosse was given its name by early French settlers, using the generic term for any game played with a curved stick (crosse) and a ball. Native terminology, however, is more apt to describe the technique (as in Onondaga *dehuntshigwa'es*, "men hit a rounded object" and in Eastern Cherokee, *da-nah-wah'uwsdi*, "little war") or, especially in the Southeast, to underscore the game's aspects of war surrogacy ("little brother of war"). There is no evidence of non-Indians taking up the game until the mid-nineteenth century, when English-speaking Montrealers adopted the Mohawk game they were familiar with from the Caugnawaga and Ak-wesasne reserves, forming amateur clubs and setting out to "civilize" the sport with a new set of rules. As the game quickly grew in popularity in Canada, it began to be exported throughout the Commonwealth, with colonial teams traveling to Europe for exhibition matches against Iroquois players. Ironically, because Indians had to charge money in order to travel, they were excluded as "professionals" from international competition for more than a century. Only with the for-mation of the Iroquois Nationals in the 1980s did they successfully break this barrier and become eligible to compete in World Games.

Apart from its recreational function, lacrosse tradi-tionally played a more serious role in Indian culture. Its origins are rooted in legend, and the game continues to be used for curative purposes and to be surrounded with ceremony. Game equipment and players are still ritually prepared by shamans, and team selection and victory are often considered to be supernaturally con-trolled. In the past lacrosse also served to vent ag-gression, and territorial disputes between tribes were sometimes settled with a game, although not always amicably. A game between the Creeks and Choctaws around 1790 to determine rights over a beaver pond broke out into a violent battle when the Creeks were declared winners. Still, while the majority of the games ended peaceably, the ceremonialism surrounding their preparations and the rituals required of the players were nearly identical to those practiced before depart-ing on the warpath.

A number of factors led to the demise of lacrosse in many areas by the late nineteenth century. Wagering on games had always been integral to an Indian communi-ty's involvement, but when betting and violence saw an increase as traditional Indian culture was eroding, it sparked opposition to lacrosse from government offi-cials and missionaries. The games were felt to interfere with church attendance and the wagering to have an impoverishing effect on the Indians. When Oklahoma Choctaws began to attach lead weights to their sticks around 1900 to use them as skull crackers, the game was outright banned.

Meanwhile, the spread of nonnative lacrosse from the Montreal area eventually led to its position as one of today's fastest-growing sports (with more than half a million players worldwide), controlled by official regu-lations and played with manufactured rather than handmade equipment, such as the aluminum-shafted stick with its plastic head. While the Great Lakes tradi-tional game died out by 1950, the Iroquois and south-eastern tribes continue to play their own forms of lacrosse. Ironically, it is the field lacrosse game of non-native women today—with its wooden stick and lack of protective gear, its undemarcated sidelines, and its tendency toward mass attack rather than field positions and offsides—that most closely resembles the Indian game of the past.

Culin, Stewart, "Games of the North American Indians," in *Twenty-fourth Annual Report of the Bureau of American Eth-nology, 1902–1903* (Washington, D.C.: Government Printing Office, 1907); Fogelson, Raymond, "The Cherokee Ball Game: A Study in Southeastern Ethnology" (Ph.D. diss., University of Pennsylvania, 1962); Vennum, Thomas, Jr., *American Indian Lacrosse: Little Brother of War* (Washington, D.C., and London: Smithsonian Institution Press, 1994).

THOMAS VENNUM, JR.
Smithsonian Institution

LA FLESCHE FAMILY

The eight children of Joseph La Flesche (1822–88)—Carey, Francis (or Frank), Louis, Lucy, Marguerite, Rosalie, Susan, and Susette (or Yosette)—were born on the Omaha Reservation near Bellevue, Nebraska, just south of present-day Omaha. Their father, a mixed blood also known as Inshtamaza or Iron Eyes, was a chief of the Omahas. Inshtamaza's father, a Frenchman named Joseph, was a trader for the Hudson's Bay Com-pany; his mother, named Watunna, was either an Omaha or a Ponca. During his early years Inshtamaza was raised among the Omahas. However, his father was often absent on extended trading expeditions, and his mother sent the younger Joseph with two of his aunts to live among the Sioux. Several years later, when his father returned, the younger Joseph rejoined his fa-ther and often accompanied him on hunting and trad-ing excursions. During this time he learned to speak French.

It was during one of these trading expeditions that the younger Joseph met Mary Gale, an Omaha, whose tribal name translated as "the One Woman." Mary Gale was the child of Nicomi, a mixed Omaha-Iowa woman and the daughter of an Iowa chief, and Dr. John Gale, an army contract surgeon. In 1827, Dr. Gale was transferred. Forced to leave his wife and daughter behind, he made provisions for their future by creating a trust, which he placed in the control of his friend

Peter Sarpy, a trader with the American Fur Company who operated near Fort Atkinson, Iowa. Four years later, in 1831, Sarpy married Nicomi. Joseph was employed by Sarpy at his trading post, where he met Mary Gale. Joseph and Mary Gale were married in 1843.

Immediately after his marriage to Mary Gale, Joseph was adopted into the Omaha tribe by Chief Big Elk, who proclaimed Joseph his "oldest son" and successor. In the following years, Joseph served the Omahas as an interpreter and a trader, and when Big Elk died in 1853, Joseph was recognized as one of the two head chiefs of the tribe. Joseph believed that for the tribe to survive it would have to adapt to the encroaching non-Indian culture that was filling Nebraska with settlers — a belief influenced by his conversion to Presbyterianism, which cost him his position as a chief.

Although he accepted Christianity, Joseph refused to abandon all Omaha traditions, and for a while he maintained three wives — Mary Gale; Tainne; and a third woman, whom he took as a wife in 1862. However, as a concession to his new religion, his third wife was sent away. He had another wife, either a Pawnee or an Oto, who died in childbirth, and probably yet another wife, our knowledge of whom is limited to a remark by a missionary that she was "giddy." Joseph also had several other children, including one possibly named Harriet, of which no record remains inasmuch as none of them reached maturity. Tainne probably died in April 1883. Mary Gale died on February 28, 1909.

Mary Gale was the mother of Louis (1848–60), Susette (1854–1903), Rosalie (1861–1900), Marguerite (1862–1945), and Susan (1865–1915). Tainne was the mother of Francis (1855 [or 1862]–1932), Lucy (1865–1923), and Carey (1872–1952). Under Omaha tradition all were considered brothers and sisters instead of half siblings. Louis La Flesche was baptized on December 27, 1850; he died while attending the Presbyterian Mission School on the Omaha Reservation. Of the four daughters of Mary Gale, Marguerite was the most beautiful and least impetuous, Susan the most active and aggressive, Rosalie the most intellectual, and Susette the most retiring.

Joseph raised his children in the traditional Omaha way. His older children lived in an earth lodge, forty feet in diameter, about one mile south of the Presbyterian Mission and its school while they were young. In 1857 Joseph decided to abandon his earth lodge and built a two-story frame house nearby. This was the first time a Plains Indian had constructed his own house.

Within four years there were eighteen other houses nearby, and the settlement became known as Joe's Village.

As a part of his belief that the Omahas had to make the transition to the non-Indian world, Joseph sent his children to the reservation's Presbyterian Mission School, where they received a preparatory education. He also refused to allow his daughters to partake of the tradition whereby Omaha women were tattooed with a "mark of honor." By the time they completed their studies, the La Flesche children could speak English as well as Omaha, were able to read and write English, and were knowledgeable in geography and arithmetic. Although Francis attended the mission school along with his sisters, he much preferred the company of a group of Omaha youths who called themselves "the Middle Five."

After completing their studies at the Presbyterian Mission School, Susette, Marguerite, and Susan were sent to a private finishing school, the Elizabeth Institute for Young Ladies, in Elizabeth, New Jersey. Susette fulfilled the requirements to be a teacher in 1875 and returned to the Omaha Reservation, where she taught in the government school, the Omaha Indian School. Susan also returned to the reservation and accepted a position as an assistant teacher. In 1884 Marguerite received a government scholarship to attend Hampton Agriculture and Normal Institute in Hampton, Virginia. Susan accompanied her, and they were later joined by Lucy. On May 20, 1886, both Susan and Lucy graduated from Hampton, with Susan giving the salutatorian address. Marguerite, whose senior paper was titled "Customs of the Omahas," graduated from Hampton in 1887 and then returned to the Omaha Reservation as a teacher at the Omaha Indian School.

In 1888 Marguerite married Charles F. Picotte, who oversaw her family's farm allottments on the Omaha Reservation. They had two sons and two daughters who reached adulthood. In 1892, Charles died and Marguerite resumed her teaching duties at the Indian school. Susan and Marguerite lived across the street from one another in the town of Walthill, Nebraska (a few miles from the Omaha Agency), where they both were respected civic leaders. Marguerite later married Walter Diddock, the Omaha Agency's industrial farmer.

Lucy married a full-blood Omaha named Noah Leaming (or Noah Stabler; the record is not clear). The son of Mahzhahkeda, he took the name La Flesche upon marriage because his family was of lower status in Omaha society than his wife's. Lucy and Noah returned to Nebraska to farm their allotment. Noah died in the winter of 1919 of the Spanish flu. In 1897 Carey married Phoeby Cline. They had five daughters and two sons. Francis married Alice Mitchell in 1877 and divorced her in the same year. He married Rosa Bourassa, a mixed-blood Ojibwa, in 1906; they probably were divorced in 1908, but the records are confusing. Susette, Lucy, and Frank had no children.

After graduating from Hampton, Susan was accepted at the Woman's Medical College of Pennsylvania, from which she received her degree in medicine in 1889. She graduated at the head of a class of thirty-three students, and was the first Native American female to become a medical doctor in the United States. After completing her training in Philadelphia-area hospitals, Susan returned to the Omaha Reservation and served as the physician at the Omaha Indian School. The hospital built by the reservation's Presbyterian church was named in Susan's honor. She also served as an interpreter and adviser to many tribal members and was an influential member of the Presbyterian church in Bancroft, Nebraska. Susan eventually married Henry Picotte, the brother of Charles Picotte. They had two sons.

When she was four years old, Rosalie was enrolled in the Presbyterian Mission School on the Omaha Reservation. She later also taught at the school, where she met Edward Farley, the school's industrial teacher. In June 1880 she married Farley. They had ten children, three girls and seven sons. She also taught Sunday school at the Presbyterian church on the reservation.

Later Rosalie and her husband oversaw "the pasture," which they held under a twenty-year lease agreement with the Omaha tribe as pasturage for cattle grazed on the Indians' land. As managers of the operation, Edward and Rosalie were responsible for fencing the land and collecting grazing fees from non-Indians. Rosalie also served as the contact person, interpreter, and adviser for the Indians, who grazed their cattle for free. Revenue from grazing fees was divided between the tribe and the Farleys. Rosalie also served as an adviser to the famed ethnologist Alice Fletcher during the course of her work to preserve Omaha traditions and heritage. Rosalie died on May 9, 1900.

While Joseph's children were receiving their formal education, they also became involved with traditional Omaha culture and heritage. This was especially true of Francis, who, as a male, had more opportunities to participate in tribal ceremonies. Delving into tribal history with zeal, when his father explained to him the importance of adapting to changing ways, he responded, "Yes, but let us save the old as we move into the new." In 1874, as a teenager, Francis participated in his first traditional Omaha buffalo hunt. Two years later, in 1876, the annual hunt was ended by federal officials and Francis lamented that "some of the boys will never get a chance [to hunt buffalo] . . . never to cut the beast open, either, and eat the raw liver with the gall over it."

In May 1877 Susette witnessed the forced removal of the Ponca tribe from its nearby homeland to a reservation in Indian Territory—present-day Oklahoma. The plight of the Poncas, who were closely allied with the Omahas, deeply affected her, and she joined her father on a visit to the Poncas before they began their trek southward. Both realized that the Omahas would probably soon follow the Poncas on the journey southward.

That same year, 1877, Susette applied for a teaching position at the Indian school on the Omaha Reservation. Informed that she would have to pass a teaching examination and receive a certificate from the School Committee of Nebraska, she applied for a permit to leave the reservation to take the examination. Although her request was refused, she left the reservation anyway and took the test without the agent's permission. After receiving a "certificate of good character" from the agent, she was hired at a salary of twenty dollars per month, half of what non-Indian teachers received.

Stories of the Poncas' suffering in Indian Territory continued to reach the La Flesches in Nebraska. Disturbed by the plight of their friends, in 1878 Susette and her father visited the Poncas on their temporary reservation among the Quapaws in Indian Territory. She returned an outspoken opponent of the government's treatment of Indians.

The following year, 1879, a group of Poncas led by Standing Bear left Indian Territory and returned to their ancient homeland, but on their arrival in Nebraska they were arrested and taken to Fort Omaha in preparation for their return to Indian Territory. While they were imprisoned at Fort Omaha, two reporters for the *Omaha Herald*, Thomas H. Tibbles and W. L. Carpenter, visited them. After hearing tales of their suffering, the reporters took up their cause and implemented a campaign to gain their release. Tibbles's *The Ponca Chiefs: An Indian Attempt to Appeal from the Tomahawk to the Courts*, published in 1879, helped win support for Standing Bear and his followers.

In April 1879, Susette became acquainted with Tibbles when, at the request of the Reverend J. Owen Dorsey, a missionary among the Indians, she wrote him describing the plight of the Poncas in Indian Territory. At the same time, she helped prepare a petition from the Omahas to "the friends of the Poncas" asking that the Poncas be allowed to return to their homeland in Nebraska. The *New York Herald* called her petition "one of the most extraordinary statements ever published in America." Their efforts resulted in Standing Bear's being brought to trial, where he was able to plead his case. Both Susette and her father traveled to Omaha to attend, with Rosalie filling Susette's teaching position temporarily. It was at this time that Susette first met Tibbles. They were elated when the court ruled in Standing Bear's favor, providing the nation with one of its most important civil rights decisions— that "an Indian is a person within the meaning of the law of the United States" and therefore has the right to seek legal redress before the courts.

Afterward, Susette quickly became involved in the Indian-rights movement and, apparently at Tibbles's suggestion, took the name Bright Eyes. At the insistence of the Omaha Committee, as the supporters of the Poncas called themselves, Joseph and Susette again traveled to the Ponca Reservation, where they learned that many of the tribe had died and most of the survivors were ill. Shocked, Susette became even more outspoken regarding the mistreatment of the Indians. Along with her brother Francis and Standing Bear, Susette undertook a speaking tour of such eastern cities as Boston and New York in an effort to end the government's policy of forced removal of the northern tribes to Indian Territory. In November 1879, Susette met Helen Hunt Jackson, who quickly became an outspoken supporter of the Indians.

Susette was convinced that the only solution to the "Indian problem" was American citizenship. Such an action would legally give the nation's Native American population equal status with its other residents. It was her belief that the effort to assimilate Native Americans into American culture was a mistake, and that the greatest error in government Indian policy was to treat the Indians as wards, incapable of caring for themselves. She made this argument before congressional committees and at the White House, and then in the fall of 1880 she made a second eastern tour.

Tibbles's wife, Amelia Owen Tibbles, died in October 1879. On July 23, 1881, in a ceremony performed by the Reverend S. N. D. Martin at the Ponca Reserva-

tion mission, Susette and Tibbles were married. Afterward she traveled widely with Tibbles, once to Europe, speaking out for Indian rights.

At Tibbles's urging, she developed her talent for writing—a means of communication that allowed them to expand their audience. In 1881 she published *Ploughed Under: The Story of an Indian Chief,* telling of the suffering of the Native Americans in a changing world. Tibbles also published a number of books describing the mistreatment of Native Americans. They included *The Ponca Chiefs,* released in 1880; *Hidden Power: A Secret History of the Indian Ring,* published in 1881; and *Buckskin and Blanket Days: Memoirs of a Friend of the Indians,* which was not printed until 1957.

Some of their views brought Susette and her husband into conflict with her siblings. She also had some problems with Tibbles's two daughters, Eda and May, who at first were resentful of their stepmother; however, these early problems were overcome. Susette spent much of her later years on the Omaha Reservation. She also maintained a residence in Lincoln, Nebraska. She died near Bancroft on the Omaha Reservation on May 26, 1903.

Francis La Flesche became active in Native American affairs as an ethnologist, working for the Bureau of Indian Affairs and the Smithsonian Institution. He was closely associated with Alice Cunningham Fletcher, a friend of Susette's, who eventually adopted him "to be my son" in the spring of 1891. Fletcher, considered the foremost woman scientist of her day, worked with Francis on *The Omaha Tribe,* published as the twenty-seventh annual report of the Bureau of American Ethnology in 1911. Previously, in 1900, he had published *The Middle Five: Indian Schoolboys of the Omaha Tribe,* in which he told about his youth at the mission school on the Omaha Reservation. He also had earned a law degree (LL.B.) in 1892 and another (LL.M.) in 1893 from National University. In 1912 he was elected vice president of the American Anthropological Association, and in 1926 he was awarded an honorary Doctor of Letters from the University of Nebraska.

Fletcher, Alice C., and Francis La Flesche, *The Omaha Tribe,* Bureau of American Ethnology, Twenty-seventh Annual Report (Washington: Government Printing Office, 1911); Green, Norma Kidd, *Iron Eye's Family: The Children of Joseph La Flesche* (Lincoln: Nebraska State Historical Society, 1969); Wilson, Dorothy Clarke, *Bright Eyes: The Story of Susette La Flesche, an Omaha Indian* (New York: McGraw-Hill, 1957).

KENNY A. FRANKS
Oklahoma Heritage Association

LAKOTA LANGUAGE

Language is vital to Lakota culture. It is our bloodline. History has demonstrated that how we handle our language, how we develop it, can cause the Lakota people to grow or can destroy us. Two hundred years ago the language built us up to a point where we were a progressive and strong people. Within two hundred years, misuse of the language almost destroyed us.

Očeti Šakowiŋ (The Seven Council Fires), most commonly referred to as the Sioux Nation, comprises seven tribes that fall into three distinct dialect groups. Four tribes speak Dakota (Mdewa-kantuŋ, Wahpetuŋ, Wahpekute, Sisituŋ), two tribes speak Nakota (Ihaŋktuŋwan, Ihaŋktuŋwaŋi), and one tribe, the Tituŋwan (People of the Prairie), the most populous of the three divisions, speaks Lakota. Today, most Lakota speakers live west of the Missouri River on various reservations within South Dakota. (The Lakota orthographic system used here was developed in 1982 by the Committee for the Preservation of the Lakota Language.)

The Lakota language, like most Native American languages, was not originally a written language. The first people to transcribe Lakota into a written alphabet were early missionaries and anthropologists. In 1834, the Episcopal missionaries Samuel W. Pond, Gideon H. Pond, Stephen R. Riggs, and Dr. Thomas S. Williamson created a Dakota alphabet. This alphabet system was adapted and extended to the "L" dialect by Ella Deloria and Franz Boas during the 1930s. Since then, three other spelling systems have been created. In 1939, the Reverend Eugene Buechel published a Lakota grammar book that contains his spelling system. In 1976 another alphabet system for the Lakota language was introduced by Allen Taylor and David Rood of the University of Colorado at Boulder.

The most recent Lakota alphabet was created in 1982 by Lakota language instructors from the South Dakota area who were frustrated by the wide variety of written forms of our language. This group of instructors—from the Rosebud Reservation, the Pine Ridge Reservation, the Cheyenne River Reservation, and Rapid City—organized the Committee for the Preservation of the Lakota Language. This committee wanted to standardize the alphabet and to learn more about the philosophy of the language from tribal elders.

In the spring of 1982, the committee members created a "recommended alphabet system" that we believe combined the best elements of the existing systems. The forty letters in our system function as a pronunciation guide for the Lakota language. Though this system is not the official alphabet system for the Sioux Nation, it does address all forty Lakota sounds and is simple enough for children to use.

After listening to tribal elders from the various reservations, the committee identified two central ideas to be emphasized in teaching the language. First, the language is *wakaŋ*, "very powerful." We use it to communicate with the other nations: the Deer Nation, the Eagle Nation, the Buffalo Nation, and so forth. We talk to the *wamakaŋkaŋ*, living beings of the earth, through spiritual communications. Language must be taught with this in mind. Second, when teaching the language to younger people, its good and evil powers must also be taught. Children need to understand that language contains great power, that it can be used to injure peoples' feelings or to compliment the achievements of another human being, that it can be used to harm or to honor and bless. Young people need to understand that language contains the power to give life or to take it away and that it therefore must be used with respect.

The committee's ideas challenged Western language teaching by emphasizing the importance of philosophy in the Lakota language. This can be seen in the Lakota use of gender endings—words at the end of the sentence that indicate whether the speaker is a woman or a man. For example, to ask if something is good, a woman says, "*Wašte he?*" while a man says, "*Wašte huwo?*" To answer "Yes, it is good," a woman responds by saying, "*Haŋ wašte kšto,*" and a man responds by saying, "*To wašte yelo.*"

These differences in male and female speech patterns reflect Lakota philosophy. Men and women have distinct roles in our society. Women represent beauty, softness, and the goodness of birth, of giving life. Though all these qualities are more gentle than those of a man, they imply just as much strength and determination. A woman's softer approach is evident by both her behavior and her speech. Traditionally, a woman lets the man address her first, out of respect for him and for his role. In addition, female expressions sound more gentle because they often contain nasal vowels.

Men, on the other hand, are the protectors of the circle and as a result, in the Lakota view they are more aggressive and rough. Their behavior and speech reflect their role in Lakota society. Men's speech tends to be loud and rugged, filled with many guttural sounds. Also, their behavior is more aggressive, especially if they are called to protect the values of the circle. Thus gender endings reinforce Lakota philosophy.

The Lakota language also reflects the Lakota environment. It affirms spirituality. It supports music, dance, good times, sad times. All those feelings are in it. Lakota teachers need to steep themselves in their language. A Lakota speaker needs to feel and understand every word in order to express true emotions.

Before World War II our people were conditioned to read and to write the Lakota language. Through this process, the language changed to reflect the Christian perspective of early missionaries. Words began to have as many as four different interpretations. For example, *wakaŋ*, used as a noun, means "energy." It teaches that all creation has the power to give life or to take it away. Christians understood this word to mean "something sacred." Anthropologists translated *wakaŋ* as "mystery." In such ways traditional Lakota meanings get corrupted and, eventually, lost. Lakota speakers in the classroom become fearful and uneasy when they hear a traditional translation. Their fear reminds me of my own struggles when I first started teaching the language. The language I spoke, although it was Lakota, reflected a Catholic philosophy. At that time I, too, was afraid of the traditional interpretation of the language. At Catholic boarding schools, I was taught that the traditional language represented evil. Once I had identified that old belief in myself, I could apply my own experience to the classroom. I could see whether a student was Catholic or Episcopalian, and then I could understand his or her perspective. Each would have a different interpretation of the language, and both would fear the traditional translation.

During the 1940s and the 1950s, communities began to deteriorate as Lakota speakers became increasingly dependent on authority figures from churches, the Bureau of Indian Affairs, or tribal programs. These circumstances created an ideal setting for alcoholism. When you drank, you could temporarily escape authority and practice a type of independence. Independence is a feature of Lakota tradition, but such alcohol-supported behavior was artificial.

By the 1960s a new culture with its own language had developed—what I call the reservation subculture and the reservation language. Young people thought that this was normal Lakota speech. When I asked students what *makuje* (I am sick) meant, they responded, "Hangover." When I asked what *oteh'i* (difficult to endure) meant, they responded, "You have one hell of a hangover. You are flat broke with absolutely no resources for another drink." This particular culture, which was aggressive and was practiced daily, challenged the other three (Catholic, Episcopalian, Lakota).

Today, in an attempt to reverse this change in language, we deliberately use words in their traditional form. Today, we have more powwows, more Sun Dances, more giveaways, more naming ceremonies, more honoring ceremonies. We use our words in settings and situations where they truly belong. It is our hope that, through these community activities, people will feel able to adjust their lifestyles to reflect the true meaning of their language.

In class, I explain the different cultures. My intention is to clarify our current situation. We are all Lakota. In the classroom, I try to explain how the different influences have conditioned students' lives and how that affects them today. I try to make students conscious of what each culture represents. You have a traditional Lakota spirituality. You have a Catholic spirituality. You have an Episcopalian spirituality. You should respect each other and honor each other's choices. I honor my people and respect them. Whatever decisions they have made I will honor.

This new approach has forced me to redefine my role as a language instructor. As an instructor, I realize that I have to demonstrate Lakota values and morals in my own daily life so that students not only learn the Lakota words but also see examples of what I am teaching. I find that this work, though challenging, frees me from concepts and uses of my language that I never chose. It is a process of deconditioning and liberation. Our language was invaded, just as our lands were. We need to bring back our language with all its spiritual values and its moral force, just as we fight to reclaim the Black Hills and the other sacred sites within our domain.

See also Languages.

Boas, Franz, "Siouan Dakota," in *Handbook of American Indian Languages* (Oosterhout: Anthropological Publications, 1969); Buechel, Eugene, *A Dictionary: Oi'e Wowapi Wan of Teton Sioux* (Pine Ridge, S.D.: Red Cloud Indian School, 1983); Buechel, Eugene, *A Grammar of Lakota: The Language of the Teton Sioux Indians* (Saint Francis, S.D.: Rosebud Educational Society, 1939).

ALBERT WHITE HAT, SR. (LAKOTA)
Sinte Gleska University

LANGUAGES

In 1929 the linguist Edward Sapir wrote:

Few people realize that within the confines of the United States there is spoken today a far greater variety of lan-

guages . . . than in the whole of Europe. We may go further. We may say, quite literally and safely, that in the state
of California alone there are greater and more numerous
linguistic extremes than can be illustrated in all the length
and breadth of Europe. . . . It would be difficult to over-
estimate the value of [the technical studies documenting
these languages] for an eventual philosophy of speech.

Sapir's words celebrate both the diversity of Native
American languages and their contribution to the study
of one of the most important capacities possessed by
human beings: the ability to construct languages. This
contribution began to influence linguistic scholarship
as early as the sixteenth century. For example, Fray
Bernardino de Sahagún and his Aztec colleagues wrote
the twelve-volume encyclopedic work entitled *General
History of the Things of New Spain* (c. 1548) entirely
in the Nahuatl language. This and other early recordings of Nahuatl gave us our first extensive written
record of a polysynthetic language.

Polysynthetic languages represent one of the important language types in Native America. We can begin to
appreciate the linguistic diversity of Native America by
comparing the polysynthetic Nahuatl with the more
analytic Hopi. Consider the following example. In
Nahuatl, the idea "I ate meat" can be rendered in a single word, *oninacaqua*. In Hopi, this would be rendered
nu' sikwit nöösa. It is the characteristic of polysynthetic languages that an entire sentence can be rendered as
a single word. A more analytic language, like Hopi,
will express the parts of a sentence as separate words.
Hopi is more like English than Nahuatl in this respect.
Interestingly, however, Hopi belongs to the same language family as Nahuatl, and both are unrelated to
English.

Let us look at the two sentences more closely, starting with the Hopi. Hopi is a verb-final language, so the
order of words in this sentence conforms to the formula *subject = object = verb*. This is often abbreviated by
linguists as "SOV," so we say, for example, that Hopi is
an SOV language. In this feature it contrasts with English, which is an SVO language.

Now let us consider the Nahuatl sentence, which appears here in the same orthography as was used for six-
teenth-century manuscripts. A more nearly phonetic
rendering would be *ooninakakwah*, where the *oo* represents a long *o*, like the sound of *oe* in English *toe*. In
order to understand the structure of this Nahuatl
"word-sentence" we must break it down into its
parts—or *morphemes*, as they are called in linguistic
jargon. Thus we have *oo-ni-naka-kwa-h*. These five ele-

ments can be glossed in English as "*past*-I-meat-eat-
perfect." Notice that *-naka-*, "meat," the object of the
verb, is "incorporated" into the verb. The verb itself is
represented by the stem *-kwa-*, "eat." The first-person
subject pronoun *-ni-*, "I," is also incorporated into the
verb, just before the object. (The subject pronoun of
Nahuatl is actually related to the independent subject
pronoun of Hopi; for example, Nahuatl *-ni-* corresponds to Hopi *nu'*.) In both Hopi and Nahuatl, the
past tense of the verb is expressed within the verb itself.
In Hopi, this is done by using the simple form of the
verb, without any affix. In Nahuatl, the past tense is
marked by the past-tense prefix *oo-* together with the
suffix *-h*, which is here glossed as "*perfect*," indicating
that the action denoted by the verb is complete or "perfected."

Polysynthesis and incorporation, both of which are
illustrated by the Nahuatl example here, are best
known to linguistic scholarship from the languages of
the Americas, and continue to be an important topic of
linguistic investigation throughout the world to this
day. The late Edward Dozier, for example, a Tewa linguist, conducted an extensive study of incorporation in
his Santa Clara dialect of Tewa, demonstrating the
richness and expressive potential of incorporation in
that language. There are many other examples of such
scholarship.

The grammatical device known as *switch reference*
was first extensively studied in the languages of North
America. Switch references can, for example, be found
in Hopi. Consider the following pair of sentences:

Pam pakit pu' pam qatuptu. (He came in and he sat
down.)
Pam pakiq pu' pam qatuptu. (He came in and he sat
down.)

The English translation of these sentences is ambiguous. We don't know whether the second *he* refers to the
same person as the first *he*. In Hopi, however, the situation is perfectly clear because of the switch-reference
system. Though the word *pam* means "he" in both
cases, we can tell from the form of the first verb
whether each occurrence of *pam* refers to the same person or to a different person. The verb *paki* bears the
suffix *-t* when the individuals are the same, but when
they are different the switch-reference suffix *-q* is used.
Switch reference is a topic of great interest in linguistic
scholarship today. Although it was first described in
Native American languages, it has also been found in

native languages of the South Pacific, such as those spoken in New Guinea and Australia.

One of the most intriguing phenomena in Native American languages, and one perhaps most closely linked to the conceptual world, is the grammatical feature known as the "animacy hierarchy" or the "great chain of being." It can be illustrated with the following example from Navajo:

Ashkii tl'ízí yizloh. (The boy roped the goat.)

This sentence is organized in the SOV order, like the Hopi sentences cited earlier: subject (*ashkii*, "boy"), object (*tl'ízí*, "goat"), verb (*yizloh* "he roped it"). The effect of the animacy hierarchy can be observed when we try to say, "The goat butted the boy." We cannot use the SOV order in this case. Instead, we must use the order OSV, with a special form of the verb (in place of the prefix *yi-* we must use *bi-*):

Ashkii tl'ízí bizgoh. (The goat butted the boy.)

The point is this: the boy ranks higher in the hierarchy than the goat, so the sentence has to be constructed so as to have the word for "boy" precede that for "goat," even though the boy is the object and the goat is the subject. In general, in a transitive sentence with subject and object expressed as nominals (nouns or noun phrases), a higher-ranking nominal must precede a lower-ranking one. The hierarchy places humans higher than animals, and animals higher than things.

The hierarchy principle in Navajo grammar provides a window into an aspect of the worldview of the speakers of that language. It must be kept in mind, however, that we cannot simply assume that it is possible to "read off" a culture from an aspect of the grammar of that culture's language. In the case of the Navajo animacy hierarchy, however, a careful study by the linguist Gary Witherspoon has linked this aspect of Navajo grammar with the structure of the Navajo philosophy concerning the origin and structure of language and thought. An important component in Witherspoon's study is the data assembled by the Navajo educator Mary Helen Creamer, who discovered a sensitive detailed hierarchy of concepts involving eight levels, with humans in the highest position and abstract concepts in the lowest position. Animals and inanimate entities are distributed among the six intervening levels. In this case, the philosophical system was studied independently of the language; the one was not derived from the other.

By virtue of its diversity and complexity, Native America presented an ideal environment for the continuing development and testing of the comparative method, which had previously been applied primarily to languages of Europe, the Middle East, and India. One of the language families that Edward Sapir helped to define was Uto-Aztecan, to which Hopi and O'odham, as well as Nahuatl, belong. The comparative method makes heavy use of the notion "regular sound correspondence," as illustrated in the accompanying table.

Hopi	O'odham	Navajo	gloss
qöya	kokda	-hé	kill
qatu	ka:c	-dá	sit/be
kiihu	ki:	kin	house
kuuki	ke'e	-hash	bite
naqvu	na:k	-jaa'	ear
maqa	ma:k	-aa ni-'aah	give
lööyöm	go:k	naaki	two
laaki	gakï	-gan	dry
wihu	gi:gï	-k'ah	fat
wu:ko	ge'e	-tsaaz	big

One can see from the table, Hopi and O'odham display a relationship of regular sound correspondences, which leads scholars to believe that those two languages belong to the same family. By contrast, Navajo has no regular sound correspondences with either language, and we therefore classify it as belonging to another language family. True, there are some accidental correspondences, as in the words for "house" and "dry," but these are not systematic—that is, they do not occur regularly. In fact, Navajo does belong to a different language family, Athabaskan.

The details of comparative linguistics involve not only noticing correspondences but also working out the details of the correspondences—that is, the "rules" for when one thing corresponds to another. For example, the O'odham *g* sometimes corresponds to Hopi *l* and sometimes to Hopi *w*. The rule is this: where there is a correspondence and O'odham has *g*, Hopi has *l* before *a* and *ö*, the original "low" vowels of the parent Uto-Aztecan language, and in all other cases has *w*. Similarly, in correspondences where O'odham has *k*, Hopi has *q* before *a* and *ö*, and in all other cases has *k*.

In addition to allowing us to determine details of construction and pronunciation, the comparative

ARCTIC
OCEAN

Eskimo

Athabaskan

Aleut

Eskimo

Eskimo

Eskimo

Hudson
Bay

Beothuk

Tlingit

Tsimshian

Athabaskan

Algonquian

Tlingit

Haida

Wakashan

Salish

Salish

Algonquian

Wakashan

Salish

Algonquian

Chimakuan

Chinookan — Salish

Salish

Siouan

Algonquian

Sahaptin–Nez Perce

Caddoan

Klamath–Modoc

Athabaskan

Uto–
Aztecan

Siouan

Siouan

Iroquoian

Pomo

Uto–
Aztecan

Uto–
Aztecan

Siouan

Algonquian

Algonquian

Miwok–Costanoan
Esselen
Yokuts
Salinan
Chumashan

Tanoan

Keres

Caddoan

Cherokee

Uto–
Aztecan

Hopi

Tanoan

Athabaskan

Siouan

Yuchi

Catawba

ATLANTIC
OCEAN

Yuman

Zuni

Caddoan

Muskogean

PACIFIC
OCEAN

Athabaskan

Comanche

Natchez

Timucua

Seri
Uto–Aztecan

Tonkawa

Atakapa
Karankawa
Coahuiltecan
Comecrudo

Chitimacha

0   500 miles

0   500 kilometers

Uto–Aztecan

Gulf of Mexico

LANGUAGES

method also permits us to "reconstruct" a common ancestor language. When we consider all of the Uto-Aztecan languages together, we can posit that in the ancestor language, the two sounds just discussed were, respectively, *w* and *k*. By custom, comparativists precede their reconstructions of linguistic elements with an asterisk. Thus *w is the Uto-Aztecan reconstruction for Hopi *l* /*w* and O'odham *g*, and *k is the reconstruction for Hopi *q* /*k* and O'odham *k*. The vowels that "condi-

tion" the appearance of *l* and *q* in Hopi are Uto-Aztecan *a and *o, the original "low" vowels of the parent language. By contrast, no such systematic reconstruction can be made for Navajo in relation to Hopi and O'odham.

Most Native American languages belong to a family to which some other languages also belong. For example, Hopi and O'odham, which belong to the Uto-Aztecan family, share that family with Nahuatl, Ute,

Paiute, Comanche, Shoshone, Yaqui, Luiseño, and many others. The family is named after the languages at its geographic extremes: Ute in the north and Aztec (Nahuatl) in the south. Navajo, as we have noted, is an Athabaskan language and as such is a member of the same family as the Apache languages of the Southwest and northern languages like Sarsi, Chipewyan, Dogrib, and Koyukon, among others. We do not know exactly how many language families there are in the New World. In North America, there are, according to a conservative estimate, approximately sixty-two language families, which belong to eight larger groupings called *phyla*. Adding Mexico and Central America brings the number of such families to eighty-four, conservatively. With the addition of South America, the total figure rises to one hundred four. These estimates are based on work that adheres to the requirement that regular repeated sound correspondences be established between languages for those languages to be considered closely related. However, this has not been always possible, because for many of the linguistic families of the Americas, the requisite data are sparse.

Much work has been done and is still being done to discover larger groupings of language families. For example, it was suggested by Sapir that Uto-Aztecan and the Tanoan family are related and form a larger grouping called Aztec-Tanoan. Similarly, Athabaskan is believed to form a larger grouping with Tlingit and Eyak, called Na-Dene. Many other groupings have been suggested as well. On the other hand, some families have only one member and are referred to as *isolates,* a term used for languages that cannot, as yet, be related to any other, like the famous Basque language of Europe. Examples of Native American isolates are Keresan, Porepecha (Tarascan), and possibly the Timucua language of Florida, now extinct.

The language just mentioned, Timucua, was spoken by as many as 722,000 people in the sixteenth century. In the early seventeenth century that number was reduced to fewer than 37,000. Today the language is no longer spoken. This was the fate of many languages following the European invasion of the Western Hemisphere. It is a sad fact that the Native American languages that survive today continue to be endangered. The danger was recognized quite early on by Native American scholars, as well as the European scholars who worked with them. A number of these native scholars spent much of their lives documenting their respective linguistic and cultural heritages. Some of these early Native American linguists included Francis La

Flesche (Omaha), Tony Tillohash (Southern Paiute), George Sword (Oglala Lakota), Ella Deloria (Yankton Sioux), William Benson (Pomo), Vi Hilbert (Skagit), William Beynon (Tsimshian), Juan Delores (O'odham), Edward P. Dozier (Santa Clara), Archie Phinney (Nez Perce), William Jones (Fox), J. N. B. Hewitt (Tuscarora), Parker McKenzie (Kiowa), George Hunt (Kwakiutl), Cora V. Sylestine (Alabama), James R. Murie (Pawnee), William Morgan (Navajo), and the Abenaki scholars Joseph Laurent, Lorne Masta, and Pial Pol Wzôkihlain.

Though the state of native languages was indeed precarious in the nineteenth century, the situation today is much more serious. Some scholars estimate that, for the world as a whole, more than half of the six thousand languages now spoken will become extinct by the end of the twenty-first century. And at that time, some 80 percent of the languages remaining will be endangered. Scholars say that a language is endangered when it is no longer being spoken by children. This benchmark has alarmed many present-day Native American communities, because many of them have no children who speak the local language. If this state of affairs continues, such languages will become extinct when the adults who now speak it die off. Many scholars, community members, and teachers, both Native American and Euro-American, are working to reverse this trend in a large number of communities. Their work involves, among other things, the establishment of community-based education programs involving Native American languages (immersion programs, bilingual-education programs, and so forth), the organization of training workshops for teachers (for example, the American Indian Language Development Institute), and the production of linguistic materials (orthographies, grammars, dictionaries).

In addition to these more traditional language-maintenance activities, political activism has been an important component of work on behalf of Native American languages. Contemporary Native America in general is heavily involved in the use of legal instruments for the promotion of its inherent rights and for the safeguarding of its cultural and intellectual traditions. Native American language scholars and educators have extended their language-maintenance efforts into the legal arena as part of this general tradition. In 1990, thanks to their efforts and those of sympathetic legislators, the Native American Languages Act passed the U.S. Congress.

In the context of this movement, a number of new traditions have developed around the written form of the languages. Among these is the tradition of using native languages to write poetry. The linguist and poet Ofelia Zepeda, for example, uses O'odham in writing a form of poetry that she has termed *cegïtoidag*, "thoughts." In contrast to the more literary uses of native languages, a number of linguists have begun to write grammatical and lexicographic essays in the native languages of which they are speakers. Representative of this genre is the work done by Albert Alvarez on O'odham, Gordon Francis on Micmac, Paul Platero on Navajo, the late Josephine White Eagle on Winnebago, Jorge Matamoros on Miskitu, and Florentino Ajpacaja Tum on Quiché Mayan.

Is the outlook for Native American languages positive or negative? The answer to this question must involve a consideration of the human energy and intellectual power being devoted to safeguarding the continent's valuable linguistic traditions. Keeping this in mind, we should recall the words of the California linguist Leanne Hinton, who, when asked in a discussion about those active in the preservation effort whether it was too late to save these languages, declared, "No. How can it be when people like these bend their efforts to saving them?"

See also Algonquian Languages; Cherokee Language; Cree Language; Iroquoian Languages; Lakota Language; Navajo Language; Ojibwa Language; Pueblo Languages; Salishan Languages.

Campbell, Lyle, and Marianne Mithun, eds., *The Languages of Native America: Historical and Comparative Assessment* (Austin: University of Texas Press, 1979); Hinton, Leanne, *Flutes of Fire: Essays on California Indian Languages* (Berkeley, Calif.: Heyday Books, 1994); Osgood, Cornelius, ed., *Linguistic Structures of Native America,* Viking Fund Publications in Anthropology, no. 6 (New York: Viking Fund, 1946).

LaVerne Masayesva Jeanne (Hopi)
University of Nevada at Reno

Laws of Indian Communities

Indian tribes, as sovereign, self-governing entities within the U.S. legal system, make and enforce a variety of laws. Tribal members, as citizens of their own governments, are subject to the laws of that tribe on the reservation. But because of historic limitations on tribal sovereignty under U.S. law, Indian tribes cannot enforce many of their laws if those laws are broken by nonmembers on the reservation. In such cases, responsibili-

ty for law enforcement over nonmembers may belong to federal or state authorities. The jurisdictional confusion that arises over the scope of tribal lawmaking authority may well mean that reservation crime and other illegal activities go unpunished and unregulated.

The scope of tribal lawmaking authority over reservation communities is defined by a complex array of treaties, congressional statutes, Executive Branch orders, administrative regulations, and court decisions. Most treatments of the topic traditionally focus on three core principles abstracted from this body of law on Indian rights and status in the United States: the Congressional Plenary Power Doctrine, the Doctrine of Diminished Tribal Sovereignty, and the Trust Doctrine.

The principle that Congress exercises a plenary power over Indian tribes explains many of the major limitations on tribal lawmaking authority and self-determination under U.S. law. The Indian Civil Rights Act, for example, passed by Congress in 1968 under its plenary power, imposes many of the restrictions contained in the U.S. Constitution's Bill of Rights on tribal governments in their dealings with their own citizens and others who come under their lawful jurisdiction. As another example, the Indian Gaming Regulatory Act, passed over the strenuous objections of many tribes in 1988, extends the plenary power of Congress to control the scope of tribal sovereignty over gambling activities on the reservation.

At the same time, Congress has used its plenary power to expand or clarify the scope of tribal self-determination over reservation affairs, as in the Indian Reorganization Act of 1934. This landmark legislation of the New Deal era established the framework for modern tribal government, enabling tribes to adopt federally approved constitutions and bylaws and setting up elective tribal councils to govern daily life on the reservation. The Indian Child Welfare Act, passed in 1978, is another example of Congress's exercise of its plenary power in Indian affairs. This important legislation placed the authority of Congress squarely behind tribal, and not state, jurisdictional control of adoption proceedings involving Indian children.

The principle that Congress possesses a unilateral power to define the limits and scope of Indian sovereignty under U.S. law has been upheld in a variety of court decisions. At its core, however, the belief that tribes must conform to American sovereign power is the product of the Doctrine of Discovery and the legacy of European colonialism.

The Doctrine of Discovery was brought to the New World by the European colonial powers, but its history extends back in time to the medieval era when Christian European crusades were fought against the "heathen and infidel" peoples who "unjustly" occupied Jerusalem and the holy lands of the Middle East.

The crusades were carried out under a legal theory that denied rights of self-rule and property to non-Christian peoples who violated church-declared precepts of natural law. This same medievally derived legal theory of a Christian European nation's superior rights to the territories occupied by "heathen and infidel" peoples was relied on by Spain in the late fifteenth century to claim rights in the "New World" discovered by Columbus, and later by other Christian European countries as well.

Most Americans would likely be surprised to learn that the basic rights of Indian governments in this country are circumscribed by a legal doctrine that evolved out of European Christian justifications for the crusades of the Middle Ages. Yet concepts derived from this doctrine such as exclusive federal authority in Indian affairs, domestic dependent nation status for tribes, and the trust responsibility have been relied on by courts and policymakers throughout our nation's history in deciding the scope and content of Indian self-governing rights.

The legacy of European cultural racism and colonialism toward American Indian peoples perpetuated by these principles is reflected in many of the limitations tribal governments face when attempting to enforce law and order in their communities. Modern-day law-enforcement problems arising from the so-called checkerboard pattern of jurisdiction on reservations can be traced, for example, to the all-encompassing program of cultural assimilation and ethnocide ushered in by the General Allotment Act of 1887. The Allotment Act, in effect, sought to encourage the destruction of tribalism and the assimilation of Indians into white "civilization" by parceling out treaty-guaranteed reservation lands to individual tribal members and "surplus" tribal lands to non-Indians. The contemporary legacy of the Allotment Act is evident in the political geography of many reservation communities and complicated rules regarding law enforcement. Tribally owned lands, individually owned Indian lands, and lands owned by non-Indians create "checkerboard" patterns of land tenure and jurisdiction.

The Major Crimes Act, another late-nineteenth-century exercise of congressional power in Indian affairs, provides further example of the lingering legacy of European cultural racism and colonialism that affects contemporary Indian tribal governments. This 1885 act authorized the exercise of federal criminal jurisdiction over felony crimes committed by tribal Indians within their tribe's reserved borders. As a consequence, federal prosecutorial authority over the major felonies committed on reservations supplants exclusive tribal control and sovereignty over member crimes. Numerous other congressional policy initiatives have perpetuated the legacy of European colonialism and racism toward Indian peoples. For example, Congress legislatively terminated 109 Indian tribes and bands in the 1950s and 1960s, and in 1953 unilaterally turned criminal jurisdiction on reservations in California, Nebraska, Oregon, and Wisconsin over to state authorities with the passage of Public Law 280. Congress also imposed on tribes both the 1968 Indian Civil Rights Act and the Indian Gaming Regulatory Act. These and numerous other legislative policies have been based on the underlying racist assumption that the majority society possesses unilateral political power over the lawmaking authority of Indian tribes on their own reservations. And no U.S. court, in applying U.S. law to Indian peoples, has dared question that assumption.

To speak of tribal "rights" of self-government in this type of historical and contemporary policy context is therefore quite misleading. It would be more accurate to speak of Indian "rights" as those privileges extended to Indian tribes as "conquered" and culturally inferior peoples, according to the unilateral whims of the majority society. In short, the courts have recognized congressional power over tribal governments by establishing a second judicial principle: the idea that tribal sovereignty has been diminished as a consequence of the European invasion of North America. The U.S. Supreme Court itself has elaborated this second principle in its most recent jurisprudence on Indian rights.

In a series of decisions, the Supreme Court has told Indian tribes that their previously assumed rights of jurisdictional control were actually privileges that the Doctrine of Discovery denied to them as Indians. In 1979 William Rehnquist, then an associate justice, wrote the majority opinion in *Oliphant* v. *Suquamish Tribe*. The court held that Indian tribes no longer possessed the inherent sovereign power to try and punish non-Indians for any crimes committed in Indian country. The decision constrained the exercise of tribal sovereign power so as not to interfere with the interests of

U.S. citizens to be protected from "unwarranted intrusions" on their personal liberty.

Justice Rehnquist's *Oliphant* opinion recalled the constraints John Marshall had placed on tribal governments in his 1823 decision in *Johnson v. McIntosh*: "Upon incorporation into the territory of the United States, the Indian tribes thereby came under the territorial sovereignty of the United States and their exercise of separate power is constrained so as not to conflict with the interests of this overriding sovereignty. Their rights of complete sovereignty, as independent nations, are necessarily diminished." Since *Oliphant*, the court has continued to define and limit the scope of tribal lawmaking authority. In *Montana v. United States*, the court denied the treaty-based rights of the Crow Tribe of Montana to regulate hunting and fishing activities of nonmembers on fee lands that had passed out of tribal ownership through the General Allotment Act. According to the court, "treaty rights with respect to reservation lands must be read in light of the subsequent alienation of those lands" under the Allotment Act. As the court reasoned, "[i]t defies common sense that Congress should intend that non-Indians purchasing allotted lands would become subject to tribal jurisdiction when the avowed purpose of their allotment policy was the ultimate destruction of tribal governments."

The court's landmark 1989 decision in the field of tribal civil jurisdiction over reservation lands, *Brendale v. Confederated Tribes and Bands of Yakima*, involved the important question of whether the Yakama Indian Nation (the current preferred spelling) in the state of Washington had the power to regulate land use on property owned by nonmembers within the allotted portions of its reservation. In this case as well, the racist premises of the Doctrine of Discovery represent the source of the court's willingness to recognize a diminished tribal sovereignty. The Supreme Court held in *Brendale* that Congress, by opening up certain portions of the Yakama Reservation to large numbers of non-Indians for settlement under the Allotment Act, had essentially divested the tribe of sovereignty over these lands. Citing its opinion in *Montana*, the court held that the Yakama Indian Nation could not regulate those areas on its reservation where the land had passed predominantly into ownership by nonmembers by operation of a nineteenth-century congressional act aimed at "the ultimate destruction" of American Indian tribal culture.

The holding of the *Brendale* case, in terms of its precedential authority in federal Indian law, is that Indian tribes lack the sovereign authority to zone or otherwise control non-Indian-owned fee lands in reservation areas where the tribe has been displaced by a significant non-Indian presence. As Justice John Paul Stevens explained in joining *Brendale*'s holding that the tribes, in spite of their treaty, no longer retained the power to regulate non-Indian fee lands in the open portion of the reservation with a significant non-Indian presence, the Allotment Act "was designed ultimately to abolish Indian reservations while attempting to bring security and civilization to the Indian." What Justice Stevens didn't even need to discuss was that the power to destroy Indian tribes was and continues to be the unassailable right of the United States, under principles derived from the Doctrine of Discovery.

It has been relatively easy for non-Indian courts and policymakers to extend the principles of congressional superiority and diminished sovereignty to establish another concept—the Trust Doctrine. The Trust Doctrine asserts that federal officials have broad discretionary authority similar to that of a guardian over an incompetent minor. In the past, this doctrine allowed the Bureau of Indian Affairs to limit a tribal government's ability to control its land and mineral resources, for example, as well as to administer educational and social-welfare programs within reservation boundaries. The Trust Doctrine was often presented as an example of federal benevolence since it justified federal protection, but only in recent decades have tribes been able to establish their own schools and courts and gain control over the reservation environment and its resources.

The legacy of European racism and colonialism toward Indian peoples is unavoidably reinscribed in modern federal Indian law whenever the principles of Indian self-government are defined, for these principles are inevitably limited by the plenary power of Congress, the principle of diminished sovereignty, and the Trust Doctrine. Each of these ideas emerged in the shadow of the Doctrine of Discovery. So long as that doctrine and its associated principles retain their vitality in federal Indian law, the extent of that law will be limited and its function will remain inescapably and irredeemably racist. A central and problematic challenge that confronts American Indian tribes in their struggle for self-determination, therefore, is to reveal to courts, legislators, and their fellow citizens in this country how U.S. law perpetuates and extends a thousand-year-old European-derived legacy of colonialism and racism toward them as indigenous tribal peoples. Any system of law that concedes to the non-Indian majority the raw racial power to determine the scope, content, and even the existence of the rights belonging to Indian tribes cannot provide a stable, much less just, foundation for protecting the cultural survival of America's indigenous tribal peoples.

See also Fishing and Hunting Rights; Water Rights.

O'Brien, Sharon, *American Indian Tribal Governments* (Norman: University of Oklahoma Press, 1989); Williams, Robert A., Jr., *The American Indian in Western Legal Thought: The Discourses of Conquest* (New York: Oxford University Press, 1990).

ROBERT A. WILLIAMS, JR. (Lumbee)
University of Arizona at Tucson

LIPAN APACHE

The Lipan Apaches were one of several southern Athabaskan-speaking tribes that ranged over the southern Great Plains during historic times. Ancestral Lipans probably constituted part of the bison-hunting "Querechos" that Spanish explorers encountered on the Great Plains in 1541. They lived in bison-hide tipis and relied on large pack dogs for transport. They organized large-scale communal hunts in the spring and fall, killing antelope, deer, and bear as well as bison. Matrilocal extended families constituted the basic social unit of Lipan society.

The Lipans apparently acquired horses soon after the Spaniards colonized the upper Rio Grande Valley in 1598. In the early seventeenth century, mounted, lance-armed Plains Apaches expanded over the southern Great Plains, pushing Caddoan-speaking horticultural peoples east—downstream—along the valleys of western tributaries of the Mississippi River. Before the end of the seventeenth century, Jicarilla, Lipan, and Kiowa Apaches had differentiated from one another. These tribes occupied the Great Plains possibly from the Black Hills to the Canadian River and began to settle the river bottoms in the region, raising maize, beans, squash, and tobacco near their summer villages.

Around 1718, Comanches from the north, armed with guns, decisively defeated the Plains Apaches, who still relied on lances, and the Lipans rapidly retreated to central Texas. Invading territory formerly occupied by small Coahuiltecan-speaking peoples decimated by Old World diseases, the Lipans rustled horses from Spanish San Antonio and eked out a living as hunters and gatherers. By midcentury, Lipans lived in a dozen bands averaging four hundred to five hundred persons each.

In the late eighteenth century armed and mounted Comanches and Wichitas continued to press the Lipans southward, but the adversaries eventually negotiated an uneasy peace. The Lipans also placated the Spaniards by requesting Roman Catholic missions. Three successive missions to the Lipans failed: in northern Coahuila in 1754, on the San Sabá River in 1757, and on the upper Nueces River in 1762–71. The Lipans continued to rely on bison meat and hides as fundamental components of their economy even as they migrated ever southward, reaching the Gulf of Mexico by 1796.

When Anglo-Texans gained their independence from Mexico in 1836, they set about expelling Lipan Apaches as well as other Native Americans from the territory. Suffering significant casualties, the Lipans retreated. A northern band fled to the Pecos River valley and the Guadalupe Mountains, amalgamating around 1860 with their Mescalero Apache kinsmen. A southern band fled to northern Coahuila, Mexico. In 1903, the nineteen surviving southern-band Lipans migrated to the Mescalero Apache Indian Reservation in south central New Mexico, and autonomous Lipan life ended.

See also Apache, Eastern; Apache, Western.

Opler, Morris E., *Myths and Legends of the Lipan Apache Indians, American Folk-Lore Society Memoirs,* vol. 36 (New York, 1940); Tunnell, Curtis D., and W. W. Newcomb, Jr., *A Lipan Apache Mission: San Lorenzo de la Santa Cruz, 1762–1771,* Texas Memorial Museum Bulletin no. 14 (Austin: University of Texas, 1969).

HENRY F. DOBYNS
Tucson, Arizona

LITERATURE BY INDIANS

In 1492 the peoples of the North American continent spoke some two thousand languages and differed greatly in their economic, social, and political forms of organization. Some tribal nations developed complex hierarchical societies; others lived nomadically, relying on hunting and gathering for subsistence; still others lived in villages, dependent on wild and domesticated plants for survival. Their cosmologies were widely diverse as well, though all were radically different from Western or European religious philosophies. Unlike European settlers, who entrusted their histories and beliefs to the written word, Native Americans preserved their cultures through oral traditions.

The first American texts were the stories, songs, chants, or ceremonials of these first nations. This traditional literature was conceived as oral performance, a language more dependent on the ear than the eye for comprehension. Many of these oral texts have survived in translations of tribal creation stories, the Navajo Night Chant, the Winnebago Trickster Tale cycles, the Iroquois condolence rituals, and so on. From creation stories to the Plains Ghost Dance songs of the late nineteenth century, oral literature recorded, for future generations, the distinct cosmology of native nations and the history of those nations' conflicts.

With the invasion of America and the subsequent negotiations by tribal peoples for their land and peace, Indian oratory became an art of survival. The eloquence and importance of the spoken word can be seen in the oratories of Pontiac, Tecumseh, Chief Joseph, and other Native American leaders from the late seventeenth to the early twentieth century. These speeches, dependent on tribal training and memory, were usually transcribed by nonnatives present at the councils between Indians and whites, and many accounts suffer from distortions common to the translation and transcription of oral materials. Also, as with all Native Americans documents, it is important to remember that such distortions often accommodated the ideology of Manifest Destiny.

In the nineteenth century the Indian autobiography became a popular literary form. However, even at the beginning of colonization there was an interest in collecting the personal narratives of Native Americans. Frontier and military expeditions, missionaries, historians, and then ethnographers attempted to record the presence and then the passing of indigenous cultures through the story of a single Indian. These autobiographies most often were the products of three authors: the Indian subject, the translator, and the writer/editor. Since few Native Americans were literate, the literary emphasis and content of the autobiography were determined by the Euro-American editor. Often, as in the autobiographies of defeated tribal leaders like Black Hawk, Geronimo, and Plenty Coups, these works served to reinforce the idea of the impending destruction and surrender of Indian nations.

Samson Occom (1723–92), William Apess (1798–1839), and Elias Boudinot (1804?–1839) were among the first Native American writers. Their writings, appearing from the late eighteenth until the mid-nineteenth century, were informed by their conversion to Christianity and their lives as Indians. Each served as a mediator between the nonliterate tribal worlds and the dominant political and social ideologies designed to destroy them. Some of these nineteenth-century writers attempted to conciliate white audiences and policies; others, like Apess and later Sarah Winnemucca, argued for the cultural and historical superiority of Native Americans. But, whatever the motives of their texts, their literacy was an important and defiant step in the reappropriation of native voices and histories.

The advent of the religious and government boarding schools for Indian children assisted the spread of literacy in Native America. Native children were taken from their homes, denied the expression of their cultures, and punished for speaking their native languages. As it had been for postcolonial intertribal interactions, English became the students' common language. Out of this tragic removal of children from their native homes and communities, contemporary Native American literature was born. The boarding schools produced not only the early writers but also the audience that would determine the content of their work.

In 1854, John Rollin Ridge published the first novel by a Native American. The subject of Ridge's first and only novel, *The Life and Adventures of Joaquín Murieta, the Celebrated California Bandit,* was a Mexican American bandit. Thirty-seven years later, Sophia Alice Callahan wrote *Wynema,* the second novel by a Native American author. Between 1854 and 1891, however, the subject of Native American literature had changed drastically. Unlike the racial masquerade penned by Ridge, Callahan's novel chose not only to narrate the experiences of Native Americans but also to protest their absence from the literary canon. The education of her mixed-blood heroine includes references to Sitting Bull and Wounded Knee as well as to Shakespeare and Dickens.

At the turn of the century, Native American literature developed themes of cultural dislocation and alienation that would be revisited by writers for decades to come. Through the short stories of Zitkala Ša (1900) and Pauline Johnson (1913) and the single novel written by Mourning Dove (1927), the questions of race and gender were raised. These questions take on further complexity for these authors (as indeed they do for all Native Americans authors) because most protagonists in native literature are mixed bloods, never defined entirely by white or Indian blood or by cultural conventions. In the first novels of John Joseph Mathews (1934) and D'Arcy McNickle (1936), the discussion remains the place and the future of mixed bloods. In each of these novels the protagonist can live neither within nor outside of tribal culture, and the consequences of such a divided life are often tragic. These early native authors attempted to define, within Western literary traditions, the often contradictory and quickly changing nature of indigenous America.

The cornerstone of contemporary Native American literature is the Kiowa author N. Scott Momaday's *House Made of Dawn,* published in 1969. It was the first major novel by a Native American to appear after decades of silence, and its publication marked the beginning of a renaissance in Native American literature. For his novel Momaday was awarded the Pulitzer Prize. The novel traces the return of Abel to his tribal community after World War II, his relocation to Los Angeles in the 1950s, and the healing process he must undergo in order to be able to return home again. It is a novel of existential exhaustion and personal and cultural division. The story of Abel's return is framed within an oral invocation to storytelling, producing a tension between oral and written literature, between traditional and assimilated lives, that inspires Abel's journey. Momaday's other prose works include *The Way to Rainy Mountain* (1969), *The Names: A Memoir* (1976), and *The Ancient Child* (1989).

Leslie Marmon Silko's *Ceremony* (1977) was the first contemporary novel published by a Native American woman. Originating from the Laguna Pueblo, her work is primarily located in the Southwest. Like *House Made of Dawn, Ceremony* traces the postwar return of its protagonist, Tayo, and the consequences of his return for himself and the community. And Silko frames the written text by oral invocations as well. However, Silko's cosmology is inclusive: Tayo's sickness or alienation is a metaphor not for his mixed-blood heritage but for his exposure to evil, produced and perpetuated by all races. In Silko's cosmology the web of life is strained or broken by individual acts. Tayo's journey to recovery necessitates a discovery that he is connected to all things. He seeks a ceremony that contains both traditional and contemporary rituals and artifacts.

Silko's work combines tribal and Western historical and literary genres. *Ceremony* is told through prose, poetry, and oral materials. Silko's second work, *Storyteller* (1981), weaves autobiographical essays, short stories, poetry, and photography into a novel. In her third major novel, *Almanac of the Dead* (1991), Silko envisions a world dedicated to violence and self-destruction.

The works of Momaday and Silko have had a profound influence on the style and themes of Native American literature. They have inspired a generation of native writers, including James Welch, Louis Owens, Joy Harjo, and Thomas King.

Two Ojibwa writers, Gerald Vizenor and Louise Erdrich, have had an enormous impact on the content and popularity of Native American literature. Vizenor's comic brilliance in his satires of urban native experience and colonial history has inspired the works of Sherman Alexie and Adrian Louis. In Vizenor the mixed blood (or *crossblood,* as he reinvents the term) becomes a postmodern liberatory space in which contradictory histories and languages can create a trickster discourse. The intent of his fiction is to demythologize and destabilize conceits about identity and knowledge. He is the most prolific Native American writer, having produced over two dozen texts, and is often the most challenging. His novels include *Griever: An American Monkey King in China* (1987), *The Trickster of Liberty* (1988), and *The Heirs of Columbus* (1991).

Though Momaday remains the only Native American writer to receive the Pulitzer Prize, few native authors have had the impact of Louise Erdrich. Her novels have received unrivaled critical and popular attention. Erdrich's first novel, *Love Medicine* (1984), outsold any novel by a Native American and received several awards, including the National Book Critics Circle Award for Fiction. Together with *Love Medicine,* three of her other novels make up a quartet; they include *Beet Queen* (1986), *Tracks* (1988), and *Bingo Palace* (1994), and have experienced similar successes. Literary critics have attributed her lyrical style and contained landscape to influences from the works of William Faulkner. Like Faulkner's work, Erdrich's novels weave people and place into interconnecting stories and genealogies. For Erdrich, as for most Native American writers, people and the land are inseparable, the land in her fiction being twentieth-century North Dakota. The mixed bloods in her novels are not so much haunted by the loss of a traditional tribal world as they are engaged in the art and acts of common survival—personal, familial, and cultural. In addition to writing short stories and poetry, Erdrich also collaborated with her husband, Michael Dorris, on a novel, *The Crown of Columbus* (1991).

Linda Hogan, a writer of poetry and prose, derives her inspiration from the red earth of Oklahoma. Like Erdrich, she returns to the land she loves and knows. And like the other writers discussed here, she is a mixed blood, a descendant of Nebraska pioneers and the Chickasaw Nation. Before Oklahoma became a state in 1907, it was Indian Territory, promised to the tribes forcefully removed from the southeastern United States. The removal and its consequences distinguish the writing that comes out of the tribal communities of Oklahoma from the literature produced by southwestern or northern native writers. Hogan depicts the repeated dispossession of Oklahoma Indians, their landless condition, and their stubborn survival. Her writing captures the land of removal, with its detritus of loss and adaptations, and the tight, never-ending weave of family and cultural histories from one generation to the next.

Hogan's first novel, *Mean Spirit* (1990), is based on the killing of the Osage people for their oil-rich land. In that novel she makes several departures from traditional beliefs about land and blood: her characters are finally dependent on the community, not the land, for continued survival, and the community is Pan-Indian, not tribally specific. Both departures are informed by Hogan's recognition of the heroism of the ordinary lives of Native Americans, fragmented and forever affected by extraordinary losses and yet maintaining continuity and affirmations of life. Her additional prose and poetry include *Calling Myself Home* (1978), *Eclipse* (1983), *Book of Medicines: Poems* (1993), and *Dwellings* (1995).

As Native American literature enters the twenty-first century, archival work and anthologies are increasing the availability of traditional and historical materials. The literature continues to develop and change to reflect the concerns and realities of late-twentieth-century tribal lives. However, Native American fiction and poetry are a literature of protest—the theft of land, language, heritage—and such protests will always be their defining characteristic. Given the current emphasis on the representation of all American cultures, Native American literature promises, in terms of content and reception, to become less isolated and marginalized in the future, to become, at last, the first of many literatures of the United States.

See also Apess, William; Arts, Contemporary (since 1960); Boudinot, Elias; Johnson, Pauline; Mathews, John Joseph; McNickle, D'Arcy; Mourning Dove; Occom, Samson; Ridge, John Rollin (Yellow Bird); Winnemucca, Sarah; Zitkala Ša (Gertrude Bonnin).

Allen, Paula Gunn, ed., *Studies in American Indian Literature: Critical Essays and Course Designs* (New York: Modern Language Association, 1983); Owens, Louis, *Other Destinies: Un-* *derstanding the American Indian Novel* (Norman: University of Oklahoma Press, 1992); Ruoff, A. LaVonne Brown, and Jerry W. Ward, eds., *Redefining American Literary History* (New York: Modern Language Association, 1990).

BETTY LOUISE BELL
University of Michigan

LITTLE BIGHORN, BATTLE OF THE

On June 25 and 26, 1876, nontreaty bands of Teton Sioux (Lakotas) and Cheyennes defended their summer hunting encampment against the U.S. Army in a battle on Montana's Greasy Grass (Little Bighorn) River. Lieutenant Colonel George Armstrong Custer commanded the attacking forces. The principal Indian leaders included Sitting Bull (Hunkpapa), Crazy Horse (Oglala), Hump (Miniconjou), and Two Moon (Cheyenne).

During the battle, approximately two thousand warriors decisively defeated Custer's troops and routed U.S. Army reinforcements under the commands of Major Marcus Reno and Captain Frederick Benteen. Custer's entire force of 215 cavalrymen were killed, while the Indians reported having lost 32 warriors themselves.

In the years prior to the battle, many Lakota tribes, including the Hunkpapas, Oglalas, Miniconjous, Sans Arcs, and Blackfeet, together with several Cheyenne and Arapaho bands, had steadfastly refused to be confined permanently to reservations. The 1868 Fort Laramie Treaty had promised that they could range the buffalo grounds of the upper Missouri as long as the herds of buffalo survived. These groups were bolstered in the summer months by reservation-based kinsmen who came north to join in the hunt. These "nontreaty" Indians frequently raided Montana tribes and white settlements. (The site of the Little Bighorn battle was actually within the boundaries of land reserved by the Crows.)

The U.S. government responded to this pattern of raiding by ordering all unsettled Sioux tribes to the Dakota agencies by January 31, 1876, declaring all who refused to be "hostile" and subject to military action. The Indians, in a coalition fashioned by Sitting Bull, a medicine chief, refused. After the battle, the peoples scattered and were relentlessly pursued by the army. This pursuit intensified after Custer's defeat so that by the winter of 1876–77, most bands had surrendered or escaped into Canada.

LITTLE CROW

(1810–63)
Mdewakanton (Sioux) chief and Dakota leader.

Little Crow was born about 1810 at the Dakota village of Kaposia, along the upper Mississippi River just below present-day St. Paul, Minnesota. His parents belonged to the Mdewakanton tribe, part of the eastern Sioux, or Dakota people. The Kaposia people occupied southeastern Minnesota. Other related Dakota tribes—the Wahpeton, Wahpekute, and Sisseton—lived west of them. Little Crow's people encountered Europeans as early as 1650 and by the time of his birth, they had already been well integrated into the fur trade.

When Little Crow was about nine years old the U.S. government erected Fort Snelling across the river from what would become St. Paul, Minnesota. The fort soon held several companies of troops and an Indian agent who urged the Dakotas to stop fighting with their old enemies, the Ojibwas, and to abandon their life of hunting and gathering. Most of Little Crow's relatives at Kaposia ignored this advice, preferring the mobility and independence of the chase. Because of overhunting, however, the Mdewakantons and Wahpekutes eventually relinquished their claims to lands in western Wisconsin and transferred these to the United States. The agreement, completed in 1837, produced the first food and cash annuities to support the tribe.

For his part, Little Crow avoided the heady business of treaty negotiation. Unlike his father, a chief named Big Thunder, the young man preferred to roam westward, trading horses, buying liquor, hunting, and gambling. But in 1846, Little Crow's father suffered a fatal accident, and the leadership of the Kaposia band fell to Little Crow's half brother. This rankled Little Crow, who quickly returned to Kaposia. In a scuffle with his half brother, Little Crow wrested the chieftainship from him, receiving severe gunshot wounds in both wrists during the melee. The wounded chief survived, and by 1849, when Minnesota had become a territory, he was the principal leader of the Mdewakanton tribe.

Little Crow's position was first seriously tested when the United States asked the Dakota people to sell their land in Minnesota in 1851. While opposed to the idea before the council opened, Little Crow knew that his father and grandfather had always been friends of the Americans and that this friendship had helped enhance their status. In addition, many of Little Crow's relatives had intermarried with whites, creating kinship ties. Reluctantly, then, but with considerable determination, Little

Crow stepped forward at the council and proposed that for the right price, the government could have the land. His efforts unquestionably tipped the balance of support in favor of the treaty and propelled Little Crow into a new role as spokesman for the Dakota people.

Little Crow expected the federal government to meet its obligations. He demanded and was promised a reservation along the upper Minnesota River. Officials also agreed that money would be set aside to pay individual debts to Indian traders and to support the Dakotas with cash and food annuities. All of these promises were broken over the next few years as Little Crow's people were forced to evacuate the eastern part of the state. Unbelievably, even the clause guaranteeing a reservation along the Minnesota River was deleted by the U.S. Senate during the ratification process. While territorial officials in Minnesota first told the Dakota people that they could stay on the lands originally set aside for them for as long as they wished, federal officials soon demanded one-half of this parcel for additional white settlement. The Commissioner of Indian Affairs told Little Crow that if he refused to agree to the treaty, the government would force his people out onto the Dakota plains as they owned nothing in Minnesota. Little Crow reluctantly agreed to the new boundaries.

The federal government did make efforts to "uplift" the Dakotas on the new reservation by teaching them farming and English-language skills. These changes in turn produced resistance as various Indian "farmer" or progressive groups soon formed and clashed with others who joined soldiers' lodges, or male societies. Little Crow maintained his distance from both groups, refusing to don the clothing of the farmer Indian while resisting the admonitions of the most angry members of the Dakota soldiers' lodge. His attempt at mediation, however, resulted in his being rejected as speaker for his people in 1861.

As opposition to government programs grew, the Civil War made it more difficult for agency officials to purchase and supply the needs of the six thousand Dakotas who lived on the upper Minnesota River. Corruption within the Bureau of Indian Affairs added to the problem, since food supplies often went to white laborers or to the cooperative, farmer Indians. On August 17, 1862, a clash occurred in which several white settlers were killed. Late that same evening, warriors from the soldiers' lodge surrounded Little Crow's house and asked him to lead them in all-out war. Most of the respected leaders among the Dakota people had by that time long since joined the progressives or

Little Crow, a leader of the Dakota conflict of 1862, in an 1858 studio portrait taken in Washington, D.C.

tle Crow's forces, badly fractionalized and difficult to control, lost a crucial engagement and promptly retreated west onto the plains. While getting ready to flee, Little Crow did what he could to preserve the one hundred odd captives held by Dakota warriors, many of whom were mixed-blood relatives.

The Dakota leader proceeded into Canada, where he found little sympathy. He eventually returned with his son to the Minnesota frontier. On July 3, 1863, a farmer living near Hutchinson, Minnesota, discovered the pair picking berries. Without ascertaining their identity, he fired on them, mortally wounding Little Crow. The Dakota leader died later that afternoon. His son dressed his body, covered it with a blanket, and left.

Little Crow should be remembered as an intelligent leader of his people who sought accommodation but found betrayal and disappointment. While he is often viewed as the tragic leader of Dakota resistance in Minnesota, in reality he tried most of his life to lead his kinsmen through the difficult transition that accompanied the American settlement of Minnesota—a sensible, though inglorious, role.

Anderson, Gary Clayton, *Little Crow: Spokesman for the Sioux* (St. Paul: Minnesota Historical Society Press, 1986).

GARY CLAYTON ANDERSON
University of Oklahoma

lacked the personal prestige necessary to lead the four Minnesota tribes. Little Crow, miffed by his demotion and angry at the federal government, agreed to join the antifarmer elements. At dawn on August 18, over a hundred Dakota warriors attacked and killed most of the government officials at the Lower Sioux Agency. The fighting became general that afternoon as more and more Indians fanned into the countryside, raiding the settlers who had recently taken up land near the reservation. Within a few days, nearly five hundred whites had perished in what is generally called the Dakota Conflict of 1862.

Little Crow's attempt to lead this rebellion proved disappointing. Although only a handful of troops remained at nearby Fort Ridgely and the German enclave at New Ulm stood largely undefended, the Dakotas were unable to capture either outpost. Minnesota state officials quickly sent a fourteen-hundred-man army into the Minnesota River valley to subdue the Dakotas. Many tribesmen fled. A month later at Wood Lake, Lit-

LITTLE TURTLE (MISHIKINAKWA)

(c. 1747–1812)
Miami war chief and political leader.

Regarded as perhaps the greatest Algonquian war leader of his time, Little Turtle grew to adulthood during the American Revolution and led Native American armed resistance to the American invasion of the Old Northwest in the late eighteenth century. A great strategist and military tactician, he was noted for his exceptional intelligence—and for his ability to debate General Anthony Wayne as an equal at the Greenville Treaty council in 1795. Little Turtle became a staunch supporter of peace in the first decade of the nineteenth century, and as a consequence he lost the support of the Miami tribe and became identified as an American chief.

Little Turtle was born in about 1747. He received the Miami name of his father, Mishikinakwa, who had signed the Lancaster Treaty with colonial Pennsylvania authorities in 1748. It is believed his mother was a Mahican woman who had moved with remnants of her tribe into the Ohio country. Little Turtle achieved war-chief status when he destroyed a small military force led by an obscure Frenchman named Augustin Mottin de La Balme west of today's Fort Wayne, Indiana, on November 5, 1780. La Balme had destroyed the Miami villages at Kekionga, the major Miami settlement, near modern-day Fort Wayne, Indiana, while attempting to aid the American cause in the Revolutionary War.

After the Treaty of Paris in 1783, American officials dictated four treaties to the tribes of the Old Northwest, each based on the premise that Indian tribes had surrendered their rights to the land with the defeat of the British. Native American resistance to these pretensions quickly escalated into border warfare as Kentucky filled with settlers who led attacks deep into Indian country in the late 1780s. Little Turtle was responsible for the security of Kekionga, which had attracted several villages of Delaware and Shawnee Indians.

Although American officials wanted to avoid war with the Ohio tribes (mainly because of the expense involved), President Washington approved an attack on Kekionga in 1790. Little Turtle led the villagers away previous to an attack by General Josiah Harmar on October 20 that destroyed all of the villages. Little Turtle then led an ambush of Harmar's forces, killing 183 Americans. The following year, General Arthur St. Clair led another American army to Kekionga. Little Turtle led the forces of the Miami Confederacy, as the allied tribes were then called, in a devastating defeat of nearly the entire American army. Some 630 officers and men, as well as many civilian camp followers, were killed in the worst defeat of an American army ever by Indian defenders.

After nearly three years of organization and planning, General Anthony Wayne led a third army against the Miami Confederacy in 1794. Little Turtle, ever the great tactician, carefully probed Wayne's forces on their advance and concluded that they could not be defeated. He called for a negotiated peace and, unable to convince his allies, left overall leadership to Blue Jacket of the Shawnees. The well-prepared Wayne, himself a master tactician, defeated the allied tribes without much loss of life on either side at Fallen Timbers, near today's Toledo, Ohio, on August 20, 1794.

Little Turtle was the principal spokesman for the eleven tribes and approximately eleven hundred Indians who gathered at Greenville the following July to conclude peace with the Americans. Little Turtle's son-in-law, William Wells, a white captive, had been a scout for Wayne's invading army, and Little Turtle was fully aware of American intentions at Greenville. At the treaty grounds he eloquently defended Native American sovereignty in the Old Northwest. He also defined Miami ownership of all of present-day Indiana, the western third of Ohio, and part of Illinois and southern Michigan. Though the Miamis had long shared this land with other tribes, "Little Turtle's Claim" was helpful to the Miamis when they filed compensation claims against the federal government in the 1950s.

At the conclusion of the Greenville Treaty, Little Turtle pledged support of peace with American authorities. That promise was sorely tested within a few years when William Henry Harrison was appointed governor of Indiana Territory. After the Louisiana Purchase in 1803, President Thomas Jefferson encouraged Harrison to press for huge Indian land sales in the Old Northwest. Little Turtle signed four treaties—in 1803, 1804, 1805, and 1809—that were disadvantageous to the Miamis, and alienated himself from the tribal leadership. He also accepted personal annuities that were thinly disguised bribes, and allowed Winimac and Topinbee, two pro-American Potawatomi chiefs, to participate in negotiations over Miami land.

American pressure for Indian land brought a new wave of Native American resistance. Tecumseh and his brother the Shawnee Prophet (Tenskwatawa) encouraged tribespeople to resist the American hunger for land and to join together to eject Americans from Indian country. Little Turtle's authority among the Miamis derived from war leadership. As he bent to American desires, hereditary leaders such as Pacanne, the Owl, and Jean Baptiste Richardville (Peshewa) rejected Little Turtle's leadership and in 1809 forced Harrison to admit that they, not Little Turtle, were the real leaders of the Miami tribe.

Little Turtle lived out the last three years of his life at his village west of Fort Wayne on the Eel River, near today's Columbia City, Indiana. He died peacefully at William Wells's house at Fort Wayne on July 14, 1812. Wells was killed a month later while leading the evacuation of Fort Dearborn, the site of modern-day Chicago. Little Turtle's pro-American stance and the neutrality of the Miami tribe did not protect his tribespeople from American attacks. Within three months of his death, Little Turtle's village and two other Miami villages were destroyed.

Little Turtle's fame rests on his brilliance as a war leader and on his defense of Indian sovereignty at the Greenville Treaty negotiations. American strategic needs and land hunger after the Louisiana Purchase eliminated the middle ground upon which Little Turtle's success depended. He ended the last decade of his life as a pliable American chief who had lost touch with the needs of his people. Among the Miamis today he is revered as a great chief despite the tragic ending of his career.

See also Miami; Richardville, Jean Baptiste (Peshewa); Shawnee Prophet (Tenskwatawa); Tecumseh.

Carter, Harvey Lewis, *The Life and Times of Little Turtle* (Urbana: University of Illinois Press, 1987); Young, Calvin M., *Little Turtle* (1917; reprint, Mt. Vernon, Ind.: Windmill Publications, 1990).

STEWART RAFERT
University of Delaware

LOFT, FRED

1861–1934
Mohawk civil servant and North American Indian political organizer.

At the conclusion of the First World War, Frederick Ogilvie Loft (Onondeyoh, "Beautiful Mountain"), a Mohawk war veteran, established the League of Indians of Canada, the country's first Pan-Indian political association. The league held its first conference at Ohsweken on the Six Nations Reserve in Ontario in December 1918. Subsequent annual meetings were held at Sault Ste. Marie, Ontario, in 1919; Elphinstone, Manitoba, in 1920; Thunderchild Reserve, Saskatchewan, in 1921; and Hobbema, Alberta, in 1922. The centuries-old league of the Iroquois inspired Loft to found the organization. In the face of determined attempts by the Canadian Department of Indian Affairs to silence the league's independent voice, he persevered to keep it alive.

Fred Loft was born on February 3, 1861, on the Six Nations Reserve near Brantford, Ontario. He grew up on his parents' hundred-acre farm on the northeastern corner of the reservation. His parents, George Rokwaho Loft (1815–1895) and Ellen Smith Loft (1830–1921), spoke English as fluently as they did Mohawk. Devoted Anglicans, George and Ellen donated three acres of their land to build Christ Church, Cayuga, in 1873. However, they remained open-minded on religious questions and allowed their children to witness ceremonies of the traditional Cayugas, Onondagas,

and Senecas, the followers of the religion of Handsome Lake.

Fred attended school near his home until the age of twelve, when he boarded for a year at the Mohawk Institute in Brantford, an Indian residential school run by the New England Company, established two centuries earlier to Christianize Native Americans. Bitterly he remembered the experience all the rest of his life: "I recall the times when working in the fields, I was actually too hungry to be able to walk, let alone work. . . . In winter the rooms and beds were so cold that it took half the night before I got warm enough to fall asleep."

Anxious to finish elementary school elsewhere, he walked from his parents' farm eight miles a day round-trip to a school in the neighboring town of Caledonia, just east of the reservation. While attending high school he did odd jobs for a local family in Caledonia in return for food and lodging. When the young Mohawk finished high school, he felt, in his own words, "equipped enough to face the world of competition — no matter at what." For several years he worked in the forests of northern Michigan, rising from lumberjack to timber inspector. Ill health forced him to leave the bush. Upon his recovery he received a scholarship to the Ontario Business College at Belleville, Ontario, where he took a bookkeeper's course. After briefly working as a journalist for the Brantford *Expositor,* Loft obtained a provincial civil service job in 1887 as an accountant in the bursar's office at the Provincial Lunatic Asylum in Toronto, where he remained for the next forty years.

In Chicago in June 1898 the thirty-seven-year-old civil servant married Affa Northcote Geare, a Canadian of British descent, eleven years his junior. Affa gave birth in Toronto in May 1899 to twin girls, one of whom died in 1902. Another daughter was born in 1904.

Fred resented the fact that his government salary remained low. He believed that the administration of the asylum was passing him over for promotion because he was Indian. For many extras the family depended on Affa, who had a sharp business sense. She bought and sold houses, rented to roomers, and owned stock.

The Lofts led a busy life in Toronto. They had season tickets to two theaters and frequented the Orphen's racetrack. Affa participated in the American Women's Club, the United Empire Loyalist Association, and the Women's Art Association. Her husband was a speaker at these clubs. The Lofts sent their daughters to the Model School, one of the most respected elementary schools in the city.

Fred participated enthusiastically in the activities of his Masonic lodge and in the United Empire Loyalist Association. He gave lectures and wrote articles on North American Indian topics. Every Sunday he attended church. Iroquois friends visited him in Toronto, and he returned regularly to the Six Nations Reserve, where his daughters spent many summers at his mother's farm. In 1907, and again in 1917, the Six Nations Council unsuccessfully requested the federal government to select him as superintendent.

A staunch supporter of Britain, Loft visited Indian reservations throughout Ontario to encourage native recruitment after the outbreak of World War I in 1914. In 1917 the volunteer with seven years' active militia service received a commission as a lieutenant. In order to qualify for overseas duty he had reduced his age on his enlistment form from fifty-six to forty-five. A physically impressive man, standing nearly six feet tall and weighing 170 pounds, the Mohawk officer looked at least ten years younger than he actually was.

Although he went to Britain with the 256th Railway Construction Battalion, Loft was later transferred to the Canadian Forestry Corps in France on account of his early lumbering experience. During his half-year absence overseas the Six Nations Council conferred on him a Pine Tree chieftanship, a rare honor given to only the most outstanding members of the confederacy. As the council's representative he had an audience with King George V at Buckingham Palace on February 21, 1918, shortly before he left England for Canada.

Upon his return the Mohawk veteran had a dream of what he could do to help the American Indians in Canada: he would work to persuade the Canadian government to improve the standard of education it offered its native peoples. This became the main thrust of the League of Indians of Canada, which he founded in December 1918.

To encourage membership and attendance at the annual meetings, the league's national president sent circulars to chiefs of bands or to any suitable person whose name he could obtain. The bands were to pay five dollars a year plus five cents per band member. While primarily concerned with education, Loft tried to deal personally with every kind of complaint he received, sending off letters to officials on behalf of bands and individual Indians alike. He did so largely at his own expense, since despite his appeals he received little financial support.

Duncan Campbell Scott, the deputy minister in charge of the federal Department of Indian Affairs, treated the league's national president as a subversive. He first tried to have Loft's Indian status under the federal Indian Act removed. After that failed, he considered criminal charges against him for attempting to raise money for Indian land-claim issues.

The department's unrelenting opposition to an organization it could not control handicapped the league's growth. The minimal resources Fred Loft could command, particularly after he retired from the Ontario civil service in 1926, prevented expansion. His own and his wife's poor health in the late 1920s and early 1930s further weakened his contribution to the league. In his early seventies, the founder could no longer coordinate the diverse Indian groups from Quebec to Alberta. By the time of his death in 1934, the league, apart from its western Canadian branches, had come to a complete halt. But his heroic attempt, taken up by others, would succeed a generation later in the form of the National Indian Brotherhood and its successor, the Assembly of First Nations.

See also Indian-White Relations in Canada, 1763 to the Present.

Kulchyski, Peter, "A Considerable Unrest: F. O. Loft and the League of Indians," *Native Studies Review* 4, no. 1–2 (1988): 95–117; Titley, E. Brian, "Indian Political Organizations," in *A Narrow Vision: Duncan Campbell Scott and the Administration of Indian Affairs in Canada* (Vancouver: University of British Columbia Press, 1986).

DONALD B. SMITH
University of Calgary

LONGHOUSE

The longhouse is a traditional Iroquois dwelling that has symbolized cultural and social solidarity since at least the fifteenth century. Constructed of sapling posts twisted into the ground at close intervals and arched to frame a roof roughly eighteen feet tall, the frame of the longhouse was covered with sheets of elm or cedar bark. Typically the floor of a longhouse was oval in shape, running up to one hundred feet long and twenty feet wide. The interior living space was divided by a long central aisle and punctuated every twenty feet by a hearth shared by the two families on opposite sides of the corridor. Each family living space contained sleeping platforms elevated one foot from the ground that were covered with bark sheets, mats, and furs. These were surrounded by storage spaces located both above the sleeping platforms and in pits dug under them.

Shared fires with smoke holes above them were the only sources of light for the longhouse until the late eighteenth century, when some basswood bark houses were constructed with sliding wall shutters. In the nineteenth century the barrel roof of the longhouse was replaced with the sharp European gable; some even had hinged wooden doors at the front and back entrances.

Ownership of the longhouse was passed down matrilineally so that the oldest woman in a dwelling would be head of household. The intimacy and physical organization of these dwellings were believed to reflect fundamental Iroquois social and political values. Today the longhouse remains a symbol of the persistence of Iroquois culture.

See also Architecture.

LOOKOUT, FRED

(1865–1949)
Osage political and religious leader.

Fred Lookout was born near present-day Independence, Kansas, in November 1865. His mother died when he was still in his infancy, and he was reared by his paternal grandmother. His father was Eagle-That-Dreams, an Osage of the Eagle clan, and the name Lookout came from a careless interpretation of the tribal-language equivalent that described an eagle, perched on a high crag or treetop, gazing into the distance and dreaming.

Little is known of Fred Lookout's reservation childhood in Kansas and Indian Territory. As an adult, he recalled accompanying his father on buffalo hunts and receiving the name Wy-hah-shah-shin-kah (Little-Eagle-That-Gets-What-He-Wants). His father was a leading figure of his clan and band, which probably explains why Osage agent Laban J. Miles chose Fred from among a dozen other Osage children to attend the Carlisle Indian Industrial School in Pennsylvania soon after it opened in 1879. After several years he returned to the Osage Reservation, shortly before his father died in 1884. Encouraged by kinsmen, Lookout refused to return to school. He soon took a wife, Julia Pryor (Mose-che-he), a member of the Bear clan, and began farming a small acreage near Pawhuska, the Osage national capital.

The Osages, a Siouan-speaking people, came to their final reservation in northeastern Oklahoma between 1871 and 1874 after the forced sale of their Kansas reservation. They had been forest dwellers, occupying villages situated along the Missouri River system west of present-day St. Louis and twice yearly venturing onto the plains to hunt buffalo, until in 1825 Anglo-American population pressure placed them in Kansas. Their Indian Territory reservation's 1.5 million acres included excellent grasslands, which they rented to Texas trail drivers. They also received cash annuities paid quarterly on a per capita basis from the interest on the $8 million paid to the tribe for relinquishing its Kansas lands. Federal agents appointed to the tribe were often troubled to find their Osage charges suffering little economic deprivation and thus little inclined toward gratitude or humility.

In 1906 the Osages became the last tribe in Indian Territory to agree to have their reservation broken up into individual allotments. As a reward for their obstinacy, the Osages were able to get over five hundred acres of surface land each (most tribes received only 160 acres for each member) and managed to retain their mineral rights as a commonly held resource. This provision was especially significant because a test well drilled in 1897 proved a harbinger of oil and natural-gas production that made the Osages a wealthy tribe after World War I. The 1906 allotment act, which paved the way for Oklahoma statehood in 1907, also established an eight-man tribal council for the Osages, headed by a principal and an assistant chief, all elected by general vote. Candidates were elected for two-year terms until 1930, when these terms were lengthened to four years.

Fred Lookout was elected to the Osage Tribal Council in 1908 as assistant principal chief. He did not run for reelection in 1910 or 1912; nonetheless, he became principal chief in 1914, appointed by Secretary of the Interior W. L. Fisher. He replaced Bacon Rind, who was removed from the position along with the entire regularly elected council when accusations of incompetence and corruption involving the approval of oil leases surfaced. The appointed council, headed by Lookout, rejected attempts to extend a disadvantageous, monopolizing blanket lease and successfully petitioned to have the federal trust control over the Osage mineral estate continued; it had been scheduled to lapse in 1931.

Lookout's reputation for honesty and reliability, which led to his entry into tribal politics, was earned by a life that combined respect for tradition with recognition of the need for change and accommodation. In the late 1890s he and his wife lost the eldest of their four children. The family grieved in the old Osage way, giving all their possessions to others and leaving their home for months to roam the reservation, sheltered and fed by fellow tribespeople.

Upon resettling on his farm, Lookout led a more public life, becoming a spiritual and political leader. He joined the peyote religion, a syncretic compromise between traditional beliefs and the white man's Christianity that had recently been introduced among the Osages. Lookout presided over ceremonies as a road man, symbolically abandoning traditional beliefs for the peyote road by allowing his roached hair to grow long, separating it into two braids. In later years photographs always show him in dress shoes, trousers, and shirt, a kerchief knotted around his neck, his hair in braids, a blanket around his shoulders or waist, and sometimes a black hat atop his head.

Lookout lost his bid for reelection as chief in late 1914, but won two years later. He and his running mate, Paul Red Eagle, presided over a council that included two other full bloods and six mixed bloods, all of whom were biologically less than one-half Osage. This was the first time in tribal history that full bloods had failed to achieve a majority on the council. The tribe's population reflected an ever-growing mixed-blood numerical advantage. This trend, however, never translated into an absence of full bloods on the council. Many mixed bloods preferred full bloods like Fred Lookout—an individual whose physical appearance, dress, and speech suggested Indianness—to lead the council's deliberations.

In 1918 the Osages elected a new principal chief, and Lookout, although a member of the council for one term, from 1920 to 1922, was not chosen to be chief again until 1924. Subsequently he was reelected in 1926 and 1928, and beginning in 1930 he won five consecutive four-year terms. In all, he served a total of twenty-six years as principal chief. Considering the divisiveness and bitter rivalries that characterized Osage politics during this era, this was an astonishing achievement. Lookout's political longevity rested in his personal reputation and in his willingness to use whatever talents his tribe could muster to deal with a world of changing realities. He urged his bicultural mixed-blood kinsmen to act as cultural brokers while reassuring the full-blood minority of their continued value to the tribe. Lookout consistently and effectually safeguarded the rights and security of future generations of Osages. He died on August 28, 1949, at Pawhuska, Oklahoma.

See also Osage.

Wilson, Terry P., "Chief Fred Lookout and the Politics of Osage Oil, 1906–1949," *Journal of the West* 23 (July 1984): 46–53.

TERRY P. WILSON (Potawatomi)
University of California at Berkeley

LUISEÑO

The term *Luiseño,* as well as the related terms *Gabrielino* and *Juaneño,* are not indigenously derived; they are Spanish misnomers used to designate Takic-speaking peoples thought to have migrated into southern California from the Great Basin. Though no definite dating estimates exist concerning when these migrations occurred, some theorists believe the appearance of Takic speakers in the region may have begun seven to eight thousand years ago. Takic is a subfamily of Uto-Aztecan.

Ecologically diverse, the territory of the Luiseños lay mostly in northern San Diego and southern Riverside counties, where more than one thousand years ago Luiseño bands founded villages with strictly delineated land and resource holdings. Only with precise permission could one group enter into another group's domain to exploit specific properties such as gardens or oak groves. Properties could be plurally or privately owned. Thus the Luiseños were not a homogeneous population. Territorial, social, political, economic, and minor dialectic differences existed between villages, and between coastal and interior populations.

Life within the village was also marked by diversity and variation. Knowledge, privilege, and power were stringently controlled by the elite: the *noot* (hereditary chief), *paxa'* (ceremonial official), and *puupulam* (village council). While the *noot* possessed the village's most sacred knowledge and ritual paraphernalia, and was assisted by the *paxa'* in his administrative duties, the members of the *puupulam* acted as advisory specialists (each held an area of ecological or supernatural expertise). Though women were sometimes chiefs or healers, religious affairs were generally the jurisdiction of men who inherited their ranked positions, often performing unusual feats—

swallowing ceremonial swords, eating fire, or dancing on hot coals—as manifestations of 'ayelkwi (knowledge/power).

'Ayelkwi was provided by Wuyoot, a powerful chief among the Hamuuluwichum 'Ataaxum (First People). Before his death, Wuyoot gave each creation its distinctive "ayelkwi. Upon his death he also cast away the 'ayelkwi that anyone can seek to accrue. Song sets or series about Wuyoot's death, the human spirit, and the relation of life and death were sung inside the waamkish (fenced ceremonial enclosure), where important observances such as Chuchamish (burning the clothes of the dead) and Towchanish (constructing, exhibiting, and burning images of the dead) were conducted.

Another religion, received from the island Gabrielinos and coastal Juaneños, was called Changichngish. Emphasizing fortitude-building initiations of male youth into secret societies, Changichngish flourished at villages associated with Mission San Luis Rey, which was established in 1798. It was based on the teachings of Changichngish, who provided remedies for illnesses and diseases, as well as prescriptions for the conservation and management of Luiseño moral and religious life. At a time when they were dealing with the effects of the Spanish invasion—servitude and rape, disease-related deaths by the thousands, and militia-enforced cultural and religious impositions that resulted in significant disruptions of traditional ways—the Luiseños seem to have waged an urgent battle for cultural continuity by adhering to the precepts of Changichngish.

Though the Luiseños waged this battle successfully, the secularization of the California missions in 1833–34 did not bring a return of lands or freedom. Luiseño lands were granted to Mexicans who proceeded to maintain—not without numerous indigenous attacks against them—a system of servitude even crueler than that of the Spanish. Retreating to interior villages, surviving families regrouped into new organizations called parties, but the Anglo-American invasion, which began in the 1840s, further disrupted their lives. By 1875, most Luiseño villages and farm lands had been expropriated by whites. No redress was available to the Luiseños, who were prohibited from testifying in court or legitimately retaining land. Nevertheless, in 1875 Chief Olegario Sal, serving the Luiseños in opposition to government-appointed Manuelito Cota, met with President Ulysses S. Grant to discuss the region's conflicts. Later that year, Grant established reserves for

some Luiseño villages. When Olegario Sal died in 1877, however, Luiseño leadership returned to the village level.

Estimated to have originally numbered from five to seven thousand, the Luiseños today number three thousand and are chiefly enrolled at six independent reservations in San Diego and Riverside Counties. Circumstances associated with drought, insufficient irrigation, and World War II prompted many Luiseños to leave those communities, but in the 1970s reservation populations increased. Water use and rights, however, remained critical concerns. In 1989, a majority of Luiseño reservations were granted restitution by the U.S. Senate for previous water diversions. Though serious community health, education, and employment concerns also exist, the reservations have created financial opportunities through the sale and lease of lands and resources. They have also instituted gaming and commercial recreation projects. Currently thirty to forty people speak the native language; and a few younger Luiseños are creating cultural and language-learning resources. In addition, many maintain indigenous orientations regarding kinship, gender issues, leadership, knowledge, and traditional activities.

See also California Tribes; Missions and Missionaries; Water Rights.

Du Bois, Constance [Goddard], *The Religion of the Luiseño Indians of Southern California*, University of California Publications in American Archaeology and Ethnology, vol. 8, no. 3 (Berkeley, 1908); Kroeber, A. L., "Gabrielino," "Juaneño," and "Luiseño," in *Handbook of the Indians of California*, Bureau of American Ethnology Bulletin 78 (Washington, 1925); Strong, William Duncan, *Aboriginal Society in Southern California*, University of California Publications in American Archaeology and Ethnology, vol. 26, no. 1 (Berkeley, 1929).

LOUISE V. JEFFREDO-WARDEN (Payomkawish; Coastal/Island Gabrielino and Luiseño)
Stanford University

LUMBEE

Located along the Lumber River in southeastern North Carolina are the Lumbees, the largest Indian tribe east of the Mississippi and the largest non–federally recognized tribe in the United States. Numbering over 40,000 enrolled members, the Lumbees have continuously occupied what is presently Robeson and adjoining counties for over two centuries.

Recent archaeological studies suggest that Indians inhabited the area along the Lumber River (the Indian name for the river was Lumbee) as long as fourteen thousand years ago. Because of the lack of written evidence, however, the actual precontact history of the Lumbees is somewhat shrouded in mystery. For over a hundred years, historians and other scholars have been examining the question of Lumbee origin. Although there have been many explanations and conjectures, two theories persist. In 1885, Hamilton McMillan, a local historian and state legislator, proposed the "Lost Colony" theory. Based upon oral tradition among the Lumbees and what he deemed as strong circumstantial evidence, McMillan posited a connection between the Lumbees and the early English colonists who settled on Roanoke Island in 1587 and the Algonquian tribes who inhabited coastal North Carolina at the same time. According to historical accounts, the colonists mysteriously disappeared soon after they settled, leaving little evidence of their destination or fate. McMillan's hypothesis, which was also supported by the historian Stephen Weeks, contends that the colonists migrated with the Indians toward the interior of North Carolina, and by 1650 had settled along the banks of the Lumber. It is suggested the present-day Lumbees are the descendants of these two groups.

Lumbee girls on the basketball team at the Indian Normal School in 1928.

Other scholars believe the Lumbees to be descended from an eastern Siouan group called the Cheraws. During the seventeenth and eighteenth centuries a number of Siouan-speaking tribes occupied southeastern North Carolina. John R. Swanton, a pioneering ethnologist at the Smithsonian Institution, wrote in 1938 that the Lumbees were probably of Cheraw descent but were also genealogically influenced by other Siouan tribes in the area. Contemporary historians such as James Merrell and William Sturtevant confirm this theory by suggesting that the Cheraws, along with survivors of other tribes whose populations had been devastated by warfare and disease, found refuge from both aggressive settlers and hostile tribes in the Robeson County swamps in eastern North Carolina.

There are other theories as well, one suggesting that the Lumbees are an amalgamation of both Siouan and Algonquian tribes. Yet despite the lack of a definitive explanation of their historical tribal ancestry, the Lumbees have always affirmed both their Indian and tribal identities.

Sustained contact with Europeans did not occur for the Lumbees until the late 1700s with the settlement of Scottish Highlanders in the area. Prior to this intrusion, the Lumbees had been self-sufficient, living a life of apparent deliberate isolation in the swamps and bottomlands of the Lumber River. Despite this solitude, it was evident that the Lumbees had been significantly influenced by Europeans. By the early eighteenth century the Lumbees, having lost their native language, were speaking an idiomatic form of Elizabethan English and had adopted much of an English lifestyle. Yet the land the Lumbees occupied was held in common. It was not until white settlement that the Lumbees realized that if they wanted to hold on to their land they would have to have legal documentation supporting their claims. As a result of this new knowledge, individual Lumbees arranged to receive land grants from King George II of England. This willingness to accept the idea of private ownership of land and the Lumbees' adoption of many European habits temporarily allowed for a degree of peaceful relations between the tribe and its new neighbors. However, as the settlers' demand for land increased, tensions between the Lumbees and their white neighbors began to mount.

By the turn of the nineteenth century, the Lumbees saw their status as free persons, as well as their rights of citizenship, begin to erode. Under the 1835 revised North Carolina Constitution, all nonwhites lost their right to vote and to bear arms. Initially, the Lumbees did not see themselves as affected by the new system, but they soon realized that their "nonwhiteness" cast them into a position of second-class citizens and their Indianness offered no protection under this new designation.

The degradation experienced by the Lumbees intensified with the onset of the Civil War. Because of their altered legal status, Lumbee men were not allowed to fight for the South, yet some were conscripted by the Confederacy and shipped to Fort Fisher on the North Carolina coast to construct defense fortifications and make salt. Conditions at Fort Fisher were extremely harsh. Starvation, disease, and unsanitary working conditions forced the Lumbees either to escape their bondage or to simply refuse to go. Many hid in the familiar terrain of the swamps and bottomlands to evade the local militia. It was not long, however, before the continued denial of basic liberties combined with increasing racial tensions within Robeson County created a volatile climate for the Lumbees that was destined to explode. This growing conflict between Indians and whites finally erupted in 1865 in what became known as the Lowrie War, one of the most violent times in Lumbee history.

There were many events leading to the Lowrie War. The most immediate cause, however, was the murder of a prominent Lumbee farmer, Allen Lowrie, and his son William. Accused of aiding Union soldiers, hiding weapons, stealing property from local plantation owners, and avoiding conscription, Allen, William, and other family members were arrested on March 3, 1865, by the local militia and carried off to a nearby field. Subjected to an extralegal trial by the home guard, Allen and William Lowrie were found guilty and summarily executed.

According to Lumbee history, the youngest Lowrie son, Henry Berry, was hiding close by in the gallberry bushes, where he witnessed the murder of his father and brother. The image of his slain family became forever seared in his mind and quickly transformed Henry's well-known hatred for the home guard into a desperate need for vengeance. Vowing to kill all who had anything to do with the murder of the two Lowries, Henry, at the age of seventeen, with his band of militants, began a lengthy war against the injustices suffered by the Lumbees. His exploits became legendary. No jail was able to hold him; the swamps shielded him from capture. He was a superb marksman who singlehandedly held eighteen militiamen at bay while shooting from behind an overturned boat in the middle of the Lumber River. Stealing from the rich while sharing with the poor, the nineteenth-century Indian Robin Hood ensured himself protection by the surrounding community.

Despite his apparent elusiveness, however, Henry Berry Lowrie disappeared in 1872 following a final raid on Lumberton, the county seat. To this day, there is no conclusive explanation of what happened. The twelve-thousand-dollar bounty for his capture offered by the state legislature was never collected. The burial site of his purportedly slain body was never found. If the surviving members of his family and band knew of his fate, they never revealed it. Yet to the Lumbees, the mystery of Henry Berry Lowrie only enhances the legend. In every Lumbee family there is an account of the "real story" of Henry Berry and the Lowrie War. And over a century later, the impact of the Lowrie War is still being felt. The indomitable spirit of Henry Berry and the Lowrie gang has become for the Lumbees a symbol of their long, continuous struggle against discrimination and injustice.

Following the Lowrie resistance, reform legislation for the Lumbees began to win support in the North Carolina General Assembly. In 1885 and 1887, under the leadership of state legislator Hamilton McMillan and a local Indian minister, W. L. Moore, the assembly enacted laws acknowledging the Lumbees as an Indian tribe—the Croatans—and establishing a separate school system for them. (Since 1885 the Lumbees have been known under several names. In 1911 their name was changed from Croatan to Indians of Robeson County, and in 1913 to Cherokee Indians of Robeson County. Finally, in 1953, at the request of the tribe, they were officially recognized as Lumbee.) The 1887 legislation created the Croatan Normal School under the direction of an all-Indian school board, with the objective of training local Indians to teach their own children in their own schools. Initially, both the Lumbees and state officials were skeptical about the school's potential for success. Still, realizing the dire need for some type of formal education for the Lumbees, tribal leaders persisted in their efforts to support the Indian schools. The creation of the Indian school system resulted in a unique triracial arrangement for the area. Until the *Brown* decision in 1954, which ended school segregation, the state of North Carolina supported three legally separate school systems in Robeson County—one for whites, one for blacks, and one for Indians.

Although the Lumbees bitterly acknowledged that their schools were the product of a closed, discriminatory society, they also realized the cultural and educational benefits of the Indian school system. Over the years, the schools produced a large number of Lumbee teachers and thereby gave the Lumbees significant control over the education of their children. Additionally, because the Indian schools were organized around individual Lumbee communities and the Lumbees were therefore forced to stay within their own social and cultural boundaries, community and tribal identities were strengthened.

To the Lumbees, however, one of their most important accomplishments is not just the founding of the Croatan Normal School but its eventual evolution into Pembroke State University, one of the sixteen constituent campuses of the University of North Carolina. Although the student body is now multicultural, from 1940 to 1953 Pembroke State University (then Pembroke State College for Indians) was the only state-supported four-year college for Indians in the United States.

In 1885, when the Lumbees were recognized by the state as a tribal entity, they began a century-long process to extend state recognition into federal recognition, and thereby establish a government-to-government relationship between their tribe and the federal government. During the 1930s their goal almost became a reality when a group of Lumbee leaders attempted to get the Lumbees organized and consequently recognized under the 1934 Indian Reorganization Act. The recognition plan, developed in conjunction with Bureau of Indian Affairs officials, actually received support from the Commissioner of Indian Affairs. However, because of BIA budget restraints, adverse departmental policies, and factionalism within the Indian community, the plan was never implemented, and attempts at federal recognition by the Lumbees failed.

Even though the Lumbees were unsuccessful in this struggle, they did not disappear from sight. In 1958, the Lumbees saw themselves thrust into the public spotlight in an armed confrontation with the Ku Klux Klan. On the cold winter night of January 18, 1958, the Lumbees came head-to-head with white supremacists. Both oral and written accounts indicate that, a week prior to the conflict, the Klan had burned crosses in the yards of two Indian families in an attempt to put an end to "race-mixing." Adding insult to injury, the Klan also had planned a rally in a field a few miles from Pembroke, the center of the Lumbee community. After years of suffering the indignities of prejudice and racism, the Lumbees were quick to take action. Hundreds of armed Lumbees charged the rally that night, shot out the lights, and sent the Klan scrambling. The incident, which received national and international news coverage, brought responses from many tribal groups offering to assist the Lumbees with their fight. The rout of the Klan that January night strengthened the Lumbees' determination to protect and preserve their rights as a people and as a tribe.

Since the turn of the century, the Lumbees have become increasingly involved in national, state, and local political activities. Determined to control their own tribal identity, they successfully lobbied for state recognition as the Lumbee tribe in 1953 and received limited federal recognition as an Indian tribe in 1956. Since the 1970s, however, their political focus has been on gaining full federal recognition, thereby acquiring status comparable to that of other federally recognized tribes in the country. A petition for acknowledgment, substantiated by ten years of research, was submitted by the Lumbees to the Department of the Interior in 1987. In 1989, the Interior Department advised the Lumbees that it was unable to process the tribe's petition in light of the restrictive language of the 1956 act. Additionally, the Lumbees have been active in trying to obtain full federal recognition through an act of Congress. No matter what the outcome of these efforts may be, however, the Lumbees are determined to maintain their cultural and tribal identity. For it is this legacy that they say they will continue to pass on to their children to ensure the survival of their people for generations to come.

Dial, Adolph L., *The Lumbee* (New York: Chelsea House, 1993); Evans, W. McKee, *To Die Game: The Story of the Lowry Band, Indian Guerillas of Reconstruction* (Baton Rouge: Louisiana State University Press, 1971); Sider, Gerald M., *Lumbee Indian Histories* (Cambridge: Cambridge University Press, 1993).

ADOLPH L. DIAL (Lumbee)
Pembroke State University

LINDA E. OXENDINE (Lumbee)
Pembroke State University

MAGAZINES
See Newspapers, Magazines, and Journals.

MANDAN

According to oral tradition, the Mandan people originated from the earth as corn itself springs from the ground. This emergence metaphor is deeply rooted in Mandan cosmology and the ceremonial practices that shape Mandan social life. Corn has been the mainstay of Mandan agriculture for thousands of years and remains a vital symbol for creation, renewal, and survival. As the keeper of seed, the Old Woman Who Never Dies recurs in the cycle of ceremonies that mark seasonal shifts in agricultural preparations, harvest, and hunting. The complex of stories and rites related to this cosmological figure directs Mandan ritual cycles by prescribing the appropriate action of cultural members. The relationship of "mother corn" to tribal sovereignty arises in contemporary land-claims cases, where knowledge about associated garden rites continues to be invoked as a means of staking legitimate claims to cultural identity. The sacred shrine of Lone Man, Creator of the Earth, stands today at the Fort Berthold Reservation as a symbolic testament to the central role Mandan religious beliefs and practices play in the cultural survival of the people.

Prior to the U.S. government's suppression of native religious practices, the apogee of Mandan ritual enactment was the Okipa Ceremony, a complex of rites linking all of creation to seasonal conditions. As part of the earth-renewal rites, the Okipa emphasized the renewal of game in the Bull Dance ceremonies, visually depicted by the nineteenth-century painters George Catlin and Karl Bodmer. The anthropologist Alfred Bowers (1950) reported that the Okipa ceremonial complex had developed along the Heart River in present-day North Dakota among all the Mandan villages by the 1700s. According to Mandan oral history, Lone Man established the ceremonial structure of the Okipa Lodge, which mirrored Mandan moiety and clan organization. In the 1980s the Okipa Ceremony underwent a revitalization, which brought with it a renewal of Mandan cultural values.

The Mandans established settlements on the Heart River in the 1600s. The villages they established there comprised mostly circular, four-post earth lodges arranged around a central ceremonial plaza. They situated the villages within naturally defensive features such as ravines or riverbanks, or built walls and ditches around them. These sites abounded with gardens of corn, squash, and beans that were controlled by women.

Before long Mandans encountered Hidatsas who had recently migrated into the area. While the Mandans had already established marriage and trade relations with the Hidatsas by the late 1700s, their reduced numbers as a result of the 1782 and 1837 smallpox epidemics forced a cultural merger with their Hidatsa neighbors that remains to this day. Thus there are many similarities between Mandan and Hidatsa social and ceremonial organization. The largest remaining Mandan linguistic groups were the Nuptadi and Nuitadi, each comprised of smaller subgroups.

Following the devastating effects of the 1837 smallpox epidemic, the thirteen clans of the Mandans were drastically reduced to two major divisions. The two extant clan divisions are the same for Mandans and Hidatsas and are generally agreed on as the Three Clan and the Four Clan. While Mandan-Hidatsa assimilation allows us to treat the two divisions as a single system, elder tribal members still distinguish between being a *chik'sa* (Hidatsa) and a *si'pucka nu'mak* (Mandan).

Contemporary Mandans follow matrilineal prescriptions for reckoning kinship by ascribing clan affiliation through the mother's side. They also follow Hidatsa rites whereby the father's clan assumes funerary responsibilities for the deceased. Language, however, remains a key feature that distinguishes Mandan from Hidatsa identity orientation. While today there are fewer than ten fluent Mandan speakers at Fort Bert-hold, one's knowledge of the Mandan language and one's genealogical links to Mandan speakers inform a range of kinship and ceremonial behavior within the cultural system that remains uniquely "Mandan." Today, the Mandan language is actively taught by elders in community-based programs, as well as in the public school at Twin Buttes, North Dakota, in the southernmost segment of the reservation.

While many Mandans have married members of other tribes and non-Indians, Twin Buttes remains the heart of the Mandan community. There many families maintain their ancestral homelands and family burial sites. Current archaeological investigations on Mandan land require compliance with tribal codes and permissions for historical inquiries into the past. The Mandan village site at Slant Village, however, is part of the North Dakota State Parks system and is open as a public site where visitors can learn about the cultural history of earth-lodge villages. Clan origin stories, such as that of the origin of the Water Buster clan, situate the Mandans at the Slant Village site.

The Water Buster clan came into the public light in 1934 when Mandan representatives went to New York City to retrieve the sacred Water Buster bundle from the Heye Foundation's Museum of the American Indian (now the Smithsonian Institution's National Museum of the American Indian). As they do in Hidatsa and Arikara societies, tribal bundles figure highly in Mandan social organization, and thus affect the efficacy of ritual performance and ceremonialism. Museum holdings of collectively controlled tribal objects were generally acquired under conditions of economic and emotional duress. Thus the Mandans' successful reclaiming of their tribal bundle almost sixty years prior to the 1990 Native American Graves Protection and Repatriation Act was a remarkable victory. The success of Mandan people in surviving the demographic decimation of their tribe and the impact of white settlement attests to their cultural tenacity and innovation.

See also Arikara (Sahnish); Hidatsa.

Bowers, Alfred W., *Mandan Social and Ceremonial Organization* (1950; reprint, Moscow, Idaho: University of Idaho Press, 1991); Catlin, George, *O-kee-pa: A Religious Ceremony and Other Customs of the Mandans* (New Haven: Yale University Press, 1967); Lowie, Robert H., *Notes on the Social Organization and Customs of the Mandan, Hidatsa and Crow Indians,* Anthropological Papers of the American Museum of Natural History, vol. 21, part 1 (New York, 1917).

TRESSA L. BERMAN
Arizona State University West

MANGAS COLORADAS

1793?–1863
Apache chief.

Mangas Coloradas (Red Sleeves) was born into a society that subsisted by hunting and gathering, as well as raiding. The Apaches were divided into several tribes, one of them being the Chiricahuas, to which Mangas belonged. That tribe, in turn, was subdivided into bands, Mangas being a member of the Eastern Chiricahuas, whose homeland stretched west from the Rio Grande to include most of what is present-day southwestern New Mexico.

We know virtually nothing about his early years, and his later career is the subject of much conjecture. It is generally agreed, however, that he was a powerfully built man, over six feet in height, who was courageous, wise, and generous. Mangas and his wife, Tu-es-seh, had a large family. One of their daughters married Cochise of the Central Chiricahuas, a chief in his own right by the 1850s and an ally of Mangas in some of his operations against Mexican and Anglo-American settlers. For generations before the United States claimed sovereignty over most of the Chiricahua homeland, these Indians alternately terrorized and traded with the settlements of the Mexican states of Chihuahua and Sonora. In the 1840s the official correspondence and the newspapers of these states were already identifying Mangas as a leading Chiricahua chief.

In 1846, the first year of the Mexican War, Mangas and other Apaches conferred with General Stephen Watts Kearney. Mangas offered to support the American campaign against the Mexicans, but Kearney declined the offer. At Las Vegas, New Mexico, Kearney had already committed the United States to a policy of confrontation by pledging that the U.S. government would assume responsibility for defending New Mexicans against the Apaches. Nevertheless, until the growth of the Anglo-American population in the area constituted a real threat, the Chiricahuas chose to view the settlers as their nominal allies against the Mexicans and to continue raiding widely in Sonora and Chihuahua.

Nevertheless, American horses and cattle proved to be an irresistible temptation to a raiding people such as the Chiricahuas. Mining settlements, outlying ranches, travelers through the area, and stagecoach stations reported increasing losses, and a Chiricahua agent was appointed in 1851. Mangas then manifested some willingness to persuade the Chiricahuas to take up farming, but he insisted that he would not give up raiding in Mexico.

The 1853 Gadsden Purchase transferred to the United States Mexico's claim to lands south of the Gila River, and miners and ranchers were attracted to the region. Mangas and his fellow Apaches, whose own claims the purchase had not extinguished, found themselves desperately trying to prevent ruthless Americans from overrunning their homeland. For attempting to divert miners from their operations in his band's territory, a group of Americans badly beat Mangas, an insult no Apache could forgive or forget.

Sometime between 1858 and 1860 Mangas concluded that resistance was the only response possible to American expansion. His efforts to improve relations with the Mexican authorities, so as to enable the Apaches to concentrate their efforts on resisting the Americans, came to naught. Mexican troops killed two of Mangas's sons as well as other Chiricahuas, and these deaths had to be avenged. Mangas and Cochise were active throughout northern Sonora and Chihuahua in 1858 and 1859, sometimes driving large herds of stock into the United States to be sold to American citizens.

But Apache thefts of American stock also continued to mount, and some of these animals were driven into Mexico to be sold. By 1860 a full-blown war was under way between the Chiricahuas and the United States, with Mangas playing a major role. The Apaches attempted to shut off all traffic through their territory, ambushing small parties and wagon trains and attacking stagecoach stations. Mangas even led a war party into the streets of Los Pinos, a mining camp in the heart of the Eastern Chiricahua homeland, but was driven out after a hard fight.

The outbreak of the Civil War made little difference to the Apaches, and they attacked, and were attacked by, both Confederate and Union troops. The Chiricahuas made movement of all but large forces through their territory very hazardous. In a major engagement in July 1862 resulting from the Chiricahuas' effort to block Apache Pass, Union forces ultimately fought their way through, but with substantial losses. Mangas was severely wounded in the fighting and was taken to a presidio in Chihuahua, where he received medical attention. The chief, however, who was now about seventy, never completely recovered.

His weakened state may have contributed to his willingness to negotiate with the Americans in January 1863. At the time, General James H. Carleton, commanding the forces charged with pacifying the Apaches, had demanded the tribe's unconditional surrender, ruling out any negotiation with Mangas. "I have no

faith in him," the general had declared. This statement had encouraged a military subordinate to track down the old chief and use a flag of truce as a ruse to capture him. Uncharacteristically, Mangas did not resist. He died sometime during the next forty-eight hours, under suspicious circumstances. The official report was that he was shot while attempting to escape, but according to an eyewitness account he had been forced to resist by means of torture with heated bayonets.

John C. Cremony, who personally knew Mangas and is the most frequently cited biographical authority, denounced the chief for exhibiting "the ferocity and brutality of the most savage savage." Nevertheless, he also described Mangas as "the greatest and most talented Apache Indian of the nineteenth century." By the very nature of Apache society, Mangas could not command even the members of his own band. Nevertheless, his reputation for bravery and sagacity enabled him to recruit large war parties, which he led effectively against both Mexicans and Americans.

See also Apache, Eastern; Cochise.

Cremony, John C., *Life among the Apaches* (Tucson: Arizona Silhouettes, 1954); Opler, Morris E., "Chiricahua Apache," in *Handbook of North American Indians*, ed. William C. Sturtevant, vol. 10, Southwest, ed. Alfonso Ortiz (Washington: Smithsonian Institution, 1983); Sweeney, Edwin R., *Cochise, Chiricahua Apache Chief* (Norman: University of Oklahoma Press, 1991).

WILLIAM T. HAGAN
University of Oklahoma

MANUELITO

(1818–93)
Navajo war and political leader.

Manuelito (Hastiin Ch'ilhaajinii) was born near Bear's Ears, Utah, into the Bit'ahni (Folded Arms People) clan of his mother and was the son of Cayetano, a prominent Navajo leader. At an early age, he distinguished himself in an ambush against Pueblo enemies and earned the war name Hashkeh Naabaah, or Angry Warrior. Other names he would be later known by were Son-in-Law of Late Texan, and Bullet Hole (for a wound in his chest).

At the age of sixteen Manuelito married the daughter of Narbona, a prominent Navajo peace leader, and relocated to his wife's camp, following Navajo tradition. In his early twenties, Manuelito became a recognized *naat'aanii* or headman, accompanying Narbona to

Manuelito and his Mexican wife, Juanita.

In 1851, Fort Defiance was established in Navajo country to guard against slave-raiding parties. When Zarcillos Largos, the appointed spokesman for the Navajos, resigned in 1855 because of increasing old age, Governor David Meriwether appointed Manuelito "official chief" and passed on to him the symbolic peace medal and cane. This would not be the only time Manuelito was selected by American government officials to lead his people.

Ironically, during this same period, Manuelito had gained tribal stature by his resistance to the Americans. Over six feet tall, with broad shoulders and a mercurial personality, Manuelito had a reputation as a clever and aggressive warrior that increased his family's herds of cattle and sheep and earned him widespread respect among his people.

Initially the Navajos tried to overlook the establishment of Fort Defiance. But eventually the tense relations between the post commander, Major William T. H. Brooks, and Manuelito made it impossible. In 1860, responding to skirmishes over grazing areas and an 1858 punitive campaign against his tribesmen, Manuelito attacked Fort Defiance directly. Nearly one thousand Navajos led by Manuelito and the Navajo medicine man and peace leader Barboncito almost succeeded in capturing the fort. Soon afterward, the army surprisingly abandoned Fort Defiance and its troops were sent east to participate in the Civil War.

In 1863, General James Carleton arrived in the Southwest from California with orders to subjugate the Indians and open an overland mail route. Determined to relocate the Navajos to Bosque Redondo, a small reservation on the plains of eastern New Mexico, Carleton appointed Kit Carson to pursue all who resisted. Under a "scorched earth" policy, fields, water holes, and animals were destroyed, hogans were burned down, and several thousand Navajos were forcibly captured and marched over three hundred miles. Eventually, eighty-five hundred Navajos would make this "Long Walk," the majority of them surrendering during the first harsh winter with no food and supplies. However, some one thousand Navajos escaped the ordeal, hiding in the Navajo Mountains, fleeing across the San Juan River to the north, or taking refuge to the south in Chiricahua Apache territory.

Manuelito was the most successful holdout against Carson and Carleton. A clever warrior who began stashing small supplies of dried corn along his routes, he would stealthily return to these caches to replenish his food supplies; sometimes he would retreat altogeth-

peace talks in Santa Fe with the governor of New Mexico. Adamantly opposed to peace, however, he soon left Narbona's side to lead many raids and retaliations against the Mexicans and Pueblos.

In 1846, American troops entered the Southwest under General Stephen Watts Kearney. Manuelito, along with thirteen other leaders, most of them much older than he, signed the Treaty of Ojo del Oso (Bear Springs), which called for lasting peace between the Navajos and the Americans and the mutual restoration of all prisoners. This would be the first of seven treaties between the United States and the Navajo tribe.

Despite their efforts, U.S. troops were unable to curtail Mexican slave raids against the Navajos, and Manuelito returned to protecting himself and his people. In 1849, his distrust of Americans grew into fierce animosity when his father-in-law, Narbona, was killed by soldiers accompanying Colonel John M. Washington during peace negotiations in the Tunicha Mountains.

er with his band to diverse places like the Grand Canyon and the Zuni Mountains. Constantly on the move, Manuelito's band was attacked not only by the Americans but by Utes, Hopis, and New Mexican raiding parties. Manuelito was able to elude capture for three bad winters and became a symbol of resistance for his imprisoned kinsmen.

After repeated attacks by his foes, and suffering wounds in his forearm and left side, Manuelito and twenty-three of his loyal supporters finally surrendered on September 1, 1866. On his way to Fort Sumner, Manuelito was marched under guard through the streets of Santa Fe because Carleton wanted the public to witness the subjugation of this most militant of Navajo leaders.

On June 1, 1868, the last treaty between the United States and the Navajos was signed by twenty-five headmen, including Manuelito. The treaty allowed the Navajos to return to their homeland instead of being relocated to Oklahoma Territory. General William Tecumseh Sherman appointed Barboncito head chief; Manuelito was appointed the subchief of the eastern Navajos, and the Navajo leader Ganado Mucho the subchief of the western Navajos.

After their long-awaited release, Manuelito took the remaining members of his family, including his Mexican wife, Juanita, his son, Manuelito Segundo, and a nephew, back to his home near present-day Tohatchi, New Mexico. In 1871, Barboncito died and the subchiefs took charge of leading the entire tribe. Manuelito still resented the Americans. Yet he accommodated himself to the demands of Western civilization. For example, after the railroad was established in 1881, Manuelito used his government-issued wagon to deliver goods made by Navajo weavers, blacksmiths, and silversmiths for shipment to eastern markets.

In August 1872, General Oliver Otis Howard organized a force of 130 men called the Navajo Calvary to stop Navajo livestock raiding. He selected Manuelito to head this police force. Two years later, Manuelito was also selected as a member of the Navajo delegation sent to Washington, D.C., to negotiate an expansion of the reservation boundaries beyond those recognized in the 1868 treaty.

Manuelito was also deeply interested in Anglo-American education. Convinced that schooling could be the ladder by which the Navajos would regain their pride and independence, Manuelito in 1880 became the first Navajo to agree to send children under his care—two sons and a nephew—to an Indian boarding school: Carlisle Indian Industrial School. Tragically, his son Manuelito Chow died of tuberculosis while at Carlisle, and Manuelito demanded that all Navajo boys at the school be brought home immediately. Unfortunately, his decision came too late to save his other son, Manuelito Chiquito, and his nephew, both of whom died at Carlisle before they could be returned.

Despondent over the deaths of his two sons and nephew, Manuelito spent the last ten years of his life seeking comfort in alcohol. In 1893, Manuelito contracted measles and tried to treat himself with a combination of traditional Navajo sweat baths and generous doses of whiskey. He caught pneumonia shortly afterward and died.

Hoffman, Virginia, *Navajo Biographies*, vol. 1 (Rough Rock, Ariz.: Navajo Curriculum Center Press, 1974).

BRENDA K. MANUELITO (Navajo)
University of New Mexico

MARTÍNEZ, MARÍA

(1887–1980)
Pueblo potter.

María Montoya Martínez was born to Tomás and Reyes Montoya of San Ildefonso Pueblo just a few years after the Southern Pacific Railroad opened its line through New Mexico and Arizona. As a child, María learn to make pottery from her mother's sister, Tía Nicolasa. As a young teen she attended St. Catherine's Indian School in Santa Fe, New Mexico, for two years, and then rejoined her family. Returning to her pueblo, located north of Santa Fe near the Jemez Mountains, María married a fellow San Ildefonso resident, Julian Martínez. Only hours after their wedding, the young couple left on a northbound train to dance at the 1904 St. Louis World's Fair. The St. Louis fair marked María's public debut as a potter. During her stay there she used her breaks between dance performances to demonstrate her pottery-making skills for curious fairgoers. Then and throughout her career María specialized in crafting various-sized coil-built bowls and water jars (ollas). As she became a world-renowned potter, María enlarged worldwide interest in Native American ceramics.

Although María and Julian Martínez are often credited with discovering the firing process associated with San Ildefonso's shiny black pottery, recent research indicates the existence of black earthenware at the pueblo during the late nineteenth century. But if María and Julian did not pioneer a new firing technique, they did perfect the skill of creating burnished black pottery with matte black designs and marketing it to non-Indians.

María created her highly prized black pots by using the bottom of an old plate or pot (*puki*) rather than a potter's wheel. Beginning by patting a tortilla-shaped piece of clay into the *puki*, María then rolled a lump of clay between her palms, creating a long clay rope of uniform thickness. Pinching and pressing this coil of clay onto a clay tortilla while turning the *puki* with her other hand, María formed the base of the olla. Successive layers of coils were similarly added until the vessel was completed. Next, using a rounded piece of gourd, María scraped, smoothed, and shaped the inside and outside of the pot. After the vessel was completely dry, she polished the outer surface with special smooth stones. Since no glaze was used, careful polishing was necessary to produce María's trademark glossy finish. Finally, she applied a thin coat of slip, a mixture of ground clay and water, to the olla. After repeating the polishing process, the piece was ready to be decorated.

Using a solution of ground clay and *guaco*, a syrupy mixture of boiled wild spinach plants, her husband Julian (and later their son, Popovi Da) decorated most of María's ollas with two designs, the "avanyu" (a mythical dragon) and the feather pattern. Once decorated, the vessels were ready for firing. These designs were later given a matte finish during a special firing process. Fueled with cattle dung, the fire was allowed to burn until the dung turned to smoldering coals. Julian and María then smothered the fire with pulverized sheep or horse dung, trapping the oxygen and turning the pottery the translucent "black on black" associated with San Ildefonso.

A pivotal point in María's career came when in 1908 she met Dr. Edgar L. Hewett, an anthropologist from the School of American Research in Santa Fe. Hewett hired a crew of men, including Julian Martínez, to help excavate the ancient Anasazi ruins on Pajarito Plateau and in Frijoles Canyon. When María, who was working as a cook at the dig site, showed an interest in the pottery shards recovered from the diggings, Hewett asked her to create reproductions of the excavated pieces. He bought the pots she and Julian made and encouraged them to continue experimenting with varying pottery-making techniques. Through this patronage and friendship María became a link between Native

American potters and non-Indians. As Hewett began promoting events to showcase contemporary Indian artists and craftspeople, her circle of admirers grew. For instance, in 1915 Hewett arranged for María and Julian to give pottery-making demonstrations at the Panama-California Exposition in San Diego.

Concurrently, María also benefited from the nation's rapidly expanding railroad systems and the increasing availability of automobiles. These transportation innovations enabled people from all over the nation to travel to the Southwest. Tourists fascinated with Indians and influenced by the aura surrounding the Taos–Santa Fe school of painters and sculptors flocked to the area. Beginning in 1921 Erna Fergusson's Koshare Tours and later Fred Harvey's Indian Detours brought scores of visitors to San Ildefonso to watch María make her unique black pottery. Many travelers returned home with an olla or bowl that María had crafted, a souvenir of their new interest in Indian ceramics. Among these buyers was John D. Rockefeller, Jr., who purchased several pieces for his famed art collection.

As María's reputation grew, she became the recipient of dozens of awards. She received a bronze medal from the Ford Foundation during the 1934 Chicago World's Fair, and the University of Colorado at Boulder honored her in 1953 with a bronze medal for achievement in the arts. Other awards included the Minnesota Museum of Art's Symbol of Man Award in 1969, the New Mexico Arts Commission's First Annual Governor's Award in 1974, and three honorary doctorates.

María's fame also spread to Europe and the Far East. For example, when the Japanese potter Shoji Hamada and the potter Bernard Leach of Hong Kong came to Santa Fe for the opening of the Museum of International Folk Art in 1952, they insisted on traveling to San Ildefonso to meet María and observe the oxidizing firing process she employed to create her black pottery. An instant friendship developed between the three masters of clay, a mutual interest in pottery overcoming all cultural barriers. In Europe, news of María's contribution to Native American ceramics prompted the French government to award her the 1954 Palme Académique. N. O. Christensen, the governor of Greenland, and Dr. Horst Hartmann, the curator of Berlin's Museum für Völkerkunde, also paid homage to María by visiting her pueblo in 1965.

María's influence on Native American pottery extended well beyond her own productions. Four generations of her descendants have practiced the craft. After Julian Martínez's death in 1943, their son, Popovi Da, began to decorate María's vessels; he also revived and experimented with polychrome designs. Next, Popovi's son, Tony Da, explored nontraditional shapes such as bear fetishes and turtles. Then María's great-granddaughter, Barbara Gonzales, began to specialize in vessels inlaid with turquoise or coral and decorated with etched spider motifs. Finally, Gonzales's sons, Cavan, Aaron, Brandan, and Derek, continue the family tradition by crafting small animal shapes and miniature bowls.

María's unparalleled acclaim as a potter, her key role in acquainting non-Indians the world over with Pueblo ceramics, and her legacy as the matriarch of San Ildefonso's pottery makers indicate her broad and enduring influence on Native American art in the twentieth century.

See also Art, Visual (to 1960).

Marriott, Alice, *María: The Potter of San Ildefonso* (Norman: University of Oklahoma Press, 1948); Peterson, Susan, *The Living Tradition of María Martínez* (New York: Kodansha International, 1989); Spivey, Richard L., *María*, rev. and exp. ed. (Flagstaff, Ariz.: Northland Publishing, 1989).

N. JILL HOWARD
Taylor University/University of New Mexico

MASCOTS AND OTHER PUBLIC APPROPRIATIONS OF INDIANS AND INDIAN CULTURE BY WHITES

When the Florida State Seminoles football team rushes onto the field, it follows the university's mascot—a stereotyped Indian warrior with colored turkey feathers and a flaming spear, which is planted in the end zone with a whoop. Florida State's fans, many in Indian costume themselves, then proceed to chant a faux-Indian melody, swinging their arms in a synchronized "tomahawk chop." The Florida State experience is a common one. "Indians"—in a variety of flavors ranging from warriors, red men, braves, and chiefs to "Fighting Sioux" and "Apaches" have been the most consistently popular mascot in American athletic history.

The University of Wisconsin at Lacrosse first named its teams Indians in 1909. In 1912, the Boston Braves baseball team followed suit, and three years later, Cleveland's baseball club also became the Indians. During the 1920s, many college and professional teams—including teams at Stanford, Dartmouth, and the University of Illinois, as well as the Chicago Black Hawks

hockey club—adopted Indian names. The practice filtered down to thousands of high schools and junior high schools seeking institutional identities. Today, professional sports boasts five major clubs that use "the Indian" as a name and mascot. In addition to Chicago and Cleveland, Atlanta has the Braves, Kansas City has the Chiefs, and Washington, D.C., has the Redskins. While some colleges and universities—including Stanford and Dartmouth—have dropped their Indian logos and mascots, many more continue to insist that their use of Indian stereotypes is harmless fun.

Americans' embrace of Indian mascots was only part of a broad, early-twentieth-century primitivist nostalgia that stamped Indian imagery on a nickel, positioned baskets and pottery in the "Indian corners" of arts-and-crafts revival homes, and permeated the rituals of Boy Scouts and Campfire Girls. At the turn of the century, many Americans perceived that the story they had been telling themselves about their origins and character—one of frontier struggle between bold adventurers and savage Indians—had lost much of its cultural power as historians and critics declared the frontier "closed." On the contemporary side of this closed frontier, Americans saw the modern world—a place of cities, immigrants, technology, lost innocence, and limited opportunity. Many Americans used a ritualized set of symbols—cowboys, Indians, scouts, and pioneers—to evoke the bygone "American" qualities of the frontier era: "authenticity," nature, community, and frontier hardiness. Through summer camp and wilderness outings in "nature," touristic contact with the "authenticity" of Indian primitivism in the southwestern deserts, and an in-

The twelve-year-old Ojibwa Patrick Battees and other protesters at the 1992 Super Bowl in Minneapolis.

creased emphasis on rugged, character-building athletic competition, they sought to reimagine "modern" compensatory experiences that might take the place of the now-lost "frontier struggle."

Bringing Indians—potent symbols both of a nostalgic, innocent past and of the frontier struggle itself—into the athletic stadium helped evoke the mythic narrative being metaphorically replayed on the field. It was no accident that many other mascots—mustangs, pioneers, and so on—were also prominent characters in the athletic rendering of the national story. Indian chiefs and braves represented the aggressiveness and fighting spirit that was supposed to characterize good athletic teams. This racial stereotyping justified an American history in which peaceable cowboys and settlers simply defended themselves against innately aggressive Indians in a defensive conquest of the continent. As mascots celebrated "Indian" ferocity and martial (read also athletic) skill, they were at the same time trophies of Euro-American colonial superiority: "Indians were tough opponents, but 'we' prevailed. Now we 'honor' them (and in doing so, celebrate ourselves)."

The performative aspects of mascot ritual bring this American narrative to life, and demonstrate to participants that their myths, enacted both on the athletic field and in the stands, remain valid. The virulent response to Indian protests against Indian mascots demonstrates the deep emotional investment many Americans have made both in their imagining of Indian people as ahistorical symbols and in their sports affiliations. In mass society, athletic spectacles have become a deeply ingrained tradition to which many Americans turn for personal and social identities. The Florida State Seminole, then, signifies not only the frontieresque American character sought by early-twentieth-century fans, but also a more contemporary longing for the relative purity, simplicity, and tradition of the early twentieth century itself.

Indian people have reacted to the use of Indian mascots differently. While many native people expressed dismay, others saw athletic rituals as truly honoring Indians. American Indian Movement (AIM) leader Dennis Banks, for example, has claimed that, until the late 1950s, Stanford and other schools promoted "positive, respectful images" of Indians. According to Banks, during the 1960s fans became more involved in a disrespectful, racist spectacle, and clubs expanded their mascot activities. In Atlanta, for example, "Chief Noc-a-homa" came out of a tipi and danced wildly each

time the Braves hit a home run. So while some Indians have always found the very idea of mascots offensive, others do not find it so even today, and still others join Banks in being most concerned about the positive or negative quality of the stereotyping.

In 1972, Banks and other media-conscious Indian activists forcibly brought the mascot issue into public discussion. AIM's Russell Means threatened the Cleveland Indians and the Atlanta Braves baseball clubs with lawsuits, and delegations from AIM, Americans for Indian Opportunity, and the National Congress of American Indians met with Washington Redskins owner William Bennett to ask him to change the team's name. Aside from cosmetic changes to mascot rituals and team songs, however, these efforts proved unsuccessful. Although Indians continued to protest, the effort to eliminate Indian mascots lost momentum for almost twenty years.

Then, in October 1991, the Atlanta Braves played the Minnesota Twins in baseball's World Series. Just a few months later, in January 1992, the Washington Redskins competed in football's Super Bowl. Both events took place in Minneapolis, a city with a high concentration of Indian people in a state that had been attempting to eliminate Indian mascots at the college and high school levels. This convergence of place, people, and issue launched a series of protests and an often rancorous national dialogue about the appropriateness of Indian mascots in American sports.

The practice of appropriating Indians as mascots, good-luck charms, or standard-bearers for nostalgia and national anxiety has not been confined to the ballpark or football field. In the late 1960s, countercultural rebels used a primitivist, antimodern version of "the Indian" to criticize American society for its perceived lack of community, spiritual values, and ecological sensibility. Environmental activists, for example, appropriated the famous "Chief Seattle speech" ("This we know. The earth does not belong to man. Man belongs to the earth"). Many Americans took these words, despite their non-Indian origins in a Southern Baptist–sponsored film script, as a representative "Indian" statement about natural balance and harmony. A well-known 1972 antipollution campaign featuring a teary-eyed Iron Eyes Cody contemplating roadside litter worked in a similar way: as American's "first environmentalists," Indians made admirable mascots for the modern environmental movement.

Like environmentalists, communitarians also borrowed the trappings of native cultures—tipis, clothing, newly constituted "family" kinship groupings, arts and crafts, and so on—to construct and evoke closely knit communal ties. For many, taking on "Indianized" names like Moonflower and Dancing Bear seemed to be a good way to acquire premodern communal identities. Spiritual and psychedelic seekers sought out their own version of enlightened Indianness. Many followed Sun Bear, Rolling Thunder, and other shamanistic leaders who promised to teach "authentic" Indian practices. A 1972 paperback edition of *Black Elk Speaks*, for example, aimed specifically at this market, promised an account of a "personal vision that makes an LSD trip pale by comparison." Political radicals opposed to U.S. involvement in Vietnam appropriated nineteenth-century Indian leaders as ancestral rebels against American colonialism. On many walls, one could find a popular series of posters featuring Geronimo, Sitting Bull, and Red Cloud—representational mascots who signified the same type of rebellion political activists themselves sought to foment. Just as Indian athletic mascots contain multiple, overlapping meanings, all of these different forms of countercultural activity blended together as people imagined and appropriated new meanings for "Indians."

None of these ideas about Indians originated or were contained in a historical vacuum. The use of "Indians" as mascots for a nostalgic antimodernism has a long history in American culture. One can trace the 1960s counterculture back through the 1950s primitivism of beat intellectuals to the early-twentieth-century antimodern criticism of New Mexico figures such as John Collier, D. H. Lawrence, and Mabel Dodge Luhan. Likewise, the same set of ideas about Indian people resurfaced later, in the 1980s and 1990s, under the auspices of the New Age and men's movements.

The continual use of Indianness as an important American symbol has raised serious questions and dilemmas for native people. Some Indians, for example, have left their communities and performed for white Americans a series of "positive" anti-modern roles—spiritual "teacher," eco-guru, community sage—in order to acquire political and economic power. While such performances indeed generate valuable cultural capital, they also force Indian people to define themselves around non-Indian criteria. For other native people, it has become increasingly apparent that, in an age of mass communication, Indians need to exert some control over—or, at the very least, constantly challenge—any and all ways they are represented in public discourse. As a result,

many Indian people—in contrast to many non-Indians—have found struggles against the use of Indian mascots and against the activities of non-Indian countercultural and New Age spokespersons to be critical and significant in terms of social, cultural, and political survival.

Banks, Dennis, Laurel R. Davis, Synthia Syndnor Slowikowski, and Lawrence A. Wenner, "Tribal Names and Mascots in Sports Issue," *Journal of Sport and Social Issues* 17 (April 1993): 1–33; Franks, Ray, *What's in a Nickname? Exploring the Jungle of College Athletic Mascots* (Amarillo, Tex.: Ray Franks Publishing, 1982).

PHILIP J. DELORIA (Lakota ancestry)
University of Colorado at Boulder

MASHPEE

The first recorded encounters between the ancestors of today's Mashpee Indians and Europeans occurred in the first decade of the seventeenth century when Martin Pring, Bartholomew Gosnold, and Samuel de Champlain explored the coastline of Cape Cod. It took another twenty years for the English to settle the area, and by that time disease had significantly depopulated the region and disrupted native society. For the remainder of the seventeenth century English settlers pressured the Indian communities into ever-decreasing enclaves or forced them to settle in villages established for them by ministers—the so-called praying towns.

The Mashpee community of Cape Cod was an example of both. The indigenous population remained in its territory, augmented by Wampanoags from other parts of the cape. By 1700, the Mashpee tribe had a recognized land base. Although much of its aboriginal belief system had been suppressed, replaced by Christian teachings, some of its aspects remained in force, including a belief in the efficacy of the culture hero Moshup, a giant to whom was attributed a range of remarkable acts, including the creation of Martha's Vineyard and Cape Cod.

Throughout the eighteenth century the Mashpee tribe continued as a self-governing community, although not without interference from Massachusetts—both the colony and, later, the commonwealth. Massachusetts declared the Mashpee settlement to be an Indian plantation, appointed overseers to assist in the management of its affairs, and alternately protected the tribe from land loss and legitimized its own illegal takings. This situation continued into the nineteenth century, until in 1834 the tribe revolted against intrusions on its land. Led by the Pequot minister William Apess, the Mashpees threw out their white minister, seized control of their meeting house, and blocked the unauthorized cutting of wood on their land. Apess and a number of Mashpee leaders were imprisoned, but were released following the restoration of order. The state legislature then changed the status of the Mashpee "plantation" to an Indian district, with a town form of government, but recognized tribal ownership and control of the land. This governmental form lasted twenty-seven years.

In 1869–70, the situation changed drastically. Without concern for tribal wishes, the Massachusetts state legislature made Mashpee a town and divided its land into individual parcels. While the Mashpees maintained control of the town government, much of their land was lost.

During the 1920s the Mashpees, along with other Wampanoag tribes in Massachusetts, participated in a revitalization movement, which continues to the present. By the 1960s, the town of Mashpee was feeling the impact of the frenetic development that was engulfing the rest of Cape Cod. Housing projects changed the town's demographics and voting patterns. By 1970, the Mashpees had lost control of the town government and access to the marine resources upon which many depended.

In reaction, the tribe incorporated and filed a lawsuit under the Trade and Intercourse Acts to recover the lands it had lost as a result of the state's unilateral disestablishment in 1870. The case went to federal court, where a jury in 1978 found that the Mashpees were not a tribe.

Despite the adverse court decision, the tribe continues its efforts to achieve federal recognition. The majority of its members live on Cape Cod and take part in tribal activities. They are governed by the thirteen-member Mashpee Wampanoag Indian Tribal Council. In addition, the tribe has two key cultural leaders, a chief and a medicine man, positions that were reestablished during the 1920s revitalization.

Brodeur, Paul, *Restitution: The Land Claims of the Mashpee, Passamaquoddy, and Penobscot Indians of New England* (Boston: Northeastern University Press, 1985); Campisi, Jack, *The Mashpee Indians: Tribe on Trial* (Syracuse, N. Y.: Syracuse University Press, 1991); Clifford, James, *The Predicament of Culture: Twentieth-Century Ethnography, Literature, and Art* (Cambridge: Harvard University Press, 1988).

JACK CAMPISI
Wellesley College

MASSACHUSETT

The Massachusetts, indigenous residents of what are now the central and northern coastal regions of the state of Massachusetts, claimed territories extending as far south and east as present-day Marshfield, Massachusetts, and west to the boundaries marked by the Charles and Seekonk Rivers. At the time of first contact with French and English explorers in the late sixteenth and early seventeenth centuries, the Massachusetts were a populous, semisedentary people dependent on marine and estuarine resources, cultivated crops, and wild game. The Massachusetts were among the hardest hit of southern New England native peoples by the European-introduced epidemic of 1616–19, which may have claimed up to 90 percent of their population.

Like most of their neighbors, the Massachusetts were organized into political units known as *sachemships,* each led by a hereditary ruler, usually male, known as a *sachem* or *sagamore.* A complex and hierarchical social order was characteristic of these sachemships, with the sachem occupying the position of highest prestige. The sachem's responsibilities included the allocation of land, diplomacy, trade, and decisions concerning warfare. The sachem's advisers, sometimes called "nobles" by English settlers, shared the burdens of leadership as well. Warriors who underwent rigorous training also occupied positions of status within Massachusett society.

Labor was divided by gender; women among the Massachusetts farmed, collected shellfish, and undertook most domestic chores. Men were hunters, deep-sea fishermen, traders, and warriors.

The Massachusett cosmos was populated by numerous beings and forces collectively and individually known as *manitou,* a term also used to describe anything strange, wonderful, or inexplicable. Manitou was sought through dreams, fasting, and visions, and its possession was linked to power, health, and well-being. The principal religious practitioners among the Massachusetts, known as *pawauog* (and called "powwows" by English travelers), encountered manitou in dreams, and thereafter served their communities as curers, prophets, and wonder workers.

Early relations between the Massachusetts and English settlers, with the exception of hostilities provoked by the Pilgrims at Wessagusset (now Weymouth, Massachusetts), were generally peaceful, but the attenuated native population was rapidly overwhelmed by the Great Migration of the 1630s. The rapid expansion of

English settlement, and the subsequent isolation of the Massachusetts from more powerful native allies, may have motivated those Massachusett people who in 1646 agreed to receive John Eliot, who then held the office of teacher at the Roxbury, Massachusetts, church, as a missionary. In keeping with the Puritan "text-based" theology, Eliot initiated efforts to establish vernacular literacy among the Massachusetts, an effort that had largely succeeded by the end of the seventeenth century.

Eliot's missionary program brought together Massachusett people with neighboring Nipmucks and Pokanokets into a number of villages that came to be known as "praying towns." These communities remained largely isolated and self-sufficient until the end of the eighteenth century. Increasingly confined to small acreages, and constrained by debt to sell much of their remaining land, the Massachusetts by the mid–nineteenth century had become largely invisible to outsiders, but continued to maintain a strong sense of ethnic identity into modern times.

Goddard, Ives, and Kathleen Bragdon, *Native Writings in Massachusett,* American Philosophical Society Memoir no. 185 (Philadelphia: American Philosophical Society, 1988); Salwen, Bert, "Indians of Southern New England and Long Island: Early Period," in *Handbook of North American Indians,* ed. William C. Sturtevant, vol. 15, *Northeast,* ed. Bruce Trigger (Washington: Smithsonian Institution, 1978).

KATHLEEN BRAGDON
College of William and Mary

MATHEWS, JOHN JOSEPH

1894–1979
Osage novelist and historian.

In the summer of 1974, a young American writer named Richard Rhodes drove to Pawhuska, Oklahoma, to see the annual dances of the Osage Indians. He had also come looking for a man whom he described as being "part Osage, former member of the tribal council, an author, an elegant man, an Oxford man." The man he sought was John Joseph (Jo) Mathews, whose family had been associated with the Osages for more than 150 years.

Mathews's great-grandmother, the full-blood Osage A-Ci'n-Ga, had married William Shirley Williams ("Old Bill Williams" of mountain-man fame), who had served as interpreter at the treaty of 1825 between the Osages and the U.S. government. And William Shirley Mathews, Jo Mathews's father, had followed the Osages to their last reservation in Oklahoma Territory, where he had established the Osage Mercantile Company and the Citizens Bank in the frontier settlement of Pawhuska.

It was there that John Joseph Mathews was born in 1894, and it was in Pawhuska's Kihekah Motel eighty years later that Rhodes would find the man whom he referred to as "the ageing chronicler of the Osages." Though Mathews was now in his eightieth year and his life's work was mainly behind him, the qualities that had made him not merely a chronicler but, more importantly, a novelist, a historian, a biographer, and, in his own way, a poet were still very much in evidence.

There in Pawhuska, in his crowded motel room, Mathews continued to work on the first volume of an autobiographical account of his early life with the Osages, tentatively entitled *Boy, Horse, and Dog.* He also continued to record on tape the journal that he had kept since April 1921, when he had left Pawhuska for England to attend Oxford University. And toward the end of almost every afternoon, he would drive his station wagon to the Osage Tribal Museum—in whose creation he had played a leading role more than thirty years before—to satisfy himself that the doors were securely locked for the night.

Only a short walk from the motel was the family house of Mathews's childhood. Its windows had commanded both the scattering of sandstone buildings that made up the little town of Pawhuska, on Bird Creek, and the rounded lodges of the Thorny Valley division of the Osages to the east. And from his childhood bedroom in those long-ago hours before dawn, the frightened boy could hear "a long drawn-out chant like the song of the wolf, like the highest pitch of the bull wapiti's moonlight challenge."

As Mathews would later write, this prayer-song was Neolithic man talking to God in a chant that always ended, before it was finished, in a sob of frustration. For the rest of his life, Mathews would search for its continuation—in the cathedrals of Europe, in desert mosques, in pre-Columbian Mexico, and finally once again in the Osage hills.

Following his service as a pilot in the First World War, and after graduating from the University of Oklahoma in 1920 with a degree in geology, Mathews received a B.A. in natural sciences from Oxford University in 1923. Subsequently he was awarded an International Relations Certificate from the University of

Geneva and worked briefly as a journalist, covering the sessions of the League of Nations for the *Philadelphia Ledger.*

It was during his European years, in the course of a hunting trip in North Africa, that Mathews rediscovered deep within himself a profound attachment to his people. This reconnection with his own cultural tradition occurred after an encounter with a group of Kabyle tribesmen who were racing across the desert firing their Winchesters in a display of joy that recalled for Mathews the vision of Osage warriors, with only their breechcloths and their guns, riding across the prairie and firing shots out of sheer exuberance. Suddenly Mathews found that he was homesick, both for the Osages and their culture, and for the old men who remembered their tribal life as it had been in the distant years before their removal to their last reservation.

Mathews's first marriage, to Virginia Winslow Hopper, took place in Switzerland in April 1924. Shortly thereafter the couple returned to the United States, living first in New Jersey and then in California, by which time they had children. But by the end of the decade he had returned alone to Oklahoma's Osage County and resumed the life he had known as a boy on the Osage prairies.

By 1930 he was fully engaged in his first extended literary effort. Drawing on personal diaries left to him by Major Laban J. Miles, an uncle of Herbert Hoover and for more than thirty years the U.S. Indian agent to the Osages, Mathews wrote *Wah'Kon-Tah: The Osage and the White Man's Road.* Published in 1932 by the University of Oklahoma Press, it earned Mathews an international reputation as a writer.

On his return to Oklahoma, Mathews had found that the survival of Osage tribal culture was gravely threatened as a result of the impact of the sudden wealth resulting from oil production on tribal lands, which had begun in 1900 and then rapidly increased in later years. During the period from 1916 to 1932—a time that Mathews characterized as the Great Frenzy—annual per capita royalties skyrocketed, rising to a peak, in 1925, of thirteen thousand dollars. But by 1932, when *Wah'Kon-Tah* appeared, each tribal head right was bringing to the holder an annual payment of $585, a small fraction of what head-right holders had received throughout the 1920s. Thus had the Great Frenzy been replaced by the Great Depression.

Because many Osage tribal members were minors or otherwise supervised by local authorities, their shares of the tribal wealth were supervised by guardians. In the 1930s press reports spoke of systematic plundering of native wealth by these guardians, and questions were raised as to the accuracy of the Osage tribal rolls. According to one later investigator, the presence of questionable enrollees on the rolls may by 1972 have cost fully qualified Osage tribal members somewhere between $100 million and $200 million.

In an interview he gave in Pawhuska in 1937, Mathews observed that locally, "the only industry is the Osage. . . . Everyone here—the doctors, the lawyers, and the merchants—is dependent on Osage money for their livelihoods. . . . Greed, the white man's greed, has caused the Indians many griefs." He became determined to devote himself to the rescue and preservation of Osage tribal culture.

This resolve ultimately found expression in five books, published between 1932 and 1961. Among them, *Talking to the Moon,* a philosophical and poetic account of his life at his hunting lodge, which he called the Blackjacks, was his favorite. *The Osages: Children of the Middle Waters* was his testament, and his most important contribution to his people. Central to his Osage preoccupations was the Osage Tribal Museum in Pawhuska, the country's first tribally owned and operated museum, whose very existence owed much to his efforts. The museum was formally opened on May 2–3, 1938, by the Osage chief at the time, Fred Lookout, in the presence of Osage tribal members and many other Indians from outside the state of Oklahoma.

In 1945, Mathews married Elizabeth Palmour Hunt, who became his coworker for the remainder of his life, particularly during the many years he devoted to research for his epic history of the Osage people. By his two marriages, Mathews had two children and two stepchildren, one of whom is the author of this essay. He took particular pride in their various literary and academic accomplishments.

John Joseph Mathews died in Pawhuska, Oklahoma, in 1979. He was buried at the Blackjacks, on the land he had received in 1906 when the Osage Reservation was divided into individual allotments. Though his hunting lodge now stands abandoned and open to the prairie winds, Mathews's immortality seems nonetheless assured, not only because of his books, which still remain in print, but also because of the Osage Tribal Museum—which, as Mathews had always hoped, now plays an increasingly important role in the cultural renewal of the Osage people.

See also Literature by Indians; Lookout, Fred; Osage.

Mathews, John Joseph, *The Osages: Children of the Middle Waters* (Norman: University of Oklahoma Press, 1961); Rhodes, Richard, "An Excursion on the Prairie," in *Looking for America* (New York: Doubleday and Company, 1979); Wilson, Terry P., *The Underground Reservation: Osage Oil* (Lincoln: University of Nebraska Press, 1985).

JOHN HUNT
Uzès, France

MATINNECOCK

The Matinnecock Indians, an Algonquian people, are the aboriginal occupants of northwestern Long Island. Among the first to feel the impact of European settlement, and seldom mentioned after the colonial period, the Matinnecocks experienced profound changes after the seventeenth century. But they did not vanish; they are still an identifiable people.

Following a massacre of local Indians by the Dutch in 1643, some Matinnecocks fled eastward to the Smithtown area. Holland's feeble attempt at the colonization of Long Island ended in 1644, and during the ensuing English period the loss of tribal domain was complete. In 1789 the Flushing courthouse was destroyed by fire, and all records of transactions with the Mattinecocks were consumed. With no supporting documents, modern descendants find it extremely difficult to trace their history or press a claim for the return of illegally seized lands.

In 1829 the village of Success was officially founded near Manhasset. The inhabitants were Matinnecock Indians, free blacks, and whites. Local tradition declares that a multiracial community had already existed there during the Revolutionary War. Descendants of these first settlers of Success (which was later renamed Lakeville) still live in the immediate area. Following their conversion to Protestant Christianity, the Matinnecocks organized independent congregations called *starlight churches*. Circuit-rider preachers traveled by night to the various Mattinecock settlements, often conducting services in homes. By the mid-nineteenth century, the starlight churches had joined black denominations, and the churches' traditional June meetings became tribal reunions.

In 1931 an Indian cemetery in Douglaston stood in the path of a proposed highway. The Mattinecocks'

chief, James Waters (Wild Pigeon), waged a well-publicized campaign against the cemetery's desecration, but the highway was built nonetheless. The bones of forty-four Matinnecocks were reinterred in the churchyard of nearby Zion Episcopal Church beside a glacial boulder that received the following inscription: "Here Rest the Last of the Matinecoc." The Daughters of the American Revolution added a bronze plaque with nearly identical wording in 1948.

During the 1950s a charismatic leader appeared. Ann Harding Murdock (Sun Tama) experienced a compelling vision in which she was commanded to lead her people out of obscurity. Her guardian spirit was probably Tackapusha, a colonial-period sachem. In 1958 the Matinnecock Indian Tribe was formally reactivated. A tribal census was taken in 1963, and approximately two hundred persons provided notarized genealogies attesting to their Matinnecock ancestry.

In 1975 the tribe began the revitalization of its ancestral religion. To date, four ceremonies have been revived. Nunnowa ("Indian Thanksgiving") is held in October, and a midwinter ceremony takes place in February; naming and pipe ceremonies are held when appropriate. Wallace Pyawasit, a traditional Menominee religious leader from Wisconsin, assisted in reviving these rites.

Tribal leadership has been a recurrent problem since the death of Ann Murdock in 1969. The Matinecoc Longhouse of Long Island, a formal organization, was chartered by the state of New York in 1985 but is now inactive, having fallen victim to factionalism. At present the tribe has a chief, but some reject his authority.

Like the Algonquian remnants of southern New England, the Matinnecocks are now involved in a regional form of Pan-Indianism. An unknown number have been assimilated by the black and white communities, but a core group cling steadfastly to their Native American identity.

Brasser, T. J. C., "The Coastal Algonkians: People of the First Frontiers," in *North American Indians in Historical Perspective,* ed. Eleanor Burke Leacock and Nancy Oestreich Lurie (New York: Random House, 1971); McMullen, Ann, "What's Wrong with This Picture? Context, Conversion, Survival, and the Development of Regional Native Cultures and Pan-Indianism in Southeastern New England," in *Enduring Traditions: The Native Peoples of New England,* ed. Laurie Weinstein (Westport, Conn.: Bergin and Garvey, 1994).

WILLIAM HAWK (MATINNECOCK)
Eastern New Mexico University

McGILLIVRAY, ALEXANDER

(1750–93)
Creek statesman.

Alexander McGillivray was an important figure in Creek history and an example of an emergent political phenomenon in the histories of all the large southern Indian groups. He was the son of Lachlin McGillivray, a Scottish trader, and Sehoy, a Creek woman of the Wind clan. But because the Creeks, like other southern Indians, were matrilineal, meaning that they reckoned kinship through the mother's line, McGillivray and those like him whose mothers were native women were in the eyes of the Indians fully as Indian as they despite their nonnative fathers and surnames.

McGillivray's contributions to Creek history owed much to the identity of both his parents. He was born in his father's trading compound at Little Tallassee, a Creek town on the Coosa River near present-day Montgomery, Alabama, and was raised there and at Augusta and Savannah, speaking and writing English from an early age. As a youth he studied in Charleston and apprenticed in business in Savannah. This early education prepared him to function in the English colonial world. At the same time, McGillivray was exposed to the world of his mother and her Wind-clan kin. From them he learned how to be a Creek. Until his death he served their interests, as he understood them, above all others.

McGillivray first appeared on the public stage in 1777, when he returned to Little Tallassee with a commission as assistant commissary in the British Indian service. Until the end of the American Revolution in 1783, he organized and directed Creek participation as allies of the Crown in the southern theater of the war. He supplied warriors for fighting in Georgia and for the defense of Pensacola, but Creek leaders made their own decisions on this internecine conflict and McGillivray never succeeded in fielding large armies against the rebels. More a politician than a warrior, McGillivray gained valuable experience during the war as he argued the British case among Creek leaders. Facile with the culture as well as the language of both sides in the struggle, he also won the respect of many who saw him as a uniquely talented interpreter of the outside world.

In 1783, Great Britain ceded to the United States and Spain its claims to all the land south of Canada. Georgia acted on that cession by expanding onto Creek lands. The Creeks were hard-pressed to respond. Best

understood as an alliance system composed of refugee groups drawn together for mutual security after the Mississippian chiefdoms were shattered, the so-called Creek Confederacy of the 1780s was a collection of autonomous towns that shared neither language, a common perception of events, nor a sense of Creek national identity. The national council provided a forum where town leaders discussed issues of mutual interest, but it lacked the mechanisms for policy making or execution that characterized European-style governments.

McGillivray responded to Georgia's expansionist policy by arguing that the Creeks had never surrendered their landed and sovereign rights to the king and that the king therefore had no authority to cede them to the United States. He also took several steps to assure that his claims of Creek sovereignty would be respected.

On the foreign-policy front, in the mid-1780s McGillivray met with representatives of the tribes of the Great Lakes and the Ohio River valley to discuss uniting with them in a massive effort to halt further American expansion west of the Appalachians. He also began negotiations with the Spanish in Florida. Formalized by the 1784 Treaty of Pensacola, the Spanish alliance guaranteed the Creeks their political and territorial rights within Florida and opened an avenue for importing goods, especially military hardware. McGillivray also corresponded with the governments of Georgia and the United States, hoping to convince both that any failure to respect Creek boundaries would be met with force. In response to continued expansion by Georgia, between 1785 and 1787 Creek armies attacked the invaders and expelled them from the contested areas. In conjunction with the Chickamauga Cherokees, McGillivray also sent parties of warriors to harass the Cumberland settlements in present-day Tennessee.

But the most important steps McGillivray took were in the direction of domestic political change. Two Creek headmen, Hoboithle Mico (Tame King) of Tallassee and Eneah Mico (Fat King) of Cusseta, responded to Georgia's claims for Creek land by selling large tracts on the Creeks' eastern border. The two leaders claimed authority over these lands because their hunters used these territories. McGillivray, on the other hand, believed that their actions threatened the survival of the Creek Nation. If they could claim the right to sell off pieces of Creek territory, then other town kings could sell the rest and the Creeks could lose their whole country. He therefore rejected the cessions as unauthorized and illegal, claiming that the tracts were part of the Creek national domain and could be sold only by the national council. But in the absence of a central government with executive powers, McGillivray had only two courses of action. He sent squads of his Wind-clan kinsmen to torment Hoboithle Mico and Eneah Mico and destroy their property. And, empowered by the Treaty of Pensacola to control the flow of trade goods, McGillivray also denied them access to weapons for their warriors. Their towns, vulnerable to the retaliatory raids of the Georgia militia, could not be defended unless they subordinated themselves to McGillivray's authority. In this way McGillivray hoped to break the historic Creek pattern of political decentralization and forge a national government. Only with political power equal to their military strength, McGillivray believed, could the Creeks protect and defend their lands and sovereignty.

The crowning moment in McGillivray's career occurred in 1790 when he completed the Treaty of New York. McGillivray exploited President George Washington's desire to bring peace to the Creek-Georgia frontier to gain federal guarantees of Creek borders and recognition of Creek sovereignty. Circumventing Georgia, the treaty established a direct relationship between the United States and the Creek Nation. The treaty also affirmed McGillivray's control over Creek trade, thereby strengthening his hold on the tribe's economy and improving his ability to subordinate Creek towns to his nationalist purposes.

On February 17, 1793, less than three years after the conclusion of the Treaty of New York, McGillivray died. Never a robust man, he suffered throughout his adult life from the effects of syphilis and rheumatism. It seems that, exhausted by the pace of his life, he simply wore out. McGillivray's death came at an inconvenient time for the Creeks. His domestic political reforms were far from complete. Indeed, factional opposition to his centralist efforts continued, in different forms, for several decades. But those who had accepted McGillivray's ideas about Creek nationalism kept them alive, and in the 1820s, as the removal crisis took shape, a new generation of Creek leaders built on McGillivray's beginnings to create a centralist political response to removal.

See also Creek (Muskogee).

Caughey, John W., *McGillivray of the Creeks* (Norman: University of Oklahoma Press, 1938); Green, Michael D., "Alexander McGillivray," in *American Indian Leaders: Studies in Diversity,* ed. R. David Edmunds (Lincoln: University of Nebraska Press, 1980); Green, Michael D., *The Politics of Indian Removal: Creek Government and Society in Crisis* (Lincoln: University of Nebraska Press, 1982).

Mɪᴄʜᴀᴇʟ D. Gʀᴇᴇɴ
University of Kentucky

MᴄIɴᴛᴏsʜ, Wɪʟʟɪᴀᴍ, Jʀ. (Tᴜsᴛᴜɴɴᴜɢɢᴇᴇ Hᴜᴛᴋᴇ)

(1775–1825)
Coweta Creek political leader, diplomat, military leader, and trader.

Alexander McGillivray's death in 1793 created a diplomatic void in the Creek Confederacy. Eighteen-year-old William McIntosh, Jr., a distant relative of McGillivray's, dreamed about becoming the tribe's next diplomat. McIntosh realized his desire for prominence when his kinsmen selected him a *micco* (chief) of Coweta in 1800. After the Creek Civil War (1813–14), McIntosh became the central diplomatic figure in the Creek Confederacy, sparking controversy among his people as he consented to land cessions to Georgia in the treaties of 1814, 1818, 1821, and 1825. He died in 1825.

William McIntosh, Jr., was born in 1775, in Wetumpka, Georgia (now Alabama). His mixed-blood lineage gave him access to two cultures. His grandfather, John McIntosh, emigrated from Scotland in 1736. John moved his family to the Georgia frontier on the Tombigbee River. John's son, William, grew up at McIntosh Bluffs on the Georgia frontier. During the American Revolution, William McIntosh achieved the rank of captain in the British army. Captain McIntosh married Senoia, a Coweta Creek. Four years after William McIntosh, Jr., was born, his father had another son, Roley McIntosh, by a second Creek wife.

Senoia raised William in Coweta, located south of Wetumpka on the west bank of the Chattahoochee River. Coweta was one of the oldest and largest towns in the Creek Confederacy. Senoia gained control of William's upbringing when her brothers thwarted Captain McIntosh's attempt to send his son to school in Scotland: they seized the boy after he had boarded a ship bound for Scotland. Captain McIntosh resigned himself to accepting Creek customs and left his son to the care of the boy's Indian uncles. The trader returned to the coast, where he married a distant cousin, Barbara McIntosh.

A lithograph by Charles Bird King of the Creek chief William McIntosh.

William taught himself to read and write English, while his mother's family taught him Creek ways. McIntosh's knowledge of both cultures led him to advocate acculturation as a strategy for Creek survival. For example, McIntosh codified Creek laws so Creeks and whites could live under a common legal system.

McIntosh had three wives and twelve children. His first wife, Eliza Grierson, a mixed-blood Creek, gave birth to Chilly McIntosh, William's oldest child, in about 1800. Susannah Roe, his second wife, was Creek, and Peggy, his third, was Cherokee. Susannah and Peggy lived together with their nine children at Lockchau Talofau, McIntosh's home on the west bank of the Chattahoochee River. Eliza and her three children lived fifty miles west on the Tallapossa River, on another plantation owned by McIntosh.

McIntosh was tall and authoritative—characteristics that, combined with his military successes, earned him the Creek name Tustunnuggee Hutke (White Warrior). The Creek Confederacy included two large geographic groupings of towns, identified as Lower Towns and Upper Towns. McIntosh's influence and popularity in Coweta and other Lower Towns coincided with his prosperity and pro-American views.

At the time of his death in 1825, McIntosh had grown wealthy. He had begun making money in 1793, when he sold beef to the American army. Later he owned a trading post, where he sold dry goods to his kinsmen in exchange for their government annuities. He also built an inn at Indian Springs and managed a ferry. His businesses allowed him to maintain two separate plantations. The twenty-five thousand dollars allotted to him in the ill-fated Treaty of Indian Springs was a restitution for his holdings.

McIntosh became widely known among Creeks and Georgians during the War of 1812, when discord erupted into civil war. Urged by Tecumseh to oppose American expansion, the Creek leader Menawa of Hillabee had led Upper Towns to ally themselves with the British in order to purge the Creek Confederacy of American influences. Lower Towns, led by McIntosh, sided with the Americans. Allying themselves with General Andrew Jackson, the Lower Towns aided Jackson in the battle of Autossee and the pivotal Battle of Horseshoe Bend, which crushed Menawa's forces. General Jackson rewarded McIntosh's loyalty with a promotion to brigadier general. Even though deep enmity existed between McIntosh and surviving Upper Towns, he was esteemed among the Lower Creeks because he led them to join the winning side.

But controversy swirled around McIntosh as he repeatedly ceded Lower Creek territory to Georgia. His actions followed a pattern of accommodation by Creek leaders to a rapidly expanding population of settlers; by 1814 Creek leaders had signed sixteen treaties to relieve the Creek Confederacy from the pressure of a burgeoning Georgia frontier. McIntosh reluctantly made land cessions by signing treaties in 1814, 1818, and 1821. Finally realizing that Georgia's hunger for land would not be satiated until it had acquired all remaining Creek territory, the Creek Confederacy enacted a law that made additional cessions by individuals a capital offense.

McIntosh believed that Georgia would inevitably get all Creek territory, so he decided to sell the remaining lands in Georgia, as well as a large tract of land in Alabama, and move his people west. Though the Upper Creeks warned McIntosh at the signing that this cession would cost him his life, the *micco* and fifty other Creeks signed the Treaty of Indian Springs on February 12, 1825. Soon afterward, the Creek Confederacy met in council and sanctioned McIntosh's execution. His nemesis, Menawa, led a force of 170 warriors to McIntosh's home. They executed him in the early morning hours of May 31, along with two other signers of the treaty.

McIntosh's historical importance is not clear-cut. Historians often portray him as either hero and patriot or villain and traitor. Saddled with the task of making difficult decisions in the face of an overpowering expansion of white settlers, McIntosh acted in the interests of his family and his town.

Congress nullified the Treaty of Indian Springs because the signers did not represent the Creek Confederacy. Ironically, Upper Creek leaders later signed a less favorable treaty and began to move west. After this defeat, Menawa and other opponents of McIntosh held him in higher esteem.

Twenty-three hundred Creeks from Coweta and other Lower Towns who had followed McIntosh began emigrating in 1828. Chilly McIntosh made repeated trips as he guided his father's people to their new land. William's half-brother, Roley, became chief of the Lower Towns in 1828—a position he held for thirty-one years, serving as first chief of the Muskogee Nation after Creek removal in 1832.

Descendants of William McIntosh continued influencing tribal affairs. After building a home in Fame, Indian Territory, his youngest son, Daniel Newnan McIntosh, formed the First Creek Regiment to fight for the South during the Civil War. Losing their land, the McIntoshes resettled in Checotah after the Civil War. His grandson, Albert Galatin McIntosh (Cheesie), practiced law in Indian Territory and represented the tribe at the Sequoyah Convention and the Oklahoma Constitutional Convention. His great-grandson, Waldo Emerson McIntosh (Tustennuggee Micco), served as principal chief of the Creek Nation, 1961–1971. His great-great-grandson, Chinnubbie McIntosh (Hacoce), served on the Creek Council and as district judge until constitutional changes limited his participation.

See also Creek (Muskogee); McGillivray, Alexander.

Chapman, George, Chief William McIntosh: A Man of Two Worlds (Atlanta: Cherokee Publishing Company, 1988); Green, Michael D., The Politics of Indian Removal: Creek Government and Society in Crisis (Lincoln: University of Nebraska Press, 1982).

KENNETH W. MCINTOSH (Muskogee)
University of Tulsa

MᴄNICKLE, D'ARCY

(1904–77)
Chippewa-Cree anthropologist and writer.

Born of mixed European and Chippewa-Cree, or Métis, heritage and enrolled on the reservation of the confederated Salish and Kutenai tribes, or Flathead, in Montana, D'Arcy McNickle reflected the current of American Indian events in the twentieth century and added to its stream.

Although not of Salish and Kutenai heritage, he grew up on the reservation, attending the Catholic boarding school at St. Ignatius and later Chemawa, an Indian boarding school in Oregon. McNickle's mixed heritage allowed him to pass for non-Indian in his youth at the University of Montana, at a time and place where an Indian identity was a disadvantage. A college mentor urged him to pursue his developing passion for writing, which took the young man to Europe and later to New York City, where he settled in 1928.

The Surrounded, McNickle's first novel, published in 1936, was written during his New York years. Set on the Flathead Reservation, it raises the issue of cultural identity for its mixed-blood protagonist, Archilde Leon. It describes how misunderstandings between a tribal culture and that of encroaching outsiders can lead to tragedy. Yet in a time when tragedy was the norm in mainstream America's perception of Indians, McNickle's *The Surrounded* also pointed the way to a reevaluation and revaluing of tribal life. The novel was not the initial success McNickle had hoped for. Needing work, he joined the Federal Writer's Project in Washington, D.C., and was then hired by John Collier, the reform-minded Commissioner of Indian Affairs.

As an employee of the Bureau of Indian Affairs, McNickle was charged with implementing the Indian Reorganization Act of 1934. His Indian heritage, it was felt, would assist him in gaining the trust of tribes suspicious of yet another federal policy ostensibly created for their own good. McNickle believed in Collier's efforts to stop the further breaking up of tribal lands under the Allotment Act and to encourage the reorganization of tribal self-government along democratic constitutional lines, and made extensive visits to various tribes to help implement the bureau's programs.

This fieldwork, coupled with the Indian Bureau's growing use of social-science scholarship, led McNickle to applied anthropology. He believed that anthropology could provide a fuller understanding of people and their problems than could politics. Anthropology, like writing, would become a lifelong interest of his. In the social-scientist style, he wrote broad overviews, intended for a non-Indian readership, that are still in use today. Among them are *They Came Here First: The Epic of the American Indian* (1949), *Indians and Other Americans: Two Ways of Life Meet* (1959; written with Harold Fey), and *The Indian Tribes of the United States: Ethnic and Cultural Survival* (1962).

Through his work in the Bureau of Indian Affairs, McNickle came into contact with a developing community of nationally oriented Indian leaders. The National Congress of American Indians, established in 1944 by this growing community, was conceived of as representing the interests of Indians in the federal system. Pan-Indian groups and groups concerned with Indians and Indian issues were not new, but the NCAI represented a rising tide of emphasis on coordination and cooperation by Indians themselves.

Disillusioned by the conservative turn of federal policy after World War II, McNickle left the Bureau of Indian affairs in 1952, turning his attention to community development at Crown Point, New Mexico, to NCAI affairs, and to education. During the 1950s congressional leaders sought to remove tribes' special status and protections. McNickle worked with the NCAI to rebut legislation that would have undone the Indian Reorganization Act and other reforms he had worked so hard to implement decades earlier. Their efforts helped to turn the tide of support against these terminationist goals.

During the early and mid 1960s McNickle hosted a series of summer leadership-training workshops for young American Indians at the University of Colorado at Boulder. These seminars were designed to address the high college dropout rate for American Indians and to nurture a new generation of Indian activism. Through them, young Indians came together with an awakened sense of value for their tribal backgrounds and a new sense of solidarity with other Indians. McNickle was also vitally involved in the pivotal 1961 American Indian conference held in Chicago. As a member of the cosponsoring NCAI's steering committee, McNickle drafted "A Declaration of Indian Purpose," a document designed to set the tone for the gathering. The final version of the document reflected a newfound sense of common conditions among American Indians. The National Indian Youth Council and other "Red Power" groups such as the American Indian Movement trace their beginnings to this 1961 conference.

During these years, McNickle was also busy as a man of arts and letters. In 1954 he collaborated with the Apache visual artist Allan Houser to produce *Runner in the Sun: A Story of Indian Maize*. This story, aimed at young adults, is possibly the first novel set in precontact America that was written by an American Indian.

In 1966 the University of Saskatchewan at Regina offered McNickle a position to develop its newly established anthropology department. He readily accepted, welcoming the attention that came with his first regular university appointment. He also spent much time traveling as a speaker and consultant about American Indians and their concerns. He retired from the university in 1971 and in the following year helped found the Center for the History of the American Indian at the Newberry Library in Chicago. McNickle served as the center's first director and remained active there until his death in 1977.

McNickle's third novel, *Wind from an Enemy Sky*, published posthumously in 1978, was the product of over forty years of labor and experience. The novel documents the seemingly unbreachable cultural gap of communication between the fictionalized Little Elk tribe of the Northwest and well-intentioned outsiders. It depicts a conflict of values that begins with the building of a dam on tribal land and culminates in misunderstanding and bloodshed. In his writing, McNickle presents embattled but viable tribal cultures. His voice is that of an American Indian assessing the state of American Indian nations, and it came to influence later generations of Indian writers and thinkers. His gritty depiction of the reality of Indian lives acknowledges the truth of tribal cultures under threat. Yet in his writing McNickle leaves room for answers to be found within tribal cultures themselves. His movement from Indian New Deal supporter to defender of Indian sovereignty and advocate of self-sufficiency sets the tone for tribal affairs today.

Parker, Dorothy R., *Singing an Indian Song: A Biography of D'Arcy McNickle* (Lincoln: University of Nebraska Press, 1992); Purdy, John L., *Word Ways* (Tucson: University of Arizona Press, 1990); Rupert, James, *D'Arcy McNickle*, Boise State Western Writers Series (Boise, Idaho: Boise State University Press, 1988).

SCOTT BEAR DON'T WALK
(Crow, Confederated Salish and Kootenai, Métis)
Denver, Colorado

MENOMINEE

The Menominee Indians, an Algonquian-speaking woodland tribe, reside on the Menominee Reservation in northeastern Wisconsin. As descendants of Copper Culture people, an ancient indigenous cultural tradition, they are Wisconsin's oldest continuous residents and one of the few tribes east of the Mississippi that inhabit part of their ancestral land. Menominee—the name was conferred on them by the Ojibwas and refers to the *manomin* (wild rice) that (along with sturgeon and maple sugar) was a staple in their diet—referred to themselves as Mamaceqtaw (pronounced *ma-ma-CHAY-tua*), meaning "the People Who Live with the Seasons."

Menominee land once consisted of 9.5 million acres stretching from Lake Michigan to the Mississippi. The modern 235,000-acre reservation, established in 1934, is home to nearly thirty-five hundred of the tribe's seventy-five hundred enrolled members. The reservation is the largest single tract of timberland in Wisconsin, with an abundance of lakes, streams, and wildlife. The Wolf River, designated for protection in the Wild and Scenic Rivers Act, winds its way through the reservation.

In A.D. 800 the Winnebago tribe began its migration from the South onto Menominee lands. Later the Potawatomis and several other tribes arrived from the East. The centuries just prior to European contact saw the arrival of the Sauk and Fox Indians. Jean Nicolet, the first European to visit what is now Wisconsin, arrived in 1634 near Green Bay, thus beginning European encroachment into Menominee territory. By 1820 sixty settlers resided on Menominee lands; forty years later their number had increased to over a million.

A structured clan system ensured the tribe's survival amid this influx of newcomers. Five principal clans—Bear, Eagle, Wolf, Crane, and Moose—were divided into various phratries and subphratries, each with specific obligations.

A 1908 photo by A. J. Kingsbury of a Menominee couple outside their bark house, she with baskets, he with gun and snowshoes. Their clothing features characteristic Menominee floral designs.

Although the clan system provided for a warrior society, the Menominee were considered peaceful. Though they sided with the British in the Revolutionary War, the Menominee were not always opposed to American actions. In 1810 the Menominee chief Tomah declined Tecumseh's invitation to join his Indian confederacy against the Americans. In the War of 1812, however, the Menominee fought alongside the British. In 1832, under Koshkenaniew, they participated with the Americans in the Black Hawk War, which drove the Sauk and Fox Indians from Wisconsin. In the American Civil War, a primarily Menominee regiment fought for the Union.

With the establishment of Fort Howard near Green Bay, Fort Michilimackinac in upper Michigan, and forts at Lake Poygan and Prairie du Chien, the tribe was always aware of the threat of force. From 1817 to 1856, a series of statutes and treaties with the federal government transferred Menominee land to European refugees and immigrant New York Indians. The first treaty, in 1817, was one of friendship; in it the Menominee were promised federal protection. Subsequent treaties involved land cessions at an average of 13.5 cents per acre, while a later agreement established the present reservation "for a home to be held as Indian lands are held." In 1854 a treaty was negotiated for the Menominee by an appointed leader, who cooperated with the Americans but stoutly resisted the government's proposed removal to Crow Wing, Minnesota. A final treaty, in 1856, set aside a portion of the tribe's land for New York's Stockbridge-Munsee Indians. Despite these concessions, however, the demand for Menominee land did not end.

In 1854, Wisconsin lumber barons lobbied for the unilateral purchase of Menominee land. The tribe was able to halt this land sale in 1871, when it obtained permission to harvest "dead and down" timber on the land, thereby using property that whites had wanted to be considered "vacant." The Menominee turned increasingly to forestry, reasoning that their timber resources could sustain them into the future. Their arguments regarding their dependence on timber enabled the tribe to survive the allotment period with their lands intact. In 1909, the U.S. Forest Service constructed the Neopit Sawmill on Menominee land; profits from the sawmill eventually supported a hospital, a clinic, schools, and other social programs for the Menominee. In 1935, the tribe charged federal authorities with forest mismanagement and sued the United States. Sixteen years later, in 1951, it was awarded $8.5 million in compensation.

In the 1950s the Menominee government consisted of a twelve-member advisory council, and a general council in which all adult members had one vote. These councils were advisory to the Bureau of Indian Affairs. On August 1, 1953, House Concurrent Resolution 108 decreed that certain tribes were sufficiently acculturated and prosperous that their federal status could be terminated; the states in which they were located would assume jurisdiction over them. Among the tribes so identified were the Menominee.

Termination was accelerated when the Menominee requested a per capita payment of one thousand dollars toward the amount owed to them as a result of their forest-mismanagement suit. In 1953 Congressman Melvin Laird introduced a House bill for the per capita payment; it passed. The bill's Senate counterpart, introduced by Joseph McCarthy, did not fare as well. Senator Arthur Watkins (Utah) broke the deadlock by attaching a termination provision to the payment bill. In 1954 Watkins informed the Menominee that they had three years to prepare for termination. In their general council, the Menominee, believing they were simply voting for their per capita payments, actually voted for termination. In May 1961, termination took effect: the tribal roll was closed, the sawmill became a state-chartered corporation, taxes were required, and the once-prosperous reservation became Wisconsin's seventy-second and poorest county. During the next few years the Menominee lost identity, livelihood, land, and assets. Modest prosperity turned into severe poverty.

Unable to pay property taxes, Menominee Enterprises, Inc. (MEI) began to sell the tribe's former holdings. A grassroots movement led by a young Menominee social worker named Ada Deer stopped the land sales and reversed termination. The Menominee Restoration Act, signed by President Nixon on December 22, 1972, redesignated the Menominee a federally recognized tribe. The campaign thrust Deer into the national spotlight and contributed to her eventual appointment as Assistant Secretary of the Interior for Indian Affairs in 1993, by virtue of which she became the first Native American woman to head the Bureau of Indian Affairs.

In the 1990s, the tribe has relied on its timber resources for its economic well-being. Lawrence Waukau, a tribal member and the president of Menominee Tribal Enterprises (MTE), has declared that the forest is more productive today than it was in 1909. Under MTE's policy of sustained development, timber harvesting is limited to 25 million board feet annually.

New trees are planted regularly to provide for the future. With its forestry and its casino, hotel, and bingo operations, the tribal government provides hundreds of jobs for tribal members and others from surrounding communities.

Menominee gaming, conducted since 1986, has supported the growth of the tribal government and community. A bus system was introduced in 1983. Recent construction has included a library, a day-care center, an elementary school addition, expansion of the Head Start program, a residential facility for the elderly, a senior-citizen center, tribal-college buildings, office renovation, a hotel, a bingo hall, youth centers, a traditional ceremonial building, and a new village—including sewer and water facilities for 150 homes.

Special events are the annual powwows: the Menominee Powwow, held during the first weekend in August; and the Veterans Powwow, held over Memorial Day weekend. Menominee Restoration Day, December 22, is celebrated annually. Other attractions drawing outsiders to the Menominee Reservation are river rafting and the tribe's Logging Camp Museum, which houses the largest collection of logging tools in the world. The Menominee welcome visitors but are careful to inform them that hunting, fishing, the harvesting of plants, and access to the forest are the exclusive rights of the Menominee people.

Kessing, Felix, M., *The Menomini Indians of Wisconsin* (Philadelphia: American Philosophical Society, 1939); Peroff, Nicholas C., *Menominee Drums: Tribal Termination and Restoration, 1945–1974* (Norman: University of Oklahoma Press, 1982); Shames, Deborah, ed., *Freedom with Reservation* (Madison, Wisc.: National Committee to Save the Menominee People and Forests, 1972).

S. VERNA FOWLER (Menominee)
College of the Menominee Nation
Keshena, Wisconsin

MERIAM REPORT

Officially entitled *The Problem of Indian Administration*, the Meriam Report was prepared by a team of social scientists led by Lewis M. Meriam (and including the Winnebago Henry Roe Cloud) and was published in 1928. It recounted the conditions for Indian peoples on reservations. The study found infant mortality rates of 190.7 per 1,000, far higher than the rate for any other ethnic group. Diseases such as measles, pneumonia, tuberculosis, and trachoma (an infectious eye disease) were rampant on the reservations, and material conditions ranging from diet to housing to health care were deplorable. The report singled out the U.S. government's allotment policy as the greatest contributor to Indian peoples' impoverishment and called for a complete overhaul of the Bureau of Indian Affairs and of national Indian policy.

See also Boarding Schools; Bureau of Indian Affairs; Diseases; Reservations.

METACOM (KING PHILIP)

(1640–76)
Wampanoag (Pokanoket) sachem.

Metacom (or Metacomet) personified native resistance to colonial power in southern New England in the seventeenth century. Puritan chroniclers celebrated his death, an event that marked the colonists' victory in the war named for him—King Philip's War—and that cemented English dominance in the region. Those who look less favorably on the Puritans' actions, on the other hand, celebrate Metacom's heroism and condemn those who pushed him to war.

Metacom grew up in what is now southeastern Massachusetts, sensitive to the swelling strength of the English newcomers. He was born a generation after a massive epidemic had decimated his people; two decades after his father, Massasoit, had become the first ally of the newly arrived Pilgrims; and two years after the colonists had established their power by destroying the Pequot tribe. When Massasoit died in 1660, his eldest son, Wamsutta, told Plymouth Colony that he was now sachem and, in accordance with native customs, asked for new names for himself and his brother as a token of this change. He was given the name Alexander, and Metacom was dubbed Philip; it is not clear, however, which names were used by other Indians, or even which were preferred by Wamsutta or Metacom. Plymouth became alarmed when the new sachem began selling land to other colonies. In 1662 an armed party captured the sachem with the intention of forcing him to testify at an inquest, but before they could do so, he sickened and died. Metacom suspected poison and, after assuming his brother's mantle, remained wary of Plymouth Colony.

A nineteenth-century engraving depicting the killing of Metacom (King Philip) in 1676. Metacom's head was exhibited in the fort at Plymouth, Massachusetts, for twenty-five years.

For a decade the new sachem maneuvered to maintain his power and to ensure his people's welfare as the English population, and English power, grew. The Wampanoag Confederacy, which consisted of many villages and allied families, apparently began to splinter, in part because of the influence of colonial authorities and missionaries. Metacom's territory formed a border zone between Plymouth Colony, Rhode Island, and the Massachusetts Bay settlement headquarted in Boston, each of which wanted the area. In part to retain influence in such a treacherous political climate, the sachem sold tracts of land in the region to various colonists. Subsequent conflicts over the borders of these lands, however, were rarely settled to his satisfaction; colonial courts seemed biased and insensitive to the Indians' concerns. The Indians were also angered by colonial efforts to shape native politics, and enraged by the disruptive effects of rum, sold by traders. Additional strife developed as English livestock wandered into Indian fields, destroying crops. Natives responded by confiscating or killing these animals—though some, including Metacom's people, began raising their own livestock, even selling the meat to colonists.

The conflict over land became acute in 1667, after Plymouth Colony violated an agreement with Metacom and authorized the purchase of land within his territory—from *any* Indian—for the town of Swansea. War parties began to appear near Swansea, possibly led by the sachem, in an effort to intimidate the colonists. In 1671 Plymouth demanded a meeting with Metacom; when he arrived, the colony's leaders compelled him at gunpoint to surrender his people's firearms and sign a treaty that bound him and, retroactively, his dead brother and father to Plymouth's authority—thereby challenging previous land sales to other colonies. Metacom complained to the rival colony at Massachusetts Bay, but instead of gaining assistance there, he was confronted with a joint commission of the two colonies that compelled him to sign a revised treaty lacking only the retroactive nature of the first.

At about this time Metacom evidently began planning a war. He sought the backing of other Wampanoag leaders, along with the support of other groups, such as the Nipmucks, who felt besieged by the colonists. His most difficult challenge, however, was in establishing an alliance with the Narragansetts, old enemies but the most powerful tribe in the region. Metacom was also forced to play a waiting game, attempting to keep his angry warriors from raiding colonial villages while maintaining their loyalty. Rumors of his efforts soon reached colonial authorities. When the bruised body of one of Plymouth's Indian informers was found in a pond, the colonists tried three Wampanoags for murder, including one of Metacom's counselors. The three were found guilty, entirely on the suspect testimony of another Indian, and on the scaffold one of the three supposedly confessed their sachem's guilt. Tension increased as the colonists' worst fears seemed confirmed and the Wampanoags, angered by recent events, became convinced that the English planned to kill Metacom and take their land.

In July 1675 Metacom's men again appeared outside Swansea, slaying cattle and convincing many that an assault was imminent. After a Swansea boy killed a warrior, the Indians attacked the town, killing several colonists. An uprising began, apparently touched off more by the rage of Metacom's people than by any plan. When a colonial army tried to besiege the sachem near his home on Mount Hope (Bristol, Rhode Island), he escaped with his warriors and their families and then, joining forces with Nipmuck allies, attacked and burned villages west and south of Boston. Indian groups in the Connecticut River valley also rose in revolt when anxious colonists overreacted to the violence. Finally, in late December the Narragansetts joined the uprising after English forces attacked their village. During the ensuing winter, joint raiding parties burned several colonial towns, sending refugees streaming into Boston. Although Metacom did not actually command this informal army—in December he had gone with his warriors to the Hudson River valley to seek the support of other native groups—the Wampanoag sachem seemed omnipresent.

But Metacom's flaming star was soon extinguished. As he discussed new alliances, Mohawks allied with colonial New York attacked his band, killing all but forty of his men and destroying the sachem's prestige. The Mohawks continued their attacks from the west,

while colonial forces, joined by other Indian allies, became more effective. Disease and hunger also began to take a terrible toll. By the spring of 1676 the informal native alliance broke apart. Many bands moved north or west out of harm's way, and some made peace with the colonists. Metacom headed for home after his allies threatened to send his head to the English as a peace offering. As the uprising dissolved, a squad including many of the sachem's former supporters began hunting the symbol of the revolt. His wife and son were captured and apparently, like most of the captured Indians, sold in the West Indies as slaves. Finally, on August 12, Metacom and his dwindling band were surrounded; he was shot by an Indian serving with the colonial forces. The sachem's head was cut off and displayed in quarters, and the pieces were sent to the colonial capitals. A Wampanoag legend holds that Metacom's warriors stole his head and secretly buried it near Mount Hope, where his spirit still periodically speaks.

The defeat of Metacom and his allies decimated the native population in southern New England. At the same time, the colonists also suffered high casualties and did not return for several decades to the towns they had abandoned. While many Indian communities survived, Metacom's death marked the end of native independence in the region.

Bourne, Russell, *The Red King's Rebellion: Racial Politics in New England, 1675–1678* (New York: Atheneum, 1990).

DANIEL R. MANDELL
University of Georgia

MIAMI

The Miamis, an eastern woodlands tribe, originally lived near the southern end of Lake Michigan. When French explorers contacted them in the 1650s, they were living in the area of today's Green Bay, Wisconsin, where they had moved in order to avoid attacks by the Iroquois. At that time there were six Miami-speaking groups, and their population probably exceeded ten thousand. When the so-called Beaver Wars ended in 1701, the Miamis moved back into today's Indiana and Ohio. Their main settlement was Kekionga (now Fort Wayne, Indiana). Two of the Miami groups, the Weas and Piankashas, eventually became separate tribes.

During the eighteenth century the Miamis enjoyed comparative security at Kekionga, where they raised a special variety of white corn that they traded to other tribes. On the border between the Ohio and Illinois country, the Miamis traded with both the French and the English, who called them "Twightwees," from *twaatwaa,* their word for the cry of the sandhill crane. As Miami wealth and trade grew, the tribe moved into European-style log houses, kept pigs and cattle, and dressed in a mixture of European and native garments. At the same time, they preserved much of their native belief system and were little affected by French missionary efforts.

As the frontier of European settlement approached the Miamis after the American Revolution, they joined the Shawnees and other tribes in border warfare with Americans. The great Miami war chief Little Turtle led the tribes of the Miami Confederacy in the defeat of two American armies in 1790 and 1791. General Anthony Wayne defeated the allied tribes at Fallen Timbers in 1794 and built Fort Wayne at the site of Kekionga. The Miamis moved to new villages along the Wabash and Mississinewa Rivers, east of today's Peru, Indiana. In 1795 Wayne negotiated the Treaty of Greenville with the Miamis and ten other tribes. The Miamis, believing that the treaty guaranteed them sovereignty of their land, pledged peace with American authorities.

After the Louisiana Purchase in 1803, Governor William Henry Harrison, eager to prepare Indiana Territory for statehood, pressured the Miamis to sign new treaties ceding most of their territory in Indiana. At the outbreak of the War of 1812, he ordered devastating attacks on neutral Miami villages. After the war, the demoralized Miamis ceded most of their remaining land in a new series of treaties from 1818 to 1840. The tribal population declined from fourteen hundred to less than eight hundred when removal came in 1846. Half of the tribe was removed, and came to be called the Western Miamis; the other half was allowed to remain in Indiana.

Many of the Western Miamis later returned to Indiana, where they were given refuge. In the late 1860s, the Kansas reservation of the Western Miamis was allotted, and those people moved to northeastern Indian Territory. In 1873 the last Indiana reservation was allotted, and in 1897 the tribal status of the Indiana Miamis was terminated administratively. Land loss accelerated, and tribal culture eroded as people moved to nearby towns.

The Western or Oklahoma Miamis were never terminated as a tribe. Today they own several businesses and offer the full services of a federally recognized tribe from their office in Miami, Oklahoma, to about fifteen hundred members. For their part, the Indiana Miamis have unsuccessfully attempted through administrative procedures, legislatively, and in federal court to regain federal recognition. They have a tribal headquarters in Peru, Indiana, and provide some services to their five thousand members.

Anson, Bert, *The Miami Indians* (Norman: University of Oklahoma Press, 1970); Callendar, Charles, "Miami," in *Handbook of North American Indians,* ed. William C. Sturtevant, vol. 15, *Northeast,* ed. Bruce Trigger (Washington: Smithsonian Institution, 1978).

STEWART RAFERT
University of Delaware

MICMAC

The Micmacs of eastern Canada and the northeastern corner of the United States (who prefer the phonetic spelling Mi'kmaq) first appeared in their homeland approximately ten thousand years ago. They call the region Mi'kma'ki. Archaeological evidence indicates that these first inhabitants arrived from the west and lived as hunters and gatherers attuned to the shifting, seasonal resources of the area. During the summer months they hunted and fished, sometimes venturing out to sea to hunt whales and porpoises. Their winter camps were inland, built along rivers and lakes so that they could augment their hunting by spearing and trapping eels and other water creatures.

The tribal territory included all of what is now Nova Scotia and Prince Edward Island, the Gaspé Peninsula of Quebec, the north shore of New Brunswick and inland to the Saint John River watershed, eastern Maine, and part of Newfoundland, including the islands in the Gulf of Saint Lawrence as well as St. Pierre and Miquelon. The Micmacs' neighbors recognized their territory and rarely violated its borders. Micmac people thought of their homeland as containing seven districts: Kespukwitk, Sikepne'katik, Eski'kewaq, Unama'kik, Piktuk aqq Epekwitk, Sikniktewaq, and Kespe'kewaq. A *keptan* or *saqmaw* (district chief) presided in each jurisdiction, doubling as local ruler and delegate to the Grand Council Sante' Mawiomi.

The Grand Council was the governing body of the nation and was led by several officers, including a *kji'saqmaw* (grand chief), a *putus* (treaty holder and counselor), and a *kji'keptan* (grand captain, adviser on political affairs). The Sante' Mawiomi determined where families might hunt, fish, and set up their *wumitki* (camp). More importantly, the Grand Council managed relations with other aboriginal nations. The Micmacs were members of the Wabanaki Confederacy, a loose coalition that included the Maliseets, the Passamaquoddy, the Penobscots, and the Eastern and Western Abenakis of present-day Maine, New Hampshire, and Vermont. At its peak, this confederacy influenced tribal life from the Gaspé Peninsula to northern New England.

The Micmacs' first contact with Europeans did not surprise them or alter their worldview. A legend in which one of their spiritual beings traveled across the Atlantic to "discover" Europe taught that blue-eyed people would arrive from the east to disrupt their lives. Micmac people also knew the story of a woman who had a vision of an island floating toward their lands; the island was decked out with tall trees on which there were living beings. Thus the Micmacs were not startled by the appearance of early explorers in sailing sips. Instead, they greeted the newcomers, set up a brisk trade with them, and looked forward to incorporating the strangers' new technologies into their own culture.

Relations with outsiders grew more complex when the Micmacs began converting to Catholicism. This process occurred over a seventy-year period, beginning with the conversion of Grand Chief Membertou in 1610. The Micmac Nation's first treaty with a European nation was an agreement with the Vatican and the Holy See. This treaty was symbolized by a wampum belt at whose center stood a black-robed priest, a cross, and a Micmac figure holding a pouch, representing the incorporation of Micmac spirituality within the context of Roman Catholicism. In the eighteenth century, the Micmacs established a series of treaties with the British Crown that gave Britain an alliance with the Wabanaki Confederacy and security across the region. During this era, the Micmacs adopted the eight-pointed star as a representation of their part of this alliance. Seven of the points represented the seven districts of Mi'kma'ki, with the eighth point standing for Great Britain and the Crown.

The first of the series of treaties between the British Crown and the Micmac Nation was signed in 1725. All were reaffirmed in 1752, and culminated in the Treaty and Royal Proclamation of 1763. The main thrust of these treaties was an exchange of Micmac loyalty for a guarantee that Micmacs would be able to continue hunting and fishing in their territory. These treaties

Micmac mother and son, Nova Scotia, circa 1865. The woman is probably Christianne Morris, who was famous for her beadwork and quillwork.

have been recognized by the Supreme Court of Canada as legal and binding through its decisions in cases that have extended well into the present century.

The Grand Council of the Micmac Nation has survived the passage of time, and its officers now have both secular and religious duties. Because of the nature of the Micmac homeland, the Grand Council's jurisdiction is international. The First Nation communities (reservations) of Canada are governed by an elected chief and council, who hold office for two years. Under the terms of a 1959 act of the Canadian Parliament, all aboriginal people of Canada are Canadian citizens and have the right to vote in federal and provincial elections.

The Micmac language is part of the Algonquian language family, and its ancestral language is Proto-Algonquian. Early forms of communication among the Micmacs included an elaborate system of runners who went from village to village relaying messages about recent or future events, treaties entered into, and even calls to war.

The earliest written language was a hieroglyphics on birchbark or animal hides. Father La Clerq, a French missionary priest, noticed children using this system as a memory aid and adapted it to translate scriptures in 1691. Silas T. Rand wrote out the sounds as he heard them spoken using the modern-day alphabet. He used his work to translate scripture as well as ordinary communication into the Micmac language and published a forty thousand–word grammar in 1894. A new orthography was developed in 1974 to give a more accurate representation of the sounds in the Micmac language. There are eleven consonants in Micmac—*p, t, k, q, j, s, l, m, n, w,* and *y.* And there are six vowels—*a, e, i, o,* and *u,* along with their corresponding long sounds, and schwa, denoted by a barred *i.*

Micmac is a polysynthetic, non-gender-specific, verb-oriented language with approximately seventy-five hundred native speakers in the Micmac Nation. Recently there has been renewed interest in the language, and it is being introduced into the reservation schools as part of the curriculum. In addition to the language, Micmacs have also focused on *waltes,* a traditional Micmac game. *Waltes* was believed by Euro-Americans to be a heathen game that promoted infidelity, promiscuity, and gambling. Indian agents and the clergy tried to stop it for decades, but it has survived as an important element in traditional tribal life. In addition, modern Micmac society has retained some of its skills in crafts such as basket making, working with hides, and using beads or quills on birch bark and hides.

The Micmac population is approximately twenty thousand, with one-third able to speak and/or write in Micmac. Unemployment is the major problem on the modern reservations. More and more Micmacs are educating themselves, with the schools incorporating the language and culture into their curricula. There is also a concentrated effort to incorporate Micmac history into the general history of the region as taught in the Nova Scotia schools. The Nova Scotia government has designated the month of October as Micmac History Month. Unfortunately, such gains are often undermined by the lack of adequate employment for young, educated tribal members. Nevertheless, Micmac elders are adamant in their belief that the key to tribal survival is the maintenance of the group's language, culture, and traditions.

Johnson, Eleanor, "Mi'kmaq Tribal Consciousness in the Twentieth Century" in *Paqtatek,* ed. Stephanie Inglis and Joy Manette (Halifax, Nova Scotia: Garamound Press, 1990); Knockwood, Isabelle, *Out of the Depths* (Lockport, Nova Scotia: Roseway Publishing, 1992).

PATRICK JOHNSON (Mi'kmaq)
University College of Cape Breton
Sydney, Nova Scotia

MINERAL RESOURCES

The natural-gas, oil, coal, and uranium reserves that lie under Indian lands represent some of the most valuable resources many tribes possess. When tribally owned lands are considered together with lands owned by individual tribal members, thirty-four Indian tribes, known collectively as the "energy tribes," can be said to possess approximately 30 percent of the coal found west of the Mississippi River, 50 percent of potential uranium reserves, and 20 percent of known natural-gas and oil reserves.

This wealth, however, has been a mixed blessing for the tribes. In the past, they rarely had meaningful control over the development of their resources, and the history of Indian mineral development is replete with stories of unfair leases extracted or coerced from unknowledgeable Indians. Many tribes have received far less income than their minerals are worth, and have seen their land bases dangerously polluted and the health of their members jeopardized. In the present day, tribes are faced with the legacy of this past. Yet today the energy tribes are in a better position than ever before to take control over mineral development decisions.

As has been the case with other Indian resources such as land, timber, and water, Indian minerals have frequently attracted outsiders. From the moment reservation boundaries were established, Indians were victims of trespass and of efforts to remove lands that contained valuable coal and oil deposits from reservation status. Tribal leaders have long fought simply to establish ownership of their lands and to survey their resources. The lack of knowledge about Indian resources has made it difficult for tribal governments and their federal "guardians" to protect Indian interests.

The first serious assault on tribal mineral resources followed the discovery of oil in the Oklahoma Territory in 1882. In 1891, the federal government began to allow the leasing of Indian lands for mining purposes, and the rich Osage, Creek, and Cherokee gas and oil fields became a significant new source of lease income for these tribes. However, this leasing and an increased interest in Indian oil followed on the heels of the General Allotment Act of 1887, and many Indians lost control of their assets. Unfamiliar with Anglo-European concepts of property and business, they were subject to outright fraud and theft, as well as federal mismanagement. By the mid-1930s, burgeoning oil interests such as Phillips, Getty, Mellon, and Standard had replaced the tribes of eastern Oklahoma as managers of the state's mineral resources.

The western tribes fared only slightly better. Although the Indian mineral-leasing act of 1891 required tribal consent for all leases, tribal leaders knew so little about their resources that they rarely understood the agreements put before them. Leases during this era too often reflected national needs for energy-yielding minerals, rather than Indian needs for a viable economic and cultural existence. The documents contained such features as fixed royalty rates, extremely long durations, a lack of requirements for renegotiation when market conditions changed, weak health and safety provisions, and a lack of requirements for restoration of the environment when mining ceased.

Federal policy generally condoned such arrangements. The relatively progressive 1891 act was followed in 1903 by the U.S. Supreme Court's *Lone Wolf* decision, which upheld congressional power to take Indian lands without tribal consent. During World War I, an increased need for oil and coal led to a rapid escalation in the leasing of Indian minerals. But when conditions changed in the 1920s, the Department of the Interior suspended leasing on Indian lands. As the demand for energy-yielding minerals slowly increased again, Congress passed a new Indian mineral-leasing act in 1938 that restated the requirement for tribal consent to leases, and standardized leasing policies in an attempt to limit unfavorable lease conditions. As demand continued to increase, however, policy again swung against the tribes, reaching an all-time nadir in 1953 with the passage of the so-called termination resolution, H.J.R. 108. The termination policy emphasized individual management of tribal resources and thus dramatically weakened the ability of tribal governments to participate in the development of their resources. The 1950s also brought the first real boom in uranium mining. For the energy tribes, these wild swings in demand, and corresponding changes in federal policy, made coherent development difficult and underscored one essential lesson: the tribes must gain control over their mineral resources.

Fortunately, Indian tribes have improved their bargaining positions in recent years. President Lyndon Johnson's War on Poverty brought an infusion of federal funds into tribal governments and organizations and strengthened tribal governments. The self-determination legislation of the 1970s also allowed tribes to expand their interests, knowledge, and capabilities, causing many to take on a much stronger role in determining the conditions of mineral development on their lands. One example of this new approach was the formation in 1975 of the Council of Energy Resource Tribes (CERT) by twenty-six tribal governments that, despite differences in their resources and development objectives, had the common goal of asserting control over the development of their mineral resources. CERT was designed to provide member tribes with the same level of information and expertise that the energy corporations possessed. Since 1975 it has worked with the tribes to assess their resources, negotiate and renegotiate lease and contract terms, and enhance tribal capacities to manage mineral resources. Success in these efforts has caused CERT to grow to more than fifty member tribes.

The market in energy-yielding minerals continues to fluctuate, and fragile tribal economies continue to be racked by painful boom-and-bust cycles. Unlike the earlier period, however, recent times have brought major changes in national policy that have not been so uniformly "for" or "against" the tribes. The 1973 oil crisis caused oil and gas prices to soar and increased pressure on Indian tribes to lease more of their minerals. Yet the 1975 Indian Self-Determination Act provided a significant boost to the independence of tribal governments. The United States experienced a second uranium boom from 1975 to 1979, followed by a near collapse in the market after the Three Mile Island accident. A number of tribes have successfully renegotiated the unfavorable terms of old leases, sometimes even canceling leases when the corporations involved refused to renegotiate in good faith. The 1982 Indian Mineral Development Act reflected this new emphasis on the independence and capability of tribal governments. The act allowed tribes to negotiate individual contracts with energy corporations, and empowered them to leave the confines of the standardized leases and strike flexible bargains that better suit tribal priorities.

The 1980s brought a combination of destructive budget cuts and increased political support for tribal sovereignty. In 1986 Congress amended several major pieces of environmental legislation, such as the Safe Drinking Water Act, the Clean Air Act, and Superfund legislation, to allow tribes to control environmental regulation on the reservations. These empowering pieces of legislation mark significant advances for tribal governments in their quest to exercise sovereign control over mineral resources.

A number of the energy tribes have managed to obtain a degree of control over the development of their mineral resources. Some tribal governments have risen to the challenge of becoming knowledgeable and skilled joint partners, or developers in their own right. The Jicarilla Apache tribe and the Fort Peck Assiniboin and Sioux tribes used the experience gained from previous joint ventures to take the risk, successfully, of drilling their own wells. The Navajo Nation set a new standard for tribal participation with its Dineh power-project agreement, in which the tribe and the private companies involved were to participate jointly in all phases of planning and operating the power plant (though the agreement fell through at the end). Today, tribes are likely to combine leases, joint ventures, and other arrangements so as to maximize tribal options.

Some tribal governments have made the equally challenging decision to slow or halt mineral development on their lands. Several tribes, including the Northern Cheyennes and the Crows, canceled or halted leases in the 1970s, despite enormous pressure from industry sources to continue them. These tribes have since maintained a cautious approach to mineral development.

But the struggle has been, and remains, one of trying to repair problems created in the past. Federal policy has immeasurably complicated the job of managing reservation resources. Despite years of mineral development, most tribes have only recently begun to receive royalties that reflect the actual value of their resources, and few tribes have had the opportunity to develop a sustainable economic plan. Virtually every tribe that possesses mineral wealth bears a legacy of past mistakes. Environmental disasters of varying degrees can be found on nearly every reservation that has experienced large-scale mining, from the water and air pollution resulting from the strip-mining of coal to the radioactive waste and spills that have accompanied uranium mining. One of the worst uranium-mining accidents in Indian Country was the 1979 collapse of United Nuclear's mill tailings dam near the Churchrock community on the Navajo Reservation. Millions of gallons of radioactive water poured into the Puerco River and contaminated the major source of water for downstream Navajo communities. From such environmental and health problems as these often flow political conflicts, as tribes find themselves in the difficult position of balancing jobs and royalty money with the health and well-being of their people and lands.

Mineral resources on Indian lands hold enormous opportunities and challenges for the tribes involved. Indian tribes are increasing their demands that their sovereignty be recognized and that they, and they alone, make the decisions about the development of their mineral resources—whether to develop them at all, how much to develop them, how fast, under what conditions. With dedication and commitment, as well as new skills and knowledge, mineral tribes may well see the future outweigh the past.

Ambler, Marjane, *Breaking the Iron Bonds: Indian Control of Energy Minerals* (Lawrence: University Press of Kansas, 1990); Churchill, Ward, and Winona LaDuke, "Native North America: The Political Economy of Radioactive Colonialism," in *The State of Native North America: Genocide, Colonization, and Resistance,* ed. M. Annette Jaimes (Boston: South End Press, 1992); Hogan, Linda, *Mean Spirit* (New York: Ivy Books, 1990).

JENNIFER W. FELMLEY
University of California at Berkeley

MINGO

Mingo is a corruption of *mingwe,* an Algonquian word meaning "stealthy" or "treacherous." English colonists used the term to describe Iroquois bands that had migrated to western Pennsylvania by 1740. Mingo villages were an amalgamation of Seneca, Wyandot, Shawnee, Conestoga, and Delaware refugees. By 1774, the Mingos acted independently of the Iroquois, frequently fighting American encroachers even when the Six Nations advocated peace. During the War of Independence the Mingos continued their western migration and crossed the headwaters of the Scioto and Sandusky Rivers. Cayugas who had sold their lands in New York joined them by 1817. In 1819, the Mixed

Band, or Lewiston Senecas, split from the main group of Mingos and shared a reservation with Shawnees. At about the same time the Sandusky Senecas, or Cowskin Senecas, left the group to establish their own reservation along the Sandusky and Cowskin Rivers.

By 1830, the Mingos had improved farms, had established schools, and were flourishing. Andrew Jackson's removal policies, however, forced the natives to sell their lands and leave Ohio. Following their removal to Kansas in 1832, the Seneca bands rejoined the group and shared the Neosho Reservation. In 1869, after the Civil War, the Mingos moved to the southern part of the Neosho tract in present-day Ottawa County, Oklahoma. In 1937, tribal members adopted the official designation Seneca-Cayuga. Today the tribe numbers over twenty-four hundred members and continues to maintain cultural and religious ties to the Six Nations.

MISSIONS AND MISSIONARIES

Christian missionaries began their work of converting the native peoples of the Americas soon after the beginnings of the European invasion, both in the north and in the south. Indeed, the missionization of native peoples in the Americas was the foundation for one of the primary European conquest strategies. In both mission and political-military documents this strategy was referred to as *pacification*.

The church or missionary responses to European and American colonialism took two general forms. One type of response, based on the view that immigrant America was the New Israel, overtly helped build the theological foundation for the political doctrine of Manifest Destiny and called for the extermination or removal of Indian communities to make room for white immigrants.

The other response, although sometimes very critical of European or Euro-American dealings with Indians or blacks, lived out its own Manifest Destiny agenda; it was most common among missionaries. Critics of colonization were openly opposed to the brutal military conquest of native peoples, preferring the gentler conquest of conversion. For them this meant conversion to what they assumed was a superior culture and its set of values and societal structures as much as it meant conversion to the gospel of Jesus Christ. For instance, both Bartolomé de Las Casas (1484–1566) and Henry Ben-

jamin Whipple (1822–1901) in different ways earned great reputations as defenders of Indian people, yet both are implicated in the cultural destruction of Indian tribes. The Catholic Las Casas first devised the famed *reducción* paradigm for missionary conquest, while the Protestant Whipple engineered the U.S. government's theft of the Black Hills from the Sioux people, which finally broke the resistance of Sioux and other Indian peoples in the upper Midwest.

In the case of Las Casas and Whipple, as with most of the missionaries among Indian peoples, the lasting devastation they caused was done with the best of intentions, albeit with a controlling dose of European paternalism. That is, they would have claimed that what they were doing was for the good of the Indian people for whom they were concerned, yet in the final analysis they always acted as the paternalistic overseer, making decisions on behalf of Indian peoples and implementing them politically.

Las Casas wrote extensively, criticizing the atrocities committed by his Spanish countrymen against Indian people in the Caribbean, Mexico, and the rest of Latin America. Yet out of a perceived need to protect these Indian people and to replace the abusive and deadly *encomienda* system, he created a mode of evangelism that ultimately dislocated Indian people from their families and from their culture, relocated them in carefully controlled mission compounds, and immersed them in European values and social systems. This new mission strategy, called the *reducción,* continued to be the preferred Catholic method of evangelizing in all colonial contexts around the world and was redesigned and implemented by Protestants in seventeenth-century New England and later in Africa and other colonial settings.

More than three hundred years after Las Casas devised *reducción,* Whipple began his efforts, sure that he was acting in the best interests of the Sioux and that the only hope of their survival lay in reducing their land holdings, thus compelling a more sedentary existence that would allow a more effective imposition of European-style agriculture. His hope was that once their land holdings had been significantly reduced, the Sioux would be forced to abandon their traditional communitarian existence and patterns of community movement and adopt nuclear-family–style farming. Nor was it merely coincidental in Whipple's mind that excess land could and would then be opened up for white settlers. He envisioned these new immigrant farmers as appropriate neighbors and role models for the newly pacified Sioux peoples.

Father Crimont, a Jesuit priest, on a visit to Crow Indians, circa 1890.

Neither Whipple nor Las Casas understood his role in the process of pacification that enabled, simplified, and enhanced the ultimate conquest of those tribes. Thoroughly blinded by their immersion in their own culture and their implicit acceptance of the illusion of European superiority, these apostles of the church, and indeed virtually every missionary of every denomination, functioned in one way or another as a participant in an unintended evil. Las Casas and Whipple served two different denominations, derived from two different European traditions. Both had genuine good intentions regarding the fate of Indian peoples, and yet both participated in the cultural, political, economic, and social demise of those same peoples.

In 1769 Junípero Serra, the Franciscan founder of the European presence in California, came with an army cohort and official orders from the Spanish vice regent to begin his missionary conquest of native peoples in California. In an analogous way, the lay Presbyterian missionary Sue McBeth arrived among the Nez Perce peoples in 1873, just when the United States needed help in the pacification of that native nation. The final success of the U.S. military in putting down Chief Joseph's valiant resistance in 1877 was aided by McBeth's efforts to keep her converts close to the Presbyterian Nez Perce mission community and out of the battle.

Beginning in 1828, Congregationalist missionaries from the American Board of Commissioners for Foreign Missions in Boston—along with the initial support of

Moravian, Baptist, and Methodist missionaries, all of whom were working with them among Cherokee peoples in northern Georgia—took a courageous stand against the state of Georgia and the president of the United States on the issue of Indian removal. The state of Georgia, wanting to extend its claim of territorial sovereignty and pressing the issue of states' rights, had hoped that the election of Andrew Jackson as president that year would finally allow the state to work toward the removal of Indians from its territory. The Jackson administration had conceived a plan to move all Indian peoples from their aboriginal territories to a place designated as "Indian Territory," west of the Mississippi River.

Siding with the Cherokees and arguing that Cherokee sovereignty should take precedence over state sovereignty, these missionaries insisted that their progress in the project of civilizing (and converting) the Indians was such that citizens of the United States and of the state of Georgia had a moral obligation to respect Cherokee occupation and ownership of their original lands. The Congregationalist missionaries continued to resist Georgia's legislative attempts to remove them from Cherokee territory and to remove the Cherokees as well. For their acts of civil disobedience in defense of the Cherokees, two of these missionaries (Samuel Worcester and Elizur Butler) were sentenced to hard labor in the Georgia state penitentiary.

While this resistance to Cherokee removal certainly indicates a moral integrity and courage on the part of the missionaries, a closer reading indicates that they too participated in their own version of Manifest Destiny: they linked their defense of the Cherokees to the success they had seen in civilizing and converting them and indicated that the continued success of the missionizing venture depended on helping the Cherokees maintain their territorial integrity. Worcester in particular argued that the pacification effort had already demonstrated success and that there was no moral legitimacy for the removal policy.

This collusion between the missionaries and the political-military institutions of the colonizers in order to achieve the important conquest goal of the pacification of Indian peoples occurred repeatedly as the European invasion moved across the Americas in both the north and the south. While this strategy often resulted in an official alliance, it was always present on a de facto basis. Hernando Cortés insisted on the conversion of Indian peoples as an officially integrated strategy of his conquest of Mexico, and in 1524 the first contingent of Franciscan missionaries arrived there. John Eliot began

his outreach to the Massachusetts peoples in 1646 under the aegis of the Massachusetts General Council and Governor John Winthrop. Shortly after the formation of the United States, Congress passed the first of a series of laws establishing the Civilization Fund, earmarked for the support of Christian missionary schools among Indian peoples. For instance, the Jesuit province of St. Louis was started with moneys from this fund in 1823. And by 1869 the Grant administration's so-called peace policy attempted to reform the federal government's Indian Service by replacing all its civil-service Indian agents with denominationally appointed churchmen. As a result, Indian country was divided up between the various denominations, accounting for many of the denominational commitments of various tribes today.

In looking at this missionizing history, it is important to keep in mind that the Indian peoples themselves participated in the process. As the reality of conquest became apparent to each native nation, American Indian peoples received Euro-American missionaries somewhat readily, doing so either as individuals and families or as whole tribal communities. The reasons for this are complex.

Of primary importance among Indian peoples of North America is the inherent and enduring cultural value of openness to the spirituality of others and a long tradition of borrowing from one another. Openness to the missionaries must be understood initially in this context. Indian people often expressed surprise as they discovered that the new spirituality of the missionaries called on them to abandon their traditional ways in favor of a wholesale adoption of the European way, since their previous experience had always been one of adding to and not replacing their own spiritual ways.

Additionally, many Indian peoples felt the power of the conquest as such an overwhelming force that conversion to the conqueror's religion seemed the only way to maintain the existence of their communities and families. Though the Flatheads of Montana had little understanding of Christianity, they acknowledged the power of the invading colonizers and apparently hoped that by inviting missionaries into their midst they too would come to experience the increase in both spiritual and political-military power that European ceremonial expertise might bring to them. Thus in the 1840s the Flatheads, interpreting missionary spirituality in terms of their own experience of traditional spirituality, expected the missionaries to be the more spiritually potent counterparts of their own spiritual performers. On the other hand, by the 1870s the Oglala leader Red Cloud was more experienced in colonial contact. He determined that the survival of his people was dependent on their learning as much as possible about Euro-American ways, and he thus invited missionaries to come to the Lakotas and start schools for Indian youth.

More common was an Indian conversion to Christianity over a period of time, during which a community's traditional culture and spirituality were constantly eroded. Church and state colluded from the founding of the United States to discourage, disallow, and even punish certain aspects of traditional culture, culminating in government policies in the 1880s outlawing specific Indian tribal rituals. Under constant pressure from both missionaries and government officials, many communities experienced the steady loss of their older ceremonies until very little was left for them except the new spiritual arrangements under the leadership of the missionaries. Mission and government schools consciously attempted to further separate Indian children from their cultural values, particularly their ceremonial traditions. Through the use of ridicule, physical and psychological abuse, and an insistence on the primacy of European-based explanations of the world, mission and government schools hoped to engender in Indian children a belief in the superiority of European ways and a turning away from the traditions of their peoples. Traditional songs, stories, explanations of reality, and ceremonies eventually fell into disuse among Indian peoples. Today, having found missionary religion to be no panacea for the ongoing state of colonialism, many of these communities have been spending much time and energy in attempting to revive, restore, preserve, and relearn the old customs and ceremonies.

In other areas, Indian peoples gave some surface acknowledgement to the imposed mission religion but still managed to preserve their own spiritual integrity and ceremonial structures. Perhaps the most pronounced example of this is the Pueblo cultures, where Catholicism and traditional ceremonies coexist. Although the two religious ways remain distinct, Pueblo peoples quite often participate in both.

A few reservations managed to withstand much of the missionary pressure and have until now, held on to many of their old ceremonial ways. The Navajo people, for instance, are only now feeling the intensity of missionary efforts to separate them from their traditions and to convert them both culturally and spiritually to various forms of Christianity—usually of the more conservative and fundamentalist sort.

Whatever the personal or ecclesiastical intentions of the missionary efforts among Indian peoples may have been, this evangelical outreach had deep political and social consequences both for the colonizer and for the colonized.

See also Religion.

Jennings, Francis, *The Invasion of America: Indians, Colonialism, and the Cant of Conquest* (Chapel Hill: University of North Carolina Press, 1975); McGloughlin, Charles, *Cherokees and Missionaries, 1789–1839* (New Haven: Yale University Press, 1984); Tinker, George E., *Missionary Conquest: The Gospel and Native American Cultural Genocide* (Minneapolis: Fortress Press, 1993).

GEORGE E. TINKER (Osage)
Iliff School of Theology

MISSISSIPPIANS

Mississippian is an archaeological term denoting those mound-building societies that flourished in North America's eastern woodlands after A.D. 700. The end of the Mississippian period is usually dated around 1550, shortly after the arrival of Europeans and Africans in the Western Hemisphere, but some peoples, such as the Natchez (in what is now the state of Mississippi), were still performing Mississippian ceremonies as late as the early eighteenth century.

The state of Mississippi was certainly one part of the mound-building region, but it was only a small part of a very large area centered along both banks of the Mississippi River from the Gulf of Mexico to Minnesota. Important centers could also be found on such Mississippi River tributaries as the Ohio, Tennessee, Missouri, Arkansas, and Red Rivers. Outside the Mississippi drainage, riverine basins along the Gulf and southern Atlantic coasts, from the Neches River in Texas to the Pee Dee River in North and South Carolina, made up the rest of the region. Thus its reach extended across most of the present-day United States from the Appalachian Mountains to the eastern edge of the Great Plains.

The Mississippian was actually the last of three mound-building epochs in the eastern woodlands. The first, which archaeologists insist upon calling the Poverty Point Culture (c. 1500–700 B.C.), was located in the lower Mississippi Valley, and the second, the Hopewellian (c. 500 B.C. to A.D. 400), had boundaries quite similar to the Mississippian. Thus from a geographical point of view one might refer to all three as

Raccoon priest's gorget, circa 1250–1350, a Mississippian artifact from the Spiro mound site in eastern Oklahoma, one of the richest sources of artifacts in the mound-building region. The design features a sun circle with ceremonial dancers—a common motif. A single raccoon appears on the upper portion, and abstracted raccoons (face and tail) hang from the cross.

"Mississippian." Archaeologists, however, insist that one must not do so, due to the confusion that it would cause them. According to their nomenclature, *Mississippian* refers not just to a geographical locale but to a specific time period and to a certain way of living that was prevalent during that period.

Much of what we know about the societies that were a part of the Mississippian cultural region has come from archaeological investigations. There are also post-1500 Spanish and Portuguese descriptions of the peoples they encountered in their largely unsuccessful efforts to conquer its lands for Spain and its souls for Christianity. They called it *Florida,* a nebulous term that referred not only to the peninsula that now bears this name, but more or less to what the Spaniards knew or imagined of the entire mound-building region. In addition, much useful information has come from seventeenth- and eighteenth-century Jesuit and French accounts of the region's peoples. Yet another source of information about Mississippian societies comes from their descendants, Native American peoples whose homelands are within what was the Mississippian region. Their oral traditions and knowledge of the region's material culture, as well as their knowledge of surviving customs, can provide an invaluable window upon the past. Some have contributed directly to our fund of knowledge, and others have served as the subjects of anthropological investigations.

During the Mississippian period the population of the mound-building region numbered in the millions. The region's southern, temperate location, along with its usually reliable rainfall, made this land an abundant provider. Although the highlands between its many river valleys might be sparsely populated, the alluvial soils of their bottomlands were covered with palisaded towns and villages. Chroniclers of the de Soto expedition (1539–43) repeatedly remark upon the density of the population and an amazing abundance of maize (corn) in such places.

Although some maize (a variety referred to as tropical flint corn) had been grown during the earlier Hopewellian period, it was only around A.D. 800, after the introduction of a new variety known as eastern flint corn, that eastern woodlands people became dependent upon this crop as the mainstay of their diet. For the most part it was the women who grew, harvested, and stored the corn, along with other crops such as beans and squash. Along with the new dependence upon agriculture came a new tool, a short-handled stone-bladed hoe. (In some areas, where suitable stones were unavailable, the blades might be made from other materials such as bone, wood, or shells.) The women also gathered a wide variety of wild fruits and vegetables.

The men managed deer herds in the forests and hunted deer and other animals to provide a supply of meat. During the Mississippian period they hunted with bows and arrows—another characteristic that distinguishes Mississippians from earlier mound-building peoples. Prior to the appearance of the bow and arrow, which spread through the region between A.D. 300 and 550 (at the end of the Hopewellian period), hunters had used the atlatl, a variety of spear thrower. The bow and arrow was also a powerful weapon, as the Spanish intruders of the sixteenth century quickly found out. Native American warriors launched arrows that penetrated the Europeans' chain-mail armor and impaled their horses. They could shoot with such speed that they were able to get off five or six arrows in the time it took a Spaniard to reload his crossbow or musket.

The largest of the Mississippian centers was located at a site now called Cahokia, eight miles east of the Mississippi River near present-day East St. Louis, Illinois. Compared with Cahokia, other Mississippian sites were considerably more modest both in size and population, but most appear to have been bustling centers of population and handicraft production. Local specialties included ceramics, engraved shells, and various goods made from stone, leather, feathers, fibers, wood, and hammered copper.

The ceremonial heart of a Mississippian center was marked by large earthen mounds. The most typically Mississippian is the platform mound, rectangular at the base, with a series of flat tiers at the top. The largest—indeed, the world's largest earthwork—can still be seen today at Cahokia. It measures about one hundred feet high, one thousand feet long, and seven hundred feet wide, and has a total volume of 804,608 cubic yards. The second largest platform mound, with a volume of 159,331 cubic yards, is at Etowah in northwestern Georgia, and the third largest, 146,496 cubic yards, is at Moundville, Alabama, near Tuscaloosa. A large wooden structure, variously referred to as a palace or temple, was built on the flat surface atop these mounds. Its interior was decorated with skillfully tanned and painted deerskins, and the roof was covered with beautiful objects such as conch shells and strings of freshwater pearls. This was the abode of a paramount chief. Most platform mounds were built in stages. Whenever a paramount chief died, his palace was destroyed, a new layer of earth was added, and a successor's palace was then constructed over it, adding to the height of the mound. In front of the mound there was a large plaza, with smaller conical or ridged mounds (shaped somewhat like loaves of bread) arrayed around it. Some of these smaller mounds contain the graves of the elite.

Accounts of Spanish expeditions and French traders both indicate that paramount chiefs were called Great Suns, and that most, if not all, were men. They were surrounded by much ceremony and were often attired in knee-length cloaks made of valuable furs or beautifully woven feathers. Only those who belonged to the paramount lineage were eligible for the position, and succession was matrilineal, which is to say that when a Great Sun died, one of his sisters' sons (a nephew) replaced him. Ranking second only to the Great Sun's lineage were allied noble lineages. Third in rank were a group of distinguished personages, variously referred to as "honored" or "principal" people by European observers. The great majority of people were commoners, and there might also be slaves, who were usually prisoners of war.

A number of sites, as far apart as Georgia and Illinois, have yielded male and female stone images.

Among the most interesting are two female figures unearthed near Cahokia. One woman is kneeling on a coiled snake, stroking or scratching its back with a hoe, while a vine of gourds grows across her back. The other woman is kneeling before a metate, a stone dish used to grind corn. Both are clearly associated with fertility and cultivation and would seem to be related to elements in the Corn Mother legend, which is widespread among southeastern peoples. There are several versions of this tradition, but all involve Corn Mother scratching or stroking her body in order to give birth to corn, and later teaching her descendants how to farm.

Ever since the Hopewellian period the Mississippian region had been knit together by an exchange network. Mound-building centers were its nodes, and large dugout canoes plying the intricate system of rivers and streams linked them together. The following were among the highly valued items exchanged within the region: tens of thousands of freshwater pearls; copper from the Great Lakes and later from southern Appalachia; Ontario silver; hematite (an ore used to make red pigment) and chert (a stone that takes a sharp edge) from various sites; galena (an ore used to make white pigment) from the upper Mississippi Valley and Missouri; mica from Appalachia; flint blades and soapstone pipes from Ohio; crystalline quartz from Arkansas; obsidian and bears' teeth from the Rocky Mountains; shell beads, whole marine shells, sharks' and alligators' teeth, barracuda jaws, and turtle shells from the Gulf of Mexico; and some varieties of pottery from southern regions.

Scholars have suggested that paramount lineages and thus mound-building centers developed in those locations that enjoyed a reliable source of foodstuffs and were well situated to amass strategic exchange items, which could then be dispersed to their allies in elaborate ceremonies of alliance that were marked by the exchange of gifts. Elite lineages situated in less strategic locations were obliged to ally with the paramount lineages and participate in the center's ceremonies in order to obtain essential materials (such as certain kinds of stone) as well as those items that displayed their closeness to the center's prestige and power. Such an interpretation is consistent with the archaeological data, which suggest differences in styles and customs at the local level but a considerable uniformity in elite ceremonial culture across the mound-building region.

Great Suns, surrounded by numerous noble allies, could muster large numbers of warriors in order to defend strategic riverine and overland routes. The

Spaniards on several occasions encountered scores of large canoes all assembled in one place, each of them sizable enough to carry dozens of warriors. One such fleet encountered by de Soto's expedition so impressed an eyewitness that he compared it to a famous armada of galleys. He reported that there were two hundred canoes. The paramount chief, who issued orders to the entire force, sat under an awning at the rear of his canoe. (The heads of allied noble lineages also were accommodated in this way.) The warriors—very large, well formed, and fine looking—were painted with ocher and wore great bunches of feathers. Armed with bows and arrows, they stood erect in the canoes from bow to stern on both sides, and held much-decorated leather shields in order to protect the oarsmen.

Mississippian military strength, on water and on land, played a major role in preventing the Spaniards from conquering the mound-building region. After many attempts, the would-be conquistadors abandoned the effort and contented themselves with a Florida shrunk to the size of the peninsula that now bears its name. Indeed, the descendants of the Mississippians, the inheritors of many of their traditions, maintained control over most of their lands until the dawning of the nineteenth century and the Industrial Revolution.

See also Cahokia; Mound Builders; Moundville.

Brose, David, James A. Brown, and David W. Penny, *Ancient Art of the American Woodland Indians* (New York: Harry N. Abrams, 1985); Hudson, Charles M., *The Southeastern Indians* (Knoxville: University of Tennessee Press, 1976); Shaffer, Lynda Norene, *Native Americans Before 1492: The Moundbuilding Centers of the Eastern Woodlands* (Armonk, N.Y.: M. E. Sharp, 1992).

LYNDA SHAFFER
Tufts University

MIWOK

The modern Miwok (or Mewuk) Indians derive from a loose aggregation of Utian-speaking groups that occupied a wide band in central California from present-day Marin and Sonoma Counties north of San Francisco Bay and the Sacramento River, extending beyond the Yosemite Valley into eastern Nevada, as far north as present-day Tehama County and as far south as the San Joaquin Valley. Generally, the Miwok groups fall roughly into the following divisions: Coast (Tomales and Bodega Bays, in Marin, Mendocino, and Sono-

ma Counties); Bay (Mount Diablo to the Sacramento Delta, in Contra Costa and Sacramento Counties); Lake (Lake and Yolo Counties); Plains (drainages of the Cosumnes and Mokelumne Rivers, in Sacramento, Amador, and San Joaquin Counties); and the Northern Sierra, Southern Sierra, and Eastern Sierra Miwoks (in the foothills and peaks of the Sierras). The Western and Sierra Miwok languages became separate over twenty-five hundred years ago, while the Plains and Sierra Miwok languages separated at the beginning of the Common Era. The modern enrollments of the Miwok and mixed-Miwok bands and tribes range from one person (Buena Vista Rancheria) to 200 (Jackson Rancheria), 300 (Tuolumne Rancheria), and nearly 600 (Mooretown Rancheria), while estimates of their precontact total populations through mission records, accounts of explorers, census records, and special federal enrollments indicate that the population was about 19,500 in 1800. In 1904, and again in 1905 and 1906, Special Indian Agent C. E. Kelsey enumerated the Miwok population at fewer than 800 persons in or near aboriginal villages. The 1910 U.S. Census identified about 700 living in distinct communities. Kelsey's successors continually monitored the population and condition of Miwok bands and tribes through the 1930s, and Cook found about 760 in 1930. By 1951, the California Senate's Interim Committee on California Indian Affairs found only 109 living on the rancherias. The 1990 U.S. Census and other recent Indian Health Service and California Office of Economic Opportunity estimates suggest that some 3,500 persons with some degree of Miwok Indian ancestry survive in California, at least 500 of whom are enrolled members of federally recognized tribes.

The Spanish explorers encountered Eastern Sierra Miwoks in the late 1700s. Before the United States acquired California in 1848, the Coast Miwok and Plains Miwok groups in particular had been the objects of early Spanish and Mexican colonization and proselytization efforts in areas surrounding the Roman Catholic missions, starting at San Francisco in 1794, and continuing at San Jose in 1811, and then at San Rafael, Solano, Sonoma, and Santa Rosa. The Lake Miwoks met the Luis Arguello expedition near Middletown in 1821. Mortality from disease and slaughter greatly reduced these populations, while the Russian fur-trading activities at Fort Ross and nearby coastal villages had a similarly negative impact. Sierra and Plains Miwoks under the leadership of hereditary patrilineal leaders known as headmen or captains—such as Ha Pipia, Estanislao, Maximo, and their relations—fought the invaders in the 1820s and 1830s and attacked Mexican coastal settlements with the support of their Yokuts neighbors. These activities played a role in the secularization of the missions, and Miwoks aided the United States in the war with Mexico. Mariano Vallejo's 1848 treaty with Lake and Coast Miwok headmen availed the tribes nothing.

The California gold rush and agricultural development brought waves of settlers into Miwok territories after 1850. U.S. treaty commissioners signed treaties that ceded most Miwok lands, while reserving several parcels for the Miwoks' permanent use. When the U.S. Senate refused to ratify these treaties, American settlers indentured or enslaved hundreds of Miwoks and murdered or drove away uncounted hundreds of others. Survivors sought employment in timber, fishing, mining, ranching, farming, and other industries, where many continue to labor. Many Coast and Lake Miwoks became fishermen and migrant farm workers throughout the Central Valley region, while Northern Sierra and the Central Sierra division of the Eastern Miwoks became ranchers and farmers, and Southern Sierra Miwoks became loggers. Over 200 Plains and Southern Sierra Miwoks worked for miners by 1860. Ghost Dance prophets like Chiplichu of Pleasanton passed through the Miwok tribes at Knight's Ferry and Ione from 1872 to the 1920s, and there remain notable surviving examples of the phenomenon, and its influence, among the Miwok rancherias.

While Miwok-speaking groups attempted to reunite as an organized body as recently as 1927, no unified Miwok national tribal organization survives. At the local level, little if anything remains of the two traditional social moieties, or "land" and "water" divisions. Modern federally acknowledged California Miwok entities reside on small rancherias (reservations under four hundred acres in area). The U.S. Congress or Bureau of Indian Affairs terminated intergovernmental relations with most of the Miwok rancherias between 1934 and 1972, but with few exceptions, these entities have obtained restoration of their status since 1984. Three of these formerly acknowledged primarily Miwok rancherias (Nevada City, Strawberry Valley, and Wilton) remain terminated.

Seven surviving rancheria-based tribes have primarily or exclusively Miwok populations. These include: Buena Vista (Plains Miwok; Amador County), Chicken Ranch (Central Sierra division of Eastern Miwok; Tuolumne County), Ione (Northern Sierra and Plains Miwok; Amador County), Jackson (Northern Sierra and Plains Miwok; Amador County), Middletown (Lake Miwok; Lake County), Sheep Ranch (Northern Sierra Miwok; Calaveras County), Shingle Springs (Plains Miwok; El Dorado County), and Tuolumne (Central Sierra Miwok; Tuolumne County). The Assistant Secretary of Interior for Indian Affairs reaffirmed the acknowledgment of the Ione band in 1994.

Most Miwok groups aboriginally traded with neighboring Miwok divisions, shared many of the same cultural and ceremonial activities and calendars, and intermarried with one another. The Coast Miwoks traditionally intermarried with Pomos as well. Lake Miwoks intermarried with Concows, Maidus, Nomlakis, Pomos, Yukis, Wailakis, and Wintus. Sierra Miwoks intermarried with Maidus and Pomos. Accordingly, at least seventeen other federally acknowledged California bands and tribes include Miwok descendants.

Traditional songs, dances, a gambling game (a form of hand game played with bone markers or sticks, to the accompaniment of singers), and other ceremonial activities remain among particular bands and rancherias. Weaving and beading, as well as the making of traditional garments and implements for ceremonial purposes, for sale, and as gifts, persist—particularly in the counties of Marin, Sonoma, Mendocino, Amador, Calaveras, Tuolumne, and Mariposa. The September Acorn Festival at Tuolumne Rancheria, the winter and spring commemorations of the hibernation and awakening of the Bear Spirit, and the Goose Dance near the winter solstice are significant examples of surviving ceremonial activities. Tuolumne Rancheria has a dance house currently in use, while one is still under construction at the Ione Reservation, and others have been constructed, destroyed, and rebuilt at Grinding Rock State Historical Park (called Chaw'se by the Miwoks.)

The Northern Sierra Mewuk Language Program has aided in the preservation of surviving Miwok language skills with the help of elders like the Ione band's Captain Nicolas Villa, Sr. The Mariposa-Amador-Tuolumne-Calaveras Indian Health Board and the Tuolumne Indian Health Center at Tuolumne Rancheria serve primarily Miwok Indians in the four named county areas. Health clinics and other Indian service agencies serve Miwoks in Sonoma, Mendocino, and Lake Counties.

ALLOGAN SLAGLE (United Keetoowah Band)
Association on American Indian Affairs
New York, New York

MOHAVE

The Ahamacav (Mohave) Nation has been described by scholars as "sometimes friendly, sometimes deadly." This characterization of fierce loyalty to friends and just retribution toward enemies summarizes the Anglo-American experience of interaction with the Mohave Nation in the period of U.S. western expansion in the nineteenth century. Although no formal treaties were signed between Congress and the Mohave Nation, the Mohave people continue to honor the gentleman's agreement negotiated in 1859 with the representatives of the United States.

The Ahamacav, or "People along the River," continue to flourish on the banks of the Colorado River in what is now known as the southwestern United States. The tribe lives in an area that currently borders the states of Arizona, California, and Nevada. The tribe maintains legal title to its critical aboriginal territory, and these areas are referred to now as the Fort Mojave Indian Reservation and the Colorado River Indian Reservation. The combined population in 1995 for both Mohave communities is approximately twenty-nine hundred.

These reservations are administered by different sovereign tribal governments under two separate legal jurisdictions. These governments were created and recognized by the Indian Reorganization Act of 1934, and the tribal-council form of government that was adopted at the time does not separate the functions of the administration, the legislature, and the judiciary. However, both governments operate civil and criminal courts that protect and assert their legal jurisdiction on the reservations over their own members.

The historic economy of the tribe consisted of a combination of gathering and agriculture by men and women and of hunting and fishing by men. The lush environment of the river valleys provided an abundance of wild foods that were seasonally gathered. The most important of these foods were the honey mesquite bean and screwbean mesquite bean, which provided a significant nourishing staple in the Mohave diet. The Mohave agriculturalists also strategically adapted their cultivation to the flood patterns of the Colorado River and raised double crops of corn, beans, squash, and melons. Spanish contact later contributed wheat as another staple food crop. Several varieties of fish provided significant protein in the diet and were gathered by means of nets, scoops, and fishing lines. Large-scale trade with surrounding tribes, in-cluding distant tribes along the coast of southern California and the Pueblos along the Rio Grande, was also an important economic activity for the Mohaves. These established Mohave trade routes were later appropriated by U.S. Army engineers and eventually served as the basis for major portions of Interstate 40 and the Santa Fe railway.

The initial integration of the Mohave people into the cash economy of the United States was problematic. Mohave women were largely displaced because there was no primary role for them in the male-dominated American labor force. However, Mohave men quickly adapted to opportunities in irrigation farming, cattle ranching, and railway or mine work. Although some Mohave women worked as domestic help, laundresses, and nannies, many selected entrepreneurial opportunities by independently producing and marketing pottery, bead ornaments, and other goods to tourists along the railway. The phenomenal business these entrepreneurs did provided significant capital to Mohave families while the legal title to Mohave land was being legally and administratively resolved.

As Anglo-American appropriation of the economic resources of the area continued, large agricultural development schemes were promoted on both reservations as a means of integrating the Mohave into the regional economy of the United States. The Colorado River Indian reservation was first funded for an irrigation system in 1868 but large-scale agriculture did not begin there until the Poston Japanese internment camp was opened in 1942. The Japanese contributed significant labor and skill in subjugating the land, until their labor was replaced by Navajo and Hopi colonists who were settled at Colorado River after the internment camp was closed in 1945. Fort Mojave financed its own irrigation system in 1976. In 1995, tribal agricultural enterprises and the leasing of irrigated farmlands to non-Mohaves provided the basis for annual tribal government revenues between eight million and ten million dollars. The development of casino-style gambling on both reservations in 1995 promised to provide significant revenue following the repayment of capital improvement loans in the early twenty-first century.

Mohave tribal identity in both reservation communities remains strong, although the pattern of intermarriage with other tribes that began in the early 1900s and a trend toward intermarriage with other races that began in the 1960s continue to challenge and change individual concepts of identity as well as the community's sense of itself. Tribal concepts of identity continue to be based on residence in the community, kinship ties, and knowledge of language. These have clashed with Pan-Indian essentialist concepts of identity concerning racial appearance, blood quantum, and manifestations of the outward appearance of "culture." Recent assertions of tribal identity in response to Pan-Indianism have taken the form of formally recognized elders' groups, increased support for scholarship in history and material culture, and legal codes defining cultural instruction and enrollment.

The most critical problem affecting the tribe today is the serious growth of diabetes among the population. The damming of the Colorado River in the 1930s and the subsequent change in economy and diet are all contributing factors to the development of diabetes in the population. Culture is affected because the time available for the transmission of knowledge decreases when the average life span is reduced by twenty to thirty years; for example, language skills have dropped significantly, and proficiency remains only in the population over thirty years of age. At present, the Mohave communities are exploring ways to resolve this problem and to mitigate the long-term impact of diabetes.

The anthropologist Alfred Kroeber noted that the Mohave people were a rare example of a true nation. When attacked or challenged, the Mohaves set aside their personal differences and coordinated their skills as a group to achieve victory. The contact history of the Mohave Nation continues to reflect this strength as they protect their people and their resources for now and the future. The Mohave people continue to properly assert themselves economically, politically, and legally in order not just to survive, but to flourish. Their ability to adapt to change on their own terms must not be mistaken for a tendency toward assimilation; rather their actions demonstrate their continued strength as a unique people and nation.

Kroeber, Alfred, "The Mohave," in *Handbook of the Indians of California* (Washington: Smithsonian Institution, Bureau of American Ethnology, 1925); Smith, Gerald, *The Mojaves: Historic Indians of San Bernardino County* (Redlands, Calif.: San Bernardino County Museum Association, 1977); Spencer, Robert F., and Jesse D. Jennings et al, *The Native Americans: Prehistory and Ethnology of the North American Indians* (New York: Harper & Row, 1965).

MICHAEL PHILIP TSOSIE
(Colorado River Indian Tribes)
University of California at Berkeley

MOHAWK

The Mohawks of the seventeenth century were the easternmost of the five Iroquois nations, keepers of the eastern door of the confederacy known as the League of the Iroquois. Their traditional territory was the Mohawk River valley of what is now eastern New York State. There were nearly eight thousand Mohawks when they were first visited by Europeans in the early sixteenth century, living in four palisaded villages of bark longhouses. They called themselves the Kanyenkehaka, "People of the Flint [or Crystal] Place." The Dutch and English called them Mohawks, a term meaning "man eaters" that they borrowed from the Indians of southern New England.

The League of the Iroquois had been formed earlier, during a period of chronic warfare, probably in the early part of the sixteenth century. The Mohawks led the creation of this political innovation and later remained dominant in its interactions with both Europeans and other Indian nations.

Like other Iroquoians, the Mohawks were strongly matrilineal in their social structure and matrilocal in their residence patterns. Longhouses were filled by clan segments made up of nuclear families that were linked through their female members.

The social organization of the Mohawks facilitated the growth of large and compact villages in which women could effectively mitigate internal strife. A horticultural system that depended upon a mix of corn, beans, and squash as staples provided basic support for the villages. Women predominated in this activity, too, being the primary food producers.

The Mohawks had begun to coalesce as a nation by the fourteenth century. Chronic warfare prompted them to increase the sizes of their villages by joining together previously separate communities. These larger villages in turn sought protection by relocating to hilltop sites remote from the main course of the Mohawk River.

The Mohawks were among the first of the Iroquois nations to come into regular contact with Europeans. Trade with Basque and French fishermen and explorers began along the St. Lawrence in the middle of the sixteenth century. Competition for access to this trade stimulated Mohawk warfare against other Iroquoians in the St. Lawrence area. A breakthrough occurred in 1609 when Samuel de Champlain explored southward toward Mohawk territory and Henry Hudson sailed northward on the river that now bears his name. Hudson's exploration led the Dutch to establish a trading post at what is now Albany by 1614. As the Dutch trade grew, so did the strength and political importance of the Mohawks. By 1626 they were the largest and most powerful of the Iroquois nations.

The first of many devastating epidemics struck the Mohawks in 1634. The initial epidemic was smallpox, followed by waves of measles, scarlet fever, influenza, and other Old World diseases to which no Mohawk was immune. The Mohawk population declined by two-thirds in one decade.

The epidemics led indirectly to increased warfare as the Mohawks and other Iroquois lashed out at their traditional enemies. Arms supplied by Dutch traders gave them a military advantage. Enemies not killed or dispersed were captured and brought home for adoption—the preferred means of counteracting the population decline. By 1650 the Huron and Neutral confederacies had been destroyed, and many residents of Mohawk villages were former refugees, captives, or their descendants.

The English took over the Dutch colony of New Netherland in 1664 and renamed it New York. After the Dutch returned briefly in 1673, the English set about winning the permanent support of the Mohawks. Governor Edmund Andros and the Iroquois League chiefs forged the Covenant Chain, an abstract symbol to bind them politically. The arrangement sought simultaneously to bring the neighboring colonies under Andros's direct control and to bring a broad range of Indian nations under the control of the League of the Iroquois.

The traditional longhouse village had disappeared by the early eighteenth century. The conversion of many Mohawks to Catholicism by French Jesuit missionaries led to their departure to the community of Kahnawake near Montreal. French attacks demonstrated the vulnerability of traditional palisaded villages. The rise of self-made men called Pine Tree Chiefs undermined the traditional leadership of clan matrons and league chiefs. This development acted in concert with the physical fragmentation of the clan segments by warfare and disease to destroy the viability of the bark longhouse as a residential unit. After 1700 most Mohawks lived in dispersed European-style cabins surrounded by fields cultivated by women using a combination of traditional and European techniques. Men continued to help with the heavy work, but they also continued to be deeply involved in diplomatic, economic, and political affairs.

Theyanoguin, a Mohawk known to the English as Hendrick, emerged as the principal Iroquois League chief in this era. Joseph Brant, a Pine Tree Chief, followed him in that role after Theyanoguin's death in the French and Indian War. The defeat of the French left the Iroquois unable to secure themselves by playing the two colonial powers off each other. A few years later the American Revolution tore the league apart. The Mohawks and many other Iroquois sided with the English and were forced out of the Mohawk Valley.

The upper-valley Mohawks followed Joseph Brant to the Six Nations reserve near Brantford, Ontario. They remain there today with the descendants of other Iroquois who sided with the English. The lower-valley Mohawks fled to Montreal, and were later granted a reserve at Tyendinaga, on the north shore of Lake Ontario.

A faction from the Catholic Mohawk reserve at Kahnawake had earlier broken away to form a new community at Akwesasne. This community now found itself straddling the new international boundary between the United States and Canada. During the nineteenth century, some Mohawks began moving to the Lake of Two Mountains Reserve (Kanesatake) and to a new community called Gibson near the eastern shore of Lake Huron. Around 1977 a small community of Mohawks was granted reservation land (Ganienkeh) by New York State in the town of Altona. Finally, in 1993, a small community of Mohawks relocated from Akwesasne back into the Mohawk Valley (Kanatsiohareke), creating a Mohawk presence there for the first time in two centuries. Mohawks continue to live in all of these communities today.

Having reached an all-time low a century ago, the Mohawks' numbers now exceed the previous high level of the early seventeenth century. A century ago, Mohawk men found a new niche as steel construction workers in the expanding industrial economy. The work has meant that once again Mohawk men engage in lucrative and prestigious work away from home while Mohawk women maintain family and community.

See also Iroquois Confederacy.

Bonvillain, Nancy, *The Mohawk* (New York: Chelsea House, 1992); Fenton, William N., and Elisabeth Tooker, "Mohawk," in *Handbook of North American Indians,* ed. William C. Sturtevant, vol. 15, *Northeast,* ed. Bruce Trigger (Washington: Smithsonian Institution, 1978); Snow, Dean R., *The Iroquois* (Cambridge, Mass.: Blackwell Publishers, 1994).

DEAN R. SNOW
The Pennsylvania State University

MOHICAN
See Stockbridge-Munsee (Mohican).

MONTAGNAIS-NASKAPI

Scholars have struggled for centuries to agree on a straightforward label for the culturally distinct people who ranged over three to four hundred thousand square miles of Canada's Labrador peninsula. The current consensus is *Montagnais-Naskapi*. The French called the hunters they met at the St. Lawrence River in the late sixteenth century *montagnais*, or "mountaineers." An early-twentieth-century student proposed that Naskapi was a word the Montagnais used to refer to the "uncivilized people" who lived to the northwest of them. Similarities in the cultural practices of these two groups and the common characteristics of their Algonquian languages have prompted anthropologists to classify the two groups together. Some Montagnais, however, especially those centered around Lake Mistassini, Quebec, are frequently referred to as Crees. Until the late twentieth century, these categorizations appear to have mattered little to the Montagnais-Naskapis themselves, who have long resisted efforts by Europeans and Canadians to bring their lives into conformity with nonnative priorities.

The problem of how to label the Naskapis and Montagnais stemmed from Europeans' misinterpretations of the Indians' social organization. French fur traders encountered Montagnais in the summers at the lakeside and riverside encampments where a few hundred tribesmen gathered for trade and festivity; they did not appreciate that for most of the year the Montagnais lived in smaller, nomadic hunting bands. A few of these summer gatherings included as many as fifteen hundred Algonquian-speaking and Inuit people who had assembled to trade with the French. The European traders, who treated these larger gatherings as the primary form of local social organization, mistakenly believed that the men whom the Montagnais designated to speak for them were chiefs, but these *ad hoc* leaders possessed no formal authority over other members of their bands.

For most of the year the Montagnais and Naskapis lived in small, fluid hunting bands. In winter these bands consisted of a few pairs of families with no more than four children each—between ten and twenty people in all. The creation of new families occurred when men left their families to live with women in other bands. The groups were generally exogamous and matrilocal, but rules for marriage were flexible.

In winter the Montagnais hunted eels, porcupine, beaver, moose, caribou, and bear. When the hunters killed a large number of animals at once, they would move the entire band to the kill site rather than haul heavy, unbutchered bodies back to camp. The Naskapis ranged across the region's northern drainage and hunted caribou nearly exclusively. The composition of the winter hunting bands varied from year to year, depending on the members' preferences and the divination of likely success through the breaking of burned bones. Hunting bands tended to travel through familiar ground during the winter, but particular families did not own the land. If a band near starvation found another band's cache of supplies or killed game in another's range, they were not begrudged the food, although it was considered polite for them to inform the people who usually hunted there.

The arrival of Europeans directly altered the lives of those Montagnais and Naskapis who dealt directly with the newcomers, and it indirectly affected all members of the group. Montagnais were among the Indians who led Samuel de Champlain through the St. Lawrence Valley in 1609; others joined the British when they tried to oust the French from Quebec in 1629. Beyond these relatively infrequent contacts, however, the European influence spread deeply into tribal life through epidemics of smallpox and measles. The desire of neighboring Iroquois to expand the lands that supported their trade with the French prompted them to attack Montagnais camps with a violence that the Montagnais still recounted early in the twentieth century. Some Montagnais joined Algonquian-speaking groups in active warfare against the Iroquois in the early seventeenth century.

During the seventeenth century the appeal of European trade caused the Montagnais to shift their winter activities from hunting to trapping. The French were particularly desirous of beaver pelts, and in fact used coins known as *Made Beaver* to pay their Indian suppliers. The Montagnais purchased copper kettles, guns, and flour with the pelts of the extra beavers they trapped, but they did not buy more than they could carry with them in the winter. Europeans expected to trade with the same people every year, and summer gatherings at particular posts became fixed features of the colonial economy. The Montagnais tried to retain their independence, however, by continuing to hunt a wide variety of animals in the winter. They still shared generously with others in need of food, but members of neighboring bands were forbidden to hunt animals valuable in the trade on each other's land.

For the Montagnais-Naskapis, the era of the fur trade continued into the twentieth century. Only when the fur trade diminished did they begin to abandon their seasonal nomadic patterns. Most Montagnais eventually accepted the Christianity offered them by the Roman Catholic priests whom they met at the summer gatherings, but they continued to celebrate their traditional religious rituals as well. The most important of these was the Shaking Tent Ritual, in which the members of the band gathered in a specially constructed tent to hear a shaman speak with the gods.

In the nineteenth century, the Canadian government encouraged the Montagnais to take up agriculture and settle down in one place, but tribesmen insisted on making their living by balancing hunting and trapping. Well into the twentieth century, the Montagnais refused to confine their hunts to the reserves. The Naskapis, however, settled at Davis Inlet, Labrador, when the caribou on which they depended failed to return to Indian House Lake in the fall of 1916.

In the middle of the twentieth century, the decline in the Montagnais-Naskapi population that had begun with the arrival of the Europeans was reversed. In 1492 there were approximately 4,000 Montagnais-Naskapis in about two dozen bands; in 1971 there were more than 11,500. But the introduction of industrialization, in the form of mining and the building of more than twenty hydroelectric dams in the Labrador peninsula, changed Montagnais culture in ways that the fur trade did not. Today less land is available for hunting and trapping than was used in the fifteenth century, and industrial wage work cannot sustain the prosperity the Montagnais-Naskapis enjoyed in the fur-trade era. Some Montagnais-Naskapis have settled into permanent buildings and receive welfare checks from the government. A few, however, balancing their experiences in hunting bands with Canadian village life, have entered the political arena. Galvanized by the Canadian government's attempts during the late 1980s to invite NATO jets onto an already noisy bomber base at Goose Bay, Labrador, and organized as the Innu Nation, some Montagnais-Naskapis now advocate alliance with Indians across Canada and the United States on behalf of the large, nonband groups to which Europeans always assumed they belonged.

Leacock, Eleanor, "The Montagnais-Naskapi of the Labrador Peninsula," in *Native Peoples: The Canadian Experience,* ed. R. Bruce Morrison and C. Roderick Wilson, 2d ed. (Toronto: McClelland and Stewart, 1995); Rogers, Edward S., ed., *A Northern Algonquian Source Book: Papers by Frank G. Speck* (New York and London: Garland Publishing, 1985).

AMANDA IRENE SELIGMAN
Northwestern University

MONTAUK

Before the arrival of the Europeans the Montauks (or Montauketts, the seventeenth-century spelling revived by tribal members in the 1990s) located their villages along the banks of freshwater streams and tidal bays in the coastal areas on the southern fork of eastern Long Island in what is now the state of New York. This rich ecosystem provided them with both woodland plants and animals and a wide variety of shellfish, finfish, and sea mammals. Although the archaeological record provides little evidence of horticulture, they probably cultivated some small plots of domesticated crops.

The Montauk artisans made disk-shaped beads from quahog (*Mercenaria mercenaria*) shells, which they used for trade and for tribute payments to the Pequots of southern New England. Purple beads made from the outer lip of the quahog were in great demand, particularly among the inland tribes. After the Montauks obtained metal awls from the Europeans, they began to make cylindrical beads and weave them into wampum, which was used as currency in the fur trade.

Following the English destruction of the Pequot villages in Connecticut in 1637, Wyandanch, a Montauk sachem, negotiated an alliance with the victors and encouraged the English to establish settlements on eastern Long Island. The English support enabled Wyandanch to become one of the most influential sachems on Long Island. By 1700, however, the English had taken possession of the Montauks' lands, leaving the Indians with only residence rights to a small area near the present-day village of Montauk.

The Montauk community adapted to the forces of change. Montauks served in the local non-Indian economy as whalers, hunting guides, cattle herders, unskilled laborers, soldiers, sailors, and domestics. As the number of Indians on Long Island declined, many Montauks married African Americans. In spite of the resulting changes in their economic base and in their physical appearance, however, the community clung tenaciously to its Indian identity.

In 1749 the Mohegan missionary Samson Occom came to Montauk, married a Montauk woman, and began his ten-year tenure as minister. In 1785 Occom led many of the Montauks to resettle in Brothertown, a Christian town he had established in central New York State. The Brothertown Indians later migrated to Wisconsin, where their descendants live today. Those Montauks who remained home came under constant harassment from the local whites who wanted them to leave. Montauk leaders complained about the abuses to the New York State Assembly in 1806 and 1811, and to the State Supreme Court in 1870, but the state declined to take any action.

During the 1880s real-estate developers pressured individual Montauks to sell their tribal residence rights and move to nearby towns. In 1909 the tribe, under the leadership of Chief Wyandank Pharaoh, a direct descendant of Wyandanch, began a court battle with the developers to regain title to their land. The developers argued that the Montauks were no longer a "tribe of Indians" because they had intermarried with African Americans and had adopted a "modern" lifestyle. The judge agreed with the defense and announced to a courtroom full of Montauks that their tribe was now extinct. The Montauks appealed the case and fought an unsuccessful eight-year battle in the courts.

In spite of their defeat in court, the Montauks have continued to meet on feast days to renew their kinship ties. Although many of their descendants today live in scattered enclaves across Long Island and as far west as Brothertown, Wisconsin, some remain in Sag Harbor and East Hampton, near the ancient homeland. Today Robert Pharaoh and Robert Cooper, both of whom are related to Wyandank Pharaoh, are in the process of reversing the cultural effects of the Montauk diaspora. Currently their primary concern is the development of a museum and learning center in the county park that is located on part of their ancient homeland.

See also Occom, Samson.

Stone, Gaynell, ed., *The History and Archaeology of the Montauk* (Stony Brook, N.Y.: Suffolk County Archaeological Association, 1993); Strong, John A., "Who Says the Montauk Tribe Is Extinct? Judge Abel Blackmar's Decision in *Wyandank* v. *Benson* (1909)," *American Indian Culture and Research Journal* 16, no. 1 (1992): 1–22.

JOHN A. STRONG
Long Island University at Southampton

MONTEZUMA, CARLOS (WASSAJA)

(1866?–1923)
Yavapai physician and reformer.

Coluyevah and Thilgeyah no doubt hoped their son, Wassaja, would live the traditional life of his people, the Yavapais of central Arizona. But by the time of his birth in about 1866, the Yavapai world had become constricted and contested. The discovery of gold, the advent of Anglo-American communities, and conflicts with neighboring American Indian tribes brought abrupt change to the community's economy and social life. Worse, in 1871 young Wassaja was captured by Pima Indians, who took him to Adamsville, near Florence, Arizona, and sold him for thirty dollars. He never saw his parents again. His purchaser, the photographer Carlos Gentile, provided him with a new name and soon with new surroundings. Wassaja became Carlos Montezuma, and he left with Gentile for the Midwest.

Given over eventually to the care of a Baptist minister, William Steadman of Urbana, Illinois, Montezuma soon demonstrated his potential for achievement. He graduated from the University of Illinois with a degree in chemistry, and then went on to earn his M.D. from the Chicago Medical College in 1889. After a stint as a physician for the Bureau of Indian Affairs, he entered private practice in Chicago. Chicago remained his home, and he continued to practice medicine, but it was as a crusader for reform of Indian policy that Montezuma gained national recognition.

Montezuma stood out as a new kind of Indian leader at the beginning of the twentieth century. He and other well-educated Native Americans, such as the Santee Sioux physician Charles Eastman, were proud of their heritage and failed to share in the gloomy predictions, common at the time, that Indians were about to disappear. Rather, they believed, with hard work, equal opportunity, and dedication, Indians could achieve great things; indeed, their own lives attested to that possibility. Montezuma and Eastman joined others in establishing the Society of American Indians in 1911. In contrast to established, white-dominated organizations like the Indian Rights Association, the society was to be for Indians themselves. Although the society's annual meetings and its journal served for a time as a useful forum for discussion and debate over important issues, its members divided eventually on some of these issues—including the merits of the Bureau of Indian Affairs—which led to its premature demise in the late

1920s. Nonetheless, the society's brief existence symbolized a brighter future and represented the kind of multitribal, national organization that more contemporary associations, such as the National Congress of American Indians, would become.

Montezuma's own involvement in the Society of American Indians was somewhat sporadic, depending in part on the degree to which the organization was likely to embrace his views. One of his mostly strongly held beliefs involved the Bureau of Indian Affairs. Montezuma thought that the bureau should be abolished. To this goal he dedicated much of his public commentary, some of which appeared in the newsletter *Wassaja,* which he published beginning in April 1916. Here Montezuma argued that the failings of the bureau were so severe that it could not be reformed or rehabilitated. Many Indians shared Dr. Montezuma's general prognosis, but refrained from endorsing his radical prescription. They worried about what would take the bureau's place.

Carlos Montezuma as a boy, with the photographer Carlos Gentile, who raised him.

At first Montezuma was influenced by the founder of the Carlisle Indian Industrial School, Richard Henry Pratt. Pratt corresponded with Montezuma while the latter was still in medical school; Montezuma worked as the school physician at Carlisle for more than two years. But in time Montezuma developed a more complicated analysis of contemporary Indian life, while Pratt remained an absolute assimilationist. Pratt believed in the potential of individual Indians, but felt that "the Indian" in the person had to be eradicated for the person to fulfill his or her promise. Thus Indian reservations, for example, had no redeeming value. As long as they existed and Indians occupied them, Indians would be held back.

By the turn of the century, Montezuma had reestablished contact with some of his remaining Yavapai relatives. His parents had died, but cousins and an aunt lived on the newly established Fort McDowell Reservation, located on the site of a former military installation to the north and east of Phoenix. As Montezuma became more familiar with the conditions at Fort McDowell and other reservations in Arizona, he protested against the prisonlike atmosphere he saw prevailing on them. He argued that agents and other bureau personnel had too much power and that they restricted the lives of reservation residents. At the same time, however, continuing contact with Fort McDowell prompted Montezuma to realize that with the passage of time reservations had become homes for the people who lived there. His relatives and his people deserved to be able to live without being forced to accept alien customs. They deserved to have access to the water they needed to farm their lands. They should not be forced off their lands or deprived of their water rights simply because non-Indians sought their land or their water.

In the final two decades of his life, then, Carlos Montezuma immersed himself in an unceasing campaign for the Yavapais. Without his help, other members of Fort McDowell have acknowledged, they might well have been evicted from their land. Montezuma looked beyond the boundaries of tribe and past prior enmity to defend the rights of local Pimas and other Indians as well. Even though he continued to have mixed emotions about the reservations as institutions, he had no doubts about native rights. At a time when most Indians were not even citizens of the United States, he stood up for their place and their future in American society. And he paid his final tribute to the people of Fort McDowell when, critically ill with tuberculosis, he returned to the land of his people. He died at Fort Mc-Dowell on January 31, 1923.

Like many leaders, Montezuma often wrote and acted with one eye on the present and the other on succeeding generations. In the last paragraph he ever wrote in *Wassaja*, published in November 1922, he declared:

> If the world be against us, let us not be dismayed, let us not be discouraged, let us up and go ahead, and fight on for freedom and citizenship for our people. If it means death, let us die on the pathway that leads to the emancipation of our race, keeping in our hearts that our children will pass over our graves to victory.

Iverson, Peter, *Carlos Montezuma and the Changing World of American Indians* (Albuquerque: University of New Mexico Press, 1982).

PETER IVERSON
Arizona State University

MORGAN, J.C.

(1879–1950)
Navajo educator, missionary, and tribal politician.

Jacob Casimera Morgan was born at Nahódeshgizh, near Crownpoint, New Mexico. He belonged to the Salt clan, and his father was a member of the Meadow clan. He had little contact with whites until his father placed him in school at Fort Defiance. A year later he transferred to a school in Grand Junction, Colorado, where he converted to Christianity, became fluent in English, and learned to play the cornet.

In 1898 Morgan enrolled at Hampton Normal and Agricultural Institute in Virginia for carpentry training. His teachers gave him high marks for his work habits, academic achievements, and musical skills. After graduating in 1900, Morgan held several temporary positions before returning to Hampton in 1901 to study business. Illness two years later forced his return home. His Hampton stay made him an outspoken advocate of Indian assimilation. Significantly, the adult Morgan always appeared in public in a suit, white shirt, and tie and usually carried a briefcase.

In 1910 Morgan married Zahrina Tso, an educated Navajo. The marriage produced three sons—Irwin Roderick, William Edmund, and Jacob Casimera, Jr., or Buddy.

After 1904, Morgan's career was always on the margin between Navajo and white society. Initially he worked for the Bureau of Indian Affairs as a financial clerk and interpreter, and later operated a trading post. In 1910 he assisted the Reverend L. P. Brink of the Christian Reformed Church (CRC) in biblical translations. Four years later, he became a shop teacher and band director at Crownpoint. His lively band gained considerable fame for its public concerts. In 1922 or 1923 he joined the staff of the San Juan Boarding School at Shiprock, New Mexico.

In 1923 Morgan won a seat on the newly formed Navajo Council. He and other returned students believed that they were being unfairly excluded from BIA jobs and other opportunities on the reservation by Chee Dodge, a prestigious older leader from Crystal, New Mexico. Morgan frequently criticized Dodge's Catholicism and immoral behavior.

In 1925 Morgan left the BIA to assist Brink at a new CRC mission in Farmington, New Mexico. Morgan plunged into the instruction of schoolchildren, camp visits, and translations. Morgan's name appeared frequently in CRC publications, and he held important posts in the church. His published writings after 1925 sometimes attacked Navajo traditions at odds with Christianity, especially Navajo medicine men and ceremonies.

After 1933 Morgan waged a bitter struggle against BIA commissioner John Collier's policy of cultural pluralism. Morgan repeatedly denounced Collier's ideas as retrogressive and a violation of the Navajos' constitutional rights. In 1934 he and fellow critics formed the American Indian Federation (AIF), in which Morgan became "First National Vice Chairman." By taking advantage of Navajos' resentment against recent livestock reductions, Morgan in 1935 conducted a successful campaign against Navajo participation in the Indian Reorganization Act. Afterward, he opposed Collier's orders to replace the existing council with a more representative body. In April 1937, Morgan bolted from a meeting of a provisional council, and he refused to serve on a committee to draft a tribal constitution.

Morgan's political allies included Protestant missionaries, some traders, the AIF, and the Indian Rights Association. Within the tribe, many returned students and, somewhat ironically, some traditional leaders backed Morgan's anti-Collier crusade. His most important ally, however, was Senator Dennis Chavez of New Mexico, who philosophically opposed Collier's policies and any attempts to expand the Navajo Reservation eastward.

In 1937 Morgan became engaged in an equally bitter controversy within the CRC. When Brink died, Morgan expected to become the missionary at Farmington and Shiprock, but the church sent an ordained replacement. The new missionary's attitude toward Indians completely alienated Morgan, and their feud led to a church decision that Morgan would have to either transfer or resign. Although Morgan formed his own congregation at Shiprock, he suffered a major financial setback and felt bitterly resentful.

Morgan's battle against council reorganization partly succeeded in 1938, when Collier ordered new elections. Morgan won the chairmanship in September by a huge margin. At his inauguration, Morgan condemned the BIA for its earlier abuses but advised the council to work together. As chairman, Morgan gradually shifted from opposing the BIA to qualified cooperation with the government. Navajo superintendent E. R. Fryer later recalled that Morgan broadened his outlook enormously once in office. Fryer also applauded Morgan's integrity and characterized him as "one of the most responsible and intelligent of all the Navajo leaders with whom I . . . worked." By 1940 Morgan even publicly supported the controversial livestock reductions. He also backed BIA efforts to start tribal enterprises such as a commercial sawmill. But Morgan's missionary ideals remained. He successfully sponsored council ordinances outlawing peyote on the reservation and forcing the Navajos into formal marriages and divorces.

World War II deeply affected Morgan. He urged the council to endorse national defense efforts. He appeared at Crownpoint in 1940 to persuade young Navajos to register for the draft. Shortly afterward Morgan wrote Collier to request an all-Navajo regiment to provide literacy training before young Navajos entered regular units. The war also brought devastating personal tragedy. His son Buddy was captured in the

J. C. Morgan (third from left) *in a photograph taken near Window Rock, Arizona, in 1939, when he participated in an investigation of the Navajo administration. The others are* (from left) *his wife, Zahrina Morgan; Thomas Jesse Jones; his granddaughter Vivienne Morgan; and Irwin Morgan, his eldest son and the father of Vivienne.*

Philippines and died in 1943 in a Japanese prison camp.

Morgan's cooperation with the BIA destroyed his political future. He could not even win a nomination for reelection in 1942. In his farewell address to the council, Morgan emphasized that he had tried to give his "best thoughts" to his people, but he admitted that his "very best friends [had] drifted away and did not want to talk [to him]."

Morgan's activities after 1942 are sketchy. A new missionary at Shiprock tried to reconcile Morgan with the CRC by reemploying him as a "native minister," but the mission board eventually rejected the scheme. He continued his ministry at Shiprock, and an interdenominational council ordained him in September 1944. He sometimes worked as a translator and Bible-camp instructor until his death on May 10, 1950.

Morgan's career represents the dramatic impact that assimilation sometimes had on Indians. He never abandoned the ideals that Hampton Institute had implanted. Even though he could accommodate aspects of Collier's cultural pluralism, he remained a zealous apostle of assimilation.

See also Bureau of Indian Affairs; Chee Dodge; Navajo.

Kelly, Lawrence C., *The Navajo Indians and Federal Indian Policy, 1900–1935* (Tucson: University of Arizona Press, 1968); Parman, Donald L., "J. C. Morgan: Navajo Apostle of Assimilation," *Prologue: The Journal of the National Archives* 4 (summer 1972): 83–98; Parman, Donald L., *The Navajos and the New Deal* (New Haven, Conn.: Yale University Press, 1976).

DONALD L. PARMAN
Purdue University

MOUND BUILDERS

The term *mound builders* arose in the eighteenth century to denote the makers of the prominent mounds and massive earthworks found scattered over lands west of the Appalachians. Since ancient earthworks were rare and inconspicuous east of the Appalachians and north of the Carolinas, recognition of this ancient American architecture had to await the westward penetration of travelers, developers, and settlers in the late colonial and federal periods. Each new discovery sparked fresh debate over the age and identity of the builders. This debate intensified over time as increasing expanses of acreage were taken up by settlers for cultivation and development.

These earthen constructions consisted of picturesque arrangements of mounds, including some impressively large and isolated examples; hilltop crests with circumvallations; and, even more startlingly, metrically precise geometric embankments in the shape of circles, squares, and octagons. As a category of landscape modification obviously of human origin, these earthworks attracted attention as indicating the deployment of numerous people in a wilderness that at the time was depopulated or lightly settled by Native Americans. Their great age was immediately apparent from the growth of large trees found on some. The identity of the people who constructed these earthworks immediately became a source of debate. Were they constructed by the ancestors of Indians, or were they built by some other people?

The Ohio Valley, where the most intensive inquiry took place, was coming under increasing pressure from settlers out of Virginia and Pennsylvania. Here Indians living in the vicinity were generally of little help. They claimed no responsibility for mound construction, which is understandable from today's perspective because we now know that these tribes were newcomers to the valley. Most travelers, missionaries, and settlers were quick to conclude that these constructions were the legacy of a race of people unrelated to the region's current Native American inhabitants. They were confirmed in their ideas by the then prevalent white attitude that Native Americans were too indifferent to labor to have been capable of devoting the effort required in the mounds' construction and would not have had the engineering knowledge to plan and execute the most demanding examples. So entrenched were early Americans in their negative perception of Native American abilities that they paid little attention to any testimony to the contrary.

Numerous theories existed about the identity of the builders of these mounds. Some were quite imaginative and focused on various "lost races." Two had strong popular support. One was that they were the descendants of the lost tribes of Israel; the other maintained that they were peoples from the south, identified with one or another of the Mexican groups. The first theory drew upon scriptural inspiration, and the latter upon the number of close correspondences between the architecture of Middle America and the mounds of the midcontinent. The former theory has been enshrined in the Book of Mormon; the latter is represented by names conferred in honor of the southern connection, such as Aztalan (Wisconsin) and Toltec (Arkansas). Al-

The Great Serpent Mound in Adams County, Ohio, constructed by either Adena or Hopewell Indians. Shaped like a serpent about to swallow an egg, it is approximately a quarter of a mile in length.

though lost-race theories were the most popular, there have always been adherents to a third view—that the earthworks were made by the ancestors of present-day Indians. This line of thinking was particularly strong in the South, where William Bartram and other travelers reported Native American use of mounds firsthand.

A broad spectrum of famous early Americans wrote on the subject of the group that came to be known as the Mound Builders. Among them were Thomas Jefferson, Albert Gallatin, George Rogers Clark, and Henry Schoolcraft. It was a primary subject of inquiry for the Smithsonian Institution in its formative years, and American archaeology cut its teeth on explorations to settle the Mound Builder question. Two studies stand out. The first of these is a monograph by Ephraim G. Squier and Edwin H. Davis, published as the initial monograph of the Smithsonian Institution in 1848. This study combined high-quality mapping with detailed field investigations at Mound City, Hopewell,

and other Ohio sites. The authors adduced information indicating a Mexican connection for the Mound Builders.

The second study was a federally supported effort to solve the Mound Builder problem under the auspices of the newly created Bureau of Ethnology. From 1881 to 1893 Cyrus Thomas led a coordinated investigation of the problem, with explorations into mounds throughout the East. A massive effort by fieldworkers in many states concluded with a definitive assessment of the Mound Builder problem based on archaeological fieldwork and a thoroughgoing search of the literature. As a result, the effort to identify the Mound Builders was abandoned, and in its place substantive evidence was offered for cultural continuity between the mound-building traditions and indigenous tribal practices. The theory of a distinct race of Mound Builders was declared to be without substance from both an archaeological and an ethnohistorical standpoint.

Archaeological fieldwork undertaken since Thomas's day has demonstrated that cultures in the East were undergoing dramatic changes long before Europeans had an opportunity to became familiar with Native American cultures. Therefore the earthworks attributed to the Mound Builders need to be seen in chronological perspective. They actually belong to a number of distinct periods. The earliest documented mounds were constructed in Louisiana about 4000 B.C., when groups in the lower Mississippi Valley established settled village life. Although these burial mounds were sometimes large, they were isolated constructions associated with distinct villages. Individual mounds and sets of associated mounds built in the millennia that followed are distributed in a manner suggestive of a similar connection with distinct communities inhabiting a particular territory over many generations. One variant of the typical circular, dome-shaped burial mound is the earthwork built in the outline of an animal. Such effigy mounds were particularly common in the upper Great Lakes area from A.D. 500 to 1000. Whatever the shape, the basic mortuary use of the mounds by small, self-contained communities continued up into the historic period.

A different function is indicated by the truly massive mounds and associated earthworks first exemplified by the Poverty Point site (Louisiana). These were mound groups that rose to prominence as a place of multigroup aggregation, where people from distant areas came together. As befitted the role that such sites have in cementing social relations among separate peoples, these assemblages of earthworks were more complicated than the mounded cemeteries of local, self-sufficient villages. At its heyday around 1000 B.C., Poverty Point covered about one hundred acres and featured six concentric rings of low embankments of earth.

Later in the Middle Woodland period, around the time of the beginning of the Common Era, aggregation centers became widely distributed from the edge of the Great Plains to the Appalachians and from southern Ontario to peninsular Florida. Among these were the impressive earthworks encountered by colonists in the upper Ohio Valley. The embankment-surrounded hill crests (such as Serpent Mound) and the massive geometric enclosures of the Ohio Valley belong to this time. These works feature the precise laying out of earthen embankments that enclosed sacred, ritual space.

Mounds and other constructions were placed in various positions within a particular location. The largest hilltop enclosure is called Fort Ancient. Encompassing about one hundred acres, it is surrounded by an embankment ranging in height from four to twenty-three feet. It is breached by seventy openings and appears, in common with other earthworks, to have been created piecemeal over a century or more. Although the location of such hilltop enclosures has inspired visions of embattled defense, their construction offers no evidence of a military objective, and all of the archaeological evidence points to mortuary and ritual use only.

The geometric earthworks laid out on broad river bottoms offer further interest because of the precision of their geometric layouts. Circles, squares, and octagons were constructed singly or in attached groups, in conjunction with round burial mounds and paths bordered by low embankments. The Newark earthworks represent an unusually large assortment of such elements, with a well-preserved octagon and an impressive great circle twelve hundred feet in diameter. The geometric works are connected by bordered pathways extending over four square miles. Each example of mounds with embankments, whether large or small, indicates the remains of mortuary and sacred architecture connected with multigroup aggregations.

With the rise of communities based on corn agriculture around A.D. 1000, the flat-topped pyramidal mound came to predominate throughout the Southeast. This construction was designed to serve as a platform for chiefly residences and shrines controlled by the chief and his priesthood. Mortuary mounds continued as members of a set of mounds at most sites that were dedicated to distinct functions. These sets of mounds were arranged in cardinal directions, and the space they delimited often defined public plazas. Fortifications with bastions accompany many of these mound-bearing towns. The largest mound in eastern North America, called Monks Mound, is one of about one hundred mounds of at least three types present at the great Cahokia site (Illinois), which is spread over two square miles. Monks Mound is one hundred feet high and has a basal area of about thirteen acres.

After A.D. 1300 mound construction declined in frequency and amount throughout the Southeast. By the sixteenth century mounds that were still in use were occupied, with little attempt to add to or alter them. Archaeology thus has demonstrated that there have been dramatic changes in the way Native Americans have made use of earth to create architectural features. The seeming disregard for earthen architecture by certain tribes during the colonial period happens to be part of an ongoing process. As a consequence, the Mound Builder label has to be regarded as a description of ancient Native American civilization rather than as something describing a fundamentally different group of people.

See also Cahokia; Mississippians; Moundville; Serpent Mound.

Fagan, Brian M., *Ancient North America: The Archaeology of a Continent* (London: Thames and Hudson, 1991); Kennedy, Roger C., *Hidden Cities: The Discovery and Loss of Ancient North American Civilization* (New York: Free Press, 1994); Silverberg, Robert, *Mound Builders of Ancient America* (Greenwich, Conn.: New York Graphic Society, 1968).

JAMES A. BROWN
Northwestern University

MOUNDVILLE

Moundville is a large Mississippian archaeological site in western Alabama that served as the capital of a large prehistoric chiefdom. Located on the Black Warrior River, south of modern-day Tuscaloosa, the site covers three hundred acres centered on a one-hundred-acre plaza surrounded by twenty paired mounds. This core area originally was surrounded by a wooden palisade.

Moundville was ruled by a theocratic elite, who were buried with finely crafted artifacts made of a variety of exotic materials, such as copper, mica, greenstone, and marine shell. From their central capital, the elite ruled an area extending seventy-five miles south from Tuscaloosa along the Black Warrior River. Within their realm were several district capitals marked by the presence of smaller, single mound centers. These district capitals funneled subsistence into Moundville, which could not support itself on locally available resources, and their elites received goods made of finely crafted exotic materials in return.

The people of Moundville engaged in a typical Mississippian economy, farming corn, beans, squash, and other starchy-seeded plants. They supplemented this diet by hunting deer, bears, raccoons, wild turkeys, and other animals, as well as by fishing. They also engaged in extensive long-distance trade, primarily in exotic materials and fine pottery, controlled by the elite.

Moundville was occupied from A.D. 900 to A.D. 1500 and reached its peak in the fifteenth century. It went into decline toward the end of that period and apparently was abandoned at or shortly after European contact in the 1540s. Moundville was probably ancestral to the Apafalaya chiefdom described by early Spanish explorers as well as the later Alabama, Pakana, and Choctaw Indians.

See also Mississippians.

MOURNING DOVE (CHRISTINE QUINTASKET)

(1884?–1936)
Salishan novelist and politician.

At the turn of this century, when few Native Americans and fewer women were authors, Mourning Dove decided to produce fiction exploring the emotional range of native peoples living in the West; in doing so, she became a pioneering Native American woman novelist. Although she earned her living as a seasonal worker and migrant laborer, her life never lacked drama.

She was born in a canoe while her mother was crossing the Kootenay River near Bonner's Ferry, Idaho, but she grew up in the lands of her people, members of Interior Salishan tribes along the upper Columbia River. Her father, Joseph, was from the Okanagans, and her mother, Lucy (née Stuikin), was from the chiefly family of the Colvilles at the important fishery of Kettle Falls. Her parents lived on a farm along the Kettle River, where they were local leaders at social and religious events, both native and Catholic. While Christine was still a teenager, her mother died, leaving the girl to run the house until her father and brother married.

Hers was never an easy life, but she sought to enrich it by creating separate personal identities. In private, she was Christine Quintasket, a woman struggling to make ends meet; in public, she was Mourning (or Morning) Dove, a writer, lecturer, and politician among the Colville Confederated Tribes and Reservation of Washington State.

Her private life was primarily spent picking crops; she would steal time to write only at night after long days in the orchards and fields. Later in life she was frequently exhausted, the result of overextending herself, and subject to repeated illnesses. During the early 1930s, as she began to publish and become politically active, at least one local white, an employee of the Bureau of Indian Affairs, denied that Christine had the education or ability to write books. In response, she drafted several versions of an autobiography, detailing a superb overview of female life among Interior Salishan tribes, but these pages were not edited and published until 1990.

Although her parents were prominent in the local culture, they had little money. In consequence, Christine chose education as a means of advancement. After about four years during the 1890s at Goodwin Catholic Mission near Kettle Falls, Washington, she spent the year of 1900 at a government school at Fort Spokane. Several years later she joined the staff at Fort Shaw School near Great Falls, Montana. There she met and married Hector McLeod, a Flathead. Humorous and easygoing like members of Christine's own family, McLeod had or developed a drinking problem and they soon were estranged.

Finally deciding to write a novel, she moved to Portland about 1912, far from family and friends. The novel, published in 1927 as *Cogewea*, is set in Montana and tries to convey a depth and range of emotions in native peoples, deliberately countering the stoic-Indian stereotype that she found so offensive. Her sisters and other members of her family appear as thinly disguised characters in the work. While producing a draft, she adopted the pen name of Morning Dove, which she began spelling "Mourning Dove" in 1921. In 1913 she moved again, enrolling at a business school in Calgary to improve her grammar and notation talents. About 1914, she met Lucullus Virgil McWhorter, a Yakima businessman and native-rights advocate, who was impressed by her dedication. Through letters and visits, he edited her novel and, after considerable delay, arranged for its publication.

Meanwhile, Christine found work where she could. About 1917, she taught on the Inkameep Okanagan Reserve in British Columbia, where she was active in local politics. She used her salary to buy a typewriter and began to record stories from Salishan elders, convinced by McWhorter and others that writing fiction was not as important as preserving "vanishing" traditions.

In 1919 she married Fred Galler, a Peskwaw also enrolled as a member of the Colville Confederated Tribes, and moved to East Omak, Washington. Childless (although she spent periods as foster mother for a niece and nephew), she set about preparing her collection of stories for publication, editing them, with the help of McWhorter and Hester Dean Guie, as bedtime tales for children. They were published in 1933 under the title *Coyote Stories*. In the process, she readily agreed with McWhorter and Guie to remove integral aspects of the stories that might seem offensive to a white audience, thereby eliminating many of the negative examples intended to provide native listeners with moral instruction about proper behavior.

Also missing from this collection is the name of the spirit—Mourning Dove—who, in the native epics, mourned her husband Salmon with such grief that he was brought back to life, returning annually to the rivers of the Northwest. This oversight is another indication of how disparate her identities as native woman and as native author could be.

In Omak, Christine formed organizations of native women to promote crafts and to intervene in legal difficulties between local natives and whites. Building on her fame as a club woman, speaker, and writer, she became in 1935 the first woman elected to the Colville Tribal Council.

Routinely overextending herself, she complained more and more of a "nevrous" (her spelling) disposition, until in 1936 she became disoriented and, after several days, died in a state hospital. Her legacies include opening the way for a succession of powerful women leaders on the Colville Tribal Council, achieving a growing fame as a writer who overcame personal and financial obstacles, and creating a body of published works that continue to help the native and nonnative communities understand each other.

See also Literature by Indians.

Miller, Jay, ed., *Mourning Dove: A Salishan Autobiography* (Lincoln: University of Nebraska Press, 1990); Mourning Dove, *Cogewea: The Half-Blood* (1927; reprint, Lincoln: University of Nebraska Press, 1981); Mourning Dove, *Coyote Stories* (1933; reprint, Lincoln: University of Nebraska Press, 1990).

JAY MILLER (Lenape)
Lushootseed Research

MOVIES

The movie Indian is a mythological creation that has existed within the minds of actors, producers, and directors since Thomas Edison previewed the kinescope at the 1893 World's Columbian Exposition in Chicago. Mythmaking can be described as an appropriation of image that interweaves fact and fiction in order to create the illusion of a true story. Because films appeal simultaneously to sight and sound, and exploit the tendency to see and then to believe, the commercial success of movies is often rooted in their ability to perpetuate invented images. Native people have long been out of this loop, relegated to the role of patrons. Native people, like all movie buffs, love a good story. Yet native people also have a stake in what is being portrayed. Try as they might to educate the nonnative public, the characterizations and stories presented onscreen are assumed by large segments of that public to represent Native America. Unfortunately, the vast majority of such images reduce native people to ignoble stereotypes.

America became enamored with novel industrial technologies in the late nineteenth century, and images of native people were among the first to be viewed on film. These images were a part of Orientalism—a public fascination with native as well as Asian peoples that tended to see them as freaks of nature and exotic curiosities. One kinescopic feature entitled *The Hopi Snake Dance* was shown at the 1893 World's Columbian Exposition. Other early features lasting sixty seconds or less included works such as *Sioux Ghost Dance* (1894), *Indian Day School* (1898), and *Buffalo Bill's Wild West Parade* (1901). These curiosities attracted thousands of nickelodeon customers.

With the advent of one-reel films, the kinescopic clips were replaced by movies that had story themes. Among the first examples of the Indian "theme" films was a 1903 Mutuscope and Biograph production, *Kit Carson*. The historical figure of Carson was quickly elevated to heroic but fictional stature in a story line that culminated in a "massacre" of trappers by savage Indians. It also depicted an Indian maiden, or "squaw," helping Kit Carson to escape his wild Indian captors. This formula of the savage male Indian and the helpful squaw was repeated countless times thereafter, perhaps reaching its peak in the B westerns produced in the 1950s.

Around the same time, the industry was producing anthropologically based films. Usually casting native people, these films were shrouded in a distinctively Rousseauesque "noble savage" cloak. Depicting the idyllic lifestyle of native people, they were made to appeal to those Americans who had missed the experience of the American frontier. Edward Curtis's *In the Land of the Head Hunters* (1917), Robert Flaherty's *Nanook of the North* (1922), and H. P. Carver's *The Silent Enemy* (1930) were among the most elaborate of these productions. In large part, they can also be credited with creating a new genre of films called the documentary.

Beginning in the 1950s, a few films tried to dispel the stereotypes. *Broken Arrow* (1950) attempted to take a humanistic view of the Apache warrior Cochise. *Walk the Proud Land* (1956) and *Cheyenne Autumn* (1964) looked sympathetically at native conditions. Many story lines of these films focused on educated, trouble-

Jay Silverheels, a Mohawk, portrayed Tonto in the 1956 film The Lone Ranger, *as well as in the subsequent television series of the same name.*

some "half-breeds"—a formula that explored the impact of tribal assimilation and cold-war xenophobia on native people. Overall, though, mainstream America had drawn on its preconceptions and experiences to appropriate elements of the exotic and primitive Indian presented to it on film. The consequent image was a subjective interpretation that saw native people as apart from their own social and community realities. And so it remained until a character named McMurphy (played by the actor Jack Nicholson) prodded a mute Indian chief (played by the Indian actor Will Sampson) into saying, "Ahh, Juicy Fruit," in the Academy Award–winning movie *One Flew Over the Cuckoo's Nest* (1975). What the audience heard was far removed from the stereotypical "hows," "ughs," and "kemosabes" of tinseltown moviedom. "Well goddamn, Chief," exclaimed McMurphy. "And they all think you're deaf and dumb. Jesus Christ, you fooled them, Chief, you fooled them. . . . You fooled 'em all!" In that simple and fleeting scene, a new generation of hope was heralded among American Indian movie-goers. Long the downtrodden victims of escapist shoot 'em and bang 'em up westerns, they were ready for a new cinematic treatment—one that was real and contemporary.

These changes paralleled the rise of Indian activism in the 1960s and 1970s. Hollywood's scriptwriters jumped onto the bandwagon with such epics as *Tell Them Willie Boy Is Here* (1969), *Soldier Blue* (1970), *A Man Called Horse* (1970), *Little Big Man* (1971), *Return of a Man Called Horse* (1976), and *Triumphs of a Man Called Horse* (1982). *Little Big Man*, in fact, established a milestone in Hollywood cinema in its human portrayal of the Lakota people, and featured what is perhaps one of the finest performances by a native actor—Chief Dan George as Chief Old Lodge Skins.

At the same time, however, Indian activism was subtly being transformed into antiwar militancy, resulting in the production of movies such as *Flap or Nobody Loves a Drunken Indian* (1970), *Journey through Rosebud* (1971), *Billie Jack* (1971), *The Trial of Billie Jack* (1974), and *Billie Jack Goes to Washington* (1977). Native Americans were portrayed as Vietnam veterans whose anti-American behavior got the better of their common sense. These portrayals helped vent the frustration of the nation's commitment to a no-cause war.

Yet in spite of their radical attempts to "correct the record," these movies all had one thing in common: their leading Indian roles were played by non-Indian actors. A few films like *House Made of Dawn* (1975; starring the Santo Domingo Pueblo actor Larry Littlebird), *When the Legends Die* (1972; featuring "the Ute tribe"), and *The White Dawn* (1975; featuring "the Eskimo People") attempted to reverse this trend. Unfortunately, producers and directors continued to seek name recognition to boost box-office appeal.

During the 1970s two Native American images were featured in popular television commercials: the teary-eyed Indian of the "Keep America Beautiful" campaign (played by the Cherokee actor Iron Eyes Cody) and the Corn Maiden of Mazola margarine's ads (played by the Chiricahua actress Tenaya Torrez). These stereotyped images and the environmental messages of the commercials they adorned etched themselves indelibly into the minds of millions of Nielsen-ratings households.

Such popular imagery was so important in movie-making that gifted native actors like Will Sampson (Creek; 1935–88) and Chief Dan George (Salish;

1899–1982) continued to be typecast in films like *The Outlaw Josie Wales* (1976; also starring the Navajo actress Geraldine Keams) and *Buffalo Bill and the Indians or Sitting Bull's History Lesson* (1976). The same fate befell others like the Mohawk actor Jay Silverheels (1912–80), who was widely recognized for his portrayal of Tonto in the 1955 movie *The Lone Ranger* and later the television series, as well as for being the first native actor to receive a star in the Hollywood Walk of Fame, in 1979.

In spite of these shortfalls, native people were poised for a mjaor breakthrough in the film industry. The Indian Actors' Workshop was begun in the early 1960s, and the establishment of the American Indian Registry for the Performing Arts soon followed. Both organizations were committed to promoting native actors in native roles. This movement, which came as a result of advocacy among the ranks of senior native actors, lost much of its momentum with their untimely deaths.

The impact of "Red Power" activism in film was sometimes uneven. In 1973, the actor Marlon Brando had the Apache actress Sasheen Littlefeather appear at the 1972 Academy Awards ceremony in his place—to decline the Oscar for Best Actor—and to protest the treatment of American Indians in film. But later that year, Littlefeather exploited her fame by appearing as a "Pocahontas-in-the-buff" in *Playboy* magazine, diminishing her credibility as a native activist.

It was not until 1989 that a major sequel to *Cuckoo's Nest*—one that featured a realistic and contemporary performance by a native person—appeared in *Pow Wow Highway*. The then-unknown Mohawk actor Gary Farmer came as close as any actor to revealing the "modern" Indian self, in much the same spirit as that in which the Choctaw producer Bob Hicks made his experimental short *Return to the Country* (1982).

Unfortunately, *Pow Wow Highway* suffered from a predictable multicultural drumbeat that had frozen solid sometime in the early 1970s. Variations on the Indian-performed-by-an-Indian motif were to be found in *Thunderheart* (1992; starring the Oneida actor Graham Green), a film loosely based on the real-life murder of a native activist, Anna Mae Aquash (played by Sheila Tousey, a Menominee-Stockbridge and Munsee actress). In spite of its casting achievement, the film's message was that "wannabes" who return to find their identity can still walk away when the going gets tougher. What was undoubtedly the finest example of this "wannabe syndrome" was soon to follow. *Dances with Wolves*—the winner of seven Academy Awards for 1990 including Best Picture—was a remarkable clone of *Little Big Man* (1971). Both films used the backdrop of the historic Lakota and Cheyenne wars. Both typecast the Lakotas and Cheyennes as hero tribes, victimized by their common archenemies, the U.S. cavalry and "those damned Pawnees!" However, unlike *Little Big Man,* with its pointed antiwar overtones, *Dances with Wolves* was devoid of any redeeming social message. Rather, it was apolitical and quietly presented a simple, New Age homily of peace and Mother Earth.

Nonetheless, *Dances with Wolves* accomplished what few other films had done. It ushered forth a wave of Indian New Age films and created a need for the film industry to employ native actors as well as to depict history from the native's point of view. Films like *War Party* (1990) and *Clear Cut* (1991) were the result. But unlike *Pow Wow Highway,* these films featured plots that were as surreal and bizarre as a Salvador Dali painting.

The most contentious example of a nonnative production was yet to come, however: the screen adaptation of the mystery novelist Tony Hillerman's *Dark Wind* (1992). A nonnative actor, Lou Diamond Phillips, was cast as the central character, the Navajo policeman Jim Chee, while the six-foot-plus Gary Farmer was miscast as a five-foot Hopi policeman. The film's odd combination of actors and the culturally offensive aspects of its story line resulted in official protests being lodged by both the Navajo and Hopi tribal governments. Fearing legal reprisal, the distributors pulled the film out of the American market and floated it instead among European moviegoers.

Still, Hollywood remained mired in mythmaking. Any strides taken were due to the efforts of a few well-placed native professionals. For instance, native playwrights and cultural consultants were finally given the opportunity to add historical precision to screenplays and to provide real native-language dialogue instead of the usual made-up words. This new treatment was evident in *Black Robe* (1991), *The Last of the Mohicans* (1992), and *Geronimo: An American Hero* (1993). At the symbolic heart of this development was the acting debut, in *The Last of the Mohicans,* of the former American Indian Movement (AIM) activist Russell Means (Oglala-Yankton Sioux). Means was cast as Chingachgook, the marathon-running sidekick of Hawkeye—although it was the Cherokee actor Wes Studi, in his role as the Huron villain, Magua, who ultimately stole the show.

Means's presence brought with it the same activist overtones as had that of his predecessor Sasheen Littlefeather a full two decades later. Both made an uneasy alliance with Hollywood, and both became hopelessly seduced by its power. Means followed his debut by playing a Navajo medicine man in *Natural Born Killers* (1994), and, in 1995, lent his voice to Chief Powhatan in the animated Disney production *Pocahontas.* Though *Pocahontas* was hopelessly flawed, Means nevertheless proclaimed it "the single finest work ever done on American Indians by Hollywood."

Yet the most interesting story lines went largely unnoticed. *Addams Family Values* (1994), for example, came as close as any film to exposing, in a few fleeting scenes, the roots of American hypocrisy and racism against Indians—an accomplishment that most Indian-dominated movies failed to achieve. The biggest sleeper, though, was a 1995 film, *The Indian in the Cupboard* (starring the Cherokee actor Litefoot). Dismissed by the film critic Roger Ebert for its lack of "entertainment" value, the film successfully explored the deconstruction of the cowboy-and-Indian myth from the perspectives of two skeptical adolescent boys.

Unfortunately, in Hollywood's treatment of native issues, very little of what has transpired over the past century is groundbreaking. As long as native people are assigned roles that are controlled by nonnatives, movie images will remain distorted and disconnected from the native experience. Dramatic change will come only when a native director and/or producer is able to break into the ranks of the Hollywood elite. In 1992, an important first step was taken with the creation of the Native American Producers' Alliance.

Friar, Ralph, and Natasha Friar, *The Only Good Indian: The Hollywood Gospel* (New York: Drama Book Specialists, 1972); Steadman, Raymond William, *Shadows of the Indian: Stereotypes in American Culture* (Norman: University of Oklahoma Press, 1982).

THEODORE S. JOJOLA (Isleta Pueblo)
University of New Mexico

MURIE, JAMES R.

(1862–1921)
Pawnee ethnographer and author.

The Pawnee tribe experienced tremendous change during the lifetime of James Rolfe Murie (Saku:rú ta', "Coming Sun"). In 1857 the tribe ceded its traditional territory in Nebraska, but at Murie's birth in 1862 it had not yet moved to Indian Territory (present-day Oklahoma), as stipulated in the land-sale treaty with the United States. James R. Murie's mother, Anna Murie, a full-blood Pawnee, raised her son in the traditional Pawnee manner as a member of the Skiri band. His father, James Murie, a Scottish-born army officer serving under Major Frank North, abandoned his wife and child in Nebraska shortly after his son's birth, moving west to California.

Murie was a pupil at the day school at the Genoa Agency in his traditional homeland for four months. In 1874 he moved to Indian Territory with his mother and most of the tribe. He continued his education there, first at the day school and then at the boarding school at the Pawnee Agency. He mastered the English language while at these schools and became an interpreter for the local agent. In October 1879 Murie, then sixteen, decided to further his education and left for Virginia, where he enrolled in the Hampton Normal and Agriculture Institute.

Murie's educational pursuits at Hampton included training in the printing trade and conversion to the Episcopal Church. After four years of training, Murie left Hampton with a diploma from the normal department. His experience at Hampton instilled in him the desire to return to his tribe to share his education. He was the first of his tribe to return to the Pawnee Nation as a graduate from an eastern school.

On his return to Indian Territory, Murie was pleased to find his tribe endeavoring to adjust to farming on individual plots of land and became determined to put his education to practical use. Before obtaining his first teaching job at the newly opened boarding school at the Pawnee Agency in 1883, however, Murie held a clerking job at a store near the agency. His duties at the boarding school included teaching, and overseeing the boys and their dormitory. He stayed at the school for one year, resigning so that he could move, along with some of his pupils, to the new Haskell Institute in Lawrence, Kansas, where he stayed for two years.

Upon his resignation from Haskell, Murie returned east to study for the ministry. He visited the Commissioner of Indian Affairs in Washington, who assured him of a teaching job at the Pawnee Agency. Unfortunately, the agent at Pawnee had not received orders for Murie's appointment and refused him the job. Murie waited for the orders to arrive but eventually became disheartened and returned to the Skiri people to farm.

In 1887 he married Mary Esau; they had eight children, four of whom survived to adulthood. In a letter in 1890 to the Hampton Institute, he related his aspirations for his young son, Fred Wallace Murie, stating, "I want my little boy to grow up in white man's ideas and become educated so he can help his people." Murie divorced Mary in 1919 and married Josephine Walking Sun, a Pawnee woman whose mother was keeper of the Morning Star bundles; they had two children.

The 1890s were crucial years for Murie. With his teaching ambition thwarted by the officials at the Pawnee Agency, Murie found a means to use his education when Alice Cunningham Fletcher, whom he had met at Hampton, arrived at the agency to study Pawnee ceremonialism. Murie became much more than an informant to Fletcher. He assisted her in her studies, clarifying, explaining, and translating Pawnee customs and introducing tribal members. Murie corresponded with Fletcher after she returned to Washington, D.C., and on occasion would visit the capital to represent his tribe and provide Fletcher with additional information on the Pawnees.

In 1902 Murie began working full-time for George A. Dorsey, the curator of anthropology for the Field Museum of Natural History in Chicago. Whereas Murie's earlier work with Fletcher had been that of an assistant, Dorsey gave the Pawnee man sole responsibility for collecting information on the customs of his people for two volumes of Pawnee mythology, to be published under Dorsey's name. Murie and his family lived in Chicago for several years while he worked for Dorsey and the Field Museum, but as the demands of field research grew, Murie found that he needed to be among the Pawnees in order to collect material objects and ethnographic data. Murie also conducted research among the Arikara tribe during the summers of 1903 and 1905. Adopted into the tribe and tutored as a priest, he recorded numerous stories and ceremonies.

Between 1906 and 1909 Murie's work with Dorsey was sporadic; it finally ended when Murie accepted a position as field researcher for the Smithsonian Institution's Bureau of American Ethnology, then headed by Frederick Webb Hodge. Murie began writing a manuscript on Pawnee ceremonialism that included detailed descriptions of the White Beaver Ceremony (the Doctor Dance) of the Chaui band and of the Bear Dance and Buffalo Dance of the Pitahawirata band.

Murie's work on the Pawnees was becoming well known, and in 1912 Robert Lowie of the American Museum of Natural History in Washington, D.C., invited the fifty-year-old scholar to work with Clark Wissler, the museum's curator of anthropology. Murie agreed to write a monograph for the museum on Pawnee ceremonial customs. Murie's manuscript was published in 1914 under his own name as *Pawnee Indian Societies*. Wissler and Murie continued to work together on their manuscript, *Ceremonies of the Pawnee*, which was finished before Murie's death in 1921.

James Murie's interest in Pawnee and Arikara ceremonialism stemmed from his Pawnee roots and his upbringing in the Skiri band. His work demonstrated a knowledge that outsiders could not fully obtain, even in the field. He was able to speak with the elders in their own language and to translate stories so that his peoples' history and culture could be preserved.

Murie's academic work did not detract from his other concerns for his tribe and their welfare. In 1915 he became president of the Indian Farmer Institute in Pawnee, Oklahoma, and continued to be active in tribal and community affairs. Murie's life exemplified American Indians' struggles to survive in a changing world. He worked to bring attention to his people and succeeded in creating a voluminous body of information on the Pawnees. He was a link between prereservation life and the twentieth century; he struggled to bring these worlds together through the education he received and was determined to share.

See also Pawnee.

Parks, Douglas R., "James R. Murie: Pawnee Ethnographer, Pawnee, 1862–1921," in *American Indian Intellectuals,* ed. Margo Liberty (St. Paul, Minn.: West Publishing, 1978).

REBECCA BALES (Choctaw/Cherokee)
Arizona State University

MUSEUMS AND COLLECTORS

Collecting is a cultural universal: all human societies have collected objects made elsewhere as well as unusual or exotic natural objects, and not only for practical uses.

There is archaeological evidence for collecting activities in North America before the arrival of Europeans. Certain types of seashell were traded far inland. Obsidian and other scarce minerals ended up distant from their points of origin, and the same is true for various perishable materials such as some kinds of feathers and well-tanned leather. The products of human art and ingenuity were also collected. Indian people acquired ob-

jects that were made by members of other tribes, through trade, gift, and capture. Foreign objects were sometimes considered superior to locally produced items of the same sort—for example, men's shirts made by Crow women, Paiute baskets, Sioux painted buffalo robes, and Haida canoes. When European goods and materials arrived, they too entered the networks of exchange and collecting.

Reciprocally, Europeans in America began collecting Indian products, both for practical uses and as curiosities and trophies. Columbus and succeeding European explorers and conquerors often returned to Europe with examples to demonstrate the wealth, ingenuity, and art of the Indian peoples they encountered. Some of these were kept as "artificial curiosities" along with artifacts from Asia, Africa, the Pacific, and the ancient world, as well as souvenirs and mementos of European history. Together with specimens of natural origin, these were exhibited in "cabinets of curiosities," parts of which survive in modern European museums. Thus a few fine Indian-made objects of the sixteenth through eighteenth centuries can still be seen in museums, especially in Europe.

The collecting of exotic curiosities was also a traditional Indian custom. One example among many is a chipped stone point from about 1500 B.C. found in southern California in the nineteenth century and then used in a Diegueño shaman's wand. Moctezuma II, the Aztec ruler at the time of the Spanish invasion in 1519, collected exotic birds, mammals, and reptiles for a zoo that was described in detail by Cortés and some of his contemporaries. The zoo's occupants, gathered from all parts of the Aztec empire, were looked after by hundreds of caretakers. Moctezuma enjoyed viewing them from "balconies very beautifully worked." This was not the only instance of an Indian ruler maintaining a collection of animals, for Nezahualcoyotl, ruler of Tezcoco, had gathered for his amusement a collection of birds, fish, and mammals from the lands that he ruled. Moctezuma's zoo came to a tragic end when Cortés ordered it and its occupants burned as part of his siege of Tenochtitlán in 1521.

The museum is an institution of European origin, one that has spread widely in modern times, along with libraries, archives, schools and universities, and other European inventions. In its modern form, the museum dates from the late eighteenth and early nineteenth centuries. One of the earliest museums in the United States, and the first operated by an Indian tribe, would have resulted when in 1826 Major Ridge and other prominent Cherokee families offered heirlooms to found a national museum at New Echota, Georgia. That the museum failed to materialize was the direct result of the oppressive conditions imposed by the state of Georgia, which soon destroyed the incipient Cherokee state and forced the people to move west of the Mississippi River to what later became Oklahoma.

During the nineteenth century museumlike collections displayed by socially prominent people often included Indian materials. Thomas Jefferson had such a collection at Monticello (mostly derived from the Lewis and Clark Expedition), and there were many others. An Indian example (from the second half of the century) is the fine collection of Iroquois arts and mementos that the Mohawk chief George H. M. Johnson and his family exhibited in their home, Chiefswood House, on the Grand River Reserve in Ontario. The well-known Ojibwa missionary Peter Jones had a collection of Delaware masks and other objects, as well as objects from his own Mississauga people, which he exhibited in England during a lecture and fund-raising tour he made in 1845.

By the mid–nineteenth century there were many private and public collections of Indian-made objects owned by Anglo-American citizens and institutions. One of the earliest systematic and comprehensive collections of this kind was gathered in the late 1840s by the early anthropologist Lewis Henry Morgan, for what eventually became the New York State Museum. He made a duplicate collection that he kept in his own house in Rochester, and acted as agent to obtain a smaller but similar collection for the National Museum of Denmark in 1860. All of these Morgan acquired with the active help of the prominent Parker family on the Tonawanda Seneca Reservation, among whom Ely S. Parker (later the first Indian Commissioner of Indian Affairs) and his sister Carolyn Parker were especially important to Morgan as collaborators and consultants. The typology of Iroquois artifacts and the descriptions of their construction and uses that Morgan presented in his publications on his collections directly reflected Iroquois concepts, terminology, and knowledge— things that were explained to Morgan by the Parkers and other Iroquois. Subsequent anthropologists followed Morgan in basing their investigations and collecting on the knowledge and assistance of native experts. The influence was often reciprocal: some of the fine clothing and other textile work surviving in the Morgan collections was made by the young Carolyn Parker; she later married John Mt. Pleasant and moved to the Tuscarora Reservation, where they are said to have displayed a large collection of Iroquois artifacts in their elegant house.

Other Iroquois who acquired things for non-Indian collectors and museums at somewhat later dates include James Jamieson (Cayuga) and John Arthur Gibson (Seneca) of the Six Nations Reserve, and Edward Cornplanter (Seneca) of the Cattaraugus Reservation. Many other Indian people during the late nineteenth and early twentieth centuries made collections for non-Indian museums, either independently or in collaboration with non-Indian anthropologists. Among the best known are Francis LaFlesche (Omaha), Louis Shotridge (Tlingit), James Murie (Pawnee), Andrew John (Seneca), William Beynon (Tsimshian), William Benson (Eastern Pomo), Juan Dolores (Papago), and George Hunt (a Tlingit who lived among the Kwakiutls).

These collectors were not the only Indian people who viewed the large non-Indian museums as suitable repositories for heirlooms, works of art, and tools and other objects become obsolete. Even ritual objects no longer needed were often sold or given to museums when it was felt the younger generation did not know how to care for such things. Other reasons, shared with non-Indians, for giving or selling things to museums have included economic motives, the prestige associated with being a donor, the wish to secure the survival of valued objects, and the desire to contribute toward preserving a record of the past history and accomplishments of a people.

Anthropological collecting and anthropology museums represent a special manner of documenting the material aspect of cultures. A full record of the accomplishments and history of a society must include an adequate sample of the material products of the society to document its artistic and technological activities. Archives and libraries preserve written evidence of cultures and societies, whereas museums preserve the artifactual record. Anthropology museums keep and display a much wider range of artifactual evidence than is preserved by museums of art and history.

Anthropology as a scientific field began in the mid–nineteenth century, and from its beginnings until about 1920 it was centered in museums. After that date, anthropological research was increasingly based at universities, and museums largely ceased collecting North American Indian materials (while continuing to collect objects from other parts of the world). Archaeological research is a partial exception to these generalizations, for museums continue to be the repositories of the material record of archaeological excavations, even though most archaeologists are no longer based in museums. The large university, national, and natural-history museums in North America and Europe still maintain and exhibit collections of North American Indian materials, and employ anthropologists to curate them and to conduct research on Indian cultures. Some of these museum anthropologists are Indians, as they have been for over a century (among the early examples are Francis LaFlesche and Louis Shotridge, already mentioned, and the Tuscarora J. N. B. Hewitt and the Seneca Arthur C. Parker).

Indian artifacts began to be appreciated and collected as art partly as a result of the establishment by the federal government of the Indian Arts and Crafts Board during the Indian "New Deal" of the 1930s. The Indian Exhibition at the 1939 International Exposition in San Francisco was organized by the board, which also sponsored the influential exhibition *Indian Art of the United States* at the Museum of Modern Art in New York in 1941. Yet only since about 1960 has there been a significant number of Indian professional artists producing paintings and sculpture for the fine-art market. Until quite recently it was very difficult for these artists to have their work shown in fine-art museums, as opposed to natural-history or anthropology museums. "Ethnic" art was considered by the mainstream fine-art world to be another kind of folk art, not meeting the international standards for fine art. This exclusionary attitude has been changing of late, although it is still difficult for many native artists to have their work accepted as art rather than crafts.

The largest collections of North American Indian materials are those in the American Museum of Natural History (New York), the Smithsonian's National Museum of Natural History (Washington), the Smithsonian's National Museum of the American Indian (Washington and New York; formerly the Museum of the American Indian, Heye Foundation), the Canadian Museum of Civilization (Hull, Quebec), the Field Museum of Natural History (Chicago), the British Museum (London), and the Milwaukee Public Museum.

Indian-controlled museums have increased in number and importance during the twentieth century. The Osage Tribal Museum, established in the 1930s, is the oldest tribally controlled museum in the United States, and serves the Osage community as both a museum and a cultural center. The next-oldest tribally sponsored museum is the Museum of the Cherokee Indian in Cherokee, North Carolina, founded in 1948 by the Cherokee Historical Association with a small collection acquired from a local citizen. The museum became a unit of the Eastern Cherokee tribal government in 1970, when plans for a new and larger facility were made.

A number of tribal museums were established in the 1960s and 1970s, largely as a result of the availability of federal funding through the Economic Development Administration. It was hoped that these museums would increase local income and provide jobs, especially by attracting tourists. Some of the museums established during this period later closed because they were not able to make the transition from EDA financing to tribal financial support. More recently some tribes have built museums using their own income from tribal economic enterprises. These museums are meant to reinforce tribal identity, preserve the cultural patrimony, and educate the young; attracting tourists is generally a secondary goal.

Tribally operated museums are quite variable with respect to size of collections, staff, exhibits, yearly operations, and intended audience. Some are modeled after local historical museums and feature exhibits of native versions of history and tribal culture; they are immersed in local priorities, local history, and community traditions. Sometimes they serve primarily as tourist attractions and outlets for native-made crafts and are not well integrated into the Indian community other than as a source of income. Other museums function as social and cultural centers and are essential institutions in their reservation communities. These museums and cultural centers do not always have exhibits, but they support a wide range of cultural activities such as instruction in music, dance, language, and crafts. And there are some museums that combine excellent exhibits, collections, and cultural activities.

Throughout the 1980s Indian interest in tribal museums and cultural centers increased, so that by 1995 there were over two hundred Indian-administered museums and cultural centers in the United States and many others in Canada. The Museum at Warm Springs, in Warm Springs, Oregon, houses one of the largest tribally owned collections in the country. Other important tribal museums are the Makah Tribal Museum in Washington State, the U'Mista Cultural Centre in British Columbia, the Seneca-Iroquois National Museum in New York State, the Cherokee National Museum (Tahlequah, Oklahoma), the Pueblo Cultural Center (Albuquerque, New Mexico), the Ashiwi A:wan (Zuni) Museum and Heritage Center (New Mexico), and the Creek Council House Museum (Muscogee, Oklahoma). When it is completed, the museum being built by the Mashantucket Pequots in Connecticut will be the largest tribally owned museum in the country and will include large exhibit galleries and an important library and archive.

Karp, I., and S. D. Lavine, eds., *Exhibiting Cultures* (Washington: Smithsonian Institution, 1991).

JOALLYN ARCHAMBAULT (Standing Rock Sioux)
National Museum of Natural History
Smithsonian Institution

WILLIAM C. STURTEVANT
National Museum of Natural History
Smithsonian Institution

MUSIC

Music is integral to Native American life. American Indians perform music every day, in public or private contexts, to preserve and perpetuate their traditional cultures, to express and affirm their Indian identities, and to honor their families and ancestors. Early European explorers and missionaries were fascinated by Native American music and described it in their chronicles with varying degrees of insight and sensitivity. By 1900, Indians had exerted a subtle but pervasive impact on world music. The field of ethnomusicology, the movement among American and Canadian composers to create national musical idioms, and the effort by American educators to foster a national identity through children's songs were all profoundly affected by Native American music.

American Indian music is richly diverse. It is unique in its nearly exclusive emphasis on singing, its palpable connection to the spiritual realm, its approach to song lyrics in which vocables (nonlexical syllables) constitute an essential part of the poetry, and its proliferation of instruments imbued with sacred symbolism that are often works of art in themselves. Native Americans perform many different genres of music in many social contexts, from private domestic activities such as singing a baby to sleep to religious ceremonials such as the Navajo Night Way that last several days and involve hundreds of songs.

Each Indian community has its own musical repertory, performance contexts, and practices, but similarities among musical and cultural characteristics within particular geographical regions have led scholars to define

six music areas in native North America: Eastern Woodlands, Plains, Southwest, Great Basin, Northwest Coast, and Arctic.

The Eastern Woodlands area includes tribes of the Southeast, Northeast, and Great Lakes regions. Their music features a moderately relaxed and open vocal style, emphasizing the middle range. Various scales and melodic contours are used, most with a range of an octave or more. Most Eastern Woodlands songs use antiphony (call and response); within native North America, antiphony is exclusive to this area. These songs use either sectional or strophic forms with intricate phrase patterns. Frequent metric changes within most songs, occasional unmetered introductions, and complex rhythmic relationships between choreography and music characterize Eastern Woodlands rhythmic structures. Drums, rattles, or striking sticks accompany singers, depending upon the specific community and musical genre. Flutes and whistles are played as solo instruments.

The Plains area includes both the prairie tribes and the tribes of the Great Plains. The Plains vocal style is nasal and extremely tense. Singers emphasize the high range, often using falsetto at the *push-up* or beginning of the song. Most Plains scales are tetratonic (four-tone) or pentatonic (five-tone). Plains melodies have an ambitus greater than an octave; they usually start high and descend by steps, a contour scholars call *terraced descent*. Singers perform in unblended monophony. Plains songs typically employ a strophic form called *incomplete repetition*: the strophe has two sections, the second of which is repeated before the singers return to the push-up, and the entire strophe is sung several times. The most characteristic Plains instrument is the large bass drum, played simultaneously by all singers in a group. Other Plains instruments include the flageolet or end-blown flute, used as a solo instrument in the performance of love songs.

The Southwest area is subdivided into the Pueblo and Athabaskan musical styles. Pueblo musicians use an open, relaxed vocal style, emphasizing the low range, in highly blended monophony. They employ various scales with an ambitus greater than an octave. Pueblo song forms are finely detailed, large-scale, and systematically integrated with choreography and ritual space. Dance songs generally contain five sections, each with four or more discrete phrases articulated by patterned pauses and long introductory and cadential formulas. Pueblo songs tend to be relatively slow; they are accompanied by large barrel drums, rattles, or other percussion instruments, depending upon the genre. Athabaskan (Navajo and Apache) musicians, by contrast, cultivate a tense, nasal voice and sing in unblended monophony, similar to the Plains style. Athabaskan songs feature numerous discrete melodic motives that are woven into elaborate, boldly patterned designs. The songs are relatively fast in tempo and are accompanied by drums or rattles, according to the genre. Unique to this area is a stringed instrument called the Apache fiddle, played as a solo instrument.

The Great Basin area includes plateau and Great Basin tribes. Their traditional vocal style is open and relaxed; singers use moderately blended monophony. Great Basin melodies are short, with a narrow range, smaller than an octave. Scholars describe the characteristic musical form as exhibiting *paired-phrase structure:* each melodic phrase is sung twice and alternates with one or two additional phrases. On the surface, Great Basin music appears to be the simplest in style of any music in native America. However, careful listening reveals delicate microrhythms articulated through special breathing techniques. In addition, Great Basin song texts employ subtle imagery and aesthetics reminiscent of haiku poetry.

Northwest Coast singers use a moderately relaxed, open vocal style. Most Northwest Coast songs are monophonic, but there are striking examples of polyphony or part singing, a characteristic not heard elsewhere in Native America. Northwest Coast songs feature long melodies with chromatic intervals, which are otherwise rare in Native America. The complicated rhythms of Northwest Coast music derive from speech rhythms, producing a declamatory effect in some songs. Northwest Coast music is best known for its tremendous variety of beautifully carved and painted musical instruments. These include many percussion instruments as well as whistles, flutes, and horns.

The Arctic area includes diverse cultures formerly identified as Eskimos. Their musical styles remain relatively unfamiliar to most outsiders, although excellent recordings and documentation have been produced since the 1970s. The vocal style here is slightly tense, and Arctic singers are known for their use of extended vocal techniques, heard in special genres such as Inuit throat games. Arctic melodies feature a narrow range and, like Northwest Coast music, may use declamatory effects. Arctic songs often use a strophic form, with repeated notes marking the ends of phrases. The most characteristic instruments from the Arctic area are large, shallow hand drums that resemble tambourines, as well as box drums, which are unique to this area.

The approach to American Indian music in terms of geographical area invites the criticism that it derives from the objectification of Indians by Euro-American scholars and results in the classification of disparate peoples into groupings that by their very nature are artificial. The main attribute of the area approach is that it permits scholars to organize a vast body of detailed musical information. Most scholars today use the area approach to introduce and contextualize individual kinds of Native American music, which then may be more fully appreciated on their own terms.

Native American sacred narratives teach that music is not a human invention, that it was first given to people by spirit beings in order to facilitate interaction between humans and the spiritual realm. This view holds significant implications for Native American musical processes, such as composition and transmission, as well as for musical concepts, such as song ownership and the purpose of music.

Each Indian community has its own processes of composition. Choctaws, for example, believe that Social Dance music was given by deities at the time of creation, and that it is impossible for humans to compose new Social Dance songs. However, Choctaw song leaders may recombine and slightly vary fixed melodic materials in prescribed ways, thereby demonstrating individuality and talent. A traditional method of composition among Plains peoples involves the assistance of spirit beings through dreams or visions. Among Pueblo peoples, the composition of certain new songs each year involves a committee process. A traditional means of acquiring new songs and repertories throughout Native America is to receive them from other human communities. The central concepts are that music comes from outside of oneself, and is a gift.

Musical transmission includes the methods by which music is taught, learned, and remembered. The way Native Americans transmit a particular piece of music depends in part on its use. Communal dance songs used primarily to strengthen social relationships are usually learned informally, by direct participation in performance. Rehearsals are optional, and the repertory is preserved through oral tradition, although contemporary singers often make recordings to ensure that new songs will be learned and remembered. Ritual music requiring absolute precision and accuracy is taught by specialists through formal, personalized instruction or apprenticeships. In these cases extensive rehearsal is mandatory, and mnemonic devices or notation systems, such as Ojibwa birch-bark rolls, help to preserve the repertory.

Native American musical concepts regarding song ownership and the purpose of music vary by community. Many Native Americans consider songs to be property, owned and used exclusively by certain individuals or groups. A healer may own songs used in his or her curing practice; initiated members of a ritual society may own the songs for a particular ceremony. Song ownership may be earned or transferred by gift, inheritance, barter, or theft. A song's value derives from its power to access the spiritual realm; thus a widespread concept about the purpose of Native American music is that it assists in communication between people and spirit beings.

Native American music is syncretic, adaptive, and adoptive in complex and sometimes contradictory ways. Indians have their own methods of constructing musical experience and shaping music history, knowledge of which is preserved in sacred narratives and oral traditions, as well as in more recent written, visual, and audio documents. Music is adapted in culturally patterned ways, permitting historical transformations that support cultural continuity or mediate change. Two common American Indian strategies for musical change are *pan-tribalism* and *revitalization*.

Musical pan-tribalism involves the adoption by one Native American community of a musical repertory indigenous to another. This process facilitates the renegotiation of ethnic boundaries and supports the perpetuation of native beliefs and expressive forms in new social and geographical environments. Some well-known types of pan-tribal music belong to the Ghost Dance, peyotism, and powwows. Ghost Dance songs employ characteristics of the Great Basin style: relaxed vocal quality, narrow melodic range, and paired-phrase structure. In the 1890s the Ghost Dance spread quickly among Plains tribes, who adopted the Great Basin musical style for use in this ceremony; the songs have survived into the twentieth century. Peyote songs, which constitute a form of prayer in the sacred rituals of the Native American Church, generally resemble Apache music. Peyote songs are monophonic and use a strophic form with a descending melodic inflection; their tempo is fast, and they are accompanied by rattle and water drum. Powwows are multifaceted intertribal celebra-

tions with historical roots in the Plains Sun Dance and Grass Dance. Powwow music features the characteristic Plains style: tense, nasal vocal quality, terraced descent in melodic contours, incomplete repetition form, and drum accompaniment. Individuals may choose to participate in one or more pan-tribal musical styles while maintaining their own tribal music in separate contexts.

Sometimes members of a community will make a deliberate effort to reconstruct a defunct or moribund repertory. This revitalization strategy provides an opportunity for the community to reshape, reinterpret, and redefine performance traditions, not by simply modifying them on the basis of feasibility, but through the expression of individual discernment and choice. Thus musical revitalization has to do with the way people make sense of their historical experience and transcend social constraints, such as the repression of traditional culture. Musical revitalization has become widespread throughout Native America as the twentieth century draws to a close.

The best way to learn about Native American music is through direct experience; respectful listeners are welcome at many public performances such as powwows, tribal fairs, Catholic feast-day celebrations, and some ceremonials. Information on musical events open to the public may be obtained from local powwow councils, urban Indian centers, and tribal administration offices. Audio recordings are available from several sources, including the Library of Congress (Archive of Folk Culture, Motion Picture, Broadcast, and Recorded Sound Division), the Smithsonian Institution (The Folkways Collection), and several private producers, Canyon Records and Indian Arts (Phoenix, Arizona) and Indian House (Taos, New Mexico).

See also Arts, Contemporary (since 1960).

Collaer, Paul, ed., *Music of the Americas: An Illustrated Music Ethnology of the Eskimo and American Indian Peoples* (New York: Praeger Publishers, 1973); Herndon, Marcia, *Native American Music* (Darby, Pa.: Norwood Editions, 1980); Nettl, Bruno, "North American Indian Music," in *Excursions in World Music,* ed. Bruno Nettl (Englewood Cliffs, N.J.: Prentice Hall, 1992).

VICTORIA LINDSAY LEVINE
The Colorado College

MUSKOGEE
See Creek (Muskogee).

MUSKRAT, RUTH (BRONSON)

(1897–1982)

Cherokee activist and national leader.

Ruth Muskrat Bronson was the fourth of James and Ida Muskrat's seven children. Her father was Cherokee, her mother of Irish and English descent. The Muskrats raised their children on a modest-sized farm in the Delaware District of the Cherokee Nation, Indian Territory. They watched as the federal government, insistent upon assimilating America's native people, dismantled Cherokee national institutions, divided up their communally held estate into family farms, and replaced Cherokee citizenship with U.S. citizenship. These changes allowed the new state of Oklahoma to absorb the lands of the old Cherokee Nation into its territory in 1907. A young Ruth Muskrat witnessed the suffering and poverty caused by the assimilation campaign. She understood why many Cherokees felt they had paid too high a price for American citizenship. By age ten, she had learned much about Indian-white relations.

In her search for answers to the problems of her generation, Muskrat left home to attend a preparatory school in Tonkawa, Oklahoma, in 1912. Later, she studied at the University of Oklahoma, the University of Kansas, and Mount Holyoke College, where she graduated with a bachelor of arts degree in 1925. Other experiences also contributed to Muskrat's education. In the summer of 1921 she organized recreational programs for Indian girls on the Mescalero Apache Reservation. It was her first experience of working with an Indian tribe different from her own. The following spring, she traveled to Asia with the American delegation of the World's Student Christian Federation. At the organization's conference in Beijing, China, she learned about race and cultural relations around the world.

During these years, Muskrat developed what would become her lifelong message of Indian self-determination: that viable solutions to Indian problems could be found only by Indians themselves. Muskrat's philosophy did not preclude receiving help from outsiders, but she remained adamant that the help offered be of a certain type. Convinced that a better future for Indians depended upon the development of a new generation of Indian leaders, Muskrat urged non-Indian friends to work for the expansion of educational opportunities for Indian youth. In one of her better-known public appearances, Muskrat requested this of a group of reformers known as the Committee of One Hundred,

Ruth Muskrat presenting President Calvin Coolidge with a book, The Red Man in the United States, *written by Protestant missionaries. She made the presentation in Washington during a 1923 meeting of the Committee of One Hundred, of which she was a member. Muskrat's clothing combined the styles of a variety of Indian tribes, including Cherokee, Cheyenne, and Mescalero Apache, to emphasize the Pan-Indian character of her message. The Reverend Sherman Coolidge (Arapaho) is to the right.*

when they met with President Calvin Coolidge in December 1923. In a brief speech Muskrat spoke of a "potential greatness" that lay "deep within the souls of the Indian students of today who must become the leaders of this new era." She told her audience that Indian students wanted to learn from the white man's culture. She also insisted, however, that Indian students wanted the chance to preserve the best in their own cultures. Education, Muskrat concluded, would offer Indian students the opportunity to achieve their goals.

Muskrat's degree from a prestigious women's college gave her choices unavailable to most Indian women of her generation. It is significant, then, that she sought a low-paying teaching job with the Bureau of Indian Affairs (BIA) after graduation. In 1925 Muskrat moved to Lawrence, Kansas, where she began teaching eighth graders at the Haskell Institute. Her position at the largest of the government's Indian boarding schools gave Muskrat an opportunity to do what she wanted most: encourage the development of a new generation of Indian leaders. In 1928, she married John F. Bronson of Connecticut in a ceremony at her childhood home in Oklahoma. Bronson fully accepted his wife's decision to pursue a career that would serve Indian people. In fact, he became her most ardent supporter.

In 1930, Ruth Bronson left Haskell to fill a new position with the BIA's emerging guidance and placement program. At first, she traveled throughout the Great Plains region in search of employment opportunities for graduates of Indian boarding schools. Then, in 1932, she began administering a new government loan program that served a modest number of Indian graduates interested in higher education or training. Bronson brought her own philosophical perspective to her work by treating loan recipients as potential Indian leaders. She also tried to give priority to those who expressed a desire to use their training in the service of their people. In 1935, Bronson moved to Washington, D.C., to oversee an expanded loan program. Three years later, the Bronsons welcomed another change in their lives when they adopted a twenty-one-month-old girl from Laguna Pueblo. Little Dolores was the daughter of a close friend who had died a tragically early death. After almost nineteen years in government service, Bronson decided to retire in 1943. She proudly recalled that during her tenure with the loan program, she helped some twenty-five hundred Indian students acquire an advanced education.

Bronson published *Indians Are People Too* in 1944. Its main theme emphasized her belief that romanticizing Indian people was as destructive to their well-being as was pinning on them the most negative of racial stereotypes. A year later, she began volunteering for the newly organized National Congress of American Indians (NCAI). A rising tide of political conservatism had revived the assimilation agenda of earlier times, and once again the government had begun pressuring American Indians to renounce their cultures and leave their reservations. Bronson established a legislative news service for NCAI members, running it out of her home for the first few years. In 1946, the NCAI elected her its executive secretary, a position she held for the next three years. All told, Bronson spent nearly a decade helping build an organization that de-

manded a hearing for native voices in the nation's capital.

In 1957, Bronson and her husband moved to the San Carlos Apache Indian Reservation, where she accepted a newly designed position in the Indian Health Service (IHS) as a health education specialist or "community worker." Believing that real improvements in Indian health would stem only from Indian initiatives, Bronson spent much of her time encouraging the development of leadership skills among Apache women. A group of women subsequently formed a hospital auxiliary called Ee-Cho-Da-Nihi and took over the outreach activities previously undertaken by the non-Indian wives of IHS workers. By 1960, Ee-Cho-Da-Nihi was planning and executing more ambitious, community-wide programs of its own design. In 1962, Bronson "retired" to Tucson, where she served as a consultant to the Save the Children Federation for the programs it sponsored in the nearby Yaqui and Tohono O'odham communities. A stroke in the early 1970s left Bronson partially paralyzed and put an end to her activism. She died on May 14, 1982.

Early in her life Bronson rejected the idea of assimilation and with it the idea that she had to choose between her Cherokee identity and her American citizenship. Instead, she developed a philosophy that accepted the fact of conquest but not the idea of powerlessness. Bronson believed that American democracy and law gave indigenous peoples a dual set of rights: those won by treaty and aboriginal occupancy, and those due them as citizens of the United States. Bronson's claim to these rights required that she work with and within the American system, all the while supporting the development of a new generation of Indian leaders who would continue the struggle. No matter what form her activism took, Bronson's commitment to empowering Indians remained constant. She should be remembered as someone who succeeded in paving the way for the more recent advances made in the movement toward tribal self-determination.

See also Cherokee.

GRETCHEN HARVEY
North Dakota State University

N

NAMPEYO

(1859?–1942)
Tewa-Hopi potter.

Nampeyo was born in Hano (Tewa Village), First Mesa, on the Hopi Reservation in Arizona. Her mother was Qotca-ka-o, of the Corn clan at Hano, and her father was Qots-vema, a Hopi farmer from Walpi, another First Mesa village. Her paternal grandmother named her Tcu-mana ("Snake Girl") because her father belonged to the Snake clan; however, because she lived at Hano, her Tewa name, Num-pa-yu ("Snake That Does Not Bite"), was more commonly used. Hano was founded in 1696 by Tewa refugees who had fled west from the Rio Grande following the Pueblo Revolt. They maintained their language, Tewa, in their new home.

Although not much is known about Nampeyo's early life, there is no question that she spent considerable time at Walpi with her Hopi grandmother, a potter who encouraged Nampeyo to learn her craft. Nampeyo's initial vessels were miniatures; however, she quickly learned pottery making, and by the time she was a young woman she was considered one of the finest potters at First Mesa. Hano women at this time produced only undecorated utility wares. In contrast, Walpi potters produced "crackle ware," pottery that was first thickly slipped (a clay solution is added to the exterior of the pot, providing a smooth finish) and then painted in the "decadent" Hopi style, incorporating a number of Zuni and possibly Rio Grande Tewa designs. A natural artist, Nampeyo showed exceptional skill in shaping, designing, and decorating her pottery. She also began finishing and/or decorating all of the vessels shaped by her grandmother.

After August 31, 1875, when Thomas Keam established Keam's Canyon Trading Post twelve miles east of First Mesa, nonnative goods formerly rare in the area became available in exchange for Hopi handicrafts. Not surprisingly, Nampeyo found a ready market for her pottery at Keam's. Encouraged by the trader and the income she could derive from the trade, Nampeyo worked to improve upon the already fine quality of her work. In the 1870s, a member of the Hayden Survey party (which was lodged and fed by Nampeyo's brother, "Captain Tom," a village chief, for whom she kept house) described Nampeyo as a gracious hostess with considerable poise, possessing exceptional natural beauty. Her beauty reportedly doomed her first marriage, to Kwi-vo-ya, in 1879: apparently fearing that her beauty would cause another man to steal her away, Kwi-vo-ya did not move to Nampeyo's home following their marriage, as was the tribal custom. In 1881 Nampeyo married Lesso, from Walpi; this union lasted and produced five children.

Lesso became interested in Nampeyo's pottery and soon began assisting her. By 1890 most of her more exceptional vessels were being produced in the Walpi "crackle ware" style. But, more importantly, she had started producing a few vessels with the yellow surface color and designs derived from prehistoric Sikyatki pottery. Art historians posit that this Sikyatki revival occurred in 1895 during the excavation of Sikyatki, a Pueblo IV ruin. J. W. Fewkes, the archaeologist in charge, noted Nampeyo and Lesso busily copying designs from mortuary vessels on all sorts of paper, including soda-cracker wrappers. It is because Fewkes "allowed" this copying that he is usually credited with the Sikyatki revival. However, other scholars suggest dates earlier than 1895 for this movement, and in fact the use of Sikyatki designs quite likely predated Fewkes's excavations.

The revival of the Sikyatki style produced a renaissance in Hopi ceramics. Perhaps copying at first, Nampeyo gradually developed complete freedom in design and mastery of the Sikyatki style. She experimented with various clays until the yellow firing clay was located, and she learned to duplicate the traditional paints, surface characteristics, and graceful shapes. Walter Hough, who accompanied Fewkes, obtained several early revival pieces in 1896 for the Smithsonian Institution.

A photograph by Edward Curtis of Nampeyo painting a small jar with a yucca brush.

Other First Mesa potters became jealous because of the material benefits accruing to Nampeyo. To combat this development, she instructed a number of interested women in the "new" techniques she had perfected. Her students were then able to raise their economic level as well. Nevertheless, Nampeyo continued to surpass all others in creative ability and mastery of the Sikyatki style. Lesso continued his search for Sikyatki potsherds and vessels with different designs at many ruins. These materials added to Nampeyo's knowledge of the style, and her skill continued to grow until her work had a flowing quality characterized by the use of open space.

As her talent increased, Nampeyo's fame spread. Although she was unable to communicate in English, Nampeyo was asked to demonstrate her ceramic techniques and to pose for numerous photographs. Later the Santa Fe Railroad and the Fred Harvey Company used her image as the symbol of Hopi culture in advertisements for the Southwest. Additionally, Nampeyo and her family demonstrated ceramics for the Fred Harvey Company twice at Hopi House, Grand Canyon (1905, 1907), and once in Chicago at the Chicago Land Show (1910). Thus Nampeyo herself became an "attraction" and was labeled "the greatest maker of Indian pottery alive." Her husband was often billed as a "famous Indian dancer."

By 1910, Nampeyo's international reputation was drawing untold numbers of people to her home to view her at work and to make purchases. Soon Nampeyo was unable to keep up with increased demands for her pottery. She began to make smaller vessels, which took less time, and to commission family members to paint them.

The tourist demand for her work did not decrease until World War I brought about a decline in domestic travel. By the time the war ended Nampeyo had aged and her sight was failing. When Ruth Bunzel interviewed Nampeyo in 1924–25, she thought the Hopi potter was totally blind. Nampeyo's daughters, however, have stated that their mother never completely lost her sight. In any case, Nampeyo's poor eyesight meant that she could no longer decorate vessels, although she continued to form them. Initially Lesso, who had mastered his wife's style, painted her vessels. When Lesso died in 1932, their daughter Fannie did the painting. Many believe that Fannie was joined in this effort by her sisters, Annie and Nellie, who also were adept at copying their mother's decorative style.

Nampeyo's final years were spent under her children's care. She became quite childlike and often sat on the bed in her room, playing with various objects. She particularly enjoyed interacting with her grandchildren, each of whom had been encouraged to make pottery. They (including Rachel, Daisy, Elva, and Leah), like their mothers, became noted potters. Nampeyo herself continued to shape vessels almost until the day of her death, July 20, 1942.

During her lifetime, Nampeyo gained an international reputation by creating a renaissance in Hopi pottery. In spite of her fame, however, Hopis continued to view her as a typical resident of First Mesa. She participated in traditional ceremonial activities, food exchanges, and work parties. As an artist and potter, and one who taught her art to numerous other women, Nampeyo made an immeasurable contribution to her people, one that continues to be appreciated and admired.

See also Art, Visual (to 1960).

Ashton, Robert, Jr., "Nampeyo and Lesou," *American Indian Art,* summer 1976, 24–33; Kramer, Barbara, "Nampeyo, Hopi House, and the Chicago Land Show," *American Indian Art,* winter 1988, 46–53; *Nampeyo, Hopi Potter: Her Artistry and Her Legacy* (Fullerton, Calif.: Muckenthaler Cultural Center, 1974).

THEODORE R. FRISBIE
Southern Illinois University at Edwardsville

NANABOZHO

A hero in Ojibwa (Chippewa) stories, Nanabozho (the name is also spelled Naanabozho and Nanabozhoo) is a man with special power. Some claim he is the product of a human mother and father, while others say his father is the wind. Though he is subject to the forces of nature such as famine and physical pain, this superman can command the wind and rain, talk to animals and plants, and slay evil spirits. Some authors have characterized Nanabozho as a trickster, though he can more accurately be described as a powerful schemer who tries to manipulate the world and the creatures of the world to his advantage with the assistance of spiritual forces. He embodies both human and supernatural qualities, reflecting the link between people and their creator. One story of this legendary man shows Nanabozho tricking the animals in the forest into feeding him and his family during a time of great famine. Even though he is not recognized as the creator of the world, Nanabozho is also credited with making a new earth after the great flood.

See also Ojibwa.

NARRAGANSETT

The Narragansetts of historic times were descended from people who archaeologists believe had occupied the region surrounding Narragansett Bay for more than ten thousand years. They spoke an Eastern Algonquian language. According to Roger Williams, who lived with them from 1636 until his death in 1683, the Narragansetts were governed by two sachems, ideally uncle and nephew. These sachems were responsible for allocating land and surplus food, for conducting diplomacy, and for making decisions regarding war.

The Narragansett territories boasted abundant natural resources, which permitted a semisedentary life based on the cultivation of maize, beans, and squash, and particularly on procuring game, fish, and especially shellfish. Whelks and quahogs, whose shells were used

for wampum, were especially abundant in Narragansett coastal regions, thus allowing the Narragansetts an important advantage in the wampum trade of the prehistoric and historic periods.

Narragansett men and women were organized according to the different patterns of their work. Men were responsible for hunting, deep-sea fishing, trade, diplomacy, and warfare. Women, on the other hand, were the farmers, and also manufactured most domestic articles. They prepared food and were responsible for child care.

Social distinctions existed in Narragansett communities. Sachems and their families were ranked highest, followed by the sachem's advisers. So-called common people had the rights of community members and might farm, whereas servants and slaves were without land rights and were said to have no names.

All Narragansetts recognized a cosmology endowed with *manitou*—an animating force found in natural phenomena, in miraculous events, and in the marvelous abilities of animals and people. All people sought access to manitou, or assistance from manitou spirit helpers, to improve their health and well-being and to bring them success in their endeavors. Religious leaders among the Narragansetts, especially the *powwaws*, had the particularly strong relations with manitou typical of North American shamans, and used their spiritual powers in curing and divination. The Narragansetts also believed that all people were possessed of two souls: one, the *animating soul*, was the special essence of each person; the other, the *dream soul*, was capable of travel or transformation during dreams or trance.

The Narragansett year was marked by a series of seasonal moves, and by festivals, games, and rituals, many of which were accompanied by a kind of sacred gambling, wherein the never-ending cycle of growth, death, and regeneration was celebrated.

After the settlement of southern New England by the English in the 1620s, Narragansetts grew rich and powerful as a result of the wampum trade. They were fortunate to escape the worst effects of the epidemics that swept the region in 1617–19 and again in 1633. Allied with the English in the Pequot War, they maintained a strong political presence in New England throughout the seventeenth century. In the succeeding centuries, although adopting the English language and participating in the local fishing and farming economy, Narragansetts retained a distinctive identity through patterns of intermarriage and continuities in ritual and folklore. They remain a powerful presence in Rhode Island today.

Bragdon, Kathleen, *The Native People of Southern New England, 1500–1650* (Norman: University of Oklahoma Press, 1996); Simmons, William, "Narragansett," in *Handbook of North American Indians*, ed. William C. Sturtevant, vol. 15, *Northeast*, ed. Bruce G. Trigger (Washington: Smithsonian Institution, 1978); Williams, Roger, *Key into the Language of America* (1643; reprint, Providence: Rhode Island and Providence Plantations Tercentenary Committee, 1936).

KATHLEEN J. BRAGDON
College of William and Mary

NATIONAL CONGRESS OF AMERICAN INDIANS

A Pan-Indian political organization, the National Congress of American Indians represents American Indians before the U.S. government, largely through lobbying in Washington, D.C. The NCAI was founded in 1944 in Denver, Colorado, by professional and college-educated Indians. Among the founding members were D'Arcy McNickle, a Flathead employee of the Bureau of Indian Affairs who held a seat on the first national council, and Napoleon Johnson, a Cherokee who served as the organization's first president. Initially, membership was restricted to "people of Indian ancestry"; later, non-Indians were offered associate membership.

In its first platform, the NCAI promised to "work toward the promotion of the common welfare of the aboriginal races of North America." The NCAI endeavored to educate non-Indians about Indian culture, preserve treaty rights, and lobby for Indian interests before the federal government. During the 1950s, the organization was the principal opponent of the policy of termination. In the 1960s the NCAI also played an important role in ensuring that federal antipoverty programs would encompass tribal communities.

In the 1980s and 1990s, the NCAI has promoted political causes and education through the efforts of its Washington office and the programs initiated at its annual national convention.

NATIVE AMERICAN CHURCH

With roots in ancient tribal traditions, the Native American Church has evolved into a twentieth-century religion. It functions like other religions, offering spiritual guidance to its members, but it employs peyote as its sacrament. The church is one important place where Christianity and indigenous beliefs intersect, although some Native American Church chapters avoid Christian references and rely entirely on traditional tribal ways.

Anthropologists and archaeologists have documented tribal use of the peyote cactus *(Lophophora williamsii)* ceremonially in pre-Columbian times in several tribes living along the coast of the Gulf of Mexico and the arid areas of northern Mexico. Legends describe peyote as a gift that first came to American Indians in peril. Some stories tell of the spirit Peyote speaking to a lone and despairing man or woman, advising the person to look under a nearby bush and eat a small cactus to be found there, after which the person would find renewed strength and the knowledge that would permit a return home.

In the late nineteenth century the peyote sacrament expanded from northern Mexico and the modern American Southwest, serving as a bridge between traditional faiths and the realities of contemporary life. In the process it became the base for a unique Pan-Indian movement. Each tribe that accepted the peyote religion did so in its own way by establishing doctrines and rituals consistent with traditional tribal beliefs and practices.

The rituals of the Native American Church allow believers to experience a revelation of mystical knowledge from the Creator. When the Creator is acknowledged as the Christian God, the peyote ritual blends traditional native beliefs and Christianity. Rituals may vary within tribes and from chapter to chapter. In the last decade of the nineteenth century, Quanah Parker (Comanche) developed a major ritual for the modern religion as it spread among his tribesmen. At the same time, Nishkuntu (Caddo/Delaware), also known as Moonhead or John Wilson, varied the design of the altar and ritual. Most Native American churches today follow either the tradition of Quanah Parker (the Half Moon Way) or that of Nishkuntu/Moonhead (the Cross Fire Way). Ministers of the Native American Church, called *road men,* officiate at prayer meetings, aided by other officials—fire men, drummers, and others. Services of the Native American Church also accompany weddings, funerals, thanksgivings, and healings.

The rituals of the Native American Church spread rapidly in the years before World War II. Faced with the suppression of many traditional rituals, native peo-

Emerson Jackson, a Navajo holy man and former president of the Native American Church of North America, performing a blessing ceremony outside the U.S. Supreme Court in November 1989. The Supreme Court was hearing arguments regarding the right of the Native American Church to use peyote in its religious practices.

ple welcomed the advent of ceremonies that took place quietly and with some legal protection. Battling alcoholism and poverty, many followers were attracted to the church's strict avoidance of alcohol and its call for monogamy and hard work. Many older religious lead-

ers among the Navajos and elsewhere opposed the new faith, but it continued to gain adherents.

Suppression of the use of peyote began early in the contact of Indians with Europeans. The king of Spain issued an edict in 1620 against the use of peyote. Beginning in 1886, federal Indian agents requested prohibition of peyote, and congressmen attempted to pass the necessary national legislation. Indian agents lobbied the Oklahoma Territorial Legislature, which adopted a law, repealed in 1908, prohibiting peyote by name.

Intense antagonism to the peyote religion, and to Indian religions in general, forced members of the Native American Church to organize formally to protect themselves. Accordingly, on October 10, 1918, the Native American Church incorporated itself in the state of Oklahoma. Led by Frank Eagle (Ponca), the group's first president, the church stated its intention to promote Christian religious belief using "the practices of the Peyote Sacrament" and to teach Christian morality and self-respect.

The 1918 charter of the Native American Church was changed through amendments in 1944 and a new charter in 1950, further amended in 1955. Most of the changes reflected the expansion of the group from Oklahoma and Mexico to the Midwest, the Great Plains, the Southwest, and even into Canada. Peyotists chartered their churches in states where the religion became active. In addition, peyotists gained the recognition of the Texas Department of Public Safety so that they could gather the cactus in that state, the only place in the United States where it grows.

In 1962 three Navajos—Jack Woody, Leon B. Anderson, and Dan Dee Nez—were arrested in California for violating laws against the distribution of peyote. Their conviction was upheld in the court of appeals, but in August 1964 the California Supreme Court held that prohibiting their use of peyote was a violation of the First Amendment's ban on state infringement of religious freedom. As a result of this ruling, federal authorities thereafter generally protected the ceremonial use of peyote, even though several states continued to list the substance as a narcotic subject to state drug laws.

To formally protect the Indian religion, Congress passed the Native American Religious Freedom Act of August 11, 1978. Though the law pledged that Indian people would enjoy the free exercise of religion, it contained no enforcement provision. In 1994, in the aftermath of conflicts between federal policy and state drug laws, Congress amended the 1978 law to include a new section that states, "Notwithstanding any other provision of law, the use, possession, or transportation of peyote by an Indian who uses peyote in a traditional manner for bona fide ceremonial purposes in conjunction with the practice of a traditional Indian religion is lawful, and shall not be prohibited by the United States or any State."

The Native American Church has tribal, regional, national, and two international organizations, with local churches, called chapters, in twenty-three states, Canada, and Mexico. The Native American Church of North America sponsors semiannual conferences as well as quarterly area meetings. Its Council of Elders, composed of past presidents, assists the organization. In addition, the presidents or chairmen of the Native American Church of North America, the Native American Church of Navajoland, Inc., and the Native American Church of the State of Oklahoma have formed a national council to provide leadership for the entire membership.

Native American Church leaders feel cautiously confident that federal law protects their religion even in states where they have no charter. They are, however, concerned that without cultivation, peyote may soon cease to exist because, unlike traditional harvesters, who take only part of the cactus, some illegal harvesters dig up the whole plant, and peyote has never been a commercial crop. In response the church is working to legalize the cultivation of peyote as well as its importation from Mexico. Their efforts are aimed at protecting ceremonies that offer believers guidance, fellowship, and contact with a spiritual power.

See also Religion.

LaBarre, Weston, *The Peyote Cult,* 5th ed. (Norman: University of Oklahoma Press, 1989); Slotkin, James S., *The Peyote Religion: A Study in Indian-White Relations* (Glencoe, Ill.: Free Press, 1956); Stewart, Omer, *Peyote Religion: A History* (Norman: University of Oklahoma Press, 1987).

CAROL HAMPTON (Caddo)
Caddo Culture and Heritage Committee
The Protestant Episcopal Church

NATIVE AMERICAN STUDIES

Native peoples have always cherished the pursuit of knowledge and wisdom in their daily lives, and Native American Studies was the first academic discipline of the Americas. Mothers, fathers, clan relatives, commu-

nity elders, and tribal leaders taught courses in Native American Studies. They offered instruction in agricultural sciences, animal husbandry, botany, and zoology. They taught medicine, pharmacy, dentistry, engineering, and psychology. They instructed young people in marketing, management, trade, and general business. In the social sciences they instructed people in law, government, political science, and sociology. They offered an array of courses in the humanities, including history, geography, literature, poetry, religious studies, philosophy, and language. Native Americans were the first to offer bilingual and bicultural education, since they felt it was important to be able to deal with neighbors who spoke different languages and followed different customs. Not everyone took every course of study, and no one took degrees in the discipline. Yet native scholars were quite accomplished in this field of study well before the arrival of Europeans.

When Europeans, Africans, and Asians arrived in America, they needed to verse themselves in Native American Studies in order to survive. For example, Jacques Cartier learned from the Wyandots along the St. Lawrence River how to cure scurvy, and the Pilgrims were taught how to plant corn, squash, and beans by Tsquantum (Squanto). At first, most nonnative peoples were interested in American Indian Studies, but after the colonial period, their descendants discounted the discipline, emphasizing the "civilized" curriculum of Western Europe. Native American Studies was ignored by nonnatives for several hundred years, until political movements of African Americans, Chicanos, and American Indians in the 1960s rekindled an interest in the field. Students demanded that institutions of higher learning offer courses in Native American Studies.

As a result of political pressure from students and community activists, colleges and universities created Native American Studies programs. Immediately, the issue arose as to the focus of the new courses: were they to foster an American Indian identity, focusing on native students and their needs, or were they to provide a general education for all students? Most programs did both, with teachers generally encouraging all students to take those courses dealing with Native American history, culture, religion, music, art, and literature. Unfortunately, in nearly all cases Native American Studies did not receive adequate academic or financial support from faculty or administrators.

Programs and departments emerged at colleges and universities in Arizona, California, Wisconsin, Minnesota, Montana, Oklahoma, Washington, North Dakota, and South Dakota. The program established at the University of Arizona in the 1970s was divided into two parts. One, an academic unit, was led by Ofelia Zepeda, Vine Deloria, Jr., Joy Harjo, N. Scott Momaday, Tom Holm, and Leslie Silko. The other unit was student- and community-oriented and helped students negotiate the culture of the university. It also served to link the university with native communities in its focus on health, medical, legal, management, and economic issues.

At San Diego State University and Washington State University the academic and student/community components of Native American Studies were not separate. Native counselors, financial-aid personnel, and recruiters worked closely with native professors. At San Diego State University John Rouillard headed a program that required him not only to teach numerous courses but at the same time to recruit, counsel, and advise native students. The same was true of Jack Forbes, David Risling, and Sarah Hutchinson at the University of California at Davis, and of Michael Dorris at Dartmouth College. The workload of Native American professors was generally higher than that of their colleagues in other departments, since native professors had a responsibility to American Indian communities. The degree to which a native instructor should provide community service continues to be debated by American Indian faculty, who are expected by their institutions to teach and publish as well as work with elementary and secondary students and serve on Native American community boards, committees, and projects. American Indian Studies professors walk a difficult line between professional and personal duties. Administrators and faculty rarely value the work of these professors in the area of community service, since they generally know little about native people and the importance of community in native culture.

Most Native American Studies programs emerged in the early 1970s, and native and nonnative students demonstrated a great interest in them. This trend has continued as many students fill the classrooms of Native American Studies courses in the United States and Canada. By 1985, a total of one hundred seven colleges and universities offered some form of Native American Studies program, but only nine of these campuses conferred departmental status on Native American Studies. Many programs were organized as part of an Ethnic Studies program or as a unit in an anthropology department. Native programs within other departments

often suffered from internal budgetary and political struggles in which American Indian Studies professors found themselves to be the minority of minorities. Often, Native Studies "fell through the cracks" within other units in which members of the faculty were hostile to American Indians. These struggles continue to characterize most American Indian Studies programs. In spite of adversity, by 1985, eighteen Native American Studies units offered majors, and forty units offered minors. In 1995, only six have graduate programs. These include the University of California at Berkeley, the University of Arizona, the University of California at Los Angeles, and Montana State University. Harvard University offers a graduate degree in American Indian Education, and the University of California at Riverside offers a Ph.D. in Native American history.

Native American Studies has always been interdisciplinary. Scholars working in the field of Native American history, for example, draw on literature, oral history, religion, sociology, anthropology, political science, ethnobotany, and other disciplines to explain and interpret native life. Several problems result from this approach, most notably in the area of the academic acceptance of Native American Studies and scholarship, a field that is viewed by many as an impure or corrupted form of history, anthropology, literature, or sociology. These suspicions make it difficult to secure funding from academic institutions as well as from the National Science Foundation, the National Endowment for the Humanities, and the National Institutes of Health. In addition, major journals in history, anthropology, literature, and sociology are often uninterested in the work of Native American scholars or the subject of American Indians. As a result, most Native American scholars and those interested in the discipline publish their scholarship in interdisciplinary journals such as the *American Indian Culture and Research Journal, American Indian Quarterly, Canadian Journal of Native Studies,* and Canada's *Native Studies Review.*

Native American Studies is accepted most widely at tribal colleges. In 1966, the Navajo Nation began Navajo Community College, the first tribally chartered institution of higher education. In 1969, Trent University in Ontario began a Native American Studies program, and a year later the Lakotas started Sinte Gleska University on the Rosebud Reservation in South Dakota. Today there are more than thirty of these institutions. All of them offer courses in Native American Studies, and all of them encourage native students to continue their formal education while maintaining a strong Indian identity.

See also Anthropology and Indians; Archaeology and Indians; Historians and Indians.

Clark, Carter Blue, "America's First Discipline: Native American Studies," in *American Indian Identity*, ed. Clifford E. Trafzer (Newcastle, Calif.: Sierra Oaks, 1989).

CLIFFORD E. TRAFZER (Wyandot)
University of California at Riverside

NAVAJO

The philosophy of a people determines that people's destiny. The foundation of Navajo life is *sq'ah naagháí bik'eh hózhóón*, a practical concept that guarantees success when applied. This concept may be translated and interpreted as *the beauty of life created by application of teachings that work*. Historically and traditionally, the Navajos have always chosen to adapt and adopt, to change and Navajoize. Their ability to embrace change has allowed them to succeed in coping with an environment that has brought them into contact with other people.

The Navajos believe that they passed through different worlds before they arrived in the Southwest, the Fourth World. Their recollections of prehistoric times portray a hunting-gathering society coming into contact with different people, interacting with them, and, finally, being asked to leave for having committed adultery or having offended their hosts in some way. A close analysis of the different prehistoric worlds in Navajo oral tradition reveals details that give merit to the Bering Strait migration theory. The First World or the Black World is, in its physical description, representative of a tundra biome, possibly the Far North. The Second World or the Blue-Green World possesses a landscape of landmarks and animals similar to that of western and central Canada. The Third World or the Yellow World touches upon mountains and plains reminiscent of the eastern slope of the Rockies and the Southwest. The Fourth World or the Glittering World brings us to Dinétah, the Gobernador region in northwestern New Mexico. Whether either the Navajo genesis story or the Bering Strait theory is true, the fact remains that the Navajos have always progressed intellectually, physically, socially, and spiritually. The story of their journey to and settlement in the Southwest is one of wanderers becoming a people. This process lies at the center of the Navajos' sense of their history.

There is also a broad area of agreement concerning the Navajo language. The Navajos speak a language that belongs to the Southern Athabaskan family, a language group that is also common to Apachean peoples, including those known as Jicarillas, Mescaleros, and White Mountain Apaches. The Southern Athabaskan language group is a subgroup of the broader language group known as Na-Dene. Other subgroups of Na-Dene are found in northern and central Canada. Stories of the Black World state that there was originally the One Language, which spoke and gave movement to creation, and that the One Language became four. The Navajo people also refer to *diné nááhódlóonii*, "the other people." The name *Navajo* is a modified Tewa word meaning "cultivated fields." The Spaniards knew the Navajo people as *Apaches de Navajó*. Eventually, the name was shortened to *Navajo*. However, the Navajo people call themselves Diné, the People.

When the People arrived in the Southwest, they left archaeological evidence indicating that they had no organized ceremonialism or belief system. The remains of their lifestyle during the Dinétah Phase (circa A.D. 1375–1650) clearly points to their way of life as a hunting-gathering society. The clan system was not in place. They knew little about planting corn and squash. They made only crude utility pots. Patterns and structures were not important. Ash piles mixed with broken pottery have been found, and evidence indicates that shelters had doors facing in all directions. Attempts to build Pueblo-style housing apparently failed.

However, linguistic evidence shows that the People were more than willing to learn from new experiences. Diné offers many examples of coined words. *Naadą́ą́*, "corn," was *anaa' bidą́ą́*—the enemy's (or alien) food. *Naayízí*, "squash," was *anaa' biyízí*—the enemy's (or alien) oval thing. *Anaasází*, "Anasazi," was *anaa' bizází*—the enemy's (or alien) ancestors. These terms attest to the People's complete experience, acceptance, and modification of an alien culture to fit the Navajo way of life. The People continue to use all these foods, together with the stories and ceremonies associated with them.

During the Gobernador Phase (c. 1650–1775), the People grew as a people. They settled down from a hunting-gathering society to an agricultural, ranching, and ceremonial people. When they moved into the Southwest, the People met the Puebloan peoples. They acquired new farming techniques that increased their crop supply. They also acquired the rituals, songs, prayers, and stories that went along with farming. Most of their ceremonial knowledge was acquired from Pueblo priests who had fled from the intrusion of the Spaniards—especially the missionaries, who were determined to convert the "Indians" to Christianity. Consequently, the People learned about ceremonial life from the best in the field. Later, when the People got wealthier through the acquisition of sheep and horses, they created entire ceremonies of their own that included songs and prayers about sheep and horses. Sheep also provided wool, which allowed the People to become great weavers of blankets and rugs. Navajo women are now widely renowned for their beautiful weaving. The People obtained sheep, horses, and cattle from the Spaniards through trading or raiding. Navajo men also developed the art of silversmithing from their knowledge of blacksmithing, which they acquired from the Spaniards. Today Navajo people are well known for their jewelry making. Horses and cattle allowed the People to have a reliable food supply and to remain semi-nomadic. The mobility of their wealth allowed the People to move out of harm's way when the need arose.

During the Canyon de Chelly Phase (c. 1775–1863), the People moved west to the present-day Four Corners area and made Canyon de Chelly their stronghold. The move was caused by hostile pressures from the Spaniards from the south, the Comanches from the east, and the Utes from the north. Whenever possible the People retreated rather than fought, and they made no exception in this case. During this time the People became prosperous materially, artistically, and ceremonially—a development that led Nathaniel Patton to write in the Missouri Intelligencer in 1824 that the People were superior to the Plains Indians because they fashioned clothes, designed jewelry, raised livestock, and cultivated land. The People also increased in numbers. Yet this was all soon to pass.

American troops moved into the Southwest in 1846 during the Mexican War. From 1846 to 1863 several treaties were signed and broken. After several years of warfare and treaties, the People were subjugated and taken to Bosque Redondo, in eastern New Mexico, by U.S. military forces. More than eighty-five hundred Navajo men, women, and children were driven to Bosque Redondo after their fields, orchards, houses, and livestock were destroyed. There they were to be civilized: they were to go to school, till and own land, and worship as Christians. After four years of hard

work and suffering on the part of the Navajos, the authorities recognized that their plan for Americanizing the People had failed. The Treaty of 1868 was negotiated and signed. Barboncito, the Navajo leader selected for the treaty negotiation, stated, "I hope to God you will not ask me to go to any other country except my own." The People went home.

The People returned to their land along the Arizona–New Mexico border hungry and in rags. Their territory had been reduced to an area much smaller than what they had occupied before the exodus to Bosque Redondo. The U.S. government issued them rations and sheep. Within a few years the People had multiplied the numbers of their livestock. The railroad arrived in 1880, and traders soon followed. The People began to trade maize, wool, mutton, hides, livestock, and crafts for food and manufactured goods. They became more sedentary and began a pastoral way of life. With the railroad came wage work, and the market economy began to emerge in Navajo country. In 1922 a business council was created to negotiate leases for natural resources found on the reservation—among them oil, natural gas, timber, uranium, and coal. This council eventually became the Navajo Nation Council, which now runs the Navajo government. The People have gained much from past experience, and today they are alive and well.

Personal growth is very significant in Navajo tradition. The stages of a person's life are recognized, accepted, and celebrated. A child's first laugh is an important event, and the person who makes a child laugh for the first time must host a dinner on the child's behalf. Relatives and friends are invited. A prayer is normally said before the feasting begins. People are served and form a line before the baby, who usually sits on the mother's lap. The mother holds a wedding basket containing earth salt. When people pass by with their plates full of food, the mother places a piece of earth salt in the child's right hand and assists the child in putting it on the food. This introduces the child to a lifelong sense of obligation to the family, the clan, and the People. The People believe that a person who has gone through this process will always share with and care for his people.

Another significant event in Navajo tradition is a girl's coming of age, which is marked by *kinaaldá*, the girls' puberty ceremony. According to Navajo tradition, when Changing Woman, a goddess, reached adulthood, Talking God performed this ceremony for her. It lasts for four days. Each morning at dawn the girl runs to the east; the last two days are reserved for singing, praying, and ritual activities. While the ceremony is going on, relatives and friends stop by to visit the girl's family, bringing food and eating. On the last night, the girl and her family, along with relatives, friends, and the local medicine person sit up all night and sing. In the morning, the girl runs to the east for the last time, and upon her return she cuts a corn cake that was prepared the day before and has been cooking underground all night long. The heart of the cake usually goes to the medicine person, and the rest goes to others who are present. After a girl has undergone this ceremony, she is ready for marriage. Recognition and acceptance are important in Navajo culture.

Many ceremonies are conducted over the course of the year. A medicine person conducts these ceremonies. Anyone can become a medicine person. One need only have the desire and patience to learn hundreds of songs, prayers, and rituals, and learn which are appropriate to which ceremony. A ceremony is a direct response to an illness. The Enemy Way Ceremony cleanses a person of foreign contagions; it is usually performed for someone who has killed an enemy and is suffering from the enemy's ghost. It lasts for three days and nights. The Night Way Ceremony, which lasts for nine days and nights, is usually performed for someone who is suffering from blindness or a physical deformity. Ideally, the Blessing Way Ceremony should be performed for a person after a ceremony for curing his or her illness has taken place.

When a person gets sick, he or she normally goes to a diagnostician first, called a *star gazer* or *hand trembler,* who tells the patient what caused the illness and recommends a particular ceremony and medicine person. Upon approval from the family, a prominent family member then goes to the medicine person and hires him or her to do the ceremony. The ceremony usually takes place at the patient's house, with the patient surrounded by friends, family members, and relatives. Depending on the illness and time of the year, the ceremony may be as short as fifteen minutes or as long as nine nights and days.

K'é—the Navajo kinship system—is the strength of the People. It keeps the Navajo people together. Navajo is a matrilineal and matrilocal society. Each Navajo belongs to four different, unrelated clans. He or she belongs to his or her mother's clan. He or she is born for his or her father's clan. He or she has maternal and paternal grandfathers' clans. Traditionally, the People were forbidden to marry into the first two clans; today

they are still strongly discouraged from doing so. *K'é* also extends to the natural world and the gods. The People are always among relatives.

To get an idea of how *k'é* works, consider the following example. A Navajo meets another Navajo from the other side of the reservation. They may never have met before. When they meet, they ask one another about their clans and thus find out how they are related to one another. For example, if they find out that they belong to the same clan, they may, depending on their ages and sex, end up being brothers, sisters, mother and daughter, grandson and grandmother, and so forth. To take another example, if an older man meets a child and finds out that the child belongs to the same clan as the older man's father's clan, the child will automatically be promoted to the status of a father. The older man will no longer treat the child like a child, but will respect him like a father.

Contemporary community life varies from place to place. The Navajo Reservation covers parts of three states: northwestern New Mexico, northeastern Arizona, and southeastern Utah. It encompasses more than twenty-five thousand square miles, an area slightly larger than the state of West Virginia. There are about 220,000 Navajos today. While most of them reside on the reservation, a good portion leave the reservation to look for jobs. Others leave to pursue an education, some returning later on to work on the reservation.

Today the People live in frame houses, traditional hogans, and trailers. They work as ranchers, farmers, teachers, lawyers, judges, mechanics, professors, carpenters, plumbers, electricians, medicine persons, and diagnosticians. They travel by horse, by automobile, and by plane. Some conduct and participate in traditional religious ceremonies, while others go to church on Sundays. A few continue to gather and cultivate food, and the majority go to nearby border towns to shop in malls and markets. They dress casually yet fashionably for comfort, formally when necessary, and traditionally for ceremonial purposes. They converse in Navajo, English, Spanish, and other languages. From weaving and silversmithing, their artistic expression has expanded to painting, literature, photography, videography, performing arts, sand painting, and ceramics, among other areas. Students attend public, Bureau of Indian Affairs, religious, and community schools. Their education extends from vocational to professional training. They receive degrees from local schools such as Navajo Community College and from prestigious universities such as Princeton. In short, the People are beginning to live again.

Bingham, Sam, and Janet Bingham, *Between Sacred Mountains: Stories and Lessons from the Land* (Chinle, Ariz.: Rock Point Community School, 1982); Iverson, Peter, *The Navajo Nation* (Albuquerque: University of New Mexico Press, 1981).

REX LEE JIM (Navajo)
Rock Point Community School
Chinle, Arizona

NAVAJO LANGUAGE

The Navajos, or Diné, as a people, and their language, have long been subjected to much study; in fact, there is more published research on this Native American tribe than any other in the United States. The Diné language belongs to the southern branch of the Apachean or Athabaskan language family. Athabaskan, Eyak, and (probably) Tlingit make up the Na-Dene family. The Na-Dene languages are widely spread—from interior Alaska to western Canada, the Northwest Coast, and the American Southwest.

Southern Athabaskan includes Jicarilla, Western Apache, Mescalero, Kiowa-Apache, and Lipan, as well as Diné. Kiowa-Apache and Lipan are close to extinction; Jicarilla has an endangered status; and even among the Diné, the most numerous of the Athabaskan tribes, only 17 percent of youngsters are speakers of the language at the time they enter school.

The traditional homeland of the Diné is a broad area bounded by the four Sacred Mountains: to the east, Sierra Blanca Peak; to the west, San Francisco Peaks; to the south, Mount Taylor; and to the north, Hesperus Peak, in the La Plata Range. The center of Diné homeland is El Capitán Peak. Most of the Diné homeland lies in northern Arizona, but it also extends into southern Utah and northwestern New Mexico.

While it is impossible to convey all aspects of Navajo in a brief description, the relationship between nouns and third-person pronouns offers a good illustration of an important element of the language. This discussion will also illuminate certain features that have often been the subject of controversy for linguists, anthropologists, and—sometimes—native speakers themselves.

The grammatical structure of Diné is vastly different from that of English. The most important of these differences lies in sentence structure: Diné sentences are built from verb stems; the resulting verb structures then function as complete sentences. The verb stems are based on about five hundred verb roots. For each root there is an underlying conceptual meaning of the verb, as well as numerous extensions of meanings, some metaphorical. For instance, the root *kaad,* with the underlying meaning of "flatness" or "expansiveness," can have extended meanings such as the following. (Sound changes in the root are irrelevant.)

si*kaad*	"It [rug, bush, blanket] is spread out flat."
na'nish*kaad*	"I am herding sheep."
ahésh*kad*	"I am clapping."
adish*ka'*	"I am playing it [cards/gambling]."
násh*kad*	"I am sewing it."

You can also see from the English meanings given here that the subject and object pronouns are incorporated into the verb.

Prefixation is widespread in Diné—unlike English, where suffixes are more common. There are as many as ten prefix position slots preceding the verb stem. Of course, not all will appear simultaneously.

Diné nouns, except for some kinship terms, have the same form for singular and plural: for example, *tl'ízí* can mean either "goat" or "goats"; the distinction is made in the verb. Also, there are no definite articles, only indefinite ones (such as *a* and *an* in English). If a noun appears without an indefinite article, the interpretation is that the noun is definite.

Another grammatical difference between English and Diné is that Diné has no gender distinctions in its third-person pronouns. Thus *sikaad,* "It is spread out flat," can also have the interpretation of someone (a male or female) flopping down or, jokingly, of someone taking up more space than necessary.

Diné makes a distinction in its pronoun system with respect to the animacy rank of the discourse participants. The belief underlying this view is that every living thing has a given volition. Volitionality distinguishes animate things from inanimate things, and within animate things, it separates humans from animals, and larger animals from smaller animals. The ranking would appear as: supernatural beings > humans > large animals > smaller animals > things. This distinction in volition divides nouns into classes whereby a being with a lower level of volition cannot act upon a being with a higher volition level. Even though Diné people know that horses can kick people, they would describe the event as a case where the person was foolish enough to let himself be kicked by a horse. In fact, this interpretation is marked by the choice of pronouns.

Native speakers can decipher sentences that contradict grammatical rules of volition ranking and pronoun choice, but these utterances clash with their worldview.

Consider the two Diné sentences that follow.

hastiin łį́į́ **bi-**ztal
man horse kicked
OBJ. SUBJ. VERB
The horse kicked the man.

łį́į́ hastiin **yi-**ztal (?)
horse man kicked
SUBJ. OBJ. VERB
(The horse kicked the man.)

There is a change in pronoun choice (in the form of the verb prefix, which in both cases indicates that the object is *hastiin*) and also a change in the order of the nouns. Although both examples describe the same event, the first would be preferred over the second. The second is not an utterable sentence; it just would be considered inappropriate, because something that is lower in volition rank is preceding a higher-ranked being.

Diné employs a very interesting strategy for circumventing unequal ranking. It uses the human third-person pronouns (in the form of verb prefixes), called the fourth-person pronouns, when a human is acted upon or when a human acts upon a lower thing. The fourth person allows lower-ranked nouns to be mentioned first for discourse prominence. Thus a native speaker who wanted to focus on the horse would use, instead of the second example, the following form.

łį́į́ **ha-**ztal
horse kicked
SUBJ. VERB
'The horse kicked him.'

If two third-person participants are of the same rank, either ordering of subject and object is permissible. The deciding factor in such cases is the topic of discussion. This is illustrated in the following examples.

hastiin ashkii **bi-**ztal
man boy kicked
OBJ. SUBJ. VERB
The boy kicked the man.

ashkii hastiin **yi-**ztal
boy man kicked
SUBJ. OBJ. VERB
The boy kicked the man.

The interplay between nouns and pronouns has been a topic of linguistic research for decades by non-speakers of Diné. In the last twenty years native speakers have initiated research on their own language that has brought about the volitionality insight. The cultural explanation of a linguistic aspect of a language provides a glimpse into the world of the speakers and how they see that world.

Griffin-Pierce, Trudy, *Earth Is My Mother, Sky Is My Father* (Albuquerque: University of New Mexico Press, 1992); Witherspoon, Gary, *Language and Art in the Navajo Universe* (Ann Arbor: University of Michigan Press, 1977); Young, Robert, and William Morgan, *The Navajo Language: A Grammar and Colloquial Dictionary* (Albuquerque: University of New Mexico Press, 1980).

MARYANN WILLIE (Diné)
University of Arizona

NAVAJO TREATY OF 1868

The Navajo Treaty of 1868 allowed about seven thousand Navajo people to return from incarceration in New Mexico to a one hundred-square-mile reservation bordering Arizona and New Mexico. The treaty ended many decades of Navajo conflict with the Spanish, the Mexicans, and U.S. forces, and began the process of unifying the Navajo people into a single legal entity.

The 1848 Treaty of Guadalupe Hidalgo established the authority of the United States in Navajo country. Fort Defiance was built in 1851 in the heart of this area, but the Navajos resisted U.S. control for two more decades. The most intense conflict occurred from 1863 to 1866 when Americans assisted by the trader Kit Carson forced the Navajos to surrender and move to the desolate Bosque Redondo region of eastern New Mexico. The infamous "Long Walk" of eight thousand tribesmen across nearly three hundred miles of New Mexico desert took place in 1864. The 1868 treaty reversed this process and promised the tribe a future of peace within the borders of its original homeland.

Two of the most prominent Navajo resistance fighters from the early 1860s, Barboncito and Manuelito, were among the twenty-nine signers of the 1868 treaty. The American negotiators were S. F. Tappen and Lieutenant-General William T. Sherman, both members of a Peace Commission established to end the frontier violence in the West. The treaty stipulated that "all war between the parties . . . shall forever cease" and that the U.S. government would "insure the civilization of Indians" by providing schools, farm equipment, clothing, and blankets.

After the treaty was signed, the Navajos experienced a period of recovery. One million acres were added to the reservation in 1875, leaders such as Barboncito and Manuelito became tribal officials, and conflicts with non-Indians ceased. During this same period sheep and cattle herds grew, trading expanded, and the tribal population rose from nine thousand in 1868 to twenty-one thousand in 1900.

See also Manuelito.

NEOLIN

(fl. 1760–66)
Delaware prophet.

Neolin (meaning "Four") was the most notable of a number of nativist prophets of the mid–eighteenth century who attributed the misfortunes of the Indians to their corruption by the whites and who advocated the restoration of aboriginal rituals, beliefs, and practices. His influence contributed to "Pontiac's Rebellion" of 1763–64.

In Neolin's time Delaware society was making considerable adjustments to the advancing colonial frontier. The Indians' material culture contained many items of European manufacture; their economy, some of it increasingly harnessed to the deerskin trade, faltered as game was reduced by overhunting and the expansion of white settlement; and the Delawares gave ground, withdrawing successively from eastern Pennsylvania to the Susquehanna, Allegheny, and Muskingum Valleys of western Pennsylvania and Ohio. Delaware communities were also damaged by European diseases, and an acquaintanceship with Christian groups—Swedish Lutherans, Quakers, Presbyterians, and Moravians—had undermined traditional Delaware theology.

Prior to contact with Europeans, the Delawares' spiritual world had been governed by the will of the spirits and was rich in rituals entreating, propitiating, or thanking them. Disasters, such as famines or sickness, were imputed to the anger of the spirits and provoked a search for the causes of the discontent. Misfortune might be redressed by a greater attention to ceremonies and practices pleasing to the spirits. In the mid–eighteenth century Indian prophets increasingly identified white interference as the source of spiritual anger and consequent misfortune. Divine favor could be restored by a rejection of alien influences and the restoration of aboriginal customs and beliefs. These "nativist" prophets were not entirely able to distinguish between cultures that were by then inextricably entangled. Not only were the material possessions of the fur trade widely prized, but Indian belief had imbibed Christian influences. Still, the prophets emphasized an independent Indian identity, albeit one composed of some white as well as Indian elements.

Neolin illustrated these complications. Described as a young man in 1766, he claimed to have experienced a vision about 1760 in which a spiritual messenger warned him of the consequences of his people's degeneration. Later Neolin apparently maintained that he had himself visited the realm of the Creator (heaven) and seen the punishments of hell. Probably Neolin's musings had been prompted by a fear that the Creator's disfavor had been evident in the smallpox outbreaks that had scourged the Indians in 1756–58. In 1762 the prophet began preaching from his home on the Cuyahoga River (Ohio), representing himself as the medium of the Creator and calling upon the Indians to exorcise white influences. The Indians, he said, must purify themselves by taking emetics, reforming, and driving the British (then just victorious in the Seven Years' War) from aboriginal land.

According to Neolin the route to heaven, once easy of access, had been obstructed by the whites. Indians neglected old sacrifices, abandoned their distinct customs, drank alcohol, wore the clothes of the Europeans and used their steel, flints, and muskets, permitted the British to occupy Indian land, and hunted to acquire trade goods instead of just for subsistence. In this new atmosphere their souls would be diverted to the realm of the Evil Spirit and be punished. Neolin's message of reform was, therefore, partly restorative, seeking a return to more traditional ways, but not entirely so. The concepts of hell and the devil, for example, were Christian inspired, the older Delaware religion contending that the souls of the wicked would simply be unable to join the Creator. And in some social strictures, such as his attack upon polygyny, Neolin would seem to have been advocating views modified by contact with Europeans.

At this time Neolin was strongly anti-British. He contended that the reformed Indian way of life would not be completed for seven years, during which time the British would be driven from the land. Unlike other

Delaware prophets, he attained widespread influence, using diagrams of his message to spread the word. His message reached the Illinois River and the Ottawas, Potawatomies, Ojibwas, and Wyandots of what is now Michigan and Ohio. Pontiac, an Ottawa chief, used it in April 1763 to support his plan to attack the British post of Detroit. Although not the principal influence behind the Indian uprising against the British in 1763, which drew upon many and varied grievances, the prophet's teachings undoubtedly played a part.

The collapse of the Indian rebellion in 1764–65 may have undermined Neolin, who had predicted victory over the British. In 1764 he was at the Shawnee village of Wakatomica on the Muskingum River, and two years later he was living at the town of the influential Delaware chief Newcomer, on the Tuscarawas River (Ohio), where he showed interest in the views of two Presbyterian visitors. This may suggest that Neolin was tempering his opinions. There are no clear references to the prophet after 1766, although in 1770 sickness in Newcomer's town led an unnamed prophet to predict disaster if the Indians did not check the progress of the Moravian missionaries and live on a diet of corn and water. Although this activity seems inconsistent with the views Neolin expressed in 1766, it may reflect the prophet's return to earlier principles or the work of a disciple.

More influential but less enduring than his Delaware contemporary, the prophet Wangomend (active 1752–75), Neolin disappeared into obscurity, but he was the most noted pioneer of a nativist prophetic tradition that spasmodically influenced Indian history for several decades. The Shawnee prophet Tenskwatawa, brother of Tecumseh, drew heavily upon the teachings of Neolin in the early nineteenth century. To whites, these prophets' activities seemed backward looking and doomed to failure. But to Indians, alarmed at the prospect of divine disfavor and the tensions produced by contact with dominant Euro-American neighbors, they were rational movements of reform.

See also Delaware; Pontiac.

Dowd, Gregory Evans, *A Spirited Resistance: The North American Indian Struggle for Unity, 1745–1815* (Baltimore and London: Johns Hopkins University Press, 1992); Hunter, Charles, "The Delaware Nativist Revival of the Mid-Eighteenth Century," *Ethnohistory* 18 (1971): 39–49; Peckham, Howard H., *Pontiac and the Indian Uprising* (1947; reprint, Chicago: University of Chicago Press, Phoenix Books, 1961).

JOHN SUGDEN
Hereward College
Coventry, England

NEW FRANCE

See Indian-White Relations in New France.

NEWSPAPERS, MAGAZINES, AND JOURNALS

The flourishing publishing industry that provides vital communications links within and among American Indian communities today had its foundation in the establishment of the *Cherokee Phoenix* at New Echota, Cherokee Nation, in 1828. Native journalists today consider its young Cherokee editor, Elias Boudinot, to be the father of American Indian journalism and see their role much as his: to reflect a self-defined image of the Indian community and to give expression to Indian thought and opinion to outside readers as well as the local community. While the traditional mainstay of native periodical publishing has been newspapers, the twentieth century has witnessed a steady growth in magazine publication and, in recent decades, the establishment of journals of American Indian thought and opinion.

Newspapers

Native newspaper publishing grew slowly and was considered an oddity until the last two decades of the nineteenth century. The *Cherokee Phoenix,* established to present the Cherokee Nation's side of its controversies with the state of Georgia during the era of Cherokee removal, closed down before the tribe's departure for the West. The Cherokee Nation established the *Cherokee* Advocate at Tahlequah in 1844. Like the *Phoenix,* the *Advocate* was published in English and Cherokee. The Choctaw and Chickasaw nations undertook similar publishing efforts: the *Choctaw Intelligencer* (Doaksville, 1850) and the *Chickasaw Intelligencer* (Post Oak Grove, 1852). All these early Indian Territory newspapers were aimed primarily at the American public as well as the local population and promoted an image of "civilization" to the outside world. Outside Indian Territory, Indian editors and publishers produced newspapers for non-Indian readers. George Copway, a Canadian Ojibwa, edited *Copway's American Indian* (1851) in New York State, while in California the volatile Cherokee John Rollin Ridge held several editorial positions, working at the *Weekly California Express* (Marysville, 1857–59), the *Sacramento Bee* (1857), and *the Daily National* (Grass

Valley), which he owned and edited (1864–67). Another Cherokee, Edward Bushyhead, was publisher of the *San Diego Union* (1869–73), and the Ojibwa entrepreneur Gus Beaulieu established The Progress (1886) at White Earth, Minnesota.

There are several reasons for the slow growth of Indian newspaper publishing during the nineteenth century. First, publishing was an index of the degree of accommodation of tribal groups or individual editors to non-Indian norms and was, therefore, concentrated in the so-called Civilized Tribes of Indian Territory. Second, although the Cherokee, Choctaw, and Chickasaw syllabaries had made publishing in these languages possible, the lack of orthographies for the other languages limited publishing in them. Thus most publishing was in English, and local Indian readerships were consequently limited. Third, Indian newspaper publishing had begun as a response to the removal crisis; once that crisis passed, there were few new incentives for the creation of additional newspapers.

In the late nineteenth century, new attacks on Indian life inspired a new phase of newspaper publishing. Again, the Civilized Tribes of Indian Territory led the way as they protested the allotment of their lands and the proposed admission of Oklahoma (which would contain Indian Territory) as a state. The Cherokees continued to publish the *Cherokee Advocate* and established a number of other newspapers such as the *Indian Chieftain* (Vinita, 1882) and the *Arrow* (Tahlequah, 1888). The Creeks established the *Indian Journal* (Muskogee, 1876), the Choctaws began the *Indian Citizen* (Atoka, 1886), and the Osages published the *Wah-shah-she News* (Pawhuska, 1893). By 1900 most towns in Indian Territory had newspapers, many of them owned, edited, managed, or typeset by American Indians. Unfortunately, however, the breakup of the tribal land titles, together with Oklahoma statehood in 1907, undermined these beginnings, and many tribal papers disappeared.

Newspaper publishing in the first four decades of the twentieth century was in many respects a product of late nineteenth-century Indian policy. Allotment, off-reservation boarding-school education, and other assimilationist policies of the late nineteenth century resulted in eroded land bases, poverty, poor health, and cultural loss that demoralized Indian communities. For the most part, newspaper publication was dominated by Indian publishers and editors who supported these destructive policies. Many were graduates of off-reservation boarding schools, where they had learned print-

ing. Their publications were not tribally oriented, but served both the local Indian and non-Indian communities. Most newspaper publishing occurred in eastern Oklahoma, formerly Indian Territory, where many former territorial editors and publishers simply directed their papers to new, statewide audiences. Elsewhere, Gus Beaulieu founded *The Tomahawk* (1903) in Minnesota; Roy Stabler, the *Winnebago Chieftain* (1907) in Nebraska; Webster Hudson, the *Quileute Independent* (1908) and the *Quileute Chieftain* (1910) in Washington State; H. C. Ashmun edited the *Odanah Star* (1912) in Wisconsin; Peter Navarre, the *Rossville Reporter* (1903) in Kansas; and William Pugh, the *Martin Messenger* (1914) and the *Shannon County News* (1930) in South Dakota.

Just as federal policy had influenced earlier developments in Indian newspaper publishing, policies during the twenty years after World War II did much to shape newspaper publishing as it exists today. Relocation policy resulted in the urbanization of native populations, a process that continues, and termination policy revealed the federal government's intent to shed its responsibility for Indian affairs. As these policies unfolded, both urban and reservation leaders realized the need to communicate with their constituents. A result was the revitalization of the tribal and native-nation press. Some newspapers that were established or grew out of newsletters in that era remain in print today, including the *Ute Bulletin* (1950) in Fort Duchesne, Utah; *Char-Koosta News* (1956) in Pablo, Montana; *Navajo Times* (1950) in Window Rock, Arizona; *Tribal Tribune* (1961) in Nespelem, Washington; *Fort Apache Scout* (1962) in Whiteriver, Arizona; and *Jicarilla Chieftain* (1962) in Dulce, New Mexico. The *Tundra Times* (Anchorage, 1962) was established to serve the Eskimo, Indian, and Aleut population of Alaska.

The decade following 1965 saw an unprecedented amount of native publishing, for several reasons. First, Great Society legislation channeled federal funds to native communities and organizations, resulting in a proliferation of newsletters and newspapers aimed at specialized audiences. Second, a rising sense of Indian nationalism and cultural awareness, and growing demands for tribal self-determination, resulted in an activist press and the establishment of the nationally circulated newspapers *Akwesasne Notes* (Rooseveltown, New York, 1969) and *Wassaja* (Los Angeles, 1973). Third, the American Indian Press Association, established in 1971, provided national Indian news stories to publishers with limited means. Finally, the Alaska

Native Claims Settlement Act of 1971, which established thirteen regional native corporations in the state, resulted in a flurry of publishing activity among Alaska Natives. However, many newspapers and other publications begun in this period were related to specific programs or policies and were funded wholly or in part by moneys from outside the native communities. Most failed to survive the slow withdrawal of federal funds from social and economic programs in the late 1970s and the periodic slashing of the federal budget in the early 1980s.

Since 1980, native publishing has begun to overcome some of the problems that have beset it throughout its history. Publications that survived federal budget cuts have become more financially secure through advertising or the commitment of local funds. An increasing number of professionally trained native journalists, improved computer technology, and the activities of the Native American Journalists Association (established in 1984) ensure better coverage of local, regional, and national native news. In addition to tribal and native-nation newspapers, some excellent independent publications have been established, including *News from Indian Country* (1977), published by Paul DeMain in Hayward, Wisconsin; *The Circle* (1979), published by the Minneapolis Indian Center; and *Indian Country Today* (1981), published by Tim Giago in Rapid City, South Dakota. Yet problems remain. Funding for tribal and native-nation publications depends on economic conditions. Independent publishers, dependent on advertising, are also vulnerable to economic trends. Editors of publications funded by local native governments or agencies often have little editorial license: tribal governments can shut down presses and remove editors, as has been demonstrated in recent years at the *Navajo Times*, the *Mandan, Hidatsa and Arikara Times*, and, most recently, *Hopi Tutu-veh-ni*.

Magazines

American Indian and Alaska Native magazine publication, basically a twentieth-century phenomenon, has been beset by most of the same problems that newspaper publishing has faced. Early efforts at magazine publishing were mounted as responses to federal policy. Ora Eddleman, a Cherokee, established *Twin Territories* (1899) at Muskogee after the United States assumed federal control over Indian Territory and the admission to the Union of a combined Indian Territory and Oklahoma Territory seemed imminent. After Oklahoma statehood, Edward Tinker, an Osage, estab-

lished the *Osage Magazine* (1909) at Pawhuska in response to the transition from Indian to non-Indian social and political domination. Both the *American Indian Magazine* (Washington, D.C, 1913), published by the Society of American Indians, and the Chickasaw Lee Harkins's *American Indian* (Tulsa, 1927) urged full citizenship rights and economic development. Others went further, stridently insisting on the abolition of the Bureau of Indian Affairs, opposing attempts by reformers to reverse assimilationist policies and to revitalize native communities, and attacking John Collier's advocacy of tribal governments. Among such publications were Carlos Montezuma's *Wassaja* (Chicago, 1916), William Paul's *Alaska Fisherman* (Ketchikan, 1923), the California Indian Rights Association's *California Indian News* (Los Angeles, 1935), and the American Indian Federation's *First American* (Washington, D.C., 1937).

Magazine publishing experienced a hiatus during the war years, from which it did not emerge until recent times. More sophisticated technologies and the aggressive pursuit of advertising have resulted in the establishment of magazines such as *Alaska Native Magazine* (Anchorage, 1982), *Navajo* (Window Rock, Arizona, 1984), *Turtle Quarterly* (Niagara Falls, 1987), and the high-quality *Winds of Change* (Boulder, 1986), published by the American Indian Science and Engineering Society.

Journals

Journal publication is a recent innovation. Though they include only a handful of titles, journals have been and continue to be generally first-rate and have been affiliated with academic institutions or professional organizations. They include *American Indian Law Review* (1973), at the University of Oklahoma; *American Indian Culture and Research Journal* (1974), at UCLA; *American Indian Quarterly* (1974), formerly at Berkeley and now published by the University of Nebraska Press; *American Indian Journal* (1975), at the Institute for the Development of Indian Law, Washington, D.C.; *Journal of Navajo Education* (1983), at the Round Rock School, Chinle, Arizona; *Akwekon* (1984), at Cornell University; *Journal of Alaska Native Arts* (1984), at the Institute of Alaska Native Arts, Fairbanks; and *Wicazo Sa Review* (1985), at Eastern Washington University.

◆◆◆

Despite obstacles, native newspaper and other periodical publishing has achieved a high degree of sophistication and professionalism. Publishers have the technical capability and expertise to focus on the major issues that confront their constituencies on local, regional, and national levels. They have established information networks among themselves and with organizations involved in the indigenous peoples' movement worldwide. As it has grown, the native press has become more authoritative and has exerted a stronger influence on behalf of the empowerment of native communities.

See also Boudinot, Elias; Copway, George; Montezuma, Carlos (Wassaja); Ridge, John Rollin (Yellow Bird).

Danky, James P., ed., and Maureen E. Hady, comp., *Native American Periodicals and Newspapers, 1828–1982* (Westport, Conn.: Greenwood Press, 1984); Littlefield, Daniel F., Jr., and James W. Parins, eds., *American Indian and Alaska Native Newspapers and Periodicals*, 3 vols. (Westport, Conn.: Greenwood Press, 1984 and 1986); Murphy, James E., and Sharon M. Murphy, *Let My People Know: American Indian Journalism, 1828–1978* (Norman: University of Oklahoma Press, 1981).

DANIEL F. LITTLEFIELD, JR.
American Native Press Archives

NEZ PERCE

The Hanyawat, or Creator, placed the Numiipu on the land at a time beyond measuring. The Numiipu honored the Hanyawat and Mother Earth through special songs and dances and gave thanks in many rituals, particularly the first feast, called the Keuuyit, which signified the first harvest of food.

The Numiipu occupied a territory that encompassed much of the land drained by the Snake River, in present-day north central Idaho, northeastern Oregon, and southeastern Washington. Communities clustered around family and extended kin groups and linked together into bands that identified with specific river drainages. Each settlement followed a variety of leaders. Some leaders organized groups to engage in hunting, others specialized in warfare, and still others focused on religious rituals, conflict resolution, or healing. Villages grouped together during the winter, but when spring came their members dispersed to gather roots and berries or to hunt for large game in the mountains. Views were generally aired in village councils, making it difficult for the entire group to establish a unified stand on any single issue. In 1800 approximately seven thousand people counted themselves Nu-

miipu, speaking a common Sahaptian language and following a common set of religious rituals.

At the end of the eighteenth century, dramatic events taking place elsewhere on the North American continent began to affect the indigenous people of the Pacific Northwest. Exploratory voyages by James Cook, George Vancouver, and the Spaniard Alejandro Malespina introduced Europeans to the geography and natural wealth of the region, and the arrival of horses and trade goods from east of the Rocky Mountains fueled native interest in new technologies. News of strange visitors and isolated trade objects may have filtered into the Snake River country, and any rumors of newcomers would have been dramatically confirmed in 1805 when an exhausted party of Americans led by Meriwether Lewis and William Clark encountered a group of young boys playing near a camas-bulb field at Musselshell, near the Clearwater River in present-day Weippe, Idaho. The explorers called the Numiipu they encountered "Nez-Percés" (in French, "pierced noses"), adopting a name common in trading circles but without apparent basis in tribal life. Outsiders referred to the group by that name ever afterward.

The newcomers who arrived in increasing numbers thereafter brought about fundamental shifts in tribal life. Village leaders felt inadequate to advise their people concerning the myriad issues that suddenly presented themselves. New diseases, unprecedented trade pressures, political pressure, and Christian evangelism each pressed on the group, and in each arena traditional leaders felt overwhelmed by the pace of change. Over time groups within the tribe turned to a variety of outside groups for help. Some Nez Perces allied themselves with missionaries, who promised to protect them from unscrupulous traders and land-hungry settlers. Others formed alliances with fur traders, who married into Indian families and offered the tribe access to guns, tools, and blankets. But there were also those who refused to cooperate or interact with anyone who came from outside the tribe. While these diverse tactics may have made sense in the short run, they gradually undermined the unity of the Numiipu.

In 1855, the newly appointed governor of Washington Territory, Isaac I. Stevens, negotiated a treaty with the tribe that created a 7.5-million-acre reservation for the Nez Perces that was closed to non-Indians. While Christian Nez Perces such as the leader Halalhot'suut ("Lawyer") accepted the new treaty and welcomed the protection of the reservation, others rejected it and refused to be bound by a paper agreement. Tribesmen liv-

The Nez Perce Women's Industrial Society. A missionary stands in the back row.

ing east of the Snake along the Wallowa and Salmon Rivers rejected both Lawyer and the new treaty, maintaining a stance of defiance that only increased after gold was discovered on Nez Perce land in the 1860s and white encroachment accelerated. In 1863 Lawyer's followers agreed to a reduction of their reservation to accommodate the gold rush, while the resisters, led by Chief Joseph and White Bird, refused to recognize the new boundaries or to remain on the new reservation.

Between 1863 and 1877 the tribe became increasingly divided between those who accepted the new reservation and those who did not. Discord arose among families and friends. Certain factions took evasive action to avoid living on or near the new reservation. Tensions mounted until in the spring of 1877 a band of young Nez Perce men attacked some local settlers, setting off panic in both the Indian and white communities; the cavalry was mobilized, and most of the antitreaty group fled into the mountains. The result was the Nez Perce War of 1877. Led by Chief Joseph, Looking Glass, White Bird, Tuhoolhut'sut, and Aloqat (or Ollokot), the escaping tribesmen crossed the Rockies and headed north for the Canadian border. Their journey ended after four months of running gun battles just a

few miles short of the Canadian border when Joseph, surrounded, and concerned that his women and children would soon fall victim to hunger and winter weather, promised to lay down his arms and "fight no more forever."

Following Joseph's surrender and imprisonment, most of the tribe resettled within the boundaries of the 1863 reservation, the only exceptions being Joseph and his most loyal followers, who were not permitted to return to Idaho. (They were forced to settle on the Colville Reservation in central Washington, where their descendants continue to live.) Forced to attend churches and government schools, the Nez Perces continued to struggle to sustain their traditions and community dignity. In 1889 the government began a process of dividing their reservation into individual homesteads, and in 1893 federal officials eagerly negotiated further sales of tribal lands to non-Indian farmers and cattlemen. Thus the tribe's original land base of 7.5 million acres (Treaty of 1855), was reduced to 750,000 acres in the Treaty of 1863. In 1893 the Dawes Act reduced the 1863 Treaty reservation to one-tenth of that, and made the present reservation resemble a checker-board. Nevertheless, tribal people continued to engage in berry and root gathering on the high plateaus, to speak their own language, and to sustain the family and band ties that had served them so well in the days before Lewis and Clark. Poverty and disease stalked the tribe, but it refused to disappear. In 1923 James Stuart, an educated Christian Nez Perce, became the first president of the Nez Perce Home and Farm Association, a group that reorganized itself in 1948 to become the Nez Perce Tribal Executive Committee, a group that has continued to this day.

In keeping with traditional practice, the executive committee is responsible to the General Council of the Nez Perce Tribe, a body that consists of all enrolled members of the tribe. While only adult members of the general council who reside within the original boundaries of the 1855 reservation may participate in the election of the executive committee, all members of the general council review and discuss reports from elected officials and departmental managers. The council also hears the executive committee's reports regarding its management of a work force of more than 250 people and a tribal budget that in the 1990s approached $2 million. One popular program administered by the committee has as its goal the reacquisition of tribal lands lost through sale or fraud.

Today over thirty-three hundred people are enrolled as members of the Nez Perce tribe. Their government is committed to ensuring a viable future for the community by providing social services, protecting treaty rights and tribal sovereignty, and securing a basis for economic development and growth. Like many other tribes, the Nez Perces have prevailed in most challenges to their treaty rights, but opposition persists. The strength of this opposition has tested the fortitude of the tribe, which continues to look to a brighter future.

See also Joseph (Heinmot Tooyalakekt).

Josephy, Alvin M. *The Nez Perce and the Opening of the Northwest* (New Haven, Conn.: Yale University Press, 1965); McWhorter, Lucullus Virgil, *Hear Me, My Chiefs! Nez Perce History and Legend* (Caldwell, Idaho: Caxton Printers, 1952); Slickpoo, Allen, Sr., *Noon Ne Mee Poo* (Boulder, Colo.: Pruitt Press, 1974).

ALLEN SLICKPOO (Nez Perce)
Kamiah, Idaho

Occom, Samson

(1723–92)
Mohegan missionary, teacher, and author; leader of the Brothertown movement.

Samson Occom (or Occum) was born at Mohegan, an Indian settlement near New London, Connecticut, in 1723. During his childhood his family lived in a wigwam, hunted and fished for a living, and had little contact with the neighboring English population. When Samson was thirteen, his mother, Sarah, converted to Christianity and encouraged him to attend Christian meetings. Three years later Samson also became a devout Christian. The following year, with his mother's help, he was admitted to a private Christian school run by the Reverend Eleazar Wheelock in Lebanon, Connecticut. Occom joined the white students there in a rigorous four-year college-preparatory program, which included the study of Greek, Latin, Hebrew, and the Bible. Although problems with his eyesight that made it difficult to read for extended periods of time prevented him from going on to college, Occom continued to study on his own and preached in many of the Indian settlements in southern New England.

In 1747 Occom spent some time in the Christian Indian settlement at Natick, Massachusetts, which had been established by John Eliot in 1651. Eliot, a missionary who translated the Bible into Algonquian, established several towns in Massachusetts for Christian Indians during the latter half of the seventeenth century. The Natick community had fallen on hard times, experiencing extreme poverty, alcohol abuse, and the gradual loss of its land to the neighboring white landowners. This visit may have convinced Occom that the only salvation for his people lay in establishing new settlements as far away as possible from the corrupting influences of the white man.

In 1749 he accepted a call to serve as minister and teacher at Montauk, a small Indian community on the far eastern end of Long Island. Occom's only source of support for the first two years came from the Montauks, who could provide him only with board and a token fee. Seeking further aid, he appealed to a London missionary society, which agreed to support his mission, setting his annual stipend at twenty pounds sterling—less than half what the society provided its white missionaries. Occom was very bitter about this disparity, but he nevertheless continued to serve the Montauk community for another decade.

Occom was an innovative teacher. When he found that the Montauk children were having trouble learning the English alphabet, he made his own teaching aid: a set of wooden blocks with letters pasted on each side. He also took a genuine interest in the Montauks and their culture. Based on what he learned from questioning them about their ancient customs, he wrote *An Account of the Montauk Indians on Long Island*. This important ethnographic study, published in 1809 by the Massachusetts Historical Society, is still used by modern scholars. In 1751 Occom married Mary Fowler, a Montauk woman, with whom he had ten children and enjoyed a lifelong relationship. Although the Montauks considered him a great success, and the Presbytery of Long Island ordained him in 1759, Occom was burdened with debt as he struggled to support a growing family on his meager stipend.

From 1761 to 1763 Occom went on three missions to the Oneida communities in New York to recruit Indians for Wheelock's school. Occom had by now earned a widespread reputation both as a missionary and as a spokesperson for his people. In the latter capacity he supported the Mohegans in their struggle to reclaim lands they believed had been seized illegally by the colony of Connecticut. Wheelock warned Occom not to lend his prestige to the Mohegan protest, fearing that such action might turn influential people in Connecticut against the missionary enterprise. One prominent white missionary, the Reverend David Jewett, who had converted Occom's mother to Christianity, actually held title to some of the land in question and stood to lose a considerable part of his estate if the Mohegan claims were upheld.

A 1772 sermon by Samson Occom that became a popular temperance tract. Nineteen editions were printed and distributed by temperance societies.

In 1765, when Wheelock was planning a fund-raising tour of Britain for a new Indian school he intended to found, a supporter in London advised him that an Indian preacher would draw enthusiastic public attention and suggested Occom, who, he said, would "get a bushel of money" for the cause. Wheelock asked Occom to accompany the Reverend Nathaniel Whitaker to Britain, but warned him not to speak out on the Mohegan land case, which was on appeal before the Privy Council in London. Although Occom deeply resented the patronizing attitudes of Wheelock and Whitaker, he embarked on the journey. He worked very hard for two years, preaching three hundred sermons and making very effective appeals for funds. The tour

was a great success, raising over twelve thousand pounds. One donor, Lord Dartmouth, made such a generous contribution that when Wheelock opened the new school in 1769, he named it after him. After the tour ended, Occom remained in England and, despite Wheelock's admonition, testified in the Mohegan land case; the appeal was denied.

Occom's disillusionment over the loss of the land, his frustration at the personal slights he felt from the white missionary establishment, and his constant struggle with debt strained his relations with Wheelock. But the final break did not come until 1773, when Wheelock ended his recruitment of Indian students and shifted his efforts to the training of white missionaries. After he had broken with Wheelock, Occom began to work on his own solution to the problems faced by the Indian settlements of southern New England and Long Island. He decided to establish a self-governing Christian Indian community as far away from white influence as possible. In 1774 he negotiated with the Oneidas for a tract of land in central New York and recruited Christian Indians to join him in building a commuity, which he called Eeayam Quittoowauconnuck (Brothertown).

The Revolutionary War interrupted Occom's plans. British troops marched through Oneida country forcing Occom and his followers to abandon the community. Most sought refuge in the Christian Indian settlement at Stockbridge, Massachusetts, and Occom returned to his home in Connecticut where he carried on a campaign urging Indians to remain neutral during the "white man's war." After the war Occom and his followers returned to Eeayam Quittoowauconnuck, officially opening the new town on November 7, 1785, with the election of five Indian trustees and a weeklong celebration. The community was to become Occom's most satisfying achievement. He served Brothertown as a spiritual leader, teacher, fund-raiser, and lobbyist until his death on July 14, 1792, at the age of sixty-nine.

Occom was an influential author. His most famous publication grew out of an occasion when he agreed to preach a funeral sermon on temperance in 1772 at the execution of Moses Paul, a Mohegan who had killed a man in a drunken rage. As a leader who himself had struggled with the destructive force of alcohol, Occom brought a special feeling to the topic. The sermon became a popular temperance tract, going through nineteen editions. Two years later, Occom published a popular hymnal, which included several of his own compositions. Although Occom's ethnographic study of the Montauks and his letters and diary were not fully appreciated in his lifetime, they have recently been rediscovered by scholars and widely admired by readers.

Occom demonstrated that a familiarity with European religious and political institutions could be useful in protecting and preserving Indian independence. His most important contribution, however, was his inspiring leadership and advocacy of Indian rights. He served the larger cause of Indians everywhere by the example of his uncompromising commitment to his people.

See also Montauk.

Blodgett, Harold, *Samson Occom* (Hanover, N.H.: Dartmouth College Publications, 1935); Love, William DeLoss, *Samson Occom and the Christian Indians of New England* (Boston: Pilgrim Press, 1899); Richardson, Leon Burr, *An Indian Preacher in England* (Hanover, N.H.: Dartmouth College Publications, 1933).

JOHN A. STRONG
Long Island University at Southampton

OCONASTOTA

(c. 1710–83)
Cherokee military leader.

Oconastota was the military commander of the Cherokee Nation throughout most of the eighteenth century. Little is known of his early life or parentage. He first appears in the historical record in 1736, when, during a French visit to the Cherokee Overhill Towns, he and other young Cherokee warriors flew French banners over their houses in defiance of the tribe's standing alliance with the British. In 1738, Oconastota received the title "Great Warrior"—the highest military position in Cherokee society. He also contracted smallpox that year during an epidemic that killed more than one thousand Cherokees.

In 1753, as a member of the Chota town council, he helped conclude a lengthy power struggle with the Tellico-Hiwassee coalition, making possible the recognition by South Carolina of Old Hop, the civil chief of Chota, as emperor of the Cherokee Nation. To solidify their alliance with South Carolina and to relieve the embattled Chickasaws, the Chota council, at the request of Governor James Glen, sent four hundred warriors under Oconastota to attack the Choctaw towns along the Tombigbee River. In 1755, Oconastota led war parties against the French Indians of the Illinois

Wabash region. In the spring of 1757, he set out with a large force of Overhills to waylay French bateaux on the Ohio and Mississippi Rivers.

At the beginning of the French and Indian War, Oconastota and other Cherokee leaders signed treaties with South Carolina and Virginia to reaffirm their loyalty to Great Britain. In turn, both Virginia and South Carolina built forts on the Little Tennessee River in 1756 to protect the power center of the Cherokee Nation from the French and their Indian allies. By the summer of 1757, the Cherokees had more warriors engaged in military service on the Virginia frontier than any other tribe aligned with the British. Nevertheless, on several occasions Cherokee veterans returning to their homes by way of the Shenandoah Valley were killed by Virginia frontiersmen, who collected bounties offered for the scalps of enemy Delaware and Shawnees. Relatives of the slain warriors, incensed by the murders and seeking revenge on English settlers, attacked closer to home, in the Carolina back country. Governor William Henry Lyttleton of South Carolina demanded that the Cherokees surrender the attackers. The Cherokee leader Attakullakulla reported in July 1759 that they could not be extradited because their leader was a relative of the "Great Warrior," who would not permit such action.

In September 1759, Oconastota and Ostenaco, in an attempt to settle the difficulties, led a peace delegation to South Carolina and proposed a treaty based on "mutual forgiveness." Refusing Oconastota's offer, Governor Lyttleton took Oconastota and his twenty-four fellow delegates hostage and demanded the surrender of the Cherokee attackers. That December, Oconastota was released because it was felt that he could convince other Cherokees to accept the harsh terms of Lyttleton's peace plan; Ostenaco was also released. The public humiliation that Oconastota subsequently suffered, however, prevented his political ascendancy when Old Hop died the following month. He and Ostenaco instead used their influence to elect Standing Turkey, a political underling with limited capabilities, as the new emperor.

Failing to secure the release of the hostages from South Carolina's Fort Prince George by diplomacy, Oconastota attempted to free them by force. He lured Lieutenant Richard Coytmore, the fort's commanding officer, into an ambush on February 16, 1760. Oconastota signaled the attack by waving his bridle, and Coytmore was shot in the first volley. Mortally wounded, he was dragged by his companions back into the fort. As the Cherokees besieged the fort, the soldiers killed the remaining Cherokee hostages. To chastise the Cherokees for the attack, Colonel Archibald Montgomery led an army into the Cherokee Nation in June 1760. After destroying seven Lower Towns in South Carolina, Montgomery's troops were stopped by warriors under Oconastota at Echowee Pass on June 27. The British losses included twenty dead and seventy wounded. With his reputation now greatly enhanced, Oconastota besieged Fort Loudoun, an outpost in what is now Tennessee. Starved into submission, the garrison surrendered the fort on August 8, 1760. Although Oconastota signed the articles of surrender promising the garrison safe passage out of Cherokee country, he did nothing to prevent the killing of twenty-three of the one hundred eighty soldiers two days later. He did, however, save the life of one soldier destined to be tortured.

On September 26, the Great Warrior hoisted the Union Jack and spoke for peace before a crowd of two thousand assembled at Nikwasi. The British were unimpressed, however, and mounted an attack on Cherokee lands the following year. During a quick trip to New Orleans to solicit French support, Oconastota received a military commission but no supplies. He returned to Cherokee country in time to direct an ambush on the lead columns of twenty-eight hundred British troops on June 10, 1761. With ammunition depleted, the Cherokees soon withdrew. The British burned fifteen Middle and Out Towns along with fifteen hundred acres of corn.

On at least three occasions in the 1760s, Oconastota requested a trip to London and an audience with King George III. Each request was denied. In late 1767, he and seven other Cherokee leaders traveled by sloop from Charleston to New York to arrange a peace treaty with the Iroquois. After a brief stay in the city, where they attended a performance of *Richard III,* they set out for Johnson Hall, near Albany, where they arrived by sledges on December 29. There Oconastota presented white belts of wampum to the Iroquois and concluded a secure peace that lasted until the outbreak of the American Revolution.

In 1768 Oconastota also signed the Treaty of Hard Labor, which established a fixed boundary with the colonies. Despite his protests about continuing encroachment by white settlers, he rejected the entreaties of northern Indians to form a military confederacy to hold off the colonists. He continued to put his faith in diplomacy. Late in 1773, on a visit to Charleston,

Oconastota was inducted into the St. Andrew's Society, a fraternal order of Scots founded in 1729. In 1775 he alienated younger warriors by agreeing to the Treaty of Sycamore Shoals, in which the Cherokees ceded 20 million acres of land in Kentucky and Tennessee to the British in exchange for trade goods worth about ten thousand pounds.

When the American Revolution began, Oconastota tried to preserve the alliance with the British and stay out of the fighting, but the war chief Dragging Canoe and his followers attacked rebel settlements on the Watauga, Nolichucky, and Holston Rivers, setting off devastating retaliatory attacks. These defeats brought Oconastota back to the role of mediator. He traveled to Virginia in the spring of 1777 and then to the Long Island of the Holston to meet with representatives of the new rebel states of North Carolina and Virginia. Before the speeches began, the old chiefs "were specially honored by the commissioners spreading three match coats on two benches, seating Oconastota and Attakullakulla thereon." The treaties resulted in more cessions of Cherokee land.

In July 1782 Oconastota, with the full consent of the whole nation, passed his leadership on to his son, Tuckese. Oconastota's last public appearance was at the signing of the Treaty of Chota, on October 10, 1782. At that time Oconastota, once a powerfully built man, was described as emaciated and almost blind. With food resources in the nation destroyed by a recent invasion, Oconastota spent the winter of 1782–83 at the home of Colonel Joseph Martin on the Long Island of the Holston. As spring came the old warrior, feeling that his time was near, asked to return home so he could be buried at his "beloved Chota." Oconastota died in the spring of 1783 and was buried in a coffin fashioned from an old canoe near the Chota council house. A string of white wampum, some vermillion, an iron sheath knife, two siltstone pipes, and a pair of eyeglasses were buried with him. His death marked the closing of a dramatic chapter in Cherokee history.

See also Cherokee.

Corkran, David, *The Cherokee Frontier: Conflict and Survival, 1740–62* (Norman: University of Oklahoma Press, 1962); Kelley, James C., "Notable Persons in Cherokee History: Oconastota," *Journal of Cherokee Studies* 3, no. 4 (fall 1978): 221–38; King, Duane H., and Danny E. Olinger, "Oconastota," *American Antiquity* 37, no. 2 (April 1972): 222–27.

DUANE H. KING (Cherokee)
Southwest Museum
Los Angeles, California

OJIBWA

The Ojibwas are spread over a thousand miles of territory from southeastern Ontario westward across the upper Great Lakes country of the United States and Canada as far as Montana and Saskatchewan. Although classed as one people in the Algonquian linguistic family, they have several alternate regional names, and are divided into about one hundred separate bands or reservation communities. The Ojibwas probably number about two hundred thousand, two-thirds of that number residing in Canada, with an estimated twenty thousand of their people fluent in one of the three or four dialects of Ojibwa.

Variant forms of the name have long been a problem. On seventeenth-century French maps, a form of the word *Ojibwa* identified a village on the north shore of Lake Superior, but use of the term expanded to include allied communities along the eastern side of Lake Superior. Depending on its division into syllables, the Ojibwa name has been interpreted as a reference either to the puckered toe of the Ojibwas' distinctive moccasins, or to their use of glyphs to inscribe historical and religious information as well as simple messages on birch bark or rock surfaces. The name has no standard spelling in English and has been corrupted into *Chippewa*, the form still used by tribal organizations recognized by the U.S. government. The French first encountered Ojibwas at the falls of the St. Marys River, the connecting link between Lake Superior and Lake Huron at the eastern end of the Upper Peninsula of Michigan. Because they were associated with this location, Ojibwas were known to the French as "People of the Falls," or Saulteurs. The form *Saulteaux* today is used in the western provinces of Canada to refer to Ojibwa people.

The heartland of the Ojibwa country is around present-day Sault Ste. Marie, Michigan. The Ojibwa migration legend, shared by Ottawa and Potawatomi people, recounts a long journey from the lower St. Lawrence River, ascending the Ottawa River at present-day Montreal, then crossing by way of Lake Nipissing to Lake Huron and continuing northwest behind Manitoulin Island to the St. Marys River. On this odyssey they were guided by a sacred *megis* (shell) that indicated stopping points. A significant place near the end of their journey was the Straits of Mackinac, the waterway separating the Upper and Lower Peninsulas of Michigan. According to the widely accepted account, it was here that members of the group separated into three divisions. The Potawatomis moved south into lower Michigan; the Ottawas made Manitoulin Island their base; and the Ojibwas continued north about fifty miles to the falls of the St. Marys River, their final destination. After several centuries of population growth, however, part of that group branched off to establish a new base on the south shore of Lake Superior at Chequamegon Bay in present-day Wisconsin, a place known historically as La Pointe.

The record of the long migration has been preserved in maps drawn on birch-bark scrolls used by leaders in the ceremonies of the Midewiwin, a physically and spiritually healing medicine society that originated among Ojibwa people. Since the scrolls were often buried with their medicine-men owners, few have survived, and the knowledge to interpret them is rare. One surviving scroll carries the time line into the late-eighteenth-century migration of a band to Leech Lake in Minnesota. Membership in the Midewiwin involved many years of dedicated study. To enter the society, the initiate has to undergo a long period of instruction to master the herbal knowledge and philosophy handed down by elders. Fasting and a vision quest are part of the preparatory ritual for admission to the first level. At one time, there were eight degrees of training in the Midewiwin, but after shamans on Madeline Island in Chequamegon Bay misused their exceptional powers sometime around 1600, training was limited to the first four levels. The Midewiwin today has a significant membership in the upper Great Lakes region and has spread from the Ojibwas to neighboring Indian people. The philosophy of the medicine society stresses the importance of maintaining balance in one's personal life, and respect for other forms of life, both plant and animal, with the goal of achieving harmony within the social order.

Situated on a major transcontinental waterway, the Ojibwas became involved in intertribal hostilities, peacemaking, and trade over a vast area of interior North America. In 1662, during Iroquois warfare to gain new hunting grounds (1649–1700), the Ojibwas and local allies decisively defeated a large war party encamped about fifteen miles west of the Sault. Thenceforth Iroquois raids were directed south of the Great Lakes. Beginning about 1680, the Missisagis and other Ojibwa bands living east of the Sault on the north shore of Lake Huron began advancing south across the Ontario peninsula, driving out the Iroquois invaders and by 1696 establishing their own communities in the area extending from present-day Detroit to the north shore of Lake Ontario. The name Missisagi continued in use in southern Ontario to identify these eastern Ojibwas. By 1750 they had moved around the bottom of Lake Huron into the Saginaw Valley of southeastern Michigan. Most of their Ottawa predecessors, who also lived around Thunder Bay, moved to the growing Ottawa concentration in northwest lower Michigan and along the north shore of Lake Michigan, or to the Ottawa village at Detroit.

Ojibwa leaders figured in all the major campaigns of eighteenth-century warfare that affected their hunting grounds and their trading connections. During the French and Indian War (1753–60) Wabojig led warriors from Chequamegon Bay to battles in upstate New York. Wasson from Saginaw contributed to General Edward Braddock's defeat near Pittsburgh in 1755, supported Pontiac's uprising at Detroit in 1763, and later met American representatives at Pittsburgh in 1775. Leaders from Sault Ste. Marie attended councils with the Shawnees on the Ohio River in the 1760s, and continued to oppose the advance of white settlement in the lower Great Lakes region until the era of the War of 1812.

While all these historical developments were in progress in the Ojibwa country east and south of Sault Ste. Marie, actions in the west were directed toward expanding hunting territory beyond Lake Superior. From the time of their first village settlement at Chequamegon Bay, Ojibwas had periodically battled two tribes who became traditional enemies: the Mesquakies (Foxes) to the south, around the headwaters of the St. Croix River in Wisconsin; and the Dakotas (Sioux) to the west, on the headwaters of the Mississippi River. By 1683, the Mesquakies had moved farther south, but conflict with the Sioux persisted until the mid–nineteenth century. Following an interval of peace and trade, aggressive warfare had resumed by 1740, leading to the advance of Ojibwa hunters into Sioux lands in present-day northern Minnesota. The Ojibwas also had the assistance of Cree and Assiniboine allies, who attacked the Dakotas from the north. After Crees living northwest of Lake Superior suffered severe population loss during the 1782 smallpox epidemic, they invited Ojibwas to come into their country.

As a result, Ojibwa communities occupied the Rainy River, Lake of the Woods, Red Lake, and lower Red River districts south of Lake Winnipeg by 1790. Pembina, on the Red River about a mile below the present-day international border, became a base for Ojibwa and Métis hunters who later made annual buffalo hunts and settled in the Turtle Mountains of the Dakota border region. An offshoot, the Little Shell Band, went farther west into Montana. In the district of future Winnipeg, the Ojibwa leader of the 1790s was Peguis from Sault Ste. Marie, who became an intermediary with early settlers and officials. Acquiring horses about 1820, Ojibwa bands advanced westward to trade near present-day Edmonton, Alberta, and the names Plains Saulteaux and Plains Ojibwa came into use, along with the Hudson's Bay Company name Bungi, referring to a begging phrase.

Ojibwa people have never formed a single organization, but the overlapping of regional groups forms a chain that ultimately links them together. Personal connections through kinship were extended by membership in patriarchal clans. Although there were originally only five or six Ojibwa clans, twenty-one were identified in the mid–nineteenth century with some geographic variations. Sault Ste. Marie has always been associated with the high-ranking Crane clan. The Marten and Loon totems have been well known around Chequamegon Bay, whereas the later-created Wolf clan was prominent in the former Sioux headquarters at Mille Lacs, Minnesota, where the Ojibwa community incorporated captive Sioux. A clan member provides hospitality for any visiting member of the same clan, even from another tribe. Common clan identities created kinship networks among Crees and Ojibwas.

Ojibwa identity has generally involved a way of life including the Midewiwin rituals; a subsistence pattern emphasizing maple sugar, fish, and wild rice with its important fall ceremonies; and travel by birch-bark canoe. The western Ojibwas for many years returned to the Red River and Lake Winnipeg districts to make maple (or box elder) syrup in the spring and gather wild rice in the fall, although some finally adopted a buffalo-hunting economic base, with its emphasis on horse herds. Today, many Ojibwas in the United States and Canada prefer to identify themselves as Anishinaabe, a term meaning "First [or Original] People." Yet they recognize that this name also refers to their eastern neighbors the Algonquins, as well as to Crees, Ottawas, and Potawatomis.

Modern Ojibwa reservations include members of mixed Indian and non-Indian heritage, with many intermittent residents who travel back and forth to cities. Economic development is a major concern. In Minnesota and along its border with Canada, Ojibwas have fought to protect their interest in the harvesting and marketing of wild rice. Although the struggle to protect tribal fishing rights has claimed public attention in Wisconsin and Michigan, other projects indicate the diversity of modern Ojibwa reservation life. A public radio station, as well as a junior college, are in operation at Lac Court Oreille, Wisconsin. The Bay Mills Reservation in the eastern Upper Peninsula of Michigan also has established a junior college. On the White Earth Reservation in Minnesota, a women's cooperative markets wild rice and crafts. The Sault Ste. Marie Tribe, officially recognized in 1972, had by 1995 enrolled twenty thousand members and developed housing projects in seven Upper Peninsula communities. Walpole Island, an Ontario reserve on the delta of the St. Clair River, has a growing historical-research center. The population there includes Potawatomi refugees from government removal efforts of the 1830s in Michigan and Indiana, and Ottawas who fled from the Toledo region and Maumee River valley of northwestern Ohio. At Walpole Island, Ojibwas emphasize their close relationship with both Ottawas and Potawatomis as the "Three Fires," invoking the memory of an alliance of the early migration era.

See also Ojibwa Language.

Johnston, Basil, *The Ojibwa Heritage* (Toronto: McClelland and Stewart; New York: Columbia University Press, 1976); Tanner, Helen Hornbeck, *The Ojibwa* (New York and Philadelphia: Chelsea House Publishers, 1992); Warren, William Whipple, *History of the Ojibway People* (St. Paul: Minnesota Historical Society Press, 1984).

HELEN HORNBECK TANNER
Newberry Library
Chicago, Illinois

OJIBWA LANGUAGE

The Ojibwa language is spoken by the Anishinaabe people, who include the Algonquins and the Nipissings of Quebec and eastern Ontario; the Ojibwas (or Chippewas) of Michigan, Minnesota, North Dakota, Wisconsin, and Ontario; the Ottawas of the Lake Huron region; and the Saulteaux of Manitoba and Saskatchewan. With its range from the eastern woodlands west across the Great Plains, and from the muskegs near Hudson Bay south across the Great Lakes, this language, known to most of its speakers as *Anishinaabemowin*, is one of the most extensive in North America and, with thirty to forty thousand speakers, one of the largest. In many northern Anishinaabe communities, people of all ages use Ojibwa as their everyday language. Elsewhere it has been replaced in varying degrees by English or French and is often spoken only by the elders, understood but not spoken by the middle generations, and neither spoken nor understood by children as a mother tongue, although they may learn it in school.

The Anishinaabe have long recorded sacred songs by incising pictographs on scrolls of birch bark; writing the language by means of symbols that stand for sounds began with European contact in the seventeenth century. Today schools teach Ojibwa orthographies that use the letters of the Latin alphabet, to which are assigned the sounds of Anishinaabemowin; for example, in one orthography, a double vowel stands for a sound that takes longer to pronounce than the sound represented by the single vowel—a difference that can distinguish words such as *agim,* "count him/her!" and *aagim,* "snowshoe." Many northern speakers write with the geometric shorthand characters, called *syllabics,* created for Ojibwa and Cree in 1840 by the missionary James Evans.

Ojibwa is not a single standardized language but a chain of linked local varieties, grouped into nearly a dozen dialects. Each dialect (and within dialects, each local variety) differs in details of pronunciation, vocabulary, and grammar from the others, with differences between nonadjacent dialects often being great enough to impede understanding between their speakers. The equivalents of the sentence "What did the children see yesterday?" in three Ontario dialects illustrate some of these differences:

Wenesh gaa-waabndamwaad binoojiinhyag jiinaago?

Wegonen gaa-waabandamowaad abinoonjiinzhag bijiinaago?

Gegonenini gaa-waabadamowaaj awaazhishag onaago?

[what/they saw it/children/yesterday]

The first sentence is Ottawa or *Nishnaabemwin,* the second is Anishinaabemowin as spoken in Northwestern Ontario, and the third is *Anishininiimowin,* also spoken there but farther north. (Other names for the language are *Ojibwemowin* in the United States and *Nakawewin* in Saskatchewan.)

A typical Ojibwa sentence contains a multipart verb, the core meaning of which is carried by a verb stem, itself composed of meaningful elements. In front of the stem may come prefixes, one of which can show the person (first, second, or third) of a subject or object; others show grammatical ideas such as tense or location, or modify the core meaning. In the verb *ningii-*

ani-maajii-babima'adoon, "I started following and following it (a road) along," the first four prefixes are *-nin-*, indicating first person; *gii-*, past tense; *ani-*, away from the speaker; and *maajii-*, "start to." The last prefix, *ba-*, which indicates that the action was extended in time or space ("following and following"), also offers an example of reduplication, a process by which a prefix takes its shape from the stem by copying its first consonant and adding a vowel: the first syllable *bi* of *bima'adoon,* "follow it along," when combined with the reduplicated prefix made from it, becomes *babi* in *babima'adoon,* "follow and follow it along."

After the stem there are more than a dozen slots for suffixes indexing grammatical ideas such as order (determining whether the verb is a main clause, subordinate clause, or command verb); the person, number, and gender of the subject and object, and their relationship; negation; and verb mode. The verb *ningii-wii-ganawaabamigosiinaabaniig,* "they didn't want to look at us (but they did)," includes a stem—*ganawaabam,* "look at someone"—and the suffixes *-igo,* indicating that the subject of the verb is a third person and that the first person referred to by the prefix *nin-* is the object; *-sii,* negation; *-naa,* "us"; *ban,* unrealized action; and *-iig,* "they."

The meanings of the stem-forming elements and their patterns of combination represent a unique Anishinaabe way of viewing human experience and the natural world. Their creative use allows speakers to talk about and name new things as well as known ones. A typical stem has two or three main parts, each selected from distinct sets of hundreds of elements. The first part is an *initial,* often a root of shape, size, color, spatial relationship, or direction, such as *azhe-,* "backwards"; *babaami-,* "going about"; *giishk-,* "severed"; *miskw-,* "red"; and, *nabag-,* "flat." The last part is a *final,* which often carries meanings close to those of English verbs. A few of these are *-aadagaa,* "swim"; *-aashi,* "blown (by the wind)"; *-batoo,* "run"; and *-shin,* "lie or fall against something." Thus there is not just one verb stem meaning "run," as in English, but many, each blending a different initial with the final *-batoo,* "run," as in *azhebatoo,* "runs backwards"; *bimibatoo,* "runs along"; *babaamibatoo,* "runs about"; and *bejibatoo,* "runs slowly."

Other finals describe the means by which something comes about, among them *-aakiz,* "by flame"; *-bood,* "by back-and-forth motion (as in sawing)"; and *-zh,* "by blade." A look at a few stems meaning "cut" can illustrate how different the Anishinaabe analysis of

events can be from that of English. The initial tells about the result of the cutting and the final about the way the cutting was done. For example, if the cutting resulted in something being cleanly cut or severed, the initial is *giishk-.* Adding the final *-zh* gives *giishkizhan,* "cut it (with a knife)"; the final *-bood* gives *giishkiboodoon,* "cut it (with a saw)"; the final *-aakiz* gives *giishkaakizan,* "cut it (with a flame, as with a welding torch)." If the result is that something is split, the initial *daashk-* is used: *daashkizhan,* "cut it (with a knife and have it split)"; *daashkaakizan,* "cut it (with a flame and have it split)." If many pieces result, the initial is *biis-,* as in *biisizhan,* "cut it (to pieces with a knife)."

An optional intervening *medial* element describes things connected with the verb. It can classify things affected, as in *giishkaabikizhan,* "cut it ([something of metal or rock] with a knife)," where the medial is *-aabik-,* "something of metal or rock"; or *daashkaakoboodon,* "cut it ([something sticklike] with a saw and have it split)," where the medial is *aako-,* "something sticklike." In the verb *giishkinikezh,* "cut off someone's arm," the medial is the more specific and nounlike *-nike-,* "arm."

Speakers of Anishinaabemowin consider their language to be precise, descriptive, and visual, and feel that it is among the greatest treasures of their cultural heritage.

Nichols, John D., and Earl Nyholm, *A Concise Dictionary of Minnesota Ojibwe* (Minneapolis: University of Minnesota Press, 1995); Rhodes, Richard A., *Eastern Ojibwa-Chippewa-Ottawa Dictionary* (Berlin: Mouton, 1985); Rhodes, Richard A., and Evelyn M. Todd, "Subarctic Algonquian Languages," in *Handbook of North American Indians,* ed. William C. Sturtevant, vol. 6, *Subarctic,* ed. June Helm (Washington: Smithsonian Institution, 1981).

JOHN D. NICHOLS
University of Manitoba

ONEIDA

The Oneida people (*On'yote'a.ka,* "People of the Standing Stone") are members of the Six Nations of the Iroquois or *Ho'da'sho'ne* (People of the Long House). Even before European invasion of the North American continent, these people were living in distinct territories in the northeastern section of the country. The Oneida territory was in what is now New York State, with the Mohawk Nation east of this land and the Onondaga, Cayuga, and Seneca territories to the west.

Today the Oneidas of Wisconsin have the largest population of the three remaining Oneida communities. The tribal enrollment in Wisconsin is 12,623, compared with approximately 1,100 in Oneida, New York, and 4,000 in Southwold, Ontario, Canada. In Wisconsin, about 4,500 enrolled members reside on the Oneida Reservation, with the remaining members living throughout the United States.

The Revolutionary War brought about significant changes in the lives of the Oneidas. Even prior to the war, there were efforts to gain the support of the Oneidas by missionaries, particularly the Reverend Samuel Kirkland, a Presbyterian missionary, as well as by other colonists and the British. At first the Oneidas wanted to remain neutral, but after their homes and fields had been destroyed, young Oneida warriors joined the war and fought on the side of the colonists while elders, women, and children fled their homes. The Tuscaroras (the sixth Iroquois nation) joined the Oneidas, and both played vital roles in the war. They not only fought alongside the colonists, but also served as lead guides and scouts for the American cause. In the winter of 1777, the Oneidas and Tuscaroras provided bags of corn for George Washington's starving army at Valley Forge even though they themselves did not have enough food.

After the war, devastation was evident everywhere. Houses had to be rebuilt and fields and orchards had to be replanted, and even though the Oneidas made attempts to regain past lifestyles, the community's traditional economic and social systems were changing rapidly. The massive immigration of Europeans onto Oneida lands disrupted hunting and endangered the food supply. Even though the Oneidas, like other Iroquois, had been a horticultural people prior to the war, the expectations after the war were that they should develop European-style agriculture.

In 1784 the Treaty of Fort Stanwix was to have guaranteed the Oneidas and Tuscaroras territorial lands in New York in exchange for their help in the Revolutionary War. This guarantee came from the Continental Congress, but the state of New York later ignored this treaty and worked actively to remove all Indians from its borders. As a consequence, the Oneidas steadily lost their lands in New York. The loss of lands was one of the most significant factors that led to the Oneida people moving out of New York. Some Oneidas remained, but most moved to Wisconsin Territory or migrated north to Ontario, Canada, where the Mohawks and other Iroquois groups had located after the war.

At the same time that white settlers pressed onto their lands, missionaries sought to change the Oneidas' beliefs. Eleazer Williams, an Episcopal missionary of Mohawk descent, was the most prominent of these. He moved to Oneida country in 1816 and established a mission that preached Christianity in the Oneidas' native language. Williams soon set about persuading the Oneidas and other Indian nations in New York to move west to the lands beyond Lake Michigan. With support from his superiors in the church as well as land speculators and the War Department, Williams pressed his case.

After his second trip to Wisconsin Territory, Williams completed an agreement with the Menominees that permitted the Oneidas to settle near Green Bay, Wisconsin. In 1822, Chief Shenandoah, grandson of the Chief Shenandoah who had helped lead the Oneida warriors during the Revolutionary War, and Chief Daniel Bread, an educated leader who spoke both Oneida and English, agreed to pay the Menominees an initial payment of one thousand dollars in goods and the same amount over the next two years in exchange for the right to settle on Menominee lands.

Over the next ten years, hundreds of Oneidas moved to their new homelands. More than one hundred men, women, and children arrived in 1823, and in 1825 they established a permanent village near Duck Creek, a settlement that still exists today. The last large Oneida group to move west arrived in 1832 under the leadership of the Oneida Methodist leader Jake Cornelius. This group settled on the southern portion of the modern reservation. This latter group resisted Christianity longer than others, but in fact the Oneidas retained many of their traditional beliefs and practices, the most prevalent being their language, foods, and medicine societies.

Though Oneida history has been marked by continual changes, the community has maintained its ability to adapt while never losing sight of its traditions. These traditions are still alive today in the way Oneidas view themselves as well as in how they are viewed by others. Past traditions include the Oneida language, which survives in the tribal school and among elders, and the Longhouse traditions that mark seasonal celebrations, which have been revived. In addition, traditional foods —particularly corn, beans, and squash—have not been forgotten and are paid respect in the community's thanksgiving celebrations.

In the late nineteenth century, the Dawes Allotment Act caused the loss of Oneida land, but the tribe was able to retain a portion of its lands. The Indian Reorganization Act of 1934 allowed the Oneidas to set up an elected form of government and begin the process of economic development. This development accelerated during the 1960s and has continued to the present, but not without the vision and hard work of the people. In recent years a successful gaming industry has brought prosperity to the Wisconsin Oneidas and provided an important source of income for community schools and social services. The community continues to struggle to defend its sovereignty rights, however, and to plan a future that includes generations of Oneidas yet to be born. In looking to the future in this way the Oneida people have a most important source of insuring their future.

Campisi, Jack, and Laurence Hauptman, eds., *The Oneida Indian Experience: Two Perspectives* (Syracuse, N.Y.: Syracuse University Press, 1988); Graymont, Barbara, *The Iroquois in the American Revolution* (Syracuse, N.Y.: Syracuse University Press, 1972); Richards, Cara E., *The Oneida People* (Phoenix, Ariz.: Indian Tribal Series, 1974).

THELMA CORNELIUS MCLESTER (Oneida)
Oneida Nation of Wisconsin

ONONDAGA

The Onondaga (People of the Hills) are one of the founding nations of the Iroquois Confederacy, a union of Indian nations that acts through a combined legislative body known as the Grand Council. Located near Onondaga Lake in central New York State, the Onondaga occupied the geographic center of a confederacy that included territories from the Mohawk Valley and the Adirondack Mountains to the Genesee River and south into present-day Pennsylvania. According to tradition the Onondaga Nation was the least numerous of the nations that formed the confederacy and a warrior chief among them—Tadodaho—was the last to join what has been variously called the Iroquois Confederacy, the League of the Haudenosaunee, and the Five Nations (after 1722, when the Tuscarora Nation joined the league, the Six Nations).

The Onondaga Nation was among the strongest voices supporting a position of neutrality which the confederacy generally followed during the wars between England and France in the eighteenth century. They were also solidly committed to neutrality as war between England and her American colonies unfolded,

but at a critical moment their town was struck by a plague, which rendered them unable to host confederacy meetings. They were later attacked by Revolutionary forces whose leadership assumed the Onondaga Nation was supporting the British war effort.

In the years immediately following the Revolution, the Onondaga Nation entered into a series of treaties with New York State that reduced their territory to some seventy-three hundred acres near present-day Syracuse, New York. The Onondaga Nation has long asserted that these treaties of land cession were improper, and tensions between the Iroquois Confederacy and the United States attributed to these and other land issues contributed to the passage of the federal 1790 Non-Intercourse Act, under which Congress committed itself to being a party to all Indian land transactions.

Beginning around 1784, some members of the Onondaga Nation relocated to the Six Nations Country on the Grand River near present-day Hamilton, Ontario. Over the years the Onondaga Nation in both locations continues to host meetings and act as "Firekeepers" of the Iroquois Confederacy. In fact, the Onondaga Nation has remained a leading force in the confederacy.

In 1815 the Seneca prophet Handsome Lake, author of the contemporary Iroquois religion, died and was buried a few yards from the Onondaga Longhouse near Nedrow, New York, and a majority of the Onondaga community continue to participate in the traditional religion. Although officially recognized by the U.S. Bureau of Indian Affairs, the Onondaga Nation has held firmly to its ancient laws and traditions, and in the 1940s rejected an initiative that would have installed a representative style of government and instead chose to retain their traditional system of participatory government convened by chiefs and clan mothers. They are one of only a few Indian nations in the United States to do so. Since the 1960s and the advent of a contemporary "Indian movement," the Onondaga Nation, under the leadership of Chief Leon Shenandoah have been a significant presence in the effort to gain recognition of indigenous sovereignty. The Onondaga Nation steadfastly opposed the military draft as an invasion of Onondaga sovereignty and has challenged every uninvited intrusion of state or federal jurisdiction, even criminal jurisdiction, into their territory. As of 1994 the Onondaga Nation has consistently refused to accept state or federal grants, which they believe would compromise their independence or infringe on their sovereignty. They have taken legal steps to reclaim significant areas of their ancient territories. Theirs is one of the oldest and largest unsettled Indian land claims in the United States and involves a significant area of central New York State, including much of the present-day city of Syracuse.

See also Iroquois Confederacy.

JOHN C. MOHAWK
State University of New York at Buffalo

OPOTHLE YOHOLO

(c. 1780–1863)
Creek political leader.

Opothle Yoholo was born at Tuckabatchee, Creek Nation (near present-day Montgomery, Alabama), probably the son of Davy Cornell and a Tuckabatchee woman, perhaps of the Potato clan. Descended from Joseph Cornells, who had entered the Creek Nation as a Carolina trader, the family was large, well connected, and influential when Opothle Yoholo was born. Opothle Yoholo's name, more correctly spelled Hoboihithli Yoholo, is best understood as a title. Creek men commonly received new names at various stages in their lives to commemorate achievements, denote changes in rank, and/or describe new responsibilities. Opothle Yoholo's name translates as "Good Child Singer [or Crier]." The meaning of *Opothle* (i.e., the "Good Child" portion) is unclear except that it indicates prestige; *Yoholo* refers to the cry uttered by the officials who managed the important Black Drink Ceremony. Because the names of adult men changed in the course of their lives, it is very hard to follow any one individual through the historical record. Opothle Yoholo's name first appears in documents in the mid-1820s, but there is no way to be sure that he was not active earlier under a different name.

Opothle Yoholo had achieved significant stature in the Creek Nation by the mid-1820s. As the speaker for Big Warrior (Tustunnuggee Thlucco), chief of Tuckabatchee and of the Upper Creeks, Opothle Yoholo was at the center of Creek political affairs. His duties included participating in council deliberations, announcing council decisions to the public, and representing Big Warrior in talks with other native groups and the United States. In negotiations with federal commissioners during the winter of 1824–25, Opothle Yoholo emerged as a prominent voice of opposition to the sale of the Creek lands claimed by Georgia. In the absence of Big Warrior, Opothle Yoholo presented the council's rejection and coordinated its arguments with the commissioners. During the critical months following those talks, the commissioners bribed William McIntosh (Tustunnuggee Hutke) and several headmen to sign a treaty, the council ordered the execution of the leading chiefs involved in the fraud, and the Creeks negotiated a new treaty in Washington. All of this occurred in the midst of a Creek leadership vacuum marked by the death of Big Warrior and the extreme age and ill health of his opposite number, Little Prince (Tustunnuggee Hopoie), chief of the Lower Creeks. Thus Opothle Yoholo was catapulted into a far more active leadership role than was normal for one in his office.

During the next several years, Opothle Yoholo led the Creek effort to resist removal to the West. To forge a united opposition, Opothle Yoholo was instrumental in an attempt to restructure council government in order to centralize its political authority and thus block voluntary emigration. Opothle Yoholo also repeatedly attempted to negotiate alternatives to removal. When all efforts failed, he masterminded a scheme to allot the lands of the Creek Nation to its citizens, hoping thereby to gain the right of the Creeks to remain in their eastern homes. This plan also failed, and in 1836 Opothle Yoholo led some fifteen thousand Creeks on the trek to Indian Territory.

Until his death, Opothle Yoholo remained the recognized leader of the Creeks who settled on the Canadian River. Although he served only one four-year term as principal chief, at times of crisis he emerged to assume a leadership role. In the mid-1850s, for example, the United States pressured the Creeks to abandon their principle of common land ownership in exchange for privately held individual tracts. Opothle Yoholo assumed a central role in the opposition, citing both tradition and the failed allotment experiment in the East.

Opothle Yoholo tended to be culturally conservative, and both contemporaries and scholars have seen him as a powerful force against the Creek adoption of Anglo-American cultural norms. But Opothle Yoholo was flexible and adaptive. Early on he recognized the value of American education, and in 1826 he enrolled his eight-year-old son in the Choctaw Academy—a famous Kentucky boarding school for Indians. He also participated actively in the market economy. He owned many slaves, managed a large plantation and ranching operation, and invested in several stores. One of these, an emporium close to his plantation on the Canadian River near

North Fork Town, was at the crossing of the Texas Road and the road that ran west from Fort Smith, Arkansas, to California. The latter was a main thoroughfare during the California gold rush, and Opothle Yoholo profited handsomely in supplying the gold seekers. On the eve of the Civil War, Opothle Yoholo was widely reputed to be the richest Creek in Indian Territory.

During the early summer of 1861, Albert Pike, an agent of the Confederate government, held talks at North Fork Town with representatives of many Indian Territory tribes. Recognizing the strategic importance of Indian Territory, the Confederacy was eager to conclude treaties of alliance with the tribes. Creek delegates agreed to such an alliance in July. Though not present at the negotiations, Opothle Yoholo let it be known that he opposed the Confederate alliance, arguing that the Confederacy represented the same southerners who had evicted the Creeks from their homes twenty-five years earlier. Furthermore, Opothle Yoholo believed that the treaties binding the Creek Nation to the United States should be respected. Hoping to avoid involvement on either side, he recommended that the Creek Nation stand neutral. Like-minded Creeks began to coalesce around Opothle Yoholo.

In November 1861, fearing an attack by Confederate Creeks, Opothle Yoholo led a group of several thousand men, women, and children north toward Kansas. On the way the Confederates attacked three times. Opothle Yoholo's party defeated them in the first two engagements, but in the third, the Battle of Chustenahlah, fought on December 26, 1861, the Confederates smashed the refugees, driving the survivors afoot into a blizzard. Forced to abandon all their possessions, Opothle Yoholo's people made their way to southeastern Kansas, where Union agents housed them in a makeshift tent encampment. Somehow Opothle Yoholo, in his eighties, survived the ordeal.

Once a neutralist, by this time Opothle Yoholo and his followers were dedicated Unionists, and several hundred men joined the Union Army. In the spring, Opothle Yoholo and the noncombatants were moved to scattered locations, but their living conditions did not improve. Housed in a tent made of rotten cloth open at both ends and sleeping on the frozen ground near Leroy, Kansas, the old speaker succumbed to the harsh winter of 1862–63, dying on March 22.

See also Creek (Muskogee).

Foreman, Grant, *The Five Civilized Tribes* (Norman: University of Oklahoma Press, 1934); Green, Michael D., *The Politics of Indian Removal: Creek Government and Society in Crisis* (Lincoln:

University of Nebraska Press, 1982); Meserve, John B., "Chief Opothleyahola," *Chronicles of Oklahoma* 9 (December 1931): 439–53.

MICHAEL D. GREEN
University of Kentucky

ORIGINS: ANTHROPOLOGICAL PERSPECTIVES

Scholars were not concerned about the origins of native groups found in North America until they realized that the "New World" was not part of Asia, as Columbus and others had originally assumed. Once the continent's separation from Eurasia was clear, however, philosophers and scientists struggled to reconcile the diversity of groups found in the Americas with biblical accounts of a single human creation. The most insightful of these early speculations was proposed in the late sixteenth century by the Jesuit missionary José de Acosta, who theorized that the Americas were originally settled before the birth of Christ by groups of hunters and their families who inadvertently passed overland from Asia to the Americas while following the animal herds they hunted.

The discovery of the Bering Strait in 1728 made a prehistoric overland migration from Siberia to North America seem improbable in spite of the evidence of similarities between Eurasian and North American mammalian populations. As geologists of the last century deciphered the traces of massive prehistoric glaciers on exposed rock, the concept of periodic Ice Ages began to develop. Then, in the early twentieth century, it was proposed that Siberia and North America had been connected by a land bridge when increasing coldness and the formation of continental glaciers lowered sea levels worldwide. Evidence now shows that the last time this bridge—the Bering Land Bridge—was in existence was between 25,000 and 14,000 years ago, near the end of the Ice Age. Anthropologists call this land bridge, together with the adjacent unglaciated areas of North America and Asia, Beringia. Less than 14,000 years ago melting glaciers and higher sea levels submerged the land bridge. Since then migration from Siberia has required boats or, in winter, a walk over sea ice.

Currently, anthropologists, biological anthropologists, and historical linguists agree with de Acosta that Native Americans are descended from northeastern

Asians, but there is heated debate over whether the first people arrived in America more than or less than 15,000 years ago. Beringian climatic and ecological conditions, the route or routes taken, and the number of prehistoric migration events are also in dispute.

Archaeologists who argue for an initial colonization less than 15,000 years ago note that the late–Ice Age animal bones found in Beringia are predominantly those of grazing animals such as bison, horses, mammoths, camels, and caribou. Beringia was part of the route from America to Asia used by horses and camels during the Ice Age. During this time mammoths, elk, moose, and caribou also used the land bridge to cross from Asia into the Americas. Therefore, less than 25,000 years ago, human groups culturally adapted to a severely cold climate could have seasonally occupied the Bering Land Bridge and followed grazing herds into the Alaskan and Canadian areas of eastern Beringia. These groups could not have moved farther south at this time because an ice sheet formed by the merging of two huge glaciers separated eastern Beringia from the rest of North America. This ice sheet stretched from the Pacific Ocean to the Atlantic Coast, creating a barrier five hundred miles long between Beringia and Alberta to the south. Less than 14,000 years ago rising sea levels prevented human groups and the animals they preyed on in eastern Beringia from crossing back to the rest of Beringia. It is at this time that melting glaciers created an ice-free corridor that allowed migration southward to the middle latitudes of North America.

Archaeological investigations into the thousands of square miles that represent the remaining Siberian and Alaskan regions of Beringia that were not submerged by rising sea levels have been limited to a few settled areas. The incomplete evidence these surveys have generated indicates that the first human settlement of eastern Siberia dates to around 18,000 years ago. By 14,000 years ago microblades and wedge-shaped cores similar to those of eastern Siberia had spread to wide areas of northeastern Siberia, perhaps as an adaptation to caribou hunting. The archaeological evidence for the earliest prehistoric settlement of eastern Beringia, as represented by modern Alaska and the Yukon, begins around 12,000 years ago with the Nenana complex of central Alaska. The earliest well-defined evidence of human occupation of North America south of where the glaciers of the Ice Age reached comes from the Clovis culture of the Paleo-Indian tradition, which begins 11,200 years ago. While this evidence supports the argument that the first human occupation of the New World occurred less than 15,000 years ago, it has not convinced all archaeologists.

Some of the archaeologists who argue for an earlier date for the initial colonization interpret the late–Ice Age pollen record of inland Beringia as indicative of a sparse tundra, or a polar desert environment, unable to sustain the large animal populations needed to support human groups. They suggest that the southern Beringian coast was more temperate and that groups subsisting on maritime resources moved along this unglaciated coastline to the west coast of the Americas sometime less than 25,000 years ago. Subsequent flooding of the land bridge and the continental shelf forced groups inland, south of the merged glaciers.

Currently there is no evidence to support this scenario, other than a few isolated and controversial North American sites dated to more than 15,000 years ago. What is needed is proof for the existence of ice-free areas south of Beringia large enough to have supported human groups, evidence of boats in this region more than 8,000 years ago, and evidence of archaeological sites on the drowned continental shelves of western North America and northeastern Asia. Unfortunately, most archaeological surveys on the inundated continental shelf areas of North America have been restricted to more temperate localities, such as Florida and the Gulf of Mexico. When the northwest coastal areas are adequately researched, evidence to confirm the hypothesis of an early coastal migration may be found.

Anthropologists who specialize in historical linguistics have tried to determine the date of the initial colonization, and the number of subsequent migrations, by organizing the more than one thousand known Native American languages into families and establishing the degree of diversity both within and between these groups. One such system suggests that most North American and South American languages, which form what scholars call the Amerind language group, are descended from the first migration, which is thought to have taken place more than 11,000 years ago. A second migration is represented by the Na-Dene family of languages found in the American Northwest and among the Navajos and Apaches of the Southwest. Inuit and Aleut language groups of the Arctic are considered to be the third, and most recent, language family. This theory of three discrete migration events has remained a minority view among anthropological linguists. The majority of linguists explain language diversity among modern Native American groups as the result of many more episodes of migration.

Some biological anthropologists have attempted to establish the number of migration events and their timing through studies of Native American dental and blood-group traits. Most of these studies confirm a late date for initial settlement and superficially agree with the linguistic data of a tripartite division among modern Native Americans. For example, dental variation between modern American Indian populations has been interpreted to suggest that members of the Amerind language family share similar dental traits and that they probably represent the descendants of an original Paleo-Indian colonization that occurred less than 15,000 years ago. These dental traits separate this group from a second group, the Na-Dene speakers of northwestern North America. This group is thought to have migrated from Siberia no later than 9,000 years ago. The third group, the Inuits and Aleuts of the Arctic, probably entered the Americas no later than about 8,000 years ago.

Blood-group studies of modern Native American populations generally support this dental and linguistic evidence. On the other hand, analyses of mitochondrial DNA (mtDNA) of modern Native American groups suggest that there are four lineages in this population. Thus the three proposed population groups do not explain all the genetic variation found in modern Native American populations. Other researchers have noted that Native Americans are about as genetically varied as any other population group. This suggests that the prehistoric peopling of the Americas was not the result of discrete migrations of a few genetically homogeneous people, as suggested by the linguistic, dental, mtDNA, and blood-group studies. It has been proposed that the genetic variation evidenced among modern Native Americans is instead the result of inadvertent migrations from western Beringia to the Americas by thousands of individuals over many thousands of years.

Other biological anthropologists have attempted to establish when the colonization of the Americas occurred by estimating the amount of time that has elapsed since Native American populations descended from a common Asian ancestor. This has been done by comparing Native American mtDNA with the mtDNA of northeastern Asian populations. The time since separation can then be determined by examining the amount of variation evidenced between these groups. This technique has proved to be problematic for two reasons. First, estimates of mtDNA evolutionary rates range, depending on the time allowed for variation to evolve, from more than 20,000 years ago to less than

15,000 years ago. Consequently, this DNA research has been inconclusive in determining whether colonization occurred more than or less than 15,000 years ago. Second, the mtDNA research assumes that the modern groups studied derive from a small, genetically similar founding population. Genetic variation in the original population would increase the estimated time of separation. Therefore, the dates generated are difficult to interpret without better demographic information on the groups ancestral to migrant populations. Further archaeological research is needed to provide this information.

See also Origins: Native American Perspectives.

Dixon, E. James, *Quest for the Origins of the First Americans* (Albuquerque: University of New Mexico Press, 1993); Fagan, Brian M., *The Great Journey: The Peopling of Ancient America* (New York: Thames and Hudson, 1987).

JOHN A. K. WILLIS
Northwestern University

ORIGINS: NATIVE AMERICAN PERSPECTIVES

The concepts of our origins and of how animals and spirit beings assist humans are reflected in the ways in which any group of human beings looks upon their place in the universe and their relationship to the world of spirits and animals. These concepts appear to be very nearly worldwide in scope. They give rise to stories of the great flood, of the twins, of Mother Earth, and of the first man and woman—themes running through the origin stories of nearly all Native American cultures. Some cultures tell of having been brought into existence by the creator; others believe they originated in the womb of Mother Earth. Common to all are animal and spiritual assistants, who, it is said, helped them through the trials and tribulations of their origins. Consider the three very basic and yet quite diverse origin stories that follow.

According to the Zunis:

In the beginning,
here were no humans in this world.
Every morning Sunfather came up in the East
and traveled high over Mother Earth,
pausing briefly at high noon.
He then descended westward and entered
the western ocean and it became night.
All night long Sunfather traveled

under Mother Earth eastward
to the eastern ocean in time to bring a new day,
but the days
were empty and devoid of joy.
There was no laughter,
there was no singing:
there were no offerings or gifts; and
there was no dancing.
Every day as Sunfather traveled high over Mother Earth
he could hear the cries of his children deep in
    the womb of
Mother Earth.
One day as he paused high overhead
he saw two columns of foam
at the base of a waterfall;
With his great power he zapped life
into the columns of foam,
thereby creating the twin gods.
He said unto the twins,
"Go, go into the womb of Mother Earth
and bring my children up to the light."
The twins obeyed and entered the womb of Mother Earth,
and after many tries they succeeded:
they brought Sunfather's children up to his light.
This was the beginning.

According to the Hopi scholar Hartman H. Lomawaima:

The Hopi Way is the continual fulfillment of the covenant made between Hisat Senom and Masau'u, the deity who facilitated the access of the long-ago-people into the present world from the underworld. The Hopi Way may be described as an ecological process; the maintenance of a proper relationship and balance between people and the universe, and of people to one another. Ritual knowledge and mutual cooperation form the basis of Hopi life.

According to the San Juan Tewa scholar Alfonso Ortiz:

The Tewa were living in "Sipofene," beneath Sandy Place Lake far to the north. The world under the lake was like this one, but it was dark. Supernaturals, men, and animals lived together at this time, and death was unknown. Among the supernaturals were the first mothers of all Tewa, known as "Blue Corn Woman, Near to Summer," or the Summer mother, and "White Corn Maiden, Near to Ice," the Winter mother.

These mothers asked one of the men present to go forth and explore the way by which the people might leave the lake. . . . After three refusals he consented to explore in every direction. . . . After each of these four ventures he reported to the corn mothers and the people that he had seen nothing, that the world above was still "ochu," "green" or "ripe."

. . . Next the mother told him to go to the above. On his way he came upon an open place and saw all the "tsiwi" (predatory mammals and carrion-eating birds) gathered there. . . . The animals gave him a bow and arrows and a quiver, dressed him in buckskin . . . and told him, "You have been accepted. These things we have given you are what you shall use henceforth. Now you are ready to go." . . . When he returned to the people he came as Mountain Lion, or Hunt chief. This is how the first made person came into being."

The foregoing are only excerpts from much longer, much more detailed accounts of origins. For example, the Zuni "Word of the Beginning" takes four nights to tell. It recounts all the major events in the migration of the people from the "beginning place" to the present "center place" and recounts the origins of the various clans and medicine societies, the rain priesthood, the bow priesthood, the kiva societies (dance societies), and other groups.

The Indians' universe contains a fixed order of social systems and structures. These include clans, medicine societies, and dance societies that have always been and always will be, because that is the way they began. The Indian worldview encompasses the physical and spiritual universe both in terms of its supporting social and religious structures and their relationship to all living things and in terms of perceptions of time, colors, space, numbers, and directions. It also encompasses a group's sense of the spiritual properties of life, death, and the hereafter. It is the expression of the whole of human experience in an ever-changing but continuous pattern.

Beliefs regarding creation are intimately intertwined with worldview but are not static. In reality, there is continuous change—small changes over time and space—whose effects, though little felt or noted at first, eventually give rise to a new "way it has always been." Large, abrupt changes are intolerable and therefore usually have little or no lasting effect on the total system—like a stone thrown into a pond that makes a splash and then, having sunk, leaves the pond free to return to its tranquil unbroken state, without any visible sign of change.

The world's systems, both "real" and "spiritual," must always be kept in balance through supplications to the spirit world. These supplications take the form of individual prayers and collective performances of various ritual acts. Such ceremonies maintain harmony between the individual and the collective universe and give joy to the gods.

This land—the four encircling oceans, the mist-covered and moss-draped mountains, the sacred springs, trails, and peaks—is the sacred dwelling place of the gods and people alike. We who originated in and came up from the four worlds below have never lost our faith in the view of our relationship to the universe. We realize how important it is that each of us, with our own methods and our own traditions, and with our collective ceremonial and ritual supplications to the gods, help maintain the universe and keep it in balance for the good of all people and for the joy of the gods.

These are the oral traditions of our people. Most, if not all, teach that human beings were born out of mother earth and upon death go to one place. Our people believe they emerged variously from two, three, four, or five worlds below, from the womb of Mother Earth, from the depths of darkness to the light and warmth of Sunfather's light and the present world. The narrative of the beginning explains all aspects of life: why things are the way they are. Retold over long winter nights and at various religious occasions, the oral traditions are cultural interpretations of the world from the tribal point of view. They tell of the place of emergence and follow our people's travels in different directions in search of the "middle place." After many years of travel all our people became settled in their own places.

It is interesting to note that the archaeologists' history agrees to some degree with the basic outline of the older cultural interpretations of origins and migrations and why cultures are the way they are, why they are where they are, and how they developed. By analysis of material cultural remains such as pottery and architecture, archaeologists have traced the movements of various peoples. Some of the ruins excavated are named in stories of the beginning and of the search for the middle place.

Lomawaima, Hartman H., introduction to *Seasons of the Hopi Kachina: Proceedings of the California State University, Hayward, Conference on Western Pueblos, 1978–88*, ed. Lowell John Bean (Hayward, Calif.: Ballena Press/California State University, Hayward, 1988); Ortiz, Alfonso, *The Tewa World: Space, Time, Being, and Becoming in a Pueblo Society* (Chicago and London: University of Chicago Press, 1969).

EDMUND J. LADD (Shiwi)
Museum of New Mexico
Santa Fe, New Mexico

OSAGE

The earliest known remains of Osage tribal culture place them as longtime residents of present-day Missouri. Forest dwellers occupying a series of villages along the Missouri River system west of present-day St. Louis, the Osages are usually characterized by social scientists as a fringe Plains tribe because they ventured onto the Great Plains for extended buffalo hunts twice yearly. Linguistically, the Osages are counted among the Dhegiha Sioux, a grouping that includes the Quapaw, Ponca, and Kansa(Kaw).

The Osages believed they were the children of the "middle waters"—the universe of sky, earth, land, and water. Wah'Kon-Tah, the spiritual force creating and guiding the tribe, ended *ga-ni-tha,* or chaos, by separating the middle waters into the separate elements: air, earth, and water. The tribespeople were divided between the *Tzi-sho,* Sky People, who descended to earth from above, and the *Hunkah,* Earth People. Ancestry was traced to one of these two divisions, which were subdivided into twenty-four clans with numerous subclans. Leadership resided in a dual-chief system, the Sky People's leader responsible for matters of peace, the Earth People's chief leading in war.

Traditionally, Osage men wore their hair roached: they shaved their heads, including eyebrows, leaving only a scalplock of hair about two inches high and three inches wide running from just above the forehead to the neck. They wore loincloths, leggings, moccasins, and buffalo or bearskin robes. They pierced their ears to accommodate numerous ornaments, wore bracelets on their wrists and forearms, and tattooed their chests and arms.

Prior to European contact, Osage women wore their long hair loosely down their backs. They wore deerskin dresses, moccasins, and leggings. Dresses were cinched with wide belts of woven buffalo calf's hair and set off by earrings and bracelets. The women also tattooed themselves, usually more elaborately than the men, and perfumed themselves with chewed columbine seed. Young females were closely guarded by older women until marriages had been arranged.

The first non-Indians to encounter the Osages were French explorers navigating southward from New France in the 1670s. The French and Osages became business partners in the fur trade. The guns and horses the Osages acquired from the French enabled the tribe to dominate its region for more than a century. The Osages helped the French and other Indians to defeat British general Edward Braddock's forces in 1755, but were inactive during the ensuing colonial war. The tribe continued to use its geographical advantage to control trade along the Missouri River system, developing an alliance with the Spanish as the French presence faded. Prolonged contact with Europeans further affected the Osages as fur traders induced a split in the tribe; as a result, about half the people, under Chief Claremore, moved to Three Forks, in Arkansas.

Once Anglo-American settlement neared the tribal villages in Missouri and Arkansas, a series of diplomatic negotiations ensued. The Osages signed a treaty in 1808, agreeing to take up a reservation existence farther west, in present-day southern Kansas. There they lived, much as before, except that continued intermarriage with Euro-Americans resulted in a population of mixed bloods that by 1890 outnumbered the full bloods. During the Civil War many Osages sporadically fought for the Union. Despite this demonstration of loyalty the Osages were forced to sell their Kansas lands in 1871 and moved south across the border into Indian Territory.

The new 1.5-million-acre reservation in the northeastern part of the territory drew many non-Indians to live among the Osages before the tribal lands were allotted in 1906. Texas cattlemen leased the rich grasslands of the reservation's west side to fatten beef driven north to meet railheads in Kansas. This lease money, coupled with interest payments on the $8 million paid to the tribe for its Kansas holdings, allowed the Osages a degree of prosperity unknown among other territorial tribes. The tribe's Quaker agents thought them unduly independent as a consequence, noting the tribespeople's preference for self-governance, which was formalized in 1881 with the adoption of a written constitution.

Pressure to open Indian Territory to white settlement and create a new state increased during the 1890s. In preparation for that event, Congress insisted that all communally held Indian reservations be allotted and that tribal governments be abolished. The Osages resisted these ideas and in the end benefitted from their intransigence. According to a 1906 agreement, unlike other tribes, which received individual allotments of 160 acres, with "surplus" land going to white settlers, the Osages received allotments of over five hundred acres each. Additionally, the Osages were able to insist on retaining their subsurface mineral estate as a tribe, rather than having the 2,229 allotted Osages individually receive mineral rights.

This latter arrangement proved fortuitous. After World War I and particularly during the 1920s, the Os-

ages became widely heralded as "the richest group of people in the world" because of tribal revenues stemming from oil and natural-gas royalties. This mineral wealth was not an unmixed blessing. Exploiters of all kinds descended upon the Osages to separate them from their money, which was distributed by the government in quarterly payments. Also, Osages born after 1907 were not included on the allotment roll, so an ever-growing class of dispossessed tribespeople was created.

During the 1930s oil prices fell and tribal incomes contracted severely. Revenues from the "underground reservation" did not recover until the 1940s, and then only temporarily. The Arab oil embargo of the 1970s brought huge profits for those tribespeople who owned "head rights" to royalties, but these dropped precipitously in the late 1980s.

The effects of the mineral wealth on the tribe are pervasive. The notoriety brought exploitation and encouraged political factionalism. On the other hand, the oil and gas money enabled the Osages to insulate themselves from many aspects of the white man's road, which they abhorred. Their relative prosperity, although now much declined, contributed to a feeling of distinctiveness, one of the features that make the Osages different from other tribes, as well as from non-Indians.

Not until 1994 did the Osages inaugurate a tribal government separate from the business council whose sole responsibility became the approval of oil and gas leases. This had the effect of enfranchising tribal members who not did own head rights and helped create renewed interest in reviving and maintaining traditional culture.

Mathews, John Joseph, *The Osages: Children of the Middle Waters* (Norman: University of Oklahoma Press, 1961); Rollings, Willard H., *The Osage: An Ethnohistorical Study of Hegemony on the Prairie-Plains* (Columbia: University of Missouri Press, 1992); Wilson, Terry P., *The Underground Reservation: Osage Oil* (Norman: University of Oklahoma Press, 1985).

TERRY P. WILSON (Potawatomi)
University of California at Berkeley

OSCEOLA

(c. 1804–38)
Seminole leader.

Osceola lived a short but dynamic life during turbulent years of war for the Indians of the Southeast. He was known throughout most of the country for his prowess as a warrior and his outspoken opposition to American expansion. He would become the best-known leader of the Seminoles.

Osceola was born in a cabin in Muskogee Creek country in present-day Alabama, in the Upper Creek town of Tallahassee, near present-day Tuskegee. Also known by the name of Billy Powell, he was the only child of William Powell, a British trader, and Polly Copinger, an Upper Muskogee Creek. Copinger, whose father was most likely an English trader, was Powell's second wife. From his previous marriage with an Indian woman, Powell had two daughters. Osceola's Indian name was derived from asi, a tealike ceremonial drink that he had a recognized ability to ingest, and *yahola,* a ceremonial cry.

In the early nineteenth century, Osceola's kinsmen at Tallahassee were pushed out of their homeland and retreated into Florida, where they joined the Seminoles, known to them as "Those Who Camp at a Distance."

Osceola was too young to fight during the Creek War or at the Battle of Horseshoe Bend, at which the Creeks were defeated by Andrew Jackson. Following these disasters he accompanied his mother to northern Florida. They traveled with a Red Stick town led by a mixed-blood relative named Peter McQueen. The Creek Confederacy consisted of Red and White towns, the former providing leadership in war and the latter providing leadership on civil matters. The youth of delicate features was still too young to fight. The young warrior-to-be and other Indians were captured by Andrew Jackson's soldiers during the First Seminole War in 1817–18. Osceola was familiar with the English language, having spent much time among traders and white settlers. Both Indians and whites knew him to be a persuasive, determined young man. His mixed blood did not hinder his advancement among his people, although his followers often feared his irrepressible ego. He loved fine ornamentation, and dressed to his personal liking.

Osceola finally settled among the Tallahassees, and as a growing young man he was called Tallahassee Tustenugee. The name was actually a title of war, meaning "Warrior of Tallahasee Town." He would become a leader in war, but his mixed ancestry limited his acceptance by traditionalists, who preferred leaders with closer ties to the tribal institutions. Nevertheless Osceola won great fame for his blunt actions of patriotism and for his anti-American stance. At the Treaty of Moultrie Creek, for example, signed in September 1823, Osceola demonstrated his opposition to land

An 1838 oil painting of Osceola, the Muskogee Seminole war leader, by George Catlin.

sales by driving his hunting knife through the document. This action became the subject of a famous painting depicting the angry Seminole warrior defying the United States.

By 1834 Osceola, five feet ten inches tall and of slender build, was a true warrior. While living in central Florida, he had witnessed numerous battles and defeats. Osceola's obstinacy got him into trouble with the Indian agent Wiley Thompson, who in June 1835 had the Seminole warrior put behind bars. At around this time some Seminoles favored signing a treaty in which they would agree to migrate westward, and Osceola and others decided to resist. Osceola gained his freedom and, on December 18, led a party that killed Charley Emathla, an advocate of removal. Holding a personal and political grudge against Thompson, Osceola killed the Indian agent on December 28, while another party massacred a military command under Major Francis Dade on Fort King Road. Their actions precipitated the Second Seminole War (1835–42).

During the early years of the war, Osceola led various bands and influenced others in successfully skirmishing against the U.S. Army. On December 31, 1835, at the Withlacoochee River, Osceola engineered a major victory even though his warriors were considerably outnumbered. Osceola was wounded in the encounter, but he was at the height of his military powers at this battle. In 1836 he recovered from his wound and worked to recruit a force large enough to score another major victory. Instead, he met with frustration as American troops pursued the Seminoles from northern Florida into the swamps to the south. In July or August 1836 Osceola came down with malaria.

In 1837 an exhausted and ill Osceola traveled to Fort Peyton, Florida, to talk peace with the Americans. On October 21, soldiers surrounded him and a delegation as he carried a white flag of truce. He was taken as a prisoner to Fort Marion, near St. Augustine. The U.S. Army considered Osceola such a magnetic figure that in the following weeks it moved him to Fort Moultrie, South Carolina.

Realizing he was near death, Osceola requested the presence of his two wives and children. One of his wives, by whom he had four children, was known by the name Che-cho-ter, "Morning Dew." The name of his other wife, the daughter of an ex-slave, is not known, but Osceola had one child by her. One of his last wishes was to be dressed in his finest clothes. The Seminole leader had always enjoyed fancy personal adornments, and, lucky for posterity, the artist George Catlin befriended Osceola just before his death and painted him in his finery. The chief received medical care from Dr. Frederick Weedon at Fort Moultrie, but on January 30, 1838, the famed Seminole warrior and leader died, still a prisoner of war. With the hope of capitalizing on Osceola's growing fame, Weedon had the corpse of the famed war leader beheaded and laid claim to many of Osceola's personal possessions and clothes. Osceola's head passed through several hands until 1843, when it came to Dr. Valentine Mott, who put it on display and later donated it to the Medical College of New York. It disappeared following a fire in 1865.

See also Seminole.

Hartley, William, and Ellen Hartley, *Osceola, the Unconquered Indian* (New York: Hawthorn Books, 1973); Mahon, John K., *History of the Second Seminole War, 1835–1842* (Gainesville: University of Florida Press, 1967); Wickman, Patricia R., *Osceola's Legacy* (Tuscaloosa: University of Alabama Press, 1991).

DONALD L. FIXICO
(Seminole, Creek, Shawnee, Sac, and Fox)
Western Michigan University

OSKISON, JOHN MILTON

(1874–1947)
Part-Cherokee journalist, editor, essayist, and novelist.

Born and raised on a cattle ranch in Indian Territory, John Milton Oskison was educated at Stanford and Harvard and eventually became involved in the major social issues of his time. He was probably always better known for his journalistic writings and editorships than for his fiction, although today critics and readers interested in early Native American writers and in new voices and fresh literary points of view are reexamining his short stories and novels. His life and writings certainly merit attention. Oskison was a scholar, a soldier, a cattleman, and an activist—a man of eclectic and cosmopolitan interests and abilities.

Oskison was born on Pryor Creek near Tahlequah, Indian Territory, on September 21, 1874, to John Oskison, an English immigrant, and Rachel Connor Crittenden, who was one-quarter Cherokee. Interestingly, their son John is listed on the Cherokee census rolls as having one-quarter degree of Cherokee blood as well. The family struggled at first to establish a livelihood in Indian Territory. At times the harsh conditions of the land and the father's strict temperament combined to keep the family's three sons out of school, but John did eventually graduate with the first class of Willie Halsell College in 1894. With the support and encouragement of his father, he attended Stanford University from 1894 to 1898 and ultimately received a bachelor's degree there; he then spent a year at Harvard doing graduate work in English. After winning first place in a writing contest sponsored by *Century Magazine* in 1899 with the story "Only the Master Shall Praise," Oskison was inspired to choose writing as a career. With his hometown newspaper and other native newspapers as enthusiastic first publishers of his essays and observations, the young man embarked on a successful career that was to last more than forty years. Besides writing newspaper editorials, essays, short stories, personal observations, speeches, and novels, Oskison was an editor for the *New York Evening Post* and *Collier's Weekly*.

In 1917, even though most of the popular journals and magazines and most of the Native American journals and newspapers of the day were publishing his writings, Oskison enlisted in the army. He was sent to France to work for and write about the relief effort under way there. After the war he directed his energies and attention to writing novels about the lives and adventures of the peoples of Indian Territory (now Oklahoma). Two in particular were set in Indian Territory: *Wild Harvest* (1925) and *Black Jack Davy* (1926). Although the vivid images and memories of those days provided the only subject matter for his novels, Oskison preferred to live in New York City or Paris, returning to Oklahoma for visits to renew his acquaintances and refresh his memories.

At the time of his death, Oskison was working on the manuscript of his autobiography. In this manuscript may be found some of his most interesting writing and glimpses of his relationships with members of his family and with other people in Indian Territory. He claims he inherited not only the restless wanderlust of his father but also his mother's love of the land and of the stories and heritage of the native peoples. These twin inheritances enabled and inspired him to travel throughout most of the United States as well as to many of the world's capitals and to record these travels with an eye and ear attuned to human experiences. The classic discord between father and sons, and between brothers, which he had observed in his own family and which had been reinforced in his worldly travels, became one of the main themes of his writings, occurring in stories such as "The Fall of King Chris," "Young Henry and the Old Man," and "Out of the Night that Covers" as well as in novels such as *Wild Harvest* and *The Brothers Three* (1935). He was also interested in themes of loyalty and perseverance, frontier justice and paradox, as may be seen in such stories as "A Schoolmaster's Dissipation," "When the Grass Grew Long," "To Younger's Bend," and "The Problem of Old Harjo."

Some readers may be disappointed that his stories are not more overtly "Indian"—that they do not depict the "noble savage" character or, conversely, the doomed victim of white encroachment. Instead Oskison's characters are almost always half-breeds or mixed bloods struggling, but ultimately surviving, on the frontier as ranch hands, newspaper writers, wives, and teachers. And in subtle, clever ways, Oskison's stories are indeed "Indian": the coyote-tale motif informs "Koenig's Discovery"; the renewal of nature and cyclic structures provide the worldview in stories such as "Tookh Steh's Mistake," "Apples of the Hesperides," and "The Quality of Mercy"; and patient, indigenous wisdom and moral law are found in "Walla-Tenaka—Creek," "The Other Partner," and "The Singing Bird."

During the years he was writing short stories, Oskison also wrote essays on Indian issues: "The President

and the Indian," "The Outlook for the Indian," "Remaining Causes of Indian Discontent," "Making an Individual of the Indian," "The Indian in the Professions," and "Acquiring a Standard of Value" to name only a few. Oskison conscientiously sought to explore the issues and alternatives while at the same time maintaining a wide audience and popular credibility as a spokesman for native people. He defended the values of the old lifestyles while presenting the opportunities of education and industry; he wrote of acculturation while simultaneously applauding the adroit jurisprudence and philosophy of tribal traditions.

Critics and readers who wish to easily summarize or pigeonhole Oskison's personal identity, political stance, or opinions on Indian issues will be disappointed. The man Oskison, as far as can be determined through his writings, is hidden and complex. He lived in the white world but knew intimately the Indian world of modern Oklahoma. He wrote for the mainstream print media but had an ear tuned to oral traditions. He was an early activist for Indian causes but never lost his influence upon or his reputation with powerful national figures in American society such as Herbert Hoover (a classmate at Stanford) and the railroad magnate Jay Gould (whose niece Florence Ballard Day he married in 1903). Oskison and Day divorced in 1920, and in that same year the author married Hildegarde Hawthorne, a granddaughter of Nathaniel Hawthorne. Oskison died in New York City in 1947. He was a man for his time—multicultured, sophisticated, and, inevitably, lonely.

Littlefield, Daniel, "Oskison, John Milton (Cherokee)," in *A Bio-bibliography of Native American Writers, 1772–1924* (Metuchen, N.J.: Scarecrow Press, 1981); Oskison, John Milton, *Black Jack Davy* (New York: Appleton, 1926); Oskison, John Milton, *The Brothers Three* (New York: Macmillan, 1935).

GRETCHEN RONNOW
Wayne State College

OTTAWA

While known to outsiders as "Ottawas," community members much prefer the term *Odawak* (singular *Odawa*). Gitche-Manitou placed the Ottawas on the land of the Great Lakes basin. The Ottawa River in the east, the shores of the lakes to the south, the Mississippi River on the west, and the height of land whence all the rivers flow northward on the north were provided by Mother Earth as boundaries of their territory. Here, guided by the surety of the Medicine Circle and the omnipresence of Gitche-Manitou, and through the benevolence of Mother Earth, the Ottawas lived.

All knowledge came from Gitche-Manitou. Contact with the spiritual world was through the medicine man and Nanabush, who spanned the gulf between Gitche-Manitou and the Ottawas. Nanabush was a paradox: while perceived as godlike, he harbored all the weaknesses of human beings. The mythology, legends, and stories painted against this backdrop formed the philosophical foundation of the Ottawa world.

Enandahgwad, the Law of the Orders, governed the Ottawas. Gitche-Manitou was foremost, and Earth, his wife, was the mother of all nature. Their natural children were the plants. The animal kind were brothers and sisters. Human beings were last in the order—the least necessary and most dependent of beings.

Teachings were formalized. The Ottawas learned of the Circle of Life, which was divided into four quadrants representing the four stages of life, the four directions, and the four seasons. Animal kind shared the circle. For an Ottawa, the east was the eagle, spring, the place of enlightenment. The south invoked the robin, summer, the place of innocence. The west depicted the buffalo, autumn, and introspection, while the north held images of the bear, winter, and the place of great wisdom. For an Ottawa, the four hills of life—infancy, youth, adulthood, and old age—were seen in relation to one another and to the responsibility pertaining to each. Only in living each hill completely did the Ottawas see their lives in balance.

The Ottawas created the tools for survival. They developed bows and arrows, the birchbark canoe, toboggans and snowshoes, buckskin clothing and footwear, wigwams, and copper tools. The knowledge of the medicinal properties of plants was given to the Ottawas for the health of the nation.

As the Ottawas survived and the environment sustained them, family units grew, communities formed, social structures became ordered, and the people organized themselves in clans. The Ottawas say they have always been here, but scientists say they came here thousands of years ago; just how many thousand is a matter of debate.

In the eighteenth century Ottawa community life was in tune with the cycles of the natural world. Spring found them at home making maple sugar to barter with traders. In summer, they planted corn, potatoes, peas, beans, and pumpkins. In July, they traveled to the nearest British garrison to receive their annual presents of clothing, blankets, and implements. The fall brought the harvest, which was followed by the annual trip to the wintering grounds on the southern shore of Lake Michigan.

Less than four hundred years ago, the *Wemitigojiwuk* (the French) entered the land of the Ottawas. This changed the Ottawa way of life forever. By 1634, they were the middlemen in the trade with the French. This precipitated conflict with the *Haudenosaunee* (Iroquoian) Confederacy and the *Assistaronon* (Algonquin) Nation and the dispersion of the Ottawas from their ancestral lands in modern Ontario. The Ottawas and *Wendot* (Hurons) pushed westward until, by 1654, the Ottawas reached Dakota Territory. War with the Dakotas sent the Ottawas back to Chequemagong Bay, Lake Superior; to Keewanaw; Manitoulin Island; and to Sault Ste. Marie. The center of Ottawa territory became Michilimackinac in 1673 with the return of the Kiskakon, Sinago, Sauble, and Nassauketon clans.

The French moved into Ottawa territory. Traders and missionaries joined the Ottawas at Chequemagong in 1665 and later at Michilimackinac and St. Ignace. In 1687, an Ottawa chief warned his people that the French intended to enslave them. The Ottawas' allegiance to the French drew them into continuous wars with the enemies of the French. In 1759, the British defeated the French at Quebec. This was a devastating blow to the Ottawas. Life would never be the same. The Ottawas were caught between two former enemies, the British and the Americans.

It has been said that the Ottawas were already a nation when the United States was taking its first breath of life. However, the Americans never treated the Ottawas as a nation. The American commissioners at Fort McIntosh, in 1785, informed the Indians that they had no rights. Subsequent American negotiators maintained the same attitude. The chiefs of the Ottawas responded by joining with other Indian nations in refusing to sign treaties unless the confederacy of tribes was involved.

The Ottawas sent a delegation to President Thomas Jefferson in 1809 and to the secretary of war, William Eustis, in 1811 explaining the desperate state of the Ottawa people and expressing disappointment in the treatment they were receiving from American officials. Their frustration led to their allegiance to the British in the War of 1812.

In 1812, Ottawa warriors defended their homes, lands, and way of life. Some of the Ottawas' greatest warriors, led by Assignack (Blackbird), included Mucketebennessy (Black Hawk), Keshigobenesse (Day-bird), Mokomanish (Knife That One Does Not Care About), and Eshuagonabe (Looking Back). These *ogemuk* (leaders) fought to protect the Ottawa villages along the Maumee from the "burn and destroy" operations perpetrated by the American troops on Indian towns on the Wabash. They defended the Niagara frontier in the mud, mosquitos, and sickness side by side with British soldiers, Canadian volunteers, and other Indian allies. They followed Tecumseh at the Battle of Moraviantown and continued to hold the line against the Americans on land and at sea until the end of the war.

The Ottawas found that in peace, their contribution was forgotten. Those on the American side of the line were left to deal with the desire of the Americans for their land, and in the 1830s many fled to Canada or were transported to the American West. Canadian Ottawas found themselves working with the British in establishing settlements devoted exclusively to the Christianization, civilization, and education of Indian

people. They returned to what they regarded as their ancestral island, Manitoulin, only to have to sign it away by treaty in 1862.

The Ottawas have survived. They have become schooled landowners and have participated in all facets of American and Canadian life. Their language has been preserved. Many follow traditional teachings, and they still believe that they are the people Gitche-Manitou placed in the Great Lakes basin.

Blackbird, Andrew, *History of the Ottawa and Chippewa Indians of Michigan: A Grammar of the Language and Personal Family History of the Author, by Andrew J. Blackbird, Late U.S. Interpreter* (1887; reprint, Petoskey, Mich.: Little Traverse Regional Historical Society, 1967); McClurken, James M., *Gah-Baeh-Jhagwah-Buk: The Way It Happened* (East Lansing: Michigan State University Museum, 1991); Tanner, Helen Hornbeck, ed., *Atlas of the Great Lakes Indian History* (Norman: University of Oklahoma Press, 1987).

CECIL KING (Odawa)
Queen's University
Kingston, Ontario

PAI

Ancestral Northeastern Pai ("people") bands inhabited the lowland desert area immediately east of the Colorado River by A.D. 700, judging from excavated pieces of ceramic pots of the kind Pai later made. These Yuman speakers gardened along the riverbanks and on spring-irrigated plots in the nearby mountains. Men hunted game, both big and small; women collected a variety of edible wild plants, seeds, and fruits. The Pai especially relished the edible fruits of one yucca species.

Sometime after A.D. 1300, the Pai expanded eastward onto the Colorado Plateau. The easternmost band (*Havasua Pa'a*, "Blue Water People") exploited the Grand Canyon south of the Colorado River. Large *agave* plants flourished on the canyon benches, where huge "mescal pits" attest to centuries of Pai pit-roasting of the sugar-rich plant hearts. The place name Indian Gardens at a spring below present-day Grand Canyon Village reflects the Pai practice of irrigated gardening; this band crossed the Little Colorado River frontier of Hopi territory to garden at Moenkopi Springs. Members of this and other Pai bands traded sun-dried mescal, flawless buckskins (from deer run to death), and red hematite to Oraibi Pueblo Hopis for ceramic vessels, textiles, foods, and, in historic times, metal tools and leather goods.

Oral tradition and linguistic evidence alike indicate that the Yavapai tribe separated from the other Pai around 1750. They spread south along the Verde River and the Agua Fría and Hassayampa tributaries of the Gila-Salt River to the frontier defended by Gila River Pimas. Pai myth attributes the split to a mud ball fight between children that spread to their parents. The Yavapai fought their bitterest battles against the Pai to their north. Warriors on both sides shouted mutually intelligible taunts in the heat of conflict. Once hostilities began, exacting vengeance for losses perpetuated lethal encounters. East of the Verde River, the Yavapai encountered Western Apache bands migrating westward. The two peoples, who spoke very different languages, mingled more than they fought, generating a border population never really understood by Euro-Americans.

The Franciscan missionary Francisco Garcés traversed northern Pai territory in 1776, from the Mojave frontier to Oraibi Pueblo and back. He noted that western Pai bands were obtaining leather and metal from Hispanic New Mexico via western Pueblo traders. New Mexican slave raiders captured a few Pai during the 1840s. U.S. Army explorers contacted the Northern Pai and Yavapai in 1853 and 1854, and members of the Western Yavapai band began seeing steamboats on the lower Colorado River during that decade.

Euro-American prospectors discovered placer gold on upper Hassayampa Creek in 1863, and the Union congress promptly created Arizona Territory. The Union dispatched troops to protect territorial officials and gold miners from the Yavapai, whose core territory the miners had invaded. Seeking to defend their economic resources, the Yavapai fought a series of skirmishes for nine years until 1872. A hundred Northern Pai scouts guided U.S. cavalrymen to the last resisting Northern Yavapai band camps in the canyon of the Santa María River. Pima-Maricopa Confederation scouts guided U.S. troops to a rock shelter in the canyon of the San River, where the last resisting Southeastern Yavapai fought to the death.

The western Pai bands had already fought and lost the "Walapai War" in 1866–69. Euro-Americans labeled all western Pai bands "Walapai," "Hualapai," or "Hualpai," versions of the native name of the western band, *Whala Pa'a*, "Pine Tree Mountain People." That conflict centered on a toll road between Fort Mohave (established in 1859) and Fort Whipple (established in 1864), which stood at the edge of Prescott, then the capital of Arizona Territory. A Prescott teamster triggered hostilities when he murdered sub-tribal chief Wauba Yuma, who carried a written pass from an army officer attesting to his good character and friendship toward Euro-Americans, along with two of his sons.

Cavalry units stationed at Fort Mohave carried out most of the search-and-destroy missions that characterized the conflict. Forces from Fort Whipple conducted a few campaigns, surprising women gathering wild grass seed in the Hualapai Valley and processing *agave* hearts near Trout Creek. Cherum, chief of the "Walapai" Cerbat Mountain band, had stockpiled firearms and ammunition before hostilities began. Protected by rocks, his warriors twice forced cavalry contingents to retreat from his home canyon located several miles north and east of the toll road. Cherum also mobilized some two hundred fifty "Walapai" belonging to several bands plus refugee Southern Paiute warriors to attack Camp Beale's Springs, on the toll road.

Once army officers forced "Walapai" chiefs formally to capitulate, they concentrated the Walapai at Camp Beale's Springs under army supervision until Bureau of Indian Affairs (BIA) officials in 1874 demanded that they be removed from their homeland to the Colorado River Indian Reservation. Members of the easternmost band—the previously mentioned *Havasua Pa'a*—evaded both concentration and removal, staying in the Grand Canyon and on the adjacent plateau. Consequently, Euro-Americans increasingly referred to these still semi-autonomous "Havasupai" as separate from the "Walapai." In 1875, the surviving Walapai fled from the unhealthy Colorado River flood plain back to their aboriginal territory. They avoided another removal by making themselves indispensable at Euro-American mining camps and ranches, which desperately needed unskilled laborers.

Meanwhile, the army had concentrated the Yavapai at Camp Verde following their defeat; there they excavated irrigation canals and began growing food crops. In 1875, the BIA had the army remove the Yavapai from their homeland to the San Carlos (Apache) Indian Reservation. Though some western band Yavapai avoided removal by working for Euro-American miners on the desert north of the Gila River, most Yavapai remained interned at San Carlos until about 1900, when the BIA allowed them to return to the Verde River valley. There they found low-paying jobs at Prescott, the smelter town of Clarkdale, and nearby abandoned Fort Verde. Some gardened once lands were reserved for them. The president created the largest Yavapai reservation in 1903 at abandoned Fort McDowell, near the confluence of the Verde and Salt rivers.

BIA policy also administratively separated the Walapai from the Havasupai. In 1882, the army officer who had led cavalry offensives during the Walapai War surveyed boundaries for a Walapai reservation on the Colorado Plateau that included five major canyons on the south rim of the western Grand Canyon. The government reserved for the Havasupai but three hundred twelve acres at Havasupai Village, at the bottom of Cataract Canyon, disregarding the fact that the Havasupai traditionally spent the winter on the plateau, where deer and firewood abounded. Not until 1975 did Congress relieve this situation, when it approved the transfer of 175,000 acres of forested plateau land from the U.S. Forest Service to the BIA for Havasupai use.

After 1934 residents of most Pai reservations organized local governments. Female chiefs from one lineage led the Prescott Yavapai group from 1940 until 1994. The Prescott and Fort McDowell governments have led Arizona tribes in establishing gambling facilities that currently finance many local reservation programs.

Dobyns, Henry F., and Robert C. Euler, *The Havasupai People* (Phoenix, Ariz.: Indian Tribal Series, 1971); Dobyns, Henry F., and Robert C. Euler, *The Walapai People* (Phoenix, Ariz.: Indian Tribal Series, 1976).

HENRY F. DOBYNS
Tucson, Arizona

PAIUTE, NORTHERN

Northern Paiutes are Uto-Aztecan speakers who spread throughout the Great Basin from Death Valley, California, in about A.D. 1000. Calling themselves Numu, "People," they displaced prior inhabitants and occupied a seventy-thousand-square-mile territory defined by the Sierra Nevada and the Columbia and Snake Rivers on the west and north, and by the territory of the linguistically related Shoshones and Owens Valley Paiutes on the east and south. Men hunted antelope, mountain sheep, and deer, as well as smaller mammals such as ground squirrels, but especially jackrabbits. They captured American coots and other waterfowl; fish were seined, netted, or speared from specially constructed willow platforms. Women, on the other hand, gathered a wide variety of roots, berries, and over 150 different types of seeds—especially pine nuts south of the Humboldt River in Nevada and camas bulbs in the north. Group names, in fact, were derived from predominant resources (e.g., the Tabooseedokadoo, "Cyberus Eaters," of the Smith and Mason Valleys in

Nevada). Following European contact, when Spanish horses were acquired Northern Paiutes organized into mounted defensive bands that were named after "captains" or "chiefs" (e.g., "The Children of Chief Winnemucca"). Residing today on federal reservations, Northern Paiutes derive their group names from topographic features (e.g., Honey Lake Paiutes, Pyramid Lake Paiutes) or from adjoining American towns or cities (e.g., the Reno-Sparks Indian Colony).

Among the Northern Paiutes, bilaterally extended families and kindreds were the primary traditional resource-gathering and residential groups; these continue to be so in many areas. Wintering in sheltered valleys near stored resources, these family units combined aboriginally to form larger sociopolitical groups in late summer, when "the People" would hunt and fish, and in early fall, when they would converge upon piñon-pine groves in the mountains to harvest what was tantamount to a staple crop. Residence with either set of parents (ambilocality), and the simultaneous existence of polygyny and polyandry, suggest a loose, flexible kinship system—one that stressed generation, relative age, and gender. "Sibling exchange" was also quite common: the practice of two brothers marrying two sisters, or a brother and sister marrying a brother and sister from another family.

Village headmen were called *poinabe,* "talkers." Other forms of leadership were usually task oriented. "Rabbit bosses," for example, coordinated family-owned nets, which were strung across valley floors in years when the population of jackrabbits soared.

Buha, "power," was a quintessential religious concept. Heritable within the family, *buha* was either acquired in dreams or deliberately sought in caves and grave sites, which otherwise were avoided. *Buha* afforded weather control, sexual prowess, gambling success, and invulnerability, but its primary use was for healing. Shamans, both men and women, used all-night cures to suck out sicknesses, which it was believed were magically intruded by witches or ghosts.

The Round Dance was the main ceremony. Held three times yearly, just before the fall pine-nut harvest, the November rabbit drive, and the May fishing season, it involved men and women dancing clockwise in a circle around a pole or (male) singer. Round Dance ceremonies affirmed social unity after months of separation, and concentrated participants' energies toward the subsistence tasks at hand.

Besides *buha* and the belief that night was the required time for shamanic cures, ceremonies, and the telling of tales, other important religious concepts stressed the sacredness of mountains and water. Job's Peak, in the Stillwater Range near the Walker River Reservation in Nevada, for example, was believed by many to be the *axis mundi.* The importance of water, which in this harsh desert still defines movement, can be seen not only in the very prefix *pa-* in Paiute, which means "water," but also in the fact that lowered lake levels today, in combination with the need to protect Northern Paiute gravesites, are among the most vital legal struggles faced by these early inhabitants of the Great Basin.

Fowler, Catherine S., and Sven Liljeblad, "Northern Paiute," in *Handbook of North American Indians,* ed. William C. Sturtevant, vol. 11, *Great Basin,* ed. Warren L. D'Azevedo (Washington: Smithsonian Institution, 1986); Miller, Jay, "Basin Religion and Theology: A Comparative Study of Power *(Puha),*" *Journal of California and Great Basin Anthropology* 5 (1983): 66–86; Steward, Julian, "Basin-Plateau Aboriginal Sociopolitical Groups," Smithsonian Institution, *Bureau of American Ethnology Bulletin* 120 (1938).

MICHAEL HITTMAN
Long Island University

PAIUTE, SOUTHERN

Southern Paiutes mostly ranged in southern Utah and southern Nevada, and followed the bend of the Colorado River southward through Arizona into California. No overall tribal organization existed historically. What usually are called "bands" include the Chemehuevis, Kaibabs, Las Vegases, Moapas, Shivwits, Pahvant Utes, Pahranagats, Panacas, Gunlocks, Saint Georges, Cedars, Beavers, Uinkarets, Panguitches, Kaiparowits, San Juans, and Antarianunts. Each is associated with a geographic territory and possesses dialectical linguistic markers within what is classified as the Southern Numic branch of the Uto-Aztecan language family. The aboriginal population was small, and remains so: the 1980 U.S. Census lists fourteen hundred Southern Paiutes. Southern Paiute occupation of the Great Basin is dated by archaeologists to A.D. 1000–1200.

Because the distribution of elk, bear, deer, antelope, and mountain sheep was erratic, small game such as rabbits, wood rats, mice, gophers, and squirrels provided most of the animal protein in the ecology of Southern Paiute territory, which varied from spruce, fir, and pine down through creosote and mesquite zones. Bird eggs, locusts, ant larvae, and caterpillars were also eaten, as well as lizards and snakes; fish were taken only at Panguitch Lake. The ownership of songs by individuals made hunting a magical as well as technical enterprise.

Plant foods, however, were more important: women gathered roots and berries on the plateau, and harvested pine nuts on Indian Peak and Charleston Mountain. Agave was another vegetable mainstay. In addition, there is evidence for early, if not precontact, irrigation agriculture: corn and squash planted near the mouths of Ash and LaVerkin Creeks, and along the Virgin River, and melons, native gourds, sunflowers, amaranth, and beans elsewhere.

Pottery and baskets, consequently, were essential for survival. Women wore twined basketry hats; men's hats consisted of tanned hides, to which tufts of quail feathers were affixed on the crown. Women also wore a double apron of skin or vegetable fiber; men wore skin breechcloths. In winter, both sexes used bark leggings and rabbit-skin blankets, which doubled as bedding. Men often went naked in hot weather. Southern Paiutes also made bark or yucca moccasins. For skin protection, as well as to celebrate rites of passage, both sexes smeared red paint on their faces and bodies. They also tattooed their faces and pierced their ears. In fact, it was believed that the demiurge Coyote had instructed Southern Paiutes that without ear piercing an individual couldn't pass to the other world.

Traditionally, a village consisted of two to ten houses and an owned spring, which was inherited by males. Elected headmen discoursed on morality and had advisory, not authority, functions. The Las Vegas band required dreaming for succession. Marriage was monogamous and patrilocal, though polygyny and polyandry existed situationally.

Birth took place in circular brush enclosures. Boys were required to surrender first kills to parents. The girls' puberty ceremony required seclusion, the use of a hot bed at night, a scratching stick, and a taboo against meat, salt, and water; afterward there was bathing, hair trimming, and painting the face and body red. Though marriage was an unimportant ritual, funerals were four-day affairs involving cremation or cave burials; the destruction of property; the killing of eagles, dogs, and horses, and sometimes even of a relative to keep the departed company; the abandonment of homes and gardens; and a naming prohibition. The Cry (or Mourning or Burning) Ceremony took place from three months to a year after each death. By 1900, Southern Paiute mourning ceremonies cut across band lines, and by the 1970s the Cry Ceremony and the funeral had coalesced.

In the late 1700s priests such as Silvestre Velez de Escalante began to baptize and enslave natives. Located as they were close to what became the Old Spanish Trail, Southern Paiutes were also subject to Ute and Navajo slave raiders. Disease followed, their population declined, and though Brigham Young ended their enslavement in the 1850s, Mormons took their best lands.

The Treaty of Spanish Forks (1865), though never ratified by Congress, resulted in the relocation of six Southern Paiute bands to the Uintah Reservation in Utah, where they lived among traditional enemies. The first Southern Paiute Reservation (Moapa) was established in 1872. A recent tragedy for the tribe was the federal government's termination of four Southern Paiute bands in 1954 and the resulting loss of 43,530 acres of land; the Utah Restoration Act of 1980, however, restored the terminated groups. In 1965 the Indian Claims Commission awarded the Southern Paiutes $8.25 million for almost 30 million acres of tribal lands lost over the years—or about twenty-seven cents per acre.

Today, new homes and economic enterprise reflect the Southern Paiutes' determination to maintain their sovereignty.

Euler, Robert C., and Catherine S. Fowler, *Southern Paiute Ethnohistory*, University of Utah Anthropological Papers, no. 78 (Salt Lake City, 1973); Kelly, Isabel T., and Catherine S. Fowler, "Southern Paiute," in *Handbook of North American Indians*, ed. William C. Sturtevant, vol. 11, *Great Basin*, ed. Warren L. D'Azevedo (Washington: Smithsonian Institution, 1986); Sapir, Edward, "Song Recitative in Paiute Mythology," *Journal of American Folklore* 23 (1910): 455–72.

MICHAEL HITTMAN
Long Island University

PALEO-INDIANS

Archaeologists study human behavior through the material remains left by human groups. In the case of the Paleo-Indians—which is the archaeologists' name for the tradition that represents the earliest widely successful human occupation of the Americas—scientists have worked to assess the continuity of stone-tool features that are used to identify the tradition and to establish how these tools changed over time. Studies of Paleo-Indian material culture usually discuss these stylistic changes in terms of the ways in which the food-getting behaviors of the people who made and used these tools also changed over time.

Archaeologists use the term *tradition* to describe distinct groups of artifacts manufactured for, or modified by, human use that are distributed over a large geographic area and persist for long periods of time. The first evidence of the Paleo-Indian tradition comes from the Great Plains of North America and indicates that the tradition lasted in this region for about twenty-seven hundred years, from approximately 11,200 to 8,500 years ago. East of the Mississippi it seems to have had a shorter duration; there it probably started around 11,000 years ago and was replaced by dozens of different Archaic projectile-point forms less than 10,000 years ago. Dating in this region is made difficult by highly acidic soils, which destroy the type of organic material usually used in radiocarbon dating.

Within traditions, differences in material culture that are more localized, or less long-lasting, than the tradition are considered to be *cultural complexes*. The cultural complexes that have been suggested as belonging to the Paleo-Indian tradition are based on differences in lithic technologies. Much of the evidence we have about Paleo-Indian lifeways comes from studies of archaeological sites occupied by the first of the Paleo-Indian groups, the Clovis cultural complex, which lasted on the Great Plains for about three hundred years. The name Clovis comes from the town in New Mexico where the first site containing Clovis lithic tools was found. The most extensive dates we have for Clovis people, approximately 11,200 to 10,900 years ago, are from the Great Plains. By 11,000 years ago Clovis groups had successfully colonized New England. Later, Clovis groups would become established as far north as the Yukon and as far south as the Andes.

Most of the stylistic evidence used to differentiate between Clovis and later Paleo-Indian cultural complexes comes from surface scatters of their distinctively fluted stone tools. In spite of the difficulty of dating this evidence, it does seem that Paleo-Indian lithic technologies increased in stylistic diversity over time. This suggests that as the colonizing Clovis groups of the Paleo-Indian tradition expanded into unoccupied regions they maintained a fairly uniform tool kit, and that over time lithic technologies diverged as groups more efficiently adapted to local environmental conditions and the subsistence resources available to them. This trend continued throughout the Paleo-Indian period, culminating in some areas of North America, such as those east of the Mississippi, with the development of the Archaic tradition, evidence of which is found in the manufacture and use, after 10,000 years ago, of dozens of different point styles.

Paleo-Indian studies began in 1926 at Folsom, New Mexico, with the discovery and subsequent excavation of fluted projectile points embedded in the ribs of an extinct and very large species of bison. Within ten years of the Folsom discovery other Paleo-Indian sites were found in the Clovis-Portales region of New Mexico, and at Lindenmeier, Colorado. Most of these sites were initially identified by the surface visibility of the bones of this extinct form of bison, or those of mammoths. Where buried and undisturbed Clovis and Folsom fluted stone tools were found at these western sites, tools identified as Folsom were excavated above those identified as Clovis, indicating that Folsom was the younger of the two cultures.

Clovis is seen to be the only continent-wide style of stone tools in North American prehistory. The rapid spread of these fluted artifacts in the Americas is suggestive of the colonization of what was an empty continent, or one that was very sparsely occupied. The Clovis culture is particularly identified with three- to four-inch-long stone tools with a distinctive fluting at the lower or shaft end. These robust tools are usually called *points* because the fluting is assumed to have made it easier to attach the blade to a wooden spear shaft. Because few western Clovis points have been found with impact fractures, which generally result from the end of a projectile point forcefully hitting an object and are common among later Paleo-Indian and Archaic bison kills, it has been suggested that Clovis points were used as knives.

Clovis tool kits were lightweight and portable, indicating that these human groups were constantly on the move and probably reliant on large territories to sustain them. These tool kits consisted of both stone and bone tools, but because acidic soils such as those found in eastern North America prevent the preservation of bone, most of the evidence of bone tools comes from west of the Mississippi. Clovis stone tools were made of fine-grained rock that came from widely separated rock outcrops. Stone-tool making started at these outcrops with the manufacture of cores called *bifaces*, large lithic pieces that were sharpened on both sides. Away from the quarry these bifacial artifact blanks could be efficiently made into a variety of smaller tools. Unmodified, the bifaces could also be used as heavy butchery knives and choppers when needed. They were constantly flaked as butchery proceeded, and the stone flakes that were struck off were also used as convenient sharp-edged tools for woodworking or for butchering animals. Clovis bone artifacts found at western sites with good organic preservation include cylindrical rod segments, points, a mammoth-bone shaft wrench, and rib sections with rounded and polished ends.

Within a few hundred years of the initial date of the Clovis culture, Paleo-Indian groups occupied most of North America and adapted to a wide variety of local environments. They also developed regional variations in the subsistence resources they utilized and the artifacts they created while at the same time maintaining similarities to the general Clovis tool kit. In the Great Plains region, the Southwest, and the Far West, Clovis was followed within a hundred years by the Folsom culture, which lasted until between 10,500 and 10,000 years ago. That culture's distinctive stone tool was thin, and fluted almost the whole length of the blade through the removal of a single flake. Most of the archaeological information we have about the Folsom people comes from kill sites. These are more abundant and larger than Clovis sites. Some, such as the Lindenmeier site in Colorado, were probably visited by a number of groups on a regular basis, indicating that Folsom groups aggregated periodically to conduct communal bison hunts.

After Folsom, western Paleo-Indian cultural complexes are defined by several different unfluted point styles. In the high plains region these include the Agate Basin, Hell Gap, Alberta, and Cody styles. It has been suggested that this proliferation of stylistic types is the result of there having been, after 10,000 years ago, several different Paleo-Indian groups in the foothills and mountains of this region that used different food resources than did groups on the Great Plains. Those on the Great Plains hunted mainly bison, whereas the groups in the foothills and mountains were generalized foragers, utilizing both plant and small-mammal resources. An alternative explanation for these stylistic differences is that they are the result not of diverging subsistence economies but of the number of times the stone tools were resharpened and reused.

In the East there is a great deal of debate about whether there was any Paleo-Indian occupation after Clovis. Although Folsom-like points have been found in the Great Lakes region, none are known from the Atlantic regions of North America. In the Northeast a number of fluted styles have been identified as occurring during the Paleo-Indian period. By 10,000 years ago, fluted tools had been replaced by unfluted lanceolate styles. This occurred first in the Deep South and later in the far Northeast. As with the later Paleo-Indian material from west of the Mississippi, changes in point forms over time could be the result of evolving cultural differences produced by the localization of subsistence economies. It has also been suggested that these stylistic differences, rather than being representative of different cultural groups, are instead the result of individuals making their own tools. This implies that during Clovis times some members of a group specialized in craft production, supplying the rest of the group with fluted tools.

Virtually all the first Paleo-Indian sites investigated by archaeologists were initially assumed to be kill sites, with Clovis subsistence being associated with mammoths, horses, and camels, and Folsom subsistence with bison. This early focus on kill sites led researchers to conclude that western Paleo-Indians were primarily big-game hunters. With the discovery that Clovis-like fluted stone tools, and associated tool kits, had been distributed over much of North America within a few hundred years, a continent-wide Paleo-Indian subsistence and settlement pattern was suggested, based on Clovis groups specializing in the efficient hunting of big game.

Recent research has questioned this model of Clovis people. Doubts regarding the big-game specialization of Clovis culture emerged because the data examined comes only from Clovis sites of the Great Plains, where the bones of large mammals were the initial focus of interest. Ethnographic and historic accounts of hunting groups show that this sort of specialization can occur only in species-poor environments where at least one species exists in large herds, such as the caribou of the Arctic or the bison of the Great Plains. Because this was not the case in North America eleven thousand years ago, other evidence of Clovis hunting practices was probably missed. Current archaeological field-research strategies at more recently discovered Clovis-age sites have been directed toward detecting and recovering evidence of plants and small mammals that might also have been included in the diet of Clovis people. These studies suggest that Clovis groups were generalized foragers rather than specialized hunters. For example, sites in Texas have yielded evidence not only for the exploitation of large mammals such as mammoths, bison, horses, and camels, but also for the hunting of coyote, bear, rabbits, turkeys, muskrats, ducks, geese, and several species of turtle.

Archaeologists have also reexamined the material evidence from western Clovis sites that were excavated earlier. Some of these classic sites show evidence of animals having been wounded by fluted materials but contain no small flakes that would indicate that these animals had been butchered. Therefore, these sites may result from unsuccessful kills in which wounded animals escaped and died undiscovered by their human pursuers. Still other sites, where butchering is evident, cannot automatically be considered as kill sites. They may also have resulted from opportunistic or systematic scavenging by human groups.

It is also evident that by focusing on western Clovis sites, where grinding stones and other plant-processing tools are rare, archaeologists have exhibited a bias against acknowledging the role of plants in Paleo-Indian diets. On sites east of the Mississippi, where the preservation of organic materials is generally poor because of highly acidic soils, Paleo-Indian sites have been found that contain unmodified stone cobbles that were probably used for grinding and pounding plant products.

This new evidence, together with the reinterpretation of evidence from earlier sites, indicates that although Clovis people opportunistically hunted or scavenged big game when it was available, for the most part they probably hunted and used a broad spectrum of other animal species. It was not until the Folsom culture of the Great Plains, when drier conditions increased the area of the grasslands and the size of bison herds, that big-game specialization was feasible.

See also Arrowheads.

Fagan, Brian M., *Ancient North America: The Archaeology of a Continent,* 2d ed. (New York: Thames and Hudson, 1995); Kopper, Philip, *The Smithsonian Book of North American Indians: Before the Coming of the Europeans* (Washington, D.C.: Smithsonian Books, 1986).

JOHN A. K. WILLIS
Northwestern University

PAN-INDIAN ORGANIZATIONS

The roots of modern Pan-Indian organizations lie in the eighteenth century in the eastern United States in what was still English colonial America. Pontiac, an Ottawa leader, attempted to create an intertribal league to resist the continued invasions of the English. His political and military vision was combined with the religious vision of the Delaware prophet Neolin, who promised the return of Indian lands by supernatural means if native people who joined the league observed a set of ethical standards that represented a mixture of Indian and Christian beliefs. Pontiac's vision, which foresaw an intertribal league committed to a program of both individual and societal reform in defense of Indian interests, was to be repeated several times during the following centuries.

In the early nineteenth century Tecumseh and his brother Tenskwatawa, also called the Shawnee Prophet, created an alliance from a number of northeastern and midwestern tribes. Tecumseh traveled widely and built a large following, but his influence was shattered when Tenskwatawa, against his brother's orders, fought William Henry Harrison at Tippecanoe and was soundly defeated. In the aftermath of that defeat the intertribal confederacy unraveled.

In the late nineteenth century two movements set the stage for the development of modern Pan-Indian organizations. The first was the attempt by tribes in Indian Territory (Oklahoma) to create an Indian state. These tribes had been relocated from the eastern and southern states to what had been described as the last refuge for Indian sovereignty, and by 1887 some were hoping that the next logical step would be a Pan-Indian commonwealth with "one common government, with common laws, officials, and institutions." Unfortunately, non-Indian economic and political forces were able to force a different future for the Oklahoma tribes.

The second movement was the Ghost Dance of the late 1880s, which attracted Native Americans with its prophecy of the restoration of an Indian world and the disappearance of whites. Wovoka's original message was pacifistic, but it was reinterpreted among the Lakotas to include power that rendered them bulletproof. This interpretation proved tragically wrong at Wounded Knee. When the new age did not come, the movement quickly died or was transformed into a less ambitious ritual. But the Ghost Dance and the human suffering that spawned it paved the way for the modern Pan-Indian organizations that developed in the twentieth century.

Pan-Indian political development was facilitated by access to mass transportation (the train and the automobile), literacy in native languages and English, mass communication (mail service and newspapers), off-reservation Indian boarding schools, and education. By

1887 there were nine nonreservation boarding schools with intertribal student bodies. The educational philosophy at some of the boarding schools deliberately fostered a nationalized Indian identity, as articulated in the 1908 annual report of the Carlisle Indian Industrial School: "The plan of mixing the tribes at Carlisle results in nationalizing the Indian."

Graduates of these schools formed prototypes of the modern Pan-Indian organization. (Some of these original bodies are still active today.) An increasing number of formally educated Indians found employment in the Bureau of Indian Affairs or in the ministry, but many still felt excluded from the American mainstream. All of them were Christian and had varying degrees of sympathy for native religions. None of them considered the restoration of an exclusive Indian world possible or even desirable, but looked to secure for Native Americans the rights held by other citizens. They were all familiar with the tragedy at Wounded Knee, and one of them, Charles Eastman, had been the attending physician at Pine Ridge at the time of the massacre. They were also aware of the attempt to establish an Indian state in Oklahoma, and some of them were from Oklahoma tribes. The organizations they created sought societal reform through political means, not supernatural acts of a divine will.

The Society of American Indians was established in 1911 to promote a broad vision of the future welfare of Indian people. The organizational goals emphasized the importance of education and the need to monitor all legislation that might have a negative impact on native interests. The leadership was drawn from the ranks of educated, middle-class Indians, and the structure was typical of American voluntary organizations, with elected officers, committees, by-laws, and a statement of purpose. It created an intertribal forum for serious discussion about Indian issues by Indians themselves, and extended that forum by publishing a journal. For a short period it supported a settlement-house experiment, the prototype of what later became the urban Indian center. The society was united on the goals of better education and securing American citizenship for Indian people, but was at odds over other issues, which ultimately led to its demise in 1924, the same year in which the Indian Citizenship Act was passed by Congress. The society provided a valuable experience for members of the urban Indian middle class, who were its principle membership and most of whom were active in subsequent Pan-Indian organizations that pursued social justice for Native Americans.

Pan-Indian religious movements found it desirable to formally organize themselves under American civil law as a protective measure against attacks by others and as a means of gaining the same legal status as that enjoyed by Christian churches. Initially, these movements were primarily reservation based. The first to establish itself as a legal entity under state law was the Indian Shaker Church of Washington, which incorporated in 1910 in order to gain "the respect and protection due them as a religious congregation." The second to seek such protection was the Native American Church of Oklahoma, which filed incorporation papers in 1918. The sacramental use of peyote by the members of the Native American Church was threatened by the possibility of federal legislation making it illegal. The issue was divisive among the Indian middle class, with supporters on both sides of the argument. Ultimately the attempt to pass federal laws failed, but the Native American Church nevertheless continued to legally incorporate new congregations as a protective measure. The Native American Church has gained followers throughout the twentieth century and now has congregations all over the country. It is the largest and most successful Pan-Indian religion of the century.

Without a doubt the most important and enduring Pan-Indian organization of the twentieth century is the National Congress of American Indians, established in 1944 and dedicated to a broad social agenda and a tribal rather than urban focus. Building upon the political support of New Dealers who championed tribal economic and cultural development, the founders of the National Congress emphasized education, legal aid, national legislation, and job training. The NCAI seeks to "confine itself to the broad problems confronting the total Indian population or large segments of it" and to attract a wide spectrum of Indian and non-Indian individuals and groups to its activities. Many of its leaders are middle-class, educated Indians, a group that has grown much larger in the late twentieth century because of the increase in educational opportunities for Indian people. The organization has been involved with every major Indian issue since its founding, and continues to play a pivotal role in national native politics.

The Bureau of Indian Affairs Relocation Program of the 1950s and 1960s created large urban Indian communities where few had existed before. Urban Indian centers, which provide a mix of social services and sociability, emerged in every relocation town in the United States. The centers became the first destination for many Indians new to an area and generally became community/self-help/counseling/social centers for many urban natives. Some of these centers are now thirty-five years old and have nurtured a generation of urban Indians. For many young people the intertribal center provides the only cultural milieu in which they can acquire an Indian identity.

The diffusion of the intertribal powwow created organizations that have provided people with opportunities for socializing with other Indians. These groups number in the thousands and tend to be short-lived, but are ubiquitous throughout urban Indian America. In any sizable urban community there will be several of these groups, which meet regularly and serve as an important outlet for Indians who wish to socialize within an intertribal context.

Beginning in the 1960s there was a dramatic increase in the number of intertribal Indian organizations that focused on particular shared concerns or were regional in focus. The National Indian Youth Council was established in 1961 to serve as a political arm for native youth, many of them college students. The organization was more militant than the NCAI and supported activities such as sit-ins and fish-ins, which were considered too extreme by some of the older leaders. United Native Americans was established in California in about 1967 to be an activist organization on behalf of both urban and reservation Indians. Many of its first members were Indian college students in the San Francisco Bay area. Although the organization had national ambitions, it was quickly overshadowed by the American Indian Movement (AIM), established in Minneapolis in 1968. AIM began as a community group committed to the welfare of urban Indians living in the Minneapolis/St. Paul area but rapidly became the most visible radical Indian organization in the country during a period of ethnic struggle and activism. A few examples of organizations that can be considered regional, professional, or special-interest groups are the National Indian Education Association (1970), the Native American Rights Fund (1970), the American Indian Registry for the Performing Arts (1983), the American Indian Law Students Association (1967), the Alaska Federation of Natives (1966), American Indian Scholarships (1969), the American Indian Science and Engineering Society (1977), Americans for Indian Opportunity (1970), and the Association of American Indian Physicians (1971). The number and range of these voluntary organizations are proof of a mature Pan-Indian commu-

nity with a wide range of interests that are best addressed in specialized associations.

See also American Indian Movement (AIM); Indian-White Relations in the United States, 1900 to the Present; National Congress of American Indians; Native American Church; Pontiac; Reformers and Reform Groups.

Cornell, Stephen E., *The Return of the Native: American Indian Political Resurgence* (New York: Oxford University Press, 1988); Hertzberg, Hazel, *The Search for an American Indian Identity: Modern Pan-Indian Movements* (Syracuse, N.Y.: Syracuse University Press, 1971).

JoAllyn Archambault (Standing Rock Sioux)
National Museum of Natural History
Smithsonian Institution

PAPAGO
See Tohono O'odham (Papago).

PARKER, ARTHUR C.
(1881–1955)
Seneca anthropologist, ethnologist, and archaeologist.

Arthur Caswell Parker was born into a powerful Seneca family on April 5, 1881, on the Cattaraugus Reservation in western New York. He was the son of Frederick Ely Parker and Geneva Griswold, a white woman who taught school on the same reservation. His paternal grandfather was Nicholas H. Parker, an influential leader of the Seneca Nation who had served as secretary to the nation and as an interpreter for the New York subagency. Nicholas's brother, Ely Parker, was a brigadier general and a military secretary to Ulysses Grant during the Civil War, and later the first Indian Commissioner of Indian Affairs. Arthur Parker lived on his grandfather Nicholas's farm, and it was Nicholas Parker who, by all accounts, was the most influential figure during his grandson's formative years.

Parker spent those years moving easily between the Seneca society of his father and the white missionary relatives of his mother. Though the Parker family was Christian, its members maintained close ties with the followers of Handsome Lake, the Seneca prophet who revitalized traditional Seneca religion around the turn of the nineteenth century.

Parker began his schooling on the reservation, but in 1892 the family moved to White Plains, where Parker entered public school. After graduating from high school in 1897, Parker was undecided about his future. He delayed going to college for two years. Eventually, however, his grandfather and the reservation minister, Asher Wright, persuaded him to enroll at Dickinson Seminary in Williamsport, Pennsylvania. He studied at Dickinson from 1900 to 1903, but left before graduation. After a short stint as a reporter, Parker decided on a career in anthropology.

How Parker came to be an anthropologist is instructive. In the years after his high school graduation and before entering the seminary, he spent many hours at the American Museum of Natural History in New York City. There he became acquainted with Frederick W. Putnam, the temporary curator of anthropology at the museum and a professor of anthropology at Harvard. It was the beginning of a long friendship, with Putnam serving as guide and mentor to the young Seneca.

Parker was also befriended by Harriet Maxwell Converse, a journalist and poet who had a special interest in anthropology. She introduced him to Frank Speck, and through Speck he met Franz Boas. Boas urged Parker to enter Columbia University's newly established anthropology program, but Parker chose Dickinson instead. While Parker was still at Dickinson, Putnam arranged for him to apprentice with the archaeologist Mark Harrington, with whom he spent two summers (1903–4) working on sites in New York State. When not digging, he worked as a reporter for the *New York Sun* and volunteered his spare time at the museum.

Arthur Parker's break came in 1904, when he was hired on a temporary basis to collect data on the Iroquois in New York State. For the next two years he collected items of material culture, folklore, speeches, and stories, as well as conducting his first archaeological research. So successful was Parker that in 1906 he was offered the newly created position of archaeologist at the New York State Museum. He promptly accepted. The position had its drawbacks, however. Parker was required to spend most of his time on archaeological projects and exhibitions. His promising career as an ethnologist was thus brought to an abrupt end.

Parker's interests extended well beyond academic research. In 1911 he joined with Charles A. Eastman and others to found the Society of American Indians, a Pan-Indian organization dedicated to educating the general public about American Indians. In 1915 he took over the editorship of its journal, the *American Indian Mag-*

azine, a post he held for the next five years. The nation's entry into World War I led to a split in the organization. For his part, Parker saw American Indian participation in the war as a means of advancing the acceptance of the Indian into American society. The young museum official was a strong supporter of the melting-pot ideal and a defender of Lewis Henry Morgan's unilinear model of social evolution. But other Indian leaders, largely western and more iconoclastic then the scholarly Seneca, opposed him. People like Carlos Montezuma believed that since Indians were not citizens, they should not become involved in another nation's war. Parker also rejected Franz Boas's cultural relativism because he feared it would place more emphasis on the aboriginal aspects of Indian life than on the monumental adjustments Indians were undergoing. In the end, however, he became disenchanted with politics and pessimistic about assimilation. In the early 1920s he returned to archaeology and museology.

For the next nineteen years Parker labored at the museum, conducting archaeological research when time allowed, but he never returned to ethnology. Much of his time was spent in the bureaucratic minutiae that seemed never to end or allow him to return to his central interest: the study of the Iroquois. In 1925 he joined the Rochester Museum of Arts and Sciences as director.

Parker retired from the Rochester museum in 1946 to continue his writing and renew his involvement in national Indian affairs, particularly the National Congress of American Indians, which he had helped to found in 1944. He died on January 1, 1955, at the age of seventy-three.

Parker was a man pulled by two distinct cultures. Able to move easily in each, he was never fully accepted by either. His connection to the matrilineal Seneca Nation was through his father's side; he was a Christian even though the things he admired and sought to understand in the Seneca world were held and protected by the followers of Handsome Lake. He entered the museum world just at the time when basic research was shifting to the university. Although an excellent researcher, he sorely felt the lack of a doctorate and was never quite accorded the status he deserved.

It is surprising that in the course of a career that spanned more than fifty years, all of his ethnographic research was confined to the years 1905 to 1913. His contributions included *Iroquois Uses of Maize and Other Food Plants* (1910), *The Code of Handsome Lake, the Seneca Prophet* (1913), *The Constitution of* the Five Nations (1916), and *The Archaeological History of New York* (1922), all published by the New York State Museum. In addition, he wrote over 250 articles and several books for children.

Of possibly equal importance was Parker's encouragement of Iroquois craftsmen and artisans. While still with the New York State Museum, he collected the works of many, including the drawings of the talented Seneca artist Jesse Cornplanter, the son of Chief Edward Cornplanter, who had provided Parker with the "Code of Handsome Lake" (his teachings). In the 1930s, Parker was active in the efforts of the Works Progress Administration to recruit and finance Iroquois artists. Perhaps his most lasting contribution, however, was to the Rochester Museum, whose collection of Iroquois material was assembled in large part through Parker's energy, support, knowledge, and foresight.

See also Cayuga; Handsome Lake; Iroquois Confederacy; National Congress of American Indians; Seneca.

Fenton, William N., introduction to *Parker on the Iroquois*, ed. William N. Fenton (Syracuse, N.Y.: University of Syracuse Press, 1968); Hertzberg, Hazel Whitman, "Nationality, Anthropology and Pan-Indianism in the Life of Arthur C. Parker (Seneca)," *Proceedings of the American Philosophical Society* 123, no.1 (1979): 47–72.

JACK CAMPISI
Wellesley College

PARKER, ELY S. (DO-NE-HO-GA-WA)

(1828–95)
Seneca sachem, military secretary to General Ulysses S. Grant, and Commissioner of Indian Affairs.

Born into a leading Seneca family and steeped in the history and lore of the Iroquois Confederacy, Ely Samuel Parker was also well educated in the white world in which he finally chose to live. Through his friendship with Ulysses S. Grant, he became the general's military secretary. In 1865 he transcribed the terms of surrender Grant offered General Robert E. Lee at Appomattox Courthouse. When Grant became president, he appointed Parker Commissioner of Indian Affairs, making him the first Indian to hold that office.

Parker's parents, William Parker (Jo-no-es-sto-wa) and Elizabeth Parker (Ga-ont-gwut-twus), lived on the Tonawanda Reservation in western New York State. William, a veteran of the War of 1812 and a chief of

the Tonawanda Senecas, had taken the name Parker from a British officer who had been adopted by the Indians. Elizabeth was a descendant of the prophet Handsome Lake and a grandniece of the Seneca orator Red Jacket. Ely Parker, one of their seven children, was born on the Tonawanda Reservation sometime in 1828 and was given the name Ha-sa-no-an-da (Leading Name), but when he attended the nearby Baptist mission school, he also acquired the name Ely (which he pronounced to rhyme with *freely*). He continued his education in western New York State, attending Yates Academy in Orleans County and Cayuga Academy in Aurora and then reading law with attorneys in Ellicottville. When he was refused admission to the New York bar because he was not a citizen, Parker turned to engineering, learning that profession by working on the New York canals.

During the course of his education, Parker also represented the Tonawanda Senecas in Albany, New York, and Washington, D.C., in a dispute with the Ogden Land Company. At the age of eighteen, Parker met personally with President James K. Polk and later boasted that he had ridden about Washington in Mrs. Polk's carriage. He also met with Presidents Franklin Pierce and James Buchanan and in 1857 helped negotiate a treaty that preserved most of the Tonawanda Reservation for the Senecas.

In 1851, Parker was elected one of the fifty sachems of the Iroquois Confederacy and was given the title Do-ne-ho-ga-wa (Open Door), the keeper of the western door of the Iroquois longhouse. Intelligent, articulate, and well versed in both Iroquois and white cultures, Parker became a valuable informant for Henry Rowe Schoolcraft and Lewis Henry Morgan in their studies of the Iroquois. When Morgan published his pioneering *League of the Ho-de-no-sau-nee, or Iroquois*, he dedicated the book to Parker, calling it "the fruit of our joint researches."

Parker's engineering skills led to positions with the New York State Canal Board, the Chesapeake and Albemarle Ship Canal in Virginia and North Carolina, and the U.S. Treasury Department in Detroit, Michigan; Galena, Illinois; and Dubuque, Iowa. At Galena, he met Ulysses S. Grant, who, during the Civil War, appointed Parker to his personal military staff. Parker remained on Grant's staff after the war, eventually reaching the rank of brevet brigadier general. He also served on two commissions to the western Indian tribes and assisted the Commissioner of Indian Affairs before his own appointment as commissioner in 1869.

As commissioner, Parker was responsible for the federal government's relations with the almost three hundred thousand Indians living in the United States and its territories. During the Grant administration the government dealt with the various Indian tribes through agents that were nominated by religious bodies. This departure, known as "Grant's Peace Policy," was intended to intensify the effort to "civilize" native people. The theory was to gather Indians onto reservations, where they could be introduced to "agriculture, to manufactures, and civilization," and to use military force on all who resisted. Parker, himself a military man, fully concurred with this approach. Working with religious bodies as well as the military, Grant and Parker hoped for justice and peace in Indian affairs.

Parker regarded his two years as commissioner as successful, particularly in preventing war with the western tribes, but his service as commissioner was clouded by controversy. The Episcopal reformer William Welsh soon brought charges of corruption against Parker, inspiring a congressional investigation. The investigating committee cleared Parker of wrongdoing but did question his judgment, and when, on the committee's recommendation, Congress passed a law limiting the commissioner's authority, Parker resigned and left Washington.

Parker retired to Fairfield, Connecticut, where he entered the business world. Business losses, however, forced him to take a minor clerical position with the New York City Police Department, a post he held for nineteen years. During his years in New York City, Parker was occasionally called upon for information about the Iroquois or to speak at major events such as the reinterment of Red Jacket's remains and a commemoration of the Delaware chief Tammany. Parker died on August 30, 1895. He was buried in Fairfield, but in 1897 his body was reinterred in Forest Lawn Cemetery in Buffalo, New York.

Physically, Parker was a strong person; he stood five feet eight inches tall and weighed two hundred pounds. He found it necessary to use his strength occasionally to defend himself against those who resented his living in white society. In personal relations, he was usually silent and reserved, although he could be assertive in public speaking or writing and was well read and exceptionally knowledgeable. Parker was active in Freemasonry and, after the Civil War, in various veterans' organizations.

In 1867, he married a younger white woman, Minnie Orton Sackett (1849–1932). The couple had one

Ely S. Parker, Seneca sachem, wearing the medal he inherited from his ancestor Red Jacket. The photograph was taken in 1855 in Elmira, New York.

daughter, Maud Theresa (1878–1956). In his later years, Parker questioned whether he had been right in abandoning his Indian heritage. Yet, had he stayed on the Tonawanda Reservation, his remarkable abilities would almost certainly have been little known, whereas his successful career in the white world demonstrated those abilities to the entire nation.

See also Indian-White Relations in the United States, 1776–1900; Peace Policy; Reformers and Reform Groups.

Armstrong, William H., *Warrior in Two Camps: Ely S. Parker, Union General and Seneca Chief* (Syracuse, N.Y.: Syracuse University Press, 1978); Parker, Arthur C., *The Life of General Ely S.*

Parker, Last Grand Sachem of the Iroquois and General Grant's Military Secretary, Publications of the Buffalo Historical Society, vol. 23 (Buffalo, N.Y., 1919).

WILLIAM H. ARMSTRONG
Burton Congregational Church
United Church of Christ
Burton, Ohio

PARKER, QUANAH

(1853?–1911)
Comanche political and religious leader.

Quanah was the only Comanche ever recognized by the U.S. government with the title "The Chief of the Comanche Indians." The son of Cynthia Ann Parker, a white captive who was taken by the Comanches in a raid on the Texas frontier in 1836, and Nocona, a Comanche warrior who died in the 1860s, Quanah (the name means "odor" or "fragrance") had two siblings: a sister, who was with their mother when she was recaptured in 1861 (both mother and daughter died within a few years), and a brother, who died before reaching manhood.

Very little is known about Quanah's prereservation life, a topic he rarely discussed with non-Indians. But by 1875 he had acquired sufficient stature to speak in band councils. In that year his band, the Quahadas, accepted defeat, and the white man who negotiated the surrender described Quanah as "a young man of much influence with his people." Quanah could have earned such stature only in the Comanche way: by distinguishing himself as a hunter and fighter. It was, however, as a political leader on the reservation that the Comanches shared with the Kiowas and Kiowa Apaches that he earned his place in history.

After the 1875 surrender, Quanah made clear his intention of walking the white man's road. He was very conscious of being of mixed blood and was eager to succeed in his changing environment without surrendering all that was traditionally Comanche. He quickly earned the approval of the reservation's Federal Indian agent who made him a band chief. That agent's successors also recognized the value of supporting a chief willing to lead his people into a new life, appointing him a judgeship on the reservation's Court of Indian Offenses. While acting as a middleman, Quanah kept many of his people's ways, wearing long hair and engaging in polygamy. In fact, he had a total of eight wives, five of them at one time, and this despite government efforts to enforce monogamy among his band. Although local agents attempted to defend him, federal authorities ultimately removed Quanah from his judgeship because of his refusal to conform to the government's expectations.

Agents were also willing to ignore the fact that this usually reliable ally of theirs was a leader in the growing peyote cult. Indeed, Quanah was the principal road man (peyote ceremony leader) among the Comanches and had a major role in the diffusion of the cult across the South Plains.

Quanah's native intelligence and leadership abilities attracted the attention of Texas cattlemen wishing to lease grazing land on the reservation. The Comanches, who occupied the portion of the reservation closest to Texas, were the most likely to be wooed by the neighboring cattlemen. Most Kiowa and Kiowa Apache chiefs opposed leasing the land, as did the government, although nearly two-thirds of the 3-million-acre reservation was underutilized. Quanah became the leading Indian advocate of leasing, speaking on its behalf in reservation councils and in Washington, D.C., which he visited from time to time. He reasoned, correctly, that Indians would benefit from the income from the pasture leases.

Quanah and other chiefs were paid by the cattlemen for their support of leasing and for the protection that they could provide vulnerable herds. Quanah's compensation was the largest, and the lessees helped him build Star House, his impressive ten-room home. They also presented him with a diamond brooch and an ivory-handled revolver, and provided junkets to Fort Worth and hunting trips to West Texas.

While most Comanches failed to take advantage of what economic opportunities there were, Quanah showed remarkable aptitude in following the example of the enterprising white men with whom he dealt. He monopolized some forty-thousand acres of the reservation, pasturing a herd of several hundred horses and cattle there and renting out the rest to white stockmen. He also sold cattle to the government, for use in providing the beef component in Indian rations.

When the government began a campaign in the early 1890s to change the system by which the Indians held property—from one of common ownership to a system of allotment in severalty—Quanah sought to delay the process. He argued that the Indians needed at least another decade to prepare themselves for the responsibilities of private ownership. Nevertheless, in 1892 the

Jerome Commission coerced the three tribes on the reservation into accepting an agreement providing for allotment and the sale of the remaining land, about two-thirds of the reservation, to the United States. During the negotiations Quanah was the only chief to demonstrate any bargaining ability. He asked searching questions about terms and pressed the evasive commissioners for answers. Quanah realized, however, that the most the Indians could hope for was to get the best terms possible and then delay the agreement's implementation. With the aid of eastern friends of the Indians and cattlemen trying to retain their leases, Quanah and his allies were able to postpone ratification of the agreement until 1900, and then on terms slightly more acceptable to the Indians.

When Congress finally acted, Quanah found his position drastically altered. He lost his income from the cattlemen and from the thousands of acres of communally held land that he had exploited. His own 160-acre allotment was only marginally productive, and the

Federal Indian agent had to find Quanah a low-paying agency position to enable him to discharge his responsibilities as chief.

Although Quanah was plagued with financial problems in his final years, his celebrity continued to grow. Communities in Oklahoma and Texas were happy to have him lead their parades mounted on a fine horse and wearing a feathered war bonnet. Visitors to the area, including Britain's ambassador, James Bryce, sought out the chief. Quanah also testified on behalf of the peyote cult before state committees. And in 190 he was one of five chiefs chosen to ride in Theodore Roosevelt's inaugural parade. When the president later visited Oklahoma, he singled out Quanah for special attention. Meanwhile, the chief had finally been able to establish contact with his white relatives in Texas, and he secured federal funds to move the remains of his mother to Oklahoma. Quanah spoke at her interment, advising his people to "follow after white way, get education, know work, make living."

The Indian agents continued to depend heavily on Quanah. To the end, he demonstrated the qualities that had led a federal investigator to declare, "Quanah would have been a leader and a governor in any circle where fate might have cast him."

When he died in 1911 two of his wives, To-nar-cy and To-pay, were with him; he was survived by sixteen of his twenty-four children. His funeral was the largest ever witnessed in the part of Oklahoma in which he had lived.

See also Comanche.

Hacker, Margaret Schmidt, *Cynthia Ann Parker* (El Paso: Texas Western Press, 1990); Hagan, William T., *Quanah Parker, Comanche Chief* (Norman: University of Oklahoma Press, 1993).

WILLIAM T. HAGAN
University of Oklahoma

The Comanche chief Quanah Parker and To-nar-cy, one of his wives, circa 1905.

PASSAMAQUODDY/PENOBSCOT

The Passamaquoddy and Penobscot Indians are the descendants of Native American peoples who inhabited Maine and western New Brunswick since well before recorded history. Traditionally they lived most of the year in family band camps that relocated on a seasonal basis, relying upon hunting, fishing, and gathering for their subsistence needs. They maintained a very fluid social organization based on patrilineal kinship that allowed multiple marriage and residence options, frequent migration, and easy division or merging of social groups. Both groups speak closely related Algonquian languages, although anthropologists generally group the Passamaquoddies linguistically with the Maliseets and the Penobscots with the Abenakis. These kinship groups were never organized as tribes during the colonial period, but English officials perceived them as such and identified them by their geographical locations. The "Passamaquoddy and Penobscot tribes" have therefore continued as entities as jurisdiction over them has passed from Massachusetts to Maine to the federal government. Currently, most Penobscots reside on Indian Island in the Penobscot River, while the Passamaquoddies are divided between two principal locations: Pleasant Point on Passamaquoddy Bay, and Indian Township near the St. Croix River.

The Passamaquoddy and Penobscot Indians were among the first Native Americans to have contact with Europeans. The wide bays along the Maine coast attracted the attention of fishermen and explorers searching for a sea route through the continent as early as the sixteenth century. Some of these first encounters were friendly, such as Samuel de Champlain's exploration and settlement of the area in 1604, while others, such as Henry Hudson's bombardment and looting of a village on the Penobscot River in 1609, were not. Instead of finding the mythical city of Norumbega, reputed to be rich in gold, silver, and pearls, these Europeans encountered an Indian confederacy consisting of twenty-two villages throughout western and central Maine controlled by Bessabez (Bashaba) from his village on the Penobscot River. A series of attacks by Micmacs in 1615 resulted in the death of Bessabez and the collapse of his confederacy, but even greater devastation stemmed from a terrible pandemic in 1617 that wiped out over 75 percent of the inhabitants along the New England coast. The surviving Passamaquoddies and Penobscots traded furs with competing English and French traders until the French established dominance in the area in the 1630s. The growing dependence of these Indians on trade goods resulted in their involvement in the so-called Beaver Wars with the Iroquois in the 1640s, 1650s, and 1660s, but peaceful relations were maintained with the English until 1677, when a series of atrocities were committed against the Penobscots.

The Penobscots' and Passamaquoddies' conversion to Catholicism by French missionaries fostered friendly relations with French officials during the colonial period, and these ties were strengthened by intermarriages,

the most famous being that between Baron St.-Castin and Pidiwamiska, a daughter of the Penobscot chief Madockawando, but the degree of French control has been exaggerated. Each of the five wars that occurred on the Maine frontier between 1689 and 1760 resulted from a combination of English insistence on sovereignty over the Indians, disputes concerning subsistence or land, and indiscriminate mutual retaliation. Most of the frontier incidents that led to the first three wars occurred to the west of the Penobscots and Passamaquoddies, but these Indians were included in blanket declarations of war against all "Eastern Indians." The third conflict, Dummer's War (1722–27), resulted in a significant merging of Abenaki refugees into the Penobscot and Passamaquoddy villages and the subsequent extension of English settlements into the Penobscot area. Although plagued by factionalism, these Indians attempted to remain neutral in the last two wars, but mutual distrust, disputes over treaty commitments, and attacks by English scalp hunters in 1745 and 1755 ultimately dragged them into the conflicts.

The strategic location of the Penobscots and Passamaquoddies during the colonial wars and their remoteness from English settlement expansion enabled these Indians to maintain their autonomy and almost all of their land until 1760. In the aftermath of the Seven Years' War, the English claimed all the tribes' lands "by right of conquest" because of their alliance with the defeated French, and English settlement quickly spread along the Maine coast. During the Revolutionary War, the Penobscots and Passamaquoddies helped the Americans defend their eastern frontier, but the Indians' loss of land continued, with large cessions by the Passamaquoddies in 1794 and by the Penobscots in 1796, 1818, and 1833. First Massachusetts, and then Maine after 1820, acquired this land and administered the affairs of these Indians by right of colonial precedent, ignoring federal law and the initial protests of federal leaders. During the 1820s, 1830s, and 1840s, the Penobscots and Passamaquoddies divided along kinship lines, producing two political groups: the Old Party and the New Party. Emotional disputes over education and traditional lifetime chiefs resulted in the collapse of tribal government, the imposition of state compromises, and a dramatic increase in state control over the Indians, which was not relinquished when tribal factionalism waned after 1860.

For the next century, a state agent handled Indian affairs in accordance with the Indian laws in the state legal code, and state policy was predicated on the assumption that the tribes would gradually disintegrate as individuals left the reservations. Tribal councils were not recognized, tribal governors were rarely consulted, and tribal decisions were thwarted. Additional land was lost as the state legislature reinterpreted treaties or granted long-term leases to non-Indians. Maine was the last state to grant reservation Indians the right to vote (1954), yet, since 1823 and 1842, respectively, the Penobscots and Passamaquoddies have each had a non-voting representative in the state legislature to articulate their concerns. These individuals, along with tribal activists, ultimately reversed state policy by thwarting termination of the tribes in 1957, gradually increasing tribal authority in the 1960s, and prompting the creation of the first state Department of Indian Affairs in 1965. In the late 1960s, the Passamaquoddies and Penobscots initiated the Maine Indian Land Claims suit, claiming that the land cessions to Massachusetts and Maine had violated the Indian Nonintercourse Act of 1790. Several favorable court rulings prompted an $81.5-million settlement in 1980, which has enabled the tribes to buy land, develop tribal businesses, employ tribe members, and foster both goodwill and profits by providing investment capital to non-Indians. This legal precedent has provided the foundation for land claims by a number of other eastern tribes.

Brodeur, Paul, *Restitution: The Land Claims of the Mashpee, Passamaquoddy and Penobscot Indians of New England* (Boston: Northeastern University Press, 1985); Ghere, David, "Abenaki Factionalism, Emigration and Social Continuity in Northern New England, 1725–1765" (Ph.D. diss., University of Maine, 1988); Morrison, Kenneth M., *The Embattled Northeast: The Elusive Ideal of Alliance in Abenaki-Euramerican Relations* (Berkeley: University of California Press, 1984).

DAVID L. GHERE
University of Minnesota

PAWHUSKA (WHITE HAIR)
Series of Osage leaders.

For one hundred years, from 1794 until 1894, the northern bands of the Osages, known as the Big Osages, were led by individuals known as Pawhuska or by the English version of the name, White Hair. A Pawhuska signed the first treaty between the Osages and the United States in 1808, and in all eight treaties that followed a Pawhuska (sometimes spelled Papuisea, Pa-hek-saw, Pa-hu-sha, or Pa-hu-sca) or White Hair participated in the treaty negotiations and signed all of

the treaties as leader of the Big Osages. The first Pawhuska began leading the Big Osages in the 1790s, and after his death in 1809, his personal name became the tribal name for the hereditary leader of the Big Osages. Thereafter, all of the hereditary Big Osage leaders took the name Pawhuska until the death of the last leader in 1894. One of the village sites on the Osage Reservation was named after this man, and today this town, Pawhuska, Oklahoma, is the home of the tribal government of the Osage people. While there were at least six Pawhuskas, the first two were the most important, for they led the Big Osages in the critical first years of the nineteenth century, a crucial time for the Osage people.

The early Osages all lived together along the upper Osage River. In the 1690s a group of Osages moved away from the Osage River and settled along the Missouri River. In the 1760s another group of Osages moved to the Three Forks region of the Arkansas River. Thereafter, the Osages living along the Missouri River became known as the Little Osages, the groups living together along the Osage River were known as the Big Osages, and the Osages in the Three Forks region were called the Arkansas Osages. The first Pawhuska assumed the leadership of the Big Osages in about 1797 and was their leader when the United States assumed possession of the Louisiana Territory in 1804. He met Lewis and Clark as they began their journey up the Missouri River, and he was the first of the western tribal leaders that the explorers sent to Washington to meet with President Thomas Jefferson. Pawhuska met Jefferson and pledged peace and friendship with the United States.

In the fall of 1806, when Zebulon Pike began his journey to the Southwest, Pawhuska welcomed Pike into his prairie villages and supplied the explorer with horses. In 1808 Meriwether Lewis, governor of the Louisiana Territory, angered by continued raiding and thefts by the Osages, summoned Pawhuska to Fire Prairie to meet with William Clark. During that meeting Pawhuska again promised to live in peace with the United States, and signed the first treaty between the United States and the Osage people. This treaty continued the promises of friendship between the United States and the Osages, and in return for this friendship and the construction of a trading post, the Osages ceded more than fifty thousand square miles of Osage land between the Missouri and Arkansas Rivers to the United States. Shortly thereafter, sometime in 1809, Pawhuska died.

Pawhuska was replaced by his son as leader of the northern bands of the Big Osages, and the new leader took the name Pawhuska. This second Pawhuska continued to foster close ties with the United States. During the War of 1812 Pawhuska II gathered his warriors to fight against the British and their Indian allies. These warriors traveled north to the Missouri, whereupon the Missouri governor, nervous about the presence of 250 armed Osage soldiers, sent them home. Before they left, however, Pawhuska II signed a treaty relieving the United States of the 1808 treaty obligation to maintain a trading post among the Osages.

After the war of 1812 Pawhuska II welcomed American traders to his villages and allowed them to establish trading posts at the Big Osage villages along the Osage River. He remained friendly with the United States and its agents, and in 1822 Pawhuska II welcomed the first Protestant missionaries of the American Board of Commissioners, and gave them land near the Big Osage villages for their mission station, Harmony. His friendliness was severely tested by the Protestant missionaries, who constantly urged Pawhuska II and his people to abandon their way of life and replace it with that of New England Protestants. Although Pawhuska II was always friendly with the missionaries, one season of living next to them was apparently enough for him. The next year he moved his villages south to the Neosho Valley, close to the newly established trading post of A. P. Chouteau and about three hundred miles from the missionaries.

In 1825 the U.S. government, eager to make room for the Native American people it was moving west from the Southeast, persuaded the Osages to cede most of their land, including Pawhuska II's village sites on the Neosho. Pawhuska II, representing the Big Osages, signed the land-cession treaty and moved his people north to the narrow strip of Osage land that remained.

In 1833 Pawhuska II died, and the new leader became the third Pawhuska. After the death of Pawhuska II it becomes difficult to distinguish who the Pawhuskas were, for throughout the 1830s the Osages splintered as more and more Osages left the parent groups and formed independent bands with new leadership. The new leaders continued to assume the Pawhuska title, and at times there were several individuals who claimed the name. During this period of political division, the Osages also became victims of epidemic diseases; simultaneous and repeated attacks of smallpox, cholera, and influenza ravaged the tribe. At this time the Osages were also being challenged by

powerful Native American rivals. Attacked by the Comanches, Kiowas, and Pawnees on the plains and outnumbered by the Cherokees, Chickasaws, and other eastern tribes forced onto Osage country by the U.S. removal policy, the Osages lost almost all of their land and resources. The remaining years of the nineteenth century were a harsh time for the Osages and the Pawhuskas who led them.

See also Osage.

Din, Gilbert C., and Abraham P. Nasatir, *The Imperial Osages: Spanish-Indian Diplomacy in the Mississippi Valley* (Norman: University of Oklahoma Press, 1983); Mathews, John Joseph, *The Osages: Children of the Middle Waters* (Norman: University of Oklahoma Press, 1961); Rollings, Willard H., *The Osage: An Ethnohistorical Study of Hegemony on the Prairie-Plains* (Columbia: University of Missouri Press, 1992).

WILLARD HUGHES ROLLINGS
University of Nevada, Las Vegas

PAWNEE

The Pawnees say they migrated from the south or southwest to their central Great Plains homes long before living memory, and that some came from a dark northern country, where they remained inanimate until the supreme being, Tirawahut, awoke them with lightning and thunder.

Archaeological evidence indicates that the Pawnees resided in the Central Plains region for several centuries before the historical period. Beginning in the late seventeenth century Pawnees occupied elevated river terraces and bluff sites along a fifty-mile stretch of the Loup and Platte Rivers. They lived in large earth-lodge band villages, gathered wild foods, grew corn, beans, squash, pumpkins, and other crops, and hunted the buffalo in semiannual hunts.

In 1541 the Spanish explorer Francisco Vásquez de Coronado discovered Wichita villages near the Great Bend of the Arkansas River. There he met a chief, said to be a Pawnee from Harahey, a place located north of Kansas or Nebraska. Pawnee hunters first saw horses in the late seventeenth or early eighteenth centuries. The hunters raced back to camp, eager to describe the tall, bizarre "man-beasts" they had seen—creatures with four legs, long tails, hairy faces, and clothing that gleamed like sun on the water.

During the seventeenth and eighteenth centuries Spain, France, and England endeavored to enlarge their

North American land possessions and aggrandize their influence through gifts and trade with the native inhabitants, including the Pawnees in present-day Kansas and Nebraska. Eighteenth-century maps and colonial records report the presence of four Pawnee bands as well as their varying names, locations, number of warriors, subsistence type, and amount of peltries produced. The bands—or tribes, as they called themselves—established loyalties to the different colonial powers according to each band's best interest. In September 1804, after the Louisiana Purchase, Pedro Vial journeyed from Santa Fe to a Pawnee village on the Chato (Platte) River. The village chiefs told him that they had refused American medals and patents and remained true friends of Spain.

A tribal delegation that included two Pawnees visited President Thomas Jefferson in Washington, D.C., in January 1806. Lieutenant Zebulon Pike, Major G. C. Sibley, Major S. H. Long, and other U.S. explorers and representatives soon visited Pawnee villages to begin a long series of councils, treaties, and agreements (1818, 1825, 1833, 1848, 1857, and 1892) that, while proclaiming friendship, eventually ended in Pawnee land cessions and the placement of Pawnees on reservations in Nebraska (1857) and Indian Territory (1875). Such occurrences disrupted Pawnee social, economic, and political life, introducing and forcing change as the U.S. government attempted to enforce its so-called civilization policy on Indian societies. To escape reservation life and maintain status, Pawnee warriors joined the U.S. Army Pawnee Scouts and saw action in the 1860s and 1870s in campaigns against their enemies, chiefly the Sioux and Cheyennes.

The four autonomous Pawnee bands—the Chauis, Pitahawiratas, Kitkahahkis, and Skiris (Skidis)—lived in present-day Nebraska and Kansas in band villages until 1857, when reservation residence forced band propinquity and tribal unity. Each village's socially elite class consisted of a hereditary head chief, subchiefs, leading warriors, and religious leaders who discussed and determined tribal matters concerning the hunt, warfare, important ceremony times, farm-plot assignments, solutions to interpersonal conflicts, intertribal visits, and foreign relations. Traditionally, marriage occurred between village members, and men then lived in their wife's household.

In spite of governmental control, the reservation Pawnees endeavored to maintain their tribal structure and traditions. In the early nineteenth century population estimates ranged from ten thousand to twelve thousand. By 1900, disease, warfare, and devastating reservation conditions had reduced their number to approximately six hundred. Continuous losses generated several cultural changes in leadership structure, residence patterns, and religious practices.

The complexity of Pawnee ceremonial life attracted the attention of many early scholars. Religious beliefs permeated most aspects of life. Ceremonies in warrior, curing, hunting, and other societies reinforced certain aspects of religious beliefs and practices. Sacred Bundles were paramount in a series of annual ceremonies that maintained life's balance and the tribe's relationship with the Sacred Beings dwelling in heavenly bodies and the sacred creatures and plants of Mother Earth. To continue essential rituals, and to compensate for members' deaths, various bands' religious societies joined together to fill vacant positions in their organizations. By this means, the Buffalo, Deer, Bear, Pipe (Adoption or Haku), and Doctor Dances, in which feats of magic and curing procedures astounded the observers, continued into the early twentieth century. Today, only the Young Dog Dance and the Kitkahahki War Dance are performed, intermittently, as are hand games, and Memorial Day, Christmas, and family-sponsored dances utilizing traditional clothing, rituals, and songs.

The Pawnees unsuccessfully resisted government reservation-land allotment in 1887 and the surplus reservation-land sale in 1892. Frustrated and demoralized, the Pawnees accepted the Ghost Dance and the sacramental use of peyote in the ongoing Native American Church. In the twentieth century, Christianity became accepted as older traditions disappeared. Today, two significant Pawnee events are the annual summer visits between the tribe and the Wichitas, their Caddoan linguistic kinsmen, and the four-day July Pawnee Homecoming, sponsored by the respected Pawnee Veterans' Association. Pawnees from many states return to Pawnee, Oklahoma, to visit relatives, camp, and take part in craft shows and evening powwows. The homecoming is a focal point for continuing tribal interaction and identity.

Institutionalized education began with the arrival of Christian missionaries among the Pawnees in the 1830s. Later, reservation school policy often forced children to leave their homes for long periods to attend schools where they lost their native language when they were prevented from speaking it. With this loss, the culture and oral history expressed in stories, songs, and ritual began to slowly disappear. Today, only a few elderly people speak Pawnee fluently.

Tribal membership currently stands at approximately twenty-five hundred, with about four hundred members living in the Pawnee, Oklahoma, area. The tribe includes teachers, artists, accountants, attorneys, and one doctor—Charles Knife Chief, M.D.

In 1936 the Oklahoma Indian Welfare Act established the Pawnee Business Council, the Nasharo (Chiefs) Council, and a tribal constitution, bylaws, and charter. In 1964, an Indian court-of-claims judgment awarded the tribe $7,316,096.55—compensation for undervalued ceded land. The Indian Self-Determination and Education Assistance Act of 1975, as well as other legislation, has assisted in improving Pawnee life. Government grants support tribal-government costs as well as health, housing, elder-care and education programs. Bingo and a tribal gas station–convenience store provide some tribal income and employment.

Bureau of Indian Affairs policies and tribal factionalism often impede tribal progress and cohesiveness. The American Indian Movement found Pawnee adherents and detractors. Today, Pawnee and other Oklahoma tribal leaders work to protect tribal sovereignty against state and federal challenges. Recently, some museum-held Pawnee remains were successfully repatriated and reburied, due largely to efforts on the part of the tribe and the Native American Rights Fund, an advocacy group whose executive director, John Echo Hawk, is a Pawnee.

Blaine, Martha Royce, *Pawnee Passage: 1870–1875* (Norman: University of Oklahoma Press, 1990); Blaine, Martha Royce, *The Pawnees: A Critical Bibliography,* Newberry Library, Bibliographical Series (Bloomington: Indiana University Press, 1980); Hyde, George, *Pawnee Indians* (Denver: University of Denver Press, 1951; reprint, Norman: University of Oklahoma Press, 1973).

MARTHA ROYCE BLAINE
Oklahoma City, Oklahoma

PEACE POLICY

After the Civil War, President Ulysses S. Grant's administration sought a quick, easy, and inexpensive way of resolving the hostilities between whites and Indians in the American West. Its answer was the "Peace Policy," which involved a reorganization of the Indian Service to address the "Indian problem." The goals of the policy were to place Indians on reservations, teach them the rudiments of Christianity and individualized farm-

ing, and eventually prepare them for citizenship. Religious men appointed by Congress would replace civil and military agents and oversee the implementation of the policy. One of the most prominent religious groups to influence the Peace Policy was the Society of Friends (Quakers); however, other denominations also participated in the "uplift of the Indians."

On June 20, 1867, Congress, in response to the growing concern over Indian affairs, created an Indian Peace Commission to investigate the conditions of the Indians. The commission's first report, drafted by Nathaniel G. Taylor, chair of the commission and Commissioner of Indian Affairs, and submitted on January 7, 1868, elaborated on the poorly functioning and corrupt agencies. It recommended a transformation of Indian policy and stressed the need for a Christian influence within the agencies and among the Indians. The result was an effort to push different tribes onto limited land bases away from ancestral homes, and a failure to protect and feed Indians while they remained on the reservations. Tribes were left with little hope. Consequently, many chose to return to their homelands and fight against the changes the government tried to force on them.

The Peace Policy faltered by the mid-1870s because of the widespread corruption in agencies and resistance by Indians. During the twenty years in which the federal government tried to implement the Peace Policy some of the most expensive and bloody Indian wars occurred.

The succession of Rutherford B. Hayes as president and the appointment of Carl Schurz as secretary of the interior signified a definite change in federal Indian policy. By 1877 the government began phasing the failing Peace Policy out of the Indian Service. In 1882 all churches relinquished their authority in the Indian Service, bringing an official end to Grant's Peace Policy.

PENOBSCOT

See Passamaquoddy/Penobscot.

PEORIA

The Peorias—one of the Illiniwek, or Illinois, tribes—have long been associated with the central Illinois River valley. Their name comes from the word *pe-wa-ri-a-ni,* meaning "one who removes on foot to another place or country." Attacks by large numbers of well-armed Iroquois after 1650 drove the Peorias, along with all the other Illinois tribes, west of the Mississippi River. The Peorias soon began visiting the French mission and trading post at Chemaquamegon Bay on Lake Michigan, where they described the Illinois homeland with its great rivers and fertile valleys. It was these descriptions that led Marquette and Jolliet to explore their country in 1673.

At the time of the Marquette and Jolliet explorations, the Peorias were living in three large villages along the Iowa River. In the meantime, the Kaskaskias, another Illinois tribe, had established a large village at the great bend of the Illinois River across from Starved Rock. As the explorers were leaving the Illinois homeland, Père Marquette promised to return to "the Grand Village of the Kaskaskias" and establish a mission, and Jolliet promised to build a fort and trading post there. By 1680 almost all the Illiniweks—including the Peorias—had moved to the Kaskaskia village, which soon had over ten thousand inhabitants. The Peorias were, at that time, the largest tribe living there. In 1691 the Illiniweks of the Kaskaskia village moved downstream to Pimeteoui, now called Lake Peoria.

The Kaskaskia fort and mission were also moved close to the new settlement. The Jesuit priest Père Gravier headed this mission and began work on a great manuscript dictionary of the Peoria language, most of which has survived. In 1700 the Kaskaskias left Pimeteoui and moved south to the Mississippi River, at which point the settlement they had left became known as Peoria, the name it still bears.

During most of the 1700s the Peorias continued to live along the Illinois River, their numbers dwindling because of constant warfare. They remained loyal to the French, and tribes allied with the English were encouraged to attack them. In revenge for the killing of a Peoria chief by the Ottawa war leader Pontiac, the Ottawa leader was in turn killed by a Peoria in 1769. This action resulted in an attack by a large coalition of tribes, who succeeded in driving the Peorias farther south.

The Peorias were among the first native communities to recognize the fledgling United States, and they provided scouts and hunters for American military operations in the Midwest. The Americans promised that, while Peoria warriors were in the field, Americans would defend Peoria villages. However, a coalition of tribes allied to the English were able to attack the Illinois villages unopposed, which resulted in a great loss of life. After the Revolutionary War, hostilities continued between the various native groups in the area.

Although the Illinois had been their allies during their fight for independence, the Americans wanted Illinois lands opened for settlement as soon as possible. At the Treaty of Edwardsville (1818), the Peorias and other Illinois tribes ceded 6,865,280 acres of land for the sum of sixty-four hundred dollars. A series of treaties with the American government gradually led to the removal of most of the Illinois Indians, including the Peorias, to lands west of the Mississippi River: across Missouri and Kansas, and eventually to Oklahoma. By the time the Peorias moved to their Oklahoma reservation at the end of the Civil War, there were only 163 adults and children on the tribal rolls. Less than twenty years later the allotment process brought even further destruction of the tribal land base as homesteads were distributed to individuals and "surplus" lands were sold to outsiders.

Under the Indian Reorganization Act of 1934, the Peorias were able to come together again as a federally recognized community. In 1939 the tribe was incorporated as the Peoria Tribe of Indians of Oklahoma. The creation of the Indian Claims Commission by the U.S. Congress in 1946 gave the tribe an opportunity to seek redress for its grievances in court. By 1994 the tribe had a total of 2,490 people on its rolls and owned 1,164 acres of land. The Peoria tribe maintains tribal offices in Miami, Oklahoma. There it conducts classes in language and traditional arts and culture in its active efforts to preserve the Peoria heritage.

See also Illinois.

Valley, Doris, and Mary Lemecke, eds., *The Peorias: A History of the Peoria Indian Tribe of Oklahoma* (Miami, Okla.: Peoria Indian Tribe of Oklahoma, 1994).

JOHN K. WHITE (Cherokee/Shawnee)
Sangamon State University

PEQUOT

At the time of first sustained contact with the Indians of southern New England—that is, the early 1600s—the Pequots controlled a sizable portion of what is now eastern Connecticut. Beginning near New London, their territory extended northward along the ridge that separates the Thames and Connecticut Rivers to the headwaters of the Thames. From that point their territory ran to the present-day border between Rhode Island and Connecticut, and from there south to Long Island Sound, including the eastern part of Long Island. The total area encompassed some two thousand square miles.

Within that area the Pequots occupied a number of small villages, each generally containing not more than twenty houses. In addition, there were smaller clusters of houses and occasional single residences separated from the villages. Throughout the year families moved to different locales to exploit a variety of resources.

The first documented encounter between the New England region's native people and Europeans occurred in 1524 when Giovanni da Verrazano sailed into Narragansett Bay. Unfortunately, Verrazano did not identify the people with whom he met. It was not until 1614, when the Dutch captain Adrian Block sailed into the same area, that mention was first made of the "Pequatoos," and it was not until the 1630s that active, regular contact was established between the Pequots and the Dutch. Trade with the English began around 1630.

That contact proved disastrous for the Pequots. By 1637 they had become embroiled in a war with the English that resulted in the destruction of their main village and the death of more than four hundred of their members. However, it was not simply the attacks by the English that defeated the tribe; equally important were the effects of disease in the early part of the 1630s that reduced tribal numbers from an estimated four thousand to nearly half that number.

Following the Pequot War, the English sought to eliminate the surviving tribal members by selling some into slavery and attaching the remainder to the neighboring Mohegans, Narragansetts, and Niantics. The effort did not succeed, however, and within twenty years two distinct groups emerged: one, under the leadership of Cassacinamon, eventually became today's Mashantucket (Western) Pequots; the other, under Harmon Garrett, was called the Paucatuck (Eastern) Pequots. The subsequent history of the Pequots is the history of these two tribes.

By 1700, both tribes had managed to secure reservations within their former territory. In 1651, the Mashantucket Pequots were granted five hundred acres at Noank (New London). Because the land at Noank was so unproductive, the tribe petitioned for additional land elsewhere, which was granted in 1666. This land was located on the northwest side of Long Pond, where the present-day town of Ledyard, Connecticut, stands. In 1683, the Paucatuck Pequots were granted a reserva-

tion in the present-day town of North Stonington, along the eastern shore of Long Pond. The Paucatuck Pequots were quick to take up residency on their reservation, unlike the Mashantucket tribe, which continued to occupy its land at Noank. It was not until 1720 that the tribe completed its removal to its new lands, which were proximate to but separate from those of the Paucatuck Pequot tribe.

Throughout the eighteenth century and for much of the nineteenth, the two tribes were known by the names of the communities in which their reservations were located. The larger of the tribes (Mashantucket) was called the Groton tribe and the smaller (Paucatuck) the Stonington tribe. The two tribes have faced similar challenges over the last three hundred years. During the eighteenth century and the first half of the nineteenth, local residents successfully applied pressure to reduce the tribal holdings, so that by 1860 each tribe had less than 250 acres left from the several thousand they owned in 1700.

Their populations similarly declined, in part because of the scattering of tribal members as a result of the loss of land and livelihoods, and in part because of an exodus in the 1770s to New York State as part of the Brothertown movement, led by Samson Occom, a Mohegan minister. By 1860, the two tribes had been reduced to fewer than fifty members each, a majority of those being women and children who made a meager living from subsistence farming, supplemented by domestic work and the sale of wild berries and homemade splint baskets. Many of the men were engaged either as farmhands or as sailors on the whaling ships that sailed from Groton and New London.

Tribal government devolved to the women. In one of the many ironies connected with these tribes, as a result of the illegal sale of their lands, the two tribes had small bank accounts, which the state-appointed overseers used to pay the expenses of the tribe. These expenses included providing for the support of indigent members as well as paying the salaries and expenses of the overseers. These funds remained active until the 1970s, when the tribes withdrew them from state control.

Little changed for the two tribes during the first half of the twentieth century, except that the numbers residing on the reservation declined steadily. By 1900, there were fewer than twenty members living at Mashantucket and about the same number at Paucatuck. By 1930, these numbers had been halved. But both tribes continued to function and control their land and resources, and both tribes had active leaders. In the case of the Paucatuck Pequots, the most prominent leaders early in the century were Ephraim Williams and, later, Atwood Williams. At Mashantucket, the leaders were two women, half sisters: Elizabeth George Plouffe and Martha Langevin Ellal. They led the tribe until their deaths in the 1970s.

The 1970s saw a major divergence in the histories of the tribes. After the deaths of the two women, the Mashantucket Pequots reorganized under the leadership of Richard Hayward, the grandson of Mrs. Plouffe, and initiated steps to recover the lands illegally lost in the previous century and to gain federal recognition. After a lengthy struggle, including an initial veto of their recognition by President Ronald Reagan, the Mashantucket Pequots prevailed and were recognized in 1983, and their land claims were settled. With the nine hundred thousand dollars it received from the land settlement, the tribe embarked on an ambitious program of economic development, land acquisition, and repatriation of its members. By 1994 tribal membership had increased to three hundred. The result of federal recognition has been a tribal renaissance.

By contrast, the Paucatuck Pequots, although they have embarked on a similar road, have been unable to achieve federal recognition or the settlement of their land claims, largely because of a factional dispute. Through the 1980s two groups emerged on the reservation, each representing a major family, and these parties have been unable to reconcile their differences. It is impossible to get a membership count to which both sides will agree. The result has been a stalemate.

See also Occom, Samson.

Hauptman, Laurence M., and James D. Wherry, eds., *The Pequots in Southern New England: The Fall and Rise of an American Indian Nation* (Norman: University of Oklahoma Press, 1990); Jennings, Francis, *The Invasion of America: Indians, Colonialism, and the Cant of Conquest* (Chapel Hill: University of North Carolina Press, 1975); Simmons, William S., *Spirit of the New England Tribes: Indian History and Folklore, 1620–1984* (Hanover, N.H.: University Press of New England, 1986).

JACK CAMPISI
Wellesley College

PHILIP, KING

See Metacom (King Philip).

PHOENIX INDIAN SCHOOL

The Phoenix Indian School in Phoenix, Arizona, opened on September 30, 1891, with an enrollment of thirty-four Pima boys. The school's first permanent structure, the "girls' building," was built in 1892. Modeled after the Carlisle Indian Industrial School in Pennsylvania, the Phoenix Indian School ostensibly offered Indian youth the opportunity to learn industrial skills with the aim of integrating them into white society as well-paid workers.

This goal, however, was not realized because of the great demand for cheap, unskilled labor on local farms and ranches. By 1900 the school was relying on its ability to place students in these menial jobs, and school authorities frequently forced local Indian children to attend the Phoenix school. The institution's authoritarian atmosphere was designed to stamp out native languages and traditions, but by the mid-1920s Indian leaders and sympathetic white reformers demanded a new approach. Change in the school's focus was slow in coming, however, and professional educators did not begin working at the school until 1935. Curriculum changes soon followed, which eliminated the placement of children in the local labor force.

In 1935 the Phoenix Indian School was operating as both a vocational training school and a regular junior and senior high school. Enrollment at the school reached its peak in 1961, but diminishing support for the school reflected a decline in support for off-reservation schools nationally. In 1990 the Phoenix Indian School was closed and developed as commercial real estate by the Collier Company of Florida.

See also Boarding Schools; Education.

PHOTOGRAPHY OF AND BY INDIANS

As the tide of nineteenth-century Manifest Destiny obliterated Native American peoples and their cultures across the continent, Europe provided an invention that made it possible to record with unprecedented accuracy what was being lost. Many Americans had from the beginning anguished over what was being sacrificed in the progress of their young country, and a vigorous tradition developed as artists and writers toiled at recording what was passing away. The camera provided a quintessentially American means of capturing what was vanishing: its cost made its services democratically

Fred E. Miller (1868–1936) photographing a Crow camp as J. H. Sharp (1859–1953) paints the scene. Crow Indians look on. This photograph was also taken by Miller.

accessible to far greater numbers than its predecessors, and its ability to record quickly and in detail on a conveniently portable medium offered new freedoms to both photographer and patron. These qualities—added to the contradictory attractions of the American Indian as both noble and ignoble savage—made the American Indian a supremely attractive subject. Nineteenth-century painters had fastened onto Indian models as a means of constructing America's own "classical" past, delighted to exploit the ethnographic parallels to minimally robed "Greek" figures. The camera, despite its direct transfer of reality, would also play a role in this romantic conceit.

It is a surprise to learn that the first instance of a Native American being photographed occurred in the Old World rather than the New. Kahkewaquonaby, also known as the Reverend Peter Jones—the son of a Mississauga mother and a Welsh father—was photographed in Edinburgh in August 1845 in Indian clothing and paraphernalia while on a British tour to raise funds for a proposed Indian school in Canada. The photographers were none other than David Octavius Hill and Robert Adamson, the most celebrated collaborative team of the medium's first decade.

In America in that same decade, some of the earliest American cameramen would capture historic images of no less than Keokuk, whose mesmerizing daguerreotype is but one of many portraits of Sauk and Fox tribesmen created by Thomas Easterly from his St. Louis base.

By the 1850s Indian leaders were traveling east as treaty delegations to Washington, their colorful diplomatic presences obvious subjects for photographers' studios in the nation's capital. McClee's was the most long-lived of these studios. Such photographers as A. Zeno Shindler and Alexander Gardner produced memorable Indian images there and occasionally ventured out to record treaty gatherings on the frontier, as Gardner did in Wyoming in 1868.

But although the Indians visiting Washington were often figures of historical importance, the remnants of the great tribal populations had been pushed far west by the time photography arrived in America. The photographers followed them. Joel Emmons Whitney made his way to Minnesota and the drama of the Sioux Revolt. Will Soule, as a resident of Fort Sill, utilized the photographic opportunity of living deep inside Indian Territory. Frederick Monsen and his camera joined Generals George Crook and Nelson Miles in the Apache campaign. Other photographers would make their way west as official members of government exploring expeditions, like Timothy O'Sullivan, on the Wheeler Survey in 1871 and 1872, who photographed in Navajo and Mojave territory. William Henry Jackson, with the Hayden Survey, focused his glass-plate mechanism on Indians farther north in the Rocky Mountains. John K. Hillers accompanied John Wesley Powell in his explorations of the Colorado River before becoming the official photographer for the Bureau of American Ethnology. The expeditionary photographers had extraordinary opportunities to record indigenous peoples before the full onslaught of acculturation clouded the cultural waters.

By the 1880s the much photographed Indian participants of the Buffalo Bill shows were evidence not only that the old ways were ephemeral, but that there was fascination enough over what was being lost to make exhibitions of it commercially successful. Photographers like Ben Wittick, A. Frank Randall, Camillus S. Fly, and George Wharton James in the Southwest, John Alvin Anderson, David F. Barry, Charles M. Bell, O. S. Goff, George Mooney, and George Trager among the Plains Indians, and Lloyd Winter and Percy Pond in Alaska are but a few of the names made illustrious by their late-nineteenth-century photography of Native Americans.

About this same time the photograph was used baldly as an item of political expediency in the "transformation" portraits produced at Indian schools throughout the nation, memorably by John Choate at the Carlisle Indian Industrial School in Pennsylvania. These photographs were meant to convince viewers, by the evidence of "before and after" shots, of the school's success in bringing about the inevitable progress from savagery to civilization—while at the same time reassuring those with funds in government and religious organizations that the goal of their subventions was worthy and possible. But to most modern eyes the photographs resoundingly proclaim just the opposite.

Like the painters that preceded them (notably Charles Bird King and George Catlin), a surprising number of photographers discovered they were not satisfied with the occasional image, but were caught up in the urgency of capturing in a comprehensive form what they believed was vanishing. Thus many photographers found themselves absorbed in ambitious schemes to produce virtual galleries of images that embraced all of the American Indian world. Prince Roland Bonaparte was one of the earlier of these, beginning in 1887 a series of photographs that resulted, by 1906, in more than seven thousand negatives. Roland Reed and Joseph Kossuth Dixon were among those who emulated the prince in his obsession with the subject. But the most ambitious and persistent was Edward Sheriff Curtis, whose enormous enterprise spanned thirty years and produced approximately forty thousand photographs. His legacy has elicited criticism from those who would have preferred documentary results rather than the photographer's romantic plan to recall what had already passed, but the response of both the general public and descendants of his Indian subjects has made him by far the most influential photographer in the shaping of the national image of the Native American.

In the twentieth century the waxing and waning of the use of the Indian as photographic subject reflects the roller coaster of public sentiment toward the Native American. Some photographers, like Adam Clark Vroman, Sumner Matteson, and Laura Gilpin, pursued their Indian interest without regard to the status of its appeal. By the second half of the century, when ethnic interests were paramount and the Indian took center stage, masters of every photographic school sought Native American subjects.

What was vanishing all along was not American Indian people, but particular expressions of their ever-evolving cultures. Native populations soared in the late twentieth century, and among them were found artists who chose the camera to do their own recording of the changing tribal civilizations.

Natives had reacted to the advent of photography as variously as the many tribes, the differing communities, and the various individuals the medium sought to "preserve." The old chestnut that Indians evaded photography because they believed that the camera captured their soul has no basis in fact for most tribal people, though metaphorically it was often on the mark. Native Americans were frequently as enamored with the idea of creating images of themselves as subjects for the camera as photographers were of controlling those same pictures. It took some time for particular communities to understand how disruptive photography could be. The ever-patient Hopis, after drawing cameramen like a magnet to their ceremonial performances at the turn of the century, had by 1915 banned photography simply to reclaim their tiny dance plazas from the crush of tripod and camera. Native communities' feelings toward photography continue to change. In an era when the people behind the camera and video recorder are often the local natives, photography has been banned as recently as 1993 at ceremonies in some of the Rio Grande Pueblos.

Despite the fact that many continue to regard the modern technology of the camera as antithetical to native ways, American Indians have been as successful behind the camera as in front of it. Since at least the early 1890s Benjamin A. Haldane, his brother Henry, and Thomas Eaton (all Tsimshians) pursued photography in the native community of Metlakatha, where some of their work was stamped as by a "Native Photographer." Horace Poolaw (Kiowa; 1906–84) documented native life from the 1920s on. Jean Fredericks (Hopi) bought his first camera in 1941. Peter Pitseolak (Inuit) began recording nomadic life on Baffin Island at about the same time. Lee Marmon (Laguna) has been photographing at Laguna and Acoma Pueblos since 1947. Paul Natonabah (Navajo) has met the demanding deadlines of the Navajo Times as its photographer since 1971. The proliferation of tribal newspapers in the 1970s created the need for numerous tribal photographers. By the 1980s the native heirs of these Indian photographic pioneers were growing rapidly in number and mastery of the medium.

In 1983 the Smithsonian sponsored *Hopi Photographers/Hopi Images,* a traveling exhibition that presented the work of contemporary Hopi photographers. In 1984, *24 Native American Photographers* was presented at the gallery of the American Indian Community House in New York City. In September 1985 a conference titled "The Photograph and the American Indian" convened at Princeton University, accompanied by an exhibition that presented examples of the entire range of photography of the American Indian but took pains to represent the work of native photographers. This conference accelerated the formation of the Native Indian/Inuit Photographers Association, which in 1986 produced the exhibition and catalog *Silver Drum: Five Native Photographers.*

The Institute of American Indian Arts in Santa Fe has attracted talented young Indian artists from all over the country since its foundation in 1962. During the 1970s its film program was dominated by George Burdeau (Blackfoot) and Larry Littlebird (Pueblo). The addition in 1992 of the photographer Larry McNeil (Tlingit/Nisga'a) to its faculty gave a new seriousness to its photography department. The 1993 opening of the institute's museum in Santa Fe provided an important new venue for the exhibition of photography by Native Americans. McNeil was also instrumental in encouraging the annual Santa Fe Indian Market to include a photographic exhibit and competition beginning in 1993.

Exhibitions of photographs by native artists proliferated in the early 1990s. Among them were *Native Visions* at the Arizona Center for the Media Arts in Tucson in 1990, *Language of the Lens at the Heard Museum in Phoenix* in 1990, *Through the Native Lens* at the museum of the Institute of American Indian Arts in 1993, and *Defining Our Realities: Native American Woman Photographers* at the Sacred Circle Gallery in Seattle. Frequently seen in these exhibitions was the work of such native photographers as Dorothy Chocolate (Diné), Jessee Cooday (Tlingit/Nisga'a), Carm Little Turtle (Apache/Tarahumara), Lee Marmon (Laguna Pueblo), Larry McNeil (Tlingit/Nisga'a), Victor Masayesva, Jr. (Hopi), Owen Seumptewa (Hopi), and Hulleah Tsinhnahjinnie (Navajo/Creek/Seminole).

Bush, Alfred L., and Lee Clark Mitchell, *The Photograph and the American Indian* (Princeton; N.J.: Princeton University Press, 1994); Gattuso, John, ed., *A Circle of Nations: Voices and Visions of American Indians* (Hillsboro, Oreg.: Beyond Worlds, 1993); Lippard, Lucy R., ed., *Partial Recall: Photographs of Native North Americans* (New York: New Press, 1992).

ALFRED L. BUSH
Princeton University

PICTOGRAPHS

The term *pictographs* generally refers to prehistoric rock or cave paintings. Pictographs can be found throughout the United States and are credited to various Native American peoples. They should be distinguished from petroglyphs, which are images that are carved on rocks. Pictographs are most abundant in Utah, New Mexico, Arizona, Nevada, Texas, and California and appear most often underneath rock overhangs or in rock shelters where the pigments have been protected. The paints used for these pictures come from minerals such as iron oxide, calcium carbonate, azurite, and ochre and are applied with fingers or with brushes made from plants. These pictures are believed to have been used for various reasons such as to commemorate the site of a hunt, to mark clan territory or sacred places, or even as mnemonic devices to recall details of tribal myths.

Pictographic expressions also appeared on hide and bark. On the Great Plains, hunters and warriors recorded their exploits in pictographic displays and leaders remembered events in large pictographs called *winter counts*. In the East, similar drawings were made on birch bark. Following contact with Europeans, pictographic paintings began to appear on cloth and paper as native people adapted this traditional art form to new conditions.

See also Art, Visual (to 1960).

PIMA
See Akimel O'odham (Pima).

PITCHLYNN, PETER (HA-TCHOC-TUCK-NEE)

(1806–81)
Choctaw political leader and diplomat.

Peter Perkins Pitchlynn, one-quarter Choctaw, exemplified the bicultural elite who dominated political and economic life among the so-called Five Civilized Tribes during the nineteenth century. Born on January 30, 1806, at Hush-ook-wa in the Choctaw homeland in Mississippi, Peter was the son of John Pitchlynn, a prosperous white farmer, and Sophia Folsom, a member of a prominent Choctaw-white family. Peter grew up in an affluent household that valued English education and Protestant Christianity. His sporadic formal schooling, begun at age fourteen, included a few months at Choctaw Academy (Kentucky) and the Uni-

versity of Nashville (Tennessee) following his marriage to his cousin Rhoda Folsom in 1824.

Pitchlynn raised livestock and crops, but his real interest lay in Choctaw politics. His life coincided with the most critical period of Choctaw history, during which the nation faced forced emigration to the Indian Territory, the Civil War, mounting threats to its sovereignty, and rapid cultural change. Many Choctaws responded to these pressures by adopting some Anglo-American ways while retaining as much of their Indian culture and nationhood as possible.

The ambitious Pitchlynn, called Snapping Turtle by his traditionalist supporters, was usually at the turbulent center of Choctaw politics. His first public service was as "colonel" of the Choctaw "lighthorse," the mounted police force established in 1820. While still a very young man, he participated in creating the Choctaw constitution of 1826.

Throughout the 1820s the federal government pressured all eastern Indians to move west of the Mississippi River. Geographically divided into three districts, the Choctaws were also divided politically over whether to agree to leave Mississippi. As they tried to decide how to deal with the crisis, the Pitchlynn family, supporting Chief Moshulatubbee of the Northeastern District, was often at odds with the Christian Party, led in part by Rhoda Pitchlynn's nationalist brother, David Folsom. Fortunately the Choctaws escaped the removal-era violence that racked the Cherokee, Creek, and Seminole nations. In the Treaty of Dancing Rabbit Creek (1830), they reluctantly agreed to exchange their eastern homeland for a reserve west of Arkansas between the Canadian and Red Rivers, in the southern third of present-day Oklahoma. Other considerations they were promised included annuities, educational funds, and federal guarantees to protect their lands and sovereignty. Peter Pitchlynn, who later claimed to have opposed the treaty, received two sections of land for his cooperation and, at age twenty-four, briefly replaced Moshulatubbee as chief of the Northeastern District.

Pitchlynn moved west with the Choctaws in 1831 over their version of the Trail of Tears. They immediately began to reestablish the Choctaw Nation in the West and to work toward creating a centralized republican Choctaw government there. Pitchlynn founded farms near present-day Eagletown and Tom in far southeastern Oklahoma, but he devoted most of his time to public life. In 1834 he helped draft the first constitution written in Oklahoma; three years later he served with the commission that negotiated a union (1837–55) with the immigrating Chickasaws.

Pitchlynn often served as a member of the Choctaw National Council, but his greatest achievement before the Civil War was the establishing of the Choctaw national school system. Although in 1841 he was named superintendent of Choctaw Academy, the Baptist boarding school in Kentucky founded by the former U.S. vice president Richard M. Johnson for Choctaw boys, Pitchlynn was also instrumental in its closing. He wanted Choctaw boys and girls educated in their own institutions in their own country and lobbied to have their educational funds redirected from Kentucky to the Choctaw Nation. As speaker of the council in 1842, he wrote a new constitution that allowed the appropriation of funds to found Spencer and Wheelock academies. Shortly afterward, Pitchlynn became president of Spencer Academy's board of trustees. Allegations that he misused school funds entrusted to him marred his record of contributions to Choctaw education and provided evidence, according to his biographer, of a tendency on his part to put personal profit ahead of Choctaw public welfare. Nevertheless, by the 1850s Pitchlynn had established himself as an able politician and "delegate" representing Choctaw interests in Washington, D.C.

During the Civil War the Choctaw Nation allied itself with the Confederacy. Pitchlynn, initially a Union man even though he owned 135 slaves, avoided conflict by withdrawing to his home deep in the mountains of southeastern Oklahoma. Still, in 1864 he was declared chief of the Choctaw Nation. As such he led the negotiations to reestablish federal-Choctaw relations through the Reconstruction Treaty (1866). Although they were forced to make important concessions, Pitchlynn and the Choctaw delegates successfully opposed federal proposals that they substitute individual landholding for traditional communal ownership of land. They also resisted the incorporation of the Choctaws into an intertribal territorial government.

Pitchlynn's major postwar concern as a politician and delegate was the "net proceeds" claim. The Choctaws insisted that the federal government owed them $3 million from the sale of 10 million acres of their former Mississippi homeland. Though Pitchlynn was tenacious in pressing the claim from 1854 until his death in 1881, his political motives were suspect given the kickbacks, excessive "attorney's fees," and collusion that were so often a part of federal dealings with the Five Civilized Tribes in the late nineteenth century.

Even so, his groundwork was primarily responsible for the successful settlement of the claim in 1886, five years after his death.

Pitchlynn led a frustrating life in which his business and political schemes rarely paid off. Opportunistic, vain, materialistic, and hot tempered, he owned brass knuckles and a brace of dueling pistols, but he was also a romantic who enjoyed Shakespeare, Milton, and Scott. George Catlin painted him as a Choctaw warrior, but Pitchlynn wrote poetry that suggested his sense of alienation from both the Anglo-American and Choctaw cultures. A loving, indulgent father, he was often away from his eight children by Rhoda Folsom, who died in 1844, and his five children by Carolyn Eckloff Lombari, a Virginian he married in 1869. In financial straits, Pitchlynn died in Washington, D.C., on January 17, 1881, and after Masonic services was buried in Congressional Cemetery. Perhaps this was a fitting resting place for a Choctaw citizen who, though absorbed in the affairs of the Choctaw Nation, lived a large part of his life at a physical and cultural distance from his people.

See also Choctaw.

Baird, W. David, *Peter Pitchlynn: Chief of the Choctaws* (Norman: University of Oklahoma Press, 1972); Debo, Angie, *The Rise and Fall of the Choctaw Republic* (Norman: University of Oklahoma Press, 1934).

MARY JANE WARDE
Stillwater, Oklahoma

PLACE NAMES

Most Native American place names are descriptive. Written in a language unknown to most of us, they often seem to be meaningless labels. Yet hidden in these names lies much of our history. When the first European settlements were made here, Native Americans had already given names to innumerable places. These names reflected what was most important to the inhabitants of a particular cultural area. For instance, in New England many place names relate to fishing.

These names sounded strange to Europeans, who had trouble pronouncing them and spelling them uniformly. In adopting native names, Europeans unfamiliar with the phonetic systems of the native languages, and unable to find in their own languages suitable letters to express native sounds, produced corrupted versions of the originals. Orthography varied according to the language of the recorder. And Europeans were not always curious about the meaning of the names. The Mississippi was "Great River," but white romantics supposed the word to mean "Father of Waters."

The invaders sought to replace many of the "heathen" names with their own. Aboriginal Shawmut (the Neck) became Boston; Waweeatunong (the Curved Channel) became Detroit (from the French *détroit*, "straits"). Europeans were less successful in renaming natural features. For these, the observation of the anthropologist T. T. Waterman is valid: "Old place names are extraordinarily likely to persist even through migration and conquest, when the spoken language shifts and one language is replaced by another."

Names of American topographic features were amazingly viable. The Rock River of Wisconsin and Illinois has retained its name in the languages of five successive occupant groups. When the frontier had been pushed far from the eastern shore, the "first people" began to appear as romantic figures. Their tribal, personal, and descriptive names became popular. Four of the Great Lakes retained aboriginal names. While only two of the original thirteen colonies took native names, by 1960 twenty-seven American states bore Indian names.

As America grew, names were transferred from one place to another, without regard to their appropriateness elsewhere. If an emigrant from Tioga, Pennsylvania, took the name of his old home to Illinois, it did not matter that there was no forked stream or trail to make this Iroquoian name fitting. However, these names, though reduced to labels, record white migration and settlement patterns as much as a native presence at another place. Place names form "layered" records of sequent occupation similar to those of the archaeologist's "horizons."

"Native" names on the map sometimes emanate from novelists, poets, and playwrights. These names may be genuine, or manufactured in part by literary fabricators. Some (for example, Horicon) originate in Cooper's novels and a great many in Longfellow's *Song of Hiawatha*. The mixed-origin name Metamora, which was adopted in four states, comes from a popular play written by John Augustus Stone in 1829.

Consistent spelling of native names is uncommon. Dakota is sometimes spelled Dacotah or Decota, while the form Lakota represents an intratribal (Teton) variation. In the absence of standardization there is no wrong way to spell a native name. Allegany, Allegheny, and Alleghany all appear on the map.

No category of native geographical names is more numerous than tribal names. These names were given to places by Europeans. Most of them probably reflect a desire to preserve colorful American names, and to avoid filling the map with endless dull European names and borrowing from classical antiquity.

Of course native names are still outnumbered by Old World names. The English traveler Frederick Marryat complained in 1837: "I detest these old names vamped up. Why do not the Americans take the Indian names; they need not be very scrupulous about it; they have robbed the Indians of everything else." Yet more than half the states have Indian names. We have their topographical names in abundance, in the original or in translation. The names of the Rocky Mountains and the Platte River, among many, are simply translations of their native names into English and French, respectively. Massachusetts did not choose a native name for any of the sixty towns founded there before 1690, while Plymouth Colony retained but two. Still, a native name was taken for Massachusetts, and native names remain for many topographical features, including the highest mountains in Maine (Katahdin) and Massachusetts (Greylock), and some of these states' principal rivers: Androscoggin, Connecticut, Kennebec, Merrimac, and Penobscot.

A tribe might be known by several names. For example, the Mesquakies (their own name, meaning "Red Earth") were also known as Outagami (People of the Other Shore), a name given them by their neighbors, and by names given them by Europeans: Foxes and Renards. The name by which a tribe was best known might not be used among tribal members themselves; for example, Navajo (as opposed to Diné), Winnebago (Hochungra), Sioux (Dakota, Nakota, Lakota), and Iroquois (Haudenosaunee, or "Longhouse People").

The Shawnee (Southerners) were named for their place of origin, while several tribes were called Wabanaki or Abenaki (Easterners) by those living west of them. Tribes or bands were sometimes known by the names of their chiefs; for instance, whites called Powhatan's tribe the Powhatan — but this name, one of two that the chief possessed, was originally a place name. A tribe might be named in derogation by whites or other Indians. Thus the Ojibwa knew both the Iroquois and the Dakota as Nodoways (Snakes). The Mohawks were given their alternate name, meaning "cannibals," by the Mahicans; the Iroquois called the Algonquins "Adirondacks" (Bark Eaters), and the

Montagnais gave the name Eskimos (Flesh Eaters) to the Inuit of Labrador.

In turn, Europeans called tribes or bands by derisive nicknames that became established names, such as Diggers, Pillagers, Puants (Stinkers), Poux (Lice), and Rogues. Often these names were misleading. The Paiutes were called Diggers because they used roots for food. The Ojibwa of Leech Lake, Minnesota, were called Pillagers because of one incident in which a trader was robbed. The Winnebago did not smell bad; their name probably came from the salty waters near which they once dwelt. And certainly the Potawatomi were no more lice prone than Europeans. In the white view, the Indians of southwest Oregon were "a peculiarly troublesome lot," and so, in lieu of their hard-to-pronounce names (Takilma, Tututni), they were simply called Rogues, a name that has been transferred to two rivers, a national forest, a town, a state park, and a community college.

Tribes were sometimes named for a supposed physical characteristic. The trader W. A. Ferris dismissed these anatomical names as applied to western tribes—Blackfoot, Nez Perce (Pierced Nose), Flathead, and Gros Ventre (Big Belly)—and showed that in no case were they correctly applied.

Other sources of names, indigenous or given, were the tribal totem, as with the Crow; a principal food, as with the Menominee (Wild Rice Eaters); a mode of travel, as with the Missouri (Canoemen); an important activity, as with the Ottawa (Traders); or a topographic feature, as with the Montagnais (Mountaineers) and Saulteurs (People of the Falls).

The names native groups gave to themselves commonly meant "people." It was not a tribal name; when natives were asked who they were, they simply asserted their humanity—not in a superior sense, as Marquette misunderstood them to be doing, but as a self-evident fact. It was not unusual for some Indians to identify themselves as Illiniwek (People), which was promptly corrupted to Illinois. The element *illeni* or *illini* appears in other tribal names—for example, the Shawnee group Pickawillany (Piqua Illeni) and Lenni Lenape, the name of the Delaware. The Navajo call themselves Diné (People), as do all other Athabascan-speaking people from Arizona to Alaska.

For egalitarian reasons, places named for individual Indians are mainly so named by whites, except in Oklahoma. Enough invaders saw heroic qualities in the foe to perpetuate their names. Among the honored are friendly Indians such as Samoset, who greeted the Pilgrims in the spring of 1621, and warriors such as Annawan, an aide to King Philip. Best remembered in New England are the Wampanoags and nearby allies, such as Massasoit, Hyannis, Ninigret, Shawsheen, Squantum (Squanto), and Wamsutta.

Since the colonial period great warriors have received as much attention from name givers as the more compliant natives. Militants such as Black Hawk, Tecumseh, Pontiac, Osceola, Red Cloud, and Geronimo are honored in place names as much as are native statesmen such as Keokuk, Oshkosh, Ouray, and Washakie.

Indian women are frequently memorialized on the map. Among them are Weetamoo (d. 1676), who died aiding King Philip, and Aliquippa (the Hat; 1684–1754), "queen" of a mixed village of Seneca and Delaware in Pennsylvania who was visited by George Washington in 1753. Others are Pocahontas (Matoaka), a Renape, daughter of Powhatan, who married John Rolfe and died in England in 1617 at age twenty-one; Sacagawea, a Shoshone (1788–1884?) who is credited with guiding Lewis and Clark to the Pacific in 1805; and Winema (1842–1932), a Modoc who saved the life of Colonel A. B. Meacham, who was attacked by Captain Jack during a peace parley in 1873. Winema is commemorated in the name of Winema National Forest and in the names of topographical features in California and Oregon.

The Siouan name Winona (First-Born Daughter) is found in twenty-eight states. Some of these place names commemorate the fictional mother of Hiawatha in Longfellow's Song of Hiawatha, while others are derived from the name of a cousin of the last Siouan chief, Wabasha; this Winona had a village on the site of present-day Winona, Minnesota. (Another legendary woman of this name was said to have thrown herself from a cliff on the Mississippi, now called Maidenrock, rather than marry a suitor favored by her parents.)

As name givers, Native Americans paid much attention to features of land and water; to foods, flora, and fauna; and to sites of important events. Indian dwellings and villages have contributed names to our map, although they are often translated into English—for example, Red Lodge, Montana; and Medicine Lodge, Kansas. Waukegan, Illinois, has the Potawatomi word for "fort," while places named Tepee, Wickiup, and Wigwam represent the Siouan, Mesquakie, and eastern Algonquian words for "lodge." Generic words for "town" are seen in the word *Canada*, of Iroquoian origin, which became the name of a country, and in the

Algonquian names of Weatogue, Connecticut, and We-taug, Illinois.

Terms related to hunting and fishing are common among native place names. The Ouachita River in Arkansas and Louisiana, and the Washita of Oklahoma, take their names from Choctaw words meaning "big hunt." Native fish names transferred to water features include Ojibwa *ashegon* (bass), *muskellunge, siscowet,* (or cisco), *winnemac* (catfish) and the generic word for fish, *keego,* seen in combinations such as *Kegomic* (Fishing Place) and *Kegonsa* (Little Fish).

Plants, including trees, furnished food and construction material and were put to other uses as well. The words *catalpa, hickory, persimmon,* and *tamarack* have become so naturalized into English and into place names that their origin has been forgotten. In Montana, the Bitterroot Mountains and River were so called by Lewis and Clark from the Salishan name of a plant food used by the natives.

No plant food was more widely used by native Americans than maize, or corn, called *mondamin* by the Algonquians, a name appropriately given to an Iowa town. Corn products are represented by Hominy, a place name in five states; Pone (or corn bread), in three states; and Sofkee (a corn gruel), on several southeastern streams. The word *menominee,* "wild rice," became a tribal name and a ubiquitous place name in the upper Great lakes region. Saskatoon, in Saskatchewan, has the Cree name of a species of cranberry. The Ojibwa name of another cranberry gave a name to Pembina, North Dakota, and to a Minnesota township. Several tuberous wild plants, sometimes called wild potatoes, were eaten by Indians and gave names to the map; these include *camas, pinicon, macoupin, topeka, tuckahoe,* and *wapato.* The largest American city bearing a native plant name is Chicago (Garlic Place), recorded in 1687 by Henri Joutel.

Manitou and Wakonda are common names on the map as Algonquian and Siouan terms for the Great Spirit. Whites often changed these names to *Devil,* and so we have Devil's Lake in Michigan, North Dakota, Wisconsin, and elsewhere.

Animals were the center of economic and religious life to those tribes that subsisted mainly by hunting. Many of their animal names became place names, including *ahmeek* (beaver), carcajou, caribou, cougar, coyote, manatee, moose, musquash, opossum, raccoon, and skunk. Buffalo, though not a native word, is in twenty-eight place names.

Indians and whites named places for important events such as battles, councils, and treaties. Battle Creek, Michigan, and Battle Mountain, Nevada, are two of the best-known examples of this group. Places named for councils or treaties with whites or other Indians include Broken Arrow, Oklahoma; Council Bluffs, Iowa; Neutral, Kansas; Purchase Line, Pennsylvania; Talking Rock, Georgia; and Treaty, Indiana.

Native names are often garbled into forms resembling English words, although robbed of their original meaning in the process. Among these are Humptulips, Washington (from the Chehalis word for "chilly"); Kitty Hawk, North Carolina (from the Algonquian *chickehauk,* of unknown meaning); Mystic River in Massachusetts and Connecticut (from the Algonquian *missi-tuk,* "big outlet," tidal estuary); Neversink, New York, from a band of Delaware called Navasink; and Lake Success, in Queens, New York, (from the Algonquian *sacut,* "creek outlet"). Similar to these are the invented names, such as Algoma and Iosco, which are mostly the work of the popular writer Henry R. Schoolcraft.

Many eye- and ear-catching names are translations of Indian names. Among these are Weeping Water, Nebraska; Medicine Hat, Alberta; Moose Jaw, Saskatchewan; and Sleepy Eye and Lac Qui Parle (Lake Which Speaks), both in Minnesota. Others, often thought of as joke material, are relatively unchanged native words, such as Walla Walla, Washington; Wahoo, Nebraska; and Podunk Lake, Michigan.

As the seemingly meaningless and inert labels on places spring to life, we see, as Henry Schoolcraft observed, that "they cast . . . a species of poetic drapery over our geography."

Donehoo, George P., *Indian Village and Place Names in Pennsylvania* (1928; reprint, Baltimore: Gateway Press, 1977); Stewart, George R., *American Place Names* (New York: Oxford University Press, 1971); Vogel, Virgil J., *Indian Names on Wisconsin's Map* (Madison: University of Wisconsin Press, 1991).

VIRGIL J. VOGEL
Northbrook, Illinois

PLATEAU TRIBES

In the Southern Plateau tribes' creation stories, which begin with the phrase "Coyote was going there," Coyote prepares the way "for the people who are coming soon." As the Nez Perce tell it, Coyote was fixing up a habitable world—smashing waterfalls so that the salmon could travel upriver; building fish traps; taking fire, stone, water, and wood to make the sweat lodge; and, in a final act of creative bravado, destroying the great Swallowing Monster of the Columbia River by building a fire under its heart. As the monster exploded, Coyote flung its body parts, blood, and bone to the corners of the plateau, from which sprang the tribes that inhabit the land today.

According to tradition, before Coyote left the world he taught the Plateau people everything they would need to know: how to fish, gather roots and berries, and hunt deer; how to obtain healing and spiritual power through the sweat lodge ceremony, vision quest, and winter Medicine Dance; and how to respect one another and the world he had prepared.

The story of Coyote and the Swallowing Monster had its counterpart in the land itself. The plateau was born in repeated violent explosions of water, fire, rock, and ash. Lying in the rain shadow of the volcanic Cascade mountain range, the plateau is a semiarid flood plain of basalt lava flow surrounded by steep forested mountains on all sides, a moonscape of deep canyons, scablands, and treeless uplands carpeted with bunch grass in the east and sagebrush in the west. Rivers of monumental force—the Fraser, Snake, and Columbia—and their tributaries course through the area, feeding and connecting its parts. The most important of these, the Columbia River, exploded through an ancient glacial ice jam, forming Lake Missoula and creating the world's greatest flood, which left in its wake boulders the size of automobiles and two monumental cuts in the basalt: the Grand Coulee of central Washington, and the Columbia Gorge.

Cataclysm seared the collective memory of Plateau people. Beginning with the smallpox pandemic of 1780, waves of deadly smallpox, fevers, influenza, and measles reduced the population by as much as 50 to 80 percent by 1850, making the region at once a burial ground and a nurturing ground for prophets and apocalyptic religious movements.

Although humans have lived on the plateau for at least ten thousand years, the names and the territories of the original peoples of the region remain obscure. When Lewis and Clark arrived in 1805–6, several dozen autonomous bands or tribes of Salishan, Sahaptian, and Chinookan language stocks resided along the major river systems and lakes of the plateau.

The names that have survived for these groups are in most instances not the names Plateau people gave to themselves, but rather European corruptions or misnomers, such as Flathead (Salish), Pend Oreille, and Nez Perce. Descendants of the bands that early Europeans and Americans called the Pend Oreilles, Flatheads, Kutenais, Coeur d'Alenes, Kalispels, Spokans, Colviles, Lakes, Okanagans, Nespelems, Sanpoils, Methows, Chelans, Wenatchis, Sinkiuses, Kititases, Klickitats, Yakamas, Palouses, Umatillas, Walla Wallas, Cayuses, Nez Perces, Cascades, Wascos, Wishrams, Wayams, John Days, Tyghs, Warm Springs, and Klamaths now affilate with tribes and confederated tribes on ten reservations.

Like their coastal Salish relatives on Puget Sound, the Interior Salishan tribes of the northern plateau and their southern Sahaptian neighbors inhabited a spiritual universe. Spiritual power was immanent in all life forms, as well as in the forces of nature, mountains, rivers and lakes, and rocks. Spirit helpers acquired during the adolescent vision quest could confer the power of chiefs and shamans, and assured success in medicine and healing, gambling, hunting and fishing, warfare, and love. People didn't talk about their spirit helpers for fear of losing them, and adolescents "forgot" them until later in life, when the spirits became lonely and demanded that their human partners dance for them in the winter Medicine Dance.

Plateau people also inhabited a physical universe. Despite extreme temperature variations and an average annual precipitation of less than ten inches at lower elevations, the plateau was an exceedingly abundant and varied subsistence habitat of river, upland, and mountain. For all but mountainous bands like the Chelans and Kalispels, who were primarily hunters, salmon and roots in equal proportion sustained Plateau peoples. Because few bands had sufficient salmon, roots, and game within their own territories, the good life on the plateau required cooperation and resource sharing with other bands. Although most Plateau bands considered the winter village their permanent home, from spring through fall people moved across the region to successively higher elevations to gather food, which they would dry and store for the winter.

Beginning in April, Nez Perce and Yakama people congregated at the great Columbia River salmon fisheries and trade centers at the Dalles and Celilo Falls in Wasco-Wishram-Wayam territory. By June, people were moving along with the salmon upriver to Walla Walla, Kettle Falls, and Spokane Falls. Parties of women meanwhile collected tule and vegetable fibers and dug the first fruit, the bitterroot. Like the arrival of the first salmon, the ripening of the bitterroot was an occasion for thanksgiving and a communal feast.

By mid-June people had left the rivers and lakes for the prairies to dig camas roots, especially abundant among the Nez Perces, Yakamas, Wenatchis, and Coeur d'Alenes. Summer was a favorite time for Plateau peoples; digging camas was hard work, and many different bands came together in this activity. Men and women traded, men raced horses in the afternoon, and the evening air resounded with the sounds of beating sticks and the songs of rival Stick Game teams.

As the late-summer heat intensified, parties of men and women moved ever higher into the mountains, to collect berries and medicines and to hunt deer. By mid-September, at the highest elevations, the huckleberries were usually ripe. By October, families had begun to pack their tule mats and dried foods for the return home, although some men spent the fall hunting bison on the plains in groups led by the Nez Perces and Flatheads. Some of these groups stayed away all winter, returning with plains-style manufactures and buffalo robes to trade in the spring.

Plateau society was extremely fluid. People from different villages and bands regularly joined together for seasonal tasks, spoke one another's languages, and intermarried, taking up residence in another village with ease. Because Plateau people were exogamous, even chiefs and their male and female offspring married across village and band lines, creating a regional network of chiefly lineages that encouraged cooperation and peace. Plateau people still trace descent in terms of these chiefly families.

Although the arrival of the horse around 1730 among the Nez Perces and its rapid spread among the neighboring Cayuses, Walla Wallas, and Umatillas created a disparity of wealth and encouraged horse raiding, Plateau people focused their hostilities outward, toward the enemy Shoshones, Blackfeet, and Crows. With only a few exceptions, peace rather than warfare characterized the plateau even after whites arrived.

The Lewis and Clark Expedition of 1805–6 provided the first recorded descriptions of the native peoples of the plateau. By 1855, the once autonomous Salishan-, Sahaptian-, and Chinookan-speaking bands had been consigned to reservations. In the fifty-year interim, Plateau peoples had been weakened by diseases, dependency on European trade goods, and resource depletion caused by the fur trade, Christian missions, forced treaty cessions, and brief wars of resistance led by the Cayuses (1847–49), the Yakamas (1855–57), and the

Spokane–Coeur d'Alenes (1860), culminating in the Nez Perce War of 1877.

The British North West Company opened the first plateau trading posts among the Kutenais and Kalispels in 1807 and 1809, respectively. Rival American Fur Company, North West Company, and Hudson's Bay Company posts proliferated along the Columbia, Fraser, and Clearwater-Snake river systems for several decades thereafter, but the southern plateau was nearly trapped out by 1825. Plateau peoples were more interested in trading horses and provisions than in trapping beaver, but a growing dependence on guns and other European manufactures, intermarriage with Indian and white outsiders, and diseases contracted at major trading posts such as Fort Walla Walla and Fort Colville created rifts in the social and political fabric.

Protestant missions to the Cayuses, Nez Perces, and Spokans established in 1836–37 and rival Catholic missions to the Flatheads, Coeur d'Alenes, Pend Oreilles, and Colviles after 1841 intensified these rifts. Urged by Catholic Iroquois and prophesies of the coming of a new spirit power that could raise the dead to life, Plateau delegations had sought missionaries during the 1830s. And although the Prebyterian mission to the Cayuses at Waiilatpu was destroyed in the 1847 Whitman Massacre, and the Flatheads abandoned St. Mary's when a mission was opened to the enemy Blackfeet, over time Christianity made substantial gains on the plateau. Simultaneously, Christian, particularly Roman Catholic, symbolism and ritual found their way into nineteenth-century Plateau revitalization movements such as the prophet Smohalla's church, founded at Priest Rapids and now called the Long House or Seven Drums religion.

The opening of the Oregon Trail in 1842 issued a flood of white settlers across the plateau. Oregon statehood in 1846, the Donation Act of 1850, allowing whites to settle anywhere in Washington Territory, and the search for a northern transcontinental railroad route to the Pacific intensified pressure on Plateau tribes. In the 1855 Plateau treaty councils at Hell Gate, Walla Walla, and Wasco (near the Dalles), which included all but the northern Salishan bands, Washington Governor Isaac Stevens and Oregon Indian Superintendent Joel Palmer threatened, bribed, and cajoled friendly tribal leaders like Lawyer of the Nez Perces to part with nearly 90 percent of their bands' ancestral homelands in exchange for reservations.

Like the Puget Sound treaties, the 1855 Plateau treaties gave tribes perpetual access to accustomed fishing and gathering grounds outside the reservations, but Plateau reservations were purposely made larger so as to encourage farming and ranching. However, white settlers invaded Yakama and Palouse lands even before the treaties were ratified in 1859, and the plateau erupted in the sporadic Yakima War of 1855–57.

As a result of treaties and executive orders, the Nez Perces and Klamaths managed to secure exclusive tribal reservations for themselves, as did the Coeur d'Alenes, Kalispels, and Spokans. Members of smaller tribes such as the Idaho Kutenais and the Chelans, Sinkiuses, and Wenatchis took homesteads or allotments in their original homelands rather than face removal to a reservation. Sparse white settlement in remote parts of the plateau also allowed hundreds of Plateau families to fish, hunt, and gather foods outside of reservation boundaries, augmenting their subsistence by occasional wage labor. By 1890, however, most of the Plateau bands had been forced onto aggregate reservations, where they are known today as the Confederated Colville Tribes, the Confederated Warm Springs Tribes, the Confederated Umatilla Tribes, the Confederated Yakama Tribes, and the Confederated Salish and Kutenai Tribes of the Flathead Nation.

The 1855 treaties intended to turn Plateau people into farmers and ranchers by offering seed, stock animals, implements, and agency instructors, but most of the southern plateau was too arid to be farmed without irrigation. In the late nineteenth century reservation Indians were surrounded by garrisoned forts designed to keep them from turning hostile. Indian agents and Indian police withheld rations and incarcerated Indians for leaving reservations without a pass, gambling, engaging in violent behavior, and practicing native religion. Industrial boarding schools run by religious denominations and the federal government were established on many of the reservations, and after 1885 many Plateau children were sent to the Chemawa Indian School, near Salem, Oregon.

Although poverty was the norm on reservations without arable lands such as Warm Springs, during the late nineteenth century some tribes made great strides toward a new economy based on farming and ranching. Tribes already horse wealthy in the 1850s like the Yakamas, Nez Perces, and Umatillas built stocks of horses, beef cattle, and hogs, as did the Coeur d'Alenes and Spokans. These same tribes, along with the Colvilles, also turned successfully to farming, putting up to twelve hundred acres under fence and building Victorian-style houses.

Other early reservation enterprises included sawmills, gristmills, and ferries; however, members of tribes without access to fisheries, timber, or arable land were often forced to become migrant workers, hiring out to white ranchers, farmers, and fruit growers or working in fish-processing plants and canneries along the lower Columbia. A barter economy still prevailed in most tribal communities, and members continued to rely on collecting fish, game, and berries, as well as traditional craft production.

Economic development on Plateau reservations was nearly snuffed out by the General Allotment Act of 1887 and land reductions mandated by executive order. Although the Yakamas lost only 10 percent of their land, shrewdly managing to hold off the sale of surplus lands while acquiring irrigation and retaining water rights through court action brought on their behalf by agents and interested white ranchers, other tribes were not so fortunate. The Umatillas lost two-thirds of their land; the Confederated Salish-Kutenais, allotted in 1904–8, lost more than half of theirs.

The twentieth century has seen a resurgence of development and autonomy among Plateau tribes. The exception is the formerly timber-rich Klamath tribe, which was terminated in 1958. Although only the Warm Springs, Colvilles, Flatheads, and Kalispels initially voted to accept the Indian Reorganization Act in 1934, the tribal governments of all Plateau reservations have become increasingly proactive in their efforts to fashion their own destinies in the areas of education, health, economic development, sovereignty, legal jurisdiction over tribal lands and resources, and intergovernmental relations at the county, state, and federal levels.

An example is the Columbia River Intertribal Fish Commission, formed in 1977 by the Warm Springs, Yakama, Umatilla, and Nez Perce tribes to address dwindling salmon runs caused by environmental degradation and the Bonneville, Dalles, and Grand Coulee dams, which flooded major Plateau fisheries. Armed with the 1974 *Boldt* decision, which restored Indian access to traditional fishing sites and allotted 50 percent of the harvestable fish to the 1855 treaty tribes, the commission in 1995 proposed that the federal government turn control of the fish and their habitat over to the tribes for whom those fish are a spiritual resource.

The managed exploitation of timber, hydroelectric, and mineral reserves, as well as tribal business complexes and industries, appear to offer equally important pathways out of persistent underdevelopment. As part of the Affiliated Tribes of the Northwest, Plateau tribes are also aiming for a piece of the tourist market. Major tribal resorts and museums attract visitors to Warm Springs, Flathead, and Umatilla, and casinos, bingo, and lotteries provide substantial revenues for these same communities, as well as those at Spokane, Coeur d'Alene, and Colville.

Gambling, particularly at the Stick Game, has a long tradition on the plateau. Though the game was banned by missionaries and government agents, it has persisted. Twentieth-century casino-style gambling is thus a reformulation of an ancient cultural tradition, and its profits are now being used by many Plateau tribes to buy back ancestral lands lost through allotment.

Anastasio, Angelo, "The Southern Plateau: An Ecological Analysis of Intergroup Relations" *Northwest Anthropological Research Notes* 6, no. 2 (1972): 109–229; S. Hunn, Eugene, *Nch'i-Wana, "The Big River": Mid-Columbia Indian People and Their Land* (Seattle: University of Washington Press, 1990); Ramsey, Jarold, comp. and ed., *Coyote Was Going There: Indian Literature of the Oregon Country* (Seattle: University of Washington Press, 1977).

JACQUELINE PETERSON
Washington State University

PLENTY COUPS (ALAXCHIIAAHUSH)

(1848?–1932)
Crow warrior and leader.

Plenty Coups, like many tribal heroes, is as famous for what he symbolized as for the life he lived. He was a visionary, a warrior, a businessman, and a promoter of education and cooperation with non-Indians. He believed that the cultural survival of the Crows depended on peace with the United States. Plenty Coups outlived all the other traditional leaders of his generation. Being the last chief placed a great burden on him, but Plenty Coups had prepared for that responsibility all his life.

As a young man, Plenty Coups was called Bull-Goes-against-the-Wind. The year of his birth was likely 1848, but this is uncertain, as no census records exist for the Crows until after 1887. He told the historian and biographer Frank B. Linderman that he was born "at the place we call The-Cliff-That-Has-No-Pass . . . not far from Billings [Montana]. My mother's name was Otter-Woman. My father was Medicine Bird."

From the beginning of his illustrious life, Plenty Coups was determined to protect his people. Born into the Sore Lips clan of the Mountain Crows, he rose to prominence by his own merits and war deeds. In play as a young boy, and later in more serious activities, he developed a reputation for fairness and generosity to his companions. A compact, athletic man, he seemed to excel at everything he attempted.

Indeed, Plenty Coups recognized his calling as a leader at a very young age when he sought power and guidance through vision quests, which were and still are famous among his people for their meanings and symbolism. In the most well known of these quests, he was taken into a lodge, where he was shown signs of many prophetic things, including his becoming a chief and the eventual disappearance of the buffalo. His vision instructed him to learn by listening, using his mind, and avoiding the mistakes of other tribes. In doing so, he would preserve Crow tribal existence. He was also warned not to fight the whites, who would come to Crow country in many numbers. Throughout his life, he was determined to abide by these visionary principles because he saw no other alternative. Well prepared by his visions and his own convictions, Plenty Coups led his people in their transition from a nomadic to a reservation existence.

Plenty Coups had risen to the challenge of postreservation leadership by becoming a war chief in battles with the Sioux during the 1860s and 1870s. Half a century later, when the Crow Reservation was in the process of being reduced from its original (1868) 38.5 million acres to 2.25 million acres, Plenty Coups became actively involved in negotiations with the United States to maintain a unified Crow position on important issues.

In prereservation times, leaders among the Crows were charged with knowing where to camp and how to protect the village, as well as with hunting, fighting, and speechmaking. Reservation leadership required a different kind of courage. Plenty Coups sought out opportunities to test himself in this new setting. At the age of thirty-two he joined a delegation of older chiefs who traveled to Washington, D.C., to represent the Crows at the Interior Department. While the agreement approved that year reduced the size of the tribe's estate, it strengthened the Crows' ability to control what they retained.

During the 1880s and 1890s, Plenty Coups's skill in uniting his fellow chiefs and maintaining a friendly but firm stance in his dealings with the United States sustained his rise in prominence. He reached independent lease agreements with local cattlemen, opposed more militant leaders within the tribe, and encouraged his friends and relatives to settle near him in what became the village of Pryor, Montana. The government built a two-story frame house for him there, part of which Plenty Coups fitted out as a store.

The Crow chief made several trips to Washington between 1880 and 1921. His most notable journey was made with the delegation of 1917 that, aided by the tribe's attorneys, defeated a bill in the U.S. Senate that proposed to purchase all unsettled land on the Crow Reservation for white homesteaders. During this occasion and on many others, Plenty Coups utilized the talents of younger Crow men who could speak English, instead of relying on government interpreters, whom he did not trust. This practice may account for Plenty Coups's consistent support for education. He was quoted as saying, "Education is your most powerful weapon. With education you are the white man's equal; without education you are his victim." It is appropriate that, today, a modern high school in Pryor bears his name.

During his visit to the national capital in 1880, the Crow chief was taken to George Washington's home at Mount Vernon. Afterward, Plenty Coups decided that he, too, would leave his house in Pryor for all to enjoy. In 1924, he turned the property over to the state of Montana for a park. It is now the site of a museum commemorating his life.

In one vision, Plenty Coups was told he would never have any children of his own. Although he did have children, by several wives, none of them survived infancy, and he has no direct descendants. Plenty Coups died on March 4, 1932. He had seen much in his long lifetime. A member of the Fox Warrior Society, he spent his youth and young adulthood fighting the tribe's old enemies: the Sioux, Northern Cheyennes, Flatheads, and Blackfeet. He knew firsthand the freedom to hunt and travel where he pleased. He saw his enemies defeated. He also saw his own freedom taken and his tribal lands reduced in size time and again, yet he never ceased to have the courage to lead. He was buried on his own home site, where in a vision he had seen himself sitting, a very old man, alone in the shade.

See also Crow.

MARDELL HOGAN PLAINFEATHER (Crow)
Sallisaw, Oklahoma

POCAHONTAS (MATOAKA)

(c. 1596–1617)

Legendary Algonquian (Powhatan) "princess" and an important peacemaker in early-seventeenth-century Virginia.

Pocahontas (the name purportedly means "the Playful One") was an active, carefree ten- to twelve-year-old girl when Captain John Smith and 103 other colonists established the first permanent English settlement at Jamestown in May 1607. As a favored daughter of Powhatan (Wahunsunacock), the most powerful chief of some thirty Chesapeake Bay Algonquian tribes along Virginia's tidal rivers, Pocahontas was destined by royal birth to play some important part in the history of her people. The arrival of the English in her father's domain, however, provided her with a unique opportunity to play a dramatic, central role in American history as an indispensable intermediary who preserved a tenuous peace between two different cultures, two distant continents, and two determined camps of armed warriors.

Pocahontas, regarded by both the Powhatans and the English as a harmless young female, was uniquely equipped by gender, high status, and tender age to serve as a peacemaker between her own people and the white strangers from a foreign land. She was a frequent visitor to the Jamestown settlement, and a mutual fascination and affection quickly developed between Pocahontas and the English. The colonist William Strachey observed that she was a "well featured but wanton young girle," best known for turning cartwheels in the nude, but Captain Smith described her first and most memorably, in 1608, as "the only Nonpareil" of Virginia, who, with her wit, wisdom, and warm personality, "much exceedeth any of the rest" of the local Indians.

Romantic images of the beguiling Powhatan maiden and the brave English captain have endured through the ages, making Pocahontas the best-known American Indian the world over. Her life story has proved irresistible to countless novelists, playwrights, and historians. The Pocahontas of legend originated in a very brief and much disputed passage in Smith's *Generall Historie of Virginia, New-England, and the Summer Isles,* which was published in 1624 but recounted an alleged event from seventeen years earlier. Smith's account described how he had been taken as a captive in December 1607 to Powhatan's capital of Werowocomoco, along the lower York River, and how, when he was about to be executed, Pocahontas suddenly threw herself across his body and "hazarded the beating out of her owne braines" to save his life.

Even if Smith's memory of what seemed to happen was accurate, he did not necessarily grasp the intent or implications of this incident. As the captured leader of the colonists, Smith was more valuable to Powhatan alive than dead, and it is virtually certain that his life was never in danger. If indeed Pocahontas interposed herself between the captain and his apparent executioners and "prevailed upon her father" to free him, she was probably performing a symbolic and highly orchestrated ceremony—a public acknowledgment that Powhatan, through his biological daughter, was adopting Smith as his "son" and making him an honorary—but subordinate—chieftain, or "werowance." It is inconceivable that Powhatan would have released Smith unless he thought that he controlled this underling and the weak, subservient English "tribe" that owed its allegiance and very survival to him.

Too much attention has been paid to the "saving" of Smith, for it obscures Pocahontas's even more vital, and verifiable, contributions to keeping the peace and preserving lives on both sides. After Smith returned to Jamestown, Pocahontas played a key role as a mutually trusted intermediary, conveying food, gifts, and important messages back and forth. Between 1608 and 1610, she negotiated the release of Powhatan prisoners held by the colonists and often shielded Englishmen from her father's wrath—risking her own life, according to Smith, to reveal "trecheries [and] preserve" the Virginia colony.

Pocahontas's best efforts, however, could not prevent the onset of the First Anglo-Powhatan War (1610–14), as the coastal Algonquians responded to unendurable coercion and effrontery by the English. Because of the war and her reputed marriage to an obscure warrior named Kocoum, Pocahontas paid no more voluntary visits to Jamestown after 1610.

Ironically, it was at the very height of violent hostility between the Powhatans and the English that Pocahontas spent more time with, and grew closer to, the colonists. Captain Samuel Argall came upon Pocahontas as she was visiting along the Potomac River in spring 1613, and with the assistance of the Patawomeke tribe, he captured her. Pocahontas remained a well-treated hostage at Jamestown for the next year, during which time she converted to Anglicanism, being baptized as "the Lady Rebecca" by the Reverend Alexander Whitaker, and became engaged to a widower

The only known contemporaneous portrait of Pocahontas. Unsigned, it was painted in England while Pocahontas was traveling there in 1616 with her husband John Rolfe, their baby son, and a group of Indians. She was twenty-one at the time, and as the inscription indicates, she had converted to Christianity, given up her Indian name Matoaka, and been baptized Rebecca.

named John Rolfe. (The Christian name chosen for Pocahontas seemed prescient: "And the Lord said to her [Rebecca] : two nations are in thy wombe, . . . the one people shal be mightier then the other, and the elder shal serve the younger" [Genesis 25:23, Geneva Bible].)

The timing of this betrothal was no accident from a diplomatic standpoint, for both the Powhatans and the English wanted to end five years of atrocity-ridden warfare without either side admitting defeat. Rolfe asked the English governor for permission to marry Pocahontas "for the good of this plantation, for the honour of our countrie, for the glory of God, for my owne salvation, and for the converting [of] . . . an unbelieving creature." Although Pocahontas may have had some affection for Rolfe, their marriage in April 1614 was a diplomatic union that suddenly ended the war and prevented a recurrence of large-scale hostilities as long as Pocahontas lived.

Officials of the financially strapped Virginia Company of London arranged a tour of England so that "the Lady Rebecca" could generate moral and financial support for future missionary endeavors. In June 1616 Pocahontas arrived in England with her husband and their infant son, Thomas. She was enthusiastically received by King James I and leading English citizens, becoming highly publicized as "*la belle sauvage*." One courtier wrote that Pocahontas "did not only accustom herself to civility, but still carried herself as the daughter of a King, and was accordingly respected . . . by . . . persons of Honor." Her friend John Smith, whom she had not seen since he left Virginia in 1609, reputedly informed the queen of Pocahontas's "extraordinarie affection to our Nation," which had been "the instrument to preserve this Colonie from death, famine and utter confusion."

Pocahontas herself was not so lucky; the cold, polluted air and foreign diseases of London all too quickly took their toll. She died on about March 21, 1617, before she was able to sail home to her beloved Virginia forests, and is buried along the Thames in the Church of St. George, at Gravesend, Kent.

Pocahontas, born into an indigenous American culture, died far from her blood relatives, among a people whose culture she had adopted and adapted to. Smith wrote that her legacy was that of a brave pioneer— "the first Christian ever of that [Powhatan] Nation, the first Virginian [who] ever spake English, or had a childe in mariage by an Englishman"—even before she left her homeland to explore new people, new customs, and new lands. Her deeds in making and preserving the peace, whether the product of childish naiveté or mature conviction, reflected a consistent effort on her part to save lives and promote tolerance amid the destruction of conflicting cultures. Ironically, she was such a powerful, virtuous, and respected symbol of harmony between the races that her sudden, premature death crushed all hope of continued intercultural cooperation in Virginia.

By the time her son, Thomas Rolfe, returned to Virginia in 1640 as a mature man, a second, even more brutal war had consumed the Powhatans and the colonists, and a third devastating conflict was just four years away. Although he would pass the blood of his mother, Pocahontas, on to later generations of distinguished Americans, Thomas followed his father's example in cultivating tobacco on the conquered lands of Powhatan, Pocahontas, and their people—thereby confirming Smith's prediction that England would achieve "a Kingdome by her meanes."

See also Powhatan.

Barbour, Philip L., *Pocahontas and Her World* (Boston: Houghton Mifflin, 1970); Mossiker, Frances, *Pocahontas: The Life and the Legend* (New York: Knopf, 1976).

J. FREDERICK FAUSZ
University of Missouri at St. Louis

POINT HOPE

Of all the continually occupied communities in North America, Point Hope, Alaska, is one of the oldest. Although its current population is only about seven hundred, it is a significant settlement both because of its rich archaeological sites and because of its vibrant modern culture. Point Hope is located at a triangular point on the Chukchi Sea, 275 miles north of Nome and 570 miles northwest of Fairbanks. The place's English name was bestowed by Captain F. W. Beechey in 1826 to honor a fellow Englishman, Sir William Johnston Hope.

Archaeologists estimate that Point Hope was first settled two thousand years ago by people who migrated over the land bridge from Siberia. In addition to an old burial ground, two prominent archaeological sites adjoin the community. One contains evidence of over five hundred houses, occupied as early as 500 B.C. This older settlement is unique because it contains no evidence of whaling, an activity that did not appear at Point Hope until the middle of the nineteenth century, at which point it transformed the community. Whaling remained profitable there until the early 1900s, but it brought with it alcohol, new diseases, and population decline. From 1894 to 1948 an unsuccessful attempt was made to introduce reindeer herding to the area. Today the forms of survival are more diverse. For many years essential supplies were delivered annually by a Bureau of Indian Affairs ship. Air travel has modified lifestyles and made the community less isolated. Inhabitants often find employment as seasonal construction workers in other locations, and as miners. Seasonal whaling and caribou hunting remain important.

Throughout its long history Point Hope has apparently functioned as a cohesive community. Historical continuity, complex kin relationships, and a regular cycle of rituals and festivals have linked the people and undergirded their sense of common identity.

POINT PLEASANT BATTLE

Following the British defeat of the French in 1763, British colonists became increasingly aggressive in pressing for Indian lands west of the Appalachian Mountains, despite the Royal Proclamation of 1763 prohibiting British colonial settlement there. In the spring of 1774, Lord Dunmore, the governor of Virginia, was locked in a dispute with Pennsylvania over control of the Ohio Valley. To bolster his position, Dunmore provoked a war with the Shawnees by circulating a proclamation throughout the upper Ohio Valley that the Shawnees and colonists were already engaged in a war. The Shawnee leader Cornstalk assured British authorities of his good intentions, maintaining that the Shawnees had "prevailed on the foolish people amongst us to sit still and do no harm till we see whether it is the intention of the white people in general to fall on us." But the British colonists along the Ohio had already begun killing Shawnees, and by mid-May, Shawnee warriors had retaliated in attacks along the frontier. Fighting continued throughout the summer, and on October 10, Cornstalk and three hundred Shawnee and Delaware warriors fought a decisive battle with a Euro-American militia under the command of Daniel Boone at Point Pleasant on the Ohio River. Puckeshinewa, the father of the nineteenth-century Shawnee leader Tecumseh, was among those who fought and died at the battle. Following the battle, the army of Virginia, led by Andrew Lewis, surrounded the Shawnee towns on the Scioto River and forced them to surrender. In the subsequent Treaty of Camp Charlotte, Cornstalk and other chiefs yielded Shawnee hunting rights south of the Ohio River to Virginia in exchange for Lord Dunmore's promise to keep colonists from crossing north into their lands.

POKAGON, SIMON

(1830–99)
Michigan Potawatomi author, entrepreneur, celebrity, and Chautauqua lecturer.

Simon Pokagon was the youngest son of Leopold Pokagon, a village headman who was for American officials the best-known speaker and negotiator for the several small, staunchly Catholic Potawatomi communities of southwestern Michigan. Little is known of his childhood years except that they were spent in his fa-

ther's village during the height of the midwestern Indian removals, which Leopold and other Michigan Potawatomi leaders skillfully resisted. In his adult years Pokagon worked at advancing his own public career through imaginative exaggerations of his father's accomplishments.

Pokagon maintained he was monolingual until age fourteen, when he was sent to Notre Dame Academy to begin his schooling. He then spent a year at Oberlin Collegiate Institute and two more at Twinsburg Academy in Ohio. Subsequently, he intimated he had been preparing for the priesthood, although how much his studies at the ardently Calvinist Ohio schools might have prepared him for such a vocation is questionable. As an adult, once established as a prominent protégé of the evangelical Protestant Friends of the Indian reformers, he turned away from his earlier Catholic heritage, apparently without formally adopting Protestantism. In his last decades, Pokagon's American publicists and sponsors billed him as the best-educated "full blooded" Indian of his day. They claimed he was fluent in five languages, including English, Latin, and Greek, and was the "hereditary principal chief" of the Potawatomi tribe.

Such press-agent puffery lacks substance. Holographic originals of his letters show that his command of written English was at best weak. None of the essays printed under his name in journals such as the *Forum, Arena, Harper's Magazine,* and the *Chautauquan* contains so much as a quote from the Latin classics or a Greek epigram. The only evidence of any exposure of his to these ancient languages is his occasional and erratic use of Greek vowel diacritics in the orthography he allegedly devised for Potawatomi, as in the title of his *O-Gî-Mäw-Kwê Mit-I-Gwä-Kî (Queen of the Woods)* (assuming that he was in fact the author of this slim volume). This book appeared posthumously in 1899, issued by Pokagon's attorney-publicist, C. H. Engle. Engle advertised *Queen of the Woods* as a true autobiographical account of events that really happened. But *Queen* is actually a clumsy mix of mawkish "vanishing frontier" fable coupled with a derivative polemic against the immorality of nicotine addiction and the evils of Demon Rum.

The first half of *Queen* purports to narrate the details of Pokagon's life following his return from school in Ohio (about 1850). Casting off the veneer of "civilization," he takes to the woods clad in buckskins, becoming a mighty deer slayer. Living a solitary life, attuned to nature, this fictive Simon encounters an unspoiled wood nymph, a "real natural" Potawatomi who speaks the languages of the birds and beasts. This was Pokagon's beloved Lonidaw, who appears in the book with her trusty (but terribly jealous) anthropomorphized companion, an albino deer. (Lonidaw, also known by her baptismal name of Angela, was the daughter of Sinagaw, a leader of the group of northern Indiana Potawatomis who broke away from the coerced westward emigration of 1837 to take refuge in southwestern Michigan.) Pokagon's sponsors called him the "king" of the Potawatomis, and in the book, upon their ill-fated marriage Lonidaw becomes his "Queen of the Woods." After living happily with Simon for some years, and delivering two babies with only Simon in attendance (there were in fact two additional children), Lonidaw drowns tragically, in an accident caused by two drunken American boatmen. (Pokagon later remarried; his second wife, Victoria, is not mentioned in *Queen of the Woods*.) Then the narrative changes course and tone entirely, as the author takes up the same popular puritanical causes Pokagon had long been advocating from various podiums.

Nonetheless, there is one substantial biographical truth in *Queen of the Woods*, whether or not Pokagon himself in any sense actually authored the manuscript. Its central theme is that of the unspoiled Savage who achieves Civilization, only to revert to nature, where the evil forces of Civilization pursue and destroy his happiness. Thereupon he again embraces Civilization, this time struggling to root out its immoral elements. This was the public image Pokagon cultivated in concert with his patrons, who were in the main the grandes dames of the Friends of the Indian reform movement. For them, Simon Pokagon was a major success story. In their eyes, he was a "master link" between Savagery and Civilization, an embodiment of their fondest hope: that Indians could traverse the great divide and serve as models of literate, Christian, smoke-free temperance for the uncouth lower-class immigrant elements of American society. There is also a substantial historical truth in this relationship. Simon Pokagon and his sponsors constituted an early version of the continuing alliance between idealistic elites and Native Americans, with images of the latter still being spun out as anti-stereotypes, moral exemplars for today's regenerative movements such as environmentalism and crime control.

C. H. Engle was also the publisher of Pokagon's several pamphlets, including "A Red Man's Greetings" and "The Lord's Prayer" (the latter in Potawatomi),

both printed on birch bark. During his speaking tours, Pokagon peddled these to his audiences, and Engle continued to market them following his death. Pokagon's several published essays were much-edited print versions of some of his public speeches. In their original oral form, these addressed a variety of issues prominent in the minds of his American sponsors and certain audiences of the day, ranging from abolition, to free silver, to temperance, to women's rights, to racial tolerance.

Along the way, Pokagon also stumped for the general allotment policy, and for the peaceful acceptance by Indians of assimilation generally. Although his skills in writing English were severely limited, he was reportedly (according to his publicists) a spellbinding orator. His style was a mix of fawning sentimentality and surrender to the inevitable, with just enough of a tinge of anger over paradise lost to titillate but not badly annoy his late nineteenth-century audiences. He was especially skilled at arousing and encouraging the growing guilt feelings of elite Americans about Indians, which he manipulated to tap their personal pocketbooks for his own expenses.

Pokagon's posthumous *Queen of the Woods* brought him some years of fame—a reputation renewed in the 1970s when, with the sudden increase in popularity of American Indian and other ethnic literatures, he was identified by uncritical enthusiasts as the first Indian novelist. But during his lifetime his career peaked on May 1, 1893, when he was invited to address the opening of the Chicago World's Columbian Exposition. He was selected to first peal the replica Liberty Bell, a key symbol of that century's Columbian celebrations, and to present an oration celebrating the progress of American civilization, with Pokagon himself standing forth both to epitomize and to eulogize the transformation of New World natives.

To be exact, Simon Pokagon was esteemed only in the eyes of his American public and patrons. Far from being the "king" or the "hereditary principal chief" of the Potawatomis, he was for some years merely an elected council member representing one of the several Michigan Catholic bands. Long before his grand 1893 Chicago performance his own constituents had come to distrust, then to depose and shun him. This was due to his efforts to collect for himself, at first unbeknown to other Potawatomis, an inordinately large share of a court-of-claims award of thirty-nine thousand dollars, which was supposed to be doled out equally to tribal members, on a per capita basis. The Catholic Potawatomis became even further incensed when they discovered Pokagon had secretly conveyed to a combine of shady Chicago attorneys and real-estate promoters a "deed" to their fancied claim to ownership of Chicago's lakefront, a claim from which the Potawatomis dreamed of extracting a huge windfall.

Simon Pokagon died suddenly and unexpectedly at his home near Hartford, Michigan, on January 28, 1899. When the Chicagoland's Daughters of the American Revolution decided to honor the deceased celebrity by interring him in that city's Graceland Cemetery, they received no complaints from the Catholic Potawatomis along Michigan's St. Joseph River. Chicago was where Pokagon enjoyed a reputation and had a following, so to them that was where his remains belonged. His metropolitan patrons further honored Pokagon and his father by persuading the Chicago Park District to erect a statue of both men in that city's Jackson Park.

Simon Pokagon's public career can be viewed as the construction of a reputation and a persona that had little to do with inherent talent or cultivated art. His inordinate need for public acclaim and compliant eagerness to seize the opportunities offered by the preferences of sponsors and mass audiences, led Pokagon to conform to elite American expectations of how a good Indian should comport himself. So it was that he became an archetype celebrity Indian, in his "army blue" suit, sometimes topped by a borrowed Sioux headdress, hawking his "Lord's Prayer" and "Red Man's Greeting," posturing dutifully before American audiences: Simon Pokagon was the Friends of the Indians' Christian counterpoint to Buffalo Bill Cody's Wild West Indian spectaculars.

Clifton, James A., *The Pokagons, 1683–1983: Catholic Potawatomi of the St. Joseph River Valley* (Washington, D.C.: Potawatomi Nation and The University Press, 1984); Clifton, James A., "Simon Pokagon's Sandbar," Michigan History 71, no. 5 (1987): 12–19; Clifton, James A., and Bernadette Rigal-Cellard, eds., *Simon Pokagon's "Queen of the Woods"* (forthcoming).

JAMES A. CLIFTON
Western Michigan University

POMO

For more than ten thousand years Pomoan people and their ancestors have lived in the hill and valley lands north of San Francisco, California, in such places as present-day Santa Rosa, Healdsburg, Ukiah, Kelseyville,

and Stewart's Point. In modern times all the people of these lands have come to be known by a single name—Pomo. However, there never was, nor is there now, one Pomo tribe. In all, about seventy-two independent tribes have been grouped together under the name *Pomo*.

The members of each Pomoan tribe spoke a dialect of one of seven related but distinct languages. Some tribes had about 125 members; others had in excess of 500. The Pomos lived an unhurried life, often talking, joking, singing, and carrying out the activities of daily life. However, on those occasions when certain plant foods—clover greens, *Brodiaea* bulbs, acorns, tarweed seeds, for example—were ready for harvest, the pace of life quickened.

In the summertime neighboring groups gathered for an event called Big Time, which featured ceremonial feasting and dancing and lasted several days. While together, the people enjoyed each other's company, shared news, gambled, engaged in sports, and traded goods.

Spirituality was part of everyday life. The elders educated each new generation, largely one-on-one, with the young learning by carefully observing, listening, and eventually doing. Values like politeness, sharing, patience, and fairness were considered important.

Some Pomoan people practiced specialized occupations, such as doctoring. Others specialized in making specific items, such as shell and magnesite beads—both valuable trade items—and certain types of baskets. The making of those things needed for daily life required great patience, precision, and technical ability.

The landing of Juan Cabrillo's ship off the coast of northern California in 1542 portended devastating changes for Pomoan peoples, even though it would be more than two hundred years before Europeans settled permanently in their homeland. In 1812 the Russians, eager to profit from the trade in sea-mammal pelts, established Fort Ross in Kashaya Pomo lands. In 1818 the Spanish established Mission San Rafael and began recruiting Pomoan peoples. Mission Indians were poorly treated, and European diseases began to devastate the population. After the Mexican government closed the mission in the 1830s, some Pomos became serfs on Mexican land grants. The Americans continued the pattern of intrusion and destruction after 1850, when California joined the Union. Not only did the Americans fail to ratify or honor the treaties they signed with Pomoan peoples, but the California state legislature passed laws that sanctioned the kidnapping and enslavement of Indian people.

Despite this tragic history, many Pomoan people have retained their cultural values and traditions. Pomoan people have distinguished themselves in many walks of life. One person has served as executive director of the California Native American Heritage Commission, while another is a judge on the Third Circuit Court. In 1992 the Santa Rosa Board of Education voted to name its newest high school in honor of the well-known Makahmo Pomo basketmaker Elsie Allen (1899–1990).

Bean, Lowell John, and Dorothea Theodoratus, "Western Pomo and Northeastern Pomo," in *Handbook of North American Indians*, ed. William C. Sturtevant, vol. 8, California, ed. Robert F. Heizer (Washington: Smithsonian Institution, 1978); McLendon, Sally, and Michael J. Lowy, "Eastern Pomo and Southeastern Pomo," in *Handbook of North American Indians,* ed. William C. Sturtevant, vol. 8, California, ed. Robert F. Heizer (Washington: Smithsonian Institution, 1978).

KATHLEEN ROSE SMITH
(Mihilakawna Pomo/Yoletamal Miwok)
Yamhuut & Associates, Walnut Creek, California

BEVERLY R. ORTIZ
University of California at Berkeley

PONTIAC

(1720?–1769)
Ottawa war leader and chief.

Robert Rogers's play *Ponteach: A Tragedy* made Pontiac the most famous Indian of the eighteenth century. Francis Parkman's *History of the Conspiracy of Pontiac* renewed and extended that fame into the nineteenth and twentieth centuries. These men created a powerful figure—a noble Indian who symbolized not only his race's fall but also the supposedly incompatible destinies of Indians and whites. But the real Pontiac was a more complicated and more interesting figure. If his life must be reduced to a symbol, then it can just as well be represented by nearly the opposite proposition: that an accommodation between Indians and Europeans was possible and that in change lay opportunity as well as danger.

Pontiac was an Ottawa war leader who took an indeterminate part in the increasingly anti-English councils and negotiations among the western allies of the French following the fall of Canada to the British in 1760. During these same years he came under the influence of Neolin, the Delaware prophet who preached a nativist message of Indian renewal. Neolin's doctrine, with its references to Christianity and its demand that Indians return to their old ways, was part of a growing movement of religious syncretism in the region. Pontiac adopted it, but only in part. He modified Neolin's anti-white message, stripped it of its renunciation of European technology, and turned it into a more specifically anti-English doctrine.

By 1763 Pontiac was an influential man at Detroit, and that spring he achieved much wider notoriety as the leader of an unsuccessful attempt to surprise the British garrison at that settlement. When the attempt at surprise failed, Pontiac became a leader of both Frenchmen and Indians in the siege that followed. Pontiac's goal was the return of his French "father," the governor of New France. He expected French soldiers to arrive to aid him.

The dramatic siege of Detroit became the centerpiece of what Europeans came to call "Pontiac's Rebellion." But the rebellion was hardly the work of Pontiac alone. His attack on Detroit was but part of the loosely coordinated attacks that were sweeping through the Great Lakes country and the Ohio River. British reinforcements eventually raised the siege of Detroit, and Colonel John Bradstreet, thinking Pontiac a broken man, refused his overtures for negotiations.

In some ways, however, Pontiac's greatest influence was yet to come. He retained a following in the Ottawa towns along the Maumee River, but he moved west to the Illinois country, where he apparently had relations. He became more than an Ottawa war leader; he came to be an important man in the towns of Wabash and Illinois country that refused to come to terms with the British.

Pontiac traveled widely, cementing loyalty to the common cause of continued resistance to British rule. He claimed to be acting for his French father, but he had made loyalty to Algonquian resistance of the British the defining quality of Frenchness. Any Frenchman who opposed him he regarded as English. The British who had dismissed him now came to regard him as a superhuman figure. In their view he was the key to peace. He had to be either gained to their interest or, as General Thomas Gage, the British commander, put it, "knocked in the head." Negotiating with him now seemed far less expensive than continued war.

Although a figure of importance, Pontiac was hardly the only influential leader in the Wabash and Illinois towns. Particularly after the Shawnees made peace in 1764, he came to take British peace overtures seriously and to use them to increase his influence with respect to more militant leaders. When in 1765 Kickapoos attacked a British delegation under the Indian agent George Croghan, they killed members of Croghan's Shawnee escort. War now threatened between the Shawnees and the Indians of the Illinois country. Indians in the Wabash and Illinois country willingly allowed Pontiac to negotiate for them. He deftly helped avert a war with the Shawnees and secured peace with the British. He had moved from being a war leader to being an influential mediator and chief.

Unfortunately, Pontiac came to believe that he was indeed the leader of a vast Indian confederation. From an Ottawa war leader seeking the return of his French father, he transmuted himself into a pretended Indian emperor in league with the British. It proved a fatal miscalculation. By 1766 he was acting arrogantly and imperiously, assuming powers no western Indian leader possessed. A French trader offered to bet that he would be dead in less than a year "if the English took so much notice of him." At Detroit he stabbed an Illinois leader; he lost virtually all influence among the Ottawas of Detroit and the Maumee River, where young warriors beat him. By 1768 he had become both the most famous Indian in the West and a man without a home. He retreated into exile among the Illinois, where his actions had made him enemies. There he belatedly proved the French trader right. On April 20, 1769, a nephew of Makatchinga, a Peoria chief of the Illinois confederation, murdered him in the streets of the French village of Cahokia. His death marked the limits of chieftainship.

Pontiac was, by all accounts, a man of great abilities and, to Europeans, great contradictions. He was an Algonquian war leader who embraced the ruthlessness which that role required. He could, particularly when in his drink, be a capricious and cruel man. In 1764 he ordered a Frenchman to drown Betty Fisher, a seven-year-old English captive who, sick and shivering from the cold, had sought to warm herself at Pontiac's fire. But in the fashion typical of Algonquian-speaking peoples, Pontiac metamorphosed from war leader to chief. Lieutenant Alexander Fraser, whose life Pontiac saved in the Illinois country, thought him "the most humane Indian" he ever saw.

In the end Pontiac aspired to a kind of chieftainship that was never really a possibility in Ottawa society. Ironically, it was only after the revolt that bore his name that he sought to unite the villages and towns of the old *pays d'en haut*, the upper country of the French,

into a single confederation under his leadership. Such pretensions cost him his life.

See also Neolin.

Peckham, Howard, *Pontiac and the Indian Uprising of 1763* (Princeton, N.J.: Princeton University Press, 1947); Quaife, Milo, ed., *The Siege of Detroit in 1763, the Journal of Pontiac's Conspiracy and John Rutherford's Narrative of a Captivity* (Chicago: Lakeside Press, 1958); White, Richard, *The Middle Ground: Indians, Empires, and Republics in the Great Lakes Region, 1650–1815* (New York: Cambridge University Press, 1991).

RICHARD WHITE
University of Washington

POOSEPATUCK (UNKECHAUG NATION)

The Poosepatucks are one of the most misunderstood Algonquian groups in southeastern New England. Recognized as the Unkechaug Nation by the state of New York, the Poosepatucks are synonymous with the fifty-two-acre reservation they occupy on Long Island, New York, in the northeast portion of the town of Mastic in Suffolk County.

The Unkechaug village of Poosepatuck is the sole remainder of 175 acres designated for the Unkechaugs by the deed of July 2, 1700, from Colonel William "Tangier" Smith. The deed allocated acreage so that Unkechaug settlements were surrounded by Euro-American land claims, thereby deliberately preventing Unkechaug unity. Further disruptions attended the arrival of the first Presbyterian missionaries in North America at Poosepatuck in 1741.

Early ethnological interest in the tribe was expressed by Thomas Jefferson, who visited Poosepatuck in 1791 to collect and translate examples of Unkechaug vocabulary. Often called one of the thirteen Long Island "tribes," the Poosepatucks initially constituted one of numerous Amerindian autonomous villages linked by kinship to a conciliar association or confederacy that stretched across Long Island and southern New England. These relationships still connect the Poosepatucks, Montauks, Shinnecocks, and Matinnecocks. Poosepatuck affiliations extend also to the Mohegans, Narragansetts, Pequots, and Wampanoags. Moreover, the Poosepatucks share cultural traits with the Lenape/Delaware and Iroquois peoples.

From 1718 to 1935, the Poosepatucks' proximity to the forty-four-hundred-acre William Floyd estate or plantation proved a serious impediment to independence and visibility. The isolation of the peninsula, the lack of opportunity, and the sentiment of the times limited Poosepatuck employment to subsistence laborers for the Floyds and other white settlers. Prior to 1799 some Poosepatucks were enslaved by the Floyds and other wealthy landowners; many became indentured ("bound out") and free laborers.

Between 1830 and 1945, most census takers and other nonnatives presumptuously assumed that European and African intermarriage among the Poosepatucks meant the death of their culture. Accordingly, their biological makeup exacerbated the lack of federal recognition. This resulted in the Poosepatucks' exclusion from voting in the Wheeler-Howard Indian Reorganization Act of 1934. Nonetheless, the Poosepatucks consistently retain a Native American identity. This has been heightened by postwar developments such as religious and cultural revitalization. Moreover, a challenge to the 1700 Smith deed was struck down in the Suffolk County (New York) court decision *William Shepherd Dana* v. *Luther Maynes, Frances Maynes, Edward Gales and Elaine Gales* (March 5, 1936), which reinforced the status of Poosepatuck as a viable New York State Indian reservation.

Important Poosepatuck rituals and social practices include the annual June Meeting (the Feast of the Dead), and the autumn Corn Festival. The June Meeting (also called the Feast of the Moon of Flowers or the Feast of the Strawberry Moon) is held at the Poosepatuck Reservation on the second weekend of June. June Meeting is a post-1790 Christian adaptation of an ancient honoring of all Long Island Amerindian ancestors. Christian and indigenous rites are observed. Traditional foods are prepared from resources available on the reservation. Flora, particularly lilacs, conveying the Poosepatuck sacred colors—including purple, white, red, green, and black—are displayed. The Poosepatuck autumn Corn Festival differs from similar eastern woodlands corn rites in its origins as a yearly tribute of "two yellow ears of corn" to the Smiths, as specified in the Smith deed. It can include powwow dancing, naming ceremonies, and the installation of tribal officers.

Currently the Poosepatuck Reservation has five core families and a population of approximately two hundred fifty. The Poosepatuck tribe is administered by a chief, land trustees, and a tribal council and headed by a titular chief who presides over tribal council meetings and ceremonies. The tribal council enforces Poosepatuck constitutional law and administers local and state Native American programs for the Poosepatucks. The

division of reservation land is by vote of the tribal trustees exclusively. Contemporary efforts at revitalization have focused on the Poosepatuck language and on sweat lodges. The issues of tax-free tobacco sales, of gaming enterprises, and of other entrepreneurial efforts on the reservation, as well as the continuing need for improvements in water and sewage services from the town of Mastic, have forced nonnative authorities to deal seriously with a previously "invisible" tribe.

Conkey, Laura E., Ethel Boissevain, and Ives Goddard, "Indians of Southern New England and Long Island: Late Period," in *Handbook of North American Indians,* ed. William C. Sturtevant, vol. 15, *Northeast,* ed. Bruce Trigger (Washington: Smithsonian Institution, 1978); Stone, Gaynell, and Nancy Bonvillain, eds., *Languages and Lore of the Long Island Indians* (Lexington, Mass.: Ginn, 1980); Treadwell, Donald (Chief Lone Otter), *My People the Unkechaug: The Story of a Long Island Indian Tribe* (Amsterdam: De Kiva, 1992).

BERNICE FORREST GUILLAUME
(Montauk/Poosepatuck)
Saint Louis University

POPÉ

(1630?–1690?)
Pueblo religious and political leader.

Popé was probably born in the Tewa village of Oke Owinge (San Juan Pueblo) around 1630. Very early in life he was likely given the name Popyn (ripe squash). His name, then, would indicate that he was from the Summer moiety. Later Spaniards wrote the name as Popé and often referred to him as El Popé. There is no reason to believe he did not grow up like any other Pueblo Indian boy of his time, following the strict rules and rhythms of the village. Native religion was inextricably woven into the patterns of Pueblo life. Even during seasons of hard work—such as planting, hoeing, irrigating, harvesting, and storing food and medicinal herbs for later use—religious observances were not neglected. Thus when ceremonials demanded it, Popé probably took part. And as the Pueblo people say, his future was already decided at the place of genesis—or heaven, as non-Indians call it.

In accordance with tradition, as a young man Popé went to a nearby river on certain mornings before sunrise to take a ceremonial bath that would make him strong both physically and mentally. Each morning he threw corn pollen to the east, toward the rising sun, and asked the deities for a good life in harmony with all creation. This was the life Popé knew, and later defended.

As he grew toward maturity Popé evidently began to serve as an assistant to the tribal war captain, helping to supervise the dances held by the tribe to entertain the people. The next step for Popé was an appointment by the village leaders as war captain, with all the responsibilities that post carried. At this time he would have become intensely aware of the pressures on the Tewa people, and other Pueblo people as well, from the Spanish, who had established the headquarters for their colonial government and missionaries in nearby Santa Fe. The colonial rulers and the missionaries who worked with them were telling the Pueblo people not to perform their traditional, centuries-old dances because they were "idolatrous."

Instead, the newcomers said, the Pueblo people were to go to the Spanish churches—many of which had been built with forced Indian labor. During the first half of the seventeenth century this pressure to abandon their native practices was resolutely, if passively, resisted by the Pueblos. How could they simply toss away the native spirituality that was for them not just a once-a-week exercise, but in fact a daily affair, interwoven into every part of their lives? Their beliefs formed the basis of their worldview. Their entire year was crowded with religious activities that kept them a peaceful people. The Spaniards were asking them to give up all this for something they did not understand.

As Popé gained stature as a leader he became increasingly aware of the Spaniards' activities and the impact they were having not only on his village but also on those that surrounded it. In this semidesert country it was hard enough to raise crops for one's own family, yet the Spanish *alcalde mayores* required certain Pueblo families to give certain Spanish families part of their crops. This practice was known as *encomienda* by the Spaniards. The Pueblo people were also required to donate their labor by working in Spanish haciendas—keeping up the Spaniards' gardens, bringing firewood, and tending animals. This was called *repartimiento*. All of these programs were instituted to assist Spanish settlers in establishing themselves in their new country.

In addition, the Spaniards regularly harassed the Pueblos and destroyed native worship centers. Although these acts were considered sacrilegious by the Indians, the Spaniards viewed the destruction as "progress"—the fulfillment of God's mandate. They considered such desecration not only legitimate but praiseworthy.

Finally, in 1675, an incident occurred that set the stage for successive events. Forty-seven Pueblo leaders were arrested for sorcery and brought to Santa Fe to be tried. The community soon learned, however, that the real reason for the arrests was the leaders' lack of success in recruiting Christian converts for the Spanish authorities. After the trial, four men were condemned to be hanged, while the rest were ordered to be whipped. The Indians watched in horror as the sentences were carried out.

Among those whipped was Popé. When he returned to his home, he nursed his wounds and found followers to commiserate with him over the indignity he had suffered. In this atmosphere Popé began to consider organizing a response to the Spaniards. He started by calling local meetings, which soon blossomed to involve a larger area. Popé and his followers concentrated on those Pueblo villages they knew were anti-Spanish. As tensions rose, Popé was accused of killing his son-in-law, who may have been pro-Spanish. Popé retreated from San Juan, moving north to Taos Pueblo.

At a meeting in Tesuque Pueblo in 1680, it was agreed to send two messengers to all the Pueblo villages participating in the planning to advise them of the date for the beginning of a movement to expel the Spaniards. A strip of deerskin tied with a specific number of knots was to be taken to each pueblo, where an exact copy would be made. Then each morning, at each pueblo, a knot would be undone, with the campaign beginning on the day the last knot was undone.

Like many plans, it almost failed. Pro-Spanish villagers at three different pueblos informed their padres about the messengers and the plans for the campaign. Governor Antonio de Otermin learned about the plans and set out to have the two messengers arrested and tried for treason. The arrest caused the messengers' fellow villagers to become alarmed, and in their fear and anger they killed a Spaniard. The next morning, when their padre, Juan Baptisto Pio, came to say Mass, he too was killed. That afternoon, with two knots still to be untied, the campaign began. It was August 10, 1680.

As the revolt spread across Pueblo country, the surviving Spanish settlers moved into Santa Fe. Indian warriors from the south laid siege to the city on August 15. They would have been wiped out quickly, but forces from the northern pueblos arrived just in time, followed by the tribes farther south in Rio Abajo.

Spanish firepower was superior, but the Indian numbers finally won. The warriors blocked the stream of water flowing to the Spanish fort, and the Spaniards' tired and thirsty animals began to die. For two nights and a day the Spaniards had no water, and on August 21 they fought their way out of their stronghold.

The tyrants with the swords had been driven away from Pueblo Indian country. The oppressors with the whips were gone. A few years later Popé was replaced as overall Pueblo leader by Luis Tupatu of Picuris Pueblo. There is no information on when and where Popé may have died.

Sando, Joe S., *Pueblo Profiles: Cultural Identity through Centuries of Change* (Santa Fe, N. Mex.: Clear Light Publishers, 1995).

JOE S. SANDO or PAA PEH (Jemez Pueblo)
Albuquerque, New Mexico

POPULATION: PRECONTACT TO THE PRESENT

There is considerable scholarly debate regarding the size of America's native population in 1492. A modest estimate is that 75 million people occupied North and South America at the time of Columbus's voyages, a figure that represents approximately 15 percent of the world's population at that time. Most of these people lived south of the Rio Grande, in what is today central Mexico and some of the countries that form Central and South America. The native population of aboriginal America north of Mexico (including Greenland) has been estimated at anywhere from less than 1 million to as many as 18 million. Early in the twentieth century, James Mooney estimated individual tribal populations for regions north of the Rio Grande and arrived at a total of only 1.15 million Native Americans (American Indians, Eskimos, and Aleuts) at the time of, in his words, "first extensive European contact." (The dates of extensive European contact, according to Mooney, varied from 1600 to 1845 across the different regions.) In subsequent decades other scholars generally reaffirmed Mooney's low estimate; Alfred Kroeber even reduced it to 900,000. In 1966, however, the anthropologist Henry Dobyns introduced the idea that European diseases may have dramatically reduced native populations long before settlers actually came into contact with Indian people. Thus, he argued, Native American population losses were far higher than Mooney and his colleagues might have imagined and, logically, Native American populations far larger.

Dobyns proceeded to use mortality rates from epidemics as well as estimates of environmental carrying capacity in specific regions to speculate that there were as many as 18 million native inhabitants north of Mesoamerica at the time of first European contact.

Since the 1960s, other scholars have arrived at estimates falling between those of Mooney and Dobyns. For example, Douglas Ubelaker summed individual tribal estimates produced by new scholars to estimate an aboriginal population north of Mexico of 1.85 million; similarly, this author concluded that the aboriginal population north of present-day Mexico numbered over 7 million people in 1492—somewhat over 5 million for the U.S. mainland and somewhat over 2 million for present-day Alaska, Canada, and Greenland combined. Another scholar, the geographer William Denevan, has produced yet another population estimate for the area north of Mexico: 3.79 million.

Despite these differences, there is a general consensus that Native American populations experienced declines that began after 1492 and continued for around four hundred years. Not until about 1900 did the native population reach its nadir, after which some population recovery occurred. At the beginning of the twentieth century—when the total population of the United States and Canada had grown to over 80 million—the two nations' census figures indicated a total of about 400,000 native people in North America.

What accounted for such a decline in the face of remarkable population growth of the groups who colonized North America after 1492? An important reason for the Native American holocaust were the diseases the Europeans and Africans brought with them to North America; other reasons included war, genocide, the destruction of traditional ways of life, and forms of colonial rule that both reduced native populations and prevented normal recovery.

The Native American population's recovery beginning around 1900 was in part a result of lower mortality rates and increases in life expectancy as the effects of Old World diseases and other reasons for population decline lessened. The recovery also resulted from adaptation through intermarriage with nonnative people and changing fertility patterns during the twentieth century, whereby Native American birth rates have remained higher than those of the general population. Census enumerations indicate nearly continuous Native American population growth in the United States since 1900; the total reported in 1990 was 1.9 million. To this may be added some 740,000 Native Americans in Canada in 1986—575,000 American Indians, 35,000 Eskimos (Inuit), and 130,000 Métis (the Métis, of mixed Indian and white ancestry, are not legally recognized as Indians)—plus some increase to 1991, and perhaps 30,000 Native Americans in Greenland. The total then becomes around 2.75 million in North America north of Mexico—obviously a significant increase from the perhaps 400,000 around the turn of the century. However, the population remains far less than the over 7 million estimated for 1492. This population is also but a fraction of the total population of the United States (around 250 million in 1990) and Canada (over 25 million in 1990).

Native Americans today are distributed unevenly throughout North America, a reflection more of events following European arrival than of aboriginal patterns. The 1990 U.S. Census reported the largest number of Native Americans in the states of Oklahoma, California, Arizona, and New Mexico. The census also indicated that slightly over half of Native Americans live in urban areas; cities with the largest Native American populations are New York, Oklahoma City, Phoenix, Tulsa, Los Angeles, Minneapolis-St. Paul, Anchorage, and Albuquerque. Around one-fourth of American Indians in the United States live on 278 reservations (or pueblos or rancherias) or associated "tribal trust lands," according to the census. The largest of these is the Navajo Reservation, with 143,405 Native Americans and 5,046 non-Indians living there in 1990. Around 60 percent of the Native American population of Alaska lives in "Alaska Native Villages."

The twentieth-century population increase for Native Americans reflected in successive U.S. Census figures was also due to changes in the U.S. Census Bureau's definition of *Native American*. Since 1960 the Census Bureau has relied on self-identification to ascertain a person's race. Much of the increase in the American Indian population—from 523,591 in 1960 to 792,730 in 1970 to 1.37 million in 1980 to 1.9 million (including Eskimos and Aleuts) in 1990—resulted from persons not identifying themselves as American Indian in an earlier census but identifying themselves as such in a later census. It has been estimated, for example, that as much as 60 percent of the apparent population growth of American Indians from 1970 to 1980 may be accounted for by such changing identifications! The political mobilization of American Indians in the 1960s and 1970s, along with other ethnic-pride movements, may have lifted some of the stigma attached to an American Indian racial identity. This would be espe-

cially true for persons of mixed ancestry who formerly had declined to disclose their American Indian background. Conversely, persons with minimal American Indian background may have identified as American Indian out of a desire to affirm a "romanticized" notion of being American Indian.

Today over three hundred American Indian tribes (excluding Alaskan villages) in the United States are legally recognized by the federal government and receive services from the Bureau of Indian Affairs. There are additionally some 125 to 150 groups seeking federal recognition, and dozens of others that might do so in the future. The Bureau of Indian Affairs has used a "blood quantum" definition—generally, one-fourth degree of American Indian "blood"—and/or tribal membership to recognize a person as an American Indian. However, each tribe has a particular set of requirements, typically including a blood quantum, for membership (enrollment) in the tribe. Requirements vary widely from tribe to tribe: a few tribes require at least a one-half Indian (or tribal) blood quantum; many others require a one-fourth blood quantum; still others, generally in California and Oklahoma, require a one-eighth, one-sixteenth, or one-thirty-second blood quantum; and some tribes have no minimum blood quantum requirement at all but require an explicitly documented tribal lineage.

Tribes located on reservations have generally required higher degrees of blood quantum for membership than those not located on reservations. This pattern of requiring low percentages of Indian "blood" for tribal membership and relying on federal authorities to certify membership may be seen as a reflection of demographic decline. As the number of American Indians was reduced and American Indians came into increased contact with whites, blacks, and others, American Indian peoples increasingly married non-Indians. As a result, American Indians have had to rely on formal certification from the federal government as proof of their "Indianness."

In the early 1980s the total membership of the three hundred recognized U.S. tribes was about 900,000. Therefore, many of the 1.37 million persons identifying themselves as American Indian in the 1980 census were not actually enrolled members of federally recognized tribes. In fact, only about two-thirds were. In the late 1980s the total tribal membership was around 1 million; hence, only about 53 percent of the 1.9 million people identifying themselves as American Indian in the 1990 census were actually enrolled. Such discrepancies have varied considerably from tribe to tribe. Most of the 158,633 Navajos enumerated in the 1980 census and the 219,198 enumerated in the 1990 census were enrolled in the Navajo Nation; however, only about one-third of the 232,000 Cherokees enumerated in the 1980 census and of the 308,132 enumerated in the 1990 census were actually enrolled in one of the three Cherokee tribes (the Cherokee Nation of Oklahoma, the Eastern Band of Cherokee Indians [of North Carolina], and the United Keetoowah Band of Cherokee Indians of Oklahoma). Thus the Navajo Nation is the American Indian tribe with the largest number of enrolled members, but more persons identifying themselves as Native American identified themselves as Cherokee in the 1980 and 1990 censuses than did persons of any other tribe. The two other largest groups in the 1990 census were the Chippewas, or Ojibwas, (103,826) and the Sioux (103,255).

Similarities and differences exist in Canada. Officially, to be an Indian in Canada, one must be registered under the Indian Act of Canada; a person with Indian ancestry may or may not be registered. Categories of Canadian Indians include "status" or registered Indians, persons registered under the act; and "non-status" or nonregistered Indians, persons who either never registered or gave up their registration and became enfranchised. Status Indians may be further divided into treaty or nontreaty Indians, depending on whether their group ever entered into a treaty relationship with the Canadian government. Of the 575,000 American Indians in Canada in the mid-1980s, some 75,000 were nonregistered and some 500,000 were registered.

The Canadian provinces with the largest number of registered Indians are Ontario, British Columbia, Saskatchewan, and Manitoba. In 1986, some 40 percent of the 740,000 Native Americans in Canada lived in cities; the largest American Indian populations were in Vancouver, Edmonton, Regina, Winnipeg, Toronto, and Montreal. Many Canadian Native Americans live on what are called *reserves*. About 70 percent of the registered Indians live on one of Canada's 2,272 reserves.

In the early 1980s, there were 578 organized bands of Canadian Indians. Most bands contained fewer than 500 members; only eight bands contained more than 3,000 members at that time: the Six Nations of the Grand River (11,172); the Bloods (6,083); the Kahnawakes (5,226); the Iroquois of St. Regis (4,098); the Saddle Lakes (4,020); the Wikwemikongs (3,493); the Blackfeet (3,216); and the Lac La Ronges (3,086).

See also Diseases.

Thornton, Russell, *American Indian Holocaust and Survival: A Population History since 1492* (Norman: University of Oklahoma Press, 1987); Thornton, Russell, *The Cherokees: A Population History* (Lincoln: University of Nebraska Press, 1990); Ubelaker, Douglas H., "North American Indian Population Size, A.D. 1500 to 1985," *American Journal of Physical Anthropology* 77 (1988): 289–94.

RUSSELL THORNTON (Cherokee)
University of California at Los Angeles

PORTER, PLEASANT

(1840–1907)
Creek political leader.

Pleasant Porter was born on September 26, 1840, in the Creek Nation (present-day Wagoner County, Oklahoma), the son of Benjamin Edward Porter and his wife, Phoebe, the daughter of Tahlopee Tustunnuggee and Lydia Perryman. The original Porters, Pleasant Porter's grandparents, were whites from Pennsylvania who settled in the eastern Creek Nation after the War of 1812. Identifying with their Creek neighbors, they supported the faction of Lower Creeks led by the McIntosh family and in 1828 voluntarily migrated to the "Creek Nation, West" in Indian Territory. Settling in the Arkansas River valley, the Porters built a plantation and enjoyed the benefits of a slave-labor force. The many Porter sons married Creek women and settled on the family plantation. From one of these unions came Pleasant Porter.

Creek matrilineal descent gave Porter the clan (Bird) and the town (Okmulgee) of his mother, and he grew up in a bicultural, bilingual, and affluent household where Anglo-American cultural values were respected. During the 1850s he attended the Presbyterian mission school, Tullahassee, and joined the Presbyterian Church. Having completed his education in 1860, he briefly clerked in a store and then herded cattle in New Mexico, but in August 1861, after the Creeks entered into an alliance with the Confederacy, Porter enlisted in Company A of the First Creek Regiment. Porter saw enough action in the Civil War to receive three wounds and win a promotion from private to first lieutenant.

The war devastated much of the Creek Nation. At war's end Porter returned to the family plantation to find his slaves and livestock gone, his buildings burned, and his fields overgrown. He set to work rebuilding his estate. Never interested in farming, at various times he owned stores, including one in Okmulgee, his town and the Creek Nation's capital, but cattle was the main source of Porter's wealth. Common ownership of Creek land meant that any Creek could use as much of the nation's land as he needed. Some Creek entrepreneurs took advantage of this, making use of thousands of acres for grazing. Though Creek ranchers ran their own cattle, they also frequently leased much of their range to Texas cattlemen. Porter, in partnership with Clarence W. Turner, made a fortune in leasing and stock raising. He also acquired a great deal of property in Muskogee, established as a shipping point on the rail line, and built his home there in 1889.

On November 25, 1872, Porter married Mary Ellen Keys, a daughter of the chief justice of the Cherokee Supreme Court. She died on January 15, 1886. Porter married his second wife, Mattie Leonora Bertholf, on May 26, 1886. The first family included three children; the second, one child.

Although Porter grew rich as a businessman, government service was his preoccupation. After the Civil War the Creek Nation underwent a political renovation whose results in many ways still mark the essential conflict in Creek political society. Formerly a decentralized alliance of autonomous towns, the nation in 1867 became a constitutional republic with an elected executive, a bicameral legislature, a tiered court system, and a concept of nationalism that seriously reduced, and in many cases obliterated, town government. Porter supported this constitutional reform and worked to preserve and strengthen Creek nationhood.

Porter's public service began in 1867 when the newly elected principal chief, Samuel Checote, appointed him superintendent of schools. Under his direction the Creeks rejuvenated and expanded a public school system shattered by the Civil War.

In 1871, Chief Checote appointed Porter commander of the national militia to put down a rebellion against the new constitutional order led by Oktaharsars Harjo (Sands). Porter's skill at defusing the volatile situation led to similar duty in 1876, when the supporters of Lochar Harjo, an impeached principal chief, launched a rebellion. On yet a third occasion, the Green Peach War of 1882–83, Porter and the national militia put down an attempted coup. Porter's dedication to Creek constitutionalism also led him into the national council, where he served four years in the House of Warriors (lower house) and eight in the House of Kings (upper house).

Much of U.S. Indian policy after the Civil War was directed at undermining tribal organization, acquiring Indian-owned land and resources, and assimilating native people into the larger American society. In response, the Creeks, along with many other tribes, kept close watch on Washington by employing lobbyists to influence congressional legislation. Beginning in 1872 and continuing for the next two decades, Porter made almost annual trips to Washington, where he became well known as an articulate and effective spokesman. Though his trips were primarily political in purpose, Porter also consulted with ethnographers at the Smithsonian Institution about Creek culture and history and supplied much of the detailed information on which scholars now depend.

But Porter and his colleagues could not derail federal Indian policy. Although the General Allotment Act of 1887 had exempted the Southern Indians, in 1893 Congress created the "Commission of the Five Civilized Tribes" to negotiate allotment agreements with those nations. Forced to respond, the Creek Council appointed a commission in 1897, chaired by Porter, to conduct the negotiations. The Creeks defeated their agreement in an 1898 referendum, but the Curtis Act, enacted the same year, empowered the congressional commission to proceed unilaterally. In 1899, in the midst of this crisis, Porter, an unsuccessful candidate for the office of principal chief in 1895, was elected to that office. His platform recognized the inevitability of allotment and argued that the nation should negotiate the best terms possible for its people. Talks began in 1900; a referendum approved the agreement in 1901 and a supplement in 1902. Under the terms of the agreement, a complex equalization formula attempted to secure a fair distribution of allotments to all Creek citizens.

Few Creeks favored allotment and the dismantling of the national government. Most, like Porter, accepted it as inevitable, but some, influenced by Chitto Harjo (Crazy Snake), resisted. Organizing a separate government at Hickory Ground in 1900, the dissidents claimed that the constitutional government was unrepresentative of the will of the Creek people and hostile to the Creeks' best interests. Chief Porter appealed to the U.S. Army to quell this latest anticonstitution movement, and in 1901 troops broke up the Hickory Ground encampment and arrested its leaders.

Porter was reelected principal chief in 1903, but because the 1898 Curtis Act had dissolved Creek government, his second term was little more than a charade.

In 1905, Porter organized the leaders of the Five Tribes to oppose a statehood plan that would link Indian Territory to Oklahoma Territory. Their solution was to create an Indian state and seek separate admission. With Porter sitting as president of a constitutional convention, delegates designed the state of Sequoyah. Congress refused to consider the idea, however, and the single-state plan was adopted, with Oklahoma joining the Union in 1907.

Though Porter's role during the allotment crisis appears to have been shaped by his desire to guide the less well acculturated Creeks through a minefield not of their making, it remains nevertheless true that Porter represented a segment of Creek society that was prepared by training and experience to succeed in an Anglo world dominated by the market economy. Wealthy by any standard, he profited under the terms of the allotment agreements he negotiated. Porter died of a stroke on September 3, 1907, in Vinita, Cherokee Nation, while on his way to St. Louis on business.

See also Creek (Muskogee).

Debo, Angie, *And Still the Waters Run: The Betrayal of the Five Civilized Tribes* (Princeton, N.J.: Princeton University Press, 1940); Debo, Angie, *The Road to Disappearance* (Norman: University of Oklahoma Press, 1941); Meserve, John B., "Chief Pleasant Porter," *Chronicles of Oklahoma* 9 (September 1931): 318–34.

MICHAEL D. GREEN
University of Kentucky

POSEY, ALEXANDER

(1873–1908)
Creek journalist, poet, satirist, educator, and political leader.

Born on August 3, 1873, in the Creek Nation close to present-day Eufaula, Oklahoma, Alexander Lawrence Posey was the first of ten children born to Lewis Henderson (Hence) Posey, a Scottish Irish farmer and herder, and Nancy Harjo Phillips, a descendant of a prominent Upper Creek family from the Tuskegee tribal town. Like his mother, Alexander belonged to the Wind clan and was associated throughout his life with his Tuskegee roots. Named by his father after Alexander the Great, Posey would, by the time of his death at age thirty-four, become one of the best-known Creek figures of his day.

Posey's writing recalls an idyllic childhood spent roaming the prairies, hills, rivers, and creeks of the area

he dubbed the Tulledegas. From his mother he learned the Creek history, language, and culture, and claims not to have learned English until age fourteen. Posey's father, well aware of the rapid changes coming to the Creek Nation, worried about his children's formal education. He began to force Alex to speak English, and enrolled him in the public school at Eufaula.

The boy progressed well in school and worked at the office of the local newspaper, the *Indian Journal*. There he learned the business that would occupy much of his adult life. At sixteen, Posey completed the course of studies at Eufaula and was selected to attend Bacone Indian University in Muskogee, where he studied for five years. There Posey read widely, concentrated on his writing, and began to gain a reputation as an orator and writer. His work, which consisted mainly of poetry, a few Creek legends, and transcripts of his commencement addresses, was often published in the university newsletter, the *Instructor*, and by other newspapers in the Oklahoma Territory. Near the end of his time at Bacone, he began to experiment with dialect writing and with the humorous style that would become his trademark.

Posey left the university in 1894 after his junior year. By this time he was already pursuing relationships with Creek elders and with literary colleagues, and had developed an interest in Creek politics. Throughout his life, Posey would align himself with the "progressive" Creeks, who saw the inevitability of change, encouraged Indian people to adapt, and supported allotment and the economic development of Indian Territory.

Posey's stance differed from that of such prominent Creek figures as Chief Pleasant Porter and Chitto Harjo. Harjo, for example, one of the leaders of the Snake faction of conservative Creeks, did not accept the abrogation of the tribal treaties, and vehemently opposed allotment and the dissolution of the tribal government. Yet despite Posey's more progressive views, in 1895 he was elected to the lower chamber of the Creek legislature, the House of Warriors, as a representative from Tuskegee. By choice he served only one term, but he would continue to be elected as a delegate to many of the important political councils and conventions held in Indian Territory.

Also in 1895, Posey was appointed superintendent of the Creek Orphan Asylum at Okmulgee. The office required little work, so Posey found time to read and develop his writing. Many of his political and lyrical nature poems from that era appeared in regional publications. At Okmulgee, Posey surrounded himself with a congenial staff and immersed himself in a pleasant intellectual life. He appointed his friend and literary colleague George Riley Hall principal of the school and hired Minnie Harris, a schoolteacher from Farmington, Alabama, as girls' matron. Before the year was out, Posey and Harris had fallen in love. They were married on May 6, 1896. The Poseys built a strong marriage; they had one daughter and two sons, the second of which died while still an infant. Posey's career in education led him to other appointments—he was for a time superintendent of public instruction for the Creek Nation—but none satisfied him as much as his first at Okmulgee.

Near the end of his tenure at the orphan school, Posey made plans to build a house, relocate, and oversee the rental of farms on tribal property he had claimed at Possum Flat, near his parents' home at Bald Hill. Such a lifestyle was common in Creek territory at the time. The Poseys moved to their new house in 1897, but Alex's time as a landlord was short. In 1898 Congress passed the Curtis Act, which dissolved common titles and authorized the allotment of Creek lands without tribal consent. Although Posey and his extended family enrolled themselves and took individual homesteads in the vicinity of Bald Hill, their allotments were limited to 160 acres per individual. In the end their tribal acreage had been dramatically reduced.

Although by 1900 his poetry had begun to gain attention beyond Indian Territory, Posey had already turned to prose and did little to capitalize on the interest. He published a few autobiographical works along with his poetry in cities like Philadelphia and Kansas City and soon was established as one of the important Indian writers of the time. In 1901 and 1902 he shifted his occupation again by purchasing the *Indian Journal,* merging it with the *Eufaula Gazette,* and becoming editor.

Posey's newspaper became a strong voice for Indian economic progress, and he developed a unique style of reporting that was liberally sprinkled with local color. In 1902, he inaugurated the "Fus Fixico Letters," a kind of humorous commentary on local events or important political debates of the day. They brought him notoriety and are the literary achievement for which he is most remembered. Fus Fixico, Posey's fictional full-blood character, spoke English with a Creek dialect. He wrote letters of opinion to the editor or reported on conversations between other characters, many of whom were caricatures of Creek figures or federal officials. Famous among Posey's characters were Wolf Warrior, a takeoff on the Creek figure G. W. Grayson, and Hotgun, the actual name of a member of the Snake

Alexander Posey, author of the "Fus Fixico Letters."

faction of Creeks. The humorous letters, seventy-two in all, became Posey's avenue for addressing controversial issues such as the restrictions placed on the sale of allotments, the bid of Indian Territory for separate statehood, and the involvement of federal officials in graft and fraudulent land deals. For example, Posey criticized the political pressure wielded by Charles Haskell, the first governor of Oklahoma, by means of this comment by Hotgun:

> Boss Haskell was a big medicine man an' had mighty influence. If he could make his men shovel dirt like he makes them vote ag'in their conscience, he could had the Panama canal dug maybe so in six weeks an' had time enough left to run for office on the independent ticket.

Although the letters gained national attention, Posey rejected suggestions that he deal with more national characters and incidents to broaden his audience. In fact, Posey had decided to sell his newspaper.

In 1904, Posey became an interpreter and agent for the Dawes Commission, the federal agency charged with enrolling and alloting members of the Five Civilized Tribes. Because of his fluency in Creek and English, his knowledge of Creek culture, and his reputation in Indian Territory, he was enlisted to find and enroll Creeks who had resisted the allotment process. For two and a half years Posey successfully served the commission, determined to convince the Creeks to accept the inevitable. Although his respect and sympathy for the conservatives grew during these years, Alex still believed that Indians must adapt to the demands of national government and participate in the development of tribal lands.

In March 1907, his work with the Dawes Commission complete, Alex Posey took what was perhaps the most controversial step of his career. He became a realtor and broker in allotted lands. Many former supporters believed he had sold out his tribespeople. At this same time, Posey again took up journalism, resuming the editorship of the *Indian Journal.* However, he would have a chance to advance neither of these ventures, because on May 2, 1908, Alexander Posey drowned in floodwaters while on his way from Muskogee to Eufaula.

Though he was passionately eulogized and memorialized through the years as a folk hero whose genius was never fully realized, Posey's literary estate received little attention after his death. His wife, Minnie, oversaw the publication of *The Poems of Alexander Posey* in 1910, but the book did not sell well, and few other excerpts from Posey's manuscripts ever saw print. He is, however, recognized today for his innovative and effective political commentary, and his "Fus Fixico Letters" are still read for their humor, historical insight, and wonderful use of dialect.

See also Creek (Muskogee); Five Civilized Tribes; Harjo, Chitto; Indian Territory.

Littlefield, Daniel F., Jr., *Alex Posey: Creek Poet, Journalist, and Humorist* (Lincoln: University of Nebraska Press, 1992).

KIMBERLY M. BLAESER (Anishinaabe)
University of Wisconsin at Milwaukee

POTAWATOMI

Closely related to the Ottawas and Ojibwas, the Potawatomis are an Algonquian-speaking people who originally inhabited the Great Lakes region. Initial French records suggest that prior to 1640 the Potawatomis occupied the southwestern quadrant of the lower peninsula of Michigan, but during the Beaver Wars, which began in the 1640s, they fled attacks by the Neutrals, first seeking sanctuary in the Sault Ste. Marie region and then crossing to Green Bay, where they joined with other tribes also seeking refuge from the Neutrals and Iroquois. By 1675 the Potawatomis had emerged as one of the dominant tribes in the Green Bay region. Through contacts with Jesuit priests and French traders they developed political and economic ties to New France. Onanguisse (Shimmering Light), a Potawatomi leader, assisted Robert Cavalier de La Salle in amassing large quantities of fur in the Potawatomis' village prior to the loss of La Salle's vessel, the *Griffon,* which sank in Lake Michigan in 1679. During the colonial period Potawatomi warriors consistently supported the French in their warfare against the British, often journeying to Montreal to join French expeditions against New England. Meanwhile, many Potawatomi women married French traders or *coureurs des bois,* and those unions produced growing numbers of mixedblood or Métis children, many of whom assumed positions of leadership within the tribe.

During the eighteenth century many Potawatomis moved back toward their old homeland, occupying the region from modern Milwaukee through Chicago and across southern Michigan to Detroit. Potawatomi tribespeople also established villages down the Illinois River as far south as Lake Peoria, and at the headwaters of the Kankakee, Tippecanoe, and Maumee Rivers in Indiana. Participants in the fur trade, Potawatomi villagers continued to raise small crops of corn, beans, and pumpkins, and to take fish from lakes and streams and deer from the forests, but by 1750 they were dependent upon European traders for muskets, gunpowder, metal instruments, and other trade goods that once had been luxury items.

During "Pontiac's Rebellion" Potawatomis at Detroit assisted in the siege of Fort Detroit, while their kinsmen on the St. Joseph River captured a British fort at that location. In the American Revolution the tribe's loyalties were split; Potawatomis from Michigan and Indiana generally supported the British, while those residing in Illinois and Wisconsin favored the Americans. In the postwar decade most Potawatomi warriors supported the Pan-Indian defense of Ohio, but following the Treaty of Greenville, Five Medals and other leaders from the Fort Wayne region welcomed Protestant mis-

A Potawatomi couple from Mayetta, Kansas, circa 1890.

sionaries into their villages. Five Medals, Topinbee (Sits Quietly), and Winimac (the Catfish) opposed Tecumseh and his brother the Shawnee Prophet (Tenskwatawa), who were staunchly pro-British, while leaders such as Nuscotemeg (Mad Sturgeon) and Main Poc (Crippled Hand) supported the Shawnee brothers and fought against the Americans in the War of 1812. Indeed, with the exception of Tecumseh, Main Poc was reputed to be the most influential pro-British leader in the Old Northwest. His raids against white settlements in Illinois and Missouri caused William Henry Harrison, the governor of Indiana Territory, to march against Prophetstown, believing that warriors in Tecumseh and the Shawnee Prophet's village on the Tippecanoe River were participating in these raids. This resulted in the Battle of the Tippecanoe.

Many Potawatomis, particularly those living in northern Indiana and southern Michigan (the Wabash band) continued to adopt white ways following the War of 1812, and a coterie of mixed bloods emerged as influential and wealthy traders. Yet as American settlement flooded the upper Midwest the Potawatomis were forced to cede much of their homeland, and between 1816 and 1832 they agreed to twelve major land cessions, relinquishing most of their territory in Indiana, Illinois, Michigan, and Wisconsin. In consequence, the federal government removed the tribe piecemeal, first resettling tribespeople from Illinois and Wisconsin (the Prairie band) in northwestern Missouri and western Iowa, then removing the Wabash band to the Osage River Subagency in Kansas. In 1846 all the Potawatomis in the West were consolidated on a new reservation along the Kansas River, just west of modern Topeka. Meanwhile, Potawatomis who had fled removal gathered at Walpole Island, across from Detroit, or scattered through the forests of northeastern Wisconsin. In addition, followers of Simon Pokagon, an acculturated Roman Catholic leader, remained on their privately owned lands near Niles, Michigan, while another smaller community continued to reside on the Huron River in eastern Michigan.

In Kansas the mixed-blood leadership from northern Indiana and southern Michigan, assisted by Catholic missionaries, dominated tribal affairs, and the Potawatomi communities, located astride emigrant trails between Missouri and Colorado, prospered. In 1854, after the Kansas-Nebraska Act was passed, Potawatomi lands in Kansas were threatened by white settlement, and in 1861 many members of the former Wabash band requested that the Kansas reservation be divided and the land be distributed to individuals. The government agreed and the land was allotted, but many members of the Prairie band refused to accept their allotments, which were consolidated into a new, smaller "Prairie Potawatomi Reservation" near modern-day Mayetta, Kansas. Within six years almost all the private plots had been sold to non-Indians. In 1867 the landless recipients of the allotments, now known as the "Citizen band," accepted a new reservation just south of modern Shawnee, Oklahoma. In 1870 the federal government established a reservation for the Hannahville Potawatomis in upper Michigan's Menominee County, and in 1913 a reservation was created for the Forest County Potawatomis near Laona, Wisconsin. On September 21, 1994, the federal government granted federal recognition to the "Pokagon band," who have continued to reside in southwestern Michigan.

Most modern Potawatomis are relatively acculturated people who transcend the differences between traditional and modern worlds. The Citizen band contains one of the most acculturated Indian communities in the United States, and its members have taken the lead in using new definitions of tribal sovereignty to champion economic development. They currently own and manage their own bank and pursue a broad spectrum of social and economic programs. Because many members of the Citizen band were dispersed during the Great Depression and World War II, their membership is scattered across the western United States. The Prairie band remains more conservative, and its reservation in Kansas continues as a wellspring for traditional values. Recently the Forest County Potawatomis have become active in promoting gaming in the Milwaukee region, and proceeds from this enterprise now fund the spectacularly successful Milwaukee Indian School. Many members of the Walpole Island community work in Detroit but continue to reside in Ontario. Though most Potawatomi people continue in the old ways, they are integrated into a modern Indian culture that has embraced the late twentieth century.

Clifton, James A., *The Prairie People: Change and Continuity in Potawatomi Indian Culture, 1665–1965* (Lawrence: Regents' Press of Kansas, 1977); Edmunds, R. David, *The Potawatomis: Keepers of the Fire* (Norman: University of Oklahoma Press, 1978); Landes, Ruth, *The Prairie Potawatomi: Tradition and Ritual in the Twentieth Century* (Madison: University of Wisconsin Press, 1970).

R. DAVID EDMUNDS (Cherokee)
Indiana University

Tlingits sumptuously dressed for a potlatch, Sitka, Alaska, December 9, 1904. In the foreground, two chiefs from neighboring villages perform a rite over a killer-whale effigy.

POTLATCH

Throughout native North America, gift giving is a central feature of social life. In the Pacific Northwest of the United States and British Columbia in Canada, this tradition is known as the *potlatch*. Within the tribal groups of these areas, individuals hosting a potlatch give away most, if not all, of their wealth and material goods to show goodwill to the rest of the tribal members and to maintain their social status. Tribes that traditionally practice the potlatch include the Haidas, Kwakiutls, Makahs, Nootkas, Tlingits, and Tsimshians. Gifts often included blankets, pelts, furs, weapons, and slaves during the nineteenth century, and jewelry, money, and appliances in the twentieth.

The potlatch was central to the maintenance of tribal hierarchy, even as it allowed a certain social fluidity for individuals who could amass enough material wealth to take part in the ritual. The potlatch probably originated in marriage gift exchanges, inheritance rites, and death rituals and grew into a system of redistribution that maintained social harmony within and between tribes.

When Canadian law prohibited the potlatch in 1884, tribes in British Columbia lost a central and unifying ceremony. Their despair was mirrored by the tribes of the Pacific Northwest when the U.S. government outlawed the potlatch in the early part of the twentieth century. With the passage of the Indian Reorganization Act of 1934 in the United States and the Canadian Indian Act of 1951, the potlatch was resumed legally. It remains a central feature of Pacific Northwest Indian life today.

POVERTY POINT
See Archaic Indians.

POWHATAN
(?–1618)
Virginia Indian leader.

The father of Pocahontas and the brother of the chief Opechancanough, who organized the great assaults on the Virginia colony in 1622 and 1644, Powhatan (a.k.a. Wahunsunacock) was the ruler and also the architect of a paramount chiefdom that covered nearly all of eastern Virginia when Jamestown was founded in

1607. As a paramount chief his powers were considerable, but they fell short of what the English expected of a "king." Powhatan's chiefly position was also inherited matrilineally; thus his children could not succeed him. His three brothers, in order of age, were his successors, followed by his two sisters, and then by their two daughters. Only the first two brothers, Opitchapam and Opechancanough, lived long enough to reign.

Powhatan governed some thirty tribes, each with its own district chief who reported to him; each district chief in turn had viceroys in the several towns within each territory. Although he often kept the "native" ruler when he took over a tribe, Powhatan placed several of his relatives in district-chief positions, especially in territories that had strategic importance. Thus the English found his sons, Pochins and Parahunt (Little Powhatan), ruling towns at the mouth and the falls of the James River, respectively (these being border territories). The chiefdom's religious heartland, which was also a major economic breadbasket of the Pamunkey River valley, was ruled by all three of Powhatan's brothers, but it was the charismatic warrior Opechancanough who dwelt closest to the piedmont, where the enemy Monacans held sway. Chiefs' sisters could rule, too, while waiting to inherit. Nothing is recorded of Powhatan's sisters doing so, but the sister of the district chief of Appamattuck (Appomattox) governed the strategically important town at that river's junction with the James. Matrilineal inheritance made for very different "royal" families than in Europe: chiefs' siblings often ruled; chiefs' children ruled only when specifically appointed.

Powhatan had many children by many wives, but the marriages of chiefs were such that all of a chief's children were half siblings of one another. Powhatan, like his fellow chiefs, married only temporarily: he would keep a wife until she had a child by him, after which she and the child would be sent back to her people. The child would be recalled to Powhatan's court at a later date, and the mother would remarry. Thus Pocahontas spent her formative years away from her father, and she had no full brothers or sisters. Powhatan had a dozen or so such temporary wives at any one time; he was said to have had over a hundred by 1607, when he was about sixty years old. Since he chose his women from a wide variety of districts that he governed, the political advantage of such an arrangement is obvious. However, by 1610 he had allowed personal feelings to interfere and was refusing to send away a favorite wife who had borne him a child. The ultimate fate of this May–

September involvement was never recorded, since the only Englishman curious enough to ask (William Strachey) soon left the Virginia colony.

Although Powhatan's private life was very different from that of European rulers, in his rise to power and the qualities he needed to achieve he bore a strong resemblance to the heads of certain families that became "royal" in earlier times on the other side of the Atlantic. Powhatan inherited a nucleus of six district chiefdoms, located along or near the fall line in the James and York River valleys. The date of his accession is unknown, but he took as his "throne name" the name of his natal town, Powhatan. From that frontier nucleus he increased his possessions, working eastward and northward and using persuasive intimidation when possible, force when necessary. He is known to have conquered the Kecoughtans at the mouth of the James by military action in 1596 or 1597. Sometime around the time that Jamestown was founded, he exterminated the Chesapeakes in what is now the city of Virginia Beach. Both had been holdouts who would neither agree to pay him tribute nor knuckle under militarily. The Chickahominy tribe, located near Powhatan's original inheritance, continued to hold out successfully because of their large and fierce body of warriors. By 1608, when Captain John Smith explored Chesapeake Bay, all the native people of eastern Virginia, including the Virginia Eastern Shore, considered themselves at least nominally under Powhatan's sway—except for the Chickahominies. Powhatan therefore had excellent reason for "acting the king" and giving "proud answers" when English emissaries came to call.

The establishment of the English colony put an end to Powhatan's expansion and instead began a process of "nibbling away" at the edges of his territory. Powhatan initially tried to draw the English "visitors" into an alliance against the Monacans; the diplomatic meetings so vividly described by Captain John Smith date from that period. But Smith left Virginia, and a new and harder-line regime began at Jamestown. Once the colony began to get regular supplies from England, it began spreading into the prime farmlands of the James River valley. The first Anglo-Powhatan War (1610–14) encouraged rather than stopped that spread; and it ended when Pocahontas was captured and held as a hostage. That capture was the beginning of the end of Powhatan's rule over his people.

Powhatan dithered for a year before making peace by allowing Pocahontas's marriage to John Rolfe in 1614. During that time his brother Opechancanough, actually the second in line of succession, appears to have superseded the old chief; eight years later he would lead many of Powhatan's possessions in a war against the English. Powhatan himself remained titular head of his organization. But after the death of his daughter in England, an epidemic that killed many of his people, and the return of his priest Uttamatomakkin with news of how many more English there were across the Atlantic (all in spring 1617), Powhatan went into retirement. He survived Pocahontas by only a year.

See also Pocahontas; Powhatan Confederacy.

Smith, John, *The Complete Works of Captain John Smith (1580–1631)*, ed. Philip Barbour, 3 vols. (Chapel Hill: University of North Carolina Press, 1986); Spelman, Henry, "Relation of Virginea," (1613?) in *Travels and Works of Captain John Smith*, ed. Edward Arber and A. G. Bradley (New York: Burt Franklin, 1910); Strachey, William, *The Historie of Travell into Virginia Britania* (1612; reprint, edited by Louis B. Wright and Virginia Freund, Hakluyt Society, 1953).

HELEN C. ROUNTREE
Old Dominion University

POWHATAN CONFEDERACY

Powhatan is a term applied variously to a seventeenth-century Indian town near the falls of the James River, the Indian leader who was born there, the thirty or so chiefdoms he eventually ruled in eastern Virginia, and the Algonquian-related language spoken by all of those people.

Confederacy is a misnomer, erroneously used by many scholars in the last two centuries. The man Powhatan acquired his power over the Virginia tribes by either conquest or intimidation, according to the English colonists who actually met him. And he was very much the leader of the resulting organization; there was nothing of a real confederacy about it.

On the other hand, Powhatan was a paramount chief (a chief who governed other chiefs), not a king. He had life-and-death power over his "subjects" only under limited circumstances; he had to listen to the advice of both priests and warrior-councilors; neither he nor those priests could make laws that interfered much with the private lives of the ordinary people; and he had even more limited control over "his" people if they lived farther away from his "capital" on the York River. After 1607 the English colonists soon wooed those more distant "subjects," like the Patawomekes (Potomacs), into their own camp.

A drawing by John White of a native village on the North Carolina coast, circa 1585–86. It is a firsthand rendering of a village similar to those occupied by Powhatan and his kinsmen in Tidewater Virginia twenty years later, complete with bark-covered longhouse and a central plaza.

Chiefs among the Powhatan Indians stood out mainly on ceremonial occasions in their towns, when they received visitors surrounded by wives, councilors, and bodyguards and feasted everyone on a grand scale. It was mainly on such occasions that status-conscious English observers saw them. Chiefs also presided at the public ceremonial that began the *huskanaw*, or initiation of boys into manhood, and at the ill-described town-wide celebrations when the first of the year's corn crop came ripe. They presided at the execution of criminals, participated in some private religious rituals, and, most importantly, decided whether to make war on enemies.

At other times, chiefs and their families lived and worked as others did, although they may have received some deference while they did it. Partly supported by tribute in the form of corn, deerskins, and ornaments, they were still working people; there was little specialization of occupation in Powhatan Indian society. All men hunted, fished, and made war; all women farmed, foraged in the woods and marshes, prepared food, and made household equipment, probably including the houses themselves. Both genders had to know the natural resources of the region well and be strong and physically fit; and both reared the children. Chiefs inherited their positions through the mother's line; inheritance among the common people is less certain, but kinship and extended family ties must have been extremely important. Chiefs were stewards over the tribal lands, which individual people could claim temporarily for farming. No one owned land outright, so no one understood what the English colonists meant by buying it permanently.

After an abortive Spanish attempt in 1570, the English established a colony on the James River in 1607 and then gradually spread out in all directions, hindered only by the later establishment of English colonies in Maryland (1634) and Carolina (1670). There were three outright wars with the Powhatan Indians (1610–14, 1622–32, 1644–46), the last resulting in a treaty, but essentially the native people had been flooded out of their territory by the 1670s thanks to tens of thousands of land-hungry settlers. Following the English internal convulsion known as Bacon's Rebellion (1675–76), another Indian treaty was made (1677) establishing civil rights for Indians within Virginia; this treaty still stands, and the Pamunkey and Mattaponi Indian reservations live under it today. Other surviving Powhatan groups, living on reservation "islands," lost their reservations in the early 1700s but stayed on as communities and became the "citizen" Indians who currently (as of 1995) have state recognition but no special treaty status (Nansemond, Chickahominy, Eastern Chickahominy, Upper Mattaponi, and United Rappahannock).

Powhatan traditional culture changed mainly after the land was all but lost. The paramount chieftaincy ceased after 1649; hereditary chiefs disappeared after 1710. The tribal communities became so small that the language could not be kept up: some young people were monolingual English speakers by the early 1700s, and a century later a handful of old people remembered only a few words of Powhatan. The native priesthood ceased to exist by the mid–eighteenth century.

Virginia's established Anglican church had little interest in evangelizing people still considered "savages," so it was itinerant Baptist preachers who converted most of the Powhatans in the late eighteenth and early nineteenth centuries. The only missions for Indians ever established in the colony or state were the Boyle legacy's school at the College of William and Mary (closing in 1777) and the Methodist mission to the Nansemonds (beginning in 1850, and now a regular Indian-white congregation). The old gender roles, as well as housing, had changed by 1800. Now women performed Anglo-Virginian "domestic" work while men did plow farming, built Anglo-style houses, and ran their communities' politics. (Women on the two reservations do not vote in tribal matters even now.)

Community politics, however informal, remained necessary for people who remembered that they were Indians, however changed their culture and language. No one tried to remove any of the Virginia Powhatans to Indian Territory in the nineteenth century; they were probably too few and too Anglicized to be considered worth transporting. Instead efforts were made in the nineteenth and twentieth centuries to make them disappear where they were, by redefining them as "people of color" and pushing them into an underclass with African Americans. They resisted successfully, transforming their groups in the process into formally organized tribes again, this time with elected "chiefs" who preside at meetings and speak for their people to the public. Increasingly the chiefs and other tribal members have become sophisticated in dealing with the media and a raft of state and federal agencies. Since the 1980s the Powhatan tribes have additionally been instrumental in creating the Virginia Council on Indians (a state agency) and the United Indians of Virginia (a purely Indian organization), both aimed at community development and education for the growing Indian population in Virginia.

See also Powhatan.

Rountree, Helen C., *Pocahontas's People: The Powhatan Indians of Virginia through Four Centuries* (Norman: University of Oklahoma Press, 1990); Rountree, Helen C., *The Powhatan Indians of Virginia: Their Traditional Culture* (Norman: University of Oklahoma Press, 1989); Rountree, Helen C., and E. Randolph

Turner III, "On the Fringe of the Southeast: The Powhatan Paramount Chiefdom in Virginia," in *The Forgotten Centuries: Europeans and Indians in the American South, 1513–1704*, ed. Charles Hudson and Carmen Chaves Tesser (Athens: University of Georgia Press, 1994).

HELEN C. ROUNTREE
Old Dominion University

POWWOWS

The term powwow is derived from the Algonquian word *pawauogs*, referring to shamans and their curing ceremonies; in the twentieth century, it has come to refer to what the anthropologist William Powers calls a "secular event featuring group singing and social dancing by men, women, and children." While the modern powwow has its origins in the social events, dances, and ceremonials of the Prairie and Plains tribes, it has developed as the creative expression of Indian identity and pride far beyond its original geographical and social range.

Most powwows are not tribally exclusive, and members of many tribal groups, as well as non-Indians, might participate in any single event. It is this aspect of the powwow that has led to its characterization as "Pan-Indian," as surpassing "tribal" exclusiveness in favor of a broader cultural identification. However, all except the largest exposition and urban intertribal powwows are sponsored by and associated with members of a particular tribal community and have an explicit, though often indirect, identification with that group.

Several variations of the powwow can be identified, based on regional history, program format, dance and song style, and costuming. Powwows range in size from small local events of a single afternoon or evening held in honor of local achievements, to three-day-weekend affairs, to annual events of a week's duration. The largest powwows are commercial expositions where the focus is not so much on a community celebrating itself as on the demonstration of generalized "Indian" dancing to a paying non-Indian audience. These include the Red Earth in Oklahoma City and the Gathering of Nations in Albuquerque, New Mexico. Other large powwows include Crow Fair at Crow Agency, Montana, and the American Indian Exposition in Anadarko, Oklahoma.

Powwows vary somewhat from region to region, but most follow the broad outlines of the southern or Ok-lahoma style of gathering. At these events, many different dances might be performed. The Round Dance is a circle dance; the dancers hold hands with their neighbors while slide-stepping to the left. The Two-Step is a couples dance; the pair hold hands side by side and follow the lead dancers through a series of figures. The southern Gourd Dance was derived from the ceremonies of the Cheyenne, Kiowa, and Comanche men's societies and is still used by the revived men's societies; its name derives from the rattle carried by the dancers, formerly a gourd, now commonly made from aluminum saltshakers. There may also be performance dances, dramatic presentations by solo or paired dancers such as the Hoop Dance, the Eagle Dance, and the Spear-and-Shield Dance. These latter are staples of performances for non-Indian audiences but are rarely seen in powwows in Indian country.

In terms of actual time spent dancing, however, most of a powwow is devoted to the so-called War Dance, whose origins are in the warrior society rituals and dances of the Prairie tribes. In the nineteenth century these ceremonials spread to other tribes, many of whom developed unique variations. The northern Plains tribes received it by the 1860s; in recognition of its southern origins they called it the Omaha Dance; it was also called the Grass Dance after the braids of sweet grass worn in the dancers' feathered bustles. The tribes of western Oklahoma received the ceremony—they called it the Crow Dance—in the early 1890s, about the same time as they received the revivalistic Ghost Dance. By the late 1890s, although interest in the Ghost Dance itself had lessened, the Crow Dance continued, often held in conjunction with other ceremonials such as the Sun Dance.

In the twentieth century these northern and southern versions of the Omaha-Grass-Crow dance and its ceremony developed in other directions. Among the Prairie tribes of Oklahoma and Nebraska it developed into the Straight Dance. Meanwhile, among the tribes of western Oklahoma the ceremony evolved toward increasingly elaborate choreography and costuming on the part of individual dancers, with the result being the Feathers or Fancy Dance. The northern tribes developed costuming in other directions. The northern Grass Dance emphasized fringes over bustles whereas the northern "traditional" style developed full face paint, animal skin headdresses, and whole bird-wing attachments at the shoulders.

The woman's role in powwow dancing has experienced similar changes. Traditionally women's choreography was supportive, providing a rhythmic descant to the men's vigorous styles, but in the late 1960s young women began participating as feathered fancy dancers, even winning several contests. While female participation as fancy dancers has declined, two women's Fancy Dances, the Shawl and Jingle Dress dances, have gained in popularity, allowing women a more expressive role in the dance.

While most attention is focused on the dances, powwows are as much community social events as they are dance performances. Powwows are sponsored by particular groups, typically a single family honoring one of its own, an extended family honoring a founding ancestor, or an entire community honoring itself. Whatever the group, the sponsors plan the event, arrange for the facilities, provide food for the participants, and select the principals.

The major principals are the head singers, the head dancers, and the Announcer. The Head Singer must know a great number of songs, from standard dance songs to special family and honoring songs. The Head Dancers lead the dancing; everyone else follows their lead. The Head Man Dancer and the Head Lady Dancer often lead Round Dances and Two-Steps as a couple. The Announcer keeps the whole affair running smoothly by alternating dances so that, as one Announcer put it, "no one gets tired, . . . so that we keep their attention." The majority of the people at a powwow are spectators; because a powwow is a social event as well as a dance performance, the interaction among the spectators is as important as are the dances themselves.

See also Dance.

Kavanagh, Thomas W., "The Comanche Pow-wow: Pan-Indianism or Tribalism," *Haliksa'i* 1 (1985): 12–27; Powers, William K., "Contemporary Oglala Music and Dance: Pan-Indianism versus Pan-Tetonism," in *The Modern Sioux*, ed. Ethel Nurge (Lincoln: University of Nebraska Press, 1970).

THOMAS W. KAVANAGH
Mathers Museum, Indiana University

PRAIRIE TRIBES

Early prairie people hunted game, fished, and gathered edible tubers, seeds, nuts, and fruits on flat and rolling grasslands and in bordering forests in regions that included present-day North and South Dakota, Nebraska, Minnesota, Wisconsin, Iowa, Illinois, Indiana, and Ohio, and also portions of present-day Missouri, Arkansas, Oklahoma, and Texas.

Far to the south, in Mexico, man first domesticated maize between 3500 and 2500 B.C. Through the centuries its cultivation and use diffused northward up the Mississippi, Arkansas, Missouri, Illinois, and Ohio Rivers and their systems into the prairie zones. The first evidence of limited maize husbandry appeared in Hopewellian sites: the Illinois Jasper Newman site (A.D. 100), the Kansas City–area sites, and the Ohio McGraw site (A.D. 200–400).

By A.D. 900, full-scale cultivation of corn, beans, pumpkins, squash, and melons had enabled inhabitants of this area to establish homesteads, camps, and villages near timber and water sources. The archaeological evidence of dwellings, pottery, deep cache pits, dibbles, and bison-bone hoes marks this period.

Complex sites such as Spiro, Fort Ancient, Aztalan, and Cahokia attest to cultural changes resulting from plant domestication. At the latter—one of the great archaeological sites, near the Mississippi River opposite present-day St. Louis—adequate agricultural food surpluses enabled a population estimated at ten thousand to flourish. Cahokia, home to a stratified society, became a major trade center, and its restored temple mounds and other edifices attest to the proliferation of cultural traits beyond those of the hunter and gatherer. Ideas and items were exchanged over a wide system of paths and river ways. Copper, obsidian, turquoise, polychrome and other pottery, and gulf-shell artifacts were found in sites far removed from their sources.

From the twelfth through the fifteen century, prairie population groups in all regions became semisedentary, developing unique patterns of social organization, religion, and economic and material culture that showed both similarities and differences.

The introduction of corn and other domestic plants brought great changes to prairie people's lives, enabling them to become farmers as well as hunters and gatherers. However, during the sixteenth and seventeenth centuries other events began to intrude upon their existence. The advent of European exploration and colonization introduced new trade items, the horse, and diseases—all of which caused continuing and often destructive cultural changes. The fur trade contributed to intertribal competition and warfare when tribes attempted to maintain their own hunting territory or to acquire others' grounds.

It was during this early historic period that prairie groups' names, locations, and populations were first recorded. Any listing of names for a particular prairie group contains a wide variety of entries because, first, tribal names were sometimes self-identifications and sometimes names given by other tribes, and second, these names were recorded by French, Spanish, English, and Dutch writers. The situation bred confusion, mistranslation, and misunderstanding.

The Illinois Confederacy tribes, the Santees (Mdewakantons and Wahpekutes), Arikaras, Mandans, Hidatsas, Pawnees, Iowas, Omahas, Poncas, Otos, Missouris, Kansas, Osages, Caddos, Wichitas, Foxes (Mesquakis), Sauks, and Prairie Potawatomis appear to be the earliest identified prairie tribes. Tribal movement occurred onto and out of the prairies. The horticultural Cheyennes migrated westward from Minnesota, eventually becoming nomadic plains hunters in the nineteenth century. Iroquois hostility and warfare drove some Ohio, Indiana, and Illinois prairie tribes from their lands. This aggression often resulted from Spanish, French, Dutch, and English alliances forged with Native Americans to further those nations' own colonial ambitions, particularly the enhancement of the profitable fur trade and the consolidation of territorial claims.

After the United States acquired Louisiana in 1803, complex rationalizations and actions expedited non-Indian possession of prairie Indian land. The United States initiated Indian treaties that resulted in land cessions and tribal removals. Illinois-dwelling tribes such as the Peorias, Weas, Piankashas, Kaskaskias, Sauks, Foxes, Potawatomis, Kickapoos, and others were forced to cede their lands east of the Mississippi River and were placed on reservations west of that river in present-day Iowa, Kansas, and Nebraska on land ceded by prairie tribes already living there. Cessions and removals continued, and between the 1870s and the 1890s many prairie tribes found themselves forced to move again, to reservations in Indian Territory (modern-day Oklahoma). The government eventually located the prairie Sioux on reservations in North and South Dakota, Nebraska, and Minnesota. The Mesquakis or Foxes, prairie entrants in the 1700s, remain on lands in Tama, Iowa; and the Omahas remain in Nebraska.

The Spanish brought horses to the New World. When the prairie tribes acquired this animal (the Pawnees named it "the large dog"), late in the 1600s and afterward, their lives and cultures changed markedly. Whereas corn and other cultigens had permitted the adoption of a semisedentary lifestyle with its concomitant social changes, the horse added another

dimension. Utilizing it as a pack and riding animal, prairie people could leave the village in early summer and/or after the autumn harvest and travel long distances to hunt bison, elk, and other animals. These animals furnished surplus food supplies, clothing and dwelling material, bone and horn implements, and robes that could be traded for metal and other articles. The horse also brought greater mobility, and (with the European-introduced gun) served to change warfare patterns. Stealing horses from other tribes enhanced a man's status and wealth, and the horse became incorporated into stories, songs, dances, and personal names.

Europeans introduced diseases to which Native Americans had no immunity. Smallpox, cholera, and other scourges passed from tribe to tribe along land or water routes, carried by tribesmen or fur traders. History records the great loss of Missouri River village populations (Mandans and Hidatsas) and other prairie dwellers living in extended family village groups—a domestic pattern that made disease transmission inevitable. The devastating loss of civil, war, and religious leaders, food producers, and child bearers often seriously altered traditional cultural patterns.

The prairie tribes' languages were Siouan (Santee, Mandan, Hidatsa, Iowa, Oto, Missouri, Omaha, Osage, Kansa, and Quapaw), Caddoan (Caddo, Wichita, Kitsai, Tawakoni, Waco, Pawnee, and Arikara) and Algonquian (the languages spoken by the Illinois tribes and, later, Fox [Mesquaki], Sauk, Kickapoo, and Prairie Potawatomi). Traditionally the tribes organized their societies in a variety of ways. Nuclear families—or, in some cases matrilineal, patrilineal, or bilineal extended families—were the basic units in clan or band organization. Individual clans or bands were designated by the name of an origin ancestor, a location, or an animal or by words denoting natural phenomena, such as Wind and Thunder. Clan members possessed certain clan names, songs, rituals, and sacred bundles. As clan members they had responsibility for certain tribal functions and protection of members, as well as rights of revenge against clan enemies. The Iowas, Osages, Omahas, Poncas, and Pawnees were composed of dual divisions (or moieties), named, for example, Summer and Winter, Sky and Earth, or Peace and War. The Kansas had phratries, divisions each of which contained a number of related clans with tribal responsibilities. Some tribal clans had more prestige and authority than others, and provided hereditary chiefs. Marriage was usually clan exogamous.

The Caddoan-speaking tribes did not have clans but maintained bands and/or villages of related and unrelated lineages. Families owned certain names, songs, and ceremonies received in dreams or vision experiences.

In all of the prairie tribes an individual's position in the kinship system determined marital choice. Band marriage was endogamous. The four Pawnee bands, for example, lived autonomously until placed together on a Nebraska reservation, at which point marriage often became band exogamous as band populations decreased and kinship-determined marriage partners were not available. Additionally, as young people met in Indian boarding schools, intertribal marriages changed traditional patterns.

Many prairie tribes maintained matrilineal and matrilocal systems, but they frequently shifted to patrilocality while on the tribal hunt. Social classes existed among prairie tribes, composed of ruling, religious, and warrior elites on one hand and commoners on the other.

Formal leadership systems existed among prairie tribes, with executive, legislative, and judicial authority held by chiefs, subchiefs, and leading men, who could be outstanding warriors or other notable figures. Some tribes had both civil and war chiefs, and chieftainship was often hereditary. Council members represented different clans, bands, or villages, and decisions regarding tribal matters were usually reached by consensus. Tribal soldiers or police kept order in the village and on the hunt.

Religious beliefs and practices dominated and determined many cultural activities. Tribes believed in a supreme power, such as Wakonda (Omaha) or Tirawahut (Pawnee), and/or in supernatural anthropomorphic beings that included animals, celestial bodies, and other features in nature. By fulfilling certain ceremonial obligations, tribal people sought to assure the beneficence of these sacred deities in the maintenance of life. Sacred bundles inherited by a village, clan, band, or family, as well as bundles that men acquired in sacred visions, contained power bestowed by a supernatural being and determined membership in some tribal groups, ritual behavior, and individual power. Medicine, war, tattooing, and other bundle types also existed.

Religious activities, which involved warrior, doctor, or other men's organizations or the whole band or village, included set ritual behavior, prayers, speeches, songs, and dances. Among some prairie tribes, the adoption of high-ranking members of neighboring

tribes occurred during the sacred pipe or calumet ceremony, during which one tribe would visit another, bestowing gifts during elaborate adoption rituals. Through this activity tribes sought to build and maintain intertribal alliances by establishing kinshiplike ties.

As the United States claimed ceded Indian land in the prairie region, it placed the inhabitants on reservation areas either within their own former possessions or on land ceded by other tribes. Reservations served mainly to segregate and control tribal peoples so that government-sponsored "civilization" programs could be initiated and tribal lands could be opened to eager white settlers and speculators. Slowly, traditional culture and languages began to disappear, and long-standing factions came forward to debate the future. Some advocated change, while others endeavored to preserve traditional ways.

By the end of the nineteenth century, frustrations had grown under inept and often corrupt agency personnel, galling restrictions, and increasing mortality caused by inadequate nutrition and continual disease. These conditions contributed to the rise of Indian prophet or messiah-led revitalization movements such as the Ghost Dance religion. Participating adherents hoped they would again see their dead kinsmen and traditional life would be restored.

Tribal hostility increased after 1887, with land allotment in severalty and the federal government's purchase of "surplus" reservation land, and its rapid occupation and ownership by white settlers. These changes also contributed to the acceptance of the Ghost Dance. Iowas were allotted in 1891, Pawnees in 1892, the resisting Southern Poncas in 1905; and Kansas Kickapoos in 1908. All prairie tribes were allotted except the Quapaws who allotted themselves in 1891. Soon laws were passed that allowed white men to lease Indian allotments and eventually buy them. The Osages held mineral rights to their reservation, so that with the discovery of oil they did not suffer the difficult economic conditions of the Pawnees, Iowas, Oto-Missouris, Poncas, Omahas, and other tribes that accepted the Ghost Dance religion.

Among the tribes that eventually were settled in Oklahoma, the sacramental use of peyote began in the late nineteenth century, at about the same time that the Ghost Dance appeared. Introduced by John Wilson, a Caddo-Delaware messiah-prophet, peyote spread from tribe to tribe among the Caddos, Wichitas, Pawnees, Otos, Missouris, Osages, Quapaws, Iowas, Poncas, Omahas, Kansas Kickapoos, and Prairie Potawatomis. Its ritualistic use formed the basis for the establishment of the Native American Church. Hallucinatory visions and healing practices harked back to traditional patterns. Tribes welcomed the presence of any tribe's member at meetings, and it is believed that this openness fostered a growing Pan-Indian movement, strengthening the relationships between tribes. As with all Indian ceremonies that were considered uncivilized, the government endeavored to prevent and obstruct the Ghost Dance and the peyote religions.

At the beginning of this century, government policy, abetted by Indian advocacy groups like the Indian Rights Association, continued to emphasize acculturation and assimilation, with the old goal of "civilizing" the Indians. In the 1920s, it became apparent that ill health, poverty, and landlessness had increased. Pressure to reform the Indian service and government policy began, eventually culminating in the passage of the Indian Reorganization Act of 1934. Among other extraordinary new provisions, the law allowed tribes to establish their own governments, constitutions, and charters. The Omahas and Santees formed governing bodies under it, whereas the Caddos, Pawnees, Poncas, Oto-Missouris, Kansas, Osages, Quapaws, Iowas, and Wichitas formed their governing bodies under a similar law, the Oklahoma Welfare Act of 1936. The Bureau of Indian Affairs and the Secretary of the Interior retained final approval of tribal-council decisions, reflecting the old paternalistic attitude—one that often continues to lead to bureau and tribal disagreements to this day.

Subsequent congressional acts pertaining to Indian health, educational improvements, and economic-development projects have improved tribal conditions in the prairie region. In 1946 Congress established the Indian Claims Commission, to which tribes could present claims against the government concerning ceded lands and monetary reparations. The Oto-Missouris were the first to win a claim judgment, in 1955.

The termination years of the 1950s are unfavorably remembered by many prairie tribes. Federal policy called for ending the government's trust responsibility (Public Law 280). Among the prairie tribes, the Northern Poncas and the Peorias were terminated, but were later reinstated when overwhelming problems caused by the policy brought it to an end.

In 1975 Congress passed the Indian Self-Determination and Educational Assistance Act. It added immeasurably to tribal autonomy and provided for tribal contracting of some government services, such as enrollment, and for land leasing. Numerous government and state agencies other than the BIA now fund health, education, economic, and elderly-assistance programs

among prairie tribes, programs that have enhanced the quality of life. Many tribes now have court systems, and cultural-renewal programs to save their languages and ceremonies. Profitable bingo, casino, and business enterprises have enabled some tribes to purchase land.

The prairie tribes continue to hold traditional dances; honor their servicemen, servicewomen, and school graduates; and resist state and federal attempts to curtail their striving toward greater sovereignty. One Pawnee leader, looking at his family's sacred bundle, said, "We are still here, Grandfather."

See also Cahokia; Caddo; Illinois; Osage; Pawnee; Sioux.

Driver, Harold E., *Indians of North America* (Chicago: University of Chicago Press, 1961); Holder, Preston, *The Hoe and the Horse on the Plains: A Study of Cultural Development among North American Indians* (Lincoln: University of Nebraska Press, 1970); Wedel, Waldo R., *Prehistoric Man on the Great Plains*, 2d ed. (Norman: University of Oklahoma Press, 1970).

MARTHA ROYCE BLAINE
Oklahoma City, Oklahoma

PUEBLO, RIO GRANDE

Running down the middle of modern New Mexico, the Rio Grande has long attracted human communities. For several thousand years, the valley's inhabitants have lived in pueblos (from the Spanish word for "towns"), where they raise corn, beans, and squash; conduct elaborate ritual dramas in open plazas and churchlike kivas to pray for rain; live communally in planned apartmentlike buildings; and govern themselves through officials who draw their authority from their membership in one or more native priesthoods.

Because the area is well watered, the Rio Grande's population has increased during recent centuries as refugees from drought and hostile conditions have joined more ancient inhabitants. When the Spanish arrived in 1540, the Pueblos belonged to two major language stocks: Keresan and Tanoan.

Keresan is a language isolate, perhaps distantly related to Hokan, and is spoken in five towns near the river (Cochiti, Santo Domingo, San Felipe, Santa Ana, and Sia), and two more (Acoma and Laguna) farther west. Although Cochiti maintains its own dialect, the other towns pair up into speech communities.

Tanoan, a branch of Uto-Aztecan, includes four living language groupings: Tewa (represented by the towns of San Juan, Santa Clara, San Ildefonso, Pojoaque, Nambe, and Tesuque); Tano, or Southern Tewa (spoken at Hopi First Mesa); Tiwa (divided into a northern dialect at Taos and Picuris, and a southern one at Sandia and Isleta); and Towa (now spoken only at Jemez, but spoken at Pecos until 1838). Tanoan languages now extinct include Piro, spoken in the middle valley; and Tompiro, spoken in the nearby highlands.

After receiving reports of multistoried adobe towns in the vast territory north of Mexico, the viceroy of New Spain authorized the expedition of Francisco de Coronado to explore the area. In 1540 Coronado and sev-eral hundred men traveled north and occupied a native town near modern Albuquerque, New Mexico. The Spaniards lived off the stored crops of local Pueblo peoples. When their food supply was nearly depleted, the Pueblos counterattacked but were defeated. From this base, Coronado and his captains explored near and far. They trekked into the plains of Kansas, lured by the promise of gold and urged on by Indian guides who hoped to lose the Spaniards in the vast grasslands. When none of these expeditions found anything worth exploiting, Coronado and his forces returned to Mexico.

Lasting Spanish settlement in the Rio Grande began in 1598, when the adventurer Juan de Oñate and a party of colonists moved north of the area devastated by Coronado and occupied the west section of San Juan, which was inhabited by members of the Pueblo's "Summer half," and was called Yunque Owinge before it was renamed San Gabriel. The "Winter half" occupied the east side of the pueblo, known as Oke (Okeh) and later dedicated to San Juan. Oñate also began a missionizing program by distributing ten friars among the towns. Pueblos that resisted—such as Acoma—were brutally subjugated.

In 1610, the Spanish moved their capital from San Gabriel to a new location called Santa Fe, a river town that has remained the political center to this day. The Spanish settlers established haciendas throughout the Rio Grande valley and in the lands to the west. Under imperial law, the occupying Spanish supported themselves with food and labor provided by native communities living within their area. In many cases, the colonists abused these *encomienda* privileges by making impossible demands on the Indians' time and labor, adding further to Pueblo resentment.

In 1680, after several unsuccessful attempts to throw off the Spanish yoke, a concerted effort by most Pueblos, under the leadership of a native priest of San Juan named Popé, succeeded. Until the 1692 reconquest by Governor Diego de Vargas, New Mexico remained under native control, a lack of unified leadership even-

tually working against the rebels and leading to their downfall. Nevertheless, the returning Spaniards were more tolerant of native religion and culture.

Pueblos were governed by an independent Mexico from 1821 until 1846, when their lands were annexed by the United States. Both nations in turn reconfirmed the land grants assigned to each pueblo by Spain. Emerging from its role as the administrative center of Spanish Catholicism, the Keresan town of Santo Domingo became the meeting site for an informal All-Pueblo Council that became reorganized in 1922.

Modern Pueblo town governments show the consequences of the historical forces that have acted upon them. Each was, and to an extent still is, ruled by a religious hierarchy. Until the Spanish arrived, each town had a dual set of leaders, concerned, respectively, with civil or military, internal or external, matters. To this pairing, a Spanish royal decree added a third set of officials headed by an annually elected governor to deal with Spanish and Catholic administrators.

Over recent centuries, constant migration to the Rio Grande has complicated the linguistic and cultural landscape. Happily, superior archaeological research has clarified most major movements. Between about A.D. 1 and A.D. 1000, some Mogollons began moving north along the Rio Grande valley, distributing members of the Tanoan family as they went. Those who stayed in the lower Rio Grande became the Piros and Tompiros, with the Tiwas settling in the central valley. Tanoans who settled in present-day Colorado near Mesa Verde became Tewa ancestors, who later congregated along the Chama River before moving south to the Rio Grande. The Tanos developed somewhat apart in the Galisteo Basin southeast of Santa Fe. During the 1680 revolt the Tanos occupied the Spanish capital, settling to the west in the Española Valley after 1692, and moving to Hopi after 1700. Most divergent of the Tanoans are the Towas, who lived in the Pecos and Jemez Valleys until they joined together in 1838 at Walatowa (Jemez). Their language developed in the Largo upland region of northwestern New Mexico, which long remained a culturally conservative area, using pit houses long after other regions had begun building stone pueblos.

The Keresans, whose ancestors left the Colorado River seven thousand years ago, founded the Oshara sequence, a part of the prehistoric Anasazi tradition. Speaking a language isolate, they developed a highly coordinated intratribal organization that led, between A.D. 800 and A.D. 1150, to the flourishing of Chaco

Canyon, a religious-pilgrimage complex with a dozen huge masonry towns and thousands of smaller hamlets. After that canyon was abandoned in the thirteenth century, towns moved east and eventually split the territory of the Tiwas living along the Rio Grande.

Between A.D. 1200 and A.D. 1400, a new religious organization emerged which served to integrate migrating groups into aggregate towns. Known as the Kachina (or Katsina) cult, this organization sponsored communal rituals that used elaborate masks to portray a variety of supernatural beings. Inspired by Mexican traditions, the Kachina cult moved into New Mexico along the Rio Grande. It flourished along the Upper Little Colorado between 1275 and 1325. Later elaborations appeared—among the Hopis about 1400, emphasizing rainmaking; and among the Jornada Mogollons of the Lower Rio Grande about 1450, with military overtones.

The modern kachina cult is distinguished by masks, group performances in the town plaza, and general membership by all townsmen (and women in half the Keresan towns). It fulfills a variety of community functions, as do the native priesthoods, but does so on a more democratic basis. In particular, the cult is associated with clouds and rain, along with curing, fertility, military strength, and ancestor worship.

Though each pueblo is distinctive if not unique, shared language, kinship, and religion establish some order amid the complexity. All pueblos are distinguished by the use of the kiva, a churchlike building that evolved from the pit houses used by Basketmakers, the archaeological predecessors of the Anasazi. Each town has one or more kivas, either round or square, entered by a ladder through a hatchway in the roof to represent the mythic opening into the underworlds. Inside, on the floor, are a hearth and standing altar, while around the sides is a built-in bench, called the *fog seat,* which represents billowing clouds and is the place where sacred items are kept. A separate development led to the style of chamber used by each of the native priesthoods, who provided the theocratic leadership of their respective towns.

Thousands of years of local development have produced a bewildering variety of cultural features among Rio Grande pueblos. Kiva shape provides a telling example. Among the northern Tiwas at Taos, kivas within the town wall are round, but those outside it are square. Among the Tewas, San Juan, Santa Clara, and Tesuque have square kivas, whereas San Ildefonso and Nambe have round ones. Kinship systems also differed in elaboration among the pueblos. The Keresans and

their close neighbors like the inhabitants of Jemez identified clan membership through the mother. Affiliation with such a unit (known to scholars as a *matriclan*) could be the basis for access to farmland, homes, and inherited offices. Tanoans largely recognized family units traced through both mother and father, either simultaneously or in alternation. Keresans in particular have elaborated a series of native priesthoods to govern, organize, or cure. Those concerned with medicine divide between those using a brushing treatment for skin diseases, believed to be caused by angry animal spirits; and those advocating the sucking out of internal illnesses, believed to be caused by witchcraft and ill will.

In all, the cultural elaborations among the pueblos can be clearly seen by focusing on the number of kivas, the gender of initiates into the kachina cult, the source of definition for basic social units, the sequence of succession to an office, and the role of native priesthoods—most of the latter inspired by the Keresans.

Each Keresan town has two kivas, called East (Turquoise) and West (Squash). Children initiated into the "secret" that it is adults who wear the kachina masks and not the spirits themselves include only boys at Cochiti, Santo Domingo, and San Felipe, but both boys and girls at the other towns. Basic social units also divide, with the three named towns emphasizing the native priesthoods and the others combining these with membership in matriclans. When an officeholder dies, he is succeeded by his "left-hand man," who in turn is succeeded by the "right-hand" one; in Keresan towns, left is valued over right—the reverse of Euro-American Christian belief.

Each Tewa town has one large kiva, which recruits for the Summer or Winter halves through the father or paternal relatives. Tewas have no kachina cult as such, but the Finishing Ceremony is held for both boys and girls so they might know that adults wear masks of their deities. The social units of Tewa society are the Summer and Winter moieties, mediated by the Made People priesthoods. Within this priestly hierarchy, right has priority over left. Thus, the right-hand assistant assumes a vacated position, and the left-hand man moves up to become the new right-hand assistant. Tewas are cured by members of the Bear (or medicine) priesthoods.

Traditionally, the Tiwas had one large kiva per town, recruiting for each moiety through both parents and initiating both boy and girls. In succession to offices, Tiwas gave priority to the right-hand helper. Tiwa moieties of Winter and Summer included smaller constituents (called *corn groups*) something like clans. Medicine priesthoods cured the sick, and Isleta also benefited from masks and rituals provided by an immigrant colony from Laguna.

The Tanos, after three centuries among the Hopis, have been influenced by neighboring matrilineal clans. Tanos now have two kivas that recruit through matriclans, and both boys and girls are inducted into the kachina cult. The Tanos also have a group of masked curers called the *sumakolih,* which seem to be uniquely their own.

For Towa speakers at Jemez, two kivas recruit paternally, and both boys and girls are initiated into the kachina cult. Each of the priesthoods is linked to a particular matriclan. Succession within the priesthoods passes to the left-hand man, then to the right-hand one.

For the larger world, all Pueblos recognize six sacred directions and four sacred mountains, variously identified. For the Keresans, each mountain and direction is associated with particular supernatural colors, weather spirits, warriors, women, animals, birds, snakes, trees, and other features. The Tewas associate them with other colors, corn maidens, mammals, birds, snakes, trees, shells, and lakes.

Because New Mexico's unique history and cultural geography foster cultural diversity, its citizens feel comfortable using English, Spanish, and many native languages. In addition, the non-Pueblo public is eager to know more about tribal traditions. In this atmosphere, Rio Grande Pueblo peoples continue to thrive on their ancestral homelands.

See also Pueblo Languages; Zuni Pueblo.

Dozier, Edward, *The Pueblo Indians of North America* (New York: Holt, Rinehart, and Winston, 1970); Dutton, Bertha, *Indians of the American Southwest* (Englewood Cliffs, N.J.: Prentice-Hall, 1975); Ortiz, Alfonso, *The Tewa World* (Chicago: University of Chicago Press, 1969).

JAY MILLER (Lenape)
Lushootseed Research

PUEBLO LANGUAGES

Like the cultures of which they are a major part, Pueblo Indian languages endure and provide a vital means of connecting Pueblo people to their traditional beliefs and practices. Despite differences in economic adaptation and social organization, the Pueblo Indians of northern Arizona and New Mexico display very similar cultures. This similarity of cultures hides structural and historical linguistic differences between the languages but also reflects a common culture of language use. Four different language families are represented in the pueblos. The eastern pueblos are dominated by Kiowa-Tanoan languages like Tewa, Tiwa, and Towa (Jemez). In the western pueblos are Hopi, of the Uto-Aztecan language family, and Zuni, often considered a Penutian language. Keresan, with no other known family members, is spoken in both eastern and western pueblos. Though each of the Pueblo languages has inherited distinctive grammatical structures, Pueblo communities speak these diverse languages in accordance with common aesthetic principles.

Along with Kiowa—a Plains Indian language— Tewa, Tiwa, and Towa compose the Kiowa-Tanoan family, which has about the same degree of interrelatedness among its members as has the Romance language family of Europe. Rio Grande Tewa is spoken in the pueblos of San Juan, San Ildefonso, Santa Clara, Nambe, Tesuque, and Pojoaque; the other Tewa language, Arizona Tewa, is spoken on First Mesa of the Hopi Reservation, brought there by Southern Tewas who left New Mexico after the Second Pueblo Revolt in 1696. The Tiwa languages are divided by geography into Northern Tiwa (Taos and Picuris) and Southern Tiwa (Isleta and Sandia). Towa is spoken only at Jemez Pueblo.

The Kiowa-Tanoan family of languages is distantly related to the Uto-Aztecan family, from which Hopi comes. All Hopi villages speak dialects of the same language, which is more closely related to such languages as Ute, Aztec, Comanche, Paiute, and Tohono O'odham than it is to any of the Kiowa-Tonoan languages.

Zuni is sometimes viewed as a Penutian language, related to such nonneighboring languages as Yokuts and Wintu—California Penutian languages—but this remote relationship is still uncertain.

The Keresan language is a continuum of dialects that range from Laguna and Acoma in the west to Cochiti, Santo Domingo, San Felipe, Santa Ana, and Sia in the east. The people of any of these pueblos can easily understand their nearest Keresan neighbors, but at the extremes of this continuum there is enough difference to preclude mutual intelligibility and to impose a true language barrier. Keresan, like Basque, is a linguistic isolate. No one has ever successfully demonstrated its connection to any recognized family of languages.

Owing to the ancestries of the Pueblo languages, it is difficult to locate common structural attributes that might be considered especially important in making claims about native grammar in relation to Pueblo worldview. Benjamin Lee Whorf, in the most famous claim of this type, found in Hopi's lack of elaboration in tense-aspect suffixes a linguistic counterpart to the Hopi emphasis on cyclical rather than linear time. However, Whorf's claim that Hopi's relative lack of suffixes distinguishing past, present, and future reflects a disinterest in linear time cannot be extended to the other Pueblo Indian languages, even though the people who speak them have many cultural similarities. Also, Whorf felt that Hopi lacked all tense distinctions corresponding to the tenses of European languages. But later scholars generally agree that Hopi does have a future tense, as in *piktani,* "he/she will make *piki.*" The *-ni* suffix indicates a future tense and is comparable to the English auxiliary *shall/will.* As for languages other than Hopi, Tewa, for example, does have tense-aspect distinctions that correspond to those made in European languages. Indeed, the structural differences within the Pueblo languages make it especially difficult if not impossible to find common structures that might provide a basis for positing a shared worldview of the Pueblo people. What these languages can do that is especially instructive in this area is to redirect our attention to shared patterns of usage that transcend linguistic differences in structure.

Among the most important of these shared cultural patterns of speaking are a reliance on traditional forms, an indigenous purism, a compartmentalization of languages, and a linguistic signaling of identity. The reliance on traditional forms can be seen in the use of cultural precedents as models of speech. For example, the Hopis chant announcements of birth celebrations or public grievances. These chants are modeled on the sacred chants of the crier chief, differing from his calls to ceremonial participation only in their closing intonation.

Indigenous purism—keeping the native language free from admixture with other languages—is exemplified in the proscription of nonnative languages in the kiva during ceremonial performances. The use of foreign languages in such settings is clearly outlawed, and violators are punished. This idea extends to everyday speech and can be seen in the restriction of loan words from other languages. Despite more than three hundred years of multilingualism in Tewa and Spanish by speakers of Rio Grande Tewa, that language has relatively few Spanish loan words—less than 5 percent of the total vocabulary.

By compartmentalization a linguistic community keeps the languages in its repertoire as distinct as possible, using each in its appropriate context. The trilingual Arizona Tewas, for example, speak Tewa in their homes and community, Hopi elsewhere on the reservation, and English in situations in which they need to participate in the cash economy of the larger society or to access federal services. Though many Arizona Tewas know each of these languages very well, they have not permitted them to mix in the form of words loaned from one to another. Despite more than two hundred years of speaking Hopi, the Arizona Tewas have only one Hopi loan word in their native Tewa language.

The linguistic signaling of identity involves a cultural emphasis on using language to convey the relevant identity of the speaker. Storytellers from the Tewa, Hopi, and Jemez Pueblos, as they tell their stories in the "so it is said" tradition, must use expressions in each narrative sentence that call attention to their role as traditional narrators. Similarly, Hopi chanters explicitly mention their status as messenger when making announcements to the village. In everyday speech, language choice itself often represents a claim to membership in the group associated with that language, as when the Arizona Tewas use Hopi to indicate their status as members of the Hopi tribe.

These shared linguistic values are often realized in their most tangible and influential forms in the ritual speech of ceremonial performance. In all pueblos, the high prestige of religious ritual makes such speech a type of cultural model for everyday speech behavior in more secular contexts. This use of ritual speech as a local model represents a fundamental difference between Pueblo Indian and Euro-American philosophies of language. Whereas Pueblo Indian conceptions of language emphasize its performative and constitutive role in creating and maintaining reality, Euro-American views of language tend to relegate it to the role of reflecting a preexisting reality. Whereas the Pueblo Indian perspective emphasizes the functions of language and its many social roles, Euro-American views emphasize the structure of language and focus on its role in cognition.

See also Languages.

Davis, Irvine, "The Kiowa-Tanoan, Keresan, and Zuni Languages," in *The Languages of Native America,* ed. Lyle Campbell and Marianne Mithun (Austin: University of Texas Press, 1979); Kroskrity, Paul V., *Language, History, and Identity: Ethnolinguistic Studies of the Arizona Tewa* (Tucson: University of Arizona Press, 1993); Whorf, Benjamin Lee, *Language, Thought, and Reality* (Cambridge: MIT Press, 1956).

PAUL V. KROSKRITY
University of California at Los Angeles

PUGET SOUND TRIBES

In folklore, Indians of the Puget Sound region explain their environment and culture as the legacy of a mythic being called Transformer. When Transformer came, the ancient world capsized like a cracked canoe. In its place he left a densely forested land, chiseled by streams draining into deep, sheltered saltwater bays. Shellfish, salmon, waterfowl, deer, and elk thrived in the waters and forests; edible roots, sprouts, and berries flourished on scattered meadows; humans congregated in cedar lodges along riverbanks and shores; and powerful spirits roamed throughout.

In partnership with spirits, the people of this lush world obtained many riches. By training and self-purification, any person could attract a spirit interested in forming a partnership. To the human who gratified its appetite for ceremony, a spirit might grant the power to catch fish, kill game, find berries, make baskets or canoes, heal the sick, kill or repel enemies, acquire wealth, or do other useful things. People did not say much about their supernatural partners, but their achievements proved that relations had been established.

In order to perform the songs and sponsor the feasts that the spirits craved, a person needed help from other humans. By meeting obligations to one's supernatural partners and wielding the powers that these spirits had bestowed, a person also earned other people's esteem. Particularly by giving away wealth that came with power—blankets, furs, canoes, slaves, shell beads—a man or woman gained prestige and influence, not only among relatives and neighbors but also in distant villages. In theory, anyone could attain eminence this way; in practice, training and wealth tended to perpetuate certain families' high status.

The spirit realm was as dangerous as it was attractive. Spirits could act malevolently for or independent of human partners. Because anyone might have undiscerned powers, there was reason to beware of everyone except close kin. Strangers especially were potential enemies. And to residents of one village the people in many other villages around Puget Sound, particularly distant villages, *were* strangers. Many spoke unintelligible languages and had unfamiliar customs.

Yet nonviolent relations with outsiders were more common than war, and most people had peaceful relations with residents of numerous other villages. Just as they desired connections with beings outside the human world, they desired connections with humans outside their closest social circle. Contacts with outsiders came principally in marriage, ceremonial gatherings, gambling games, trade, and seasonal excursions to fishing and gathering sites.

Kinship through marriage entitled people to live or travel and to take resources in their relatives' territories. For this reason, and because in-laws exchanged foods and manufactures, exogamy expanded the merged families' sources of wealth. Since they also required wealth to arrange, exogamous marriages were most common among the well-to-do. By marrying outsiders and inviting in-laws to ceremonies which validated family members' achievements, the well-to-do forged bonds which transcended local loyalties. They thus drew the region's diverse communities into a web of overlapping kinship ties. On the other hand, by making their ceremonies occasions for displaying material and cultural specialties of particular families or villages, they reinforced local pride.

History has obscured the names, configurations, and relations of local groups that existed before English explorers entered Puget Sound in 1792. By then smallpox epidemics had reduced village populations 20 to 80 percent, compelling survivors to relocate and regroup. In addition, the maritime fur trade had furnished northern peoples such as the Kwakiutl with guns, equipping them for raids, which prompted some Puget Sound villagers to move or form new alliances.

Early European and American colonists sorted indigenous peoples into a few dozen territorial groupings. Names assigned to these so-called tribes did not all reflect the named peoples' usages or important affiliations. Few if any of the groups had unifying political institutions, although some shared language, resources, and cultural traditions. Today most descendants of the region's first peoples claim affiliation with a handful of organized tribes—Klallam, Skokomish, Squaxin, Suquamish, Nisqually, Puyallup, Steilacoom, Muckleshoot, Duwamish, Snoqualmie, Snohomish, Tulalip, Stillaguamish, Skagit, Sauk-Suiattle, Swinomish, Samish, Lummi, Nooksack—that evolved in varied ways from the more numerous groups listed in nineteenth-century records. But social ties to other communities, including non-Indians, have remained the norm for members of these tribes. Largely for this reason, the criteria of Indian and tribal identity have been at issue for one hundred fifty years.

Interest and experience in relations with impressive outsiders enabled Puget Sound's inhabitants to devise successful strategies for dealing with fur traders and early colonists. When Hudson's Bay Company opened land-based trade at Fort Langley in 1827 and Fort Nisqually in 1833, many Indians seized opportunities to increase their wealth and enhance their status by marrying, trading with, and working for the newcomers. Thousands of native people, probably hoping to learn what powerful spirit gave Europeans wealth and resistance to disease, also welcomed Catholic missionaries after 1839.

American settlers—the first came in 1845—met with similar hospitality. Indians appeared proud to incorporate settlers into their communities and to participate in economic enterprises, such as stores and sawmills, that settlers organized. Because Indians met people from other indigenous communities at trading posts, missions, and towns, colonization also prompted them to extend their network of relations with each other.

As long as colonists depended on Indians for food, transportation, and labor, Indians played a major part in defining the terms of their relations with non-Indians. Conventions developed that still governed relations in lightly settled areas at the century's end. One vital feature of this bridge culture was the Chinook jargon, a limited trade language that facilitated communication not only between Indians and others but also among Indians of different groups.

The United States assumed sovereignty north of the Columbia River in 1846. In 1850, without first extinguishing Indian title, the government authorized settlers to claim land in the territory. After immigrants streamed in and organized Washington Territory, the responsibility for appeasing resentful local tribespeople fell to Governor Isaac Stevens. On Christmas Eve, 1854, Stevens launched a whirlwind campaign to get treaty cessions from all tribes in his jurisdiction. In an effort to draw autonomous villages into manageable confederations, Stevens appointed and dealt primarily with a few head chiefs, including the now famous Seattle. By February 1855 he had negotiated three treaties covering lands surrounding Puget Sound.

These treaties were among the first in the United States to clear the way for colonization by reducing Indians' land base to small areas within their original territories. Stevens had hoped to consolidate Puget Sound groups on two or three reserves, but at the meetings with local leaders he reluctantly consented to eight: Skokomish, Squaxin Island, Nisqually, Puyallup, Suquamish, Tulalip-Snohomish, Swinomish, and Lummi. Because Americans needed Indian labor and wanted to minimize expenditures for Indians' support, Stevens

also agreed that they could leave the reservations to fish, hunt, and work.

Only a few people in the southeastern sector of the region—horse-raising Indians who needed more grazing land than their treaty provided—violently resisted Stevens's plan. Although the brief war of 1855–56 and the execution of war chief Leschi became symbols of Indians' subjugation, the rebels won larger and more numerous reservations. Furthermore, neither treaties nor war changed Indians' lives as significantly as did immigration, which increased exponentially after 1880. Until then settlers were few, government was weak, reservations held few attractions, and established patterns of intercultural intercourse still met people's needs. Therefore, most Indians did not move to reservations until the 1880s; and as late as World War I thousands of people of aboriginal descent still lived elsewhere.

Wherever they lived, most Indians moved freely and found opportunities in the larger society, selling food and raw materials or working at sawmills, logging camps, and farms. Many combined these activities with accustomed subsistence pursuits. By such strategies all but the feeblest supported themselves without government aid. Mobility and interaction with other culture groups contributed to increasing diversity in Indians' social and religious practices, economic orientations, and family ties.

Against their desire for good relations with whites, Indians weighed the fact that most whites regarded them as inferior. One remarkable product of this and other tensions was the Indian Shaker Church, which began on South Puget Sound in the 1880s when an off-reservation logger had a messianic vision. Unlike the cults that revitalized other Indian societies during this period, Shakerism did not militantly reject white influence in favor of aboriginal customs. Indeed, Shakers condemned most practices that made Indians obnoxious to many whites, including shamanism and gambling. Their conviction that the holy spirit gave individuals the power to heal was a syncretic fusion of Christian and aboriginal beliefs. Shakers simultaneously claimed membership in the Christian fold and asserted that Indians needed different religious instructions than whites. The Indian Shaker religion, which spread throughout the Pacific Northwest after the 1890s, still has many adherents.

Twentieth-century developments undermined the ability of Indians to live comfortably alongside non-Indians. Dwindling employment opportunities for unskilled and seasonal laborers, discrimination, poor education, and prejudicial state fisheries management reduced Indians' economic options and condemned increasing numbers to poverty. Hoping to hold the government accountable for their distress, members of reservation and off-reservation communities organized the Northwest Federation of American Indians in 1914. Led by Thomas Bishop, scion of an off-reservation biracial family, the NFAI identified thousands of people who considered themselves Indians but were not on government rolls. The federation's main project—a court of claims case tried in 1927—gave many people a forum to demand land and protest breaches of treaty promises, but it ended in defeat.

NFAI activists also led Puget Sound groups' response to the Indian Reorganization Act. Apparently confident that they could govern themselves, residents of all reservations but one accepted the IRA with little recorded controversy, even though the concepts of majority rule and corporate organization departed from their tradition of informal association in interlinked, fluid groups. On the Swinomish and Tulalip Reservations, still-distinct bands voted to confederate. Descendants of Puyallup allottees, who had become citizens and disbanded in 1903, formed a new government. Two Klallam bands that had refused to move to the Skokomish Reservation finally secured reservations of their own. But other Indians who had never settled on reservations, despite their continuing ties to reservation communities, did not have an opportunity to organize or acquire land under the IRA. Twenty years later officials decided that most such people had forfeited their tribal status.

During the twentieth century another of the NFAI's concerns—state interference with Indian fishing—moved to the top of activists' agendas. After 1890 non-Indian commercial fishing and state regulation made it increasingly difficult for Indians to take salmon—a staple of the aboriginal diet. Especially outside reservations, Indians risked arrest by fishing without licenses and out of season. The state supreme court, declaring that the treaties did not secure special rights, sanctioned regulations that effectively discriminated against Indians. But because lower courts sometimes acquitted Indian fishers, because federal court decisions contradicted state rulings, and because fishing remained vital for many Indians' subsistence, questions about the treaties' meaning persisted.

The issue gained urgency in the 1950s, when state repression escalated as many Indians' economic position deteriorated. During the 1960s protest fish-ins on some western Washington rivers attracted national attention and spurred the United States and several tribes to seek a definitive federal interpretation of the treaties. In February 1974, District Court Judge George Boldt vindicated the Indians, recognizing their right to take half the harvestable salmon and barring the state from imposing regulations not essential to preserving fish runs. State officials and non-Indian fishers responded with five years of extraordinary, often violent resistance; but in 1979 the U.S. Supreme Court upheld Boldt's ruling in all important respects.

As construed, treaty fishing rights belong to tribes, which determine their own membership and regulate members' fishing. After 1974, this fact, together with the federal policy of funding tribes directly, focused Puget Sound Indians' attention on their tribal organizations to an unprecedented extent. Even very small tribes developed thriving governments that administer conservation, law-enforcement, and social-service programs. Thanks largely to their participation in the treaty-rights struggle, four landless groups—the Nooksacks, Upper Skagits, Sauk-Suiattles, and Stillaguamishes—won federal recognition of their tribal status in the 1970s. On the other hand, federal courts denied the Samish, Snohomish, Snoqualmie, Duwamish, and Steilacoom tribes treaty rights because the United States did not recognize them as Indian polities. These groups subsequently submitted petitions for federal acknowledgment.

Proving the unrecognized tribes' historical continuity with aboriginal tribes involves telling a complex story of people who have never fitted into neat ethnic, racial, or political categories. It is a story inseparable from the stories both of other Indians and of non-Indians. It is a tale of many peoples who have contributed distinctive threads to a rough but seamless social fabric that has blanketed the Puget Sound region.

Cohen, Fay G., *Treaties on Trial* (Seattle: University of Washington Press, 1986); Collins, June M., *Valley of the Spirits: Upper Skagit Indians of Western Washington* (Seattle: University of Washington Press, 1974); Elmendorf, William W., *Twana Narratives: Native Historical Accounts of a Coast Salish Culture* (Seattle and Vancouver: University of Washington Press and University of British Columbia Press, 1993).

ALEXANDRA HARMON
Seattle, Washington

Q

QUAPAW

When the French explorers Marquette and Jolliet descended the Mississippi River in 1673, the Quapaws (from Ugaxpa, meaning "downstream people") occupied four villages near the confluence of the Mississippi and Arkansas Rivers. The only Dhegiha Sioux speakers in the lower Mississippi Valley, the Quapaws were sedentary hunters and farmers whose population numbered between fifteen thousand and twenty thousand.

Dhegiha oral tradition refers to migration from a homeland in the lower Ohio River valley: a larger group ascended the Mississippi and Missouri Rivers, whereupon successive division gave rise to the Osages, Omahas, Kansas, and Poncas. The remaining group went down the Mississippi and became the Quapaws.

Archaeological sites attributed to precontact Quapaws, however, are similar to late prehistoric Mississippian sites. Thus, some contemporary archaeologists dismiss the oral tradition and derive Quapaw culture from local Mississippian sequences. Whatever their origin, the Quapaws lived in a universe structured by reciprocal relationships among communities of living beings and powerful spiritual forces. Ceremonies for planting and harvesting crops, hunting and warfare, curing, naming, marriage, adoption, and mourning and burying the dead were performed to sustain positive relationships between human and spiritual communities and to ensure that the power of Wahkondah—a dynamic, mysterious, and creative life force—imbued important events and undertakings.

Members of Quapaw society belonged to descent groups traced through the father's line. Twenty-one named clans were divided into two divisions called Sky People and Earth People. Each clan possessed a unique relationship with spiritual powers, through which rights to perform specific rituals were secured. Earth People clans performed rituals that sustained the physical and material well-being of the community, while Sky People clans performed rituals involving spiritual affairs. Together these rituals maintained the total set of cosmological relationships that structured the Quapaw world.

The division between Sky People and Earth People also regulated marriage; the two intermarrying sides symbolized the idea that tribal subdivisions made up a unified whole that was greater than the sum of its parts. Kinship relations were extended to outsiders via the calumet ceremony, which employed sacred pipes to symbolize the themes of unity and reciprocity.

The Quapaws built bark-covered longhouses (forty were observed at one village in 1700), each occupied by several related families. Longhouses were arranged around an open plaza where ceremonies and public events were held. A meetinghouse stood near the plaza, along with an open-sided arbor where community leaders sat during public ceremonies. Some Quapaw villages had sacred temples where religious specialists presided; there ritual paraphernalia was kept and troubled individuals could find sanctuary. Quapaw villages had one or two leaders whose offices were inherited through the male line, although decision making involved a council of male elders.

With penetration of the fur trade into the lower Mississippi Valley in the eighteenth century, the Quapaws supplied forest products to European traders at Arkansas Post (permanently established in 1721) in exchange for manufactured goods. During the French (1699–1763) and Spanish (1763–1803) regimes, Louisiana governors made annual distributions of presents to strengthen Quapaw support of colonial objectives. The Quapaws viewed warfare and other services to their European allies as reciprocal exchange for these considerations.

Some European introductions—particularly infectious diseases and alcoholic beverages—had extremely deleterious effects. The Quapaws suffered catastrophic population losses, which necessitated village consolidation and modification of the clan system. However, traditional political institutions and religious beliefs persisted, and associated ceremonies continued to punctuate the annual cycle.

When U.S. representatives replaced the Spaniards at Arkansas Post after 1804, the Quapaws attempted to continue their policy of reciprocal interaction. However, the Americans wanted land, not forest products or military assistance, and the Quapaws were forced in 1818 and 1824 to cede their Arkansas homelands and relocate on reservations established first along the Red River and then in Indian Territory (now Oklahoma).

Crop losses, disease, and hardships suffered at the hands of inept federal agents determined to impose new lifestyles and values plagued the Quapaws throughout the removal period. The population scattered into different parts of Indian Territory, but cultural identity was maintained through get-togethers for annuity distributions and the annual Green Corn Ceremony.

After the Civil War large numbers of Quapaws hoped to better their circumstances by joining the Osages in southeastern Kansas. By 1880, the "home band" had declined to the point where it was in jeopardy of losing the reservation. This was avoided, however, by the adoption of "homeless" members of other tribes, intermarriage, and the return of many Quapaws from other reservations. Passage of the General Allotment Act in 1887 brought more Quapaws back to the reservation. The Quapaws voted in favor of allotment; 234 enrolled members each received 240 acres (two additional members received 40-acre tracts), mostly in contiguous parcels, which preserved a substantial land base.

Many Quapaws converted to Catholicism during the reservation years. In 1896, John "Moonhead" Wilson, a Caddo-Delaware holy man, introduced the peyote religion, which the Quapaws combined with elements of Catholicism. The new religion, which promoted generosity and "right living," was embraced by full-blood owners of allotments in the western part of the former reservation, an area that provided lucrative returns from lead and zinc mining.

Many traditional ceremonies endured, including those associated with child naming, mourning, and burying the dead. At the end of the nineteenth century, however, the Green Corn Ceremony was replaced by an annual picnic. By the 1920s this picnic was transformed into a powwow that provided opportunities for wealthy full bloods to foster community solidarity through the distribution of gifts. This group also gained control of the Quapaw Tribal Council, the governing body created under the General Allotment Act. In 1956, the tribal council was replaced by the Quapaw Business Committee. The distribution in 1961 of money awarded under a federal judgment stimulated interaction among Quapaws long separated from each other, and promoted increased involvement in tribal affairs.

Today there are about two thousand Quapaws, most living near a tribal center in Miami, Oklahoma. An industrial-park development, a convenience store, and a bingo parlor are managed by the business committee. The annual powwow is the major social and ceremonial event of the year. The community is a dynamic one, carrying its distinctive but always changing identity into the future.

Baird, W. David, *The Quapaw Indians: A History of the Downstream People* (Norman: University of Oklahoma Press, 1980); Sabo, George, III, *Paths of Our Children: Historic Indians of Arkansas* (Fayetteville: Arkansas Archeological Survey, 1992).

GEORGE SABO III
University of Arkansas

R

RADICALS AND RADICALISM, 1900 TO THE PRESENT

During the first two-thirds of the twentieth century, *radicalism* was a term largely inapplicable to Indians in the United States. The more famous advocates of native rights prior to 1960—people like Charles Eastman (Santee Dakota), Carlos Montezuma (Yavapai), and Ella Deloria (Lakota)—tended to exhibit an essentially liberal cant, endeavoring to secure relief for their people from at least the worst aspects of dominant-society oppression by appeals to public sympathy and reliance upon channels of due process offered by the U.S. government. Others, such as Rupert Costo (Cahuilla), adopted attitudes drawn mainly from the discourse of conservative Republicanism. The organizations created by such figures—the Indian Rights Association, the National Congress of American Indians, the National Tribal Chairmen's Association, and others—conformed for the most part to the outlooks of their founders. Only in the rarest of instances was direct confrontation an aspect of their relationship to federal authority.

By the mid-1960s, however, things had begun to change decisively. Spurred by the draconian impact of government termination and relocation policies beginning in the early 1950s, and inspired by the example of the civil rights movement a few years later, a new generation of Indians began to forge a uniquely indigenous radical politics for North America. In the process, they openly rejected the accommodationist stance of officially sanctioned Indian leaders—whom they derided as sellouts and "Uncle Tomahawks"—while striving to link themselves to their own deeper traditions of national and cultural sovereignty. Simultaneously, they sought to integrate this heritage with contemporary theories of decolonization and anti-imperialism.

Perhaps the first overt expression of this trend occurred at a national conference, the American Indian Chicago Conference, called at the University of Chicago in 1961. During the proceedings, a youth caucus broke off and issued its own independent and fiery statement of purpose. Within a year, the primary instigators of this insurrection—student activists led by Clyde Warrior (Ponca), Herb Blatchford (Navajo), Shirley Hill Witt (Mohawk), Mel Thom ("Mao Tse-Thom," a Paiute), Mary Natani (Winnebago), and Vivian One Feather (Navajo)—had established their own organization, the National Indian Youth Council (NIYC), complete with a monthly newsletter entitled *ABC: Americans Before Columbus*. The latter quickly became a major vehicle for the voicing of radical Indian thought, while NIYC membership swelled from its original handful to several hundred.

Beginning in 1965, the NIYC set out to engage its steadily evolving liberationist ideology in direct action. This assumed the form of participation in the fishing-rights struggles of the Quillayute, Nisqually, Muckleshoot, and other indigenous nations of the Pacific Northwest. There, an extended series of physical confrontations with state and federal authorities—dubbed "fish-ins"—and attendant courtroom actions resulted not only in the eventual reaffirmation of Indian treaty rights in the region, but also in national attention for several key local activists, among them Janet McCloud (Tulalip), Sid Mills (Yakima), Ramona Bennett (Puyallup), and Hank Adams (Assiniboin/Lakota).

The very sharpness of the fishing-rights conflict attracted public support from celebrities like Jane Fonda and Marlon Brando, and stimulated broad popular interest in native issues for the first time in decades. Rising public concern in turn created a context in which genuinely radical Indian writers could finally see their ideas put before a national audience. Notable in this regard was the Lakota writer Vine Deloria, Jr., whose first two books, *Custer Died for Your Sins* (1969) and *We Talk, You Listen* (1970), offered a searing indictment of conventional attitudes and government policies. Another prime medium for the spread of indigenous radicalism was *Akwesasne Notes,* a quarterly newspaper published on the St. Regis Mohawk Reservation. *Akwesasne Notes* attained a circulation of more than fifty thousand after several of its staff played key roles in dramatizing U.S. and Canadian violations of Mohawk treaty rights during the 1968 occupation of the Cornwall Bridge, a span linking upstate New York with Canada. Soon, its editors would include John Mohawk (Seneca), whose insights into social ecology would, along with those of Onondaga leader Oren Lyons, have a profound effect on shaping the outlook of native radicals.

The momentum created by all these developments led to ever more militant groups displacing the NIYC and extending the list of radical concerns. For example, in 1969 a group calling itself Indians of All Tribes (IAT) organized the occupation of Alcatraz Island in San Francisco Bay. Nominally headed by Richard Oaks (Mohawk), IAT defined itself as being committed to the use of direct confrontation to "recover Indian lands illegally taken by the United States of America." The group sustained its occupation for more than a year, by which time it had inspired a number of similar actions, including the successful takeover of an abandoned military site at Fort Lawton, near Seattle. In the wake of the Alcatraz occupation, IAT became involved in supporting the Pit River land struggle in northern California, but the organization rapidly dissolved after Oaks was murdered in September 1972.

Meanwhile, the American Indian Movement (AIM) —an organization founded in Minneapolis in 1968 by several Anishinabes including Dennis Banks, George Mitchell, and Mary Jane Wilson—was expanding steadily and articulating an increasingly hard-line approach to indigenous rights. Its early success was due primarily to the efforts of Russell Means (Oglala Lakota), a man acknowledged even by his adversaries as being "possessed of a bizarre knack for attracting media attention to Indian grievances." In short order, Means master-minded a series of spectacular actions— a demonstration conducted at Mount Rushmore National Monument on July 4, 1971, for instance, and the "capturing" of the *Mayflower* replica at Plymouth, Massachusetts, on Thanksgiving Day the same year— that placed AIM squarely at the forefront of Indian radicalism. This development was greatly reinforced by the contributions of John Trudell (Santee Dakota), considered by many to be a truly gifted orator.

In 1972, AIM launched the Trail of Broken Treaties, a cross-country caravan involving several hundred people and designed to "inject an Indian agenda" into that year's presidential race. The plan was to arrive in the nation's capital and conduct a mass demonstration on the eve of the election, during which the group would deliv-

er a twenty-point manifesto to incumbent president Richard M. Nixon. As it turned out, the Bureau of Indian Affairs (BIA) headquarters building in downtown Washington was also occupied, an event that garnered almost continuous press coverage for several days and forced official agreement to a formal review of the Indians' proposals. Afterward, many native people referred to the AIM activists as "the shock troops of Indian sovereignty." Such attention also attracted the FBI.

The events that followed have been described as an example of "the continuing Indian wars" of the United States. Indeed, the FBI itself has, in its internal documents, referred to its anti-AIM campaign as an exercise in "domestic counterinsurgency." The locus for this campaign was the Pine Ridge Reservation in South Dakota, where, in early 1973, residents requested AIM assistance in a land-recovery effort and in combatting the policies of the BIA-installed tribal government. The upshot was that a specially assembled force of several hundred U.S. marshals and FBI agents, augmented by BIA police and a federally funded (and tribal council–supported) paramilitary group calling itself Guardians of the Oglala Nation (GOONs), surrounded an AIM contingent at the reservation hamlet of Wounded Knee on February 28.

Thus began a seventy-one-day siege that saw the deployment of armored military vehicles and Pentagon advisers against the Wounded Knee defenders. More than a half million rounds of military ammunition were fired into the AIM perimeter, killing two Indians and wounding several others before the siege ended. Perhaps a dozen more were intercepted by roving GOON patrols and murdered as they attempted to backpack supplies into Wounded Knee under cover of darkness. In the aftermath, the FBI had nearly 550 felony charges—all but fifteen of which were ultimately unsuccessful—filed against AIM members, in particular against the movement's leaders.

Even as these "leadership trials" were going on, the FBI fostered what the U.S. Commission on Civil Rights later termed a "reign of terror" on Pine Ridge. This resulted in the murder of more than sixty AIM members and supporters on the reservation during the three years following Wounded Knee. Nearly 350 others suffered serious physical assaults. Most if not all of these crimes were apparently committed by GOONs, whose membership included many of the local BIA police. The FBI seemed to do nothing to stop the violence. On the contrary, according to one former police official and GOON commander, Duane Brewer (Oglala Lakota),

An American Indian woman wrapped in an upside-down flag, amid a group of West Coast Indians (some five hundred in all) who occupied the Bureau of Indian Affairs in Washington, D.C., in 1972 to protest broken treaties and other injustices.

and others, the FBI actively collaborated in it, providing equipment, field intelligence, and virtual immunity from prosecution to the killers.

Under these conditions, AIM adopted a posture of armed self-defense. On June 26, 1975, tensions culminated in a massive firefight near the reservation village of Oglala, during which two FBI agents and an AIM member were killed. The FBI then brought a further 250 militarily equipped agents onto Pine Ridge and finally overwhelmed the Indian resistance. A year later, two AIM members, Bob Robideau (Anishinabe) and Dino Butler (Tuni) were tried for killing the agents. They were acquitted by an all-white jury in Cedar Rapids, Iowa, on the basis that, given the FBI's performance on the reservation since 1973, the accused had acted in self-defense. A third man, Leonard Peltier (Anishinabe/Lakota), was then tried, convicted, and sentenced to double life imprisonment. Subsequent rev-

elations concerning the government's fabrication of evidence and other misconduct during the Peltier trial have eturned his ongoing incarceration into an international cause célèbre.

After Pine Ridge, AIM drifted into a period of relative ineffectuality, its surviving members scattered and exhausted. Flashes of the old brilliance continued, however—for example, the "Longest Walk" from San Francisco to Washington, D.C., in 1978. In 1981, Russell Means and his brother Bill started what became a four-year occupation of an 880-acre parcel in the Black Hills dubbed "Yellow Thunder Tiyospaye," near Rapid City, South Dakota. They were able to achieve a landmark federal court opinion concerning Indian rights to sacred areas, but the victory was voided by the Supreme Court's "G-O Road" decision a short time later. All things considered, AIM was in no condition to play a significant role in opposing the forced relocation of Navajos at Big Mountain during the mid-1980s or the federal impoundment of Western Shoshone livestock in Nevada a few years later. The same circumstance pertained to the series of armed confrontations between the Mohawk Warriors Society and U.S. and Canadian authorities, which congealed in a standoff at the Mercier Bridge, outside Montréal, during the summer of 1990.

On another front, several female AIM members—notably Madonna (Gilbert) Thunderhawk, Lorelei DeCora Means, and Phyllis Young, all Lakotas—formed an offshoot entitled Women of All Red Nations (WARN) during the second half of the 1970s, mainly to confront an involuntary sterilization program administered by the BIA's Indian Health Service and other issues of specific interest to native women. Although WARN experienced a brief prominence at the end of the decade, it later slid into decline. By the late 1980s, however, a variant known as the Indigenous Women's Network (IWN) had been organized by Ingrid Washinawatok (Oneida) and others. At present, IWN publishes a journal, *Indigenous Woman*, and seems to be growing at a healthy pace.

Probably the most successful radical endeavor of the late 1970s and early 1980s was the creation of the International Indian Treaty Council (IITC). Under the direction of Jimmie Durham (Cherokee), who brought in a raft of younger activists like Winona LaDuke (Anishinabe), "AIM's international diplomatic arm" was able to put together the initial United Nations–sponsored convocation of indigenous peoples in Geneva, Switzerland, during the summer of 1977. The IITC then played a key role in forming the United Nations Working Group on Indigenous Populations (WGIP) in 1982. The WGIP was charged with drafting a Universal Declaration of the Rights of Indigenous Peoples for submission to the U.N. General Assembly by 1992, thus affording native nations a standing in international law they had previously lacked.

With the departure of Durham in 1981, however, the IITC began an ongoing period of decay, increasingly divorcing itself from the "indigenist" or "Fourth World" vision of AIM while aligning itself ever more closely with an assortment of socialist or Third World revolutionary governments. During the Sandinista/Indian conflict of the mid-1980s, for example, the IITC openly sided with the Nicaraguan government against that country's native people. Predictably, this stance caused the IITC to lose much of its hard-earned status as a leading advocate of indigenous rights.

Currently, with the reconstitution of active AIM chapters in many places, there are signs that Indian radicalism is revitalizing itself. In Denver and San Francisco in particular, this process had progressed to the point that, by 1992, demonstrations of sufficient scale could be mounted to put a stop to planned celebrations of the Columbus Quincentennial. In December 1993, representatives of a dozen functioning AIM chapters across the United States conducted a "summit" in the village of Edgewood, New Mexico, to hammer out a statement of reorientation and purpose for the movement as a whole. Although the effects of the Edgewood Declaration are as yet unknown, it seems certain that indigenous North American radicalism, forged in the crucible of the late twentieth century, will continue to exert an influence well into the twenty-first.

See also Alcatraz, Occupation of; American Indian Movement (AIM); Reformers and Reform Groups; Wounded Knee Takeover, 1973.

Deloria, Vine, Jr., *Behind the Trail of Broken Treaties*, 2d ed. (Austin: University of Texas Press, 1985); Matthiessen, Peter, *In the Spirit of Crazy Horse*, 2d ed. (New York: Viking Press, 1991); Steiner, Stan, *The New Indians* (New York: Harper and Row, 1968).

WARD CHURCHILL (Keetoowah Cherokee)
University of Colorado at Boulder

RANCHING
See Herding and Ranching.

RED CLOUD (MAKHPYIA-LUTA)
(1821/22–1909)
Oglala chief.

Although Red Cloud was one of the most celebrated of all the Oglalas, the facts of his early life, including the date and place of his birth, are obscure. All that can be said with some certainty is that he was born near the forks of the Platte River in 1821 or 1822. Similarly, his rise to a position of leadership is difficult to document. It is clear, however, that as a young man he developed a reputation for both bravery and cruelty, particularly in expeditions against the Pawnees. By the middle 1860s he was a leading Oglala warrior and was recognized by the whites as a chief. (The whites insisted in their dealings with the Indians that someone speak for each tribe as a chief.)

Red Cloud's principal military achievement lay in forcing the United States to abandon the Bozeman

Trail between the North Platte River and the gold-fields of Montana. Following the failure of the Fort Laramie conference of 1866, which Red Cloud left in a huff, the Indians stopped virtually all civilian travel on the trail. The little forts—Reno, Phil Kearny, and C. F. Smith—that the army had established to protect travelers could hardly protect their own garrisons. On December 21, 1866, the Sioux massacred Lieutenant Colonel W. J. Fetterman and eighty men sent out from Fort Phil Kearny to protect a train sent out to gather wood. The Fetterman massacre dramatized the failure of the army's Indian policy and gave new impetus to calls for negotiating peace with the Sioux, and particularly with Red Cloud. Red Cloud, however, refused to negotiate until the Bozeman forts were abandoned. The army abandoned the forts in August 1868, but Red Cloud did not arrive at Fort Laramie to discuss peace until November 4; he had sent word that he would make his winter's meat before coming in. After three days of haggling he "put his mark" on the treaty.

The Fort Laramie negotiators dealt with various Sioux tribes throughout the summer of 1868. In signing the treaty, the Indians, in exchange for presents and the promise of annuities and other benefits, agreed to abandon the warpath and locate on a large reservation north of the state of Nebraska and west of the Missouri River. The Treaty of 1868 was a long and complicated document that the Indians found difficult to understand. There is little evidence that its most celebrated signatory understood the treaty, or, if he did, that he had any intention of abiding by it. From the beginning Red Cloud made it clear that he had no intention of living north of the Platte Valley. Indeed, he had signed the treaty because he thought it would make it possible for him to return to the area around Fort Laramie.

There followed a decade of frustrating negotiations in which representatives of the government tried to explain the terms of the treaty to Red Cloud and persuade him to abide by them. He made four trips to Washington to visit with the president. These trips, extensively covered by the press, provided Red Cloud with a splendid platform from which to criticize the government's Indian policy, and he used it effectively. He was an imposing figure with a flair for the dramatic, and he spoke with rare eloquence, even through indifferent interpreters. On his first trip east, in 1870, he visited New York City as well as Washington. He spoke to deafening applause before an overflow crowd at the Cooper Institute. He was lionized by various reform groups but

was a thorn in the flesh of those who were trying to carry out the government's "peace policy." He was a central figure in the conflict between the army and the Interior Department over who should have authority over the Plains Indians. He resisted all efforts to locate his people away from the Platte Valley, although not with force. He also made life difficult for most of the agents assigned to the tribe.

Finally, in 1878 Red Cloud agreed to locate on the Pine Ridge Reservation in western South Dakota. He soon engaged in a much-publicized controversy with the agent, Dr. Valentine T. McGillycuddy, which concluded with the agent's resignation.

Despite his many difficulties with the government, Red Cloud kept the peace he had agreed to at Fort Laramie in 1868; one of the results of his trips to Washington was an appreciation of the overwhelming power of the white man. He recognized the folly of going to war, but he tried to win as many concessions as possible. He opposed the movement of gold seekers and settlers to the Black Hills, for example, but he did not participate in the Custer massacre. He lent encouragement to the "hostiles," however, and his son Jack was in the Little Bighorn fight. Red Cloud also retained some influence with Crazy Horse. It was he who persuaded the noted war chief to come in to Fort Robinson. In 1890 Red Cloud discouraged participation in the Ghost Dance, trying to avert the troubles that led to the Wounded Knee massacre.

As the years wore on, Red Cloud had increasing difficulty with those younger members of the tribe who wanted to resume the warpath. They felt that he no longer was an effective leader. At the same time, there were those who felt that he was an obstructionist who impeded his people's progress along the white man's road. Both judgments have some validity. The noted frontiersman Captain James H. Cook observed that "during Red Cloud's life, he and his people had to meet such conditions as never before had confronted his tribe." With the old guideposts gone, he made his way as best he could. He, more than any of the other old chiefs, was associated with the erosion of the traditional way of life. He was perhaps one of the most important transition figures in the history of the American Indian.

Hyde, George E., *Red Cloud's Folk* (Norman: University of Oklahoma Press, 1937); Olson, James C., *Red Cloud and the Sioux Problem* (Lincoln: University of Nebraska Press, 1965).

JAMES C. OLSON
University of Missouri

Red Jacket (Segoyewatha)

(c. 1750–1830)
Seneca orator and political leader.

As a child and young man, the figure whites knew as Red Jacket was called Otetiani, usually translated as "Always Ready." Born into the Wolf clan in a Seneca village near present-day Geneva, New York, he came of age during the most stressful era of his people's history. The American War of Independence deeply split the Six Nations of the Iroquois, of which the Senecas were both the westernmost and the most populous member. Ultimately, however, most of the Iroquois nations—including nearly all Seneca factions—sided with the British. That choice was disastrous. As fighting ended in the early 1780s, several thousand refugees were living near British Niagara, their villages destroyed by U.S. forces in 1779. When the Treaty of Paris was signed in 1783, they had only begun to reoccupy homes that European diplomats had placed within the victorious state of New York.

During the war, Red Jacket had been a messenger for British officers and, so the story goes, received his namesake coat as a reward. On the whole, however, his military career was undistinguished, if not, as the political opponents who called him Cow Killer alleged, cowardly. His talents lay instead in diplomacy, and particularly in oratory, a skill long prized in Iroquois political culture. Sometime in the 1780s he assumed the ceremonial role of council orator, and with it the name Segoyewatha, traditionally translated as "He Keeps Them Awake," but more accurately rendered "He Makes Them Look for It in Vain."

Red Jacket's oratory marked nearly every major treaty council between whites and Senecas from the 1780s to the 1820s. Iroquois traditions of political consensus required him to pose as spokesman for all Senecas. But usually he articulated a diplomatic middle course between two competing factions. On one side were the followers of his fellow Seneca Cornplanter, who pursued accommodation with U.S. and state authorities; on the other were the supporters of the Mohawk Joseph Brant, who continued his wartime alliance with the British and in 1785 led nearly half of the Six Nations population to new homes on the Grand River in present-day Ontario. Between these extremes, Red Jacket's positions were consistent: the Iroquois Confederacy should remain neutral in disputes between the United States and British Canada; broker an honest peace between the new republic and the Shawnees, Mi-amis, and other western Indians with whom it remained at war; resist Christian proselytization; and—above all—maintain a land base within the boundaries claimed by the state of New York.

His success was mixed. Red Jacket was at his best with stirring speeches that inspired his followers and rebuked Euro-Americans. In 1792, for instance, when President Washington summoned him to Philadelphia in hopes that the Senecas would bring the western Indians to peace, the orator minced no words. "The President has assured us that he is not the cause of the hostilities," he said. "Brother, we wish you to point out to us . . . what you think is the real cause." Similarly blunt was the most famous speech attributed to Red Jacket, an 1805 response to a Christian missionary. "The Great Spirit . . . has made a great difference between his white and red children," he declared. "We do not wish to destroy your religion or take it from you. We only want to enjoy our own."

Oratory alone, however, could not solve the Senecas' problems. Moreover, a long tradition of factionalized, decentralized politics ensured that no single policy could be pursued consistently and that federal, state, or private interests could always find leaders who could be coerced or bribed into surrendering Iroquois lands. By these means, treaties at Fort Stanwix in 1784, Big Tree in 1797, and Buffalo Creek in 1826 created a paper trail depriving Senecas of all but a tiny fraction of western New York. Despite his vigorous opposition during and after treaty councils, Red Jacket signed the Big Tree and Buffalo Creek documents and occasionally accepted cash from white negotiators. Perhaps, as some alleged, he sold out. Or perhaps his resistance was outweighed by his commitment to Iroquois unity and his ambition to remain at the center of power.

Whatever the case, Iroquois politics remained anything but unified. In 1801, for example, Cornplanter's half brother, the prophet Handsome Lake, accused Red Jacket of witchcraft and nearly had him executed. Four years later, Red Jacket's quarrel with Brant climaxed during a dispute between Canadian officials and the Grand River Iroquois over the terms of their royal land grant. While Brant's ally, the adopted Mohawk John Norton, sought support at Whitehall, Red Jacket helped convene a rump council that repudiated Norton's transatlantic mission and briefly deposed Brant. After the latter's death in 1807, Red Jacket's principal factional foes were Seneca Christians. In 1824, his "Pagan" faction used an obscure state law to win the temporary expulsion of the missionary Thompson S. Harris and to close his school on the Buffalo Creek Reservation. Three years later, the Christian faction retaliated with a written document ousting Red Jacket as orator.

By the time a subsequent council reinstated him, Red Jacket had become a celebrity among white audiences captivated by stereotypes of the "Vanishing Indian." Charles Bird King, George Catlin, and others painted portraits of the man people were calling "the last of the Senecas," yet his final decade was hardly happy. To the devastating results of the Buffalo Creek Treaty and his battles with political enemies were added the indignity of public appearances that resembled carnival sideshows, the humiliation of his wife's conversion to Christianity, the pain of ill health, and, probably, the demon of alcoholism. His last trip eastward, in 1829, took him to Washington, D.C., where he met the newly inaugurated president, Andrew Jackson. While en route home Red Jacket appeared before an Albany, New York, audience made up largely of Jacksonian state legislators. In a rambling speech that inspired most of the assembled worthies to walk out, he compared Old Hickory unfavorably with the nation's first president.

Home at Buffalo Creek, knowing the end was near, Red Jacket made a round of farewell visits. "Let my funeral be according to the customs of our nation," he reportedly said. "Be sure that my grave be not made by a white man; let them not pursue me there!" When death came on January 20, 1830, however, the Christian faction appropriated his corpse, prepared it for a Protestant service, and interred it in a grave indeed dug by whites. These acts were bitter symbolic blows to the causes Red Jacket had stood for. Yet, paradoxically, his enemies' need to appropriate him in death as they could not in life affirms the magnitude of his legacy.

See also Brant, Joseph; Cayuga; Cornplanter; Seneca.

Robie, Harry, "Red Jacket's Reply: Problems in the Verification of a Native American Speech Text," *New York Folklore* 12 (1986): 99–117; Stone, William L., *The Life and Times of Sa-go-ye-wat-ha, or Red Jacket* (Albany, N.Y.: J. Munsell, 1866); Wallace, Anthony F. C., *The Death and Rebirth of the Seneca* (New York: Alfred A. Knopf, 1970).

DANIEL K. RICHTER
Dickinson College

RED STICK WAR

By 1811 a group had emerged within the Muskogees (Creeks) that was hostile to the United States because of its invasion of their territory. This faction—called Red Sticks by whites—was influenced by Tecumseh, the Shawnee advocate of resistance. The Red Sticks joined Tecumseh's confederacy in 1812. Red Sticks were young soldiers who were inspired both by political allegiance and religious devotion to help their people in the struggle against the whites.

In August 1813, promises of Spanish and British help, together with raids by white frontiersmen, provoked the Red Sticks to attack Fort Mims, an American post near Mobile, Alabama. Their action, which resulted in the deaths of nearly 250 whites and their Indian allies, gave the United States an excuse to mount a military campaign to crush the rebellious Muskogees. In the ensuing war, the U.S. Army, headed by Andrew Jackson, defeated the Red Sticks with help from some Muskogees and other Indians. The culmination of the Red Stick War came at the Battle of Horseshoe Bend on the Tallapoosa River on March 27, 1814.

In the Treaty of Fort Jackson, signed after the battle, the Creek Nation ceded 14 million acres to the United States. The treaty paved the way for the removal of Indians from the East and crushed the religious fervor that had given the Red Sticks hope for a better future.

See also Creek (Muskogee).

REFORMERS AND REFORM GROUPS

From the outset of the European invasion of North America, critics pressed the newcomers to alter both their cultural attitudes and their formal policies toward the continent's native peoples. These reformers called on their contemporaries to view American Indians as fellow human beings and to deal with them peacefully. In the colonial era, these reformers were generally men and women of the church who based their arguments on Christian theology; in the nineteenth and twentieth centuries, they advocated justice for Native Americans by stressing the practical advantages of peaceful relations and by calling on their leaders to live up to their democratic ideals.

It is possible that there were dissenters among the earliest travelers to the Americas, but the first to speak out publicly about his concerns was Bartolomé de Las Casas (1474–1566), the son of a Seville merchant who, inspired with Christian zeal, traveled to Hispaniola in 1502 to missionize the island's Indians. Later ordained into the priesthood (and subsequently named bishop of Chiapas), Las Casas became disillusioned with the

Spanish enterprise in the New World. He attacked the Spanish conquests and argued that Christians should proceed peacefully and with the consent of their native adversaries.

In New France, the hostility of the Canadian environment and the settlers' limited resources placed a premium on friendly relations with native people and encouraged the idea that the empire might be based on mutual self-interest. Early in the seventeenth century Jesuit missionaries cloaked this theme in religious terms and urged their hosts to accept Christianity and to ally themselves with the French. The deaths of early Jesuit missionaries such as Isaac Jogues (1607–46) and Jean de Brebeuf (1593–1649) elevated them to martyrdom and encouraged faithful colonists to repeat their preachings through the Iroquois wars of the 1640s and the imperial rivalries of the ensuing century.

The English colonies were neither so well supported by a state church nor so well supplied with missionaries. Along the Atlantic Coast the call for peaceful relations with the Indians generally came from dissenting clerics who opposed both imperial brutality and local colonial officials. Roger Williams (1603–83), for example, opposed both the rule of the Puritan fathers in Boston and the Bay Colony's ambitions to control all of New England. His tract *Christenings Make No Christians* (1645) was a plea for peaceful diplomacy and tolerance. Later in the seventeenth century, the Quaker followers of George Fox (1624–91) who settled in William Penn's Pennsylvania colony in 1685 extended their policy of nonviolence to the region's tribes. They insisted on purchasing land for settlement and pledged to deal honorably with their Indian neighbors. Williams and the early Pennsylvania colonists were followed in the eighteenth century by other dissenters such as David Brainerd (1718–47) in New England and Samuel Kirkland (1741–1808), who lived and worked with the Oneidas and Tuscaroras of New York State.

At the end of the eighteenth century, the weakness and poverty of the United States, together with the new nation's idealistic self-image, inspired a secular version of the religious reformers' plea for peaceful relations between Indians and whites. Henry Knox (1750–1806), the country's first secretary of war, was the most articulate spokesman for this view. When the national government was organized in 1789, Knox pointed out the financial and human cost of military campaigns against the tribes that opposed American expansion and urged President George Washington and his colleagues to avoid bloodshed by negotiating with their adversaries.

In the early nineteenth century, the national debate over Indian removal fused the religious ideals of the colonial missionaries with the practical concerns of secular leaders like Knox. The opponents of removal believed that Indian and white communities could coexist peacefully and that treaties and statutes could regulate relations between the groups. The leading advocates of this position were members of the American Board of Commissioners for Foreign Missions and Whig opponents of President Andrew Jackson.

In the wake of the removal debate and a series of unsuccessful legal challenges to removal, journalists and commentators described the forced expulsion of the Cherokees and other tribes in the 1830s as a national disgrace. Non-Indian reformers such as the Baptist missionary Isaac McCoy (1784–1846) used the removal tragedies to press for policies that would follow the principles of humanity, democracy, and the rule of law. Among government officials, such as Indian Commissioner Luke Lea (1810–98), who served from 1851 to 1853, and his successor, George Manypenny (1808–90), "reservations" in California, the Southwest, Oregon, and the Great Plains became popular alternatives to removal or warfare.

In the aftermath of the Civil War, optimism inspired by the destruction of slavery caused critics of the government to organize for the first time into national reform organizations. Many of these critics were veterans of the abolition campaign, such as Lydia Maria Child and Wendell Phillips. Others were newcomers. Congress created the Board of Indian Commissioners to investigate corruption in the Indian Office. Led from its founding in 1869 by William Welsh (1807–78), a wealthy Philadelphia merchant, the board created a cadre of national reform leaders who within a decade or so would found the Boston Indian Citizenship Committee, the Women's National Indian Association, and, in 1882, the Indian Rights Association.

Between 1881 and 1883 Indian reformers launched a new era of activism. First, Helen Hunt Jackson's *A Century of Dishonor* (1881) condemned government cruelty and called for Indian citizenship. In 1882 William Welsh's nephew, Herbert Welsh (1851–1941), founded the Indian Rights Association, a group that conducted independent investigations of conditions among the tribes and supported a Washington lobbyist. The following year, the Lake Mohonk Conference of the Friends of the Indian began meeting at a resort near New York City. Chaired by Albert Smiley, a Quaker member of the Board of Indian Commissioners, the annual conference brought together all the major actors in the reform movement: religious leaders, civil reformers, women's groups, and writers.

Although reformers continued to be prominent actors in Indian affairs after the turn of the century, it gradually became apparent that the reform activity of the previous century had not improved native life as much as the activists had promised. New laws and humanitarian rhetoric had produced little besides dispossession and poverty. The Indians' aggressive neighbors had used the reformers' policy of peace to buy up native resources and silently divide tribal communities into scattered constellations of individuals whose circumscribed economic and political power could not threaten non-Indians. To oppose this trend, a new generation of reformers arose in the first decades of the twentieth century. These people turned away from the humanitarian rhetoric of the nineteenth century and embraced the interest-group language of the twentieth. Modern reformers argued that Indian people *as a group* shared certain common interests and that *all* Native American tribes should have a say in the shaping of their futures.

Two groups were vital to the rise of this twentieth-century reform agenda. English-speaking Indians who had become familiar with American society forcefully presented native interests to the general public. Men like the physicians Charles Eastman (1858–1939) and Carlos Montezuma (1867–1923) and women such as the writer Zitkala-Ša (Gertrude Simmons Bonnin) (1875–1938) stepped forward to criticize the white man's "civilization" and celebrate their tribal past. In 1911 these three joined with other "red progressives" to found the Society of American Indians (SAI), an organization pledged to improving the lives of native people by opposing government paternalism and defending the legal rights of tribesmen. Political and religious differences divided and ultimately doomed the SAI, but it established the principle that Indian leaders should have a say in policymaking. In 1944 a more long-lived Pan-Indian reform group was founded in Denver, Colorado. The National Congress of American Indians had deeper roots than its predecessor, but it shared the SAI's commitment to broad representation and outspoken advocacy.

The second group of reformers consisted of social scientists and their political supporters, who began to argue in the early twentieth century that there was no single definition of culture or civilization. "Cultures" were functionally equal, men like the anthropologist Franz Boas (1858–1942) argued, and should not be arranged in an imaginary pecking order that placed Europeans at the top and tribal people at the bottom. Boas and his students produced detailed studies of American Indians that revealed the complexity of their lifeways, their ancient origins, and their ability to adapt to new circumstances. These ideas inspired sympathetic accounts of native life (such as the one contained in Oliver Lafarge's novel *Laughing Boy,* which won the Pulitzer Prize for fiction in 1929) and prompted non-Indians to form new organizations such as the Association on American Indian Affairs (1936) that worked to assist and defend tribal interests rather than to convert and destroy native peoples.

The contributions of both educated Indian leaders and social scientists to Indian reform came sharply into focus between 1933 and 1945, when a former New York City social worker, John Collier (1884–1968), served as Commissioner of Indian Affairs. Collier set out to repeal the General Allotment Act and reduce the influence of religious leaders on Indian affairs. He opposed bans on traditional religious rituals and favored school curricula that were consistent with community values. The Indian Reorganization Act, the centerpiece of his reform efforts, brought Indian people dramatically into the decision-making process.

In the wake of Collier's administration, Indian reform came to be equated with support for tribal values and tribal authority. Efforts in the 1940s and 1950s to reduce the federal role in Indian affairs, for example, were met with statements from both Indian and white reformers that stressed the government's statutory and moral obligation to native people. During the 1960s criticism of the tribal governments Collier had helped put in power focused on questioning the extent to which these governments were in touch with community desires and community traditions. Radical Indian leaders and their non-Indian supporters urged tribal officials to protect the prerogatives spelled out in their treaties and agreements with the United States and to defend traditional rituals and beliefs no matter what the cost. The National Indian Youth Council, formed in 1961, and the American Indian Movement, founded in Minneapolis in 1968, were leaders in this effort. More moderate figures—lawyers involved in litigating treaty rights, elected officials who participated in groups such as the National Tribal Chairmen's Association and the Council on Energy Resource Tribes, educators who formed the National Indian Education Association, and religious figures—echoed this position, urging their adversaries to accept the existence of modern Indian communities and to respect native values, ambitions, and religious practices.

By the end of the twentieth century the definition of *reform* in Indian affairs had shifted completely from the meaning Las Casas and his followers had given it in the time of Columbus. Rather than referring to non-Indian attitudes and methods of treatment, the term now implied a recognition of Indian interests and aspirations. Instead of being rooted in Christian ideas regarding the common humanity of all God's children, the term now emanated from a concern for equity and a practical balance of group interests in a multiethnic, democratic society. At the same time, however, reformers continued to believe in the possibility of peaceful and mutually respectful relations between Native Americans and those who had immigrated to North America.

Hoxie, Frederick E., *A Final Promise: The Campaign to Assimilate the Indians, 1880–1920* (Lincoln: University of Nebraska Press, 1984); Prucha, Francis Paul, *The Great Father: The United States Government and the American Indians* (Lincoln: University of Nebraska Press, 1984).

FREDERICK E. HOXIE
Newberry Library
Chicago, Illinois

REIFEL, BEN (WIYAKA WANJILA)

(1906–90)
Brulé Sioux civil servant and U.S. Congressman.

Benjamin Reifel was born on September 19, 1906, in a log cabin near Cut Meat (now Parmalee), on South Dakota's Rosebud Reservation. He was the oldest of the five sons born to Lily Lucy Burning Breast and William Reifel. Growing up bilingual, he at times would translate for his full-blood Sioux mother and his German-American father.

His early school years were disorganized, and at the age of sixteen, shortly after starting the seventh grade, he dropped out. As fortune would have it, however, his teacher approached the boy's farming parents and offered to tutor him. Young Reifel completed the seventh and eighth grades in one year. After this experience, he was determined to learn more and channel his education toward improving conditions on the reservation. After spending the next two years farming, and clerking at the Anderson store in Rosebud, he used his

"Sioux benefits" of $550 to pay his tuition and expenses to attend "Winter" or "Aggie" School, and later, college at South Dakota State College. Until this time, he had never been farther than forty miles from home; but his determination would carry him further than he had ever envisioned.

Reifel completed three terms of a special Winter School program before gaining admission to the college's School of Agriculture, where he majored in biochemistry and dairy management. He was elected student-body president, and was a member of the ROTC; he was commissioned a second lieutenant in the U.S. Army in 1931. Upon graduating in 1932, he became the boys' adviser at Hare School, an Episcopal school for Indian boys in Mission, South Dakota. In December 1933 he married Alice Johnson, a fellow graduate of South Dakota State College. They had one daughter, Loyce Nadine.

Reifel began his career with the Bureau of Indian Affairs in 1933, as a farm agent at Oglala, South Dakota, on the Pine Ridge Reservation. In 1935, as an organization field agent, he worked with the tribes throughout the plains area in setting up self-government organizations to administer tribal affairs. His fluency in the Lakota language was a considerable asset in this predominantly Siouan area. After serving four and a half years of active duty (1942–46) in a military police unit of the U.S. Army, he was discharged a lieutenant colonel. In 1946, Reifel was appointed superintendent of the Fort Berthold Reservation in North Dakota. During his tenure there, the reservation experienced geographical changes as a result of the Garrison Dam Project, and much of his time was spent in negotiation with the Bureau of Reclamation on behalf of the Three Affiliated Tribes (the Mandans, Arikaras, and Hidatsas).

In 1949 Reifel was awarded a scholarship to Harvard's Littauer School of Public Administration, and in 1950 he received a master's degree from that institution. He was then awarded a John Hay Whitney Fellowship, and received a doctorate in public administration from Harvard in 1952. His six-hundred-page thesis was titled "The Relocation and Rehabilitation of the Ft. Berthold Indian Reservation."

Returning to the Bureau of Indian Affairs, Reifel served at Fort Berthold as superintendent and in 1954 transferred to the Pine Ridge Agency. Just as he had been the first person from his reservation to attend South Dakota State College, he was the first Sioux to be superintendent at a tribal agency. In 1955, he became the first Indian to be appointed area director of the BIA's Aberdeen office in South Dakota. All Indian agencies and nonreservation boarding schools in North Dakota, South Dakota, and Nebraska came under the jurisdiction of his office.

Throughout his career Reifel could not resist a speaking invitation if the occasion might allow for some "educating." He used his sense of humor and speaking ability to explain the cultural differences that exist between Indians and whites, believing that with awareness of the respective dignities of the two cultures, a better relationship could develop. He stressed that the concepts of time, work, and savings were radically different in these cultures, and expressed his belief that the only way out of poverty and prejudice was through education regardless of race.

In 1960 the South Dakota Republicans selected Reifel to run for a seat in Congress representing the eastern half of the state. Although only three years from retirement, he resigned from the BIA (under the Hatch Act, a government employee cannot be politically active) and won the election with a sizable plurality. He would win the next four elections by even larger margins. During his tenure in Congress Reifel served on the House's Agriculture and Appropriations Committees. He retired voluntarily at the end of the Ninety-first Congress, on January 2, 1971.

After retiring from Congress, Reifel served, without salary, as an assistant on Indian programs to the director of the National Park Service, as chairman of the National Capitol Planning Commission, and as president of the American Indian National Bank. In 1976 he served as Commissioner of Indian Affairs in the last few months of the Ford administration. He was on the board of directors for the Lower Brulé Sioux's irrigation project, and served as chairman of the Eastern Band of the Cherokee Nation's grand council to help draft a constitution (1979). He was a member of the National Advisory Council for the Education of Disadvantaged Children and served as national president of ARROW, Inc., an Indian service organization; as vice president of Easter Seals; as a member of the national and state boards of the Boy Scouts of America; and as an Episcopal lay reader.

In 1956, Reifel received the Outstanding American Indian Award and the Indian Council Fire Achievement Award. In 1971, he received an honorary doctorate in humanities from South Dakota State University and an honorary doctorate in law from the University of South Dakota. In 1960, the Boy Scouts of America honored

him with the Silver Antelope Award and, subsequently, the Silver Beaver, the Silver Buffalo, and, in 1984, the Gray Wolf. Reifel is the only South Dakotan to receive all four awards.

Following the death of his first wife in 1972, Reifel married Frances Ryland Colby. He died on January 2, 1990, in Sioux Falls, South Dakota. On May 11, 1991, the South Dakota Badlands National Parks Visitors Center was renamed the Ben Reifel Visitors Center.

Fielder, Mildred, "Ben Reifel, Sioux Congressman," in *Sioux Indian Leaders* (Seattle: Superior Publishing Company, 1975); Gridley, Marion E., "Ben Reifel (Dakota-Brulé), United States Congressman," in *Indians of Today* (I.C.F.P., 1971); Paulson, T. Emogene, and Lloyd R. Moses, "Ben Reifel," in *Who's Who Among the Sioux* (Vermillion: Institute of Indian Studies, University of South Dakota, 1988).

LOYCE REIFEL ANDERSON (Brulé Sioux)
Saratoga, Wyoming

RELIGION

The phenomena referred to by the term *Native American religions* pose an interesting and complex problem of description and interpretation—one that has consistently captured the imagination of European immigrant peoples. These phenomena have been misunderstood, maligned, romanticized, and misappropriated. In almost every case the authoritative and definitive analyses of particular Native American religious traditions have been written by non-Indians, and thus nonadherents, who lacked any lifelong experiential basis for their analyses. It seems that now, at the end of the twentieth century, deeply held Indian traditions and beliefs have been politicized—on the one hand by academic experts, and on the other by New Age aficionados who have mistakenly seen Indian spirituality as a new trade commodity. It has become increasingly clear that those phenomena we call Native American religions were and are yet today very complex socially and philosophically and are therefore not easily represented or described by means of either popular interpretation or the critical categories of academic analysis, especially when those categories have been constructed in a cultural context alien to the traditions themselves.

Most adherents to traditional American Indian ways characteristically deny that their people ever engaged in any religion at all. Rather, these spokespeople insist, their whole culture and social structure was and still is

The Hunka-Alowanpi Ceremony of the Oglala Sioux, 1907. The ceremonial pipe is consecrated before a painted buffalo skull lying on a bed of holy sage.

infused with a spirituality that cannot be separated from the rest of the community's life at any point. The Green Corn Ceremony, the Snake Dance, kachinas, the Sun Dance, sweat-lodge ceremonies, and the sacred pipe are not specifically religious constructs of various tribes but rather represent specific ceremonial aspects of a world that includes countless ceremonies in any given tribal context, ceremonies performed by whole communities, clans, families, or individuals on a daily, periodic, seasonal, or occasional basis. Whereas outsiders may identify a single ritual as the "religion" of a particular people, the people themselves will likely see that ceremony as merely an extension of their day-to-day existence, all parts of which are experienced within ceremonial parameters and should be seen as "religious."

For instance, among the *Ni U Konska* (Osages), what ethnographers would classify as "religion" pervades even the habitual acts of sleeping and putting on shoes. All the ceremonies and prayers of the Osages reflect the principle of the simultaneous duality and unity of all existence. Prayers commonly begin with an address to the Wakonda Above and the Wakonda Below (manifested in Sky and Earth, respectively), the two great fructifying forces of the universe. This principle is mirrored in the architectural structure of Osage towns and in the marriage customs of the people. Each Osage town was divided by an east-west road into two "grand divisions" representing Sky and Earth. Just as Osages perceived the necessity of these two forces coming together in order for life to be sustained, so too they saw the two grand divisions of the people as sustaining the life of the whole. To insure that the principle of spiritual and political unity in this duality would be maintained, Osages were mandated by social custom to marry someone from the other grand division. To further enforce this religious sense of wholeness, members of each of the two grand divisions developed distinct personal habits that helped remind them of their own part in the communal whole. For instance, those from the Honga grand division customarily slept on their right side and put on the right shoe first, whereas those from the Tsizhu grand division functioned in the opposite manner. As a result, even in sleep the two divisions performed a religious act that maintained their unity in duality as they lay facing each other across the road that divided the community.

Thus the social structures and cultural traditions of American Indian peoples are infused with a spirituality that cannot be separated from, say, picking corn or tanning hides, hunting game or making war. Nearly every human act was accompanied by attention to religious details, sometimes out of practiced habit and sometimes with more specific ceremony. In the Northwest, harvesting cedar bark would be accompanied by prayer and ceremony, just as killing a buffalo required ceremonial actions and words dictated by the particularities of tribal nation, language, and culture. Among the Osages the spiritual principle of respect for life dictated that the decision to go to war against another people usually required an eleven-day ceremony—allowing time to reconsider one's decision and to consecrate the lives that might be lost as a result of it. Because to be successful the hunt required acts of violence, it was also considered a type of war. Hence the semiannual community buffalo hunt, functioning on the same general principle of respect for life, also required a ceremony—one that was in all respects nearly identical to the War Ceremony.

Perhaps the most distinctive aspect of American Indian religious traditions is the extent to which they are wholly community based and have no real meaning outside of the specific community in which the acts are regularly performed, stories told, songs sung, and ceremonies conducted. Vine Deloria, Jr., described the communitarian foundations of American Indian existence in his 1973 book *God Is Red*, his point being that ceremonies are engaged in not primarily for personal benefit but rather for the benefit of an entire community or nation. The most common saying one hears during the Lakota Sun Dance is "That the people might live!" This sentiment becomes the overriding reason for and

purpose of this ceremony. Likewise, violations of the sacred become threatening to the whole community and not merely to the one who commits the error. The communitarian nature of Indian ceremonies represents a key distinction between Native American religious traditions and modern Euro-American New Age spirituality, with its emphasis on radical individualism.

Some would argue that the so-called vision quest is evidence of the quintessential individualism of Plains Indian peoples. However, just the opposite can be argued, because in Plains cultures the individual is always in symbiotic relationship with the community. This ceremony involves personal sacrifice: rigorous fasting (no food or liquids) and prayer over several days (typically four to seven) in a location removed from the rest of the community. Yet in a typical rite of vigil or vision quest, the community or some part of the community assists the individual in preparing for the ceremony and then prays constantly on behalf of the individual throughout the ceremony. Thus by engaging in this ceremony, the individual acts on behalf of and for the good of the whole community. Even when an individual seeks personal power or assistance through such a ceremony, he or she is doing so for the ultimate benefit of the community.

Unfortunately, the traditional symbiotic relationship between the individual and the community, exemplified in ceremonies such as the vision quest, has become severely distorted as a shift in Euro-American cultural values has begun to encourage the adoption and practice of Indian spirituality by the general population no matter how disruptive this may be to Indian communities. The resulting incursion of Euro-American practitioners, who are not a part of the community in which the ceremony has traditionally been practiced, brings a Western, individualistic frame of reference to the ceremony that violates the communitarian cultural values of Indian peoples. The key concern for Indian people in preserving the authenticity and healthy functioning of the relationship between the individual and the community is the question of accountability: one must be able to identify what spiritual and sociopolitical community can rightly make claims on one's spiritual strength. In the Indian worldview, this community— this legitimate source of identity—is intimately linked to, and derives directly from, the significance of spatiality, of space and place.

In *God Is Red* Deloria clearly identified and described another characteristic feature of American Indian religious traditions: spatiality. Indian ceremonial life

A Hopi kachina doll, circa 1900, from First Mesa, Arizona. Called tihu *by the Hopis, they are given as ceremonial gifts to young girls. Each signifies a prayer wish for good health, growth, and fertility.*

and all of Indian existence are rooted in a profound notion of space and place. The spatial layout for any ceremony takes on paramount importance. As with the structure of the Osage village, most Osage ceremonials are structured around a north-south, Sky-Earth division. In a similar manner, the structure for a Green Corn Ceremony, the subterranean location of a kiva, the design of a sweat lodge, or the direction one turns in a pipe ceremony all have tribally specific cosmic representational value that reflects the spiritual relationship of a particular people with the spatial world around them. This understanding of the importance of spatiality also emerges in the longstanding identification of places that are known to a tribe to be particularly powerful spiritually. For most Indian communities, there are one or more such places that they have long identified as powerful: the Black Hills for the Sioux Nation; Blue Lake for Taos Pueblo; Mount Gra-

ham for the San Carlos Apaches; the mountains that mark the territorial boundaries of any pueblo—to mention but a few examples.

Indian peoples, then, tend to locate sacred power spatially—in terms of places or in terms of spatial configuration. This is in stark contrast to European and Euro-American religious traditions, which tend to express spirituality in terms of time: a regular hour on Sundays and a seasonal liturgical calendar that has become more and more distanced from any sense of the actual flow of seasons in particular places and is therefore both more abstract and more portable than Native American traditions. In the Southern Hemisphere, for instance, Christians celebrate Lent (named for springtime and the lengthening of the days) and Easter during the antipodean autumn. It would be an exaggeration to argue that Indian peoples have no sense of time or that Europeans have no sense of space. Rather, spatiality is a dominant category of existence for Native Americans whereas time is a subordinate category. Just the opposite is generally true for European peoples.

The identification of places of particular spiritual power points to yet another important aspect of Indian religious traditions: these places are experienced as powerful because they are experienced as alive. Not only are they sentient; they are intelligent manifestations of what Native Americans call the Sacred Mystery or the Sacred Power. The Sacred Mystery, sometimes simplistically and badly translated as "the Great Spirit," is typically experienced first of all as a great unknown. Yet this unknown becomes known as it manifests itself to humans spatially: as the Mystery Above and Mystery Below; as the Mystery (or Powers) of the Four Directions; as the Sacred Mystery in its self-manifestation in a particular place, in a particular occurrence, in an astronomical constellation, or in an artifact such as a feather. All of the created world is, in turn, seen as alive, sentient, and filled with spiritual power, including each human being. The sense of the interrelationship of all of creation—of all two-legged, four-legged, wingeds, and other living, moving things (from fish and rivers to rocks, trees and mountains)—may be the most important contribution Indian peoples have made to the science and spirituality of the modern world.

In conclusion, the religious traditions of Indian peoples are communitarian and have no meaning outside the particular community of reference. Unlike Euro-Americans, Indian people do not choose which tribal religious traditions they will practice. Rather, each of them is born into a community and its particular ceremonial life. Indian traditions are fundamentally spatial in nature and in configuration, which makes them peculiarly difficult for temporally oriented peoples to understand. Because of cross-cultural misunderstandings, distortions are now threatening Native American religious traditions on several fronts. Many Native American religious traditions are undergoing a transformation under intense pressure from New Age would-be adherents. The modern Euro-American appropriation of native traditions is introducing a mutation that is now shaping those traditions in the image of European individualism. Moreover, the systemic pressures of the colonial experience, which have worked variously to eradicate, suppress, or at least erode Native American religious traditions, continue today in the legal and economic activities of corporate and government interests; for example, American Indians have little legal recourse for protecting places of traditional spiritual value to them. Yet the religious traditions and indeed the cultural whole of many Indian peoples continues today to give those peoples hope and life.

See also Ghost Dance; Missions and Missionaries; Native American Church; Religious Rights.

Deloria, Vine, Jr., *God Is Red: A Native View of Religion,* 2d ed. (Golden, Colo.: Fulcrum Publishing, 1994).

GEORGE E. TINKER (Osage)
Iliff School of Theology

RELIGIOUS RIGHTS

The U.S. government has always valued religious freedom. The freedom to worship is a right that is basic to our national life and history. Ironically, however, the colonizers who first came to North America to escape religious persecution routinely violated the religious freedom of the continent's native people. This practice devastated Native American communities, whose strong religious beliefs underlay all aspects of their lives and cultures. European colonizers perceived native cultures as barbaric and godless, and therefore felt justified in condemning and destroying them.

The denial of Indian religious liberty arose from the clash of European and Native American worldviews. Christian colonizers evaluated Indian religions from the perspective of their own particular faiths. They searched for sacred texts, written histories, and church institutions in Indian societies, and were appalled when

tribal religions did not display these characteristics. Because the colonizers failed to recognize the complexity, diversity, and richness of native religions, they intruded upon Indian religious rights without feeling any guilt or self-doubt.

In colonial America, Christianity and Western civilization were intertwined, and when these concepts were imposed upon native people the process was called "education." In colonial Indian schools, civic and religious leaders were the Indians' overseers, and they continually undermined tribal religions and prohibited their practice. Christian Indian "praying" towns, established by John Eliot in 1646, segregated natives from both frontiersmen and non-Christian tribal members, forcing native residents to completely repudiate their culture and traditional ways of worship.

Nineteenth-century Americans expected the federal government to follow the colonial tradition of suppressing tribal religions, and thus to "civilize" native people. Through the Civilization Act of 1819, the government agreed to subsidize missionaries in their civilizing efforts and to support the active destruction of native religions. In 1870 President Grant's "Peace Policy" expanded this federal support by inviting Christian denominations to nominate people to serve as federal agents to the tribes. Under this policy entire Indian nations were placed under the administrative control of particular churches, many of which had had no previous contact with the tribes they were selected to oversee. President Grant's own denomination, the Methodists, received the "rights" to several agencies.

Government persecution of native religions accelerated in the late nineteenth century. U.S. forces killed Sioux Ghost Dance participants at Wounded Knee, South Dakota, in 1890, and two years later arrested Ghost Dance leaders in Oklahoma. On most reservations the federal Indian Office's Courts of Indian Offenses investigated, convicted, and punished natives who persisted in following their ancient tribal religions. The Sun Dance, for example, which had long sustained a variety of Plains groups, was deemed offensive and was banned.

At the turn of the twentieth century many museums—operating on the assumption that native people were "vanishing"—began gathering ceremonial and secular objects for their collections. As a result, many museums have in their collections objects from the Ghost Dance, the Sun Dance, and other tribal religions, despite the fact that the rightful owners of these objects continue to hold them sacred, and need them for religious practices.

Infringements upon Indian religious traditions continued well into the twentieth century. Even as late as 1921, the Office of Indian Affairs issued Circular 1665, with a supplement, to all reservation superintendents. The circular banned native ceremonies and traditional rites, and encouraged missionaries and government officials to turn the public against Indian dances. However, Indian people continued their formal ways of worship surreptitiously.

It was not until the passage of the Indian Reorganization Act in 1934 that restrictions against native religions ended. With a vigorous movement toward Indian reform, a new era of understanding and acceptance of Indian culture and religion permeated Indian policies. This change, however, was short-lived. The nation's misconception of native religions resurfaced after World War II with the implementation of the federal government's termination and relocation policies, which aimed at completely integrating Indians into American society. These policies resulted in the loss of sacred lands and the destruction of native cultures; reservation lands no longer had federal status, and Indians were removed from the reservations and placed in urban areas.

A brief revival of native religious acceptance occurred, however, in the tumultuous sixties when Americans shifted their moral and religious attitudes in response to the Vietnam War and domestic unrest. As Americans groped for a broader religious understanding of the world, many sought answers in native religions. However, attitudes and policies became unstable in later years.

In the seventies, concern for the preservation of endangered species and fear of Indian religious revivals led to the arrest of traditional Indians for possession of sacred objects such as eagle feathers, and to criminal prosecutions of individuals for using peyote. Government agents also denied tribal members access to sacred sites on public lands and interfered with religious ceremonies they deemed "criminal." These confrontations produced Indian protests that culminated in the 1978 Congressional hearings on American Indian religious freedom.

Those hearings documented three specific types of infringements on Indian religious rights: the disruption of ceremonies and traditional rites; the seizure of ceremonial objects (sacred objects, including those that museums possessed); and the denial of access to sacred sites. In response, Congress concluded that native ways of worship were an integral part of Indian life, ac-

knowledging in the process that many federal statutes, regulations, and enforcement policies infringed upon native religious liberties. That same year Congress passed the American Indian Religious Freedom Act (AIRFA), which promised to protect and preserve American Indian religious liberties.

AIRFA was applauded as a reversal of the antagonistic policies toward Indian religions that had been in force for so long. Unfortunately, however, the statute has proved to be "toothless": its provisions are vague, and enforcement procedures are virtually nonexistent.

Congress's intent to protect American Indian religious freedom has been further distorted in recent years by two landmark U.S. Supreme Court cases. In 1988, in *Lynq* v. *Northwest Cemetery Protection Association,* the high court limited a tribe's ability to protect aboriginal sacred sites on federal land; and in 1990, in *Smith* v. *Oregon Department of Human Resources,* the justices decided that the First Amendment's free exercise of religion clause did not protect the sacramental use of peyote in religious services of the Native American Church. In *Smith* the court further concluded that if the Indians' "minority religion" deserved legal protection, it would have to win that protection in the state legislatures.

Native people have responded to the *Smith* and *Lynq* decisions by proposing new legislation that would strengthen AIRFA. Their proposal charges federal authorities with protecting Native American sacred sites, defending the religious use of peyote in Native American Church services, securing the religious rights of Native American prisoners, and streamlining federal permit systems to allow for the religious use of eagle feathers. Further, any government proposal that might threaten native religious freedom would have to pass the "compelling state interest test" (discarded by the Supreme Court in *Smith*) before it could become law.

In the past five hundred years Indians have fought many battles, both to defend their right to worship and to have their religions be accepted by the Christians who live among them. Unfortunately, however, Indian religions have been actively hindered or only partially protected. Nevertheless, irrespective of this sad history of governmental insensitivity, the struggle for Indian religious freedom continues, fueled by a belief that the defense of religious liberty will ensure the preservation of all ways of life.

See also Ghost Dance; Missions and Missionaries; Native American Church; Peace Policy; Religion.

Beck, Peggy V., and Anna L. Walters, *The Sacred: Ways of Knowledge, Sources of Life* (Tsaile, Ariz.: Navajo Community Press, 1977); Vecsey, Christopher, ed., *Handbook of American Indian Religious Freedom* (New York: Crossroad Publishing, 1991).

IRENE S. VERNON (MESCALERO APACHE/YAQUI)
Colorado State University

REMOVAL

Shortly after the acquisition of the Louisiana Purchase, American leaders began to view that region as a potential homeland for Native Americans living east of the Mississippi River. Early American explorers such as Zebulon Pike and Stephen H. Long gave impetus to Indian removal when their reports classified the Great Plains as "the Great American Desert," an area unfit for farming. If the land could not be farmed, why not place the Indians there? President Thomas Jefferson was one of the first advocates of this policy. He viewed removal as voluntary, but following the War of 1812 western politicians urged federal officials to remove the tribes by force. By 1825, most of the tribes in the Old Northwest had been removed westward. That year, federal authorities withdrew from the public domain all land from Missouri and Arkansas westward to the one-hundredth meridian. This area, bounded on the north by the Platte River and on the south by the Red River, was classified as "Indian Territory."

Voluntary removal continued until the election of President Andrew Jackson in 1828. A westerner and a veteran of Indian campaigns, Jackson promised to force the remaining eastern tribes across the Mississippi. Spurred by this new attitude, state officials began to extend state laws over the Indians. Congress, in turn, passed the 1830 Indian Removal Act, which authorized the president to negotiate with the tribes. Appeals to the U.S. Supreme Court proved fruitless, and the removal policy went into effect. The result was the infamous Trail of Tears and forced removal. Not all tribes went peacefully. Several resisted but were crushed in the Black Hawk War, the Creek War of 1835–36, and the Second Seminole War.

A second removal took place following the Civil War. Under the terms of the Reconstruction treaties with the Five Civilized Tribes, western Oklahoma was granted to the federal government as a homeland for the Plains tribes. Although the Kiowa, Cheyenne-Arapaho, and Plains Apaches accepted reservations in

the area as provided in the 1867 treaties of Medicine Lodge, almost two decades of warfare followed before the plains were pacified. Additional wars were fought with the Nez Perces and the Modocs in the Pacific Northwest to force their removal to Indian Territory. One band of Apaches remained prisoners of war at Fort Sill until 1913.

By the close of the nineteenth century, more than one hundred tribes, bands, and clans of Indians had been removed to Oklahoma, making the state home to more tribes than any other. Largely as a consequence of removal, twenty-five tribes still maintain their headquarters in Oklahoma.

REPATRIATION

The repatriation movement of the 1980s and 1990s represented a historic and fundamental shift in the relationship between the native and museum communities in the United States. It culminated in two key pieces of federal legislation: the National Museum of the American Indian Act (NMAIA), enacted on November 28, 1989; and the Native American Graves Protection and Repatriation Act (NAGPRA), enacted on November 16, 1990.

To understand the repatriation movement and its immediate and longer-range consequences, it is necessary to draw upon both the past and the present. First, we need to consider the histories of the native and museum communities, as well as their relationship with each other. Second, in looking to the future as well as the past, we need to examine the ripple effects of the movement for both communities, something that will probably prove to be as significant as repatriation itself.

During the late nineteenth century two cultural phenomena were occurring that subsequently would intertwine and eventually set the stage for the repatriation movement. The development of museums as large and prominent private and public institutions of collecting and culture was in full flower. The Victorian age, and the European expansion and colonization that it signified, had expanded the art of collecting beyond private palaces to arenas more accessible to the wider public in the form of museums. These institutions were focusing considerable attention on the culturally unusual and exotic as America and Europe encountered indigenous peoples and cultures in various parts of the world.

Ceremony in the Bronx, New York, marking the repatriation of eighty-six objects from the National Museum of the American Indian by a delegation of leaders from Jemez Pueblo in October 1993.

At the same time, the native peoples of the Western Hemisphere were at their cultural nadir. Decimated by hundreds of years of imported disease and military conquest, the native populations of North and South America had experienced demographic devastation. And military oppression had had a distinct cultural analogue. As the result of overt and explicit federal policies in the United States, much of the ceremonial and religious ritual life that had sustained native communities over millennia was forbidden. Native children were routinely removed from parental care at an early age and sent to federal boarding schools for the specific purpose of deculturalization.

The confluence of these two historical and cultural trends had a very particular result. Large amounts of native cultural patrimony, often viewed as the last physical vestiges of dead or dying cultures and peoples, began moving into museums through means fair and foul—some of it sold by native people to collectors and much else literally stolen. In a more grisly collateral development, significant numbers of native human remains began making their way from the battlefields of the West into medical collections of the U.S. Army and eventually into the physical anthropological collections of museums. Thus, by the early twentieth century several large public and private museums, including the Smithsonian Institution's National Museum of Natural History, New York's Heye Foundation Museum of the American Indian and American Museum of Natural History, and the Field Museum in Chicago held collections of native objects that, cumulatively, numbered in the millions.

The problem with this cultural confluence was that native peoples, although frequently on the brink of physical and cultural extinction, persisted and, indeed, survived beyond their early-twentieth-century nadir.

Furthermore, federal policies in the United States eventually changed and, although always challenging from a native standpoint, became culturally more responsive and at times even supportive. A native cultural stabilization, or at least retrenching, took root from the 1930s through the 1950s and developed into a cultural renascence in the 1960s. Native communities began to focus more on the material culture that historically had been associated with the ceremonial and religious rituals that continued to define their cultural worlds. This focus led inevitably to interest in the cultural materials that sat in museum collections.

For a period native communities attempted to approach museums directly to gain access to cultural materials or to obtain their return. For a variety of reasons museums as a whole were not initially responsive to these requests regarding human remains, funerary objects, and sacred and ceremonial materials. After a time of stalemate, native interests ultimately sought redress from Congress; the results in 1989 and 1990 were, respectively, the NMAIA and the NAGPRA.

The philosophical underpinnings of the NMAIA and the NAGPRA reflect, legally and figuratively, a fundamental shift in the trust obligations of museums with respect to the collections of native cultural material they hold. Historically museums have viewed themselves, under existing legal theory and practice, as holding collections for the benefit of the broader public rather than of specific constituent groups. The NMAIA and the NAGPRA represent an acknowledgment that cultural institutions holding the patrimony of living peoples have an obligation, as yet not perfectly defined, of support, collaboration, and interaction with respect to those particular constituents.

This philosophical base resulted in a set of fundamental provisions in the NMAIA and the NAGPRA. The NMAIA, which also authorized the founding of the Smithsonian's National Museum of the American Indian, related only to the collections held by Smithsonian museums. The NAGPRA applied, with the exception of the Smithsonian and museums receiving no federal funds or support, to virtually all museums in the United States. While the NMAIA covered only human remains and funerary objects, the NAGPRA included human remains, funerary objects, sacred objects, and cultural patrimony. The Smithsonian's National Museum of Natural History and National Museum of the American Indian, although technically not covered by the NAGPRA, subsequently adopted policies that follow or are closely aligned with that legislation.

Under the provisions of both pieces of legislation, the human remains and cultural materials covered must be returned, upon request, to those native communities—a term that also covers Native Hawaiians in addition to Native Americans in the continental United States—that continue to be culturally affiliated with the materials and objects. Using legal standards of proof that are specified in the NMAIA and the NAGPRA, native applicants also must demonstrate that the materials of sacred or ceremonial significance are essential to the contemporary religious and ceremonial life of the community.

The legislation is complex and, throughout the early 1990s, remained in the preliminary stages of implementation. Under the NAGPRA, museums were obliged to provide native communities with certain kinds of information regarding their collections so that the communities could begin to determine where cultural materials relating to them were physically located. Most museums also appeared to be focusing initially, often at the behest and request of native communities themselves, on human remains and funerary objects rather than sacred and ceremonial materials.

Completely apart from encouraging the physical act of returning to native peoples portions of their material cultural heritage, the repatriation movement also has had broader and more far-reaching implications regarding museums and native communities. From the standpoint of museums, the very issue of repatriation has resulted in a focus, as a programmatic matter, on the concept of highly diverse native cultures as continuing cultural phenomena that reach from a deep and distant past through the present and into the future. With respect to public programming, exhibitions, and basic research, the impact of repatriation also has added impetus to the systematic inclusion and participation of native people in these areas.

From the standpoint of native communities, the results of repatriation are proving to be equally fundamental. The era of the removal and withholding by museums of vast amounts of material cultural patrimony has come to an end, and portions of museum collections relating to contemporary religious and ceremonial life will soon become a part of native communities again. Even with respect to collections not repatriated, the sharing of them and their associated information with native communities will soon be on a new footing that contributes, in significant ways, to the continuation of this vital element of American culture.

Bray, Tamara L., and Thomas W. Killion, eds., *Reckoning with the Dead: The Larsen Bay Repatriation and the Smithsonian Institution* (Washington, D.C.: Smithsonian Institution Press, 1994); Echo-Hawk, Roger, *Battlefields and Burial Grounds: The Indian Struggle to Protect Ancestral Graves in the U.S.* (Minneapolis: Lerner Publications Company, 1994); Goldstein, Lynne, "The Potential for Future Relationships between Archaeologists and Native Americans," *Quandaries and Quests,* Occasional Paper no. 20 (1992): 59–71.

W. Richard West, Jr. (Southern Cheyenne)
National Museum of the American Indian

RESERVATIONS

Reservations were first created by seventeenth-century English colonizers and imposed on American Indian nations to remove them from the path of white settlement. Reservations also provided a place where missionaries could show Indians how to live, work, and worship like themselves. The United States took up this practice, employing military might, fraud, and deception to create hundreds of tribal reserves established by treaty, executive order, or congressional decree. Despite the reservations' grim origins, Indian people have been able to adapt to reservation environments while preserving many of their traditional values, beliefs, and customs. In fact, many Indians now regard reservations as homelands.

The interplay of Indian aspirations and outside interests is central to an understanding of reservations. Notwithstanding the oppression and land loss associated with their founding, reservations also represent a valiant struggle on the part of Indians for autonomy, self-sufficiency, religious freedom, and cultural identity.

Before Europeans arrived, Indians occupied all of what became the United States. They practiced self-government, lived in accordance with revered customs, and worshiped as they saw fit. The English immigrants who began to arrive in North America in the seventeenth century lacked the strength to dislodge and subjugate the more powerful Indian nations. As a consequence, the newcomers established two fundamental land policies with regard to Indians. First, they established borders between themselves and native people. After clearly delineating which areas were "Indian country," the British allowed residents on both sides of the boundaries to maintain their own laws, customs, and institutions. Imported diseases, however, soon shifted the balance of power in favor of the Europeans,

giving rise to the second policy: as they pushed inland, the invaders placed remnant native groups that had been decimated by pestilence and warfare on small reservations and in settlements of Christian converts called "praying towns."

After the founding of the United States, federal officials continued these earlier practices. Treaties established borders between "Indian country" and the new nation. During the early nineteenth century these borders were frequently moved as government agents used bribery, coercion, and trickery to "remove" tribes from lands east of the Mississippi. And although the removed tribes were promised new, permanent borders in lands in Iowa, Missouri, Arkansas, and Oklahoma, in 1854 federal officials preparing to "open" Kansas and Nebraska to "settlement" began relocating tribes again, this time to Oklahoma. Local Plains nations such as the Pawnees, Poncas, and Otos retained, at least temporarily, small reservations in their homeland, but many new tribes were resettled nearby. After the disruption of the Civil War this process continued. The official goal of deadly military campaigns against nations such as the Sioux, Cheyennes, Arapahos, Navajos, Comanches, and Apaches was to confine them to permanent reservation homes.

Expected by federal officials to become Christian farmers, reservation Indians encountered policies that restricted their movement, autonomy, and religious freedom. Bureau of Indian Affairs agents called on U.S. troops and federally supported reservation police to quash native religious movements, arrest traditional religious leaders and healers, and place children in distant boarding schools. The Indian Office established the Court of Indian Offenses on many reservations in order to undermine traditional mechanisms of resolving disputes and administering justice. Missionaries also operated on reservations with federal approval, and often with federal funds.

In the last decades of the nineteenth century, the passage of the General Allotment Act and the Curtis Act began the process of dividing reservation lands into individual homesteads. These laws had a profound impact on reservations. Economically, many Indian nations—particularly those on the Great Plains, in Oklahoma, and in the Pacific Northwest—lost most of their land. After allotting reservations to tribal members, federal officials sold the "surplus tracts" to non-Indians, and Congress amended the allotment acts to facilitate the sale of allotments. As a consequence, and because reservation residents were often compelled to

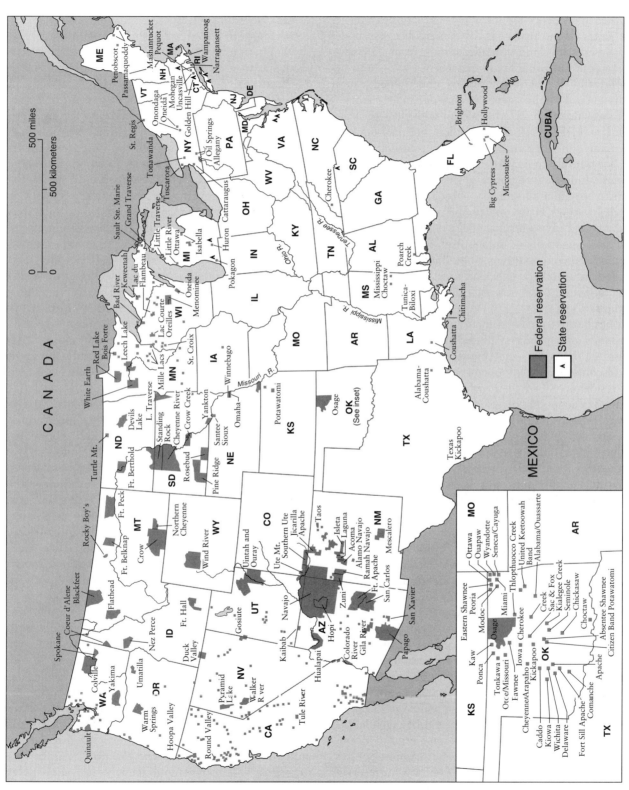

FEDERAL AND STATE RESERVATIONS

sell their allotments for income or to pay delinquent state taxes or mortgages, many Indians became landless. Reservation land holdings shrank from 138 million acres in 1887 to 48 million acres in 1934.

Politically, the allotment policy undermined tribal sovereignty. Federal agents began dealing primarily with individual Indians rather than with their governments, with the result that outsiders assumed control over many functions once provided by traditional leaders. Socially, the policy encouraged federal agents to pressure Indians into moving from their traditional towns to isolated allotments. Thus, rather than living in tribal settings, many Indians began to reside in culturally mixed environments, where racism often heightened discrimination and antagonism. Facing a bleak future under these conditions, some Indians educated in non-Indian schools began migrating from their home areas to distant cities in search of work and other opportunities.

Tribes began to reassert their authority over reservation lands after Congress passed the Indian Reorganization Act (IRA) in 1934. Among other things, the new law discontinued the allotment policy, allowed reservation residents to form their own governments, provided funds for economic development, protected Indian culture, and promoted traditional arts and crafts. It also enabled Indian governments to purchase small amounts of land they had lost during the allotment era. Eventually, about half the reservations adopted IRA governments, but many of those that refused to change their existing governing bodies also became eligible for IRA benefits.

The IRA was neither a panacea for Indian problems nor an unconditional endorsement of Indian sovereignty. It did little to alleviate the problems created in the allotment era: poverty, deprivation, shoddy housing, and poor health. Nor did it prevent additional assaults on reservation life during the termination era of the 1940s and 1950s. Termination deprived thousands of persons access to Indian Health Service medical care, educational assistance, and other services and led to a direct attack on several reservation governments that federal officials believed should be "free" of federal protection. Because their private state holdings became subject to state taxation, terminated tribes such as the Menominees and the Klamaths became even more impoverished and virtually landless. Termination policies also extended state criminal and civil law to reservations under the terms of Public Law 280, passed in 1953. Under its terms most reservation Indians in Min-

nesota, Nebraska, California, Oregon, and Wisconsin lost the right to police their own communities.

Termination proved to be disastrous for reservation residents. In its wake, the Kennedy and Johnson administrations began listening to Native American calls for a return to the earliest notion of reservations: areas where self-governing tribes could live undisturbed. With reservations plagued by continuing problems of poverty and despair, Congress supported presidential initiatives by opening antipoverty programs to reservation participation. Congress also passed legislation that enabled Indian governments to contract educational programs and services formerly provided by the Bureau of Indian Affairs, to determine the disposition of children in adoption and placement cases, and to compete for federal grants.

Reservation leaders responded quickly to these government initiatives and also embarked on economic-development programs ranging from tourism to attracting industry. Unfortunately, the results of these efforts have been less than successful in many instances. Strings attached to federal contracts and grants required Indian governments to spend money and administer programs in accordance with federal guidelines rather than local priorities and customs. Business partners were not always willing to make long-term investments in reservation businesses, and tribes often lacked the necessary training to fulfill their goals.

During the 1970s and 1980s, Republican and Democratic administrations alike reduced federal appropriations for reservation development, and federal opposition to Indian rights increased. At the same time, federal and state agencies often restricted Indian access to off-reservation sacred sites and opposed the extension of Indian government jurisdiction to non-Indians who commit crimes on reservation land. U.S. officials have also shown a willingness to employ force to resolve disputes on reservations. In 1992, for example, armed federal agents raided six Arizona reservations, confiscating hundreds of video gambling machines and ignoring the protests of the tribal governments.

Today, Indian lands, whether called reservations, rancherias, communities, or pueblos, comprise less than 2 percent of their original area. These reservations also vary widely in size and demographic composition. In 1990, the federal government recognized 278 Indian land areas as reservations. The Navajo (Diné) Reservation consists of some 16 million acres in Arizona, New Mexico, and Utah, while others contain less than a hundred acres. Some 950,000 Indians, slightly less than

50 percent of all Indians, lived on or near reservations. About half of the land on contemporary reservations belongs to Indians; significant portions are owned and inhabited by non-Indians. The Indian-owned land is usually held "in trust" by the federal government, meaning that this property is exempt from state and county taxes and can be sold only in accordance with federal regulations.

Although both paternalism and anti-Indian racism persist, Indian governments have reinvigorated their reservations by adopting tax codes, establishing profitable enterprises, organizing courts, drafting law-and-order codes, controlling their resources, and demanding a right to worship in customary ways. Nonetheless, many small, landless, and isolated native nations have been able to gain few benefits. As a result, economic, health, and social problems still haunt many reservations. The challenge facing Indian governments and federal policymakers continues to be to devise ways of improving reservation living conditions in ways that support tribal self-government, traditional culture, and religious freedom.

See also Bureau of Indian Affairs; Termination.

Deloria, Vine, Jr., and Clifford Lytle, *The Nations Within: The Past and Future of American Indian Sovereignty* (New York: Pantheon Books, 1984); O'Brien, Sharon, *American Indian Tribal Governments* (Norman and London: University of Oklahoma Press, 1989); Trafzer, Clifford E., "Earth, Animals, and Academics: Plateau Indian Communities, Culture, and Walla Walla Council of 1855," *American Indian Culture and Research Journal* 17, no. 3 (1993): 81–100.

JAMES RIDING IN (Pawnee)
Arizona State University

RICHARDVILLE, JEAN BAPTISTE (PESHEWA)

(1761?–1841)
Miami political leader and entrepreneur.

Born near modern-day Fort Wayne, Indiana, around 1761, Jean Baptiste Richardville (Peshewa, "the Wildcat") was the son of Joseph Drouet de Richardville (originally Richerville), a French trader, and Taucumwah, a sister of the prominent Miami civil and war chief Pacanne. In 1770 Joseph Richardville left Indiana Territory to return to Canada, and the younger Richardville periodically resided with his father there, at Three Rivers, where he attended school. Taucumwah

remained in Indiana, maintaining her own trading ventures, and eventually married Charles Beaubien, another trader. Richardville spent many of his formative years with his mother and stepfather at Kekionga, the Miami village at Fort Wayne, becoming versed in trade. Although well educated (Richardville spoke French, English, and Miami), he was a shy young man; when given the opportunity to speak in council, he was at first reticent. In his early twenties he identified with French Creole traders who lived in the region, dressed in European clothing, and developed a preference for European music. In about 1800 Richardville married Natoequah, a Miami woman. The union produced at least one son, Joseph, and three daughters: LaBlonde, Catherine, and Susan. Following the War of 1812, Richardville began to identify more with his Native American heritage, speaking only in the Miami language at public meetings and usually dressing as an Indian.

During the American Revolution, Richardville seems to have favored the Crown, for his stepfather served as a British agent among the Miamis. It is likely that in November 1780, after a party of pro-American Creoles led by the Frenchman Augustin Mottin de La Balme seized trade goods belonging to his family, Richardville joined with the Miami war party that pursued and defeated the raiders. In the immediate postwar years, when Pacanne moved his village down the Wabash to the Vincennes region, seeking a closer association with the new United States, Richardville remained at Kekionga, assuming a more active role in Miami politics and maintaining commercial and political ties with the British at Detroit. There is no evidence to suggest that he fought in either Harmar's Defeat (1790) or St. Clair's Defeat (1791), and he favored peaceful negotiations with the Americans prior to the Battle of Fallen Timbers (1794), and in 1795 he signed the Treaty of Greenville as a chief of the "Miamis and Eel Rivers."

After 1795, Richardville's influence increased. Closely associated with the Miami war chief Little Turtle, he utilized his position as an intermediary between the Miamis and the United States not only to protect the interests of the Miami tribe, but also for his own personal advantage. He operated trading posts at the forks of the Maumee and at the forks of the Wabash; his posts dominated the portage between the two rivers, and he charged traders and other travelers to transport goods between the two watersheds. In addition, as a "government chief" he exercised considerable control over the disbursement of annuity payments to his fellow tribesmen for the cession of Miami lands. Richardville capitalized on this economic power to reward friends and punish enemies. Renowned for his generosity, Richardville used his largesse to increase his political influence, which he then parlayed to further his business interests. He kept his profits in an iron-bound safe, and in 1816, when Indiana entered the Union, Richardville was reputed to be the wealthiest man in the state.

After 1800, Richardville's ties to the government increased. In 1802 and 1803 he signed treaties relinquishing Miami claims to lands in southern Indiana, and in 1808, accompanied by Little Turtle and several chiefs from other tribes, Richardville journeyed to Washington, D.C., where he met with Thomas Jefferson. Upon his return, he opposed the growing influence of the Shawnee Prophet (Tenskwatawa) and Tecumseh, whose assertions of pan-tribal land ownership threatened Miami claims to the Wabash Valley. He initially opposed the cession of Indian lands at negotiations for the Treaty of Fort Wayne (1809), but he signed the document after federal officials increased their offer of compensation and recognized Miami claims of lands south of the Wabash. Although Richardville sought sanctuary in Canada during the War of 1812, William Henry Harrison, then the governor of Indiana Territory, considered him to be friendly and instructed American troops not to destroy Richardville's Indiana property.

Following the War of 1812 Richardville emerged as the dominant leader among the Miamis in Indiana. Although the Miamis were forced to sign the Treaty of St. Mary's (1818), ceding much of their land, Richardville persuaded federal officials to exempt an area called the Miami National Reserve, an 875,000-acre tract in central Indiana. In the land cessions he also received, as his personal property, seven sections of land along the St. Mary's River near Fort Wayne and two sections at the forks of the Wabash. During the following two decades, in four subsequent land cessions, he received another thirty-five sections, and cash payments totaling almost thirty-two thousand dollars.

Although Richardville has been criticized for his role in these land cessions, he used his influence to obtain high prices for the Miamis for those lands. Moreover, as the Miami land base shrank, he offered many of the displaced tribespeople refuge on his property. Meanwhile, his mercantile activities prospered, and in 1824 he built an additional trading post near the mouth of the Mississinewa River. For the next sixteen years

Richardville lived at two amply furnished residences, one at Fort Wayne and the other near his trading post on the Mississinewa.

Richardville initially opposed federal plans to remove the Miamis to the West, but in 1838 and 1840 he signed two treaties that ceded most of the Miami National Reserve and provided for Miami removal. The treaties also provided Richardville with cash payments and additional lands, and exempted him and his heirs from the removal process. He died one year later, on August 13, 1841, at his home in Fort Wayne.

Richardville exemplified the mixed-blood leaders who emerged among the midwestern tribes after the War of 1812. Most were relatively well educated men, experienced in the fur trade. Skillful negotiators, they attempted to protect tribal interests, and when removal became inevitable, they exacted the highest possible prices for tribal lands. Yet they also used their political leadership for personal gain, and sometimes seemed to be motivated by personal expediency. Jean Baptiste Richardville was successful in both of these realms.

See also Miami.

Anson, Bert, *The Miami Indians* (Norman: University of Oklahoma Press, 1970); Chaput, Donald, "The Family of Drouet de Richerville: Merchants, Soldiers, and Chiefs of Indiana," *Indiana Magazine of History* 74 (June 1978): 103–16; Rafert, Stewart, *The Miami Indians of Indiana* (Indianapolis: Indiana Historical Society, 1995).

R. DAVID EDMUNDS (Cherokee)
Indiana University

RIDGE, JOHN ROLLIN (YELLOW BIRD)

(1827–67)
Oklahoma Cherokee newspaper editor, novelist, and poet.

Born just a few years prior to the crisis surrounding the Cherokee removal from Georgia, John Rollin Ridge experienced firsthand the most traumatic moments in the tribe's history. In 1830, the Indian Removal Act established the process that allowed for the removal of Cherokees from their homes in the Southeast. The Cherokees resisted this process, but federal officials exploited splits within the Cherokee Nation over relocation to advance their policy. In 1835 the government convinced twenty-one Cherokees, including Major Ridge (John Rollin Ridge's grandfather), John Ridge

(John Rollin Ridge's father), Elias Boudinot, and Stand Watie, Boudinot's younger brother, to sign the Treaty of New Echota. The treaty provided for the cession of all Cherokee lands east of the Mississippi and the subsequent removal of the tribe to the West.

Within months of removal, tribal leaders held general meetings to establish a new government. Negotiations between the pro-removal treaty faction and the Ross anti-removal faction quickly broke down, and on June 22, 1839, Major Ridge, John Ridge, and Elias Boudinot were murdered by their political enemies. As a twelve-year-old boy, John Rollin Ridge witnessed his father's murder, an event that deeply affected him. Because of continuing hostilities between the two factions, John Ridge's widow, a white woman, and her son immediately left Indian Territory for Fayetteville, Arkansas. In 1843, young Ridge was sent to the Great Barrington School in Massachusetts, where he stayed until 1845. He then returned to Fayetteville and began studying law.

In 1847, Ridge married Elizabeth Wilson, a white woman he had met in Massachusetts, and one year later they had their first and only child, Alice. His years in Arkansas, however, were also marked by conflict. He became involved in Cherokee politics, closely following the internecine struggles of the nation. On one occasion, he expressed his desire to avenge his father's death by killing one of the men implicated in the murder, the anti-removal leader John Ross. Ridge's involvement reached a climax in 1849 when he killed David Kell, a Cherokee he believed was one of his father's assassins.

In 1850, largely because of Kell's murder, Ridge left for California. He worked briefly in the gold mines there and soon afterward began writing. His poetry, dealing primarily with love and nature, was published in various magazines; it was collected and published posthumously in 1868. His major literary accomplishment, however, was his first and only novel, *The Life and Adventures of Joaquín Murieta, the Celebrated California Bandit* (1854), whose story gave Ridge a chance to verbally avenge his father's death. His hero committed murders in the name of justice and stood up to all who resisted him. Ridge's novel also condemned American racism, particularly the hatred he saw being directed toward Mexican Americans. He declared in the book's conclusion that "there is nothing so dangerous in its consequences as injustice to individuals—whether it arises from prejudice of color or any other source; that a wrong done to one man is a wrong to society and to the world." *Joaquín Murieta* is considered

"historical fiction," given the fact that the novel was based on the life of an actual California bandit. Ridge utilized newspaper articles extensively, and he claimed to have interviewed those close to Murieta. Several California historians later used the novel as a source in their own works.

From 1857 to 1862, Ridge worked as an editor for several California newspapers, including the *Sacramento Bee,* the *California Express, the National Democrat, the San Francisco Herald,* and the *Red Bluff Beacon.* As an editor he often advocated assimilationist policies and federal protection for American Indians. Like his father, he felt that American Indians needed the guidance and assistance of the federal government to maintain their rights. Also like his father, he often ignored the ways in which the federal government abused those rights. In regard to California Indians, Ridge felt they were inferior to the Indians of the Southeast and Northeast, and supported policies that confined them to reservations while upholding the claims of Euro-Americans to California lands.

During his years as an editor, Ridge also became increasingly involved in national politics. As a slave-owning southerner, he found himself sympathetic to the "Copperheads," a politically conservative faction of the Democratic Party. His critics accused him of establishing several chapters of the pro-slavery Knights of the Golden Circle. He worked for Democratic newspapers and openly supported the party's platform in his writings.

With the coming of the Civil War, Ridge expressed the sentiment that the Union should be preserved at all costs. While working for the *Red Bluff Beacon* in 1862, he protested the election of Abraham Lincoln and, later, insisted that the Emancipation Proclamation subverted democratic principles. In addition, while working for the *National Democrat,* he spoke in favor of the Confederacy and blamed the Civil War on abolitionists.

With the end of the Civil War, Ridge was given the opportunity to work toward his political goals for Cherokees. Invited by the federal government to head the Southern Cherokee delegation in postwar treaty proceedings, Ridge eagerly traveled to Washington, D.C. He worked diligently but failed to acquire Cherokee admission into the Union. In December 1866 Ridge returned home to Grass Valley, California. He died there on October 5, 1867.

Much of John Rollin Ridge's significance lies in his status as the first professional American Indian writer.

More importantly, his life demonstrates that it was not only Euro-Americans who supported contradictory positions and detrimental policies toward American Indians and African Americans. Ridge, an American Indian writer whom we might expect to have thought otherwise, clearly helped to reinforce systems of thought and practice whose violent reverberations continue to be felt today.

See also Cherokee; Ridge, Major.

Parins, James W., *John Rollin Ridge: His Life and Works* (Lincoln: University of Nebraska Press, 1991).

LIZA E. BLACK (Oklahoma Cherokee)
University of Washington

RIDGE, MAJOR

(c. 1771–1839)
Cherokee chief, planter, diplomat, and soldier.

Major Ridge was born circa 1771 at Hiwassee in what is now Polk County, Tennessee. Of the Deer clan, he had six brothers and sisters, several of whom died young. In his boyhood he was known as Nung-noh-hut-tar-hee, or, "the Pathkiller," and in his maturity as Kah-nung-da-tla-geh, or, in the truncated English version, "the Ridge"—the name by which whites knew him. Later still, he took Major as his first name, the military title and rank he had earned while serving with General Andrew Jackson's forces during the Creek War.

As a youth, the Ridge was trained in turn as hunter and warrior, and when border warfare with the whites erupted in 1788, he fought intermittently until peace was established in 1794. He settled then at Pine Log, Georgia, where neighbors chose him to represent the town at the council in Oostanaula, then the Cherokee capital. About 1792, he married Susanna Wickett, or Sehoya, as the Cherokees addressed her. They settled in the Oothcaloga Valley in northern Georgia, where she bore him five children. The second child, a son born in 1803 and named Skah-tle-loh-skee, or John Ridge, would later become a noted Cherokee leader and, like his cousins, the brothers Elias Boudinot and Stand Watie, a staunch political ally of the Ridge. Meanwhile, to support his flourishing family, the Ridge planted peach and apple orchards on his fertile bottomlands. He also raised stock with the help of a growing crew of African slaves.

As an affluent planter, Ridge was often called upon by the Cherokee council. For example, he was named ambassador to the Creek Confederation. In that capacity he so impressed the Creeks that they adopted him as a chief of their own and assigned him a seat on their council. But he sided with the Americans when Congress declared war against Great Britain on June 18, 1812, and helped to muster Cherokee warriors to march with backwoods soldiers from Tennessee against the Red Stick forces. The Ridge served on the American side throughout the Creek War, emerging with the rank of major.

After his military exploits, he became a top-flight Cherokee diplomat, going to Washington on several tribal missions. He did not hesitate to work for the Creeks as well, helping them on one occasion to forge a treaty with the federal government that retrieved for them all the land in Georgia that the United States had secured by subterfuge and fraud. In 1826 the grateful Creeks rewarded him with a gift of ten thousand dollars, a windfall that enabled him to build a fine house and undertake other improvements at Ridge's Ferry on the Oostanaula River—the new house replacing the one at Oothcaloga as the principal residence of the Ridge family until their removal west.

By 1827 the Ridge had gained such prestige among his countrymen that after the successive deaths of both principal and second Cherokee chiefs he served temporarily as acting head of the nation. But changing times had caused that position to require more formal education than was his lot, and so in 1828 he was satisfied to see the educated and nearly all-white John Ross elected as principal chief, with himself as the first of three councilors.

For decades the Cherokees had sold so much land to the federal government and reduced the area of their domain so drastically that they now found it imperative to halt all further cessions. Major Ridge assumed a leading role in the drive to keep this anticession policy in place, notwithstanding Georgia's retaliation with massive oppression aimed at all Cherokees living within the state. Such harassment did not deter the Ridge from riding horseback through Cherokee territory there and making a careful assessment of the deteriorating condition of his people. As a result of his survey, he reached the unexpected conclusion sometime in 1832 that the Cherokee cause in the East was lost. By coincidence, John Ridge and Boudinot came to the same conclusion at about the same time during a mission they had undertaken together in Washington and certain states in the Northeast; and on their return home, they joined Major Ridge in launching the cause of removing all eastern Cherokees to the West.

Thereafter a seesaw contest between the Ross majority and the Ridge minority factions intensified under the stimulus of Georgian persecution. A state lottery set in motion on October 22, 1832, a steady transfer of Cherokee acreage to "fortunate drawers" among the Georgian whites. The upshot was that, after a series of desperate and fruitless councils over a period of more than three years, the Ridge faction arranged that still another council be convened at the abandoned Cherokee capital of New Echota, Georgia, on December 22, 1835—its object being to enable the Cherokees to treat with the American commissioner, John F. Schermerhorn, who had been sent to the Cherokee Nation for that express purpose. The deliberations that followed, though boycotted by Chief John Ross and the majority faction, resulted in the signing of a treaty of dubious legality that provided, among its various measures, for the removal of all the eastern Cherokees to the West and for the purchase of their lands for the twice upwardly adjusted sum of $6,647,067. Though the Ross faction rejected the treaty as fraudulent, the U.S. Senate ratified it on May 17, 1836.

The following March Major Ridge requested federal authorities to transport him and his family west by riverboat, and upon arrival there, though seriously ailing, he took up land on Honey Creek in the northeast corner of the western Cherokee domain, where he was soon joined by Stand Watie. Later his son John joined Boudinot in independently moving their families west by horse and carriage, and upon their arrival, Boudinot settled at Park Hill, while John Ridge followed his father's example and took up land on Honey Creek.

The time mandated for the mass removal of the Cherokees came on May 23, 1838, and federal troops began a twenty-five-day roundup of 12,500 or more Indians. Negotiations initiated by Chief Ross, however, led to the transfer of subsequent operations from federal control into Cherokee hands and to the allowance of sixty-five dollars a head to enable the Cherokees to meet the cost of a self-directed migration. Unfortunately, unprecedented drought dried up most of the springs along the way, and conditions grew so dire that the emigrants perished in wholesale numbers, causing the route to the West to become known as the Trail of Tears.

Meanwhile the Ridges, Boudinot, and Watie had abstained from Cherokee politics. But when a general council was scheduled to meet at Takatoka on June 3, 1839, to effect a formal union of the recent arrivals with the old settlers, an indiscreet curiosity lured all four to the council ground on June 14. Their presence so infuriated a splinter group of the Ross faction that it convened a secret rump council on the evening of June 21, the date of the adjournment of the general council, and condemned all four treaty leaders to death. The "executions" followed the next morning, June 22, with the triple murders of both the Ridges and Boudinot. Stand Watie was warned of danger, however, and lived to succeed the Ridges as chief of the treaty faction of the nation, later known as the Southern Cherokees.

See also Boudinot, Elias; Cherokee; Watie, Stand.

McLoughlin, William G., *Cherokee Renascence in the New Republic* (Princeton, N.J.: Princeton University Press, 1986); Wilkins, Thurman, *Cherokee Tragedy: The Ridge Family and the Decimation of a People*, rev. ed. (Norman: University of Oklahoma Press, 1986).

THURMAN WILKINS
Bandon, Oregon

RIEL, LOUIS

(1844–85)
Métis leader and founder of the province of Manitoba, Canada.

National hero of the Métis, Louis Riel is a key figure in Canadian history. In formulating the aspirations of his people during the difficult years following the confederation of Canada (1867) and acting to realize them, he became a catalyst in the French-English and Catholic-Protestant rivalries that dominated the Canadian political scene of the period.

Of Franco-Chipewyan descent, he was the grandson of Marie-Anne Gaboury, the first white woman in western Canada. Riel was born in the Red River Settlement (at that time under the governance of the Hudson's Bay Company), and went to Montreal to study for the priesthood but turned to law instead. He returned to the West the year following the confederation of Ontario, Quebec, New Brunswick, and Nova Scotia as the Dominion of Canada. An immediate challenge to the fledgling government was the transfer of the huge expanse of Rupert's Land (essentially present-day Northwest Territories) from Hudson's Bay Company (HBC) administration to that of the new dominion. The date set for this was December 1, 1869.

The Métis communities of the Northwest, the product of the fur trade that was still flourishing in those regions, had been developing for more than two centuries. Far removed as they were from the centers of colonial government, they already had a well-established tradition of independent self-sufficiency. Nowhere was this more evident than at Red River. Years earlier, in 1816, when the HBC had sought to enforce regulations that the Métis considered to be against their interests, the people of Red River under the leadership of Cuthbert Grant (c. 1793–1854) had mounted successful resistance in a confrontation known as the Battle of Seven Oaks. It was a moment of truth that confirmed the Métis in thinking of themselves as a "new nation," a people neither Amerindian nor white, but a combination of both. Beginning in the 1840s, the Métis at Red River presented a series of petitions to the HBC and to the imperial government in London, asking for recognition as a separate people and a voice in government. Officials dragged their heels, suspicious of these people who did not fit into established social categories.

As the date for the transfer of the HBC lands to Canada drew closer, tensions mounted in Red River. When government surveyors arrived unannounced and set to work, Riel and a group of Métis stopped them, on October 11, 1869. The alarmed Métis then organized the Comité National des Métis (National Committee of the Métis) to defend their interests. In the meantime, Canada had named a former commissioner of crown lands with a dubious record regarding his dealings with aboriginal territories, William McDougall (1822–1905), as lieutenant governor of Rupert's Land. When he arrived at Red River, his entry was blocked by Riel and the Comité, on the grounds that the settlement had not been consulted about his appointment. On November 2, the Métis took peaceful possession of Lower Fort Garry, the HBC's regional headquarters—a move that symbolized the Métis' control of Red River. All this they accomplished without firing a shot.

A furious McDougall, unwilling to accept what had happened, slipped into the settlement during a snowstorm on December 1, the day that had been scheduled for the transfer, and read the proclamation that had been prepared to announce Canada's takeover. His action formally ended HBC authority without providing any effective official authority to take its place; in effect, he created a political vacuum. Under the circumstances, the Métis were legally free to form a provisional government, which they did, with Riel as president.

Opposition was not long in developing, however, its major manifestation being a group calling itself Canada First, based in English-speaking Protestant Ontario. The aggressive behavior of some of the Canada Firsters in Red River led to arrests, and eventually to the court-martial and execution of one of them, Orangeman Thomas Scott. As Ontario cried for vengeance and Quebec sprang to the defense of the Métis, Ottawa rushed the Manitoba Act through Parliament, carving a new province—Northwest Territories—out of Rupert's Land that guaranteed equal rights to French and English speakers and provided for a separate Catholic school system; in addition, 1.4 million acres of land were set aside for Métis.

For Riel, the consequences were not so happy. In spite of Ottawa's promise of amnesty, Ontario contin-

Louis Riel, leader of the Métis rebellions.

ued to demand that he be brought to justice for the execution of Scott. Although Riel was twice elected to Parliament, in 1873 and again the following year, hostility against him was such that he was never able to take his seat. In 1875 he was banished from Canada for five years, with the promise of amnesty afterward. Nervously exhausted from the strain of his position, he began to see himself as a prophet of a new form of Christianity that would be based in Canada—an unorthodox position that lost him support among the Catholic clergy. Under the name of Louis R. David, he was hospitalized in Quebec for a little more than a year and a half. Upon his discharge he returned west to work as a trader and interpreter, and to become involved in regional politics. In 1881 he married a Métis woman, Marguerite Monet. In 1883 he became a U.S. citizen, and the following year he accepted an invitation to teach at the Jesuit mission at Sun River, Montana. Soon after he settled there, a delegation of Canadian Métis arrived to ask his help in a crisis that had been precipitated by the passing of the buffalo herds.

The situation in the Canadian Northwest in 1884 was very different from what it had been in Red River in 1869–70. In addition to the disappearance of the herds, the transcontinental Canadian Pacific Railway was nearing completion, and the federal North-West Mounted Police were a strong presence. But in one unfortunate respect, things were all too much the same: Ottawa was still having trouble hearing the voice of the West, particularly that of the Métis. Frustrated at the slow pace of negotiations over the place of the Métis in the province, Riel, on March 8, issued a ten-point bill of rights for the North-West Territories. The manifesto included provisions recognizing the rights of Amerindians and white settlers as well as the rights of the Métis. When Ottawa did not respond, Riel proclaimed a provisional government on March 19 (the name day of Saint Joseph, the patron saint of the Métis) and seized the parish church at Batoche, on the Saskatchewan River. Within a week, with the help of the new railway, federal troops were on the scene.

The armed conflict that followed was quickly over, but the same cannot be said for its consequences. The repercussions from the hanging of Riel for high treason on November 16, 1885, are still being felt. The cause of the Métis had received a severe setback, but it was not destroyed. It has in fact been regaining momentum in the closing decades of the twentieth century. A testimony to this was the inclusion of the Métis as one of Canada's three aboriginal peoples in the Constitution of 1982, and the federal government's recognition, in 1994, of the aboriginal right to self-government.

Flanagan, Thomas, ed., *The Diaries of Louis Riel* (Edmonton: Hurtig, 1976); Lussier, A. S., ed., *Louis Riel and the Métis* (Winnipeg: Pemmican Publications, 1988); Stanley, George F. G., *Louis Riel* (Toronto: McGraw-Hill Ryerson, 1963).

OLIVE PATRICIA DICKASON
University of Alberta

RIGHTS

See Fishing and Hunting Rights; Religious Rights; Water Rights.

ROGERS, WILL

(1879–1935)
Cherokee author and humorist.

William Penn Adair Rogers was born on November 4, 1879, near Oolagah, Cherokee Nation. While the Cherokee allotment roll listed him as one-quarter-degree Cherokee, his family genealogy indicated that he was probably eleven-thirty-seconds Cherokee. The Rogerses were a wealthy mixed-blood ranching family who, prior to the Civil War, had been slave owners. William's father, Clement Vann Rogers, had served as a captain in the Cherokee Confederate regiment. Active in politics, he had later been a delegate from the Cherokee Nation to the Dawes Commission, which allotted Indian Territory, and a delegate to the Oklahoma state constitutional convention. William's mother, also Cherokee, was Mary America Scrimsher. In personality he was said to have taken after his mother, who died when he was ten years old. His relationship with his serious-minded and stern father was often strained.

A poor student with discipline problems, Rogers was in and out of a number of schools in Indian Territory and Missouri: Drumgoole School, Willie Hassell School, Harrell Institution, Cherokee Seminary, and Scarritt Collegiate Institute. In 1898, with money borrowed from his sister, he ran away from Kemper Military School in Missouri to become a cowboy on a Texas ranch. When he returned to Oolagah, his father made him foreman of the family ranch, the Dog Iron. Restless and social, young Will was more interested in contest roping and fiddling than ranching.

Will Rogers and cast members of his Follies, *circa 1925.*

In 1902 his father gave him three thousand dollars for the purpose of going to Argentina to buy a ranch. His funds quickly dissipated, and, finding himself in Argentina without enough money to purchase a ranch, he took a job on a cattle boat headed for South Africa. In South Africa he first broke horses for the British army and then, calling himself the Cherokee Kid, joined a Wild West show. In Australia, he joined the Wirth Brothers Circus. In 1904 he arrived back in Oolagah broke, and left almost immediately to join Zack Mulhall's Wild West show as a trick roper. After appearing in Madison Square Garden in 1905, he left the show to form his own vaudeville act. In 1906 Rogers played the Wintergarten Theater in Berlin and the Palace in London. Returning to the United States, he was soon hired by the Ziegfeld Follies.

In 1908 he married Betty Blake, from Rogers, Arkansas. Roping came to play a subordinate role in his act as audiences were increasingly attracted to his humorous social and political commentaries. Although he was one of the greatest trick ropers ever, it was his humorous monologues that made him one of the biggest stars in vaudeville. By the eve of World War I he commanded a salary of thirty-five hundred dollars a week. So great were his popularity and appeal that he became a major fund-raiser for the American Red Cross during the war and began to consider expanding his career into writing and the movies.

His popular stage monologues were readily transferable to the written word. In 1919 he published his first two books: *The Cowboy Philosopher on the Peace Conference* and *The Cowboy Philosopher on Prohibition.* In late 1922 he began writing a weekly newspaper column, and in 1923 his national syndicated column began to appear daily. In 1923 he published his *Illiterate Digest. The Saturday Evening Post* sent Rogers to

Europe in 1926 as an unofficial ambassador for President Calvin Coolidge. The articles he wrote for the *Post* were later published in book form as *Letters of a Self-Made Diplomat to His President.* In 1927 *Not a Bathing Suit in Russia* was published, based on Rogers's travels in the Soviet Union.

His movie career was not initially successful. Rogers's popularity was based on his use of words, and films were still silent at the time. Beginning in 1918 he starred in several films, but none were box-office hits. He then produced and bankrolled three movies of his own, also failures. In 1920 he returned to the stage and the Ziegfeld Follies to help pay off the creditors from his failed movies. In 1923 he made some short comedies with Hal Roach, but within a year he was back in the Follies. In 1929 he made his first talking picture and began a moderately successful movie career.

However, in 1930 he began his radio program, *The Gulf Refining Company Hour.* Modeled after his stage monologues and columns, it consisted of humorous but pointed comments on major social and political issues. It was through his radio program that Rogers reached his broadest audience and gained his strongest influence on public opinion.

He became the voice of the average American commenting on the world. In his humorous, highly entertaining editorializing of the current news, he covered the full range of national and international events. Although he publicly and regularly identified himself as a Cherokee, only rarely did he directly comment on Indian issues. However, when he did make such comments, they were frequently pointed, dealing with exploitation and abuse:

I hear the Navajos have struck oil on their reservation. That will give the white man a chance to show his so-called 100 percent Americanism, by flocking and taking it away from the Indians.

They sent the Indians to Oklahoma. They had a treaty that said: "You shall have this land as long as grass grows and water flows." It was not only a good rhyme, but looked like a good treaty; and it was, till they struck oil. Then the government took it away from us again. They said the treaty only refers to "water and grass; it don't say anything about oil."

In regard to a 1935 controversy over the actual landing place of the Pilgrims in Massachusetts, he said:

Now in the first place I don't think that this argument . . . [is] so terribly important. The argument that New England has to settle . . . is "Why was they allowed to land anywhere?" . . . That's what we want to know. . . . Now I

hope my Cherokee blood is not making me prejudiced. I want to be broadminded, but I am sure that it was only the extreme generosity of the Indians that allowed the Pilgrims to land. Suppose we reversed the case. Do you reckon the Pilgrims would have ever let the Indians land? Yeah, what a chance! What a chance! The Pilgrims wouldn't even allow the Indians to live after the Indians went to the trouble of letting 'em land.

Mild but pointed, Rogers was able to poke fun at some of America's most sacred historical icons. Engaged as he was in popular culture, he struck a pose of democratic informality. Knowing the tragic history of his family and region, he was able to give his humor a pungency few could deny or forget. He wrote, for example, that "you've never . . . seen a picture of one of the old Pilgrims praying when he didn't have a gun right by the side of him. That was to see that he got what he was praying for."

Rogers died in a plane crash near Point Barrow, Alaska, on August 15, 1935. Although he had become an international celebrity and had lived most of his life in New York or California, he never forgot he was a Cherokee. He became the champion and the voice of the underdog, the abused, the dispossessed, and the powerless. His salary from his radio program was given to charity. He was buried in Claremont, Oklahoma, about ten miles from the Dog Iron Ranch.

Ketchum, Richard, *Will Rogers, His Life and Times* (New York: American Heritage, 1973); Rogers, Will, *The Autobiography of Will Rogers* (Boston: Houghton Mifflin, 1949); Yagoga, Ben, *Will Rogers: A Biography* (New York: Alfred A. Knopf, 1993).

GARRICK BAILEY
(Euro-American, Cherokee, and Choctaw)
University of Tulsa

ROBERTA GLENN BAILEY
Tulsa, Oklahoma

ROMAN NOSE (WOO-KA-NAY)

(1835?–68)
Cheyenne warrior.

One of the most esteemed warriors of the Great Plains, Roman Nose fit the white man's romantic notion of an ideal Indian warrior, and his story highlights both the tragic clash of cultures on the plains and the ignorance and misunderstanding with which white observers approached the "Indian problem."

Roman Nose, or, more precisely, "Arched Nose," came to prominence during the Plains Indian wars of the 1860s, and when he was killed at Beecher's Island in 1868, he had become the most famous Indian of the plains. The white troops admired his fearlessness and leadership, qualities they assumed were connected with high political office and tribal authority. Numerous accounts describe him as a chief with a chief's powers, but in fact he was not a chief and had no official political authority. Unlike the white man, the Cheyennes did not admire individualism and ambition—a cultural difference that inevitably led to conflict and misidentification. After Roman Nose became prominent, the U.S. Army tended to identify any unknown Cheyenne male in a position of authority as Roman Nose. And since engaging in battle against the notorious Roman Nose conferred prestige on American military leaders, almost every raid and skirmish in the central plains was said to be "led by Roman Nose."

Another conflict of values lay in the area of religion. Roman Nose, like other Indians, placed complete faith in the spiritual power of sacred objects and ceremonies. Among Indian people, such power was held in awe. Warring tribes respected the sacred medicines of their opponents, and the Indians were appalled and dumbfounded that the white man did not.

Roman Nose's most powerful medicine was the magnificent headdress he wore in battle; made with one buffalo horn and a long tail of red and black eagle feathers, this war bonnet was believed to have absolute protective powers. It was not unusual for him to arrive at a battle site after the skirmish had begun, because a long and complicated ceremony had to be performed before he could put on his headdress. Strict rules were followed, and certain actions were proscribed; among the most significant proscriptions for Roman Nose was that he was never to eat food that had been in contact with metal, a white man's object.

A common battle tactic of his was to ride up and down the line of army troops within rifle range, getting them to discharge their weapons and waste their ammunition. He would repeat this maneuver several times without injury, protected by his strong medicine.

During this time, U.S. Army policies dictated burning villages as well as killing buffalo and destroying other food sources, thus leaving the Indians destitute and dependent on rations from the government. The Indians, however, turned to a different means of livelihood based on raiding the homesteads of white settlers.

The winter of 1864–65 saw increased raiding and military conflicts by Indians in retaliation for the Sand Creek Massacre, the army's brutal and unprovoked attack of a friendly Indian camp promised protection by the U.S. government. Under increasing assault, the army toughened its tactics. It was at this time that Roman Nose first appeared in military accounts. His bravery and fearlessness were recounted in descriptions of the Battle of Platte Bridge and the Powder River Expedition, both in 1865.

Another episode frequently mentioned is Roman Nose's encounter with General Winfield Scott Hancock. Feeling snubbed by the Indian's absence at a meeting with chiefs at Fort Larned, Kansas, Hancock brazenly marched his troops to the Cheyenne camp, heedless of warnings that he was frightening the women and children. When Roman Nose confronted him, harsh words of war were exchanged. But meanwhile the camp dwellers fled, and a major incident was avoided.

The Indian wars of the central plains continued through 1868, and on September 17, a party of Cheyennes and Sioux attacked the fifty troops of Major George A. Forsyth's "first-class frontiersmen" on the Republican River near the Colorado-Kansas border. Most of the scouts retreated to a small sandbar in the dry bed of the Arickaree Fork, which became known as Beecher's Island. The Indians greatly outnumbered the scouts, but the whites were well protected on the island, with its high grass and willows, as well as a hastily dug line of rifle pits in the sand, with packs and a growing number of dead horses and mules lined up for breastworks. In addition, two or three scouts found holes hidden by tall grass in the sand onshore, and used their position as an ambush site.

The scouts were equipped with modern weaponry: new Spencer repeating rifles, Colt army revolvers, and boxes of extra ammunition. Aside from a few heavy carbines and old Sharps rifles, most of the Indians were armed only with bows and lances. The open prairie at streamside offered no shelter.

When Roman Nose arrived at the battle site late in the day, he felt vulnerable. His medicine had been weakened, he said, for during a feast, a Sioux woman had unknowingly contaminated his food with metal when she fed him bread from a skillet with an iron fork. His purification ceremonies had not yet begun when he was called to battle. He consulted with the war leaders about his concerns, but when chastised by an old man for cowardice, Roman Nose unhesitatingly agreed to lead a charge. It was very late when he painted himself, put on his headdress, and rode to the front of the Indian line. Roman Nose approached the sandbar. As he rode past the ambush site of the white scouts on the riverbank, he was shot in the small of the back. Even in death, Roman Nose was misidentified by virtue of his body's lack of symbols for rank or prestige. Soldiers mistakenly identified at least two other bodies as Roman Nose because of one's elaborate funerary attire and the other's burial in a lodge.

Roman Nose's body was actually placed on a scaffold and exposed to the winds and sky with the bodies of other dead warriors. Troops later discovered the bodies and pulled them to the ground, leaving the carcasses for the wolves.

When he died, Roman Nose was in the prime of life. His friend George Bent described him as "strong as a bull, tall even for a Cheyenne, broad-shouldered and deep-chested." He had two wives; the first, Island, gave him a daughter named Crooked Nose Woman, and the second, Woman with White Child, also gave him a daughter. Other warriors had counted more coup, but the fearless Roman Nose and his famous headdress have continued to be sources of awe and legend.

Grinnell, George Bird, *The Cheyenne Indians: Their History and Ways of Life,* 2 vols. (New York: Cooper Square Publishers, 1962); Grinnell, George Bird, *The Fighting Cheyennes* (New York: Charles Scribner's Sons, 1915); Hyde, George E., *A Life of George Bent: Written from His Letters,* ed. Savoie Lottinville (Norman: University of Oklahoma Press, 1968).

JOHN HARTWELL MOORE
University of Florida

SHELLEY A. ARLEN
University of Florida

ROSEBUD, BATTLE OF THE

In the spring of 1876, the U.S. Army moved against the so-called hostile Lakotas and Cheyennes who had not complied with the ultimatum to return to the agencies in the Dakotas and Nebraska after negotiations to acquire the sacred Black Hills had failed in the fall of 1875. General George Crook moved his forces north into the Rosebud Valley after his Crow and Shoshone scouts reported a huge concentration of Lakotas and Cheyennes there. On June 17, one thousand to fifteen hundred warriors led by Crazy Horse attacked Crook's force of about thirteen hundred, which included some one hundred seventy-five Shoshone and Crow scouts. The swirling, fragmented battle over broken, rough terrain evolved into three separate fights marked by charge and countercharge. There were many incidents of note and acts of bravery on both sides, perhaps the

most famous being a Cheyenne girl's rescue of her brother, whose horse had been shot out from under him. Thus do the Cheyennes call this battle Where the Girl Saved Her Brother. The Lakotas and Cheyennes called off the fight after six hours, with both sides expending much ammunition and suffering relatively few casualties. Though Crook claimed victory because he believed he had driven the Indians from the field at the end of the day, his claim was hollow: the fight was at best a draw, and Crook's bloodied column later withdrew to its base camp on Goose Creek. As a result of the battle, one of the three army columns converging on the Indians was effectively incapacitated and taken out of the campaign for two months.

The Battle of the Rosebud was an unusually large battle in the annals of the Plains Indian wars. In this regard, it was similar to, and a prelude to, the Battle of the Little Bighorn, which took place thirty miles away and eight days later. To students of the battle and to Native Americans today, the Rosebud is recognized as another episode in the Lakota and Cheyenne defense of their lands and way of life. On the other hand, to the Crows and Shoshones who scouted for the Americans, the battle was also an attempt to defend their lands and way of life from the Lakotas and Cheyennes, who were expanding into their territories. All Indians involved in the battle felt they were fighting for their own people against the invasion of outsiders.

ROSS, JOHN
(1790–1866)
Cherokee leader.

John Ross served his people, the Cherokees, for more than fifty years, most importantly as principal chief during one of the most turbulent periods in the tribe's history. From the time the Cherokees established a constitutional government in 1827 until his death in 1866, Ross was repeatedly elected to the highest office. He was tapped for leadership because of his devotion to their primary cause, the maintenance of the tribal homeland. His shrewd negotiating style enabled him to bargain with the United States to the tribe's advantage over the years, but he was unable to win on the most important point—the preservation of the national homeland. After losing that cause in the 1830s, Ross continued as a major presence, working to reunite the tribe in the West after its bitter breakup over the issue of removal. He steered his people through the vendettas and civil disturbances of the postremoval period until peace and unity were restored. He then guided the Cherokees during their golden years before they became caught up in the American Civil War and split anew over the issue of slavery. Ross died shortly before a new treaty with the United States was signed in 1866, but with the knowledge that his efforts had succeeded and that his people would be reunited once again.

Ross was born at Turkey Town, Cherokee Nation (near present-day Center, Alabama), on October 3, 1790. He was the son and grandson of Scottish traders who married Cherokee women. Only one-eighth Cherokee and with little ability in the native language, Ross nonetheless gained the support of the tribe's full-blood majority because of his devotion to maintaining the homeland in the American Southeast. Ross initially chose the world of his father and grandfather and went into the merchandising business. At Ross's Landing (present-day Chattanooga, Tennessee) he operated a ferry and warehouse, then moved south to present-day Georgia and turned to a planter's life. At Head of Coosa—today's Rome, Georgia—he built a comfortable home, increased his slave holdings, ran a ferry, and worked nearly two hundred acres of choice farmland. By the 1830s he was one of the wealthiest men in the Cherokee Nation.

The move to a central location in the nation reflected his growing interest in Cherokee political affairs, and Ross gradually became involved in tribal government. In 1816 he served as clerk to the Cherokee chiefs and that same year made his first trip to Washington, D.C., as a tribal delegate. Three years later he became president of the Cherokee national legislature, and in 1827 he was elected president of the Cherokee constitutional convention and helped write the finished document—the first constitution among Native Americans. The following year Ross was elected first principal chief of the new government, a position he held for nearly forty years. He had committed himself to the Cherokee way.

In the 1830s the Cherokees faced external forces that would deprive them of their lands and internal dissension that would leave them divided. As principal chief, Ross confronted Georgians who, backed by their state government, were pushing onto Cherokee lands. Ross found the state and federal courts of little help. Despite landmark decisions in such cases as *Cherokee Nation* v. *Georgia* (1831), the Cherokees got no relief. Ross also had little solace from the federal executive. President Andrew Jackson was in sympathy with Georgia and pressed the southeastern Indians to move west. Ross,

John Ross in 1862.

however, was determined to keep the Cherokees in their homeland, and he had the support of the traditionalist, full-blood majority in his resolve. But reformist dissenters called "mixed bloods," led by Major Ridge and his followers, considered removal the more reasonable solution. They signed a treaty at New Echota, Georgia, in 1835 that relinquished all Cherokee lands for new homes in the West.

Ross fought the fraudulent Treaty of New Echota, but to no avail. After a military removal of the tribe began in 1838, the chief relented and led his people to Indian Territory (present-day Oklahoma). At least one-quarter of the tribe, perhaps five thousand people, died during the removal period and along the route later called the Trail of Tears. Afterward near civil war erupted as the Cherokees tried to reorganize their national affairs. Assassinations were carried out against treaty signers by non-treaty Cherokees and several members of the Ridge family were killed. Ross probably neither ordered nor approved of the killings, but neither was he aggressive in trying to bring the perpetrators to justice. Peace finally returned in 1846 when

Ross and the surviving Ridge followers reconciled and signed a new treaty with the federal government.

The two decades following 1846 were a golden age for the Cherokees and a time of peace and prosperity for Ross. He built a splendid home near Tahlequah, the capital of the Cherokee Nation, and looked forward to tranquillity in his last years. Ross could also feel pride in Cherokee accomplishments carried out under his leadership: the founding of a national newspaper, the introduction of free public schools, and the establishment of a stable political system.

The American Civil War disrupted the Cherokees' peace and renewed factional quarrels, this time over the issues of slavery and of loyalty to the Union. Ross tried to withstand the pressures of Southern agents and their Cherokee sympathizers, but eventually he acquiesced and the tribe sided with the South. Ross probably made the decision under duress, fearing internal division and Confederate invasion. Within a year he fled east, where he lived out the war working for the tribal cause. At war's end he came back to a defeated nation, but turned east one last time to oppose the disintegration of his tribe in retributive postwar treaties. Shortly before his death, Ross learned that a new treaty had been signed guaranteeing that the Cherokee Nation would remain intact.

Ross married twice. His first marriage, in 1813, was to Elizabeth Brown Henley (called Quatie), who died on the Trail of Tears in 1839. She and Ross had six children, five of whom survived into adulthood. In 1844 Ross married Mary Brian Stapler, a Quaker of Wilmington, Delaware, and a woman thirty-five years his junior. Ross and Mary settled in Tahlequah at their spacious Rose Cottage and had two children; she died in Philadelphia in 1865. Ross's four sons by Quatie served in Indian regiments during the Civil War and one died during the conflict. His daughter lost her husband in the war. Several of the children attended private academies in the East.

Ross's life cannot be measured solely by the fact that he lost some of the great contests of his career: the Cherokees were removed, and they were forced into the American Civil War. Rather, he must be assessed with respect to his times and judged for his integrity and his devotion to his people and their cause. It was not chance that won him the highest office in his tribe, nor was it by accident that he gained the enduring devotion of his people. Such achievements stand as a monument to his character.

See also Cherokee; Civil War in Indian Territory, The.

Moulton, Gary E., *John Ross, Cherokee Chief* (Athens: University of Georgia Press, 1978); Moulton, Gary E., ed., *The Papers of Chief John Ross,* 2 vols. (Norman: University of Oklahoma Press, 1985); Wilkins, Thurman, *Cherokee Tragedy* (Norman: University of Oklahoma Press, 1986).

GARY E. MOULTON
University of Nebraska at Lincoln

S

SACAGAWEA

(1786/88–1812/84)
Shoshone (Snake) interpreter of the Lewis and Clark Expedition.

Sacagawea (Sacajawea, Sakakawea) was born in a Northern Shoshone village in the vicinity of the Lemhi River valley in what is today Idaho; it is likely that she was a member of the Agaiduka or Salmon Eater band of the Shoshone tribe. Around 1800, while her tribe was engaged in a hunting or war expedition east of their home territory in the Three Forks area of the Missouri River (Montana), she was captured, most likely by the Hidatsas from the Knife River village of Metaharta (North Dakota). Sacagawea was twelve to fourteen years old at the time of her capture. By 1804 she had become the property of Toussaint Charbonneau, a French-Canadian trader and trapper.

In the winter of 1804–1805, Captains Meriwether Lewis and William Clark wintered at Fort Mandan on the Missouri River in what is today North Dakota, where they encountered Charbonneau and Sacagawea. Before leaving Fort Mandan in April 1805 to continue their westward journey, Lewis and Clark hired Charbonneau as an interpreter, requesting that he bring one of his Shoshone wives with him. Charbonneau brought Sacagawea, who had given birth to their son, Jean Baptiste, on February 11, 1805, at the fort; the infant became the youngest member of the expedition.

While much popular literature portrays Sacagawea as the pilot of the Lewis and Clark Expedition, her role as expedition guide has been greatly exaggerated. She was unfamiliar with most of the terrain through which the expedition traveled, and so could not have led the expedition to the Pacific Ocean. Sacagawea's geographical knowledge was limited to the region near her homeland in the Three Forks area of the upper Missouri River; here she recognized landmarks and provided some direction to Lewis and Clark.

While it is not likely that Sacagawea acted as the expedition's guide, her services certainly contributed to the success of the expedition. She acted as an interpreter (her most important role), collected wild foods, boosted morale, and on occasion pointed out landmarks and possible routes (such as the Bozeman Pass on the return trip). She even saved valuable instruments and records from being lost overboard when the expedition was traveling on the Missouri River. William Clark was impressed by Sacagawea's service and strength, and nicknamed her Janey in his expedition journals. He became attached to Sacagawea's son, Jean Baptiste, and assumed responsibility for the education of the boy, whom he fondly nicknamed Pomp. Clark's journal also indicates that the presence of a woman with an infant served as a sign that the intentions of the expedition were peaceful.

Much of the success of the expedition hinged on Sacagawea's presence as an emissary and liaison. In August 1805, west of the Continental Divide in present-day Lemhi County, Idaho, she was unexpectedly reunited with her brother Cameahwait, who had become Shoshone band chief during her many years of absence. He provided the expedition with horses and guides for the journey across the Bitterroot Mountains and through the Salmon River country to the navigable waters of the Clearwater and Columbia Rivers.

Sacagawea, Charbonneau, and their son left Lewis and Clark at Fort Mandan, their starting point, on August 17, 1806. Charbonneau was paid $500.33. Because Sacagawea was an unofficial member of the expedition, she received no monetary compensation. Little is known of her life after the expedition. Historical records, however, suggest that Charbonneau, Sacagawea, and Jean Baptiste went east to St. Louis, Missouri, around 1810 to accept Clark's offer of 320 acres of land and additional pay, and to finance the education of their son. But city life did not agree with Charbonneau, and he and Sacagawea left St. Louis to return to the upper Missouri country to work for the famous Missouri Fur Company trader Manuel Lisa. Jean Baptiste most likely remained behind in St. Louis to begin his education under the patronage of William Clark.

Most historians believe that Sacagawea died at Fort Manuel (Manuel Lisa's post) on the Missouri River in what is today South Dakota on December 20, 1812; they base their conclusions on three recorded accounts that suggest this as the date of her death. One account is that of Henry Brackenridge (author, statesman, and lawyer) of Pittsburgh, who records in his journal on April 2, 1811, that a wife of Charbonneau who had accompanied Lewis and Clark to the Pacific was on board a trading boat with him in the vicinity of Fort Manuel. His journal entry indicates that she was ill and wanted to return to her people. Over a year later, on December 20, 1812, John Luttig, head clerk of the Fort Manuel trading post, wrote in his journal: "This Evening the Wife of Charbonneau a Snake Squaw, died of a putrid fever she was a good and the best Woman in the fort, aged about 25 years she left a fine infant girl." Finally, somewhere between 1825 and 1828, Clark wrote "dead" next to Sacagawea's name (listed as "Se-car ja we au") on the cover of his cash or accounting book, along with the known whereabouts of the other members of the expedition.

An alternative version of Sacagawea's later life, however, persists. Shoshone, Comanche, Mandan/Hidatsa, Gros Ventre, and other oral traditions maintain that Sacagawea lived to be an old woman (ninety-six to ninety-eight years old) and died on April 9, 1884. According to these oral traditions, Sacagawea (Bird Woman in Hidatsa; Boat Pusher in Shoshone), also known as Porivo (Chief Woman), Wadze Wipe (Lost Woman), and Bo-i-naiv (Grass Woman), left Charbonneau (perhaps around 1810) and wandered from tribe to tribe in the area that is now the states of Kansas and Oklahoma, finally settling with the Comanches, among whom she married and had children. Upon the death of her Comanche husband, Jerk Meat, she traveled up the Missouri River in search of her own people. Reunited with her son, Jean Baptiste (now Baptiste), and an adopted nephew, Bazil, she helped her Wind River Shoshone people in their transition to life on their newly created reservation. Venerated by her tribe, she was buried on the tribe's Wyoming reservation in 1884. Tribal historians argue that Charbonneau had at least two Shoshone wives and that Brackenridge and Luttig (who never named Sacagawea) misidentified the correct wife; they also contend that Clark's information about Sacagawea's whereabouts as recorded on the cover of his account book was inaccurate. The works of Charles

Eastman (Sioux) and Grace Hebard, while somewhat inconsistent and subjective, provide evidence to support this position.

Sacagawea has become an appealing figure in the history of the American West, and she continues to capture the romantic imagination of both Indian and non-Indian Americans. It has been said that there are more monuments, memorials, rivers, lakes, and mountain areas named after her than after any other American woman. Novelists, poets, historians, anthropologists, and feminists have resurrected, re-created, and immortalized the mystique of Sacagawea. Controversies and romance aside, however, Sacagawea emerges as a courageous, determined, and admirable Indian woman, and the ongoing disputes have served to keep the memory of this extraordinary woman alive.

Anderson, Irving W., "A Charbonneau Family Portrait," *The American West* 17, no. 2 (1980): 4–13; Howard, Harold, *Sacajawea* (Norman: University of Oklahoma Press, 1971).

SALLY MCBETH
University of Northern Colorado

SACHEM

The word *sachem,* of Algonquian origin, was used among some northeastern tribes to refer to their leaders. In contrast to chiefs, who were chosen for their skill in battle or oratory, sachems held hereditary, civil positions and ruled by consensus. Their responsibilities included the distribution of land, the dispensation of justice, the collection of tribute, the reception of guests, and sometimes the direction of war or the sponsoring of rituals. Only the rare sachem, such as Tispaquin, the "Black Sachem" of Assowampset, was also a shaman. Among the Narragansetts, sachems held sway over villages, which formed the basic political, territorial unit of the society. Villages were governed by a pair of patrilineally related older and younger sachems. Leaders among other northeastern tribes were sometimes also called sachems, but their authority was shared in a council, and some were appointed.

Most sachems were men, but many women are known to have been sachems as well. The most famous of the female sachems was the Narragansett sachem Quaiapen, also known as Magnus or Matantuck. In addition to establishing her own sachemdom after she was widowed in 1658, Quaiapen was the sister, wife, and mother of several other Narragansett sachems. Rumors among white colonists of her marriage in 1649 to the sachem Mixanno aroused fear of an Indian conspiracy. That fear took on a new form in 1675, when the Massachusetts Bay Colony went to war against the Wampanoag sachem Metacom, whom whites called King Philip. In an attempt to limit Philip's resources, the Bay Colony called on the Narragansetts to swear neutrality. When the Narragansetts failed to turn over any Wampanoag refugees, they too came under attack. Quaiapen was killed on July 2, 1676, in a battle with Major John Talcott's troops in a swamp near Nipsachuck; killed with her or captured in that battle were 171 of her followers.

The last of the Narragansett sachems was George Sachem, who ruled in the early nineteenth century. In keeping with its preference for employing Indian words, the infamous New York City political machine Tammany Hall called its local leaders sachems. But after the Indian Reorganization Act of 1934, the Narragansetts took the title back when they reincorporated their tribe and restored the ancient office.

SALISHAN LANGUAGES

The Salishan languages were spoken aboriginally along the Pacific Coast of British Columbia and Washington and eastward into western Montana. The homeland of the protolanguage was probably the delta of the Fraser River—the center of the coastal language distribution and the head of a route into the interior. Kootenay, a language isolate, may have a common ancestry with proto-Salish, based on two dozen similarities.

By 1800 the Salishan family consisted of twenty-three interlinked languages, separated by the Cascade Range into Coast (sixteen members) and Interior (seven members) divisions. Each member language also included several internal dialects.

The four branches within Coast Salish include Bella Coola (northernmost), Central, Tsamosan, and Tillamook (on the Oregon coast). Central Coast Salish, centered in the border homeland, includes Comox, Sechelt, Pentlatch, Squamish, Nooksak, Halkomelem (including Chilliwack, Musqueam, and Cowichan), Straits (including intergrading Sooke, Saanich, Songhees, Lummi, Samish, Semiahmoo, and Klallam, the most distinct), Twana, and Lushootseed (Puget). Tsamosan, sometimes called Olympic, includes Cowlitz, Upper (including Satsop) and Lower Chehalis, and Quinault.

Interior Salish, which arose later, consists of St'at'imcets (Lillooet), Nlakapamuxcin (Thompson), and Sexwepemuxcin (Shuswap) in British Columbia; the three Columbia River dialect chains of Methow-Okanogan-Nespelem-Sanpoil-Colvile-Lakes, Chelan-Entiat-Wenatchi-Columbian, and Kalispel-Spokan-Selish (Flathead); and, in Idaho, Coeur d'Alene.

As an example of internal diversity, Lushootseed, spoken north and south of modern Seattle, has two dialect chains: southern (Sahewamish-Nisqually-Puyallup-Duwamish-Suquamish-Snoqual-mi) and northern (Snohomish-Stillaguamish-Skagit). The Skykomish, about whom we know little, seem to have been intermediary between these two chains. Culturally, the most important distinction is the use of four as the pattern number in the north and of five in the south, presumably a borrowing from the Columbia River Chinook and upriver Plateau tribes.

Salishan languages consist overwhelmingly of verbs, with secondary additions to suggest that nouns are merely verbs made to hold still, and of consonants—often the same sounds spoken in both plain and glottalized (pronounced in the throat) versions. While three to five vowels are used, in rapid speech the vowels drop out so words with strings of four to six consonants are common. Indeed, Bella Coola, the first branch to separate, has many words without vowels. Further, particular sounds are characteristic of certain branches, such as the *ng* sound that occurs only in Straits.

As a family, Salish employs numerous suffixes and syllable copying (reduplication) to express shades of meaning. Unlike English, prefixes and infixes are uncommon.

The major categories of Salish grammar are aspect, transitivity, voice, person, gender, and control, with tense and number optional, depending on the individual language. Aspect indicates the manner or way in which something is done. In Salish, at least, aspect includes whether or not something is ongoing (durative), stative, or active. Transitivity—taking an object or not—is indicated by suffixes. Both active and passive voices occur, as do person (first, second, third) and gender (as female or other). Tense, to mark time, and number (singular or not) occur in many of these languages. Control, which is distinctive but not unique to Salish, automatically specifies the degree of involvement or care a speaker has in an action, ranging from the accidental to limited or full control. In English, lack of or limited control is often translated as "managed to," as in *I poured it* (full control), *I managed to pour it* (limited), *I spilled it* (lack). In Salish, all three ideas can be expressed by the same word modified by syllables indicating degree of control.

These languages create analogies and metaphorical extensions through compound words that include terms referring to some body parts (mouth, nose, foot), geography (beach, stream, path), and artifacts (thread, house, canoe). For example, the word for a headland jutting into the water derives from "nose," as does one of the terms for a leader, "the one who 'noses' ahead."

As an example of local innovations and specializations, Lushootseed is characterized by an ancient reworking of the two sets of transitive person markers, regularization of the suffix system, and an elaboration of prefixes. Over a century ago, Lushootseed and neighboring non-Salishan languages (Twana, Chimakum, and Southern Nootkan) shifted away from nasals so that former *m* became *b* and former *n* changed to *d*. Thus, any snowcapped mountain is now called *takoba,* which is developed from the name that settlers heard as *takoma* (Tacoma) and attributed to Mt. Rainier and a nearby city. Since the Lummis and Klallams—nasal-using Straits Salish—were expanding their territories around 1800, the shift from nasals by Lushootseeds, Twanas, Chimakums, and Southern Nootkans may have been a response to Straits depredations. Speakers of Nooksak, Twana, and Lushootseed were displaced, to some extent, by Klallam colonies.

Technical and teaching grammars, dictionaries, and stories exist for almost all Salishan languages. Only Pentlatch and Nooksak, virtually extinct, are documented solely in manuscripts. Nevertheless, English and television are seriously eroding the perpetuation of these languages, which survive better in Canada, with its polyglot governmental policies, than in the United States. In Canada, some Salishan languages became extinct not because they were replaced by English but because so many speakers of another Salishan language had married into the community that the old language was replaced by another Salishan example; for instance, Halkomelem replaced Nooksak, and Pentlatch shifted to Comox.

Most linguists prefer to treat Salish as a distinct family, finding relations with other major native language groups hard to substantiate. Several decades ago a grouping was proposed to combine Salish with the neighboring Wakashan family and the transcontinental stock of Algonquian or Algic languages, but this superstock seems unlikely.

Among young people, Salish survives in disconnected words for particular kin, native foods, and special places. Names, still expressed in Salish rather than translated into English, continue to be passed on with feasting and formalities. Prayers and hymns to local spirits and the Creator also remain in these languages, and probably will do so forever.

Kinkade, Dale, "Salish Evidence against the Universality of 'Noun' and 'Verb,'" *Lingua: International Review of General Linguistics* 60, no. 1 (1983): 25–39; Thompson, Laurence, "Salishan and the Northwest," in *The Languages of Native North America: Historical and Comparative Assessment,* ed. Lyle Campbell and Marianne Mithun (Austin: University of Texas Press, 1979).

JAY MILLER (Lenape)
Lushootseed Research

SAND CREEK MASSACRE

On November 29, 1864, approximately 450 Southern Cheyennes following Black Kettle, and 40 Southern Arapahos under Left Hand, camped on Sand Creek, about fifty miles north of present-day Lamar, Colorado. At dawn, Colonel John M. Chivington's 700 Colorado volunteers, along with Major Scot Anthony's command of 125 regular army troops, attacked the unsuspecting villagers. These Plains Indian peoples thought themselves under U.S. Army protection, but the deaths of over 70 Indians, and the horrible mutilation of many of their bodies, proved otherwise.

This unwarranted attack came after mounting numbers of freighters, overlanders, and military personnel had, with their thousands of stock animals, destroyed the bison economy of the Plains Indians. Recently arrived farmers and ranchers had little regard for the Indians' plight. Retaliatory raids launched by a few Plains warriors inflamed the settlers' irrational fears and sparked demands for the eradication of all Indian peoples in the region.

After the Sand Creek Massacre, Black Kettle and his people abandoned the Colorado plains, and white Coloradans hailed Chivington as a hero. But when detailed news of the attack reached the East, many reacted with disgust. Both an army and a congressional commission investigated Chivington's actions, but no official censure resulted.

In the summer of 1993, as a result of federal legislation passed in 1989 directing the Smithsonian Institution to repatriate its Indian remains, a delegation of

Southern Cheyennes traveled to Washington, D.C., and retrieved the remains of six Sand Creek victims for a ceremonial burial at Concho, Oklahoma.

SAND PAINTING

Sand painting is a spiritual art form that emerged among the Pueblo peoples and spread westward to the Navajos, Apaches, Tohono O'odhams (Papagos), Zunis, and southern California tribes during the seventeenth century. Today the Navajos are the most active practitioners of this art. The traditional materials used in sand painting include sands of natural colors, cornmeal, flower and corn pollen, and powdered roots and bark. Individuals sprinkled these materials on the ground to form sacred symbols and representations of supernatural beings. All sand paintings are prescribed and complex; only a chanter/singer may create a sand painting in ceremonies such as the Navajo Blessing Way or curing rituals. Sand paintings were never meant to be permanent or to be marketed commercially. They are ritual objects that bring the past, present, and future into a single moment in order to unite a patient with time in the universe. Traditionally they would be erased immediately upon conclusion of the ceremony. Those who practice traditional sand painting oppose keeping sand paintings intact and permanent because the power generated by the designs can bring harm to those who encounter them.

Recent interest in sand painting as a popular art form has led to decorative innovations. Commercial artists use nontraditional materials and employ sand painting motifs in textiles and other objects. Despite this popularization, sand painting remains an important part of ceremonial life for southwestern tribes, and concerns about the art form's exploitation continue.

See also Art, Visual (to 1960).

SANTEE NORMAL TRAINING SCHOOL

The Santee Normal Training School was a missionary boarding school located in Santee, Nebraska, on the Santee Indian Reservation. It was established by Alfred L. Riggs of the American Board of Commissioners for Foreign Missions in 1870 to train native teachers. The school functioned until 1938.

The Santee Normal Training School soon became a center of education for all the Sioux. It reached its high points in enrollment and influence in the early 1890s. It published *Iapi Oaye/Word Carrier,* a bilingual monthly periodical, from 1875 to 1937. The school originally used Dakota as its primary teaching language. Dakota was replaced by English in 1887 in response to a threat from the Bureau of Indian Affairs to end its financial subsidy for the school. (The BIA eventually withdrew funding anyway, in 1893.) Though Dakota was no longer spoken in the classroom, it did continue to be used in *Iapi Oaye.*

See also Boarding Schools; Education.

SAUK

The Sauks call themselves *asa-ki-waki,* meaning "people of the outlet" in their Algonquian language. "The outlet" refers to the Saginaw River of Michigan, and denotes the area where they first gathered together as a people and from which they were driven by the Iroquois in the early seventeenth century. French missionaries found the Sauks near Green Bay in the 1660s. They remained in what is now Wisconsin until 1733, when they incurred French enmity for sheltering Fox refugees from the Fox-French war. The Sauks and their neighbors the Foxes fled to Iowa, but after 1737 they moved their villages back across the Mississippi to the lower Rock and Wisconsin Valleys. Early nineteenth-century U.S. settlers encroached upon Sauk and Fox lands, and the tribes shifted to Iowa, but in 1832 Black Hawk, a Sauk war chief and the leader of a pro-British band within the tribes, led a Sauk minority back to Saukenak, near Rock Island, Illinois. Federal and Illinois territorial officials launched an armed expedition against Black Hawk. The Black Hawk War ended at the mouth of the Bad Axe River, where 150 of the chief's followers were slaughtered, followed shortly by the killing of more people by Sioux warriors. Keokuk, the leader of the pro-American party within the tribe, and Fox chiefs negotiated a series of cession treaties for the tribes' Iowa land, after which they were assigned a reservation in Kansas. In 1869 all but Mokohoko's band moved to Oklahoma. That band finally moved to Oklahoma in 1886, sharing a reservation until 1891, when what was officially called the Sac and Fox Tribe of Oklahoma was placed on 160-acre allotments. In 1902 new federal legislation permitted many tribal members to sell their trust land; in 1951 the Oklahoma Sauks and Foxes retained only 30 percent of their allotted land.

Early Sauk population figures are only estimates and vary from six hundred in 1734 to four thousand in 1822. Since Sauk and Fox people intermarried very frequently, the joint Sauk-Fox population is easier to approximate. The numbers of Sauks and Foxes are given as sixty-four hundred in 1825, twenty-two hundred in 1845, nine hundred seventy-five in 1909, eighteen hundred in 1950, and thirty-five hundred in 1990. The latter two numbers include those people, predominantly Foxes, who resettled and purchased land near Tama, Iowa.

A horticultural and hunting people, the Sauks traditionally lived in a spring and summer village when not dispersed for fall and winter hunting. Villages often consisted of groups of extended families and were usually identified by outsiders as the collective residences of a "band." Summer shelter consisted of substantial pole-and-bark longhouses, while hunting-camp shelters were portable pole-and-reed mat lodges. Corn was the principal food crop, supplemented by squash, beans, wild rice, and meat, including buffalo. In the nineteenth century Sauk women were reported to have produced about eight thousand bushels of corn, selling some to traders. Men hunted for pelts and hides, trading them for blankets, guns, ammunition, knives, and camp equipment. When living in northwestern Illinois, the Sauks engaged in surface lead mining, smelting some ore but selling most of it to traders. On their Oklahoma reservation, the Sauks resisted government efforts to transform them into farmers, preferring small-scale ranches and subsistence gardens. Their reluctance to farm is demonstrated by the rapid sale of their allotted land. The development of the Cushing oil field after 1912 brought wealth to a few Sauk families.

Descent among the Sauks was patrilineal, and their clans were exogamous. Two divisions or moieties existed: *aškaša* (black) and *ki·ško·ha* (white). Early on, these divisions likely referred to warrior organizations, but by the mid–nineteenth century parents assigned their first child to the *aškaša* and the second to the *ki·ško·ha,* alternating later children among the divisions. At dances and ceremonies, division members assembled together and competed during games. Naming or clan bundles were primarily used well into the twentieth century at children's naming ceremonies, when an elderly man of the father's clan conferred a name and announced to which division the child belonged. Males retained the given name until acquiring another after a memorable war exploit.

The political organization of the Sauks was complex. The Sturgeon clan traditionally supplied a principal chief, but other clans also had chiefs assisted by criers or runners; all of these offices were hereditary. People also gathered about band chiefs such as Keokuk, Black Hawk, Grey Eyes, and Mokohoko. There was in addition a war chief for each of the divisions. One war chief, Keokuk, was able to overshadow the hereditary chiefs, acquiring support from government officials and American Fur Company agents. He incurred the hostility of the other chiefs, especially when federal officials entrusted him with the distribution of annuities and recognized him as tribal chief. After Keokuk's death in 1848, Moses, his son, succeeded him, serving as tribal chief until his death in 1903.

Traditional leadership was abolished in 1885 by a constitution that provided for a multiple executive, a representative assembly, and court and police systems. Never thoroughly accepted, the executive was replaced in 1891 by two chiefs and eight councilmen, who in turn were dismissed in 1909. For about ten years a three-man business committee was appointed by the Sac and Fox Agency superintendent. Finally, in 1937 the Sac and Fox Tribe of Oklahoma adopted a constitution, as provided for by the 1936 Oklahoma Indian Welfare Act, that incorporated the tribe and created an elected business committee and principal chief.

Contemporary Sauk society little resembles the old way of life. Gone are the medicine dances, naming ceremonies, and war and medicine bundles. Christianity began replacing the veneration of spirits after 1876, when Moses Keokuk converted to Christianity. Early in the twentieth century the peyote ceremony was practiced simultaneously with Christian observance; today only a few peyotists remain among Sauk people. Tribal members intermarried extensively with members of other tribes and with non-Indians. Many are not unlike the "world's greatest athlete," Jim Thorpe, who could claim descent from Black Hawk but whose father was half Sauk and half Irish and whose mother was of Potawatomi, Kickapoo, and white descent. Education, the experience of living and working in non-Indian communities, and an inherent ability to adapt speeded acculturation so that many tribal members are now indistinguishable from their white neighbors. A diminishing minority of the tribe live within the boundaries of their former Oklahoma reservation, but many assemble for the annual Sac and Fox Powwow, held near Shawnee, Oklahoma, on tribal land.

See also Fox/Mesquakie.

Hagan, William T., *The Sac and Fox Indians* (Norman: University of Oklahoma Press, 1958); Skinner, Alanson, *Observations on the Ethnology of the Sauk Indians* (1923–25; reprint, Westport, Conn.: Greenwood Press, 1970).

DONALD J. BERTHRONG
Lafayette, Indiana

SAVAGE, SAVAGES, SAVAGISM

The concept of the savage predates the European colonization of North America by several millennia. The word has its root in the Latin *silvaticus*, meaning "in a state of nature," "of a woodland," or "wild." (*Silvaticus* itself is linked to silva, "wood" or "forest"). In Spanish, the Latin word became *salvage*; in French, *sauvage*. Closely related words that are instructive in this context are *pagan*, from the Latin *paganus*, "villager," "rustic," "not of the city"; *heathen*, from an Old English word meaning "of the heath," "a person of a vast wasteland"; and *barbarian*, from a Greek root meaning "one whose language and customs differ [from the speaker's]."

The antecedents of the word *savage* suggest an ideology that holds people who are different or who live in the woods or rustic settings to be inferior or primitive. When one recalls that European treatment of so-called primitive people was based on the ancient Aristotelian formulation that some peoples are, by their nature, candidates for slavery, while superior peoples are within their rights to enslave them, then the real-world consequences of these categories of us and them become self-evident.

As a corollary to these ancient concepts and connotations, one should also consider the situation in Europe in 1492. In that year the Spanish had finally concluded Europe's efforts to expel the Jews and the darker, non-Christian Moors from the continent, and virtually all of Europe was in the throes of religious anxiety. Witch-hunts, inquisitions, and sectarian conflict bubbled forth throughout the continent.

Europe's protracted war against witches had taken on a new dimension in 1486 with the publication of the Malleus Maleficarum. The book was written by two Dominican monks, Johann Sprenger and Heinrich Kraemer, and was sanctioned by Pope Innocent VIII. It was widely popular and set off a renewed and feverish wave of witch-hunting that lasted for two centuries. Its authors had three aims: first, to prove that witches did indeed exist; second, to provide a manual for the detection of witches along with a recounting of their activities; and third, to furnish a legal guide for the torture of suspected witches and their subsequent punishment or execution.

Under torture, suspected witches admitted to all sorts of encounters with Satan and his cohorts; some sexual, many mocking the established religion, and all invariably taking place in the woods far from public view. The image of the devil that emerged from such confessions is often that of a being with a dark or red visage and, if not naked, clothed in the skins of animals or decorated with feathers. Such a description stands in sharp contrast to the biblical image of Lucifer, the beautiful archangel, the Prince of Light. Further complicating the issue was the fact that most often the suspected witches were women whose alleged crime was often associated with their knowledge of unauthorized herbal healing.

It is of little wonder, then, that when Columbus encountered the indigenous people of the Caribbean he applied the current Eurocentric interpretation to their "devilish" mein: the natives were darker than Columbus and his men, they lived in a decidedly rural and rustic environment, and they decorated themselves with the feathers of colorful tropical birds and the skins of animals. In addition, they healed with herbs and the women and men enjoyed equal status. Columbus, the first to actually describe these people, did so by cataloging the things they lacked. To him, it appeared the native people had no clothes, no laws, no religion, no weapons, no customs, and no private property. Consequently, he believed they were indeed barbarians and savages. As Columbus fit what he saw into his own linguistic and intellectual framework, he invented the notion of the savage native.

Columbus applied one further descriptive term to the people he encountered: he called them *Los Indios*—Indians. In the Europe of 1492, *India* was synonymous with the land east of the Indus River, and the term Indians was therefore applied to all of the area's Indian and Asian people. Indeed, Columbus was certain that he had discovered the "Indies." The effects of this misapplication go far beyond the confusion it engenders in attempting to distinguish between Asian and American Indians. Use of this all-embracing term masked the distinctive characteristics of the various indigenous peoples long after Europeans came to recognize that they had encountered hundreds of unique and autonomous native groups. From the European perspective, the most important quality of these many groups was their difference from "civilized" norms.

By the Papal Bull of 1493, the church granted the kings of Spain and Portugal the right to settle and possess vast tracts of what is now Africa and the Americas. As these two ambitious states expanded their realms, they encountered hundreds of new societies, the humanity of whose members became the topic of vigorous debate. This debate reached its peak in 1550 at the Spanish court in Valladolid, when Bartolomé de las Casas, a Spanish priest, and Juan Gines Sepulveda squared off to settle the matter once and for all.

Sepulveda had gained influence in the Spanish court by writing a treatise justifying war against the native people of the Americas. Indians, he stated, "are inferior to the Spanish, just as children are to adults, women to men, and, indeed, one may even say, as apes are to men." Las Casas had spent several years in the Caribbean and Central America and had gained his understanding of the native people firsthand; Sepulveda had never visited the Americas and based his argument on popular stereotypes. The debate revolved around the question of whether the peoples of the New World were in possession of a soul. If so, they were worthy of humane treatment and of attempts to convert them to Christianity; if not, they were destined for conquest and enslavement.

Although a final verdict was never reached, the special Spanish court convened to hear the case seemed to side with Las Casas, and the court issued a directive counseling more humane treatment of the hemisphere's native people. But the directive was widely disregarded. In the colonies, imperial ambition created its own definition of the Indians. When native people refused to accept the Christian religion and rejected the continuing Eurocentric view of their cultures, European soldiers and governors insisted that their resistance proved their ignorance and inferiority. For example, after the Acoma Pueblo refused to supply food to Spanish colonists under Juan de Oñate in 1599, the Spanish commander punished them for their impudence by decreeing that all males over the age of twenty-five would have one foot cut off and would be required to give the Spanish twenty years of servitude.

The English defeat of the Spanish Armada in 1588 opened North America to a new wave of colonizing Europeans. By the time of the Pilgrims' arrival in 1620, most Europeans had accepted the belief in the savage nature of the continent's peoples. Despite the efforts of

las Casas and others, the Plymouth Colony's future governor, William Bradford, expressed this deeply embedded notion when he declared in 1617: "The unpeopled countries of America [are] devoid of all civil inhabitants, where there are only savage and brutish men, which range up and down, little otherwise than the wild beasts of the same." Bradford made this statement three years before the landing at Plymouth Rock. This view of the "savage" Americans was coupled with the Pilgrims' belief in a divinely mandated mission to found a new civilization upon this "empty land."

The concept of savagery imputed diabolical motives to New World peoples, whose acceptance of Christianity was thus equal to their salvation and civilization. The Native Americans' resistance to English proselytizing and their refusal to accept British ways only served to reinforce the European view of them as being in league with the devil. For example, the Indian uprising in Virginia in 1622 was put forth as proof of native savagery. The Native Americans' defense of their homeland in the face of English encroachment was transformed by the English notion of savagism into an assault on civility and Christianity. Consequently, after the Jamestown attack, the English—as a demonstration of their faith and in defense of civilization—declared a war of annihilation. As with the Spanish, the English colonists found in the notion of savagery a justification for their own imperial ambitions.

Over time, the equation of Indians with savagery became formalized into a philosophy scholars now refer to as *savagism*. According to the tenets of this outlook, Indians are (1) emotional rather than rational; (2) morally and culturally deficient; (3) uncivilized; (4) genetically inferior; (5) untrustworthy (although individuals have the potential to be "noble"); (6) generally lazy and indolent; and (7) often immorally sensual in their nature. The logical outcome of this array of qualities was the belief that Indians belonged to a vanishing race, one that must necessarily perish in the face of civilized "progress." The succession of savagery by civilization also served as an additional justification for "civilizing" (that is, dismantling) native societies. From this perspective, converting "savages" to "civilization"—which often entailed destroying their ancient traditions—could be understood as humanitarian. Invaders could thus recast themselves as civilizers dedicated to the salvation of native barbarians. The internal logic of these concepts required non-Indians to be seen as rational, civilized, moral, trustworthy, hard working, and triumphant.

At times, white society became convinced that the Indian could not be "civilized." In the early nineteenth century many argued that the savage Indian had to be isolated—set apart from the non-Indian. They proposed a federal policy of removal under which all of the Native American people who lived east of the Mississippi—even the so-called Five Civilized Tribes of the Southeast—were to be forced west, to evolve and progress on their own.

Later in the nineteenth century, Indians who were shown to have accepted the "civilizing" notions of white society were given the option of rejecting all tribal connections. Thus Native people could gain U.S. citizenship (which was not granted to all native people until 1924). Any faithful reading of American history will reveal that attempts to "civilize savages" through an insistence on English language usage, Christian conversion, and so forth never abated. Yet the concept of savagism is not restricted to Native American experience. Today terms such as "war lord," "tribes," and "clan violence" are a common feature of descriptions of non-Western peoples. In contrast, discussions of European countries refer to "presidents" and political "parties." The division of the world into "settled" and "wild" communities persists.

While terms of inferiority such as *pagan, heathen, barbarian,* and *savage* are now generally avoided in the United States, the Eurocentric psyche continues to reflect the tradition of viewing others through the lens of savagism. Even though both the negative stereotypes devised by non-Indians and the popular image of the savage can be shown to rest upon false representation of indigenous people, we cannot assume that the savage formulation has disappeared. Abolishing the habit of casting others as inferiors will require a fundamental shift in Euro-American identity. Consequently, we should not think of the concept of the savage and the formal philosophy of savagism as mere historical anomalies. Current popular conceptions of the world's "other people"—American Indians included—continue to embrace these false and destructive beliefs.

Berkhofer, Robert F., *The White Man's Indian: Images of the American Indian from Columbus to the Present* (New York: Knopf, 1978); Pearce, Roy Harvey, *Savagism and Civilization: A Study of the Indian and the American Mind* (Baltimore: Johns Hopkins Press, 1967); Todorov, Tzvetan, *The Conquest of America: The Question of the Other* (New York: Harper and Row, 1984).

PHIL BELLFY (White Earth Anishinaabe)
Sault Ste. Marie, Michigan

SCALPS AND SCALPING

Before the 1960s most Americans believed that scalping was a distinctive military custom of the American Indians. History books and the popular media all attributed scalping to Indians, who collected the scalplocks of enemies as war trophies and proof of their valor in battle.

But with the advent of the Red Power and other countercultural movements in the 1960s, many people, Indians and non-Indians alike, began to argue that Native Americans had never scalped until they were taught and encouraged to do so by European colonists, who offered them monetary bounties for the scalps of the settlers' enemies. Since this new version of Indian history sounded plausible and suited the anti-Establishment tenor of the times, it was quickly adopted by many as conventional wisdom.

To be accurate, however, we must acknowledge the following. First, the only non-Indians known to have scalped their enemies were the Scythians, nomadic Eurasian peoples who flourished from the eighth to the fourth century B.C. The ancient Greeks regarded them as "barbarians" for their practice of making napkins from head scalps and for decorating their persons and their horses' bridles with them. When Europeans of the sixteenth and seventeenth centuries wished to terrorize their enemies, rather than scalping the dead they decapitated them and mounted the heads in prominent places, a practice they continued in America.

Second, there is no evidence that colonial officials ever taught their Indian allies to take scalps. In the seventeenth century, European traders did introduce to native markets so-called scalping knives. But these were ordinary, all-purpose butcher knives, which the natives used more for cutting meat, wood, and skins than for lifting scalps. They were bought by Indian women as well as men because they were more durable and held an edge longer than knives of flint, reed, or shell.

Finally, while there is no evidence for European knowledge of scalping before the arrival of Europeans in the New World, we have abundant evidence that scalping took place in native America well before Europeans arrived. There are four different kinds of evidence, the best of which is archaeological. Two kinds of skulls from precontact sites east and west of the Mississippi, from as early as 2500 to 500 B.C. right up to contact, provide evidence of scalping. The majority of these skulls exhibit circular or successive cuts or scratches just where scalps were traditionally lifted.

Some tribes took only a small patch of skin attached to a male victim's specially braided and decorated scalplock at the hair's whorl or vertex, which left little mark on the skull. But many tribes took larger scalps, sometimes from the middle of the forehead or hairline all the way back to the neck, with or without the ears. To extract such a scalp, the warrior probably put one foot on the prone victim's back, pulled back his or her head by the hair, made an incision with a knife across the forehead and around the sides to the back, and then cut or tore the whole skin away from the skull. A nonmetal knife used forcefully to cut away the skin often scratched the bone, leaving telltale marks.

Even better evidence is provided by lesions on the skulls of victims who survived scalping long enough to allow the bone tissue to partially regenerate, leaving a distinctive dark ring where the skull had been cut and infected. Contrary to popular belief, scalping was not necessarily fatal. The historical record is full of survivors, so many that in 1805–6 a physician published "Remarks on the Management of the Scalped-Head" in a Philadelphia medical journal.

The most familiar kind of evidence for pre-Columbian scalping comes from written descriptions by some of the earliest European observers, who saw the Indian cultures of the eastern seaboard in virtually aboriginal condition. On his voyage up the St. Lawrence in 1535–36, Jacques Cartier was shown by the Stadaconans at Quebec "the skins of five men's heads, stretched on hoops, like parchment." In 1540, two of Hernando de Soto's men, the first Europeans to reach west Florida, were seized by Indians. The killers of one "removed his head, or rather all around his skull . . . and carried it off as evidence of their deed." Twenty years later, another Spanish *entrada* reached the Creek town of Coosa on the Alabama River and accompanied local warriors on a raid against an enemy town. They found it abandoned, but in its plaza was a war pole "full of hair locks of the Coosans. It was the custom of the Indians to flay the head of the enemy dead," wrote a chronicler, "and to hang the resulting skin and locks insultingly on that pole." Much angered, the Coosans cut down the pole and carried the scalps home to bury them with proper respect and ceremony.

Virtually every major group of European explorers found scalping among the eastern Indians in the earliest stages of contact, before native customs had changed appreciably or at all. Later descriptions closely resembled earlier ones. The first characteristic they share is an expression of surprise at the discovery of such a novel practice. The nearly universal highlighting of scalping in the early literature, the search for comparisons intelligible to European readers (such as parchment or vellum), the detailed anatomical descriptions of the act itself, and the total absence of any suggestion of European precedence or familiarity with the practice at all suggest that scalping was unique to native America.

These descriptions also indicate that the actual taking of a scalp was firmly embedded in other customs whose forms and patterning varied markedly from tribe to tribe and area to area. In some areas of North America and most of South America, scalping was not in vogue before contact. But in the Southeast, the Northeast, parts of the Southwest, and on the Great Plains, scalping was richly associated with a wide variety of customs.

Scalps were elaborately prepared by drying, stretching on hoops, painting, and decorating. Warriors gave special scalp yells when a scalp was taken and when it was carried home on a raised pole, bough, or bow. Men grew scalplocks to symbolize their soul or personhood; these were never touched without grave insult, because their loss was tantamount to social death, even if physical death did not occur. Young males earned status by taking the scalp of an enemy, which then could be adopted by a family, like a living captive, to replace a dead member or to avenge the dead person's restless spirit. Scalps were given to chiefs or loved ones or worn on a horse's bridle or as fringe on a buckskin war shirt. At a warrior's death, his accumulated scalps might be buried with him or hung on his grave marker. Scalps were routinely displayed on palisades, cabins, and canoes to intimidate enemies and to impress allies. And scalps were always treated ritually, most often in dances to celebrate victory and to thank the appropriate gods.

There is also pictorial evidence for Indian scalping. The most important picture is Theodore de Bry's engraving of Jacques Le Moyne's drawing *Treatment of the Enemy Dead by Outina's Forces*. Based on Le Moyne's observations in Florida in 1564, the 1591 engraving was the first public representation of Indian scalping, one faithful to Le Moyne's written description and to subsequent accounts from other regions of eastern America. The details of using sharp reeds to remove the scalp, then drying the green skin over a fire, displaying the trophies on long poles, and later celebrating the victory with established rituals by the native priest lend authenticity to de Bry's rendering.

Indian pictographs, carved on trees as messages to following tribesmen, add to the evidence. The usual symbol for a scalping victim was a stylized figure without a head. This makes sense because scalping probably developed from head taking when skulls were too heavy or cumbersome to carry home as trophies. Scalps were occasionally lifted at home from head trophies or from live prisoners undergoing torture.

Finally, Indian languages contain many specialized expressions for the scalp, the act of scalping, and the victim of scalping. Muskogean languages in the South, Iroquoian in the Northeast, and Algonquian around the Great Lakes possess ancient root words for "scalp" that are cognate with equally ancient words for "head" or "hair," and verb forms for "lifting" the scalp, which is probably the source, by loan translation, of the colonial English expression "to lift hair" and the French *enlever le chevelure*. Ojibwa warriors distinguished between "scalp" and "Sioux scalp." Eastern Abenakis had words to tell the difference between an enemy scalp that had already been taken and one that was being or could be taken.

Although the American Indians took scalps long before 1492, Europeans promoted the spread and frequency of scalping by trading the natives guns (leading to more deaths) and knives (making scalp removal easier) and, from 1637, by offering bounties for Indian and, after 1688, European scalps.

Axtell, James, "Scalping: The Ethnohistory of a Moral Question," and Axtell, James, and William C. Sturtevant, "The Unkindest Cut, or Who Invented Scalping?: A Case Study"; in Axtell, James, *The European and the Indian: Essays in the Ethnohistory of Colonial North America* (New York: Oxford University Press, 1981).

JAMES AXTELL
College of William and Mary

SCHOLARSHIP

See Anthropology and Indians; Archaeology and Indians; Bibliographies; Historians and Indians; Museums and Collectors; Native American Studies.

SCOUTS

When Europeans came to the New World in the fifteenth century, they were in the midst of a significant and quite deadly revolution in warfare at home. Gunpowder had brought numerous changes in the dealing of death on the battlefield, not the least of which was the ability to kill people, notably upper-class knights, at greater distances and in ever-increasing numbers. Although small arms and cannon had been used on European battlefields in the fourteenth century, their tactical and strategic value was not fully realized until after they had gone through a fairly lengthy period of technical development. These weapons were effective in routing closely packed, pike-wielding infantry formations and reducing to rubble the old feudal castles; but they were also cumbersome, slow firing, and extremely expensive. European armies, although they could deliver a strong initial punch on the battlefield, lacked mobility and were unable to use the topography of a given region particularly well. Consequently, European battles in the three hundred years between 1500 and 1800 were either sieges or sanguinary affairs in which two armies met on a fairly level piece of ground literally to slug it out with cannon or musket balls until one side or the other was driven from the field.

On the surface, the native peoples of the New World appear to have been disadvantaged in the extreme when it came to fighting off the European invaders. Native Americans utterly lacked firearms. Moreover, most native people viewed warfare in very different terms than did Europeans. Native American nations might have looked upon warfare as a disruptive force, a method of gaining a degree of economic gain in raiding, a ritual of manhood, part of a cycle of ceremonial mourning and retribution, or a spiritual contest between two traditional enemies. Rarely did Native Americans see warfare as a means of conquering vast territories or obliterating entire societies.

On the other hand, Native Americans knew their environments and how to use topography to their advantage in battle. Young native males, taught from childhood to track game and deal with the hazards, fatigue, hardships, and frustrations of the hunt, were also taught that their hunting skills were useful in combat. Native Americans for the most part were lightly armed, highly mobile, and extremely resourceful in terms of supplying themselves while on campaign, and they had a knowledge of terrain that the Europeans could not hope to gain within a short span of time.

Europeans, then, certainly had the advantage of firepower over Native Americans, but they lacked tactical knowledge of the New World's natural environments. Except for a small minority of officers, European battlefield commanders were locked into a particular tactical and strategic mindset. To be used effectively, musketry and cannon presumably had to be concentrated and synchronized to fire great volumes of projectiles at the same time. Battles had to take place on open ground in set positions, and firepower was to be used against an enemy's concentrated force. When Native Americans began to obtain firearms and adapt them to traditional battlefield tactics used in raiding other tribes, Europeans incrementally lost whatever advantage firearms had secured for them in the first place.

As they began to lose their firepower advantage, the Europeans realized that in order to conquer Native American nations they would have to modify both their tactics and their strategies to suit warfare in the New World. Consequently, each of the imperial powers sought to secure native allies and auxiliaries. Soon these colonial powers—Spain, Great Britain, France, the Netherlands, and Portugal—were locked into great struggles for control of New World resources. In their numerous wars with each other, all utilized native allies as shock troops, skirmishers, and, most importantly, scouts.

Intelligence gathering was and is of enormous strategic and tactical importance. Knowing enemy troop movements, weapons capabilities and emplacements, fortifications, and numbers gave commanders in the field advantages that could win battles and even wars, provided, of course, that these bits of information were reported accurately and quickly. Colonial military leaders began to understand that Native American scouts, utilizing their stalking skills and other outdoor abilities to the utmost, could locate, pinpoint, and report on enemy activities without endangering their own troops. They also learned that spying on and defeating Native American warriors in battle required the expertise and tactical knowledge of other Native Americans.

Native scouts and native tactical knowledge became legendary. Americans seem always to have attributed their victory in the Revolutionary War to their use of Indian tactics and stealth, previously learned during their numerous wars against the tribes. In 1799 Captain James Smith, a former captive of the Caugnawagas and commander of a commando-type American unit during the Revolution, wrote a treatise on Indian warfare admonishing his countrymen not to become entirely complacent in their military capabilities just because

they had defeated their British adversaries. Native Americans, he stated, were still capable of inflicting defeat after defeat on the new American nation, primarily because of their knowledge of the land and because "war is their principal study."

Although it is typically ignored as such, the recruitment of Native American allies and scouts was a major American policy decision every bit as calculated and beneficial to the federal government as Indian removal, the allotment of tribal lands, or the reservation system. It was predicated on the idea that traditional intertribal enmities could be used against tribes hostile to U.S. expansionism. It was also eventually seen as a method of gradually acclimating native scouts and allies to American customs and practices. In short, the militarization of Native Americans became what was called a "civilizing force."

The policy worked well for the Americans. In its first decisive victory over a large Native American force, the new U.S. Army in 1791 defeated an intertribal confederacy in the old Northwest Territory that had previously inflicted over nine hundred casualties on American troops. The leader of the victorious American army, General "Mad" Anthony Wayne, purposely brought along a contingent of Choctaw and Chickasaw warriors as light infantrymen and scouts. Later Andrew Jackson would employ Cherokee "guides" against the Creeks and Seminoles. By the outbreak of the Civil War, Indian scouts had been used in nearly every continental American conflict, including the Mexican War of 1846–48. Native Americans also served in the Civil War on both sides, but as scouts they acted primarily against other Native American tribes.

Historically, Congress usually cuts military spending following a major American conflict. An urge to impose austerity on the military followed the Civil War, despite the fact that the army was to aid in reconstructing the South and was engaged in a series of wars with Native American tribes in the Southwest, in California, and on the Great Plains. Badly needing personnel knowledgeable about these new territories and about the tribes living in them, the army pressured Congress into passing a statute in 1866 that provided for the establishment of a branch of the military called the Indian Scouting Service. Army officers on the frontiers knew exactly which intertribal enmities would benefit their mission and duly began to recruit scouts from among the enemies of the tribes hostile to the United States. Soon Pawnees were scouting against the Lakotas and the Cheyennes in the North;

Osages led expeditions against the Comanches and Kiowas on the southern plains; Klamaths were employed as scouts in the war on the Modocs in Oregon and California; and Crow and Arikara scouts were with George A. Custer prior to the Battle of the Little Bighorn. In Texas, a number of black freedmen of Seminole-African heritage were utilized as scouts against several tribes. And in the Southwest, Apaches were enlisted to follow and fight other Apaches who chose to escape the living conditions and confinement of the reservation.

Unlike the previous policy of simply employing scouts from allied tribes who would be dismissed after the conflict was over, the newly formed Scouting Service was a permanent branch of the army. The scouts were enlisted personnel on the army payroll, and subject to military discipline and training. On the other hand, the Indian Scouting Service was always subject to budgetary restrictions and was brought together on a piecemeal basis whenever a crisis arose. For example, in 1876, the year Custer met his demise, Congress had appropriated only enough money for the army to maintain three hundred scouts. It was soon realized that the army did not have the wherewithal to combat the hostile tribes with such limited personnel, and Congress immediately repealed the limiting provision in spite of its interest in austerity.

As a military branch, the Indian Scouting Service stayed intact for seventy-seven years. Members of the organization fought in the Spanish American War and were utilized by General John Pershing in the campaign against Pancho Villa in 1916. Pershing brought a contingent of Apache scouts to France when the United States entered World War I. The military record of the Scouting Service is without parallel: between 1872 and 1890, sixteen Native American members of the branch were awarded Congressional Medals of Honor. The scouts were disbanded in 1943, but in the previous year the Army Special Forces, an elite branch, adopted the service's crossed-arrow insignia. The last scout, Sergeant William Major, an Apache, retired from the army in 1948.

Downey, Fairfax, and Jacques Noel Jacobson, Jr., *The Red Bluecoats* (Fort Collins, Colo.: Old Army Press, 1973); Grinnell, George Bird, *Two Great Scouts and Their Pawnee Battalion* (Cleveland: Arthur H. Clark, 1928); Utley, Robert M., and Wilcomb E. Washburn, *Indian Wars* (Boston: Houghton Mifflin, 1987).

TOM HOLM (Cherokee/Creek)
University of Arizona

SEATTLE (SI'AŁ)

(c. 1786–1866)
Duwamish, Suquamish, and Lushootseed war leader and diplomat.

Seattle, born on Blake Island in Elliot Bay (fronting what would become the city named for him), built upon his ancestral rank among the native nobility to rise to prominence in the aftermath of Euro-American settlement in the Pacific Northwest.

Traditionally, each river draining into Puget Sound was occupied by a tribe sharing a common language, foods, and customs. All of these tribes spoke languages belonging to the Lushootseed (Puget) branch of the Coast Salish family. Interlinking this entire region was a system of three social classes composed of nobility, commoners, and slaves, the latter either war captives or their descendants. Nobility was based on an unblemished genealogy, intertribal kinship, the wise use of resources, and the possession of knowledge about the workings of spirits and the world, whispered only to family members in closely guarded circumstances. The free born also looked different because their mothers carefully shaped their heads as babies by binding them into stiff cradle boards, which produced a steep slope to the forehead.

Whereas everyone worked to hunt game and fish, especially salmon, the leaders of a household, town, or tribe worked as executives, making sure that economic and social activities ran smoothly. When things went well, members of the community provided the leading families with fresh food to compensate for time spent giving help and advice instead of getting provisions. Leaders were expected to have several wives, all of good families, to increase their supply of stored food and hospitality. Of course, leaders also had slaves who did much of the routine work of getting water, firewood, and food.

Seattle was born into this intertribal nobility. His father, Shweabe, was a Suquamish from the west side of Puget Sound, and his mother, Sholitza, was a Duwamish from the White River of the eastern sound. Her family has passed on the name Si'ał for generations.

At the end of the eighteenth century, the introduction of guns, together with depopulation from epidemics, destabilized native society in the Northwest, resulting in increased raiding and some territorial expansion by native aggressors. A series of Suquamish war leaders arose in the wake of those events. The first was Kitsap, who led a huge intertribal flotilla that attacked the Cowichans on Vancouver Island. Walak succeeded Kitsap, but he was better known as a speaker. About the time of the 1855 treaties imposed by Governor Isaac Stevens, Seattle replaced Walak, who interpreted for Seattle at the Point Elliot Treaty because Seattle never used Chinook jargon, the international trade jargon of the Northwest both before and after European traders arrived. Denying knowledge of this jargon was a curious step for an intertribal figure to take, though in doing so Seattle called attention to his stature since he then required, and was provided with, a special interpreter to translate from jargon into Lushootseed for him.

As a child Seattle was sent out to quest for spirit power, and he was successful at least once: Thunder, a powerful being, gave him abilities as a warrior and orator.

One of the signs of effective leadership was the ability to direct the labor and resources needed to construct a shed-roofed, cedar-plank longhouse. Usually this construction was undertaken by a set of brothers, who then "owned" the house and led the household. Seattle was associated with one of the longest plank houses in the entire region, known as Oleman House, on Agate Pass at Suquamish; his fame served to attract many followers, who expanded the house, first built about 1800. During Seattle's prime, this house was a thousand feet long.

Seattle had at least two wives. The first, Ladaila of the Duwamishes, was the mother of Angeline (Kikisoblu), a famous figure in her old age and the ancestor of the Deshaw, Thompson, and Fowler families still prominent among the Duwamishes. The second, Owiyał, was the mother of at least two boys—George and Jim—and three girls. Jim Seattle was the father of Moses Seattle, a dwarf often seen at public functions. Jim briefly succeeded his father, but was found to lack calm judgment. He eventually became a subchief under Jacob Wahalchu.

When Fort Nisqually was built by the Hudson's Bay Company in 1833, Seattle, known there as Le Gros or See yat, was a frequent visitor and occasional troublemaker. By this time, Seattle had led many successful raids and gained prestige throughout southern Puget Sound. At the fort, he familiarized himself with European ways while insisting on his prerogatives as the leader of a loose Lushootseed confederacy.

Other allegiances increased his status. In 1838, Catholic priests baptized Seattle, giving him the name

Seattle, holding a rain hat.

Noah because he enjoyed the parallels between the biblical and Suquamish stories of the Flood.

Seattle led a last major attack in about 1847. One of his sons had killed a fellow Suquamish, and, to regain the loyalty of the Suquamishes, Seattle led a force against the Chemakum (non-Salish) village at Hadlock. During the massacre, the murderous son was also killed. Grieving, Seattle decided to give up being a warrior and became a diplomat. His fame, augmented by the support of pioneers, now gave him greater authority. Seeking overall native leaders, Governor Stevens appointed Seattle a head chief for the region when he arrived to organize American rule.

During the war that followed the negotiation of treaties with the Americans, Seattle warned the white settlement that took his name of an impending attack by Leschi, an old friend. To some extent, this friendship among leaders of hostile factions was a balancing act to assure native survival whatever the outcome of the war.

Renowned as an orator among natives even now, Seattle is reported to have given a speech in 1854, since become famous, that has been much debated by scholars. An eloquent defense of Indian lands and traditions, the speech is frequently cited by environmentalists and contemporary native leaders. Because popular English versions of the speech have been distributed so widely, however, many dispute its authenticity. It is significant, then, that it has recently been translated back into Lushootseed and found to convey much the same intent as the English version without its Victorian flourishes.

Among the Lushootseeds the name of a person who had died was not spoken for a year or more after the death, until it had been transferred to a descendant. By taking the name of Seattle, supposedly to honor his support for their settlement in 1853, city fathers unknowingly guaranteed that an important cultural rule would be violated after Seattle's death. Later, in compensation, they feasted and potlatched the chief before his death in 1866.

Today, the memory of Seattle is still honored. Though the Si'ał name is held sacred, a diminutive form, Si'si'ał, has been bestowed on a male descendant at Lummi. When the Native American galleries were dedicated at the new Seattle Art Museum in 1993, natives sang Seattle's Thunder song in public for the first time in over a century.

Anderson, Eva Greenslit, *Chief Seattle* (Caldwell, Idaho: Caxton Printers, 1943); Hilbert, Vi, "When Chief Seattle (Si'ał) Spoke," in *A Time of Gathering: Native Heritage in Washington State,* ed. Robin K. Wright (Seattle: University of Washington Press, 1991).

JAY MILLER (Lenape)
Lushootseed Research

SEMINOLE

The Seminole Indians, an offshoot of the Creeks, emigrated into northern Florida beginning in the early 1700s and established full autonomy by 1800. Their name, derived from the Spanish *cimarrón,* means "wild" or "runaway."

The earliest proto-Seminole settlers came from the Lower Creek towns on the middle Chattahoochee River along the modern-day Georgia-Alabama border. Many early settlers belonged to groups incorporated by the Creeks, including Apalachis and Yamasees. Other Lower Creeks joined them during the eighteenth century. The Seminoles also conquered or incorporated Yamasees, Apalachis, and other Indians who fled to northern Florida from South Carolina after the Yamasee War of 1715. From the 1770s to the 1820s, the Seminoles also incorporated escaped slaves, who lived in independent communities. Upper Creek refugees joined the Seminoles following the Red Stick War of 1813–14.

Seminoles established towns identical to those of the Creeks and maintained Creek social practices and matrilineal clan structure. Following earlier Creek practice, Seminoles organized their towns into larger chiefdoms or confederacies ruled by paramount chiefs. The towns in the Apalachee area formed one such chiefdom. The chief of Cuskowilla headed a chiefdom in north central Florida known as the Alachua or Seminoles. By the late 1700s, Europeans applied the latter name to all Florida Indians. Around 1800, the towns in the forks of the Apalachicola River formed a similar chiefdom.

The Seminoles relied on farming, supplemented by hunting (primarily for deer), fishing, and the gathering of wild plants. They also adopted livestock raising and traded with Europeans for manufactured goods such as tools, weapons, cloth, and ammunition. The Seminoles acknowledged the authority of Kawita and the Creek Confederacy during most of the eighteenth century. The Alachua settlements began acting independently during the American Revolution and were largely autonomous afterward. The Apalachee settlements began pursuing autonomy during the late 1780s. None of the Seminoles participated in the Red Stick War, but the Apalachee settlements adopted the Red Stick cult and aided the British during the War of 1812.

The Seminole and Red Stick towns engaged in continuing hostilities with American border settlements until 1818. The settlements on the lower Chattahoochee, as well as Chiaha, Hichiti, and Yuchi villages on the Flint River—all of whom had accepted the Red Stick cult—joined them. General Andrew Jackson used these hostilities as a pretext to invade Florida, destroy half a dozen Indian and Negro towns, and conquer the Spanish posts at St. Marks and Pensacola. Spain formally ceded Florida to the United States in 1821. Two years later, under the Treaty of Moultrie Creek, the Seminoles agreed to locate on a reservation in central Florida. A separate agreement allowed five chiefs and their towns to remain on the Apalachicola and lower Chattahoochee Rivers. Most western Seminoles did not move until 1825. The first unified Seminole government, which replicated the governments of the towns and older chiefdoms, was formed at that time.

Under pressure from the American government, the Seminoles signed another treaty at Paynes Landing in 1832 and agreed to consider emigration to Indian Territory. Mounting tensions over removal culminated in the Second Seminole War, the longest and costliest Indian war in U.S. history. It began in the winter of 1835 and did not end until the fall of 1842. Though most Seminoles actively resisted emigration, a few towns (mostly Red Stick and Apalachicola towns) refused to fight and voluntarily emigrated to Indian Territory in 1838. The remainder were captured and sent west as prisoners of war.

The majority of Seminoles (more than twenty-five hundred) had been removed by the end of 1839. At the end of the war in 1842 there were 3,612 Seminoles in Indian Territory. Additionally, about 350 to 500 Seminoles remained in Florida, concentrated in the Big Cypress Swamp, distributed around Lake Okeechobee, or scattered in the Everglades.

After removal, the Seminoles in Indian Territory reestablished their communities and their government under adverse conditions. Prior to 1861, they relocated their settlements several times and suffered other hardships. At least one Indian town, under Kowakochi (Wildcat), and one black town, under John Horse (Gopher John), emigrated to northern Mexico in 1849. Also in 1849, a party of Florida Seminoles immigrated to Indian Territory under Kapichochi. Another group, under Holata Mikko (Billy Bowlegs) and Fushachi Hacho, immigrated in 1858.

The Seminole tribe signed a treaty with the Confederacy in August 1861, after Union officials abandoned Indian Territory and Confederates seized the forts there. That fall, dissident elements in the tribe allied with the Union and fled to Kansas. Both Union and Confederate Seminoles participated in and suffered greatly from the Civil War, and the Seminole Nation was laid to waste. A treaty signed by the Seminoles after the Civil War ignored the tribe's efforts on behalf

Cow Creek Seminole women, circa 1917. Their skirts were made of strips of cotton sewn together.

of the Union and treated the whole group as national enemies. The Seminoles relinquished their existing lands for a tract one-tenth the size, which they purchased from the Creeks for three times the price per acre paid by the federal government for their old lands.

The Seminoles reestablished their towns and government on the new reservation and entered a period of prosperity and peace that lasted until 1898. The number of towns declined from over twenty-four in 1845 to fourteen (including two black towns) by 1880. A written constitution was adopted in 1871 but did not change the government's basic structure. Christian missionaries opened schools and missions in 1848 but met with little success during the nineteenth century. Most

Seminoles retained their traditional religion, and few spoke English or were literate before 1900.

In 1898, the Seminoles signed an agreement under the General Allotment Act that divided the Seminole lands among the three thousand tribal members and formally dissolved the tribal government. The Seminoles became citizens of the United States in 1901 and six years later became citizens of the newly formed state of Oklahoma. Protections contained in the Allotment Act proved inadequate. By 1920 the Seminoles had lost 80 percent of their lands, and today they retain less than 10 percent of their original treaty-protected territory.

Many other changes occurred after allotment. Most Seminoles converted to Christianity, primarily the Baptist faith, and many ceased speaking their native language. The old town settlements broke up, and many Seminoles emigrated out of the area. There are between ten thousand and eleven thousand Oklahoma Seminoles today, including about nine hundred to eleven hundred blacks, most of whom live in Seminole County. Educational and income levels remain low among most Seminoles, and economic-development projects by tribal, federal, and state governments have had little success. The tribal government was formally reestablished in 1935 and reorganized in 1970 along traditional lines.

Back in Florida, the remaining Seminoles withdrew into scattered settlements around Lake Okeechobee, in the Big Cypress Swamp, and in the Everglades, south of their former territory, generally avoiding Americans. The American government's efforts to persuade the Florida Seminoles to remove met with little success. In 1911, Executive Order 1379 created three reservations in Florida: Brighton, northwest of Lake Okeechobee; Big Cypress, on the northeastern edge of Big Cypress Swamp; and Dania, outside Hollywood, Florida. Other Seminoles lived along the Tamiami Trail (U.S. Highway 41) and south in the Everglades.

In 1957, the Seminole Tribe of Florida was organized. The Miccosukee Tribe of Florida incorporated separately in 1965, establishing a reservation along the Tamiami Trail. Today there are about twelve hundred Seminoles and Miccosukees (Mikasukis) in Florida. Most, except those on the Hollywood Reservation (Dania), still live apart from other Americans. A number of economic-development strategies have been attempted, including cattle raising, tourism, and retailing, but so far have met with little success. The recently established high-stakes-bingo enterprise at the Holly-

wood Reservation, however, has been extremely successful.

Fairbanks, Charles H., *Ethnohistorical Report on the Florida Indians* (New York: Garland Publishing, 1974); Kersey, Harry A., Jr., *Pelts, Plumes, and Hides: White Traders among the Seminole Indians, 1870–1930* (Gainesville: University of Florida Presses, 1975); McReynolds, Edwin C., *The Seminoles* (Norman: University of Oklahoma Press, 1957).

RICHARD A. SATTLER
Newberry Library
Chicago, Illinois

SENECA

The Senecas call themselves *onǫtowá'ka·'*, "People of the Big Hill." Their name in Iroquois Confederacy councils is *Ho-nan-ne-hó-ont,* "the Door Keeper." Historically, they were the westernmost nation of the League of the Iroquois and are depicted as being the "western door" of the figurative extended longhouse of the confederacy, reaching across New York State, with the Mohawks as the "eastern door" and the Oneidas, Onondagas, and Cayugas extending westward in that order to the Senecas. Foreign ambassadors wishing to approach the Iroquois were reminded to enter by one of the doors, through which they or their messages could pass to the other nations.

The Senecas, Mohawks, and Onondagas are the Elder Brothers of the Iroquois Confederacy and have reciprocal relationships within league councils with the Oneidas and Cayugas, the Younger Brothers. The Senecas have eight chiefs in the confederacy.

At the time of first contact with Euro-Americans, the Senecas occupied what is now western New York State. The western Senecas lived near the Genessee and Allegheny Rivers, and the eastern group near Canandaigua Lake. They resided in two large, and one or two smaller, agriculturally based villages. Agriculture was supplemented by hunting, fishing, and the gathering of fruits and vegetables.

From 1641 to 1684, the Senecas, together with other Iroquois, warred against nations to the northwest, west, and south of them to control trade, to forge alliances, and to "fill the places" of the dead among them. Captives from as far away as Canada and the Great Lakes region were often absorbed among the Senecas and other Iroquois. Conflict with the French, who were expanding westward, also ensued. A peace treaty with the French in 1653 opened the door for the Jesuit missionary Joseph Chaumonot, who visited the Senecas in 1656. The Senecas preferred traders to missionaries, however.

Another peace treaty was signed in 1665. Nonetheless, relations with the French remained tense. The Senecas were invaded unsuccessfully by a French force under the command of Joseph-Antoine Le Febvre de La Barre in 1684, and successfully in July 1687 by another led by Jacques René de Brisay, marquis de Denonville, which resulted in the burning of Seneca villages and cornfields. Hostile feelings between French and Senecas continued until treaties of neutrality were signed between the Iroquois and the French, and the Iroquois and the English, in 1701.

During King George's War (1744–48) and the Seven Years' War (1754–63), Seneca warriors, especially western Senecas and others who had begun to settle in multicultural villages in the Ohio region, often supported the French, largely because of the influence of a trader, Louis-Thomas Chabert de Joncaire, who had been raised as a captive among the western Senecas.

The defeat of the French by the English in 1763 left Senecas with no diplomatic foil for the advancement of English colonists into Indian country. In that year Senecas in the Ohio region and the western Senecas joined the nationalistic Pan-Indian movement led by the Ottawa war leader Pontiac. Pontiac's failure to capture Detroit in 1763 weakened the Senecas' negotiating position with the English. They were induced to cede strategic land at Niagara.

During the American Revolution, Senecas such as the warriors Cornplanter, Blacksnake, and Red Jacket aggressively supported the British as the best option against land-hungry Americans. The Americans retaliated in 1779, when General John Sullivan led an expedition that burned their crops and villages, and forced communities to flee northward.

After the war, some Senecas settled with other Iroquois on the Grand River in Ontario, Canada, at Six Nations Reserve. Many returned to their homeland, with a number settling at Buffalo Creek (near present-day Buffalo, New York), others on the Genesee River, and still others at Tonawanda (near present-day Akron, New York). Their lands were quickly whittled away, however. The Treaty of Fort Stanwix in 1784 forced the Senecas to cede lands west of New York and Pennsylvania to the United States. From 1788 to 1810 portions of reservation land were acquired by speculators: Oliver Phelps and Nathanial Gorham; Robert Morris

and the Holland Land Company; and David Ogden and the Ogden Land Company. At the Treaty of Big Tree (1797) they lost the last of their lands on the Genessee River.

In 1799 and 1800 alienation caused by loss of land, lack of access to hunting grounds, and pressure on Iroquois men by Christian missionaries (Quakers and other Protestants) to enter the domain of women—to take up farming—provided fertile ground for the spread of teachings based on visions of the Seneca Handsome Lake. The prophet exhorted his people to remain true to Iroquois ways by maintaining their practice of calendric ceremonies such as Midwinter, Strawberry, and Green Corn, and by giving thanks to the Creator. The Handsome Lake religion is still practiced on Iroquois reservations, although not all traditionalists adhere to the Code of Handsome Lake and not all Senecas are traditionalists. Many are Christian.

Efforts to remove Senecas from their lands culminated in the Treaty of Buffalo Creek in 1838, by the terms of which the four remaining Seneca reservations—Buffalo Creek, Tonawanda, Cattaraugus, and Allegany—were sold and provisions were made for the Senecas to remove to Kansas. The corrupt proceedings were protested, however, and a new Treaty of Buffalo Creek was signed in 1842. The new agreement stipulated the sale of Buffalo Creek and Tonawanda, but retained Allegany and Cattaraugus. As a result of the Buffalo Creek treaties, some Senecas moved to Kansas. Most did not, however, and of those who did, all but two returned.

Senecas of Tonawanda, who had not been present at the treaty proceedings in 1842, objected. By a treaty signed in 1857, they bought back most of their reservation with money set aside for their removal to Kansas. The Tonawanda Senecas maintain their government by hereditary chiefs, practice the Longhouse religion, perform traditional calendric rituals, and have medicine societies (a tradition separate from the Longhouse religion) for preventative and curative purposes.

In 1848, people of the Allegany and Cattaraugus reservations formed the Seneca Nation, with a written constitution and an elective system of government. They retain that system of government today. In the 1960s, one-third of the Allegany Reservation was lost in the Kinzua Dam project in western New York State. The Senecas received monetary compensation, but this did little to replace the loss of land and homes.

In 1991, ninety-nine-year leases to land at Salamanca on the Allegany Reservation, obtained in 1892 by non-Indians for commercial and residential purposes, were renegotiated, with the Seneca Nation taking a firm stand, insisting on fair rents for the land. Attempts to maintain control over their land and resources continued. An acceptable agreement for forty-year leases was reached. For example, the modern Seneca Nation has resisted attempts by New York State to tax the sale of cigarettes and gasoline to non-Indians at the Allegany and Cattaraugus reserves.

By the beginning of the nineteenth century, Iroquois in the Ohio region, many of whom were Senecas, had settled on the Little Sandusky River in Ohio, forming two reservation communities in 1817 and 1818. In 1831, they ceded their Ohio land in return for the Neosha Reservation in Oklahoma. Beginning in 1887, most Iroquois land in Oklahoma was allotted to individuals, with some kept as tribally owned property for ceremonial and burial grounds. In 1934, the group adopted the name "Seneca/Cayuga Tribe of Oklahoma" and established an elective tribal council. Traditional calendric rituals and medicine societies are found among Senecas in Oklahoma, but the Handsome Lake religion is not.

Diversity, along with persistent cultural identity, has been fostered among the Senecas through time.

Wallace, Anthony F. C., *Death and Rebirth of the Seneca* (New York: Vintage Press, Random House, 1972).

MARY DRUKE BECKER
Iroquois Indian Museum
Howes Cave, New York

SEQUOYAH

c. 1770–1843
Inventor of the Cherokee syllabary.

Sequoyah is one of the most celebrated of all Native Americans, but his fame rests less on his bravery as a warrior or his skills as a diplomat than on his intellectual achievement. Knowledge of Sequoyah is slight, and anecdotes about him lend themselves to mythmaking. He was born about 1770, and his paternity is unknown. The only thing we know for sure is that Sequoyah never knew his white father. Sequoyah's Cherokee mother belonged to an important lineage that included several prominent chiefs. As Cherokee society was matrilineal, Sequoyah's place in the social structure was secure despite his mixed parentage. Little is known of his childhood. As a young man, he was alternately a farmer, a blacksmith, a silversmith, and something of an artist given to sketching animals and people. He was popular with women and enjoyed drinking bouts with male friends. Military records indicate that he served in the war against the Creek Red Sticks in 1813.

In later years Sequoyah was reported to have been unimpressed with the white man's ability to communicate by means of "talking leaves." He boasted that he, too, could etch symbols on stones that could have meaning. While his idea of writing was influenced by contact with whites, perhaps Sequoyah was also stimulated by the example of petroglyphs that abounded in Cherokee country. In response to the derision of his friends, Sequoyah took up his project in earnest. He spent much time alone in a shed making marks on scraps of paper and wood chips. He tried to devise marks for different Cherokee words. His friends despaired of his obsession, and many suspected him of practicing sorcery. His wife eventually burned down his workshop in a fit of desperation. According to oral tradition, Sequoyah supposedly shrugged off this setback and decided to begin anew.

Following the loss of his workshop, Sequoyah claimed he had a better idea. Instead of a mark for each Cherokee word, he carefully set about listening to the sounds of the Cherokee language until he could differentiate distinctive units. This was no mean feat: to isolate the sounds of one's own language is a bit like a fish discovering water, a bird finding air, or human beings discovering culture. Sequoyah eventually reduced Cherokee to eighty-six, later eighty-five, minimal sound units, to each of which he attached a particular symbol, thereby producing his syllabary. He derived many of the symbols from figures he copied from English print. However, these common symbols have no correspondence in sound value and many of the signs are completely original.

It must be emphasized that Sequoyah created a *syllabary,* not an alphabet. The eighty-five symbols in the syllabary appear at first glance to be more forbidding and cumbersome than the twenty-six letters of the English alphabet. Yet the syllabary is a much more efficient means of transforming spoken Cherokee into a written form. A Cherokee speaker can learn to read and write as soon as the eighty-five symbols are mastered, often after a few days of study. This is in marked contrast to the many years it takes to learn to read and write English. The Sequoyan script has certain technical linguistic limitations, but it has nevertheless proved to be an effective means of written communication for a variety of purposes.

Sequoyah's first student was his young daughter, Ahyokeh. Father and daughter gave public demonstrations in which, standing several hundred yards apart, they would encode and decode written messages. Some people thought trickery was employed; others suspected conjury. When the significance of the syllabary was realized in 1821, literacy spread rapidly throughout the Cherokee Nation. In 1822 Sequoyah went to join kinsmen who had voluntarily emigrated to the Arkansas Territory. Communications between the eastern and western groups of Cherokees could now be maintained through written correspondence.

Missionaries quickly recognized the advantages of the syllabary over the awkward orthography they had tried to impose on the Cherokee language. In 1827, the Reverend Samuel A. Worcester of the American Board of Foreign Missions had the syllabary typeset in Boston and sent to the Cherokees, along with a white printer. An active program of translating the Bible and various religious tracts ensued, and a short-lived tribal newspaper, the *Cherokee Phoenix*, arose. In contrast to their staggered historical development in Western civilization, the discovery of writing and printing and the flourishing of mass or unrestricted literacy happened nearly simultaneously among the Cherokees.

Sequoyah remained in the West while his fame spread among Cherokees and whites alike. After the traumatic forced removal of the remainder of the tribe in 1838, Sequoyah became an active advocate of the political reunification of the Cherokee Nation, calling for an end to factional strife.

Sequoyah's death, like his birth, is surrounded in mystery and conjecture. In 1843 the aged leader set out with a small group of men to find a detached band of Cherokees who had emigrated to northern Mexico. After an arduous journey, the party lost their way. Sequoyah remained sequestered in a cave when the others went for help. He was never seen again, living or dead.

Sequoyah's accomplishment made him a culture hero, in all senses, to both Cherokees and whites. As noted before, the Cherokees published Christian religious materials, printed a tribal newspaper, and corresponded with one another via letters; laws were codified, other legal materials were recorded, and various ledger account books were employed for business transactions. All these efforts clearly contributed to elevating the Cherokees to what whites termed a "civilized" state.

But the syllabary also functioned as a means of cultural conservation by preserving traditional beliefs and

The Cherokee syllabary invented by Sequoyah.

practices. Curers and conjurers recorded in the syllabary many esoteric ceremonies for healing a wide range of native disorders, for divination, for love magic, for war and ball games, for sorcery, and for a variety of other specific purposes. This large corpus of handwritten sacred texts affords an unparalleled glimpse into an exceedingly complex Native American medico-magical system.

For some theorists the advent of literacy marks a watershed in cultural evolution and brings about a dramatic restructuring of thought. While the possession of a syllabary brought the Cherokees much prestige and an enhanced sense of self-worth, writing for the Cherokees tended to be more of an advanced mnemonic system and a device for focusing thought rather than a mental move into a more enlightened level of cultural development. According to a contemporary, George Lowery, Sequoyah is reported to have said, "When I have heard anything, I write it down, and lay it by and take it up again at some future day. And there find all that I have heard exactly as I heard it." This may be as close as we can ever come to discerning the intent of the inventor. Literacy was a retention technique that made possible future use of inscribed information. It also freed the mind for other pursuits. But we must also recognize what Cherokees *did not* do with writing. They did not suddenly blossom into a nation of poets; they did not write short stories, novels, biographies, and autobiographies or other genres recognized as literature in the West; they did not record their myths or the oratory of their great leaders, although they did record ceremonies of great eloquence and style.

But the Cherokees' failure to develop an indigenous literature should not demean the magnitude of Sequoyah's achievement. Sequoyah's genius must be understood in Cherokee terms as the accomplishment of a native intellectual who brought honor and hope to his people and who provided both a vehicle for cultural adaptation to difficult times and a means for promoting cultural continuity and survival.

See also Cherokee Language.

RAYMOND D. FOGELSON
University of Chicago

SERPENT MOUND

The largest known serpent effigy in the world, Great Serpent Mound is located in rural Adams County, Ohio, and is the centerpiece of a state park (see photograph on p. 399). Some scholars believe the earthwork to be a product of Adena culture; though no human artifacts have been found in the earthwork itself, a nearby burial mound has yielded Adena objects. The mound's form is of an undulating serpent, uncoiling and opening its mouth to swallow a large oval. The height of the mound ranges from four to six feet, and its width ranges from four to twenty feet. The serpent proper is a little over twelve hundred feet long but, including the oval, extends for roughly fourteen hundred feet; the ends of the jaws are seventy-five feet apart. There are seven undulations in the body of the snake, as well as three coils in its tail. Great Serpent Mound differs from many other native earthworks in that it ex-

tends down a gently sloping, crescent-shaped hill. Thus, its overall appearance is visible from the ground.

Most scholars interpret the oval as an egg, though others interpret it as a frog; because the serpent extends to the west, some think the oval represents the setting sun. In recent years, the idea that this mound was created by prehistoric European travelers or Central American tribesmen has faded in popularity. Though its exact origins are unclear, most scholars believe the mound was constructed by North Americans.

See also Mound Builders.

SHAWNEE

An Algonquian people whose native language (now threatened) is most closely related to Kickapoo, the Shawnees were noted historically for their extensive migrations and a formidable resistance to Euro-American expansion into the Ohio Valley. Three recognized groups of Shawnees now live in Oklahoma: the Eastern Shawnees of Ottawa County; the Absentee Shawnees, with headquarters at Shawnee; and the Loyal Shawnees, who became part of the Cherokee Nation in 1869, located around Whiteoak.

Their name, which signifies "southerners," and other evidence suggest an early location on the Savannah River (South Carolina), but in the 1670s and 1680s the Shawnees were being dislodged from the Ohio and Cumberland Valleys by Iroquois raids. By 1730, after a period of dispersal, they had regrouped—most in western Pennsylvania, but others in what is now Alabama. In the ensuing decade the Pennsylvania Shawnees, seeking better game and freedom from English and Iroquois interference, withdrew down the Ohio toward the Scioto, reclaiming the territory they had occupied a century before. Such fragmentation destroyed what little tribal organization had existed among them.

Prior to European contact the Shawnees had been a confederacy of five patrilineal divisions (Mekoche, Pekowi, Chillicothe, Kispoko, and Hathawekela) that appear to have functioned in independent villages with their own civil and war chiefs. Each division also exercised some overall tribal responsibility. The Mekoches, for example, handled external political affairs, and their head civil chief was effectively the tribal chief. Dispersal dismantled this system.

In 1787 many Ohio Pekowi and Kispoko Shawnees, tiring of conflict with the United States, fled westward to

Spanish territory (Perry County, Missouri), where they were joined in about 1814 by the Alabama Shawnees, primarily Hathawekelas. These were the groups that formed today's independent Absentee Shawnee tribe.

Under leaders such as Cornstalk and Blue Jacket, the Shawnees on the Ohio defended the region against successive intruders with outstanding ingenuity and courage. In 1746 Shawnees tried to build an intertribal alliance against the French. They participated in "Pontiac's Rebellion" in 1763, and in 1774 they challenged the advance of the Virginians into Kentucky. During the Revolutionary War, Ohio Shawnees enlisted British support for their attempt to clear their Kentucky hunting ground of white settlers. Thereafter they were the nucleus of an Indian confederacy that resisted the seizure of Ohio by the United States and defeated the armies of Josiah Harmar (1790) and Arthur St. Clair (1791). Nevertheless, by the Treaty of Greenville (1795) the Shawnees and their allies were compelled to cede southern and central Ohio.

After the peace the Ohio Shawnees, largely Mekoches and Chillicothes, established two towns north of the treaty line, Wapakoneta (Auglaize County, Ohio) and Lewistown (Logan County, Ohio), from which the modern Loyal and Eastern bands of Shawnees, respectively, are descended. Up to this time Shawnee society, while imbibing some influences of groups with whom they associated, had been quite conservative. European trade had created tensions by causing the spread of new diseases and encouraging the excesses of the liquor traffic. These damaging effects inspired the reforms of the Shawnee Prophet (Tenskwatawa) in 1805, even as they accompanied an improvement in the tribe's material culture. This trade was incorporated into the tribe's existing economic pattern of spring and summer planting and fall and winter hunting.

More systematic absorption of Euro-American culture began in 1802, when the Ohio Shawnees sought the aid of Quaker missionaries and the U.S. government to develop their economy. The government's policy required the group to maintain peace with the United States, and both bands of Ohio Shawnees rejected the overtures of a Kispoko band under Tecumseh and Tenskwatawa, who revived militant Pan-Indianism before the War of 1812. Despite their commitment to peace, however, the Ohio Shawnees were confined to three reservations in 1817, and in 1831 they were persuaded to sign removal treaties.

The Lewistown band went directly to Oklahoma, became part of the Quapaw Agency, and in 1940 organ-

ized as the Eastern Shawnee tribe. Most Ohio Shawnees, however, migrated to a reservation in Kansas, where they prospered until pressure from the United States, difficulties with white neighbors, and the disruption of the American Civil War (in which the band earned the name Loyal Shawnee for its fidelity to the Union) led them to relinquish their lands and join the Oklahoma Cherokees in 1869. Among modern Shawnees cultural conservatism is strongest among the Absentee band, which had not participated in the Ohio development policy. They surrendered their territory in Missouri in 1825, but not all followed the prescribed course of relocating on the Kansas reservation, many scattering to Arkansas, Oklahoma, and Texas. When the Kansas reservation was alloted in 1854, they were designated the Absentee Shawnees. These Indians regrouped on the Canadian River in Oklahoma, where they were recognized by the U.S. government and their lands confirmed in 1872.

Modern Shawnees participate conventionally in mainstream American society, and the three groups remain politically independent. But a tribal pride and sense of identity has been preserved. Ceremonial grounds are maintained by both Absentee and Loyal Shawnees, and the annual community rituals with their attendant beliefs reflect traditions of considerable antiquity. A distinguishing feature of Shawnee culture is the significance it has accorded women. In the eighteenth century female war and civil chiefs (one of them Tecumapease, Tecumseh's sister) were recognized, while the Creator (Waashaa Monetoo) was held to have been aided by an old Shawnee woman and her grandson. Sometime after 1824 Shawnees raised the Grandmother (Kokomthena) to the position of their supreme deity, and it is from her that it is now believed the tribe received its skills, laws, and ceremonies, and for whose favor religious observances ultimately make appeals. Less unusually, many of the subordinate deities are also female, including Earth Mother, Corn Woman, and Pumpkin Woman; their support is considered essential to the vitality of Shawnee harvests.

The most important community ceremonies observed today, the spring (May) and fall (October) Bread Dances, commemorate the old Shawnee economy, entreating blessings for forthcoming crops and hunts and returning thanks for bounties already received. Both the men-versus-women football match, which opens the spring Bread Dance, and the Green Corn Ceremony, celebrated by the Loyal Shawnees in August, were recorded as early as the 1790s. Although modified, current versions of such rituals as the War Dance and feasts for the dead likewise testify to a desire to protect the Shawnee cultural heritage.

About six thousand Shawnees now live in Oklahoma, and a small band that had resided in Canada recently returned to Ohio and is seeking federal recognition.

Alford, Thomas Wildcat, *Civilization and the Story of the Absentee Shawnees, As Told to Florence Drake* (Norman: University of Oklahoma Press, 1936); Downes, Randolph C., *Council Fires on the Upper Ohio: A Narrative of Indian Affairs in the Upper Ohio Valley until 1795* (Pittsburgh: University of Pittsburgh Press, 1940); Howard, James H., *Shawnee! The Ceremonialism of a Native American Tribe and Its Cultural Background* (Athens: Ohio University Press, 1981).

JOHN SUGDEN
Hereward College
Coventry, England

SHAWNEE PROPHET (TENSKWATAWA)

(1775–1836)
Kispoko Shawnee religious and political leader.

One of a set of triplets, the Shawnee Prophet was born at Old Piqua, a Shawnee village on the Mad River in western Ohio. His mother was Methoataske (Turtle Laying Its Eggs), a Creek woman. His father, Puckeshinewa, a Shawnee war chief, was killed at the Battle of Point Pleasant prior to the triplets' birth. The triplets were the youngest siblings in a large family (they had at least six older brothers and sisters), and one of the triplets died in infancy. The other triplet, Kumskaukau, lived at least until 1807.

In 1779 Methoataske left Ohio. The two remaining triplets and Tecumseh, a brother born in 1768, were left in the care of Tecumapease, an older, married sister. Their upbringing also was supervised by Chiksika, a brother in his late teens. Both Tecumapease and Chiksika favored Tecumseh, an athletic youth who excelled at the contests and games popular among Shawnee boys. In contrast, the boy who would become the Prophet was an awkward, corpulent youth who accidentally gouged out his own right eye while fumbling with an arrow. Because he often boasted and complained, he was called Lalawethika (the Noisemaker), a name he disliked. He married in his teens, but was unskilled as a hunter and became an alcoholic. He did not participate in the Indian victories over Josiah Harmar (1790) or

Arthur St. Clair (1791), but he did join a war party of Shawnees led by Tecumseh who fought at the Battle of Fallen Timbers. Following the Treaty of Greenville (1795) he lived with a band of Shawnees led by Tecumseh who resided at several locations in western Ohio and eastern Indiana. In 1798 they moved to the White River near Anderson, Indiana, where Lalawethika, still an alcoholic, unsuccessfully attempted to assume a role as a healer and shaman.

In the decade following the Treaty of Greenville socioeconomic conditions among the Shawnees and neighboring tribes deteriorated. Game and fur-bearing animals declined, while frontiersmen encroached upon Indian land, poaching the few remaining animals and establishing new settlements. White juries protected Americans accused of crimes against tribespeople while systematically convicting Indians. Meanwhile, many Indian people contracted new diseases for which they had no immunity. Under considerable stress, tribal communities were plagued with apathy and dysfunction, and alcoholism increased. Considerably alarmed, many Shawnees believed that their troubles were caused by witches spreading chaos in the Shawnee world.

During April 1805, in the midst of this crisis, Lalawethika underwent a religious experience in which he appeared to fall into a trance so deep that his family at first believed him to be dead. After a few hours he recovered and informed his neighbors that he had died, had been taken to a location overlooking heaven and hell, and had been shown how the Shawnees could improve their situation. He stated that although Indians had been fashioned by the Creator, Americans were the children of the the Great Serpent, the source of evil in the world. Aided by witches (Indians who accepted American cultural values), the Americans had spread chaos and disorder. In consequence, he championed a new religious revitalization, urging the Shawnees and other Indians to minimize their contact with the Americans. He admonished tribespeople to relinquish American food and clothing, most manufactured goods, and alcohol. Firearms could be used for defense, but game should be hunted with bows and arrows. If Indians followed such doctrines, their dead relatives would return to life and game would reappear in the forests; if they refused, they would be condemned to a fiery hell reminiscent of Christian doctrines. He also announced that thenceforward he should be known as Tenskwatawa (the Open Door), a name befitting his new role as a prophet.

Tenskwatawa's teachings found many adherents among the Shawnees and neighboring tribes, particularly after he successfully predicted an eclipse of the sun in June 1806. By 1807 so many Indians had traveled to his village near Greenville, in western Ohio, that they exhausted food supplies in the region. White officials became alarmed at this influx, and in 1808 the Prophet led his followers to Prophetstown, a new village near the juncture of the Tippecanoe and Wabash Rivers, near modern Lafayette, Indiana.

In 1809, after the Treaty of Fort Wayne, Tecumseh attempted to transform the religious movement into a centralized political alliance designed to retain the remaining Indian lands in the West. From Prophetstown Tecumseh traveled throughout the Midwest. In November 1811, while Tecumseh was recruiting allies in the South, William Henry Harrison, the governor of Indiana Territory, led an expedition against Prophetstown. Forced to protect his village, Tenskwatawa promised his followers that they would be immune from American firearms and instructed them to attack Harrison's camp. In the resulting conflict, the Battle of the Tippecanoe, the Indian attack was repulsed. Although both sides suffered losses, the Prophet's influence was broken. When Tecumseh returned from the South in January 1812 he assumed sole command of the Indian alliance

Never a warrior, the Prophet took little part in the War of 1812. In December 1812 he fled to Canada, then accompanied Tecumseh back to northern Indiana. In the following spring they led a large party of western warriors to the Detroit region. The Prophet accompanied the British and Indian forces that unsuccessfully besieged Fort Meigs during May 1813, but he took no part in the fighting. On October 5, 1813, he was present at the Battle of the Thames, but he fled with the British when the battle started. Tecumseh was killed in the battle.

Following the War of 1812, the Prophet remained in Canada for ten years, unsuccessfully attempting to regain a position of leadership. In 1825, at the invitation of Lewis Cass, the governor of Michigan Territory, he returned to the United States and used his limited influence to promote Indian removal. One year later he accompanied a party of Shawnees from Ohio who were traveling via St. Louis to Kansas. The Prophet settled at the site of modern-day Kansas City, Kansas, where he posed for the artist George Catlin in the autumn of 1832. He died there four years later, in November 1836.

The Prophet's experiences and teachings reflect a general pattern of Native American response to American aggrandizement. During periods of economic, political, and social stress, Indian people often have sought a religious deliverance, and the Prophet's syncretic, nativistic doctrines of revitalization fit into a pattern of similar solutions offered by Handsome Lake, Kennekuk, Smohalla, and Wovoka. Although white contemporaries and subsequent historians have credited Tecumseh with founding the Indian resistance movement prior to the War of 1812, it originated with the religious revitalization championed by the Shawnee Prophet.

See also Shawnee; Tecumseh.

Dowd, Gregory, *A Spirited Resistance: The North American Indians' Struggle for Unity, 1745–1815* (Baltimore: Johns Hopkins University Press, 1992); Edmunds, R. David, *The Shawnee Prophet* (Lincoln: University of Nebraska Press, 1983); Kinietz, Vernon, and Erminie Wheeler-Voegelin, eds., *"Shawnese Traditions": C. C. Trowbridge's Account,* Occasional Contributions from the Museum of Anthropology of the University of Michigan, no. 9 (Ann Arbor: University of Michigan Press, 1939).

R. DAVID EDMUNDS (Cherokee)
Indiana University

SHINNECOCK

Shinnecock (originally called *shinni-auk-it,* meaning "at the level land"), in eastern Long Island, New York, is the year-round home to approximately 450 Native Americans. Over a thousand additional tribal members are scattered through the country. Of the approximately 400 to 450 people living year-round on the reservation, 50 percent have married within or had children by tribal members; 25 percent are married to outside Indians; and 25 percent are married to whites, Hispanics, African Americans, and others.

In 1640, English colonists entered Shinnecock land. There they met peaceful, resourceful people who had been in the same geographical area for thousands of years. The Shinnecocks' land extended eastward to the Easthampton town line and westward to the Brookhaven town line, with the Atlantic Ocean to the south and Peconic Bay to the north.

In a gesture of friendliness, the Shinnecocks parceled out eight square miles of land to the settlers. Numerous unfair land transactions had by the 1850s reduced the tribe's holdings to its present eight hundred acres. A legislative act in 1859 designated this small neck of land as the Shinnecock Indian Reservation. It is located two miles west of the village of Southampton, New York, in Suffolk County.

In 1857, Ferdinand Lee, a tribal member, rose from fourth mate to captain on various whaling ships. As captain of the bark *Callao* out of New Bedford, Massachusetts, many of his crew members were Shinnecock natives who followed the call of life at sea.

In 1792, at a town meeting, the first tribal governing system was introduced. Three male members of the tribe were selected to conduct tribal affairs. Only men were allowed to vote or have a voice in tribal meetings; it was not until 1993 that women acquired these privileges. The Shinnecocks have the oldest ongoing Native America church in America. Most tribal members are Presbyterians. Close-knit family ties have kept them united.

Ancient June Meeting spiritual gatherings continue on the first Sunday in June, an indication of the tribe's determination to remain traditional. The Shinnecocks celebrate "Indian Thanksgiving" a week before the nationwide observance as a demonstration of their cultural awareness and tenacity.

The annual three-day Shinnecock Labor Day Powwow, with over fifteen thousand daily attendees, generates a fair amount of capital for the tribe, whose income is supplemented by state grants. Young people maintain their heritage by making their own dance regalia and by practicing beadwork and other crafts.

A tribal council with a few ad hoc committees enlivens the progressive political and business status of the community. Several programs have enriched the social structure. The Shinnecocks have recently renewed their traditional skills of herb gathering, hunting, and fishing.

Today many professionals and entrepreneurs operate both within and outside the confines of the reservation. Launcelot Gumbs, known as "Fierce Eyes," is the proprietor of the Shinnecock Outpost, a highway deli, gifts, and smoke shop; he employs eighteen members of the tribe in this enterprise.

The Shinnecocks are proud people, determined to hold on to their identity and the last of their tribal land bases. A tribal enrollment list is being prepared for an application by the tribe for federal recognition.

HARRIET CRIPPEN BROWN GUMBS (Shinnecock)
Shinnecock Indian Outpost,
Southampton, New York

SHOSHONE

The Shoshone people belong to the Numic branch of the larger Uto-Aztecan language family. During the past two centuries the Shoshone people have been identified in print as "Snake Indians," "Shoshone," and "Shoshoni," but older members of the tribe refer to themselves in writing as "Soshonies." The spelling of the singular form of the name throughout this entry will be *Shoshone*, but the word itself should be pronounced *sho-SHO-nee*.

The two largest groups of Shoshone people are the Eastern Shoshones, who reside in central Wyoming on the Wind River Indian Reservation, near Lander; and the Shoshone-Bannocks and Lemhis, who live on the Fort Hall Indian Reservation, on the Snake River and the surrounding plains in southern Idaho. The Shoshones who live on the Fort Hall Indian Reservation have been identified as Northern Shoshones, Bannocks, and Lemhis. But because of intermarriage, the development of close family relationships, and the placement of several bands on the Fort Hall Reservation by the U.S. government, they now officially identify themselves as the Shoshone-Bannock Tribes of the Fort Hall Reservation. The Eastern Shoshones, who are related to the Shoshone-Bannocks, officially identify themselves as members of the Eastern Shoshone Tribe. (During the treaty-making period of 1863–68, they were called the Washakie band.) Another group, the Northwestern Band of the Shoshoni Nation, lives on a small tract of land near Brigham City, Utah (and was included in the Washakie band in the Treaty of 1863). The Paiute and Ute Indians also speak Uto-Aztecan languages, and intermarriage has always been common among Shoshones and these groups, who reside in the states of Wyoming, Utah, Idaho, Nevada, Oregon, Arizona, and California. As a result, in addition to the Eastern Shoshone tribe and the Shoshone-Bannock tribe, there are also the Duckwater Shoshone tribe, the Ely Shoshone tribe, and, in Nevada, the Fallon Paiute Shoshone tribe.

The Shoshone tribe is also related through language and intermarriage to the Comanches of the southern plains. In 1700 the Shoshones acquired the horse from their relatives the Comanches, and they expanded their hunting territory from the North Texas plains to the plains of Saskatchewan, Canada. The Shoshone people lived and hunted on the Green River, Sweetwater River, Wind River, and Popo Aggie River and also inhabited the Wind River Mountains of central Wyoming. The boundaries of the Shoshone tribe thus were pushed east to the slopes of the Bighorn Mountains, north to the Yellowstone River and the adjoining plains of Montana, and west to the Salmon Mountains and the plains where the Snake River and its tributaries flow west to the Columbia River in Washington. Traditionally, the southern boundary of the Shoshone lands comprised the Uinta Mountains of Utah, the Yampa River and Brown's Hole in northwestern Colorado on the Green River, and the Great Basin.

The Bannocks are Northern Paiutes who migrated from western Oregon into the Snake River plains of Idaho and lived with the Northern Shoshones. The term *Northern Shoshones* is used by anthropologists to distinguish the Shoshones of the upper Columbia River drainage from the Western Shoshones of Nevada and Utah and the Eastern Shoshones of Wyoming. The Bannocks left their relatives, the Northern Paiutes in western Oregon, when they acquired the horse during the late seventeenth century. With the acquisition of the horse the Bannocks became mounted warriors and hunters who roamed the Snake River basin and the Wind River valley.

The most striking cultural difference between the Bannocks and the Northern and Western Shoshones was their adoption of the plains culture. The Bannock culture is more closely related to that of the Eastern Shoshones and the Lemhis. The basis of the Shoshone and Bannock religion was a belief in dreams, visions, and a Creator. Shoshone religious belief fostered individual self-reliance, courage, and the wisdom to meet life's problems in a difficult environment. Most of the Northern Shoshone and Bannock ceremonies are dances similar to the Great Basin Round Dances. The Bannocks shared the warfare practices of the Plains Indians, which included counting coups and taking scalps of enemies. They adopted the Scalp Dance from the plains tribes and during the reservation period began dancing the Sun Dance. Today the Sun Dance, a very important event, is held each summer.

In 1750 the Blackfeet, Bloods, Piegans, and Crows to the north and the Sioux, Cheyennes, and Arapahos to the east were well armed and had an abundant supply of horses. They began hunting to the south and west of their original homelands, and they defeated the Shoshones whenever they came upon them. They moved the Shoshones south from the northern plains and west of the Continental Divide. By 1840 the presence of the Shoshones east of the Continental Divide was limited to hunting parties that would remain in the area for a very short time. During this same period the Shoshone tribe was also beset by epidemics of smallpox, which decimated the tribe and also diminished its power. In the nineteenth century the Northern Shoshones and Bannocks hunted in the Snake River valley, the Kansas Prairie, and the Portneuf and Sawtooth Mountains, while a Shoshone group called the Sheepeaters lived primarily in the Yellowstone country and the Eastern Shoshones spent most of their time in the Wind River and Bighorn Mountains. By the 1850s the Crows began hunting regularly in central Wyoming, and the Eastern Shoshones, under the leadership of Chief Washakie, challenged their right to hunt and camp there. In March 1866 the Crows were camped near the present site of Kinnear, Wyoming, on the north side of the Big Wind River, when the Eastern Shoshones drove them out of the valley and thus ended the Crow intrusion into Shoshone country.

The reservation period of the Eastern Shoshones' and the Shoshone-Bannocks' history began when the United States realized that some agreement had to be reached with the Indian tribes whose territory lay astride the Oregon and California Trails. In 1863 the United States negotiated the Fort Bridger Treaty and subsequent agreements that opened the area to travelers and set aside lands for Shoshone bands. During the period between 1863 and 1939, the Eastern Shoshone and Shoshone-Bannock tribes saw their reserved lands, which once covered five states, reduced to parcels making up an area one-twentieth the size of the original reserves. The Treaty of 1868 between the Eastern Shoshones, the Shoshone-Bannocks, and the United States included a provision that the United States would provide a reservation for the Shoshone-Bannocks whenever they requested one of their own.

The Wind River Reservation now consists of 2,268,008 acres, or approximately 3,500 square miles, and is located in Fremont and Hot Springs Counties in west central Wyoming. The Fort Hall Indian Reservation of the Shoshone-Bannock tribes is located in southeastern Idaho, and the counties of Bannock, Bingham, Caribou, and Power lie within its boundaries. The cities of Blackfoot and Pocatello are on the northern and southern ends of the reservation, respectively. The Fort Hall Reservation originally consisted of 1.8 million acres of land but now consists of only 544,000 acres. Its size was decreased in order to accommodate white settlement in the Fort Hall area and also because of a surveying error in 1872. The General Allotment Act of 1887 further divided the lands of the Shoshone-

Bannocks—into 160-acre tracts for adults and 80-acre tracts for children. After the land had been allotted among tribal members, the surplus was turned back to the government. In 1888 an executive order created the city of Pocatello, and 1,840 acres of treaty land were ceded to accommodate this change.

With the discovery of gold at South Pass in the Wind River Mountains, the Eastern Shoshones were given no choice but to cede to the United States the southern portion of their reservation, including all of the land south of the Popo Aggie River. Another form of loss occurred in 1878 when the U.S. military escorted 938 starving Arapahos to what was then called the Shoshone Reservation. They were to stay temporarily, but they remained, despite the Shoshone people's protests. In 1896 U.S. Inspector James McLaughlin was sent to the Shoshone Indian reservation to negotiate for ten square miles on its northeastern boundary. Within this ten square miles lay great mineral hot springs, which white men wanted.

In 1891 Chief Washakie protested the presence of the Arapahos on the Shoshone Reservation and the loss of the hot springs, but these decisions were not reversed. Later the Eastern Shoshones sued the U.S. government for compensation for the placement of the Arapahos on their lands. They won the suit in 1939, but the settlement gave the Arapahos official title to half of the Shoshone Reservation and officially renamed the reserve the Wind River Reservation of the Shoshone and Arapahoe Tribes.

Other losses accompanied white settlement. In 1904 McLaughlin negotiated an agreement to cede 1,472,844 acres of reservation land for an irrigation district. Lands were to be sold under the Homestead Act, and the proceeds were to be paid to the tribes for per capita payments, expenses, and improvements for the benefit of the tribes. Portions of these ceded lands were restored to the tribes in 1939, 1947, and 1959, but valuable resources were permanently lost.

The present structure of the Wind River tribal government was created in 1901 by the Indian agent H. G. Nickerson. The Eastern Shoshones elect (to two-year terms) a tribal council—the Shoshone Business Council—consisting of six members, one of whom is elected chairman. Its members conduct the day-to-day business of the tribe. Any matter that is not within the jurisdiction of the business council is acted upon by the Shoshone General Council, which consists of all enrolled members of the tribe over eighteen years of age. The business council meets weekly, and must also meet jointly with the Arapaho tribe for matters that affect the reservation and are not specific to the Shoshone tribe.

The Eastern Shoshones did not accept the provisions of the Indian Reorganization Act, but the Shoshone-Bannocks did so, adopting a constitution and becoming a reorganized tribe. The Shoshone-Bannocks elect seven members to their governing body—the Fort Hall Business council—for four-year, staggered terms. They also have a general council of all enrolled members, but its actions must be ratified by the business council. The business council legislates laws put into effect either by general-council resolution or by ordinances the business council itself has passed.

The Eastern Shoshones and the Shoshone-Bannocks can enter into agreements, memoranda of understanding, and compacts with the states of Wyoming and Idaho, respectively, and with the federal government. The respective business councils oversee and provide services through various tribal departments and offices. Those services range from federal Indian Health Service programs to planning, zoning, education, a credit program, and water management. Each reservation has its own police department and a state recognized judicial system.

In the more than one hundred years since the signing of the Fort Bridger Treaty, the Eastern Shoshones and the Shoshone-Bannocks have preserved most of their traditional lands and also their traditional ceremonies. Each summer on the Fort Hall Reservation and the Wind River Reservation the annual Sun Dance is held, and throughout the year tribal members engage in sweat ceremonies to pray for individuals, families, or the tribe. Each tribe hosts an annual powwow, featuring dancing contests in which tribal members participate in fancy dancing and traditional dancing. In July the Eastern Shoshone tribe sponsors the Eastern Shoshone Fair and Rodeo, and in August of each year the Shoshone-Bannocks sponsor the annual Shoshone-Bannock Festival, which includes dancing, singing, stick games, Indian arts, and Indian relay racing. All are welcome to attend the Shoshone-Bannock Festival and the Eastern Shoshone Fair and Rodeo.

Areas in which tribally sponsored activities have developed over the past hundred years include education, religion, health, employment, treaty rights, water rights, and housing. Unemployment represents one of the most perplexing problems faced by the Eastern Shoshones and the Shoshone-Bannocks; it varies from 65 to 75 percent of employable males and females. The primary occupation of the Eastern Shoshone and Shoshone Bannock people is agriculture. But a large number of tribal members depend upon the tribal government, the Bureau of Indian Affairs, the Indian Health Service, and the local schools for employment. The Shoshone-Bannocks and the Eastern Shoshones are active citizens of Idaho and Wyoming, respectively, and of the United States, but they exercise their tribal sovereignty, which was guaranteed to them by the treaties they entered into with the United States.

Madsen, Brigham, *The Northern Shoshoni* (Caldwell, Idaho: Caxton Printers, 1980); Murray, Larry G., *The Wind River Reservation, Yesterday and Today* (Riverton, Wyo.: Riverton Ranger, 1972); Trenholm, Virginia, *The Shoshonis* (Norman: University of Oklahoma Press, 1964).

LARRY G. MURRAY (Eastern Shoshone)
Economic Development
Eastern Shoshone Tribe

SIGN LANGUAGE

American Indian nations of the Great Plains spoke so many different languages that vocal communication between them was difficult. As extensive trade networks developed and political alliances became necessary, an elegant language of the hands developed that cut across spoken language barriers. This language became known as Indian Sign Language or, more accurately, Plains Sign Language.

Details of the origin of Plains Sign Language are unknown, but historical records show that when Spanish explorers in Coronado's expedition entered the southern plains in 1541–42, they encountered Indians who were using signs. Captain William Clark, who carried out extensive field research in the 1870s and used the sign language fluently, was of the opinion that, whatever its origin, the language had particularly flourished during the eighteenth and nineteenth centuries, along with many other aspects of Plains cultures, as horse nomadism arrived and the permanent population of the plains increased. Clark learned the sign language from Indian scouts of the Pawnee, Shoshone, Arapaho, Cheyenne, Crow, and Sioux Nations, who were employed by the U.S. Army in 1876–77 and who conversed with each other entirely in signs.

Garrick Mallery, a former army officer turned ethnologist, collected evidence that showed that despite many regional variations in signed vocabulary in the nineteenth century, such dialect differences did not prevent skilled sign talkers from understanding each other across the whole plains area. In his book *The Indian Sign Language* (1885), Clark suggests that long-term alliances between powerful nomadic tribes like the Cheyennes and Arapahos encouraged sign-language use because their spoken languages were so different and Arapaho was difficult for the Cheyennes to master. Tribes like the Kiowas, who moved great distances and thus frequently made new contacts, also became very proficient in the language. The Crows, who created alliances with many surrounding nations, became good sign talkers in the process and passed their knowledge on to tribes from the eastern plateau such as the Nez Perces, Shoshones, and Bannocks.

Although we do not know exactly how and why Plains Sign Language developed, there are a number of factors that shed some light on the subject. First, no one nation in the plains area was economically or politically dominant, and so no particular spoken language was imposed upon neighboring groups. Perhaps the Plains peoples of long ago simply maximized the pan-human tendency to resort to gestures when in the company of equals who do not share a spoken language.

Second, in contrast to the kinds of philosophical and religious biases against the human body that had existed for over two thousand years in European thought, Native Americans did not consider gestures to be "primitive" or less sophisticated than speech, and so manual gestures (signs) were not considered to be of less value than vocal gestures (speech) as a means of communicating.

Third, sign languages generally have properties that make them easier to learn than spoken languages. In Plains Sign Language, for example, extensive use is made of signs that look like the objects and actions they refer to (iconic signs), in addition to signs that are grammaticalized pointing gestures (indexical signs). Such properties make signs quicker to learn than the abstract sound combinations of a spoken language (arbitrary signs). Nevertheless, Plains Sign Language is not a "universal" language. It is one of many sign languages in use around the world, most of which are not mutually intelligible, despite popular misconceptions to the contrary.

Fourth, with increasing travel and trade, and with the formation of new political alliances, gestures common to two or more nations may have undergone a gradual process of acceptance or rejection for use in intertribal contexts, the product of which was a standard sign system that became a common language. Skilled sign talkers would probably be those who were well traveled and who represented their nations frequently in intertribal contexts. It is possible that at first a number of signed pidgins were used in trading or diplomatic contexts, just as spoken pidgins were used in other complex linguistic areas. Frequent users would extend the vocabulary and create rules for the grammar until a full-fledged sign language evolved.

The sign language was of great practical value for economic and political purposes, but was also important in social contexts in which people shared their life experiences with friends and allies and entertained visitors with jokes and stories. Although the impetus for its widespread standardization undoubtedly came from its intertribal functions, the sign language was also used by people from the same tribe. Signing became part of a person's everyday language use, adding meaning to speech in numerous everyday contexts, especially during instances of storytelling and public oratory. Some outside investigators claimed that only men knew the sign language, but this perception may have resulted from the fact that men were much more visible to them in the public sphere.

This author found that by the 1980s, Plains Sign Language was no longer commonly used on the northern plains because forced accommodation to the English language had led to its gradual replacement. Its decline mirrors that of many spoken languages of the Plains Indians. In the late twentieth century fluent sign talkers are few, but they can be found in several communities where elders learned the language at an early age, where traditional storytelling keeps it alive, or where deafness in a family has preserved its practical function. Signing remains in use among the Assiniboins, Stoneys, Blackfeet, Piegans, Bloods, Crows, and Northern Cheyennes, in contexts involving such activities as religious ceremonies, drumming, and storytelling. This author has also noted that, in speaking their native language, Plains people frequently use gestures from the sign language to accompany their speech in everyday interactions. The revival of interest in indigenous languages, and the efforts to preserve them, have led to a renewed interest in the Plains Sign Language. Among the Assiniboins at Fort Belknap, and on the Blackfoot, Crow, and Northern Cheyenne Reservations in Montana, for example, the sign language is being incorporated into language-maintenance programs.

Clark, William P., *The Indian Sign Language* (1885; reprint, Lincoln: University of Nebraska Press, 1982); Farnell, Brenda, *"Do You See What I Mean?": Plains Indian Sign Talk and the Embodiment of Action* (Austin: University of Texas Press, 1995); Umiker-Sebeok, Jean, and Thomas A. Sebeok, eds., *Aboriginal Sign Languages of the Americas and Australia,* 2 vols. (New York and London: Plenum Press, 1978).

BRENDA FARNELL
University of Iowa

SIOUX

The large group of people collectively identified as the Sioux existed on the northern plains prior to European contact and the eventual conquest of their lands. Today this same group of people, having survived many attempts at cultural genocide, continue their struggle to regain and maintain a culture that has had to adapt to a changing environment.

The term *Sioux* is a fragment of the French and Ojibwa word *nadouessioux,* which is generally believed to be a derogatory term meaning "little snakes." The name resulted from a history of territorial conflicts between the Sioux and the Ojibwas, who were located to the east of the Sioux. Contemporary Sioux prefer the terms *Dakota, Nakota,* and *Lakota* when referring to themselves as a people and a nation, for these are the names of the group's different dialects, regions, and economies.

Before European contact the Sioux Nation consisted of seven major divisions, which called themselves the Oceti Sakowin, or Seven Council Fires. The Dakotas comprised the Mdewakantonwan (People of Spirit Lake), Wahpekute (Shooters among the Leaves), Wahpetonwan (Dwellers among the Leaves), and Sisitonwan (People of the Swamp). The Dakota dwelling place was to the east and northeast in the lakes region within the vast territory that the Oceti Sakowin commanded. The majority of the Dakota economy centered around fishing and the harvesting of wild rice and herbs. The Dakotas were known and recognized as the People of the Herbs.

To the southwest of the Dakotas were the Nakotas. They included the Ihanktonwan (Campers at the End), and Ihanktonwanna (Little Campers at the End). The Assiniboines (Cook with Stones), although not one of the original divisions of the Oceti Sakowin, became a band associated with the Nakota divisions in the pre-reservation era. The Nakotas resided to the southeast and south within Oceti Sakowin territory. The Nakota economy centered around pipestone quarrying, and they were known and recognized as the caretakers and protectors of the pipestone quarries.

Although the third group, the Lakotas, were but one division within the Oceti Sakowin, they consisted of seven smaller subdivisions called bands. The seven Lakota bands were the Sicangu (Burnt Thighs), Oohenunpa (Two Kettles), Itazipacola (Without Bows), Miniconjou (Planters by the Water), Sihasapa (Black Feet), Hunkpapa (End of the Horn or Entrance), and Oglala (Scatter Their Own). The Lakotas were known as the People of the Prairie and the Pte Oyate (Buffalo People). They resided on the Great Plains region to the west, northwest, and the southwest of the main Oceti Sakowin territory. Their economy was based on the buffalo and the wild fruits and vegetables of the plains. They were also known and recognized as the caretakers and protectors of the Black Hills, which they themselves and the Oceti Sakowin referred to as He Sapa.

The Oceti Sakowin were greatly dependent upon each other for survival. Their commerce reflected their locality and what they were able to provide in trade with the other groups. The different groups were in constant communication with one another, whether they were twenty miles apart or four hundred. Their lifestyles were ideally suited to their climate and could be adjusted to sudden shifts in conditions. Such an adjustment occurred annually at the time of the religious and social gathering, when the entire nation came together. It was a time for family socializing and for the various leaders to meet for major decision making.

The Sioux contend that they have always lived in the northern Great Plains area. If there was a migration that occurred, they say, it was outward from the Black Hills into the outlying regions. The Black Hills have a strong religious significance for the Oceti Sakowin—particularly the Lakotas, the chosen caretakers and protectors of the Black Hills—because the Black Hills are the traditional birthplace of the Sioux Nation.

According to tribal tradition, the Sioux originated within the Black Hills themselves. The story goes back to a time in history when they lived underground beneath the Black Hills. Eventually they were enticed to the surface of the earth, emerging through Wind Cave, in the southern Black Hills. Once they had emerged, they were unable to return to the place that had been their home for thousands of years. Their leader, whom they had left behind underground, foresaw the fate of his people and the hardships they would encounter and,

sacrificing his safe existence, came to the surface in the form of the buffalo. And it was the buffalo that sustained the people during that early period; it provided food, clothing, shelter, tools—all the necessities of life.

The entire Black Hills region has always been known to the Oceti Sakowin as "the heart of everything that is," because within the Black Hills lie the psychological and physical curing elements for the people. Other places within the Black Hills of religious significance are Harney Peak, Devil's Tower, and Bear Butte. Stories tell of the creation of these particular formations. Religious ceremonies were conducted at these sites, beginning in the spring and continuing throughout the summer in accordance with the movement of the constellations. The Oceti Sakowin as a whole never resided in the Black Hills for long periods of time, but they did return annually for the religious and social gathering.

Throughout the rest of the year, the Oceti Sakowin resided in their respective regions. They never lived in one large encampment, but rather in smaller groups called *tiospaye,* which consisted of family members, extended family, and others who chose to live with that particular *tiospaye.* There were many *tiospaye* within any given division of the Oceti Sakowin; *tiospaye* were located near enough to each other that they were never isolated, yet they maintained the privacy and space needed for comfortable living.

Within the Oceti Sakowin, every individual had a role and was greatly respected for his or her contributions. Each sex was aware of and recognized the importance of the other. Both sexes shared the responsibility of creating the nation and sustaining it. Both the men and the women were expected to exemplify the values of respect, generosity, bravery, fortitude, and wisdom in their everyday lives.

In any event, that peaceful life, although far from the idealistic existence that many people have since perceived it to be, was dramatically altered with the arrival of the newcomers from abroad.

The first encounter took place in the Rockies and was with the Spanish, from whom the Sioux acquired horses. This began what became known as the horse culture. Because of the horse's outstanding ability to do many things, the Sioux called it *sunkawakan,* meaning "sacred/holy dog." It was also considered sacred or holy because it had been revealed to the people through prophecy. Their encounter with the Spanish thus allowed the Oceti Sakowin to make positive changes within their culture.

A prison camp of Sioux at Fort Snelling in Dakota Territory after the Sioux uprising in 1862. Although the seventeen hundred Sioux held at the fort were not involved in the uprising, they were imprisoned there during the winter of 1862–63 and then relocated to a reservation in Nebraska.

The second encounter occurred with French traders and trappers at the confluence of the Mississippi and Missouri Rivers. This led initially to a friendly and undemanding alliance of the two cultures, and when the trade moved up the Missouri River, the strong alliance continued. Marriages between French traders and Oceti Sakowin women became common and acceptable. Guns were introduced, as well as household wares—a development that eventually resulted in a lesser dependence on the buffalo. Because the traders often lived and interacted within the bands and learned the language, they and their offspring later served as interpreters. Many of the decendants of these traders and Oceti Sakowin women continue to live in Sioux communities as tribal members.

The Indian trade continued with American traders, reaching its height between 1825 and 1835. During that time, American companies attempted to monopolize the Indian trade. Alcohol was employed as a means of attracting and gaining the trust and business of the bands. This had a negative effect within the structure of the Oceti Sakowin. The combination of alcohol and guns proved to be the beginnings of a breakdown in their value system. Whereas prior to the introduction of alcohol, decisions were made only for minor infractions of tribal laws, the leaders now had to deal with alcohol-related crimes such as assault, theft, and even murder.

For a time, the Oceti Sakowin bands continued to struggle for control and management of their governmental system and their territory. The Euro-American westward expansion continued, however, and the Oceti Sakowin gradually lost control over their once vast territory.

The United States seized land through treaties. These documents set boundaries for tribes and constrained their natural lifestyle and freedom. The first major treaty for the Oceti Sakowin was the 1851 Fort Laramie Treaty, which called for peace among the northern tribes, the establishment of roads and military posts, protection for Indians, and the establishment of boundaries. This document was ill conceived, because many of the tribes included in it had been enemies who did not make peace. In addition, the Oceti Sakowin bands had become severed into two factions—one that cooperated and sanctioned change, and one that abhorred white encroachment and resisted it. The latter refused to sign any treaties.

The second major treaty was the 1868 Fort Laramie Treaty. Its terms reduced the boundaries set in the 1851 treaty to the western half of present-day South Dakota, an area to be called the Great Sioux Reservation. It also called for the overall acculturation of the people by means of Christianity and education.

The U.S. government ceased treaty making in 1871, but when gold was discovered in the Black Hills, located within the boundaries of the Great Sioux Reservation, federal authorities attempted to negotiate with the Oceti Sakowin for the sale of the Black Hills region. Unable to conclude a legal agreement, the government rammed a document through an unrepresentative gathering and withdrew the Black Hills region from the Great Sioux Reservation. The Oceti Sakowin have continued to dispute the violation and have refused to accept any monetary payment.

In the attempt to enforce the 1868 treaty, the government ordered the Oceti Sakowin bands to relocate to the established reservation by January 31, 1876. Some complied, while others, under the leadership of Crazy Horse and Sitting Bull, resisted and remained at large until forced to return to South Dakota following their confrontation with the U.S. Army at the Little Bighorn.

The establishment of settled reservations in the 1880s was marred by fear and distrust of the U.S. government. Nevertheless, the conditions that were thrust upon the Oceti Sakowin were taken in stride and marked the beginnings of a new, sedentary lifestyle. A land "agreement" in 1889 reduced the land base of the Great Sioux Reservation dramatically. In addition, the new policy of allotment enrolled tribal heads of household, their spouses, and children and assigned them to individual homesteads. Once all enrolled tribal members received their allotments, the surplus lands were opened to homesteaders, further reducing the size of Indian lands.

Many more U.S. policies that followed were aimed either at assimilation and acculturation, or at rectifying previous policies. According to U.S. policy, the Oceti Sakowin or Sioux are a sovereign nation, but the United States has as yet failed to recognize and deal with these tribes as such.

The 1990 U.S. Census indicated that there are 103,255 enrolled members of the Oceti Sakowin or Sioux. They reside on reservations in South Dakota, North Dakota, Minnesota, Nebraska, and Montana. The census figure does not include the Sioux who reside in Canada or nonenrolled tribal members.

Bernotas, Bob, *Sitting Bull, Chief of the Sioux,* North American Indians of Achievement (New York and Philadelphia: Chelsea House Publishers, 1992); Garst, Doris Shannon, *Crazy Horse, a Great Warrior of the Sioux* (Boston: Houghton Mifflin Company, 1950); Goodman, Ronald, *Lakota Star Knowledge: Studies in Lakota Stellar Theology* (Rosebud, S. Dak.: Sinte Gleska University, 1992).

KAREN D. LONE HILL (Oglala Lakota)
Oglala Lakota College, Kyle, South Dakota

SITTING BULL (TATANKA IYOTANKA)

(1831?–90)
Hunkpapa military, religious, and political leader.

Sitting Bull was probably born in 1831 on the Grand River in present-day South Dakota. His father bore the name Sitting Bull; his mother, Her-Holy-Door. They named their son Jumping Badger.

Jumping Badger inherited his father's name at age fourteen as part of the ceremonies celebrating his accession to warrior status. Accompanying a raiding party, he had counted a first coup on a Crow warrior, thus earning the coveted measure of bravery in combat. His new name connoted a stubborn buffalo bull planted firmly on his haunches.

As young Sitting Bull matured into adulthood, he accumulated a superlative war record in fighting with Assiniboins, Crows, Flatheads, Blackfeet, and other enemy tribes. This led in 1857 to his designation as a tribal war chief. At the same time, he mastered the sacred mysteries of the Lakotas and rose to eminence as a holy man. Profound spirituality characterized his entire life, and scars on his chest, back, and arms testified to repeated sacrifices in the Sun Dance. The Hunkpapas came to look on him as the embodiment of the cardinal virtues of the Lakotas—bravery, fortitude, generosity, and wisdom. His name and fame spread to all seven Lakota tribes.

Sitting Bull's name captured the attention of white people, too, as growing numbers intruded into the Hunkpapa domain. In the 1860s white gold seekers

Sitting Bull and Buffalo Bill Cody in a publicity photo taken in Montreal in 1885. Sitting Bull was a star attraction in Cody's Wild West show during the 1885 season.

came up the Missouri River headed for the mines of western Montana, and at the same time shock waves from the Dakota Sioux uprising of 1862 rolled west from Minnesota. In fighting with the armies of Generals Henry H. Sibley and Alfred Sully in 1863 and 1864, Sitting Bull emerged as the leading Hunkpapa war chief. When the army planted forts along the river, he waged a deadly war on them that lasted for five years.

Sitting Bull rose to more powerful leadership as the seven Lakota bands confronted the provisions of the Treaty of 1868. This accord, which few of the signatory chiefs truly understood, defined a "Great Sioux Reservation" embracing all of present-day South Dakota west of the Missouri River. Here all Lakotas promised to reside. For those who wished to delay, however, the treaty identified an "unceded territory" west and north of the reservation. Portions of each Lakota band settled on the reservation and grew dependent on government rations.

Others remained in the buffalo ranges of the Powder and Yellowstone Valleys.

These "nontreaties" who continued to follow the buffalo accorded allegiance to Sitting Bull and the powerful Oglala war chief Crazy Horse. A staunch foe of government programs, Sitting Bull wanted no part of treaties, agents, rations, or any course that would interfere with the old life of following the buffalo and warring against enemy tribes. The people designated him supreme chief of all the Lakotas, a post that had never before existed and that ran counter to the loose Lakota political structure. When all the band chiefs gathered in council, however, they recognized Sitting Bull as the one "old-man chief" entitled to deference.

With the firm support of Crazy Horse, Sitting Bull broke off the war against the upper Missouri forts but vowed to defend the buffalo ranges to the west against all white intrusions. When intrusions occurred, his warriors fought back. In 1872 and 1873, they skirmished with troops escorting surveyors of the Northern Pacific Railroad in the Yellowstone Valley.

The most damaging intrusion took place on the Great Sioux Reservation itself, when the discovery of gold in the Black Hills set off a rush that blatantly violated the treaty of 1868. The government tried to buy the hills, but the Indians would not sell. From this dilemma sprang a comprehensive military campaign aimed ostensibly at punishing the Sitting Bull bands for aggressions against tribes friendly to the United States, but which in reality was aimed at forcing them to give up their freedom and settle on the reservation.

The Great Sioux War of 1876 featured the stunning disaster to U.S. troops at the battle of the Little Bighorn. But "Custer's last stand" prompted a massive offensive that ended Lakota freedom. Most of the "hostiles" surrendered and settled on the reservation. Sitting Bull and a diehard remnant took refuge in Canada. As the buffalo dwindled, starvation set in. On July 20, 1881, Sitting Bull surrendered at Fort Buford, Dakota Territory.

After two years as a prisoner of war, Sitting Bull settled on the reservation at the Standing Rock Agency in present-day North Dakota. Here he resisted the government's objective of transforming the Lakotas into imitation whites. At the same time, he sampled innovations that he thought beneficial. He became a successful farmer and stockman, and he sent his children to government schools. In 1885 he traveled with Buffalo Bill's Wild West show.

The reservation years gave Sitting Bull leisure to

enjoy his family, to all of whom he was deeply devoted. His first wife had died in childbirth in 1857. Of two successors, he had expelled one from his tipi, and the other had died. Finally, in 1872, he married sisters, Four Robes and Seen-by-the-Nation. Of many children by these wives, he especially treasured in his final years a son, Crow Foot, and a daughter, Standing Holy. Sitting Bull's father had been killed by a Crow warrior in 1859, but his mother was a powerful presence in his tipi until her death in 1884.

Sitting Bull's last years found him in the familiar stance of opposing government aims. He battled the land agreements of 1888 and 1889, which threw half the Great Sioux Reservation open to white settlement and divided the rest into six separate reservations. When this and other grievances laid the groundwork for a powerful religious revitalization movement, he emerged as the leading apostle of the 1890 Ghost Dance on the Standing Rock Reservation. Agent James McLaughlin urged his removal from the reservation. On December 15, 1890, Indian police stormed into his cabin on the Grand River and took him into custody. His followers intervened, and in a bloody shootout police fire cut him down; he was shot and killed, ironically, by men of his own race garbed in blue uniforms.

Today Sitting Bull is remembered as one of the greatest of all Indian chieftains, a man of power and renown among his own people, an uncompromising foe of white encroachments on his land and his way of life. His rocklike dedication to the principles that ordered his life ensured failure in the great purpose he set for himself but also awarded him stature as one of American history's greatest patriots.

See also Sioux.

Utley, Robert M., *The Lance and the Shield: The Life and Times of Sitting Bull* (New York: Henry Holt & Co., 1993); Vestal, Stanley, *Sitting Bull, Champion of the Sioux* (Norman: University of Oklahoma Press, 1957).

ROBERT M. UTLEY
Moose, Wyoming

SKOLASKIN

(1839–1922)
Sanpoil prophet.

When Skolaskin became a prophet to the Interior Salish–speaking Sanpoils, they were a peaceful people who occupied the north bank of the Columbia River from its confluence with the Spokane River to the Sanpoil Valley in today's lower Ferry County, Washington. For years the Sanpoils had followed the teachings of the dreamer Michael, but when he died at an early age sometime in the mid–nineteenth century, Skolaskin assumed power and control over them.

In the years when white encroachment had become alarming to the Indians, Michael had adopted white soldiers' hymns and the preaching of missionaries to offer the Sanpoils hope that the Great Spirit would deliver them, but after Michael died, Skolaskin adopted other tactics. Unlike those tribal leaders who had risen to high positions through heredity and valorous deeds, Skolaskin assumed his leadership role through prophecies and manipulation. After "dying" and remaining motionless for one to three days (accounts vary), he awakened and told the Sanpoils that he had gone to heaven and received a mandate to preach to them. He further validated his authority by predicting both the earthquake of 1872 and its aftershocks. These, he warned, were signs that the Great Spirit and the Earth Mother were displeased with the people for failing to observe proper traditional ceremonials.

Skolaskin's prophecy occurred in the year that the Colville Indian Reservation was established in an area that included the Sanpoils' lands, and he claimed that the placement of Indians on the reservation was yet another sign of the deities' anger. He also opposed the Sinkiuse (Columbia) chief Moses, who had helped settle Chief Joseph and his weary band of Nez Perces in 1885 on the Colville Reservation following their capture in 1877 by government troops and subsequent exile in Oklahoma Territory.

Playing on his people's anguish at the loss of their land and way of life, Skolaskin won many followers with sermons of hope. Salvation, he said, would be possible if they followed him. To exert further control, he developed his own law and justice system, which included a police force, a court, and a crude jail (a pit dug into the ground to receive those who resisted him).

Skolaskin's most bizarre means of controlling people involved a plan to build an ark that would save his followers from a flood he had predicted. The ark was never built, but he used the plan to build it as a ruse to lure attractive women. After commanding their husbands to gather logs for the ark at distant places, he could pursue these women without fear of reprisal. Men who refused were threatened with imprisonment in the prophet's jail.

Skolaskin within a few years of his death in 1922. A blanket covers his contracted legs, which kept him from standing erect or mounting his horse on his own.

Initially, women considered Skolaskin unattractive because of a deformity that caused him to walk about with his hands on his knees and to mount a horse only from a stump or other elevated object. Later, though, the women were mesmerized by his preaching, and eventually he had six wives and many affairs.

When Skolaskin was at the height of his power, no fellow Indians were able to unseat him, but in 1889 the federal government intervened. Believing Skolaskin to be a threat to its policies on the Colville Reservation, the government shipped him off to Alcatraz, then a military prison where troublesome Indians were often sent. At Alcatraz the prophet lived in a dark cell until 1892.

Upon his release—accomplished through the efforts of Indian-rights advocates—he was forced to pledge not to "make any trouble amongst the Indians nor between them and the white people, nor give any advice or talk to the Indians that will make them discontented or not willing to obey the agent."

Once home, a broken but still resentful Skolaskin ignored the pledge and made a few last attempts to stir up reservation Indians against the federal government. However, during his absence new tribal leaders had emerged, and Skolaskin found that his authority had waned.

By this time the government had already traded off the northern half of the reservation to accommodate miners and settlers. Skolaskin called meetings of his people to oppose any further allotting of reservation land, and in 1911 he journeyed to the nation's capital to petition the government directly. His efforts on both fronts were futile.

Despite Skolaskin's loss of power, some of his followers remained loyal to him until his death, even citing the great Columbia River deluge of 1894 as evidence that his prophecy of a flood had been fulfilled. A similar claim was made in 1939, when Roosevelt Lake filled with water behind the newly built Grand Coulee Dam. Ironically, the waters of that lake covered Skolaskin's home, forcing the removal of his grave.

This was not the first irony in the prophet's life. Although he was anathema to the Roman Catholic Church, which considered him a devilish pagan, Skolaskin used song, prayer, hand bells, and other symbols of Catholic worship in his church house. Later, on May 30, 1918, he became a Catholic convert at a church in Keller, Washington, took the name of Frank, and cut his long hair to symbolize his rift with a nativist past. It seems he was hoping through conversion to find a peace in heaven that he was never able to enjoy on earth.

See also Colville Tribes.

Ray, Verne F., *The Sanpoil and Nespelem: Salishan Peoples of Northeastern Washington*, University of Washington Publications in Anthropology, no. 5 (Seattle, 1933); Ruby, Robert H., and John A. Brown, *Dreamer-Prophets of the Columbia Plateau* (Norman: University of Oklahoma Press, 1989).

ROBERT H. RUBY
Moses Lake, Washington

JOHN A. BROWN
Wenatchee, Washington

SLAVERY

For Native American peoples, *slavery* describes three distinct experiences: the aboriginal practice of holding war captives; the capture or purchase of native peoples by Europeans for use in plantation agriculture; and the acquisition of African Americans by southern Indians for use on their own plantations.

Except along the Northwest Coast, in most precontact Native American societies war captives served social rather than economic purposes. Torture awaited some, while others became adopted members of their captor's family and tribe. Torture enabled Indians to fulfill a sacred obligation by avenging the deaths of kin. Adoption, on the other hand, enabled a family to replace members who had died, and adopted war captives enjoyed all the privileges extended to relatives by birth. A few captives underwent neither torture nor adoption but remained on the fringe of society. This status most closely resembled the institution that Europeans called "slavery," because these people often performed menial tasks and strenuous work. Nevertheless, because most native peoples lived at the subsistence level and placed no premium on the accumulation of material wealth, these captives did not contribute economically in the way "slaves" commonly do. Certainly they contributed to the overall productivity of the group, and their sale or ransom might bring desirable goods into the community, but they did not represent a capital investment. Native economies did not depend on slave labor, nor did they value it.

Captives may well have served an important social function in traditional societies. Their anomalous situation—they had no kin ties—served to reinforce the importance of kinship. That is, a person without kin was a slave. On the Northwest Coast, where material wealth assumed greater significance, slaves did acquire a value unknown elsewhere and became a species of property to be bought, sold, and given away.

The arrival of Europeans in North America radically changed the aboriginal institution of slavery. Early Spanish slave raiding along the Atlantic Coast seriously depleted populations through seizure and the introduction of disease. Ponce de Leon sought slaves as well as the fountain of youth when he explored Florida in 1513, and Hernando de Soto's *entrada* in 1540 introduced thousands of native peoples in the Southeast to the European concept of slavery when the conquistador impressed Indians into service as pack carriers for his expedition. Bartolomé de Las Casas sharply criticized the enslavement of Indians, and most Spaniards adopted labor systems technically distinct from slavery. The native people who were subject to the *encomienda*, or tribute, system or were forced to labor on missions probably would not have recognized the distinction. Furthermore, in areas such as northern Mexico, where silver mining demanded a large labor force, Indian slavery endured, and the Spanish depended on the native peoples for their labor force.

The English also enslaved native people, particularly once the 1622 Powhatan uprising in Virginia enabled the colonists to define Indians as hostiles. Colonial Indian wars usually degenerated into slaving expeditions, if they had not actually started that way. New Englanders, for example, enslaved substantial numbers of Indians in the aftermath of the Pequot War (1637) and King Philip's War (1675–76). Colonists either put their native captives to work in the fields alongside African Americans or exported them to the West Indies, where they could not escape and return home. Archaeological evidence reveals a Native American influence on the material culture of slaves, and names and cultural practices (such as matrilineal kinship) hint at the extent of enslavement.

The English slave trade severely disrupted the native Southeast in the late seventeenth and early eighteenth centuries as Indians turned on each other to satisfy the insatiable English appetite for labor and their own desire for English manufactured goods. The Choctaws, for example, may have lost over two thousand men to other native people armed with English firearms who sold captives to British traders. The old social functions of captives gave way to the economic imperatives of trade. When the French arrived on the Gulf Coast in 1699, they pledged to end the slave trade and provided arms to vulnerable tribes. But the growing relative importance of the deerskin trade—difficult to sustain in a conflagration—and a growing number of African-American slaves did more to curtail slave raiding than did the French overtures. Furthermore, the French themselves precipitated slave raiding on the Great Plains, a fact that calls into question their sincerity about ending an institution so linked to colonial exploitation of the Western Hemisphere.

The shift from Indian slave to Indian slaveholder, in the European sense, grew out of the cultural impact of Europeans on native peoples. Some Indians, particularly in the South, began to adopt European attitudes toward Africans in the early eighteenth century. Treaties that required the capture of runaway slaves and paid bounties for their return drew Indians into the slave system of the southern colonies. Never isolated from colonists or their ideas, Indians became aware of the racial antipathy European colonists felt toward Africans. Unwilling to risk identification with these despised people, many native southerners began to distance themselves from Africans. Furthermore, some Indians began to find Africans useful as translators or laborers, and a few purchased slaves.

The Indian adoption of racial slavery, however, dates primarily from the 1790s, when George Washington and his secretary of war, Henry Knox, began to implement a "civilization" program designed to convert Indians culturally into white men. In the South, Indians who embraced the tenets of the "civilization" program took white planters as their role models and began to acquire African-American slaves to work in their fields. The adoption of slave labor in agriculture also conformed to "civilization's" division of labor. Women, who traditionally had farmed, could now leave the fields and take up their duties as housewives, while men, for whom routine farming traditionally was anathema, could avoid agricultural labor. The practice of holding land in common enabled native planters to invest capital in labor, and they quickly became an economic elite in the southern Indian nations. They also wielded a disproportionate share of political power, and their interests came to dominate political decisions. As time went on, they developed slave codes to regulate and protect their property and grew ever more like their role models.

The Seminoles provide an exception to the pattern of race relations that developed among southern Indians in the early nineteenth century. When the Red Stick Creeks joined the Seminoles in Florida following the Creek War (1813–14), they took many slaves with them. Together with runaway slaves from white plantations, these African Americans maintained a semiautonomous existence, with their own towns and leaders, and merely offered tribute to the Seminoles. The traditional values of the Seminoles may help explain this divergent pattern, but the shift in racial attitudes that took place in the United States after the War of 1812 may also account for the difference. In the eighteenth century, Europeans had tended to explain differences in human beings in terms of culture, learned practices, and beliefs, which can change, rather than racial characteristics, inherited features that cannot be altered. By separating themselves from the "civilization" program and American thought in the early nineteenth century, the Seminoles apparently did not imbibe the racism

that increasingly influenced the actions of other southern Indians.

In the Seminoles' armed resistance to removal (1835–42), African Americans fought alongside them. When captured Seminoles arrived west of the Mississippi, they resisted settlement among the Creeks, as the United States had planned, because they feared that the Creeks would enslave their black comrades. Although most relented, some refused to leave their encampment in the Cherokee Nation, where the independent status of the black Seminoles contributed to a rebellion by Cherokee slaves. Finally, in the 1850s, the Seminoles received their own nation, where they no longer had to defend the African Americans among them against the Creeks.

Removal west of the Mississippi in the 1830s had little effect on the status of the slaves of southern Indians, but the Civil War wreaked havoc on both native people and their bondsmen. All southern Indian nations signed treaties with the Confederacy, but profound divisions within the Creek and Cherokee Nations soon brought about internal civil wars. Southern partisans with their slaves fled to the Choctaw Nation or Texas, while Union sympathizers took refuge in Kansas. Southern Indians served on both sides in the war, and the end of hostilities left all their nations devastated. In the treaties negotiated with the United States following the war, the southern nations freed their slaves and promised to extend privileges of citizenship, including land, to the freedmen. Most freedmen, abandoned outside their nations and ignorant of the provision or powerless to force compliance, found the promise empty.

Although slavery ended in 1865, the institution's offspring—debt peonage and forced labor—subsequently trapped many Indians, as well as African Americans, in economic bondage. Ensnared by debt or arrested for minor crimes and then forced to work off their obligations, Indians from North Carolina to California have lived in the shadow of slavery for well over a century. Isolated, nonreservation Indians have been particularly vulnerable to this form of exploitation. Slavery indeed has many meanings for native people and remains a part of their lives as well as their histories.

Littlefield, Daniel F., Jr., *Africans and Seminoles: From Removal to Emancipation* (Westport, Conn.: Greenwood Press, 1977); Perdue, Theda, *Slavery and the Evolution of Cherokee Society, 1540–1866* (Knoxville: University of Tennessee Press, 1979).

THEDA PERDUE
University of Kentucky

SMITH, REDBIRD

(1850–1918)
Cherokee religious and political leader.

Redbird Smith was born in the Cherokee Nation just west of Fort Smith, Arkansas, to a Cherokee father and a half-Cherokee, half-German mother. His father, Pig Redbird Smith, was a blacksmith—thus the name Smith. Smith grew up in a highly conservative family, but by the 1850s most traditional Cherokee institutions had disintegrated. The clan system and the division of the political arena into White (peace) and Red (war) moieties had all but disappeared. Christianity had replaced the traditional tribal priesthood and community religious ceremonies. The sacred fires were no longer maintained; the stomp dances were no longer performed. Even the tribal wampum belts had been entrusted to the elected chief, John Ross. The only Cherokee religious rites still actively practiced were those related to healing, conjuring, and witchcraft. In most ways, the lifestyle of even the traditional tribesmen bore more resemblance to that of their white neighbors in Arkansas than to that of their ancestors.

Despite these changes, however, the western Cherokees were a deeply divided people. "Full-blood," Cherokee-speaking families lived primarily as subsistence farmers and hunters. They formed the core of a group that resisted further cultural change. Opposing them were acculturated, "mixed-blood" families, whose leaders were usually wealthy slave owners. Their plantation lifestyle was indistinguishable from that of wealthy southern whites. The two groups had divided in the 1830s over the issue of removal to Indian Territory. The "mixed-blood" leaders had signed the removal treaty of New Echota in 1835, and the "full bloods" had been forced west. In the years immediately following the removal, a virtual civil war of recrimination and revenge had raged within the Cherokee Nation. With the approach of the American Civil War, political issues imposed on the Cherokees from outside once again amplified the differences between these two groups.

In 1859 a white Baptist missionary, Evan Jones, revived the Keetoowah Society. The purpose of this secret society was to reestablish the moral life of the tribe. More social and political than overtly religious, the society quickly found favor among the conservative "full bloods" of all religious persuasions: Baptists, Methodists, Presbyterians, Quakers, and non-Christians. Their main cause was their opposition to slavery and to

the power of the wealthy Cherokee planters. Pig Smith was an early member of the Keetoowah Society.

At the outbreak of the Civil War the Smith family, together with some other Keetoowah families, joined Opothleyaholo and the neutral Creeks and Seminoles in their disastrous flight to Kansas during the winter of 1861–62. Eventually most of the Keetoowah families ended up in the refugee camps in Kansas; Keetoowah men formed the core of the Cherokee regiments that opposed their government's alliance with the Confederacy and fought for the Union.

By the end of the war, Pig Smith had emerged as a major leader of the Keetoowahs, particularly among the most conservative, non-Christian element of the tribe. In 1867 he was elected to the Cherokee Senate and served as president. Pig Smith argued that the divisions and rivalry that had plagued the tribe since removal had been caused by the loss of traditional Cherokee values and beliefs. Foreseeing that his life would be too short to fulfill his mission (he in fact died in 1871), he took his son Redbird to Creek Sam, a Natchez religious leader, so that he could be educated to act as his adviser. Notchee (Natchez) town, located in the Illinois District of the Cherokee Nation, south of Tahlequah, was one of the most conservative communities in all of what is now Oklahoma. The Natchez had brought their sacred fire with them from the East, and their home in the Illinois District became the gathering place for religiously conservative kinsmen. It was in this community, with its living ties to preremoval Cherokee life, that Redbird Smith came of age.

In the years after the Civil War, the Keetoowahs became the major force in Cherokee politics. Tribal rivalries continued, however, and the "mixed bloods" gained control of the Cherokee government in 1887. That same year, pressure on all Indians to conform to Anglo-American norms increased as Congress adopted the General Allotment Act and pressed for tribes to divide up their lands. By 1889 many of the Keetoowahs believed that their society had become too political and had lost its original moral purpose. Meeting together, these dissenting Keetoowahs broke away from the old society and formed a new Keetoowah Society that would be religious as well as political. Redbird had been a "little captain" (community leader) in the old society. He now became a head captain of the Illinois District. In 1890 he was elected to the Cherokee council.

During the 1890s, as pressures from the federal government to allot the lands of the Five Civilized Tribes mounted and the number of non-Indians living in Indian Territory grew, conservatives such as the Keetoowahs and their supporters started banding together in opposition. The Four Mothers Society was established in the Illinois District, with the Natchez and their sacred fire forming its core. Redbird Smith, together with many other Cherokees as well as Creeks, became active in this new society. Some followers thought the society should be more overtly political, while others believed that it should withdraw entirely from society and focus exclusively on religion.

Redbird Smith sided with those who believed that the divisions in Cherokee society would not be healed until political opponents stopped resorting to violence and witchcraft. He argued that the Cherokees had brought their problems upon themselves by turning away from the teachings of their Creator. Only the Creator could save the Cherokee people. As he spoke out on the need to revive traditional religious practices, Smith called for the general adoption of the "White Path," the path of nonviolence and righteousness. To accomplish this goal, he instructed his followers to rekindle their sacred fires, revive the stomp dances, and take back their wampum belts.

Redbird Smith scored his first success when one of John Ross's sons gave the Keetoowahs seven tribal wampum belts. The interpretations of these belts became the basic teachings of a new religion. In 1896 Smith and his followers revived the Cherokee stomp dance. In 1902 they rekindled the first of the new Cherokee sacred fires. By 1906 there would be twenty-two sacred fires among the Cherokees. Finally, Smith and his followers formally broke with the earlier, political Keetoowah Society and became the Nighthawk Keetoowahs.

In spite of the opposition of the conservative Cherokees, the official tribal government agreed in 1900 to the allotment of Cherokee lands. As a member of the Cherokee Senate, Smith refused to vote on the agreement, and when it was presented for approval he declared he would not sign it. Smith encouraged his followers to resist allotment by refusing to register for their lands. It was estimated that over five thousand Cherokees followed his lead. In frustration, the Dawes Commission, the body charged with overseeing the allotment process among the Five Civilized Tribes, ordered the arrest of Smith and several other Nighthawk Keetoowah leaders. They were jailed briefly, but the Dawes Commission released them and proceeded to add their names to the allotment roll and assign them allotments.

In 1906 Redbird Smith appeared before a special U.S. Senate investigating committee in Tahlequah, asking that the federal government stop the process of allotment and honor its treaty obligations to the tribe. Although allotments had been assigned to the Nighthawks, hundreds refused to recognize their new titles or to live on their allotments. In 1910, seeing that the government was not going to change its position and that resistance was no longer in his followers' interest, Smith accepted an allotment. Although he continued to try to find a peaceful way to restore traditional beliefs, the power and influence of the Nighthawks began to wane. By the time of his death in 1918, many of the sacred fires had been consolidated and the Nighthawk Keetoowah Society had become primarily a religious movement; its days as an active political force were over.

Hendrix, Janey B., *Redbird Smith and the Nighthawk Keetoowahs* (Park Hill, Okla.: Cross Cultural Education Center, 1983).

GARRICK BAILEY
(Euro-American, Cherokee, and Choctaw)
University of Tulsa

ROBERTA GLENN BAILEY
Tulsa, Oklahoma

SMOHALLA

(c. 1815–95)
Wanapam shaman and prophet.

Born in a Wanapam village near present-day Walla Walla, Washington, Smohalla came to speak for a large contingent of Plateau Indians who faced dispossession during the nineteenth century. In the process, he created an ideology that continues to influence Plateau affairs to this day.

We know almost nothing of Smohalla's childhood and early career. Some claim that his given name was Wak-wei (Arising from the Dust of the Earth Mother), though some called him Waip-shwa (Rock Carrier). Physically distinctive—he had a hunchback, unnaturally short legs, and a head disproportionately large for his body—he experienced an adolescent vision quest that confirmed his peculiar nature: in it he was granted the powers to become a shaman. After his vision, he changed his name to Smohalla ("Dreamer"), a reference to the means by which spirits communicated with him.

Smohalla's reputation grew quickly. Like all successful Plateau shamans, Smohalla could accurately predict the arrival of the annual salmon runs, foretell where root diggers would find fertile grounds, and direct hunters to game herds; but he also had a reputation for being able to predict earthquakes and eclipses. Skeptical whites claimed that Smohalla got this information from an almanac, but the shaman claimed that spirits told him of these things because he was faithful to the traditional religion of his people.

Smohalla's continuing commitment to native traditions brought him into conflict with progressive elements in his village. In about 1850 he debated with a Wallawalla political leader named Homily over accepting white requests to use tribal land. "You do not own this land, our Mother Earth," he told Homily. "It is not your land to barter to the white people like a piece of salmon." But Homily chided, "Look at you, you are a poor man. Where are all your horses? You are no fit leader for your people. . . . You always talk of the old customs while up and down the river others accept the new ways and they grow rich." Homily's speech won the village over, and Smohalla and a small group of followers were forced to flee. They moved to the foot of the Priest Rapids near the present-day town of Vernita, Washington. There they were free to live as the shaman taught them, but their independence was short-lived.

Taking advantage of factional tensions between groups, Washington Territory officials convinced the largest and most powerful local Indian groups to settle on large reservations in 1855, ceding thousands of square miles of land belonging to outlying groups. Although the land occupied by his village had been sold out from under him, Smohalla refused to relocate onto the new reserve. He also refused to join an alliance that warred against the treaties, putting him at odds with all the contending parties in Plateau diplomacy. Growing resentment over Smohalla's position finally led to a confrontation between the shaman and a Sinkiuse political leader named Moses. Some witnesses claimed that the two men fought and that Smohalla died of his wounds. According to another story, at about this same time Smohalla's favorite daughter died of European diseases and the shaman died of grief at her graveside.

Accounts of Smohalla's death were particularly important to the role he would play in Plateau life. Tradition among Plateau peoples called for prophets to experience death and then return to life bearing important messages for the living. Smohalla always claimed that this was how he had learned his religious ideology, the Washani (dancer's) Creed.

The fundamental message in the Washani Creed was that of the organic unity between people and the earth. Smohalla often repeated the basic articles of faith:

> You ask me to plough the ground! Shall I take a knife and tear my mother's bosom? Then when I die she will not take me to her bosom to rest.
> You ask me to dig for stone! Shall I dig under her skin for her bones? Then when I die I cannot enter her body to be born again.
> You ask me to cut grass and make hay and sell it, and be rich like white men, but how dare I cut off my mother's hair?

Smohalla also taught his followers that they should not work as white people did, but should accept the fish, game, and bulbs that were nature's gifts. "Men who work cannot dream," he said, "and wisdom comes to us in dreams." Finally, he taught that "those who cut up the lands or sign papers for the lands will be defrauded of their rights, and will be punished by God's anger."

In essence, Smohalla was advocating passive resistance to the forces of modernization and cultural disintegration. Rather than resorting to armed rebellion, Smohalla counseled his followers to withdraw into the world of dreams to await supernatural events that would bring relief and salvation. "After a while," Smohalla proclaimed, "when God is ready, he will drive away all the people except the people who have obeyed the laws." Then those who obeyed the Washani Creed would experience new life. "All the dead men will come to life again," Smohalla asserted. "Their spirits will come to their bodies again."

Smohalla's message had great appeal for Plateau groups who, like the prophet's own band, had been excluded from treaty settlements in 1855. The most prominent of these, the Wallowa band of the Nez Perces, led by young Chief Joseph, never joined the Washani faith, but often referred to Smohalla's creed as a reflection of the truth. Such references led white policymakers to conclude that Smohalla was a latter-day Tenskwatawa — the Shawnee Prophet — and Joseph a reborn Tecumseh, a perception that led to the Nez Perce War in 1877.

Smohalla weathered the violence of the 1870s virtually unscathed. Although continuing pressure by Indian agents and military men carved the plateau region into a checkerboard of reservations and homesteads, hundreds refused to "sign papers for the land." They continued to

A rare photograph showing an aged Smohalla, foreground, dressed in white, *surrounded by priests of the Washani cult. Despite his advanced age (he was about eighty when this photograph was taken), the prophet remained a commanding presence.*

move about the plateau harvesting the gifts of nature, protected by provisions in the 1855 treaties that granted them the right to gather foods in their "usual and accustomed places." Various government agents tried to enlist Smohalla in the allotment process, but he apparently refused to cooperate. As he aged and grew increasingly blind, the prophet withdrew from public life.

Smohalla died in 1895, but the Washani ideology lived on. Outside the plateau, Indian groups who heard about Smohalla's religion incorporated aspects of the Washani Creed into resistance ideologies like the Ghost Dance. In the Pacific Northwest, both whites and Indians found meaning in Smohalla's teachings, but an essential irony resulted. In the 1960s, white conservationists found a powerful rhetoric in the Washani Creed and used it to lobby for laws designed to control hunting, fishing, and other such practices. At the same time, both reservation and nonreservation Indians cited the prophet's creed as a justification for disregarding those very conservation measures on the grounds that they violated not only treaty rights, but the prophet's religious laws as well.

See also Joseph; Plateau Tribes.

Miller, Christopher L., *Prophetic Worlds: Indians and Whites on the Columbia Plateau* (New Brunswick, N.J.: Rutgers University Press, 1985); Relander, Click, *Drummers and Dreamers: The Story of Smowhala the Prophet and His Nephew Puck Hyah Toot, the Last Prophet of the Nearly Extinct River People, the Last Wanapums* (1953; reprint, Seattle: Pacific Northwest National Parks and Forest Association, 1986); Ruby, Robert H., and John A. Brown, *Dreamer-Prophets of the Columbia Plateau: Smohalla and Skolaskin* (Norman: University of Oklahoma Press, 1989).

CHRISTOPHER L. MILLER
University of Texas, Pan American

SPIRO

Spiro is a large Mississippian archaeological site in eastern Oklahoma, near the town of the same name, and belongs to the Caddoan archaeological tradition. The site, covering about fifty acres, contains a circle of six low mounds, two large, pyramidal platform mounds, and a large pyramidal charnel mound. The low mounds originally served as the bases for communal charnel houses, and the large charnel mound served the same purpose for the elite, who were buried alongside large quantities of finely crafted grave goods. The two platform mounds originally served as the bases for large public structures. The site also contains residential areas and cemeteries.

People occupied Spiro between A.D. 700 and A.D. 1450, and the site reached its peak between A.D. 1200 and A.D. 1400. During this time, Spiro was the capital of a large theocratic chiefdom centered on the Arkansas River. Unlike many Mississippian capitals, Spiro served primarily as a ceremonial center and supported a relatively small resident population. The chiefdom also contained ten subordinate district capitals.

The people of Spiro and its chiefdom relied primarily on farming, supplementing their diet by hunting, fishing, and gathering wild plants. They also engaged in an extensive trade that brought them copper, mica, greenstone, and marine shells from as far away as the Appalachian Mountains and the Gulf Coast. Spiro's geographic location probably allowed it to control trade between the Southwest and the southern plains and other Mississippian chiefdoms in the southeastern woodlands.

Though it experienced no contact with early Spanish explorers, Spiro was probably similar to the Caddoan-speaking chiefdoms of western Arkansas encountered by the de Soto expedition in the early sixteenth century. By the time the first Europeans arrived in northeastern Oklahoma, the site had been abandoned.

See also Mississippians.

SPORTS MASCOTS
See Mascots and Other Public Appropriations of Indians and Indian Culture by Whites.

SPOTTED TAIL (SINTE GLESKA)
(1823?–1881)
Brulé Sioux warrior, civil leader, and negotiator.

As a young man Spotted Tail (or, in Lakota, Sinte Gleska) demonstrated bravery in battle. He was called Spotted Tail because of a raccoon tail he received as a gift from a white trapper. During the last twenty-five years of his life he was best known as a negotiator, seeking peace with the whites who were dominating North America. He considered education, including the effective use of the English language, a key to Native American survival. At the same time he insisted on the preservation of traditional culture.

Spotted Tail was born in 1823 or 1824 near present-day Pine Ridge, South Dakota. His father was a Blackfoot-Sioux and his mother a Brulé. His earliest recognition came from warfare with the Pawnees over hunting lands. By the time he was thirty he was a Shirtwearer — adorned with over one hundred locks of hair that represented scalps, coups, and captured horses. Little else is known of his life until 1854, when he participated in the retaliation against Lieutenant J. L. Grattan near Fort Laramie. In September 1855 Spotted Tail was wounded in a battle on Bluewater Creek in Nebraska in which cavalry forces led by General William S. Harney killed eighty-six Brulés and took others captive, including Spotted Tail's wife and baby daughter.

In October 1855, Spotted Tail and four others surrendered at Fort Laramie to prevent further conflict. Expecting execution, they were in fact sent to Fort Leavenworth in Kansas, and later to Fort Kearney; they were set free about a year afterward. From that point Spotted Tail would evaluate the long-term interests of his people differently. Having witnessed the strength and numbers of the white military forces, he recognized that survival required coexistence and that diplomacy had to be substituted for battle.

Upon Spotted Tail's return, he kept the status of Shirt Wearer and head soldier. Conflict with the Pawnees continued. Spotted Tail was pulled into an intertribal alliance with the Cheyennes, Arapahos, and three Sioux bands (the Sicangu, Oglala, and Miniconjou) in late 1864. The alliance was formed following restric-

Spotted Tail and his wife, photographed in Washington, D.C., in 1872.

tions on Sioux movement along the Platte River and the Chivington Massacre of Cheyennes and Arapahos at Sand Creek. Early the next year he led warriors in an assault on Julesburg, Colorado.

Shortly thereafter Spotted Tail brought his people to Fort Laramie to seek a peace settlement. He advised accommodation with white settlers during the conflicts along the Bozeman Trail from 1866 to 1868, and he agreed to the Treaty of Fort Laramie in 1868. In accordance with the treaty, Spotted Tail's band and a group called the Loafers, who had lived a life of dependence near Fort Laramie for nearly twenty-five years, moved to an area on Whetstone Creek near the Missouri River in the late summer of 1868. Not pleased with his band's new location, Spotted Tail chose to live over thirty miles from the agency.

Part of the history of this period was documented by the agent D. C. Poole, who admired Spotted Tail. Poole recounted the conflict between Spotted Tail and Big Mouth, the Loafer leader, who resented the Brulé's authority: following a drunken threat by Big Mouth, Spotted Tail shot and killed him; he then calmly went to the agency office to report the event and to present a brief lecture on temperance. (Spotted Tail's firm opposition to drinking and smoking was one of the reasons he had chosen to live at a distance from the agency.)

Spotted Tail soon requested a meeting with the U.S. president and initially expected a meeting to be set at some geographical point halfway between them. In 1870 he traveled with Poole and several others to Washington, D.C. He was annoyed by the sightseeing diversions, wishing to convey as quickly as possible his message about a future reservation and hunting rights for the Brulés. In his encounter with the secretary of the interior, Spotted Tail displayed "melancholy dignity" in responding to the secretary's dismissal of government violations of the 1868 treaty. When told by the official that he should "expect some trouble in his life" and not complain, Spotted Tail laughingly replied, "Tell [the secretary] that if he had as much trouble in his life as I have had in mine, he would have cut his throat long ago." He also declined President Grant's offer to arrange for his sixteen-year-old son to live in Washington as a student. Later on in the trip he told a New York City audience, "Leave us alone."

Spotted Tail openly wondered why the president had only one wife whereas he himself had four. His favorite wife died during his month of absence in the East, and upon his return to his camp he disposed of all of the materials he had collected while he was away. He also refused to tell his people of all the things he had witnessed on the trip, fearing that he would not be believed and might consequently lose his authority.

Spotted Tail's last battle with the Pawnees took place in July 1873. A year later General George Custer would complete his exploratory venture into the Black Hills and, with the confirmation of the presence of gold there, establish a rationale for further exclusion of Indians from their own lands. The U.S. government offered to lease or purchase the Black Hills. Spotted Tail conducted his own inspection of the region in 1875 and told a federal commission, "As long as we live on this earth we will expect pay. . . . The amount must be so large that the interest will support us." An ultimate demand for $60 million was rejected by government representatives. Over a century later, another financial settlement was refused by the Sioux tribes of South Dakota, and no final agreement has as yet been attained.

In early December 1875 President Grant set the impossible goal of having all Indians placed on agencies within two months. The climactic victory at the Little Bighorn in June 1876 did not insure a glorious future for the victors. Repression would in fact be more complete. In early 1877 Spotted Tail journeyed to visit the remaining hostiles, including Crazy Horse, and encouraged submission. Although Crazy Horse avoided a direct meeting, he too surrendered at Fort Robinson in May of that year.

In the aftermath of the plains wars, Spotted Tail agreed to send four of his sons, two grandchildren, and thirty-four other students from the Rosebud Reservation to the Carlisle Indian Industrial School in Pennsylvania. Secure in the belief that learning English would be of benefit to his people, he was outraged when he found that they had been baptized as Episcopalians, given Christian names, dressed like soldiers, and made to farm and do industrial work. In 1880 he personally withdrew his family members from the school and immediately lost favor with many Easterners. The Lakota scholar Victor Douville writes: "Although this was a major setback for Sinte Gleska [Spotted Tail] he, nevertheless, raised one of the first and significant issues of bilingual and bicultural education. It was this concern that set the stage for the founding of Sinte Gleska College [on the Rosebud Reservation] 100 years later."

Meanwhile, Spotted Tail was facing opposition at home. Crow Dog, a cousin of his and a long-time friend, was becoming his most serious adversary. Crow Dog issued charges against Spotted Tail to the secretary of the interior. The conflict ended when Crow Dog shot Spotted Tail on August 5, 1881. There are several contradictory accounts of the event; court records suggest that both men were armed at the time.

A 1995 family history by Crow Dog's grandson Leonard Crow Dog offers a new perspective on the reasons for the tragedy. In it Spotted Tail is praised for trying "to save his people from being wiped out" or removed to Oklahoma Territory. According to Leonard Crow Dog, Spotted Tail "tried to beat the wasichus [whites] at their own game, playing politics." But his grandfather "thought that Spotted Tail was too soft on the wasichus, too ready to give in."

Although a customary punishment for the offense might have resulted in a quicker resolution, the situation became complicated by the arrest of Crow Dog and a subsequent trial, in which he was found guilty of murder and sentenced to be hanged. A successful appeal to the U.S. Supreme Court, *Ex Parte Crow Dog* (1883), determined that the federal government did not have jurisdiction over crimes involving Indians on Indian land, and he was released. A period of ostracism followed, and only now are four generations of condemnation of the Crow Dog clan coming to an end.

Spotted Tail left a complex and significant legacy. He skillfully avoided the full restraints of reservation life, finally settling in a favored location, and was able to retain much tribal culture and authority. Unlike Sitting Bull and Crazy Horse, he demonstrated a flexibility that largely avoided confrontation. It is appropriate that a tribal university established on the Rosebud Reservation in 1971 bears his name. Its curriculum combines Lakota values and language with the unique survival tools of the twentieth century.

See also Sioux.

Hyde, George E., *Spotted Tail's Folk: A History of the Brulé Sioux* (Norman: University of Oklahoma Press, 1961); Poole, DeWitt Clinton, *Among the Sioux of Dakota: Eighteen Months' Experience as an Indian Agent, 1869–70* (St. Paul: Minnesota Historical Society, 1988).

KEITH A. WINSELL
Sinte Gleska University
Rosebud, South Dakota

SQUANTO (TISQUANTUM)

(c. 1590–1622)
Wampanoag translator, guide, and emissary for the early Plymouth Colony.

Squanto was born in the Wampanoag community of Patuxet, a village of about two thousand inhabitants on present-day Plymouth Bay, Massachusetts. Patuxet was linked by kinship, ethnicity, and political alliance to other Wampanoag communities between the eastern shore of Narragansett Bay and the tip of Cape Cod and on the islands of Martha's Vineyard and Nantucket.

As Squanto entered adulthood, European explorers began frequenting Patuxet and adjacent shores in search of trade, sites for settlements, and a passageway to the Pacific. The best documented of these visits were made by the French colonizer Samuel de Champlain in 1605 and 1606. The Patuxets began producing surpluses of maize and furs for exchange with friendly visitors while warding off those who were hostile. Although Squanto's position among his people at this time is unknown, he was almost certainly a person of prominence, perhaps a sachem or potential sachem.

A visit in 1614 by the English colonizer John Smith set in motion the events that changed Squanto's life. After skirmishing against and then making peace with the Patuxets, Smith returned to England, leaving a second ship to fish for cod under the command of one Thomas Hunt. Luring Squanto and about twenty other Wampanoags on board, Hunt kidnapped them and then seized about seven others on Cape Cod before sailing for Málaga, Spain. There Hunt began selling his captives as slaves until some priests intervened and redeemed the rest, including Squanto, in hopes of converting them to Christianity. Squanto's movements are unclear for the next three years—until 1617, by which time he had somehow gotten to London. Living in the home of John Slany, the treasurer of the Newfoundland Company, he became immersed in the English language and culture, and he began to see in the colonial ambitions of Slany and his associates the means by which he could return home.

Squanto's plans moved closer to realization when, on an expedition to Newfoundland, he became reacquainted with Thomas Dermer, an officer under John Smith in 1614. Like Smith, Dermer had left Patuxet before the fateful kidnapping. Dermer took Squanto back to England to meet Sir Ferdinando Gorges, then the most determined would-be colonizer of New England. Although he had already failed in several attempts to use kidnapped Indians to advance his endeavors, Gorges was persuaded by Squanto's evident knowledge of the region, his apparent standing among his people, and his professed loyalty. With Dermer at the helm, Squanto finally sailed for home in the spring of 1619.

During Squanto's absence the New England coast from Cape Cod northward had been ravaged by one or more epidemics of European origin to which Indians lacked adequate immunity. As a result, Patuxet and most other Wampanoag villages had been abandoned, and the survivors, 10 to 25 percent of the earlier population, had joined together in a few smaller communities. These communities were hard-pressed to defend themselves against tribute demands by Narragansetts and attacks by Micmacs, both of whom had avoided the epidemics, as well as hostile English and French expeditions. Squanto therefore confronted a very different world from the one he had been torn out of five years earlier.

Although native hostility to the English was intense, Squanto at first smoothed the way for Dermer with the Wampanoags, including the Pokanoket sachem, Massasoit, now the most prominent Wampanoag leader.

But returning the following year, the expedition was attacked at Martha's Vineyard, the center of anti-English sentiment. Dermer was mortally wounded, while Squanto was captured and turned over to the Pokanokets.

The second turning point in Squanto's life came the following November, when about a hundred English settlers arrived at Patuxet aboard the *Mayflower* to establish Plymouth Colony. Struggling to survive, half the unprepared colonists succumbed to starvation and disease during the harsh winter. Finally in March, the Pokanokets and Nemaskets dispatched Samoset, a visiting Abenaki with ties to English traders, to sound out the beleaguered colonists. Finding them receptive, Samoset returned a few days later with Squanto, whose knowledge of the English and their language exceeded his own.

Squanto's first contributions to the English were to teach them how to use fish fertilizer with their crops and to help arrange a treaty of alliance binding the Pokanokets and Nemaskets to Plymouth. As a reward for the latter, the Pokanokets allowed him to live among the English, at the site of his native Patuxet. While Massasoit and the Pokanokets welcomed the treaty, the Nemaskets resisted the paramount authority it accorded the English and the supremacy among Indians claimed by the Pokanokets. Some Nemaskets seized Squanto, who had to be rescued by heavily armed Plymouth soldiers. Squanto then helped the Plymouth colony secure treaties with some Wampanoag villages on Cape Cod and some Massachusett Indians north of Plymouth.

As critical as he was to Plymouth's fortunes, Squanto's usefulness was limited because he had no power base among the remaining Wampanoags or other local natives. In the summer of 1621 the colony invited a second Indian, a Pokanoket named Hobbamock, to live among them. Squanto attempted to undermine the Pokanokets by telling Wampanoag audiences that he alone had the ear and loyalty of the colony's leaders and that they should abandon Massasoit's leadership for his. He also attempted to mislead the English into thinking that Massasoit, with the Narragansetts and Massachusetts, was conspiring against them. His effort backfired when the English and Pokanokets discovered the truth. Because of his past services to them, the English protected Squanto from Massasoit's wrath, but for his own safety he thereafter remained close to the English at all times. A few weeks later, he was stricken by a severe fever and died.

Squanto's historical reputation rests largely on his role in helping the Plymouth Pilgrims establish their colony. The actual story of his life reveals a man who adapted heroically to new circumstances and indeed aided the English, but at the price of alienating himself from most other Wampanoags. Seeking to establish or reestablish himself as a native political leader, he ended his life a stranger in his own land.

Salisbury, Neal, *Manitou and Providence: Indians and Europeans, 1500–1643* (New York: Oxford University Press, 1982); Salisbury, Neal, "Squanto: Last of the Patuxets," in *Struggle and Survival in Colonial America,* ed. David G. Sweet and Gary B. Nash (Berkeley: University of California Press, 1981).

NEAL SALISBURY
Smith College

SQUAW

The literal meaning of the word *squaw* is obscure, and its connotations have changed over time. Its origins are found among the northeastern tribes. In Massachusett, *squà* referred to a younger woman. In Narragansett, *sunksquaw* meant "queen" or "lady." Despite these Algonquian-language origins, however, nonnatives applied the term to native women throughout North America. Over time it took on derogatory connotations as travelers referred to native women as *squaw drudges* and often used the term in opposition to *Indian princess.* Nonnatives often referred to women leaders as *squaw sachems* and nonnative men who married native women as *squaw men.* By the twentieth century the word *squaw* had developed multiple derogatory associations that had no connection with the word's original meaning.

See also Women.

STANDING BEAR, LUTHER

(1868?–1939)
Brulé Sioux author and film actor.

Placing his birth in or around 1868—the "winter" known to his *tiospaye,* or extended family group, as the "breaking up of camp" and five years later than is indicated by Bureau of Indian Affairs records—Luther Standing Bear was from the last generation of Sicangus or Brulé Sioux who could claim to have been reared in the ways of the prereservation Lakotas. As he was later to write, "My first years were spent living just as my forefathers had lived—roaming the green, rolling hills of what are now the states of South Dakota and Nebraska." At the same time, according to Standing Bear, these were "troublous days . . . when the Sioux were succumbing to the trickery of the whites and the undermining of their own tribal morale."

The "troublous days" began for the Sicangus the year of Standing Bear's birth, directly after Spotted Tail and other Lakota chiefs had "touched the pen" to a treaty at Fort Laramie, Wyoming. Although the Lakotas believed that this agreement granted them the right to continue their customary practices, its intentionally ambiguous contents in fact consigned them to life on a reservation as federal wards. The transformation of the Sicangus into a reservation people almost immediately influenced the direction that Standing Bear's life would take. In 1879, his father enrolled him in the Carlisle Indian Industrial School, Captain Richard H. Pratt's Indian boarding school in Carlisle, Pennsylvania. Although he was initially entered on the school rolls by his birth name, "*Ota Kte* [Plenty Kill], son of Standing Bear," once at Carlisle he was assigned the Anglo name Luther Standing Bear. This was only the first of many changes that would be thrust upon him during his career at Carlisle. In writings and lectures Standing Bear would later recall the odd mixture of traumas and pleasures he experienced in contending with the school's assimilationist curriculum and unremitting assault on its students' Indian identities. His response to being groomed and outfitted as an "imitation white man" was typical of this ambivalence. Of the required haircut he wrote, "When my hair was cut short, it hurt my feelings to such an extent that tears came into my eyes." However, concerning how he and other Sioux students reacted to Euro-American clothing, he stated, "How proud we were with clothes that had pockets and boots that squeaked! We walked the floor nearly all that night."

Notwithstanding his later criticism of Carlisle, Standing Bear not only survived but seems to have thrived under the school's challenges. He apparently was able to transvalue painful conditions by facing them with a warrior's courage. Upon leaving for Pennsylvania he had vowed that he would not return alive "unless [he] had done something very brave."

In 1884, following his final term at Carlisle, Standing Bear moved back home to the Rosebud Reservation. Like most other returned students, he soon discovered that the vocational training he had received in the East (tinsmithing) was totally ill suited to life on the reservation. Nevertheless, he realized that there "would be no more hunting—[Indians] would have to work for [their] food and clothing . . . like the Garden of Eden after the fall of man." With the help of a letter of recommendation from Pratt, Standing Bear was eventually hired as an assistant at the reservation's government school. In 1891 he visited the neighboring Pine Ridge Reservation. The local agent (a former employee at Carlisle) offered him command of one of that reservation's day schools. The young graduate took charge of the school at Allen, South Dakota, and managed at the same time to operate a small ranch. He later worked as a store clerk, post-office assistant, and minister's aide.

In 1902 Standing Bear successfully auditioned for a role in Buffalo Bill's Wild West show and spent eleven months performing in England. A second season with the troupe in 1903, however, was cut short by a train accident in which several cast members died and Standing Bear was severely injured. In 1905 he was chosen to replace his deceased father as the chief of his *tiospaye*. Although this was undoubtedly the greatest honor that could be accorded a Lakota male, Standing Bear wrote, "with all my title of chieftain, and with all my education and travels, I discovered that as long as I was on the reservation I was only a helpless Indian, and was not considered any better than any of the uneducated Indians . . . according to the views of the white agent in charge of the reservation. . . . If I tried to better conditions of my people, while on the reservation, I found it was an utter impossibility."

In order to escape from under the thumb of the reservation agent, Standing Bear traveled to Washington, D.C., to win his citizenship and control of his allotment and trust moneys. Later he would describe his feelings on the "happy day" his petition was granted as follows: "When I got my freedom from the iron hand of . . . the Indian agent at my reservation, I began to feel that I had been raised higher than a chieftainship." Citizenship accorded Standing Bear the freedom to come and go from the reservation without first receiving permission from the agent. He spent most of the remaining years of his life in non-Indian environments, first working in Sioux City, Iowa, at a dry-goods firm and then at the 101 Ranch in Oklahoma. In 1912 he moved to California, where he found employment as a film actor at the studio of Tom Ince and was eventually elected president of the Indian Actors' Association. He costarred with such notables of the silent screen as William S. Hart and Douglas Fairbanks. His sound movies, mostly grade-B "oaters" of the Stetson vs. warbonnet ilk, included *The Santa Fe Trail* (1930), *Texas Pioneers* (1932), *Circle of Death* (1935), *Cyclone of the Saddle* (1935), and *Fighting Pioneers* (1935). He died in Huntington, California, on February 19, 1939, during the filming of the movie *Union Pacific*.

Among all his pursuits and accomplishments, Luther Standing Bear is today best remembered for his contributions to Indian literature. In addition to numerous essays and articles, between 1928 and 1934 he wrote four important books with the help of his niece Waste Win (Good Woman): *My People, the Sioux* (1928), *My Indian Boyhood* (1931), *Land of the Spotted Eagle* (1933), and *Stories of the Sioux* (1934). Although varied in content, all of Standing Bear's works reflect the central purpose that inspired his writing: to defend the worth and dignity of Indian cultures. In pursuing this goal, he can be said to have raised the art of autobiographical apologetics to new heights. While both *My People, the Sioux* and *My Indian Boyhood* may be read simply as accounts of his life, their common subtext is an attack on the conception of Indians as savages and of assimilation as a process for turning Indians into whites. His labors as a writer were in perfect harmony with his participation in such groups as the League for Justice to the American Indian and on the lecture circuit as an outspoken advocate for Indian rights. Toward the conclusion of *Land of the Spotted Eagle* Standing Bear eloquently summarized his position on America's obligations to its Indians when he exhorted the "white brethren" to "look upon the Indian world as a human world; then let him see to it that human rights be accorded to the Indian. And this for the purpose of retaining for his own order of society a measure of humanity."

See also Movies.

Ellis, Richard N., introduction to *My People, the Sioux,* by Luther Standing Bear (Lincoln: University of Nebraska Press, 1975); Ellis, Richard N., "Luther Standing Bear: 'I Would Raise Him to Be an Indian,'" in *Indian Lives: Essays on Nineteenth- and Twentieth-Century Native Americans,* ed. L. G. Moses and Raymond Wilson (Albuquerque: University of New Mexico Press, 1985); Standing Bear, Luther, *Land of the Spotted Eagle* (Boston: Houghton Mifflin, 1933).

HARVEY MARKOWITZ
Newberry Library
Chicago, Illinois

STARR, EMMET

(1870–1930)
Cherokee historian and medical doctor.

Emmet Starr dreamed of becoming "the Herodotus of the Cherokees." Ironically, however, even though his *History of the Cherokee Indians* (1922) remains in print and has been called the "single most valuable source of authentic material on the personal history and biography of the Cherokee people," the historian died in a two-room walk-up apartment in St. Louis, convinced that he was a failure.

In many ways Starr was typical of the citizens of the Cherokee Nation who were born in the period immediately following the American Civil War. The independent political entity that was the Cherokee Nation was coming to an end as young Starr was approaching manhood. The invasions of railroads and white intruders were under way, and both sought to destroy the prewar Indian empire. By 1907 the Cherokee Nation had become a part of the state of Oklahoma. Students of Cherokee history know of the removal of the tribe from Georgia over the "Trail of Tears," but few realize that the influx of settlers following the Civil War was equally disastrous for the ultimate survival of the tribe.

Emmet Starr, the eldest son of Walter Adair Starr, was born in the Going Snake district, Cherokee Nation, Indian Territory, on December 12, 1870. Both his parents were mixed-blood Cherokees well versed in the history and traditions of their distinguished families. Starr was educated in the Cherokee public schools and graduated from the Cherokee Male Seminary in 1888. He received a degree in medicine from Barnes Medical College at St. Louis in 1891. Starr devoted himself to a variety of careers and never married.

Starr began gathering materials for his *History of the Cherokee Indians* in about 1891. For five years he practiced medicine, but in 1896 he began to devote himself full-time to becoming the Cherokee Nation's historian. Starr also served one term on the Cherokee National Council as a representative of the Cooweescoowee district and as a delegate to the Indian Territory statehood meeting known as the Sequoyah Convention. Active in the movement to avoid the abolition of Indian territory and create a separate Indian state, Starr considered the congressional rejection of the proposed state of Sequoyah and the subsequent creation of the state of Oklahoma a major blow to the Indian people. With the admission of Oklahoma to the Union in 1907, the Cherokee Nation ceased to exist; this marked the end of an era for the Cherokee people. Though some Cherokee leaders successfully made the transition from tribal government to statehood, many more did not. Hundreds who might have been leaders in Cherokee district government or prominent in the Cherokee National Council chose not to participate in the affairs of the new state. Gradually, the Cherokees began to lose their sense of being a nation.

Despite the Cherokees' loss of tribal status, however, Starr continued the preparation of his histories. He often worked with the support of the Cherokee National Seminaries and Normal School (now Northeastern State University) in Tahlequah. He published four books. His first, *Cherokees West* (1910), is essentially a reprint of the memoirs of the Western Cherokee missionary and leader Cephas Washburn and a collection of Cherokee laws. A very rare volume among his works is his second book, *Encyclopedia of Oklahoma* (1912). Prior to the publication of *History of the Cherokee Indians* (1922), without doubt his most significant and valuable contribution, he published a smaller volume, *Early History of the Cherokees* (1917), concerned primarily with the Arkansas or Western Cherokees.

In a sense, Starr's 1922 *History* is not a history at all. Its major value is as a source of primary documents and genealogical data on the Cherokee tribe. It includes descriptions of early colonial wars, Cherokee removal and civil war, the role of the Cherokees in the Texas Revolution and in the American Civil War, and hundreds of other events in Cherokee history. Much of this history comprises the texts of the laws, constitutions, and treaties of the Cherokee Nation. Many of these had never before been printed; others could be found only in Cherokee Nation publications, often printed in Sequoyah's Cherokee syllabary.

Starr began his research by turning to oral sources, supplementing them with exhaustive research using primary documents and books. He was both a field and a library researcher. As a Cherokee, Starr had access to oral and manuscript material that no white historian could ever have acquired. The tribe's confidence in Starr is reflected in his book's inclusion of previously unrecorded traditionalist Keetowah letters and pictures. Perhaps the most striking of these illustrations is one of the Keetowah Council of 1916 that shows the ancient Cherokee wampum belts, never previously exhibited.

Because of his commitment to Cherokee traditions, Starr was frequently at war with the Oklahoma historical establishment. At a time when much Indian history, especially the history of the Five Civilized Tribes, was being written as the story of inevitable "civilized progress," Emmet Starr wrote about the traditionalist Knighthawk Keetowahs as well as the Cherokees' frequently ignored achievements in government and education. At a time when the historian Grant Foreman cast Cherokee history as a tribute to acculturation, Emmet Starr dared to write of the pernicious influence of Baptist missionary groups on tribal life and to criticize the continuing power of missionaries.

Starr's 1922 *History* was in many ways a book of the turn of the century, although it was not published until later. It reflected an overwhelming concern with family and genealogy that was a part of the enrollment process for the Five Civilized Tribes. What today may seem an unreasonable concern with family was at the time the central issue of tribal existence. Starr began gathering material for his family histories as early as the 1890s, assembling genealogical data from Cherokee district courthouses, taking detailed statements from individual family Bibles, and tracing family lineage through wills, birth certificates, and property transactions. There are few Cherokee families who do not have at least one member who recalls Starr coming for a visit in his old buggy and staying for a night or even a week. Tribal tradition has it that "the Doctor" talked and listened, and talked and listened. Starr wrote, "I was afforded at an early age the opportunity of listening to the conversations and reminiscences of many of the most brilliant minds among my own people. I listened as a boy to . . . many . . . who were born raconteurs and savants." This childhood delight became the historian's principal method.

Having abandoned his medical career, Starr moved from job to job. The Indian Bureau office in Muskogee, the Northeastern Normal School (formerly the Cherokee Seminary) in Tahlequah, and the public schools of Rogers County furnished him with temporary employment. Starr sought more permanent employment with a variety of Oklahoma state agencies, especially with the Oklahoma Historical Society. The simple truth was that Starr was a man whose country was gone, destroyed as completely as if it had been bombed from the face of the earth. For Starr, and for other Cherokees of his age, the end of the nation was a blow from which they never recovered.

As is often the case, the merit of Starr's achievement was not widely recognized during his lifetime. Though he was, in fact, sad and lonely, some considered him eccentric. He was a man who, according to a friend of thirty-five years, "died as he had lived—misunderstood and, therefore, disappointed." Starr left Oklahoma for St. Louis sometime after World War I. There is poignancy in his letters written from St. Louis—a constant sense of his being in the wrong place. Again and again he writes of hearing little of Oklahoma, of the Cherokees. In 1929 he lamented, "I hear and know just as much about Oklahoma now as I do about China." And yet he never stopped thinking or writing or talking about his people and the state of Oklahoma, into which their political destiny had been merged. A friend from his last days in St. Louis recalled: "He liked to talk politics, especially as concerned Oklahoma. . . . He could tell stories concerning territorial and early statehood days in Oklahoma for hours at a time, and nothing seemed to please him more than to have an interested listener to these stories."

Emmet Starr was the Cherokee historian for all times. He performed one of the greatest services possible for the Cherokee people. Sequoyah, it is said, gave his people "talking leaves." Starr gave his people a recorded history. Starr's *History of the Cherokee Indians* is of more significance today than ever before. Those who can remember the historic greatness of Cherokee tribal government, education, and culture are almost gone. For the new generation, and for generations yet to come, Starr's *History* is a constant reminder of Cherokee achievements.

See also Cherokee.

"Death of Dr. Emmet Starr," *Chronicles of Oklahoma* 8 (1930): 129–30; Harper, William R., "Dr. Emmet Starr—A Tribute," *Chronicles of Oklahoma* 8 (1930) 130–31; Strickland, Rennard, and Jack Gregory, "Emmet Starr: Heroic Historian," in *American Indian Intellectuals*, ed. Margot Liberty (St. Paul, Minn.: West Publishing Company, 1976).

RENNARD STRICKLAND
Oklahoma City University

STEREOTYPES

See Mascots and Other Public Appropriations of Indians and Indian Culture by Whites; Savage, Savages, Savagism.

STOCKBRIDGE-MUNSEE (MOHICAN)

The headquarters for the Stockbridge-Munsee Band of Mohicans is in Shawano County in northeastern Wisconsin. The tribe's forty-six-thousand-acre reservation encompasses two townships, Red Springs and Bartelme. Approximately sixteen thousand acres of this land are held in trust for the tribe by the U.S. government.

The history of the Stockbridge-Munsee people is punctuated by repeated migrations and removals. Tradition says that originally a great mass of people moved from the north and west seeking a place where the waters were never still. They established a homeland on both sides of the Mahicanituk (later called Hudson's) River. The earliest known contact between these "Mahican" people and Europeans was with Dutch fur traders in the early seventeenth century. In 1734, the Mahicans agreed to let Protestant missionaries come among them; the missionaries were followed by teachers, farmers, and other colonials. A church and a school were built, and a village named Stockbridge, Massachusetts, grew up around them. The Christian Mahicans who lived there became known as Stockbridge Indians.

Stockbridge Indians fought on the side of the Americans in the Revolutionary War, but by war's end they found that their land titles were not recognized by the new federal government. They were landless. They moved west to lands in New York State provided them by the Oneida tribe, another largely Christian group that had fought against the British. During the following 150 years, the Stockbridge people were forced to move from New York to Indiana and later to several places in Wisconsin, where some Munsee Delaware families joined them. These removals and disruptions created insecurity and tensions that still affect the people today. Resisting removal west of the Mississippi River, the Stockbridge-Munsees moved to a reservation in Shawano County, Wisconsin, in 1856. By 1920, the distribution of their lands dictated by the terms of the General Allotment Act again rendered the group landless and destitute.

In 1934 the Indian Reorganization Act gave the Stockbridge-Munsees an opportunity to re-form into a tribal entity. Carl Miller provided the leadership for this tribal rebirth. The new tribe acquired approximately fifteen thousand acres of submarginal timberland and began establishing a tribal presence on the new reservation. Harry A. Chicks was elected the first tribal president. The second president, Arvid E. Miller, led the people for twenty-six years. He was a charter member of the National Congress of American Indians (1944) and helped establish the Great Lakes Intertribal Council in 1961.

Today about half of the tribe's fourteen hundred members reside on or near the reservation in northeastern Wisconsin. The tribe is led by a seven-member council, which is responsible for upholding the tribal constitution and ordinances and managing a variety of social-service programs. Located on the reservation are tribal offices, a clinic, a residential facility for the elderly, a family community center, a historical library and museum, a campground and powwow grounds, and several tribal enterprises, including a bingo hall, casino, and golf course. Several small private businesses also operate within the reservation.

The Stockbridge-Munsee people, having survived centuries of movement and political struggle, have adopted as their symbol the Many Trails, designed and made by tribal member Edwin Martin. It symbolizes the strength, hope, and endurance of the Mohican people.

See also Indian-White Relations in the United States, 1776–1900; Oneida.

Brasser, T. J., "Mahican," in *Handbook of North American Indians,* ed. William C. Sturtevant, vol. 15, *Northeast,* ed. Bruce Trigger (Washington: Smithsonian Institution, 1978); Frazier, Patrick, *The Mohicans of Stockbridge* (Lincoln: University of Nebraska Press, 1992); Savagian, John C., "The Tribal Reorganization of the Stockbridge-Munsee: Essential Conditions in the Re-Creation of a Native American Community, 1930–1942," *Wisconsin Magazine of History* 77, no. 1 (autumn 1993): 39–62.

DOROTHY W. DAVIDS (Mohican)
Stockbridge-Munsee Historical Committee

SUBARCTIC TRIBES

The subarctic region of the North American continent extends from Labrador to Alaska. The indigenous languages of this region belong to the Athabaskan and Algonquian language families. Linguists have divided the Athabaskan language family into three subfamilies: Apachean, Pacific, and Northern Athabaskan. Northern Athabaskan is composed of twenty-three distinct languages, eleven of which are spoken by indigenous people living in Alaska. The remainder are used by people living in the Yukon Territory, northern British Co-

Two Ahtna girls, Mary Ann and Natsannilna, from the lower Copper River Valley, Alaska.

lumbia, northern Alberta, northern Saskatchewan, northern Manitoba, and the Northwest Territories. The two Algonquian languages spoken in the subarctic region are Cree and Ojibwa. Language experts have separated Cree into three major dialects: Cree, Montagnais, and Naskapi. These languages are spoken by indigenous people living on the Quebec-Labrador Peninsula, in the Hudson Bay coastal region of Ontario, and in central Manitoba, Saskatchewan, and Alberta. Ojibwa is divided into eight dialects found in southwestern Quebec, north central Ontario, southern Manitoba, and southern Saskatchewan.

Traditionally, the Athabaskan and Algonquian people of the subarctic based their economy on hunting, fishing, and gathering. In addition, many groups conducted trade in various foodstuffs, wood products, furs, native copper, and obsidian. Caribou, moose, and fish were the primary resources, followed by small game and plants. In Alaska and western Canada, the two most reliable animal resources that also provided the greatest return of protein and usable products were salmon and barren-ground caribou. Farther east cari-

bou remained important, but people fished for lake trout, northern pike, and whitefish instead of salmon. Moose and woodland caribou were of major significance to people inhabiting the full boreal forest.

Like hunters and gatherers everywhere, subarctic people fixed their economic activity to the seasonal availability of resources. Late winter and early spring were often the most difficult time of year because stocks of fish or meat harvested and stored the previous season were gone. Furthermore, the annual migrations of birds, fish, and game had not yet begun. At this time hunters often left their families in the winter camps as they searched for scattered groups of caribou, moose, black bears, or small game. When successful, hunters either carried game to the family camp or moved the whole family to the kill. In mid-spring, after the days lengthened but before warm weather made it difficult to travel across muskeg swamps, families moved from winter camps to the shores of frozen lakes and streams, where they set fishnets and beaver snares under the ice. Open water along the lakeshores offered habitat for migrating waterfowl and muskrats, which hunters added to the larder. After the ice was completely gone people moved to fishing sites, where they remained most of the summer, drying and storing fish for the coming winter. Intermittently, women and children picked roots, wild rhubarb, wild celery, blueberries, cranberries, and rose hips. In the meantime, the men went hunting for big and small game.

In the western subarctic, where salmon was a major staple, a successful harvest of fish provided the basis for a stable supply of food. This resource enabled people to live a relatively sedentary existence during the winter months. Yet, even with abundant supplies of fish, the coming fall meant a major shift in activity. Groups left their summer fish camps to secure a supply of fresh meat and skins. Where caribou was the major staple, the fall migration was a significant event, even more important than the annual runs of fish. After a summer of feeding, the caribou were fat and their hides in prime condition, good for clothing and bedding. By intercepting the migrating herds at strategic locations, the people were able to kill large numbers of caribou, whose meat they dried and then stored in caches for use during the winter. In mountainous regions, the fall was a good time for hunters to set snares for mountain sheep.

At the approach of winter, people retired to winter accommodations located either close to large caches of fish and meat or near areas with abundant game. If the summer and fall harvests had been particularly successful, the people remained in and around their camps for much of the winter. To supplement stored foods, women set snares for rabbits in the immediate vicinity of camp while the men made periodic forays to hunt caribou, moose, or a bear in its den. The harvest of hibernating bears meant meat, fat, and hides for a community. If food shortages occurred, the whole camp might move to a new location. During December, January, and February, the deep cold made movement difficult, and greater effort was required to find moose or caribou, which tended not to move about in the cold. Without big game animals the people were forced to subsist on rabbits or the lower legs and hooves of the caribou they had killed previously. During the winter, hunters and their families required approximately forty-five hundred to five thousand calories, or about four pounds of flesh, per day. Of this, a substantial portion needed to be in the form of fat in order to secure the necessary calories. Since rabbit flesh could not provide the requisite fat, it was possible to starve to death if rabbits were the only source of food.

Conditions improved with the arrival of spring. Increased daylight and warmer temperatures made traveling easier for both humans and animals until breakup. Then the people settled down in their spring camps to fish under the ice, hunt for returning waterfowl and muskrats, and wait for the summer fishing to begin.

Across the subarctic, subsistence techniques varied according to environmental conditions and the type of game sought. On large salmon rivers, such as the Yukon, fishermen built weirs fifty to one hundred feet out from the bank and set large cone-shaped wooden basket traps into the water parallel to the shore. Men tended the traps in birch-bark canoes. As the traps filled, the fish were brought to shore and processed by the women. In smaller salmon streams, the people built weirs across the stream with an opening in the middle for either a fish trap or dip net. A similar technique, using a weir, dip net, or trap, was used by some groups in harvesting whitefish. Gill nets, set in lakes for trout, sucker, and pike, were more commonly used in the central and eastern subarctic. In all cases practically every part of the fish was used, from the head and eggs to the intestines, and the flesh was eaten roasted or boiled, or was dried. Rendered fish oil was added to berries to preserve them, the mixture being stored in birch-bark containers.

Barren-ground caribou were hunted by groups of people using drift fences and corrals constructed of brush. In the corrals, hunters set snares made out of rawhide called babiche. The approaching caribou instinctively followed the drift fence into the corral, where they were then caught in the snares and killed by hunters using spears, bows and arrows, or knives. Another method of taking caribou, often used in the central and eastern subarctic, was to intercept the herds as they crossed a lake or river. Hunters paddled into a throng of swimming caribou and pushed their canoes up onto the backs of the animals, stabbing them in the kidney with a spear.

Moose, being generally solitary animals, were stalked by lone hunters or by hunting partners. Staying downwind of the animal, the hunters moved in a series of arcs intersecting the moose's trail at intervals until they lost the trail. At that point the hunters knew the moose had doubled back on its trail and had bedded down. The hunters then approached the moose with the wind in their face and shot it with arrows tipped with serrated heads that worked into the flesh as the moose moved. This stalking method was particularly effective during the winter, when trails were easy to follow and deep snow hindered the moose but not the men, whose snowshoes enabled them to move easily across the country. In some places moose were also snared, the snare being set in a fence across a game trail.

Snares were also used to catch rabbits, Dall sheep, and even bears. During the fall some people conducted rabbit drives. The people gathered on an island or peninsula, the women and children assembling at one end and driving the rabbits toward the men at the other end. The rabbits were clubbed or shot with blunt-tipped arrows. In the spring ducks, geese, and swans were killed with bows and arrows tipped with pronged points.

To a great extent the spiritual and ritual life of subarctic people involved solving the philosophical question of being simultaneously dependent on the goodwill of powerful animals and the need to kill and eat them to survive. This problem was resolved by demonstrating respect for the animals. All animals and all things were believed to have a spiritual essence or soul. As sentient beings, animals were believed to consciously give themselves to hunters. In return, hunters were expected to properly care for the animal's flesh and to respect its soul; otherwise the animal would make itself unavailable, with dire consequences for the hunter. To placate the animal's soul, hunters conducted small personal rituals. For example, after a moose was killed, the hunter punched out the eyeballs so that the moose's spirit could escape and so the moose could not see what was then done to its body. A similar custom was followed for bears. To placate the souls of salmon, and thus to ensure the abundance of the annual runs, the very first salmon caught was shared by everyone in camp.

Since all things were believed to have a spiritual essence, the world was thought to be alive. Within this animate world, hunters negotiated their way through unseen dangers by enlisting spiritual allies and abiding by numerous taboos. Assistance or luck was obtained either by dreaming of animal spirits or through divination techniques such as scapulimancy. Using this technique, the hunter scorched the bone of a rabbit to determine the whereabouts of animals. Hunters ensured their luck by following a wide variety of restrictions and leading a good life. While hunting rituals were often carried out privately, shamans practiced semipublic or public ceremonies to call game during times of starvation. Shamans sought cures by entering a trance state, singing, and drumming, using native medicines and removing objects of affliction by sucking them out of the patient's body.

In the western subarctic, a distribution of gifts called a potlatch was held to commemorate various events, particularly a person's death. Accompanying the potlatch were days of singing, dancing, oratory, and feasting. Through the distribution of gifts as well as dancing and singing, the potlatch participants expressed their grief for the dead and attempted to reinstate a balance in the universe, which had been upset by the death of the individual.

Throughout the subarctic, people lived in small, mobile, autonomous groups. These groups ranged in size from the local band or hunting group, composed of a few nuclear families related through the primary ties of kinship and marriage, to the regional band, consisting of two hundred to four hundred people. The household unit was usually two or more closely related families who resided together in a single dwelling. Relations within the local band were characterized by mutual assistance and the sharing of material goods and food. Each band had affiliations with other groups adjacent to it but formed no lasting political alliances. Depending upon circumstances, regional bands might or might not assemble for seasonal hunting, fishing, or ritual activities. Both regional bands and hunting groups had an amorphous quality because of constantly shifting allegiances and associations within and between the bands.

Families and individuals often moved between bands out of personal inclination.

Among Athabaskan and Algonquian speakers of the central and eastern subarctic, kinship was bilateral. In a bilateral system, the major kinship linkages are lateral rather than lineal, allowing for greater variety of kin relationships among members of the same generation. By contrast, Athabaskans living in far western Canada and Alaska had a matrilineal kinship system. Within this system, descent was reckoned lineally and society was divided into moieties or halves, with each half composed of a number of exogamous clans. Clans were not localized entities but occurred throughout a wide region. More localized groups or lineages were composed of two intermarrying clans. In bilateral as well as matrilineal systems cross-cousin marriage was preferred, which created linkages between widely dispersed groups. Across the subarctic, polygyny was practiced by leading men who were good providers.

There were no powerful chiefs in the subarctic region. More typical were leading men, whose power rested on their abilities as hunters and on personal qualities such as generosity and demonstrated wisdom and judgment. While leadership was rather diffuse in the eastern and central subarctic, it was less so in the west. Leaders there were called *rich men* and were identified precisely in the genealogical record. The status of a rich man was both ascribed and achieved. Ascribed status came from clan membership, which gave the rich man access to certain spiritual knowledge, including certain types of hunting magic. To retain his status, however, a rich man had to demonstrate his ability to manage resources and provide for the welfare of his people.

In the eastern subarctic initial encounters between native people and Europeans occurred in the sixteenth and seventeenth centuries. In the west contact began in the late eighteenth or early nineteenth century, and some Alaska Athabaskans did not meet white people until the last decades of the nineteenth century. First encounters usually took place between native people and traders interested in bartering manufactured goods such as guns, knives, clothing, and beads for furs. Native people quickly integrated these objects into their culture, not only as utilitarian items but as symbols that reflected indigenous concepts of wealth, prestige, respect, and influence.

Following the traders came various Christian missionaries who attempted to convert the people and settle them into permanent communities. Today many subarctic Athabaskan and Algonquian people consider themselves faithful Christians, but their beliefs are a synthesis of Christian and native traditions.

Although traders and missionaries influenced native people, in the western subarctic it was the discovery of gold in the late nineteenth century that brought the greatest change. With mineral development came an influx of people who had no interest in native people but an intense interest in developing and owning the land. The laws created to administer these developments excluded native people from owning property, restricted their ability to hunt in the traditional manner, and formed the framework for future conflicts between natives and whites.

A central problem in native and white relations across the subarctic was, and continues to be, control and ownership of land and resources. In Canada, the government made treaties with some Athabaskan and Algonquian people in the late nineteenth century. In Alaska, the U.S. government settled the aboriginal claims of native people in 1971 when Congress passed the Alaska Native Claims Settlement Act (ANCSA). In return for relinquishing aboriginal claim to 325 million acres and aboriginal hunting and fishing rights, Alaska Natives received $962.5 million and 44 million acres of land. The money and the land were allocated to twelve regional and over one hundred village corporations set up by ANCSA. The Canadian government reached similar settlements with the James Bay Crees of northern Quebec and the Athabaskan people of the Yukon Territory. Despite their cost, however, none of these settlements has been entirely successful in healing the wounds wrought by the clash of cultures. Outside business interests and reformers continue to penetrate native communities, and subarctic people continue to struggle over how best to adapt traditional practices to modern conditions.

Today subarctic Athabaskan and Algonquian people live in permanent communities with some modern conveniences. They no longer live completely off the land but have developed a mixed economy that includes both hunting and fishing and wage labor. The people use money to buy food, clothing, televisions, and the items necessary to continue their hunting life: gasoline to run outboard motors and snow machines, fishnets, guns, and bullets. Native children attend school, wear the latest fads in clothing, and play sports like hockey and basketball. Yet modern subarctic peoples continue to regulate their lives by the seasonal availability of resources, they continue to express values that stress community over individualism, and they strive to maintain their identity as native people.

See also Indian-White Relations in Alaska; Indian-White Relations in Canada.

Helm, June, ed., *Subarctic*, vol. 6 of *Handbook of North American Indians*, ed. William C. Sturevant (Washington: Smithsonian Institution, 1981); Tanner, Adrian, *Bringing Home Animals: Religious Ideology and Mode of Production of the Mistassini Cree Hunters* (New York: St. Martin's Press, 1979).

WILLIAM E. SIMEONE
Alaska Department of Fish and Game

SUN DANCE

Like many other aspects of Indian life and culture, the Sun Dance has evolved since the first European observers described it in the early nineteenth century. When the anthropologist Robert Lowie completed his overview of Plains Indian culture in 1954, he concluded that some twenty of the region's tribes maintained or once participated in a religious ceremony known as the Sun Dance.

The format of the Sun Dance has always varied from community to community. Nevertheless, there are certain features of the dance that many tribes share, although they attach different levels of significance to each. Often, the dance must be initiated by an individual sponsor, someone who takes a vow in the hope of being relieved of a worry, or being blessed in the coming year. It is almost always performed in the late spring and early summer, near the time of the summer solstice. Most Sun Dances begin with the erection of a circular lodge or corral around a solemnly chosen and cut central pole. During the next three or four days, periods of dancing, accompanied by singing, drumming, or whistling, are interspersed with periods of rest and meditation. Dancers do not eat or drink during the three or four days of the dance, although some do chew on bear root to keep their mouths moist. Toward the end of the Sun Dance, participants experience visions and receive blessings.

Early European witnesses to the Sun Dance were repulsed by some tribes' practice of self-mortification in the ceremony. Male dancers had their breasts or backs skewered and tied to a central lodge pole. Dancing and straining against the ropes, they eventually tore loose from the skewers that held them fast. Through this ritual, participants literally suffer on behalf of their community and call upon the Creator to pity and assist them in the fulfillment of their vows. This aspect of the ritual was the principal reason federal officials prohibited it between the end of the Plains wars and 1935. Despite the ban, however, many tribes continued to hold the Sun Dance surreptitiously in remote areas of their reservations or to enact it without its objectionable features.

For many Indians today, the use of modern technology (cars, tents, loudspeakers) does not take away from the solemnity or integrity of the Sun Dance, which has always been undergoing transformation. Whether they have reinvigorated the ritual (as the Lakotas have done), adopted it anew (as many Great Basin groups have done), or called it back into being after having lost it as a result of government prohibitions (as the Crows have done), it provides a central focus for community devotion and renewal.

Sᴡᴇᴀᴛ Lᴏᴅɢᴇ

One of the most common structures in Indian communities, the sweat lodge is typically made of young saplings bent to shape a half dome and covered with blankets, skins, or canvas. The lodge is used for ritual sweat baths that are believed to bring both spiritual

Big Medicine (1857–1926), Alligator Stands Up (1845–1909), and Hunts the Enemy (1841–1935), Crows, outside a sweat lodge on their Montana reservation. Photograph by Fred E. Miller (1836–1936).

and physical health. Hot stones are brought into the structure, and water is then poured over them to create steam. Another type of sweat lodge uses no water; the structure often serves as both a sweat lodge and a dwelling place in which a fire is lighted in the center. California tribes used this type of sweat lodge. A third type of sweat lodge, the *temescal,* was found among Mesoamerican peoples. It was built of stone or clay and was heated by channeling heat through exterior ducts.

Ceremony and ritual surround the construction and use of the sweat lodge. Traditionally, men and women use the sweat lodge separately. Participants sing, pray, and meditate. Sweats are also an opportunity for friends and kinsmen to spend time together in a quiet, contemplative setting. For many, the sweat lodge itself represents the universe and connects participants to the past, the earth, and the spiritual world.

As reservations were established in the nineteenth century, government officials outlawed the sweat lodge among tribes, forcing the ceremonies underground. However, the lodge's simplicity and ubiquity ensured its survival, and today it is a feature of Native American life in all parts of the United States.

SWORD, GEORGE

(c. 1847–1910)
Oglala Lakota scholar and leader.

George Sword (Miwakan), a member of the Oglala division of the Teton Sioux, was born in about 1847 in the region that now comprises western South Dakota. Through a rare combination of innate talent and ambition, he distinguished himself in the buffalo chase and in war—the two most important pursuits of Oglala males. In an autobiographical sketch that Sword recorded later in his life, he recalled, "I was . . . a *blota hunka* (commander of war parties) and have led many war parties against the enemy, both of Indians and white men. The scars on my body show the wounds I have received in battle." In recognition of his outstanding achievements, while he was still a young man the members of his *tiospaye,* or extended family camp, selected him to be one of their *wakiconze* (magistrates) "and so," Sword explained, "I [knew] all the customs of the camp and of the march."

In addition to his accomplishments on the warpath and the hunt, Sword achieved great renown as a *wicasa*

wakan (holy man or shaman) and *pejuta wicasa* (medicine man). Concerning his knowledge of Lakota religion, he declared, "I know the old customs of the Lakotas, and all their ceremonies for I was a *wicasa wakan* and I have conducted all the ceremonies. I have conducted the Sun Dance, which is the greatest ceremony of the Lakotas, and no Lakotas will dispute my word. I was also a *pejuta wicasa* and belonged to the Bear medicine people."

As increasing numbers of white settlers invaded Lakota lands during the last third of the nineteenth century, the Oglalas came under mounting pressure from the U.S. government to cede their territories and relocate on reservations. Sword was a major participant in the alternating bouts of warfare and diplomacy that characterized this era. Because of his reputation as a civil and religious leader, he was included in several delegations to Washington and other eastern cities to negotiate with the "Great Father" (the president) and other administrators of U.S. Indian affairs. The government carefully orchestrated these diplomatic excursions to awe Indian leaders with the numbers and technical achievements of whites, thereby rendering them more pliable to government demands for their lands and submission. While this strategy failed to achieve its desired effect on many Lakota leaders, it succeeded with Sword. He stated, "I went to Washington and to other large cities, and that showed me that the white people dug in the ground and built houses that could not be moved. Then I knew that when they came they could not be driven away."

Sword's gloomy prognosis concerning the Lakotas' struggle to rid their country of whites convinced him to settle on the Red Cloud Agency—the first of the Oglalas' federal reservations—to begin the process of adopting their customs and, as he observed, "to persuade my people to do so." It was at this point that he changed his name from Tokicuwa (which the Dakota ethnologist Ella Deloria has translated as "Enemy Bait") to Miwakan ("Sword" or "Long Knife") "because," as he explained, "the leaders of the white soldiers wore swords." He served as a scout for General George Crook and Colonel Ranald Slidell Mackenzie. As part of his military service Sword participated in Mackenzie's attack on a Cheyenne village in 1876 and, following the Battle of the Little Bighorn that same year, was sent as an envoy to convince Crazy Horse and his camp to lay down their arms.

Soon after the Indian Bureau relocated the Oglalas on their permanent homeland of Pine Ridge in 1878,

Sword accepted an appointment as the captain of the agency's fifty-man Indian police force, and remained so, as he noted, "until the Oglalas ceased to think of fighting the white people." His wages were five dollars a month. After retiring from the police force he served as a judge on the reservation's Court of Indian Offenses and was also ordained a deacon in the Episcopal Church. In February 1891 Sword returned to Washington, D.C., to take part in a council held by a delegation of Lakotas with the Commissioner of Indian Affairs on the causes of the massacre at Wounded Knee and ways to improve conditions on the Indian agencies. He died on the Pine Ridge Reservation in 1910 at the age of sixty-three.

Though Sword realized that life on the reservation spelled the end for many Lakota customs, he nonetheless sought to preserve for posterity as many Lakota beliefs and practices as possible. Sword's most enduring contribution to the preservation of Lakota culture came through his collaboration with James R. Walker, a government doctor who ceaselessly compiled information on traditional Oglala beliefs and practices during his residence on the Pine Ridge Reservation from 1896 to 1914. There is good reason to believe that without Sword's assistance, Walker would never have been privy to the kinds of esoteric information on Lakota religion and society that he was ultimately able to collect. As Walker himself wrote, Sword

> argued to the holy men that soon they would go from the world and all their sacred lore would pass with them unless they revealed it so that it could be preserved in writing; that future generations of the Oglalas should be informed as to all that their ancestors believed and practiced; that the Gods of the Oglalas would be more pleased if the holy men told of them so that they might be kept in remembrance and that all the world might know of them.

As a result of Sword's pleadings, the holy men agreed to share their mysteries with Walker, on the condition that he become a member of the Buffalo medicine society, comply with the requirements of that order, and "not divulge what [he] learned until after there were no longer any holy men among the Oglalas so that their Great Judge of Spirits would not hold against them that they had done wrong to make the sacred things common."

Sword, however, not only served as a facilitator for Walker's investigations, but was also among the physician's chief informants. As a member of the Bear medicine society, he claimed to know "all the medicine ceremonies that other kinds of medicine men [had] and much more." This "much more" included the rituals Lakotas performed before embarking on the warpath and the hunt as well as many of the *ehanni wicowoyake* or sacred narratives that constituted the core of Lakota cosmology and metaphysics. It is important to stress that in his role as informant, Sword also acted as Walker's principal mentor, guiding him through the complexities of Lakota thought and etymology. The fact that Sword had learned to read and write the Lakota language as an adult, and could supply Walker with written as well as oral testimony on various aspects of Lakota culture, contributed in no small measure to his success as a tutor.

At first glance, Sword's efforts to preserve Lakota culture may appear at odds with his decision to follow the white man's road and to encourage his people to do likewise. However, a more considered reflection suggests that his accommodation to white culture was consistent with the cardinal Lakota value that obligated civil and religious leaders to utilize their talents for the welfare of their community. Viewed in this light, Sword's activities as agency policeman, judge, and deacon were pragmatic transformations of his earlier roles of warrior, magistrate, and holy man by means of which he hoped to shepherd his people through the traumatic transformation from political autonomy to an existence as federal wards on the reservation. Thus, despite his apparent submission to the assimilationist goals of federal Indian policy, at the most fundamental level Sword remained thoroughly Lakota.

Parks, Douglas R., and Raymond J. DeMallie, "Plains Indian Literature," *Boundary 2* 19 (1992): 107–45; Walker, James R., *Lakota Belief and Ritual*, ed. Raymond J. DeMallie and Elaine Jahner (Lincoln: University of Nebraska Press, 1980); Walker, James R., *Lakota Myth*, ed. Elaine Jahner (Lincoln: University of Nebraska Press, 1983).

HARVEY MARKOWITZ
Newberry Library
Chicago, Illinois

T

Taboos

Native Americans believed that balance and harmony should pervade their relationships with the environment, from the sky to the underworld and all beings in between. For that reason, the negative was as important as the positive. The Polynesian term for the dangerously charged sacred, there spelled *tabu,* is used by Native Americans to refer to forbidden or circumscribed relationships, which can involve special beings, places, and times.

Overly intense identification between beings was controlled by the imposition of taboos. Throughout the Pacific Northwest, the parents of newborn twins were forbidden to take them near water, because the words for "twins" and "salmon" were the same. Since both symbolized dualities (such as return and rebirth), their equation was particularly strong, and, at least until the twins became mature human beings, the infants had to be kept spatially and emotionally separated from the fish to prevent their fusing. Parents were willing to make the arduous overland detours that this taboo entailed because twins, once fully grown, could use their special relationship with salmon to bring bounty to their communities.

In general, taboos served to temper such intensities of connectedness among beings. For example, a Dunne-za (called Beaver by whites), a hunter of British Columbia, blessed by power from the Spider spirit, avoided the sound of plucked strings, as from a fiddle or guitar, because the strings on such instruments were much like spider webbing and their sound could cause the hunter to be overwhelmed by his or her identification with Spider, often fatally. Indeed, a being's most characteristic feature was often most subject to the moderating influences of taboo. Spider webbing, for example, gained attention rather than the creature's eight legs or some other less distinctive feature.

Among farming nations with large populations and complex institutions, taboos define memberships in corporate groups such as clans. Thus those belonging to the Deer clan had to be especially careful with that species, often avoiding killing or eating venison so as not to consume what was in some sense an ancestor. In consequence, of course, each clan thereby contributed its totemic life form to the sustenance of the larger community. In some cases, taboos defined tribal membership—as for example, did the ban on murder among Cheyennes. By following that injunction tribesmen ensured that they would not pollute their national Four Sacred Arrows.

Shrines and other sacred places in the landscape, particularly so-called holy homes, where a spirit was believed to dwell, were approached with all caution. General taboos applied to them, included fasting, thirsting, and praying so as to appear "pure" to the supernatural being inhabiting such places. Some places could not be looked at, except under special circumstances, and most required that some offering be left as a gesture of respect.

Not all taboo relationships lasted a lifetime. In certain cases—for example, when hunting, fishing, or gardening—special injunctions lasted about four days. Similarly, at life-cycle events like birth, puberty, marriage, and death, taboos applied to the person directly affected—along with relatives considered close enough to be equally intensely involved in the process—for only a set time.

JAY MILLER (Lenape)
Lushootseed Research

Tamany

One of a number of village chiefs or band leaders of the Delaware (Lenape) Indians in the late seventeenth century, Tamany is often referred to as "the chief of the Delawares." It is unclear why white observers and recorders of history credited Tamany with so much power. Some writers speculate that it may have been due to Tamany's charismatic personality. In reality, however, Tamany wielded no more power than any other village chief. Tradition has it that Tamany was one of the spokesmen for the Delawares during the negotiation of their peace treaty with William Penn in 1682. Little else is known about the Indian leader, yet white Americans fabricated legends about his political prowess and power. In 1798, members of a political society in New York "canonized" Tamany when they named themselves the St. Tammany Society or Columbian Order. Though the "St." was later dropped, Tamany's name stuck and later became attached to the political machine—Tammany Hall—that ran New York City government in the late nineteenth and early twentieth centuries.

TATTOOING

Most native peoples of the Americas practiced tattooing to some extent. It served a variety of purposes depending on location, gender, and the state of intertribal relations.

A variety of methods were used to create tattoos. Among the Sioux, for example, women would draw a circle or line on a person's skin with clay, punch the design with an awl, and then rub blue clay over it. By the time the clay was dry it had penetrated beneath the awl holes. Among California natives an older woman would scratch the skin of a subject and rub charcoal dust or plant juice into the scratches for color. Following contact with Europeans, the Ojibwas drew on the skin with a stick dipped in gunpowder dissolved in water. The figure was then pricked with needles dipped in vermillion and the skin was seared with punkwood to prevent festering. The area would then be treated with an antiseptic herbal wash. These processes often took a number of days.

Tattoos held different meanings for different tribes. In the Northwest, from California to Washington, tattoos identified a woman's village. In Alaska certain tattoos indicated that a man had killed an enemy in battle, and among the Yokuts of California tattoos marked the location of a person's supernatural power. As is the case in other parts of the world, Native American tattooing reflected (and reflects) a variety of concerns and attitudes related to the human body.

TECUMSEH

1768–1813
Shawnee war chief and pan-tribal political leader.

Born at Old Piqua, a Shawnee village on the Mad River in Ohio, Tecumseh (Panther Springing across the Sky)

was the fifth of nine children born to Puckeshinewa, a Shawnee warrior, and Methoataske, a Creek woman. Puckeshinewa was killed in 1774 at the Battle of Point Pleasant, and in 1779 Methoataske emigrated to Spanish Louisiana. Tecumseh remained in Ohio, living with Tecumapease, an older, married sister, but was influenced by Chiksika, an older brother who opposed white settlement of the Ohio Valley. Chiksika and Tecumseh fought against the Americans in 1782 and 1783, and raided settlements south of the Ohio in the postrevolutionary period. In 1788, after Chiksika was killed in Tennessee, Tecumseh remained in the South and did not oppose Josiah Harmar's campaign into Ohio and Indiana (1790). In 1791 he led a party of Shawnee scouts who monitored Arthur St. Clair's march up the Miami River, but he did not participate in the attack upon St. Clair's encampment. On June 30, 1794, he joined in the attack upon Fort Recovery, and two months later he led a party of Shawnee warriors at Fallen Timbers, but he refused to participate in the Treaty of Greenville (1795).

Following the signing of the treaty, Tecumseh and a small band of Shawnees withdrew. They first settled on Deer Creek, a tributary of the Mad River, and then in 1796 moved to the Great Miami River in western Ohio. In 1797 they moved to the Whitewater River in eastern Indiana, and one year later they settled on the White River, near modern Anderson. Tecumseh remained in this village for seven years, until in 1805 he moved to a new village, near Greenville, Ohio. During this period Tecumseh was married twice. His first marriage ended in a formal separation. His second marriage, to a woman older than he named Mamate, produced one son, Pachetha. Mamate died soon after Pachetha's birth, and the boy was raised by Tecumapease, Tecumseh's sister.

In April 1805, Lalawethika (the Noisemaker), a younger brother of Tecumseh, sustained a religious experience in which he claimed to have died and been given a doctrine of revitalization. Changing his name to Tenskwatawa (the Open Door), he argued that the Americans were the children of the Great Serpent, the Shawnee epitomy of evil, and he advised the Shawnees and neighboring tribes to relinquish all contact with them. After this "prophet" successfully predicted an eclipse of the sun, his influence expanded, and during that summer he and Tecumseh established a new village, near modern Greenville, Ohio.

Tecumseh played almost no role in the rapidly spreading religious revitalization, but he did provide political leadership to the large number of Indians who flocked to the village at Greenville. By 1808, however, he began to transform the religious movement into a political alliance, urging Indians to accept a common ownership of their remaining land base and to sell no more land to the Americans. He also championed a unified political structure that would prohibit village chiefs from negotiating independently with state or federal officials. Meanwhile, local settlers had become alarmed by the large influx of Indians at Greenville, and Tecumseh and Tenskwatawa moved their village to a new site, Prophetstown, at the mouth of the Tippecanoe River, near modern Lafayette, Indiana.

Tecumseh spent the next three years promoting his political confederacy. Traveling across Ohio, Michigan, Indiana, and Illinois, he urged younger warriors to abandon village chiefs friendly to the United States and join in his alliance. He also visited British officials in Canada, seeking political and logistical support. Angered by the Treaty of Fort Wayne (1809), in August 1810 Tecumseh met with William Henry Harrison, the governor of Indiana Territory, and proclaimed that he was "the acknowledged head of all the Indians." He also warned the Americans against occupying the territory ceded in the Fort Wayne Treaty. He then visited the British in Canada, and in July 1811 he passed through Vincennes, meeting with Harrison while en route to recruit warriors from the Five Southern Tribes—the Cherokees, Creeks, Choctaws, Chickasaws, and Seminoles. He met with the Chickasaws, Choctaws, and Creeks, but only the Creeks received him favorably.

In November 1811, while Tecumseh was in the South, Harrison marched on Prophetstown, defeated the Prophet at the Battle of the Tippecanoe, and subsequently burned the Indian village. Tecumseh returned to the Wabash in January 1812, where he assured American officials of his friendship but secretly rebuilt his alliance. In July 1812, when war was declared between Britain and the United States, Tecumseh was in Canada. There he helped the British repulse an American invasion, led a mixed force of British and Indians who ambushed an American relief force at Brownstown, and was wounded in the subsequent Battle of Monguagon. In early August he assisted the British in their capture of Detroit, then participated in Major Adam Muir's unsuccessful campaign in the Maumee Valley.

Tecumseh spent the winter of 1812–13 in northwestern Indiana, but in late April 1813 he led the Indians who accompanied Colonel Henry Procter's ill-fated siege of Fort Meigs, near modern Toledo. On May 5,

1813, he intervened to stop the killing of American prisoners after the Indians captured a party of Kentucky militia, but he was disappointed when the British eventually abandoned the siege and withdrew to Canada. During the following summer he assisted the British in their unsuccessful attempts to capture Fort Meigs and Fort Stephenson.

In September 1813, after the American naval victory on Lake Erie, Tecumseh opposed British preparations to abandon Amherstburg and withdraw to Niagara. Embittered, Tecumseh denounced Procter as a coward and demanded that the British either stand and fight or surrender their guns and ammunition to the Indians. Procter reluctantly agreed to make a stand on the Thames River, near modern Moraviantown, Ontario, but on October 5, 1813, when the American forces advanced, the British army fired only three volleys and then fled. Tecumseh and his warriors fought on, but in the subsequent battle Tecumseh was shot and killed, probably by Colonel Richard M. Johnson. After the battle Kentucky militiamen skinned and mutilated Tecumseh's body. He was buried in a mass grave near the battlefield.

Tecumseh advocated Pan-Indian political unity, but during his lifetime many of his political concepts seemed alien to other Indians, most of whom still viewed their world from a tribal perspective and were wary of his attempts to centralize political leadership. Since his death Tecumseh has been portrayed by both historians and the general public as an idealized "noble savage." Enshrouded in myth (e.g., that his mother was a white captive, that he predicted the great earthquake of 1811, that he was in love with a white woman, that he was a member of the Masons), Tecumseh has emerged as an American folk hero. Unquestionably Tecumseh was one of the most gifted and admirable of all Native American political and military leaders, but his career stands on its own merits. His biography should not be embellished with the romanticism of non-Indian historians.

See also Shawnee; Shawnee Prophet (Tenskwatawa).

Dowd, Gregory, *A Spirited Resistance: The North American Indians' Struggle for Unity, 1745–1815* (Baltimore: Johns Hopkins University Press, 1992); Drake, Benjamin, *Life of Tecumseh and His Brother the Prophet* (1841; reprint, New York: Kraus Reprint Company, 1969); Edmunds, R. David, *Tecumseh and the Quest for Indian Leadership* (Boston: Little, Brown and Company, 1984).

R. David Edmunds (Cherokee)
Indiana University

TEEDYUSCUNG

(1700–1763)
Delaware chief.

Teedyuscung (Teddyuscung) grew up in the "Forks of the Delaware" region, where the Lehigh River flows into the Delaware's main stream. As a young man he witnessed the conferences between Pennsylvania's Proprietaries and Delaware Indian landowners in which John and Thomas Penn swindled the Indians out of the so-called Walking Purchase lands in what is now Bucks County, Pennsylvania. Teedyuscung's Delaware parents were dispossessed in consequence, and when a Moravian colony settled on their former lands, they protested. The Moravians were at first willing to compensate the Indians, but then became fearful that an outright purchase would be at odds with the Penns' arrangements and draw down the powerful brothers' wrath.

Perhaps it was Moravian goodwill that made Teedyuscung a temporary convert (he even adopted a new name, "Gideon"), but he chafed under mission discipline and soon left. He emerged to historical notice when the Seven Years' War broke out. In 1755, an assembly of scattered Delaware bands—Teedyuscung called them "five nations"—resenting the degree of control the Iroquois League had over their affairs, chose Teedyuscung as their chief. At about the same time, they raided isolated European homesteaders, especially in the territories that had been taken by fraud.

Pennsylvania's pacifist Quakers were alarmed that the Indians had become hostile, and arranged a conference to placate them. At this time, Teedyuscung emerged into view as a tall, portly man with a commanding presence, who had by this time become addicted to rum, which he could consume in great quantities. The Quakers' intervention had angered William Johnson, who demanded exclusive management of all Indians as Royal Superintendent of Indian Affairs for the Northern Department. Proprietary Thomas Penn was also angered, for fear that the fraudulent Walking Purchase deal might come to light as the cause of Delaware hostilities and prompt the British crown to revoke his charter of propriety.

The Quakers persisted in trying to negotiate peace with the Indians, against all the objections of Johnson and Penn. The two men then attempted to minimize the Delawares' grievances by asserting that Teedyuscung was merely a stupid drunk being used by the Quakers to smear Penn. If, in fact, there was any "using" going on, Teedyuscung was the perpetrator:

he understood perfectly how valuable the Quakers were to his cause.

In April 1756, Iroquois chiefs tried to discipline the wavering Delawares but were rebuffed by Pennsylvania Indians' new spirit of independence. Saving face, they formally recognized Teedyuscung's position of leadership and authorized him to negotiate with Pennsylvania for his own people. Pennsylvania's provincial council accepted the chief in that capacity also, pairing him with the Seneca leader Newcastle to represent the Iroquois. At this point historical records become deliberately misleading, with Penn's partisans alleging that Teedyuscung, upon Newcastle's death, put himself forward as "king" of the Iroquois—a death sentence for the Delaware chief, had it been true. In fact, Teedyuscung was careful to consult regularly with the Iroquois chiefs.

Meanwhile, Johnson, now Sir William Johnson, a baronet, tried in June to shunt Teedyuscung aside by "recognizing" a feeble old man named Nutmus as Delaware "king," but the Delawares would have none of it.

In November, Quaker leaders forced the provincial governor to confer with Teedyuscung at Easton, Pennsylvania, where Teedyuscung blurted out that "this very land has been taken from me [i.e., the Delawares] by fraud." Thus the secret of the Walking Purchase was exposed; thereafter it became a hot issue in provincial politics. Opponents of Thomas Penn blamed his policies as the cause of Indian attacks. His defenders tried to discredit Teedyuscung. Meanwhile, Teedyuscung explored options. He looked in on the French commander Captain Pierre Pouchot at Niagara but discovered few available resources of arms and food, so he turned back to the English, whose promises to redress grievances prompted him to make peace with them on behalf of the eastern Delawares.

Despite Teedyuscung's reconciliation, the Delawares of the "Ohio country" remained fiercely on the warpath. French officers at Fort Duquesne, at the forks of the Ohio River, incessantly instigated raids by these western kinsmen, and Teedyuscung, sensing disaster, attempted to mediate. If successful, he would have become a very great chief indeed. But his wampum belts inviting the Ohio group to counsel were diverted by pro-French Senecas, and the western Delawares remained hostile. When the western group sent delegates Pisquetomen and Keekyuscung to Teedyuscung in 1758, they were met, by coincidence, by two emissaries from Philadelphia, Frederick Post and Charles Thomson. Post and Thomson persuaded the diplomats to come to Philadelphia directly and begin peace negotiations without Teedyuscung.

There the provincial governor and secretary gave a peace message to the Ohio visitors, Pisquetomen and Keekyuscung, who were well known to the secretary, Richard Peters. Post returned west with them as a sort of validation for the message, Peters having blocked Teedyuscung's efforts to insert himself into the proceedings. The upshot was a great treaty signed at Easton in 1758, whereby the previously hostile Delawares agreed to abandon their French sympathies in return for a promise of a firm boundary between Indians and Englishmen. The French, thus abandoned, withdrew from Fort Duquesne and burned it, but the English boundary promise was not kept.

In 1762, Sir William Johnson negotiated with Teedyuscung about the Walking Purchase. After much disputation, Johnson talked to the chief "in the bushes"—away from the scribes. In return for a cash compensation, paid by Thomas Penn, Teedyuscung would withdraw his charge of fraud, and Penn would keep his province. (Ironically, Benjamin Franklin had first proposed this cash purchase six years earlier.) Teedyuscung also extracted a promise for houses to be built for his people in the Wyoming Valley of the Susquehanna River's north branch, and Quaker builders fulfilled that promise. Unfortunately, this agreement was also short-lived. The Susquehannah Company of Connecticut claimed the land, and Teedyuscung died when unknown persons set fire to his cabin less than a year after it had been built.

See also Delaware; Iroquois Confederacy.

Jennings, Francis, *Empire of Fortune: Crowns, Colonies and Tribes in the Seven Years War in America* (New York: W. W. Norton & Co., 1988); Wallace, Anthony F. C., *King of the Delawares: Teedyuscung, 1700–1763* (Philadelphia: University of Pennsylvania Press, 1949).

FRANCIS JENNINGS
University of North Carolina at Chapel Hill

TEKAKWITHA, KATERI

(1656–80)
Mohawk religious figure.

Kateri Tekakwitha ("She Who Pushes All before Her"; Mohawk pronunciation: GAH-teh-lee deh-gah-QUEE-tah) was born in what is now Auriesville, New York (near Albany), to a religiously traditional Mohawk chief father and a Catholic Algonquin mother. The facts of her life come to us through the chronicles of seventeenth-century missionaries; few modern scholars, either Mohawk or non-Indian, have examined and interpreted this data. Until recently, information about her life had been published mainly in devotional literature (in which Catholic hagiography often takes precedence over scholarly detachment).

The life of this extraordinary young Mohawk woman was originally recorded by Jesuit priests in Canada, who included her exploits in the annual reports they compiled and sent to their superiors and benefactors in France. They described her exemplary Catholic devotions, including daily attendance at Mass, daily prayer in solitude, works of mercy, looking after elders, visiting the sick, and instructing young people in their religious obligations. Despite their admiration, however, the priests were concerned that her penances, although conforming to the Catholic asceticism of the times, were extreme. Her dying words typified her devotion to Jesus and her indomitable faith: "*Iesos konoronkwa,*" she declared in Mohawk. "Jesus, I love you."

Tekakwitha's life was unremarkable until 1660, when a smallpox epidemic swept through her village and killed all the members of her immediate family. She survived, but her health was permanently weakened. The disease left her body ravaged; she was nearly blind and could never again endure exposure to bright sunlight. In addition, her face was scarred by the disease's telltale pockmarks. In the aftermath of the epidemic, Tekakwitha's paternal uncle took her into his lodge and made her a part of his household. Although she was fed and housed by her kin, the young girl's movements were tightly controlled, and she was frequently mistreated. Her disfigurement undermined her appeal as a marriage partner, yet when her aunt and uncle arranged a match, she refused to cooperate.

In 1676 Jacques de Lamberville, a Jesuit missionary to the Mohawks, visited Tekakwitha's longhouse and found the twenty-year-old woman eager to learn from him. Tekakwitha had met other Jesuits as she was growing up and had loved to hear their stories about Jesus and the Catholic religion. For her, it all suggested a new way of being. After a period of instruction, Lamberville christened Tekakwitha "Catherine." But the young convert's life grew even more difficult. Her family opposed her new faith, and the majority of her village harassed and ostracized her. After eighteen months of hardship, she ran away to Canada, settling at the

Christian Mohawk community of Kahnawake at Sault St.-Louis, near Montreal, where she lived for the remainder of her life.

At Kahnawake, Tekakwitha lived the ordinary life of a Mohawk woman of her day. She was part of a long-house headed by an elderly woman, and initially she joined in the expected activities: family celebrations, hunting, and farming. But her devotion to Catholic rituals grew increasingly intense. She stopped participating in the winter hunt because it deprived her of the chance to attend daily Mass and to receive Communion from the Jesuit priests. She again refused the opportunity to marry, declaring that she would have "no other spouse but Jesus Christ." During her final years at Kahnawake, Tekakwitha modeled her behavior on that of the nuns of nearby Montreal and the priests she had encountered. She performed numerous penances: she walked barefoot in the snow, fasted, slept on a bed of thorns, and burned herself with hot coals.

Tekakwitha, her already frail constitution weakened by her asceticism, grew sick and eventually died on April 17, 1680, at the mission of St. Francis Xavier at

A portrait of Kateri Tekakwitha painted by Father Claude Chauchetière in the 1680s, after Tekakwitha's death.

Kahnawake in Canada. She was twenty-four years old. Upon her death, the Jesuits present recorded an incident that quickly made its way into Catholic folklore. Moments after her last breath, the pockmarks on her face reportedly disappeared and her skin became fresh and youthful. This miracle, along with the witness of her life, led to a devotional following for her that spread throughout North America and has continued to the present. In 1980, the Jesuit accounts of Tekakwitha's life and death were used as the basis for a papal declaration that the Mohawk woman was "blessed," which in the Roman Catholic tradition meant that after serious research and investigation, the church had concluded that extraordinary holiness had illumined her.

Recently, devotion to Kateri Tekakwitha has deepened and taken on new meaning among Catholic American Indians. Though the basic known facts of her life are few, Catholic native people of all tribes accept her spiritual presence and identify with her as a holy Mohawk woman and a saint. Her life appeals to contemporary native Catholics because of its elements of heroic survival in situations of human suffering and its evidence of spiritual transformation and personal spiritual power. After all, their own history has been one of suffering through removal and separation, and the communal and personal tragedies that attended these enormous losses.

Thus North American Indians see parallels between Tekakwitha's experience and their own history. Both reflect a common experience of oppression. First, her life was marked by the desolation of her being separated at an early age from all that was known and familiar to her. Second, following the disease there was misunderstanding, cruel treatment, and persecution by her own relatives because of her appearance. Third, in the face of adversity, she endured bravely.

In addition, Native Americans have been drawn to Tekakwitha's feminine qualities. Precisely because of these characteristics, Catholic Indians of all tribes have rallied around this Mohawk woman, in spite of a heavily patriarchal and paternalistic Christian history and experience. The reality of Tekakwitha as a dynamic gathering symbol for Catholic natives can be seen particularly in the Tekakwitha Conference, a national association for native Catholics founded in 1939. Thus in recent years Tekakwitha's life story has become a means for native Catholics to come to terms with their own history. With her as a spiritual model and guide, they pursue the integration and inner convergence of their own native spiritual traditions with the practices of the Roman Catholic Church.

See also Missions and Missionaries; Mohawk; Religion.

Béchard, Henri, *The Original Caughnawaga Indians* (Montreal: International Publishers, 1976); Weiser, F. Xavier, *Kateri Tekakwitha* (Kahnawake, Quebec: Kateri Center, 1972).

MARIE THERESE ARCHAMBAULT
(Hunkpapa Lakota)
National Tekakwitha Conference
Great Falls, Montana

TERMINATION

The word *termination* describes U.S. policy toward Native Americans during the 1950s and 1960s. Reacting to Commissioner of Indian Affairs John Collier's policy of cultural pluralism and the Indian New Deal (1934–1945), conservative congressmen led by westerners such as Utah senator Arthur Watkins sought to "emancipate the Indian" by terminating federal ties to Indian communities and withdrawing federal support for tribal governments. House Concurrent Resolution no. 108, sponsored by Watkins, was adopted on August 1, 1953, to codify federal policy. It called for Congress to initiate sixty separate termination bills, the last in 1962. Generally, the statutes called for the preparation of a final roll of tribal members, the distribution of tribal assets to members, and the removal of Indian lands from federally protected trust status. Implementation was to take from two to five years to complete.

Among the groups affected by this policy were the Menominees of Wisconsin, the Klamaths and other, smaller tribes in Oregon, the Ute and Paiute Indians of Utah, and the Alabama-Coushattas of Texas. Termination undermined health and economic conditions and accelerated the decline of traditional cultural practices. In the wake of these negative outcomes, several tribes have campaigned successfully to reverse their termination. These include the Menominees, the Klamaths, the Oregon Siletzes, and the Alabama-Coushattas.

TEXTILES

The story of textile evolution in prehistoric North America begins in about 200 A.D. Woven textile fragments from this era found in the arid southwestern part of the United States point to hundreds of years of simple finger weaving, whereby vegetal fibers and human and animal hairs were twisted into threads that were then plaited, interlooped, braided, or netted into small textile objects such as sashes, belts, bandoleers, small bags, and footgear. Although these woven objects were limited in size, they often carried surprisingly sophisticated woven designs—sometimes colored by vegetal or mineral dyes and paints.

Scholars have determined that this preloom stage lasted until sometime between A.D. 500 and 700, when rudimentary loom forms—now believed to have come from Mexico—began to appear in the Southwest. The suspension-bar "loom" brought control of many more strands of weaving threads than finger manipulation could manage. This early development involved the attachment of a horizontal wooden pole between two stationary uprights, from which many hand-spun threads were suspended, allowing the weaver to interweave the hanging threads together, using one or more finger-weaving techniques.

The next significant technical advance—more in the direction of the true loom—came in the form of the belt loom, which provided for threads to be attached in warp fashion to a body-wide bar, which was in turn attached to a belt worn around the weaver's waist on the near end and affixed to a similar bar attached to a vertical fixed pole or some rigid object on the far end. This contraption allowed the weaver to lean forward or backward to control the tension of the warp threads for a more convenient crosswise insertion of flexible weft threads.

The true loom, with other advanced auxiliary weaving paraphernalia—heddles, shuttles, and battens—is believed by some authorities to have arrived full-blown in southwestern North America from Mexico sometime between A.D. 700 and 1000. The vertical or upright version of the true loom consists of a rectangular frame—two sturdy vertical uprights crossed at the bottom and top by horizontal crossbeams—to which smaller crossbars can be attached. Warp threads are attached to the smaller crossbars, which in turn are lashed to the permanent crossbeams at top and bottom, providing for the stretching of a rectangle of vertically strung warp threads between them. The size of this rectangular body of taut threads determines the size of the finished textile. With the help of auxiliary devices and hand tools, the taut warp threads can be conveniently separated to facilitate the right-angled, under-and-over insertion of movable weft threads. This mechanical setup allows for the interweaving of warp and weft, and illustrates the basic technical principle of weaving

A Navajo woman in Keam's Canyon, Arizona, weaving a blanket on a horizontal loom during the winter of 1892–93. The child, Nedespa, cards wool; the woman on the left spins wool; and the woman on the right weaves at a belt frame.

that underlies the production of most woven textiles today.

Access to the true loom came at about the same time as knowledge of how to domesticate cotton plants. A dependable supply of cotton fiber and blanket-sized looms enabled the weaver to produce wider, longer, and smoother fabrics than ever before. By A.D. 1000 the vertical loom had spread extensively throughout the Southwest; it remains the loom in general use by Native American hand weavers today.

The story of handwoven textiles has continued in North America at varying levels and locations. Many textile collectors and aficionados believe the richly designed and crafted dance blankets of the Chilkat weavers of the Tlingit tribe of southeastern Alaska represent the epitome of weaving art in North America. However, the most significant story of textile development in the United States is that of the Pueblo In-

dians and their Anasazi ancestors, who have been in the Southwest for untold centuries, and of the Navajos, who migrated to the Southwest from vaguely established origins in the great Northwest over a period of time ranging from roughly A.D. 1000 to 1500. It is generally believed that Navajos learned weaving and many other cultural ways from the Pueblo people, who had been weaving on upright looms since the tenth century.

Pueblos and their Anasazi ancestors had been proficient weavers even in preloom times. However, Pueblo weaving waned considerably after contact with the Spanish, the Americans, and the flood of tourists who appeared with the coming of the railways. Once prolific weavers, only a few Hopi (Pueblo) men currently produce an occasional woolen wearing blanket. A once flourishing production of sets of twilled bridal cotton mantas and sashes, as well as sets of brocaded cotton dance kilts and sashes, made for sale to members of other Pueblo villages, has dwindled extensively within the past three decades. Several other Pueblo groups have discontinued weaving altogether.

By 1700 the newcomer Navajos, with access to the vertical loom adopted from Pueblos and wool from Spanish-introduced sheep and goats, had begun an astounding three-century saga of weaving. By 1800 women members of hundreds of Navajo families had become flock owners, proficient weavers, and major family breadwinners. During the nineteenth century Navajo women, using the upright loom and the tapestry-weave technique, produced a body of fine wearing blankets of design, color, craftsmanship, and beauty not equaled elsewhere in American Indian art—the best of which were quickly bought up by appreciative traders and collectors. Today the finest blankets and rugs from this period sell, in an ever more demanding market, at prices that run well into six figures.

By 1900, however, fine blanket weaving had given way to poor-quality coarsely woven rugs made at the behest of traders to accommodate the demands of an ever increasing tourist trade. Today, rapidly changing cultural and economic lifestyles have thrown the Navajo weaving arts into further decline, in terms of both quantity and quality.

Native American hand-weaving arts are waning on all fronts—a trend that is likely to keep pace with the decline of Indian traditions in general. However, the strong cultural renaissance that is now under way among all Indian groups offers hope that many cultural traditions will soon be updated to fit new cultural realities. Harbingers of such change can be found in the increasing number of Native American students who have enrolled in arts and cultural institutions in order to reacquaint themselves with fading traditions. Thus as old textile traditions disappear, new, vital ones, fitted to the realities of changing times, will arise.

See also Arts, Contemporary (since 1960).

Berlant, Anthony, and Mary Hunt Kahlenberg, *Walk in Beauty: The Navajo and Their Blankets* (Boston: New York Graphic Society, 1977); Dockstader, J. Frederick, *Weaving Arts of the North American Indian* (New York: Thomas Crowell, 1978); Kent, Kate Peck, *Navajo Weaving: Three Centuries of Change* (Santa Fe, N.M.: School of American Research Press, 1982).

LLOYD KIVA NEW (Cherokee)
Indian Arts and Crafts Board
Santa Fe, New Mexico

THORPE, JIM

(1887–1953)
Sauk and Fox football and baseball player and Olympic athlete.

James Francis Thorpe (Wa Tha Huck, Bright Path) was born on May 22, 1887, in Keokuk Falls, south of what is now Prague, Oklahoma, on the Sauk and Fox Indian Reservation. He and his twin brother, Charlie, were baptized on November 17, 1887, at Sacred Heart Catholic Church, in what is now Konawa, Oklahoma, their mother's home.

Jim was one of eleven children born to Hiram P. Thorpe, a man of mixed Sauk and Fox and Irish ancestry; and Charlotte Vieux, of mixed Potawatomi, Kickapoo, Menominee, and French ancestry, the great-granddaughter of Jacques Vieux, a French fur trader. Jim's father was a horse breeder and trainer and occasional bootlegger. Life was a struggle for the family, and only five of the eleven children grew to adulthood. Jim used to run down the horses on their ranch on the banks of the North Canadian River, an activity that developed his strength and stamina, and helped him hone the athletic skills that would later make him famous.

Like many other Indian children, Thorpe went off to Indian boarding schools. He began at the Sauk and Fox Mission School at age six, and went on to Haskell Institute and the Carlisle Indian Industrial School in Pennsylvania. While the government's assimilationist lessons were imperfectly learned—Thorpe never forgot that he was an Indian—he never again lived in an Indian community.

It was while he was at Carlisle that Thorpe gained international fame. An outstanding football player, he was so skilled at running and place-kicking that he was chosen for the 1911 and 1912 all-American teams. In 1912 he participated in the Olympics in Stockholm, Sweden, where he won both the decathlon and pentathlon—a feat that has never been equaled.

Barely a month after his Olympic victories, however, Olympic officials demanded the return of Thorpe's medals. They had discovered that he had played semiprofessional baseball with the Rocky Mount League, in North Carolina, during the summers of 1909 and 1910. Seventy years later, in 1983, the International Olympic Committee president Juan Samaranch of Spain apologized and returned the gold medals to Thorpe's heirs. They are now displayed under a portrait of Thorpe that hangs in the rotunda of the state capitol in Oklahoma City.

Jim Thorpe at bat during the New York Giants' spring training in 1916.

Jim Thorpe's personal life was not a happy one. At age nine he lost his twin brother. Jim's mother died of childbirth complications when he was attending Haskell, and he became an orphan at age sixteen when his father died of gangrene poisoning after a hunting accident. His first son, Jim Jr., died in his arms at age two, from pneumonia. Iva Margaret Miller, his first wife, divorced him after the birth of four children: Jim Jr., Gail, Charlotte, and Grace. His second wife divorced him after the birth of four sons: Carl Phillip, William, Richard, and John. He was later married to Patricia Agnew, with whom he lived until he died. Through it all he learned to overcome tragedy and still perform. Losing the Olympic gold medals was only one tragedy he overcame.

After the 1912 Olympics, Thorpe returned to Carlisle and played his last season of amateur football. In 1913 he turned professional, signing a contract with the New York Giants baseball team. Two years later he started playing part-time professional football in Ohio for Jack Cuzak's Canton Bulldogs. He was paid $250 a game, an unheard-of sum at the time. For the next fifteen years, he played baseball in the spring and football in the fall.

In 1920, when Thorpe became the first president of the American Professional Football Association (now the National Football League), professional football was in its infancy. Thorpe's talent and enthusiasm drew the public to the game and helped establish it as a national pastime. Perhaps this is why the first image to greet visitors at the Pro Football Hall of Fame in Canton, Ohio, is a statue of Thorpe, with a football under his arm, charging down the field toward another touchdown.

In the early 1930s, when Thorpe became too old for sports, he turned to acting, playing small movie roles in California. Working also as a casting director for various studios, Jim rounded up Indians for westerns. He insisted that only Indians should play Indian roles, but was frequently overruled.

Big salaries and pension benefits for players in professional sports did not exist during the time of Thorpe's career, and even with his film jobs it was difficult for him to make a living during the depression years. Strapped for cash, he sold his life story to Warner Bros. for less than three thousand dollars. The film company released *Jim Thorpe, All-American,* starring Burt Lancaster, in 1951. Thorpe was paid as a part-time consultant during filming, but he never received royalties or further payments for the film, which continues to be shown. Ahead of his time as a professional athlete, he was unable to reap any substantial monetary benefits from his unprecedented sports achievements.

Running as a constant through Thorpe's life was a love of sport and competition. His daughter Grace remembers her father standing at center field at the Haskell Institute football stadium in Lawrence, Kansas, when she was five years old. He kicked a football through one goal post, then turned around and easily kicked another ball to the goal post at the other end of the field. When asked what sport he preferred, Thorpe would often reply that he liked hunting and fishing best of all. He kept many coon dogs in his small backyard in Hawthorne, California, and made frequent trips to the fishing piers at El Segundo and Redondo Beach.

Jim Thorpe died of a cerebral hemorrhage on March 28, 1953, in Long Beach, California. Despite the fact that he never capitalized on his fame, Thorpe's athletic achievements continued to impress the sporting public. In Associated Press polls of sportswriters taken in 1950 and 1975, Thorpe was judged not only America's greatest all-around athlete, but also America's greatest football player. In 1955, the town of Mauch Chunk, Pennsylvania, changed its name to Jim Thorpe, and his body was reinterred there. The words King Gustav V of Sweden spoke in 1912 are inscribed on Thorpe's rose granite sarcophagus: "You, sir, are the greatest athlete in the world."

Newcombe, Jack, *The Best of the Athletic Boys: The White Man's Impact on Jim Thorpe* (Garden City, N.Y.: Doubleday & Company, 1975); Richards, Gregory B., *Jim Thorpe, World's Greatest Athlete* (Chicago: Children's Press, 1984); Thorpe, Grace F., "The Jim Thorpe Family: From Wisconsin to Indian Territory," parts 1 and 2, *Chronicles of Oklahoma* 59, no. 1 (spring 1981): 91–105; no. 2 (summer 1981): 179–201.

GRACE THORPE (Sac and Fox)
Stroud, Oklahoma

TIPI

The word *tipi* comes from the Siouan family of languages and means "used to dwell." Based on archaeologists' findings and Indian oral tradition, tipis were used by North American Indians as long ago as 2000 B.C. Spanish explorers in the late sixteenth century were the first to note the round structures of poles and animal skins that could be packed up quickly and transported, initially by dogs and later by horse travois.

Among the Plains Indians, the tipi varied in construction from north to south. In the north, among the Crows, Nez Perces, Crees, Blackfeet, Mandans, Arikaras, and Hidatsas, a four-pole base was common. These four central poles (usually made from pine saplings) were fastened together and partially buried in the ground. Several additional poles were arranged around them. Four-pole tipis are generally larger than the three-pole frames common to southern tribes such as the Shoshones, Cheyennes, Pawnees, Sioux, Kiowas, Kiowa Apaches, and Arapahos.

The traditional tipi covering was of bison hides carefully prepared and sewn together with sinew by the women of the tribe. Canvas became available in the nineteenth century, allowing tipis to be much larger and lighter. Most tipis in use today are covered with canvas. Smoke was ventilated through the roof of the tipi and could be directed with flaps that were opened and closed by poles outside of the covering. Doorways consisted either of holes cut into the hide

covering and flapped open, or of triangular slits held in place by thongs. The bottom of the tipi was secured either by stakes or rocks, and the central pole frame was anchored to the ground by a rope tied to a stake in the earth. A three-foot-high liner of separate material was typically lashed to the poles inside the tipi to provide insulation and protection against seeping or dew.

Tribal beliefs and customs were incorporated into tipi technology and tipi use. In many tribes, for example, honored individuals were placed against the wall directly across from the entrance. Many tribes, like the Blackfeet of Montana and Canada, painted their tipis with images of guardian spirits and medicine or clan symbols. Though most Plains Indians no longer use tipis as their permanent dwellings, many retain them for use during good weather and on special occasions such as the Sun Dance, powwows, and annual fairs.

See also Architecture.

TIZWIN

Tizwin (or *tiswin*) is one of two potent alcoholic beverages traditionally brewed by the Chiricahuas and Western Apaches. Although early observers often confused *tizwin* with *tula-pah*, the corn beer made by the western bands, the two drinks have distinct cultural and botanical origins. *Tizwin* originated among the Chiricahuas (who passed the recipe on to the Western Apaches) and comes from the heart of the mescal plant. Like *tula-pah*, it required considerable preparation time, and the concoction was extremely perishable: it spoiled within twenty-four hours. Accordingly, the Apaches usually brewed *tizwin* only for ceremonial occasions and large social gatherings, consuming it rapidly and in large quantities. Whites who sampled the beverage generally found it distasteful.

After the Apaches were forced onto reservations in the late nineteenth century, the production and consumption of *tizwin* caused numerous confrontations between the Indians and the government. Concerned with the boisterous and sometimes violent nature of "tizwin drunks," General George Crook outlawed the consumption of the beverage. The Apaches treated his order with scorn, however. In 1885, the superintendent of the San Carlos Agency, Britton Davis, attempted to enforce the ban and thereby sparked Geronimo's second breakout from the San Carlos Reservation. Agency officials never succeeded in abolishing the use of *tizwin*, and many Apaches still brew it for ceremonial occasions, particularly the "coming out" (puberty) ceremonies of adolescent girls.

TLINGIT

The Tlingit Indians of southeastern Alaska developed one of the most complex cultures to be found among the indigenous populations of North America. With their vast stores of surplus resources, they extended their commerce east into the Canadian interior regions to trade with neighboring Athabaskan tribes. To the west, they traded with the Eyaks and Chugach Yupiks along the coast of the Gulf of Alaska. In their large canoes, they traveled south to the Queen Charlotte Islands to trade, and sometimes to war, with the Haidas and the Tsimishians. By the mid-1800s, the Tlingits expanded their fur trading expeditions as far south as the Puget Sound. Today they trade on an international scale.

The Tlingits maintained absolute control over their homeland, which stretched over four hundred miles along the coastal mainland and islands from Portland Canal in British Columbia and northward to the Yakutat region. Major river ways provided access into the interior region, where a smaller group of inland Tlingits established themselves. At the time of first contact with Westerners, the Tlingits were expanding their northwestern frontier across the Gulf of Alaska. Today, as in the past, their communities dot the coastal mainland and the mountainous islands of the adjacent eighty-mile-wide archipelago. The protected waterways through the maze of islands allow easy maritime transportation between these communities.

The warm Japanese Current produces moderate temperatures and heavy precipitation along the western coast of North America. This climatic condition nourishes an environment rich in natural resources. Dense stands of forests blanket the region, and thick underbrush provides a variety of berries, plants, and roots that are used for food and medicine. The sea produces even greater riches: abundant salmon, herring, smelt, halibut, cod, seals, sea lions, and sea otters. Shellfish, clams, mussels, sea urchins, seaweed, and herring spawn add to this variety and broaden the Tlingit diet. Waterfowl and gulls provide meat and eggs.

Every Tlingit is a member of one of two groups (referred to as *moieties*), and identifies himself or herself as a Raven or an Eagle. Members of one moiety refer to the other as "the opposite side." Marriage was formerly allowed only between persons from opposite moieties, but today this rule has been relaxed. Each moiety comprises smaller kinship groups known as clans.

The clan is the enduring organization that unifies the Tlingits into a cohesive, functioning unit. Clans govern the social, ceremonial, and political life of the Tlingits and link them to their ancestors and future generations. Tlingit individuals die, but the clan persists through the birth of new clan members. Names are owned by clans, and a child receives a name that was held by one of his or her ancestors. This naming system, and the belief that a Tlingit may be reborn, mean that, through continued rebirth, clans in essence retain their original membership. Today, the primary function of clans is ceremonial.

Among the Tlingits, the house is a subunit of the clan. In the past, houses were occupied by several closely related families. The term *house* refers in Tlingit society to both a physical structure and the matrilineage associated with that structure. Each house has a formal name. In the past, the house group consisted of a house leader, his brothers, their wives and children, and the house leader's matrilineal nephews. Members of the house joined forces to hunt, to fish, and to gather and preserve food and supplies. Today, Tlingit people live in nuclear-family houses, while group ceremonies and potlatches are held in the remaining clan houses.

The Tlingit kinship system is matrilineal. Children are born into their mother's moiety, clan, and house rather than their father's. Although they are not members of their father's clan, they maintain a special relationship with his clan. Through his or her birth into a clan and house, an infant has all the rights to land and property held by the clan. The child does not inherit privileges, rights, or property as under American law, but is entitled to these rights through his or her membership in a clan.

The Tlingits held slaves until American law banned slavery. A large number of slaves were owned by the Tlingits, with wealthy chiefs possessing as many as twenty to thirty. Slaves were captured in war or purchased from southern tribes and did much of the hard and tedious labor. They were sacrificed in ceremonial activities that validated the ownership of property and the transfer of office to new leaders.

Among the most distinctive features of Tlingit culture are the visual arts. Though their art has gained international renown, the Tlingits believe it embodies more than aesthetic qualities. For them its visual features—including clan crests—symbolize their social organization and depict their spiritual relationship to wildlife and the environment. Each clan owns as its sole property one or more crests that depict the origin and history of the clan; the crests also serve as titles to land. They adorn ceremonial objects and regalia, jewelry, totems, screens, house posts, and house fronts, as well as utilitarian objects.

The Tlingit potlatch has been described as a ritualized competition in which clan leaders increase their status through the opulent consumption and distribution of goods and the destruction of property. While these activities were part of the traditional ceremonial activities of a potlatch, they are not its central elements. Basically, the Tlingit social and spiritual order is acted out in the traditional potlatch. In modern-day potlatches, the reciprocal relationship between clans is demonstrated when the host clan provides food and gifts for guest clans. The relationship between the dead and the living is demonstrated as well, in solemn speeches and songs, and through the distribution of food—including the feeding of the dead. Through these actions the dead are mourned and the living are honored. There are several types of modern potlatches, but they all relate to memorials to the dead.

The Tlingits used the Peace Ceremony to resolve legal disputes between clans. In it, negotiations were held to establish settlement terms, whereupon hostages were exchanged. Then, through a dance, the hostages were ritually transformed into deer, who acted as peacemakers. Their function was to ensure that the terms of peace were maintained for their yearlong period of captivity with the other clan.

The Tlingits' first contact with Westerners began with the arrival of Russians in 1741. Within a generation, European and American traders followed in the Russians' wake. The explorers and traders introduced both Western goods and Western diseases. The trade goods enriched the society and culture of the Tlingits, and the diseases reduced their numbers. Their aboriginal population, which has been estimated at near fifteen thousand at first contact, was reduced by more than 50 percent after the smallpox epidemics of 1835–40. Once the Tlingits learned that their shamans' powers could not heal the new diseases and observed that the Russians who had been vaccinated against smallpox survived, they clamored to be vaccinated. The consequence was that many Tlingits accepted the Russian Orthodox faith and began to discount the role of the shaman.

The establishment of American jurisdiction in 1867 and the arrival of the military brought further social diseases and vices. The Tlingits' loss of land and of control over streams and seas was devastating, the result of permanent American settlements in the area and economic expansion into Tlingit territory. In 1878 one salmon cannery was established in Sitka and one in Klawock, followed by ten more in the area over the next decade. A Tlingit who unknowingly led a white man to the Tlingits' source of gold unleashed the 1880 gold stampede into southeastern Alaska. The traditional hunting and fishing economy that had supported the rich culture of the Tlingits gave way to a new economic order in which they would no longer share in its wealth as owners of the land.

Despite the decline in their numbers, the Tlingits never abandoned their claims of land ownership, which they had avowed since the arrival of the first visitors to their shores. They removed the cross the Spaniards left in 1775 as a sign of a Spanish claim to Alaska. They resisted the Russians' claim to their land and resources. In the nineteenth century they hired a lawyer and argued that if the United States wanted to purchase Alaska, it should pay the Tlingits, who were the rightful owners, rather than the Russians. They claimed that the Tlingits had owned and occupied the land since time immemorial. They entered the twentieth century undaunted by their losses—epidemics, economic losses, bombardments of their villages by the U.S. Navy, depletion of fish and wildlife resources, dispossession of their land, and suppression of their culture. Under the leadership of the first Tlingit lawyer, William Paul, they moved to regain title to their land and compensation for the destruction of their fishery resources.

The Alaska Native Brotherhood was organized in 1912, and in 1929 it initiated efforts to reclaim Tlingit land. The Tlingits joined with the Haidas to pursue their first land settlement. In 1968, they were awarded $7.5 million by the U.S. Court of Claims, far short of the originally proposed amount of $80 million. The Central Council of Tlingit and Haida Indians established a trust fund, whose earnings are used to promote the social and educational welfare of tribal members.

A second Tlingit land settlement, part of a settlement unprecedented in American Indian history, occurred in 1971, when Congress, rather than establishing reservations, transferred Alaska tribes' communally owned land to corporations in accordance with the Alaska Native Claims Settlement Act (ANCSA). With tribal members enrolled as individual shareholders in corporations that hold title to tribal land and manage tribal capital, the intent was clearly economic assimilation. Under this act, Southeast Alaska Indians have reclaimed ownership of more than six hundred thousand acres of land. They have established a region-wide corporation and twelve village and urban corporations. They were compensated approximately $200 million for the 2 million acres of land that were not covered by the first land claims settlement. Five communities, however, did not receive their land entitlement, and they continue to seek their land.

The Tlingit and Haida Indians were not satisfied with ANCSA, since it violated their traditional ideas of communal land ownership and posed the potential loss of land. They brought their concerns to Congress. ANCSA did not allow for the perpetual enrollment of their children into the corporations, a policy that conflicts with ancient laws that recognize that children have rights to land because of their membership in the tribe. They argued that their grandparents and parents did not pursue the land-claims settlement for only one generation of Tlingits and Haidas. In addition, corporate laws do not allow for unequal distributions and benefits to one class of shareholders. The Southeast Indians wanted to give special benefits to their elders. More importantly, they opposed the option to sell stock and the concomitant threat of loss of their land; although there was a restriction in place on the sale of stock, it was to be in effect only through December 1991.

The Tlingits joined with other Alaska Natives and successfully amended ANCSA. Shareholders must vote to enroll new Alaska Natives or children born after the 1971 enrollment; to provide special benefits to elders; and to lift restrictions on the sale of stock. Sealaska Corporation, the regional corporation, voted to establish a settlement trust for tribal elders. As each shareholder reaches the age of sixty-five, he or she receives a special dividend of two thousand dollars.

Perhaps the single most pressing issue for the Tlingits and other Southeast Alaska Indians during the 1990s has been the protection of their hunting and fishing rights. While federal legislation protects subsistence hunting for rural residents, it does not provide protection for urban Indians. The Alaska constitution and state laws, on the other hand, do not allow a subsistence hunting and fishing priority for rural residents. As a result, when the state failed to comply with the federal legislation by recognizing the rural subsistence priority, the federal government in 1990 reassumed the management of fish and game on federal lands. Since native people living in urban communities are not protected under the federal legislation, the Tlingits and Haidas organized the Southeast Native Subsistence Commission to advocate for the protection of their hunting and fishing rights for both rural and urban natives.

Left unresolved by ANCSA were the sovereign rights of Alaska Natives. The corporations and the statewide organization, the Alaska Federation of Natives, took the lead in seeking federal recognition of a government-to-government relationship with Alaska Native tribes. On the closing day of the Bush administration in January 1993, the Department of the Interior concluded that Congress intended in ANCSA to extinguish all tribal territorial jurisdiction, but nine months later the department reversed itself and acknowledged that native communities have the same status as tribes in the contiguous forty-eight states, including the same governmental status as other federally acknowledged Indian tribes. And while ANCSA did not terminate Alaska Native tribes, neither did it extend to them jurisdiction over native corporate lands; it was essential that the Tlingits continue to be vigilant guardians of their rights.

Considerable changes have occurred within their culture, but the Tlingits' persistence has challenged earlier assumptions that it was only a matter of time before the Tlingits and other American Indians would be absorbed into the dominant society. True, the Tlingit language has all but disappeared except among those who are in their late fifties and older. However, significant elements of traditional Tlingit culture have been maintained through potlatches and funerary practices. The strict prohibition against marriage within the same moiety is no longer adhered to by all Tlingits, but the clan remains strong in the ceremonial domain, and the clans are still fiercely protective of their ownership of crests, names, and songs.

See also Indian-White Relations in Alaska; Potlatch.

deLaguna, Frederica, *Under Mount Saint Elias: The History and Culture of the Yakutat Tlingit,* Smithsonian Contributions to Anthropology, vol. 7 (Washington: Smithsonian Institution Press, 1990); Kan, Sergei, *Symbolic Immortality: The Tlingit Potlatch of the Nineteenth Century* (Washington: Smithsonian Institution Press, 1989); Worl, Rosita, "History of Southeastern Alaska since 1867," in *Handbook of North American Indians,* ed. William C. Sturtevant, vol. 7, *Northwest Coast,* ed. Wayne Suttles (Washington: Smithsonian Institution, 1990).

ROSITA WORL (Tlingit)
Juneau, Alaska

TOBACCO

The leaves of various species of the plant (genus *Nico-tiana*), native to the Americas, commonly called "to-bacco" (from a Caribbean Arawak Indian word for "cigar") were smoked, chewed, snuffed, drunk, and held sacred by most Indian peoples of the Americas. A carving from the Mayan city of Palenque shows a priest, circa A.D. 400, puffing a tubular "straight" pipe.

Among North American Indians the common method of smoking was to use stone pipes. Early evidence of pre-Columbian tobacco ceremonialism comes from Ohio's Hopewell culture (200 B.C. to A.D. 500). At Mound City, along the Scioto River, the Mound of the Pipes yielded over two hundred so-called platform-pipe bowls carved from local soapstone into animal, bird, and reptile shapes. Suggestive of elaborate smoking rituals, this "effigy pipe" tradition continued into Mississippian times. One masterfully sculpted example, known as the Big Boy pipe, was excavated from Oklahoma's Spiro Mound and has been dated at A.D. 1200–1350. It shows a seated warrior wearing elaborate headgear and special ear ornaments that portray what archaeologists call the "Long-Nosed God."

The first recorded Indian use of tobacco appears in Christopher Columbus's journal entry for November 15, 1492. In subsequent European observations of Indian life, tobacco use or ceremonialism was reported throughout the North American continent and was practiced during social, economic, diplomatic, and religious occasions. Among southwestern Indians, smoking empowered prayers in the kivas, and smoke was blown to bless stone hunting fetishes. Calling their tubular pipes "cloud blowers," the Hopis equated their tobacco smoke with the clouds that brought rain to their fields. In the Southeast the Cherokees referred to their tobacco (*Nicotiana rustica*) as "father" or "grandfather" and believed it to be the earthly incarnation of heavenly bodies. Before contact with Europeans introduced the use of pipes, Northwest Coast tribes like the Tlingits blended tobacco leaves with lime, added the burned inner bark of cedar, and chewed the resulting mixture.

The most elaborate Indian smoking practices developed on the southern plains. Possibly influenced by earlier Mississippian-period rites, these practices were dubbed by seventeenth-century French visitors *calumet* ceremonies, from the Norman word meaning "reed." The name pointed to the greater symbolic importance accorded the elaborately decorated pipe stems with their eagle-fan pendants than the actual stone bowls. Exacting protocols were associated with smoking such pipes in order to seal friendship or trade contracts (hence the stereotypical term *peace pipes*) but also to declare war, to assure safe passage through dangerous regions, to greet strangers, and to make appeals or offerings to supernatural beings. Originally documented among Caddoan-speaking tribes, this smoking rite apparently diffused eastward to be incorporated into rituals of other tribes, notably the Cherokee and Iroquois Eagle Dances.

Most Indian peoples felt that smoking together helped to create a spirit of congeniality and cooperation. "See our smoke has now filled the room," said a Delaware Indian from Oklahoma named Jesse Moses to the anthropologist Frank Speck. "First it was in streaks and your smoke and my smoke moved about that way, but now it is all mixed up into one. That is like our minds and spirit too, when we must talk. We are now ready, for we will understand one another better."

Throughout the historical period the shared use of tobacco in red stone pipes with quill-wrapped and feather-festooned stems became an important rite for creating temporary zones of amity that allowed the often-feuding Plains Indian peoples to trade and negotiate military alliances. Smoking etiquette might include the removal of moccasins; the proper circulation of the pipe around the circle, which usually consisted of men only; and the addressing of the pipe to the cardinal directions before and after an appropriate number of puffs.

The brick-red soapstone that was the preferred material for sawing, filing and sanding to produce pipe bowls came to be called *catlinite,* after the artist George Catlin, who visited the major quarry, in western Minnesota, in 1830. Since precontact Hopewell times this spot had served Indian craftsmen far and wide; blanks of catlinite were probably traded to the Middle Missouri villagers as early as A.D. 900. Older catlinite bowls were shaped in flat discs or "elbow" shapes, but soon the predominant form was the elegant, inverted-T-shaped bowl. By the early 1800s the bowls were being inlaid with lead, the stems were often intricately carved with animal symbols, and the tobacco mixtures were kept inside beaded, quilled, and fringed pipe bags, which were obligatory accouterments in formal Plains warrior attire.

In tribal folklore the sacred origins of tobacco and its potential as a mediator between Indians and supernatural beings were common themes. Some narratives emphasized its association with creation, others with fertility. According to Ho-Chunk (Winnebago) tradition, the animals first gave humankind "a weed, pleasant to the sense of smell," to compensate for the incapacity of people to foresee the future—a gift the animals already enjoyed. Thereafter this plant linked humans to their creator, Earthmaker, who was so pleased that he satisfied any requests that were accompanied by tobacco offerings. While humans might not share with animals knowledge of the future, in this way they could influence it.

Among the Fox Indians, the gift of tobacco was made by the Great Manitou to offset the brutal fact of the short lifespan of human beings. With tobacco Fox tribespeople could obtain special blessings from the spirit world. When the Creator passed the sacred plant to the neighboring Menominee tribe, it is said, "they liked it so much that they wanted more and more, and he made them dance before he would give it to them." Their Tobacco Dance pleased the Creator, and established this plant as a bonding medium between them and their gods.

In the Southeast, tribal folklore stressed the connection between tobacco and human fertility. According to oral tradition, the first tobacco plant was discovered growing on ground where a man and woman had had sexual intercourse. After finding this plant and smoking its leaves, an elderly tribesman shared that man's experience. "That's a mighty good thing," his people responded. "We had better take that and smoke it." Thereafter special tobacco plots were cultivated alongside the other crops.

Rituals for germinating tobacco were found across Indian country. Among the Karoks of northwestern California, growing rites originated when a race of supernatural predecessors caused the first tobacco to sprout along the river bottoms, which cut through steep mountains. "Human will smoke this," they said. "Human will sow this. . . . Behold, he will be feeding his tobacco to the mountains." Thereafter special plots were tended by ritual practitioners. Then the plant was smoked in wood-plank sweathouses and "fed" to the mountains, thereby sealing a pact between human beings and the supernatural beings who were embodied in these peaks.

Among many Plains Indians tobacco was grown with special care. Horticultural tribes such as the Hidatsas, Mandans, and Arikaras cultivated plots of *Nicotiana quadrivalvis* not far from their vegetable gardens along the river flood plains. The Sarsis and Blackfeet gave greater ritual attention to their *Nicotiana rustica* seeds and seedlings. In their early days as a farming people the Cheyennes grew tobacco, but upon fully embracing the horse culture they obtained their tobacco in trade.

Among the Crow Indians of south central Montana, however, the reverence for their home-grown tobacco elevated the plant to the status of a tribal totem. An offshoot of the Missouri River–dwelling Hidatsas, the Crows claim that their emergence as a separate people was actually triggered when a long-ago chief dreamed of tobacco seeds. After leading his wandering people from present-day North Dakota on an epic circuit of the plains, he settled with them in the Bighorn Mountains, where they became the Crows. There divine instructions told them that their survival was dependent on their annual growing of this rare form of tobacco—*Nicotiana multivalvis*. The cultivation of this plant in sacred gardens, and the adoption of tribal members into the Crow Tobacco Society, became rituals that distinguished this new equestrian tribe from its neighbors. Furthermore, the Crows observed a taboo against ever using this ceremonial tobacco, instead obtaining their smoking mixtures via trade with their old kinfolk, the Hidatsas.

Special mixtures of tobacco were common, producing in the eastern United States and Canada the blend called *kinnikinnick*, from an Algonquian word meaning "that which is mixed"; sumac leaves and the inner bark of dogwood were the additives. Among the Crees of central Canada dried bearberry leaves were blended in, and for Crows "bear root" lent a special flavor.

As an offering, however, tobacco did not need to be smoked to be efficacious. Early French missionaries among the Hurons noticed the Indians throwing tobacco on the fire before speaking to the spirits. Today tobacco is tightly wrapped in tiny red cloth pouches and left to hang as offerings at sacred sites such as Bear Butte, South Dakota. Prayers during meetings of the Native American Church are accompanied by the smoking of cigarettes made of loose-cut commercial tobacco wrapped in wetted corn husks. Yet it is through sacred pipe ceremonialism that the offering of tobacco smoke remains most hallowed for many contemporary Indian peoples. "To the red man," said Assiniboin chief Dan Kennedy in 1939, "the Pipe of Chiefs symbolizes what the Magna Carta and the Ark of the Covenant stand for with other races."

Paper, Jordan, *Offering Smoke: The Sacred Pipe and Native American Religion* (Moscow, Idaho: University of Idaho Press, 1988); West, George A., *Tobacco, Pipes and Smoking Customs of the North American Indians*, Bulletin of the Public Museum of the City of Milwaukee 17 (Milwaukee, Wis.).

PETER NABOKOV
University of Wisconsin at Madison

TOHONO O'ODHAM (PAPAGO)

The Tohono O'odhams, known to many as the Papagos, live in southern Arizona and the northern part of the Mexican state of Sonora. The Tohono O'odhams

say that Elder Brother, known as I'itoi, led them into this land from the underworld. Their domain once extended from the San Pedro River to the Colorado and from the Gila River down past the Altar in Mexico.

A Piman-speaking people, the Tohono O'odhams are directly related to two neighboring O'odham groups. To survive in the desert environment, each of the three groups developed a unique lifestyle. The Akimel O'odhams (River People) settled in sedentary villages along perennial rivers and developed irrigation agriculture. Some Akimels, known as the Subiapuris, lived along the San Pedro and Santa Cruz Rivers, while others, known as the Pimas, located on the Gila River. The Hia C'ed O'odhams (Sand People) lived west of the Tohono O'odhams. One of the few truly nomadic peoples in the

Tohono O'odham women of the 1940s participating in the game of toka. *This women's athletic contest pits one village against another. The "ball" is made of two pieces of wood or cactus rib attached by a leather cord. The sticks are of catclaw—cut to the height of the player, with a curve at the end.*

United States, the Hia C'eds developed a hunting and gathering lifestyle specially adapted to that extremely dry part of the desert.

The Tohono O'odhams (Desert People) settled between the Akimels and Hia C'eds. This group of desert dwellers survived by migrating between two locales—a mountain-spring village in the winter and a flood-farming village in the summer. Their semiannual move ended in the early twentieth century when the government drilled deep wells. As a result, the farming village became permanent.

An individual Tohono O'odham gave his or her loyalty to one of eleven village complexes. These village clusters originated in the nineteenth century when the Apaches forced the Tohono O'odhams to band together for defense. With the disappearance of the Apache threat at century's end, the large defensive villages broke up and the inhabitants established new kin-based communities. The newly formed villages became the central social unit of the Tohonos, but the ties and loyalties of the old fortified villages remained. The Tohonos maintained their village groupings through ceremony, marriage, economic cooperation, social interaction, and limited political association.

Water has always been key to the Tohono O'odhams' survival as desert farmers and ranchers. One of their most important ceremonies, the *vi:gida,* centers around the bringing of rain. In late summer, the Tohonos gather saguaro fruit, which they ferment into a wine—*nawait.* The *vi:gida* is marked by the drinking of *nawait,* which brings the annual rains. The *vi:gida* also marks the beginning of the Tohono O'odham New Year.

Spaniards were the first Europeans to make contact with the Tohono O'odhams. Starting in the 1690s, the Jesuits under Father Eusebio Francisco Kino established a series of missions for the Tohonos in what is today northern Sonora and southern Arizona. The Spanish also established garrisons, such as Tucson, to protect themselves and the missions from the Apaches. The Tohonos adopted wheat, cattle, and horses from the Spaniards. They also mixed Catholism with their I'itoi faith to create Sonoran Catholism, which is still the predominant faith among the Tohonos.

By the early 1800s, European diseases and Apache pressure had decimated the Subiapuris along the San Pedro and Santa Cruz Rivers, pushing the survivors eastward. When the Americans arrived in southern Arizona in the 1850s, only the Subiapuri village of Wa:k, on the Santa Cruz, remained. The Tohono O'odhams moved to Wa:k and intermarried with the surviving Subiapuris.

The situation changed when the Gadsden Purchase of 1853 divided the Tohono O'odham homeland. North of the new border, the Tohonos cooperated with the Americans to defeat the Apaches and restore peace by the 1870s. Unfortunately, American newcomers coveted Tohono O'odham land. In response, the U.S. government established several small reservations, starting with San Xavier in 1874 and Gila Bend in 1884. Nevertheless, the Tohonos used a much larger area. At the same time, white miners and ranchers were encroaching on the Desert People's land. As a solution, in 1916, President Woodrow Wilson issued an executive order establishing the Papago Reservation (later renamed the Tohono O'odham Reservation). It has gone through several adjustments, including a 1917 change that gave the Tohonos surface rights but left the subsurface minerals in the public domain. A final addition in 1937 made for a total land area of 2,774,370 acres, giving the Tohono O'odhams the second-largest reservation in the United States. The government finally returned subsurface mineral rights to the Tohonos in 1955.

The Tohono O'odhams in Mexico did not fare as well. After Mexico became independent, ranchers and miners encroached on Tohono land. Many of the Tohonos either mixed into Mexican society or moved to the United States. In 1928, the Mexican government granted an *ejido* (a community land holding) to the village of Pozo Verde, but it covered only 7,600 acres. A 1979 census identified only two hundred Tohono O'odhams still living in Sonora.

At the turn of the century, Tohonos in the United States followed the village headman system. After several unsuccessful attempts in the 1910s and 1920s, the Tohonos in 1937 formed a single tribal government under the Indian Reorganization Act. The new constitution divided the reservation into districts that matched the former village groupings, all of which were united under a tribal council. In 1986, the tribe adopted a new constitution that better reflected Tohono O'odham society.

Except for a few ranching and mining operations, the reservation was comparatively undeveloped until the 1930s. Through government public-works projects, the Tohonos built roads, strung telephone wire, dug deep wells, and constructed schools and other buildings. World War II brought even more changes. Some 250 young men served in the armed forces, while many families moved off the reservation to take war-industry jobs. Veterans returned with new skills and knowledge that helped the people. One such individual, Thomas Segundo, served six consecutive terms as tribal chairman.

Today there are sixteen thousand members of the Tohono O'odham Nation. Over half live on the San Xavier, Gila Bend, and Tohono O'odham reservations. Most are Sonoran Catholics, although a significant number have joined the Presbyterian Church. Ranching, basket making, and government employment are the leading economic activities on the reservations. Jobs are limited, however. Consequently, many young Tohonos migrate to Tucson, Phoenix, and elsewhere in search of jobs. To improve their economic situation, the Tohono O'odhams recently opened the Desert Diamond Casino. Profits from this project are helping the tribe provide better social services. Although the people have seen many changes in the world around them, many aspects of Tohono O'odham culture remain intact: an economically diversified lifestyle, strong family ties, a love of the desert, a willingness to share, and a richly distinctive identity.

See also Akimel O'odham (Pima).

Erickson, Winston P., *Sharing the Desert: The Tohono O'odham in History* (Tucson: University of Arizona Press, 1994); Fontana, Bernard L., *Of Earth and Little Rain: The Papago Indians* (Flagstaff, Ariz.: Northland Press, 1981; reprint, Tucson: University of Arizona Press, 1989); Underhill, Ruth, *Social Organization of the Papago Indians* (New York: Columbia University Press, 1939).

PETER MACMILLAN BOOTH
Purdue University

TOLOWA

The Tolowas are the southernmost of five groupings of Athabaskan-speaking peoples of modern-day southwestern Oregon and northwestern California, all with similar cultures. Historic Tolowa territory comprised over six hundred square miles in extreme northwestern California, more or less coinciding with present-day Del Norte County, California, but extending slightly north across the Oregon border. The land encompasses ocean coastline, a narrow, dense strip of redwood forest as well as fir and oak forests, and Lake Earl and the Smith River and its tributaries.

Prior to the arrival of Europeans, there seems to have been no strong sense of tribal identity among the Tolowas. They referred to themselves as simply *Hush* or *Huss*—their word for "person" or "people." The name Tolowa came from Yurok neighbors to the south, and referred to only one of three bands, the other two being the Hennaggi and the Tataten. According to contemporary Tolowa, *Tolowa* may be translated as "Those People Who Live at Lake Earl." However, the Tolowas did have a strong sense of village identity. The basic unit of their society, the village consisted of family houses made from redwood planks, occupied by patrilineal kin groups having exclusive rights to the food resources of their area. Tolowa villages were located along the coast but were abandoned during the summer months, when the Tolowas traveled to beaches to harvest smelt and inland to harvest acorns.

Villages were autonomous, and were governed by headmen determined by individual wealth in chipped obsidian, redheaded-woodpecker scalps, and dentalium. Village lineage tended to be centered around the headmen. Formal ties between villages occurred through blood kinship or marriage. Marriages were typically between men and women from different villages, with the couple residing in the man's village. Frequently Tolowa men even married women from neighboring Yurok, Karok, or Chetco tribes.

The Tolowas' first recorded contact with Europeans occurred in 1828 when they encountered Jedediah Smith as he traveled through California and Oregon. At that time the tribe was located in eight different villages. The precontact Tolowa population may have been as large as 2,400, but it had declined significantly by the mid-1800s because of epidemics of cholera, measles, and diphtheria (and perhaps smallpox). The population declined further in the next several decades, largely because of massacres suffered at the hands of Euro-American settlers. In 1870, the Tolowa population was estimated at only 200, and in 1910, at less than 150.

Between 1852 and 1855, the Tolowas were relocated to what they refer to as the Klamath Concentration Camp on the Klamath River, to the south of their territory. In 1860, they were removed to the Siletz Reservation in western Oregon as a result of the Rogue River War. In 1872, the 1870 Ghost Dance reached the Tolowas via the Siletz Reservation, and developed into a local Dream Dance cult among them. In 1929–30, the Tolowas became involved in the Indian Shaker movement.

In the twentieth century the Tolowa population has recovered somewhat; today there are perhaps 500

Tolowas. During the last two decades, the Tolowas have experienced a resurgence; they have revived their language and some cultural practices. The tribe has petitioned the Bureau of Indian Affairs for formal federal recognition. Their application is pending.

Gould, Richard A., "Tolowa," in *Handbook of North American Indians,* ed. William C. Sturtevant, vol. 8, *California,* ed. Robert F. Heizer (Washington: Smithsonian Institution, 1978); Thornton, Russell, "Social Organization and the Demographic Survival of the Tolowa," *Ethnohistory* 31 (1984): 187–96.

RUSSELL THORNTON (Cherokee)
University of California at Los Angeles

TOMAHAWK

Derived from the Algonquian word *tamahak,* which denoted a utensil used for cutting, the word *tomahawk* generally refers to a light, hatchetlike implement with a stone or metal head. Early Euro-Americans described Indian axes and war clubs made of stone or wood as tomahawks, but eventually the term came to be applied exclusively to metal hatchets. Because of their versatility and superiority to native equivalents, European-manufactured tomahawks quickly became prized trade items and remained so well into the nineteenth century.

Though frequently employed as a weapon, the tomahawk also served as a tool, a ceremonial object, a decorative item, and a symbol of leadership. One of the most popular versions of the tomahawk doubled as a pipe. A blade and a pipe bowl balanced each other at either end of the tomahawk's handle. When smoked in council or given as gifts, pipe tomahawks helped to seal alliances or treaties between different groups.

Along with the tipi, the totem pole, and the war bonnet, the tomahawk has become a popular symbol of Indian culture, especially among nonnatives. Plastic tomahawks can be found at many souvenir stands and toy stores. And in the early 1990s, the "tomahawk chop" performed by fans of the Atlanta Braves became a target of protests by Native Americans, who argued that the cheer belittled Indian people and their history.

TONTO

A character in the radio and television western *The Lone Ranger,* Tonto represented the "good" Indian who supported his masked partner. The relationship between the two was characterized by interdependence and an implicit equality. However, during the "Red Power" movement of the 1960s, Indian activists assailed Tonto as an "Uncle Tomahawk" who did the bidding of the white man. Ironically, Jay Silverheels, the Mohawk actor who played Tonto, was instrumental in forming the Indian Actors Guild in the 1960s, a group that worked to develop Indian talent and to lobby studios for better scripts and productions featuring Indian life. The word *Tonto* was first applied by the Spanish to a group of western Apaches and is still used by them as a self-designation.

See also Movies.

TOTEM POLES

Among the tribes of the Pacific Northwest, totem poles symbolize several features of tribal life. Usually carved from red cedar trees, the poles contain family and clan crests, represent wealth within a family, and portray important mythical and historical figures. Just as important as its construction are a totem pole's decay, fall, and eventual return to its environment, which symbolize the cycle of life and change to northwestern tribes. Carving styles and functions of totem poles vary according to tribe and family. Tribes that carve totem poles range from Alaska to Vancouver Island and include the Haidas, Kwakuitls, Tsimshians, Tlingits, Coast Salishes, and Bella Coolas. The antiquity of carved poles has not been established, but they were noted in 1778 by Captain James Cook.

Ceremony and ritual surround the creation of a totem pole, from the selection of the tree to the erection of the finished work; a potlatch was often held in conjunction with the completion and erection of a totem pole. Types of totem poles include house posts, commemorative poles, welcome figures, and mourning posts. The carving of poles increased dramatically during the nineteenth century. A decline in pole carving at the end of the century accompanied a decline in tribal populations and economies.

Between 1920 and 1950 the preservation of totem poles became a priority for non-Indians, who often moved them into museums without permission from tribes. During the 1950s carving once again emerged as a spiritual and sometimes commercial art form. That revival continues into the present.

Haida totem poles at Old Kasaan Village, southeastern Alaska, in 1885.

TRAIL OF TEARS

The term *Trail of Tears* refers to the removal of the Five Civilized Tribes from their ancient homeland in the East to present-day Oklahoma. Though all of the tribes —Cherokees, Choctaws, Chickasaws, Creeks, and Seminoles—were forcibly uprooted and herded westward, the removals varied in severity.

The Choctaws were the first to be removed. In October 1831 approximately four thousand Choctaws started on foot, by wagon, or on horseback, then by steamboat, and finally overland to Oklahoma. The migration took place during the winter over snow-covered trails. Shelter was inadequate. Food was scarce. The Choctaws moved westward in groups of between five hundred and two thousand. Hundreds died. Entire families, and in some instances whole communities, perished of disease, exposure, exhaustion, and accidents. It was from the Choctaws' experience that the name Trail of Tears was derived. A second mass removal took place in 1832, and another in 1833.

The Muskogee or Creek Nation followed the Choctaws, but not as peacefully. Following the signing of the Muskogee removal treaty in 1832, conservative factions of the tribe refused to leave their homeland. The result was the Creek War of 1836–37. Under the command of Winfield Scott, the American army captured more than fourteen thousand five hundred Creeks and marched them overland to Oklahoma. Two thousand five hundred made the trip in chains. No accurate count was made, but many died during the trip, and thirty-two hundred died of exposure and disease after their arrival.

The Chickasaws probably had the easiest removal. There were fewer tribal members, and better preparations were made for the trip. Nonetheless, they suffered. Observers were horrified as the Chickasaws marched past, and one remarked, "Money cannot compensate for the loss of what I have seen." Five hundred died of smallpox alone.

The Cherokees suffered the most. Supporters of the removal, numbering about two thousand, moved west between 1835 and 1838 in relative ease, but about fourteen thousand others opposed removal. Georgia militia invaded the Cherokee Nation, destroying crops, burning homes, and scattering families. To control the militia and bring order to the removal process, federal troops rounded up the remaining Cherokees and herded them into concentration camps. Disease spread rapidly. Many died, and others were sick when they started westward in 1838. Eventually one-quarter of the tribe perished.

Deceived by government agents into signing a removal treaty, the Seminoles fought when federal authorities insisted they honor the fraudulent treaty. The result was the Second Seminole War. Fighting started in 1835 as the U.S. Army moved into Florida to remove the Seminoles. The last band of Seminoles were forced westward in chains in February 1859.

TRAVEL AND TRANSPORTATION ROUTES

River systems and mountain ranges created the Indian transportation routes, many used later by railroad and highway engineers. Lengthy routes developed throughout the vast drainage of the Mississippi River between the Appalachians and the eastern slopes of the Rocky Mountains, with links to the regional systems of the Pacific, Gulf, and Atlantic Coasts. Sparse networks existed in the thinly occupied desert and plateau area of the West, while California's mountainous terrain curtailed long journeys between pockets of tribal people.

Streams were the main highways in the interior of North America, with well-marked portages to detour around rapids or waterfalls and connect watercourses. In the north country, where birch trees were available, the ideal craft was the bark canoe, but the dugout made

from a fire-hollowed log was the watercraft common to most of the United States. Trails followed river valleys or kept to the ridges in hilly country. Buffalo and deer are given credit for marking out many pathways that became major trails.

The Mississippi River has always been the main artery for north-south travel through the populous central section of what is now the United States. Segments of the river also were utilized as parts of lateral routes from the region east of the Mississippi to the western plains along the river's major tributaries: the Wisconsin, Illinois, and Ohio Rivers entering from the east; and the Minnesota, Missouri, and Arkansas Rivers entering from the west. Overarching this river system, a separate east-west water highway, most heavily used during the fur trade era of 1640–1840, connected Montreal and the lower St. Lawrence River in a virtually straight line to the region west of the Great Lakes. This thoroughfare went up the Ottawa River and across the Mattawa River portage to Lake Nipissing, then descended the French River to Georgian Bay of Lake Huron, continuing through the channel north of Manitoulin Island, and finally ending either at the St. Mary's River outlet to Lake Superior or the north-country transportation hub at the Straits of Mackinac. At the western end of Lake Superior, the Grand Portage route continued through the Rainy River to Lake of the Woods on the Minnesota-Manitoba border and Lake Winnipeg. An extension of this water route connected the upper Great Lakes with Hudson's Bay. Alternatively, by way of present-day Duluth and the St. Louis River, Indian travelers crossed the Savannah River portage to Sandy Lake and the headwaters of the Mississippi River.

From the Straits of Mackinac, additional travel routes fanned out through Lake Huron and Lake Michigan. Of primary importance was the main line westward by way of Green Bay and the Fox and Wisconsin Rivers to the Mississippi River at present-day Prairie du Chien. A jog northward reached the Minnesota River, at whose western headwaters on the South Dakota border trails led to the Missouri River. By following the Lake Michigan shoreline to the lake's southwest end, travelers gained access to the Chicago River and the Des Plaines River portage to the Illinois River, entering the Mississippi close to the mouth of the Missouri River. On the southeast side of Lake Michigan, an alternative route to the Illinois River followed the St. Joseph River upstream to present-day South Bend, Indiana, with a portage to the Kankakee River and the Illinois.

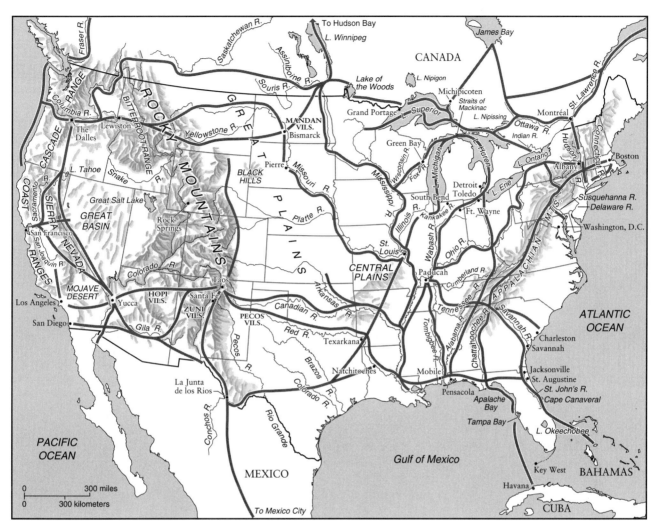

MAJOR TRADE ROUTES

The Straits of Mackinac was also a starting point for two north-south routes to the southern tribes, both commencing with a canoe journey down Lake Huron and the Detroit River to Lake Erie. At that point, the straight-south route required an island-hopping passage across western Lake Erie to Sandusky Bay, then on to the Sandusky and Scioto Rivers to the Ohio River. In a southwesterly direction from Lake Erie, at modern-day Toledo, travelers ascended the Maumee to present-day Fort Wayne, portaging to the Wabash River and descending to the Ohio River entrance about one hundred miles above the entrances of the Ohio's southern tributaries, the Cumberland and Tennessee Rivers. The southward journey continued by going up the Tennessee River to its head branches in the southern Ap-

palachians. Where the Tennessee bends eastward, a major trail led directly south to Mobile Bay. This trail, and the Tombigbee and Alabama Rivers, converging north of the bay, contributed to making Mobile a major transportation hub, the Gulf Coast equivalent of the Straits of Mackinac.

Travel often involved a combination of canoe routes and land trails. For intervillage communication, trails crisscrossed the terrain. Along the eastern seaboard, paths extended the length of the Appalachian chain from New York to Georgia in high valleys and along the fall line, with auxiliary prongs and feeder routes. Portions are preserved today as the historic Appalachian Trail. A significant north-south corridor linked Montreal and the St. Lawrence River with New York

Harbor and the Atlantic Coast by way of the Richelieu River, Lake Champlain, and the Hudson River.

Strategic rivers and mountain passes connected Indian settlements on the Atlantic seaboard and the trans-Appalachian interior. At the northern edge of mountainous country, the Mohawk River entering the Hudson at present-day Albany provided access to Lakes Ontario and Erie. At the southern end of the Appalachians, the Savannah River flowing into the South Atlantic originates only about five miles from the Hiawassee River, at the headwaters of the Tennessee River. With the expansion of the British Indian trade from Savannah and Charleston, packhorses pounded out westward trails that crossed the Mississippi River into present-day Oklahoma.

The Florida peninsula's main transportation route is the St. Johns River, which rises south of Cape Canaveral and flows northward, bending at present-day Jacksonville to enter the Atlantic Ocean. From St. Augustine on the Atlantic shore, a main trail crossed the peninsula to Apalache Bay and the mouth of the Apalachicola River. The Apalachicola-Chattahoochee River was part of a long route from interior Georgia to the Gulf Coast, continuing southward along the shore to Tampa Bay and over open water to Cuba. The inland trail west from Apalache Bay around the Gulf Coast went through Mobile to Natchez and Vicksburg, crossing points on the Mississippi to the east-flowing Red and Arkansas Rivers. From Natchitoches, Louisiana, a trade center on the lower Red River, parallel and braided trails along rising ground at the edge of the coastal plain traversed Texas to present-day Presidio on the middle course of the Rio Grande, opposite the mouth of the Rio Conchos entry to the Mexican Plateau. A more southerly crossing of the Rio Grande at Eagle Pass became the *camino real* of the Spanish era. Diagonal trails from the St. Louis area and the mouth of the Arkansas River led southwest to fording points on the bend of the Red River near present-day Texarkana, Arkansas, then joined the *camino real* near Nacogdoches, Texas.

In the Southwest, Santa Fe and Taos became focal points of trade in the densely populated Pueblo country of the upper Rio Grande valley. From Texas, a difficult trail followed the course of the Colorado River, then crossed arid and broken plains. Trails followed the Red and Arkansas-Canadian Rivers to the pass through the Sangria Mountains, reaching the head of the Rio Grande, itself an important north-south travel route that extended by trails to Mexico City. To the north of

Santa Fe, traders followed overland routes across the plateau to modern-day Idaho as well as the Dakota Territory north of the Missouri. These journeys were feasible only in summer, when streambeds were dry, or in winter, when they were frozen. The availability of Spanish horses, by purchase or theft, drew tribes to make excursions across the plains to Santa Fe.

Long-distance travel from the western plains to the Pacific Coast was limited by water sources and passes through the mountains. Three main routes funneled travelers into modern-day California. On the south, the desert crossing led to the present-day San Diego–Los Angeles region. From the central plateau district, a narrow band of alternative passes crossed the mountains around Lake Tahoe. On the north, one main entry to the California country was the Klamath River valley; another led to San Francisco Bay by way of the Sacramento River.

Transcontinental travel in a westerly or northwesterly direction from the central Mississippi Valley began on the lower Missouri River, continued up the Yellowstone River, and ultimately utilized the Lolo Pass through the mountains at Lewiston on the Idaho-Washington border to reach what is now the state of Washington.

In the Northwest coastal region, The Dalles, located upstream on the Columbia River, has long been the major transportation hub for exchange between the numerous small population clusters on the bays and river mouths of Puget Sound. The Columbia and Fraser Rivers connected the Pacific Coast with a vast hinterland on both sides of the present-day Canadian border. The Willamette River served as an interior water highway in Oregon. Along the coast, travel was not restricted by the ocean shorelines. Specially designed seagoing canoes were devised by the whaling Indians of the Northwest Pacific Coast, who traveled to offshore islands.

Although the continent-wide communications network served traders, it was also used by war expeditions, messengers, diplomatic parties, visiting delegations, and exploratory travelers.

Meyer, William E., *Indian Trails of the Southeast,* Bureau of American Ethnology, Forty-second Annual Report (Washington: Government Printing Office, 1928); Swagerty, William R., "Indian Trade in the Trans-Mississippi West to 1870," in *Handbook of North American Indians,* ed. William C. Sturtevant, vol. 4, *History of Indian-White Relations,* ed. Wilcomb E. Washburn (Washington: Smithsonian Institution, 1988); Tanner, Helen Hornbeck, "The Land and Water Communications Systems of the Southeastern Indians," in *Powhatan's Mantle: Indians in the Colonial Southeast,* ed. Peter H. Wood, Gregory A. Waselkov, and M. Thomas Hatley (Lincoln and London: University of Nebraska Press, 1989).

HELEN HORNBECK TANNER
Newberry Library
Chicago, Illinois

TRAVOIS

A travois (from the French *travail,* which refers to the shaft of a cart) was a form of transportation that resembled a wheelless chariot. It consisted of two long poles joined by a netting. When laid over the back of a dog or horse, it could hold a load of household items, firewood, hunting gear, game, or trade goods. The poles' tips converged at the animal's shoulders and were secured by leather strips or rope. An extremely important aspect of transportation and mobility on the Great Plains, the travois was ideally suited to the treeless northern plains. It allowed easy and quick transit to different areas during seasonal movements. Originally pulled by dogs, the travois was adapted to horses when the larger animals appeared on the plains in the eighteenth century. Horses allowed the travois to carry heavier loads and disabled people.

TREATIES

In 1776, thirteen American colonies declared their independence from England. One of the first significant acts by those colonies was the decision to negotiate an agreement with militarily powerful Indian tribes, either to gain the tribes' alliance or, at least, to ensure the tribes' neutrality in the imminent revolutionary war. That act set the stage for dealing with the tribes through formal government-to-government agreements such as treaties.

In 1778 the first treaty — between the new American confederation and the Delaware tribe—was signed. Between 1789 and 1871 the primary instrument for relations between the United States and Indian nations was the treaty. The U.S. Constitution granted the executive branch the power to negotiate treaties and granted the Senate the power to ratify treaties, while the House of Representatives carried the burden of appropriating

money to carry out the United States's obligations under the treaties. The last treaty between the United States and an Indian tribe was negotiated in 1868. Feeling that the treaty process was unfair to Indians, the House attached a rider to the 1871 Appropriations Act officially ending treaty making with Indian tribes.

Between 1789 and 1871, the United States and Indian tribes negotiated approximately eight hundred treaties. However, the Senate ratified fewer than four hundred. History illustrates that the Indian tribes believed that each treaty became effective upon the solemn exchange of rights and obligations during the negotiations with government officials rather than after the document was ratified by the U.S. Senate. The Indian tribes generally complied with all eight hundred treaties. No tribe ever negotiated a treaty with the United States only to subsequently renege on the grounds that the tribe's lawmakers did not ratify it.

President George Washington negotiated the first treaty with an Indian tribe on behalf of the United States. Because they involved two parties in equal bargaining positions, the first negotiations led to treaties of peace, not surrender, between the United States and Indian tribes. Both sides were militarily powerful, and each was economically dependent on the other. President Washington urged the first Senate to ratify the treaties to ensure peace on the western frontier, to provide for an orderly westward expansion, and, most important, to establish the treaty-making authority of the new national government over Indian affairs. State control of treaty making would have undermined federal control. In other words, treaties with tribes served to establish the legitimacy of the U.S. government as much as they did that of tribal governments.

Later, as the United States grew and advanced, treaty negotiations indicated a shifting of bargaining positions, concluding in treaties not of mutual peace but of surrender imposed on militarily defeated tribes. The negotiations themselves were not always conducted in an ethically or morally defensible manner. The unequal bargaining position of the parties in later negotiations resulted in some treaties being signed by only a part of the tribe without the whole tribe's authority or consent. In some cases a significant portion of the tribe were absent, perhaps on a hunting party. Sometimes a recognized leader of the tribe was offered extra amenities, or drink, to persuade the leader to convince the tribe to negotiate. The result was that the more powerful United States, often acting in bad faith, became comfortable with breaking treaties it had signed.

Members of a Winnebago delegation displaying what are believed to be treaties.

After 1871, negotiations between the United States and tribes were labeled *agreements*. Nevertheless, the president and Congress continued to deal with tribes through executive orders and statutes. The Supreme Court has ruled that, for the most part, agreements are the same as treaties under the law. In other words, a tribe entered into a political relationship with the United States on an equal footing with that body regardless of the instrument. Today, both treaties and agreements are in full force and effect under the law.

Treaties generally included a heading setting forth the names of the parties involved, the terms of agreement, and any exchanges of commercial items. Over 60 percent of the treaties required tribes to give territory to the United States. Through treaties, tribes gave to federal authorities virtually the entire territory we now know as the United States. For example, in 1795 the Treaty of Greenville granted the United States a "piece of land at the mouth of the Chikago river, emptying into the south-west end of Lake Michigan, where a fort formerly stood." Of course, this small chunk of territo-

ry quickly became one of America's commercial transportation hubs: Chicago.

These grants of territory by tribes were made in exchange for solemn lasting promises and commitments. In exchange for territory the United States offered money, food provisions for a specified number of years, education to the tribes' young, health provisions, and (with no concern about separating church and state) missionaries. Most importantly, in the treaties, the United States typically sought alliances with tribes and offered to extend the Union's protection to them.

Treaties between the United States and Indian tribes raise questions of international law and constitutional law. Therefore, to understand treaties between the United States and Indian tribes, we must first have some general knowledge of international and American law and of four important concepts embodied in the terms *treaty, sovereignty, republican democracy,* and *federalism.*

Treaties are documents used to formalize relations between two or more international states. Only international states may enter into treaties. To be recognized as a state by the United States, an entity must have territorial boundaries and a self-governing people. Generally, treaties provide the method for legalizing comprehensive agreements and understandings between international states. The terms of the treaty may serve to alter the international relationship of the signatory states, such as creating alliances or exchanging protections. After declaring independence but before creating the Union, the original thirteen states of the United States were international states, each capable of entering into international treaties.

The fact that the United States entered into treaties with Indian tribes is evidence that American leaders imagined an international relationship between the United States and tribes. Like the original thirteen states, the Indian tribes were viewed as international states with territorial boundaries and self-governing peoples. However, the terms of every treaty between the United States and an Indian tribe served to alter the parties' original international relationship. Every treaty between the United States and tribes provided for overlapping spheres of political sovereignty between the United States and those tribes.

The word *sovereignty* represents a difficult concept. Sovereignty is the basis upon which a government arises and exists, defining the scope of the government's power. In a *republican democracy* such as the United States, sovereignty is shared by the people and the state. The people may grant the government certain express powers or the state may exercise its own implied powers, subject to the consent of the people. The governments of the fifty states of the Union exercise varying degrees of sovereignty along the continuum between democracy and republican democracy. All American citizens possess inherent sovereignty either to authorize or at least to consent to their respective state's government. Also, they have either authorized or consented to the Union's federal government through their representatives in Congress.

Because the same people authorize or consent both to states and to the Union, the spheres of sovereignty of the states and the Union overlap, just as the spheres of sovereignty of the United States and the Indian tribes overlap because of treaties. In other words, like every American, every Indian who is a citizen of a tribe possesses the inherent sovereignty to authorize and consent to that tribe's government. Significantly, treaties have also brought Indian tribes and their people into the Union with their inherent sovereignty intact, so that individual citizens of tribes are also citizens of the United States and, like state citizens, authorize and consent to the Union's federal government as well.

Federalism is the word used to describe the relationship established under the Constitution between the Union and the states and arising from their overlapping spheres of sovereignty. Often the interests of the Union, the states, and their people come into conflict. Republican democracy guides American federalism to ensure that when such conflicts arise, the Union, the states, and their people maintain their respective powers of self-governance within the American system. The Tenth Amendment to the federal Constitution embodies this logic: "All powers not granted in this Constitution shall be reserved to the States, or to the people."

Like the Constitution, treaties, when they establish overlapping spheres of sovereignty, give rise, based on America's principles of republican democracy, to a federal relationship between the United States and the other signatory states, such as Indian tribes. In its role as interpreter of the Constitution and treaties, the U.S. Supreme Court has declared that, in accordance with republican democracy, the tribes and their people are the source of their government's power. Tribes are therefore a part of a federal system.

A treaty gave rise to a relationship of compact federalism based on good faith. When the American Constitution was written, this was the common understanding of the educated persons who drafted the document.

The political principles and legal logic that guide the relationship between the Union and the states therefore guide the relationship between the Union and the Indian tribes as well. In a statement remarkably similar to the Tenth Amendment, the Supreme Court rendered perhaps the most important statement about the treaty relationship between the United States and Indian tribes, reflecting America's highest principles of federal republican democracy: "Treaties are to be construed as a grant of rights from the Indians, not to them—and a reservation of those not granted."

The U.S. Constitution provides that treaties entered into by the national government shall be the "supreme law of the land." No state may act to violate a federal treaty. Treaties between the United States and tribes have given rise to some of the greatest conflicts between the national government and the states, testing all of America's notions of federalism, separation of powers, and republican democracy.

Over the course of history the Supreme Court has addressed the legal effect of treaties between the United States and tribes. Generally, the court has found such treaties to be similar to treaties between the United States and foreign nations. However, the Supreme Court has given special attention to the unique circumstances surrounding many treaties with tribes, developing "canons of construction" to interpret and apply Indian treaties. First, the court has declared that treaties are to be interpreted as the tribes would have understood them at the time of the negotiations. Second, the justices have said that any ambiguities are to be construed in favor of the tribes. These "canons" have been the cornerstone of many Supreme Court opinions.

Thus, to understand treaties between the United States and Indian tribes, it is important to keep several things in mind. First, treaties were made between sovereign governments. Second, because treaties were made between governments, the United States made treaties with tribes, not individual tribal citizens. Therefore, when the tribes reserved rights in treaties, they reserved the use of those rights for their governments as governments would use them. In short, governments regulate rights, and individuals use them. For example, when treaties reserved fishing rights, those rights were vested in the tribal government for the use of its members.

And, finally, treaties are made and treaties are broken. Any country can unilaterally abrogate a treaty to which it is a party. Congress can abrogate any treaty to which the United States is a party, including treaties with Israel, England, or Indian tribes. When treaties are broken, they are not rescinded; only a subsequent treaty or agreement can relieve the signatory parties of the original treaty. When the United States breaks a treaty, it reflects on the integrity of the country. Treaties are as old and venerable as the U.S. Constitution. Age does not impair their validity or legality.

See also Treaties of Fort Stanwix (1768 and 1784); Treaty of Dancing Rabbit Creek (1830); Treaty of Fort Laramie (1851); Treaty of Fort Laramie (1868); Treaty of Greenville (1795); Treaty of Medicine Lodge Creek (1867); Treaty of New Echota (1835); Treaty of New York (1790); Treaty of Prairie du Chien (1825).

RICHARD MONETTE (Chippewa)
University of Wisconsin at Madison School of Law

TREATIES OF FORT STANWIX (1768 AND 1784)

The Royal Proclamation of 1763 forbade the settlement of colonists west of the Appalachian crest, but by then decades of warfare over control of the North American interior had reduced the power of the native people to keep settlers out of these lands now designated "Indian Territory." The Iroquois in particular faced tremendous pressure to cede lands to the advancing colonists, and through the Fort Stanwix Treaty of 1768 they did just that, ceding to British authorities land south of the Susquehanna and Ohio Rivers, land they claimed as theirs but did not occupy. It was a convenient pact. Lands of other tribes were sold in order to secure for the Iroquois their ancestral lands in New York State. Unfortunately for the Iroquois, however, this situation did not last: the American Revolution increased the pressure to dispossess native people of their land, and most tribes (including the Iroquois) supported Great Britain in order to hold off American settlers. When the United States was victorious, the Americans forced some Iroquois into new cessions in the Fort Stanwix Treaty of 1784, whereby natives agreed to cede western Pennsylvania and Ohio to the new American government. The pattern of 1768 had been repeated. The 1784 treaty was considered by almost all native people—including many Iroquois—as being signed under duress by people who were not recognized by the native people as having authority to sign treaties with the government. The questionable legality of the 1784 cessions and subsequent American encroachment on

the ceded land in Pennsylvania and Ohio led directly to the Indian wars of the 1780s and 1790s. Control over these disputed lands was not settled until after the War of 1812.

TREATY OF DANCING RABBIT CREEK (1830)

During the first three decades of the nineteenth century the Choctaw tribe of Mississippi signed treaties with the United States guaranteeing their rights to remain on their land and hold lands in common. When the state of Mississippi extended its laws over the Choctaw Nation and refused to acknowledge these agreements, the Choctaws hoped federal authorities would help them settle the dispute in a peaceful manner. Unfortunately, they placed their trust in the administration of Andrew Jackson, a president committed to the removal of all southeastern Indians to lands west of the Mississippi River.

U.S. Secretary of War John Eaton and a group of Choctaw leaders signed the Treaty of Dancing Rabbit Creek on September 27, 1830, in which Choctaws agreed to remove to the West. Although the terms of the treaty promised the Choctaws protection "from domestic strife and from foreign enemies," more than one-quarter of the tribe perished in the long trek to Indian Territory. For those who remained in the East, treaty provisions allowing individual Choctaws to claim homesteads were undermined by settlers and corrupt state officials, who conspired to dispossess them. Finally, although the treaty pledged that the United States would "forever secure said Choctaw Nation," federal officials later encouraged the state of Oklahoma to organize in an area that encompassed what had previously been recognized as tribal land.

TREATY OF FORT LARAMIE (1851)

The treaty between the United States and northern Plains tribes signed in 1851 at Fort Laramie, in southeastern Wyoming, had as its objectives peace between Indians and whites as well as intertribal peace among the Indian signatories. Prior to the treaty, Indians had protested against the tide of settlers who passed through their lands on the trail to Oregon and California. They raided and stole from the wagon trains in frustration over the decimation of game along the trail and the frequent introduction of diseases among their populations.

During the summer of 1851, approximately ten thousand Sioux, Cheyenne, Arapaho, Crow, Shoshone, Assiniboine, Mandan, Hidatsa, and Arikara representatives met in the greatest council in recorded history— on surprisingly peaceful terms. On September 8, after much fanfare and pageantry and days of discussions with the treaty commission and among themselves, the chiefs signed the treaty. Under its terms, the Indians guaranteed safe passage for westward-bound settlers along the Platte River, and the chiefs accepted responsibility for the behavior of their followers in specified territories. In return, the government promised annuity goods worth fifty thousand dollars each year for fifty years. Congress later cut appropriations for the treaty to ten years' annuities, and several tribes never received the commodities promised them. Although the treaty produced a brief period of peace, rivalry among tribes, the fluidity of Plains societies, and the persistent growth of American emigration soon rendered the agreement moot.

TREATY OF FORT LARAMIE (1868)

An agreement made by the United States with several bands of Sioux (the Brulés, Oglalas, Miniconjous, Yanktonais, Hunkpapas, Blackfeet, Cutheads, Two Kettles, Sans Arcs, and Santees) and Arapahos, the 1868 Treaty of Fort Laramie brought temporary peace to the northern plains following "Red Cloud's War" of 1866–68.

Fighting had broken out along the Bozeman Trail in 1866. The Bozeman carried gold seekers from the Oregon Trail in southern Oregon to the mines near the Continental Divide. Teton Sioux bands under Red Cloud and Crazy Horse claimed to control the Bighorn region and pledged to drive out anyone who challenged them. In 1866 the U.S. Army erected several forts to defend the trail, but these were quickly surrounded by well-armed warriors. In December of that year at one such garrison, Fort Phil Kearny, near modern-day Sheridan, Wyoming, a war party under Crazy Horse wiped out a detachment of eighty soldiers who had ridden out to pursue them. In the ensuing panic Congress established a Peace Commission to negotiate a settlement with the region's tribes.

Set up in July 1867, the commission was led by the Civil War hero William Tecumseh Sherman and populated with politicians and Christian reformers such as John T. Sanborn and Samuel F. Tappan. It invited friendly Indian leaders to assemble at Fort Laramie, in southeastern Wyoming, in spring 1868. A single session had been envisioned, but by the end of the year three separate treaty negotiations had taken place. In April and May, Spotted Tail of the Brulés and American Horse of the Oglalas came to Fort Laramie and signed the agreement, but other Sioux leaders stayed away. In July the commission met with Hunkpapa, Blackfoot, Two Kettle, Sans Arc, and Miniconjou leaders aboard the steamboat *Agnes* on the Missouri River. The spring agreement was approved by these chiefs and a new provision was added: the government would abandon its Bozeman Trail posts. The order to disband the forts was given in September. Finally, on November 6, Red Cloud and his followers appeared at Fort Laramie and added their consent to the document. Congress ratified the treaty on February 16, 1869.

The 1868 treaty had four parts. The first pledged both sides to peace. The second reserved the area west of the Missouri River and east of the Rockies for the "absolute and undisturbed use" of the Sioux. The third and longest section described several mechanisms by which the government would support the tribes: it would establish schools, provide seed and clothing for Indian farmers, and set up agencies for the distribution of aid. The treaty further stipulated that no revisions would be made in the agreement without the approval of three-quarters of the adult males of the tribe. Finally, the treaty recognized the Bozeman Trail area as "unceded Indian territory" where whites would not be allowed to settle and within which there would be no military posts.

Because the 1868 Fort Laramie treaty tacitly recognized Sioux power in the Bighorn region, it was viewed by war leaders like Red Cloud as a ratification of their victory over the United States. At the same time, the agreement's extensive provisions for government assistance to those who settled on the new Sioux reservation and took up farming satisfied government officials that the Sioux would soon be "pacified." These divergent views underlay conflicts between the Sioux and the United States until the Battle of the Little Bighorn eight years later. A much longer dispute would surround the treaty's "three-fourths rule" regarding future changes. Congressional leaders would insist that the government was not perpetually bound by it, whereas tribal officials would argue for decades to come that this provision was a continual mark of tribal sovereignty and an ongoing bar to federal power over the tribes.

TREATY OF GREENVILLE (1795)

Signed by eleven tribes on August 3, 1795, the Treaty of Greenville placed much of the Ohio Valley in American hands and forever changed tribal boundaries in that area. After General Anthony Wayne's campaign against the Indians of the Ohio Valley, which culminated at the Battle of Fallen Timbers in August 1794, the Wyandots, Shawnees, Delawares, Ojibwas, Ottawas, Potawatomis, Miamis, Weas, Piankashas, Kickapoos, and Kaskaskias met and negotiated with American officials to secure some tribal lands and cede others. The tribes that participated in this treaty were familiar with Greenville, the treaty site, because it had often served as a refuge center for tribes fleeing the Iroquois wars of the seventeenth and eighteenth centuries.

The Treaty of Fort Stanwix (1768) had established a borderline between whites and Indians in the Ohio River valley, but the Kentucky lands conveyed in that agreement did not belong to the Six Nations of the Iroquois who signed the treaty. In the following years hostilities developed because the Indians of the Ohio Valley did not recognize the Fort Stanwix document and resented white intruders on their lands.

Following Wayne's victory at Fallen Timbers, the Ohio tribesmen's British allies announced that they had made peace with the Americans. Under the provisions of a new agreement, Jay's Treaty, the British promised to withdraw from Ohio and stop supplying their Indian friends with arms. Faced with this new condition, Indian leaders began preliminary discussions with the Americans in January 1795. They met at a small fort in western Ohio and planned the official treaty council for June. The Treaty of Greenville established a boundary line between the tribes of the Ohio Valley and the Americans and granted the Americans control over key trading and transportation sites. In return for these concessions, the Americans guaranteed the tribes a territory large enough to serve the eleven tribes and to keep whites from intruding into their territory. The agreement was quickly undermined by white settlers, but it was not completely abandoned until the American victory in the War of 1812.

TREATY OF MEDICINE LODGE CREEK (1867)

Negotiated at a council held in 1867 near Fort Larned in southern Kansas, the Treaty of Medicine Lodge Creek attempted to end hostilities on the southern plains. Approximately five thousand Comanches, Kiowas, and Plains Apaches and six hundred white soldiers, officials, and onlookers gathered at the treaty grounds. The Indians were led by Ten Bears of the Comanches, Satanta of the Kiowas, and others, and the United States was represented by members of a Peace Commission set up by Congress the previous spring and charged with securing agreements with all the western tribes. The commission included Commissioner of Indian Affairs Nathaniel Taylor, Senator John Henderson of Missouri, General William S. Harney, a veteran of several Indian campaigns, and the Civil War hero William Tecumseh Sherman, who was not present at Medicine Lodge Creek.

The government's negotiators persuaded the assembled tribes to cede land to the United States in exchange for secure reservations. The Kiowas and Comanches exchanged a claim to 90 million acres for a firm title to 2.9 million acres in what is now south central Oklahoma. Both parties promised to live in peace and to punish anyone who violated the new reservation's boundaries. The government also promised to provide the tribes with agency buildings, schools, clothes, a doctor, a farming instructor, and a physician. To ensure the permanence of the treaty's provisions, the signatories also agreed that the treaty could not be altered except by a vote of three-fourths of the adult male population of the tribes.

The Medicine Lodge agreement did not bring peace to the region. Many Kiowa and Comanche leaders rejected the treaty and did not consider it binding; others claimed not to have been present at the negotiations or considered the treaty nullified as soon as whites began violating the boundaries described within it. Sporadic fighting continued until 1875, when federal forces eliminated both Comanche and Kiowa resistance and forced the tribes to remain within their reservations. Despite its casual enforcement, however, the treaty continued to define the relationship of the Comanches and Kiowas to the U.S. government. Thus, when a new group of negotiators, the Jerome Commission, appeared in 1892 seeking to open a portion of the 1867 reservation to whites, the tribes objected. They preferred to continue living under the Medicine Lodge agreement. The federal officials' decision to go through

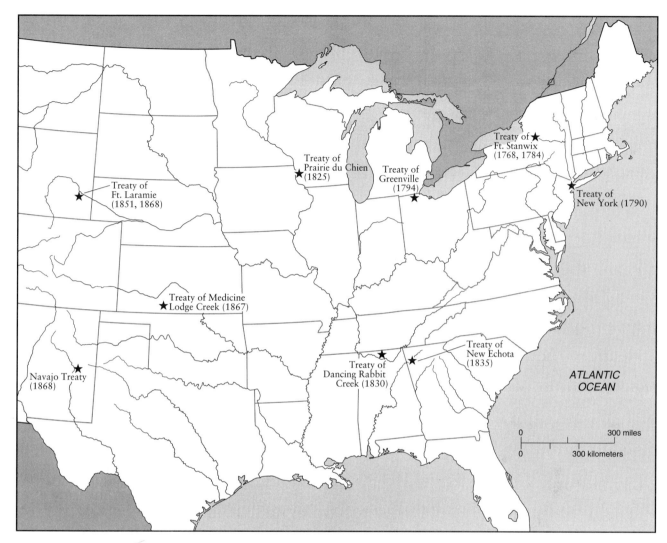

TREATY SITES

with a new agreement despite their failure to secure the approval of three-quarters of the Kiowas formed the basis for *Lone Wolf* v. *Hitchcock,* a suit that eventually reached the U.S. Supreme Court. The tribe's legal defeat in 1903 did not end its veneration of the 1867 treaty, which remains a symbol of the group's sovereign status and unbending national pride.

TREATY OF NEW ECHOTA (1835)

On May 28, 1830, President Andrew Jackson signed the Indian Removal Act, formalizing his administra-

tion's policy of sending to the West Indians living east of the Mississippi River on lands desired by whites. During the next decade, the U.S. government pursued removal of the southeastern tribes through treaties negotiated in an atmosphere of intimidation and coercion. The effort to force Cherokees from their lands in Georgia produced the Treaty of New Echota, signed by a small faction of the Cherokee Nation in 1835.

The majority of the Cherokees refused to leave their homes in Georgia and sued the state of Georgia in the U.S. Supreme Court in order to prevent their removal. When Secretary of War Lewis Cass and President Jackson grew impatient with the Cherokees, they acted unilaterally by authorizing the Reverend John F. Schermerhorn to sign a treaty with a group of Cherokees who had concluded that further resistance was futile. Led by Major Ridge, his son John Ridge, and his nephews Elias Boudinot and Stand Watie, this group signed a treaty at New Echota, Georgia, on December 29, 1835. The agreement exchanged title to all Cherokee lands east of the Mississippi for $5 million and a large tract in Oklahoma. Despite protests by the Cherokee National Council and John Ross, the principal chief, the U.S. Senate ratified the Treaty of New Echota in May 1836.

After signing the New Echota treaty, Ridge and his group left for Oklahoma. Chief Ross and the majority of the tribe continued to resist, however, arguing that the treaty was invalid because it had not been properly ratified. In April 1838, Ross submitted a petition containing 15,665 signatures to Congress, requesting that the United States void the Cherokee removal treaty. In May the War Department sent General Winfield Scott to Georgia to round up the resisting tribesmen and begin their removal. This began the migration known as the Trail of Tears, during which the tribe moved west, losing one quarter of its number in the process. In June of the following year, three of the men who had signed the Treaty of New Echota—John Ridge, Elias Boudinot, and Major Ridge—were killed by Cherokee assailants as punishment for selling the tribe's lands in Georgia.

See also Boudinot, Elias; Cherokee; Removal; Ridge, Major; Ross, John; Trail of Tears.

TREATY OF NEW YORK (1790)

In the summer of 1790, twenty-six Creek leaders led by Alexander McGillivray traveled to New York and signed a treaty on behalf of the "Upper, Middle, and Lower Creek and Semanolies composing the Creek nation of Indians." Creek leaders ceded a significant portion of their hunting grounds to the United States and agreed to turn runaway slaves over to federal authorities, although the Creek leaders averred that convincing the Creek people to honor the new boundary lines or to return African Americans would be difficult at best. The United States granted the Creeks the right to punish non-Indian trespassers in their territory but refused to allow the Creeks to punish non-Indians who committed crimes on Creek lands. For their part, the Creeks agreed to turn over Creek people accused of crimes to the U.S. courts. In a secret side agreement to the treaty, McGillivray received a commission as a brigadier in the U.S. Army and was granted permission to import goods through the Spanish port of Pensacola without paying American duties.

TREATY OF PRAIRIE DU CHIEN (1825)

Negotiated by the Indian agent Lawrence Taliaferro, the Prairie du Chien Treaty of 1825 was intended to bring peace to the western Great Lakes. The treaty did not involve cessions of land to the United States. Instead it set out terms of peace and established definable territories for several Indian nations. Although the treaty was signed by representatives of the Sauk and Fox, Menominee, Iowa, and Winnebago tribes, and of some portions of the Ottawa and Potawatomi tribes, the treaty's main signatories were the Sioux and the Ojibwas. These protagonists had been waging a territorial battle for control of large areas west of the Great Lakes since precolonial times. The treaty fixed the line between these nations as the Red River, which later became the boundary between the states of North Dakota and Minnesota. Unfortunately, the signatories did not respect the borders established by the 1825 agreement, and the rapid onset of white settlement made many of its provisions moot. Disputes over territory continued and were addressed by a series of treaties that established several Ojibwa reserves in Wisconsin and Minnesota and culminated at Traverse des Sioux in 1851, where the remaining Dakota bands in Minnesota ceded the bulk of their lands in the state.

TUSCARORA

Several thousand Tuscaroras were living in Virginia and North Carolina when Europeans arrived in the sixteenth century. Speaking an Iroquoian language, a fact that indicates a probable northern origin, they were the most powerful Indians in the region, occasionally raiding neighboring Algonquins. The Tuscaroras brokered furs, rum, and other trade items between Europeans and Native Americans. They established agriculture, permanent settlements, and a strong political organization. In winter they moved to hunting quarters, bringing with them corn that the women had cultivated, with some help from the men.

Tuscarora Indians William Rickard, left, *and Wallace "Bad Bear" Anderson,* bottom right, *protesting in 1958 against the New York State Power Authority's plan to create a reservoir that would flood their reservation. Despite legal measures and public protest, the reservoir was eventually built.*

Peaceful relations prevailed during the first two centuries of European colonization. But Tuscarora territories were increasingly seized by whites. Tuscaroras were frequently cheated, abused, and captured and sold into slavery. Bent on vengeance, southern Tuscaroras attacked several white settlements, killing families and capturing some women. North Carolina whites appealed to Governor Edward Hyde for protection. Though Hyde asked Virginia for help, he received little because of North Carolina–Virginia boundary disputes. He petitioned South Carolina, and an expedition of whites and British tributary Indians ruthlessly devastated several Tuscarora villages.

The Tuscaroras and their Iroquoian allies—the Merherrins, the Nottaways, and several smaller bands—were defeated, but later regrouped and continued the Tuscarora War (1711–13) under the leadership of Hancock (Hencock). This conflict provided the English with an opportunity to exterminate the Tuscaroras or drive them from North Carolina. The Northern Tuscaroras, led by the ambitious, accommodationist Tom

Blount, professed neutrality but soon joined the English in the war against their southern kindred. Pretending friendship, Blount betrayed Hancock to the English, who promptly executed him. Another expedition under James Moore finally vanquished the Tuscaroras.

Starved into submission, their power broken, the Tuscaroras experienced the end of hostilities in 1713. Some were forced onto a small reservation in North Carolina and the rest fled north, some settling in Virginia where Blount was now the English-recognized Tuscarora leader. Over the next ninety years North Carolina Tuscaroras migrated in clusters of families or small bands into Virginia, Pennsylvania, and ultimately to the homeland of their linguistic and cultural relatives, the Iroquois in New York State. The League of the Iroquois admitted them as its sixth member nation in 1722. The last Tuscaroras left the South for New York in 1804.

During the American Revolution Tuscaroras and Oneidas sided with the colonists, but the other Iroquois groups joined the English. Although at war's end George Washington ordered the punishment of pro-British Indians, Tuscarora villages were also destroyed. The Tuscaroras rebuilt their cabins but these were later burned by the British in the War of 1812. The Tuscaroras finally settled on a reservation adjacent to Lewiston, close to Niagara Falls. The reserve was later enlarged by Seneca grants and land purchased by the Tuscaroras themselves and eventually encompassed ten square miles.

In the early nineteenth century many Tuscaroras were converted to Christianity. A few practiced the Handsome Lake religion until Christians burned their longhouse. Despite their unequal status in the Iroquois League, the Tuscaroras retained their chiefs' council, matrilineal kinship system, and many other aboriginal traits, while adopting many aspects of white material culture. They vigorously resisted the New York State Power Authority's plan to construct a reservoir that flooded hundreds of acres of their reserve (1957–60). Though they lost the struggle, it gave them and other Iroquois peoples a renewed sense of identity and helped to inspire the Red Power movement of the 1960s.

Swanton, John R., *The Indians of the Southeastern United States,* Smithsonian Institution, Bureau of American Ethnology Bulletin 137 (Washington, D.C., 1946); Trigger, Bruce G., ed., *Northeast,* vol. 15 of *Handbook of North American Indians,* ed. William C. Sturtevant (Washington: Smithsonian Institution, 1978); Wallace, Anthony F. C., *The Modal Personality Structure of the Tuscarora Indians,* Smithsonian Institution, Bureau of American Ethnology Bulletin 150 (Washington, D.C., 1952).

DAVID LANDY
University of Massachusetts at Boston and
University of North Carolina at Wilmington

UMATILLA

The Umatillas believe that the first creation brought plants, animals, mountains, rivers, and lakes into being and the second brought native people into existence. Coyote is a major character in the Umatilla creation story, placing the people near the lower Umatilla River upstream from the Columbia, in present-day eastern Oregon. They spoke Sahaptin and intermarried with Cayuses, Walla Wallas, Palouses, Nez Perces, and others. Umatillas lived off camas, cous, and other roots. The women gathered berries, seeds, and nuts, while the men fished and hunted. Salmon, venison, and mussels were major foods. Their religion reflected the Umatilla reverence for the earth, plants, and animals. Umatillas gave thanks in first-foods ceremonies. They lived in A-frame mat lodges and tipis, traveling across the Columbia Plateau in seasonal rounds.

Around 1750 the Umatillas acquired horses from the Shoshones. Umatillas rode to the buffalo plains to hunt and to fight Paiutes, Shoshones, and Blackfeet. Scholars estimate their population in 1780 at fifteen hundred, a figure that later dwindled because of smallpox and other diseases. The Umatillas met Lewis and Clark in 1805–6, dealt with fur trappers at Fort Nez Perces, and watched Marcus Whitman build a mission on Cayuse land at Waiilatpu (Walla Walla). In 1847, Catholic missionaries established St. Anne (later called St. Joseph and then St. Andrew) near Pendleton, Oregon, where some Umatillas converted to Christianity. A year later, the Umatillas joined Cayuses fighting against Oregon volunteers during the Cayuse War. They watched as hundreds of Americans moved west across their lands on the Oregon Trail, and they learned in 1850 that Congress had passed the Donation Land Law, permitting non-Indians to settle native lands not yet ceded to the United States. The next year, the Office of Indian Affairs established the Utilla Agency on the Umatilla River near present-day Echo, Oregon.

In 1855, the United States forced the Umatillas and other Indians of the Columbia Plateau to negotiate treaties with federal officials. On June 9, 1855, the Umatillas, Cayuses, and Walla Wallas secured for themselves a small portion (245,699 acres) of their former 4-million-acre domain from Superintendent of Indian Affairs Isaac Stevens of Washington Territory and Joel Palmer of Oregon Territory. The government ratified the relevant treaty in 1859, establishing the Umatilla Reservation in northeastern Oregon. Between 1855 and 1858 some Umatillas resisted this resettlement by fighting against the U.S. Army and volunteer troops in the "Yakima War." They also fought Paiutes, some of whom were forced onto the Umatilla Reservation in the nineteenth century.

On the reservation, the Umatillas, Cayuses, and Walla Wallas formed a confederated tribe with a constitution and bylaws, approved by the federal government in 1949. In the early twentieth century, the government had allotted over 156,000 acres on the reservation, and much of it fell into the hands of white ranchers. By 1969, only 95,000 acres remained in Umatilla hands. In the 1950s and 1960s, the Umatillas won claims cases against the United States that brought them $172,000, but they did not recover any of their lands. Today the Umatillas sponsor education, forestry, ranching, farming, and recreational enterprises. Approximately two thousand people live on the Umatilla Reservation, many of whom are descendants of Umatillas. Powwows and rodeos are major events, and many Umatillas are Christians, Shakers, or believers in their native *washat* religion.

Trafzer, Clifford E., *Yakima, Palouse, Cayuse, Umatilla, Walla Walla, and Wanapum Indians: A Historical Bibliography* (Metuchen, N.J.: Scarecrow Press, 1992); Zucker, Jeff, Kay Hummel, and Bob Hogfoss, *Oregon Indians: Culture, History, and Current Affairs, an Atlas and Introduction* (Portland: Oregon Historical Society, 1983).

CLIFFORD E. TRAFZER (Wyandot)
University of California at Riverside

UNKECHAUG NATION
See Poosepatuck (Unkechaug Nation).

URBAN INDIANS

Contrary to popular stereotypes, American Indians have a long history of urban settlement. Before the arrival of Europeans, various Pueblo and Mississippian peoples lived in densely populated communities in parts of the Southwest and the Mississippi River Valley. When the numbers of Europeans increased during the seventeenth century, especially in the English colonies of what is now the eastern seaboard of the United States, small numbers of American Indians moved into the villages of the colonial settlers. Some of these urban Indians settled in colonial villages to be near the trade for manufactured goods from Europe. Others were converts to Christianity and lived in non-Indian communities to be near mission schools and churches.

As the United States expanded in the nineteenth century, the federal government adopted policies that forcibly resettled American Indians on isolated reservations, distant from the rapidly growing cities. As a result of their removal to reservations, American Indians are still heavily concentrated in rural areas. Nevertheless, for much of the twentieth century, and especially since 1945, the number of American Indians living in cities has been increasing. In 1930, when about half of all Americans lived in cities, barely 10 percent of American Indians were city dwellers. By 1990 about 51 percent of American Indians were living in urban areas.

The First and Second World Wars had a profound impact on the urbanization of American Indians. As the United States entered World War I, American Indians became involved in the war effort in many ways. Most significantly, approximately eight to ten thousand American Indians served directly in the armed forces. Participation in the war gave these Indians exposure to mainstream urban America as well as the skills to cope with the cultural expectations of white society—important prerequisites for urban settlement.

World War II involved an unprecedented number of American Indians. Approximately twenty-five thousand American Indians served in the military in World War II, including combat soldiers as well as men and women in technical support positions. An even larger number of American Indians were involved in the war effort at home, working in defense plants and related activities. Not all of these individuals returned to their rural origins after the war.

The experience of World War II affected the American Indian population in many important ways. It exposed native people to urban American culture and to the industrial society outside their reservations; it provided many with job skills and work experience; and it was an impetus for many to leave their communities for extended periods and in some cases permanently. An equally important outcome of World War II was that the GI Bill provided a large number of American Indians with the chance to attend college, an opportunity never before available. Many of these college graduates remained in cities to find employment because reservations offered few job prospects.

Postwar federal policy also played a direct role in moving American Indians to cities. In the early 1950s the federal government established special programs to encourage American Indians living on reservations to move to cities such as Los Angeles and Chicago. These relocation programs resettled thousands of American Indians in urban areas. One of the principal justifications for urban relocation was that economic opportunities were more plentiful in cities. However, the economic benefits of urban relocation have proved questionable. Some studies have shown that American Indians have thrived as a result of urban relocation, while other studies have found few benefits. After many years of controversy about the effectiveness and desirability of these programs, they were sharply reduced in the 1970s.

Of course the federal government's policy of relocating reservation Indians was not the only factor involved in the urbanization of American Indians. For most of this century the population of the United States as a whole has been moving away from rural areas and toward the cities. Like other Americans, American Indians have also been more inclined to move to cities than to stay in rural areas.

For a large segment of the American Indian population, the transition to urban life has not been a simple one. Many elements of urban life fundamentally contradict the ethics of tribal culture and lifestyles. These conflicts have led some observers to predict that urban American Indians would eventually surrender their culture and identity as American Indians and blend into urban society. But these predictions have yet to materialize, and the widespread American Indian resistance to Euro-American ways has caused many social scientists to rethink their expectations.

One explanation for the persistence of tribal culture among urban American Indians can be found in the ways they are able to transform ordinary urban landscapes to make them suitable for cultural expression. In New York City, for example, the dangers and physical

Mohawk ironworkers on the fifty-fourth story of the Equitable Life Assurance Building in Manhattan, which was completed in 1985.

vide urban analogues to the off-reservation bars and tribal headquarters of reservation life.

Another important factor in the persistence of urban Indian ethnicity has been the emergence of pan-Indianism. This is a supratribal ideology that unites the interests of American Indians by virtue of their common heritage, independent of the social and political agendas of particular tribes. Pan-Indianism is particularly important as a unifying force because urban Indian populations are often composed of many different tribes.

The spread of Pan-Indianism since 1950 has been extremely important as an organizational basis for urban Indian social life. With few exceptions, community events and social gatherings for urban Indians are typically Pan-Indian affairs—all tribes are welcome. Furthermore, the ideology of Pan-Indianism has been important for political activism. Organizations such as Women of All Red Nations (WARN), the National Indian Youth Council (NIYC), and the American Indian Movement (AIM) have mobilized support for a variety of issues that supersede the interests of individual tribes, including educational and employment opportunities, improved health care, and other matters related to social justice for all American Indians, regardless of their tribe.

Sorkin, Alan L., *The Urban American Indian* (Lexington, Mass.: Lexington Books, 1978); Thornton, Russell, Gary D. Sandefur, and Harold G. Grasmick, *The Urbanization of American Indians: A Critical Bibliography* (Bloomington: Indiana University Press, 1982); Weibel-Orlando, Joan, *Indian Country, L.A.: Maintaining Ethnic Community in Complex Society* (Urbana: University of Illinois Press, 1991).

C. MATTHEW SNIPP (Cherokee and Choctaw)
University of Wisconsin at Madison

demands of high steel construction work has allowed Mohawk men opportunities to exhibit the bravery and risk-taking traditionally expected of them. Urban American Indians also have developed a variety of institutional settings that help them preserve what many consider essential elements of tribal culture.

Four institutions that are particularly important arenas of social interaction and cultural expression are bars, powwows, Indian centers, and churches. Urban powwows are tribal events imported directly from reservation traditions. On reservations powwows are held in ceremonial locations, while in urban areas they are most often sponsored by informal groups or Pan-Indian organizations and held in gyms or public auditoriums. Similarly, urban Indian churches resemble reservation missions, and bars and Indian centers pro-

U.S. BOARD OF INDIAN COMMISSIONERS

The Board of Indian Commissioners was created in 1869 as a part of President Ulysses S. Grant's "Peace Policy" and lasted until 1933, when it was disbanded by President Franklin D. Roosevelt. The board was created to investigate allegations of fraud and corruption at the Indian Bureau and to place the agency under the direction of an independent and objective group of prominent Christian men.

Unfortunately, Congress never clarified the board's powers. Board members claimed, for example, that their authority extended over the Commissioner of Indian Affairs, yet neither President Grant nor Congress agreed with this view, and the board eventually accepted an advisory role. During the late nineteenth century, members were religious leaders who used the board as a platform for publicizing their assimilationist agenda. The board's first chairman, William Welsh, was an Episcopalian layman and wealthy Philadelphia businessman who typified the group's philanthropic mission. Unwilling to serve without power, Welsh resigned only a month after accepting his appointment.

Throughout its sixty-four-year history, the board maintained a pious, largely Protestant identity. No American Indians were appointed to the board, and no Catholics served until 1902. (Only one woman, Flora Warren Seymour, ever served, taking office just before the group's disbandment in May 1933.) At its demise, the board opposed Roosevelt's New Deal for Indians and called Commissioner John Collier too emotional and melodramatic to be of any practical use to Indians.

UTE

The first relatively extensive account of European contact with Utes is to be found in the journal of Fray Escalante, a Franciscan, who traveled through Ute territory in northern New Mexico, western Colorado, and central Utah in 1776. In the late eighteenth century Ute Indians were organized into several large equestrian hunting and gathering bands that were named for the territory they inhabited or things they exploited on it. The Great Basin to the west, the Snake River and Wind River drainages to the north, and much of the Colorado River drainage to the southwest were inhabited almost exclusively by Uto-Aztecan relatives of the Utes—Shoshones, Panamints, and Paiutes.

For at least a century after Escalante's visit, the Utes spent parts of the spring and summer in large bands of two hundred or more family camps. The far western portion of Ute territory was occupied by the Tumpanuwaches on the north and the Pahvants on the south. The central portion was occupied by the Parusanuches, the northeastern by the Yamparkas, and the central eastern by the Taviwaches. The Muwaches occupied Ute territory in the southeast, the Kapotas the region of the San Juan River in northern New Mexico, and the Wiminuches the territory around the four corners of what are now Utah, Colorado, New Mexico, and Arizona.

With time, more bountiful environments, the acquisition of horses, and greater opportunities to raid and trade facilitated larger populations, somewhat more complex social organizations, and a richer ceremonial calendar for the Utes than what their Great Basin counterparts had.

During the winter months, aggregates of Ute families dispersed into local communities of sixty or more persons; in the summer, three or four such communities convened—rather informally—into large residential units or bands that recognized common territories. Each such unit was directed by a band chief, who gained his position through competence and who led by precept and suasion. There were no warrior societies or other groups that were not based on kinship among the Utes. Moreover, no person in any band possessed the authority to allocate strategic resources, civic duties, or scarce food.

Bands provided for common defense and sponsored some public ceremonies. Special groups would split off from bands during the summer periods for raiding, trading, and hunting ventures. The communities in the eastern areas, whose environments were less arid, had larger and more complex band organizations than those in the center and west. They also suffered more aggressive and contentious neighbors—Arapahos, Cheyennes, Comanches—who raided Ute encampments for horses.

While the Utes had generally maintained friendly contacts with the Spanish in the seventeenth and eighteenth centuries, they often attacked the mule trains that brought white settlers west across the Santa Fe Trail from the San Luis Valley in Colorado to southern California.

In 1847 the first wave of Mormon settlers passed through the Bridger Valley and then into the Salt Lake Valley, where they squatted in Shoshone territory. The closest Ute settlements were in the Utah Lake Valley, thirty miles to the south. Within ten years Mormon pioneer communities comprising forty thousand people had been established along the north-south axis of the Wasatch Mountains. The expropriation of resources and the domination of Utes by Mormons were resisted by Chief Wakara through a series of depredations and skirmishes known as the Walker War, which took place from the late 1840s through the mid-1850s, and by Chief Black Hawk through another series of skirmishes and depredations in the 1860s known as the Black Hawk War.

In 1855, with the Mormons expanding throughout Ute territory along the Wasatch front, the Utah territorial government set aside three temporary "farms" for the western Ute bands, and then supported the negotiation of new treaties in 1861 that required the removal of Utes from the farms to the 2-million-acre Uintah Valley Reservation in eastern Utah. There they became known as the Uintah Utes. Provisions, goods, and annuities were not delivered as promised, however, and the Utes refused to remain on the reservation. Some men, under Black Hawk, conducted raids. Others begged for food at Mormon households. By 1879 the Uintah Ute population had dropped to eight hundred—less than 20 percent of its prereservation size.

In 1870, Uintah Utes, Bannocks, Northern Paiutes, Eastern Shoshones, Western Shoshones, and Yamparka and Taviwach Utes convened in the Bridger Basin in present-day southwestern Wyoming to participate in the Ghost Dance religion, which Bannock missionaries promised would rid the world of whites, resurrect deceased ancestors, and solve the ubiquitous problems facing all Utes, Shoshones, and Northern Paiutes. Utes sponsored Ghost Dances in 1871 and 1872 to no avail before losing interest in them.

The eastern Utes of Colorado and northern New Mexico were pushed from their territories more slowly than were the western Utes. The skirmishes with whites occurred in the 1860s, the major battles in the 1870s. The climax came in 1879, when agent N. C. Meeker of the White River Agency in Colorado, in an effort to stop Utes from gambling and to encourage them to begin farming, plowed up their race track and prime pasturage to make way for gardens. The Ute response triggered several events that came to be known as the Meeker Massacre, in which thirty-seven Utes, twelve U.S. cavalrymen, and eight agency personnel, including Meeker, were killed.

In response, Governor Pitkin of Colorado called for the extermination of all Utes, and the federal government relocated 665 White River Utes to the Uintah Reservation in eastern Utah. In addition, 1,360 Uncompahgre Utes were relocated on 2 million acres adjacent to the Uintah Reservation, even though the Uncompahgres had not participated in the White River revolt. Muwach, Kapota, and Wiminuch Utes were relocated to a narrow strip of land along the southwestern Colorado border. These actions opened over 12 million acres in Colorado to prospectors and miners.

Since 1880, the Uintah, White River, and Uncompahgre Utes have been known collectively as the Northern Utes. The Muwaches and Kapotas came to be known collectively as the Southern Utes. The Wiminuches, following a struggle over the federal expropriation of Mesa Verde for a national park enabled by the Antiquities Act in 1906, gained a 513,000-acre reservation in the Four Corners area and came to be known as the Ute Mountain Utes.

Reservation subjugation was difficult for Utes. They resisted allotment under the Dawes Severalty Act. Small farms would have made it impossible for them to maintain their 12,500 horses and perhaps 15,000 sheep and goats, and so on two occasions Northern Ute groups numbering over three hundred fled the reservation in hopes of returning to their hunting-herding existence. In 1887 a group of White Rivers and Uncompahgres fled to western Colorado, and in 1906, a large group of Uintahs and White Rivers fled to South Dakota. Most of both parties later returned, destitute.

In the late 1880s, Uintah Utes attended Sun Dances on the Wind River Shoshone Reservation. Shamans there had revised the purpose and many ritual acts of the Sun Dance from prereservation forms to assist people in achieving the power to cure themselves and others of maladies. In either 1889 or 1890, General Grant, a Uintah Ute, sponsored the first Sun Dance at the Northern Ute Reservation. Although outlawed by the federal government, the Sun Dance was soon diffused to the Southern Ute and Ute Mountain Ute Reservations, where, as at the Northern Ute Reservation, it was sponsored annually, albeit surreptitiously.

The political and economic histories of the three reservations from 1880 to the passage of the Indian Reorganization Act in 1934 are quite similar. Each reservation was affected by the same federal Indian laws, and each was affected by the agrarian Anglo communities that grew up in their midst and dominated local production and trade. Tuberculosis and trachoma were endemic among reservation populations, and measles epidemics ravaged students in reservation boarding schools. By 1934, allotment of land in severalty had reduced the Northern Ute Reservation from 3.97 million acres to 355,000 acres and the Southern Ute Reservation from about 1 million acres to 40,600 acres. The Ute Mountain Utes successfully resisted allotment.

Population nadirs were reached on each reservation in 1924–30. Between 1880 and 1930 the Northern Ute population had decreased by 68 percent, from 2,825 to 917; the Southern Ute by 33 percent, from 500 to 334; and the Ute Mountain Ute by 30 percent, from 650 to 462. Livestock, principally sheep, goats, and horses, decreased from about ten per capita in 1880 to about five per capita in 1934. About 75 percent of Indian allotments were leased and cultivated by non-Indians. On the reservation, full-time employment for Utes was extremely rare (3 percent in 1912; 2 percent in 1920); in off-reservation towns it was nonexistent. All Ute employment was provided by the federal government.

The three Ute reservation populations ratified constitutions in 1934 and charters in 1935 under provisions of the Indian Reorganization Act (IRA). Business committees were formed pursuant to IRA charters to govern reservation affairs and to create and oversee tribal businesses. All of the committees foundered for a host of reasons, and through 1975 no successful business was ever established on any of the three reservations. On the other hand, as a provision of the IRA, the federal and tribal governments repurchased and placed in trust some of the erstwhile reservation land that, following general allotment proceedings, had been purchased or acquired through government programs such as the Homestead and Desert Land Entries Acts. By midcentury the Southern Ute Reservation had increased to 310,000 acres (up from 40,600 in 1934), and the Northern Ute Reservation had increased to 1.06 million acres (up from 355,000 in 1934).

Between 1951 and 1962, in three decisions by the Indian Claims Commission, the "Confederated Ute Tribes" (Northern, Southern, and Ute Mountain Utes) were awarded a total of $47.7 million for treaty violations by the federal government (the expropriation of treaty land from Utes in Utah and Colorado in the 1850s, 1860s, and 1870s). Attorneys' fees ($5 million) and offsetting costs (about $4 million claimed by the federal government for overseeing and maintaining reservation land and providing services to Utes) were deducted. Moneys to the Utes were paid out over fourteen years. Between 1951 and 1959 some of the judgment funds were allotted per capita into individual accounts controlled by Bureau of Indian Affairs employees, who had to be petitioned to relinquish portions of those funds. After 1960, judgment funds were allocated for tribal uses, including youth recreation and education projects, livestock and farming operations, and other business projects.

From the time the Utes organized into corporations under the IRA through 1975, full-time employment seldom reached 10 percent on any of the reservations. The Arab oil embargo of 1973 and the increase in worldwide oil prices brought energy companies to the three Ute reservations in quest of the abundant reserves of oil, gas,

and coal to be found there, and to the Northern Ute Reservation for its oil sands and oil shale as well.

From about 1978 the tribes began receiving royalties—the Northern Utes from oil and gas leases, the Southern and Ute Mountain Utes from gas and coal leases. Attempts to diversify—motels, restaurants, cattle operations, chemical plants, fabrication plants, furniture plants, crafts, a race track, an industrial park—were funded by oil, gas, and coal royalties. Most of these business ventures were defunct by 1984, and all required tribal subsidies until they were finally closed. The single success at the Northern Ute Reservation was a bowling alley that operated in the black, though barely, through 1991. The Southern Utes, following a widespread trend among western tribes, opened a bingo casino, which was operating in the black in the early 1990s.

For each of the three reservations, similar factors have contributed to business failures. As agriculture withered near all of the reservations, the regions became heavily dependent on energy-resource extraction and tourism. Both industries are vulnerable to outside economic forces. In 1990 Ute families enjoyed about half the average income of other American families and about 60 percent of the average income of households adjacent to their reservations.

The Bear Dance, which was the grandest of the precontact rituals performed by Ute bands, is still performed by each Ute community on each reservation (e.g., three Bear Dances, each at a different locale, are sponsored annually—one each by Uncompahgres, White Rivers, and Uintahs—on the Northern Ute Reservation). The Sun Dance religion flourishes on all three reservations, its rituals performed for the same reasons as and in a fashion similar to the Sun Dances first sponsored by Utes in the 1890s. The peyote religion, which was introduced to the Northern Utes in 1914 and to the Colorado (Southern and Ute Mountain) Utes in 1917, also flourishes on all three reservations.

Callaway, Donald G., Joel C. Janetski, and Omer C. Stewart, "Ute," in *Handbook of North American Indians*, ed. William C. Sturtevant, vol. 11, *Great Basin*, ed. Warren L. D'Azevedo (Washington: Smithsonian Institution, 1986); Jorgensen, Joseph G., *The Sun Dance Religion: Power for the Powerless* (Chicago: University of Chicago Press, 1972); Smith, Anne M. Cook, *Ethnography of the Northern Ute*, Museum of New Mexico Papers in Anthropology, no. 17 (Santa Fe, 1974).

JOSEPH G. JORGENSEN
University of California at Irvine

V

VISION QUEST

A vision quest is one of the means by which various Indian cultures seek knowledge or answer questions. A person may choose to participate in a vision quest in order to discover what path his or her life should take, or perhaps to find an answer to a specific problem. The visions, or dreams, experienced in the quest can help shape a person's understanding of events, remove conflict, clear up a situation, provide a spirit helper, or possibly even reveal the future. Whatever the purpose of the quest, the desired goal is usually to bring peace and restore harmony.

A person usually undertakes a vision quest in an isolated area, generally without food or water. The person remains isolated as long as it takes to achieve the desired goal, and the quest may last up to three or four days. The design of the quest varies according to the tribe's culture and the purpose behind seeking a vision. A successful quest will produce contact with a spirit helper or guide, whose presence is often signaled by a visionary experience or contact with an animal or some other being.

VOTING

The right to vote is arguably the most significant characteristic of American citizenship. Though not explicitly guaranteed in the U.S. Constitution, the right to vote has been declared fundamental by the U.S. Supreme Court since it "is preservative of other basic civil and political rights." But despite its significance, the franchise has been denied to many groups throughout our nation's history, including blacks, women, and Indians. However, whereas blacks were formally enfranchised with the Fifteenth Amendment (1870) and women with the Nineteenth Amendment (1920), Indians cannot claim one defining historical moment when their right to vote was constitutionally secured. Rather, the struggle for Indian suffrage has been an extraordinarily prolonged, complex, and piecemeal process that has yet to be fully resolved.

Given the political and symbolic importance of the franchise, it might seem incredible that the Constitution does not explicitly grant anyone the right to vote. Except for their needing to adhere to constitutional provisions pertaining to the electoral process and to the specific prohibitions against discrimination in voting based on race (Fifteenth Amendment), sex (Nineteenth Amendment), failure to pay poll taxes (Twenty-fourth Amendment), and age (Twenty-sixth Amendment), the states are free to set reasonable requirements in determining who is eligible to vote in both state and national elections.

Armed with this power, many states, especially those with large Native American populations, imposed severe restrictions on the right of the Indian to vote. For example, some states, such as Colorado, Montana, Nebraska, Oregon, South Dakota, and Wyoming, required that voters be citizens. Although this requirement appears neutral on its face, its discriminatory implications become clear considering the fact that many Indians were not citizens until 1924, when Congress passed the Indian Citizenship Act. Prior to 1924, this requirement barred from the polls all reservation Indians who had not yet been granted citizenship and all nonreservation Indians who could not prove "to the satisfaction of the courts" that they had abandoned their tribal relations.

The states of California, Minnesota, North Dakota, Oklahoma, and Wisconsin imposed a somewhat different but equally burdensome restriction on Indian suffrage, requiring that voters be "civilized." North Dakota's constitution, for example, contained a provision that extended the franchise only to "civilized persons of Indian descent who shall have severed their tribal relations." In *Opsahl* v. *Johnson,* decided by the Minnesota Supreme Court in 1917, the state's requirement that voters be "civilized" was defined more specifically. "Tribal Indians," the justices explained, might demonstrate their eligibility "by taking up [their] abode outside the reservation and there pursuing the customs and habits of civilization." Though the discriminatory implications of this decision are obvious, it takes on a larger significance in that it reflected the deep-seated belief that a traditional, tribal lifestyle was inherently inconsistent with, and inferior to, the more "civilized" white way of life.

Other states, such as Idaho, New Mexico, and Washington, disenfranchised the Indian by inserting provisions into their constitutions that disqualified from the polls all "Indians not taxed." These states apparently subscribed to the notion that Indians should not be entitled to full and equal participation in the political community since they did not contribute to the fiscal well-being of the state. This argument seems disingenuous at best, however, considering the fact that whites not taxed were allowed to vote and that Native Americans, though generally exempt from paying taxes on tribal property, frequently paid sales taxes, licensing fees, and other levies.

The states that set the most stringent restrictions on voter eligibility were Arizona, Nevada, and Utah. These states required that voters be not only citizens, but residents and taxpayers as well. In Arizona, the state supreme court in *Porter v. Hall,* decided in 1928, ruled that Indians should be disqualified from voting because they were under "federal guardianship," a status construed by the court to be synonymous with "persons under disability." This decision stood for twenty years until the court finally reversed itself in *Harrison* v. *Laveen.*

State residency requirements were also used to preclude Indian participation at the polls. The state of Utah, for example, disenfranchised the Indian by claiming that Indians residing on reservations did not qualify as residents of the state. Despite an 1881 U.S. Supreme Court decision that declared all Indians to be residents of the state where their reservations were located, the Utah Supreme Court ruled in 1956 in *Allen* v. *Merrill* that Indians living on reservations did not meet residency requirements as stipulated in state law. Before the U.S. Supreme Court had time to vacate the decision, which it did in 1957, the Utah state legislature repealed the statute on which the case had been based. In so doing, Utah became the last state to abolish its discriminatory methods of withholding suffrage from Indian people.

In addition to these types of invidious election laws, other tactics and devices, such as literacy tests, poll taxes, and voter intimidation and harassment, were used to discriminate against the Indian at election time. All of these practices were declared illegal, however, when Congress passed the Voting Rights Act of 1965. Though originally enacted to prevent black disenfranchisement, the Voting Rights Act as amended in 1970, 1975, and 1982 had significant implications for Indian voting. When the act was renewed in 1975, for example, Congress inserted a provision designed to protect Native Americans that required twenty-four states to provide bilingual ballots and voter assistance at the polls for linguistic-minority voters. When the act was extended again in 1982, section 2 was amended so as to prohibit any voting law or practice that resulted in discrimination on account of race, color, or linguistic-minority status.

Not surprisingly, manifest attitudes of racial animus clashed with the amended provisions of the Voting Rights Act to produce a dilemma for opponents of Indian voting: how could they continue to disenfranchise the Indian without violating the newly established dictates of federal law? Their solution was simple: they shifted their attention from vote denial to vote dilution.

Perhaps the most predominant method of vote dilution today is the misuse of at-large elections. Under these types of systems, the majority of the residents in a given district can prevent minority voters from electing representatives of their choice if the majority votes as a bloc. This practice was challenged by several Crow and Northern Cheyenne Indians in 1986 in *Windy Boy* v. *County of Big Horn.* In that case, the federal district court of Montana ruled that the county's at-large election scheme violated section 2 of the Voting Rights Act and ordered the county and school district to be reorganized into single-member districts.

Single-member districting is not always effective, however, when minority populations are dispersed. In those circumstances, cumulative voting schemes provide a more potent preventative against the devastating effects of vote dilution. Because voters are allowed to cast multiple votes in a cumulative system, they do not have to be part of a majority of the electorate to get a candidate of their choice elected. In *Buckanaga* v. *Sisseton School District,* the Sisseton Wahpeton Sioux tribe challenged its district's voting system after years of unsuccessful attempts to elect Indians to the school board. On remand in 1985, a cumulative voting system was adopted that gave voters the option of casting their allotted votes in any combination they wished, thereby providing Indian voters with a more meaningful opportunity for political participation. That this was so can be seen in the results of the May 1990 election: three of the nine school-board members elected were Indians.

Problems of vote dilution have also developed in connection with reapportionment plans. In 1982, a New Mexico court found in *Sanchez* v. *King* that the state's reapportionment plan violated the one-person, one-vote rule and ordered the state to redraw its districts. Two years later, in response to Indian and Hispanic claims that the new scheme unlawfully diluted minority voting strength, the court imposed its own redistricting plan so as to bring the state into compliance with the requirements of the Voting Rights Act.

As recent cases suggest, the struggle for Indian suffrage is an ongoing, politically contested process that contains within it the whole panoply of conflicting opinions concerning the Indian's position within society. And though many conflicts remain unresolved, there is reason for cautious optimism as American Indians continue not only to vote in record numbers but to get elected to local, state, and federal offices as well.

Deloria, Vine, Jr., ed., *American Indian Policy in the Twentieth Century* (Norman: University of Oklahoma Press, 1985); Hoxie, Frederick E., "Redefining Indian Citizenship," in *A Final Promise: The Campaign to Assimilate the Indians, 1880–1920* (Lincoln: University of Nebraska Press, 1984); Wolfley, Jeanette, "Jim Crow, Indian Style: The Disenfranchisement of Native Americans," *American Indian Law Review* 16 (1991): 167.

SUZANNE E. EVANS
University of California at Berkeley

WAMPANOAG

The Wampanoags were sometimes referred to as Pokanokets, in reference to the sachemdom or territory centered at Sowams (now Warren, Rhode Island). *Pokanoket* means "Place of the Clear Land," and *Wampanoag* means "People of the East." At the beginning of the seventeenth century between twenty-one and twenty-four thousand Wampanoags inhabited the southeastern portion of present-day Massachusetts, Martha's Vineyard, the Elizabeth Islands, Nantucket, and the eastern part of Rhode Island. Their grand sachem was Massasoit, who had authority over all the Wampanoag sachemdoms. Wampanoag men built their people's circular homes, engaged in politics, traded, hunted, and fought. Women cultivated the land, caught shellfish, cooked, cared for children, and manufactured mats, baskets, and clothing. The Wampanoags were competent farmers, fishers, hunters, and gatherers, and performed their tasks according to a seasonal schedule. Today there are two bands of Wampanoags—one in Mashpee, Massachusetts, and the other on Martha's Vineyard.

Hunters were living on Martha's Vineyard as early as 2270 B.C. The direct ancestors of today's Gay Head Wampanoags were firmly established on Martha's Vineyard by A.D. 1380.

In 1641, Thomas Mayhew purchased Martha's Vineyard, Nantucket, and the Elizabeth Islands from the British for forty pounds. According to the first English settlers, the Martha's Vineyard Wampanoags numbered about 3,000 in 1602 and about 2,500 in 1674. Because of a host of deadly diseases brought by the white newcomers and the overwhelming pressure to conform to a society so alien to their traditional values, the Martha's Vineyard Wampanoags today number only about 700; of these, some 250 live on the island.

In 1870 the main Indian settlement on the island, centered at Gay Head, was officially given town status by the state of Massachusetts. This action took away all of the community's Indian rights and facilitated the destruction of its culture and lifestyle. In 1987, the Gay Head Wampanoags were granted federal tribal status.

The Gay Head Wampanoags believe that the giant Moshup created Martha's Vineyard and its neighboring island, taught their people how to fish and to catch whales, and still presides over their destinies. They also believe that a hundred million years of history are imprinted in the Gay Head cliffs.

Cranberry Day (the second Tuesday in October), though no longer a festival lasting three or four days, is still more important and meaningful to the Gay Head Wampanoags than any other holiday, including Christmas. Moshup Pageant (in August) honors and reenacts the story of Moshup's life until his disappearance, weaving together narration, music, and drama.

Though regaining Wampanoag sovereignty over all of Gay Head is a goal yet to be fulfilled, the Gay Head Wampanoags have recovered a measure of self-government over their daily affairs, especially as regards health services, scholarship programs, and local environmental policies. The tribal council, consisting of a chairperson and twelve council members, is elected by the Gay Head Wampanoags to represent them in all affairs pertaining to the tribe. The Gay Head Wampanoags also have a multipurpose building that houses various offices and provides a place where they can gather for council meetings (twice a month) and general membership meetings (four times a year).

During the nineteenth century, a whole social fabric, and the traditions that supported it, were obliterated by the dominant American culture. Of the Wampanoag language, little has survived. Nonetheless, a hopeful trend is rising today, together with a new determination to preserve what is left of the Wampanoag legacy and pass it along to following generations. Though the Gay Head Wampanoags do not have their own schools, school curricula and activities are being progressively redesigned so as to make room for the teaching of native history and culture. Wampanoag women's groups have been formed to revive the traditional gathering of foods and medicinal herbs and to preserve Gay Head Wampanoag arts and crafts.

See also Mashpee.

Banks, Charles Edward, *History of Martha's Vineyard*, 2 vols. (Edgartown, Mass.: Dukes County Historical Society, 1966); Ritchie, William A., *The Archaeology of Martha's Vineyard* (Garden City, N.Y.: Natural History Press, 1969); Simmons, William S., *Spirit of the New England Tribes: Indian History and Folklore, 1620–1984* (Hanover, N.H.: University Press of New England, 1986).

HELEN VANDERHOOP MANNING
(Gay Head Wampanoag)
Education Department
Wampanoag Tribe of Gay Head/Aquinnah

WAMPUM

In contemporary American English, wampum is a slang term meaning "money." And indeed, its use as a medium of exchange was one of the historically evolved functions of wampum—originally a collective term for small cylindrical marine-shell beads, either white or dark purple. Among the Indians of the northeastern woodlands, wampum's use as legal tender was its least culturally significant function; for them wampum was and still is both the medium and the message of social communications.

Wampum is one of many words belonging to the Eastern Algonquian language family that came to be incorporated into modern American English beginning in the early seventeenth century via a trade language, or pidgin, that was primarily derived from the languages of coastal Delaware. It is a shortened form of *wampumpeag* or *wampumpeake*, an Algonquian word of southern New England origin meaning a string of white shell beads. The term appears in contemporary documents, as do the full form and another shortened form, *peag* or *peake*. The form *wampum* prevailed in usage in the Anglo-American colonies to such an extent that it was also borrowed in English translation by neighboring non-Algonquian-language-speaking Indian populations, including speakers of Iroquoian. For example, the Iroquois continue to use the term in English translation, but in its plural form, *wampums*, when referring to wampum strings and belts.

In the contemporary Dutch colony of New Netherland these shell beads were known as *sewant* or *ze-want*, a Narragansett Algonquian term. This word referred to the beads in their unstrung state. The word also appears in *Sewanhacky*, a name by which Long Island was known in 1636 and which no doubt refers to the manufacture of these beads by Corchaug, Montauk, and Shinnecock Algonquins residing on the eastern half of the island. Wampum manufacture centered here, particularly at Peconic Bay, and across Long Island Sound, where it was carried out by Mohegan, Narragansett, Niantic, and Pequot Algonquians of coastal Connecticut and Rhode Island.

White wampum beads were made principally from the central spiraled columella of periwinkles, knobbed whelks (*Busycon carica*), and channeled whelks (*Busycon canaliculatum*). Dark purple beads were manufactured solely from the dark purple spot of the hard clam, or northern quahog (*Mercenaria mercenaria*). The scientific name of this mollusk acknowledges its former role in the manufacture of wampum for use as money. Reportedly, because of the relative difference in bead yield per unit of raw material, in economic and other exchange contexts each dark purple bead was considered equal in value to two white beads.

In contemporary New France the French applied the word *porcelaine* to these shell beads. The French term acknowledged the resemblance in color and substance between the white beads and the rare and highly valued translucent ceramic referred to by that name that was then being imported into Europe from China and Japan. The French name was itself derived from the Italian term for this ceramic, *porcellana*.

The term *wampum* or, more properly, *wampumpeag* specifically refers to white marine-shell beads, which historically conformed to a certain size and shape. These beads were more or less cylindrical and of a relatively small diameter and length. In the early seventeenth century they averaged about one-quarter inch in length and one-eighth inch in diameter. By the late eighteenth century wampum beads had become somewhat longer, but also more uniform in size and shape. This uniformity was directly related to the beads' economic uses: they were usually exchanged in strung fathom lengths, but were increasingly used in the form of woven "belts" as well. Bead standardization was also related to the shift from the beads' aboriginal style of manufacture in the early seventeenth century to their increasing cottage-industry manufacture within Anglo-Dutch communities as far inland as Albany in the mid-eighteenth century, and to their subsequent manufacture in wampum factories.

Wampum belt. This belt was presented by representatives of the Six Nations of the Iroquois at the Treaty of Fort Stanwix on October 22, 1784.

The last of these factories, the Campbell Factory, closed in Bergen County, New Jersey, in the 1880s, when the raw materials for wampum making could not be obtained in sufficient quantity to make wampum manufacture economically viable. This factory depended upon a steady supply of northern quahog shells for bead manufacture, and a decline in the public's taste for these shellfish led to a decline in their harvesting and market availability.

Accompanying the evolution in the size and shape of wampum beads was a shift in bead-drilling techniques. American Indians originally used stone-tipped tools and drilled from either end of the bead. By the middle of the seventeenth century, wampum holes were drilled from either end using an iron awl or drill of European manufacture. Subsequently, holes were drilled straight through from one end only, using a metal drill. The size, shape, and drilling pattern of wampum beads, as revealed by X-ray analysis, can be used to roughly date individual beads or to relatively date a series of beads. But an object made with or decorated with one or more beads cannot be so easily dated: wampum beads were frequently recycled, and extant bead strings and bead belts often incorporate "old" beads as well as "new" ones.

White marine-shell beads conforming in size and shape to wampum beads have been found at archaeological sites of northeastern woodlands Indians spanning the past four thousand years. Dark purple wampum beads, on the other hand, have not been found at prehistoric sites; rather, they make their appearance in the archaeological and documentary record around the turn of the seventeenth century. It is very probable that these purple beads were initially manufactured by coastal Indian communities to imitate the dark blue glass beads of similar size and shape then traded along the coast by Europeans.

Written records of the seventeenth and eighteenth centuries and a few rare contemporary illustrations document the many functions of wampum, a term that increasingly came to mean both the white and the dark purple beads. Individual wampum beads were inlaid on a variety of wooden objects, including bowls, the handles of stone or iron celts (aboriginal "tomahawks"), and ball-headed war clubs. Individual beads were also used for body ornamentation—suspended as pendants from the ears or nose or strung on necklaces. Hundreds and even thousands of beads were woven into headbands, collars, and sashes and attached to other articles of clothing and accessories. Wampum could be owned by individuals, clan lineages, clans, tribes, nations, and confederacies of tribes or nations.

Archaeological evidence suggests that all composite woven forms of wampum such as headbands, collars, sashes, and belts date no earlier than the seventeenth century. While the earliest historic reference to wampum may have been Jacques Cartier's observation of the highly valued, snow-white shell beads in use among the St. Lawrence Iroquois in 1535, the earliest reference to what were likely shell beads woven into a "strap-like" form was in the 1609 report of "stropes of beads," presumably wampum, being proferred to Henry Hudson by Mahican Algonquins.

The most culturally significant function of wampum among the northeastern woodlands Indians has been its use, in the forms of strings and belts, in rituals of kinship affirmation and rituals of condolence. It is in these contexts that it is possible to see the primacy of color in communicating meaning—whether it be the color of wampum; the color of the feathers decorating the calumet, or peace pipe; or the color of other ritual materials.

Color—specifically white, red, and black (or dark purple)—is fundamental to the symbolic meaning of wampum among these Indians. White wampum forms the background for a system of symbolic contrasts with red-painted wampum and dark purple wampum. In ritual contexts, white wampum beads symbolize social states of being, exemplifying the desire of the individual or community for physical, social, and spiritual well-being. White wampum in its ritual use stands in potential contrast both to black wampum, which most frequently symbolizes ritual asocial states of being, such as the "darkness" of mourning, and to red-painted wampum, which most frequently symbolizes antisocial states of being— specifically, war. In addition, one or more pictographs are frequently woven into the belt in beads of a contrasting color and serve as a mnemonic for the belt's message or, in some cases, as an intensifier. For instance, black-fielded belts featuring the pictograph of an ax or hatchet also symbolize war. Furthermore, wampum belts could be painted to change their communication functions. A white-fielded "peace belt" might be made into a "war belt" by a coat of red paint, or a black-fielded "war belt" might be changed to a "peace belt" by a coat of white or, in the upper Great Lakes, blue-green paint.

By the end of the seventeenth century another white substance had been incorporated into this system of communication. The metal silver came to symbolize social relations between the Iroquois and the Anglo-American colonies—"the Silver Covenant." This symbolic permutation of white shell into white metal is also evident in the eighteenth-century correspondence between circular marine-shell gorgets and silver gorgets of similar size and shape, known as *wampum moons*. Albany Dutch silversmiths would list such an ornament in their records as a *schulp* (shell). Across the continent, a similar analogy in substance and form, and perhaps symbolic meaning, appears to be reflected in the southwestern *concho*.

While the manufacture, functions, and functional contexts of white wampum extend far back into prehistory, its use in the form of wampum belts is an early seventeenth-century innovation. Wampum-belt ceremonialism and iconography developed and flourished in the cross-cultural exchanges of American Indians and Euro-Americans, in which peace and trade were perceived as one. While the beads and belts never assumed the symbolic significance among Euro-Americans that they had among Indians, by the late eighteenth century most wampum beads were probably the product of non-Indian manufacture. Furthermore, theoretically, half of the wampum belts in circulation at this date were made by Euro-Americans, or on their behalf, for presentation to Indians.

While wampum beads, strings, and belts are identified with "traditional" northeastern woodlands Indian religious, social, and political practices, they were also incorporated into mission Catholicism in the seventeenth century, as exemplified among the Christianized Huron (formerly of southwestern Ontario and later of Lorette, near Quebec City). Wampum beads sometimes functioned as rosary beads. Wampum belts and other wampum objects were made as gifts to the Society of Jesus or to mission churches, where they were displayed above the altar. Latin inscriptions woven into extant belts record their dedication to the Virgin Mary. One of the more interesting syncretisms is evident in a wampum belt offered to Saint Michael, the Archangel, to elicit his assistance on the warpath.

It was Jacques Cartier who stated in 1535 that the white shell beads that he found in use among the St. Lawrence Iroquois were regarded by them as the most precious articles in the world. It was also Jacques Cartier who first asserted an analogy between the uses of these beads by the Indians and the uses of gold and silver among Europeans. Cartier's observation should not be taken at face value, however, for he and subsequent commentators also recognized the analogy between the symbolic functions and meaning of these white shell beads and the functions and meaning of silver, gold, and diamonds in Western European traditions. In the Western world these substances have served as tangible metaphors of highest cultural value: not simply wealth in the economic sense, but wealth as a visible symbol of well-being.

One might speculate that, cross-culturally, white, bright, and light things serve as material metaphors for those abstractions of greatest cultural value, such as life itself—animacy and consciousness—and their correlated states of physical, social, and spiritual well-being. In the context of contemporary American English, the value of "a gem of wisdom" or of "the Golden Rule" is not in its monetary worth, but in its reflective virtue.

Hamell, George R., "The Iroquois and the World's Rim: Speculations on Color, Culture, and Contact," *American Indian Quarterly: Journal of American Indian Studies* 16 (1992): 451–69; Hewitt, John N. B., "Wampum," in *Handbook of American Indians North of Mexico*, vol. 2, ed. Frederick Webb Hodge, Smithsonian Institution, Bureau of American Ethnology Bulletin no. 30 (Washington, D.C., 1910); Williams, Lorraine E., and Karen A. Flinn, *Trade Wampum: New Jersey to the Plains* (Trenton: New Jersey State Museum, 1990).

GEORGE R. HAMELL
New York State Museum
Albany, New York

WARRIOR, CLYDE

(1939–68)
Ponca activist, writer, and cofounder of the National Indian Youth Council.

Clyde Warrior was one of the most prominent leaders of the Indian youth movement that arose during the early 1960s. As such, he rallied young Indian people to ideas of native nationalism and cultural, social, and economic development. As head of the National Indian Youth Council (NIYC; founded in Gallup, New Mexico, in 1961), he influenced the direction of national Indian advocacy groups, helped provide organizational structure for an emergent generation of Indian youth, and articulated ideas of nationalism that came to take center stage during the following decade.

He was highly confrontational and favored engaging in direct political action, despite the discomfort many of his peers felt with such a strategy. Warrior's desire to embrace protest became most clear in 1963 and 1964, when he helped maneuver the NIYC into becoming involved in fishing-rights protests in the Pacific Northwest. The group enlisted the aid of the actor Marlon Brando for the protests, a move that ensured national press exposure.

The radical figures who followed Warrior were mostly from cities and often had prison records. In stark contrast, Warrior was raised by his grandparents in the most traditional of Ponca environments. His first language was Ponca, and from his youth he was immersed in traditional Ponca life. By his late teen years he was an accomplished powwow fancy dancer.

Warrior began making a name for himself politically while he was in college, in regional and national programs for Indian students. When the handsome young Ponca pointed out the growing fissures in American life, his mostly conservative fellow students whispered in disbelief, "He can't say that!" But he continued to speak his mind, becoming in the process a lightning rod for controversy as well as a leader whom many saw as overbearing. He attended Northeastern State University in Tahlequah, Oklahoma, and graduated in 1966.

In the early 1960s, Warrior's fame and constituency grew. Perhaps his most well known work was a 1964 essay, "Which One Are You?: Five Types of Young Indians." The five types he described were the Hood (the young person who lives up to the status of being the problem society has defined him or her to be); the Joker (the young person who makes a fool of himself or herself in front of non-Indians in hopes of gaining acceptance from them); the Sellout (someone who ingratiates himself or herself to non-Indians and accepts the values of non-Indian society); the Ultra-Pseudo-Indian (one who is proud of being an Indian but doesn't have an experiential base in Indian communities and so copies popular images of Indianness); and the Angry Young Nationalist (one who rejects American society but whose arguments are too ideological and abstract to have an impact among local Indian people).

"It appears that what is needed," Warrior went on to say in the essay, "is genuine, contemporary, creative thinking, democratic leadership to set guidelines, cues, and goals for the average Indian. The guidelines and cues have to be *based on true Indian philosophy geared to modern times.*" Warrior further contended that new programs for Indian people were not ends in themselves, but needed to be taken into account as Indian communities came to an understanding of the fundamental realities they faced.

Warrior himself was a prime example of his own ideals. College educated and a keen student of national and international politics, he was also a walking library of tribal songs. Some of those songs were Ponca, but many others were intertribal songs that people shared with him as he traveled around the country. He was living proof that tribal traditions were vital and alive, and he firmly believed those traditions to be a central component in building an Indian future.

But as Warrior's commitment to more radical change increased, the NIYC drifted toward the center. The group still had a reputation for being on the cutting edge of Indian politics, but by 1966 Warrior and others were beginning to see it as little more than a springboard for young people seeking permanent positions in the National Congress of American Indians or the Bureau of Indian Affairs.

Still, Warrior predicted that the growing instability of mainstream America would continue to foster unrest and that newer, more radical Indian groups would emerge. "As I see it," he told one interviewer, "before we change things are going to get worse. There are going to be more riots. And if [society] doesn't change, then the students and the Indians might just smash it, and change it themselves."

Though still in his mid-twenties, Warrior by 1966 was himself changing. He had married Della Hopper (Oto) in July 1965, and the couple would soon have two daughters. Increased family responsibilities and a significant weight gain forced him to give up fancy dancing for slower-paced events.

The weight gain was more than likely related to a drinking problem, Warrior's capacity for consuming bourbon being legendary. The weight gain, coupled with Warrior's addiction to alcohol, caused or at least exacerbated a liver condition, and doctors warned the still-young man that his next drink might be his last. Twice, friends arranged for him to enter alcohol-rehabilitation programs. Both times, he emerged resolved to stay sober. As long as he stayed home, according to his wife, he was fine. But when he once again entered into the fast-paced lifestyle of Indian-affairs meetings, he lost whatever resolve he had had and began drinking once again. In July 1968 his liver failed, and he died.

Associates and friends from around the country flew in for the funeral—an affair that was carried out according to strict Ponca tradition. Family and friends gathered for four days at his grandparents' home for services. On the final day a feast was held, at which food prepared over open fires was served to mourners by Warrior's male relatives. Afterward, Warrior's widow gave away blankets, shawls, and other gifts to those who had supported her. Finally, the body was laid to rest in a nearby cemetery.

During his life, he had asked, "How long will Indians tolerate this? Negroes, Mexican Americans, and Puerto Ricans could only take colonialism, exploitation, and abuse for so long; then they did something about it. Will American Indians wait until their reservations and lands are eroded away, and they are forced into urban ghettos, before they start raising hell with their oppressors?" In the years following his death, his questions were answered in the Indian protests that erupted—protests from which, at least in retrospect, his unique brand of analysis and insight appears to have been conspicuously absent.

Smith, Paul Chaat, and Robert Allen Warrior, *Like a Hurricane: The Indian Movement from Alcatraz to Wounded Knee* (New York: New Press, forthcoming); Warrior, Clyde, "We Are Not Free," in *Red Power,* ed. Alvin Josephy (New York: McGraw-Hill, 1971; reprint, Lincoln: University of Nebraska Press, 1985); Warrior, Clyde, "Which One Are You?: Five Types of Young Indians," *ABC: Americans before Columbus* 2, no. 4 (December 1964): 1–3; reprinted as an appendix to *The New Indians,* by Stan Steiner (New York: Harper and Row, 1968).

ROBERT ALLEN WARRIOR (Osage)
Stanford University

WARRIORS AND WARFARE

Warfare in aboriginal North America was not necessarily a political act. Native Americans certainly developed their own unique forms of combat and, in some cases, elevated warfare to ritualistic contests of great spiritual significance, but they did not develop warfare to its most destructive and sanguinary potential. In general, tribes raided or engaged in pitched battles to obtain material goods, take revenge on traditional enemies for the killing of relatives, seize captives, or vent aggression. Although a few groups, like the Aztecs and the League of the Haudenosaunee, or Iroquois, were able to assemble large numbers of warriors into very real armies, territorial conquests and instances of mass slaughter on the scale of those habitually carried out by the Assyrians, Greeks, Romans, Huns, Ottomans, and Spanish did not occur in aboriginal America. It seems that Aztec armies were bent more on acquiring a limited number of captives for sacrifice in religious ceremonies than on the annihilation of other tribes. And the Iroquois appear to have been much more concerned with adopting captives taken on raids than on the acquisition of territory and the destruction of entire societies. In fact, the Iroquois constitution guaranteed that each tribe within the league would maintain its internal sovereignty.

Native American intertribal warfare, in short, took on many forms and was undertaken for a very complex set of reasons. Territoriality was a motivating factor, but only in certain instances. It has been argued that populous tribes that engaged in big-game hunting, agriculture, or even large-scale seasonal gathering developed highly organized war complexes to defend their territorial boundaries. Tribes in areas where subsistence was difficult and population densities were low might not have had to resort to warfare to maintain large territories. On the other hand, raiding, which occurred even in areas with low population densities, might have forced tribes into organizing for warfare purely for the sake of protecting goods or tribal members.

Most tribes viewed the possession of land in a unique way. Tribes had well-defined, sacred territorial boundaries that literally defined who they were; but these areas were relatively small and did not necessarily abut other areas. Local spirits and deities existed within these central areas, and the tribes' traditions reinforced the connection between identity and place. Territories surrounding these particular lands were shared hunting grounds or ranges, claimed by numerous groups. In effect, they were no man's lands, owned by no one but used by all. Tribal warriors might meet in pitched battles or intercept another tribe's raiding party in these neutral lands; but colonizing them, even for the sake of defense, would have been an unwarranted disruption of the natural order, necessitating a redefinition of the tribe's identity.

Raiding was by far the most predominant form of organized human violence in native North America. It was an activity that accomplished several things but did not necessarily require the acquisition of new territory or the recasting of tribal identity. In the first place, raiding added to tribal wealth. Apaches, Comanches, Kiowas, and numerous other tribes raided for foodstuffs, material goods, and, later, livestock. But there was another meaning placed on raiding, in addition to the simple acquisition of property: raiding was a means of gaining social rewards for the individual raider or that person's family. Consider the potlatches of Northwest Coast tribes, for example. Often the family or clans offering these formal displays of generosity obtained the goods they gave as gifts during the potlatches by raiding other tribes. Similarly, Kiowas placed a great deal of emphasis on stealing horses. Those warriors who had acquired a number of horses often gave them away to less fortunate younger men. The recipients, in turn, could take part in mounted raids on enemy tribes for more horses. They could then pay back their benefactors and become benefactors themselves. In a like manner, when Cherokee warriors returned from a successful war they gave the booty they had collected to their female relatives for redistribution among those women who had no close male relatives who could participate in raids.

While Native American raiding and warfare served both an economic and a social function, two other dynamics were also at work: kinship and spirituality. Many tribes practiced what has been termed "mourning" warfare—a highly ritualized form of blood vengeance or spiritual indemnification. When a kinsman or kinswoman died or was killed in battle, some groups believed, the clan's, tribe's, or nation's collective spiritual power was diminished directly in proportion to that of the slain person. Retaliatory raiding took place to take captives and/or kill a certain number of enemy warriors. In numerous cases, captives were adopted as replacements for deceased relatives. Killing an enemy or torturing a captive to death was intended to repair the metaphysical imbalance caused by a

death. Some Native American women literally "dried their tears" with the scalps of enemies killed in battle. All in all, mourning warfare kept populations relatively stable, promoted group cohesion, and reaffirmed the tribal sense of superiority.

The spiritual dimension in Native American warfare cannot be overlooked. Most tribes believed in a rigid distinction between the activities of war and those of peace. Consequently, ceremonies were devised to aid individuals and entire communities in making the transition from peace to war and back again. Warriors were ritually prepared for war and offered protective medicine to assure their safe return to the community. In addition to preparation rituals, many tribes used purification ceremonies to restore individual warriors, as well as the rest of the community, to a peaceful state. Unless the returning warriors were purged of the trauma of battle, it was felt, they might perpetuate unacceptable patterns of behavior within the community.

Most native people felt that, like the line drawn between the activities of war and peace, there was a distinct separation between male and female physical and spiritual powers. In many tribal societies female power was associated with the ability to reproduce and nurture. Menses was, in itself, a force that could, according to numerous tribal legends, block or negate male powers. Women not only gave birth and nurtured children but among several tribes became the principal sowers and reapers of the soil. Women, then, could perform most or even all essential economic activities. Males were born without such power and had to acquire it through the intervention of the supernatural. This often led to the establishment of distinct male and female activities: female power was frequently associated with the activities of life (child bearing, cultivation); male power, with death (warfare, hunting).

Aboriginal North American warfare was also seen as an outlet for youthful male aggression. In this sense it resembled an elaborate game in which young males gained status within their group under a strict set of guidelines. The practice of counting coups (or "blows") among the tribes of the Great Plains supports this idea in many ways. Coups were war honors that emphasized bravery, cunning, and stealth over the actual killing of an enemy. According to some tribal elders the best coup was touching an enemy in the heat of battle and thus leaving him alive to wallow in shame and self-reproach. In effect, the warrior had captured the enemy's spirit. Other tribes possessed the same ideas but were less formal in recognizing war honors. While the Apaches of the Southwest appear not to have had specific war honors for feats of bravery, they nevertheless honored their warriors for stealing goods and livestock and thus for adding to (and redistributing) wealth within the band. Apache warriors were also given respect in stories and song for either their stealth or their extreme valor in capturing livestock or obtaining goods from enemy peoples.

Because going to war was one of two principal occupations for young tribal males (the other being hunting), warfare and the ceremonies linked to warfare became traditions in and of themselves. Warriors gained status not only by going to war but also by participating in the rituals of war. Some tribes basically reinforced their own sense of peoplehood through conflict with traditional enemies. In the early 1700s, when whites were urging the Cherokees to make peace with the Tuscaroras, the Cherokees explained that they could not live without war and that the nation would be forced to find someone else to fight. Implicit in the Cherokee argument was the idea that the Tuscaroras, while hated, were worthy and needed opponents. In 1802 the Muskogee Creek elder Efau Harjo summed up the need for traditional warfare and warned the whites not to interfere with it:

> There is among us Four Nations [Muskogee Creek, Cherokee, Choctaw, and Chickasaw] old customs, one of which is war. If the young men, having grown to manhood, wish to practice the ways of the old people, let them try themselves at war, and when they have tried, let the chiefs interpose and stop it. We want you to let us alone.

There were other, more practical reasons to participate in regular combat with long-time foes. Traditional enemies were known quantities, and tribal leaders and warriors therefore had little cause to be suspicious of novel tactics, new weapons, or even of the size of a given enemy's force. Native Americans faced each other on the battlefield symmetrically armed. Ritual warfare with traditional foes was not all that expensive in terms of either lives lost or time spent in the search for more destructive weaponry. Tribal warriors either equipped themselves or sought out skilled artisans who fashioned arms. These weapons makers might also be endowed with magical powers that could be transmitted into their handiwork. In addition, the numbers of combatants in tribal encounters were usually low. Armed with muscle and spiritually powered weapons, using face paint, ritualized gestures, and vocalizations to frighten the enemy, and fighting in limited numbers,

tribal warriors were likely not, after all, seeking the utter destruction of their traditional foes. In fact, the ultimate annihilation of an enemy, or even his capitulation, might very well have been antithetical to the goals of tribal warfare.

The word *warrior* in many Native American languages is often translated as a gender-specific term for males who fill a traditional social role. But in several tribal societies there were female warriors who received many specific war honors. The term *warrior*, then, could in some cases be a label that did not carry a specific gender identity. Thus such a warrior did not act out a specific role so much as he or she developed a relationship with the community that sustained and reaffirmed tribal identity. By participating in war-related ceremonies the warrior cemented the tribe's special relationship with the spirit world. The warrior replaced lost kin and dried the tears of mourning relatives. Equally, the warrior's generosity contributed significantly to tribal wealth, prosperity, and continued harmony. In turn, the society offered the warrior ceremonies, a place in the tribe's sacred history, and honor.

See also Wars: Colonial Era; Wars: 1776–1850; Wars: 1850–1900.

Driver, Harold E., *Indians of North America* (Chicago: University of Chicago Press, 1975); Kroeber, Clifton, and Bernard L. Fontana, *Massacre on the Gila: An Account of the Last Major Battle between American Indians, with Reflections on the Origins of War* (Tucson: University of Arizona Press, 1986); Richter, Daniel K., "War and Culture: The Iroquois Experience," *William and Mary Quarterly* 40 (October 1983): 529–37.

TOM HOLM (Cherokee/Creek)
University of Arizona

WARS: COLONIAL ERA

Colonial wars evolved in type and function through several phases. The wars of the eighteenth century differed greatly from those of the sixteenth. In the earliest conflicts—initiated by Spanish mercenaries—military conquest was made possible by superior weaponry. Thus Columbus and his successors at Hispaniola overbore and terrorized the Tainos and Caribs of the West Indies.

This method had limits. When Hernán Cortés landed in Mexico in 1519, he ran afoul of the great numbers and fighting abilities of Aztec soldiers. After tentatively accepting his troops in their twin cities of Tenochtitlán-

Tlatelolco, the Aztecs furiously inflicted heavy casualties and drove the Spaniards out. Cortés had to solicit thousands of allies from the city of Tlaxcala and other native enemies of the Aztecs in order to maintain a Spanish presence in Mexico. Thus early on, the pattern was set by which European invaders divided Indian peoples against themselves in order to conquer.

In 1521, Juan Ponce de León, ignorant of this strategy, invaded Florida with only his mercenaries, and was killed by the Calusas. Similarly, between 1536 and 1539, Hernando de Soto depended on his hired killers to ravage the Gulf Coast regions of North America, ultimately losing both the campaign and his life. A year later Francisco Coronado led an invasion of the Rio Grande that carried him as far east as modern-day Kansas, but, finding neither gold nor allies, he retreated back to Mexico City.

Different patterns appeared farther north. The people most worrisome to Spaniards along the Atlantic Coast were their European rivals rather than Indian natives. When French Huguenots founded Fort Caroline with native allies, Pedro Menéndez de Avilés led a massacre of the French in 1565 as Indians looked on awestruck. Menéndez de Avilés promptly founded San Agustin (later St. Augustine) as a base to ward off future European colonization of Florida. All European invaders (particularly those supported by sea power) were cockily confident that they could handle Indian threats.

Patterns changed substantially in the seventeenth century. In the St. Lawrence Valley, Samuel de Champlain, understanding the potential riches of trade with neighboring tribesmen, carefully allied himself with those who held the greatest economic potential. This required him to take up arms against those enemies France had in common with its Indian allies—tribes such as the Mohawks. By these actions he inaugurated New France's network of alliances with tribes who accepted French leadership, a system that lasted for more than 150 years—as long as did New France itself.

The French never permitted any Indian tribe to act as intermediary in relations with other tribes. French officials, agents, and traders invariably negotiated directly with all Indians. Governors-general insisted on being addressed as *father,* and called the Indians *children.* The Dutch and English colonies operated differently. They gave certain client tribes authority over "tributaries" and held them responsible for desired conduct. For these Europeans, their Indian clients were *brethren.*

New Netherland began in this fashion by negotiating with the Mohawks in 1643. In consequence, the Dutch broke with colonial precedent by selling four hundred guns to the Mohawks, who shared them with Seneca allies to the west. The partners attacked and dispersed the French-allied Huron Confederacy, disrupting the great cycle of Huron trade that had so enriched New France. The Mohawks and Senecas, as well as their Dutch patrons, benefited from these attacks on the French and their trading partners. The lesson was plain: no tribe could defend itself without guns, and guns could be obtained only through trade with Europeans.

Almost simultaneously with the Dutch-Mohawk agreement, trouble arose in Chesapeake Bay between Maryland's English colonists and the powerful Susquehannock tribe. Although the tribes of the Chesapeake Bay area's Powhatan Confederacy had tried to rid themselves of Englishmen in 1622, they had killed too few in this uprising, and the survivors harried them mercilessly. Marylanders suspected the upstream Susquehannocks of similar hostile intent, and marched against them in 1643. They won a battle, but not the war. From nearby Delaware Bay, the men of New Sweden, alarmed at the prospect of losing their best Indian trading partners, provided guns and training to the Susquehannocks, who then trounced Maryland's second campaign against them.

Again the lesson was plain: even the mighty European colonists could be defeated when competing colonists helped the Indians with arms and encouragement. In an atmosphere of colonial expansion, tribes could not survive in total independence. They had to accept clientage to a colony in order to survive a war. And client tribes were obliged to help their patrons in return. New alliances thus generated numerous occasions for tribal hostilities and increased casualties. The historian Douglas Edward Leach remarks that "groups of colonists and Indians formed relationships and attachments that were to become the warp and woof of an intricate pattern whose central theme was deadly strife."

On the other hand, the fact that the Indians showed great resourcefulness in obtaining arms meant colonists could no longer simply smash annoying Indian neighbors without fear of retaliation. For security, each colony needed at least one client tribe. Struggles between colonies became, like struggles between tribes, conflicts involving a partnership of colony and tribe pitted against a similar opposing partnership. For this reason, "race wars" were not a part of the colonial landscape.

In New England, Massachusetts Bay set out to imitate the French. The Puritans established a Protestant mission among the local Indian communities and, in 1669, sent armed "praying Indians" against the Mohawks. This was in effect war by surrogates against New York. Massachusetts hoped to gain so-called rights of conquest over the upper Hudson Valley, but the New Yorkers supported the Mohawks and indirectly inflicted grievous defeat on Massachusetts. Such efforts to establish rights of conquest became a common feature of frontier life throughout the entire colonial era.

The period 1675–77 marked a general transition to these new policies all across North America. Two distinct wars broke out at the same time: Virginia marched against the Susquehannocks, with Maryland joining in for fear of losing territory to Virginia; and New Englanders warred to gain rights of conquest to lands belonging to the Wampanoags and Narragansetts. New York's governor, Edmund Andros, first sent the Mohawks to crush the New England tribes, then gave them refuge when the Bay Colony carried the day. Similarly, Andros gave refuge to the Susquehannocks who fled Virginia. Thus he gained manpower and trading hunters for his own colony of New York.

In negotiations that ended these wars in 1677, all the parties agreed to the so-called Covenant Chain—a network of multiple alliances—with the Iroquois League as the representative body for the allied tribes and New York as the mediator for the colonies. The Covenant Chain, which endured through many alterations until the American Revolution, gave the Iroquois hegemonic leadership among the eastern tribes.

In 1680, Pueblo Indians in the Rio Grande valley rose against Spanish overlords and drove them out. For a time, the colony headquartered at Santa Fe was abandoned. But the Spaniards returned in 1693 and beat the rebels down harshly. In the outcome, the Pueblos accepted clientage and accommodated to the Spaniards in order to resist Indian raiders from the north and east who were beginning to obtain guns from French traders.

After 1700 the European colonists' numbers grew because of continuous immigration, while Indian populations declined because of epidemics and battle. Two grand frontiers—one in the North and one in the South—formed east of the Mississippi. In the North, New France faced against New England, New York, and Virginia. In the South, Louisiana faced against Georgia and South Carolina. In both frontier regions, Indians were sandwiched between rival empires.

As this situation took form, the Iroquois threw themselves against New France; but, inadequately supported by New York, they were unsuccessful. Opposing Canadian Frenchmen organized and armed great numbers of their Indian allies from the Great Lakes region and drove the Iroquois out of the Ontario region, compelling them to accept French terms in the treaty of 1701.

The southern frontier took different shape. South Carolinian traders pushed westward all the way to the Mississippi, alarming the French crown, which feared the loss of its trans-Appalachian tribes and territories. To preserve them, the French ordered Fort Biloxi (Mississippi) built in 1699, and expanded their operations into Louisiana. Surrogate wars here were fought between the Carolina-allied Chickasaws and the Louisiana-allied Choctaws. Indians on both sides experienced thousands of casualties, but the empires' traders prospered.

During the eighteenth century, these frontier regions were affected by great conflicts involving England, France, and their European allies: King William's War (1689–97); Queen Anne's War (1701–13); King George's War (1744–48); and finally the global Seven Years' War (1754–63), which was called the French and Indian War in the Colonies. In the end England triumphed and acquired legal "sovereignty" over all Indians east of the Mississippi, but the Indians asserted independence. The tribes launched fierce resistance movements that once more became entangled in world conflicts when England's colonies rose in a war for independence—a war that marked the end of the colonial era in America.

Jennings, Francis, *The Invasion of America: Indians, Colonialism, and the Cant of Conquest* (Chapel Hill: University of North Carolina Press, 1975); Jennings, Francis, *Empire of Fortune: Crowns, Colonies and Tribes in the Seven Years War in America* (New York: W. W. Norton & Co., 1988); Leach, Douglas Edward, "Colonial Indian Wars," in *Handbook of North American Indians,* ed. William C. Sturtevant, vol. 4, *History of Indian-White Relations,* ed. Wilcomb E. Washburn (Washington: Smithsonian Institution, 1978).

FRANCIS JENNINGS
University of North Carolina at Chapel Hill

WARS: 1776–1850

Between the arrival of Columbus and the end of the nineteenth century, warfare was a major part of Indian-white relations, resulting in more than one thousand battles and wars. From 1776 to 1850, the woodlands tribal nations and the United States waged wars of deliberate destruction, with heavy cost in human life on each side. Both sides operated at a comparable level of power, but they usually applied different strategies of warfare.

From 1776 to about 1790, the eastern Indian nations usually engaged the new United States in skirmishes and battles for domination and territorial control, but other motives were also at play. These included struggles over trade routes and revenge for past actions. In some instances, Indians fought as allies of the United States, and in some situations tribes fought other tribes, but the Indian wars usually pitted Native Americans against the United States. At first, Indian nations had the advantage against inexperienced local American militia. Unequal to their foes in terms of technology and adequate sources of arms and ammunition, however, the eastern Indian nations fell gradually before American guns, leading to the westward migration of an estimated thirty eastern tribes.

The Great Lakes region witnessed numerous battles between 1778 and 1794, the majority of them in what is now Ohio and Indiana. The British in Canada frequently armed the Americans' Indian adversaries with British muskets and ammunition. With this support, a confederacy of Miamis, Shawnees, and Delawares in northern Ohio won major victories over General Josiah Harmar, his ill-trained 320 regular troops, and 1,133 Kentucky militiamen in October 1790. A year later, Ohio governor Arthur St. Clair led 2,300 men against this same enemy and was routed. The loss of 647 men under St. Clair's command was the worst military defeat American troops would ever suffer in a battle with Native Americans. Fortunes were reversed at the Battle of Fallen Timbers in August 1794. In that battle, internal divisions and British indifference undermined the Indian forces, whereas "Mad" Anthony Wayne's disciplined American Legion seized the strategic portage point at the mouth of the Maumee River, near modern-day Toledo, Ohio.

Gradually, American soldiers abandoned European battlefield formation and adopted the Indian style of fighting, using smaller forces that relied on camouflage, ambush, and retreat. In this manner, knowledge of the environment became an advantage. In Ohio, war clubs and hunting knives were used in hand-to-hand combat, resulting in some of the most violent scenes of American warfare and producing a level of bitterness and racial hatred that would last for the rest of the century.

Farther south, as American settlers crossed the Appalachian Mountains following folk heroes like Daniel Boone, deadly encounters became legendary. Kentucky became a battleground with the Shawnees. In 1780, the British Loyalist Colonel William Byrd led an Indian army of one thousand to defeat Kentucky settlements at Martin's and Ruddle's Stations. In the latter battle, two hundred men, women, and children were killed. In 1782 Loyalists defeated and killed seventy Kentuckians at the Battle of Blue Licks. In retaliation, Major George Rogers Clark and his army marched across the Ohio River and destroyed Shawnee and Delaware villages, notably at Chillicothe and Piqua in 1782. Retaliation from the Shawnees, Delawares, and Senecas on American settlements in western Pennsylvania provoked the American slaughter of nearly ninety peaceful Christian Delaware men, women, and children at Gnaddenhutten Mission. Colonel William Crawford paid for this action when Indians defeated him and his army from Fort Pitt; Crawford himself was later captured and tortured to death.

During the War of 1812—a conflict that stretched from 1811 to 1815 in America—about 150 hostile actions occurred. Supported by his brother the Shawnee Prophet, Tecumseh had gathered a massive Indian force on the banks of the Wabash River in what is now north central Indiana. His followers used the latest technology in guns and operated in tandem with other Indian allies and regular British units. That force was scattered by William Henry Harrison's attack on Prophetstown in 1811, and the alliance ended with Tecumseh's death in 1813 at the Battle of the Thames, in southern Ontario.

With the British removed as a factor in Indian-white relations in the United States and the Spanish on the decline in the Southeast, the United States realized the need for diplomacy in its contact with tribes in other areas. Indian agents often worked to negotiate peace with frontier tribes, but settlers desiring Indian lands usually produced conflict. Diplomacy at intertribal councils often divided and weakened Indian opponents. During the Creek War of 1813, for example, particularly at the decisive American victory at Horseshoe Bend, the Americans were aided by friendly Indian nations and "loyal" Creeks. Similarly, during the Seminole War of 1817–18 (fought in northern Florida), the Red Bird War of 1827 (waged in southwestern Wisconsin), and the Black Hawk War of 1832, former allies of the warring tribes either remained neutral or sided with the Americans. The Black Hawk War was particularly tragic as it pitted an aging Sauk leader with a dwindling following against an unruly American force that eventually cornered and massacred the Indians along the Bad Axe River in southern Wisconsin. Abraham Lincoln served as a disgusted recruit during the conflict.

From about 1776 to 1835, the continued expansion of the United States meant that fighting Indians became the steady task of the U.S. Army. Americans now produced leaders who rose to political prominence as Indian fighters. Two of these heroes, William Henry Harrison and Andrew Jackson, became presidents of the United States.

From 1835 to 1850, the Indian nations continued to engage the U.S. Army east of the Mississippi, even though the balance of power had tipped heavily in favor of the United States. The last major war during this period, the Second Seminole War (1835–42), involved the Seminoles of Florida. A third Seminole war occurred from 1855 to 1858, but the second was more notorious. In it, twelve generals of the U.S. Army were sent to defeat the Seminoles and prepare them for removal to the West. This second war symbolized the ability of Indian strategy to pin down a large and well-supplied army. These same years found hostilities spreading in the West, repeating the patterns first seen in Ohio in the 1790s. Texas Rangers organized to repel attacks from the Comanches on white settlements in 1835, and other settlements in Missouri and Iowa stood ready to defend themselves.

War between the United States and Mexico over the American claim to Texas spurred larger conflicts. From 1847 to 1850, the Cayuses warred against the Oregonians wanting their land. Gold discovered in 1849 in California brought a slaughter of Indian groups in massacres, and in 1851 the Miwoks and Yokuts fought California miners in the Mariposa War.

Dowd, Gregory, *A Spirited Resistance: The North American Indian Struggle for Unity, 1745–1815* (Baltimore: Johns Hopkins Press, 1992); Utley, Robert M., and Wilcolm E. Washburn, *Indian Wars* (Boston: Houghton Mifflin, 1977).

DONALD L. FIXICO
(Seminole, Creek, Shawnee, Sac and Fox)
Western Michigan University

WARS: 1850–1900

The lure of mineral wealth, vast territories for the taking, and numerous other natural resources brought whites west of the Mississippi in droves—nearly 8 million people between 1850 and 1890. The majority of these immigrants saw Native Americans simply as barriers to progress, and Native Americans immediately became locked in a struggle to save themselves from obliteration. The viciousness and sanguinary excesses of the resulting wars between tribes and whites that took place in the ensuing few years matched in intensity and ferocity all of the wars fought between the two groups in the previous 350 years.

Among the first to feel the weight of the American onslaught were the tribes of California. The gold seekers who came to the Sierra Nevada mountain range to pry the precious metal from the ground were perhaps less tolerant of Native Americans than most others. During the early 1850s the tribes, who subsisted primarily by hunting, fishing, and gathering, suffered heavily under a local policy of genocide. The native population of California declined by as much as 70 percent over the course of the next ten years. Meanwhile, the mining and timber industries precipitated conflicts in New Mexico, Arizona, Colorado, Washington, and Oregon as well as along the trails that the whites followed westward to the goldfields, forests, and fertile plains. Most of the tribes in these areas were better armed for war and more inclined to fight the intruders than were the natives of California.

In 1853, Secretary of War Jefferson Davis urged the enlargement of U.S. Army forces in order to garrison the forts that were to protect trails and mount punitive raids on Native American tribes suspected of harming white miners, lumberjacks, and farmers. The clashes were intermittent but deadly. Nearly every war between whites and tribes in the 1850s followed the same tragic pattern: white intrusion, tribal rejection, and white counterattack.

In Oregon Territory (present-day Oregon and Washington) the army conducted numerous punitive raids against the people of the Rogue River between 1851 and 1856 and attacked Yakima, Walla Walla, and Cayuse villages sporadically throughout the decade. In New Mexico Territory (present-day New Mexico and Arizona) the army clashed with the Apaches at Cienguilla and Rio Caliente in 1854 and at the Gila River in 1857. The Utes were attacked at Poncha Pass in 1855. On the Great Plains, General William Harney mounted a bloody raid on a Lakota encampment in Nebraska in 1854; Colonel Edwin V. Sumner attacked a large contingent of Cheyenne warriors on the Solomon Fork in Kansas in 1857; and Major Earl Van Dorn fought the

Comanches at Rush Spring in present-day Oklahoma in October 1859 and along Crooked Creek in Kansas in 1860.

The Civil War marked a change in the nature of Indian-white conflicts. When the war broke out, the American officer corps was deeply divided. Several of its members simply left their posts in the West to offer their services to the Confederacy. Other officers remained in place, but large contingents of their units were sent to join the Union forces operating in Missouri, Kentucky, and Tennessee. The federal government, concentrating on winning (but in fact primarily losing) battles in Virginia, more or less ignored its relations with Native Americans. Lacking leadership, direction, and personnel, what was left of the regular army in the West had difficulty in controlling anything. Native American–white relations, already at a low, reached their nadir when irregular white forces (volunteers) began to take over the army's responsibilities.

What followed was a series of military blunders, cruel roundups, and horrific massacres. In 1861 an American military force attacked previously peaceful Chiricahua Apaches under Cochise, precipitating a running conflict that continued for twenty-five years. The very next year, the Santee Dakotas in Minnesota, who had nursed long-festering grievances against intruding traders, missionaries, lumber mills, and settlers, launched a war that would eventually take the lives of nearly a thousand whites and hundreds of their own people. A largely volunteer white force under Henry Sibley, a former fur trader who was Minnesota's first governor, met the Dakotas in a pitched battle at Wood Lake. Cannon fire eventually won the day for Sibley's force, and the Dakotas were rounded up. Sibley, acting as if the Dakotas were a part of some grand rebellion, convened a military tribunal that tried, convicted, and sentenced to death 303 Santees. Abraham Lincoln, suspecting that justice had taken a wrong turn in the turmoil, commuted the sentences of all but thirty-eight, who were hanged en masse at Mankato in December 1862. Those Santees who escaped Sibley's wrath went among their Lakota relatives farther west to confirm the Lakotas' already grave concerns about white intruders.

Meanwhile, the all-volunteer California Column, under Union colonel James Carleton, descended on New Mexico Territory to rid it of Confederate influence. Finding few Southerners there, Carleton turned his patriotic fervor on the local tribes. His army fought several engagements with the Apaches, which, in turn, provoked raiding and killing throughout Arizona. Army volunteers and even citizen groups retaliated by attacking Apache bands, usually people who had not previously molested anyone. The Navajos were similarly engulfed by the tide of war. When they mounted punitive raids on whites in 1863, Carleton moved against them with a vengeance. Colonel Kit Carson led the attacks against the Navajos, killing dozens of tribesmen at Canyon de Chelly in 1864 and capturing more than five hundred. Following the fighting, thirty-five hundred Navajos were rounded up and marched some three hundred miles into imprisonment at Bosque Redondo in eastern New Mexico.

In the same year that the Navajos were forced on what came to be called the Long Walk, the Cheyennes and Arapahos suffered a massacre of chilling ferocity and barbarism. On November 29, 1864, Colonel John M. Chivington led his volunteer Third Colorado Cavalry Regiment in an attack on a Cheyenne and Arapaho camp at Sand Creek, a tributary of the Arkansas River in southeastern Colorado. Black Kettle, the Cheyenne leader, had just concluded negotiations on a new peace treaty when Chivington's men attacked. Two hundred Cheyennes died in the onslaught, but, what was worse, Chivington's men dismembered Cheyenne corpses and brought hundreds of body parts back to Denver to be put on display at the local theater. Attacks on tribes by civilian irregulars, however, were even more horrible than those made by regular army troops. In 1871 at Camp Grant, Arizona, for example, a Tucson citizens' group killed and scalped most of the Apache males in the camp, and then raped, murdered, and scalped the women. They took the children to be sold into slavery.

The horrors of Sand Creek led to renewed and even more intensive rounds of warfare on the Great Plains that would last beyond the end of the Civil War. The Cheyenne survivors held a great council with Arapaho and Lakota leaders soon after the slaughter and launched a war against the whites along the South Platte and in the region of the Powder River. In 1865 the tribes sacked Julesburg, Colorado, twice, cut telegraph lines, drove cavalry units back into their forts, and destroyed a military supply train.

The next year General William Tecumseh Sherman took over the direction of the "Indian Wars." Sherman's strategy rested on continued punitive attacks on villages, the destruction of tribal horse herds, and the pursuit of Indians even during the winter months. In maneuvers, the army was to follow the general plan of "convergence." The idea was to send out several (usually three) different forces by different routes who would then converge on an Indian village in a well-timed and coordinated attack.

During June 1866, the Oglala Lakotas Red Cloud and Crazy Horse began to prove themselves the equals of Sherman on the battlefield. An immigrant road, the Bozeman Trail, lined with forts, ran directly through the heart of Oglala land. Red Cloud and Crazy Horse eventually besieged the forts, raided the outlying settlements, destroyed an entire troop of cavalry under William J. Fetterman, and effectively closed the road. After he signed the Fort Laramie Treaty in 1868, Red Cloud did not make war on the whites again. Of Crazy Horse, on the other hand, the whites would hear a great deal more.

During the "peace policy" years of the 1870s, whites continued to encroach on Indian land, and miners were still coming in wagonloads to extract wealth from tribal territories. In addition, the railroads were building across tribal lands and the whites were slaughtering the buffalo herds. Many of these civilian actions had military consequences. The Kiowas and Comanches, for example, struggled to protect their hunting grounds, but military authorities worked to confine them to an Oklahoma reservation. These efforts culminated in an assault on the tribes' stronghold in Palo Duro Canyon, which destroyed their horse herd and forced them to return to their agencies. In southern Oregon and northern California, the Modocs escaped their reservation only to end up fighting for their lives in the lava beds of Tule Lake. In 1876, bands of off-reservation Lakotas, Dakotas, and Cheyennes were engaged in similar resistance when they destroyed the Seventh Cavalry at the Little Bighorn.

Outbreaks continued throughout the decade. In 1877, the Nez Perces were forced to move from their homelands in Oregon to an Idaho reservation whose boundaries had been reduced in response to pressure from local miners. Their desperate attempt to escape this reservation and flee to Canada produced brilliant military tactics, but it ended in surrender and imprisonment. During the next year a group of Cheyennes escaped from their reservation in Indian Territory in an effort to return to their homelands in Montana. Relentlessly pursued and lacking provisions, half of the Cheyennes surrendered to the army at Fort Robinson, Nebraska. The Cheyennes were treated as prisoners,

and when they attempted another escape, more than fifty men, women, and children were gunned down in the snow.

The Apache wars in Arizona and New Mexico continued throughout the late nineteenth century, despite a lull in the mid-1870s when several bands concluded treaties with General George Crook. Under the able leadership of men like Cochise, Mangas Coloradas, and Geronimo, the Apaches had fought an effective guerrilla campaign that took full advantage of the mountain and desert terrains of the region. It was only when the U.S. Army began to recruit and utilize Apache scouts that the direction of the war shifted. Still, Geronimo, who had tried on several occasions to live on a reservation, held out until 1886, when Crook negotiated the Apache leader's final surrender.

Four years later, unrest broke out again on the several Sioux reservations in North and South Dakota, where many were captivated by the Ghost Dance's promise of the return of the buffalo and freedom for the tribes. The movement frightened local government agents, who called for federal troops to quell the "disturbances." The Standing Rock agent even ordered the arrest of Sitting Bull, who was killed during a melee at his home. Another Lakota leader, Big Foot, left the Cheyenne River Reservation with a large contingent of Ghost Dance followers for the Pine Ridge agency. They made it as far as Wounded Knee Creek, where they were surrounded by infantry, artillery, and cavalry units. While Big Foot's band was being forcibly disarmed, a small fight broke out between a warrior and a few soldiers, and a full army attack on the band ensued. Officially, 150 Sioux were killed in the incident, but the Lakotas have always maintained that at least double that number perished.

Although several outbreaks of warfare between Indians and whites occurred after Wounded Knee, all were small and easily quelled. The "Indians Wars" were over.

See also Cochise; Crazy Horse; Geronimo; Little Bighorn, Battle of; Mangas Coloradas; Peace Policy; Red Cloud; Sitting Bull; Treaty of Fort Laramie (1868); Wounded Knee Massacre, 1890.

Andrist, Ralph K., *The Long Death: The Last Days of the Plains Indian* (New York: Macmillan, 1964); Brown, Dee, *Bury My Heart at Wounded Knee: An Indian History of the American West* (New York: Holt, Rinehart and Winston, 1970); Utley, Robert M., and Wilcomb E. Washburn, *Indian Wars* (Boston: Houghton Mifflin, 1977).

TOM HOLM (Cherokee/Creek)
University of Arizona

WASHAKIE

(1804?–1900)
Shoshone chief.

Chief Washakie of the Eastern Shoshones proved to be a forceful yet complex leader who managed the pressures of the nineteenth-century American West, defending his followers against an array of adversaries for nearly six decades. Sometimes criticized for his willingness to cooperate with whites, Washakie was an exceptional warrior, military strategist, and orator. His greatest legacy, however, was his political leadership, which produced both victories and defeats for his tribe—the Shoshones of Wyoming's Wind River Reservation.

The precise date of Washakie's birth is in dispute; some place it as early as 1798. His mother was Shoshone but his father was Flathead, and he was reared with a Northern Shoshone band that resided in the Lemhi Valley of modern-day Idaho. Washakie does not seem to have joined the Wyoming Shoshones until he was about thirty years old. Around six feet tall and strikingly handsome, the young man quickly established himself as a war leader. His reputation as a warrior grew rapidly among whites and opposing tribes. The fur trader Osborne Russell reported in 1840 that Washakie's name caused the Blackfeet to quake with fear. By 1843 Washakie had become the head of a Shoshone band and was perhaps even recognized as the principal chief of the Shoshone camps in modern-day southwestern Wyoming.

Through adroit political skill and effective war leadership, Washakie came to dominance by uniting the dispersed bands of Shoshones into a cohesive entity. Playing the role of a generous leader who distributed goods to his followers, Washakie used resources that came his way to consolidate his personal power. At the treaty conference held near Fort Laramie in 1851, for example, Washakie used the sponsorship of trapper Jim Bridger to gain entry to the gathering. Previously unrecognized by federal authorities, he became a participant, although not a signatory, in the negotiations.

Washakie's true leadership qualities were most evident in the delicate course he pursued in trying to maintain the support of his people while cooperating with the U.S. government, and in keeping enemy tribes at bay. In complex settings where doing anything or nothing at all carried great risk, Washakie was repeatedly able to turn circumstances to his favor. During the 1850s, for example, Washakie cultivated a reputation as a friend to the U.S. Army and the emigrants of the Oregon Trail. In 1859 Washakie's Shoshones received an especially strong commendation from Colonel Frederick Lander, who noted that a "paper bearing over nine thousand signatures" declared that the signatories had been most kindly treated by the Indians. Washakie capitalized on this perception of Shoshone amity by arranging compensation for his tribe's friendship in the form of government annuities and military support.

Not all Shoshones were satisfied with the course that Washakie pursued, and in 1862 some dissidents joined the neighboring Bannocks in raiding emigrant groups. Indeed, rumors quickly circulated that Washakie had been deposed by malcontents. In January 1863, Colonel Patrick Connor attacked a Shoshone village occupied by the raiders on Bear River. The ensuing conflict subdued the group and, incidentally, buttressed Washakie's claims to leadership. Washakie rebuked those who returned from the Bear River defeat, not for the error of their hostile ways but for losing the battle.

In the aftermath of the Civil War, discussions began concerning the establishment of a Shoshone reservation along Wyoming's Wind River. While government agents believed Washakie was willing to move onto a reservation, the chief used his record of cooperation to advantage by noting the dependence of his tribe on whites now that the life of the hunt had been eliminated. He argued that unless the government supplied provisions, the Shoshones could not afford to move to a new permanent home. While the agency superintendent reported that Washakie would accept a reservation in the Wind River Valley, he noted that the Shoshones would require extra protection against attack by both the Crows and the Sioux. The result was a delay in the establishment of a new Shoshone reservation. During these negotiations Washakie also agreed to encourage the Shoshones to farm and to send their children to government schools. Despite these promises, however, the chief is said to have dramatically repudiated the white man's sedentary life by declaring before his followers, "God damn a potato." Ambivalent or paradoxical, Washakie managed time and again to prevail in complex circumstances by convincing those who counted on him—whites and Indians alike—that their confidence in him was well placed.

In 1868, Washakie finally signed a treaty establishing the Shoshone Reservation. This treaty, negotiated at Fort Bridger, Wyoming, reduced the size of the territory originally assigned to the Shoshones in 1862 and stipulated in addition that Washakie and his followers would remain permanently within the preserve's borders. Washakie liked the location of the new agency, and he was optimistic about the future.

During the 1870s, the Shoshones continued to migrate northward to the Big Horn Basin every year to hunt for buffalo. They also joined U.S. Army troops in a battle against Arapahos who had camped near Fort Brown, and they scouted for General George Crook in his campaign against the Sioux. Despite these diversions, however, the Shoshones found reservation life dreary and oppressive. In 1878, in one of the more eloquent statements made by any native on the frustrations of reservation life, Washakie described the reservation as a culmination of tragedies inflicted upon his society. The reservation was a failure for Indians, Washakie argued, and a betrayal of white promises.

The circumstance that occasioned Washakie's lament was a government proposal to settle the Shoshones' ancient enemies, the Northern Arapahos, on the Shoshone Reservation. Washakie resisted the Arapahos' resettlement, not only on the grounds of the two tribes' long-standing enmity, but also because the sparse supplies provided to the Shoshones would have to be divided with the newcomers. Despite these protests, however, the government gave the Arapahos permission to reside indefinitely on the Shoshone Reservation. In the wake of this decision, Washakie again found it necessary to weigh the power of the federal government against the desires of his followers. The chief cooperated, and yet he was able to retain his influence until 1891, when, approaching the age of ninety, he was challenged by Black Coal, an Arapaho war leader whom he had faced on the battlefield in 1874. Black Coal protested his tribe's junior status on the reservation and successfully argued that the Arapahos should be equal partners on the preserve. (In 1937, the name of the reservation was changed to Wind River.) Despite this setback, Washakie remained the reservation's dominant leader until his death in 1900.

See also Arapaho; Shoshone.

Fowler, Loretta, *Arapaho Politics, 1851–1978* (Lincoln: University of Nebraska Press, 1982); Hebard, Grace Raymond, *Washakie: An Account of Indian Resistance of the Covered Wagon and Union Pacific Railroad Invasions of Their Territory* (Cleveland: Arthur H. Clark, 1930); Thomas, David H., ed., *A Great Basin Shoshonean Source Book* (New York: Garland, 1986).

MICHAEL CASSITY
University of Wyoming

WATER RIGHTS

In the American West, most rights to use water are regulated by state laws founded on the principle of "first in time, first in right": in times of water shortage, the oldest water right is satisfied in full before junior water rights are satisfied. In the East, most rights to use water are governed by each state's common-law-based riparian system, in which water runs with land ownership. In addition to these state water rights, the U.S. Supreme Court has long recognized that federal Indian water rights also exist and must be satisfied in the water priority system.

Federal Indian water rights are defined and governed by a body of federal law that recognizes that Indian tribes have unique property and sovereignty rights to the water on their reservations. Generally, the Supreme Court has upheld tribal government jurisdiction over both tribal members and activities on the Indian reservations. And, within the last twenty years, tribes increasingly are quantifying and using their federal water rights, subject to tribal and federal laws governing the regulation of the water. Because Indian reservations were established before most water uses began in the West, tribes often hold the oldest, and thus most valuable, water rights. In both the West and the East, Indians have occupied land since time immemorial and thus have strong ancient priority claims to water for tribal uses in these areas. The state and federal courts examine what water was reserved for use on the Indian reservations, how tribal water rights are quantified and used, and how these water rights are regulated and enforced. Because of the great value of federal Indian water rights in times of increasing water scarcity, Indian water rights are under attack in the courts and in political arenas. The core doctrines of Indian water law, however, will likely remain undisturbed.

Federal Indian water rights are substantively governed by federal law and characterized in three ways: aboriginal rights, Pueblo rights, and *Winters* rights. Federal water rights for lands that tribes have occupied since time immemorial are accorded a priority date of time immemorial and are known as *aboriginal water rights*. New Mexico Pueblo water rights also have early priority dates derived from Spanish land grants and the 1848 U.S. Treaty of Guadalupe Hidalgo with Mexico. Most federal Indian water rights, however, are based on *Winters v. United States* (1908). That decision held that when tribes agreed to the creation of reservations by federal authorities, they made vast land cessions in return for guarantees that certain lands would be permanently reserved for their use and occupation. The tribes reserved to themselves every aspect of ownership and, implicitly, sovereignty not expressly relinquished to the federal government or unequivocally abrogated by the federal government. In *Winters,* the U.S. Supreme Court held that when Indian reservations were established, the tribes and the United States implicitly reserved, along with the land, sufficient water to fulfill the purposes of the reservations. In reaching this decision, the court reasoned as follows:

> The Indians had a command of the lands and the waters — command of all their beneficial use, whether kept for hunting, "and stock," or turned to agriculture and the art of civilization. Did they give up all this? Did they reduce the area of their occupation and give up their water which made it valuable or adequate?

Some courts have held that non-Indians who purchase former Indian allotment lands pursuant to the General Allotment Act (1887) acquire the right to use whatever federal water right the Indian allotment had, with the same priority date as the reservation. Indian lands held in trust by the United States for individual Indians, known as allotments, are entitled to a reasonable share of any tribal water right, computed on the basis of agricultural needs. To ensure that federal Indian water is used primarily for the benefit of the tribes, however, special rules apply to the use by non-Indians of tribal *Winters* water rights on former allotments.

Indian water rights, although created and vested as of the date of the reservation — or earlier, in the case of aboriginal rights — are not quantified unless litigation or congressional action has determined the size of the right. Between 1908 and 1963, tribes' water rights rarely were quantified. In addition, a few congressional quantifications and one judicial quantification were inadequate in that they were not based on standards that would provide tribes with water for all present and future needs. (In water adjudications, water rights are determined with finality and, in the case of Indians, for all time.) The federal McCarran Amendment (1986) waives the United States's sovereign immunity from suit for purposes of adjudicating Indian water rights in state-court general-stream adjudications. (A general stream adjudication determines the rights of all claimants to water from a particular water source.) As a result, Indian water-rights litigation and negotiation abound throughout the country. *Winters* water rights have been found to exist for a variety of purposes, including those of agriculture and fisheries as well as general homeland purposes.

In the case of *Big Horn I* (1988), the first state general-stream adjudication to reach the U.S. Supreme Court, the court found that the tribes were not entitled to a reserved right for ground water, as compared with surface water, in that case; other cases, in which the matter was addressed more directly and comprehensively, have found that tribal *Winters* rights may be satisfied from both surface and ground water. Satisfaction of *Winters* rights from either ground or surface water is logical, since in most instances surface and ground water are interrelated.

The U.S. Supreme Court has recognized that to achieve the important goal of finality in water adjudications, Indian water rights must be quantified for both present and future uses. The most commonly used method for quantifying Indian water rights is the practicably irrigable acreage (PIA) method. This method quantifies the amount of water needed to irrigate arable lands on the reservation.

Big Horn I was the most widely watched Indian water case before the U.S. Supreme Court of its time. In 1989 the court, in a tie vote, affirmed the Wyoming Supreme Court's comparatively large award of 1868 priority water rights to the Shoshone and Arapaho tribes. The PIA method was the issue before the U.S. Supreme Court, but the Wyoming Supreme Court had ruled on many Indian water issues. The final dimensions of Indian water rights are unclear, however, since the Wyoming case continues as part of an ongoing general-stream adjudication, and Indian water issues continue to be litigated in many parts of the country.

Importantly, tribes can dedicate their reserved water, once quantified, for uses other than the purpose upon which the right was originally defined. Thus PIA and other quantification methods are a basis for quantifying but not restricting the use of the *Winters* rights. As noted above, one badly divided court has concluded that certain restrictions may exist on the use of tribal water rights.

In some instances, tribes have been awarded water based on future need although those tribes have no present use for the water. In such circumstances, tribes have sought to lease their water to nontribal users to create needed tribal income. Congress in several instances has expressly authorized such leases, and some case law supports tribal rights to lease tribal water for nontribal use, especially on the reservations. The federal Non-Intercourse Acts, however, require congressional permission for Indian property interests to be alienated even on a temporary or lease basis. Indian rights to lease their *Winters* water have proved quite controversial in the water-scarce western states, because non-Indian junior-priority water users have become accustomed to using Indian water for free.

A debate continues regarding which sovereign has jurisdiction over water use on the reservations, where there may exist state, federal, and tribal concerns or any combination thereof. In *Colville Confederated Tribes* v. *Walton* (1981), the tribe was held to have jurisdiction over federal Indian reserved water rights to the exclusion of the state. In controversies over the Bighorn River, in Montana, the court established a seemingly dual administration scheme that appears to be under judicial supervision, whereby the tribes administer tribal water rights and the state monitors non-Indian and Indian on-reservation water rights, along with off-reservation rights to a stream that flows both on and off the reservation.

Some courts are wary of granting tribal administration over non-Indians in certain areas where non-Indians are the majority. In *Brendale* v. *Confederated Tribes and Bands of Yakima Indian Nation* (1989), the Yakima Nation was found not to have authority to zone fee land areas on the reservation owned in significant part by nonmembers, but to have authority to regulate areas owned predominantly by Indians. On the other hand, the *Walton* decision expressly recognized important tribal interests in regulating both Indian and non-Indian water use on the reservation, regardless of reservation land ownership patterns. Significantly, many other decisions, following the lead case of *Montana* v. *United States* (1981), have held that tribes have sovereign authority over all persons on a reservation, including non-Indians on fee lands, when significant tribal interests are at stake.

Tribes contend that they have regulatory authority over water use by non-Indian successors to allottees, or *Walton* rights holders, because of basic principles of tribal sovereignty in matters that directly affect the tribes' welfare, and because the non-Indians have entered into a consensual relationship with the tribes to share in the use of those tribes' treaty-based water. Also, tribes argue that treaty-based water rights derive from the tribes' ownership—an ownership that has never been abrogated. The U.S. Supreme Court has long confirmed tribal sovereignty in these instances.

The regulation of the use of reservation water and of its quality by tribes, and not states, is essential to pro-tecting the significant interests tribes have in reservation water resources. Principles of sound water regulation compel tribal regulation of all users along a river, not just Indian users. Moreover, tribes have special congressional mandates supporting tribal regulation of water quality on the reservation as part of a national scheme for protecting water quality.

See also Fishing and Hunting Rights; Treaties.

Getches, David, Charles Wilkinsen, and Robert A. Williams, Jr., *Federal Indian Law Cases and Materials,* 3d ed. (Minneapolis, Minn.: West Publishing Company, 1993).

SUSAN M. WILLIAMS
(Sisseton-Wahpeton Dakota Nation)
Gover, Stetson & Williams

WATIE, STAND (DE-GA-TA-GA)

(1806–71)
Cherokee political leader, Confederate general, and principal chief of the Confederate Cherokees.

Born on December 29, 1806, at Oothcaloga, Cherokee Nation, Georgia, Stand Watie was given the tribal name De-ga-ta-ga ("He Stands"). He was the son of Oo-wa-tie ("The Ancient One"), a full-blood Cherokee, and Oo-wa-tie's half-blood wife, Susanna Charity Reese. Watie had an older brother, Kilakeena (also known as Buck Watie or Elias Boudinot) and seven younger siblings: Thomas Black, John Alexander, Charles Edwin, Nancy, Mary Ann, Elizabeth, and Susan. After accepting Christianity, Oo-wa-tie dropped the *Oo* from his Cherokee name to form the surname Watie and was known as David Watie. He gave Stand Watie the Christian name Isaac, and, although his son called himself Isaac S. Watie for a while, he eventually dropped Isaac and became known as Stand Watie.

In 1815 Watie was dispatched, along with his brother Buck, to the Moravian Mission School at Springplace, Georgia, where Watie was baptized into the Moravian Church. Upon completing his education, Watie returned home to oversee the family farm, while Buck continued his training for a leadership position among the Cherokees. Prior to removal, Watie married the first three of his four wives—Eleanor Looney, Elizabeth Fields, and Isabel Hicks. None of these marriages produced children. His fourth marriage was to Sarah Caroline Bell in 1843.

Watie's early career was overshadowed by his more politically active relatives such as his brother; his uncle,

Major Ridge; and his cousin, John Ridge. As a member of the Ridge-Watie-Boudinot faction, Watie became embroiled in the question of Cherokee removal. Watie's "mixed-blood" faction was convinced that the only way to maintain tribal sovereignty was to accept removal to the West. This position, however, was unpopular among most "full-blood" Cherokees, who constituted a majority of the tribe and were led by Principal Chief John Ross.

In 1834 Major Ridge and Elias Boudinot negotiated a removal treaty with the federal government. This unsanctioned sale of tribal land was a violation of Cherokee law and was punishable by death. However, the treaty was rejected by the U.S. Senate. Undaunted, another pro-removal council was called at Running Waters, Georgia, in November 1834. That assembly asked the government to remove the Cherokees to the West. Watie was among the fifty-seven Cherokees who signed the petition, which was the final break between the pro- and anti-removal factions.

In August 1835, Watie was named editor of the *Cherokee Phoenix*, a Cherokee-language newspaper that called for a removal treaty. Three months later, on December 1, Watie left for Washington, D.C., as a member of a pro-removal delegation. While he was absent another pro-removal council, led by Boudinot and the Ridges, convened at New Echota, Georgia, and negotiated the Treaty of New Echota. Signed on December 25, the agreement traded the Cherokee Nation in Georgia for $5 million and a new home in present-day Oklahoma. As soon as Watie returned to Georgia he added his name to this document.

Watie moved to the Cherokee Nation West in 1837 and settled on Honey Creek just across the Oklahoma-Missouri border southwest of Southwest City, Missouri. He maintained a farm there and operated a general-merchandise store at nearby Millwood. Meanwhile, the majority of Cherokees, led by John Ross, worked against the agreement and vowed to remain in Georgia. But by 1838, it was clear that resistance was futile. The federal government had ordered the military to enforce the removal treaty, and the rest of the tribe began to move west over what came to be called the Trail of Tears. An estimated four thousand Cherokees—one-fourth of those undertaking the journey—died along the way.

The bitterness over removal dominated Cherokee politics for decades to come. In June 1839 Ross's followers gathered at Takuttokah near the Grand River to punish the pro-removal party under Cherokee law. The gathering condemned Watie, Boudinot, Major Ridge, and John Ridge to death, and on June 22, 1839, the Ridges and Elias Boudinot were assassinated. Watie barely escaped. With the murder of his brother, uncle, and cousin, Watie assumed the leadership of the Ridge-Watie-Boudinot group within the Cherokee tribe. Another brother, Thomas, was murdered in 1845. Civil war raged among the Cherokees until federal officials intervened and forced the Cherokee Treaty of 1846 upon the tribe. Although this agreement supposedly reunited the Cherokees, bitterness and hatred continued to smolder until the outbreak of the Civil War.

In the decade and a half between the Cherokee Treaty of 1846 and the Civil War, Watie and Sarah Caroline Bell Watie had three sons—Saladin Ridge (1846), Solon Watica (1849), and Cumiskey (1851)—and two daughters—Ninnie Josephine (1852) and Charlotte Jacqueline (1857). Watie also served as the Delaware District's representative to the Cherokee National Council, rising to the position of speaker. In addition, he began his legal practice and was active in the Knights of the Golden Circle, an avidly pro-slavery group.

The false peace imposed on the Cherokees by the Treaty of 1846 ended with the secession of the South from the United States in 1861. Commissioned a Confederate colonel in July of that year, Watie raised the Cherokee Regiment of Mounted Rifles, which he hoped to use to seize the leadership of the Cherokees from the pro-Union Ross. Forced by Watie either to sign an alliance with the Confederacy or to face a Southern coup, Ross reluctantly sided with the South. The alliance was purely one of convenience, however, and in 1862 the chief fled the Cherokee Nation for Philadelphia. Shortly afterward, in August 1862, Watie was elected principal chief of the Confederate Cherokees.

Watie saw action at Wilson's Creek (1861), Chustenahlah (1861), Pea Ridge (1861), Cowskin Prairie (1862), Old Fort Wayne (1862), Webbers Falls (1863), the First Battle of Cabin Creek (1863), and a myriad of skirmishes. Promoted to brigadier general on May 6, 1864, he was given command of the First Indian Cavalry Brigade. He was the only Confederate Indian to achieve the rank of general in the Civil War. Watie became best known for guerrilla warfare. His two greatest victories came in 1864 with the capture of the federal steamboat *J. R. Williams* and the seizure of $1.5 million worth of supplies in a federal wagon supply train at the Second Battle of Cabin Creek. Watie surrendered on June 23, 1865, the last Confederate general to do so.

After the war Watie served as a member of the Southern Cherokee delegation during the negotiation of the Cherokee Reconstruction Treaty of 1866 and as a delegate to the General Council for Indian Territory in 1870 and 1871. However, after Ross's death in 1866 he began to retreat from politics and joined with Elias Cornelius Boudinot, Buck Watie's son, to form the Boudinot and Watie Tobacco Company. Their claim of exemption from the federal excise tax on tobacco was denied in the Cherokee Tobacco Case in 1871, in which the U.S. Supreme Court ruled that congressional action took precedence over the sovereignty implied in Indian treaties.

Tired of tribal politics, Watie longed to return to his home on Honey Creek, where he spent much of his time refurbishing the family farm. While he worked there, his family remained in a temporary home in Webbers Falls. He was at his Honey Creek farm when he died on September 9, 1871. At the time the Grand River was flooding, and his family found it impossible to return his body to Webbers Falls. As a result he was buried in the Old Ridge Cemetery (also called Polson Cemetery) in Delaware County.

Watie left no direct descendants. None of his children married, and all died without issue. After Watie's death Sarah moved to a cabin near the junction of Horse Creek and Grand River. She died there in 1883 and was buried near her home. Nearly a century later she was reinterred next to Watie in Polson Cemetery.

The conflict between Watie and Ross characterized Cherokee politics for almost half a century and continued to influence the Cherokee Nation long after their deaths. The bitterness over removal, the suffering of the Trail of Tears, and the destruction of the Civil War still divide the tribe. The tribal divisions that Watie helped to sustain have been impressed indelibly on the history of the Cherokees.

See also Boudinot, Elias; Civil War in Indian Territory, The; Ridge, John Rollin; Ridge, Major; Ross, John; Trail of Tears.

Dale, Edward E., *Cherokee Cavaliers: Forty Years of Cherokee History as Told in the Correspondence of the Ridge-Watie-Boudinot Family* (Norman: University of Oklahoma Press, 1939); Franks, Kenny A., *Stand Watie and the Agony of the Cherokee Nation* (Memphis, Tenn.: Memphis State University Press, 1979); Knight, Wilfred, *Red Fox: Stand Watie's Civil War Years in Indian Territory* (Glendale, Calif.: Arthur H. Clark, 1988).

KENNY A. FRANKS
Oklahoma Heritage Association

WHITE DOG CEREMONY

The sacrifice of a white dog by the Iroquois has been variously described as a ritual of thanksgiving, an offering for success in war or in hunting, or a ceremonial marking of the New Year. Most accounts of the ceremony tend to support the sacrifice as a "New Year" ritual, a central part of a longer cleansing and renewal ritual cycle lasting several days. The New Year renewal ceremony took place on the fifth day of a ritual cycle that began on the first day of the second new moon following the winter solstice, placing the ceremony in late January or early February. In midwinter the earth appeared to the Iroquois to be in a weakened or dying state, and the migration of birds, the hibernation of animals, and the inability of humans to cultivate plants portended disaster and famine if the forces of restoration were not triumphant over those of the Winter God. The ceremony offered at least one dog to Hawenniyo ("He Who Rules") to ensure that the earth would be restored and that the health and welfare of the people would again be assured. The ritual required that the dog be as white as possible and that it be strangled to death so as not to mar its perfection. Before its immolation, it was painted with several red dots and bedecked with many ribbons of various colors, and had feathers and a belt of wampum attached to its neck. The ceremony required that a quantity of tobacco also be offered to Hawenniyo during the dog's immolation on a newly kindled sacrificial fire. Subsequent to the ceremony, all fires in the community would be rekindled with embers from this ceremonial fire.

WIGWAM

Although often used to refer to the dwelling of virtually any Native American, *wigwam* originally referred only to the dwellings of the Algonquian-speaking peoples of the northeastern woodlands. The word is Abenaki in origin. Perfectly adapted to the seminomadic lifestyle of the woodland people, the wigwam could be easily constructed in less than a day. The typical wigwam was oval and consisted of saplings set in the ground and bent into arches and lashed with basswood or cedar fiber. Crossbars were lashed to these arches for strength. The resultant frame was covered with large bark strips (usually of white birch, less often of elm, ash, or cedar), leaving a smoke hole in the center and one end open for a doorway, which was covered with a hide or a woven rush mat. In some cases the lower, vertical portions would also be covered with woven mats. Long ropes of cedar fibers, weighted on either end by stones, would be used to keep the bark and mats secure. The finished structure could be up to twenty feet long and fourteen feet wide, with walls six or seven feet high and an overall height of fourteen feet at the arch. The sleeping areas were arranged around the central fire and consisted of mats or cedar boughs and animal skins. A storage area was established at the rear of the structure.

Woodland peoples used the wigwam for sleeping, for storing possessions, and as an escape from inclement weather. All other activity was generally conducted outdoors. At the end of the season, the valuable bark strips, mats, and ropes would be removed and carried to the next site. The frame was left standing. When a person died, the body was removed from the wigwam through a hole made in the west wall, since this was the direction in which the dead were believed to travel. The doorway was always to the east so that one would greet the sun upon arising.

See also Architecture.

WILKINSON, GERALD
(1939–89)
Cherokee and Catawba Indian-rights activist.

Gerald Thomas Wilkinson was the executive director of the Albuquerque-based National Indian Youth Council from 1969 until his death in 1989. In that capacity, he spearheaded a number of efforts to address issues facing Indian people, including the reform of the federal bureaucracy and the protection of Indian religious freedoms, environments, and treaty rights. He also worked to improve Indian education and to increase Indian employment opportunities and political power.

Wilkinson was born on February 9, 1939, in Statesville, North Carolina, the son of Virginia and Harold Curtis Wilkinson. He spent much of his youth in Greer, North Carolina, later returning with his family to Statesville, where he attended high school and distinguished himself as a student and athlete. Wilkinson injured his left eye during a football game, and because of medical complications he eventually lost the eye. This loss appears to have contributed to his eventual

loss of interest in athletic pursuits, but certainly did not result in any loss of ambition toward intellectual growth.

Wilkinson attended Duke University on scholarship and graduated in 1961 with a bachelor's degree in history. He later engaged in graduate studies in international relations at Columbia University. He continued his education with study at the University of Limoges, near Paris, where he also taught English. While at Limoges Wilkinson became fluent in French and acquired a broad appreciation for the arts, literature, and world affairs that continued to animate his intellect through the later parts of his life.

It might well be that Wilkinson entertained his first thoughts of devoting his life to activism and change while a student in France. There he became embroiled in student politics and the burning issues confronted by students and people of conscience in the late 1960s. Even though he was a foreigner, he assumed a leadership role in major student demonstrations.

Upon his return to the United States, Wilkinson focused his attention on the concerns of Indian people. In 1968, he became the youth coordinator for Oklahomans for Indian Opportunity, an organization based in Norman, Oklahoma. A year later, he was named the executive director of the National Indian Youth Council (NIYC), a position he accepted without any guarantee of monetary compensation. The NIYC had been formed several years earlier by a group of young, mostly college-educated Indians who, proclaiming a credo of Indian self-determination and cultural survival, sought broad reforms in government policies and programs concerning Indian people. When Wilkinson became the executive director of the NIYC, the organization had its headquarters in a small office in Albuquerque and operated on a shoestring. For some time, Wilkinson lived in the basement of the building that housed the office.

Wilkinson was innovative in his leadership of the NIYC, taking the organization in new directions and employing new strategies. He established a direct-mail campaign that served both to educate targeted individuals about Indian issues and to raise funds for the organization. As it increased its financial resources, the organization took on a legal arm in order to take its battles into the courts. Under Wilkinson's leadership, NIYC attorneys challenged government and private action threatening the environmental security of Indian lands and sacred sites.

Wilkinson encouraged the NIYC to utilize the United Nations as a forum for drawing international attention to indigenous peoples' concerns. The NIYC became one of the first indigenous nongovernmental organizations to gain official consultative status at the United Nations. Under Wilkinson's direction, the NIYC used that status to press for international standards to protect the rights of indigenous peoples and to expose the problems facing indigenous communities throughout the world.

Wilkinson believed that Indian empowerment required native participation in all levels and forms of government that affected Indian people. He orchestrated a coordinated program of voting-rights lawsuits, voter-registration drives, and polling to gauge Indian opinion on issues of concern to non-Indian politicians. In the aftermath of numerous successful lawsuits challenging practices disadvantageous to Indian voters in the 1980s, Indian people were elected to local and state governing bodies in unprecedented numbers. Wilkinson himself also became active in national politics. He was a frequent adviser to Senator Edward Kennedy, and he counseled Michael Dukakis on Indian issues during Dukakis's unsuccessful 1988 bid for the presidency.

Through his extensive writing and public speaking, Wilkinson displayed the passion he held for his work and the depth of his commitment to improving the lives of Indian people. He contributed regularly to the NIYC's monthly publication, *Americans before Columbus,* and his writing also appeared in numerous other periodicals, including *La Confluencia, Akwesasne Notes,* and *Country Magazine.* Wilkinson spent the final weeks of his life working on a book on the contemporary Indian movement in North America. He died of a heart attack on April 27, 1989, which he suffered in the Washington, D.C., office of Americans for Indian Opportunity while working there on his book.

S. JAMES ANAYA
College of Law
University of Iowa

WINNEBAGO

The Winnebago people call themselves Ho-Chunk, "People of the First Voice." They trace their origins to modern-day Kentucky, where groups speaking a common Siouan tongue emerged in the first centuries of the common era. About A.D. 200, ancestors of the Winnebagos, Otos, Iowas, and Missouris began to move northward. The Winnebagos' forerunners arrived in Wisconsin about A.D. 700. Linguistic, archaeological, and oral evidence supports this tale of the migration of the Chiwere Sioux tribes.

Modern Winnebago people first made contact with Europeans in 1614, when they encountered French explorers near the eastern borders of Lake Superior. In 1634, at the time of Jean Nicolet's visit to the Great Lakes, the tribe numbered around twenty-five thousand people. By 1640 it had been reduced to a little over a hundred souls. This population loss was due to three massive smallpox epidemics and war with surrounding Algonquian tribes.

In 1687 a revived Winnebago tribe allied itself with the French in a war on the Iroquois League. When the Iroquois sued for peace in 1697, the Winnebago tribe joined the Mesquakies (Foxes) in two wars with the French (1701–16 and 1723–37). These wars, fought partly to decide who would control the fur trade, had a dramatic impact on traditional Winnebago tribal culture, and in 1728, the tribe's Grand National Council elected Hopoe-Kaw, the first female chief of the Winnebagos. This event caused a split to develop within the tribe, because Hopoe-Kaw wanted peace with the French, and the other group of Winnebagos did not. The factions were reunited in 1755, when both the Green Bay and the Rock River Winnebagos joined the French against the British in the "French and Indian War," the final struggle for empire, which eliminated the French from North America and thus removed the tribe's ally from the Great Lakes area.

In 1776, when war broke out between Britain and her colonies, the two Winnebago groups joined the British. They allied themselves with the British again in the War of 1812, when 90 percent of the tribe left Wisconsin to fight alongside the Shawnee brothers Tecumseh and Tenskwatawa. With the American victory in 1814, the factional split that had developed in 1728 finally broke up the tribe for good. The Hopoe-Kaw or Green Bay group of Winnebagos signed the 1816 peace treaty, while the Rock River group refused.

The year 1816 also saw the breakup of the traditional political structure of the tribe. Before the War of 1812 the Winnebago tribe relied on a clan system to manage tribal affairs. The tribe had twelve patrilineal clans arranged in two moieties. The Sky moiety consisted of the Thunder, Eagle, War, and Pigeon clans. The Earth moiety contained the Bear, Wolf, Buffalo, Water

Spirit, Deer, Elk, Snake, and Fish clans. After 1816 the tribe used the clan system only in religious ceremonies and naming feasts.

With the arrival of American soldiers and settlers in Wisconsin, both factions of the Winnebago tribe signed three territorial treaties—in 1825, 1827, and 1828. When American miners invaded the southern portion of their homeland in 1827, the Prairie La Crosse band, led by Chief Red Bird, went to war with the Americans. The war ended in 1828, and in 1829 the American government forced the Winnebagos to sign their first cession treaty. By signing the treaty at Prairie du Chien, the tribe relinquished further claims to lands in Illinois and Wisconsin south of the Fox and Wisconsin Rivers.

When the Black Hawk War broke out in 1832, most Winnebagos remained neutral. However, because some members of the tribe aided Blackhawk, the tribe had to sign another cession treaty in 1832, ceding land between the Wisconsin and Rock Rivers to Lake Winnebago. In 1837, through government trickery, the tribe signed its last cession treaty and lost all its homeland east of the Mississippi.

The years between 1840 and 1863 were the removal period for the Winnebagos. They were moved to the Neutral Ground in northeastern Iowa, where they remained from 1840 to 1846; to Long Prairie, Minnesota (1846–55); to Blue Earth, Minnesota (1855–63); to Crow Creek, South Dakota (1863–65); and finally to the Nebraska Winnebago Reservation in 1865. During this period of turmoil, the tribe lost some seven hundred people on its own "trail of tears." In 1866 the tribe sold its Crow Creek lands and purchased land in northeastern Nebraska from the Omaha people.

During the allotment era of 1887–1934, the Winnebago tribe lost more than three-fourths of its reservation land. Also, half of the tribe had moved back to Wisconsin in 1880 to form their own political unit. Those remaining in Nebraska reorganized as the Winnebago Tribe of Nebraska under the 1934 Indian Reorganization Act. However, the most dramatic change for the tribe during the early reservation period was the boarding school experience. This alone brought about the almost total destruction of traditional Winnebago culture. Reservation children were sent to schools in Hampton, Virginia; Carlisle, Pennsylvania; Genoa, Nebraska; Chilocco, Oklahoma; and Haskell, Kansas. There they were forced to give up their language, religion, culture, and tribal traditions.

Today, the Winnebago Tribe of Nebraska numbers forty-one hundred people, with sixteen hundred living on the Nebraska reservation. Another sizable community of Winnebagos exists in Wisconsin. This eastern group, which began to take shape in the late nineteenth century, was formed from people who had refused to move west in the nineteenth century, those who had moved back in 1880, and those who had drifted back later on in search of work. The Wisconsin Winnebagos formed their own tribal government in 1963 and now count more than five thousand members on their rolls. In 1975 both groups received $4.6 million from the Indian Claims Commission as compensation for the inadequate payment made to the tribe in the 1837 cession treaty with the United States. The Nebraska Winnebago people voted to put 65 percent of their money into three tribal programs: land acquisition, credit, and burials.

The town of Winnebago, Nebraska, is home to an Indian Health Service hospital, a Bureau of Indian Affairs agency office, tribal offices, schools, churches (both native and Christian), and businesses such as a tribally owned grocery store, a gas station, and the new Winna-Vegas Casino, where 30 percent of the tribe is employed. Most of the people live in housing provided by the tribe. Winnebago children attend St. Augustine's Elementary School and Winnebago Public Elementary and High School. After high school many Nebraska Winnebago students attend the local Nebraska Indian Community College, and young people from both communities attend local colleges and universities.

English is spoken in all homes, but the traditional native language and religious celebrations are on the rise. The tribe is also busy trying to recover its human remains and sacred objects from museums across the country. The Winnebagos also support a community of Native American Church adherents.

With casino money and the new tribally owned Ho-Chunk Corporation, which is buying land and businesses, both groups hope to achieve economic self-sufficiency by the year 2000.

Lurie, Nancy O., "Winnebago," in *Handbook of North American Indians,* ed. William C. Sturtevant, vol. 15, *Northeast,* ed. Bruce G. Trigger (Washington: Smithsonian Institution, 1978); Radin, Paul, *The Winnebago Tribe* (1923; reprint, Lincoln: University of Nebraska Press, 1970).

DAVID LEE SMITH (Winnebago)
Nebraska Indian Community College

WINNEMUCCA, SARAH

(1844?–91)
Northern Paiute activist and educator.

Born about 1844 near the Sink of the Humboldt River in what is now western Nevada, Sarah Winnemucca (later Sarah Winnemucca Hopkins) played an active role in the transition of the Northern Paiute from the independence of pre-contact life to full containment on reservations. Part of her childhood and much of her early married life was spent among the white settlers and soldiers who had moved into her people's country, giving her the opportunity to observe non-Indian systems of education and government. Later she lectured extensively in the East and Far West on reservation conditions, inequities in federal Indian policy, and corruption by government agents. She established and operated for two years her own school for Northern Paiute children near Lovelock, Nevada—an early attempt at self-determination in Indian education. And she wrote a book about her life and circumstances (*Life Among the Piutes: Their Wrongs and Claims*), being one of the first, if not the first, Native American woman to do so.

Sarah Winnemucca was the daughter of Old Winnemucca, a Northern Paiute headman from a district north of Pyramid Lake in western Nevada. Her mother's name and affiliation are not recorded, other than that she was the daughter of Captain Truckee, another early Northern Paiute headman apparently from near Lovelock, Nevada. Truckee served as a guide for various emigrant parties traversing the Sierra Nevada, fought in California for John C. Frémont in his Mexican campaigns in the 1840s, and generally befriended white settlers throughout northern Nevada and parts of California. In the early 1850s Truckee took Sarah and her mother and sister to California for several months, where she had her first intensive experiences with white settlers while living on the ranch where Truckee worked. She would recall later in her book being impressed by all of the material things that she saw, but being terrified of the whites themselves. Truckee, Old Winnemucca, and Sarah continued to feel that some type of accommodation to white ways was in the best interest of their people, although it is clear at least in Sarah's case that she felt that Indian people should direct the accommodation.

Following her initial experiences in California, Sarah learned to speak and ultimately to read the English language through her associations with whites in western Nevada. Largely self-taught, she acted periodically as interpreter for the military at Fort McDermitt in Nevada and at Camp Harney in Oregon between 1866 and 1875. It was at Fort McDermitt that she met her first husband, Lieutenant Edward C. Bartlett, whom she married in 1871. After a few years the marriage dissolved, and Sarah settled with some of her people on the Malheur Reservation in Oregon. From 1875 to 1878 she acted as interpreter there and also as teacher's aide. During the Bannock War of 1878, which involved some of the people of Malheur, including her father, she again worked for the military. With the cessation of hostilities she went to Yakima Reservation in Washington where some of the Paiute prisoners from the war were interned. When their expected release and the restoration of lands to them at Malheur were not forthcoming, Sarah went on a lecture tour in the West to publicize their plight. With her father and her brother Natches she went to Washington, D.C., in 1880 to plead for their release and for the restoration of Malheur with the Secretary of the Interior, Carl Schurz. When that attempt failed she again went on the lecture circuit, and in 1883 expanded her efforts to the East Coast.

Between April 1883 and August 1884 Sarah gave nearly three hundred lectures from Boston and New York to Baltimore and Washington, D.C. She spoke in the homes of many prominent Indian advocates of the day, including Ralph Waldo Emerson, John Greenleaf Whittier, Massachusetts senator Henry Dawes, and Elizabeth Palmer Peabody and her sister Mary Mann, the wife of Horace Mann. Her speeches, along with the work of this group, supported the passage of the General Allotment, or Dawes, Act in 1887. It was also during this period that Sarah wrote her book, which was edited by Mary Mann and published in Boston in 1883.

Although she was defeated in getting the lands at Malheur restored or the prisoners at Yakima released, Sarah's contacts in the East ultimately led her to found her own school in Lovelock, Nevada, on a parcel of her brother Natches's land. Backed by Elizabeth Peabody, a pioneer in kindergarten education, Sarah successfully operated the school for two years (1886–87). However, attempts by Peabody to have the school federally funded came to nothing. Discouraged and despondent over the breakup of her marriage—to Lewis H. Hopkins, an ex-military man—Sarah went to Idaho to be with her sister Elma. She died in Henry's Lake, Idaho, in 1891, at the approximate age of forty-seven.

Sarah Winnemucca, dressed as she appeared on tours to Boston and other East Coast cities.

to their welfare. She was an activist who felt strongly that her people could and should run their own lives without the interference of federal authorities. She tried under several circumstances to show that her ideas could work, but the reality of conditions in the nineteenth-century West ultimately limited her achievements.

Canfield, Gae W., *Sarah Winnemucca of the Northern Paiutes* (Norman: University of Oklahoma Press, 1983); Fowler, Catherine S., "Sarah Winnemucca, Northern Paiute, ca. 1844–1891," in *American Indian Intellectuals,* ed. Margot Liberty (St. Paul, Minn.: West Publishing Company, 1978); Hopkins, Sarah Winnemucca, *Life Among the Piutes: Their Wrongs and Claims* (Boston: Cupples, Upham, 1883).

CATHERINE S. FOWLER
University of Nevada, Reno

WOMEN

Women have traditionally been the "hidden half" in the voluminous ethnographic reporting on the native peoples of North America. The thrust of the reporting by early observers—traders, trappers, missionaries, and pioneering anthropologists—was decidedly male centered and therefore carries a deep androcentric bias. To compound the situation, some tribes, such as the Lakotas and Cheyennes, restricted females from speaking to male strangers. As a result, few outsiders have appreciated the range of activities in which women played a role in traditional Indian societies and little attention has been paid to the world of native women—the associations, rituals, and material culture that characterized women's relationships with each other and that functioned next to, but apart from, the world of men.

When descriptions of women's experience have appeared, they have generally been extrapolations from a small body of data. For example, many observers viewed the range of activities engaged in by Native American women—farming, trading, household provisioning—and concluded that these women functioned within their communities as beasts of burden and as servants of their lazy husbands. Such a view also confirmed the European judgment that native society was "uncivilized" because it exploited women and excused men from the role of principal breadwinner and community benefactor. At the other extreme, writers like the Jamestown settler John Smith projected their own cultural expectations onto women, who appeared free

Sarah Winnemucca was a remarkable woman whose life and works had a direct impact on the course of nineteenth-century Indian affairs. Although her accommodationist positions, and particularly her association with the military, did not make her universally popular among her own people, she nonetheless was dedicated

Five generations of Navajo women: Jenny Manybeads, Blanche Wilson, Mae Wilson Tso, Betty Tso, and Fiona Tso in 1986 at Mosquito Springs of Big Mountain, Navajo Reservation, Arizona. Photograph by Ronnie Farley.

from restrictive European gender roles. Romantics wrote of the duskily alluring Indian "princess" who was free from the restraints of "civilized" society. As a result of these patterns, a polar typology emerged in which Native American women were characterized as either degenerate "squaws" or lithesome maidens. Both images were the products of limited information and substantial imagination.

Explorers, trappers, and early traders were all intruders into Native American society. Newcomers in an alien environment, and living far from home, they survived in large part because they formed alliances with native people and became kin to native families. Relationships with Indian women were an essential part of their strategy. Typically, the explorers themselves and the male historians who recorded their exploits assumed that liaisons with native women were the product of the explorers' masculine charm and wit. More

recently, however, scholars who have examined these formative relationships from the perspective of the women involved have begun to appreciate that native families frequently brought the strangers into their circle as a way of establishing a reliable tie to the power and technology of the outside world. The Crees of the northern Great Plains and the Cherokees of the Southeast, for example, frequently sealed alliances by drawing a white trader or diplomat into one of their leading families. Such ties often had long-term consequences, particularly in matrilineal communities such as the Cherokees', where descent was traced through women and the children of white traders and native mothers could easily be incorporated into tribal life.

Scholars have also overlooked the role of women in early diplomatic relations between Indians and whites. Beginning with the story of Pocahontas and continuing with Mary Musgrove of the Creeks, Molly Brant of the

Mohawks, and modern figures such as the Navajo Annie Wauneka, women have been successful intermediaries between contending powers and cultural traditions. Pocahontas served as both interpreter and emissary in the early years of the Jamestown settlement in Virginia, while Musgrove — sent by her family to be educated with whites in eighteenth-century Charleston — served as James Ogelthorpe's principal interpreter and adviser during the early years of the Georgia colony. Brant brought powerful Mohawk kinsmen into the English camp when she began living with the British Indian agent Sir William Johnson in 1759; she served as adviser and interpreter for Johnson as well as for her brother Joseph throughout the remainder of the eighteenth century. A twentieth-century figure, Wauneka has been a tireless advocate of improved health care for rural Navajos while serving as a steady supporter of tribal traditions and practices. She has used her prominence as the daughter of the tribal leader Chee Dodge to connect the worlds of white doctors and native healers.

Just as male historical actors and scholars have often failed to recognize the contributions of women in encounters between Indians and whites, so have legislators and bureaucrats overlooked native traditions regarding gender when shaping policies for the administration of national policy. As a result, legal systems and policy decisions have often reinforced the positioning of females in subordinate administrative roles. In both the United States and Canada federal governments have ignored native kinship patterns by imposing patrilineal kinship definitions of descent on all tribes. Though this definition is appropriate for the Ojibwa (Anishinaabe) and Sioux (Lakota), it comes into conflict with the matrilineal traditions of such tribes as the Iroquois, the Cherokees, and many Pueblo communities of the Southwest. In recent times many tribal councils that have adopted this imposed patrilineal model have allowed enrolled males to marry nonnatives or women from other tribes and defined their children as "Indian," while at the same time barring female members who marry outside the group from gaining the same status for their children. Caught in the snare of these rules, such children of native women become "white" in the eyes of tribal officials.

In the United States the case of *Santa Clara* v. *Martinez* (1978) brought the conflict between government rules and traditional practices sharply into focus. In this case Julia Martinez, a woman in the matrilineal community of Santa Clara, wished to leave her house to her daughters. The tribal council opposed her deci-

sion, noting that her Navajo husband was an outsider and that by the definitions adopted by this tribal authority in the twentieth century her children were not members of the Santa Clara Pueblo. Pueblo officials declared that their position was not intended to penalize Mrs. Martinez, but to sustain the tribe's right to establish its own membership criteria. In response, Martinez and her supporters argued that Pueblo leaders were simply enforcing a European definition of descent and tribal membership. The fact that the tribe prevailed in the U.S. Supreme Court only underscores the fact that distinctive patterns of kinship — particularly ones that highlight a central role for women — are rarely recognized by policymakers and those who do their bidding. A Canadian case in which native women marrying European men lost their band affiliation is yet another example of this practice. Only in 1985 was this inequity eradicated in Canada (an inequity that allowed European women marrying native men to become full-fledged band members).

Although women's historical experience and distinctive roles have frequently been denigrated or overlooked, it is counterproductive simply to decry the lack of data on women in the ethnographic record. It is possible to extract information from tribal profiles, linguistic texts, and aspects of expressive culture such as folktales and legends to obtain some indication of the differing status of males and females in aboriginal cultures and to explore the distinctive aspects of relations between the sexes within those societies.

Whether native societies were matrilineal or patrilineal or bilateral, male and female work seems to have been egalitarian. For example, many horticultural societies tended to be matrilocal. Men moved into the female's household after marriage. However, among the Iroquois, men cleared the fields for planting, whereas women planted and harvested the crops and were the distributors of produce; females chose the sachems or leaders in civic activities, and clan mothers could remove them for malfeasance.

In the "warrior" societies of the Great Plains "man the hunter" syndrome on the part of ethnographers often obscured the important role of women in the arduous tasks of tanning, preparing tipis and clothing, and processing food for storage. Throughout North America, aboriginal men and women seem to have valued and appreciated each other's contributions to traditional life; their complementary roles seem to have provided both community stability and mutual satisfaction.

Ethnographies also illuminate the beliefs and folk knowledge of a group of people, thus opening a window on the contours of tribal society. For example, *Waheenee,* an autobiography of a Hidatsa woman recorded in the early twentieth century, draws a poignant description of the dyadic relationship between males and females in that agricultural society. She declared that she was a "contented Indian girl, obedient to my mothers. . . . I learned to cook, dress skins, embroider, sew and make moccasins, clothing, and tent covers." On the other hand, she noted that she was not expected to take on tasks "beyond my strength. My father did the heavy lifting, if posts and beams were to be raised. 'You are young, daughter,' he would say. 'Take care you do not overstrain.'" The author of *Waheenee* also noted that her husband insisted on taking on the tasks that required physical strength. When he came upon her struggling with a heavy load, he declared, "That is foolish . . . you will hurt your back." Such personal accounts extracted from interviews give a native female perspective and speak to the complementarity of gender roles in the maintenance of lifeways.

Recent autobiographies such as Mary Crow Dog's *Lakota Woman* (1990), Mark St. Pierre's *Madonna Swan: A Lakota Woman's Story* (1991), and the Haida woman Florence Edenshaw Davidson's *During My Time* (1982) show a number of different patterns. Nevertheless, questions also have arisen with these narratives. Lakota people, for example, raised doubts concerning the authenticity and truth of Crow Dog's account. Davidson's book, compiled by the anthropologist Margaret Blackman, appears more culturally based and methodologically rigorous. These narratives make it exceedingly difficult to generalize about the role of native women in contemporary society, and they illustrate the fact that women's experiences have taken many forms and have been filtered through the experiences of many role models: mothers, aunts, sisters, and grandmothers.

With such a diverse and varied range of living examples, one can also see a variety of ways of presenting the role of native women in caring for children and passing on cultural knowledge. The commonly held and frequently expressed belief that women are "the carriers of native culture" has reached sloganlike status at conferences and community gatherings. As appealing as this theme is, however, it poses some dilemmas for understanding women in both traditional and modern Indian societies. Many native women reject the call

to political activism in the wider women's movement while praising the importance of women in the maintenance of traditional tribal life. Similarly, Indian women are prone to say that their preeminent concern is with community survival—treaty rights, the protection of native resources, and child welfare—rather than with making common cause with other women in the struggle for equality.

In the last century schools and government agencies sought to educate Indian people away from tribal lifeways. Though these efforts were sometimes successful, women have continued to be the principal socializers of children into native traditions and native languages. Whether producing children who followed a Euro-American path, tried to maintain tribal traditions, or sought to be bicultural, women have passed their values on to the next generation. Women who have earned advanced university degrees are often exhorted to "work for their people," to "take the best from two worlds," or to "raise their children the Indian way." Indian women are often seen as culture brokers as well as the primary transmitters of indigenous culture. As a consequence, Indian women—often assisted by men—have maintained the mechanisms both for adaptation and for encouraging the continuity of traditional cultures in the modern age. These complex roles cannot be summarized easily or reduced to a single theme.

Many Lakota women have acted as revitalizers of ritual, as in the Sun Dance, where they mentor younger women in ritual performance. They also advise their peers regarding proper behavior for wives and mothers. Navajo female educators have held puberty ceremonies for their daughters—even if the fathers are non-Navajos. These rites have instilled in the child knowledge of the menarche, which allows the child to make the transition into womanhood with the knowledge of proper sexuality, taboos, and child-care practices. Many indigenous women who become medical doctors utilize native knowledge and collaborate with traditional healers.

In each of these settings, Native American women demonstrate their diverse roles in Indian societies as well as their ability to adapt to new conditions. Their actions also illustrate the ways in which women affect all corners of tribal life and frequently renew community traditions—in a creative and compelling way.

Editors of Time-Life Books, *The Women's Way* (Alexandria, Va.: Time-Life Books, 1995): Medicine, Beatrice, and Patricia Albers, *The Hidden Half: Studies of Plains Indian Women* (Lanham, Md.: University Press of America, 1983); Wilson, Gilbert L., *Wa-*

heenee: *An Indian Girl's Story Told by Herself* (St. Paul: Minnesota Historical Society, 1921).

BEATRICE MEDICINE (Lakota)
Wakpala, South Dakota

WOODLAND PHASE INDIANS

The umbrella term Woodland is a confusing one. Like *Archaic* and *Paleo-Indian*, *Woodland* has a special meaning in American archaeology. It is important here to distinguish the archaeological term *Woodland tradition* from another, quite useful term, *eastern woodlands*. The latter is a geographic designation generally indicating the eastern half of native North America, those millions of acres of primeval forests cut by countless coursing "river roads."

Woodland tradition, by contrast, refers to a widespread archaeological manifestation, traditionally defined by the presence of three key traits: the manufacture of distinctive ceramics, the incipient development of agriculture, and the construction of funerary mounds. Throughout much of eastern North America —including the Midwest, the Southeast, the Northeast, and the eastern Great Plains—the Woodland period follows immediately after the Archaic tradition (which, of course, lacks the three hallmarks listed above). Although their age varies considerably by location, most Woodland characteristics appeared in most areas by about 1000 B.C.

The Woodland people of eastern North America can be traced to their Paleo-Indian roots. At present, most archaeologists believe that the Paleo-Indians, the First Americans, arrived via the Bering Strait sometime prior to 11,000 B.C. The Paleo-Indians of the American West were hunters of large game animals such as mammoths, extinct forms of bison, and the American horse and camel. But in eastern North America Paleo-Indians probably followed a more generalized ecological adaptation, one not as easily disrupted by the disappearance of one or two key resources. As it turned out, this broadspectrum lifestyle preadapted their descendants to the more focused plant-collecting economies that characterized the eastern woodlands during later periods.

As Archaic populations increased, people of eastern North America became more efficient, intensifying their own food-collecting strategies, increasing economic exchanges with others, and improving their ability to store food for the future. In this way, even as their

food-producing economy escalated, they learned to protect themselves against year-to-year resource fluctuations. Inevitably some groups harvested more effectively and produced more food than their neighbors. Others excelled at trade and barter. As time passed, primary access to the more valued exotic items came to rest in the hands of a relatively small elite. In response to growing competition over scarce resources, the older, more egalitarian social forms of Archaic society came to be more rigid and controlled.

The Archaic adaptations at Poverty Point, Louisiana, foreshadowed the creativity that would soon be evident elsewhere across the eastern woodlands. Between 2000 and 1000 B.C., native people began a long-term interaction with local plant species they found growing wild—especially squash, sumpweed (marsh elder), sunflowers, and goosefoot. As people harvested the wild bounty, they usually selected only the best plants and kept only the best seed for replanting. Given sufficient time, such selection would activate genetic pressures for such seeds to germinate more quickly than did those of untended plants in the wild.

The Woodland farmers of eastern America came to be inextricably involved in the life cycles of these plant crops. Their gardens, so informally planted at first, became increasingly significant by providing a dependable, managed food supply that could be stored for use in late winter and even into early spring.

So it was that these early Woodland pioneers initially domesticated the native annual plants of eastern North America. Seasonally occupied campsites, surrounded as they were by organically rich trash deposits, provided ideal habitats for wild plants and incidental domesticates. These new and vigorous seedbeds in turn attracted further human attention. Tethered to the major river-valley trenches, Native American people reoccupied special places and key locales over extended periods of time. As human populations increased, the interaction between people and plants intensified.

Note something special here. Archaeologists once spoke of a "Neolithic revolution," the time when humans took control over nature, domesticating plants and animals to provide a predictable and secure food source and to escape the uncertainties of nature. With the invention of agriculture, the thinking went, the requirements of storing grain created a demand for durable, heat-resistant storage vessels—and therefore, some genius thought up pottery. So viewed, agriculture and pottery were seen as together paving the road to the great civilizations of the past.

Yet no such overnight food-producing rebellion ever happened—at least not in eastern North America. The entire process of initial plant domestication was extremely casual, without any radical change in human diets or human habits. The effects of such incidental plant domestication can readily be seen at a place like Russell Cave (Alabama), where foraging Archaic people lived and worked beneath the cave's huge overhang for thousands of years. Then, sometime between about 1000 B.C. and A.D. 500, the character of Russell Cave changed markedly as the site became tied to the changing lifestyles of settled village farmers.

Just as agriculture did not develop overnight, neither did the manufacture of fired pottery. Pottery showed up in parts of South Carolina, Georgia, and the Florida coastal lowlands toward the end of the preceding Late Archaic period. The earliest ceramic vessels look like flowerpots, remarkably similar to the earlier steatite (soapstone) bowls from the same area. Some of these early ceramic pots were even tempered with steatite fragments, and it is tempting to assume that early southeastern potters were consciously imitating these early stone bowls. Although the evidence is difficult to interpret, many archaeologists think that these early northeastern ceramics were invented locally and then spread throughout the eastern woodlands between 2500 B.C. and 500 B.C.

Russell Cave reflected the changes that characterized much of the eastern United States during this time. Apparently these farming people left their settled villages when food supplies ran low and transformed Russell Cave into a temporary winter campsite. When they quit the cave in the springtime, they probably rejoined other Woodland groups at summer encampments, settlements far larger than any known during the preceding Archaic period.

Like agriculture and pottery, the third defining Woodland characteristic—burial ceremonialism—actually shows up during the late Archaic period (at Poverty Point, for instance). Before long, the funerary-mound complex was to sweep across the eastern United States. In fact, one burial mound of this period stands only a few hundred feet from the entrance to Russell Cave.

The Adena culture is the most visible manifestation of the new American ceremonialism. Distributed across the American midlands to the Atlantic Coast, at least five hundred Adena sites have been documented, most of them dating after 500 B.C. In the early Adena period, burial ceremonialism was relatively simple. The deceased was commonly laid out in a shallow, sometimes bark-lined pit, and a small mound was erected over the spot. During later Adena times the dead were generally interred in more elaborate log tombs. The original mound often grew in size as subsequent bodies were interred and covered over. Sometimes burials were sprinkled with red ocher or other colored pigment.

The Adena Mound, excavated in 1901, is located near Chillicothe, Ohio. Its earlier stage began with construction of a large, subsurface bark-lined tomb containing extended and cremated burials, and continued with the addition of log tombs and more burials. The second stage was composed of distinctly different soil that had been heaped over the dead who were not buried in log tombs.

The famous Hopewell complex (200 B.C.–A.D. 500) was first recognized at a sprawling mound group near Chillicothe, Ohio. This astonishing site initially contained at least thirty-eight conical mounds, most enclosed by an extensive geometric embankment, obviously laid out with great precision. As nineteenth-century investigators began to explore the strange constructions, it became immediately clear that the ancient people who had built these mounds had cared deeply about their ancestors. Not only had they built huge earthen monuments to encase their dead, but their respect was reflected in the magnificent objects prepared especially for the graves. Mica was brought in from the distant Appalachian Mountains, volcanic glass from Yellowstone, chert from North Dakota, conch shells and shark's teeth from the Gulf of Mexico, copper from the Great Lakes. They fashioned mystical and exotic artworks from these raw materials, then placed these offerings inside tombs to memorialize their dead. Unfortunately, many of the Ohio mounds were later mined and looted for their treasures.

Denoting neither a particular culture nor a political power, the term Hopewell is today used to describe North America's first Pan-Indian religion—stretching from Mississippi to Minnesota, from Nebraska to Virginia—as well as the broad network of contacts among different Native American groups in these areas between about 200 B.C. and A.D. 500. For the first time these native people, who shared neither language nor culture, were drawn together by a unifying set of beliefs and symbols. For centuries, the Hopewell network dominated eastern North America.

While the Hopewell people enjoyed a certain degree of agricultural productivity, even this marginal abundance created problems. By A.D. 400 the Hopewell population had grown so large that it threatened to outstrip and degrade its environment. Towns got bigger, and as new communities sprang up, they built on top of the critical agricultural hinterland. No longer was there plenty of unused land encircling each village. Living in sedentary villages became a risky strategy, particularly because the Hopewell people did not store up much extra food. What if the gardens failed? What if the local acorn did not mature? What if a particularly harsh winter killed off the local deer herd, or if the local fish run failed because of droughts or floods? Every Hopewell community experienced, at one time or another, occasional shortages. Starvation was not unknown.

As their new lifestyle posed more problems, the Hopewell people responded by banding into huge networks of reciprocal trading partners. Far-flung communities joined forces, looking to one another for support in lean years.

Exotic raw materials were funneled into regional Hopewell centers, where artists crafted them into fine objects of art that today represent some of the most impressive Native American art ever made. These items were in turn distributed to distant leaders. Food may also have been traded, following established lines of trade.

This so-called Hopewell interaction sphere developed into the first large-scale trade network in precontact North America. It not only forestalled famine but also dispersed tons of exotic items across the eastern half of the continent.

Hopewell culture was in decline by A.D. 400. Although carrying on for a time in a few core areas, the trade network eventually collapsed, perhaps from competition by more advanced agricultural systems, perhaps because a drying climate depressed overall food production.

By A.D. 800 a new cultural development took hold in the eastern woodlands. This new tradition, known as Mississippian, was based on new strains of maize imported from Mexico. Elsewhere, on the Great Plains, the Plains village tradition succeeded the Woodland tradition. In the Northeast, the Woodland lifeway persisted, with great diversity, up to and beyond European contact in the sixteenth and seventeenth centuries. Most archaeologists believe that Iroquois-speaking people developed out of the local Woodland tradition. Elsewhere, as in the Far West, so-called Archaic lifeways continued for millennia, extending into the historic period; in such places, Woodland characteristics never appeared at all.

See also Archaic Indians; Mound Builders; Paleo-Indians.

Keegan, William F., ed., *Emergent Horticultural Economies of the Eastern Woodlands* (Carbondale, Ill.: Center for Archaeological Investigations, 1987); Struever, Stuart, and Felicia Antonelli Holton, *Koster: Americans in Search of Their Prehistoric Past* (New York: Doubleday, 1979); Thomas, David Hurst, "Harvesting the Eastern Woodlands," in *Exploring Ancient Native America: An Archaeological Guide* (New York: Macmillan, 1994).

DAVID HURST THOMAS
American Museum of Natural History

WORDS THAT HAVE ENTERED ENGLISH USAGE

Few Americans, it is safe to say, realize just how frequently they use and encounter words borrowed from American Indians. The English language possesses about one thousand American Indian loan words, mostly nouns. These borrowed words constitute a fascinating chapter in the growth of the English vocabulary. But the rate and kind of verbal borrowing also reflect key developments in white-Indian relations (see graph).

The struggle to understand Indian words began, for English speakers, with Thomas Harriot (1560–1621). This renaissance man ably assisted Walter Raleigh in several expeditions to explore and settle Virginia. Harriot learned a Virginia Algonquian dialect from two Indians Raleigh's first expedition carried back to England in 1584. It is not certain that Harriot went on that expedition, but he did accompany a second expedition the following year, as a navigator, translator, naturalist, and historian. His *Briefe and True Report of the New Found Land of Virginia* (1588) records the first American Indian loan words adopted directly into the English language. (Several loan words had already come, indirectly through other languages, from the West Indies.) Harriot appears to have introduced *cushaw* (the crook-necked squash) and *manitou* (deity) in his classic *Report*.

Harriot's words and other loan words borrowed from the Indians in the early days of English exploration and settlement belong to the Algonquian family of languages. About fifty languages in this family were spoken along the Atlantic seacoast from North Carolina to the far north and across much of northern North America to the Great Plains. Because of their initial impact and great range, the Algonquian languages have

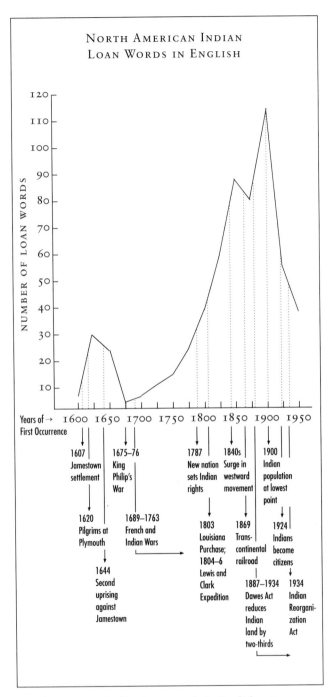

NORTH AMERICAN INDIAN
LOAN WORDS IN ENGLISH

Years of → 1600 1650 1700 1750 1800 1850 1900 1950
First Occurrence

1607
Jamestown
settlement

1675–76
King
Philip's
War

1787
New nation
sets Indian
rights

1840s
Surge in
westward
movement

1900
Indian
population
at lowest
point

1620
Pilgrims at
Plymouth

1689–1763
French and
Indian Wars

1803
Louisiana
Purchase;
1804–6
Lewis and
Clark
Expedition

1869
Trans-
continental
railroad

1924
Indians
become
citizens

1644
Second
uprising
against
Jamestown

1887–1934
Dawes Act
reduces
Indian
land by
two-thirds

1934
Indian
Reorgani-
zation
Act

*North American Indian loan words in English, 1600–1950.
The peaks and troughs of loan-word borrowing from North
American Indian languages generally correspond to historical
fluctuations in white-Indian relations. Borrowing was greatest from 1875 to 1900, but Indian population and cultural
influence were by then already starting to decline.*

provided English with as many loan words as have all
the other Indian languages together.

After Harriot, the next infusion of loan words came
from the voyage of George Waymouth in 1605 to what
is now Maine. He kidnapped five Indians, and his
sailors taught them "some English" on the way back to
England. Words garnered from the Waymouth voyage
apparently come from several northern Algonquian
languages and give linguistic evidence of life in the New
World: *caribou, moose, pone* (corn bread), *powwow,
sagamore* (chief or leader), and *tomahawk.*

The most informative of the early-seventeenth-century travelers to America was John Smith. Still in his
twenties but with experience as a soldier of fortune in
Europe and the Middle East, Smith helped found
Jamestown in 1607. "I be no scoler," he apologetically
wrote his employers back in London. But he plunged
into the Virginia wilderness to meet the Indians there—
a venture that led to his capture by Powhatan's followers and his famed rescue by Pocahontas. Smith's inquis-
itiveness helped him learn enough of the local Indian
language to qualify as a translator for other settlers.

The first published fruit of Smith's efforts was a letter
printed in 1608. In it he introduced *raccoon,* spelling it
rahaughcum. In 1612, Smith published an account of
his adventures, *Map of Virginia, with a Description of
the Countrey*—a thirty-nine-page volume. There he introduced his readers to more loan words, including
chinquapin (a tree similar to the chestnut), *hickory,
hominy, maracock* (a passionflower), *muskrat, persimmon,* and *tuckahoe* (arrow arum root). Other early-
seventeenth-century visitors to the New World recorded words redolent of the continent—*moccasin* (1609),
opossum (1610), and *terrapin* (1613).

The landing of the Pilgrims in 1620 led to no such
harvest of loan words in the early years after their arrival. Four years before, a plague had wiped out the Indians in the area the Pilgrims chose for Plymouth Plantation. Furthermore, two English-speaking Indians
showed up who relieved the Pilgrims of any immediate
need to learn Indian languages. Governor William
Bradford's *Plimoth Plantation* employs fewer than ten
different Indian loan words in that lengthy history of
the Pilgrim settlement. Bradford does, however, introduce *wampumpeag* (1627), or wampum, from Massachusett *wampompeag,* literally "white strings." In a
similar vein, *Mourt's Relation,* an account of the first
years of Plymouth Colony, introduced only the loan
words *sachem* (an Indian chief) and *squaw* in 1622.
The few other new New England loan words of the pe-

riod include *wigwam* (1628), *papoose* (1634), and *skunk* (1634).

Roger Williams stands out as an amazing exception to the tendency of early New Englanders to keep Indians at arm's length. He is best known as the founder of Rhode Island on the principle of religious freedom. But Williams's other great achievement deserves equal renown—a description of the Narragansett people (with whom he had warm relations) and their language, *A Key into the Language of America* (1643). This pioneering work of linguistics introduced into English the loan words *squash, succotash,* and *quahog.* Williams also introduced the names of fish that the coastal Narragansetts caught—among them the *menhaden, mummichog, scuppaug* (later scup), and *tautog.*

A Key demonstrates that the borrowing of words in America was not all one-sided. Williams gives several examples of the way the Narragansetts took over English words for objects they had not been familiar with: *Monéash* for "money"; and *Côwsnuck, Gôatesuck,* and *Hógsuck* or *Pígsuck* for the farm animals the whites introduced.

But Indian resentment at white intrusions had been steadily rising. The Indians in Virginia exploded in 1622 with a rebellion that killed hundreds of settlers. The peace that followed the white victory was shattered in 1644 with another uprising—this one suppressed with a finality that left the Virginia Indians permanently broken as a political power. Then King Philip's War in 1675–76 brought another white victory that ended Indian independence in New England as well.

One result of the bloodshed was a lasting cultural breach between settlers and Indians in the affected regions. The borrowing of Indian loan words by colonists declined (see the deepest trough on the graph). More than a century passed before loan-word borrowing returned to its previous level—and then the nature of this borrowing changed.

Of the approximately ninety Indian words adopted during the eighteenth century, a third are of non-Algonquian origin, whereas *all* previous loan words had been Algonquian. Some of the century's new words betrayed the early thrust of whites into the Southeast—such as the Creek *catalpa* (1731) and *tupelo* (1731) and the Choctaw *bayou* (1763). Others indicated the beginning of northward and westward population movements— *pecan* from the Illinois language (1712), *pemmican* from Cree (1743), *tipi* from Dakota (1743), *Canada jay* from Huron-Iroquoian (1772), and *Seneca oil* probably from Mahican (1795).

With the nineteenth century came the massive white migration west that led to a continent-wide meeting and clashing of cultures. The Lewis and Clark Expedition of 1804–6 set the stage. This expedition brought back, in its reports, words that were a foretaste of more far-western words to come—such as *camas,* a plant of the lily family eaten by Plateau Indians.

Increasingly, Indian words entered English from all parts of the continent. The names of inland peoples used in loan words and loan terms registered the nation's geographical shift. The *Osage orange,* an ornamental tree with orangelike fruit, became known by that name in 1817. The *Navajo blanket* was so called in 1834. *Choctaw,* a derogatory term meaning a strange language, appeared in that sense in 1839. The *cayuse,* a range horse, was named in 1841 after the people living in today's Oregon and Washington.

Cold-weather words reflect white trading and settlement in the north. *Canada,* first adopted as a place name, gave rise to *Canada goose* (1806), *Canada lynx* (1836), and other loan terms. *Toboggan* comes from *tophagan,* a Micmac word for a kind of sleigh (1820). *Mackinaw,* the heavy woolen blanket that the U.S. government distributed to the Indians, acquired its name in 1822 from the Fort Mackinac trading post in Michigan, named after Mackinac Island—from the Ojibwa *michilmachinak,* "island of the large turtle."

It seems paradoxical that the peak period of borrowing occurred during the second half of the nineteenth century. The Indian wars in that period were as ferocious as ever and became more widespread with white expansion. Before the century was over, the American Indians had been defeated and largely confined to reservations—a development that curtailed contact with whites.

But about two hundred still-current Indian loan words entered English in that period, a record number. One reason seems to be that the quality of white-Indian relations went beyond battles and land grabbing. Whites and Indians were trading, hunting, and parleying with one another throughout the West and elsewhere in the nation. Even during episodes of war, Indian scouts worked closely with whites in campaigns against other Indians. More than thirty years after General George Custer's death, for example, Chief Plenty Coups of the Crow Nation still spoke with admiration of Custer, who had been aided by Indian scouts.

The new influx of loan words came from both the West and other parts of the country. What follows are some of the most significant new words, by region.

Pacific Northwest

Traders augmented the loan words that Lewis and Clark had started borrowing from this fertile region. The Chinook Indians lent their name to the *chinook* (1860), a warm, dry wind blowing eastward from the Rocky Mountains. The *Chinook salmon* (1851), largest of the species, became a prime article of trade in the region. So did the *sockeye salmon* (1869), named by folk etymology from Salish (dialectal) *suk-kegh*. Another name from Salish for a related fish is *kokanee* (1875), referring to a landlocked kind of sockeye salmon. Chinook jargon further gives us *potlatch* (1861, as a noun) and *high muckamuck* (1856). The naturalist John Muir noted the *totem pole* as such in 1879. Evidence of a seamier side of white-Indian relations in the Northwest is the word that became *hooch* (1897), ultimately named after the Hootsnuwu Indians, whom U.S. soldiers taught how to make a molasses-based brew. Other Northwest Indian names adopted for plants and animals are too numerous to mention here, but it should be noted that *Oregon,* of obscure Indian origin, was used in names such as *Oregon cedar* (1872).

Southwest

Distinctive Indian words from the Southwest reflected a growing national interest in the cultures there. From Hopi came *kiva* (1871), referring to the sacred room where the Indians held meetings; *kachina* (1873), naming an ancestral spirit or a masked dancer impersonating one; and *kachina doll*. From Navajo came *hogan* (1871), a kind of dwelling. The *Gila monster* (1877), one of the only two venomous lizards in the world, was named after Arizona's Gila River, named in turn after an Indian tribe. The *saguaro* (1856) cactus bears a name probably of Piman Indian origin. *Texas,* derived through Spanish from a Caddo word, yielded several new loan terms such as *Texas bluegrass* (1882).

East

The most common sources of new Indian loan words or loan terms in the East were place names of Indian origin of already existing Indian loan words. But *Tammany* or *Tammany Hall* (1871), as a term for political corruption, came from a once-idealistic patriotic society named after Tammany — or Tamenend, "The Affable" — a seventeenth-century Delaware chief friendly to the whites. *Honk,* expressing the call of Canada geese, appeared in Henry David Thoreau's *Walden* in 1854; it may proceed from the Wampanoag or Narragansett *honck,* naming the bird. *Chautauqua* (1873),

meaning an institution that combines education with entertainment, can be traced to New York's Indian-named Chautauqua Lake, on which the great Chautauqua Institution was founded. The *tuxedo* (1889) received its name from a country club in Tuxedo Park, New York, with an Algonquian name that may mean "wolf." The *Manhattan cocktail* (1890) borrowed its name, of course, from the New York borough that harks back to the original Indian inhabitants.

The number of Indian loan words and loan terms entering English remained high between 1900 and 1909. But borrowing fell off abruptly starting in 1910. Some of the interesting additions since then are *appaloosa* (horse; 1924), *Sasquatch* (1929), *Idaho* (potato; 1934), and *Tex-Mex* (1949). The explanation of why only about seventy others can be counted between 1910 and 1970 (using *Webster's Third New International Dictionary* as a standard) seems to be complex. Among the possible reasons for the decline in borrowing are:

- the attrition of Indian languages, leaving ever fewer potential sources;
- fewer North American phenomena lacking names in English;
- the change from a rural to a predominantly urban population, making the traditional Indian experience less relevant to the rest of the nation;
- an apparent decline in white-Indian communication resulting from the reservation system.

Nevertheless, the *Oxford English Dictionary* and other major reference works are monitoring the writings of modern Indian authors and noting other sources as well for possible new loan words. English, already permanently enriched by Indian loan words, may yet gain many more.

Cutler, Charles L., *O Brave New Words! Native American Loanwords in Current English* (Norman: University of Oklahoma Press, 1994).

CHARLES L. CUTLER
Rockfall, Connecticut

WOUNDED KNEE MASSACRE, 1890

The situation on Lakota Sioux reservations in 1890 was desperate. Promises to increase rations, made by

Wounded Knee, New Year's Day, 1891. The corpses of the victims of the massacre, bloody and frozen, were pulled from beneath the snow for burial in a mass grave.

U.S. officials in 1889 in order to secure signatures to reduce Sioux treaty lands by half, and to create six separate reservations, had proved false. Instead, rations had been cut precipitously, and the people were nearly starving.

Against that backdrop of despair, the millenarian vision of the Paiute prophet Wovoka presented a beautiful alternative. Many Lakotas left their homes in search of a better future through the Ghost Dance. In the badlands of the Pine Ridge Reservation in southwestern South Dakota, three thousand Lakotas, Oglalas from Pine Ridge, and Sicangus from neighboring Rosebud camped together in a remote and rugged natural fortress called the Stronghold. They danced and experienced visions of dead ancestors and loved ones returning, of the buffalo that once sustained them coming back to the plains, and of the disappearance of whites, whose actions had destroyed their way of life. Some believed the Ghost Shirts they wore would deflect the bullets of the whites, but most danced because they harbored dreams of renewal and an end to the oppression of the reservation system.

The Ghost Dance frightened many whites in the region, and rumors were rampant. Although there were no incidents of raiding outside the newly established reservation boundaries, many whites left their isolated homesteads and took up temporary residence in towns. The U.S. government's response to the Ghost Dance was to send over half the entire U.S. Army to the reservations.

The troop buildup was a serious worry for Lakota leaders, who wanted to insure peace. In December 1890, Oglala leaders on the Pine Ridge Reservation, including Young Man Afraid of His Horses, Little Wound, and Turning Hawk, made numerous efforts to bring the Ghost Dancers out of their camp. By month's end, most did come in, making camp near the Pine Ridge Agency.

To the north, on the Cheyenne River Reservation, Chief Big Foot's band, traveling to the agency headquarters to pick up supplies, was alarmed by an approaching contingent of U.S. Army troops. After they stopped to consider whether the troops posed a threat, they learned that the respected Hunkpapa Lakota leader Sitting Bull had been killed the previous day (December 15, 1890) by Indian police at his home. A group of Hunkpapa Lakota men, women, and children, in terrible condition, starving and suffering from frostbite, joined them and told the story of Sitting Bull's murder. Fearing for their safety, Big Foot and his people fled southward toward the Pine Ridge Agency, traveling some two hundred miles over frigid, wind-swept prairie. The military did not find them until December 28, when they surrendered to the Seventh Cavalry under Major Samuel Whitside. As they camped along Wounded Knee Creek, Whitside's detachment was reinforced by troops led by the Seventh Cavalry commander, Colonel James Forsyth.

In the camp, the 106 warriors were separated from the approximately 250 women and children. Their separate camps were surrounded by 470 soldiers and 30 Indian scouts. On a hill overlooking the camp, four rapid-fire Hotchkiss cannons, capable of firing fifty two-pound explosive shells per minute, were trained on Big Foot's band. That night there was elation in the soldiers' camp over the capture of Big Foot. James Asay, a local trader, procured a barrel of whiskey for the troops, and their late-night celebrations kept many of the Lakotas awake.

On the morning of December 29, Forsyth ordered the disarmament of Big Foot's band. The search for weapons added to the tension. Soldiers treated the women roughly and disrespectfully. Captain Charles Varnum reported that one "squaw" was thrown on her back to make accessible the rifle she had under her dress. Joe Horn Cloud recounted how soldiers took off the blankets the women had around them against the chill, raised their dresses, and laughed. The alcohol the soldiers had consumed the previous night probably contributed to the situation. Horn Cloud testified that Captain George Wallace warned him that Colonel Forsyth was drunk and that anything could happen. Searchers collected rifles, bows and arrows, hatchets, axes, and knives. Anything that could conceivably be used as a weapon was confiscated. Even sewing awls were taken.

After the women were searched, and the tipis ransacked for guns, the men were subjected to a body search. About forty rifles were seized in all. What happened next is not certain, but one man apparently refused to relinquish his weapon. Soldiers grabbed for it, and in the struggle a shot went off. Shooting immediately began on both sides. Half of the warriors were killed on the spot. Others ran to rescue their families, and a few broke through the line of troops.

Many women and children standing by their tipis under a white flag of truce were cut down by deadly shrapnel from the Hotchkiss guns. The rest fled under withering fire from all sides. Pursuing soldiers shot most of them down in flight, some with babes on their backs. One survivor recalled that she was wounded but was so scared she did not feel it. She lost her husband, her little girl, and a baby boy. One shot passed through the baby's body before it broke her elbow, causing her to drop his body. Two more shots ripped through the muscles of her back before she fell.

The warrior Iron Hail, shot four times himself but still able to move, saw the soldiers shooting women and children. One young woman, crying out for her mother, had been wounded close to her throat, and the bullet had taken some of her braid into the wound. A gaping hole six inches across opened the belly of a man near him, shot through by an unexploded shell from the guns. Others told of women, heavy with child, shot down by the soldiers. Bodies of women and children were found scattered for three miles from the camp.

On New Year's Day, a pit was dug on the hill that the Hotchkiss guns had been on, and the frozen bodies of 146 men, women, and children were thrown into the pit like cordwood until it was full. The whites stripped many of the bodies, keeping as souvenirs the Ghost Shirts and other clothing and equipment the people had owned in life, or selling them later in the thriving trade over Ghost Dance relics that ensued. One member of the burial party remarked that it was "a thing to melt the heart of a man, if it was of stone, to see those little children, with their bodies shot to pieces, thrown naked into the pit." Besides the 146 buried that day, others who had been wounded died soon afterward, and relatives removed many of the bodies before the government burial party arrived. Estimates of the number of Lakotas slain vary, but many authorities believe that the figure is around three hundred men, women, and children. Not many escaped.

General Nelson Miles was outraged by the deaths of women and children, and he removed Colonel Forsyth from command. Besides the women and children, a large number of the warriors had no firearms. In addition, contended Miles, it would be difficult to conceive of a worse disposition of troops than Forsyth had made. Because of his blunder, some of the thirty-one soldiers lost at Wounded Knee died from friendly fire.

Colonel Forsyth was oblivious to any problem. His report, written on New Year's Eve, expressed his admiration for "the gallant conduct of my command in an engagement with a band of Indians in desperate condition, and crazed by religious fanaticism." The secretary of war evidently agreed with Forsyth, and Forsyth was reinstated, later rising to the rank of major general. U.S. approval of the action was further emphasized by awards of the Medal of Honor to three officers and fifteen enlisted men for their heroism at the "Battle of Wounded Knee Creek." Today, Tilly Black Bear, a Sicangu from the Rosebud reservation, continues to advocate for the rescission of those medals, the most ever awarded for a single engagement in the history of the U.S. Army.

Some historians say Wounded Knee 1890 heralded the end of the Indian Wars. It could perhaps better be seen as the last well-known large-scale massacre in the long history of massacres of Indian people in North America. One of the first was documented by Bartolomé de Las Casas in 1502 on the island of Hispaniola, where the Spanish variously dismembered, beheaded, and raped three thousand Indians in one day. One feature Wounded Knee shared with Hispaniola was racism. What else but race-driven hatred could explain the fact that women and children were slaughtered so far from the camp? Another factor may have been a thirst for vengeance on the part of the Seventh Cavalry. A report published in the *Nebraska State Journal* on December 10, 1890, under the headline "The Redskins Retreat—War Cloud Grows Darker," claimed that the Seventh Cavalry was fairly itching for a fight. "These are the same Indians who mercilessly shot down the gallant Custer and 300 of the Seventh Cavalry on that memorable day of June 25, 1876 . . . and it is safe to say the Sioux will receive no quarter from this famous regiment should an opportunity occur to wreak out vengeance for the blood taken at the battle of the Little Big Horn." That prophetic piece reflected the vengeful mood, and the racism, of much of the country.

Not all the soldiers were bent on the annihilation of Big Foot's band. One Lakota survivor reported that after one soldier, shouting "Remember Custer," shot an elderly woman and followed his action up by shooting a child, one of his fellow troops shot him. Similarly, not all of Lieutenant William Calley's men participated in murdering the 347 Vietnamese, mostly women and children, who were killed in the My Lai massacre in 1968.

Some people retain their humanity. Nations need to retain theirs too. The Lakota people have asked the United States for an apology, but to date none has been given.

See also Wounded Knee Takeover, 1973.

Brown, Dee Alexander, *Bury My Heart at Wounded Knee: An Indian History of the American West* (New York: Holt, Rinehart & Winston, 1971); Flood, Renee Sansom, *Lost Bird of Wounded Knee: Heroic Spirit of the Lakota* (New York: Scribner, 1995); Mooney, James, *The Ghost Dance Religion and the Sioux Outbreak of 1890* (Lincoln: University of Nebraska Press, 1991).

PAUL M. ROBERTSON
Oglala Lakota College
Kyle, South Dakota

WOUNDED KNEE TAKEOVER, 1973

On February 27, 1973, in the village of Wounded Knee on the Pine Ridge Sioux Reservation in South Dakota, about two hundred Sioux Indians led by American Indian Movement (AIM) activists seized control of a Catholic church, a trading post, and a museum near the gravesite of the Lakotas killed in the 1890 Wounded Knee Massacre. It was a reaction to and an outgrowth of the difficulties generally faced by Indians in the United States, but it was prompted by events on and near the Pine Ridge Sioux Reservation.

On January 21, 1973, in Buffalo Gap, South Dakota, a young Lakota named Wesley Bad Heart Bull was stabbed to death, and the white man suspected of the killing was charged with only second-degree manslaughter. The charge, it seemed, would inevitably lead to a blatant and racially biased miscarriage of justice— something all too familiar to Indians in South Dakota. To make matters worse, white law-enforcement officials refused to take the testimony of an Indian who had witnessed the stabbing of Bad Heart Bull or to consider a more serious charge. The situation led to a confrontation between AIM protestors and white authorities in Custer, South Dakota, which in turn led to a riot. Twenty-seven Indians were arrested, and eleven police officers were seriously injured.

As AIM members and local and state officials met nearby in Rapid City to discuss the problems of white discrimination against the Lakotas in South Dakota, a fight between whites and Indians erupted elsewhere in town. Forty Indians were arrested and charged with rioting. Among them was Bad Heart Bull's mother. Her situation seemed to exemplify the double standard of

Members of the American Indian Movement standing guard outside the Sacred Heart Catholic Church during the occupation of Wounded Knee in 1973.

justice in South Dakota. She faced forty years in prison if convicted, while her son's killer faced a maximum of ten years in prison if convicted of second-degree manslaughter.

Meanwhile, the feelings between Indian factions on the Pine Ridge Reservation did nothing to lessen the overall tension of the moment. Tribal chairman Dick Wilson had secured a tribal court order to prevent any member of AIM from attending or speaking at any public gathering. Months earlier he had described AIM members as "lawless" and "social misfits." Wilson, intentionally or not, effectively heightened the rapidly growing tension on and around the already polarized reservation by making sensational threats against AIM leaders and by apparently ignoring the legal and social

implications of the incidents related to the Bad Heart Bull killing. Consequently, AIM was heavily supported by the more traditional members of the reservation's Lakota community, traditional leaders and elders among them. The traditionalists also took the occasion to charge Wilson with the mismanagement of tribal funds, nepotism, and corruption. Wilson's apparent indifference to the Bad Heart Bull murder also created a feeling that the chairman favored white ranchers and nontraditional Indians. In response, Wilson expanded his campaign of intimidation and harassment against his opponents by organizing a group of young supporters locally known as the "goon squad." Meanwhile, Bureau of Indian Affairs officials—both at the Pine Ridge agency and at the Aberdeen (South Dakota) Area office—stood aside, claiming that the disputes were internal, tribal questions.

The Oglala Sioux Civil Rights Organization, formed by traditionalists opposed to Wilson's administration, invited AIM to meet with them. From that meeting emerged a consensus that some type of action was necessary. But a specific course was not initially decided until a few Lakota women suggested that a stand be made at Wounded Knee and challenged their men to take action. The decision to move into the Wounded Knee settlement was taken spontaneously and with little forethought.

After the initial takeover at the end of February, the activists built fortifications and took stock of their supplies and arms. Meanwhile, Wilson's supporters and the federal government swung into action. Over two hundred armed men—FBI agents, U.S. marshals, and BIA police officers—moved in to surround the occupied area. They were supported by .50 caliber machine guns, armored personnel carriers, and helicopters. In comparison, an initial inventory of firearms inside the Wounded Knee compound yielded about two dozen rifles with mismatched ammunition.

Wounded Knee II immediately became an international media event. Federal forces tightened their perimeter around the occupation site, installed tripwire flares, and brought in specially trained dogs and sharp shooters with night-vision scopes. They were a well-supplied, well-armed, largely military-type force pitted against a meagerly armed, sporadically supplied group that included women and children. The parallels with the first Wounded Knee incident in 1890—armed soldiers and destitute Indians—were striking and inescapable. Most Indians were chagrined to see that politicians and government officials from the local to the national level offered self-serving pronouncements on the crisis but few solutions. Of the two senators from South Dakota, only one seemed interested in resolving the crisis fairly, while the other hinted that if the federal government was not able to oust the occupiers, the white citizens of South Dakota would certainly be willing to do the job.

Activists in the village never numbered more than two hundred at any one moment. The insurgents faced cold and hunger, but the supposedly tight perimeter around the occupation site was not particularly effective. The Indians' knowledge of the terrain enabled them to move in and out of Wounded Knee almost at will. Consequently, perhaps as many as two thousand people, mostly Indians, participated in the occupation.

Supporters provided food and medicine; two deliveries were even made by light airplanes landing inside or near the occupied area.

Not unexpectedly, the frequent sniping and gunfire resulted in death. Two activists were killed: Buddy LaMonte, a Lakota; and Frank Clearwater, a Cherokee. Ironically, in the midst of the constant threat of death there was also one birth: a baby boy, a Lakota, was born inside the occupied area.

From the beginning, the activists knew they could not win a confrontation and that it would probably be only the publicity and public support for their cause that would prevent federal forces from completely overrunning them. Indeed, AIM was able to momentarily focus widespread attention on the problems faced by all Indians in the United States. For seventy-one days the group of beleaguered activists captured the attention of the world. Led by Russell Means, an Oglala Lakota, and Dennis Banks, a Chippewa, the group demonstrated the courage and commitment that Indian men and women could bring to a cause, to the point of dying if necessary to bring about positive change for their people.

In the end, the leaders of the takeover signed a "peace pact" with the government that contained stipulations guaranteeing fair treatment of the activists involved in the occupation as well as a fair review of treaties and of the state of Indian affairs. Unfortunately, the stipulations of the agreement were never fully honored, and the Bureau of Indian Affairs did little to fully investigate the Wilson administration. Violence against and persecution of traditionalists continued on the Pine Ridge Reservation for years afterward. But the AIM takeover had great symbolic value. The dramatic setting and stark confrontations brought new attention to the social, legal, and economic conditions of Indian life, conditions that have not yet been satisfactorily addressed.

See also American Indian Movement (AIM); Wounded Knee Massacre, 1890.

Crow Dog, Mary, and Richard Erdoes, *Lakota Woman* (New York: Grove Weidenfeld, 1990); Deloria, Vine, Jr., *Behind the Trail of Broken Treaties: An Indian Declaration of Independence* (New York: Delacorte, 1974); Matthiessen, Peter, *In the Spirit of Crazy Horse* (New York: Viking, 1983).

JOSEPH M. MARSHALL III (Sicangu Lakota)
American Indian Nations Arts and Cultural Organization
Santa Fe, New Mexico

WOVOKA (JACK WILSON)

(c. 1858–1932)
Northern Paiute (Numu) founder of the 1890 Ghost Dance movement.

Wovoka (The Woodcutter) lived his entire life in the Smith and Mason Valleys of western Nevada, though the reverberations from his Ghost Dance religion were felt throughout the Indian world of the late nineteenth century. According to contemporary sources, Wovoka was sick with fever when, while cutting wood in the Pine Grove Hills during the solar eclipse of January 1, 1889, he received his Great Revelation. In his vision he reportedly died and entered heaven, where he saw dead ancestors alive and well and received instructions from God: he was to abstain from fighting; to work for the *taivo*, or white man; and to dance the traditional Round Dance. If he complied, Wovoka was told, he, and by extension other Indians, would be rewarded in the next life. During the vision Wovoka also received twin powers: control over the natural elements, and the political status of the co-presidency of the United States.

However, the inauguration of the Ghost Dance—a term Plains Indians applied to the new religion, Paiutes calling it by their familiar name of Round Dance—did not occur until Wovoka predicted rain during the severe drought of 1888–90. The Paiutes who were farming on the Walker River Reservation, in the adjacent Walker Lake Valley, had been adversely affected by the drought and were naturally interested in this "weather prophet." In his own natal valleys, Wovoka had gained a following by feats reported variously as causing ice to appear in the Walker River on a hot summer day or to fall from a cottonwood tree, as well as by his alleged ability to reenter heaven via public trance states. He also provided spectacular demonstrations of his alleged invulnerability to gunpowder, linking the Nevada experience of the 1890 Ghost Dance with "Ghost Dance shirts" worn at the tragic Wounded Knee massacre of December 29, 1890, in which some two hundred Lakota men, women, and children, many wearing the sacred shirts they believed would protect them, fell under federal soldiers' bullets. A Lakota delegation had visited Wovoka earlier that year, drawn by reports of a messiah promising a new life for Indian peoples. Ironically, the Lakotas' interpretation of Wovoka's message was more consistent with the teachings of the earlier Paiute prophet Wodziwob, or Fish Lake Joe, whose 1870 Ghost Dance religion on the Walker River Reservation

Wovoka leaning against a post outside a bank belonging to his benefactor Joe Wilson in Yerington, Nevada.

foretold the widespread destruction of whites and the resurrection of Indian dead, along with a return to the traditional Indian way of life. Though it is unclear whether Wovoka believed his own revelation to be intended for Paiutes alone or for all Indians, he gladly entertained all Indian visitors, and the vision itself emphasized cooperation with whites in this world and equality with them in the next.

Wovoka's father was named Numuraivo'o (Northern Paiute White Man). Characterized as "wild and quarrelsome" and "wont to steal cattle and horses," Numuraivo'o was most likely imprisoned as a result of participation in the 1875 Bannock War, after which many Paiutes were sent to the Malheur Agency in eastern Oregon. Returning to Nevada with a wife, Numuraivo'o lived past the turn of the century. Significantly, he was said to be a prophet who could make rain and was "bulletproof." His wife, Wovoka's mother, was named Teeya. Described as "very intelligent," she was said to have been a powerful influence on her son. And since Teeya worked for whites, as did Wovoka himself, it is not surprising that a Protestant-type work ethic was part of the 1890 Ghost Dance religion. Wovoka had two other male siblings who survived to maturity. Wovoka's wife was named Mary (or Mattie or Maggie); her tribal name was Tuuma, a Northern Paiute word that denotes a woven basket used for cooking pine nuts. Wovoka and Tuuma had several children who survived to maturity.

James Mooney, of the Bureau of American Ethnology (BAE), interviewed Wovoka two years to the day after his vision and described the 1890 Ghost Dance prophet as a "tall, well-proportioned man with piercing eyes, regular features, a deep voice and a calm and dignified mien. He stood straight as a ramrod, spoke slowly, and by sheer projection of personality commanded the attention of any listener. He visibly stood out among his fellow Indians like a thoroughbred among a bunch of mustangs." Wovoka's English name, Jack Wilson, was taken from the family name of the original settlers of Mason Valley: David and Abigail Wilson. The young Paiute was raised on the Wilsons' ranch and developed a close friendship with their sons. It was while cutting wood for a mine the Wilsons owned in Pine Grove that Wovoka had his vision. Exposure to the Wilsons' frontier brand of Presbyterianism, which included prayers before meals and daily Bible readings as well as "saddlebag preachers" who conducted revivalistic camp meetings, presumably influenced both the form and ideology of the 1890 Ghost Dance in Nevada. For example, an Indian agent reported that "at least 200 Indians to say nothing of the squaws and papooses [who] turned out yesterday [on the Walker River Reservation] in the face of a driving snow storm to see and hear him . . . took up a collection of $25 for his benefit . . . and they talk of nothing but Jack Wilson and the miracles he performs."

Discredited by local whites as a fraud, subject to threats of violence from his own people, and probably disturbed by the reinterpretation placed on his religion by Lakota and other Plains Indians, Wovoka broke off proselytizing in 1891 or 1892. "Jack Wilson is in Mason Valley on a rabbit hunt, and seemingly happy," another Indian agent wrote in 1902. In contrast to his predecessor Wodziwob, however, Wovoka continued to

believe in his vision, entertaining visitors from all over the country practically until his death. For the remainder of his life, Wovoka supported himself by selling eagle and magpie tail feathers, red ocher, and ten-gallon Stetsons such as those he wore in the many remunerated photographs taken of him. Followers nationwide believed that these items had healing powers. He also received payment locally for his services as a shaman. In addition, the retired prophet traveled frequently. He went to Oklahoma in 1906 and 1916, for example, and returned with suitcases full of gifts such as buckskin suits and gloves.

In the twentieth century, Wovoka's efforts to obtain land were twice rebuffed by the government. In 1912 he apparently failed to receive an allotment on the Walker River Reservation. The Indian agent wrote: "You wanted land here and I thought it would be a good thing as we could work together, and help each other, I have been holding land for you and wrote you long time ago to come over, but if you do not come pretty soon I will give it to someone else." And in May 1916 his claim of a five-acre plot on the Wilson ranch resulted in this letter from a county clerk: "Mr. Dyer [Robert Dyer, the brother of Ed Dyer, the owner of a grocery store in nearby Yerington; Ed Dyer, who spoke Paiute, interpreted for the BAE's Mooney, and subsequently became Wovoka's business partner and amanuensis] does not know of your ever having title to any land, but says that the Wilson Bros. allowed you the use of some of their land."

The political repercussions of the 1890 Ghost Dance religion never entirely disappeared. Its prophet was reported to be thinking of assisting President Wilson during the First World War by freezing the Atlantic and sending Indians over to fight the Germans with ice. Wovoka also apparently threatened to quell an Indian incident in Utah "with a word." Other political activities of his included joining the local temperance movement, participating in Warren G. Harding's presidential campaign, and sending a telegram in 1929 to Herbert Hoover's newly elected vice president, Charles Curtis, congratulating the Kaw politician on his achievement while extending the hope that "someday you will be president."

Two other prophecies of Wovoka's are part of his legacy. In the first, he told his grandson that he would "one day fly in the sky" and be a "captain of men." The boy, who grew up to become Captain Harlyn Vidovich of the Flying Tigers, was shot down over China in 1944 while flying against the Japanese. Wovoka's second prediction was that an earthquake would occur following his death, as a sign that he had reentered heaven. According to the coroner's report, Wovoka died on September 29, 1932, at age seventy-four, of "enlarged prostate cystitis." The earthquake that rocked the Smith and Mason Valleys three months later is believed by his descendants today to have been a fulfillment of that prophecy.

See also Ghost Dance.

Dangberg, Grace, "Letters to Jack Wilson, the Paiute Prophet," in *Anthropological Papers,* Smithsonian Institution, Bureau of American Ethnology Bulletin 164 (Washington, D.C.: 1957); Hittman, Michael, *Wovoka and the Ghost Dance: A Sourcebook* (Carson City, Nev.: Grace Dangberg, 1990); Mooney, James, "The Ghost Dance Religion and the Sioux Outbreak of 1890," 14th *Annual Report of the Bureau of American Ethnology,* part 2 (Washington, D.C., 1896).

MICHAEL HITTMAN
Long Island University

WYANDOT
See Huron/Wyandot.

YAKAMA

Before the arrival of humans, the Wahteetash (Plant and Animal People) put the world into motion and prepared life for the Yakamas. Spilyáy (Coyote) was a primary actor in the creative drama, establishing "laws" by causing the first camas, kouse, bitterroots, and other roots to grow, directing the salmon to travel upriver each spring to spawn, separating certain mountains into singular formations, destroying destructive monsters that ruled the rivers and lands, and establishing rules through which humans could learn to behave. Traditional Yakama Indian "law" is based on lessons learned from the Wahteetash and Indian interaction with these people.

Yakama Indians (who changed the spelling of their name from Yakima to Yakama in 1994) speak the Sahaptin language. Salish-speaking Indian neighbors along the Columbia River called the people who lived along the Yakima River *Yah-ah-ka-ma* ("A Growing Family"), but Yakamas say their tribal name is a Sahaptin word meaning "the Pregnant Ones." Yakama people were divided into two major groups: the Lower Yakamas, *Waptailmin* ("Narrow River People"), and the Upper Yakamas, *Pswanwapum* ("Stony Rock People"). Most Yakamas did not view themselves as members of a "tribe" but identified with their village.

The Yakamas shared a common culture with many Indians living on the Columbia Plateau of present-day Washington, Oregon, and Idaho. They lived through a seasonal round that took them to different areas of the plateau at different times of the year. Throughout the winter, people lived in villages constructed of A-frame tule-mat lodges along inland rivers. In March they traveled (by horse after about 1750) to root grounds, visiting and camping with other Indians until May or June, by which time the salmon had begun to move up the Columbia River. Then Yakamas moved to their fisheries along the lower Columbia, harvesting and preserving salmon in great numbers. In the fall they hunted and gathered berries in the Cascade Mountains, drying their foods for the winter. Yakamas gave thanks for the foods through sacred rituals that tied them to the Creation. This was and is a critical element of their religion.

In 1805 Yakamas met Meriwether Lewis and William Clark at Quosispah, a village near the junction of the Yakima and Columbia Rivers. Less than a year later the British trapper David Thompson traveled down the Columbia. British and American fur trappers introduced manufactured goods to Yakamas, and the Catholic missionary Charles Pandosy instructed the people in Christianity. Yakamas refused to join their Cayuse Palouse neighbors to the south in fighting Oregon volunteers during the Cayuse War (1848). The Yakamas became concerned about the intentions of the United States after 1853, when the government separated Washington Territory from Oregon Territory and Isaac I. Stevens became governor of Washington Territory and Superintendent of Indian Affairs.

In 1854–55 Stevens liquidated Indian title to thousands of acres and created reservations in western Washington. On June 9, 1855, he concluded the Yakama Treaty, but not without opposition from Chief Kamiakin. The treaty created the Yakama Reservation and directed Indians from fourteen tribes and bands—speaking three distinct languages—to remove to the reservation. Kamiakin opposed the agreement and reservation. When miners discovered gold north of the Spokane River, whites invaded the inland Northwest through Yakama lands. After miners killed and raped Yakama people, the Yakama leader Qualchin killed the culprits. Learning of these deaths, the Indian agent Andrew Jackson Bolon rode into Yakama territory, but Kamiakin's brother Skloom warned Bolon that his life was in danger. A few Yakamas killed Bolon at Whak-Shum, triggering the Yakima War (1855–58). In 1858 Colonel George Wright executed the Yakama chiefs Owhi and Qualchin as well as several warriors, ending the war.

Most Yakamas removed to the reservation, but some filed for off-reservation homesteads. In the twentieth century, Yakamas lost all of their homesteads. Life on the Yakama Reservation was precarious. James Wilbur and other agents ruled the reservation like big-city bosses, dictating policies designed to "civilize" and Christianize. The Office of Indian Affairs established a school at Fort Simcoe to assimilate and acculturate Indian boys and girls into white society, jailing recalcitrant parents. Agents forced Indians to cultivate wheat, corn, and oats. Yakamas eagerly raised horses and cattle, but farmed grudgingly. Many continued to fish, hunt, and gather, but with great difficulty.

Non-Indian ranchers and farmers "settled" former Yakama lands. In 1894 P. McCormick began allotting the reservation into eighty-acre parcels. By 1914, 4,506 tribal members retained 440,000 acres (over half of it owned today by non-Indians), with another 780,000 acres tribally owned. During the twentieth century, nearly all agricultural lands fell out of Indian ownership, and government agencies and private companies threatened to take all Indian water. Whites allowed their animals to graze on roots and berries. Their plows destroyed plant and animal habitats, and irrigation projects destroyed salmon runs on the Yakima River. At the expense of Native Americans, state, federal, and county governments supported development, including ranching and the building of roads and railroads as well as the huge Wapato Development Project. Wapato, Toppenish, and other towns emerged on lands purchased from Indian allotments. Whites pressured government authorities to limit the movement of Yakamas on the Columbia Plateau. Yakamas also lost access to territories rich in roots and berries as well as to fishing and hunting lands.

Their confinement to the reservation contributed to ill health, anomie, alcoholism, and other problems among the Yakamas. Tuberculosis, pneumonia, and gastrointestinal disorders killed hundreds of Yakamas, particularly infants. Death rates and infant-mortality rates for the Yakamas skyrocketed in comparison to the rates for other U.S. populations until after World War II, when heart disease, suicide, and diabetes became the leading causes of death among the Yakamas. Politically, the Yakamas refused to participate in the Indian Reorganization Act and instead organized the Confederated Tribes of the Yakama Nation. The Yakama Nation has committees dealing with timber, grazing, housing, education, cultural-resource management, roads, recreation, farming, irrigation, health, and wildlife management.

Since World War II, the Yakamas have emphasized self-determination and economic development. The United States recognized Yakima fishing rights in 1855, but state and county officials opposed native fishing rights. As a result of *United States* v. *Winans* (1905), *Sohappy* v. *Smith* (1969), *United States* v. *State of Washington* (1974), and other legal battles, the government reaffirmed aspects of Yakama fishing rights. The tribe maintains and manages 1,118,149 acres, including 600,000 acres of valuable timber. It owns its own furniture business and enjoys 15,000 acres of cultivated tribal farmland. In addition, the tribe irrigates 90,000 acres of Indian-owned lands from the Wapato Project and leases acreage to non-Indians for farming and grazing. The people support their own police force and tribal court. They stress academic excellence, providing scholarships to gifted students. Each summer the Yakamas sponsor Camp Chaparral, motivating their children to continue their education yet maintain their native identity.

The Yakamas proudly retain many aspects of their culture. The Yakama dialect of Sahaptin is taught in public schools for children and in adult education classes. On June 9, 1980, the Yakama Nation opened its Cultural Heritage Center, complete with museum, library, gift shop, restaurant, theater, meeting hall, lodge, and offices. The culture center hosts numerous tribal projects designed to maintain traditional language, literature, crafts, history, arts, skills, and so forth. Yakama people host numerous powwows and celebrations throughout the year as well as sporting events such as rodeos, basketball tournaments, and softball games. More important, Yakama people worship in many ways, remembering the great powers surrounding their homeland. Some participate in First Foods celebrations, partaking of salmon, roots, and berries in sacred rituals. Some worship at the three longhouses located on the reservation, while others participate in the Feather religion. Other Yakamas are members of Christian faiths, including the Indian Shaker Church. Páhto, their sacred mountain (known to Euro-Americans as Mount Adams), towers over nearly eight thousand members of the Yakama Nation, comprising men, women, and children of fourteen tribes and bands, including the Yakamas.

See also Kamiakin.

Schuster, Helen H., *Yakima* (New York: Chelsea House Publishers, 1990); Trafzer, Clifford E., and Richard D. Scheuerman, *Renegade Tribe: The Palouse Indians and the Invasion of the Inland Pacific Northwest* (Pullman: Washington State University Press, 1986).

CLIFFORD E. TRAFZER (Wyandot)
University of California at Riverside

YELLOWTAIL, ROBERT

(1889?–1988)
Crow political leader and reservation superintendent.

Robert Summers Yellowtail was born about four miles south of Lodge Grass, Montana, in 1889—or perhaps two years earlier, if some church records found in the last years of his life are accurate. Yellowtail was a member of the Whistling Water clan, and his paternal clansmen were of the Big Lodge clan.

Robert Yellowtail's father, Yellowtail, was a Crow and his mother, Elizabeth "Lizzie" Frazee Chienne, was descended from Crows and a French Canadian fur trader named Pierre DeChienne. As a child, Yellowtail attended the Catholic church and later the Crow Indian Baptist church in Lodge Grass, but as an adult he would go to all six Christian churches in town and participate in the Crow tribal religious activities as well. Yellowtail was taken from home at the age of four and put into the Crow Agency boarding school. After completing most or all of grade school, he transferred to the Sherman Institute boarding school in Riverside, California. He completed high school there in about 1907 and remained in Riverside, studying law.

Soon after he returned home from California in 1910, Yellowtail became involved with the first Crow Business Committee. When the business committee reformed in 1918, he was not only one of the representatives from the Wyola district, but also the committee's secretary. However, more significant than his business-committee involvement—and instrumental to his achieving the first great success of his political career—were his efforts, along with those of several of the old-time chiefs and other young men, to defeat the attempts of Montana congressmen to open the Crow Reservation to general homesteading.

Serving as an interpreter for the old chiefs and perhaps increasingly as a spokesman in his own right, Yellowtail traveled to Washington, D.C., with Crow delegations each time the bill came up in hearings in 1915, 1916, and 1917. When the Montana delegation would propose the general opening of the reservation, the Crow delegation would counter with offers to divide up the remaining Crow communal lands by allotting most of them among tribal members. After the congressional committee studying the proposed bill voted at the end of the 1917 hearings not to send the bill to the Senate, it asked the Crows to prepare their own bill. The Crow delegates, including Yellowtail, worked with Senator Thomas Walsh and the Indian Office on what would become the 1920 Crow Act, which divided unallotted land.

In the period from the passage of the Crow Act until 1934, Yellowtail was active in tribal politics. He also continued to be involved in national politics, serving on the Indian Office's "Committee of 100" and making a run for a seat in Congress as an independent in 1926. During this period he also concentrated on developing his ranching and farming interests.

Yellowtail's career shifted dramatically in 1934, when he was appointed superintendent of his own reservation by Commissioner of Indian Affairs John Collier. Though the Crows accepted the appointment of Yellowtail as superintendent, they did not accept the centerpiece of Collier's new Indian policy, the Indian Reorganization Act of 1934 (IRA). Documentary evidence strongly suggests that Yellowtail vigorously supported the act as a way to consolidate and end the loss of remaining Crow land. However, oral history indicates that he opposed the act because he felt that the general-council political system and the Crow Act itself served the needs of the Crows and protected the Crows better than would the IRA.

Yellowtail began to implement new programs soon after he assumed the superintendency in the fall of 1934. He brought in different types and breeds of horses and cattle to strengthen Crow livestock and secured permission to transplant bison and elk from Yellowstone National Park to the reservation.

As superintendent, Yellowtail controlled leasing on the reservation. He worked with and helped the larger lessees, viewing this policy as cooperation for effective governance. Yellowtail's critics charge that he compromised the interests of his people and often gained advantages for himself—that he worked mainly for his own interests. His acquisition of a fine ranch only increased suspicion and jealousy.

Support for Yellowtail on the reservation was greater than opposition, however, particularly from the many Crows who benefited from the programs brought in under his administration. Beginning in 1935, activities took place over the entire reservation, such as the building of reservoirs, roads, and mountain trails. His tenure also saw the emergence of logging, the improvement of health care, the introduction of the Shoshone Sun Dance, and the revival of the annual Crow Fair. During this period Yellowtail also introduced initiatives to increase agricultural activities and ranching. Though some improvements were made, the vast majority of land was still leased and the reservation economy controlled by whites.

Yellowtail resigned the superintendency in 1945 but remained a prominent reservation figure. The extent and nature of his role in the formation, writing, and passage of the 1948 Crow tribal constitution is unclear. He himself stated that he wrote it. Regardless of authorship, it is clear that the constitution advocated by Robert Yellowtail was the one that was adopted by the Crows.

Robert Yellowtail was elected tribal chairman in 1952, when he was in the midst of leading the fight against a proposed dam on the Bighorn River. In 1944, Congress had authorized the construction of the dam for purposes of irrigation and hydroelectric power. Many Crows were opposed to it because it would flood beautiful mountain valleys. In 1951, the government began in earnest to pressure the Crows to agree to the construction of the dam. By this time, people had begun referring to the project as Yellowtail Dam in spite of the opposition to the dam by Yellowtail—its greatest enemy. The tribe began to divide over the project: Mountain Crows, led by Yellowtail, opposed any sale of land, and River Crows favored it.

In 1955, the Mountain Crows proposed to lease the dam site for fifty years, whereas the River Crows proposed a sale for $5 million. In January 1956, the Mountain Crow resolution was defeated in tribal council and the River Crow resolution passed. Congress authorized a $5-million tax-free payment to the Crows, but President Eisenhower vetoed this action. The Montana delegation introduced it again in 1957 but accepted an amendment lowering the payment to $2.5 million with the right to sue for additional compensation. The president signed this agreement into law on July 15, 1958. Yellowtail Dam was completed in 1964.

After he resigned as superintendent, Yellowtail began ranching nearly full-time. He continued to be involved in politics until nearly the end of his life, though after the Yellowtail Dam issue he reduced his level of activity and began to enjoy life as an elder statesman. Yellowtail died on June 18, 1988, at his home on the Little Horn Ranch south of Lodge Grass. A tough old fighter to the last, he had refused offers to move him to an old-age institution in his last years and died as he wished, only yards away from where he had been born on the Little Bighorn River.

See also Crow; Indian-White Relations in the United States, 1900 to the Present.

Bradley, Charles Crane, Jr., *The Handsome People: A History of the Crow Indians and the Whites* (Billings, Mont.: Council for Indian Education, 1991); Hoxie, Frederick E., *Parading through History: The Making of the Crow Nation in America, 1805–1935* (New York: Cambridge University Press, 1995); Poten, Constance J., "Robert Yellowtail, the New Warrior," *Montana; the Magazine of Western History* 39, no. 3 (summer 1989): 36–41.

TIM BERNARDIS
Little Big Horn College
Crow Agency, Montana

YUMA (QUECHAN)

The Yumas, or Quechans (kwuh-TSANS), as they prefer to be called, probably lived in their present locale at the confluence of the lower Colorado and Gila Rivers before Spanish explorers arrived in 1540. They trace their original home to a sacred mountain, Avikwamé (near Needles, California). After being taught vital skills by their creator's son, they moved southward to the confluence. Well before the Spanish intrusions this was a strategic spot, a relatively narrow river crossing, giving those who controlled it an important role in trade between the Pacific Coast and the interior. Spaniards, then Mexicans, then Euro-Americans grappled with the Quechans for control of the crossing. In 1852 the U.S. Army finally fought the people and starved them into submission.

Historically, in the fall, winter, and spring the Quechans lived in as many as six settlements or rancherias, located on high ground, away from the river's flooding. After the late spring floods receded, extended families fanned out from the rancherias to plant corn, beans, squash, and grasses in the cracks of the drying silt. Wild plants, especially mesquite beans, and fish made up about half of their yearly diet. Each rancheria had its own leaders and a distinct identity. Several hundred people lived in each. In 1774 Spaniards estimated that one of the largest, Xuksíl, about eleven miles below the confluence, contained about eight hundred people.

For major warfare and for rituals of harvest or mourning the rancherias came together to form the Quechan "tribal" group. Depending on the purpose of the gathering, the group was then led by gifted benevolent ritualists (called *kwaxót*) or by wise, brave warriors (*kwanamí*). Each person also belonged to a patrilineal clan having totemic references (e.g., Corn, Snake,

Frog). Clans once may have performed as distinctive units in tribal mourning rituals. Men could not marry women from their own clan. Most Quechans today know their clan affiliation, but many now say it is "just a name."

There was—and is—an active belief in a special individual power that comes through dreams. There was also a tribal power, one that could be enhanced by taking enemy scalps in battle. The power of war and the importance of mourning were combined themes in the major tribal mourning ceremony, the *karúk*, which featured a mock battle and the cremation of effigies of deceased loved ones; it is infrequently performed today. The Quechans are currently trying to ensure that their ritual knowledge does not become irretrievably lost.

The Quechans have continually fought to retain their land. In 1884 the dispersed rancheria groups were amalgamated within a forty-five-thousand-acre reservation along the Colorado. By 1950 all but about eighty-five hundred acres had been taken or sold by the federal government. Through long-term legal action, plus some aggressive confrontations with non-Indians in 1960 and 1972, the Quechans regained twenty-five thousand acres in 1978—unfortunately, without the tract's rights to vital river water.

The Quechans' struggle for land has coexisted with a sophisticated quest for federal moneys and programs for community development. A seven-member council oversees tribal housing, employment, health, education, and business ventures (including two trailer parks). Most of the arable acreage on the reservation is leased to non-Quechan farmers. About half of the three thousand tribal members live on the reservation, their home sites scattered on ten-acre tracts allotted to their elders in 1912.

See also Water Rights.

Bee, Robert L., *Crosscurrents along the Colorado* (Tucson: University of Arizona Press, 1981); Bee, Robert L., *The Yuma* (New York: Chelsea House, 1989); Forbes, Jack D., *Warriors of the Colorado* (Norman: University of Oklahoma Press, 1965).

ROBERT L. BEE
University of Connecticut

ZITKALA ŠA (GERTRUDE BONNIN)

(1876–1938)

Yankton Sioux author, musician, and political activist.

Gertrude Simmons was born to Ellen Simmons, a Yankton Nakota woman, and a white trader. She was raised by her mother, who gave the child the last name of another of her husbands and instilled in Gertrude a distrust of the "heartless paleface." At the age of eight, and speaking no English, Gertrude was enticed to leave her mother's home in South Dakota by the promise of "red, red apples" at the Quaker-sponsored White's Indian Manual Labor Institute in Wabash, Indiana. She continued her schooling at Earlham College, in Richmond, Indiana, where she developed prize-winning skills as an orator and a musician.

Hired in 1898 by Colonel Richard H. Pratt to teach at the Carlisle Indian Industrial School in Carlisle, Pennsylvania, she found her education and literacy leading to an estrangement from her mother and her people. She recounted these tensions in a series of autobiographical articles published under her self-given Lakota name, Zitkala Ša (Red Bird), in the *Atlantic Monthly* (1900 and 1902), *Harper's Magazine* (1901), and *Everybody's Magazine* (1902); these articles were later collected and published as *American Indian Stories* (1921). The articles, particularly the essay titled "Why I Am a Pagan" (retitled "The Great Spirit" in *American Indian Stories*), revealed a divergence between Richard Pratt's policy of total assimilation and Gertrude's ethnic pride, as well as her indignation toward injustices. Validating her Yankton heritage, Zitkala Ša published *Old Indian Legends* (1901), illustrated by a fellow Carlisle teacher, Angel DeCora (Winnebago). The book, a collection of Iktomi (trickster) stories, was intended to demonstrate the value of a particular Native American culture. That same year she was engaged to the activist physician Carlos Montezuma (Yavapai). She intended to study the violin at the Boston Conservatory of Music, but the ill health that plagued her for much of her life forced her to abandon her music studies.

Gertrude's commitment to maintaining tribal connections led her to leave the Carlisle School in 1902 in order to return to Yankton to gather more stories. She broke off her engagement to Montezuma, who was living in Chicago and would not relocate, and married Raymond T. Bonnin, a Yankton Sioux and an employee of the Indian Service (a forerunner of the Bureau of Indian Affairs).

The Bonnins were assigned to the Uintah Ouray Ute Agency in Duchesne, Utah, where they lived from 1902 until 1916. Their only child, Raymond Ohiya, was born in 1903. Gertrude taught, clerked, did public speaking, and performed community service. She became affiliated with the Society of American Indians (SAI), organized in 1911, which sponsored her later work.

In 1913 Gertrude collaborated with Professor William Hanson of Brigham Young University in composing and transcribing traditional native melodies for a production called *The Sun Dance Opera*. A mixture of romance and ritual, the opera had several successful performances in Utah. Zitkala Ša participated in these performances, playing a flute that had been a wedding gift from her husband. The New York Light Opera Guild performed the work in 1938, shortly after Zitkala Ša's death.

While in Utah, Gertrude was a firsthand witness to the growing popularity of peyote rituals. Ironically, she and her former employer, Colonel Pratt, with whom she had often disagreed, united in opposing the use of the peyote plant. In 1916 Zitkala Ša was elected secretary of the SAI and the Bonnins moved to Washington, D.C., where she actively campaigned against the use of peyote, developing skills and connections as a lobbyist that would serve her the rest of her life. She edited the SAI's *American Indian Magazine* in 1918 and 1919, contributing editorials condemning peyote and advocating policy reform in recognizing Indian servicemen in World War I, and promoting citizenship for Indians. She became a popular public speaker, often appearing in her traditional buckskin dress.

Zitkala Ša, 1921. At the time of the photo she was attending a suffrage meeting in Washington sponsored by the National Women's Party. She often wore traditional dress during public presentations.

Internal dissension led to the dissolution of the SAI after 1920, and its magazine ceased publication. Raymond, who had earned the rank of army captain during World War I, pursued law studies. Together, the Bonnins continued their campaign for Indian citizenship and justice. In 1921 Zitkala Ša met and worked with Stella Atwood of the General Federation of Women's Clubs to form the Indian Welfare Committee. She also worked with the Indian Rights Association and the American Indian Defense Association (AIDA), coauthoring a report of abuses entitled *Oklahoma's Poor Rich Indians* (1924).

After citizenship was granted to American Indians in 1924, the Bonnins continued their work with Pan-Indi-

an organizations. In 1926 they formed the National Congress of American Indians (NCAI), with Zitkala Ša as president and Raymond as secretary. Local chapters were established on numerous reservations. Of the various Pan-Indian groups, only the NCAI maintained Indians as executive officers, with Gertrude and Raymond keeping their positions until Gertrude's death. The Bonnins lobbied Congress and the Bureau of Indian Affairs on behalf of individual claimants; they also attempted to establish political power through voting blocs, incorporating an Indian-rights plank in the 1928 Republican platform and supporting the Democrats in 1932. They maintained close ties with the Yankton tribe, arguing strongly for an independent agency in Yankton after the passage in 1934 of the Howard Wheeler (Indian Reorganization) Act. Their efforts were ultimately defeated, in part by ideological differences with John Collier, Commissioner of Indian Affairs. Raymond, though not an attorney, also represented the Uintah Ouray Ute claims before Congress.

Although the NCAI shared offices with the AIDA until 1932, the Bonnins never had the financial support of other Indian-rights organizations. Most of their money came from Zitkala Ša's speaking engagements, small book royalties, and Raymond's paralegal work. The couple established a pattern of summer travel to reservations and winters in Washington, D.C., where they answered volumes of correspondence and preserved political contacts.

Zitkala Ša died in Washington, D.C., in January 1938; she is buried in Arlington Cemetery. Raymond died in 1942. The legacy she leaves is as vast as the changes she experienced in her lifetime. As an author she transcribed the oral tradition and experience, fiercely guarding her Indian identity and defying the aims of assimilationist education. She articulated historical injustices with an eloquence and emotional rhetoric that enchanted sympathetic readers and audiences. Like Charles Eastman and Luther Standing Bear, she recorded the transition from a traditional culture via an Indian boarding school to the modern world, but she did so with a female voice. She utilized the education that had at first alienated her from her roots to politically empower her fellow Native Americans.

See also Carlisle Indian Industrial School; Literature by Indians.

Willard, William, "Zitkala Ša: A Woman Who Would Be Heard!" *Wicazo Sa Review* 1, no. 1 (spring 1985): 11–16; Zitkala Ša, *American Indian Stories* (Washington, D.C., Hayworth Publishing House, 1921; Lincoln: University of Nebraska

Press, 1985); Zitkala Ša, *Old Indian Legends* (Boston: Ginn and Co., 1901; Lincoln: University of Nebraska Press, 1985).

P. JANE HAFEN (Taos Pueblo)
University of Nevada, Las Vegas

ZUNI PUEBLO

The antecedents of the A:shiwi (Zunis), in their search for the "Middle Place," migrated into the Zuni River valley and settled in several small villages along the banks of the little intermittent stream that is the Zuni. The stream forms a tributary of the Little Colorado River, which it joins near the present-day town of St. Johns, Arizona. The A:shiwi were eventually joined by other migrating Puebloan people from the south, west, north, and east by about A.D. 1000. Culturally, the Zunis are not unlike many of the other Pueblo groups in the Southwest. Linguistically, however, they are not related to any other group in Arizona, New Mexico, or perhaps elsewhere in the world. They speak a unique language, classified by anthropologists as Zunian.

In the spring of 1539, the A:shiwi were living in six villages along the banks of the Zuni River, at Kyakima, Matsa:kya, Pinna:wa, Ku/akinna, Kechipa:wa, and Hawikuh; all are in ruins today. Halona:itiwanna—present-day Zuni Pueblo—at that time was a shrine called Hepatinn/a. During this period, the A:shiwi acquired news of strange people raiding villages and taking young men and women captive to work as slaves in the silver mines. So, when in June 1539 a dark-skinned man and his attendants arrived at the village of Hawikuh demanding food, the villagers became suspicious. At first the A:shiwi accepted the stranger, but he made more demands and stated that he was the leader of "white men" who were more powerful than he. At this point the A:shiwi concluded that he was a spy and killed him.

The stranger was Estevanico, a Moor from Morocco, who had been with the Spanish explorer Alvar Núñez Cabeza de Vaca on an expedition to Florida and had returned to Mexico in 1536 with stories about large cities to the north. Unbeknownst to the A:shiwi, Estevanico's companions returned to Mexico City after he was killed and told a story of the fabulous cities they had seen. In February 1540, three hundred foot soldiers and a thousand native allies departed from the outpost of Compostela, in northern Mexico, under the command of Francisco Vásquez de Coronado. They hoped to find and conquer the Seven Cities of Gold (which did not in fact exist).

As the Spaniards headed north, the A:shiwi were preparing for a sacred religious ceremony—a pilgrimage to a sacred lake in the west—to commemorate the summer solstice. In 1540 the kiva group from Hawikuh was to take the lead in conducting the ceremonies. Starting on the third of July, everyone from the villages to the north who could travel went to Hawikuh. Early on the morning of July 4, those making the pilgrimage departed amid solemn prayers and rituals. Traditionally, it takes four days to complete the pilgrimage and ceremony. While the pilgrims are on their way, no one is allowed to cross their path.

On July 7, 1540, the day set for the pilgrims' return from the sacred lake, the village of Hawikuh was bursting with people from the other villages, who were gathered on the house tops and on the plains below the village in great anticipation. Smoke signals from the little Firegod were spotted early in the morning, and it looked as if the pilgrims would be arriving at the village shortly past noon. Suddenly there appeared a huge cloud of dust to the west—the direction from which the pilgrims were expected to arrive. Amid the dust, waving flags, and shining armor could be seen something—or someone—that was interfering with the ceremony. The bow priest (warchief) and other village elders immediately convened in an emergency council. Under the direction of the bow priest, all the males, visitors and residents alike, gathered on the plain to watch the strange "apparition."

The first thing the bow priest did was sprinkle white cornmeal so that it formed a line on the ground, across the path of the advancing intruders. Its message was "Do not cross this line at this time. Do not enter. This is a sacred area." The Spanish intruders misinterpreted the sacred cornmeal line, taking it as a hostile challenge, and a battle ensued. The A:shiwi, outnumbered and outgunned, retreated. The invaders failed to find any gold, silver, or other precious metal among the A:shiwi, however, and soon returned to Mexico, broken in spirit and with empty pockets.

A number of other exploration parties came north, but most traveled along the Rio Grande and did not disturb the Zunis. In 1680 the pueblo was drawn into a major revolt against the Spanish that was organized by the Rio Grande groups. During that uprising, the A:shiwi took refuge atop their sacred mountain, Towa:yallane. After the Spanish reconquest in the 1690s, the A:shiwi came down from their mountain

Zuni women at an intertribal ceremony in Gallup, New Mexico.

and settled at modern-day Zuni Pueblo, where they have lived for nearly three hundred years.

In 1848 the Americans asserted their authority over the Mexican Southwest, and in 1877 federal officials created the Zuni Reservation. The Southern Pacific Railroad reached nearby Gallup, New Mexico, in 1881, signaling a new era of non-Indian expansion and settlement. Missionaries accompanied the newcomers: Mormons arrived and settled east of the village in the Zuni mountains in 1876, and Presbyterians a year later; a Christian Reformed mission opened in 1897. Traders also arrived, encouraging the Zunis to raise sheep and cattle for shipment east. A new economy based on cash began.

Accompanying these social and economic changes was a struggle for political control between the bow priests, who traditionally protected the community from attack, and rivals, who accused the priests of

abusing their power. Early in the twentieth century one of the insurgents, Nick Tumaka, successfully challenged the bow priests, encouraging the rise of a large tribal council as the community's governing body. In 1964 the Zunis adopted a written constitution that called for the election of a tribal council by secret ballot. Today, despite the legal power of the tribal council, leadership in Zuni cultural affairs depends on the United States Bureau of Indian Affairs and the New Mexico state government.

In 1994 the Zuni Reservation comprised nearly 640 square miles. Zuni culture encompasses a complex socio-political-religious system based on fifteen matrilineal, matrilocal, exogamous clans. Clans form the entire underpinning of the religious system; clan membership cuts across all other organizations, which include six kiva groups, (male societies); priestly orders concerned with medicine, curing, and rain; and the bow priesthood. All Zuni societies work in concert to keep the religious ceremonial system working. Different groups are responsible for certain festivals and are charged with particular aspects of community life. The best-known ceremony is the Shalako, part of the forty-eight-day winter solstice ceremony. While elected officials lead the tribe's civil government, the installation of the tribal council is performed by the Rain Priest of the East.

As a rule, the ten thousand people who are Zuni tribal members are bilingual: in the home they speak their first language, Zuni; elsewhere they speak English. Some of the elders also speak Spanish, as well as other native dialects. While some of the younger people are losing their native-language skills, the tribe has sought to bring language instruction into tribally run schools. Other schools include a government day school, St. Anthony's Mission (Catholic) School, the Christian Reform Mission school, and two large independent elementary schools. A branch of the University of New Mexico is located at the old Zuni Day School. A Zuni hospital is operated and maintained by the BIA through the tribal government.

The modern Zuni economy is based on cottage industries, mainly arts and crafts, although some Zunis have found employment in nearby communities such as Gallup, New Mexico, and Flagstaff, Arizona. Forest-fire fighting during the spring and summer months brings additional income to the community, as do ranching, tribal-government employment, and truck farming. Ranching and farming are very minimal, however, mainly because there is not enough land to make those activities worthwhile.

The village of Zuni has spread out from its center at Halona, particularly in the years since World War II. New, modern building materials have taken the place of stone and adobe, and two- and three-bedroom homes now cluster near the pueblo in a subdivision. House trailers have sprung up like mushrooms, providing inexpensive housing for young people. House trailers are the only kind of housing the banks in Gallup will finance because they can be moved off the reservation if a purchaser defaults on a loan. The village has become an architectural hodgepodge of design and materials, some compatible and others not. In general, the pueblo suffers from the ills of any U.S. town. But despite it all the Zunis have managed to retain their land, their religion, their language, and their culture.

See also Pueblo, Rio Grande.

Crampton, C. Gregory, *The Zunis of Cibola* (Salt Lake City: University of Utah Press, 1977); Ferguson, T. J., *A Zuni Atlas* (Norman: University of Oklahoma Press, 1985).

EDMUND J. LADD (Shiwi)
Museum of New Mexico
Santa Fe, New Mexico

LIST OF CONTRIBUTORS

CREDITS

CONTRIBUTOR INDEX

GENERAL INDEX

CONTRIBUTORS

KATHRYN A. ABBOTT received her Ph.D. from the University of Massachusetts at Amherst in 1996. Her dissertation is a history of alcohol use among the Anishinaabe Indians of Minnesota. She has also been a contributor to the *Reader's Encyclopedia of the American West* and the *Western Historical Quarterly*.

FREDA AHENAKEW, head of the Department of Native Studies at the University of Manitoba, was born in 1932 on the Atâhk-akoph (Sandy Lake) Reserve in central Saskatchewan, where she grew up with Cree as her first language. She holds an M.A. in Cree linguistics from the University of Manitoba, and is the author-editor of numerous books on Cree language and literature.

S. JAMES ANAYA is a professor of law at the University of Iowa, where he specializes in the fields of international law, human rights, and Native American rights. He is the author of *Indigenous Peoples in International Law* (Oxford University Press). Prior to joining the Iowa law faculty in 1988, he was the staff attorney for the National Indian Youth Council in Albuquerque, New Mexico. A graduate of the University of New Mexico and Harvard Law School, Professor Anaya has Apache and Purépecha ancestry.

GARY CLAYTON ANDERSON is a professor of history at the University of Oklahoma. He has written and edited several books on the eastern Sioux, including *Kinsmen of Another Kind: Indian-White Relations in the Upper Mississippi Valley, 1650–1862* (1984). His biography of Sitting Bull will appear in 1996, published by Harper Collins. He has been a research fellow at the Newberry Library, Chicago; at the Huntington Library, San Marino, California; and with the National Endowment for the Humanities.

LOYCE REIFEL ANDERSON (Brulé Sioux, enrolled at the Rosebud Reservation in South Dakota) graduated from South Dakota State University, married Emery G. Anderson, raised three daughters—Lisa K. Moss, Laurie N. Anderson, and Valerie J. Cox—and is currently living in Saratoga, Wyoming.

JOALLYN ARCHAMBAULT (Standing Rock Sioux Tribe), Ph.D., is director of the American Indian Program at the National Museum of Natural History, Smithsonian Institution. Her research specialties are art, material culture, and Plains Indian history and culture.

MARIE THERESE ARCHAMBAULT (Hunkpapa Lakota) was born in Fort Yates, North Dakota, on the Standing Rock Reservation. A Franciscan sister, she holds degrees in theology and spirituality, as well as a licentiate in scripture from the Pontifical Biblical Institute in Rome. She recently earned an M.A. in religious studies, with a concentration in Lakota/Catholic expressions.

SHELLEY A. ARLEN, an associate librarian with the University of Florida Libraries, holds degrees from Barnard College and the University of Oklahoma. Her research interests include myth/ritual studies and visual anthropology (notably, historical photographs). Her publications include *The Cambridge Ritualists*.

WILLIAM H. ARMSTRONG is the minister of the Burton Congregational Church, United Church of Christ, in Burton, Ohio. Previously he served as associate director of the Peace Corps in Ethiopia and director of the Peace Corps in Swaziland. He has written biogra-

phies of David Tannenberg, Ely S. Parker, and Edward Parmelee Smith.

JAMES AXTELL is Kenan Professor of Humanities at the College of William and Mary. A graduate of Yale and Cambridge, he is the author of several books on Native American and colonial American history; the most recent is *Beyond 1492: Encounters in Colonial North America* (Oxford University Press, 1992).

GARRICK BAILEY (Euro-American, Cherokee, and Choctaw) is a professor of anthropology and the director of Native American Studies at the University of Tulsa. His publications include *Humanity: An Introduction to Cultural Anthropology* (with James Peoples), *A History of the Navajos* (with Roberta Glenn Bailey), and *The Osage and the Invisible World* (in press).

ROBERTA GLENN BAILEY, a historian and an independent scholar and writer, has been involved in ethnohistoric research projects on the Blackfeet, Pawnees, Poncas, and Navajos. Her publications include *Historic Navajo Occupation of the Northern Chaco Plateau* (with Garrick Bailey) and *A History of the Navajos* (with Garrick Bailey).

REBECCA BALES is of Choctaw, Cherokee, and Hispanic descent. Her father, Walter H. Bales, was born and raised in Oklahoma; her mother, Julia (Franco) Bales, in Texas. Rebecca received her B.A. from the University of California at Santa Cruz and her M.A. from the University of Colorado at Boulder. She is currently a doctoral candidate at Arizona State University.

LOWELL JOHN BEAN, anthropologist, is professor emeritus at California State University, Hayward, as well as vice-president of Ballena Press and president of Cultural Systems Research, Inc. He is the author of more than a dozen books, including *Mukat's People,* a history of the Cahuilla Indians.

SCOTT BEAR DON'T WALK, of the Crow, Métis, and Salish and Kootenai peoples, studied philosophy at the University of Montana. As a Rhodes Scholar he studied history at Oxford University. Currently he writes plays and screenplays.

MARY DRUKE BECKER, Ph.D., is a research associate at the Iroquois Indian Museum, Howes Cave, New York. She has written a number of articles about Iroquoian culture; was associate editor of *The History and Culture of Iroquois Diplomacy* (1985); is preparing a bibliography of recent writing (1991–1995) about Native American history and culture; and is completing a book on mid-eighteenth-century Mohawk and Oneida leadership.

ROBERT L. BEE is a professor of anthropology at the University of Connecticut. He has studied in the Quechan and Prairie Potawatomi communities and that of federal Indian policymakers in Washington, D.C. He continues his research on tribal governance/development and the interaction between tribes, states, and the federal government.

MANLEY A. BEGAY, JR. (Navajo), is the executive director of the Harvard Project on American Indian Economic Development, John F. Kennedy School of Government, Harvard University, and the co–executive director of the National Executive Education Program for Native American Leadership. He serves as a member of the board of trustees of the National Museum of the American Indian, Washington, D.C.; of the board of directors of the North American Indian Center of Boston, Inc.; and of the faculty of the Graduate School of Education, Harvard University.

BETTY LOUISE BELL is an assistant professor of English, American culture, and women's studies at the University of Michigan. She is the author of a novel, *Faces in the Moon.* Currently, she is working on a book on Native American women writers and serves as a coeditor of *The Norton Anthology of Native American Literature.*

PHIL BELLFY is a member of the Crane clan of the White Earth band of Minnesota Chippewas and lives in Sault Ste. Marie, Michigan. Phil is the coauthor (with Judith Dupré) of *First Americans* (a desk calendar published by Random House) and has earned a Ph.D. in American studies from Michigan State University.

MARILYN BENTZ, M.S.W., Ph.D., spent her childhood on the Fort Belknap Reservation in Montana, and was a faculty member at the University of Washington from 1968 to 1994, first in the School of Social Work and later in the Department of Anthropology. She was also the director of the University of Washington's American Indian Studies Program for thirteen years.

TRESSA L. BERMAN is an assistant professor of anthropology at Arizona State University West. She also holds a research appointment in the Anthropology Department of the National Museum of Natural History, where she has implemented repatriation policy. She has published articles in various books and journals, including *Cultural Survival Quarterly* and *American Indian Quarterly.* She is currently at work on a book that explores the work and family experience of Mandan, Hidatsa, and Arikara women.

TIM BERNARDIS is the library director at Little Big Horn College, the Crow tribal college in Montana. The author of *Baleeisbaalichiweé (History) Teacher's Guide,* he is both adopted and married into Crow families. Tim holds bachelor's degrees from the University of California at Berkeley in history and Native American studies, and an M.Ed. in adult and higher education from Montana State University at Bozeman.

DONALD J. BERTHRONG is professor emeritus at Purdue University. He has written extensively on the history of the Cheyenne-Arapaho Tribes of Oklahoma. On a number of occasions he served as a consultant and expert witness on historical or legal issues related to the Cheyenne-Arapahos and other tribes.

GARY BEVINGTON is a professor of linguistics at Northeastern Illinois University and a linguist for tribal languages at NAES College in Chicago. He and his wife, Emily, conduct linguistic and ethnographic fieldwork among the Mayas in Cobá, Mexico. He is the author of *Maya for Travelers and Students* (University of Texas Press).

LIZA E. BLACK (Oklahoma Cherokee) received her B.A. in history from the University of California at Santa Cruz. She is currently a Ph.D. candidate in American Indian history at the University of Washington and a Dorothy Danforth-Compton and Ford Foundation fellow.

KIMBERLY M. BLAESER (Anishinaabe), an enrolled member of the Minnesota Chippewa Tribe, is currently an associate professor at the University of Wisconsin at Milwaukee. Blaeser's book *Trailing You* won the 1993 Native Writers' Circle Award for Poetry, and her critical study, *Gerald Vizenor: Writing—in the Oral Tradition,* is forthcoming from the University of Oklahoma Press.

MARTHA ROYCE BLAINE has taught anthropology and sociology and served as head curator of the Oklahoma State Historical Society and as director of its Archives and Manuscripts Division. She married Garland J. Blaine, head chief of the Pawnees. With his invaluable assistance, she has written about Pawnee history and culture.

A member of a long-time Western family, PETER MACMILLAN BOOTH received his bachelor's in history from the University of Texas, his master's in history from the University of Arizona, and is working on his doctorate in history through Purdue University. To complete his dissertation, Peter has moved back to his adopted home of Tucson, Arizona. Peter is currently the assistant education director at the Arizona Historical Society.

DANIEL L. BOXBERGER is a professor of anthropology at Western Washington University, where he has taught since 1983. He is the author of several books and articles, including an ethnohistorical study of Lummi Indian commercial fishing entitled *To Fish in Common* and a popular textbook, *Native North Americans: An Ethnohistorical Approach.*

KATHLEEN J. BRAGDON, Ph.D., is an anthropologist with research interests in the Algonquian-speaking peoples of the Northeast. Her publications include *Native Writings in Massachusett* (with Ives Goddard, 1988) and *The Native People of Southern New England 1500–1650* (1996). She is currently an associate professor of anthropology at the College of William and Mary.

ELIZABETH A. BRANDT is a professor of anthropology and linguistics in the Department of Anthropology at Arizona State University in Tempe, Arizona. She has worked with Apache people since 1978 and also with other tribes in the Southwest. Her major concerns are ethnohistory, language revitalization, and cultural preservation, especially the protection of traditional cultural properties.

JAMES A. BROWN, Ph.D., is a professor of anthropology at Northwestern University. He specializes in the prehistory of eastern North America and has excavated at Mound City (Ohio) and conducted research on the Spiro Mounds (Oklahoma) and other ancient earthworks.

JOHN A. BROWN was born in Burlington, Washington. He received B.A. and M.A. degrees in history from the University of Washington and went on to teach history at Wenatchee Valley College for thirty years. His publications include a 1989 bibliography of written materials of the Greater Wenatchee area, where he lives. He has coauthored numerous publications with Dr. Robert H. Ruby.

JON L. BRUDVIG is a Phi Beta Kappa graduate of Marquette University. He is currently a Ph.D. candidate in history at the College of William and Mary.

ALFRED L. BUSH, curator of the Princeton Collections of Western Americana, has taught courses on the American Indian in Princeton University's departments of Anthropology, Religion, and American Studies. He is the coauthor of *The Photograph and the American Indian,* and the publisher of a series of books in Native American languages.

COLIN G. CALLOWAY, a British citizen, is an associate professor of history at the University of Wyoming. His publications include *The Western Abenakis of Vermont, 1600–1800* (1990), *Dawnland Encounters: Indians and Europeans in Northern New England* (1991), and *The American Revolution in Indian Country* (1995).

LESLIE CAMPBELL (Hoopa) is the tribal historian for the Hupa tribe.

JACK CAMPISI is an associate professor of anthropology at Wellesley College. He holds a Ph.D. in anthropology from SUNY Albany. The author of *The Mashpee Indians: Tribe on Trial,* he has written numerous articles, coauthored half a dozen books, and done legal work with approximately thirty-five tribes.

MICHAEL CASSITY, an administrator and historian at the University of Wyoming, has published several books and numerous articles, including two in the *Journal of American History,* in American social history. Active in community history, he received the 1993 Wyoming Humanities Award from the Wyoming Council for the Humanities.

BRENDA J. CHILD is an assistant professor in the Department of History at the University of Wisconsin at Milwaukee. Child is a member of the Red Lake band of the Chippewa Tribe in northern Minnesota. She has a forthcoming book, *A Bitter Lesson: Boarding Schools and American Indian Families, 1890–1940.*

WARD CHURCHILL (enrolled Keetoowah Cherokee) is an associate professor of American Indian studies and associate chair of the Department of Ethnic Studies at the University of Colorado at Boulder. From 1983 to 1993, he served as codirector of the American Indian Movement of Colorado. He has also served as national spokesperson for the Leonard Peltier Defense Committee, as a delegate for the International Indian Treaty Council, and as vice-chair of the American Indian Anti-Defamation Council. An award-winning writer, he has published a number of books, among them *Marxism and Native Americans* (1983), *Struggle for the Land* (1993), and *From a Native Son* (1996).

Currently the executive vice president of Oklahoma City University, C. B. CLARK, a member of the Muskogee (Creek) Nation of Oklahoma, taught American Indian studies for nearly twenty years in the northern plains and on the West Coast.

A social anthropologist, JAMES A. CLIFTON is known for his ethnographic and ethnohistorical studies of Indians, mainly tribes of the Great Lakes region. He has published fourteen books and monographs and more than one hundred essays, and has served as expert witness and research consultant in thirteen Indian treaty-rights cases.

GEORGE L. CORNELL (Sault Ste. Marie Chippewa) is an associate professor of English and history at Michigan State University. He has published works on Great Lakes Indian populations and the influence of American Indians on the rise of modern conservation. He currently serves as a trustee for the National Museum of the American Indian, Smithsonian Institution.

Articles by CHARLES L. CUTLER, an independent scholar, have appeared in *American History* and *American Heritage.* Cutler is the author of *Connecticut's Revolutionary Press* (Pequot Press, 1975) and *O Brave New Words!* (University of Oklahoma Press, 1994). He is married, with a son and a daughter. His pastimes include judo and collecting dinosaur tracks.

JERE DANIELL is a professor of history at Dartmouth College. He specializes in the history of New England, writes mostly about New Hampshire, and gives dozens of public lectures annually on a wide range of regional topics. He has worked closely with Dartmouth's Native American Studies Program since its inception.

DOROTHY W. DAVIDS, a retired educator (elementary through university), chairs the Stockbridge-Munsee (Mohican) Historical Committee. Long active in national, state, and local organizations, she is currently elder adviser to the Indigenous Women's Network and is a multicultural consultant specializing in women's and indigenous issues. She now resides on the Stockbridge-Munsee Reservation in Wisconsin.

LEE DAVIS is an anthropologist who has lived and worked with the Hupa Indian people of California for twenty years and is currently the assistant director for Cultural Resources at the National Museum of the American Indian. She has written over twenty publications on Native American worldview, ethnogeography, and precontact mapping.

DENYS DELÂGE is chair of the Department of Sociology at Laval University in Quebec City, where he teaches North American Indian history. Most of his writings deal with Indian-white relations in New France and in British North America.

PHILIP J. DELORIA is a member of a prominent Lakota family. He completed a Ph.D. in American studies at Yale University and is a member of the history faculty at the University of Colorado at Boulder. Deloria is a coauthor of *The Native Americans* (Turner, 1993).

ADOLPH LORENZ DIAL, Ph.D., is professor emeritus at Pembroke State University, where he also serves on the board of trustees. Dial has published two books on Lumbee history, *Lumbee* (Chelsea House, 1993) and, with David Eliades, *The Only Land I Know* (Indian Historian Press, 1975). A former state legislator, he has published numerous articles on Lumbee Indians and is recognized as a Lumbee leader in education, business, and politics.

OLIVE PATRICIA DICKASON, professor emeritus at the University of Alberta, is of Métis ancestry. She is the author of *Canada's First Nations: A History of Founding Peoples from Earliest Times* (1992), which was awarded the Sir John A. Macdonald prize by the Canadian Historical Association. Several of her works have appeared in French.

HENRY F. DOBYNS has taught anthropology at Prescott College, Cornell University, and the universities of Kentucky, Wisconsin-Parkside, Florida, and Oklahoma. He is the author of thirteen books and coauthor of twenty-three books and sixty-three scholarly journal articles reporting research in Peru, Mexico, and the United States.

R. DAVID EDMUNDS (Cherokee), a professor of history at Indiana University, is the author of seven books and over sixty articles. He has served as the acting director of the D'Arcy McNickle Center for the History of the American Indian, Newberry Library, and currently holds a Guggenheim Fellowship.

ANYA DOZIER ENOS is a member of Santa Clara Pueblo, where she lives with her husband, Terry, and their children, Lisa and Pasquala. Ms. Enos is a teacher, a Ph.D. candidate, and a writer whose poetry has appeared in several magazines nationwide.

SUZANNE E. EVANS is a doctoral candidate at the University of California at Berkeley. She received a B.A. in history from the University of California at Los Angeles and a J.D. from Western State University College of Law, where she was the lead-articles editor and book-review editor for the law review.

JOHN FAHEY, professor emeritus at Eastern Washington University, writes on the inland Pacific Northwest. His books include historical accounts of the Flathead and Kalispel tribes.

BRENDA FARNELL is a sociocultural anthropologist at the University of Iowa. Her teachers of Plains Sign Talk and spoken Assiniboine were elders of the Fort Belknap community, Montana; especially helpful to her were James Earthboy and Rose Weasel. Her special interests include dance and other forms of expressive culture, as well as language revitalization.

PHOEBE FARRIS-DUFRENE (Powhatan), Ph.D., is an associate professor of art and design at Purdue University. As the recipient of a Fulbright grant to Mexico, a Midwestern Universities Consortium International Association grant to Brazil, and two Purdue travel grants to Cuba, Farris-Dufrene has established an international reputation in art disciplines. She is the coauthor of two books, *Art Therapy and Psychotherapy: Blending Two Therapeutic Approaches* and *Portfolios: Native American Artists.*

J. FREDERICK FAUSZ is dean of the Pierre Laclede Honors College in Saint Louis. He earned his Ph.D. in history, Phi Beta Kappa, from the College of William and Mary and has researched European-Indian relations, from the seventeenth-century Chesapeake wars to the nineteenth-century Missouri fur trades.

CHRISTIAN F. FEEST received his Ph.D. in anthropology from the University of Vienna in 1969 and was curator of the North and Middle American collections of the Museum of Ethnology in Vienna from 1963 to 1993. He is now a professor of anthropology at the University of Frankfurt.

JENNIFER W. FELMLEY is a political-science graduate student at the University of California at Berkeley. Her dissertation work is on tribal governments, including aspects of decision-making, participation, and local control. In 1993 and 1994, she was the tribal energy policy and science fellow for the Council of Energy Resources.

DONALD L. FIXICO (Sac and Fox, Shawnee, Creek, and Seminole) is a professor of history at Western Michigan University at Kalamazoo. He has been a visiting lecturer/professor at the University of California at Berkeley, UCLA, San Diego State University, and the University of Nottingham. He has written *Termination and Relocation: Federal Indian Policy, 1945–1960* and *Urban Indians,* and edited *An Anthology of Western Great Lakes Indians.*

RAYMOND D. FOGELSON is a professor of anthropology and psychology (human development) at the University of Chicago. He specializes in the study of Southeastern Indians and has done fieldwork with Cherokees and Creeks.

CATHERINE S. FOWLER is a professor of anthropology at the University of Nevada at Reno. Her special interests are in the cultures and languages of the native peoples of the Great Basin. These have led her into Uto-Aztecan (particularly Northern Paiute) historical and comparative studies, museum studies, and major emphases in descriptive and theoretical aspects of ethnobiology.

LORETTA FOWLER is a professor of anthropology at Indiana University. Her book *Arapahoe Politics, 1851–1978* won the American Society for Ethnohistory's Erminie Wheeler-Voegelin Prize for 1982. She has also published *Shared Symbols, Contested Meanings: Gros Ventre Culture and History, 1778–1984, The Arapaho,* and several articles in professional journals.

S. VERNA FOWLER (Menominee) is president and founder of the College of the Menominee Nation, co-owner of Wolf River Trading Post, and a founder of Sisters of a New Genesis, a Catholic religious order. She received her Ph.D. in education administration from the University of North Dakota.

KENNY A. FRANKS received his Ph.D. from Oklahoma State University and is the director of education and publications for the Oklahoma Heritage Association. The winner of several national awards, he has written, cowritten, or contributed to twenty-nine books and is the author of numerous articles and book reviews that have appeared in twenty-seven different historical journals.

THEODORE R. FRISBIE, against family wishes, left his Connecticut home in 1958 to study anthropology at the University of New Mexico (B.A., 1963; M.A., 1967). He continued his specialization in Pueblo ethnology and archaeology at Southern Illinois University at Carbondale. After receiving his doctorate there in 1971, he took a professorial position at the sister campus in Edwardsville, where he continues to teach and direct the Anthropology Teaching Museum. He has received numerous grants and authored over fifty publications.

GEORGE FRISON is a professor of anthropology at the University of Wyoming. He has published eight books and numerous articles on Great Plains prehistory. His interests include Plains Paleo-Indians, prehistoric large-mammal hunting, and prehistoric high-altitude cultural adaptations. He was a Wyoming rancher before beginning academic studies at age thirty-seven.

LOUIS GARCIA is a carpentry instructor with the Fort Berthold Community College, New Town, North Dakota. He became interested in the Native Americans as a Boy Scout at age eleven in New York City. His main fields of interest are the Grass Dance and American Indian place names. He is an avid powwow dancer, singer, and craftsman. His wife of twenty-five years, Hilda Redfox, is a member of the Devils Lake Sioux Tribe. Mr. Garcia has over a dozen articles to his credit, published mostly in *Whispering Wind Magazine.* In 1976, Mr. Garcia was appointed honorary historian for the Devils Lake Sioux Tribe.

JEANNINE GENDAR is the managing editor of *News from Native California,* a quarterly magazine devoted to California Indian history and ongoing culture, and is the author of *Grass Games and Moon Races* (Heyday Books, 1995), a book about California Indian games and toys.

DAVID L. GHERE is an assistant professor of history in the General College at the University of Minnesota. He has received an M.Ed. from the University of Illinois, a Ph.D. in history from the University of Maine, and a predoctoral fellowship at the Newberry Library.

WARREN GOLDSTEIN is the author of *Playing for Keeps: A History of Early Baseball* (Cornell University Press, 1989) and coauthor of *A Brief History of American Sports* (Hill and Wang, 1993). He teaches American studies at the State University of New York/College at Old Westbury.

MICHAEL D. GREEN teaches Native American history at the University of Kentucky. His research and publications have dealt with the history of the Creeks, and he is currently working on a book about their adjustment to Indian Territory after removal. With Theda Perdue, he has also written a book on Cherokee removal.

BERNICE FORREST GUILLAUME was born in Chicago in 1950. She received a Ph.D. in U.S. history from Tulane University, and her honors include the Newberry Library, NEH, and Fulbright-Hays awards. Guillaume, who compiled and edited *The Collected Works of Olivia Ward Bush-Banks* (Oxford University Press, 1991), is a maternal great-granddaughter of Olivia Bush-Banks, a Montauk tribal historian and author possessing Poosepatuck and African-American heritages. Guillaume is currently completing a Poosepatuck ethnohistory.

HELEN CRIPPEN BROWN GUMBS (Princess Starleaf) is a blood member and tribal historian of the Shinnecock Tribe. She is the twelfth descendant of Chief Wyandanch (Montauk) and Chief Nowedonah (Shinnecock). She received a B.A. in history and education from Southampton College and paralegal training at Antioch School of Law, Washington, D.C. A retired schoolteacher, she is now a lecturer and consultant on Native American affairs.

P. JANE HAFEN (Taos Pueblo) is an assistant professor of English at the University of Nevada at Las Vegas. She received a Frances C. Allen Fellowship from the D'Arcy McNickle Center for the History of the American Indian at the Newberry Library in Chicago.

WILLIAM T. HAGAN is the author of six books, the best known of which is *American Indians,* a brief survey and one of the first of its genre. A past president of the American Society for Ethnohistory and of the Western History Association, in 1989 he was the recipient of the Western History Association Prize.

OTIS HALFMOON is a full-blood member of the Nez Perce Tribe. His family bloodline includes participants in the Nez Perce campaign of 1877. He is currently employed by the National Park Service and has worked for the Nez Perce Tribe in various capacities.

For thirty years, GEORGE R. HAMELL has had an interest in Iroquois myth, ritual, and material culture. Its seeds were planted in boyhood and nurtured by a sense of place: the Genesee Valley region—the historic homeland of the Seneca Iroquois. This interest has since been transformed into a series of professions: senior museum exhibits planner in anthropology at the New York State Museum (since 1981); curator of anthropology at the Rochester Museum and Science Center (1974–1980); and interpretive naturalist for the Monroe County Parks Department (1962–1969).

CAROL HAMPTON (Caddo) is currently field officer for congregational ministries for the Episcopal Church, with responsibility for multicultural ministry. She serves on the Heritage and Culture Committee for the Caddo Nation and previously served as councilwoman. She received her doctorate in history from the University of Oklahoma.

SUZAN SHOWN HARJO (Cheyenne and Hodulgee Muscogee) is president of the Morning Star Institute in Washington, D.C. Poet, writer, lecturer, and curator, she also has developed federal Indian policy in areas including religious/cultural rights, repatriation, land protection, and the establishment of the National Museum of the American Indian, which she serves as a founding trustee.

After graduating from Yale Law School, ALEXANDRA HARMON worked for sixteen years for Indian tribes in Washington State. A desire to explain her clients' histories outside the adversary system prompted her to enter the University of Washington, where she earned a Ph.D. in 1995.

HOWARD L. HARROD became interested in Native Americans during his childhood in Oklahoma. After earning his Ph.D. at Yale University, he taught in the areas of sociology of religion and Native American religions. He is the author of three books on Native American religions and teaches at Vanderbilt University.

SAMUEL C. HART is currently a member of the Koinonia Mennonite Church, Clinton, Oklahoma, and is a past employee of the Cheyenne-Arapaho Tribes of Oklahoma. He belongs to the Elk Horn Society, of which his daughter Statia and son David are also members, and is active in community affairs of the Cheyennes in Oklahoma. He is also a member of the State of Oklahoma Planning Council for Developmental Disabilities.

GRETCHEN HARVEY is writing a biography of Ruth Muskrat Bronson. It builds upon her doctoral dissertation, entitled "Cherokee and American: Ruth Muskrat Bronson, 1897–1982." She lives in Fargo, North Dakota, where she teaches American Indian history at North Dakota State University.

LAURENCE M. HAUPTMAN is a professor of history at SUNY College at New Paltz, where he has taught for a quarter of a century. He is the author, editor, or coeditor of ten books on the American Indian history of the Northeast. In 1987 he received the Peter Doctor Memorial Award from the Iroquois for his research and writing on American Indians. In 1990 he served as the expert witness for congressional committees attempting to resolve the Seneca Nation-Salamanca lease controversy, testifying before both houses of Congress.

WILLIAM HAWK's ancestors, the Matinnecocks of the Smithtown area of Long Island, were known as Nissequogues. He is currently an associate professor of anthropology at Eastern New Mexico University. He also serves as faith keeper for the Matinnecock people.

SUZANNE HECK is an assistant professor of mass communication at Central Missouri State University. A descendant of the Sac and Fox of the Missouri, she is researching the tribe's history as part of her doctoral work in American studies at the University of Kansas.

JOSEPH B. HERRING has held various governmental positions, serving stints with the navy, the U.S. Postal Service, the National Archives, and the National Endowment for the Humanities. A native of Washington, D.C., Herring attended colleges in Maryland and Texas, earning a Ph.D. in history at Texas Christian University.

KATHLEEN SHAYE HILL, an enrolled member of the Klamath Tribes, was responsible for the archival research and writing for the Klamath restoration effort and has served in tribal government. She earned a law degree in 1994 and an advanced law degree in 1995. She has published both fiction and nonfiction.

CURTIS M. HINSLEY is the author of The Smithsonian and the American Indian: Making a Moral Anthropology in Victorian America (1994) and, with Melissa Banta, From Site to Sight: Anthropology, Photography, and the Power of Imagery (1986). With David R. Wilcox, of the Museum of Northern Arizona, he is currently at work on a multivolume history of the Hemenway Southwestern Archaeological Expedition (1886–89). Professor Hinsley lives and works in Flagstaff, Arizona.

MICHAEL HITTMAN received his Ph.D. from the University of New Mexico. He considers his ethnohistorical studies of the Yerington Paiute Tribe and the body of fiction he has produced so far to be his life's work. He won the Society for Humanistic Anthropology Award for Best Short Story in 1990 and was a recent Newberry Center scholar.

TOM HOLM (Cherokee/Creek) was born and educated in Oklahoma. He received a Ph.D. from the University of Oklahoma and has been a faculty member at the University of Arizona since 1980. A Vietnam veteran himself, he has recently completed a book on Indian veterans entitled Strong Hearts, Wounded Souls.

JONATHAN B. HOOK is a member of the Cherokee Nation of Oklahoma. He has traveled from Nicaragua to South Africa to the former Soviet Union. A member of the Alabama-Coushatta Powwow Association, he enjoys golf, camping, and singing. His research interests include ethnic studies, cross-cultural athletics, and Nicaraguan Indians.

JOSEPH D. HORSE CAPTURE (A'ani') is a member of the White Clay Society. He worked on Visions of the People, an exhibition of Plains Indian pictorial art at the Minneapolis Institute of Arts, and has been published in American Indian Art Magazine. He is currently finishing his B.A. at Montana State University in Bozeman. As a recipient of the Honors Program's Presidential Scholarship, he is pursuing a master's degree in American history and hopes to enter the museum field.

N. JILL HOWARD is an instructor at Taylor University and a research assistant at the Center for the American West at the University of New Mexico. She has compiled Native Americans of the Southwest: The Navajos, the Apaches, and the Pueblos: A Selective Bibliography and is coeditor, with Richard W. Etulain, of A Bibliographical Guide to the Study of Western American Literature.

FREDERICK E. HOXIE received his B.A. from Amherst College and his Ph.D. in history from Brandeis University. He has taught Native American history at Antioch College and Northwestern University. He has written A Final Promise: The Campaign to Assimilate the Indians, 1880–1920 (1984) and Parading through History: The Making of the Crow Nation in America, 1805–1935 (1995) and edited With the Nez Perces (1981), Indians in American History: An Introduction (1988), and Discovering America (1994).

JOHN HUNT, stepson of John Joseph Mathews, is a novelist who makes his home in the south of France.

R. DOUGLAS HURT is the editor of Agricultural History and a professor and the director of the Graduate Program in Agricultural History and Rural Studies at Iowa State University.

LEE IRWIN is the director of the Religious Studies Program in the Philosophy and Religion Department at the College of Charleston. He holds an interdisciplinary Ph.D. from Indiana University and has attended ceremonies and social events among the Lakotas, Absarokees, Wind River Shoshones, and Oklahoma Cherokees. He is part Mohawk-Delaware.

PETER IVERSON is a professor of history at Arizona State University. His interest in Indian history began with his grandfather's stories and developed through his teaching at Navajo Community College and his association with native individuals and communities. He has written or edited seven books, including, most recently, When Indians Became Cowboys.

LaVERNE MASAYESVA JEANNE, a Hopi, received her Ph.D. in linguistics from the Massachusetts Institute of Technology. She is currently an associate professor in the Anthropology Department at the University of Nevada. She resides in Reno with a daughter, Juliette; a son, Po'kyaya; and her husband, Richard.

A writer, folklorist, anthropologist, environmentalist, and award-winning poet of coastal/island Gabrielino/Luiseño descent, LOUISE V. JEFFREDO-WARDEN is completing her doctorate in anthropology at Stanford University. Her graduate work has focused on creating, with the late Luiseño elder Villiana Hyde, an extensive archive and dictionary for the Luiseño community. Ms. Jeffredo-Warden is a member of the Temecula/Pechanga band of Luiseños.

FRANCIS JENNINGS teaches at the University of North Carolina, Chapel Hill. The title of his first book, *The Invasion of America*, has been generally adopted in place of the former "settling of America." His most recent revisionist book is a general synthesis of American Indian history called *The Founders of America*.

REX LEE JIM, a Navajo educator, lives in Rock Point, Arizona. He is a poet and playwright. Most of his writing and publication is in the Navajo language. He travels frequently to lecture on his writings and Navajo-related materials in philosophy, literature, history, and culture. Currently he works for Navajo Community College in Tsaile, Arizona, doing what he loves most: working with young Navajo people.

JENNIE R. JOE, Ph.D., M.P.H., is a medical anthropologist and a member of the Navaho Nation. She is currently an associate professor in the Department of Family and Community Medicine at the University of Arizona, where she serves as the director of the Native American Research and Training Center, an organization involved in health-related research projects with Indian tribes throughout the United States.

PATRICK JOHNSON, director of Mi'kmaq Student Services at the University College of Cape Breton, is a member of the Mi'kmaq Nation of Nova Scotia. Mr. Johnson graduated with an honors B.A. in 1990, majoring in Mi'kmaq studies, political science, and English. His goal in life is to promote Mi'kmaq language, culture, and traditions.

TED JOJOLA is an associate professor at the University of New Mexico, where he is director of Native American Studies and acting director of the Masters Program in Community and Regional Planning. He is a lifelong resident and enrolled member of the pueblo of Isleta. His current work encompasses the role of identity in tribal community development.

JOSEPH G. JORGENSEN, a professor of anthropology at the University of California at Irvine and a native of Utah, was an employee of the Northern Ute Tribe in eastern Utah in the early 1960s. His interest in Ute political economic history, culture, and language grew during that experience and prompted him to pursue a Ph.D., his research for which focused on the Utes.

ALVIN M. JOSEPHY, JR., has written more than a dozen well-known books on American Indians, including *The Patriot Chiefs*, *The Nez Perce Indians and the Opening of the Northwest*, *The Indian Heritage of America*, *Now That the Buffalo's Gone*, and *500 Nations*. A former associate editor of *Time* and editor in chief of *American Heritage*, he has also been active for more than forty years in supporting Indians in their struggles for self-determination, treaty rights, and sovereignty.

THOMAS W. KAVANAGH, Ph.D., is curator of collections at the William Hammond Mathers Museum, Indiana University. His recent work has focused on Comanche ethnohistory and politics. He has served as director of the Hopi Tricentennial Project at the Hopi Cultural Center Museum, and as contractor for several projects at the Smithsonian Institution.

CLARA SUE KIDWELL (Choctaw/Chippewa) is assistant director of Cultural Resources at the National Museum of the American Indian, Smithsonian Institution, Washington, D.C., and professor of Native American studies at the University of California at Berkeley. She has published articles on Choctaw history, Indian women, and Indian science and medicine.

CECIL KING, Ph.D., an Odawa scholar, has researched his people's story for over twenty years. He is fluent in Ojibwa and interviews elders and translates hitherto untranslated historical texts from Ojibwa to enhance the contemporary understanding of the Odawa people.

DUANE KING is executive director of the Southwest Museum in Los Angeles, and former assistant director of the National Museum of the American Indian. He has worked at the Museum of the Cherokee Indian, the Cherokee National Historical Society, and the Middle Oregon Indian Historical Society, and taught at Western Carolina University, Northeastern State University, and the University of Tennessee, Knoxville/Chattanooga.

DARRELL ROBES KIPP is the great grandson of Chief Heavy Runner, leader of the band of Blackfeet slain during Baker's Massacre in 1870. His Blackfoot name is Morning Eagle. Kipp researches the Blackfoot language full-time, and is the founder of the Piegan Institute, located in Browning, Montana.

BENJAMIN R. KRACHT received his Ph.D. in anthropology at Southern Methodist University. He currently teaches anthropology and Native American studies at Northeastern State University, Tahlequah, Oklahoma, and is writing an ethnohistory of Kiowa belief systems. Kracht resides in Broken Arrow, Oklahoma, with his wife, Kelly, and their daughter, Elena, and son, Robbie.

PAUL V. KROSKRITY is currently a professor of anthropology at the University of California at Los Angeles, where he has served as chair of the Interdepartmental Program in American Indian Studies since 1985. Since earning his doctoral degree in anthropology from Indiana University, he has conducted long-term ethnolinguistic research with both the Arizona Tewas and the Western Monos of Central California.

REBECCA KUGEL teaches Native American history at the University of California at Riverside. She did her undergraduate work at the University of Iowa and her graduate work at UCLA. Her research explores the political strategies pursued by nineteenth-century Minnesota Ojibwas to retain their autonomy when faced with Euro-American domination.

EDMUND J. LADD is a Shiwi (Zuni). Educated on the Zuni Reservation, he served in the armed forces during World War II and earned his degree in anthropology from the University of New Mexico. He retired from the National Park Service in 1984 and returned to New Mexico. He is active in the federal repatriation program (NAGPRA). He and his wife, Delphine, reside in Santa Fe.

HOWARD R. LAMAR, Sterling Professor of History at Yale University, has devoted his career to teaching and writing about the American West. He is the general editor of *The Reader's Encyclopedia of the American West* and the author of *The Far Southwest, 1846–1912: A Territorial History*, *Dakota Territory, 1861–1889*, *Texas Crossings*, and many articles, and has contributed to many edited works.

DAVID LANDY is an adjunct professor of anthropology at the University of North Carolina at Wilmington; emeritus professor and former departmental chair at the University of Massachusetts at Boston; and professor in the Department of Anthropology and the Graduate School of Public Health at the University of Pittsburgh. His publications include *Tropical Childhood: Culture, Disease, and Healing* and *Halfway House*, along with numerous journal articles.

ADRIAN LeCORNU (Haida) is the former president of Hydaburg Cooperative Association Tribal Council, a former city administrator for Hydaburg, Alaska, and a Vietnam veteran. He currently works for Shaanseet Inc., an Alaskan Native corporation.

VICTORIA LINDSAY LEVINE is an associate professor at Colorado College, where she teaches ethnomusicology and Southwest studies. As a specialist in American Indian music, she has coauthored a book on Choctaw music and dance and has published several articles on Choctaw and other American Indian musical cultures.

JERROLD E. LEVY received a Ph.D. in anthropology from the University of Chicago. He worked on the Navajo reservation from 1959 to 1964 as an anthropologist with the Indian Health Service, and has been a professor of anthropology at the University of Arizona since 1972.

DANIEL F. LITTLEFIELD, JR., is an internationally recognized scholar in American Indian studies. He is a professor of American literature and director of the American Native Press Archives at the University of Arkansas at Little Rock.

HARTMAN H. LOMAWAIMA, associate director of the Arizona State Museum, University of Arizona, traces his interest in museums to his days as a graduate student at Harvard. Hartman is Hopi, from the village of Sipaulovi, on Second Mesa, Arizona. In addition to his career as an administrator, he has worked in the area of Native American material-culture studies. He has written and presented papers on the subject and has developed and consulted on many museum exhibits throughout the United States.

KAREN D. LONE HILL, an enrolled member of the Oglala Sioux Tribe, resides in Porcupine, South Dakota, on the Pine Ridge Reservation, with her daughter, Kimberly Dawn Wilson.

Karen is chair of the Lakota Studies Department at Oglala Lakota College. She has coauthored *Pine Ridge Reservation: Yesterday and Today* (1992), contributed an article, "Anpetu Otanin Win and Mni Aku Win," to *Portraits of Ft. Phil Kearney* (1993), and written a student text, *Lakota Language I* (1989). Karen's source of inspiration is her people, the Lakota Oyate, and their struggle and need to tell their history.

BONNIE LYNN-SHEROW is currently an instructor in the Department of History at Kansas State University and is finishing a dissertation in environmental history for Northwestern University. She holds a B.A. in history from the University of Windsor in Ontario, Canada, and received a master's degree in American Indian history from Purdue University in 1990. Her dissertation research is a cross-cultural study of Indians, blacks, and whites in Oklahoma at the turn of the century.

PETER C. MANCALL, an associate professor of history at the University of Kansas, received his Ph.D. from Harvard University in 1986. He is the author of *Deadly Medicine: Indians and Alcohol in Early America* (1995) and *Valley of Opportunity: Economic Culture along the Upper Susquehanna, 1700–1800* (1991), and the editor of *Envisioning America: English Plans for the Colonization of North America, 1580–1640* (1995).

DANIEL MANDELL, Ph.D., is senior lecturer of history at Suffolk University, Boston, and has taught at the University of Georgia and DePauw University. He has published several articles on Indians in eighteenth-century Massachusetts, and his book on that topic will be published in 1996 by the University of Nebraska Press. Mandell is now researching Indians in nineteenth-century southern New England.

HELEN VANDERHOOP MANNING, a member of the Wampanoag Tribe of Gay Head/Aquinnah, received an M.A. from New York University in 1952. She has worked as an elementary school teacher and is currently the education director of the Wampanoag Tribe of Gay Head/Aquinnah, in Gay Head, Massachusetts. She has served on the Wampanoag Tribal Council of Gay Head, was awarded a fellowship at the Newberry Library in 1984, and since 1986 has headed the Massachusetts Commission on Indian Affairs.

BRENDA MANUELITO (Navajo) is of the Towering House clan born for the Salt clan. A former assistant director of the D'Arcy McNickle Center for the History of the American Indian, she is a doctoral candidate in anthropology at the University of New Mexico and

has received fellowships from the Smithsonian Institution and the Wenner-Gren Foundation.

HARVEY MARKOWITZ is associate director of the D'Arcy McNickle Center, head librarian of Native American Educational Services in Chicago, and a doctoral candidate at the University of Chicago. He recently served as the consulting editor for *Ready Reference: American Indians.*

JOSEPH M. MARSHALL III (Sicangu Lakota) was born and raised on the Rosebud Sioux Reservation. He speaks Lakota and handcrafts primitive Lakota bows and arrows. Currently a freelance writer, he has published *Soldiers Falling into Camp, Winter of the Holy Iron,* and *On Behalf of the Wolf and the First Peoples.*

SALLY MCBETH, a native of Detroit, Michigan, currently resides in Colorado and teaches anthropology and multicultural studies at the University of Northern Colorado. She is the author of *Ethnic Identity and the Boarding School Experience* (1983) and is currently working with Esther Burnett Horne on a life history of Horne, a Shoshone educator and historian who is a descendent of Sacagawea.

MICHAEL N. MCCONNELL is an associate professor of history at the University of Alabama at Birmingham. He is the author of *A Country Between: The Upper Ohio Valley and Its Peoples, 1724–1774* and essays on the early history of the Ohio Valley.

Born in 1952 in Tulsa, Oklahoma, KENNETH W. MCINTOSH, Ph.D., is a member of the Muskogee Nation. He is the son of Chinnubbie McIntosh (Hacoce) and Nancy Fortner. His grandfather, W. E. Dode McIntosh (Tustenuggee Micco), was principal chief of the Creek Nation from 1961 to 1971. In addition to an M.A. and Ph.D. in American history, he also holds an M.Div. from Brite Divinity School. He is married to Eulaine King; they have two sons.

THELMA CORNELIUS MCLESTER, an enrolled Oneida of the Turtle clan in Wisconsin, is an Oneida singer and speaker, and a lecturer on Oneida history. Her essay on Oneida women leaders appeared in *Oneida Indian Experience: Two Perspectives,* and she has published articles on Oneida history in *Voyageur* magazine and *Museletter.* She is a member of the board of regents of Haskell Indian Nations University.

BEATRICE MEDICINE (Lakota) has a Ph.D. in anthropology and is an emerita associate professor at California State University in Northridge. She lives near Wakpala, South Dakota, on the Standing Rock Reservation.

JAMES H. MERRELL teaches history at Vassar College. He has held fellowships from the Newberry Library, the Institute of Early American History and Culture, and the John Simon Guggenheim Memorial Foundation. His book, *The Indians' New World,* won the Bancroft Prize, the Frederick Jackson Turner Award, and the Merle Curti Award.

MELINDA MICCO (Seminole/Creek/Choctaw) is an assistant professor and the chair of the Ethnic Studies Department at Mills College. She received her Ph.D. in ethnic studies from the University of California at Berkeley. Her research interests are black and Indian communities. She has served as consultant to the Seminole Nation and to the attorney for the Seminole Freedmen.

CHRISTOPHER L. MILLER is an associate professor in the Department of History at the University of Texas, Pan American. His most prominent publications include *Prophetic Worlds: Indians and Whites on the Columbia Plateau* 1985) and, as coauthor, *Making America: A History of the United States* (1995).

DAVID REED MILLER, Ph.D., is a professor of Indian studies at Saskatchewan Indian Federated College–University of Regina. Trained as both an anthropologist and a historian, Miller is a former dean of instruction at Fort Peck Community College and associate director of the D'Arcy McNickle Center for the History of the American Indian at the Newberry Library.

JAY MILLER (Lenape) has worked as a linguist, anthropologist, ethnohistorian, and expert witness, and is the author of over thirty articles, twenty chapters, ten edited collections, and five books. His research topics have included New Mexican Pueblos, British Columbia Tsimshians, Washington State Salishans, Nevada Numics, Ontario Ojibwas, Wisconsin Menominees, and, in Oklahoma, Delawares, Caddos, and Creeks.

MARIANNE MITHUN is a professor of linguistics at the University of California at Santa Barbara. She is a specialist in North American Indian languages, particularly Mohawk, Oneida, Cayuga, Seneca, Tuscarora, Central Pomo, and Barbareño Chumash. She is currently completing *The Native Languages of North America,* to be published by Cambridge University Press.

JOHN C. MOHAWK (Seneca), Ph.D., is former editor of *Akwesasne Notes* (1976–1983) and currently edits *Daybreak* magazine. He is an assistant professor of American studies at the State University of New York at Buffalo.

RICHARD MONETTE currently teaches at the University of Wisconsin Law School. Prior to that he was staff attorney for the United States Senate Committee on Indian Affairs. He also spent a year in Washington, D.C., as the director of the Office of Congressional and Legislative Affairs for the Bureau of Indian Affairs, Department of the Interior. Professor Monette grew up on the reservation of the Turtle Mountain Band of Chippewa, where he is an enrolled member.

TED MONTOUR is a writer and consultant from the Six Nations of the Grand River Territory in Southern Ontario. Of Delaware, Mohawk, and Oneida extraction, he is a descendant of Joseph Brant, Mohawk war chief of the Iroquois Confederacy. Mr. Montour gratefully acknowledges the assistance of the staff of the Woodland Cultural Centre in Brantford, Ontario.

JOHN HARTWELL MOORE, chair of the Anthropology Department at the University of Florida, has done extensive fieldwork among the Plains Indians since receiving his doctorate from New York University in 1974. His publications include *The Cheyenne Nation* and *Political Economy of North American Indians.*

In spite of attending college in the heart of Cherokee country, GARY E. MOULTON did not become interested in Cherokee history at that time. Eventually, he wrote a biography of Chief John Ross, then edited his papers. He is now the editor of the Lewis and Clark journals.

LARRY G. MURRAY, a member of the Eastern Shoshone Tribe, resides on the Wind River Reservation. He earned his master's degree from Chadron State College and did postgraduate work at the University of Wyoming. He is a member of the Wyoming Indian Affairs Council and is the director of economic development for his tribe. His publications include "The Wind River Reservation: Yesterday and Today."

PETER NABOKOV is an assistant professor in the Department of Anthropology at the University of Wisconsin at Madison. His books include a collection of Indian narratives on Indian and white relations, entitled *Native American Testimony: From Prophecy to the Present, 1492–1992* (1992), *Native American Architecture* (with Robert Easton; 1989), *Indian Running* (1987), and *Two Leggings: The Making of a Crow Warrior* (1967). Currently he is conducting research into the sacred geographies of various American Indian groups.

JUNE NAMIAS is an associate professor of history at the University of Alaska at Anchorage. Her books include *White Captives: Gender and Ethnicity on the American Frontier* (1993) and an edition of James E. Seaver's *A Narrative of the Life of Mrs. Mary Jemison* [1824] (1992). Her annotated edition of Sarah F. Wakefield's *Six Weeks in the Sioux Tepees* [1864] is forthcoming.

LLOYD KIVA NEW (Cherokee) received a B.A.E. from the School of the Art Institute of Chicago and did graduate work in arts management at Harvard University. He is an artist, arts educator, fabric/fashion designer, and entrepreneur, and also serves as president emeritus of the Institute of American Indian Arts and as chairman of the Indian Arts and Crafts Board.

JOHN D. NICHOLS is a graduate of Hamilton College and holds a Ph.D. in linguistics from Harvard. He first studied the Ojibwa language with Maude Kegg (Naawakamigookwe) and other elders of the Mille Lacs band of Ojibwas in Minnesota, and has since studied many other varieties of that language and other Algonquian languages. The editor of several volumes of transcriptions of Ojibwa oral literature and Ojibwa language dictionaries, he is a professor of native studies and linguistics at the University of Manitoba.

ROGER L. NICHOLS, a professor of history at the University of Arizona, has also taught at Wisconsin State University and the universities of Georgia and Maryland. His books examine frontier and Indian issues; in 1992 he won the Benjamin Shambaugh Award for *Black Hawk and the Warrior's Path.*

SHARON L. O'BRIEN teaches at the University of Notre Dame. She is the author of *American Indian Tribal Governments,* published by the University of Oklahoma Press, and other works concerning the status and rights of tribal governments and Indian people. She and her husband, Donald Fixico, have one son.

BARRY O'CONNELL first taught in an elementary school in Roxbury, Massachusetts. Since then he has taught in public housing projects, libraries, prisons, high schools, colleges, and universities, here and abroad. He is currently a professor of English at Amherst College. His scholarly interests focus on the history and culture of the many peoples who have, in conflict as well as in common, shaped the United States.

BARNEY OLD COYOTE is an enrolled member of the Crow Tribe. He was educated in Montana, Kansas, and Iowa. He served on the Crow Culture Committee, was the director (and founder) of Indian Studies, Montana State University, and was the principal spokesman for the American Indian Religious Freedom Act.

JAMES C. OLSON is president emeritus of the University of Missouri. Before joining Missouri, he taught history and held various administrative posts at the University of Nebraska. He has written a number of books and articles about higher education, Nebraska, and the West, some of them with Vera Farrington Olson.

BEVERLY R. ORTIZ, a Ph.D. candidate in anthropology at the University of California at Berkeley, is an ethnographic consultant, skills and technology columnist for *News from Native California,* and park naturalist. She has published one book and more than seventy-five articles about California Indians. She is currently writing a life history of the Pomo/Miwok elder Milton Lucas.

LINDA E. OXENDINE, a Lumbee, is associate professor and chair of the American Indian Studies Department at Pembroke State University. She received her Ph.D. in American studies, with a concentration in American Indian studies, from the University of Minnesota. During her twenty-five-year tenure in Indian affairs she has worked in several educational and cultural positions at both tribal and national levels.

DONALD L. PARMAN holds degrees from Central Missouri State University, Ohio University, and the University of Oklahoma. Since 1966 he has taught at Purdue University. He has published *Navajos and the New Deal, Indians and the American West in the Twentieth Century,* and numerous articles and book chapters.

STEVE PAVLIK is now in his twentieth year as a teacher of American history and American Indian studies at Chinle High School on the Navajo Reservation in Arizona. He holds a master's degree in

American Indian studies from the University of Arizona, has published over twenty papers, and has spoken extensively throughout the United States and Canada on Native American topics and issues.

DAVID H. PENTLAND teaches linguistics and anthropology at the University of Manitoba, and writes on a variety of topics concerning the Algonquian languages. A graduate of the universities of Manitoba (B.A.) and Toronto (M.A., Ph.D.), he began his research on Cree and related languages in 1969.

THEDA PERDUE is a professor of history at the University of Kentucky. She is the author of *Slavery and the Evolution of Cherokee Society, Native Carolinians,* and *The Cherokee.* She is editor of *Nations Remembered* and *Cherokee Editor.* Most recently, she coedited *The Cherokee Removal* with her husband, the historian Michael D. Green.

JACQUELINE PETERSON teaches history and Native American studies at Washington State University at Vancouver. She has published extensively on the Métis, Indians of the Great Lakes and the plateau, and has authored a catalog and scripted several award-winning video productions associated with a five thousand-square-foot traveling museum exhibition titled "Sacred Encounters: Father De Smet and the Indians of the Rocky Mountain West," which she directed and curated. She lives in Portland, Oregon.

MARDELL HOGAN PLAINFEATHER (Big Lodge Clan Crow) is retired from the National Park Service, where she was chief ranger at the Fort Smith Historic Site in Fort Smith, Alabama. The grandmother of three, she lives with her husband in Sallisaw, Oklahoma, and does consultations and presentations about historic sites and Native American history.

WILLIAM K. POWERS is Distinguished Professor of Anthropology at Rutgers University. He is the author of fifteen books on American Indians, including the popular *Oglala Religion* (1977) and *Yuwipi: Vision and Experience in Oglala Ritual* (1982). He began studying Lakota language and culture in 1948, and was adopted by Frank Afraid of Horse in 1950.

GORDON L. PULLAR, a Kodiak Island Sugpiaq, is the director of the Alaska Native Human Resource Development Program at the University of Alaska, the past president of the Kodiak Area Native Association, and the current national president of Keepers of the Treasures: Cultural Council of American Indians, Alaska Natives and Native Hawaiians.

STEWARD RAFERT has worked with the Indiana Miami tribe for many years as a consultant on federal recognition. He has written a book on the tribe to be published by the Indiana Historical Society. He and his wife and daughters Samara, Kyla, and Jesse live in Newark, Delaware.

DANIEL K. RICHTER teaches history and American studies at Dickinson College. He is author of *The Ordeal of the Longhouse: The Peoples of the Iroquois League in the Era of European Colonization* (1992) and the coeditor, with James H. Merrell, of *Beyond the Covenant Chain: The Iroquois and Their Neighbors in Indian North America, 1600–1800* (1987).

JAMES RIDING IN (Pawnee) is an assistant professor of justice studies at Arizona State University. A historian by training, he has focused his research on the relationship between Indians and whites, particularly in the areas of repatriation, federal policy, and cultural survival. He teaches courses on social and Indian (in)justice.

DAVID RISLING (Hupa), senior lecturer emeritus at the University of California at Davis and interim president of D-Q University, Davis, is cofounder and former board chairman of the California Indian Education Association, California Indian Legal Services, the Native American Rights Fund, and D-Q University. He has received numerous awards, including one recognizing him as California's Outstanding Indian Educator.

PAUL M. ROBERTSON holds a Ph.D. in cultural anthropology and is currently an instructor at Oglala Lakota College, a tribal college on the Pine Ridge Reservation in South Dakota. He and his wife, Eileen H. Iron Cloud, are active in the reservation community, having worked on issues ranging from family violence to land reform.

ROBERT A. ROESSEL, JR., has lived and worked on the Navajo Reservation for forty-four years. He was the founding father of the Rough Rock Demonstration School. He was the founding father and first president of Navajo Community College. He has been a school superintendent and administrator, and teaches in public, BIA, and contract schools.

J. DANIEL ROGERS, curator of anthropology and head of the Division of Archaeology at the National Museum of Natural History, received B.A. and M.A. degrees in anthropology from the University of Oklahoma and a Ph.D. in anthropology from the University of Chicago. He has worked in archaeology for nineteen years, specializing in the prehistory and early history of the North American Great Plains and Southeast. His most recent books include *Objects of Change* (Smithsonian Institution Press, 1990) and *Ethnohistory and Archaeology: Approaches to Post-Contact Change in the Americas* (coedited with Samuel M. Wilson; Plenum Press, 1993).

WILLARD HUGHES ROLLINGS, part Choctaw, is married to the graphic artist Barbara Williams-Rollings. An associate professor of history at the University of Nevada at Las Vegas, he has written *The Osages* and *The Comanche.* Rollings was a Newberry Library Fellow and won a Fulbright to New Zealand.

GRETCHEN RONNOW received an M.A. degree in English from Utah State University and a Ph.D. degree in comparative American literatures from the University of Arizona. She is currently an associate professor of English at Wayne State College and is frequently a visiting professor of English and comparative indigenous literatures at Barnaul State Pedagogical University in Siberia.

HELEN C. ROUNTREE, a cultural anthropologist and Virginia native, has been studying eastern Virginia's Native Americans, historic and modern, since 1969. She is an honorary member of two present-day Virginia Indian tribes, and her more popularized writings include *Young Pocahontas in the Indian World* (1995), a book for children.

ROBERT H. RUBY was born in Mabton, Washington, where he received his public education. He graduated from Washington University School of Medicine, St. Louis, Missouri, in 1945. After a tour of duty during World War II, he served two years in the Public Health Service on the Pine Ridge Indian Reservation in South Dakota. He currently teaches a course on Indians of the Pacific Northwest at Big Bend Community College, in Moses Lake, Washington, where he resides. He has coauthored numerous publications with John A. Brown.

A. LAVONNE BROWN RUOFF, professor emerita of English at the University of Illinois at Chicago, has published *American Indian Literatures* (1990), *Redefining American Literary History* (coedited with Jerry W. Ward, Jr., 1990), and *Literatures of the American Indian* (1990). She directed NEH seminars for college teachers on American Indian literature in 1979, 1983, 1989, and 1994.

GEORGE SABO III is an associate archeologist at the Arkansas Archeological Survey and an associate professor of anthropology at the University of Arkansas at Fayetteville. His research is on the prehistoric and historic development of Native American cultures in the trans-Mississippi South.

VELMA "VEE" SALABIYE (Navajo) is head librarian at the American Indian Studies Center Library, UCLA. A published poet and bibliographer, she is a founding member of the American Indian Library Association and a member of the American Library Association (ALA) Council, in which capacity she will serve the interests of American Indians until her term ends in 1998.

NEAL SALISBURY was born in Los Angeles and received his undergraduate and graduate education at UCLA. A member of the History Department at Smith College since 1973, he is the author of *Manitou and Providence: Indians, Europeans, and the Making of New England, 1500–1643* (1982) and coauthor of *The Enduring Vision: A History of the American People* (3d ed., 1995).

JOE S. SANDO was born at Jemez Pueblo, New Mexico. After graduating from the Santa Fe Indian School and serving three years in the navy during World War II, he graduated from Eastern New Mexico University and Vanderbilt graduate school. He taught at two post high schools before retiring. He has written five books and has appeared in many television documentaries. Currently he is the director of the Institute of Pueblo Indian Research and Study in Albuquerque.

RICHARD A. SATTLER received his Ph.D. in anthropology from the University of Oklahoma and is on the staff of the D'Arcy McNickle Center for the History of the American Indian at the Newberry Library. He has conducted extensive ethnographic and ethnohistorical research and published on the Seminole and Creek Indians.

AMANDA IRENE SELIGMAN is a research assistant for *The Encyclopedia of Chicago History* and a Ph.D. candidate in United States urban history at Northwestern University.

LYNDA NORENE SHAFFER, associate professor of history at Tufts University, received her Ph.D. in East Asian and American history from Columbia University. The author of *Native Americans before 1492: The Moundbuilding Centers of the Eastern Woodlands,* she would like to see Native American history become an integral part of world history.

JAMES E. SHEROW, PH.D., is an associate professor of history at Kansas State University, where he teaches environmental history, ethnohistory, and the history of Kansas and the American West. He is the author of *Watering the Valley* (University Press of Kansas, 1990) and numerous journal articles. As a fellow at the Newberry Library he helped initiate a collaborative class exchange between Haskell Indian Nations University and Kansas State University—the first exchange of its kind.

FRED J. SHORE was raised in Montreal, Quebec. He moved to Manitoba, where he worked as a housing officer for the Manitoba Métis Federation until 1981. He studied Métis history and received his Ph.D. in 1991. Currently he is an assistant professor and head of the Native Studies Department at the University of Manitoba.

WILLIAM E. SIMEONE has lived in Alaska for twenty-five years. During that time he spent extended periods in two Alaska Native communities. In 1990 Simeone received a Ph.D. in anthropology from McMaster University. Since then he has taught classes in anthropology at the University of Alaska at Anchorage, conducted fieldwork in northern Alaska and Canada, and prepared a forthcoming book on the Northern Athabaskan potlatch.

ALLOGAN SLAGLE, since 1989 the federal acknowledgment project director for the Association on American Indian Affairs, has published over fifty articles on law, policy, history, and ethnography. A member of the United Keetoowah Band (UKB), he has served on the UKB Tribal Council since 1992. He earned a J.D. from Loyola Law School, Los Angeles, in 1979, and is a member of the California State Bar.

ALLEN SLICKPOO served in elective offices of the Nez Perce tribal government for twenty-six years. He is recognized as an authority on Nez Perce tribal history and culture by his own people. Slickpoo is the author of *Noon Ne Mee Poo,* a history of the Nez Perces, and coauthor of *Nu Mee Pum Tit Wah Tit,* a book of Nez Perce legends. He is currently employed as an ethnographer for the tribe. His prime interests are native American history and the preservation of traditional culture.

DAVID LEE SMITH is a member of the Winnebago Tribe of Nebraska. He holds an M.A. from UCLA and is director of Indian studies at the Nebraska Indian Community College. David is also the cultural preservation officer for the tribe. He is a lifelong resident of Winnebago, and is a direct descendant of Hopoe-Kaw.

Born and raised in Ontario, DONALD B. SMITH has taught Canadian history at the University of Calgary since 1974. For over a quarter of a century he has had a special interest in the perceptions of North American Indians held by both English-speaking and French-speaking Canadians in the nineteenth and twentieth centuries.

The artist and writer KATHLEEN ROSE SMITH (Mihilakawna Pomo/Yoletamal Miwok) received her B.F.A. from the San Francisco Art Institute. Her work has been shown throughout California and Russia (1995). She has served on several boards and commissions, and taught Native American art at Sonoma State University (1993 and 1994).

SHERRIE SMITH-FERRI, her husband, David, and their daughter, Rachael, live in Dry Creek Valley, California, the ancestral home of her grandmother's people, the Dry Creek Pomos, and close to Bodega Bay, where her grandfather's Coast Miwok people lived. She believes it is the most beautiful country on earth.

CHUCK SMYTHE conducted his doctoral fieldwork among aboriginals in the western desert of Australia, an experience that led him to an interest in applied anthropology. He has lived and worked in Alaska for the past fifteen years, where he has carried out research in ethnography and ethnohistory among Arctic and Northwest Coast peoples. Recently, he accepted a position as anthropologist in the Repatriation Office of the National Museum of Natural History at the Smithsonian Institution.

C. MATTHEW SNIPP is a professor of rural sociology and has been a fellow at the Center for Advanced Study in the Behavioral Sciences. He has published numerous works on American Indian demography, economic development, poverty, and unemployment, including *American Indians: The First of This Land* and *Public Policy Impacts on American Indian Economic Development.* His tribal heritage is Oklahoma Cherokee and Choctaw.

DEAN SNOW is a professor and the head of anthropology at Penn State University. While previously at the State University of New York at Albany, he directed the Mohawk Valley Archaeological Project. He is the author of *The Iroquois,* which covers the Mohawks and the other nations of the League of the Iroquois.

RUBIE SOOTKIS (Northern Cheyenne) is a writer and filmmaker focusing on Cheyenne history and culture. She cowrote the Emmy-nominated 1984 HBO documentary *Paha Sapa: A Struggle for the Black Hills.* She is a direct descendant of Chief Morningstar (Dull Knife) and American Horse.

SHEILA STAATS is a Mohawk from the Six Nations Reserve in Ontario. She attended Huron College at the University of Western Ontario and received a B.A. in 1978. She currently works at the Woodland Cultural Centre in Brantford, Ontario, as the center's historical researcher.

BLAIR STONECHILD (Plains Cree) is of the Muscowpetung First Nation. He studied at McGill and Regina, and teaches Indian history. He has been the head of Indian Studies and dean of academics at the Saskatchewan Indian Federated College, and president of the Canadian Indian/Native Studies Association. He is married, with three children.

RENNARD STRICKLAND, a legal historian of Osage and Cherokee heritage, is currently dean and professor of law at Oklahoma City University School of Law. He has been honored by the Oklahoma Indian Affairs Commission for his role as an expert witness in cases advancing the cause of tribal sovereignty and by the American

Indian Heritage Association for his scholarly contribution to the understanding of the relationship between Indian law and history. He is the author of *The Indians in Oklahoma* (1981) and *Fire and the Spirits: Cherokee Law from Clan to Court* (1975).

JOHN A. STRONG, professor of history at the Southampton Campus of Long Island University, has written extensively on the Indians of Long Island. His most recent work, *The Indians of Long Island: From Earliest Times to 1700,* was published in 1995 by the Long Island Studies Institute at Hofstra University.

WILLIAM C. STURTEVANT is curator of North American Ethnology in the Department of Anthropology, National Museum of Natural History, Smithsonian Institution. He is also general editor of the encyclopedic *Handbook of North American Indians.* He is especially interested in the cultures of eastern North America and in the history of anthropology.

JOHN SUGDEN, Ph.D., formerly director of studies at Hereward College, Coventry, England, is currently completing studies of Tecumseh and the Shawnees. His publications, which include *Tecumseh's Last Stand* (1985), have won acclaim in Britain and North America. In 1988–89 he was Ford Foundation Fellow at the Newberry Library, Chicago.

WILLIAM R. SWAGERTY, an associate professor of history at the University of Idaho, is the former associate director of the D'Arcy McNickle Center for the History of American Indians. His specialties include the Indian trades and fur trades of North America.

EDWIN R. SWEENEY, a native of Boston, graduated from the University of Massachusetts at Amherst with a B.S. in accounting. He has published several articles and two books on the Apaches: *Cochise: Chiricahua Apache Chief* (University of Oklahoma Press, 1991) and *Merejildo Grijalva: Apache Captive, Army Scout* (Texas Western Press, 1992). He lives in St. Charles, Missouri, with his wife, Joanne, and his daughters, Tiffani, Caitlin, and Courtney.

Born near the confluence of the Snake and Columbia Rivers, MARGARET CONNELL SZASZ studied at the University of Washington and the University of New Mexico, where she is a professor of history. Working with native and nonnative students in the U.S. and Britain encouraged her most recent publication, *Between Indian and White Worlds: The Cultural Broker.*

HELEN HORNBECK TANNER holds a doctoral degree from the University of Michigan. She has taught and has served as an expert witness and consultant in litigation involving treaties with American Indians. Since 1976 she has also been associated with the Newberry Library.

JASON M. TETZLOFF received his B.A. and M.A. degrees from the University of Wisconsin at Eau Claire and will complete his Ph.D. in American history from Purdue University in 1996. His special areas of research are nineteenth- and twentieth-century Native American history and the Age of Reform in America (1880–1940). His dissertation is a biography of Henry Roe Cloud. He is currently teaching at Western Washington University in Bellingham, Washington.

A curator at the American Museum of Natural History in New York for twenty-five years, DAVID HURST THOMAS, Ph.D., is a specialist in Native American archaeology. He has written and/or edited more than one hundred books and is a founding trustee of the National Museum of the American Indian, Smithsonian Institution, and a member of the National Academy of Sciences.

RUSSELL THORNTON is a professor of anthropology at the University of California at Los Angeles and a registered member of the Cherokee Nation of Oklahoma. He is the author of *We Shall Live Again* (1986), *American Indian Holocaust and Survival* (1987), *The Cherokees: A Population History* (1990), and many other publications.

GRACE THORPE, or No Teno Quah (Wind Woman), of the Sauk and Fox tribe, is Jim Thorpe's daughter. She has served as health commissioner of the Sauk and Fox tribe, as tribal judge, and as the president of the National Environmental Coalition of Native Americans. She lives in Prague, Oklahoma, with her daughter Dagmar and granddaughter Tena Malotte.

GEORGE E. TINKER (Osage) teaches on the faculty of Iliff School of Theology in Denver, Colorado. He is the author of *Missionary Conquest: The Gospel and Native American Cultural Genocide* (Fortress Press, 1993) and numerous articles on American Indian issues.

ELISABETH TOOKER is professor emerita of anthropology at Temple University, and is the author of a number of publications on Northern Iroquois culture and history, including *An Ethnography of the Huron Indians, 1615–1649* (1964), *The Iroquois Ceremonial of Midwinter* (1970), and *Lewis H. Morgan on Iroquois Material Culture* (1994).

CLIFFORD E. TRAFZER (Wyandot) is a professor of history and ethnic studies at the University of California at Riverside, where he is director of Native American Studies. He has been a member of various Native American studies programs for eighteen years, serving thirteen of those years as chair. Among his books are *The Kit Carson Campaign, Chief Joseph's Allies,* and *Renegade Tribe.* Trafzer is currently vice-chair of the California Native American Heritage Commission.

MICHAEL TSOSIE, an enrolled member of the Colorado River Indian Tribes, is currently a Ph.D. candidate in the Anthropology Department at the University of California at Berkeley. After serving as director of planning and development for the Chemehuevi Indian tribe, he was selected in 1990 by the National Museum of Natural History as a Native American Community Scholar. In 1993, in recognition of his accomplishments as a tribal community leader, Mr. Tsosie was awarded a Kellogg Fellowship.

WILLIAM E. UNRAU received his Ph.D. from the University of Colorado and is Endowment Association Research Professor of History at Wichita State University. He is the author or coauthor of eight books on Indian-white relations, including his latest, *Indians of Kansas: The Euro-American Invasion and Conquest of Indian Kansas* (Kansas State Historical Society, 1991).

ROBERT M. UTLEY is a former chief historian of the National Park Service and the author of many books and articles on western history, including a two-volume history of the frontier army, biographies of General Custer and Sitting Bull, and *The Indian Frontier of the American West, 1846–1890.*

As a Smithsonian researcher since 1975, THOMAS VENNUM, JR., has published widely on American Indian music and specifically on the music and culture of the Ojibwas. His study, *The Ojibwa Dance Drum: Its History and Construction,* won the Society for Ethnomusicology's Klaus Wachsmann prize in 1989.

IRENE S. VERNON (Mescalero Apache/Yaqui), Ph.D., is a professor of ethnic studies and English at Colorado State University. Professor Vernon specializes in Native American studies and is trained in various fields: Native American history, law, and literature; American ethnicity; and American history.

GERALD VIZENOR (Anishinaabe) is a professor of Native American Indian literatures at the University of California at Berkeley. He is the author of *The People Named the Chippewa,* narrative histories, *Interior Landscapes,* an autobiography, and five novels. *Griever: An American Monkey King in China,* his second novel, won the American Book Award.

VIRGIL J. VOGEL (1918–1994) was born near Keota, Iowa, and moved to Chicago at age eight. He received his Ph.D. in history from the University of Chicago and was a professor of history at H. S. Truman College. A noted scholar in American Indian history, he was the author of many books and articles, including several on Indian place names in Illinois, Iowa, Wisconsin, and Michigan.

MARY JANE WARDE, who received her doctorate in 1991 from Oklahoma State University, is a historical consultant from Stillwater, Oklahoma. Her specialty is the Indian Territory, with emphasis on the Muskogee (Creek) Nation. She has published several articles, designed a course in Oklahoma history, and is active in historic preservation.

ROBERT ALLEN WARRIOR (Osage) teaches in the English Department at Stanford University. He is the author of *Tribal Secrets: Recovering American Indian Intellectual Traditions* (University of Minnesota Press, 1994) and, with Paul Chaat Smith, *Like a Hurricane: The Indian Movement from Red Power to Wounded Knee* (New Press, 1996).

JACK WEATHERFORD is a writer and professor of anthropology at Macalester College in St. Paul, Minnesota. His books include *Indian Givers: How the Indians of the Americas Transformed the World, Native Roots: How the Indians Enriched America,* and *Savages and Civilization: Who Will Survive?*

GLORIA CRANMER WEBSTER is a member of the 'Namgis tribe of Alert Bay, British Columbia. Before becoming the founding director of the U'mista Cultural Centre, she was an assistant curator at the Museum of Anthropology, University of British Columbia. Her interests include oral history and developing museum exhibits.

W. RICHARD WEST JR. was appointed director of the Smithsonian's National Museum of the American Indian on June 1, 1990. West is a Southern Cheyenne and a member of the Cheyenne and Arapaho Tribes of Oklahoma. He is the son of the renowned Southern Cheyenne artist Walter Richard (Dick) West, Sr., and Maribelle McCrea West. He has devoted his professional and much of his personal life to working with American Indians on cultural, educational, legal, and governmental issues.

JOHN K. WHITE is a cultural anthropologist and traditional storyteller of Cherokee, Shawnee, and Scots ancestry. He attended Bacone Indian College and has graduate degrees from the University of Chicago and Stanford University. He and his wife, Ela, who is of French and Kaskaskia ancestry, teach traditional culture at their school, the Ancient Lifeways Institute, in Michael, Illinois.

RICHARD WHITE teaches history at the University of Washington in Seattle. He is the author of *Roots of Dependency, The Middle Ground,* and *It's Your Misfortune and None of My Own: A New History of the American West.*

GARY WHITE DEER (Choctaw) is a visual artist, Native American festival coordinator, and the former director of the Department of Cultural Resources for the Chickasaw Nation. He lives in Ada, Oklahoma.

ALBERT WHITE HAT, SR., an enrolled member of the Rosebud Sioux Tribe, lives in St. Francis, South Dakota. He began teaching the Lakota language in 1971 and has been a full-time instructor at Sinte Gleska University since 1982. Though Albert has a high-school diploma and an associate's degree in Lakota studies from Sinte Gleska University, most of his formal education comes from being Lakota and from listening to the words of elders and medicine men. He has published *Lakota Ceremonial Songs* (Sinte Gleska University Press, 1983) and is currently working on a Lakota language textbook with Jael Kampfe, who also contributed to Albert's article in this encyclopedia.

THURMAN WILKINS, a Guggenheim fellow, the author of four biographies of American figures, and professor emeritus of English at Queens College of the City University of New York, was born in

1915 in Malden, Missouri, but grew up in southern California. He earned degrees at UCLA, the University of California at Berkeley, and Columbia University, where he taught American literature for thirteen years before moving on to Queens College.

ROBERT A. WILLIAMS, JR. (Lumbee), is a professor of law and American Indian studies at the University of Arizona. He is the author of *The American Indian in Western Legal Thought: The Discourses of Conquest* (Oxford University Press, 1990) and coauthor, with David Getches and Charles Wilkinson, of *Federal Indian Law: Cases and Material* (3d ed., West, 1993), the leading casebook in the field of Indian law and policy. Professor Williams has received numerous grants and awards, and serves as a judge for the court of appeals for the Pascua Yaqui Tribe and as judge pro tem for the Tohono O'odham Nation.

SUSAN M. WILLIAMS is a shareholder in Gover, Stetson & Williams, P.C., an Indian-owned law firm, and an enrolled member of the Sisseton-Wahpeton Dakota Nation. Susan is a graduate of Radcliffe College and Harvard Law School. She currently represents numerous Indian tribes on water and gaming matters. Susan serves on several national and regional boards of directors and national advisory committees on state-tribal relations, resource development, and environmental protection, including the World Wildlife Fund/Conservation Foundation, the American Bar Association Water Resources Committee, and the American Indian Resources Institute.

RAY A. WILLIAMSON earned his Ph.D. in astronomy from the University of Maryland. In 1977–78, he was named a Smithsonian Fellow to study the astronomical practices of pre-Columbian and historic Native Americans. He has published numerous articles on Native American astronomy and ritual, and has written or edited more than six books on anthropology, archaeology, and folklore.

MARYANN WILLIE (Navajo) received her Ph.D. in linguistics from the University of Arizona in 1991. She is currently assistant professor of linguistics and American Indian studies. Her main research interest is the structure of Navajo, on which she has published articles. She lives in Tucson, Arizona.

JOHN A. K. WILLIS is a doctoral candidate in the department of anthropology at Northwestern University. His bachelor's and master's degrees are from Hunter College in New York City. Currently he is researching the prehistoric origin and historic ethnogenesis of the Illinois Indians using archaeology, ethnohistory, and a comparative analysis of the ceramics of Midwestern Algonquian Indian groups.

TERRY P. WILSON, Potawatomi, is professor emeritus of Native American studies at the University of California at Berkeley. He has published numerous books and articles about American Indians, including *The Underground Reservation: Osage Oil* (University of Nebraska Press, 1985) and *Teaching American Indian History* (American Historical Association, 1993).

KEITH A. WINSELL is director of the library at Sinte Gleska University, on the Rosebud Sioux Reservation in South Dakota. He has a doctorate in American history and a library degree. He has taught in Indiana, Ohio, Kansas, Georgia, and Minnesota. Past administrative positions have included director of American Minority Studies at St. Olaf College and associate director of the Amistad Research Center at Tulane University.

ROSITA WORL is a Tlingit from the Eagle Thunderbird clan of Klukwan, Alaska. She serves on the board of directors of Sealaska Corporation, which holds the regional lands of the Southeast Indians. She teaches anthropology at the University of Alaska Southeast and conducts research on Alaska Native societies.

ALVIN J. ZIONTZ is a Seattle lawyer whose firm has specialized in the practice of Indian law. He is the author of numerous articles on Indian law topics. He has also been a visiting professor of law at the University of Iowa and at Durham University in England.

CONTRIBUTORS OF BRIEF ENTRIES

Kathryn A. Abbott
Rebecca Bales
Teresa Bales
Carol Behl
Phil Bellfy
Tim Bernardis

Jon Brudvig
Elizabeth A. Carney
Cary Christie
J. Daniel D'Oney
Kathy M. Evans
Andrew H. Fisher

Kenny Franks
Bonnie Lynn-Sherow
Rosalyn LaPier
Jaako Puisto
Dan Eagle Boy Rowe
Richard A. Sattler

Amanda Irene Seligman
James E. Sherow
Keith A. Winsell
Scott C. Zeman

⋈⋈⋈ CREDITS ⋈⋈⋈

MAPS: Sanderson Associates, Peterborough, New Hampshire

TEXT: Dance © Charlotte Heth 1992. Adapted from the introduction to *Native American Dance: Ceremonies and Social Traditions* (Golden, Colorado: Fulcrum Publishers, 1992; Washington, D.C.: National Museum of the American Indian, Smithsonian Institution, 1992).

PICTURE CREDITS:

Abenaki Peabody Museum Harvard/copy negative no. N31034 by Hillel Burger; **African Americans and American Indians** Chicago Albumen Works of Housatonic, Massachusetts, Fred E. Miller Collection/© Nancy Fields O'Connor; **Agriculture** Minnesota Historical Society/photo by Adrian J. Ebell/negative no. 36703; **Alcatraz** AP/Wide World Photos; **Alcohol and Indians** American Antiquarian Society; **Aleut** UPI/Corbis-Bettmann Archive; **Architecture (tipi)** Montana Historical Society, Gift of Mrs. A. C. Berglund/negative no. 955-523; **Architecture (pueblo)** Photo Researchers, Inc./photo by M.B. Duda; **Architecture (wickiup)** National Museum of the American Indian, Smithsonian Institution/negative no. 26403; **Arrowheads** Courtesy of George C. Frison; **Art, Visual (to 1960) (Chilkat mask)** Cincinnati Art Museum, Gift of Dr. and Mrs. W. W. Seely/accession no. 1889.294; **Art, Visual (to 1960) (pottery)** Museum of New Mexico/photo by Arthur Taylor, negative no. 98598; **Arts, Contemporary (since 1960)** Courtesy of Fritz Scholder/photo by Bill McLemore; **Basketry** Courtesy of Victoria Patterson, Redwood Valley, California/photo by Scott M. Patterson; **Beads and Beadwork** Photo Researchers, Inc./photo by Paolo Koch; **Black Elk** Smithsonian Institution, National Anthropological Archives, Washington, DC/negative no. 3303-C; **Blackfoot** Whyte Museum of the Canadian Rockies, Banff, Alberta, Canada/negative no. V469/2771; **Boarding Schools (before)** Cumberland County Historical Society, Carlisle, Pennsylvania/negative no. PA-CHI-19; **Boarding Schools (after)** Cumberland County Historical Society, Carlisle, Pennsylvania/negative no. PA-CHI-31; **Brant, Joseph** National Archives of Canada/negative no. C11476; **Bureau of Indian Affairs** Library of Congress/negative no. LCUSZ62-56003; **California Tribes** Southwest Museum, Los Angeles, California; **Cherokee** Corbis-Bettmann Archive; **Cheyenne, Northern** Smithsonian Institution, National Anthropological Archives, Washington, DC/negative no. 270-A; **Child Rearing** Smithsonian Institution, National Anthropological Archives, Washington, DC/negative no. 76-4346; **Crazy Horse** Beinecke Rare Book and Manuscript Library, Yale University; **Curtis, Charles** Kansas State Historical Society; **Dance** Smithsonian Institution, National Anthropological Archives, Washington, DC/negative no. 42019-D; **Eskimo** The Granger Collection, New York; **Families (Bannock)** Smithsonian Institution, National Anthropological Archives, Washington, DC/negative no. 1713; **Families (Apache)** Photo Researchers, Inc./photo by Lawrence Migdale; **Fishing** Oregon Historical Society/negative no. OrHi4463; **Food and Cuisine** Smithsonian Institution, National Anthropological Archives, Washington, DC/negative no. 1878-B; **Fur Trade** Provincial Archives of Alberta, Ernest Brown Collection/negative no. B1700; **General, Alexander** Brantford Expositor, Brantford, Ontario; **Geronimo** National Archives and Records Administration/negative no. 165-AI-46; **Ghost**

Dance Milwaukee Public Library; **Hand Game** Nevada Historical Society/negative no. E-535; **Harjo, Chitto** Archives and Manuscript Division of the Oklahoma Historical Society/negative no. 3905; **Hatathli, Ned** Amon Carter Museum, Fort Worth, Texas/photo by Laura Gilpin, Navaho Book: 4301.1, "Arts and Crafts Guild: Ned Hatathli," 4"x 5" safety negative, September 1954; **Herding and Ranching** Contact Press Images/photo by Eric Haase; **Hole-in-the-Day** Minnesota Historical Society/photo by J. E. Whitney/negative no. 8161; **Hopi** The Picture Cube/photo by Cynthia Sterling; **Horses and Indians** Stock, Boston/photo by John Eastcott; **Hunting** Photo Researchers, Inc./photo by Lawrence Migdale; **Indian-White Relations in Canada** Canapress Photo Service/photo by Tom Hanson; **Indian-White Relations in the U.S., 1776–1900** Smithsonian Institution, National Anthropological Archives, Washington, DC/negative no.690-B; **Iroquois Confederacy** Smithsonian Institution, National Anthropological Archives, Washington, DC/negative no. 961-C-1; **Ishi** Phoebe A. Hearst Museum of Anthropology, University of California, Berkeley/negative no. 15-5414; **Johnson, Pauline** Brant County Museum & Archives, Brantford, Ontario, Canada; **Jones, Peter** Amon Carter Museum/calotype by David Octavius Hill, c. 1845/negative no. P1979.38; **Joseph** Courtesy of Dr. James Brust/photo by John Fouch; **Kwakiutl** Smithsonian Institution, National Anthropological Archives, Washington, DC/negative no. 3946; **Little Crow** Smithsonian Institution, National Anthropological Archives, Washington, DC/negative no. 3505-B; **Lumbee** Pembroke State University, Native American Resource Center, Pembroke, North Carolina; **Manuelito** Courtesy of the School of American Research at the Museum of New Mexico/photo by Ben Wittick/negative no. 16332; **Mascots** Contact Press Images/photo by Eric Haase; **McIntosh, William, Jr.** Smithsonian Institution, National Anthropological Archives, Washington, DC/negative no. 45,111-B; **Menominee** Smithsonian Institution, National Anthropological Archives, Washington, DC/negative no. 56826; **Metacom** American Antiquarian Society; **Micmac** Smithsonian Institution, National Anthropological Archives, Washington, DC/negative no. 56827; **Missions and Missionaries** University of Oklahoma Library, Western History Collections, Campbell Collection; **Mississippians** University of Oklahoma, Oklahoma Museum of Natural History, Norman, Oklahoma/negative no. LF CRi I 108-4; **Montezuma, Carlos** Arizona State University; **Morgan, J. C.** Navajo Nation Museum, Window Rock, Arizona; **Mound Builders** Photo Researchers, Inc./photo by Mark C. Burnett; **Movies** Courtesy of Broadway Video Entertainment, L. P. and George Eastman House, International Museum of Photography, Rochester, N.Y.; **Muskrat, Ruth** Library of Congress/negative no. LCUSZ62-107775; **Nampeyo** National Archives of Canada/photo by Edward S. Curtis, negative no. PA-39513; **Native American Church** AP/Wide World Photos; **Nez Perce** Schlesinger Library, Radcliffe College, Cambridge, Massachusetts; **Occom, Samson** American Antiquarian Society; **Osceola** National Museum of American Art, Washington, DC/Art Resource, New York; **Parker, Ely S.** Western Reserve Historical Society, Cleveland, Ohio; **Parker, Quanah** Smithsonian Institution, National Anthropological Archives, Washington, DC/negative no. 1754-A-2; **Photography** Chicago Albumen Works of Housatonic, Massachusetts, Fred E.

Miller Collection/© Nancy Fields O'Connor; **Pocahontas** Library of Congress/negative no. LCUSZ62-39316; **Posey, Alexander** Archives and Manuscript Division of the Oklahoma Historical Society, Barde Collection/negative no. 4213; **Potawatomi** Detroit Institute of Arts, Photographer unknown, Mayetta, Kansas/photo by Richard A. Pohrt; **Potlatch** University of California, Berkeley, Bancroft Library; **Powhatan Confederacy** Library of Congress/negative no. LCUSZ62-00582; **Radicals** UPI/Corbis-Bettmann Archive; **Religion (ceremony)** Smithsonian Institution, National Anthropological Archives, Washington, DC/negative no. 55940; **Religion (kachina)** The Brooklyn Museum, *Kachina Doll*, Museum Expedition 1905, Museum Collection Fund; photo by Justin Kerr/accession no. 05.588.7193; **Repatriation** National Museum of the American Indian, Smithsonian Institution/photo by Pamela Dewey; **Riel, Louis** National Archives of Canada/negative no. C-6688; **Rogers, Will** Brown Brothers; **Ross, John** Nebraska State Historical Society/collection no. R539; **Seattle** Washington State Historical Society; **Seminole** Smithsonian Institution, National Anthropological Archives, Washington, DC/negative no. 45836-D; **Sequoyah** Smithsonian Institution, National Anthropological Archives, Washington, DC/negative no. 999; **Sioux** Minnesota Historical Society/photo by B. F. Upton/negative no. 3475; **Sitting Bull** McCord Museum of Canadian History, Notman Photographic Archives, Montreal, Canada; **Skolaskin** Collection of Robert H. Ruby; **Smohalla** Smithsonian Institution, National Anthropological Archives, Washington, DC/negative no. 2903-A; **Spotted Tail** Smithsonian Institution, National Anthropological Archives, Washington, DC/negative no. 3121; **Subarctic Tribes** Smithsonian Institution, National Anthropological Archives, Washington, DC/negative no. 75-5337; **Sweat Lodge** Chicago Albumen Works of Housatonic, Massachusetts, Fred E. Miller Collection/© Nancy Fields O'Connor; **Tekakwitha, Kateri** Mission St. Francis Xavier, Kahnawake, Canada; **Textiles** Smithsonian Institution, National Anthropological Archives, Washington, DC/negative no. 2433; **Thorpe, Jim** UPI/Corbis-Bettmann Archive; **Tohono O'odham** Arizona Historical Society Library/negative no. 8847; **Totem Poles** Smithsonian Institution, National Anthropological Archives, Washington, DC/negative no. 4320; **Treaties** Smithsonian Institution, National Anthropological Archives, Washington, DC/negative no. 3793-A; **Tuscarora** Buffalo and Erie County Historical Society; **Urban Indians** Sipa Press/photo by Catherine Leroy; **Wampum** Courtesy of the New York State Museum, Albany, New York/negative no. NYSM 37415; **Winnemucca, Sarah** Nevada Historical Society; **Women** "Five Generations, Mosquito Springs of Big Mountain, Arizona," from *Women of the Native Struggle* by Ronnie Farley, New York City; **Words That Have Entered English Usage** Anne Chalmers/reproduced by permission of Charles L. Cutler from his book *O Brave New Words! Native American Loanwords in Current English*, Norman: University of Oklahoma Press, 1994; **Wounded Knee Massacre** Smithsonian Institution, National Anthropological Archives, Washington, DC/negative no. 47,685-B; **Wounded Knee Takeover** UPI/Corbis-Bettmann Archive; **Wovoka** Nevada Historical Society; **Zitkala Ša** UPI/Corbis-Bettmann Archive; **Zuni Pueblo** The Picture Cube/photo by Ernesto Burciaga.

CONTRIBUTOR INDEX

GENERAL INDEX

Page numbers in **boldface type** refer to the major article for an entry.